Psychology

Second Edition

Psychology

Second Edition

HENRY GLEITMAN
UNIVERSITY OF PENNSYLVANIA

W · W · NORTON & COMPANY · NEW YORK · LONDON

Copyright © 1986, 1981 by W. W. Norton & Company, Inc.

Published simultaneously in Canada by Penguin Books Canada Ltd,
2801 John Street, Markham, Ontario L3R 1B4
Printed in the United States of America
All Rights Reserved
Second Edition

Library of Congress Cataloging-in-Publication Data

Gleitman, Henry.
    Psychology, 2nd Edition.

    Bibliography: p.
    Includes index.
    1. Psychology. I. Title.
BF121.G58   1986   150   85-15476
ISBN 0-393-95378-5

The text of this book is composed in Times Roman, with display type set
in Times Roman Bold.
Composition by New England Typographic Service, Inc.
Manufacturing by R. R. Donnelley & Sons Company
Book design by Antonina Krass.

Cover illustration: *David,* by Michelangelo (reprinted by permission of Scala/Art
Resources, New York).

Acknowledgments and copyrights appear on pages A66–A70, which constitute a
continuation of the copyright page.

W. W. Norton & Company, Inc., 500 Fifth Avenue, New York, N. Y. 10110

W. W. Norton & Company Ltd., 37 Great Russell Street, London WC1B 3NU

1 2 3 4 5 6 7 8 9 0

To three who taught me:

    Edward Chace Tolman, to cherish intellectual passion
    Hans Wallach, to recognize intellectual power
    Lila Ruth Gleitman, to admire intellectual elegance

The Contents in Brief

Contents

PART II

Cognition

CHAPTER 5

CHAPTER 6

PART IV   Development

CONTENTS

Preface

This is a revised version of my book *Psychology.* One reason for the revision is the obvious fact that like any other science, psychology advances and develops and a text must necessarily keep pace with the field. Another reason is the response to colleagues and students who used the text and whose suggestions prompted a number of changes, including a separate section on development.

THE OVERALL AIM: COHESION IN A DIVERSE FIELD

Before describing these changes, let me briefly review what has not changed: my original aims. In writing *Psychology,* I sought to present the field in all its diversity while yet conveying the sense in which it is a coherent intellectual enterprise. In pursuit of this goal, I did the following:

1. To present the different sub-areas of psychology, I organized the book around five main questions: How do humans (and where relevant, animals) act, how do they know, how do they interact, how do they develop, and how do they differ from each other?

2. To provide some intellectual cohesion, I considered each topic against the backdrop of one or two major ideas that could serve as an organizing and unifying framework. Thus the chapter on the biological bases of behavior opens with Descartes's conception of the organism as a machine, and the next chapter treats various aspects of motivated behavior as manifestations of negative feedback. To relate the material across chapters, I used several overarching themes. For example, the various chapters that deal with cognition (Sensory Processes, Perception,

Memory, Thinking, and Language) all involve variations on the twin controversies of nature versus nurture and psychological atomism versus organization.

3. In many cases, the attempt at integration required taking a step backward to look at psychology's intellectual history, for a number of the field's endeavors are hard to explain unless one points to the paths that led up to them. Why did Thorndike study cats in puzzle boxes? Why did his conclusions have such an important effect on American psychology? Why were they challenged by Köhler and Tolman? It still pays to take a serious look at the work of such pioneers before turning to the present. Much as a river's water is clearer when it is taken from its source, so issues which have become more and more complex as detail has piled upon detail become more plain and evident when traced back to their origin.

GENERAL ORGANIZATION

The most obvious difference between this and the previous edition is the inclusion of an entire part on development. In the previous edition, I had concentrated on two complementary forms of explanation in psychology—one centering on mechanism, which tries to understand how something works; another focusing on function, which tries to explain what something is good for. By adding a developmental section, I now give greater emphasis to a third approach to explanation which asks how various psychological phenomena came into being. I had previously dealt with such developmental issues by considering them separately in the context of such topics as thinking, language, and personality. In the new edition, the developmental aspects of these areas are expanded and brought together under one intellectual roof.

Most other revisions are best described within an outline of the overall structure of the book. After an introductory chapter, the book is divided into five parts that reflect the perspectives from which most psychological phenomena can be regarded: Action, Cognition, Social Behavior, Development, and Individual Differences. In brief outline, they cover the following topics:

Part I: Action

This part focuses on overt behavior and its physiological basis. It begins by considering the biological underpinnings of human and animal action, leading to a discussion of the nervous system and its operation (Chapter 2) and some phenomena of motivation (Chapter 3). It then asks how organisms can modify their behavior to adapt to new circumstances, a topic which leads to a discussion of classical and instrumental conditioning and modern behavior theory (Chapter 4).

In Chapter 2 *(Biological Bases of Behavior),* there is now a greater stress on neurotransmitter processes, including work on endorphins. The organization in Chapter 3 *(Motivation)* has been simplified and includes a discussion of some recent approaches to the study of obesity as well as a new section on food selection. Chapter 4 *(Learning)* now merges what were formerly two chapters on learning into one. In this new chapter, the organization has been simplified, with a greater stress on more recent approaches (e.g., contingency) and applications of behavior theory in clinical settings (e.g., behavior therapy, behavioral medicine).

Part II: Cognition

This part deals with knowledge and how it is gained and used. We begin by asking how the senses provide us with information about the world outside (Chapter 5), and how this information is organized and interpreted to lead to the perception of objects and events (Chapter 6). Further questions concern the way this knowledge is stored in memory and retrieved when needed (Chapter 7), the way it is organized through thinking (Chapter 8), and the way knowledge is communicated to others through the medium of language (Chapter 9).

Many of the changes in this part reflect a greater concern with recent information-processing approaches. In Chapter 5 *(Sensory Processes)* the organization has been simplified by eliminating a chapter appendix on signal-detection theory and incorporating its most important parts within the chapter. Chapter 6 *(Perception)* gives more prominence to the theories of James J. Gibson and now has a new section on perception as problem solving. Chapter 7 *(Memory)* covers a number of new approaches (e.g., encoding specificity, the workbench conception of short-term memory, memory reconstruction as exemplified by studies of hypnosis in the courtroom). Chapter 8 *(Thinking)* includes new material on spatial thinking, reasoning, and a discussion of some of Tversky and Kahneman's analyses of decision making. The material on cognitive development has been expanded and moved into the Development section. Chapter 9 *(Language),* written by Lila Gleitman and myself, has been simplified but is augmented by discussions of new approaches to the way language is processed by both speaker and listener. The material on language acquisition is now dealt with in the Development section.

Part III: Social Behavior

This part concerns our interactions with others. It begins with a discussion of built-in social tendencies in humans and animals, a topic to which ethology and evolutionary theory have made major contributions (Chapter 10). It proceeds by considering the complex way in which adult humans interpret and cope with social situations, a subject which is the main concern of modern social psychology (Chapter 11). It then turns to the first influential attempt to understand how childhood affects human socialization by considering Freud and psychoanalytic concepts (Chapter 12), thus paving the way for the discussion of modern approaches to social development taken up in the new section on Development.

There have been several changes in this section. Chapter 10 *(The Biological Bases of Social Behavior)* includes an expanded section on biological altruism. In addition, most of the material on infant attachment has been moved to become part of the new Development section. Compared to its counterpart in the first edition, Chapter 11 *(Social Psychology)* has a greater coverage of such topics as attitudes and attitude change, attribution processes, attraction, and recent work on the nature of emotions.

Part IV: Development

This entire section is new, though as already mentioned, many of its components were drawn from discussions formerly distributed through separate parts of the book. In writing this section, my aim was the same as that which prompted my work throughout the entire book: to find some intellectual cohesion in a sprawling field. Toward this end, Chapter 13 *(General Issues in Development)* sketches the historical background, outlines some conceptual issues that run through many of the subtopics of the field, and then tries to exemplify these issues by discussing physical and motor development. Chapter 14 *(Cognitive Development: Thought)* takes up the child's mental growth, beginning with the work of Jean Piaget, and then considering more recent and quite different approaches, including some influenced by Gibsonian perception theory, and some based on an information-processing analysis of cognition. Chapter 15 *(Cognitive Development: Language),* written by Lila Gleitman and myself, and takes up language development. Chapter 16 *(Social Development)* discusses social growth and development, considering such topics as attachment, theories of socialization, sex roles, moral development, and adult development.

Part V: Individual Differences

This part begins with a chapter on mental testing in general and intelligence testing in particular (Chapter 17), and then turns to various issues in personality assessment (Chapter 18). It continues by looking at several varieties of psychopathology and asking how they arise (Chapter 19), and concludes by examining various methods of treatment and therapy (Chapter 20).

Chapter 17 *(Intelligence)* now includes a section on recent attempts to understand differences in intelligence-test performance in information-processing terms. Chapter 18 *(Personality)* includes a discussion of recent developments in the trait-situationism debate. Chapter 19 *(Psychopathology)* has been modified to reflect the new diagnostic taxonomy and nomenclature of DSM-III, and it describes some of the reasons that prompted the change from the old diagnostic manual.

THE READER AND THE BOOK

It is sometimes said that students in the introductory course want to learn about things that are relevant to themselves and to their own lives. But why should this be a problem? When you come right down to it, there is something odd about the idea that psychology is *not* relevant to anyone's particular life history—specialist and nonspecialist alike. Psychology deals with the nature of human experience and behavior, about the hows and whys of what we do, think, and feel. Everyone has perceived, learned, remembered and forgotten, has been angry and afraid and been in love, has given in to group pressure and been independent. In short, everyone has experienced most of the phenomena that psychology tries to explain. This being so, psychology cannot fail to be relevant.

It surely is relevant, but its relevance has to be pointed out. I've tried to do so by a liberal use of examples from ordinary experience and a frequent resort to metaphors of one kind or another, in the hope that in so doing I would show the direct relation of many psychological phenomena to the reader's own life.

In these attempts, the most important guide has been my own experience as a classroom teacher. There is little doubt that one of the best ways of learning something is to teach it, for in trying to explain to others, you first have to clarify it to yourself. This holds for the subject matter of every course I have ever taught, but most especially for the introductory course. Students in an advanced course will come at you with tough and searching questions; they want to know about the evidence that bears on a theory of, say, color vision or language acquisition, and about how that evidence was obtained. But students in an introductory course ask the toughest question of all. They ask why anyone would ever want to know about color vision (or language acquisition or whatever) in the first place. And they also ask what any one topic has to do with any other. They ask such questions because they—unlike the advanced students—have not as yet accepted the premises of the field. They wonder whether the emperor is really wearing clothes. As a result, they made me ask myself afresh what the field of psychology is all about—what the emperor's clothes are really like when you look at them more closely.

This book as well as its predecessor grew out of my attempts to answer such questions over the years in which I taught the introductory course, to answer them not only to satisfy the students but also to satisfy myself.

SUPPLEMENTARY MATERIALS

To help serve the needs of students, instuctors, and teaching assistants, several supplementary materials are available with this text.

1. *For the student:*

There is a complete *Study Guide* for students, prepared by two of my colleagues and collaborators, John Jonides of the University of Michigan and Paul Rozin of the University of Pennsylvania. This *Study Guide,* a revised version of the guide the same authors wrote for the first edition of *Psychology,* should prove very useful to students who want some help and guidance in mastering the material in the text. Moreover, for every chapter, it provides experiments and observational studies that the students can carry out on their own to get some first-hand experience with psychology's subject matter.

2. *For the instructor:*

There is an *Instructor's Manual,* prepared by Christine Massey and Hilary Schmidt of the University of Pennsylvania, Alan Silberberg of the American University, and myself, which offers specific suggestions for every textbook chapter, including discussion topics as well as demonstrations and experiments that are described in detail for easy classroom use. The manual also includes an annotated film and media guide prepared by James B. Maas of Cornell University.

John Jonides of the University of Michigan and I have prepared a *Test Item File* with the help of Susan Scanlon of Indiana University, Harvey Weingarten of

McMaster University, and Tibor Palfi of Syracuse University, whch includes questions for all chapters and the statistical appendix. This *Test Item File* is also available on computer tape. Among other features, the computer program allows the instructor to include his or her own questions.

Acknowledgments

There remains the pleasant task of thanking the many friends and colleagues who helped so greatly in the various phases of writing this book and its predecessor. Some read parts of the manuscript and gave invaluable advice and criticism. Others talked to me at length about various issues in the field which I then saw much more clearly. I am very grateful to them all. These many helpers, and the main areas in which they advised me, are as follows:

BIOLOGICAL FOUNDATIONS

Norman T. Adler *University of Pennsylvania*
Robert C. Bolles *University of Washington*
Brooks Carder
John D. Corbit *Brown University*
Alan N. Epstein *University of Pennsylvania*
Charles R. Gallistel *University of Pennsylvania*
Harvey J. Grill *University of Pennsylvania*
Jerre Levy *University of Chicago*
Martha K. McClintock *University of Chicago*
Peter M. Milner *McGill University*
Douglas G. Mook *University of Virginia*
Allen Parducci *University of California, Los Angeles*
Judith Rodin *Yale University*
Paul Rozin *University of Pennsylvania*
Jonathan I. Schull *Haverford College*
W. John Smith *University of Pennsylvania*
Paul G. Shinkman *University of North Carolina*
Edward M. Stricker *University of Pittsburgh*

ACKNOWLEDGMENTS

Ruth Ostrin *University of Pennsylvania*
Ted Suppala *University of Illinois*
Kenneth Wexler *University of California, Irvine*

SOCIAL PSYCHOLOGY

Solomon E. Asch *University of Pennsylvania*
Joel Cooper *Princeton University*
Phoebe C. Ellsworth *Stanford University*
Frederick J. Evans *Carrier Foundation, Bellemead, N.J.*
Alan Fridlund *University of Pennsylvania*
Larry Gross *University of Pennsylvania*
Michael Lessac
Clark R. McCauley, Jr. *Bryn Mawr College*
Stanley Milgram
Martin T. Orne *University of Pennsylvania*
Albert Pepitone *University of Pennsylvania*
Lee Ross *Stanford University*
John Sabini *University of Pennsylvania*
Philip R. Shaver *University of Denver*
R. Lance Shotland *Pennsylvania State University*

DEVELOPMENT

Thomas Ayres *Clarkson College of Technology*
Anne L. Brown *University of Illinois*
Justin Aronfreed *University of Pennsylvania*
Edwin Boswell
Carol S. Dweck *University of Illinois*
Margery B. Franklin *Sarah Lawrence College*
Rochel Gelman *University of Pennsylvania*
Frederick Gibbons *Iowa State University*
Philip J. Kellman *Swarthmore College*
Ellen Markman *Stanford University*
Elizabeth Spelke *University of Pennsylvania*
Douglas Wallen *Mankato State University*
Sheldon White *Harvard University*

PERSONALITY

Jack Block *Massachusetts Institute of Technology*
Lewis R. Goldberg *University of Oregon, Eugene, Oregon*
Ruben Gur *University of Pennsylvania*
Judith Harackiewicz *Columbia University*
John Kihlstrom *University of Wisconsin*
Lester B. Luborsky *University of Pennsylvania*
Carl Malmquist *University of Minnesota*
Jerry S. Wiggins *University of British Columbia*

INTELLIGENCE

James F. Crow *University of Wisconsin*
Jonathan Baron *University of Pennsylvania*
Daniel B. Keating *University of Minnesota*
Robert Sternberg *Yale University*

PSYCHOPATHOLOGY

Lyn Y. Abramson *University of Wisconsin*
Lauren Alloy *Northwestern University*

xxix

ACKNOWLEDGMENTS

Kayla F. Bernheim *Livingston County Counseling Services*
John B. Brady *University of Pennsylvania*
Gerald C. Davison *University of Southern California*
Robert J. DeRubeis *University of Pennsylvania*
Leonard M. Horowitz *Stanford University*
Steven Matthysse *McLean Hospital*
Ann James Premack *University of Pennsylvania*
Martin E. P. Seligman *University of Pennsylvania*
Larry Stein *University of California, Irvine*
Hans H. Strupp *Vanderbilt University*
Paul L. Wachtel *College of the City University of New York*
Richard Warner *University of Southern California*
David R. Williams *University of Pennsylvania*
Julius Wishner *University of Pennsylvania*

INTELLECTUAL HISTORY

Mark B. Adams *University of Pennsylvania*
Alan C. Kors *University of Pennsylvania*
Elisabeth Rozin
Harris B. Savin

To state in detail how each of these persons helped me is impossible. But I do want to express special thanks to a few of them. Among those who helped me to see whole topics in a new light for this new edition were several friends and colleagues: Robert Rescorla and Barry Schwartz for penetrating comments on the field of learning; Jacob Nachmias for wise counsel on matters sensory and perceptual; Ruth Ostrin for incisive criticism of several drafts of the chapters on language and language acquisition; Margery Franklin, Rochel Gelman, and Philip Kellman for countless and invaluable discussions of the field of development.

Yet another kind of thanks goes to Neil Macmillan who wrote "Statistics: The Collection, Organization, and Interpretation of Data," an appendix for *Psychology* which was also revised for this edition. I admired his clear exposition then, and admire it no less today.

Three persons contributed in a special way: Lyn Abramson, John Jonides, and John Sabini. All three are distinguished scientists as well as dedicated teachers with considerable experience in the introductory course. They served as an editorial advisory group who advised me on all aspects of the new edition, sharing their knowledge of the subject matter as well as their experience in communicating it to beginning students. Lyn Abramson contributed a unique combination of clinical insight and sharp, analytic reasoning, which was particularly helpful in discussions of individual differences and psychopathology. John Jonides provided sharp criticisms and new perspectives, especially in the area of cognition. John Sabini shared his wide-ranging scholarly perspective, which was of particular help in the area related to social processes. I owe a great debt to all three, and so does this edition.

To two persons I owe a special debt—in matters professional, collegial, and personal. One is my friend and colleague Paul Rozin, who served as a general adviser on this edition as he did on the previous one. He gave me many new ideas and helped me see various facets of the field in a new light, especially its biological aspects. The other is my wife, colleague, friend, and collaborator, Lila R. Gleitman, who did what she always does to the things I write and think about—she makes them better.

Several persons helped me in other ways. Annette Luzon and Linda Taylor typed repeated drafts, xeroxed many articles, checked up on many reference lists, and tried to help me remember what I always forgot. Kathy Hirsh-Passek, Philip Kellman, and Hilary Schmidt took photographs of infants and children at home and in the developmental laboratory. Further thanks go to my publisher, Norton, specifically to Roy Tedoff who managed the production of the book, to Antonina Krass who designed it, to Roberta Flechner who arranged the layouts, to Amanda Adams who helped with many aspects of the book, and to Amy Cherry and Ruth Mandel who searched for photo illustrations and always managed to find the unfindable.

I am particularly indebted to two Norton editors. One is Don Fusting, who provided constant advice and encouragement and whose personal contact with many psychology instructors throughout the entire country was of great benefit. Another is Sandy Lifland, who served as project editor throughout the entire process of writing this edition, a person of exquisite taste, great personal tact, and extraordinary judgment and competence. It was a pleasure to work with her.

My final thanks go to the man who first gave me the idea to write this book over twenty years ago: Donald Lamm of Norton. I can only repeat what I said in a previous preface: He served as sharp-eyed critic, brilliant adviser, occasional psychotherapist, and patient (oh, how patient) literary midwife; in the course of this enterprise he has become my friend. I value him greatly and owe him much.

H. G.

Merion, Pennsylvania
September 1985

Psychology

Second Edition

CHAPTER 1

Introduction

What is psychology? It is a field of inquiry that is sometimes defined as the science of mind, sometimes as the science of behavior. It concerns itself with how and why organisms do what they do. Why wolves howl at the moon and sons rebel against their fathers; why birds sing and moths fly into the flame; why we remember how to ride a bicycle twenty years after the last try; why humans speak and make love and war. All of these are behaviors and psychology is the science that studies them all.

THE SCOPE OF PSYCHOLOGY

The phenomena that psychology takes as its province cover an enormous range. Some border on biology, others touch on social sciences such as anthropology and sociology. Some concern behavior in animals, many others pertain to behavior in humans. Some are about conscious experience, others focus on what people do regardless of what they may think or feel inside. Some involve humans or animals in isolation, others concern what they do when they are in groups. A few examples will give an initial sense of the scope of the subject matter.

Electrically Triggered Images

Consider the relation between biological mechanisms and psychological phenomena. Some investigators have developed a technique of electrically stimulating the brains of human patients who were about to undergo brain surgery. Such operations are generally conducted under local rather than general anesthesia. As

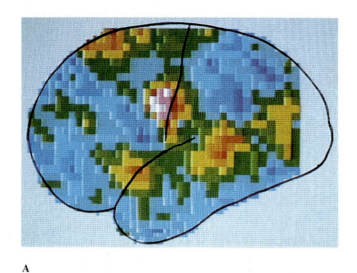

A

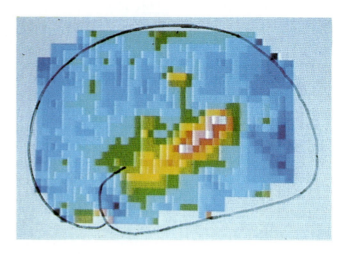

B

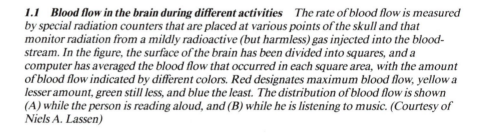

1.1   Blood flow in the brain during different activities   The rate of blood flow is measured by special radiation counters that are placed at various points of the skull and that monitor radiation from a mildly radioactive (but harmless) gas injected into the bloodstream. In the figure, the surface of the brain has been divided into squares, and a computer has averaged the blood flow that occurred in each square area, with the amount of blood flow indicated by different colors. Red designates maximum blood flow, yellow a lesser amount, green still less, and blue the least. The distribution of blood flow is shown (A) while the person is reading aloud, and (B) while he is listening to music. (Courtesy of Niels A. Lassen)

1.2   Reversible figure   Photograph of a vase celebrating the twenty-fifth year of the reign of Queen Elizabeth in 1977. Depending on how the picture is perceptually organized, we see either the vase or the profile of Queen Elizabeth and Prince Philip. (Courtesy of Kaiser Porcelain Ltd.)

a result, the patients are conscious and their reports may guide the neurosurgeon in the course of the operation.

These and other procedures have shown that different parts of the brain have different psychological functions. For example, when stimulated in certain portions of the brain, patients have visual experiences—they see streaks of color or flickering lights. When stimulated in other regions they hear clicks or buzzes. Stimulation in still other areas produces an involuntary movement of some part of the body (Penfield and Roberts, 1959; Penfield, 1975).

Related findings come from studies that look at the rate at which blood flows through different parts of the brain. When any part of the body is especially active, more blood will flow to it—to deliver oxygen and nutrients, and carry away waste products—and the brain is no exception. The question is whether the blood flow pattern depends on what the patient does. The answer is yes. When the patient reads silently, certain regions of the brain receive more blood (and are thus presumably more active) than do others. A different blood flow pattern is found when the person reads aloud, yet another when he watches a moving light, and so on (see Figure 1.1; Lassen, Ingvar, and Skinhoj, 1978).

Ambiguous Sights and Sounds

Many psychological phenomena are much further removed from issues that might be settled by biological or medical investigations. To attack them, one pro-

A

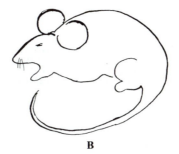

B

C

1.3 Perceptual bias *(A) An ambiguous form that can be seen either as (B) a rat or (C) a man with glasses. (After Bugelski and Alampay, 1961)*

A	B
ZYP	RED
QLEKF	BLACK
SUWRG	YELLOW
XCIDB	BLUE
WOPR	RED
ZYP	GREEN
QLEKF	YELLOW
XCIDB	BLACK
SUWRG	BLUE
WOPR	BLACK
SUWRG	RED
ZYP	YELLOW
XCIDB	GREEN
QLEKF	BLUE
WOPR	GREEN
QLEKF	BLUE
WOPR	RED
ZYP	YELLOW
XCIDB	BLACK
SWRG	GREEN

1.4 Automatization of reading *The two lists, A and B, are printed in five colors— black, blue, green, red, and yellow. To observe the Stroop effect, go down the list of nonsense words in A, and say aloud the color in which each nonsense item is printed, going from top to bottom. Then do the same for the words in list B—say the color in which each word is printed, again from top to bottom. This will probably be easier for list A than list B because we all find it hard not to read what's there to be read, even if we don't want to.*

ceeds at the psychological level alone. An example is the perception of ambiguous visual patterns. Consider Figure 1.2 which is a photograph of a vase created for Queen Elizabeth on the occasion of her Silver Jubilee. It is usually seen as a vase, but it can also be seen as the profiles of the queen and her consort, Prince Philip.

The way ambiguous figures are perceived often depends on what we have seen just before. Take Figure 1.3 which can be seen as either a rat or an amiable gentleman with glasses. If we are first shown an unambiguous figure of a rat, the ambiguous picture will be seen as a rat. If we are first exposed to an unambiguous face, the ambiguous figure will be perceived as a face.

What holds for visual patterns also holds for language. Many utterances are ambiguous. If presented out of context, they can be understood in several different ways. An example is the following sentence:

The mayor ordered the police to stop drinking.

This sentence may be a command to enforce sobriety among the population at large. It may also be a call to end drunkenness among the police force. Just how it is understood depends on the context. A prior discussion of panhandlers and skid row probably would lead to the first interpretation; a comment about alcoholism among police officers is likely to lead to the second.

Automatization

The reactions to ambiguous patterns illustrate the effects of the immediately preceding past upon our interpretations of the present. But behavior is obviously affected by the individual's entire past, of which the just preceding recent past is but a fraction. An example is the effect of acquiring skills—such as handling knife and fork, or reading and writing. With increasing practice, such skilled activities become virtually automatic; once set in motion, they are difficult to stop. When we see a billboard on the highway, we can't help but read what it says, whether we want to or not. The letters on the sign trigger a by-now automatized reading routine that can't be denied.

A striking demonstration of the automatization phenomenon is the so-called ***Stroop effect*** illustrated in Figure 1.4. In the left panel, there is a column of unrelated letter sequences printed in different colors. The subjects are asked to name the colors in which the letter sequences are printed, and to do so as quickly and accurately as they can. It's easy enough to do, and so the subjects rattle off the colors in quick succession: "red, blue, green . . ."

The task becomes vastly more difficult, however, when the subjects have to deal with the right panel of Figure 1.4. For here the letter sequences constitute words that in fact are color names. But unhappily for the subject, these names are *not* the names of the color in which the word is printed. Thus GREEN is printed in red, BLACK in blue, and so on. Under these circumstances, the subjects respond very much more slowly. They are asked to name the colors in which the letters are printed, to say: "red, blue, green . . ." But they can't help themselves from reading what the words say, that is: "yellow, green, blue . . . ," for reading is an automatized skill that can't be turned off at will. As a result, they are under a powerful conflict: the color pulls in one direction, the word pulls in the other, and so there are errors, stammers, and long hesitations.

The Perceptual World of Infants

Phenomena such as these document the enormous effect of learning on what we see and do. But this does not mean that all psychological accomplishments are acquired by past experience. Some seem to be part of the innate equipment that all of us bring into the world when we are born. An example is the infant's reaction to heights.

Crawling infants seem to be remarkably successful in noticing the precipices of everyday life. A demonstration is provided by the so-called *visual cliff*. This consists of a large glass table, which is divided in half by a wooden center board. On one side of the board, a checkerboard pattern is attached directly to the underside of the glass; on the other side, the same pattern is placed on the floor three feet below. To adults, this arrangement looks like a sudden drop-off in the center of the table. Six-month-old infants seem to see it in much the same way. When the infant is placed on the center board and called by his mother, his response depends on where she is when she beckons. When she is on the shallow side, he quickly crawls to her. But when she calls from the apparent precipice, discretion wins out over valor and the infant stays where he is (Figure 1.5).

A  B

1.5 The visual cliff (A) An infant is placed on the center board of a heavy sheet of glass and his mother calls to him. If he is on the "deep" side of the cliff, he will not crawl across the apparent cliff. (Courtesy of Richard D. Walk) (B) A similar reaction in a kitten (Courtesy of William Vandivert)

1.6 Courting birds *Birds have evolved many diverse patterns of courtship behavior that are essentially built-in and characteristic of a particular species. (A) The peacock displays his tail feathers. (Photograph by Keith Gunnar, Bruce Coleman) (B) The blue bird of paradise shows off his plumage while hanging upside down from a branch. (Photograph by B. Castes, Bruce Coleman) (C) The frigate bird puffs up his red throat pouch. (Photograph by E. R. Degginger)*

This result suggests that, to some extent at least, the perception of depth is not learned through experience, but is built into our system at the very start.

Displays

Thus far, all our examples have dealt with individuals in isolation. But much of the subject matter of psychology is inherently social. This holds for animals no less than humans. For virtually all animals interact with others of their species, whether as mates, parents, offspring, or competitors.

In animals, many social interactions depend on largely innate forms of communication. An example is courtship in birds. Many species of birds have evolved elaborate rituals whereby one sex—usually the male—woos the other. Just what this wooing consists of depends on the species. Some males court by making themselves conspicuous: The peacock spreads his magnificent tail feathers, the blue bird of paradise displays his plumage while hanging upside down from a branch, and the red frigate bird inflates his reddish throat pouch. Other males take a more romantic approach: The bower bird builds a special cabin that he decorates with colored fruit and flowers, and the males of many species offer gifts. In all cases, the fundamental message is the same: "I am a male, healthy, and willing peacock (or bird of paradise, or frigate bird, or whatever), and hope that your intentions are similar to mine" (Figure 1.6).

Such social communications are based on built-in signals called ***displays*** which are specific to a particular species. They are ways by which one individual informs another of his current intentions. Some are mating displays, as in the case of courtship displays. Others are threats ("back off or else!"; see Figure 1.7A). Still others are attempts at appeasement ("Don't hurt me. I am harmless!"). Some built-in displays form the foundation of emotional expression in humans. An example is the smile, a response found in all babies, even those born blind who couldn't have learned it by imitation. It is often considered a signal by which humans tell each other: "Be good to me. I wish you well." (See Figure 1.7B.)

1.7 Displays *(A) Threat display of the male mandrill, a large West African baboon. (Photograph by George H. Harrison, Grant Heilman) (B) The human smile. (Photograph by Suzanne Szasz)*

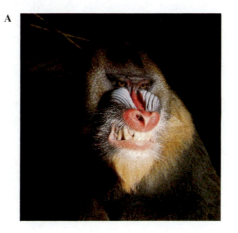

1.8   Panic   In June of 1985, a riot broke out at a soccer match in Brussels resulting in the collapse of a stadium wall that killed 38 persons and injured more than 200 others. The photo gives a glimpse of the resulting panic. (Photograph by Eamonn McCabe, The Observer)

Complex Social Behavior in Humans

Human social interactions are generally much more subtle and flexible than those of animals. Male peacocks have just one way of going courting: They spread their tail feathers and hope for the best. Human males and females are much more complex, in courtship and many other social interactions. They try one approach, and if it fails, they will try another and yet another. If these fail, too, the partners will do their best to save the other's face. For much of human social life is based on the individual's rational appraisal of how another person will respond to his own actions: "If I do this . . . he will think this . . . then I will have to do this . . . ," and so on. Such subtleties are beyond the peacock. If his usual courtship ritual fails, he has no alternate strategy. He won't try to build bowers or offer flowers; all he can do is to display his tail feathers again and again.

While human social behavior has a strong element of rationality, there are some apparent exceptions in which we seem to act with little thought or reason. This is especially likely when we are in large groups. Under some circumstances, people in crowds behave differently than they do when alone. An example is panic (see Figure 1.8). When someone shouts "Fire" in a tightly packed auditorium, the resulting stampede may claim many more victims than the fire itself would have. At the turn of the century, a Chicago theater fire claimed over six hundred victims, many of whom were smothered or trampled to death by the frantic mass behind them. In the words of a survivor, "The heel prints on the dead faces mutely testified to the cruel fact that human animals stricken by terror are as mad and ruthless as stampeding cattle" (Brown, 1965). The task for psychology is to try to understand why the crowd acted differently from the way each of its members would have acted alone.

A SCIENCE OF MANY FACES

These illustrations document the enormous range of psychology, whose territory borders on the biological sciences at one end and touches on the social sciences at the other. This broad range makes psychology a field of multiple perspectives, a science of many faces.

To make this point concrete, we will focus upon one psychological phenomenon and show how it can be approached from several different vantage points. This phenomenon is *dreams*. Dreaming is a topic interesting in its own right, but it is also an especially good illustration of how psychology approaches any single phenomenon—not just from one point of view but from several.

Let us start out by describing dreaming as we all experience it. A dream is a kind of nocturnal drama to which the only price of admission is falling asleep. It is usually a series of scenes, sometimes fairly commonplace, sometimes bizarre and disjointed, in which the dreamer often figures as a participant. While this dream play unfolds, it is generally experienced as real. It seems so real in fact, that on waking one sometimes wonders whether the dream events might have happened after all. As a Chinese sage wrote over two thousand years ago, "Once upon a time, I, Chuang-tzu, dreamed I was a butterfly, fluttering hither and thither. . . . Suddenly I was awakened. . . . Now I do not know whether I was a man dreaming I was a butterfly, or whether I am a butterfly now dreaming I am a man" (MacKenzie, 1965).

How can such delicate, transient events ever become a suitable topic for scientific inquiry?

Dreams as Mental Experiences

One way of looking at dreams is as conscious, mental experiences. According to an old account which goes back to the Greek philosopher Aristotle, the dream happenings are mental re-evocations of sights and sounds that occurred during the dreamer's waking life. Aristotle believed that the succession of these dream images from the past is experienced as real while it occurs because during sleep there is no competition from the clamor of waking reality and because the intellect is "dulled" during sleep (Aristotle, ca. 330 B.C.).

Later investigators tried to relate what people dream about to what happens to them both before and during sleep. One question concerns the effect of recent waking experiences. Aristotle was apparently correct in his belief that such recent events often re-emerge in dreams. This is especially so when the recent waking experience was highly emotional. For example, soldiers who have just gone through intense battle stress may relive their combat terrors in nightmare dreams (Pai, 1946).

Some writers have suggested that the dream images from the past are supplemented by external events that impinge upon the sleeper in the present. A widely cited example is the alarm clock which is often said to turn into a peal of church bells or a fire engine in the dream.

To test this hypothesis, several investigators have studied the effects of applying various forms of external stimulation during sleep. Numerous sleepers have been shaken, tickled, splashed with water, and shouted at—all to discover whether they would later report a dream that referred to these experiences. Sometimes they did. An example is a dream reported on awakening after an experimenter shouted "Help" into the sleeper's ears: "I was driving along the highway at home. Heard yelling and we stopped. A car was turned sideways in the road. I went down and saw the car was turned over on the side of the road. . . . There was a

Henri Rousseau, **The Dream** (Collection, the Museum of Modern Art, New York. Gift of Nelson A. Rockefeller)

woman badly cut. We took her to the hospital" (Hall, 1966, p. 6). It is hard to resist the conclusion that, at some level, the dreamer heard and understood the shout "Help" even while asleep and then incorporated it within his dream narrative.

Dreams as Behavior

Dreams as conscious, mental experiences are essentially private; they go on "inside" the individual. As such, dreams can be regarded as a form of behavior that is looked at from within, as if the actor were observing his own actions. Yet psychologists study most aspects of behavior from "outside," for much of what we do is directly apparent and overt and can therefore easily be seen by others. Humans and animals act. They run and fly and scurry about; they eat and fight and mate; they often perform new acts to attain their ends.

OVERT BEHAVIOR

Can we study dreaming by taking this action-oriented view from the outside? On the face of it, the prospects don't seem too bright, for during sleep the body is by and large immobile. Even so, there is a way. For there is one thing that the sleeper does while dreaming that is overt and can be observed from the outside: He moves his eyes.

This fact emerged after it became clear that there are two kinds of sleep: quiet sleep and active sleep. During quiet sleep, both breathing and heart rate are slow and regular while the eyes are motionless. But during active sleep the pattern is different. Breathing and heart rate accelerate, and—most characteristic of all—the eyes move back and forth behind closed eyelids in quick irregular darts. Periods of quiet and of active sleep (often called REM sleep because of the rapid eye

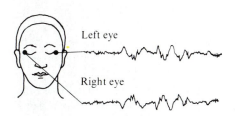

1.9 Quiet and active sleep *Record of eye movements picked up by electrodes at the side of each eye. The record shows the eye-movement pattern during active sleep, the period when sleepers dream. Both eyes move rapidly and in synchrony. (After Dement, 1974)*

AWAKE

QUIET SLEEP:

REM SLEEP (dreaming)

1.10 Sleep and the EEG *The figure shows EEG records during waking, during increasingly deep stages of quiet sleep, and during active sleep. (Courtesy of William C. Dement)*

movements) alternate throughout the night, with a total of perhaps ninety minutes devoted to REM (Figure 1.9).

The crucial fact about REM sleep is that this is the period during which dreams occur. When subjects—the persons whose behavior is being studied—are aroused during REM sleep, about 85 percent of the awakenings lead to reports of a vivid dream. In contrast, subjects awakened from non-REM sleep recall dreams much less often (Dement, 1974).

There is little doubt that the rapid eye movements go along with dreaming. But some investigators take a further step. They suggest that these movements provide a clue to what the sleeper is dreaming of. In their view, the eye movements indicate that the sleeper is "looking at" whatever he sees in his dream world. Some evidence for this intriguing (though quite controversial) hypothesis comes from studies which show that the direction of the eye movements observed during a given REM period is appropriate to what the subject recalls having seen while dreaming. For example, when the predominant direction of eye movements was up and down, one subject dreamed that he had thrown basketballs, looking up at the net and shooting, then looking down to pick another ball off the floor. In contrast, another REM period in which the eye movements were mostly from side to side, produced a dream in which the subject watched two people throwing tomatoes at each other (Dement and Kleitman, 1957).

BIOLOGICAL UNDERPINNINGS OF BEHAVIOR

Evidence based on eye movements is one clue to the nature of dreaming. Another clue concerns its biological basis. Most psychologists take it for granted that whatever we do or think has some physical basis in the activity of our brains. Some promising first steps in this direction pertain to dreams. These came after the development of a number of methods for monitoring what people do when they are fast asleep. An important tool is the electroencephalogram, or EEG, which measures the overall activity of the sleeper's brain. The EEG traces the quick fluctuations of electrical activity over time, and its graphic record is sometimes called brain waves. Happily for sleep investigators, it soon proved possible to attach the multitude of required electrodes to the subjects without disturbing their sleep (Figure 1.10).

The results showed that the EEG patterns of sleep and waking differ markedly. As the subject falls into deeper and deeper stages of sleep, the brain waves become slow, large, and rather regular, indicating a lower level of brain activity. But this only holds for periods of quiet sleep. As this is interrupted by active (that is REM) sleep, the EEG becomes quite similar to that found when the subject is awake. This makes good sense, for it suggests that during REM sleep the brain is reasonably aroused and active—as well it should be since this is the time when we are busily engaged in dreaming.

Dreams as Cognition

Like many other psychological phenomena, dreams reflect what we know, what we have experienced, remembered, or thought about—activities that psychologists call cognition. To be sure, the dream happenings didn't really take place. We didn't really fly through the air or have tea with Queen Elizabeth. But the components of the dream were surely drawn from the dreamer's own knowledge, which contains information about flying and the queen of England. How was this knowledge retrieved and woven into the dream story? How was the dream recalled on later awakening? And why is it that most of us remember so few of our dreams?

Some psychologists have tried to attack these and related questions by asking about the factors that make for better dream recall. They have come up with some evidence that people who remember more of their dreams are more likely to have better and sharper visual mental images in their waking life; perhaps their dreams are more memorable because they are experienced in a more vivid pictorial form (Cory et al., 1975). Another factor is the extent to which the dream experience is interfered with by what happens immediately after the sleeper awakes. In one study, subjects were asked to call the weather bureau immediately after waking up; after this, they had to write down a detailed description of any dreams they had that night. The results showed that weather reports and dreams don't mix. The subjects who made the call generally remembered that they had had a dream, but most of them could not remember what it was that they had dreamed about (Cohen and Wolfe, 1973).

Dreams and Social Behavior

Human life is rarely solitary but is spent among a world of others—strangers and friends, partners and rivals, potential and actual mates. What holds for waking existence, holds for dreams as well. Most of them involve interaction with others. Some feature themes of aggression, such as competition, attack, and submission. Others concern friendship and sometimes sex. But whatever the plot, the cast usually includes some others. More than 95 percent of our dreams are peopled with others, and most revolve around our relations with them (Hall and Van de Castle, 1966).

DREAMS AND THE CULTURE

Dreams concern major themes in the person's own life, but they take place within a larger framework, the dreamer's own culture. In our own society, a common dream is of appearing naked among strangers and being embarrassed. But such a dream would be unlikely among Australian aborigines who wear no clothing. Nor are many urban Americans likely to have nightmares in which they are chased by cows, which happens to be a common dream in western Ghana (Barnouw, 1963).

The culture affects not only what the dream is about but also how the dreamer thinks about it when she recalls it later on. In some societies, including our own, dreams are generally dismissed as nonsensical fancies, irrelevant to real life. Many preliterate cultures have a different view (Figure 1.11). Some regard dreams as supernatural visions and behave accordingly. Others take dreams very seriously even though they think of them as naturally occurring events. The Senoi, a tribe in Malaya, act as if they had all taken several courses in psychoanalysis. They believe that dreams indicate something about their inner lives and can provide clues for heading off problems before they become serious. Every morning Senoi children tell their father what they had dreamed about the night before.

1.11 Iroquois cornhusk mask for dream ceremony   The Iroquois Indians regarded dreams as an important means for revealing hidden desires and held formal dream-remembering ceremonies during which special masks were worn. (Courtesy the Smithsonian Institution)

The father then helps the children interpret their dreams. These may reveal some incipient conflict with others, as in a dream of being attacked by a friend. If so, the father may advise the child on how to correct matters, for example, by making his friend a present (Stewart, 1951).

DREAMS AND INTERNAL CONFLICT

The social aspect of dreaming lies at the heart of a famous (and controversial) theory of dreams proposed by Sigmund Freud. According to Freud, dreams are the product of an elaborate clash between two contending forces—the unconscious primitive urges of our biological heritage and the civilizing constraints imposed by society. In dreams we sometimes see one, sometimes the other side of the battle. Various forbidden impulses—mostly sex and aggression—emerge, but they are soon opposed by the thou-shalt-nots of our early upbringing. The result is a compromise. The forbidden material breaks through but only in a stealthy, censored masquerade. This disguise explains why dreams are so often odd and senseless. Their senselessness is only on the surface, a cunning mask that lets us indulge in the unacceptable wish without realizing that it is unacceptable (Freud, 1900).

According to Freud, some distortions involve various transformations of the unacceptable themes. One is symbolism. For example, he believed that sexual urges often emerge in symbolic guises. Thus, in his view, dreams of riding horses or walking up a staircase often mask erotic wishes. Here the symbols presumably bear some resemblance to that which they symbolize. The rhythmic movements of rising and falling in the saddle are similar to those of sexual intercourse, while ascending a staircase may be reminiscent of the way in which sexual passion mounts to a peak (Figure 1.12).

Freud argued that these and many other symbolic transformations are the dreamer's way of smuggling the forbidden wish past the inner censor's eye. He believed that such defenses refer back to early childhood when the parents set up the

1.12 Symbolism in dreams A film about Freud's early career includes a dream sequence in which he enters a deep tunnel that eventually leads him to a cavern where his mother sits, smiling, on a Cleopatra-like throne. The dream is a compact symbolic expression of how Freud saw himself: an explorer of subterranean unconscious motives who uncovered the hidden childhood lusts of all men and women. (From John Huston's 1963 film, Freud, *with Montgomery Clift. Courtesy The Museum of Modern Art/Film Stills Archive)*

various prohibitions that still haunt the adult in the present. Seen in this light, dreams reflect important social processes that pertain to the past, to the way in which the major social commandments were instilled in each of us by society's first agents, our parents.

Dreams and Human Development

Thus far we have discussed dreams as they are experienced by adults. But of course dreams occur in childhood as well as in adulthood. Psychologists who are concerned with the course of human mental development have considered the different ways in which children and adults think about their dreams.

Developmental psychologists want to know how children acquire the basic intellectual operations that are part of adult human thought—how they learn to count, to understand that events have causes, and so on. For example, they ask how children learn that there is a difference between two realms of phenomena, those which we call subjective (thoughts, beliefs, and of course, dreams) and those which we call objective (the world of tangible things "out there"). To ask how this distinction is made is another way of asking how we attain our adult notion of objective reality, how we come to know that the tree in the garden—unlike a dream —will still be there after we blink our eyes.

This distinction is by no means clear in early childhood. Thus young children initially have great trouble in distinguishing dreams from waking life. A three-year-old awakes and tells her parents how much she loved the elephants at the circus yesterday. The parents correct her; she had not been at the circus yesterday. But the child indignantly sticks to her story and appeals to her brother for corroboration, for "he was there too." When her brother shakes his head in denial, she begins to cry, angrily insisting that she told the truth. Eventually she learns that there is a whole group of experiences that older people call "just dreams," no matter how real they seem to her (Levy, J., 1979).

The fact that the child finally recognizes the circus elephants—and the nightmare robbers and witches—as dreams does not mean that she has acquired an adult conception of what dreams are. Young children tend to think of them as physical objects. When asked whether dreams can be tall, a four-year-old replied, "*Yeah.* How tall? *Big, big, big* (spreads arms). Where are dreams? *In your bedroom.* In the daytime? *No, they're outside. . . .* What are they like? *They're made of rock.* Could they be heavy? *Yeah; and they can't break either*" (Keil, 1979, pp. 109–10).

It's quite a while before children think of dreams the way adults do. By six or seven, they believe that dreams are sent through the air, perhaps by the wind or by pigeons. Eventually of course they recognize that, as one eleven-year-old put it, "You dream *with the head* and the dream is *in the head*" (Piaget, 1972).

This realization that dreams are subjective events is no mean achievement. As we will see later, it is not limited to dreams, but extends to many other conceptual attainments about the basic nature of the physical and psychological universe.

Dreams and Individual Differences

There is a further aspect of dreams: they are a reflection of the fact that people are different. People vary in what they characteristically do and think and feel. And

That very night in Max's room a forest grew

and grew—

The distinction between dreams and waking reality is not always clear in childhood *(From Sendak, 1963)*

Wilhelm Wundt (1832–1920) *(Courtesy Historical Pictures Service, Chicago)*

William James (1842–1910) *(Courtesy The Warder Collection)*

some of these differences between people are reflected in their dreams. Some simply pertain to the differing circumstances in the dreamers' lives. This point was made some two thousand years ago by the Roman poet Lucretius who noted that at night lawyers plead their cases, generals fight their battles, and sailors wage their war with the winds (Woods, 1947).

More interesting are differences that reveal something about the personalities of the dreamers. An example is a comparison between the dreams of normal people and of patients with a diagnosis of schizophrenia, a condition generally regarded as the most serious psychiatric disorder in our time. The difference between the two groups was enormous. The schizophrenics reported dreams that were highly bizarre and often morbid. The dreamer is eaten alive by an alligator; there are nuclear wars and world cataclysms. Themes of bodily mutilation were fairly common, as in a dream in which a woman killed her husband and then stuffed parts of his body into a camel's head. In contrast, the normals' dreams were comparatively mild and ordinary. This result fits in with what we know about schizophrenia. Schizophrenics often jump from one idea to the other without maintaining a firm line of thought. As a result, their behavior often appears bizarre. It seems that their extremely bizarre and morbid dreams are simply an exaggeration of a condition already present in their waking life (Carrington, 1972).

THE TASK OF PSYCHOLOGY

We have seen that dreams can be looked at as conscious, mental experiences, as overt behaviors, as aspects of cognition, as indications of social patterns, as reflections of human development, and as expressions of the dreamer's individuality. What holds for dreams holds for most other psychological phenomena: They can all be viewed from several perspectives. Each perspective is valid but none is complete without the others, for psychology is a field of many faces and to see it fully, we must see them all.

Given the many-faceted character of psychology, it is not surprising that those who have contributed to it came from many quarters. Some had the proper title of psychologist with appropriate university appointments in that discipline, including two of its founding fathers, Wilhelm Wundt of Germany and William James of the United States. But psychology was not built by psychologists alone. Far from it. Among its architects are philosophers, beginning with Plato and Aristotle and continuing to our own time. Physicists and physiologists played important roles and still do. Physicians contributed greatly, as did specialists in many other disciplines, including anthropology, and more recently, linguistics and computer science. Psychology, the field of many faces, is by its very nature a field of many origins.

In presenting the subject matter of psychology as it is today, we must try to do justice to this many-sidedness. In an attempt to achieve that, this book has been organized around five topics that emphasize somewhat different perspectives on the field as a whole. These five mirror the different ways in which we have just looked at dreams: action, cognition, social behavior, development, and individual differences.

General Principles and Unique Individuals

Before starting, a word about a widespread misunderstanding. Psychology is sometimes popularly regarded as a field that concentrates on the secret inner lives of individual persons—why Mary hates her mother and why George is so shy with girls. But questions of this sort are really not psychology's main concern. To be sure, there is an applied branch of psychology that deals with various adjustment problems, but it is only a special part of the field. The primary questions psychology asks are of a more general sort. Its purpose is not to describe the distinctive characteristics of a particular individual. Its main goal is to get at the facts that are general for all of humankind.

The reason is simple. Psychology is a science and, like all other sciences, it looks for general principles—underlying uniformities that different events have in common. A single event as such means little; what counts is what any one event—or object or person—shares with others. Ultimately of course, psychology—again, like all other sciences—hopes to find a route back to understand the individual event. It tries to discover, say, some general principles of adolescent conflict or parent-child relations to explain why George is so shy and why Mary is so bitter about her mother. Once such explanations are found, they may lead to practical applications: to help counsel and guide, and perhaps to effect desirable changes. But, at least initially, the science's main concern is with the discovery of the general principles.

Is there any field of endeavor whose primary interest is in individual persons, with the unique George and Mary who are like no other persons that ever lived or ever will live? One such field is literature. The great novelists and playwrights have given us portraits of living, breathing individuals who exist in a particular time and place. There is nothing abstract and general about the agonies of a Hamlet or the murderous ambition of a Macbeth. These are concrete, particular individuals, with special loves and fears that are peculiarly theirs. But from these particulars, Shakespeare gives us a glimpse of what is common to all humanity, what Hamlet and Macbeth share with all of us. Both science and art have something to say about human nature, but they go about it from different directions. Science tries to discover general principles and then applies them to the individual case. Art focuses on the particular instance and then uses this to illuminate what is universal in us all.

Science and art are complementary. To gain insight into our own nature we need both. Consider Hamlet's description:

> What a piece of work is a man, how noble in reason, how infinite in faculties; in form and moving how express and admirable, in action like an angel, in apprehension like a god: the beauty of the world, the paragon of animals! (*Hamlet,* Act II, scene ii).

To understand and appreciate this "piece of work" is a task too huge for any one field of human endeavor, whether art, philosophy, or science. What we will try to do here is to sketch psychology's own attempts toward this end, to show what we have come to know and how we have come to know it. And perhaps even more important, how much we have not learned as yet.

We will begin with the topic of action. Our first question is what makes humans and animals move.

PART I

Action

The study of mind has many aspects. We may ask what human beings know, we may ask what they want, and we may ask what they do. Much of psychology is an attempt to answer the last question: What is it that humans do and why do they do it? In this section we will deal with the approach to mind that grows out of an interest in what all animals do, an approach that emphasizes behavior as the basic subject matter of psychology. We will focus on the particular version of this approach that is based on the notion that mind can be understood as a reflex machine. We shall see how the reflex notion has led to impressive achievements in our understanding of the structure and function of the nervous system, and how this notion has been modified to encompass the phenomena of motivation and of learning in animals and humans.

CHAPTER 2

Biological Bases of Behavior

The ancients, no less than we, wondered why men and beasts behave as they do. What is it that leads to animal movement, impels the crab to crawl, the tiger to spring? Prescientific man could only answer *animistically:* There is some inner spirit in the creature that impels it to move, each creature in its own fashion. Today we know that any question about bodily movement must inevitably call for some reference to the nervous system; for to us it is quite clear that the nervous system is the apparatus which most directly determines and organizes an organism's reactions to the world in which it lives. We will soon ask many detailed questions about the structure of this apparatus and the way it functions. But we begin with a more general question. Broadly speaking, what must such a system accomplish?

THE ORGANISM AS MACHINE

René Descartes (Courtesy National Library of Medicine)

This question was first raised seriously by the French philosopher René Descartes (1596–1650), and his answer provides the broad outline within which we think about such matters even now. Descartes lived in a period that saw the beginning of the science of mechanics. Kepler and Galileo were beginning to develop ideas about the movements of the heavenly bodies which some thirty years later led to Newton's *Principia.* Radically new views of man and his universe were being put forth. There were laws of nature that determined the fall of stones and the motions of planets: rigid, precise, and immutable. The universe was run by a system of pushes and pulls originally set in motion by God, the Great Watchmaker. At a more lowly level, these natural laws were mirrored in the workings of ingenious mechanical contrivances that were all the rage in the wealthy homes of Europe:

2.1   Reflex action as envisaged by Descartes   *In this sketch by Descartes, the heat from the fire, A, starts a chain of processes that begins at the affected spot of the skin, B, and continues up the nerve tube until a pore of a cavity, F, is opened. Descartes believed that this opening allowed the animal spirits in the cavity to enter the nerve tube and eventually travel to the muscles which pull the foot from the fire. While the figure shows that Descartes anticipated the basic idea of reflex action, it also indicates that he did not realize the anatomical distinction between sensory and motor nerves. (From Descartes, 1662)*

clocks with cuckoos that would call the hour, water-driven gargoyles with nodding heads, statues in the king's garden that would bow to the visitor who stepped on a hidden spring. The action of a lever, the release of a spring—these could explain the operation of such devices. Could human thought and action be explained in similar mechanical terms?

Descartes and the Reflex Concept

To Descartes all action, whether human or animal, was essentially a response to some event in the outside world. His human machine would work as follows. Something from the outside excites one of the senses. This transmits the excitation upward to the brain, which then relays the excitation downward to a muscle. The excitation from the senses thus eventually leads to a contraction of a muscle and thereby to a reaction to the external event which started the whole sequence. In effect, the energy from the outside is *reflected* back by the nervous system to the animal's muscles—the term ***reflex*** finds its origin in this conception (Figure 2.1).

Conceived thus, human doings could be regarded as the doings of a machine. But there was a problem. The same external event produces one reaction today and another tomorrow. The sight of food leads to reaching movements, but only when we are hungry. In short, the excitation from one of the senses will excite a nerve leading to one muscle on one occasion, but on another occasion it will excite a different nerve that may move an entirely different muscle. This means that Descartes's mechanism must have a central switching system, supervised by some operator who sits in the middle to decide what incoming pipe to connect with which pipe leading to the outside.

To describe these behavioral options mechanically was very difficult. Descartes was deeply religious and he was extremely concerned over the theological implications of his argument should he bring it to its ultimate conclusion. In addition he was prudent—Galileo had difficulties with the Inquisition because his scientific beliefs threatened the doctrines of the Church. So Descartes proposed that human mental processes were only semiautomatic. To handle the switching function he provided a soul (operating through a particular structure in the brain), which would affect the choice of possible nervous pathways.

Descartes shrank from taking the last step in his own argument, the reduction of human beings to the status of machines. Animals might be machines, but humans were more than mere robots. Later thinkers went further. They felt that the laws of the physical universe could ultimately explain all action, whether human or animal, so that a scientific account required no further "ghost in the machine"—that is, no reference to the soul. They ruthlessly extended Descartes's logic to human beings, arguing that humans differ from animals only in being more finely constructed mechanisms (Figure 2.2).

The Basic Nervous Functions: Reception, Integration, Reaction

Psychologists today agree with Descartes that much of behavior can be understood as reactions to outside events: The environment poses a question and the organism answers it. This approach, like Descartes's, must lead to a tripartite

A

B

2.2 Automata in the eighteenth century (A) A mechanical "scrivener" who could dip a pen into an inkwell and write a number of words. (B) The scrivener's mechanical insides. (Courtesy Musée d'Art et d'Histoire, Neuchâtel, Switzerland)

classification of nervous functions: *reception* through the senses, *reaction* from the muscles and glands, and a *conduction* and *integration* system that mediates between these two functions.

The chain of events that leads to action typically begins outside of the organism. A particular physical energy impinges upon some part of the organism sensitive to it. This event we call a *stimulus* (a term that derives from the name of a wooden implement with a nail at one end used by Roman farmers some two thousand years ago to goad their sluggish oxen). The stimulus excites *receptors,* specialized structures capable of translating some physical energy into a nervous impulse. Once a receptor is stimulated, the excitation is conducted farther into the nervous system. Bundles of nerve fibers that conduct excitation toward the brain or spinal cord are called *afferent nerves* (from the Latin, *affere,* "to bring to"). These fibers transmit their message still farther; in the simplest case, to other fibers that go directly to the *effectors,* the muscles and glands that are the organs of action. Nerve fibers that lead to the effectors are called *efferent nerves* (from the Latin, *effere,* "to bring forth").

The transmission path from receptors to effectors is usually more circuitous than this, however. The afferent fibers often bring their messages to intermediate nerve cells, or *interneurons,* in the brain or spinal cord. These interneurons may transmit the message to the efferent nerve cells or send it on to yet other interneurons. Typically, many thousands of such interneurons have been "consulted" before the command to action is finally issued and sent down the path of the efferent nerve fibers.

We now turn to a more detailed discussion of the nervous system. We will deal with progressively larger units of analysis, first discussing the smallest functional and structural units of nervous activity (the nerve impulse and the nerve cell), then the interaction among different nerve cells (the synapse), and finally, the functional plan of the major structures of the nervous system.

NERVE CELL AND NERVE IMPULSE

Neuroscientists know that the basic building block of the nervous system is the nerve cell or *neuron,* and that the basic unit of nervous function is the *nerve impulse,* the firing of an individual neuron. This impulse is today considered in physical and chemical terms. But this conception was not attained for centuries. Animistic conceptions of nerve function were not easily abandoned and the ghost in the machine was not exorcised until the nineteenth century.

From Animal Spirits to Nerve Impulse

It was known even in ancient times that bodily motion depends upon the muscles. But what makes the muscles move? The Greeks proposed an immaterial soul *(anima)* that "animated" the body but was made of different stuff. By 100 A.D. it was clear enough that the whitish threads called nerve fibers were somehow critical. The Roman physician Galen proposed that the critical agent was a gaseous substance, the *animal spirits,* distilled from the blood in the brain and transmitted through the nerves to the muscles.

Galen's views were frozen into a medical dogma which prevailed until the seventeenth century. This doctrine was accepted even by Descartes, although evidence against it was gradually being accumulated. The most convincing argument was raised finally by the Dutch naturalist Jan Swammerdam (1637–1680), who removed a frog's leg muscle together with a piece of the nerve connected to it. He found that if the nerve is pinched or irritated, the muscle will contract. Swammerdam then asked whether the muscle increases in volume while contracting. After all, if contraction is caused by animal spirits that enter the muscle, there should be an increase of volume; the muscle should expand as does a balloon when inflated by air. But nothing of the kind took place. Given this finding, the concept of animal spirits became difficult to entertain.

Animal spirits were rejected, but what was to take their place? No one could deny that muscular contraction depended on transmission of an impulse. No matter how strong the stimulus, a muscle whose nerves were cut would not contract. But if no "substance" was transmitted through these nerves, how then did they carry their message to the muscles? In 1780, the Italian scientist Luigi Galvani found that when a frog's severed leg is touched by two wires, each of which is connected to a different metal (thus forming what we now know is an electric battery), the leg muscle twitches. This discovery paved the way for the recognition that the nerve impulse is at bottom electrical. While the details of this process took two more centuries to unravel, it was already clear that nerve transmission no longer needed be conceived in spiritual, nonsubstantial terms but could be explained in terms of the same physical laws that govern the rest of the universe.

Before turning to modern conceptions of the nervous impulse, we must take a brief detour into anatomy to consider the microscopic structure in which this impulse occurs—the neuron.

The Neuron

The neuron is the simplest element of nervous action. It is a single cell, with three subdivisions: the *dendrites,* the *cell body,* and the *axon.* The dendrites are usually branched, sometimes enormously so. The axon may extend for a very long distance, and its end may fork out into several end branches. Impulses from other cells are received by the dendrites; the axon transmits the impulse to yet other

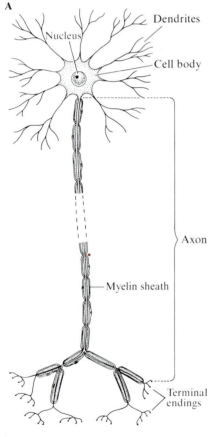

A

Dendrites

Nucleus

Cell body

Axon

Myelin sheath

Terminal endings

2.3 Neurons (A) A schematic diagram of the main parts of a "typical" neuron. Part of the cell is myelinated; that is, its axon is covered with a segmented, insulating sheath. (After Katz, 1952) (B) Highly magnified nerve cell in the human brain showing cell body and several dendrites. The long diagonal bands are branches from other nerve cells. (Nilsson, 1974)

B

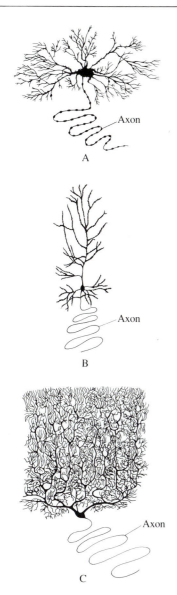

2.4   Different kinds of neurons in the human nervous system   *(A) A motor neuron of the spinal cord. (B) A neuron in the cerebral cortex, the part of the brain concerned with such higher mental functions as perception and memory. (C) A specialized neuron in the cerebellum, a part of the brain which controls motor coordination. This kind of cell has been said to gather impulses from as many as 80,000 other neurons. (After Kolb and Whishaw, 1980)*

neurons or to effector organs such as muscles and glands. Thus, the dendrites are the receptive units of the neuron, while the axon endings may be regarded as its effector apparatus (see Figure 2.3).

A few details about neurons will give a feeling for their size and number. The diameter of an individual neuron is very small; cell bodies vary from 5 to about 100 microns in diameter (1 micron = 1/1,000 millimeter). Dendrites are typically short; say, a few hundred microns. The axons of motor neurons can be very long; some extend from the head to the base of the spinal cord, others from the spinal cord to the fingers and toes. To get a sense of the relative physical proportions of the cell body to the axon in a motoneuron, visualize a basketball attached to a garden hose that stretches the whole fourteen-mile length of Manhattan Island. The total number of neurons in the human nervous system has been estimated to be over a 100 billion. While this number seems prodigious, it is somewhat sobering to realize that there is no way of getting more, at least in adulthood; a neuron, once lost, can never be replaced.

The gap between the axon terminals of one neuron and the dendrites and cell body of another is called the *synapse;* this is the gap the nerve impulse must cross for one neuron to stimulate the next. Such junctions often involve many more than two cells, especially in the brain.

TYPES OF NEURONS

Different kinds of neurons are specialized for different tasks. We will mention only a few of the varieties. Some neurons are attached to specialized *receptor cells* that can respond to various external energies, such as pressure, chemical changes, light, and so on. These receptor cells can translate (more technically, *transduce*) such physical stimuli into electrical changes, which will then trigger a nervous impulse in other neurons. Receptor cells are like money changers, exchanging the various energies impinging from the other world into the only currency acceptable within the nervous system—the nervous impulse.

Neurons that convey impulses from receptors toward the rest of the nervous system are called *sensory neurons.* Sometimes the receptor is a specialized part of the sensory neuron; an example is the neurons that are responsible for sensing pressure on the skin. But in many cases, transduction and transmission are separate functions that are entrusted to different cells. In vision and hearing, there are receptor cells which transduce optic stimulation and air pressures into electrical changes in the cell. These changes in the receptors trigger impulses in sensory neurons that then transmit their information to other neurons in the nervous system.

Other neurons have axons that terminate in effector cells. An important example is the *motoneurons* which activate the *skeletal musculature,* the muscles which control the skeleton, such as those of the arms and legs. The cell bodies of the motoneurons are in the spinal cord or brain, and their long axons have terminal branches whose final tips contact individual muscle cells. When a motoneuron fires, a chemical event is produced at its axon tips which causes the muscle fibers to contract.

In complex organisms, the vast majority of nerve cells are *interneurons,* which have a functional position that is between sensory neurons and motoneurons. Interneurons come in many shapes and forms. They usually show considerable branching, which produces an enormous number of synaptic contacts (see Figure 2.4).

THE ELECTRICAL ACTIVITY OF THE NEURON

The description of the electrical events that occur when a neuron fires required several advances in scientific instrumentation. One of these was the development of ever finer **microelectrodes,** some of which have tips tapered to a diameter of 1 micron. Such electrodes can pick up currents from within a neuron without squashing the cell they are supposed to study. Equally important was the development of the **oscilloscope,** a device whose electrical response is amplified by vacuum tubes which send forth a stream of electrons that are swept across a fluorescent screen, leaving a glowing line in their wake. The pattern on the screen indicates what happened electrically during the entire (very brief) interval of the cell's activity. Yet another contribution was made by evolution, which provided the squid, an animal that contains several axons with giant diameters up to 1 millimeter—a great convenience for electrophysiological work on the nervous impulse.

Resting and action potentials Figure 2.5 shows how one microelectrode is inserted on the inside of a squid axon while the other records from the surface of the fiber. In this manner one can record the **electrical potential** (the voltage) across the cell membrane. One fact emerges immediately. There is a difference in potential between the inside and the outside of the fiber when the cell is at "rest" (that is, not firing). The inside is electrically negative with respect to the outside. This **resting potential** is about −70 millivolts relative to the outside of the cell. This means that in its normal state the cell membrane is **polarized.** Its outside and inside are like the electrical poles of a miniature battery, with the outside positive and the inside negative.

What happens when the neuron is aroused from rest? To find out, the surface of the fiber is stimulated by means of a third microelectrode which applies a brief electrical pulse. This pulse reduces the potential across the membrane for a brief instant. If the pulse is weak, nothing further will happen; there is no impulse. If the strength of the pulse is slowly increased, the resting potential drops still more, but there is still no impulse. This continues until the pulse is strong enough to decrease the potential to a critical point, the **threshold.**

Now a new phenomenon occurs. The potential suddenly collapses; in fact, it overshoots the zero mark and for a brief moment the axon interior becomes posi-

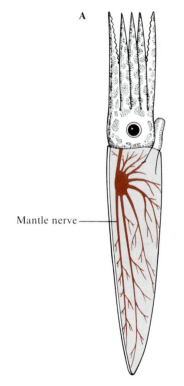

2.5 The nerve impulse and the squid *(A) A drawing of the nerve in the squid that contains the giant axons. When dissected from the animal and placed in sea water, the axons will conduct nerve impulses for 12 hours or so. (Eccles, 1973) (B) A schematic drawing of how the impulse is recorded. One electrode is inserted into the axon, the other records from the axon's outside. (After Keynes, 1958)*

A

Mantle nerve

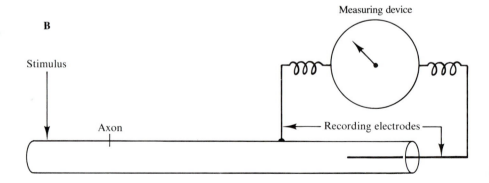

B

Measuring device

Stimulus

Axon

Recording electrodes

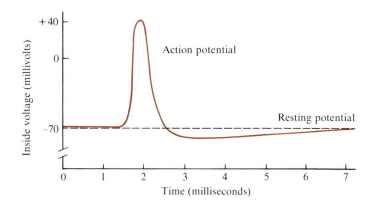

2.6 *The action potential* Action potential recorded from the squid giant axon. (After Hodgkin and Huxley, 1939)

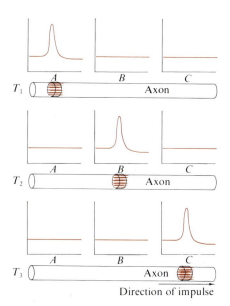

2.7 *The action potential as it travels along the axon* The axon is shown at three different moments in time—T_1, T_2, and T_3—after the application of a stimulus. The electrical potential is shown at three different points along the axon, A, B, and C.

tive relative to the outside. This brief flare lasts about 1 millisecond and quickly subsides. The potential then returns to the resting state. This entire sequence of electrical events is called the ***action potential*** (Figure 2.6).

The action potential is recorded from only one small region of the axon. What happens elsewhere in the fiber? Consider Figure 2.7. An ***adequate stimulus***—that is, one which is above threshold—is applied to point A and the potential is measured at points A, B, and C. At first, an action potential is observed at A; at that time B and C are still at rest. A bit later, A returns to normal, while B shows the action potential. Still later, B returns to normal but an action potential is found at C. (Of course, these time intervals are exceedingly brief.) The change of potential is evidently infectious: each region sets off its neighbor much as a spark travels along a fuse. (These phenomena are based on physical and chemical interactions at the cell membrane that are beyond the scope of this book.)

The all-or-none law   One point must be stressed. The size of the reaction is unaffected by the intensity of the stimulus, once the stimulus is at threshold level or above. Increasing the stimulus value above this level will not increase the intensity of the action potential or affect its speed of conduction to other points in the fiber. This phenomenon is sometimes referred to as the ***all-or-none law*** of neuron stimulation. The all-or-none law clearly implies that the stimulus does not provide the energy for the nervous impulse. It serves as a trigger and no more. Given that the trigger is pulled hard enough, pulling yet harder has no effect. Like a gun, a neuron either fires or does not fire. It knows no in-between.

STIMULUS INTENSITY

We have seen that the axon obeys the all-or-none law. It appears that stimulus intensity has no effect once threshold is passed. Does this law make sense? Much of our everyday experience seems to deny it. We can obviously tell the difference between the buzz of a mosquito and the roar of a jet plane, even though both sounds are above threshold. How can we square such facts with the all-or-none law?

The number of neurons stimulated   In many cases what happens is that the more intense stimulus excites a greater number of neurons. This is precisely what we should expect, for we know that different neurons vary enormously in their

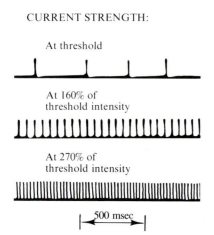

CURRENT STRENGTH:

At threshold

At 160% of
threshold intensity

At 270% of
threshold intensity

|← 500 msec →|

**2.8 Stimulus intensity and firing
frequency** *Responses of a crab axon to a
continuous electric current at three levels
of current intensity. The time scale is
relatively slow. As a result, the action potentials show up as single vertical lines or
"spikes." Note that while increasing the
current intensity has no effect on the
height of the spikes (the all-or-none law) it
leads to a marked increase in the frequency of spikes per second. (After Eccles,
1973)*

thresholds. Thus, a strong stimulus will stimulate more neurons than a weak
stimulus. The weak stimulus will stimulate all neurons whose thresholds are
below a given level; the strong stimulus will stimulate all of those, plus others
whose threshold is higher.

Frequency of impulse   While remaining strictly obedient to the all-or-none law,
the individual neuron is nevertheless affected by stimulus intensity. This becomes apparent when we apply a continuous stimulus for somewhat longer intervals. Now we obtain not one impulse but a whole volley. We notice that the size of
the action potentials remains the same whatever the stimulus intensity. What
changes instead is the impulse frequency. The stronger the stimulus, the more
often the axon will fire. This effect holds until we reach a maximum rate of firing,
after which further increases in intensity have no effect (Figure 2.8). Different
neurons have different maximum rates; the highest in man is of the order of
1,000 impulses per second.

INTERACTION AMONG NERVE CELLS

In a way, the neurons of our nervous system are like 100 billion speakers, endlessly prattling and chattering to one another. But each of them has only one
word with which to tell its story, the one and only word it can utter. It can choose
only whether to speak its word or keep silent, and whether to speak it often or
more rarely. Looked at in isolation, the individual speakers seem like imbeciles
with a one-word vocabulary, babbling and being babbled at. But when taken as a
whole, this gibbering becomes somehow harmonious. The trick is in the integration of the individual messages, the interplay of the separate components. The
really interesting question for psychology, then, is not how a neuron manages to
produce its word, but rather how it can talk to others and how it can listen.

The Reflex

To study the interactions among different neurons, we begin with the simplest illustration of such interactions—the ***reflex.*** Descartes had pointed out that some
of our actions are automatic—controlled by mechanical principles and not by
the "will." Later progress in neuropsychology was made by studying animal
motion that persists after the brain is gone. (What farmer had not seen a chicken
running around the barnyard after its head was cut off?) Around 1750, the Scottish physician Whytt showed that such movements are controlled by the spinal
cord. He found that a decapitated frog will jerk its leg away from a pinprick; but
when deprived of *both* brain and spinal cord it no longer responded. Presumably,
the frog's leg movement depended on the spinal cord.

   The study of reflexes received some additional impetus during the French Revolution. Pierre Cabanis, friend and physician to some of its leaders, wondered
whether consciousness survives beheading. He concluded that it does not and
that the body's twitches after execution are mere reflex actions, automatisms
without consciousness. This grim business was taken up again some forty years
later by the German scientist Theodor Bischoff who performed a series of rather

macabre experiments on the freshly separated head of an executed criminal. Even fairly intense stimuli produced no effects during the first minute after decapitation. Among the stimuli Bischoff employed, with perhaps greater devotion to science than human sensitivity, was the word "Pardon!" shouted into the ears of the severed head (Fearing, 1930).

Today we can list a host of reflexes, built-in response patterns executed automatically, without thought and without will. Vomiting, the rhythmic contraction of the intestines (peristalsis), erection of the penis, blushing, limb flexion in withdrawal from pain, sucking in newborns—the catalog is very large.

Can we classify these reflexes in any sensible fashion? There are several criteria. We can ask how many steps are part of the *reflex arc*—the reflex pathway that leads from stimulus to response. Some reflexes represent a chain of only two components, as in the case of an afferent neuron which contacts a motoneuron directly. More typically the chain is longer, and one or more interneurons are interposed between the afferent and efferent ends. We can also ask whether the reflex involves the brain (and if so, which part) or the spinal cord. When considering *spinal reflexes* we may want to distinguish further between those of *flexion* and those of *extension*. Flexion reflexes are typically associated with withdrawal, as when one pulls back one's arm from a burning fire. Extensor reflexes are often involved in postural reactions which uphold the body against gravity. Pressure on the soles of the feet stimulates the extensors, which thrust the leg upright.

Inferring the Synapse

Until the turn of the century, most neurologists believed that the reflex pathway was across a long and essentially continuous strand of nervous tissue. The notion of the *synapse,* a gap between neurons across which they must communicate, is relatively modern. The critical studies which established the existence of the synapse and its role in nerve interaction were performed at the turn of the century by the English physiologist Sir Charles Sherrington (1857–1952). Sherrington's work was conducted at the level of behavior rather than that of electrophysiology. What he observed directly was reflex action in dogs, cats, and monkeys. How the synapse worked, he inferred.

Sherrington set out to study the *simple reflex,* that is, the reflex considered in splendid neurological isolation, unaffected by activities elsewhere in the nervous system. Of course he was well aware that such simplicity does not really exist, for even the lowliest spinal reflex is modified by higher centers in the spinal cord or the brain. An itch in your side will initiate a scratch reflex, but if you are the catchman in a trapeze act you will probably inhibit it. To remove the effect of higher centers, Sherrington used the *spinal animal,* usually a dog, whose spinal cord had been completely severed in the neck region. This cut all connections between the body (from the neck down) and the brain, so that spinal reflexes could be studied pure.

Sir Charles Sherrington (Courtesy National Library of Medicine)

EXCITATION

Sherrington's method was simple. He applied mild electric shocks to some point on the spinal animal's skin and observed whether this stimulus evoked a particu-

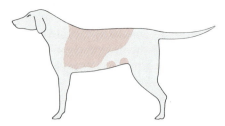

2.9   Saddle-shaped area of spinal dog   *When a stimulus whose strength is above threshold is applied at any point in the "saddle," the animal will perform a scratching movement. (After Sherrington, 1906)*

lar reflex response (Figure 2.9). His results indicated that there had to be conduction across at least two neurons—a sensory neuron from the skin receptor and a motoneuron that activates muscle fibers. Sherrington had asked whether conduction across neurons had the same characteristics as conduction within neurons. He discovered that it did not.

One line of evidence came from ***temporal summation.*** Sherrington showed that while one stimulus below threshold will not elicit the reflex, two or more of them (all equally subthreshold) may do so if presented in succession. The important point was that such temporal summation effects occurred even when the individual stimuli were spaced at intervals of up to half a second or thereabouts. But summation over such comparatively long time intervals does not occur within an individual axon fiber. The fact that temporal summation takes place anyway suggests that the summation process occurs somewhere else, presumably at the crossover point between neurons. The differences between conduction in reflex arcs and conduction in individual nerve fibers point to different mechanisms operating at the synaptic junction.

Sherrington supposed that there is some kind of excitatory process (presumably caused by the liberation of a then still undiscovered chemical substance from the ends of the axon) which accumulates at the synapse and builds up until it reaches a level high enough (the threshold level) to trigger the next neuron into action. This hypothesis clearly accounts for temporal summation. Every time cell *A* fires, a tiny amount of the excitatory substance is liberated into the synaptic gap between cell *A* and cell *B*. With enough repetitions of the stimulus, the total quantity of what Sherrington called the ***central excitatory state*** exceeds the threshold of cell *B* which then fires (Figure 2.10A).

Further evidence for Sherrington's general approach derives from the phenomenon of ***spatial summation,*** which highlights the fact that several neurons may funnel in upon one output. Consider two fairly adjacent points on a dog's flank, *A* and *B,* such that stimulating either of them alone will elicit a particular reflex if the stimulus is intense enough. Sherrington showed that subthreshold stimulation at *both* points will yield the reflex, even though this same weak stimulation would not suffice for either of these points in isolation. This indicates that two groups of nerve fibers converge upon one neural output—the ***final common path.***

2.10   Further arguments for synaptic transmission   *(A) Temporal summation. A subthreshold stimulus will not elicit the reflex but two or more stimuli will if presented successively at intervals of up to half a second. This indicates that the effects of the first stimulus were somehow stored and added to the effects of the second. (B) Spatial summation. Subthreshold stimuli applied to different points in the saddle area will not evoke a reflex if presented separately, but they will if presented simultaneously. This indicates that the excitatory effects from different regions are all funneled into the same common path.*

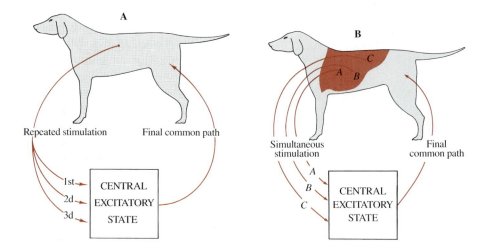

At this juncture, the several converging neurons generate excitatory processes whose effects summate (Figure 2.10B).

INHIBITION

So far it would appear that neurons either vote "aye," thus adding to the central excitatory state at the synapse, or else abstain altogether. However, some neurons may signal "nay" and set up an inhibitory effect, actively opposing and preventing excitation.

One of the clearest demonstrations of such an effect is the phenomenon of *reciprocal inhibition.* Skeletal muscles typically come in antagonistic pairs—flexor and extensor (Figure 2.11). What happens to the flexor muscle when the extensor is excited and conversely? Patently, the antagonists must not both contract at the same time, like wrestlers straining against each other. For maximum mechanical efficiency, the force of the excited muscle should encounter no opposition whatever from its antagonist.

Using a spinal animal, Sherrington provided an experimental demonstration. He found that stimulation of a sensory site that caused the flexor to contract had a further effect. It also caused the extensor to relax so that it actually became limp —limper in fact than it was in the normal resting state. Sherrington concluded that this subzero level of muscular contraction could only be explained by assuming that there was a counteracting process that nullifies the excitatory messages to the muscle fibers—*inhibition.*

These facts suggest that a neuron can receive both excitatory and inhibitory messages. The two processes summate algebraically; they pull in opposite directions and thus have opposite signs (with excitation positive, inhibition negative). Whether an efferent neuron fires (and thus activates a muscle fiber) depends upon many other neurons that form a synapse with it. Each of these cells gives a positive or negative signal or remains neutral and thereby determines whether the excitatory threshold of the efferent neuron is reached, whether it fires or does not.

DISINHIBITION

Impulses that have an inhibitory effect may derive from centers higher up than the spinal cord. The inhibitory effect of such brain centers is often discovered directly, by noting an *increase* in the strength of a reflex after the influence of this higher center is removed. Such an effect is calld *disinhibition.* A classic example is spinal reflexes in frogs, which are more vigorous when all brain structures have been removed.

A rather ghoulish instance of disinhibition is provided by the love life of the praying mantis. The female mantis is a rapacious killer. She seizes and devours any small creature unfortunate enough to move across her field of vision. Since the male mantis is smaller than the female, he too may qualify as food. This cannibalism is quite puzzling. How can the mantis survive as a species given a behavior tendency that counteracts successful fertilization?

According to one hypothesis, the female's predatory pattern is triggered almost exclusively by moving visual stimuli. The courting male's behavior is delicately attuned to this fact. As soon as he sees her he becomes absolutely immobile. Whenever she looks away for a moment he stalks her ever so slowly, but immediately freezes as soon as her eyes wheel back toward him—an inhibitory effect

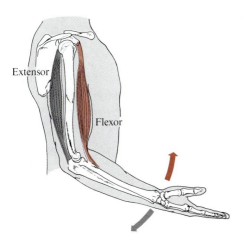

2.11   An example of muscle antagonists *The figure shows how the members of an antagonistic muscle pair (triceps and biceps) oppose each other in flexing and extending the forearm.*

Extensor

Flexor

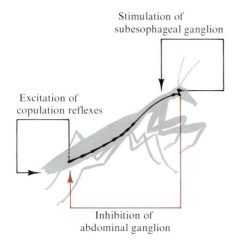

Stimulation of
subesophageal ganglion

Excitation of
copulation reflexes

Inhibition of
abdominal ganglion

2.12   The disinhibitory mechanism in the praying mantis   *Excitation of the abdominal ganglion leads to copulatory movements in the male. But the sight of the moving female stimulates the subesophageal ganglion in the male's head. This in turn inhibits the abdominal ganglion so that copulation stops. Decapitation severs the subesophageal ganglion. The result is disinhibition and copulation resumes. (After Roeder, 1967)*

upon overall reflex activity. When close enough to her, he suddenly leaps upon her back and begins to copulate. Once squarely upon the female's back he is reasonably safe (her normal killer reflexes are elicited only by moving visual stimuli and he is mostly out of sight). But the dangers he must surmount to reach this place of safety are enormous. He must not miss her when he jumps; he must not slip while upon her. Should he fall, he will surely be grasped and eaten. Fairly often he does lose his balance, but even then all love's labour is not lost—for his genes, if not for him. The female commences to eat her fallen mate from the head on down. In almost all instances, the abdomen of the male now starts vigorous copulatory movements that are often successfully completed. Clearly, the male performs his evolutionary duty whatever his own private fate. But what is the mechanism?

It appears that the intact male's copulatory reflexes are inhibited by the subesophageal ganglion, located in his head. When this nerve cluster is removed, the animal will engage in endless copulatory movements even when no female is present. The same thing happens if the female chances to seize her mate and eat him. She first chews off his head and with it the subesophageal ganglion, thus disinhibiting the male's copulatory pattern which now resumes in full force—proof positive that love can survive beyond the grave (Roeder, 1935; see Figure 2.12).*

The Synaptic Mechanism

Sherrington could only guess at the specific physical mechanism that governs transmission at the synapse, but he did sketch some general guidelines. There had to be excitatory and inhibitory processes, accumulating over time, pooling effects from various neural inputs and adding algebraically. But what was their nature?

SYNAPTIC TRANSMISSION

By now, quite a bit is known about the way in which this transmission occurs. Let's begin by distinguishing between the *presynaptic* neuron and the *postsynaptic* neuron: the first sends the neural message, and the second is the one the message is directed to. The process begins in tiny swellings of the axon terminals of the presynaptic neuron. Within these swellings are numerous tiny sacs, or *vesicles,* which contain chemical substances called *neurotransmitters.* When the presynaptic neuron fires, the vesicles release their transmitter load into the synaptic gap that separates the two cells. The transmitter molecules diffuse across this gap and come to rest upon a dendrite or the cell body of the postsynaptic cell (see Figure 2.13).

How do the transmitters transmit the impulse from one neuron to another? Essentially, by decreasing the resting potential of the membrane of the postsynaptic cell. As more and more transmitter molecules are hurled across the synaptic bridge, the resting potential of the second cell drops further and further. When

* A recent study suggests that this cannibalistic pattern may only occur under artificial conditions of captivity and when the female is virtually starved. Under more natural circumstances, males seem to manage to mate quite successfully without losing their heads in the process. But even if induced artificially, the phenomenon is an interesting if macabre illustration of the effect of disinhibition (Liske and Davis, 1984).

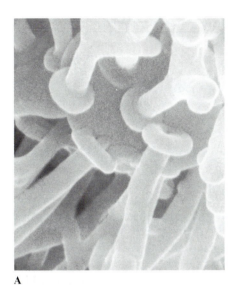

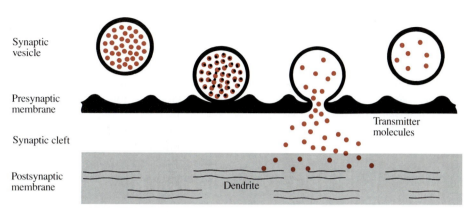

Synaptic
vesicle

Presynaptic
membrane

Synaptic cleft

Postsynaptic
membrane

Transmitter
molecules

Dendrite

A

B

2.13 The synapse *(A) Electron micrograph of synaptic knobs, magnified 11,250 times. (Lewis et al., 1969) (B) As the neuron fires, the synaptic vesicles travel to the presynaptic membrane, open into the cleft, discharge their transmitter load, and are eventually resupplied. (Adapted from Rosenzweig and Leiman, 1982)*

the drop gets large enough, the cell's threshold is reached, the action potential is triggered, and the impulse will now speed down the second cell's axon.

The changes in potentials in the dendrites and cell body which are produced by the transmitters are quite different from the action potential in the axon. For unlike the action potential, they are **graded** rather than all-or-none. They can be small or they can be large because the small changes will add up as the presynaptic neuron keeps on firing and more and more transmitter molecules affect the postsynaptic cell (temporal summation). They will also add up in space. Most neurons receive inputs from a great many presynaptic cells—in the brain, often from a thousand or more (spatial summation). As a result, transmitter molecules will arrive at several different regions of the postsynaptic membrane, and their effects will summate (see Figure 2.13).

A similar mechanism accounts for inhibition. At some synapses, the presynaptic cell liberates transmitter substances that produce an *increase* in the resting potential of the postsynaptic neuron. As a result, a larger drop in resting potential will now be necessary to set off the action potential in the postsynaptic cell. Since most neurons make synaptic connections with neurons that excite them as well as others that inhibit them, the response of a given postsynaptic cell depends on a final tally of the various excitatory and inhibitory effects that act upon it. If the net value is excitatory (and if this value exceeds the threshold), the cell will fire.

NEUROTRANSMITTERS

On the face of it, one might think that the nervous system only needs two transmitters: one excitatory and the other inhibitory. But nature, as so often, turns out to be exceedingly generous, for in actual fact there are a great number of different transmitter substances. Over a dozen have been isolated thus far, and many more are sure to be discovered within a decade or two.

We will mention only a few of these neurotransmitters, to which we will return in later discussions. One is **acetylcholine**, which is released at many synapses and at the junction between motor neurons and muscle fibers (a junction which is a

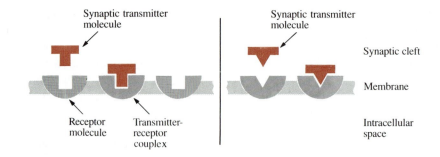

2.14 Lock-and-key model of synaptic transmission *Transmitter molecules will only affect the postsynaptic membrane if their shape fits the shape of certain receptor molecules in that membrane much as a key has to fit into a lock. The diagram shows two kinds of transmitters and their appropriate receptors. (From Rosenzweig and Leiman, 1982)*

kind of synapse) and makes the fibers contract. Others include *norepinephrine, dopamine,* and *serotonin.* The important point is that neurons differ in the transmitters they release, as well as the transmitters that affect them. Thus, neurons sensitive to serotonin will not respond to dopamine, and vice versa. It is as if different groups of neurons spoke different languages: some speak Dopaminese, others Serotonese, and so on. These differences in the kinds of chemical languages neurons speak and understand have become an important way of classifying neural systems in the nervous system. An attempt to explain these differences in chemical responsiveness is the so-called *lock-and-key model.* This proposes that transmitter molecules will only affect the postsynaptic membrane if their shape fits that of special receptor molecules in that membrane much as a key has to fit into a lock (see Figure 2.14).

DRUGS AND NEUROTRANSMITTER ACTIVITY

The fact that the communication between neurons depends on different neurotransmitter substances has wide implications for many aspects of psychological functioning. One is the effect of various drugs that enhance or impede the activity of transmitters at the synapse.

Curare and acetylcholine   A well-known example is *curare,* a substance discovered by certain South American Indians who tipped their arrows in a plant extract that contained it, with deadly effect on animal prey and human enemies. Curare blocks the action of acetylcholine at the synaptic junctions between motor neurons and muscle fibers. The result is total paralysis and eventual death by suffocation, since the victim is unable to breathe.

Chlorpromazine and dopamine   The transmitter blockade produced by curare leads to catastrophic results. But other blockades may be beneficial. An example is the effect of *chlorpromazine* on the symptoms of schizophrenia, a serious mental disorder that afflicts about one percent of the population. In its more extreme forms, schizophrenia is characterized by delusions (believing what isn't so, such as conspiracies and persecution), hallucinations (perceiving what isn't there, such as hearing voices), or bizarre mannerisms and unusual postures that may be maintained for many hours. According to one hypothesis, schizophrenia is produced by an oversensitivity to the transmitter dopamine. Neurons that liberate dopamine have an arousing function in many parts of the brain. Adherents of the dopamine hypothesis believe that people who are overly responsive to this transmitter will be continually overaroused, which may ultimately lead to the symptoms of schizophrenia. One of the arguments for this theory comes from the fact that chlorpromazine, which blocks the effect of dopamine, has a pronounced effect in alleviating schizophrenic symptoms. While the dopamine hypothesis of schizophrenia is still a matter of dispute, many investigators do agree that disturbances in transmitter function play a role in the production of this and other mental disorders (see Chapter 19 for further discussion).

Amphetamine and norepinephrine   Curare and chlorpromazine exert their effects by blocking a neurotransmitter. Other substances do the very opposite: They enhance the activity of a transmitter at a synapse. An example is **amphetamine,** which stimulates the release of norepinephrine. Neurons whose transmitter is norepinephrine have to do with general bodily and psychological arousal. The greater the activity of such neurons, the more active and excited the individual is likely to be. It is therefore understandable that amphetamine acts as a powerful stimulant ("speed"). In moderate doses, it leads to restlessness, insomnia, and loss of appetite; larger doses and continued use may lead to frenetic hyperactivity and delusions.

ENDORPHINS AND ALLEVIATION OF PAIN

Some recent discoveries have implicated neurotransmitter substances in yet another psychological process: the alleviation of pain (Bolles and Fanselow, 1982).

There is little doubt that the perception of pain can be alleviated or even abolished by psychological means. There are many stories of athletes or soldiers at war who suffer injuries but don't feel the pain until the game or the battle is over. Somewhat related effects are obtained by acupuncture, an ancient Chinese treatment in which needles are inserted in various parts of the body to produce certain therapeutic results. One result is the alleviation of pain, an effect which seems fairly well established (Mann, Bowsher, Mumford, Lipton, and Miles, 1973). A related phenomenon is the reduction of pain by a *placebo.* This is a chemically inert substance which the patient believes will help him (such as the old family doctor's little sugar pill). Such placebos often have some beneficial effects and can lessen pain (see Chapter 20). In all these cases the question is why.

The answer seems to be a matter of brain chemistry. It is of course well known that the experience of pain can be dulled and sometimes entirely eliminated by the administration of various drugs—in particular, morphine and other opiates. These drugs are typically applied from the outside. But on occasion, the brain can be its own pharmacist. For when assailed by painful stimulation, the brain seems to produce its own brand of opiates, which it then administers to itself. These are the so-called **endorphins**, a group of neurotransmitters that are secreted by special cells located within the brain. The effect of these endorphins is to stimulate certain neurons, which in their turn disrupt messages from the pain receptors. Regular opiates such as morphine are chemically very similar to the endorphins and will therefore activate the same pain-inhibiting neurons (Snyder, 1977; Snyder and Childers, 1979).

To prove that the endorphins are involved in many phenomena in which pain is reduced by "psychological" means, investigators turned to **naloxone,** a drug which is known to inhibit the effect of morphine and similar opiates. Recent studies have shown that naloxone also blocks the pain alleviation normally produced by acupuncture (Mayer, Price, Rafii, and Barber, 1976; see Figure 2.15).

2.15 Acupuncture Acupuncture is a complex system of treatment that grew up in ancient China and was based on the idea that disease is a disturbance in the balance of certain vital energies which were thought to circulate in certain channels. Their balance was to be restored by manipulating metal needles at special points along these channels. The figure is from a seventeenth-century Chinese treatise and illustrates the liver tract with twenty-eight special points. (From Blakemore, 1977, p. 42)

The same holds true for placebos administered to patients who believe they are taking a pain killer. Under normal conditions such placebos lessen the patients' pain, but when the patients are given naloxone in addition to the placebo, this effect disappears (Levine, Gordon, and Fields, 1979).

Some authors suggest that the exhilarating effect of repeated stressful exercise, such as jogging or marathon running, has a similar cause. The runner continues to exert himself until he is exhausted and in pain. This builds up endorphins, which counteract the pain and produce a mood swing in the opposite direction. Eventually there may be something akin to an addiction—the jogger has to have his jogging fix to enjoy the endorphin-produced euphoria. Whether this interpretation is correct is as yet unknown. (It would be interesting to see whether the joy of jogging is diminished by naloxone.)

INTERACTION THROUGH THE BLOODSTREAM: THE ENDOCRINE SYSTEM

Thus far, we have considered the one primary instrument of communication within the body: the nervous system. But there is another organ system that serves a similar function: the *endocrine glands* (see Figure 2.16 and Table 2.1). Various endocrine glands (for example, the pancreas, adrenal glands, and pituitary) release their *hormone* secretions directly into the bloodstream and thus exert effects upon structures often far removed from their biochemical birthplace. As an example, take the *pituitary gland*. One of its components secretes a hormone that tells the kidney to decrease the amount of water excreted in the urine, a useful mechanism when the body is short of water (see Chapter 3).*

On the face of it, the integration that the endocrine glands give us seems to be very different from that which is provided by the nervous system. In the nervous system, messages are sent to particular addresses through highly specific channels. In contrast, the chemical messengers employed by the endocrine system travel indiscriminately to all parts of the body until they finally reach the one organ that is their destination. But at bottom, the two communication systems have a good deal in common, for ultimately they both use chemical substances to transmit information. In the nervous system, these are the neurotransmitters that excite or inhibit the postsynaptic cell; in the endocrine system, they are the hormones that affect specially sensitive cells in the target organ. To be sure, there is an enormous difference in the distance these messengers have to travel. In the one case, it is the synaptic cleft, which is less than 1/10,000 mm wide; in the other, it may be half the length of the entire body. But the fact that in both cases the medium of their message is chemical leads to a number of important similarities. Thus, several substances turn out to serve both as hormones and as neurotransmitters. For example, norepinephrine is the transmitter released by certain neurons that make blood vessels constrict; it is also one of the hormones secreted by the adrenal gland and has similar results.

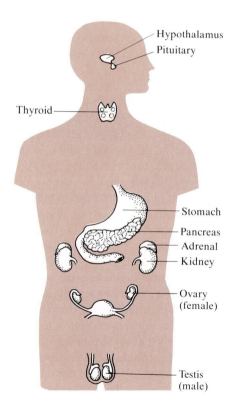

2.16   Location of major endocrine glands and hypothalamus   *(After Keeton, 1972)*

Hypothalamus
Pituitary
Thyroid
Stomach
Pancreas
Adrenal
Kidney
Ovary (female)
Testis (male)

---

* In addition to the endocrine glands, there are also *duct glands* (for example, salivary and tear glands), which have ducts that channel their secretions to the proper region of application.

Table 2.1   THE MAIN ENDOCRINE GLANDS AND THEIR FUNCTIONS

Gland	Functions of the released hormones
Anterior pituitary	Often called the body's master gland because it triggers hormone secretion in many of the other endocrine glands.
Posterior pituitary	Prevents loss of water through kidney.
Thyroid	Affects metabolic rate.
Islet cells in pancreas	Affects utilization of glucose.
Adrenal cortex	Various effects on metabolism; some effects on sexual behavior.
Adrenal medulla	Increases sugar output of liver; stimulates various internal organs in the same direction as the sympathetic branch of the ANS (e.g., accelerates heart rate).
Ovaries	One hormone (estrogen) produces female sex characteristics. Necessary for sexual behavior in mammals other than humans. Another hormone (progesterone) prepares uterus for implantation of embryo.
Testes	Produces male sex characteristics. Relevant to sexual arousal.

THE MAIN STRUCTURES OF THE NERVOUS SYSTEM

Our general approach has been to move from the simple to the increasingly complex. We first looked at the operation of the smallest functional unit of the nervous system, the neuron, and then considered the way in which two or more neurons may interact. We now turn to a third and still more complex level of analysis to discuss the function of large aggregates of neurons. What can we say about the function of those clumps of nervous tissue, each made up of millions of neurons, which comprise the gross structures of the brain and spinal cord?

The Evolution of Central Control

The nervous system is analogous to a government, and its evolution can be understood as the gradual imposition of central control over local autonomy. A first step was the establishment of regional rule. Early in evolutionary history the cell bodies of many interneurons began to clump together to form *ganglia* (singular, *ganglion*). At first, these ganglia served primarily as relay stations that passed on sensory messages from the receptors to the muscles. But eventually they became much more than mere relay stations. The close proximity of the cells within these clumps of neural tissue allowed an ever-increasing number and complexity of synaptic interconnections. As a result, the ganglia became local control centers which integrated messages from different receptor cells and coordinated the activity of different muscle fibers. These regional centers were usually located close to the sites where important sensory information is gathered or where vital activity takes place.

As evolution progressed, the initial loose federation of ganglia gradually became increasingly centralized; some ganglia began to control others. The dominant ganglia were those that were located in the head. Their eventual preeminence grew out of the fact that the head contains the major receptors. To integrate the messages from the various receptors in the head, more and more neural machinery was required and the ganglionic centers which processed the incoming information became increasingly complex. They eventually started to coordinate the activity of ganglia elsewhere in the body until they finally emerged as the head ganglia in status as well as location—in short, they became the brain.

This tendency toward increasing centralization continued within the brain itself. The various structures of the brain tend to function hierarchically; there are higher centers which command lower centers, which in turn command still lower centers, and so on.

The Peripheral and Central Nervous Systems

Taken as a whole, the human nervous system consists of a fine network of fibers that gradually merge into larger and larger branches which converge upon a central trunk line, like the tributaries of a stream. This system is composed of the central and peripheral nervous systems. The *central nervous system* (usually abbreviated *CNS*) is made up of the brain and spinal cord. The *peripheral system,* as its name implies, comprises all nervous structures that are outside of the CNS.

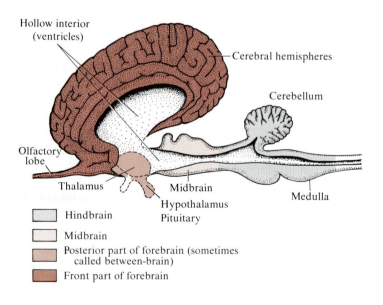

2.17 The central nervous system This diagram is a highly schematic representation of the main parts of the brain. (After Lickley, 1919)

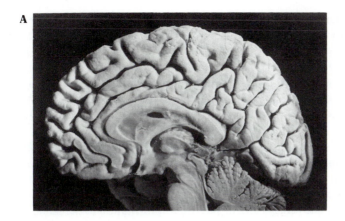

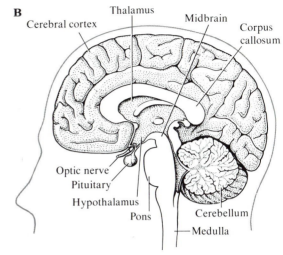

2.18   The human brain   *(A) A photograph of the brain taken from the side.
(Courtesy The Warder Collection) (B) A
diagram of the brain, cut lengthwise.
(After Keeton, 1980)*

Anatomists distinguish between two divisions of the peripheral nervous system
—the somatic and the autonomic. The ***somatic division*** is primarily concerned
with the control of the skeletal musculature and the transmission of information
from the sense organs. It consists of various nerves that branch off from the CNS
—efferent fibers to the muscles and afferent fibers from the skin, the joints, and
the special senses. The ***autonomic nervous system (ANS)*** serves the many visceral
structures that are concerned with the basic life processes, such as the heart, the
blood vessels, the digestive systems, the genital organs, and so on.

The central nervous system can be described as a long tube that is very much
thickened at its front end. The portion of the tube below the skull is the ***spinal
cord,*** while the portion located in the skull is the ***brain stem.*** Two structures are
attached to the brain stem. One is the pair of ***cerebral hemispheres,*** which are very
large and envelope the central tube completely; the other is the ***cerebellum*** (literally, "little brain"), which is located lower down and is much smaller (see Figure
2.17).

THE ANATOMY OF THE BRAIN

Neuroanatomists find it convenient to consider the brain in terms of three major
subdivisions: the ***hindbrain, midbrain,*** and ***forebrain*** (see Figures 2.17 and 2.18).

The hindbrain   The hindbrain includes the medulla and the cerebellum. The
medulla is the part of the brain stem closest to the spinal cord; it controls some
vital bodily functions such as heartbeat, circulation, and respiration. The ***cerebellum*** is a deeply convoluted structure that controls bodily balance and muscular
coordination. It functions as a specialized computer whose 30 billion or more
neurons integrate the enormous amount of information from the muscles, joints,
and tendons of the body that are required both for ordinary walking and for the
skilled, automatic movements of athletes and piano players.

The midbrain   The midbrain contains several neural centers that act as lower
level control centers for some motor reactions and that also have some limited

auditory and visual functions (such as controlling eye movements). Of particular interest is a rather diffuse structure known as the ***reticular formation,*** which extends through the entire length of the brain stem from medulla to thalamus but is particularly prominent in the midbrain region. One of its functions is to serve as a general activator whose excitation arouses other parts of the brain, particularly the cerebral hemispheres. Its deactivation seems related to sleep. We will return to these issues in a later section (see Chapter 3).

Forebrain: Thalamus and hypothalamus   Two of the forebrain structures represent the topmost region of the brain stem. They are the thalamus and the hypothalamus. The ***thalamus*** is a large system of various centers that serves as a kind of reception area to the cerebral hemispheres. Fibers from the eyes, the ears, the skin, and some motor centers, pass their information to the thalamus, which then forwards it upward to the cerebral cortex. The ***hypothalamus*** is intimately involved in the control of behavior patterns that stem from the basic biological urges (e.g., feeding, drinking, maintaining an appropriate temperature, sexual activity, and so forth; see Chapter 3).

Forebrain: Cerebral hemispheres   We finally turn to the structures that have traditionally been regarded as the functional summit of the behaving organism (or at least, of the thinking organism): the ***cerebral hemispheres.*** Anatomists usually distinguish several large parts within each hemisphere, called ***lobes.*** There are four such lobes, each named for the cranial bone nearest to it: the ***frontal, parietal, occipital,*** and ***temporal.***

The outer layer of the cerebral hemispheres is called the ***cerebral cortex,*** and it is this region rather than the hemispheres as a whole that is thought to represent the pinnacle of neural integration. The cells in the cortex are densely packed and intricately interconnected; they are therefore capable of the most complex synaptic interconnections. While the cortex is only about 3 mm thick, it comprises a substantial proportion of the entire human brain. This is because the cerebral hemispheres are deeply folded and convoluted. Thus crumpled up, the cerebral surface that can be packed into the cranial cavity is very much increased (see Figure 2.19). The cortex is generally believed to be critical for the so-called "higher mental processes" (thinking, many aspects of memory, planned and voluntary action) and is the most recent to emerge in the course of evolution. Fish have none at all, reptiles and birds have but a poor beginning, while in mammals there is considerable enlargement, especially in the primates.

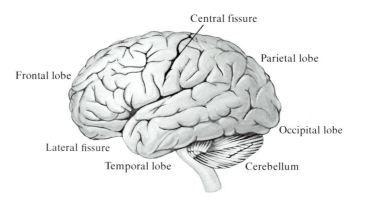

2.19   The cerebral hemispheres, side view

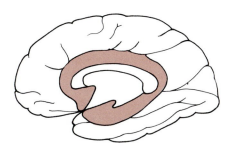

2.20   The limbic system   *(After Russell, 1961)*

A word or two should be added about the subcortical regions of the cerebral hemispheres. Some important structures are located near the center of the hemispheres, in a region that borders on the brain stem. These are often grouped together under the term *limbic system* (from *limbique,* "bordering"). Many limbic structures are part of what in evolutionary terms is an older unit, the "old cortex," which has close anatomical ties with the hypothalamus, and is involved in the control of emotional and motivational activities (see Figure 2.20). Another subcortical structure is the *corpus callosum,* a large band of fibers that connects the two hemispheres and plays an important role in integrating their functions (see pp. 41–44).

Hierarchical Function in the Nervous System

The various structures in the brain tend to function hierarchically; there are higher centers which command lower centers, which in turn command still lower centers, and so on. This hierarchical principle is the rule throughout the entire system (Gallistel, 1980).

To see how this hierarchical system operates, we will consider the behavior of cats whose brain has been cut (technically, "transected") at various anatomical levels of the system. Such transections sever the part of the nervous system below the cut from all control by the portion above. The question is what the part below the cut can do now that it is on its own.

Let's begin with a transection that leaves the animal with spinal cord and hindbrain and nothing else. The resulting "hindbrain animal" can still make the various limb and trunk movements that are required for standing, crouching, or walking. But it can't put them together. As a result, it is unable to stand or make walking movements unless supported by straps. Without support, it will collapse, unable to come up with more than disorganized reflex twitches if stimulated. Reduced to a hindbrain, the animal has become a mere biological marionette without a puppet master. As one author put it, the animal can move, but it cannot act (Gallistel, 1980).

Such acts are possible, however, if the transection is made just above the midbrain. Now the animal can stand without support, can walk, can shiver, chew, swallow, and hiss. The midbrain clearly performs some integrating function, for it somehow pulls the individual muscle movements together to form coordinated acts. But these acts don't fit into any larger behavioral scheme. The acts of a normal cat are organized into sequences that serve a larger goal. A hungry cat will walk to search for prey, will stalk the prey if one is found, and will then pounce, kill, and eat it. But a midbrain cat can't put its acts together. If starved, it won't look for food; if attacked, it won't flee. It acts, but it acts without point or purpose.

When the transection is made at a still higher level, so that the animal is left with most of its limbic system, lacking only the cortex, its separate acts are organized toward some purpose. It searches for food when hungry, looks for a warmer place when cold, escapes when harmed, and so on. In many ways, it behaves much as a normal cat. But there is a difference—its performance is inept. When attacked by another cat, it will strike back, but quite ineffectively. Its blows will be poorly directed and easily avoided by its enemy. The limbic animal can coordinate its acts into a sequence that has an aim. But that sequence and the environment in which it is enacted must be very simple. If it is at all complex, the animal will fail. The limbic animal can act, and its acts have some purpose. But lacking a cortex, it is stupid (Bard and Rioch, 1937; Wetzel and Stuart, 1976; Gallistel, 1980).

THE CEREBRAL CORTEX

We now turn to the cerebral cortex, the part of the nervous system that allows us to be intelligent. In cats, its presence may not be utterly necessary, although as we saw they are certainly in a bad way without it. But in our own species, its absence is catastrophic. For without a cortex there can be no planning, no complex sequence of motor movements, no perception of organized form, and no speech—in short, no semblance of anything that we call human.

Projection Areas

Among the first discoveries in the study of cortical function was the existence of the so-called *projection areas.* These serve as receiving stations for sensory information or as dispatching centers for motor commands. *Sensory projection areas* are those regions of the cortex where the messages that come from the various senses (usually through some other relay stations) are first received and upon which this input is "projected." *Motor projection areas* are those from which directives that ultimately go to the muscles are issued.

MOTOR AREAS

The discovery of the cortical motor areas occurred when several physiologists opened the skull of a lightly anesthetized dog and then applied mild electric currents to various portions of its cerebral cortex. They discovered a region in the frontal lobe that controls movement. Stimulating a given point led to motion of the forelimb, stimulating another point led to motion of the trunk, and so forth. Exciting the left hemisphere led to movements on the right side of the body; exciting the right hemisphere caused movements on the left. This made good anatomical sense because most of the major efferent pathways from the brain cross over to the opposite side just as they leave the hindbrain.

Similar studies have been conducted on human subjects by the Canadian neurosurgeon, Wilder Penfield. The stimulation is administered in the course of a brain operation. Such operations are usually administered under local rather than general anesthesia and patients are therefore able to report their experiences. Electrical stimulation applied to the open brain produces no pain. While pain receptors are located throughout the body and send their messages upward to the brain, the brain itself contains no such receptors.

The results of Penfield's studies showed that the cortical motor area in humans is in a region of the frontal lobe that is quite similar to that found in dogs. Stimulation there led to movement of some parts of the body, much to the surprise of patients who had no sense of "willing" the action, or of "performing it themselves." Systematic exploration showed that for each portion of the motor cortex,

A
MOTOR PROJECTION
AREA

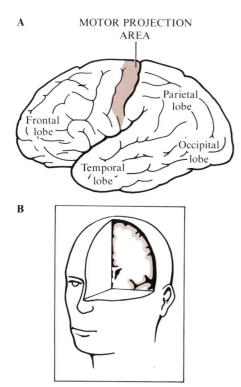

B

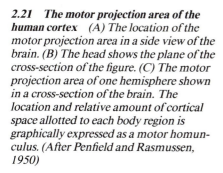

C

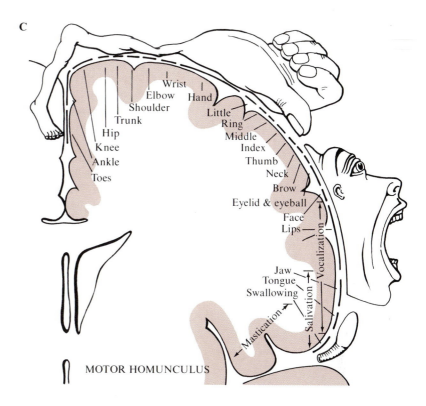

MOTOR HOMUNCULUS

2.21   The motor projection area of the human cortex   (A) The location of the motor projection area in a side view of the brain. (B) The head shows the plane of the cross-section of the figure. (C) The motor projection area of one hemisphere shown in a cross-section of the brain. The location and relative amount of cortical space allotted to each body region is graphically expressed as a motor homunculus. (After Penfield and Rasmussen, 1950)

there was a corresponding part of the body that moved when its cortical counterpart was stimulated, with each hemisphere controlling the side of the body opposite to it. The results are sometimes expressed graphically by drawing a "motor homunculus," a schema of the body as it is represented in the motor projection area (Figure 2.21).

Inspection of the motor homunculus shows that equal areas of the body do not receive equal cortical space. Instead, parts of the body that are very mobile and capable of precisely tuned movement (for instance, the fingers, the tongue) are assigned greater cortical space compared to those employed for movements that are more gross and undifferentiated (for instance, the shoulder). What matters is evidently function, the extent and complexity of use (Penfield and Rasmussen, 1950).

Some related findings with various animals fit neatly into this picture. For example, consider the cortical representations of the forepaw in dogs and raccoons. Unlike the dog, the raccoon is a "manual" creature which explores the world with its forepaws; neatly enough, the forepaw cortical area in raccoons dwarfs its counterpart in dogs (Welker, Johnson, and Pubols, 1964).

SENSORY AREAS

Analogous stimulation methods have demonstrated the existence of cortical sensory areas. The **somatosensory area** is located in the parietal lobes. Patients stimulated at a particular point of this area report a tingling sensation somewhere on the opposite side of their bodies. (Less frequently, they will report experiences of cold, warmth, or of movement.) Again, we find a neat topographic projection.

37

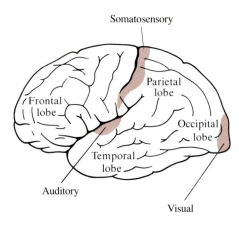

2.22 **Sensory projection areas of the human cortex** *The location of the somatosensory, auditory, and visual projection areas in the brain. (After Cobb, 1941)*

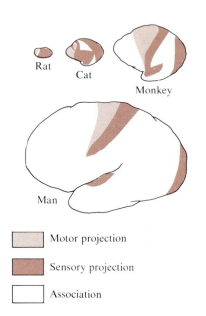

Motor projection

Sensory projection

Association

2.23 **Projection and association areas in animals and humans** *There is an orderly progression in the amount of cortex devoted to association areas. As we ascend the animal series from rat to man, both the absolute amount of cortical association area and the ratio of association to projection areas increases dramatically. In rats, cats, and to some extent even monkeys, the bulk of the cortex is devoted to making the animal agile and perceptive; in humans, most of it is devoted to making us smart. (After Thompson, 1973)*

Each portion of the body's surface is mapped onto a particular region of the cortical somatosensory area but again with an unequal assignment of cortical space: The parts of the body that are most sensitive to touch such as the index finger and the tongue enjoy a disproportionately larger space allotment in the brain.

Similar projection areas exist for vision and for hearing. They are located in the occipital and temporal lobes respectively (Figure 2.22). Patients stimulated in the visual projection area report optical experiences, vivid enough, but with little form or meaning—flickering lights, formless colors, streaks. Stimulated in the auditory area, they hear things, but again the sensation is meaningless and rather chaotic—clicks, buzzes, booms, hums. Some psychologists might argue that here we have "pure" visual and auditory input, the crude, disembodied raw materials of sensation, to be shaped and interpreted as the excitation is transmitted to other areas.

Association Areas

Less than one-quarter of the human cortex is devoted to the projection zones. The remaining regions have traditionally been called *association areas,* a term that grew out of an earlier notion that these areas somehow link events arising in different projection zones, whether motor or sensory. There is good reason to believe that these areas are implicated in the higher mental processes such as planning, remembering, thinking, and speech. One source of this belief stems from a comparison of the anatomy of the cortex found in different mammals. In the rat, the bulk of the cortex is taken up by projection zones; in the cat, more space is devoted to the association areas; more yet in monkeys; and most in man (Figure 2.23).

APRAXIA AND AGNOSIA

Most of the evidence on the function of the association areas comes from studies of human patients who have incurred cortical damage (technically, *lesions*) through tumors, hemorrhage or blockage of cerebral blood vessels (popularly known as a stroke), or accident. Lesions in the association areas seem to impair the organization of messages that come from the sensory projection areas or that go to the motor areas.

An example is *apraxia* (Greek, "inability to act"), a serious disturbance in the organization of voluntary action. In one form of apraxia, actions that normal persons regard as quite simple and unitary become utterly fragmented and disorganized. When asked to light a cigarette, the patient may strike a match against a match box, and then strike it again and again after it is already burning; or he may light the match and then put it into his mouth (Luria, 1966). These defects are in no sense the result of a motor paralysis, for the patient can readily perform each constituent of the sequence in isolation. His problem is in selecting the right components and fitting them together.

Apraxia is evidently some impairment of a neurological system that organizes individual movements into coherent, larger actions, and also initiates them. We encountered this hierarchical principle when we looked at the behavior of transected cats and saw how different levels of the brain organize limb movements into acts, and acts into simple goal-directed sequences. The same idea applies to

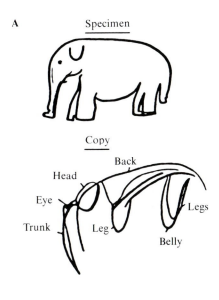

A · Specimen

Copy

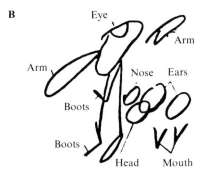

B

2.24 Drawings by a patient with visual agnosia *(A) Trying to copy an elephant. (B) Production when asked to draw a man. (From Luria, 1966)*

cortical action. The association region whose lesion leads to apraxia is perhaps analogous to the command post of a regiment that draws up the battle plan and orders an attack. If the command post falls and no other takes its place, there can be no organized attack, even though the individual soldiers are still able to fire their guns and throw their hand grenades. There is considerable debate over just where this neural command post is localized, or for that matter, whether there is one such center or several (Geschwind, 1975). Some neurologists argue that the relevant regions are roughly adjacent to the motor projection zone in the frontal lobe. As evidence, they point to the fact that certain apraxias are caused by lesions in the association areas of the frontal lobe (Luria, 1966).

Another disorder caused by lesions in certain association areas is *agnosia* (Greek, "ignorance"). Whereas apraxia represents a disrupted organization of action, agnosia is characterized by a disorganization of various aspects of the sensory world. In visual agnosia, patients can see, but are often unable to recognize what they see. They may have 20/20 vision, but they nevertheless suffer from what neurologists have called "psychic blindness." In less severe cases, patients may be able to perceive each separate detail of a picture, but be unable to see the picture as a whole. When shown a drawing of a monkey, one patient painstakingly identified several parts and then ventured an appropriate guess: "Eyes . . . mouth . . . of course, it's an animal." Or for a picture of a telephone: "A dial . . . numbers . . . of course, it's a watch or some sort of machine!" (Luria, 1966, p. 139). He had similar difficulties when asked to copy a drawing he was shown. The individual parts were rendered reasonably well, but they couldn't be integrated into a coherent whole (Figure 2.24).

It is perhaps not surprising that visual agnosias of this sort are usually produced by lesions of the association areas surrounding the visual projection zone, for it is not implausible to believe that the elaboration and organization of messages from a given projection area is the primary business of neighboring association regions.

APHASIA

Certain lesions of cortical association areas lead to serious disruptions of the most distinctively human of all human activities—the production and comprehension of language. A disorder of this kind is called *aphasia* (Greek, "lack of speech").

In one form of aphasia, *expressive aphasia,* the patient's primary difficulty is with the expression of speech—in effect, a language apraxia. In extreme cases, a patient with expressive aphasia becomes virtually unable to utter or to write a word. Less extremely, a few words or phrases survive. These may be routine expressions such as "hello" or emotional outbursts such as "damn it!" They may also be words uttered just prior to the event that caused the lesion. An example is a woman who suffered a cerebral stroke while ordering boiled beef and subsequently could express her entire range of ideas in only one word—"horseradish" (Ruch, 1965). In less severe cases, more of the spoken vocabulary remains intact but the patient's speech becomes fragmented, as finding and articulating each word requires a special effort. The result is a staccato, spoken telegram: "Here . . . head . . . operation . . . here . . . speech . . . none . . . talking . . . what . . . illness" (Luria, 1966, p. 406).

The similarity to the apraxias we have discussed before is very striking. There is no paralysis of speech muscles, for the patient is perfectly able to move lips and tongue. What is impaired is the ability to organize and plan these movements

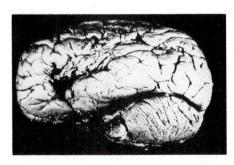

2.25 Tan's brain *The embalmed brain of Broca's famous aphasic patient "Tan," so-called because this was the only syllable he was able to utter. Note the area of damage on the lower side of the left frontal lobe, now known as Broca's area. (Courtesy Musée Dupuytren, Paris)*

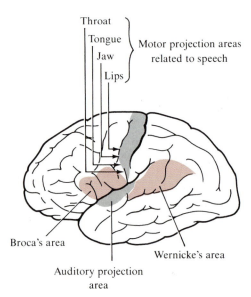

2.26 Broca's and Wernicke's areas *The diagram shows the two association areas most relevant to language. Destruction of Broca's area generally leads to expressive aphasia; destruction of Wernicke's area leads to receptive aphasia. Note the proximity to the relevant projection areas: Broca's area is closest to the regions that control the speech muscles, while Wernicke's area borders on the auditory projection zone.*

into a unified sequence, the ability to synthesize individual movements so as to form a word or to put one word after another so as to create a coherent sentence.

Expressive aphasias of the kind described here are generally produced by lesions in a region of the left frontal lobe called **Broca's area** (after a French physician, Paul Broca, who first noted its relation to speech in 1861; see Figures 2.25 and 2.26). This is an association area that borders on the part of the motor projection zone which controls the various speech muscles (jaw, tongue, lips, larynx, and so on) and presumably plays an important role in orchestrating their separate functions.

In expressive aphasia, patients understand what they hear but cannot answer. In **receptive aphasia,** the patient's problem is that they don't understand, though they often try to answer anyway—in effect, a language agnosia. In consequence, they are usually impaired in both comprehension and expression. A relatively mild version of receptive aphasia is sometimes called word deafness. Patients can hear but they can no longer differentiate the complex acoustic patterns that make up speech. These are now perceived as a disorganized jumble, much as we perceive a rapid conversation in a language we don't know. As one patient described his condition, "Voices, come, but not words. I can hear, sounds come, but words don't separate" (Brain, 1965, p. 106).

Other cases of receptive aphasia are even more catastrophic, for in them the patient has an impaired appreciation of the meaning of the words she hears (or sees in print). She can perceive the sound patterns, for she can repeat them; but they often lack their former symbolic value. Thus, when asked to point to a spoon, one patient said, "Spoon, poon, yes," and then pointed to an irrelevant object. When asked to touch her nose, she replied, "Stuch, tux news, nose," and then did nothing (J. W. Brown, 1972, p. 65).

The previous examples illustrate the fact that severe receptive aphasia affects speech production as well as comprehension, for one can hardly speak normally if one doesn't understand one's own utterances. In marked contrast to expressive aphasia, patients with receptive aphasia talk very freely and very fast, but while they utter many words, they say very little. The sentences are reasonably grammatical but they are largely composed of filler words that provide little information. A typical example is, "I was over the other one, and then after they had been in the department, I was in this one" (Geschwind, 1970, p. 904).

In many cases, there are substitutions of one sound for another ("spoot" for "spoon") or of one word for another ("fork" for "spoon"). Occasionally, the entire speech output becomes an almost unintelligible jargon. In some cases, most of the key words are incomprehensible: "Then he graf, so I'll graf, I'm giving ink, no, gefergen, in pane, I can't grasp, I haven't grob the grabben, I'm going to the glimmeril, let me go" (J. W. Brown, 1972, p. 64). In others, each individual word is clear enough, but the phrase as a whole is gibberish, as in the reply of a patient when shown a bunch of keys and asked to name it: "Indication of measurement of pieces of apparatus or intimating the cost of apparatus in various forms" (Brain, 1965, p. 108).

Receptive aphasia is usually associated with left-hemisphere lesions (in right-handers) in various association areas of the temporal and parietal lobes. Many authorities believe that the crucial locus is **Wernicke's area,** a region that borders on the auditory projection zone and is named after a nineteenth-century neurologist who first described word deafness and other receptive aphasias (Figure 2.25).

One Brain or Two?

Anatomically, the two cerebral hemispheres appear to be quite similar, but there is abundant evidence that their functions are by no means identical. This asymmetry of function is called *lateralization,* and its manifestations include such diverse phenomena as language, spatial organization, and the superior dexterity of one hand over the other (Springer and Deutsch, 1981).

We have already seen that in right-handers aphasia is usually associated with lesions in the left hemisphere. Until recently, neuroscientists interpreted this fact to mean that one hemisphere is dominant over the other. As a result, they called the (right-hander's) right hemisphere the "minor hemisphere," for they believed that it is essentially a left hemisphere without language functions and with a lesser capacity for fine motor control.

More recent evidence has rescued the right hemisphere from this poor relation status, for it now appears that it has some important functions of its own. Right-handers with lesions in the right hemisphere seem to suffer from various difficulties in the comprehension of space and form; they concentrate on details but cannot grasp the overall pattern. Some have trouble recognizing faces. Some have great difficulties in dressing themselves; they put their arms in a pants leg or put a shirt on backwards (Bogen, 1969).

The results are more ambiguous for the 12 percent or so of the population that is left-handed (and also left-footed, and to a lesser extent, left-eyed and left-eared as well; Porac and Cohen, 1981). Somewhat more than half of them have speech predominantly localized in the left hemisphere; in the rest, language is usually represented in both hemispheres. A further fact concerns the relation between speech and other language functions such as reading and writing. In right-handers, these are all represented in the left hemisphere. But in left-handers, the situation is less clear-cut, for speech and reading or writing are often localized in different hemispheres (Gloringen, Gloringen, Haub, and Quatember, 1969). All told, there seems to be less lateralization in left-handers than in right-handers, so that the functional capacities of left-handers' two hemispheres are more on a par. As a result, in left-handers, aphasia may often be produced by lesions to either hemisphere. There is also, however, a greater likelihood for ultimate recovery from aphasia, for the intact hemisphere is better able to take over the responsibilities formerly assigned to the one that suffered damage (Brain, 1965).

EVIDENCE FROM SPLIT BRAINS.

Some of the most persuasive evidence on lateralization comes from studies on persons with *split brains.* These are people whose *corpus callosum* has been surgically severed. The corpus callosum is a massive bundle of nerve fibers that interconnects the two hemispheres so that they can pool their information and function as a harmonious whole. This neurological bridge (and some other less important ones) is sometimes cut in cases of severe epilepsy so that the seizure will not spread from one hemisphere to the other. Once confined to a small cortical area, the seizures are much less severe and, in fact, much less frequent. The operation clearly relieves suffering, but it has a side effect—the two hemispheres

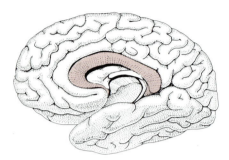

2.27 The split brain *To control epilepsy, neurosurgeons sometimes sever the two hemispheres. This is accomplished by cutting the corpus callosum and a few other connective tracts. The corpus callosum is shown here in a lateral cross-section.*

of the split brain become functionally isolated from each other and essentially act as two separate brains (Figure 2.27).

The effect of the split-brain operation is best demonstrated by setting a task which poses a question to one hemisphere and requires the answer from the other one (Figure 2.28). One method is to expose a picture so that the neural message reaches only one hemisphere. This is done by flashing the picture for a fraction of a second to either the right or the left side of the patient's field of vision. If it is to the right, it is projected to the left hemisphere; if to the left, to the right hemisphere (Figure 2.29). The patient simply has to say what he sees. When the picture is on the right, he easily does so, for the information is transmitted to the same hemisphere that can formulate a spoken answer—the left. This is not so when the picture is flashed on the left. Now the visual image is sent to the right hemisphere, but this hemisphere can neither provide a spoken reply, nor can it relay the news to the left hemisphere which has the language capacity. In consequence the patient is unable to answer. Sometimes, there is a haphazard guess. When this happens, the patient may frown or shake his head immediately after he has given the incorrect answer. The right hemisphere evidently does have some limited language capacity after all. It sees the pictured object, and while it cannot produce the correct name, for instance, "ashtray," it at least understands that this name is not "coffee pot" (Gazzaniga, 1967).

Another demonstration of the fact that the right hemisphere understands what is shown even though it cannot talk about it, comes from the observation of a patient who was unexpectedly shown a picture of a nude girl. When this picture was flashed to the left hemisphere, the patient laughed and correctly described what she had seen. When the same picture was presented to the right hemisphere, the patient said that she saw nothing, but immediately afterward she smiled slyly and began to chuckle. When asked what was so funny, she said, "I don't know . . . nothing . . . oh—that funny machine" (Gazzaniga, 1970, p. 106). The right hemisphere knew what it was laughing at; the left hemisphere heard the laughter but couldn't tell its cause.

An elegant demonstration of hemispheric differences uses stimuli that are composites of two pictures, in which the left half of one is joined to the right half

2.28 A setup sometimes used in split-brain studies *The subject fixates a center dot and then sees a picture or a word on the right or left side of the dot. He may be asked to respond verbally, by reading the word or naming the picture. He may also be asked to respond without words, for example, by picking out a named object from among a group spread out on a table and hidden from view, so that it can only be identified by touch. (After Gazzaniga, 1967)*

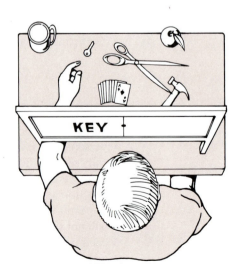

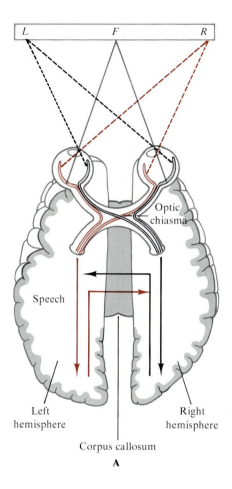

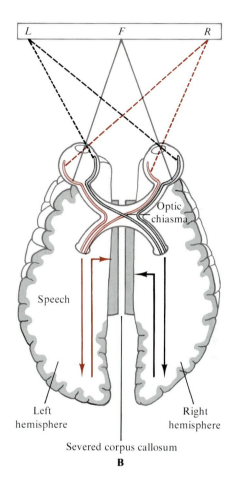

2.29   Restricting visual input to only one hemisphere   (A) This illustration shows how visual information is sent to the brain in normals. A person looks at a point—the so-called fixation point or F—of a picture. Points to the left of F, such as L, will fall on the right side of each retina (the receptor region of each eye). Points to the right of F, such as R, will fall on the left side of each retina. The reason is simple optics: Our lens reverses up and down, right and left. We next have to consider a special anatomical fact. As the figure shows, half of each retina sends its information to the hemisphere on the same side. But the other half feeds into a part of the optic nerve that crosses over to the opposite hemisphere. This arrangement guarantees that if the eyes are fixed at F, the entire left side of the field (including point L) will be sent up to the right hemisphere; the entire right side of the field (including point R) will be dispatched to the left hemisphere.

As a result of all this, point L goes to the right hemisphere; point R to the left hemisphere. But this only works if the eyes stay fixed at point F. In actuality, it is hard to keep the eyes stationary. To get around this, investigators use a special trick. They flash the picture very briefly, say, for 150 milliseconds. They can now be sure that there are no eye movements while the picture is exposed, for such eye movements take longer to execute (about 200 milliseconds) than the time the picture is in view to the person.

(B) These procedures ensure that certain points in the visual field go to only one hemisphere. Normals have an intact corpus callosum which serves as a bridge between the two hemispheres over which information can be passed in both directions. But this isn't so in split-brain patients whose corpus callosum is cut so that their right and left hemispheres can't exchange information. As the figure shows, in a split-brain patient point L only gets to the right hemisphere and can't be relayed back to the left which has the language capacity. As a result, the patient is unable to say what he saw on the left side of the field. (Gazzaniga, 1967)

2.30 Composite figures used to test for hemispheric differences in split-brain patients *(After Levy, Trevarthen, and Sperry, 1972)*

of the other (Figure 2.30). These are briefly exposed, with their midline centered in the field of vision. Normal subjects see such pictures as they really are—bizarre monstrosities, such as the left half of a bee stuck onto the right half of an eye. In contrast, split-brain patients never seem to notice anything unusual. They either see a bee or they see an eye, but never both. Which of the two they choose depends upon which hemisphere is asked. Suppose the stimulus is the bee-eye combination, with the bee on the left (thus in the right hemisphere), the eye on the right (hence in the left hemisphere). In one condition, the subjects have to indicate what they just saw by pointing to one of several objects that are shown to them after the brief flash of the bee-eye combination. The choice objects include both a bee and an eye (drawn in complete form) and can be inspected at the subjects' leisure. In this task, language is irrelevant, for the subjects have to recognize only the similarity between two forms, regardless of the names. We have already seen that the right hemisphere is probably more critical for the perception of complex forms than the left. If so, the patients should point to the bee, for that is the only stimulus that the right hemisphere saw. This is just what happens.

In another condition, the task calls on language functions. Patients are again presented with a brief flash of the bee-eye combination. They are then shown pictures of several objects, such as a key and a pie, and they have to select the one whose name *rhymes* with the object they just saw. When tested in this manner, the patients will almost invariably choose the pie, an object whose name rhymes with the name of the only stimulus that was shown to the left hemisphere, the eye (Levy, Trevarthen, and Sperry, 1972; Levy, 1974).

LATERALIZATION IN NORMAL SUBJECTS

All the evidence for lateralization we've discussed thus far has come from patients with certain neurological deficits: some with lesions in one or the other hemisphere, others with a severed corpus callosum. Can lateralization be demonstrated in normal populations? A great deal of recent research has shown that it can.

Selective stimulation of the hemispheres One approach uses the same experimental procedure that was so successfully employed with the split-brain patients. Various stimuli are presented to either the right or the left visual field of normal subjects at very brief exposures. As we've already seen, when subjects fix their eyes at a point straight ahead, everything to the left of this fixation mark will be sent to the right hemisphere; everything to the right goes to the left hemisphere. Some of the stimuli are items that are presumably better dealt with by the left hemisphere: words or letters. Others are items that call on the special capacities of the right hemisphere: complex forms or faces. The subject's task is to recognize the items and to indicate his response as quickly and as accurately as possible.

In studies of this sort, the experimenters' primary interest is in the subject's **reaction time,** that is, in how long it takes him to respond. The logic is simple. Suppose the stimulus is appropriate to the capacity of the hemisphere to which it is presented: words to the left, faces to the right. If so, this hemisphere can get to work immediately, decipher the stimulus, and come up with an answer. But suppose the stimulus is sent to the wrong cerebral address: words to the right hemisphere, and faces to the left. This calls for an extra step, for now the visual

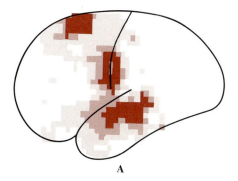

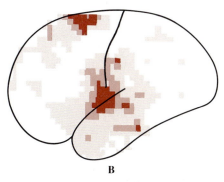

2.31 Computer-derived maps of the surface of the brain *These maps show the rate of blood flow in different regions of the brain while subjects are speaking. In these maps, the brain surface was divided into squares, and a computer averaged the blood flow that occurred in the area indicated by each square. The rate of blood flow is indicated by the degree of shading; the deeper the shading, the greater the rate. (A) Left hemisphere activity. Note that maximum blood flow occurred in the lower portion of the motor and somato-sensory projection areas (the regions that control or receive sensory input from the mouth, tongue, and larynx), the auditory projection area, and Broca's area. (B) Right hemisphere activity. There is considerably less activity in the mouth, tongue, and larynx region, in Broca's area, and in the auditory projection zone. (After Lassen, Ingvar, and Skinhoj, 1978)*

message must be forwarded to the other hemisphere by way of the corpus callosum. But this additional transmission step takes a certain amount of time. As a result, we would expect that subjects will be faster in recognizing words presented to the left hemisphere than to the right hemisphere. By the same token, we would expect them to respond more quickly to faces that are shown to the right hemisphere rather than to the left. By now, a fair number of experiments have shown that this is essentially what happens (e.g., Geffen, Bradshaw, and Wallace, 1971; Moscovitch, 1972, 1979).

Monitoring the two hemispheres The reaction time studies just described show lateralization effects in normal subjects. But these effects have to be inferred from the subject's responses in a rather roundabout way. In recent years, neuroscientists have tried to observe the operation of the two hemispheres more directly and have devised a number of techniques to look in at the cortex from the outside.

A recent technique measures the blood flow in different cortical areas while the subject is engaged in various mental operations. This method is based on the assumption that an increase in the activity of brain cells in a certain part of the cortex will call for an increase in the blood supplied to that region. To determine the distribution of blood flow in the cortex, a mildly radioactive gas is injected into an artery (or is inhaled) and special radiation counters are placed at various points on the subject's skull. The subject is fully conscious and is asked to perform various tasks: to speak, read, follow a moving light, and so on. The distribution of counter readings at the various points on the skull will then give an index of the rate at which blood flows through a given region (Ingvar and Lassen, 1979).

The results of such studies provide a graphic proof that different cortical regions become activated during different tasks. In particular, they document the asymmetry of hemispheric functions. Figures 2.31A and B show the rate of blood flow in the two hemispheres while subjects were speaking. In the left hemisphere, the blood flow was more extensive in just the areas where one would expect it to be: the lower portions of the motor and somatosensory cortex (which control and receive sensory information from the mouth, tongue, and larynx), the auditory projection zone, and Broca's area. In the right hemisphere, the activity was much less, especially in the mouth and auditory areas (Lassen, Ingvar, and Skinhoj, 1978).

TWO MODES OF MENTAL FUNCTIONING

The preceding discussion indicates that language and spatial organization are usually handled in two different areas of the brain. Some psychologists believe that this difference in localization goes along with a distinction between two fundamentally different modes of thought: one that involves words, the other spatial processes. This distinction is certainly in line with everyday observation. We often think in words—about scientific problems, about politics, about who likes whom; the list is endless. But we also mentally manipulate the world with little benefit of language—as when we visualize our living room with rearranged furniture or when we work a jigsaw puzzle. Many problems can be solved by either mode: We may find our way to a friend's home by referring to a mental map, or by memorizing a verbal sequence such as "first right turn after the third traffic light." But the two modes are somehow not intersubstitutable. How a corkscrew

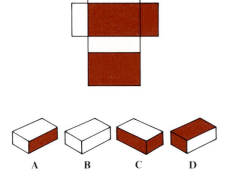

2.32 An item from a test of spatial relations *The subject has to decide which of the figures, A, B, C, or D, can be made by folding the pattern above. (The correct answer is* D. *After Cronbach, 1970a)*

works is hard to describe in words; the pros and cons of a two-party system are impossible to get across without them.

The difference between verbal and spatial modes of thought is explicitly recognized in the construction of many tests of intelligence. Different test items are provided to assess each mode separately. Verbal aptitude may be gauged by questions that involve vocabulary ("What does *formulate* mean?") or the abstraction of underlying similarities ("In what ways are waterpipes and streets alike?"). Spatial ability may be tested by items that require the subject to construct a design by arranging a set of colored blocks, or to visualize how a two-dimensional shape will appear when folded into a box (see Figure 2.32). In line with our previous discussion, performance on the various verbal tests is more impaired by lesions to the left hemisphere; that on spatial tests by lesions to the right (Levy, 1974).

The difference between the functions of the two hemispheres goes beyond the verbal-spatial distinction. For there is also the fact that, at least in right-handers, the same hemisphere that is dominant for language—the left hemisphere—is also superior in the organization of skilled motor acts. Thus, in right-handers, the left hemisphere's control of bodily movement on the side of the body opposite to it leads to a more dexterous right side. (The Latin adjective *dexter* means "situated on the right," and thus also "skillful.")

Is it just an accident that the same hemisphere that handles language is also the one that is responsible for fine motor control? Some neuroscientists feel that it is not. On the contrary, they believe that it gives a clue to a more fundamental difference in the functions of the two hemispheres. In their view, the right hemisphere is specialized for the organization of space, whereas the left hemisphere concentrates upon organization in time. This formulation of the left hemisphere's function is relevant both to language and to motor dexterity, for both require a precise appreciation of temporal order. The person who is insensitive to what comes first and what comes second cannot possibly speak or understand the speech of others. *Tap* is not the same word as *pat,* and the sentence "Wellington beat Bonaparte" is crucially different from "Bonaparte beat Wellington." This is also true of skilled manual acts, which consist of organized sequences of wrist and finger movements whose order must not be disrupted. To summarize this view, the right hemisphere is concerned with what goes where, the left with what comes when (Bogen, 1969).

Some Problems in Localizing Brain Function

The preceding discussion has sketched some recent advances in our understanding of the localization of function in the human cortex. But there are various problems that complicate the analysis of any correlation between anatomical site and psychological function.

WHAT IS THE PSYCHOLOGICAL FUNCTION?

Much of our knowledge of human cerebral function comes from the study of lesions. But the fact that we know that the destruction of a given site leads to a particular deficit doesn't tell us how that site contributed to the function that was lost. An important first step toward an answer is to ask what that underlying function really is. Sometimes this is fairly clear, as in lesions of the sensory projection

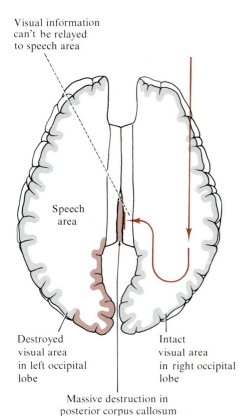

Visual information
can't be relayed
to speech area

Speech
area

Destroyed
visual area
in left occipital
lobe

Intact
visual area
in right occipital
lobe

Massive destruction in
posterior corpus callosum

2.33 A disconnection effect The figure
shows lesions in the left occipital cortex
and the posterior corpus callosum. Given
these effects, vision depends entirely on
the visual projection area in the right
hemisphere. But this information can't be
related to the speech area of the left
hemisphere because the hemispheric
bridge for visual messages is the posterior
corpus callosum. As a result, the patient
sees the word, but only as a meaningless set
of forms. (After Geschwind, 1972)

areas which cause defects in vision and hearing. But in some other cases, the explanation is much less obvious.

A good example is a famous case reported by the French neurologist Dejerine in 1892 (Geschwind, 1972). Dejerine's patient woke up one morning to discover that he could no longer read. He could speak and understand speech as before; in fact, he could write, though he could not read what he had written. His vision was unaffected with one exception—he could no longer see the right half of his visual field. Given the anatomical arrangement of the visual pathways, one neurological inference was inescapable: There was serious damage to the visual projection area of the left hemisphere (see Figure 2.33). Should we conclude that this region is a "reading center"? Such an interpretation is wildly improbable. Man roamed earth for eons before the advent of writing and we could hardly expect the evolutionary process to provide neurological machinery for a purpose some million years ahead.

To explain the phenomenon we must first consider what reading is. In virtually all modern writing systems, the written word is a visual transcription of the spoken one. (The great exception is Chinese.) The child learns to read by associating certain visual forms with speech sounds and, through them, with meanings. Since the speech sounds and meanings are dealt with in the language areas of the left hemisphere, it is plausible to assume that these areas must participate in the act of reading. According to this view, the visual information has to be passed on to the language areas of the left hemisphere in order to be interpreted as language symbols—in order to be read. But suppose the pathway between the visual and the speech areas is no longer there? At postmortem examination, Dejerine found that his patient suffered such a disconnection. A large portion of his corpus callosum was destroyed, as was the visual projection area of the left hemisphere. This solved the riddle. The *right* visual cortex was unimpaired and so the patient could see. The language areas of the left hemisphere were intact, and so he could speak and comprehend. The motor system was unaffected, so he could write. But the destruction of the corpus callosum isolated the visual cortex of the right hemisphere from the language areas of the left. As a result, the patient saw printed text but could not read it (Figure 2.32). This effect is obviously quite similar to what is observed in split-brain patients.

This example highlights the fact that we must try to understand both terms of a psychoanatomical correlation. To understand the neural underpinnings of some aspect of behavior, whether language, memory, or whatever, we must understand something about that behavior itself, quite apart from its relation to cerebral anatomy. For psychology and neurophysiology go hand in hand. To claim that psychology will not progress until we know more about the brain is to assert only half the truth because the search for a neurophysiological underpinning necessarily requires some knowledge of what it is an underpinning of.

WHO'S IN CHARGE?

A related problem concerns hierarchical control. Who is in ultimate charge? We have previously seen that the nervous system is organized along the lines of a hierarchy, with higher centers controlling lower centers, which control yet lower ones. But where does the cortex fit in? Some nineteenth-century neurologists supposed that some regions of the cortex are at the very top of the hierarchy and hand down orders to all the rest. This notion fits in with our view that those functions that are most severely disturbed by cortical lesions—language, thinking, memory, and perception—are the "higher" mental processes, which presumably govern the "lower" ones. But many modern neuroscientists believe that this conclusion doesn't really follow. For the cortex does not control many of the lower functions. For example, rats—and for that matter, humans—continue to eat and seek food even though they may have suffered extensive cortical damage. Foods that they found highly palatable or distasteful before the lesion will still be palatable or distasteful afterwards (Grill and Berridge, 1985). This is not to say that the cortex does not play any role in food seeking (or drinking, or sexual behavior, or any other so-called "lower" functions). But there is no evidence that it governs them.

The best guess is that the nervous system is not organized according to a single hierarchy. It is not an absolute monarchy, with a cortical king who governs all else below (e.g., Arbib, 1972). Instead, it is composed of a number of hierarchies whose controls and functions overlap, with some in the cortex and some in subcortical structures. These hierarchies interact continuously, with one in charge on one occasion but not on another. So it probably makes no sense to say that any one of them is ruler. For the operation of the nervous system may well be analogous to that of a complex twentieth-century society such as ours. The United States in 1980 is not governed by *one* hierarchy, but by a number of interlocking ones. There are the three branches of the federal government, as well as the armed forces, the bureaucracies of the government agencies, the hierarchies of the large corporations, the labor unions, the media, and so on and so on. We are governed by a complex interaction of them all, and who will decide depends on many factors, including what it is that is to be decided.

Who's in charge? As yet, we know too little to be sure of any answer. But the best guess is: Nobody. Everybody. It depends.

SUMMARY

1. Since Descartes, many scientists have tried to explain human and animal movement within the framework of the *reflex* concept: A stimulus excites a sense organ, which transmits excitation upward to the spinal cord or brain, which in turn relays the excitation downward to a muscle or gland and thus produces action. Descartes's general classification of nervous function is still with us as we distinguish between *reception, integration,* and *reaction.*

2. Later investigators showed that the smallest unit of the nervous system is the *neuron,* whose primary anatomical subdivisions are the *dendrites, cell body,* and *axon.*

3. The main function of a neuron is to produce a *nerve impulse.* This is an electrochemical disturbance that is propagated along the membrane of the axon. The impulse is triggered by stimuli that are above some *threshold value.* The impulse obeys the *all-or-none law* of neuron stimulation: Once threshold is exceeded, further increases of stimulus intensity have no effect on the magnitude of the impulse. But the nervous system can nevertheless distinguish between different intensities of the stimulus. One means is *impulse frequency:* The more intense the stimulus, the more often the neuron fires.

4. To understand how neurons communicate, investigators have studied *reflex action,* which is necessarily based on the activity of several neurons. Results of studies with *spinal dogs* led Sherrington to infer the processes that underlie conduction across the *synapse,* the

gap between the axon of one neuron and the dendrites and cell body of the next. Conduction within neurons was shown to obey different laws than conduction between neurons (that is, across the synapse). Evidence included the phenomenon of *temporal summation.* Sherrington concluded that the excitation from several neurons funnels into a common reservoir to produce a *central excitatory state.*

5. Further studies argued for a *central inhibitory state.* Evidence came from *reciprocal inhibition* found in antagonistic muscles. Further work showed that a reflex can be activated either by increasing excitation or by decreasing inhibition. An example of the latter is the *disinhibition* produced by the destruction of higher centers which inhibit the reflex.

6. Sherrington's inferences of synaptic functions have been confirmed and extended by modern electrical and chemical studies. Today we know that transmission across the synapse is accomplished by *neurotransmitters,* chemical substances that are liberated at the axon terminals of one neuron and exert excitatory or inhibitory effects on the dendrites and cell body of another. Examples include *norepinephrine* and *dopamine.* Some recent discoveries concern a group of neurotransmitters called *endorphins,* whose activity serves to alleviate pain.

7. In addition to the nervous system, there is another group of organs whose function is to serve as an instrument of communication within the body. This is the *endocrine system,* whose glands secrete their *hormones* directly into the bloodstream, which will eventually carry them to various target organs.

8. A crude anatomical outline of the vertebrate nervous system starts out with the distinction between the *peripheral (somatic* and *autonomic)* and *central nervous systems.* The central nervous system consists of the *spinal cord* and the *brain.* Important parts of the brain are the *hindbrain* (including *medulla* and *cerebellum*), *midbrain* (including the *reticular formation*) and *forebrain* (including *thalamus, hypothalamus, cerebral hemispheres,* and *cerebral cortex*).

9. In general, the brain tends to function hierarchically, with higher centers commanding lower centers. Animals whose brain is cut so that they lack both midbrain and forebrain can still move but don't integrate their movements. Animals that lack the forebrain show integrated movements but without any goal.

10. The *cerebral cortex* is generally believed to underlie the most complex aspects of behavior. The *projection areas* of the cortex act as receiving stations for sensory information or as dispatching centers for motor commands. The remaining regions of the cortex are called *association areas.* Their function concerns such higher mental processes as planning, remembering, thinking, and speech.

11. Certain lesions of association areas lead to *apraxia,* a serious disturbance in the organization of voluntary action. Other lesions produce *agnosia,* a disorganization of perception and recognition. Still others cause *aphasia,* a profound disruption of language function, which may involve speech production, speech comprehension, or both.

12. In many ways, the two hemispheres are mirror images of each other. But to some extent, their function is not symmetrical. In most right-handers, the left hemisphere handles the bulk of the language functions, while the right hemisphere is more relevant to spatial comprehension. One source of evidence for this difference in hemispheric function, or *lateralization,* comes from the study of *split-brain patients* in whom the main connection between the two hemispheres, the *corpus callosum,* has been surgically cut. Further evidence is provided by the reaction times of normal persons when stimuli calling on verbal or spatial abilities are presented to either hemisphere. Direct observation of the operation of the two hemispheres can be obtained by measuring different rates of blood flow in the two hemispheres.

CHAPTER 3

Motivation

In this chapter, we will examine some of the simple motives that human beings share with other animals. These motives steer our behavior in certain directions rather than others; toward food, say, rather than toward shelter.

Our main concern will be with motives that are essentially unlearned and that pertain to the individual alone rather than to his interaction with others. Examples are hunger and thirst, the desire for safety, the need for rest. We will later take up two other kinds of motives. One concerns desires that are acquired through learning, such as the need to achieve, to attain prestige, or to amass possessions (see Chapters 12 and 15). The other group is no less biologically based than hunger and thirst, but it involves motives that transcend the individual alone and focus on his relations with other persons, such as sex, filial love, and aggression (see Chapter 10).

MOTIVATION AS DIRECTION

Most human and animal actions are directed. We don't simply walk, reach, shrink, or flee; we walk and reach *toward* some objects, shrink and flee *away* from others. The objects that are approached or withdrawn from may be in the organism's here and now, as when a kitten jumps toward a rolling ball. But often enough, the object exists in an as yet unrealized future. The hawk circles in the sky in search of prey, but there is none in sight as yet. In such a case, an inner motive (a purpose, a desire) leads to actions that bring the hawk closer to its food.

Directed action seems difficult to reconcile with Descartes's notion of humans and animals as reflex machines, however complex their internal wiring. This problem is most pronounced for actions that are directed toward some future goal, for it is hard to see how an automaton can be imbued with purpose or desire. But difficulties arise even in the simplest case in which the direction is toward (or away from) an immediately present object. Consider the kitten reaching for the ball. What matters is not whether this flexor muscle is contracted or that extensor muscle relaxed, but rather whether the overall pattern of muscular activity gets the creature closer to the final end state—near the ball. The kitten may swipe at the ball with its right paw or its left, it may crouch more on one side or the other —all that matters is that, whatever the specific motor response, it will be toward the ball. Descartes's statues walked out and bowed when a visitor stepped on a hidden spring, but did they bow *to* the visitor? Suppose the visitor were to push the spring and then jump quickly to the left. The statue would surely lumber through its prescribed routine exactly as before, in stony disregard of the altered circumstance.

It is evident that a simple automaton is incapable of directed action. Can the machine be modified to overcome this lack? The answer is yes.

Control Systems

Modern engineers have developed an immense technology based on machines that control their own activities and are in that sense directed. The basic principle upon which these devices are built is the notion of a ***feedback system.*** When a machine is in operation it performs some kind of action which may be mechanical, electrical, thermal, or whatever, but which in all cases engenders some changes in the external environment. If these changes in turn influence the further operation of the machine—if they feed back upon the machine—we have a control system based on feedback.

In ***positive feedback systems,*** the feedback strengthens the very response that produced it. The result is an ever-increasing level of activity. A technological example is a rocket that homes in on airplanes. It is designed to increase its velocity the closer it gets to its target.

Of greater relevance to our present concern is ***negative feedback*** in which the feedback stops, or even reverses, the original response of the machine that produced the environmental change. Negative feedback underlies a large number of industrial devices called ***servomechanisms*** that can maintain themselves in a particular state. A simple example is the system that controls most home furnaces. A thermostat closes an electric contact for all temperatures below a given setting and opens it for all that are above it. The contact controls the furnace, which only operates when the contact is closed. In the winter, the result is a steady house temperature, for the furnace will burn fuel only if the temperature is below the critical level; once this is reached, the furnace shuts off, deactivated by its own negative feedback (Figure 3.1). In a sense, the thermostatically controlled furnace has a goal: It "aims" at a particular temperature.

Negative feedback systems exist at all levels of the nervous system and are responsible, at least in part, for directed action. In this chapter we will see how such systems underlie motivated actions of many kinds. Some concern the organism's regulation of various vital functions—temperature maintenance, food and water intake, and the like. Others involve the organism's reaction to threats from outside, whether fearful escape or raging attack.

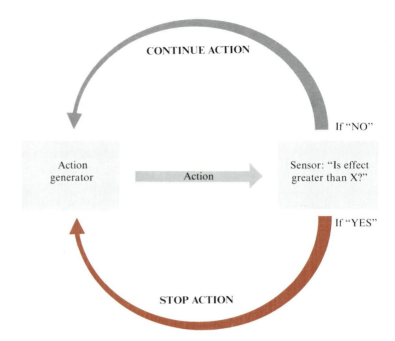

3.1 Negative feedback *In negative feedback systems, the feedback stops or reverses the action that produces it. A sensing device indicates the level of a certain stimulus. If that level exceeds a certain set-point, the action stops. The effect is self-regulation.*

SELF-REGULATION

Can we apply the principles of negative feedback to the understanding of motivated action in which the direction is imposed from within? We will begin by considering those motives which grow directly out of the organism's regulation of its own internal state, such as its temperature, its water level, and its supply of food nutrients.

Homeostasis

Claude Bernard (*Courtesy National Library of Medicine*)

Some two hundred years after Descartes, another Frenchman, the physiologist Claude Bernard (1813–1878), emphasized the fact that the organism exists in an internal environment as well as an external one—the organism's own body fluids, its blood and its lymph. Bernard pointed out that this *internal environment* is kept remarkably constant despite considerable fluctuations of the environment outside. The striking constancy is shown by the salt and water balance of the body, its oxygen concentration, its pH (a measure of acidity), its concentration of various nutrient substances such as glucose, and its temperature (in warm-blooded animals). In healthy organisms, all of these oscillate within very narrow limits, and these limits define the organism's conditions for health and survival. Thus 60 to 90 milligrams per 100 cubic centimeters of blood is the acceptable range for the glucose concentration in the bloodstream of a healthy person. A drop below this level means coma and eventual death; a prolonged rise above it indicates disorders such as diabetes. The modern term for this stable internal equilibrium is *homeostasis* (literally, "equal state") and the mechanisms whereby it is achieved are sometimes said to reflect the "wisdom of the body" (Cannon, 1932).

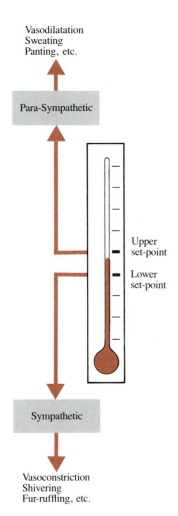

Vasodilatation
Sweating
Panting, etc.

Para-Sympathetic

Upper
set-point

Lower
set-point

Sympathetic

Vasoconstriction
Shivering
Fur-ruffling, etc.

**3.2   Reflexive temperature regulation in
mammals**   *When the temperature
deviates from an internal set-point, various
reflexive reactions will occur to restore the
temperature to this set-point.*

Temperature Regulation

A rather simple example of homeostatic balance is temperature regulation in birds and mammals. These animals are called warm-blooded because they have a large repertoire of homeostatic adjustments that keep their internal body temperatures at a fairly constant level, despite wide temperature variations in the surrounding environment.

TEMPERATURE CONTROL FROM WITHIN

If the internal temperature of a warm-blooded animal is too high, various reflexive reactions produce heat loss. One is peripheral *vasodilatation,* a widening of the skin's capillaries. This sends warm blood to the body surface and results in heat loss by radiation. Other reactions that lead to cooling are sweating (in humans) and panting (in dogs), both of which produce heat loss by evaporation.

An opposed pattern is called into play when the internal temperature is too low. Now there is no sweating or panting, and instead of peripheral vasodilatation there is *vasoconstriction.* The capillary diameters narrow, so that the blood is squeezed away from the cold periphery and heat is conserved. Other reflexive reactions include *piloerection,* a ruffling of fur which creates a thick envelope of protective air. (The gooseflesh feeling is our feeble remnant of this reflex response, of little use to us now in our naked condition.)

These and other reflexive reactions are called into play when the temperature deviates too far from some internal temperature set-point (Figure 3.2). But in some animals this set-point can be changed. For example, a certain ground squirrel spends the winter in hibernation. As the outside temperature gets colder and colder, his internal set-point drops, so he finds a secluded burrow and falls into a torpor—a useful mechanism in times when food is very scarce. But while his new set-point is low, it still functions. When the weather gets cold enough, he wakes up to keep from freezing to death (Heller, Cranshaw, and Hammel, 1978).

TEMPERATURE CONTROL BY BEHAVIOR

The homeostatic mechanisms we have just described are essentially involuntary. They may be actions, but we don't feel that they are *our* actions; in fact, some of them concern only a fraction of the body's subsystems. For example, vasodilatation and vasoconstriction do not involve the skeletal musculature at all. But there is no question that when the need arises, these reflexive mechanisms are supplemented by voluntary actions that involve the organism as a whole. If a rat is placed in a cold cage, it will search for suitable materials and build a nest. That humans perform similar voluntary acts in the service of temperature regulation goes without saying: They wear coats when they are cold and wear as little as custom permits (or turn on an air conditioner if they have it) when they are hot. The important point is that these voluntary actions are still in the service of that same internal environment whose constancy is so crucial to survival. But there is one important difference: Now the organism actively changes its external environment so that its internal environment can stay the same.

THE AUTONOMIC NERVOUS SYSTEM AND TEMPERATURE CONTROL

To understand how the nervous system marshals its forces to protect us against extreme heat and cold, we'll begin by looking at the involuntary side of temperature regulation. What controls the various reactions of the internal organs that accomplish this? The most direct control is exerted by the autonomic nervous system (ANS), which sends commands to the **glands** and to the **smooth muscles*** of the viscera (internal organs) and the blood vessels. The ANS has two divisions: the **sympathetic** and the **parasympathic**. These two divisions often act as antagonists. Thus, the excitation of the sympathetic division leads to an acceleration of heart rate and inhibition of peristalsis (rhythmic contractions) of the intestines. Parasympathetic activation has effects that are the very opposite: cardiac deceleration and stimulation of peristalsis. This same antagonism is seen in temperature regulation. The sympathetic division acts to counteract cold; it triggers vasoconstriction, shivering, and fur-ruffling. In contrast, the parasympathetic helps to cool the body when it is overheated; it stimulates panting, sweating, and vasodilatation (see Figure 3.16, p. 68). We'll have more to say about the tug-of-war between the two autonomic divisions when we discuss fear and rage. For now, we merely note that the autonomic nervous system is an important agent in directing the control of the internal environment.

SENSING THE INTERNAL ENVIRONMENT: THE HYPOTHALAMUS

The sympathetic and parasympathetic divisions control the various reflexive levers that help to maintain the internal environment. But what governs *them*? A crucial control center is the hypothalamus, which represents a certain triumph of anatomical miniaturization, for within its few cubic millimeters are the controls for many of the biological motives (see Figure 3.3).

Two regions within the hypothalamus have been shown to be control centers for temperature regulation. One is in the anterior (toward the front of the body) hypothalamus and cools the body down, the other is in the posterior hypothalamus and heats the body up. Electrical stimulation of the anterior, cooling region leads to panting and vasodilatation.; its destruction may cause death by overheating (Andersson, Grant, and Larsson, 1956).

These two temperature control centers of the hypothalamus presumably control the two divisions of the autonomic nervous system whose excitation leads to the cooling and heating effects. The next question is how the hypothalamus decides which of the two centers should act and by how much. Under normal conditions, temperature regulation is nearly perfect. This means that the organism somehow knows its own body temperature, can sense deviations from the normal level, and can then determine in which direction it must throw the autonomic two-way switch (for example, vasoconstriction versus vasodilatation) to restore the thermal balance. How does it do this?

The answer is that the hypothalamus contains its own thermometer: receptor cells which respond to the temperature cells which respond to the temperature of

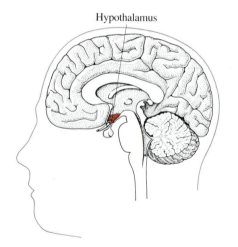

Hypothalamus

3.3   The hypothalamus   *Cross-section of the human brain with the hypothalamus indicated in color. (After Keeton, 1980)*

---

* The individual fibers of these muscles look smooth when observed under a microscope, in contrast to the fibers of the skeletal muscles which look striped.

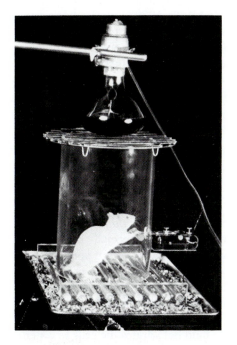

3.4 Performing a learned response to keep warm *A rat kept in a cold environment will learn to press a lever which turns on a heat lamp for a few seconds after each lever press. (Weiss and Laties, 1961)*

the body fluids in which the brain is bathed. These thermoreceptors are hooked up to the reflex controls so as to yield negative feedback—a hypothalamic thermostat. If this is so, one should be able to fool the hypothalamus by changing its temperature independently of the temperature of the skin and body; a hot hypothalamus should then cause sweating, regardless of the actual body temperature. This is just what happens. When a cat's anterior hypothalamus is heated by a warm wire, there is panting and vasodilatation despite the fact that the cat's body temperature may be well below normal (Magoun et al., 1938). The effect is analogous to what happens when hot air is directed at a home thermostat. The furnace will shut itself off, even though the house is actually freezing.

Vasoconstriction and vasodilatation are involuntary reflexes, more in the domain of physiology than that of behavior. Does the hypothalamic feedback device have similar effects upon actions that reach out into the external world (for instance, wearing a fur coat)? Indeed it does. As one example, consider a study that utilized the fact that rats in a cold chamber will press a bar for a brief burst of heat (Weiss and Laties, 1961; see Figure 3.4). The question was whether rats that had learned this skill in a cold environment would bar-press for heat if one cooled their brains rather than their bodies. The test was to run cold liquid through a very thin U-shaped tube implanted in the anterior hypothalamus (Satinoff, 1964). The rats turned on the heat lamp when their brains were cooled even though the outside temperature was reasonably neutral.

Tricking the hypothalamus can evidently affect integrated behavior patterns just as it does autonomic reactions like vasodilatation. The hypothalamus defines an internal need state for the rest of the nervous system, and this need state will then become an important criterion for the appropriateness of any given act.

THIRST

What holds for temperature holds for most other homeostatic regulations as well. An example is the body's water supply. The organism continually loses water—primarily through the kidneys, but also through the respiratory system, the sweat glands, the digestive tract, and occasionally, by hemorrhage.

How does the system act to offset these losses? One set of reactions is entirely internal. Thus, a loss of water volume leads to a secretion of the so-called *antidiuretic hormone (ADH)* by the pituitary gland. ADH instructs the kidneys to reabsorb more of the water that passes through them. As a result, less water is passed out of the body in the urine.

But as with temperature regulation, internal readjustments can only restore the bodily balance up to a point. ADH can protect the body against further water loss, but it cannot bring back what was lost already. Eventually, the corrective measures must involve some behavior by which the organism reaches out into the external world so as to readjust its internal environment. This behavior is drinking—in humans, an average of two to three quarts of water per day.

Volume Receptors

How does the body know about its own condition? How does it know that what it needs is water? There are a number of receptors that provide this information.

55

Some are located in the brain and monitor the total volume of blood and other body fluids outside of the cells. According to some investigators, the receptors perform this task by responding to a substance called **angiotensin,** which is produced by the kidneys when there is a decrease in the total amount of liquid that passes through them (Epstein, Fitzsimons, and Rolls, 1970). Other volume receptors are located inside of the heart and its surrounding veins, and they are excited by drops in blood pressure set off when there is a decrease in the total amount of body fluid. Their effect was shown by studies on dogs in which a small balloon was inserted into the large vein that leads to the heart. When this balloon was inflated, the dogs drank copiously. The balloon impeded the blood flow into the heart and caused a decrease in fluid pressure. This set off the pressure receptors which sent the brain the signals that led to drinking (Fitzsimons and Moore-Gillow, 1980; Rolls and Rolls, 1982).

Osmoreceptors

Still another group of receptors keep track of the water *within* the body's cells. This depends on the concentration of certain minerals (especially sodium) that are dissolved in the fluid outside of the cell. Suppose the sodium content of the outside fluid is markedly increased (for example, by drinking salt water). While water can pass freely through the cell's membrane, many dissolved minerals cannot. The water will now flow in the direction that keeps the total concentration of dissolved materials equal on both sides of the membrane. As a result, any increase in the sodium content of the outside fluid dehydrates the cells as water is drawn out of them—a process called **osmosis** (see Figure 3.5).

A number of studies have shown that there are receptor cells in the brain that are sensitive to these osmotic processes (and are therefore called **osmoreceptors**). They respond to the concentration of their surrounding fluid solutions. Proof comes from studies in which tiny drops of salt water are injected into certain regions in or around the hypothalamus of a rat. The injection immediately leads to drinking. This is because the injection changes the concentration of the fluid that surrounds the receptor cell. It will now contain more dissolved materials (here, sodium) than the cell itself. As a result, water leaks out by osmosis, the receptor fires, and the animal begins to drink (Blass and Epstein, 1971; Rolls and Rolls, 1982).

It appears that there are at least three separate receptor systems that monitor the body's water levels; future research may find even more. Why so many? Here, as in the case of other disruptions of the organism's internal environment, we find that evolution has provided us with multiple defenses. There is a redundancy of mechanisms, so that if one fails another can take its place. We will find even greater redundancy when we turn to a more complex system of self-regulation: maintaining the body's nutrient levels by feeding.

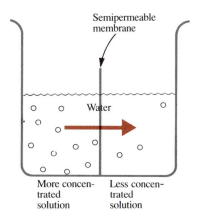

3.5 Dehydration by osmosis *If two solutions are separated by a membrane that allows the free flow of water but impedes the flow of substances that are dissolved in the water, water flows from the less concentrated region into the more concentrated one.*

HUNGER

All animals have to eat and much of their lives revolve around food—searching for it, hunting it, ingesting it, and doing their best not to become food for others.

There is no doubt that feeding is ultimately in the service of homeostasis, for no matter what food an animal eats or how he gets it, the ultimate biological consequence is always the same—to maintain appropriate nutrient supplies in the internal environment. But what are the actual mechanisms that determine whether humans and animals eat or stop eating? To put it another way, what is hunger and what is satiety?

The Signals for Feeding

There are numerous signals that control food intake. Among the most important of these are stimuli that arise from within the animal's own body and somehow inform the brain of the current state of the nutrient supplies. That some such messages are sent is certain. Without them, neither humans nor animals would be able to control their food intake, and they generally do. If food is freely available, they usually tend to eat just about the right amount to keep a roughly constant weight as adults. What is regulated is calorie intake rather than the total volume of food that is eaten. This was demonstrated in a study in which the experimenter varied the calorie level of the diet he fed to rats by adulterating their food with nonnutritive cellulose. The more diluted the food, the more of it was eaten, in a quantity roughly adequate to keep the total calorie content constant (Adolph, 1947).

This self-regulation of food intake persists even when there is no guidance from taste and smell receptors. One experiment used rats whose food was always delivered directly into the stomach. The animals learned to press a bar that squirted a few drops of liquid food through a special tube which led into the stomach. The rats injected themselves with just about the right number of squirts to keep a level weight. When the food was diluted with an equal amount of water, they doubled their intake (Epstein and Teitelbaum, 1962).

SIGNALS FROM WITHIN

Receptors in the brain How does the animal manage to adjust its food intake to its calorie needs? From the start, investigators focused on *glucose* (or blood sugar) which is the major source of energy for bodily tissues. They believed that somewhere in the body are receptors which detect changes in the way this metabolic fuel is utilized.

Many authors believe that some of the relevant receptors are in the brain itself, most likely the hypothalamus. These *glucoreceptors* are thought to sense the amount of glucose that is available for metabolic use (Mayer, 1955). Evidence comes from studies in which the hypothalamus was injected with a chemical that made its cells unable to respond to glucose. The result was ravenous eating. This treatment presumably silenced the glucoreceptors whose failure to fire was then interpreted as a fuel deficiency, which led to feeding (Miselis and Epstein, 1970).

Receptors in the stomach Why does an animal stop eating? The receptors in the brain can't be the only reason. For they respond to fuel deficiency in the bloodstream, and this deficiency will not be corrected until after the meal has been at least partially digested. Yet, humans and animals will terminate a meal much before that. What tells them that it's time to stop?

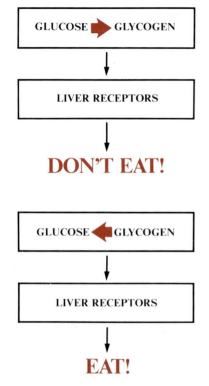

3.6 *The relation between the glucose-glycogen balance in the liver and eating*

Common sense suggests that feeding stops when the stomach is full. This is true enough, but it is only part of the story, for animals will stop eating even when their stomach is only partially full. This will only happen, however, if they have ingested a nutritious substance. If the stomach is filled with an equal volume of nonnutritive bulk, the animal will continue to eat. This suggests that the stomach walls contain receptors that are sensitive to the nutrients dissolved in the digestive juices. They signal the brain that nutrient supplies to the internal environment are on their way as food is about to enter the intestines. The result is satiety (Deutsch, Puerto, and Wang, 1978).

Receptors in the liver Yet another source of information about the body's nutrient levels comes from the organ that acts as the manager of the body's food metabolism—the liver.

Immediately after a meal, glucose is plentiful. Since the body can't use it all, much of it is converted into other forms and put in storage. One such conversion goes on in the liver, where glucose is turned into **glycogen** (often called animal starch). Glycogen cannot be used up as a metabolic fuel. This is fine right after a meal, but eventually the stored energy has to be tapped. At that time, the chemical reaction goes the other way. Now the glycogen is turned into usable glucose.

Several recent studies suggest that the liver contains receptors that can sense in which direction the metabolic transaction goes, from glucose cash to glycogen deposits, or vice versa. If the balance tips toward glycogen manufacture, the receptors signal satiety and the animal stops eating. If the balance tips toward glucose production, the receptors signal hunger and the animal eats (Figure 3.6). The evidence that this happens in the liver comes from hungry dogs that were injected with glucose. If the injection was into the vein that goes directly to the liver, the dogs stopped eating. If the injection was anywhere else, there was no comparable effect (Russek, 1971; Friedman and Stricker, 1976).

Such evidence suggests that the internal stimuli for hunger and satiety arise at a rather earlier stage in the process of food extraction and storage than had been traditionally believed. If so, food-related homeostasis is not a last-ditch affair in which the system waits until the internal environment is already in precarious imbalance. Instead, the built-in hunger mechanism seems to be more prudent. It has an anticipatory character that corrects metabolic insufficiencies before they can possibly affect the internal environment that bathes the brain.

SIGNALS FROM WITHOUT

The self-regulation of food intake is remarkable, but it is not perfect. Humans and animals eat to maintain nutritive homeostasis; put another way, they eat because they are hungry. But they sometimes eat because they like the taste of a particular food. We eat dessert even though we may be full; our hunger is gone, but not our appetite.

Such facts show that eating is not solely determined by stimuli that come from within the body. For these are supplemented by various external signals. We clearly do not eat for calories alone. Taste—and also smell and texture—is a powerful determinant of food intake for humans as well as animals. But palatability is not the only external signal for eating. Other signals are determined through learning. The expected mealtime is one example; the company of fellow eaters is another. A hen who has had her fill of grain will eagerly resume her meal if joined by other hens who are still hungry (Bayer, 1929).

Hypothalamic Control Centers

We have seen that there are many different signals for food intake. It was natural to suppose that these various messages are all integrated at one point in the nervous system where a final decision is made to eat or not to eat. The natural candidate for such a "feeding center" was the hypothalamus, which was already known to house controls for temperature regulation and water balance and which gave evidence of containing glucoreceptors. Psychophysiologists soon devised a theory of hypothalamic control of feeding that was analogous to the temperature system. It postulates two antagonistic centers, one corresponding to hunger, the other to satiety.

DUAL-CENTER THEORY

According to dual-center theory, the hypothalamus contains an "on" and an "off" command post for eating. Two anatomical regions are implicated. One is located in the ***lateral zone*** of the hypothalamus; it was said to function as a "hunger center" whose activation leads to food search and eating. The other is the ***ventromedial region*** which was thought to be a "satiety center" whose stimulation stops eating (Figure 3.7).

To buttress their claims about the functions of these regions, dual-center theorists pointed to the effects of lesions. Rats whose lateral hypothalamus has been destroyed suffer from ***aphagia*** (Greek, "no eating"). They refuse to eat and drink and will starve to death unless forcibly tube-fed for weeks (Teitelbaum and Stellar, 1954). Interestingly enough, eventually there is some recovery of function. After a few weeks the animals begin to eat again, especially if tempted by such delectables as liquid eggnog (Teitelbaum and Epstein, 1962).

The reverse occurs after lesions to the ventromedial zone. Animals with such lesions suffer from ***hyperphagia*** (Greek, "excess eating"). They eat voraciously and keep on eating. If the lesion is large enough, they may become veritable mountains of rat obesity, finally reaching weights that are some three times as great as their preoperative levels. Tumors in this hypothalamic region (although very rare) have the same effects on humans (Miller, Bailey, and Stevenson, 1950; Teitelbaum, 1955, 1961).

While ventromedial lesions lead to rapid weight gain, this levels off in a month or two, after which the animal's weight remains stable at a new (and of course much greater) level. Once this new weight is reached, the animal eats enough to maintain it but no more (Hoebel and Teitelbaum, 1976). This suggests that the lesion produced an upward shift in the ***set-point*** for weight regulation—the point that defines a kind of target value that determines food intake. As we will see, this interpretation may be relevant to explain some of the phenomena of human obesity (Nisbett, 1972; see Figure 3.8, p. 60).

Details aside, dual-center theorists regard the two hypothalamic regions as mutually inhibitory centers, of which one serves as an on-switch for eating, the other as an off-switch. These switches are in turn activated by a number of internal and

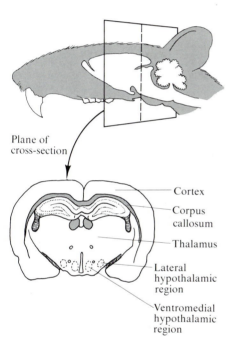

3.7   The lateral and ventromedial hypothalamic regions   *A schematic of the lateral and ventromedial regions of the hypothalamus. The top part of the figure shows a side view of a rat's head and indicates the plane of the bottom figure, which is an ear-to-ear section of the brain showing the two hypothalamic regions. (After Hart, 1976)*

Plane of
cross-section

Cortex

Corpus callosum

Thalamus

Lateral hypothalamic region

Ventromedial hypothalamic region

A

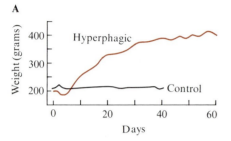

B

3.8 Hyperphagia (A) Curve showing the weight gain of hyperphagic rats after an operation creating a hypothalamic lesion. The weight eventually stabilizes at a new level. (After Teitelbaum, 1955) (B) Photograph of a rat several months after the operation. This rat weighed over 1,000 grams. (Courtesy Neal E. Miller, Rockefeller University)

external signals. All of these signals act upon the feeding centers—some to trigger eating, others to inhibit it. Whether the organism eats will then depend on the summed value of them all: the level of various available nutrients in the bloodstream, satiety signals from the stomach, food palatability, learned factors, and so on (Stellar, 1954).

DUAL CENTERS RECONSIDERED

The dual-center theory of feeding has held center stage for several decades. But it has been seriously questioned in recent years. The main grounds concern the effects of hypothalamic lesions. Some critics believe that some of the effects of these lesions are not directly on behavior, but rather on food metabolism (Stricker and Zigmond, 1976).

An example of this approach is a reanalysis of the effects of ventromedial lesions. According to the dual-center view, rats with such lesions overeat because of damage to some off-switch for feeding. But an alternative interpretation lays the blame on a disruption of fat metabolism.

Under normal conditions, animals store some of their unused nutrients in the form of fats. This tendency to save for later use can sometimes go too far, however. One effect of ventromedial lesions is that they produce an overreaction of certain branches of the parasympathetic system. This in turn increases the proportion of usable nutrients, especially glucose, that are turned into fat and cached away as adipose tissue. The trouble is that so much is stored that not enough is left over to serve as metabolic fuel. As a result, the animal stays hungry; it has to eat more to get the fuel that it needs. But since most of what it eats is turned into fat and stored away, the process continues and the animal has to keep on eating. It is in the position of a rich miser who has buried all of his possessions and has therefore no money to live on.

Evidence in favor of this general approach comes from studies which show that animals with ventromedial lesions get fatter than normals even when both groups are fed the identical amount. Whether such results are a decisive disproof of the dual-center theory is still a matter of debate (Friedman and Stricker, 1976).

Food Selection

We've seen that the mechanisms that determine feeding are at least partially under the control of homeostasis. To that extent they resemble those that govern drinking and temperature regulation. But in many ways they are considerably more complex. One reason is that the control of food intake depends on two decisions. The animal (or its nervous system) must not only decide whether to eat, but also *what* to eat. How do animals and humans make this selection?

To some extent the selection is built into the nervous system. An example is the response to sweet and bitter tastes. When a human newborn's mouth is moistened with a sweet solution (say, sugar water), the infant's facial expression suggests pleasure; when the solution is bitter (say, quinine water), the newborn screws his face into a grimace and turns away (Steiner, 1974; see Figures 3.9A and B). This selectional bias makes good biological sense, for it leads to the best nutritional bet: In general, sweet substances have more nutritional value than others. In contrast, bitter tastes are found in many poisonous plants. Occasionally, the

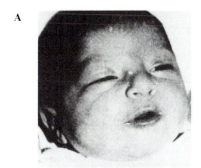
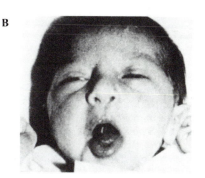

3.9   The response of newborn human babies to different tastes   *Drops of different solutions were placed on the infants' mouths to record their reaction to (A) a sweet taste (sugar solution) and (B) a bitter taste (quinine solution). (From Steiner, 1977; photographs courtesy of Jacob Steiner)*

3.10   A koala in its native Australian habitat   *This animal looks like a living teddy bear, but it is really not a bear at all, but a marsupial that spends the early part of its life in its mother's pouch. Its diet is almost exclusively composed of eucalyptus leaves, which provide its nutrients as well as its water. (Courtesy Australian Information Service)*

nutritional bet is lost: Saccharin is sweet and is generally preferred to less sweet substances, but it contains no calories whatsoever.

Can built-in preferences account for all of an animal's food choices? They might, if the animal lives on one (or only a very few) food items, such as the koala, whose diet consists almost entirely of eucalyptus leaves (Figure 3.10). But the majority of animals are less specialized than the koala; their diet is made up of all sorts of foods. How do these animals know which substances in the world provide calories and which do not? Furthermore, how do they identify the various nutrients they require over and above calories: various vitamins, minerals, amino acids, and so on? For carnivores, the food selection problem is relatively easy. Since the animals they feed on have nutritional needs like their own, carnivores are assured of getting a balanced diet. Lions run no risk of vitamin deficiency unless they insist on eating vitamin-deficient zebras (Rozin, 1976, 1982).

The food selection problem is more difficult for omnivores like ourselves who are culinary generalists and eat a wide variety of plant foods. The problem is that many plants lack some essential nutrient that is necessary for survival. Worse yet, other plants contain poisons—an adaptive device that protects them from plant-eaters. To get the necessary nutrients, the omnivore must somehow identify a large range of edible plants which, taken together, will satisfy all of its dietary needs, but it must also identify those that are toxic. The number of possible foods they might properly select is now too large to be programmed into the nervous system. Under the circumstances, how do we and other omnivores decide what is edible and what is not? The answer is learning.

NEOPHOBIA AND FOOD

Learning about food has to be of a special kind. It must allow the animal to learn about things that can be eaten so it can enlarge the range of its possible diet, for yesterday's food may not contain all the ingredients the body needs. But the animal must also learn to avoid certain substances that are poisonous. On the face of it, the animal's problem seems insoluble. To find out whether an unknown substance is nutritious, it must eat it and risk death. To protect itself against poisoning, it must shun it and risk starvation. But some animals (and we're probably among them) have found a rather simple solution. When it comes to food, they are ***neophobic***—that is, afraid of anything that is new. When rats (who like humans are food generalists) are confronted with some substance they've never tasted before, they will initially shy away from it altogether. But eventually, they'll taste a very small amount, as it were, to "test" it. If it is a poison, they will

3.11 Food-avoidance learning in birds *In contrast to rats and humans, whose learned food aversions are usually based on taste and odor, most birds rely on visual cues. The figure shows the reaction of a bird who has just eaten a monarch butterfly, which contains distasteful and poisonous substances. The distinctive wing pattern of this butterfly provides the cue for an immediately acquired food aversion, for after one such mistake the bird will never again seize another monarch. Several species of other butterflies have copied the monarch's distinctive patterning, which affords them a certain protection since some of the bird's acquired food aversion will generalize to them as well. (Courtesy of Lincoln P. Brower, University of Florida)*

The transmission of food preferences *(Photograph by Suzanne Szasz)*

get sick. But since they only ate a little, they will most probably recover. They will later associate the taste of that food with their sickness and will avoid this taste from then on (see Figure 3.11).* On the other hand, if the food turns out to be safe, the animals will return in a day or two, take larger bites, and add this particular taste to their repertoire of acceptable food flavors (Rozin, 1976).

Many human children exhibit a somewhat similar neophobia about foods once they are about two years old. From then on, they tend to be culinary conservatives who stick to foods they know and make sour faces if confronted with something new. But in humans this neophobia is less pronounced than it is in rats and is not too hard to override. One factor is built-in taste preferences, particularly for sweets. Babies may dislike new foods, but they are certainly willing to make exceptions for chocolate pudding. But even more important is the fact that unlike rats, people live in a culture, which allows them to benefit from the pooled experience of previous generations. Each rat has to learn anew whether a given food is safe, but a human child can rely on her mother. The child may fuss and scream about the spinach and cauliflower on her plate, but at least she doesn't have to worry that they might be poisonous. After a while, she will learn to eat the foods her culture prefers (Mother's apple pie), and to avoid those to which the culture has aversions or taboos (pork to Muslims and Jews).

HUMAN CUISINES

The food preferences and aversions of a culture are generally institutionalized in the form of a *cuisine,* a special pattern of preparing and flavoring food that gives it a distinctive cultural character. Examples are Chinese cuisine in which food is often flavored with soy sauce and ginger, and Middle Eastern cuisine that relies on a combination of olive oil, tomato, and cinnamon (E. Rozin, 1982). Like

* Such acquired taste aversions have some important implications for our understanding of the learning process which will be discussed in a later section (see Chapter 4, pp. 122–24).

many other cultural practices, cuisines provide a means of identifying members of the culture and setting them off from others. Thus in India, the relations between different castes are represented in the rules about who may eat what and when (Appadurai, 1981).

Cuisines may also provide a means for overcoming food neophobia, since new foods can be made to appear comfortably familiar when prepared in old and well-known flavor contexts. An example is the reaction to the potato when it was introduced in France in the eighteenth century. Initially rejected, it was eventually accepted and ultimately hailed when prepared according to customary French practices; for example, with butter, cheese, and herbs (Rozin, 1976; E. Rozin, 1982).

How do cuisines arise? The sources are often utilitarian. Take Chinese cuisine in which many foods are prepared by brief, and very rapid heating (stir-frying). The reason is simple. Stir-frying is a very efficient method of utilizing fuel, a scarce commodity on the Chinese mainland on which there are relatively few trees. The origin of soy sauce is no less utilitarian. While the soybean is an excellent source of protein and is fairly abundant, its nutrient value is hard to extract by ordinary means. To achieve this end, the Chinese developed a fermenting process whose product serves as the base of the sauce. A final example is the fact that Chinese cuisine shuns most milk products. In part, this aversion has its origins in digestive biology, for many adult Chinese lack the enzyme that digests milk sugar (Johnson, Kretschmer, and Simoons, 1974).

Built-in taste preferences, neophobia and learned food aversions, and even cuisine, can all be considered as ways through which we maintain our nutrient levels, and to that extent they all serve as vehicles for homeostasis. But that is not all there is to it. For there are a number of motives whose basis is not homeostasis (for example, sex). This holds even for feeding, for Man does not eat for nutrition alone. Consider Mexicans who spice their food with hot chili peppers. If asked why, they answer "It provides zest." Once basic, homeostatic needs are met and safety is assured, humans often seek stimulation for its own sake. Some of the ways for providing such nonutilitarian stimulation become increasingly elaborate and stylized, at which point we call them art forms. And one such art form is human cuisine, which serves the palate as well as the stomach.

Obesity

Both homeostatic and nonhomeostatic determinants of food intake are relevant to a problem partially created by the affluence of modern society which prior eras would have suffered only too gladly: obesity. Obesity is sometimes defined as a body weight that exceeds the average for a given height by 20 percent. Judged by this criterion, about one-third of all Americans are obese. Most of them would rather be slim, and their wistful desires offer a ready market for a vast market of diet foods and fads. In part, the reason is health (at least it is sometimes said to be). But more important are social standards of physical attractiveness. There are no corpulent matinee idols, no fat sex goddesses (Stunkard, 1975).

Most authorities agree that there are several reasons why people become fat. In a minority of cases, the cause is a bodily condition. In others, it is a matter of eating too much.

BODILY FACTORS IN OBESITY

Oversecretion of insulin   One reason for obesity is a metabolic malfunction. For whatever reason, some persons secrete too much insulin. This ultimately leads to excess fat storage because insulin affects the glucose-glycogen balance; the more insulin is secreted, the more glucose will be converted into glycogen. People who suffer from a serious hypersecretion of insulin will eventually be in the position of rats with ventromedial hypothalamic lesions. They are continually hungry because they can't help converting most of what they eat into fat. In consequence, they don't have available glucose to fuel their bodily functions. As a result, they keep on eating to obtain more glucose. Rather than getting fat because they eat too much, such people eat too much because they are fat. And eating too much makes them get even fatter.

Fat cells in the body   Another bodily factor concerns the fat cells in the body. In obese people, their number is some three times larger than that found in normals (Hirsch and Knittle, 1970). To the obese person, these cells are an adipose albatross that cannot be removed. If a fat person diets, the fat cells will shrink in size but their total number will remain unchanged. Some investigators suspect that the brain receives some signals that urge further eating until the shrunken fat cells are again refilled. If this is so, the once-fat can never truly escape their obese past. They may rigorously diet until they become as lean as a friend who was never fat, but their urge to eat will always be greater.

Some recent studies suggest that the number of fat cells in the body is partially determined by feeding patterns during early childhood. If rats are overfed before weaning, they develop many more fat cells. In contrast, overfeeding in adulthood leads to an enlargement of the fat cells that are already there but does not change their number (Knittle and Hirsch, 1968). These results fit in with the fact that obesity often begins in childhood: the fat boy is father to the fat man (Collip, 1980).

BEHAVIORAL FACTORS

In some persons, obesity is evidently produced by a bodily condition. But for many others, the cause lies in behavior: they eat too much and exercise too little. The question is why. It is virtually certain that there is no one answer, for there are probably many reasons for chronic overeating.

The externality hypothesis   Some years ago, a number of investigators subscribed to the **externality hypothesis,** which held that obese people are comparatively unresponsive to their own internal hunger state but are much more susceptible to signals from without (Schachter and Rodin, 1974). One line of evidence came from studies in which people were asked how hungry they are. In normal subjects, the response depended on the time since their last meal. But in obese people, there was no such correlation between the subjective experience of hunger and the deprivation interval. Further evidence came from experiments that seemed to show that obese subjects are rather finicky when it comes to food. If offered a fine grade of vanilla ice cream, they eat more than normal subjects. But if offered vanilla ice cream that has been adulterated with bitter-tasting qui-

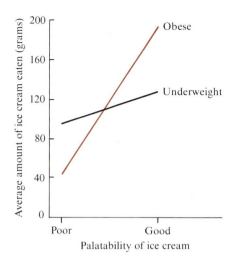

3.12 Eating, palatability, and obesity *In the experiment, obese and underweight subjects were given the opportunity to eat ice cream. If the ice cream tasted good, the obese subjects ate more than the underweight ones. The reverse was true if the ice cream did not taste good. (After Nisbett, 1968)*

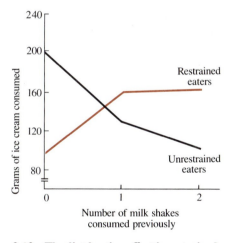

3.13 The diet-busting effect in restrained eaters *In the experiment, restrained (color) and unrestrained eaters (black) were asked to consume 0, 1, or 2 milk shakes in what they thought was an experiment on taste perception. They later were asked to judge the taste of ice cream and allowed to sample as much of it as they wished. The figure shows that restrained eaters ate considerably more ice cream if they had previously consumed one or more milk shakes. (After Herman and Mack, 1975)*

nine, they eat *less* of this mixture than do normals (Nisbett, 1968; see Figure 3.12).

According to some advocates of the externality hypothesis, this discrepancy in the sensitivity to external and internal cues for eating might be a contributing cause of obesity. Since he is presumably rather insensitive to his internal body state, the obese person will eat even though his body needs no further calories as long as there are enough external cues that prompt him on. And in food-rich twentieth-century America, such cues are certainly plentiful (Schachter, 1971).

The restrained-eating hypothesis More recent studies have thrown doubt on the externality hypothesis. To begin with, the evidence for the greater sensitivity of obese persons to external cues turns out to be rather inconsistent. But to the extent that this oversensitivity does exist, its explanation may be quite different from what it was originally; it may be an *effect* of the obesity rather than its cause (Nisbett, 1972; Rodin, 1980, 1981).

In our society many people who are overweight consciously try to restrain their eating. After all, obesity is a social liability, so they make resolutions, go on diets, buy low-calorie foods, and do what they can to clamp a lid on their intense desire to eat. But the clamp is hard to maintain, for any external stimulus for eating will threaten the dieter's resolve. This is especially so when it comes to ending a meal. Anyone who has ever tried to diet knows that it's much easier to refrain from eating than to stop after eating has already begun. At this point, all the external signals for eating are at full strength, and the inhibition on further eating is easily overridden. In effect, there is disinhibition (Herman and Polivy, 1980).

An interesting demonstration of the disinhibition of eating is provided by a study of "restrained" and "unrestrained" eaters. Persons judged as restrained said they were on a diet or expressed concerns about their weight. The subjects participated in what was described as an experiment on the perception of tastes. Initially, some subjects had to taste (and consume) one or two 8 oz. milk shakes, while control subjects tasted none. After this, the subjects were asked to judge the taste of ice cream. While performing this task, they were left alone with an unlimited supply of ice cream. How much would they eat? Unrestrained eaters ate a sensible, homeostatically appropriate amount: the more milk shakes they previously had consumed, the less ice cream they ate in the subsequent test. But the exact opposite was true of the restrained eaters. The more milk shakes they previously consumed the more ice cream they ate now. The prior exposure disinhibited their restraint and led to a motivational collapse—a phenomenon all too familiar to would-be dieters which some investigators have dubbed the "what the hell" diet-busting effect (Herman and Mack, 1975; see Figure 3.13).

The subjects in the milk shake study were deliberately selected so that the average weight of the restrained and unrestrained eaters was the same. This indicates that the disinhibition effect results not from the person's weight as such, but rather from his efforts to keep this weight under control. But in general, overweight people are more likely to feel that they should restrain their eating than are normal persons. This might explain some of the previous results that show a greater sensitivity to external food signals in obese people.

The same reasoning may help to explain how eating is affected by anxiety or stress. When unrestrained eaters (who tend to be of normal weight) are made anxious in various laboratory situations, they are likely to eat less. But in restrained eaters (who are more likely to be overweight), anxiety has the opposite effect: it leads to overeating. Similar effects are found in patients who suffer from depression. If they are unrestrained eaters, the depression makes them lose weight. If they are restrained eaters, their weight goes up. Once again, the cause is probably disinhibition. The emotional disturbance distracts the restrained eater and loosens his self-imposed food controls (Schachter, Goldman, and Gordon, 1968; Herman and Polivy, 1975; Polivy and Herman, 1976).

The set-point hypothesis   The restrained-eating hypothesis tries to explain some of the effects of obesity. But it has little to say about its cause. One possibility is that people differ in their set-points for weight. These may reflect differences in constitution (for example, in the number of fat calls, or insulin metabolism), which in turn may be partially determined by heredity (Foch and McClearn, 1980). Set-points may also result from feeding experiences in childhood. Whatever their cause, these set-points determine the weight an individual's system aims at as it regulates its internal economy. But if so, then many a person who is fat by the standards of official what-your-weight-should-be tables may weigh just the right amount considering his own particular set-point. If he starves himself, he'll drop to a weight level below that level. But in the long run he probably won't stay there, for there'll always be a tendency to go back to the set-point weight (Nisbett, 1972).

THE TREATMENT OF OBESITY

What can be done to help people who are overweight? Everyone knows that it's relatively easy to lose weight over the short run; the problem is to keep it off for good. Can it be done? Some authors are optimists and believe that obesity is a behavioral problem that can be remedied by retraining people to develop self-control and acquire appropriate habits of diet and exercise. Other authorities are more pessimistic, for they believe that weight depends largely on a person's set-point, which he can't escape from in the long run. Attempts at treatment include psychoanalysis, various forms of behavior therapy (techniques for modifying the individual's behavior by the systematic use of certain principles of learning; see Chapters 4 and 20), and self-help groups (for example, Weight Watchers International). There is considerable dispute over the extent to which any of these methods lead to long-term changes although there is some suggestion that the self-help groups do a fairly good job, especially for those who are only mildly overweight (Booth, 1980; Stuart and Mitchell, 1980; Stunkard, 1980; Wilson, 1980).

At this point it is difficult to decide whether the optimists have a better case than the pessimists. Thus far, the outcomes of the various procedures have not been studied systematically enough. For all we know, more effective treatment methods may be developed in the future. But suppose the pessimists turn out to be correct—suppose that there is a set-point which decrees that weight is fate. If so, can we offer any hope to those who are overweight?

To begin with, one may question the widely held belief that being overweight is necessarily a disorder. It is often asserted that being overweight is a health hazard, and that over one-third of the U.S. population are too heavy (U.S. Public Health Service, 1966). But apart from cases of gross obesity, the relation between overweight and life expectancy is still a matter of debate (Fitzgerald, 1981; see Figure 3.14). Some authors argue that for the great majority of individuals, obesity is a social and aesthetic problem, rather than a problem of physical health. (This is

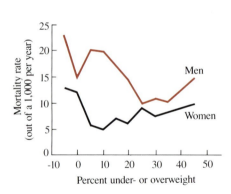

3.14   Relation of obesity to mortality
The figure suggests the mortality rate in a sample of 5,209 persons in Massachusetts for men and women between 45 and 74 years old between 1948 and 1964. The percent overweight is calculated by reference to mean weights for a given height. The figure shows that overweight does not increase the overall mortality risk, at least not for overweight percentages that are less than 50. (From Andres, 1980)

A

B

C

3.15 Changing conceptions of the relation between body weight and attractiveness Is slender beautiful? It depends. (A) The Venus of Willendorf, a prehistoric statuette, unearthed near Willendorf, Austria, that was sculpted some 30,000 years ago. Some archeologists believe that it depicts a fertility goddess; others, that it represents the female erotic ideal of the ice age. (Courtesy American Museum of Natural History) (B) The Three Graces, painted by the Flemish master Peter Paul Rubens in 1639 (Courtesy Museo del Prado) (C) A model in a 1984 issue of Vogue. (Courtesy Vogue)

especially so for women, who are much more likely to regard themselves as overweight than are men; Gray, 1977; Fallon and Rozin, 1985). Seen in this light, being slender is a social ideal, but we should not forget that it is an ideal of *our* society. Other cultures set different standards. The women painted by Rubens, Matisse, and Renoir were considered beautiful by their contemporaries; today they would be considered overweight (see Figure 3.15). But does it really make sense to aspire to the body form of a fashion model if it is not one's own and perhaps can't be?

Many people who regard themselves as overweight try to become lithe and slender but often fail anyway. Perhaps the best advice to them is to accept themselves as they are.

FEAR AND RAGE

Thus far, our emphasis has been on motives that are largely based on internal, homeostatic controls, in which there is a disruption of the internal environment, and the organism performs some action that ultimately restores its internal balance. But there are a number of motives that do not fit this pattern. Sex is one example. While internal states such as hormone levels play an important role, the desire is essentially aroused (as it were, "turned on") by external stimuli of various kinds; homeostatic imbalances have nothing to do with it. We will discuss this in a later chapter that deals with motives that are primarily social (see Chapter 10). Here we will consider another example of a motive that is instigated from without rather than within: the reaction to intense threat, which results in attempts to escape or to fight back in self-defense and is often accompanied by the violent emotions of rage and fear.

Threat and the Autonomic Nervous System

What are some of the biological mechanisms that underlie these intense reactions? We'll begin our discussion by looking at the functions of the autonomic

3.16 The sympathetic and parasympathetic branches of the autonomic nervous system *The parasympathetic system (shown in black) facilitates the vegetative functions of the organism: It slows the heart and lungs, stimulates digestive functions, permits sexual activity, and so on. In contrast, the sympathetic system (shown in color) helps to place the organism on an emergency basis: It accelerates heart and lung actions, liberates nutrient fuels for muscular effort, and inhibits digestive and sexual functions.*

Note that the fibers of the sympathetic system are interconnected through a chain of ganglionic fibers outside of the spinal cord. As a result, sympathetic activation has a somewhat diffuse character; any sympathetic excitation tends to affect all of the viscera rather than just some. This is in contrast to the parasympathetic system whose action is more specific. (After Cannon, 1929)

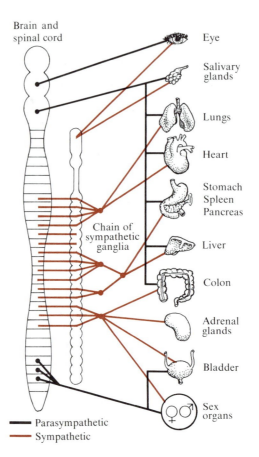

Brain and spinal cord

Eye
Salivary glands
Lungs
Heart
Stomach Spleen Pancreas
Liver
Colon
Adrenal glands
Bladder
Sex organs

Chain of sympathetic ganglia

— Parasympathetic
— Sympathetic

PARASYMPATHETIC SYSTEM

Constriction of pupil

Secretion of tear glands

Salivation

Inhibition of heart action

Constriction of respiratory passages

Stomach contraction: secretion of digestive fluids

Intestinal peristalsis

Contraction of bladder

Erection

SYMPATHETIC SYSTEM

Dilation of pupil

Inhibition of tear glands

Inhibition of salivation

Acceleration of heart action

Opens respiratory passages

Inhibits stomach contractions and digestive secretion

Inhibits intestinal peristalsis

Relaxes bladder

Inhibits erection

Walter Cannon (Courtesy National Library of Medicine)

nervous system (see Figure 3.16). We have previously seen how the interaction of sympathetic and parasympathetic excitations permits adjustments of the visceral machinery in the control of temperature. But the opposition between the two autonomic branches is more fundamental yet. According to the American physiologist Walter B. Cannon (1871–1945), they serve two broad and rather different functions. The **parasympathetic system** handles the *vegetative* functions of ordinary life: the conservation of bodily resources, reproduction, and the disposal of wastes. In effect, these reflect an organism's operations during times of peace—a lowered heart rate, peristaltic movements of stomach and intestines, secretion of digestive glands. In contrast, the **sympathetic system** has an *activating* function. It summons the body's resources and gets the organism ready for vigorous action (Cannon, 1929).

As an example of this opposition, consider the role of the two autonomic divisions in governing the delivery of nutrient fuels and oxygen as well as the removal of waste products to and from the musculature. Parasympathetic excitation slows down the heart rate and reduces blood pressure. Sympathetic excitation has the opposite effect and also inhibits digestion and sexual activity. In addition, it stimulates the inner core of the adrenal gland, the so-called **adrenal medulla,** to pour epinephrine (adrenalin) and norepinephrine into the bloodstream. These have essentially the same effects as sympathetic stimulation—they accelerate the heart rate, speed up metabolism, and so on. As a result, the sympathetic effects are amplified yet further.

THE EMERGENCY REACTION

Cannon pointed out that intense sympathetic arousal has a special function. It serves as an *emergency reaction* that mobilizes the organism for a crisis—for flight or fight.

Consider a grazing zebra, placidly maintaining homeostasis by nibbling at the grass and vasodilatating in the hot African sun. Suddenly it sees a lion approaching rapidly. The vegetative functions must now take second place, for if the zebra does not escape it will have no internal environment left to regulate. The violent exertions of the skeletal musculature require the total support of the entire bodily machinery and this support is provided by intense sympathetic activation. There is more nutrient fuel for the muscles which is now delivered more rapidly. At the same time, waste products are removed more quickly and all unessential organic activities are brought to a halt. If the zebra does not escape, it is not because its sympathetic system did not try.

Cannon produced considerable evidence suggesting that a similar autonomic reaction occurs when the pattern is one of attack rather than of flight. A cat about to do battle with a dog shows accelerated heartbeat, piloerection (its hair standing on end—normally a heat-conserving device), and pupillary dilation—all signs of diffuse sympathetic arousal, signs that the body is girding itself for violent muscular effort (Figure 3.17). But some later studies have suggested that, despite their many similarities, the autonomic reactions that accompany fear and anger may not be entirely identical. In one experiment, human subjects were either frightened by the possibility of an intense electric shock or were angered by a rude technician who insulted them. Both fear and anger led to intense sympathetic arousal, but the hormonal secretions were not the same. In frightened subjects, there was a high level of epinephrine, but in angered subjects there was an increase in norepinephrine, which has similar but not identical physiological effects (Ax, 1953).

Cannon emphasized the biological utility of the autonomic reaction, but his principle cannot tell us which choice the animal will make—whether it will choose fight or flight. This depends in part upon built-in predispositions, in part upon the specific situation. For example, a rat first tries to escape, but fights when finally cornered. Emergency situations may produce still different reactions from those we have already seen. Some animals become paralyzed by fright and stand immobile—an adaptive reaction since predators are more likely to detect a prey that is in motion. Other animals have even more exotic means of self-protection. Some species of fish pale when frightened, which makes them harder to spot against the sandy ocean bottom. This effect is produced by the direct action of epinephrine upon various pigmented substances in the animal's skin (Odiorne, 1957).

Bodily concomitants of intense emotion are of course found also in humans. In fear, our hearts pound, our palms sweat, and we sometimes shiver—all sympathetic activities. It is hardly surprising that such autonomic responses (for example, pulse rate, respiration, and the so-called galvanic skin response) are often used as indicators of emotional states. The *galvanic skin response (GSR)* is a particularly favored measure. It is a drop in the electrical resistance of the skin, particularly of the palm (related to, but not identical with, the activity of the sweat glands), that is a sensitive index of general arousal.

The GSR and other indices of autonomic activity are used in lie-detector tech-

3.17 Sympathetic emergency reaction *A cat's terrified response to a dog as drawn in Charles Darwin's classic work on emotional expression,* The Expression of the Emotions in Man and Animals *(Darwin, 1872; Courtesy the New York Public Library)*

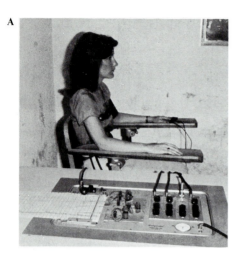

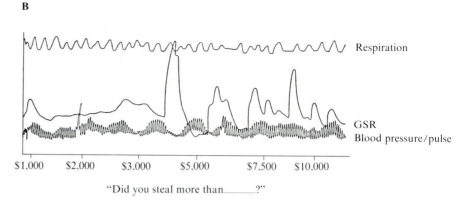

"Did you steal more than_____?"

3.18 Lie detection by use of autonomic measures *(A) Various devices measure autonomic arousal—a tube around the chest measures respiration rate, electrodes attached to the hand measure GSR, and an armband measures blood pressure and pulse. (Photograph by Mary Shuford) (B) A recording of respiration, GSR, and a measure of blood pressure and pulse. The record was obtained from a store employee caught stealing merchandise. At issue was the amount of the theft. To determine this, all parties agreed to be guided by the results of a lie-detector test. The subject was asked questions about the amount, such as "Did you steal more than $1,000?" and "Did you steal more than $2,000?" The record shows a high peak just after $3,000 and before $4,000. Later the subject confessed that the actual amount was $4,000. (After Inbau and Reid, 1953)*

nology. Lie detectors obviously cannot detect lies as such, rather they uncover autonomic arousal to certain key questions or phrases. The responses to these critical items (e.g., "Did you stab anyone with a knife on . . . ?") are then compared with the responses to control items—questions that are likely to produce an emotional reaction but are irrelevant to the issue at hand (e.g., "Before age nineteen did you ever lie to anyone?"). The fundamental assumption on which the lie-detection enterprise rests is that innocent persons will be more concerned by the control items than by the critical questions, and will therefore show more intense autonomic arousal to the former than to the latter (Figure 3.18). But this assumption is currently under serious dispute (Smith, 1967; Podlesny and Raskin, 1977; Lykken, 1979).

CENTRAL CONTROLS

The autonomic nervous system is by no means as autonomous as its name implies, rather it is largely guided by other neural centers. Some of these are among the oldest and most primitive portions of the cerebral cortex. These primitive cortical structures, together with parts of the hypothalamus and some surrounding regions, comprise the so-called *limbic system,* which is intimately involved in the control of the emotional reactions to situations that call for flight, defense, or attack (Figure 3.19). Electrical stimulation of certain portions of the limbic system transforms a purring cat into a spitting, hissing Halloween figure. Stimulation of the same region in humans often produces feelings of great anxiety or of rage, as in a patient who said that she suddenly wanted to tear things to pieces and to slap the experimenter's face (Magnus and Lammers, 1956; King, 1961; Flynn, Vanegas, Foote, and Edwards, 1970).

Psychologically there seem to be different kinds of attack, and they are evi-

3.19 The limbic system of the human brain *The limbic system (shown in color) is composed of a number of anatomically different structures of the brain, including relatively primitive parts of the cortex. These structures are intimately related to the control of various emotional reactions, especially those that concern flight and attack. (After Keeton, 1980)*

dently initiated by different control centers. In cats, the stimulation of one hypo-thalamic region produces predatory attack: quiet stalking followed by a quick, deadly pounce. The stimulation of another region leads to the Halloween pattern: a counterattack in self-defense (probably related to what in humans is called rage). When this rage pattern is triggered, the cat ignores a nearby mouse and will spring viciously at the experimenter, by whom it presumably feels attacked. (Egger and Flynn, 1963; Clemente and Chase, 1973). The lion who pounces on the zebra is probably not at all enraged but is merely engaged in the prosaic business of food gathering. (Whether the zebra is comforted by the fact that the lion is not angry at it is another question.)

STIMULUS CONTROLS

What are the stimuli that produce fear and lead to flight or to counterattack? Some of them obviously acquire their significance through learning. However, some stimuli seem to produce fear without any prior experience. We will briefly note two such innate triggers of fear.

Stimulus intensity   By and large, animals flee from any stimulus that is very intense, especially if its onset is sudden. These tendencies are probably built into the organism's reaction system and do not depend upon experience. They are certainly found at a very early age. Puppies and human infants are terrified by loud, sudden noises, young rats by high-pitched sounds, and colts by the sight of an abrupt movement. Another fear-evoking stimulus is pain. In part, this may simply be a special case of stimulus intensity, for pain sensations are generally quite intense.

Stimulus novelty   Both animals and humans are afraid of the unknown. Infant monkeys shake with fright when placed in a large, empty room or when confronted by a strange, mechanical toy that makes clanking noises; they immediately run to their mothers and cling desperately (Harlow and Zimmerman, 1959). Similarly, chimpanzees go into paroxysms of terror when they come across an unfamiliar object such as a stuffed toy animal, or—eerier yet—the trunkless head of a chimpanzee (actually a plaster cast; Hebb, 1946). In humans, there is the well-known fear of strangers observed in most infants between eight and twelve months of age. A built-in disposition to fear novelty and change makes good biological sense, given a world full of myriad, hidden dangers in which it generally pays to keep the unknown at a safe and healthy distance (Figure 3.20). This fear is most apparent in the young who have had little opportunity to get used to new situations and to learn that they are safe enough. The unfamiliar, however, is only feared if recognized as a change from the familiar. To the newborn, all faces are strange but none of them are feared. The fear of strangers begins only *after* the child recognizes and responds to one or both parents (Schaffer, 1966; see Chapter 16).

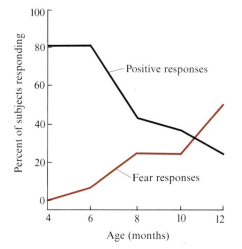

3.20   Fear of strangers in infancy   *Infants' reactions to a stranger's first approach. As shown, positive reactions such as smiling decline with age, while negative reactions such as frowning, whimpering, or crying increase. (Data from Morgan and Ricciuti, 1969)*

Disruptive Effects of Autonomic Arousal

Our preceding discussion emphasized the biological value of the emergency system. But strong autonomic arousal can also be disruptive and even harmful to the organism. This negative side of the matter is especially clear in humans. In our day-to-day lives we rarely encounter emergencies that call for violent physical effort. But our biological nature has not changed just because our modern world contains no sabertooth tigers. We still have the same emergency system that served our primitive ancestors, and its bodily consequences may take serious tolls.

The disruptive effect of fear and anger upon digestion or upon sexual behavior is a matter of common knowledge. During periods of marked anxiety there are often complaints of constipation or other digestive ills. The same holds for impotence or frigidity. This is hardly surprising, since digestive functions and many aspects of sexual activity (for example, erection) are largely controlled by the parasympathetic system and are thus inhibited by intense sympathetic arousal.

A more puzzling phenomenon is weeping. This is usually a concomitant of the more unpleasant emotions; by and large, tears are shed in grief and sadness. But this is not the whole story. A bereaved person rarely weeps when most depressed by the loss; weeping comes later, when there is some relief or comfort mingled with the grief. A common example is a man whose wife dies suddenly. For several days he shows no emotion except deep depression, but he breaks into tears when a friend brings a beautiful wreath. A similar pattern holds in various forms of psychopathology. The most depressed and agitated patients rarely weep; tears are much more likely when the patient's condition is transitional, moving from a depressed to a more elated state (Lund, 1930).

These phenomena are by no means understood, but some of their aspects may reflect the interaction of parasympathetic and sympathetic excitation. The tear glands are activated by parasympathetic fibers. Their uncontrollable discharge seen in weeping may be in part the result of a *parasympathetic overshoot.* Given strong sympathetic excitation (for instance, the fear that someone we love may die) and the concomitant inhibition of parasympathetic action, what happens when this excitation is suddenly withdrawn? The effect is analogous to a tug-of-war in which one of the contestants abruptly lets go of the rope—the opponent falls backward. Thus the parasympathetic division overshoots its normal level after the inhibition from its sympathetic antagonist is suddenly lifted.

The aftereffects of emotional arousal are sometimes more permanent, causing profound and long-lasting bodily harm. Various disorders such as peptic ulcer, colitis, asthma, and hypertension can often be traced back to emotional patterns in the patient's life and are then considered psychophysiological disorders in which a psychological cause produces a bodily effect (see Chapter 19). But the wages of autonomic arousal can be even more grievous and irrevocable; they may be death.

Anthropologists have long noted instances of mysterious and sudden death in members of various preliterate cultures who believed that they were victims of sorcery. Some of these cases were examined by competent physicians who found no signs of ordinary disease or of poisoning. Under the circumstances, there was some reason to believe that death was brought on by psychological factors, including the victim's belief in his persecutor's supernatural powers. Several such cases were studied by Walter Cannon. He describes a vivid example:

> I have seen more than one hardened old Haussa soldier dying steadily and by inches because he believed himself to be bewitched; no nourishment or medicines that were given to him had the slightest effect either to check the mischief or to improve his

condition in any way, and nothing was able to divert him from a fate which he considered inevitable. In the same way, and under very similar conditions, I have seen Krumen and others die in spite of every effort that was made to save them, simply because they had made up their minds, not (as we thought at the time) to die, but that being in the clutch of malignant demons they were bound to die (Cannon, 1942).

Needless to say, such reports have to be viewed with considerable caution; they are essentially anecdotes whose details are difficult to check. But a similar effect has been observed in some animal studies—sudden death that is somehow linked to violent fear.

In one experiment, wild rats were placed in large vats filled with water (Richter, 1957). To survive, the animals had to keep on swimming. Some of them died within a few minutes after they were placed in the vat. Instead of swimming (which should be no problem, for rats are very good swimmers) they gave up, dropped to the bottom of the vat, and died. A few rats died even before immersion, when held in the experimenter's hand. Why did these animals die so suddenly? No doubt they were intensely frightened, but surprisingly enough they did not die because of sympathetic overstimulation. Quite the contrary. Autopsy showed that at death the heart was *over*expanded (a parasympathetic effect) rather than constricted (a sympathetic effect). Death was therefore produced by an excess of parasympathetic activity, by an excess of cardiac relaxation. A further fact fits in neatly. If the rats were first injected with atropine, a drug that blocks the parasympathetic division, they generally continued to struggle and did not die a sudden death.

This effect may well be the result of a more violent form of the parasympathetic overshoot we have already discussed. Initially, the organism is in utter terror and its sympathetic emergency apparatus operates at its absolute peak. When this system comes to a sudden halt, there is a correspondingly massive rebound in the other direction. But why this sudden stop in sympathetic action? One possibility is that the animal has given up hope and stops struggling. In line with this interpretation is what happened to rats that were first immersed in the water, then taken out, then immersed again, and so on. When later tested in the same situation that produced sudden death in the others, these rats did not succumb. They had learned that they could cope in the situation by continued swimming; as a result, they kept on struggling and managed to survive. They stayed alive because they did not become helpless. (For a further discussion of the profound consequences of feeling helpless in the face of threat, see Chapters 4 and 19.)

SLEEP AND WAKING

Thus far, our main concern has been with the *directive* function of motives. This direction can be primarily imposed from within, as in the case of the homeostatic motives such as thirst and hunger. It can also be initiated by conditions from the outside, as in fear and rage. Either way, the effects on behavior are readily described in terms of a negative feedback system. In the case of homeostatic motives, the organism acts so as to change the state of the internal environment; it eats or drinks until its water balance or nutrient levels are restored. In the case of rage and fear, it acts to change the conditions of the external environment that prompted the disturbance. The cat runs away to remove *itself* from a barking dog, or it hisses and scratches in a frantic attempt to remove the *dog*.

Motives have another function in addition to direction. They *arouse* the organism, which then becomes increasingly alert and vigorous. A given motive will thus act like both the tuner and the volume control of a radio. A thirsty animal seeks water rather than food or a sexual partner. And the thirstier it is, the more intensely it will pursue its goal. Psychologists have used various terms to describe this facet of motivation. Some call it **activation;** others prefer the term **drive.** They all agree that increased drive states generally lead to increased behavioral vigor. Thus, rats will run faster to water the longer they have been water-deprived.

We will now look at some of the biological mechanisms of activation as we consider its two extremes. One is a state of intense waking arousal, perhaps best typified by fear and rage. The other is sleep.

Waking

In a sense, we may consider the sympathetic branch of the autonomic nervous system as an arousal system for the more primitive physiological processes of the body. Similar arousal systems operate to alert the brain. They activate the cortex so that it is fully responsive to incoming messages. In effect, they awaken the brain.

One of the most important of these is the **reticular activating system** or **RAS**. This neurological system has its origin in the upper portion of the recticular formation, a network of interconnected cells that extends throughout the brain stem and has branches that ascend to much of the rest of the brain (Figure 3.21). Sleeping cats whose RAS is electrically stimulated will awaken; cats whose RAS is destroyed are somnolent for weeks (Lindsley, 1960). RAS activity not only leads to awakening but it also produces increasing levels of arousal once awake. Stimulation of the RAS in waking monkeys jolts them into an alert state of attention in which they look around expectantly.

What triggers the RAS? One factor is sensory stimulation. On the face of it, this is hardly surprising, for we all know that sleep comes more readily when it is quiet and dark. But the neurological chain of events that explains why intense stimuli lead to awakening is fairly complex. Oddly enough, the direct input from the sensory pathways to the cortex is not the primary cause of wakefulness. In one study, the investigators severed virtually all of the sensory tracts to the cortex in cats (Lindsley et al., 1950). When the cats were asleep the experimenters presented a loud tone and the cats woke up. But how could this be, if the path from ear to cortex was cut so that the cortex was isolated from any auditory input? The answer is that there is another, indirect pathway that leads through the RAS. All of the sensory pathways to the cortex send collateral side branches to the RAS. The information the RAS receives in this manner is very meager and unspecific; it amounts to no more than a statement that a sensory message is on its way up to the cortex without any further indication of what that message might be. But this is enough for the RAS which now functions as a general alarm. It arouses the cortex which can then interpret the specific signals sent over the direct sensory pathway. In effect, the RAS is like a four-year-old who has just been handed a telegram while his mother is asleep. The child cannot read but he awakens his mother who can.

3.21 The reticular activating system *The figure indicates the location and function of the reticular structures in the hind- and midbrain. When a sense organ is stimulated, its message is relayed to a particular region of the cortex, typically a projection area. The sensory stimulation also triggers the reticular system which then arouses the cortex. As a result, the areas of the brain that receive the specific sensory message are sufficiently activated so that they can interpret it. (After French, 1957)*

Nonspecific stimulation

Reticular formation

Specific stimulation

Stimulation of one or more sense organs

Sensory stimulation is not the only source of RAS activation. Another comes from the cortex itself. There are descending fibers from the cortex that may excite the RAS which will then activate the cortex more fully. This circuit—cortex to RAS to cortex—probably plays an important role in many phenomena of sleep and waking. We sometimes have trouble in falling asleep because we "can't shut off our thoughts." Here cortical activity triggers the RAS which activates the cortex which again excites the RAS and so on. The importance of cortical activation of the RAS is also shown by the fact that some stimuli are more likely to wake us than others, regardless of their intensity—a baby's cry, the smell of fire, the sound of one's own name.

Sleep

The primary focus of this chapter is on motivation, and thus on the direction and activation of behavior that motives bring about. In this context, sleep is of considerable interest because it seems to represent the very opposite of arousal. But it has a more direct relevance as well. The desire for sleep is one of the most powerful of motives; if kept awake long enough, the urge to sleep will eventually take precedence over most other motives (which is one of the reasons why jailers sometimes use enforced sleeplessness to force confessions out of prisoners). What can we say about this state in which most of us spend a third of our lives?

SLEEP AND BRAIN ACTIVITY

Sleep cannot be observed from within, since it is by definition a condition of which the sleeper is unaware. We must perforce study it from without. One way of doing this is by observing what the brain does while its owner is asleep.

Eavesdropping on the brain of waking or sleeping subjects is made possible by the fact that the language of the nervous system is electrical. When electrodes are placed at various points on the skull, they pick up the electrical changes that are produced by the summed activity of the millions of nerve cells in the cerebral cortex that is just underneath. In absolute terms these changes are very small; they are therefore fed to a highly sensitive amplifier whose output in turn activates a series of pens. These pens trace their position on a long roll of paper that moves at a constant speed (Figure 3.22). The resulting record is an *electroencephalogram* or EEG, a picture of voltage changes over time occurring in the brain.

Figure 3.23 shows an EEG record. It begins with the subject in a relaxed state, with eyes closed, and "not thinking about anything in particular." The record shows *alpha waves,* a rather regular waxing and waning of electrical potential, at some eight to twelve cycles per second. This alpha rhythm is very characteristic of this state (awake but resting), and is found in most mammals. When the subject attends to some stimulus with open eyes, or when he is involved in active thought

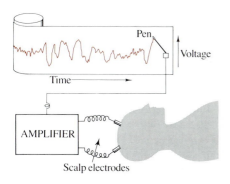

3.22 Schematic diagram of EEG recording *A number of scalp electrodes are placed on a subject's head. At any one time, there are small differences in the electrical potential (that is, the voltage) between any two of these electrodes. These differences are magnified by an amplifier and are then used to activate a recording pen. The greater the voltage difference, the larger the pen's deflection. Since the voltage fluctuates, the pen goes up and down, thus tracing a so-called brain wave on the moving paper. The number of such waves per second is the EEG frequency.*

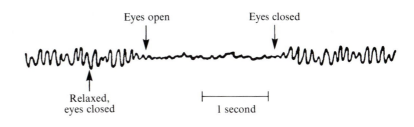

3.23 Alpha waves and alpha blocking *(After Guyton, 1981)*

| AWAKE | | QUIET SLEEP | | | ACTIVE SLEEP |
| | (Stage 1) | (Stage 2) | (Stage 3) | (Stage 4) | Dreaming |

3.24 The stages of sleep *The figure shows EEG records taken from the frontal lobe of the brain, during waking, quiet sleep, and active sleep. (Courtesy of William C. Dement)*

(for instance, mental arithmetic) with his eyes closed, the picture changes. Now the alpha rhythm is *blocked;* the voltage is lower, the frequency is much higher, and the pattern of ups and downs is nearly random.

THE STAGES OF SLEEP

Several decades of work involving continuous, all-night recordings of EEGs and other measures have shown that there are several stages of sleep and that these vary in depth. Just prior to sleep, there tends to be an accentuated alpha rhythm. As the subject becomes drowsy, the alpha comes and goes; there are increasingly long stretches during which the pattern is random. The subject is now in a light, dozing sleep, from which she is easily awakened (Stage 1 in Figure 3.24). Over the course of the next hour she drifts into deeper and deeper stages, in which the EEGs are characterized by the complete absence of alpha and by waves of increasingly higher voltage and much lower frequency (Stages 2 through 4 in Figure 3.24). In the last stages, the waves are very slow. They occur about once every second and are some five times greater in amplitude than those of the alpha rhythm. At this point the sleeper is virtually immobile and will take a few seconds to awaken, mumbling incoherently, even if shaken or shouted at. During the course of the night, the sleeper's descent repeats itself several times. She drops from dozing to deep, slow-wave sleep, reascends to Stage 1, drops back to slow-wave sleep, and so on for some four or five cycles.

The oscillations between different sleep stages are not merely changes in depth. When the sleeper reascends into Stage 1, he seems to enter a qualitatively different state entirely. This state is sometimes called *active sleep* to distinguish it from the *quiet sleep* found during the other stages. Active sleep is a paradoxical condition with contradictory aspects. In some ways it is as deep as sleep ever gets. The sleeper's general body musculature is more flaccid and he is less sensitive to external stimulation (Williams, Tepas, and Morlock, 1962). But judged by some other criteria, the level of arousal during active sleep is almost as high as during alert wakefulness. One sign is the EEG, which in humans is rather similar to that found in waking (Jouvet, 1967).

Of particular interest are the sleeper's eye movements which can be recorded by means of electrodes attached next to each eye. During quiet sleep, the eyes drift slowly and no longer move in tandem. But during active sleep a different pattern suddenly appears. The eyes move rapidly and in unison behind closed lids, as if the sleeper were looking at some object outside. These jerky, rapid eye movements (REMs) are one of the most striking features of active sleep, which is often called *REM sleep.* Young human adults enter this stage about four times each night (Figure 3.25).

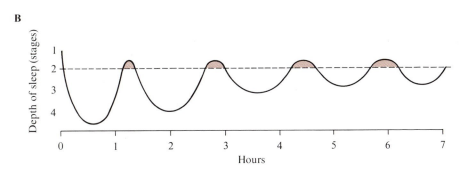

3.25   REM and non-REM sleep   (A) Eye movements during non-REM and REM sleep. The REM periods are associated with dreaming. (B) The alternation of non-REM and REM periods throughout the course of the night (REM periods are in color). Rapid eye movements and dreams begin as the person repeatedly emerges from deeper sleep to the level of Stage 1. (After Kleitman, 1960)

DREAMS

REM sleep was discovered fairly recently, but its discoverers almost immediately related it to a phenomenon known to humans since prehistoric times: dreaming. When sleeping subjects are awakened during REM sleep, they generally report a dream: a series of episodes that seemed real at the time. Not so for quiet (that is, non-REM) sleep. When awakened from quiet sleep, subjects may say that they were thinking about something, but they rarely relate the kind of inner drama we call a dream (Cartwright, 1977). Further evidence links the duration of the dream events to the length of the REM period. Subjects who are awakened five minutes after the onset of REM tend to describe shorter dreams than subjects awakened fifteen minutes after the REM period begins. This result argues against the popular notion that dreams are virtually instantaneous, no matter how long they take to relate when later recalled. In actual fact, the dream seems to take just about as long as the dream episode might have been in real life (Dement and Kleitman, 1957; Dement and Wolpert, 1958).

These findings suggest that the average adult dreams for about one and a half hours every night, the time spent in REM sleep. How can we square this statement with the fact that in everyday life many people seem to experience dreams only occasionally, and that some deny that they ever dream? The answer is that dreams are generally forgotten within minutes after they have occurred. In one study, subjects were awakened either during REM sleep or five minutes after a REM period had ended. In the first condition, detailed dream narratives were obtained on 85 percent of the narratives; in the second, there were none (Wolpert and Trosman, 1958).

Why dreams leave such fragile memories is something of a puzzle. One possibility is that the memory of the dream is ordinarily inaccessible because of a failure to relate the dream episode (when it occurs) to the many other memories of waking life (Koulack and Goodenough, 1976). This interpretation may explain some odd experiences in which we seem to remember something that we know did not occur. These may be recollections of a dream without the realization that it was a dream and not a real event.

THE FUNCTIONS OF SLEEP

What functions are served by sleep, whether in its active or quiet form? Surprisingly enough, the answer is still unknown.

Sleep deprivation   One way of trying to assess the benefits that sleep may bring is to observe what ills befall if it is prevented. This is the logic of sleep-deprivation experiments in which humans and animals are kept awake for days on end. The results suggest that there is indeed a need for sleep. If deprived of sleep, the organism seeks sleep just as it seeks food when it is starved. When sleep is finally allowed, the subjects sink down upon the nearest cot and try to make up for the sleep they have lost.

The need of the sleep-deprived person is not just for sleep in general but also for the two major sleep states that comprise it. This is shown by studies on selective sleep deprivation in which the experimenter prevents one kind of sleep (for example, REM) but not the other. If he wants to deprive the subjects of REM sleep only, he simply wakes them up whenever the EEG and eye movements signal the beginning of a REM period. After the subjects wake up, they go back to sleep, are reawakened when they next enter the REM state, go back to sleep, are reawakened, and so on through the night. After a few nights of this, the subjects are allowed to sleep freely. They will now spend more time in REM than they normally do, as if to make up for the state of which they were deprived (Figure 3.26). The same holds for selective deprivation of the deep, slow-wave sleep of Stages 3 and 4. If lost one night, it is made up on another (Webb, 1972).

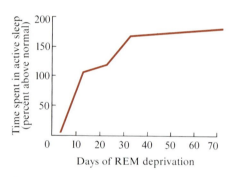

3.26   The effect of lost REM sleep   *The figure shows an increase in the time cats spend in REM sleep after various periods of REM-sleep deprivation. The animals were deprived of REM sleep (but not non-REM sleep) for from 5 to 72 days by being awakened as soon as their EEG indicated the beginning of a REM period. On the first day when the animals were finally allowed to sleep undisturbed, there was an increase in the proportion of time spent in REM sleep rather than non-REM sleep. (Data from Cohen, 1972)*

Sleep as a restorative process   The sleep-deprivation experiments suggest that there is a need for sleep, but they do not tell us why. One possibility is that sleep is restorative, that it is a period during which some vital substance is resynthesized in the nervous system. But just what is this substance? Various candidates have been proposed. One is a growth-promoting hormone whose secretion seems to go up during sleep (Takahashi, 1979). Another concerns certain proteins in the brain that are synthesized much more rapidly during sleep—especially REM sleep—than while awake (Drucker-Colin and Spanis, 1976). But thus far these are only leads for the future and controversial ones at that. The restoration hypothesis may well be correct, but as yet we don't know what it is that is restored and why it is so vital.

Sleep as an evolutionary relic   Some investigators argue that while the desire for sleep is clearly an insistent motive, there is no reason to believe that it serves a vital bodily need. They agree that the sleepless person seeks sleep just as the starved one craves food. But they point out that while starvation eventually leads to death, there is no evidence that even prolonged sleep deprivation will have such dire effects; it will make people drowsy, a bit confused, and desperately anxious for sleep, but little more. One interpretation is that sleep is an evolutionary relic of former times, a built-in response system that once had an important adaptive function although it no longer does. A daily period of enforced near-immobility spent in some hiding place may have been quite useful to our animal ancestors; it would have helped them to conserve their energies and kept them out of the way of possible predators. Thus, according to some authors, human sleep may be nothing but a remnant of such an ancestral adaptive pattern. It is of little use to us now that we have electric light bulbs and need fear no predators except those of our own kind, but it is no less powerful even so (Webb, 1974).

To sum up, while we know a great deal about the phenomena of sleep and some of the mechanisms that bring it about, we can do little more than speculate about its functions. The desire for sleep is a powerful motive, and some twenty-five years of an average lifetime are devoted to it. But it's still unclear what, if anything, it is good for.

WHAT DIFFERENT MOTIVES HAVE IN COMMON

The preceding sections have dealt with a number of motives that impel to action —hunger, thirst, fear, and so on. Some such as hunger are in the service of homeostasis and serve to maintain the internal environment. Others such as rage are triggered by stimuli in the environment and are relevant to self-preservation. For a few others—the main example is sleep—the function is still unknown. These various motives are clearly very different, as are the goals toward which they steer the organism—food, water, escape from threat, a good night's sleep. But despite the differences between them, is there something that all these motives and these goals have in common?

Level of Stimulation

A number of theorists have suggested that all—or at least most—motives can be described as a search for some *optimum level of arousal* or of general stimulation. One of the early controversies in the area was over the question of what this optimum level is.

DRIVE-REDUCTION THEORY

According to the drive-reduction theory proposed by Clark L. Hull some forty years ago, the optimum level of arousal that organisms seek is essentially zero. Hull and his students were impressed by the fact that many motives seem directed at the reduction of some internal state of bodily tension which if continued would lead to injury or even death. Examples are food deprivation, water deprivation, pain, and so on. Hull believed that this is true for all motives. In his view, all built-in rewards produce some reduction of bodily tension (or, as he called it, of drive). This position amounts to the assertion that what we normally call pleasure is at bottom nothing else but the reduction of pain or discomfort. According to this view, what organisms strive for is the absolute minimum of all arousal and stimulation, a biopsychological version of the Eastern search for *Nirvana*.

In some ways, Hull's theory can be regarded as a homeostatic conception carried to its extreme form. As Hull saw it, anything an organism does is ultimately directed at getting rid of some noxious state—pain, nutrient deficit, or whatever. One immediate difficulty is posed by sex, a motive that is clearly not homeostatic in the sense in which hunger and thirst are. To explain sexual satisfaction in drive-reduction terms, Hull and his students argued that what is rewarding about sexual activity is the drop in tension that occurs during orgasm (Hull, 1943).

Seeking stimulation Hull's drive-reduction theory suggests that, in general, organisms seek minimum levels of stimulation, preferring peace and quiet to states of tension and arousal. But, in fact, this does not seem to be true. For there is little doubt that some experiences are actively sought after. One example is the taste of sweets or erotic stimulation. These are both felt to be positive pleasures rather than the mere removal of some irritant. One example concerns saccharin, a sweet substance that has no nutritive value and thus no effect on the bodily tension and deficit that underlies hunger. But rats and other animals will nevertheless drink a saccharine solution avidly (Sheffield and Roby, 1950).

Other findings concern sexual activity. In one study, male rats were run in a maze that had two end boxes. One was empty, while the other contained a sexually receptive female. When the male encountered the female, he usually mounted her. But an unsympathetic experimenter invariably separated the pair before ejaculation could occur. This meant that sexual tension was increased rather than decreased. But the males nevertheless chose the side of the maze that held the female. This shows that sexual stimulation is rewarding in its own right. Whether this point really required experimental substantiation is debatable, considering that so many humans engage in sexual foreplay and try to lengthen the time before orgasm (Sheffield, Wulff, and Backer, 1951).

Curiosity and manipulation Such evidence suggests that drive reduction is not the only goal. Similar conclusions emerge from work on curiosity and manipulation. Monkeys will go through considerable lengths to puzzle out how to open latches that are attached to a wooden board. But when the latches are unlocked, nothing opens, because the latches never closed anything in the first place (see Figure 3.27). Since unlatching gets the animal nothing, the response was presumably its own reward. In this regard, monkeys acted much like human beings, who in countless ways indicate that they often do things as ends in themselves, rather than as means to other ends.

AN OPTIMUM AROUSAL ABOVE ZERO

According to Hull's theory, organisms always seek to diminish their level of arousal. But as we have seen, the evidence says otherwise. To be sure, we do try to reduce arousal if our arousal level is unduly high, as in intense hunger or fear or pain. But in many other cases we apparently try to increase it. This suggests that there is an above-zero optimum level of arousal. If we are above this optimum (for example, in pain), we try to reduce arousal. But if we are below it, we seek stimulation to ascend beyond it. This optimum undoubtedly varies from time to time and from person to person. According to some authors, some people are "sensation seekers" who generally look for stimulation, while others prefer a quieter existence (Zuckerman, 1979; see Chapter 18).

Drugs and addiction Occasionally, we are aroused to rather high-pitched levels —by prolonged sex play, by watching an effective horror movie, by riding on a roller coaster. These are ways of inducing high arousal states by external stimulation. But there is another way of getting "high." One can use drugs that artificially excite the brain's arousal systems.

Examples of drugs that have this effect are the amphetamines and cocaine. They boost the activity of the reticular arousal system and other structures in the

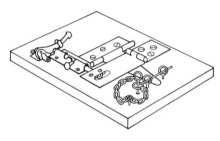

3.27 Mechanical puzzles which monkeys solve without special reward *The complex puzzle presented to monkeys was basically a hinge which was restrained by a variety of devices: a bar, a pin, a bolt, and so on. The monkeys received no special reward for their labors, but even so, learned to open many of these devices "for the fun of it." (After Harlow, 1950)*

A   B   C

Seeking stimulation *People have invented many activities to experience the paradoxical joy of fear and danger. (A) Some of these activities induce excitement but are known to be safe in reality, such as riding on roller coasters. (B) Others are more dangerous but provide greater thrills, such as skydiving. (C) In yet other activities the fear and danger are experienced vicariously, as in watching horror movies. The figure shows Boris Karloff as the monster in the 1931 classic* Frankenstein. *(Photographs by Kent Halsell, and José A. Fernandez, Woodfin Camp; movie still courtesy of the Museum of Modern Art/Film Stills Archive)*

brain by artificially increasing the amount of available norepinephrine at the relevant synaptic junctions. The result is greater activation. The individual is almost literally "turned on"—alert, sensitive, and extremely energetic. This overactivation is often experienced as very pleasurable, sometimes to the point of extreme euphoria.

Of course, the drug user pays a substantial price. To begin with, the arousing drugs have certain unpleasant side effects. If the activation is intense enough, there may be high anxiety and extreme suspiciousness. Even more important is the fact that in many individuals repeated drug use leads to *addiction.* The consequences of this are two-fold. One is an increased *tolerance* for the drug, so that the addict requires ever-larger doses to obtain the same effect. A second consequence of addiction goes hand in hand with increased tolerance. When the drug is withheld, there are *withdrawal symptoms.* In general, these are the precise opposites of the symptoms produced by the drug itself. For instance, amphetamine addicts deprived of their drug often feel intensely depressed and sluggish.

The Opponent-Process Theory of Motivation

Our discussion of the controversies that followed in the wake of Hull's drive reduction theory made it clear that relief from pain and pleasure are not really equivalent. Pain and pleasure are opposites, but pleasure is more than the absence of pain, and pain more than the absence of pleasure. The fundamental opposition of the various emotional feelings associated with pain and pleasure (such as fear and terror on the one hand, and joy and euphoria on the other) is the focus of an influential recent formulation, the *opponent-process theory.* This asserts that the nervous system has a general tendency to counteract any deviation from motivational normalcy. If there is too much of a swing to one pole of the pain-pleasure dimension, say toward joy and ecstasy, an *opponent process* is called into play that tilts the balance toward the negative side. Conversely, if the initial swing is toward terror or revulsion, there will be an opponent process toward the positive side. The net effect is that there will be an attenuation of the emotional state one happens to be in, so that ecstasy becomes mild pleasure and terror loses some of its force. A further result occurs when the situation that originally led to joy or to extreme fear is withdrawn. Now the opponent process is unopposed by the motivational condition that first evoked it. The consequence is a shift toward the opposite side of the emotional spectrum (Solomon and Corbit, 1974; Solomon, 1980).

Opponent-process theory may account for some of the phenomena of drug addiction we have just discussed. Consider tolerance and withdrawal effects. According to this theory, the emotional reaction produced by a drug such as amphetamine generates an opponent process that pulls in the opposite direction. As a result, there is increased tolerance, so that ever larger doses of the drug are required to produce an emotional high. The effect of the opponent process is revealed more starkly when the drug is withheld and there is no further pull toward the positive side of the emotional spectrum. All that remains is the opponent process, which pulls the reaction in the opposite direction, resulting in withdrawal symptoms such as depression (Solomon, 1977).

Another example comes from a study of sky divers. These people presumably parachute for the fun of it, but not on their first jump. Judging from photographed facial expressions and autonomic measures, they initially seem to be in a state of panic. When they land safely, they act stunned and stony-faced. But after several successful jumps, their reaction changes. Prior to the jump, they are no longer terrified; at worst, they are a bit tense. But when they land safely, they feel exuberant and intensely happy (Epstein, 1967).

This pattern of results fits in with the opponent-process view. With repeated experiences, the parachutists' original terror is counteracted by an opponent process that tilts the scale toward the positive side. As a result, there is less and less fear prior to the jump (a phenomenon akin to increased drug tolerance). The opponent process reveals itself more clearly after several safe landings. This is the analogue of a withdrawal effect, but in this case it is all to the good, since what is withdrawn is the occasion for the initial terror. After the jump, all that's left is the opponent process. Since this is now unopposed and pulls toward the positive side of the emotional axis, there is exhilaration.

What is the physiological basis of the mood shifts studied by opponent-process theory? Some of them may be caused by the secretion of endorphins. As we saw in the previous chapter, endorphins are neurotransmitters that act as self-administered opiates; they are secreted in conditions of stress and counteract the perception of pain. Some authors suggest that they can also produce an opponent-process change in the opposite direction. An example is the exhilarating effect of repeated stressful exercise such as jogging or marathon running. The runner continues to exert herself until she is exhausted and in pain. This builds up endorphins which counteract the pain and produce a mood shift in the opposite direction. Eventually there may be something akin to an addiction—the jogger has to have her jogging fix to enjoy the endorphin-produced euphoria.

Are There Pleasure Centers in the Brain?

Thus far, we have discussed various attempts to determine what the various satisfactions that humans and animals strive for have in common psychologically.

3.28 Self-stimulation in rats *The rat feels the stimulation of a pulse lasting less than a second. (Courtesy of Dr. M. E. Olds)*

Another approach to this question has been through studies of the brain processes that come into play when an organism is rewarded. A number of investigators have asked whether there is a special region of the brain whose activation gives rise to what humans call "pleasure," a so-called "pleasure center" that is triggered whenever a motive is satisfied, regardless of which motive it is. They have tried to answer this question by studying the rewarding effects of electrical stimulation of various regions in the brain.

This general area of investigation was opened up in 1954 when James Olds and Peter Milner discovered that rats would learn to press a lever to give themselves a brief burst of electrical stimulation in certain regions of the limbic system (Olds and Milner, 1954; see Figure 3.28). Similar rewarding effects of self-stimulation have been demonstrated in a wide variety of animals, including cats, dogs, dolphins, monkeys, and human beings. To obtain it, rats will press a lever at rates up to 7,000 presses per hour for hours on end. When forced to choose between food and self-stimulation, hungry rats will typically opt for self-stimulation, even though it literally brings starvation (Spies, 1965).

SPECIFIC AND GENERAL PLEASURE CENTERS IN THE BRAIN?

What is the mechanism that underlies the rewarding effect of self-stimulation? Two possibilities suggest themselves. One is that brain stimulation mimics certain *specific* natural rewards. Stimulation in one region might fool the brain into assuming there had been eating, stimulation in another that there had been copulation, and so on. Another possibility is that self-stimulation provides a more *general,* nonspecific kind of pleasure, something that all rewards share. Drinking, eating, and copulating are obviously different, but perhaps the different motivational messages they send to the brain ("have just drunk, eaten, copulated") ultimately feed into a common neurological system that responds to all of them in much the same way ("that sure felt good").

There is evidence that the stimulation of certain areas provides rather specific rewards. For example, animals will work to obtain electrical stimulation of the lateral zone of the hypothalamus (the "hunger center"). The extent to which they will work to get this reward depends on their hunger level. If they haven't eaten for a while, they will work much harder than they would otherwise. This suggests that the brain regards stimulation in this region as equivalent to food. Analogous effects are found for regions that are concerned with drinking or sexual behavior (Olds and Fobes, 1981).

The case for nonspecific reward effects is somewhat weaker. To begin with, there are a number of regions that lead to self-stimulation, but at a rate that is uninfluenced by food or water deprivation, sex hormones, and the like. Further evidence comes from studies of self-stimulation in human patients—schizophrenics or persons suffering from severe epilepsy. When asked to describe what the stimulation felt like, some patients showed specific reward effects. Most of these were sexual. The stimulation of one region made one patient feel that he had built up to a sexual orgasm. Other patients reported a more nonspecific, pleasurable feeling. They said they "felt good," "wonderful," and then they smiled, laughed, and continued to stimulate themselves by pressing the "happy button." Such results suggest that there might be a nonspecific reward system, a kind of general "pleasure center," that exists in addition to those specific to a particular motive (Heath, 1964; Rolls, 1975).

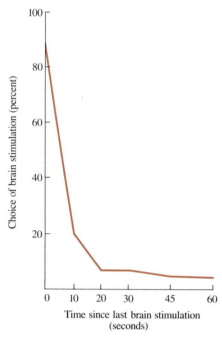

3.29 Priming and rewarding brain stimulation *Very thirsty rats were given a choice between two arms of a maze: one led to brain stimulation, the other to water. This choice was made either immediately after a burst of brain stimulation, or from 10 to 60 seconds after stimulation. The figure shows that the animals were much more likely to ignore their thirst and choose brain stimulation if they had been primed with such stimulation shortly before the choice. (Data from Deutsch, Adams, and Metzner, 1964)*

PRIMING

The notion of pleasure centers is hotly debated among current physiological psychologists (e.g., Gallistel, 1983). One problem is that the same rats who initially responded with such wild frenzy will ignore the lever altogether when put back in the experimental chamber after an interval of an hour or less. But they will resume their wild pressing if first given a few free brief electric pulses. It seems as if something in the brain has to be "primed" in order to reinstate the desire for the brain stimulation (Figure 3.29). But why? There are a number of interpretations. One is that rewarding brain stimulation is not just rewarding. It also starts a *positive* feedback cycle in which every stimulation strengthens the tendency to get yet another stimulation and so on. (For discussion, see Deutsch, 1960; Gallistel, 1973; Rolls, 1975.)

In this regard, the effect of self-stimulation seems to be similar to the effect of many natural rewards. When we start to eat, the first taste increases our desire for more food rather than decreasing it. In sexual behavior, this effect is even more striking. Each stimulation heightens the desire for further stimulation as sexual passion mounts to a higher and higher pitch. Of course, the positive feedback system is shut off eventually; feeding is finally stopped by satiety signals from the stomach and elsewhere, and sexual passion subsides with orgasm. The priming effect in self-stimulation may well be just another instance of this general phenomenon. The difference is that the poor (or perhaps enviable) rat with a self-stimulating electrode in its head has no shut-off mechanism. There is no satiety signal and no orgasm, and so the rat keeps on self-stimulating and self-stimulating until the experimenter finally tears it away from the lever or it falls to the ground in sheer exhaustion.

The Nature of Motives

To sum up. During the past fifty years, there has been enormous progress in our understanding of the psychology and the physiological basis of the biological motives. But as yet, there is no agreement on one mechanism that explains their action. It may be that such a unitary mechanism doesn't really exist (although advocates of a general pleasure center would probably disagree). Like all scientists, psychologists are much happier when they get neat explanations, and one underlying mechanism would be so much neater than many different ones. But nature did not design organisms to make psychologists happy. And she may well have provided multiple mechanisms rather than just one.

A final point. This chapter was concerned with a number of built-in motives—the biological goals we must seek in order to survive. But whenever we looked at a motive in detail (as in the case of human food selection), we saw that the specific nature of these goals depends not only on our biology but also on what we have learned and have been taught. Just what we drink is not only a matter of our water balance: except for Count Dracula, none of us drink blood. By the same token, we have to maintain certain nutrient levels, but this doesn't mean that we'd be satisfied with a diet of grasshoppers. Similar concerns apply to what we fear and hate, or how we behave in sexual matters and when, where, and with whom. In all these cases, experience builds upon biology and gives form to the built-in basics with which we start. We learn—from the experience of our own lifetime, and through culture, from the lifetime of hundreds of prior generations.

Evolution gave us a set of built-in, biological goals, and a few built-in mechanisms for attaining them. Learning provides the way to modify these goals and to find ever more complex means to achieve them. We turn next to the mechanisms by which such learning occurs in humans and animals.

SUMMARY

1. Most human and animal actions are motivated. *Motives* have a two-fold function: They *direct* behavior toward or away from some goal. They also serve to *activate* the organism, which becomes more aroused the greater the strength of the motive.

2. The biological basis of directed action is *negative feedback* in which the system "feeds back" upon itself to stop its own action. Built-in negtive feedback is responsible for many reactions that maintain the stability of the organism's internal environment or *homeostasis.* Special cells in the hypothalamus sense various aspects of the body's internal state. An example is temperature. If this is above or below certain *set-points,* a number of self-regulatory reflexes controlled by the sympathetic and parasympathetic divisions of the autonomic nervous system are triggered (for example, shivering). In addition, directed, voluntary acts (such as putting on a sweater) are brought into play.

3. Similar homeostatic mechanisms underlie a number of other biological motives. An example is *thirst.* The organism is informed about its water balance by *volume receptors* that monitor the total volume of its body fluids, and by *osmoreceptors* that respond to the concentration of certain minerals dissolved in these fluids. Water losses are partially offset by reflex mechanisms, including the secretion of the *antidiuretic hormone* (ADH), which instructs the kidneys to reabsorb more of the water that passes through them. In addition, the organism readjusts its own internal environment by directed action—drinking.

4. The biological motive that has been studied most extensively is *hunger.* Some stimuli for feeding come from the internal environment: the nutrient levels in the bloodstream and metabolic processes in the liver. Other stimuli are external, including the *palatability* of the food.

5. Many authors believe that the control of feeding is lodged in two antagonistic centers in the hypothalamus whose excitation gives rise to hunger and satiety respectively. As evidence, they point to the effect of lesions. Destruction of the supposed hunger center leads to *aphagia,* a complete refusal to eat. Destruction of the supposed satiety center produces *hyperphagia,* a vast increase in food intake.

6. Homeostatic factors determine *that* an animal feeds, but they have less of an effect on *what* it feeds on. Food selection is determined by a variety of factors, including built-in preferences and learning. Many animals are *neophobic*—afraid of anything that is new. They will only sample new foods in small amounts, developing a learned *taste aversion* if they turn out to be poisonous, and adding them to their diet if they prove to be safe. In humans, food preferences are generally institutionalized in the form of a *cuisine,* which is a special cultural pattern of preparing and flavoring food.

7. A feeding-related disorder is *obesity.* Some cases are produced by bodily malfunctions, including an oversecretion of insulin and an overabundance of fat cells. Others are

the result of various behavioral factors. According to the *externality hypothesis,* overweight people are comparatively insensitive to internal hunger signals and oversensitive to external ones such as palatability. An alternative is the *set-point hypothesis,* which asserts that overweight people have a higher internal set-point for weight.

8. In contrast to thirst and hunger, which are largely based on homeostatic factors from within, a number of motives are instigated from without. An example is the intense reaction to external threat. Its biological mechanisms include the operations of the *autonomic nervous system.* This consists of two antagonistic branches. One is the *parasympathetic nervous system,* which serves the vegetative functions of everyday life, such as digestion and reproduction. It slows down the heart rate and reduces blood pressure. The other is the *sympathetic nervous system,* which activates the body and mobilizes its resources. It increases the available metabolic fuels and accelerates their utilization by increasing the heart rate and respiration. Intense sympathetic activity can be regarded as an *emergency reaction,* which underlies the overt reactions of *fight* or *flight* and their usual emotional concomitants, rage or fear.

9. The sympathetic emergency reaction is not always biologically adaptive. It is sometimes disruptive as in psychophysiologically produced ailments and certain cases of "sudden death."

10. While the sympathetic system arouses the more primitive physiological processes of the body, a structure in the brain stem, the *reticular activating system,* or *RAS,* arouses the brain. The RAS awakens the cortex and is opposed by an antagonistic system which leads to sleep.

11. During sleep, brain activity changes as shown by the *electroencephalogram* or *EEG.* Each night, we oscillate between two kinds of sleep. One is *quiet sleep,* during which the cortex is relatively inactive. The other is *active sleep,* characterized by considerable cortical activity and *rapid eye movements* or *REMs,* a pattern of internal activity which is experienced as *dreams. Sleep-deprivation* studies show that when one or the other kind of sleep is prevented, it is to some extent made up later on. This suggests that there is a need for each of the two sleep states, but the biological functions served by either are as yet unknown.

12. According to *drive-reduction theory,* all built-in motives act to reduce stimulation and arousal. Today most authors believe instead that organisms strive for an *optimum level of arousal.* If below this optimum, they try to increase arousal by various means, including the use of certain drugs. The *opponent-process theory of motivation* points out that all shifts of arousal level produce a counteracting process that acts to moderate the ups and downs. When the original instigator of the shift is removed, the opponent process is revealed more clearly, as in the *withdrawal effects* in a drug addict.

13. Work on the rewarding effects of certain regions of the brain has led to speculations about possible *pleasure centers* in the brain. There is evidence that the stimulation of certain areas leads to specific reward effects, although this interpretation is challenged by the fact that self-stimulation requires some *priming.* The evidence for a nonspecific rewarding effect is somewhat weaker.

CHAPTER 4

Learning

Thus far, our discussion has centered on the built-in facets of human and animal behavior, the general neural equipment that provides the underpinning for everything we do, and the specific, innate feedback systems that underlie directed action. But much of what we do and are goes beyond what nature gave us. It is acquired through experience in our lifetime. People learn—to grasp a baby bottle, to eat with knife and fork, to read and write, to love or hate their neighbors, and eventually, to face death. In animals, the role of learning may be less dramatic, but it is still enormously important even so.

What can psychology tell us about the processes whereby organisms learn? Many investigators have tried to reconcile the phenomena of learning with the reflex-machine conception that goes back to Descartes. The adherents of this approach, whose modern exponents are sometimes called **behavior theorists,** argued that the organism's *prewired* repertory of behaviors is supplemented by continual *rewirings* that are produced by experience. Some of these rewirings consist of new connections between stimuli. Thus, the sight of the mother's face may come to signify the taste of milk. Other rewirings involve new connections between acts and their consequences, as when a toddler learns that touching a hot radiator is followed by a painful burn. The behavior theorists set themselves the task of discovering how such rewirings come about.

The behavior theorists' interest in the learning process was admirably suited to the intellectual climate during the first part of this century, especially in the United States. For here was a society that was deeply committed to the individual's efforts to improve himself by pushing himself on to greater efforts and acquiring new skills—in numerous public schools and colleges, night classes for recent immigrants, dance classes for the shy, courses for those who wanted to "win friends and influence people," and martial-arts classes for those less interested in winning friends than in defeating enemies. There was—and in many ways, still is—an enormous faith in the near-limitless malleability of human beings, who were thought to be almost infinitely perfectable by proper changes in their environment, especially through education. This attitude is well expressed in a widely quoted pronouncement by one of the founders of behavior theory, John B. Watson:

> Give me a dozen healthy infants, well-formed, and my own specified world to bring them up in and I'll guarantee to take any one at random and train him to become any type of specialist I might select—doctor, lawyer, artist, merchant chief, and yes, even beggar-man thief, regardless of his talents, penchants, tendencies, abilities, vocations, and race of his ancestors (J.B. Watson, 1925).

How should the learning process be studied? Most behavior theorists feel that there are some basic laws of learning that come into play regardless of what it is that is learned or who does the learning—be it a dog learning to sit on command or a college student learning integral calculus. For in their view, even the most involved learned activities are made up of simpler ones, much as complex chemical compounds are made up of simpler atoms. Given this belief, behavior theorists have concentrated their efforts on trying to understand learning in simple situations and in (relatively) simple creatures like dogs, rats, and pigeons. They have sought to strip the learning process down to its bare essence so that its basic, atomic laws might be revealed. This search has led to some major discoveries to which we now turn.

HABITUATION

The simplest of all forms of learning is **habituation.** This is a decline in the tendency to respond to stimuli that have become familiar due to repeated exposure. A sudden noise usually startles us—an adaptive reaction, for sudden and unfamiliar stimuli often spell danger. But suppose the same noise is repeated over and over again. The second time, the startle will be diminished, the third time it will hardly be evoked, and after that, it will be ignored altogether. We have become habituated. Much the same holds for many other everyday events. We have become so accustomed to the ticking of a clock in the living room that we are utterly unaware of it until it finally stops. By the same token, city dwellers become completely habituated to the noise of traffic but are kept awake by the crickets when they take a vacation in the country.

Habituation is found at virtually all levels of the animal kingdom. Birds, fish, insects, and snails perform various escape reactions when they first encounter a novel stimulus, but after several repetitions they come to ignore it. Thus, marine snails initially withdraw their gills at the slightest touch on the body but will stop responding after repeated stimulation.

What is the adaptive significance of habituation? One of its major benefits is that it narrows down the range of stimuli that elicit escape reactions. After all, organisms have to eat and drink and mate to survive, and they can't do so if they spend all their time running away from imaginary enemies. Habituation allows them to ignore the familiar and focus their emergency reactions on things that are new and may signal danger (Wyers, Peek, and Hertz, 1973).

Alarm

↑

↓

No alarm

4.1 Innate fear of hawks or habituation? Young turkeys run for cover when a silhouette model is pulled in the direction of the model's short end which makes it look like a bird of prey, but not when it is pulled in the opposite direction which makes it look like a goose. (After Tinbergen, 1951)

Ivan Petrovich Pavlov (Courtesy Sovfoto)

An interesting example of the role of habituation in focusing escape reactions is the response of ground-living birds to the sight of birds flying above. Some early experiments had studied the reaction of young turkeys to a cardboard silhouette of a bird pulled overhead on a string. The silhouette had a short end and a long end (see Figure 4.1). When pulled so that the long end pointed forward (which made it look like a goose with an outstretched neck), the young turkeys were nonchalant. But when it was pulled in the opposite direction, the birds became terrified and ran for cover. Now the short end pointed forward and the silhouette resembled a hawk. Some authors took this result as evidence that ground-living birds have a built-in fear reaction to birds of prey (Tinbergen, 1951). But further studies suggested that the effect was a result of novelty and habituation. In the turkeys' environment, long-necked geese and ducks flying overhead were fairly common, while hawks were hardly ever seen. As a result, the turkeys had become habituated to the one and not to the other. The young birds begin with a fear reaction to just about everything. Given time and habituation, this reaction gradually narrows down to the rather infrequent stimuli that the animal really has reason to fear (Schleidt, 1961).

CLASSICAL CONDITIONING

In habituation, an organism learns to recognize an event as familiar, but he doesn't learn anything about the relation between that event and any other circumstances. Such learned relationships are called **associations.** There's little doubt that much of what we learn consists of various associations between events: between thunder and lightning, between the nipple and food, between the sound of a thumping motor and a large automobile repair bill. The importance of associations in human learning and thinking has been emphasized since the days of the Greek philosophers, but the experimental study of associations did not begin until the end of the nineteenth century. A major step in this direction was the work on conditioning performed by the great Russian scientist, Ivan P. Pavlov (1849–1936).

Pavlov and the Conditioned Reflex

Ivan Petrovich Pavlov had already earned the Nobel Prize for his work on digestion before he embarked upon the study of conditioning which was to gain him even greater fame. His initial interest was in the built-in nervous control of the various digestive reflexes in dogs; most important to us, the secretion of saliva. He surgically diverted one of the ducts of the salivary gland, thus channeling part of the salivary flow through a special tube to the outside of the animal's body where it could be easily measured and analyzed. Pavlov demonstrated that salivation was produced by several innate reflexes, one of which prepares the food for digestion. This is triggered by food (especially dry food) placed in the mouth.

In the course of Pavlov's work a new fact emerged. The salivary reflex could be set off by stimuli which at first were totally neutral. Dogs that had been in the laboratory for a while would soon salivate to a whole host of stimuli that had no such

4.2 Apparatus for salivary conditioning *The figure shows an early version of Pavlov's apparatus for classical conditioning of the salivary response. The dog was held in a harness, sounds or lights functioned as conditioned stimuli, while meat powder in a dish served as the unconditioned stimulus. The conditioned response was assessed with the aid of a tube connected to an opening in one of the animal's salivary glands. (After Yerkes and Morgulis, 1909)*

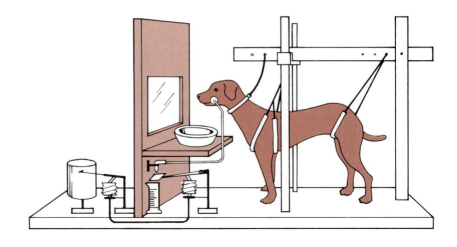

Pavlov watching an experiment (Courtesy Sovfoto)

effect on their uninitiated fellows. Not only the taste and touch of the meat in the mouth, but its mere sight, the sight of the dish in which it was placed, the sight of the person who usually brought it, even that person's footsteps—eventually all of these might produce salivation. Pavlov soon decided to study such effects in their own right, for he recognized that they provided a means of extending the reflex concept to embrace learned as well as innate reactions. The approach was simple enough. Instead of waiting for accidental events in each animal's history, the experimenter would provide those events himself. Thus he would repeatedly sound a buzzer and always follow it with food. Later he observed what happened when the buzzer was sounded and no food was given (Pavlov, 1927; Figure 4.2).

The fundamental finding was simple: Repeated buzzer-food pairings led to salivation when the buzzer was presented alone. To explain this, Pavlov proposed a distinction between unconditioned and conditioned reflexes. ***Unconditioned reflexes*** he held to be essentially inborn; these would be unconditionally elicited by the appropriate stimulus regardless of the animal's history. An example is salivating to food in the mouth. In contrast, ***conditioned reflexes*** were acquired, thus conditional upon the animal's past experience, and, according to Pavlov, based upon newly formed connections in the brain. An example is salivating to the buzzer. Every unconditioned reflex is based upon a connection between an ***unconditioned stimulus (UCS)*** and an ***unconditioned response (UCR);*** in our example, food-in-the-mouth (UCS) and salivation (UCR). The corresponding terms for the conditioned reflex are ***conditioned stimulus (CS)*** and ***conditioned response (CR).*** The CS is an initially neutral stimulus (here, the buzzer) that is paired with the UCS; the CR (here, again salivation) is the response elicited by the CS after some such pairings of CS and UCS. Typically, the CR is very similar to the UCR, but the two are not necessarily identical, a point we shall return to later on. These various relationships are summarized in Figure 4.3 and constitute what is now known as ***classical conditioning.****

---

* The adjective ***classical*** is used, in part, as dutiful tribute to Pavlov's eminence and historical priority, and in part, to distinguish this form of conditioning from ***instrumental conditioning,*** to which we will turn later.

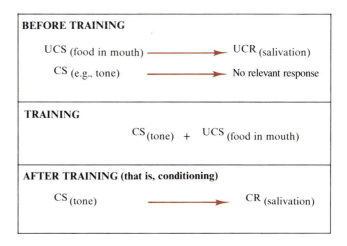

4.3 Relationships between CS, UCS, CR, and UCR in classical conditioning

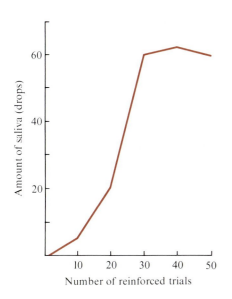

4.4 Learning curve in classical conditioning *The figure shows the increase in the amount of saliva secreted (the CR) as reinforced trials proceed. The CS was a tone, the UCS was meat powder, and the strength of the CR was measured by the number of drops of saliva secreted by the dog during a thirty-second period in which the CS was presented alone. (Data from Anrep, 1920)*

The Major Phenomena of Classical Conditioning

ACQUISITION OF CONDITIONED RESPONSES

Pavlov noted that the tendency of CS to elicit CR goes up the more often CS and UCS have been paired together. Clearly then, presenting UCS together with (or more typically, subsequent to) CS is a critical operation in classical conditioning. Such a pairing is said to *reinforce* the connection; trials on which UCS occurs and on which it is omitted are called *reinforced* and *unreinforced* trials respectively.

Figure 4.4 is a typical *learning curve* in which magnitude of CR is plotted against successive test trials. In this and other conditioning curves, the general trend is very clear and unsurprising: Response strength increases with the number of reinforced trials. Response strength can be measured in several ways. One is response *amplitude:* here, the amount of saliva secreted when presented with CS (which increases with increasing number of CS-UCS pairings). Another is response *latency:* the time from the onset of CS to the CR (which decreases with increasing number of CS-UCS pairings).

Once the CS-UCS relation is solidly established, the CS can serve to condition yet further stimuli. To give one example, Pavlov first conditioned a dog to salivate to the beat of a metronome, using meat powder as the UCS. After many such pairings, he presented the animal with a black square followed by the metronome beat, but without ever introducing the food. Eventually the sight of the black square alone was enough to produce salivation. This phenomenon is called *higher-order conditioning.* In the present case, conditioning was of the second order. The metronome which served as the CS in first-order conditioning functioned as the UCS for a second-order conditioned response. In effect, the black square had become a signal for the metronome, which in turn signaled the appearance of food.

In most cases, higher-order conditioning is fairly weak. Pavlov found that the second-order response was about half the strength of the first-order one, that third-order responses could be established only with great difficulty, while fourth-order conditioning was impossible altogether. We can readily understand why, if we consider the specifics of the experimental procedure. The black square is paired with the metronome, but on these occasions the metronome is never followed by food. The square becomes indeed a signal for the metronome, but while this happens the metronome loses *its* signal relationship to food. Put more precisely, the CR to the metronome *extinguishes* (see below). Since higher-order CRs stand upon the shoulders of now unreinforced lower-order ones, the pyramid can never attain any appreciable height. As the higher-order CRs are established, the ones below necessarily start to crumble.

EXTINCTION

The adaptive value of conditioning is self-evident. A zebra's chance of future survival is enhanced by conditioning. There's much to be gained by a conditioned fear reaction to a place from which a lion has pounced some time before (assuming, of course, that the zebra managed to survive the CS-UCS pairing in the first place). On the other hand, it would be rather inefficient if a connection once established could never be undone. The lion may change its lair and its former prowling place may now be perfectly safe for grazing.

Pavlov showed that in fact a conditioned reaction can be undone. He demonstrated that the conditioned response will gradually disappear if the CS is repeatedly presented without being reinforced by the UCS; in his terms, the conditioned reflex undergoes *experimental extinction.* Figure 4.5 presents an extinction curve from a salivary extinction experiment. As usual, response strength is measured along the *y*-axis, while the *x*-axis indicates the number of extinction trials (that is, trials without reinforcement). As extinction trials proceed, the salivary flow dries up. In effect, the dog has learned that the CS is no longer a signal for food.

A conditioned response that has been extinguished can be resurrected. One means is through *reconditioning,* that is, by presenting further reinforced trials. Typically, reconditioning requires fewer reinforced trials to bring the CR to its former strength than were necessary during the initial conditioning session, even if extinction trials had been continued until the animal stopped responding altogether. The conditioned response was evidently not really abolished by extinction but instead was somehow masked.

GENERALIZATION

So far our discussion has been confined to situations in which the animal is tested with the *identical* stimulus which had served as CS during training. But of course in the real world the stimuli are never really identical. The master's voice may signal food, but the exact intonation will surely vary from one occasion to another. Can the dog still use whatever it has learned before? If it can't, its conditioned response will be of little benefit. In fact, animals do respond to stimuli other than the original CS, so long as these are sufficiently similar.

This phenomenon is called *stimulus generalization.* A dog may be conditioned to a tone of 1,000 hertz (cycles per second); nevertheless, the CR will be obtained not just with that tone, but also with tones of different frequencies, like 900 or 1,100 hertz. The CR evoked by such new stimuli is weaker than that elicited by the original CS, diminishing progressively the greater the difference between the

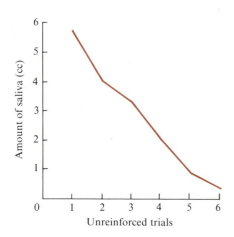

4.5 Extinction of a classically conditioned response *The figure shows the decrease in the amount of saliva secreted (the CR) with increasing number of extinction trials—that is, trials on which CS is presented without UCS. (After Pavlov, 1927)*

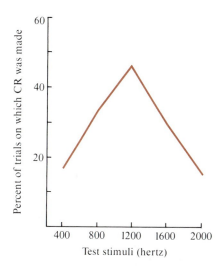

4.6   Generalization gradient of a classically conditioned response   The figure shows the generalization of a conditioned blinking response in rabbits. The CS was a tone of 1,200 hertz and the UCS was electric shock. After the conditioned response to the original CS was well established, generalization was measured by presenting various test stimuli, ranging from 400 hertz to 2,000 hertz and noting the percent of the trials on which the animals gave the CR. The figure shows the results, averaged over several testing sessions. (After Moore, 1972)

new stimulus and the original CS. The resulting curve is called a ***generalization gradient*** (Figure 4.6).

DISCRIMINATION

Stimulus generalization is not always beneficial. A kitten may be similar to a tiger; but a man who generalizes from one to the other is likely to be sorry. What he must do instead is discriminate.

The phenomenon of ***discrimination*** is readily demonstrated in the conditioning laboratory. A dog is first conditioned to salivate to a CS, for example, a black square (CS⁺). After the CR is well established, reinforced trials with the black square are randomly interspersed with nonreinforced trials with another stimulus, say, a gray square (CS⁻). This continues until the animal discriminates perfectly, always salivating to CS⁺, the reinforced stimulus, and never to CS⁻, the nonreinforced stimulus. Of course the dog does not reach this final point immediately. During the early trials it will be confused, or more precisely, it will generalize rather than discriminate. It will tend to salivate to CS⁻ (which, after all, is quite similar to CS⁺); by the same token, it will often fail to salivate when presented with CS⁺. Such errors gradually become fewer and fewer until perfect discrimination is finally achieved. Not surprisingly, the discrimination gets harder and harder the more similar the two stimuli are. As similarity increases, the tendency to respond to CS⁺ will increasingly generalize to CS⁻, while the tendency not to respond to CS⁻ will increasingly generalize to CS⁺. As a result, the dog will require many trials before it finally responds without errors.

One might think that the difficulty in forming discrimination is that the animal has trouble telling the two stimuli apart. But that is generally not the reason. The dog's problem is not that it can't form a sensory discrimination between CS⁺ and CS⁻. What is at fault is not its eyesight, for it can distinguish between the dark-gray and light-gray squares visually. Its difficulty is in discovering and remembering which stimulus is *right,* which goes with UCS and which does not. Eventually the animal learns, but this doesn't mean that it has learned to see the stimuli differently. What it has learned is their significance; it now knows which stimulus is which.

The Scope of Classical Conditioning

Thus far, our discussion has been largely restricted to the laboratory phenomena that Pavlov looked at: dogs salivating to buzzers, lights, and metronomes. Needless to say, conditioning would be of little interest if it only applied to those phenomena. But in actual fact, its scope is very much larger than that.

To begin with, classical conditioning has been found in a large variety of animal species other than dogs, including ants and anteaters, cats and cockroaches, pigeons and people. Any number of reaction patterns have been classically conditioned in animals. Thus, crabs have been conditioned to twitch their tail spines, fish to thrash about, and octopuses to change color. Responses conditioned in laboratory studies with humans include the galvanic skin response (where the UCS is typically a loud noise or electric shock) and the blink-reaction of the eyelid (where the UCS consists of a puff of air on the open eye; Kimble, 1961).

Nor is classical conditioning restricted to the laboratory, for there is little doubt

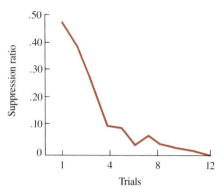

.50
.40
.30
.20
.10
0

Suppression ratio

1   4   8   12
Trials

4.7 Response suppression *Lever pressing in rats upon successive presentations of a 3-minute light CS which is immediately followed by an electric shock. The suppression ratio is a measure that compares lever pressing rates while CS is presented with intervals when it is not presented. When the ratio is .50, there is no suppression: the animal responds as readily in the 3 minutes after the CS is presented as it does otherwise. When the ratio is 0, suppression is complete: the animal doesn't respond at all in the 3 minutes during which the CS is presented. The figure shows that response suppression is almost complete after 4 CS-shock pairings. (After Kamin, 1969)*

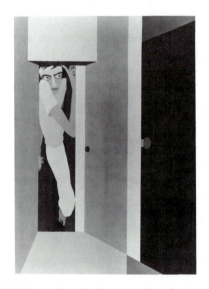

Phobias *An artist's conception of claustrophobia, the fear of enclosed spaces. (Painting by Vassos)*

that it plays a considerable role in our everyday life. Many of our internal feelings and urges are probably the result of classical conditioning. We tend to feel hungry at mealtimes and less so during the times between; this is so even if we fast a whole day. Another example is sexual arousal. This is often produced by a partner's special word or gesture whose erotic meaning is very private and is surely learned.

CONDITIONED FEAR

Of special importance is the role of classical conditioning in the formation of various emotional reactions, especially those concerned with fear. Fear is readily conditioned in the laboratory, a fact known all too well to scores of rats, cats, dogs, and pigeons that have been exposed to a neutral CS paired with a painful UCS (typically, an electric shock). After several such trials, the CS will produce various bodily reactions appropriate to fear—crouching, trembling, urination, defecation, and similar indications that the CS is a signal for impending shock.

A common consequence of a conditioned fear reaction is *response suppression.* Suppose a hungry rat has been taught to press a lever for food. If hungry, it will press at a steady clip for an occasional food reward (see pp. 110 in this chapter). But its behavior changes drastically if it suddenly sees a light that had previously been paired with an electric shock. Now the rat stops pressing, at least for a while. The light makes the rat afraid because of its association with the painful UCS. Since fear interferes with hunger, lever pressing declines (see Figure 4.7).

It is a plausible guess that many adult fears are based upon classical conditioning, acquired in much the same way that fear is acquired in the laboratory. These fears may be relatively mild or very intense (if intense enough, they are called *phobias*). They may be acquired in early childhood or during particular traumatic episodes in later life. An example is an Air Force pilot who bailed out of his plane but whose parachute failed to open until the last five seconds before he hit the ground. In such traumatic episodes, conditioning apparently occurs in a single trial. This seems reasonable enough, for it would certainly be unadaptive if the pilot had to bail out on ten separate occasions, each time barely escaping death, before he finally developed a conditioned fear reaction (Sarnoff, 1957).

CONDITIONING AS AN ADAPTIVE REACTION

The relation between CR and UCR In many cases of classical conditioning, the CR is quite similar to the UCR. This was certainly true in the situations Pavlov studied, where the dogs salivated both to UCS (that is, to the food) and to the CS (the buzzer or the metronome). But on closer examination, the two responses were by no means identical. When the dog responded to the UCS, its saliva was more copious and much richer in digestive enzyme than when it reacted to the CS. This difference is even more pronounced for other aspects of behavior. Given the UCS, the animal lunges forward to the food pan and eats; given the CS it looks as if it is "expecting" the UCS, but it doesn't make any chewing responses. All of this makes good biological sense. The CR prepares an organism, while the UCR actually performs the task for which the organism is now so well prepared (Zener, 1937).

Conditioning and drug effects   Some recent studies show that the CR is sometimes the precise opposite of the UCR. This effect is often encountered in studies on the conditioning of drug effects. Suppose a person gets many doses of insulin, which depletes blood sugar. It turns out that after a number of such insulin injections, the bodily reaction to various conditioned stimuli that accompany the drug is the exact opposite of the response to the drug itself: Given the CS, the blood-sugar level goes *up*. It is as if the body prepares itself for the chemical agent it is about to receive and does so by adopting a compensatory reaction that tilts the other way (Siegel, 1977).

This compensatory-reaction hypothesis has some important consequences for our understanding of drug addiction. Consider opiates such as morphine or heroin. These have various effects, such as relief from pain, euphoria, and relaxation. But after repeated administrations, stimuli that usually precede the injection of these drugs (for example, the sight of the hypodermic needle) produce effects that go in the opposite direction: depression, restlessness, and an increased sensitivity to pain. Some authors believe that these effects represent a compensatory reaction in which the response to the CS counteracts the reaction triggered by the UCS. As a result, the user develops drug tolerance. To make up for the conditioned compensatory reaction, he must inject himself with increasingly larger doses of the drug to obtain the same effect that was produced when he took it for the first time. But this will only work if he takes the drug under familiar circumstances, for if he takes it in a new environment, he runs the risk of a dangerous overdose. The reason is simple. He has increased his drug dose to overcome the compensatory reaction of various conditioned stimuli. But in a new environment, many of the old conditioned stimuli are missing so that there is a much weaker compensatory response. The result may be death by overdose—a lethal side effect of classical conditioning (Siegel, 1977, 1979; Siegel, Hinson, and Krank, 1979).

The compensatory-reaction hypothesis is still a subject of considerable debate, for as yet it's unclear under what conditions a CR will be similar to the UCR and under what others it will be the very opposite. In all likelihood both phenomena occur, and they depend on a number of different mechanisms, many of which are still unknown.* But whatever the ultimate upshot, it is clear that classical conditioning is much more than a laboratory curiosity limited to dogs, metronomes, and saliva. It is a phenomenon of enormous scope, a basic form of learning that pervades much of our life and is shared by flatworms and people alike (Eikelboom and Stewart, 1982; Hollis, 1982; Rescorla and Holland, 1982).

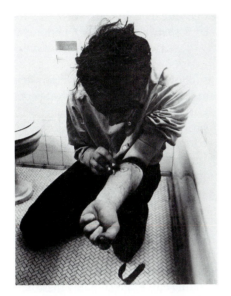

The compensatory-reaction hypothesis and drug use   *In an addict, the sight and feel of the hypodermic needle (or other drug-related stimuli) have become a CS for the counterreaction to the drug. If so, then a larger dose of the drug is needed to get the high. This may account for some overdose deaths, especially if the too-large dose was taken in an unfamiliar environment. (Courtesy of the Museum of the City of New York)*

What Is Learned in Classical Conditioning?

What is learned when a human or animal is classically conditioned? According to Pavlov, an association is set up between two stimuli, the CS and the UCS. But what led to this association? In line with many philosophers who had thought

---

* The compensatory-reaction hypothesis is similar to the opponent-process theory discussed in the previous chapter in assuming that various drug reactions are accompanied by processes that pull in the opposite direction. According to one hypothesis, such compensatory reactions are equivalent to conditioned opponent processes (Schull, 1979).

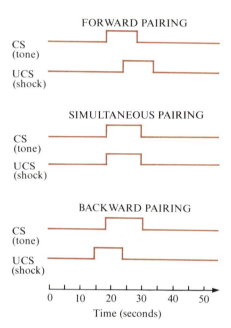

FORWARD PAIRING

CS
(tone)

UCS
(shock)

SIMULTANEOUS PAIRING

CS
(tone)

UCS
(shock)

BACKWARD PAIRING

CS
(tone)

UCS
(shock)

0   10   20   30   40   50

Time (seconds)

4.8   Some temporal relationships in classical conditioning

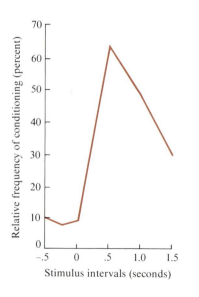

4.9   The role of the CS-UCS interval in classical conditioning   *The figure shows the results of a study on the effectiveness of various CS-UCS intervals in humans. The CR was a finger withdrawal response, the CS a tone, and the UCS an electric shock. The time between CS and UCS is plotted on the horizontal axis. Negative intervals mean that the UCS was presented before the CS (backward pairing), a zero interval means that the two stimuli were presented simultaneously, and a positive interval means that the CS began before the UCS (forward pairing). The vertical axis indicates the degree of conditioning. (After Spooner and Kellogg, 1947)*

about association, Pavlov believed that the linkage is forged by mere **contiguity,** that is, togetherness in time. But as we will see, the answer is not quite as simple as that.

TEMPORAL RELATIONS BETWEEN CS AND UCS

One way of finding out whether the CS-UCS association is based on contiguity in time is to vary the interval between the two stimuli as well as the order in which they are presented. A number of procedures do just that. In some, CS precedes UCS *(forward pairing),* in others it follows UCS *(backward pairing),* and in yet others the two stimuli are presented at exactly the same time *(simultaneous pairing)* (Figure 4.8).

The general result of these procedures is as follows: Conditioning is best when the CS *precedes* the UCS by a small optimum interval (whose precise value depends on the particulars of the experimental situation). Presenting CS and UCS simultaneously is much less effective, and the backward procedure is even worse. On the other hand, the effectiveness of forward pairing declines rapidly when the CS-UCS interval increases beyond the optimum interval (Spooner and Kellogg, 1947; Moeller, 1954; Schneiderman and Gormezano, 1964; see Figure 4.9).

How can we make sense of these facts? A reasonable suggestion is that the CS serves a signaling function: It prepares the organism for a UCS that is to come. Let us consider forward, simultaneous, and backward pairing in this light by likening the subject's situation to that of a driver setting out upon an unfamiliar road. Suppose our driver wants to go from Denver to Salt Lake City, and that some 150 miles out of Denver there is a dangerous hairpin turn over a ravine. How should the driver be warned of the impending curve? Presumably there will be a sign, "Hairpin Turn," which should obviously appear just a bit before the turn (analogous to forward pairing with a short CS-UCS interval). If the interval is too long it will be almost impossible to connect the sign with that which it signifies. We will lose some of our faith in the Highway Department if it sets up the sign, "Hairpin Turn," just outside the Denver city limits while the turn itself is three hours away (forward pairing with a long CS-UCS interval). Our faith will be really shaken if we see the sign prominently displayed just at the sharpest bend of the turn (simultaneous pairing). We finally begin to suspect a degree of malevolence if we discover the sign innocently placed on the road a hundred feet or so beyond the turn (backward pairing), though we should probably be grateful that we did not find it at the bottom of the ravine.

It is clear that in classical conditioning an organism learns something about the relationship between stimuli. As Pavlov saw it, what was learned was an association between two stimuli, for to Pavlov, associative conditioning was a glue that could bind just about anything to anything else. All that mattered was that the two stimuli were contiguous in time, with the CS preferably a bit before the UCS.

CONTINGENCY

It would seem that in classical conditioning an organism learns that one stimulus is a signal for another. But this poses another problem. How does the animal ever manage to discover this signal relationship?

Consider a dog in Pavlov's laboratory who is exposed to several presentations of a beating metronome followed by some food powder. The poor beast doesn't know that he is supposed to form a CS-UCS connection. All he knows is that every once in a while food appears. There are all sorts of stimuli in the laboratory situation. Of course he hears the metronome, but he also hears doors slamming, and a babble of (Russian) voices in the background, and he feels the strap of the conditioning harness. How does he discover that it is the metronome which is the signal for food rather than the scores of other stimuli that he was also exposed to? After all, no one told him that metronome beats are Professor Pavlov's favorite conditioned stimuli.

A useful way of trying to understand what happens is to think of the animal as an amateur scientist. Like all scientists, the dog wants to predict important events. (When his human counterparts succeed, they publish; when the dog succeeds, he salivates.) How can he predict when food will appear? He might decide to rely on mere contiguity, and salivate to any stimulus that occurs along with food presentation. But if so, he'd have to salivate whenever he was strapped in his harness or whenever he heard voices, for these stimuli were generally present when he was fed. But if the dog had any scientific talent at all, he would realize that the harness and the voices are very poor food predictors. To be sure, they occur when food is given, but they occur just as frequently when it is not. To continue in his scientific quest, the dog would look for an event that occurs when food appears and that does not occur when food is absent. The metronome beat is the one stimulus that fulfills *both* of these conditions, for it never beats in the intervals between trials when food is not presented. Science (or rather classical conditioning) has triumphed, and the dog is ready to announce his findings by salivating when the CS is presented and at no other times.

Contingency in classical conditioning   The preceding account is a fanciful statement of an influential theoretical analysis of classical conditioning proposed by Robert Rescorla. According to Rescorla, classical conditioning depends not only on CS-UCS pairings, but also on pairings in which the absence of CS goes along with the absence of UCS. These two experiences—metronome/meat, and no metronome/no meat—allow the dog to discover that the occurrence of the UCS is **contingent** (that is, dependent) upon the occurrence of the CS. By determining this contingency the animal can forecast what is going to happen next (Rescorla, 1967).

Contingency need not be perfect. In nature it rarely is. A dark cloud generally precedes a storm, but it doesn't always. As a result, our weather predictions are never perfect. But we can nevertheless make some predictions about the weather that are better than chance, for it's more likely to rain when the sky is dark than when the sun is shining. The same holds in the conditioning laboratory in which we can arrange whatever relationship between CS and UCS we choose. We could

Table 4.1 CONTINGENCY IN
CLASSICAL CONDITIONING

The table shows the number of trials on which each of the four stimulus combinations were offered. Each table presents a different tone/meat contingency based on twenty trials for each of the three conditions. The column labeled p shows the probabilities that meat will occur under a particular stimulus condition.

Meat contingent upon tone

	Meat	No meat	*p*
Tone	8	2	.80
No tone	2	8	.20

Meat contingent upon absence of tone

	Meat	No meat	*p*
Tone	3	7	.30
No tone	7	3	.70

Meat and tone independent

	Meat	No meat	*p*
Tone	5	5	.50
No tone	5	5	.50

decide that the metronome will be followed by food on say 80 percent of the trials, but that food will occur unheralded by the metronome on 20 percent of the trials. We have now created an imperfect contingency that will be harder to detect. But it is a contingency even so, for food is more likely after the CS than otherwise. To recognize such imperfect contingencies, the animal must keep track of four possible stimulus combinations that he will encounter. If the metronome is the CS, and meat is the UCS, these combinations are: metronome/meat, metronome/no meat, no metronome/meat, no metronome/no meat. To determine if getting meat is contingent upon the metronome, the animal must somehow compute two probabilities: the probability of getting meat when the metronome is sounded and the probability of getting meat when it is not. If the first probability is greater than the second, then getting meat is contingent on the metronome. If it is smaller than the second, getting meat is contingent upon the absence of the tone. Such a negative contingency is analogous to the relation between a sunny sky and rain—rain is more likely when the sun is *not* shining. An important final possibility is that the two probabilities are identical. If so, there is no contingency, and the two events are independent (see Table 4.1).

Rescorla has argued that conditioning will only occur if there is a CS-UCS contingency. To prove his point, he first trained dogs to jump back and forth over a hurdle in a shuttle box to avoid shocks that occurred without any signals at all. The rate at which the animals jumped back and forth provided a yardstick by which he could later estimate the extent to which a CS had become conditioned to a UCS (see Figure 4.10).

The next step was a classical conditioning procedure in which the animals were exposed to various CS-UCS pairings, with tones as the CS and shock the UCS. For one group of dogs, the tones and shocks occurred randomly and independently. Pure accident produced a number of CS-UCS pairings, but the CS had no predictive power, for shock was equally likely during or after the tone as at any other time. A second group received the same number of CS-UCS pairings as did the animals in the first group. The important difference was that for this group, the CS did have predictive power. For the animals in this group, shock was more likely shortly after the tone than at other times. But this difference was not created by adding more shocks. On the contrary. The second group received the same number of shocks as the first group during the half-minute after the tone but fewer shocks in the period thereafter (see Figure 4.11).

If conditioning depended merely on CS-UCS contiguity, both groups should come to fear the tone equally, since both were exposed to an equal number of tone-shock pairings. But a contingency approach would lead one to expect a different result. Conditioned fear should be shown by the second group, for whom the tone predicted an increased likelihood of shock. But the tone should have no effect in the first group, for it had no predictive power.

To decide between these alternatives, Rescorla put all dogs back in the shuttle box. When they were jumping steadily, he introduced the tone that had been paired with shock in the conditions just described. If this stimulus had become conditioned to fear, it should make the dogs jump faster by increasing their fear.

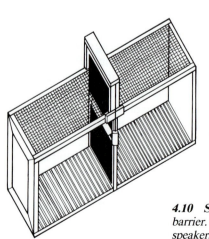

4.10 Shuttle box for dogs   *The dog is first trained to jump back and forth over the barrier. During classical conditioning, the drop gate is closed, and tones are presented by speakers mounted at each end. (After Solomon and Wynne, 1953)*

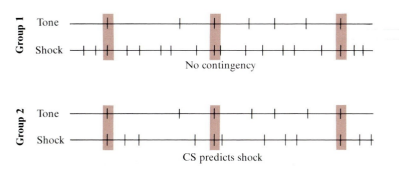

4.11 Contingency in classical conditioning *The figure is a schematic outline of Rescorla's experiment on contingency. Two groups of dogs were run. Both received tones and shock. Sometimes the tone and shock occurred together; such pairings are indicated in color. Note that the number of such CS-USC pairings is identical in the two groups. Note also that the total number of shocks is less in Group II than in Group I. The tone-shock contingency is created by making a shock more probable after a tone than at other times. It is not achieved by increasing the absolute number of shocks. (After Rescorla, 1967)*

The results were in line with the contingency approach. If the CS was previously associated with an increased likelihood of shock, its presentation made the dogs jump twice as often as they had before. But if shock had been just as likely during or after the tone as at other times, the animals' jumping rate was unaffected. Thus, it appears that conditioning depends on contingency rather than on contiguity alone (see Figure 4.12).

The absence of contingency What happens when there is no contingency whatsoever? On the face of it, there is nothing to learn. But in a situation in which there is fear and danger (for example, electric shock) the animal does learn something after all: It can never feel safe at any time.

Consider two situations. In one, there is a CS that signals that shock is likely to follow. When the CS appears, the animal will become more fearful. But there is a compensation. When there is no CS, the animal can relax, for now shock is less likely. The absence of the CS has become a ***safety signal.***

The situation is quite different when there is no stimulus that predicts when shock will occur. Now the animal is worse off than it is when there is a CS-UCS contingency, for it now has good reason to be afraid at all times. This unpleasant state of affairs is mirrored by a number of harmful physiological consequences. For example, rats who are exposed to unsignaled electric shock are much more likely to develop stomach ulcers than rats who receive just as many shocks, but with a signal that predicts their occurrence (Seligman, 1968; Weiss, 1970, 1977).

The difference between signaled and unsignaled shock may be related to the distinction between *fear* and *anxiety,* made by clinical psychologists concerned with human emotional disorders. As they use the terms, fear refers to an emotional state that is directed at a specific object—of flying in airplanes, of snakes, or whatever. In contrast, anxiety is a chronic fear that has no particular object but is there at all times. A number of authors suggest that this unfocused anxiety state is in part produced by unpredictability. Patients whose dentists tell them "this may hurt" but at other times assure them "you won't feel anything now" will probably have fewer dental anxieties than those whose dentists never tell them anything (Seligman, 1975; Schwartz, 1978).

OVERSHADOWING AND BLOCKING

We've seen that an animal in a conditioning experiment can be likened to a scientist who tries to predict something in the world around him. To predict the occurrence of the UCS, the animal must discover a contingency between this UCS and

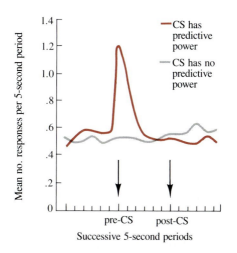

4.12 Contingency and classical conditioning *The figure shows the shuttle box jumping rate of dogs that were previously exposed to pairings of tones and electric shock. The first arrow shows the point at which the 5-second tone is introduced during the test; the second arrow indicates the end of the 30-second period thereafter. Dogs for whom the CS had predictive power (color) jumped much faster immediately after the tone was introduced; dogs for whom the CS had no such power (black) showed no effect. (After Rescorla, 1966)*

some other stimulus event (the CS). Such a contingency is a necessary requirement without which conditioning will not occur. But as it turns out, contingency alone is not sufficient. Animals, just like scientists, don't pay equal attention to everything in the world around them; they have various prejudices about what is important and what is not.

A simple illustration of the role of attention in classical conditioning is the phenomenon of *overshadowing.* Suppose dogs are given a number of trials on which two stimuli are presented simultaneously: a bright light and a soft tone. This stimulus compound is then followed by the usual food UCS. When later tested with each of these stimuli presented alone, the dogs salivate to the light but not to the tone. It's not that they are unable to hear the tone, for control experiments show that when the UCS is preceded by this tone alone, it serves as a perfectly adequate CS. The reason is that this soft and unobtrusive stimulus is accompanied by the much more noticeable light. As a result, it is overshadowed and not attended to.

What determines which stimulus overshadows which? In the study just described, it was simply a matter of relative intensity. But stimuli may command attention even if they are weak. Suppose prior experience makes us believe that a given event causes another. This may make us ignore some other aspects of the situation that are no less important. Consider the early biologists who asked themselves where maggots come from. Whenever they saw rotting meat, they saw maggots, and they never saw maggots anywhere else. As a result, they assumed that the maggot's appearance was contingent upon the rotting meat (which they took as proof for the theory that life is generated spontaneously). Once having discovered a contingency (which fit in with their prior beliefs), they were blinded to other contingencies that were also present—such as the fact that the meat had been lying around for a while (so flies could lay their eggs in it). Something similar holds for animals in classical conditioning laboratories. If they've already found a stimulus that signals the appearance of the UCS, they don't attend to other stimuli that are additional signals but provide no further information. The old stimuli overshadow the recognition of the new, much as a scientist's old theory prejudices her to further facts.

The effect of prior experience on attention was demonstrated by a study in which rats first received a series of trials during which a sound was followed by shock. Not surprisingly, this sound became a CS for conditioned fear. In a later series of trials, the shock was preceded by *two* stimuli that were presented simultaneously: one was the same sound that had previously served as a CS for shock, the other was a light. After this, they were tested with the light alone to see whether this would produce a conditioned fear reaction. The results showed that the animals were completely undisturbed by the light even though it had been a perfect predictor of shock. What had happened? The answer is that the light did not provide any new information. The sound already told the animals about the impending shock, and so they never paid attention to the light. The sound overshadowed the light because of the animals' prior experience, a learned overshadowing effect that is technically known as *blocking.* To prove that this effect was indeed caused by the animals' previous experience, a control group was run. These control rats started out with the composite trials (light + sound, followed by shock) from the very outset, with no previous exposure to the sound alone. When these animals were later tested with the light alone, they exhibited a substantial conditioned fear response (Kamin, 1969; see Table 4.2 and Figure 4.13).

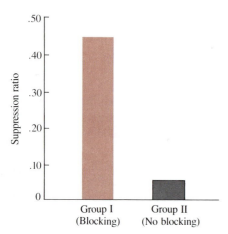

4.13   The effect of blocking   *The figure shows the animals' behavior in the final test phase of the experiment outlined in the text and in Table 4.2, when the animals were presented with the light alone. Conditioning to the light was measured by the suppression ratio (see Figure 4.7, p. 94). When that ratio is .50, there is no suppression and thus, no fear conditioning. If the ratio is zero, suppression is complete and fear-conditioning is at a high level. As the figure shows, there was virtually no suppression for Group I (color): the initial pairing of sound and shock in Stage I had blocked the animals' recognition of the light-shock contingency during Stage II. The control animals in Group II (black), which had no such prior pairings, showed no such blocking effect: they showed almost complete suppression during the test phase, indicating that the light had become a potent CS during Stage II. (After Kamin, 1969)*

Table 4.2 BLOCKING

Group	Stage 1	Stage 2	Test	Result
I	Sound, then shock	Sound + Light, then shock	Light alone	No conditioned fear
II	—	Sound + Light, then shock	Light alone	Conditioned fear

MECHANISM FOR COMPUTING CONTINGENCIES

To sum up. In classical conditioning, animals and humans learn that certain stimuli are signals for impending events. They do so by noting a contingency between these stimuli and the events they forecast (that is, the UCS's). But while contingency is necessary, it alone is not sufficient. To become an effective signal, a stimulus must also be one that provides information which the animal did not have before.

How does the animal manage to combine all the information he gets in the conditioning experiment to determine which stimulus it is that he'll respond to? We have repeatedly likened him to a scientist who tries to infer cause-and-effect relations. But of course this is just a metaphor. For it's very unlikely that the rats, dogs, and pigeons in classical conditioning laboratories keep a conscious mental record of their experiences, tallying trials in which CS was followed by UCS and trials on which CS occurred and UCS did not, and then computing probabilities and making appropriate deductions the way scientists do. Although in some ways they behave as though they do just that, the means by which they achieve their results are almost certainly more automatic and less intelligent than those employed by the human scientist.

To be sure, classical conditioning may achieve results that sometimes resemble those of human analytical thinking. But there are other indications that it is a rather primitive form of learning. Thus, in many cases of human classical conditioning, the CR will be made even when the subject knows perfectly well that the UCS won't follow the CS. An example is conditioned fear. Consider a concentration camp survivor who visits the site of the camp four decades later. He probably will still feel his heart race and his mouth dry up. He knows that Hitler is dead and the camp is in ruins. But this does not change his actual reaction—which is essentially blind, automatic, and under involuntary control.

The best guess is that classical conditioning is based on rather simple processes which somehow combine to produce a complex result. Just what those simple mechanisms are and how they combine is still under debate (e.g., Rescorla and Wagner, 1972; for discussion, see Schwartz, 1984).

INSTRUMENTAL CONDITIONING

Habituation and classical conditioning are two of the main forms of simple learning. Another is *instrumental learning.* An example of instrumental learning comes from the zoo. When a seal learns to turn a somersault to get a fish from the zoo attendant, it has learned an *instrumental response.* The response is instrumental in that it leads to a sought-after effect; in this case, the fish.

On the face of it there are many similarities between this form of learning and

101

classical conditioning. (This is one reason why instrumental learning is often called *instrumental conditioning.*)* Compare the seal with a dog that has acquired a salivary CR to a bell while meat powder served as the UCS. In both cases, we have a response which occurs more frequently with increased training (on the one hand, salivation, on the other, the somersault). In both cases, we have a stimulus that is somehow important in determining whether the response is made (the bell and the sight of the attendant). In both cases, finally, we have reinforcement without which the response will soon disappear (the meat powder and the fish).

Yet, despite these many similarities, there are some important differences. Perhaps most important is the fact that in instrumental learning, reinforcement (that is, reward) depends upon the proper response. For the seal the rules of the game are simple: no somersault, no fish. This is not true for classical conditioning. There the UCS is presented regardless of what the animal does. Another difference concerns response selection. In instrumental learning, the response must be selected from a sometimes very large set of alternatives. The seal's job is to select the somersault from among the numerous other things a seal could possibly do. Not so in classical conditioning. There the response is forced, for the UCS unconditionally evokes it.

We could loosely summarize the difference between the two procedures by a rough description of what is learned in each. In classical conditioning the animal must learn about the relation between two stimuli, the CS and the UCS: Given CS, UCS will follow. In instrumental learning, the animal has to learn the relation between a response and reward: Given this response, there will be reinforcement. But such statements are only crude descriptions. To get beyond them we must discuss instrumental learning in more detail.

Thorndike and the Law of Effect

The experimental study of instrumental learning began a decade or two before Pavlov. It was an indirect consequence of the debate over the doctrine of evolution. Darwin's theory was buttressed by impressive demonstrations of continuity in the bodily structures of many species, both living and extinct. But his opponents could argue that such evidence was not enough. To them the essential distinction between humans and beasts was elsewhere: in the human ability to think and reason, an ability that animals did not share. To answer this point it became critical to find proof of mental as well as of bodily continuity.

For evidence, the Darwinians turned to animal behavior. At first, the method was largely anecdotal. Several British naturalists (including Darwin himself) collected stories about the intellectual achievements of various animals as related by presumably reliable informants. Taken at face value, the results painted a flattering picture of animal intellect, as in accounts of cunning cats scattering bread crumbs on the lawn to entice the birds (Romanes, 1882). But even if such observations could be trusted (and they probably could not) they did not prove that the animals' performances were achieved in the way a human might achieve the same thing: by reason and understanding. To be sure of that, one would have to

Edward L. Thorndike (Courtesy The Granger Collection)

* Another term for this form of learning is *operant conditioning.*

study the animals' learning processes from start to finish. To see a circus seal blow a melody on a set of toy trumpets is one thing; to conclude from this observation that it has musical understanding is quite another.

There was clearly a need for controlled experimental procedures whereby the entire course of learning could be carefully scrutinized. That method was provided in 1898 by Edward L. Thorndike (1874–1949) in a brilliant doctoral dissertation that became one of the classic documents of American psychology (Thorndike, 1898).

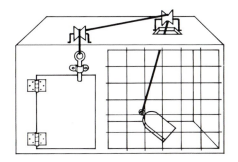

4.14 Puzzle box *This box is much like those used by Thorndike. The animal steps on a treadle which is attached to a rope, thereby releasing a latch that locks the door. (After Thorndike, 1911)*

CATS IN A PUZZLE BOX

Thorndike's method was to set up a problem for the animal. To gain reward the creature had to perform some particular action determined by the experimenter. Much of this work was done on hungry cats. The animal was placed in a so-called **puzzle box,** an enclosure from which it could escape only by performing some simple action that would unlatch the door, such as pulling a loop or wire or pressing a lever (Figure 4.14). Once outside, the animal was rewarded with a small portion of food and then placed back into the box for another trial. This procedure was repeated until the task was mastered.

On the first trial, the typical cat struggled valiantly; it clawed at the bars, it bit, it struck out in all directions, it meowed, and it howled. This continued for several minutes until the animal finally hit upon the correct response by pure accident. Subsequent trials brought gradual improvement. The mad scramble became shorter and the animal took less and less time to perform the correct response. By the time the training sessions were completed the cat's behavior was almost unrecognizable from what it had been at the start. Placed in the box, it immediately approached the wire loop, yanked it with businesslike dispatch, and quickly hurried through the open door to enjoy its well-deserved reward. The cat had certainly learned.

How had it learned? If one merely observed its final performance one might credit the cat with reason or understanding, but Thorndike argued that the problem was solved in a very different way. For proof he examined the learning curves. Plotting the time required on each trial (that is, the response *latency*) over the whole course of training, he usually found a curve that declined quite gradually (Figure 4.15). Had the animals "understood" the solution at some point during training, the curves should have shown a sudden drop with little change thereafter (for one would hardly expect further errors once understanding was reached).

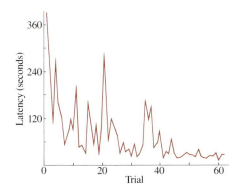

4.15 Learning curve of one of Thorndike's cats *To get out of the box, the cat had to move a wooden handle from a vertical to a horizontal position. The figure shows the gradual decline in the animal's response latency (the time it takes to get out of the box). Note that the learning curve is by no means smooth but has rather marked fluctuations. This is a common feature of the learning curves of individual subjects. Smooth learning curves are generally produced by averaging the results of many individual subjects. (After Thorndike, 1898)*

THE LAW OF EFFECT

Thorndike proposed that what the animal had learned was best described as an increase in the strength of the correct response. Initially, the cat has the tendency to perform a large set of responses, perhaps because of prior learning, perhaps because of built-in predispositions. As it happens, virtually all of these lead to failure. As trials proceed, the strength of the incorrect responses gradually weakens. In contrast, the correct response, which at first is weak, increasingly grows in strength. In Thorndike's terms, the correct response is gradually "stamped in" while futile ones are correspondingly stamped out. The improvements in the

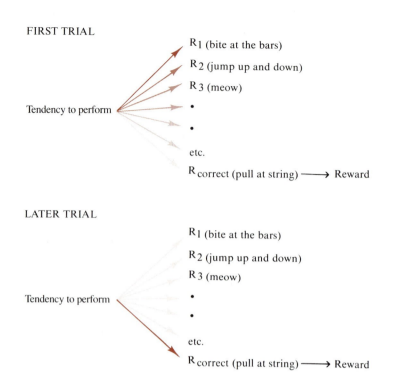

4.16 The law of effect *The figure is a schematic presentation of Thorndike's theory of instrumental learning. On the first trial, the tendency to perform various incorrect responses (biting the bars, jumping up and down) is very strong, while the tendency to perform the correct response (pulling the string) is weak or nonexistent. As trials proceed, the strength of these responses change. The incorrect responses become weaker and weaker, for none of these responses is immediately followed by reward. In contrast, there is a progressive strengthening of the correct response because this is followed more or less immediately by reward.*

learning curves "represent the wearing smooth of a path in the brain, not the decisions of a rational consciousness" (Thorndike, 1911).*

According to Thorndike, some responses get strengthened and others weakened as learning proceeds. But what produces these different effects? Thorndike's answer was a bold formulation called the **law of effect.** The relevant features of his analysis are schematized in Figure 4.16, which indicates the tendency to perform the various responses, whether correct (R_c) or incorrect (R_1, R_2, R_3, etc.). The critical question is how the correct response gets strengthened until it finally overwhelms the incorrect ones that are at first so dominant. Thorndike's proposal, the law of effect, held that the consequences (that is, the effect) of a response determine whether the tendency to perform it is strengthened or weakened. If the response is followed by reward, it will be strengthened; if it is followed by the absence of reward (or worse yet, by punishment) it will be weakened. There was no need to postulate any further intellectual processes in the animal, no need to assume that the animal noticed a connection between act and consequence, no need to believe that it was trying to attain some goal. If the animal made a response and reward followed shortly, that response was more likely to be performed at a subsequent time.

This proposal neatly fits into the context of evolutionary thinking so dominant at the time. Thorndike emphasized the adaptive nature of the animal's activity which is gradually shaped to serve its biological ends. But the relationship to evolutionary theory is even closer for, as Thorndike pointed out, the law of effect is

* This description of Thorndike's interpretation is a highly simplified description that is closer to the spirit of B. F. Skinner's later analysis of instrumental learning than to Thorndike's own. The account presented here ignores certain aspects of his theory that are no longer held, in particular, the belief that instrumental learning is based on the formation of new connections between stimuli and responses.

an analogue of the law of the survival of the fittest. In the life of the species, the individual whose genetic makeup fits it best for its environment will survive to transmit its characteristics to its offspring. In the life of the individual, learning provides another adaptive mechanism through the law of effect which decrees that only the fittest *responses* shall survive. As Thorndike put it, "It is a process of selection among reactions . . . by eliminating the unsuitable reaction directly by discomfort, and also by positively selecting the suitable one by pleasure. . . . It is of tremendous usefulness. . . . 'He who learns and runs away, *will live* to learn another day' " (Thorndike, 1899, p. 91).

As we have seen, the anecdotalists tried to support their evolutionary convictions with accounts of high animal intelligence. But Thorndike seemed to show that animal learning proceeds in another way altogether, without reason or understanding.* Did this do violence to the evolutionist's belief in an ultimate continuity between the mental processes of humans and animals?

The eventual upshot was ironic. The belief that humans and animals learn in much the same way won many adherents among psychologists of Thorndike's general persuasion, but hardly in a way that Darwin or the anecdotalists had in mind. These thinkers had suggested that animals learn like humans; Thorndike and his theoretical descendants proposed that humans learn like animals! Eventually many psychologists began to believe that the laws of learning discovered with cats in a puzzle box (or dogs in Pavlov's harness) hold for all other situations and for all animals including human beings. This belief in the essential equivalence of both learners and learning tasks dominated much of the research on learning produced during the five or six decades following Thorndike's original work and commands considerable allegiance even now.

Skinner and Operant Behavior

Thorndike initiated the experimental study of instrumental behavior, but the psychologist who shaped the way in which most modern behavior theorists think about the subject is B. F. Skinner (1904–   ). Unlike Thorndike who believed that classical and instrumental conditioning are much alike, Skinner was one of the first theorists to insist on a sharp distinction between classical and instrumental conditioning. In classical conditioning, the animal's behavior is *elicited* by the CS; to that extent, the salivation is set off from the outside. But Skinner insisted that in instrumental conditioning the organism is much less at the mercy of the external situation. Its reactions are *emitted* from within, as if they were what we ordinarily call *voluntary.* Skinner calls these instrumental responses **operants;** they operate on the environment to bring about some change that leads to reward. Like Thorndike, Skinner believed in the law of effect, insisting that the tendency to emit these operants is strengthened or weakened by its consequences (Skinner, 1938).

Behavior theorists have always searched for ever-simpler situations in the hope that the true laws of learning will show up there. Skinner's way of simplifying the study of operant behavior was to create a situation in which the same instrumen-

B. F. Skinner (Photograph by Nina Leen, Life Magazine, © Times Inc.)

* Thorndike's insistence that animals are unable to use reason may seem puzzling considering our discussion of the way in which animals extract the contingencies between CS and UCS in classical conditioning. The fact is that Thorndike's work predated modern discussions of contingency by over seventy years.

tal response could be performed repeatedly. The most common example is the experimental chamber (popularly called the Skinner box), in which a rat presses a lever or a pigeon pecks at a lighted key (Figure 4.17). In these situations, the animal remains in the presence of the lever or key for, say, an hour at a time, pressing and pecking at whatever rate it chooses. All of the animal's responses are automatically recorded; stimuli and reinforcements are presented automatically by automatic programming devices. The measure of response strength is ***response rate,*** that is, the number of responses per unit time.

The Major Phenomena of Instrumental Conditioning

Many of the phenomena of instrumental learning parallel those of classical conditioning. Consider ***reinforcement.*** In classical conditioning, the term refers to an operation (establishing a CS-UCS contingency) that strengthens the CR. In the context of instrumental learning, reinforcement refers to an analogous operation: having the response followed by a condition that the animal "prefers." This may be the presentation of something "good," such as grain to a hungry pigeon. The grain is an example of a ***positive reinforcer,*** a state of affairs which, in Thorndike's terms, is one that the animal does everything to attain and nothing to avoid. It may also be the termination or prevention of something "bad," such as the cessation of an electrical shock. Such a shock is an example of a ***negative reinforcer,*** a situation that the animal does everything to avoid and nothing to attain.

As in classical conditioning, the probability of responding increases with an increasing number of reinforcements. And, again as in classical conditioning, the response suffers ***extinction*** when reinforcement is withdrawn, and the extinguished response can be reconditioned.

A

B

4.17 Animals in operant chambers (A) A rat trained to press a lever for water reinforcement. (Courtesy Pfizer, Inc.) (B) A pigeon pecking at a lighted key for food reinforcement. Reinforcement consists of a few seconds' access to a grain feeder which is located just below the key. (Photo by W. Rapport, courtesy B. F. Skinner)

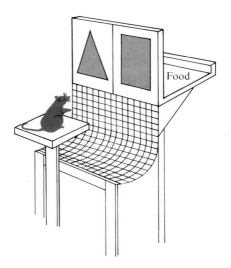

4.18 Studying discriminative stimuli with the jumping stand *The rat has to jump to one of two cards, say, a triangle or a square, behind which is a ledge that contains food. If the choice is correct, the card gives way and the animal gets to the food. If the choice is incorrect, the card stays in place, the rat bumps its nose and falls into the net below. (After Lashley, 1930).*

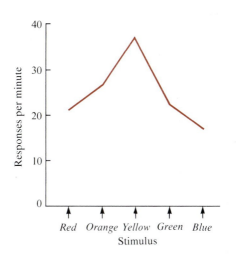

GENERALIZATION AND DISCRIMINATION

The instrumental response is not elicited by external stimuli but is, in Skinner's terms, emitted from within. But this doesn't mean that such stimuli have no effect. They do exert considerable control over behavior, for they serve as *discriminative stimuli.* Suppose a pigeon is trained to hop on a treadle to get some grain. When a green light is on, hopping on the treadle will pay off. But when a red light is on, the treadle-hopping response will be of no avail, for the pigeon gets no access to the food container. Under these circumstances, the green light becomes a positive discriminative stimulus and the red light a negative one (here indicated by S^+ and S^- respectively). The pigeon will hop in the presence of the first and not when presented with the second. But this discrimination is made in an instrumental and not a classical conditioning context. The green light doesn't signal food the way a CS^+ might in Pavlov's laboratory. Instead, it signals a particular relationship between the instrumental response and the reinforcer, telling the pigeon as it were "If you hop now, you'll get food." Conversely for the red light, the S^- tells the animal that there's no point in going through the treadle-hopping business right now.

A variety of techniques have been used to study the role of discriminated stimuli in affecting learned instrumental behaviors. Many of the results mirror those obtained in the study of generalization and discrimination in classical conditioning (see Figure 4.18).

An example is the study of stimulus generalization using operant techniques. Figure 4.19 shows a typical stimulus generalization gradient for color in pigeons. The animals were trained to peck at a key illuminated with yellow light, after which they were tested with lights of varying wavelengths. The resulting gradient is orderly. As the test light became less similar to the original S^+, the pigeons were less inclined to peck at it (Guttman and Kalish, 1956).

SHAPING

How does an animal learn the particular instrumental response that will lead to reinforcement? The law of effect tells us that once that response has been made, then reinforcement will act to strengthen it. But what happens if that response isn't ever made in the first place? As it happens, pecking and lever pressing are fairly easy as such responses go; many animals hit upon them of their own accord. But we can make the response much more difficult. For example, we could set the rat's lever so high on the wall that it must stretch up on its hindlegs to depress it. Now the animal may never make the response on its own. But it can learn this response and even ones more outlandish if its behavior is suitably shaped. This is accomplished by the method of *successive approximations.*

4.19 Stimulus generalization of an instrumental response *Pigeons were originally reinforced to peck at a yellow light. When later tested with lights of various colors, they showed a standard generalization gradient, pecking more vigorously at colors more similar to yellow (such as green and orange) than at colors farther removed (such as red and blue). Prior to being reinforced on the yellow key, their tendency to peck was minimal and roughly equal for all colors. (After Reynolds, 1968)*

4.20 The little pig that went to market
The figure shows a pig trained by means of operant techniques to push a market cart. The animal was first taught to push with its snout, a response which it is innately prepared to perform, and was then trained to use its forelegs and stand upright. (Courtesy Animal Behavior Enterprises)

4.21 Conditioned reinforcement in chimpanzees *Chimpanzee using token to obtain food after working to obtain tokens. (Courtesy Yerkes Regional Primate Research Center of Emory University)*

Take the problem of the elevated lever. The first step is to train the animal to approach the tray in which the food is delivered whenever the food-dispensing mechanism gives off its characteristic click. At random intervals, the click sounds and a food pellet drops into the tray; this continues until the rat shows that it is properly trained by running to pick up its pellet as soon as it hears the click. Shaping can now begin. We might first reinforce the animal for walking into the general area where the lever is located. As soon is it is there, it hears the click and devours the pellet. Very soon it will hover around the neighborhood of the lever. We next reinforce it for facing the lever, then for stretching its body upward, then for touching the lever with its paws, and so on until we finally complete its education by reinforcing it for pressing the lever down. The guiding principle throughout is immediacy of reinforcement. If we want to reinforce the rat for standing up on its hindlegs we must do it the instant after the response; even a one-second wait may be too long, for by then the rat may have fallen back on all fours and if we reinforce it then we will reinforce the wrong response.

By means of this technique, animals have been trained to perform exceedingly complex response chains. Pigeons have been trained to play Ping-Pong and dogs to plunk out four-note tunes on a toy piano. Such successes encouraged some enterprising psychologists to develop live advertising exhibits, featuring such stars as "Priscilla, the Fastidious Pig" to promote the sale of certain farm feeds (Breland and Breland, 1951). Priscilla turned on the radio, ate breakfast at a kitchen table, picked up dirty clothes and dropped them in a hamper, vacuumed the floor, and finally selected the sponsor's feed in preference to Brand X—a convincing tribute to the sponsor and to the power of reinforcement (Figure 4.20).

CONDITIONED REINFORCEMENT

According to the law of effect, reinforcement is a necessary condition for instrumental learning. But since the days of Thorndike, it has become clear that this law requires a number of amendments. One of these is the extension of the law to cover learned as well as unlearned reinforcers.

So far, our examples of reinforcement have included food or water or termination of electric shock. These are instances of *primary reinforcers* whose capacity to reinforce responses is presumably based upon built-in mechanisms of various kinds. But instrumental learning is not always reinforced by events of such immediate biological consequence. For example, piano teachers rarely reinforce their pupils with food or the cessation of electric shock; a nod or the comment "good" is all that is required. How does the Thorndikian approach explain why the word *good* is reinforcing?

The answer is that a stimulus will acquire reinforcing properties if it is repeatedly paired with a primary reinforcer. It will then provide *conditioned reinforcement* if administered after a response has been made.

Numerous experiments give evidence that neutral stimuli can acquire reinforcing properties. For example, chimpanzees were first trained to insert poker chips into a vending machine to acquire grapes. Having learned this, they then learned to operate another device which delivered poker chips (Cowles, 1937; see Figure 4.21).

Examples of this kind indicate that the critical factor in establishing a stimulus as a conditioned reinforcer is its association with primary reinforcement. It is then not surprising that the effect increases the more frequently the two have been paired. As we might also expect, a conditioned reinforcer will gradually lose its powers if it is repeatedly unaccompanied by some primary reinforcement. All of this argues that conditioned reinforcement is established by a process that is akin to, if not identical with, classical conditioning. The secondary reinforcer serves as a CS that signals some motivationally significant UCS.

If conditioned reinforcers are so readily extinguished in the laboratory, why do they seem so much more permanent in human life? Nods do not lose their reinforcing value just because they haven't been paired with any primary reinforcer for a month or more. In part, the answer may be that the nod or the smile has enormous generality. It is associated not with one but with many different desirable outcomes. Even if extinguished in one context, it would still be maintained in countless others.

DELAY OF REINFORCEMENT

The law of effect requires a second amendment. This concerns the role of the time interval between the response and the reinforcement that follows it. Specifically, a reinforcer becomes less and less effective the longer its presentation is delayed after the response is made.

The relation between the delay and the effectiveness of a reward has been experimentally studied in various ways. One experimenter trained several groups of rats to press a lever which was withdrawn from the box immediately after the correct response. Food was delivered after different delays of reinforcement ranging from 0 to 30 seconds for the various groups. Learning was clearly faster the shorter the interval. These results are summarized in Figure 4.22 which shows the declining effectiveness of reinforcement with increasing delay. Note that in this study there was no learning at all when the interval was as large as 30 seconds; in instrumental learning, late is sometimes no better than never (Perin, 1943).

To what extent does the delay of reward principle apply to humans? It depends upon which aspects of human behavior we consider. At one level there is an enormous gap between what we see in the rat and what we know of ourselves. Rats and humans live according to different time scales entirely. Reinforcement may come months or even years after an action and still have effect, because humans can relate their present to their past by all sorts of symbolic devices. A politician wins a close election, looks carefully at the returns, and realizes that a speech he gave a month ago turned the tide. Unlike the rat, humans can transcend the here and now.

The fact that people sometimes overcome long delays of reinforcement should not blind us to the fact that they often do not. Many of our actions are dictated by immediate reward, regardless of the long-term outcome. To give only one example, consider cigarette smoking. By now, most smokers are probably convinced of the ultimate dangers they are courting. In fact, they may experience some discomfort: They may cough and have trouble breathing when they wake up. Yet, despite all this, they continue to smoke. The problem is that the *immediate* reinforcement of the act is positive while discomfort or worse comes later. Transcending the gradient of reward is no easy task.

SCHEDULES OF REINFORCEMENT

So far, we've only dealt with cases in which reinforcement follows the response every time it is made. But outside of the laboratory, this arrangement is surely the exception and not the rule. The fisherman does not hook a fish with every cast,

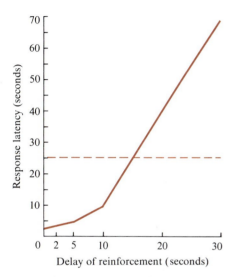

4.22 The effect of a delay in reinforcement *The graph shows the response latency for rats pressing a lever after 50 trials on which they received food reward after a delay of 0, 2, 5, 10, or 30 seconds. The dotted line indicates the animals' average latency at the very first trial. It is clear that animals trained with delays up to 10 seconds improved over trials, and the shorter the delay the greater was their improvement. But animals trained with a delay of 30 seconds did not improve; on the contrary, their performance was markedly worse after 50 trials than it was initially. (Data from Perin, 1943)*

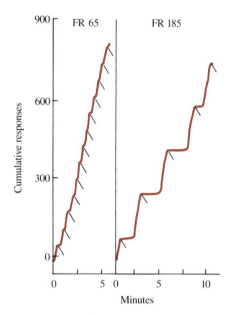

4.23 Performance on two fixed-ratio schedules *The figure records the pigeon's cumulative responses—how many key pecks it has made after 5 minutes in the operant chamber, after 10 minutes, and so on. The steeper the record, the faster the response rate. The left-hand panel shows performance on FR 65, the right on FR 185. The small diagonal slashes indicate times when the animal received reinforcement. Note the characteristic pause after the fixed ratio has been run off, and that the duration of this pause increases with increasing ratios. (Adapted from Ferster and Skinner, 1957)*

and even a star tennis player occasionally loses a match to one of her less accomplished rivals. All of these are cases of ***partial reinforcement*** in which a response is reinforced only some of the time.

One way of studying phenomena of this kind is in the operant situation. Here reinforcement can easily be *scheduled* in different ways—after every response, after some number of responses, after some interval, and so on. The ***schedule of reinforcement*** is simply the rule set up by the experimenter which determines the occasions on which a response is reinforced.

Behavior on a schedule One example of such a rule is the so-called ***fixed-ratio schedule*** (abbreviated FR 2, FR 4, FR 50, as the case may be) in which the subject has to produce a specified number of responses for every reward, like a factory worker paid by piecework. Such schedules can generate very high rates of responding but to get the organism to that level requires some finesse. The trick is to increase the ratio very gradually, beginning with continuous reinforcement and slowly stepping up the requirement. By such procedures, pigeons (and probably factory workers) have been led to perform at schedules as high as FR 500.

When the fixed-ratio gets high enough, a new pattern develops. Following a reinforcement, the pigeon will pause for a while before it starts to peck again. The higher the ratio, the longer the pause (see Figure 4.23). In a way, the pigeon is like a student who has just finished one term paper and has to write another. It is very hard to start again, but once the first page is written, the next ones come more readily. In part, this effect is the result of a discrimination. A peck (or a page) is only reinforced if it is preceded by other pecks (or pages). Not having pecked before is then a stimulus associated with lack of reinforcement, an S⁻ which inhibits the response. The pause following reinforcement can be eliminated by changing the schedule to a ***variable ratio*** (VR). In VR schedules, reinforcement still comes after a certain number of responses but that number varies irregularly, averaging out to a particular ratio (for example VR 50). Now there is no way whereby the pigeon can know which of its pecks will bring reward. It might be the first, the tenth, or the hundredth peck following the last reinforcement. Since the number of prior pecks is no longer a clue, the pause disappears. A glance at a gambling casino gives proof that VR schedules affect humans much as they do pigeons. The slot machines are set to pay off occasionally, just enough to maintain the high rate of behavior that keeps the casino lucrative to its owners and not to its clients.

Partial reinforcement and extinction Some of the most dramatic effects of partial reinforcement are seen during subsequent extinction. The basic fact can be stated very simply: A response will be much harder to extinguish if it was acquired during partial rather than continuous reinforcement. This phenomenon is often called the ***partial-reinforcement effect*** (Humphreys, 1939).

A good illustration is provided by an experiment in which several rats were trained on a runway for food (Weinstock, 1954). All animals received the same number of trials but not the same number of reinforcements. One group was reinforced on every trial, another only on 30 percent of the trials. Figure 4.24 shows what happened to these two groups during extinction. The rats reinforced 100 percent of the time gave up very much sooner than their partially reinforced fellows. Numerous other experiments have given substantially the same result, on all manner of subjects, including humans.

On the face of it, the partial-reinforcement effect is paradoxical. If the strength

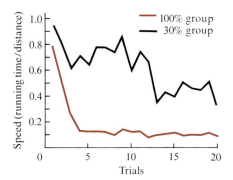

4.24 The partial-reinforcement effect
The figure shows runway speeds during extinction of two groups of rats. One group had previously been reinforced on every trial; the other had only been reinforced on 30 percent of the trials. The figure shows that the group trained under full reinforcement (in black) stops running considerably before the group that was trained under partial reinforcement (in color). (After Weinstock, 1954)

of an instrumental response increases with increasing reinforcements, we should expect that groups reinforced 100 percent of the time would continue to respond for longer than those reinforced only partially. In fact, the very opposite is true. The question is why? Speaking loosely, we might suggest that the partially reinforced rat has come to expect that reward may occur even after several unrewarded trials; it has learned that "if you don't succeed, try, and try again." In contrast, the rat reinforced 100 percent of the time has never encountered unreinforced trials before. If this interpretation of the partial reinforcement effect is correct, we would expect an irregular sequence of reinforcements to be harder to extinguish than a regular one, even if the proportion of reinforcements is the same in both cases. This is precisely what happens. Thus ratio schedules engender greater resistance to extinction if they are variable rather than fixed.

To see the partial-reinforcement effect in action, consider a simple problem in child rearing. Many parents find that their six-month-old does not want to go to sleep; put into his crib at night, he howls his vehement protests until he is lifted out again. Sooner or later his parents resolve that this has to stop. The baby is put away and the wails begin. The parents stay firm for a while but eventually they weaken (after all, the baby might be sick). Brought out of his crib, the baby gurgles happily and the process of partial reinforcement has begun. Next time, the parents will have an even harder time. According to one study (and to common sense) the answer is consistent nonreinforcement. Two determined parents plotted an extinction curve for their twenty-one-month-old child's bedtime tantrums. One day they simply decided to put their little tyrant to bed and then leave the bedroom and not go back. On the first occasion, the child howled for forty-five minutes; the next few times the cries were much diminished, until finally after ten such "trials," the child went to sleep smiling and with no complaints at all (Williams, 1959).

AVERSIVE CONDITIONING

So far, our discussion of instrumental learning has largely centered on cases where reinforcement is positive, of the kind we normally call reward. But there is another class of events that is no less relevant to instrumental learning than is reward; it represents the opposite side of the coin—the stick rather than the carrot, punishment rather than reward. These are negative reinforcers, sometimes called ***aversive stimuli,*** such as swats on the rear for infants, and electric shock for laboratory rats. There is little doubt that both organisms learn whatever they must to minimize such unpleasantries, to get as few shocks, swats, and insulting reproofs as they possibly can.

Punishment Psychologists distinguish between several kinds of instrumental learning that depend on the use of negative reinforcers. The most familiar from everyday life is ***punishment training.*** Here, a response is followed by an aversive stimulus, which will then tend to suppress the response on subsequent occasions. One factor that determines the resulting response suppression is the extent to which reinforcement is delayed, which we've already discussed in the context of reward. Consider a cat that has developed the unfortunate habit of using a large indoor plant as its private bathroom. The irate owner discovers the misdeed an hour or so later, and swats the cat severely when he sees it in the kitchen. It's hardly surprising that the punishment will not produce the hoped for hygienic re-

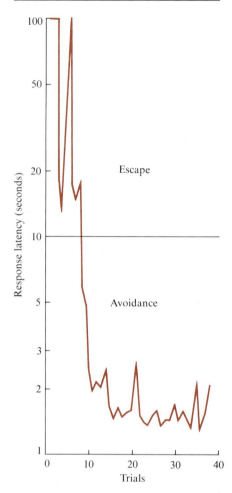

4.25 The course of avoidance learning in a dog *The figure shows response latencies in a shuttle box (where latency is the time from the onset of CS to the animal's response). A warning stimulus indicated that shock would begin 10 seconds after the onset of the signal. For the first nine trials the dog escaped. It jumped over the hurdle* after *the shock began. From the tenth trial on, the dog avoided: It jumped* before *its 10 seconds of grace were up. The jumping speed increased even after this point until the animal jumped with an average latency of about 1½ seconds. (Latency is plotted on a logarithmic scale. This compresses the time scale so as to put greater emphasis on differences between the shorter response latencies.) (After Solomon and Wynne, 1953)*

sult, for the animal has no way of connecting the crime with the punishment. For punishment to have its desired effect, it must be administered shortly after the unwanted response was performed. While humans are much better than cats at linking events that are separated in time, they too are subject to the delay of reinforcement principle. The young child who steals a cookie is more likely to refrain from further thefts if punished immediately than if told "Just wait until your father comes home."

Escape and avoidance Negative reinforcers can weaken response tendencies (as in punishment training), but they can also be used to strengthen them. This happens in *escape* and *avoidance learning.* In escape learning, the response stops some aversive event that has already begun. In avoidance learning, the subject can forestall it altogether. An example of escape learning is when a rat learns to press a lever to get rid of an electric shock. An example of avoidance learning is when a dog learns to jump over a hurdle in a shuttle box when it hears a tone that signals impending shock; if it jumps within some grace period, it will manage to avoid the shock entirely (see Figure 4.25).

Aversive reinforcement and the law of effect Both punishment training and escape learning readily fit into the Thorndike-Skinner conception of instrumental learning. Punishment training simply represents the opposite side of the law of effect: Where positive reinforcers strengthen the response that precedes them, negative reinforcers weaken it. The interpretation of escape learning is even easier: The response is followed by the termination of an aversive stimulus, which then serves as reward.

The interpretation of avoidance learning is more difficult. Consider a dog who jumps back and forth over a hurdle to avoid shock. What is the reinforcement? It is not the *cessation* of shock as it is in escape learning, for the animal doesn't get shocked to begin with. Could it be the *absence of shock*? This too won't work, for *not* receiving punishment can only be a source of satisfaction if punishment has been threatened. (After all, most of us spend our entire lives without being drowned, beaten, or otherwise put to bodily harm, but we don't therefore regard ourselves as being in a state of perpetual bliss.) It's not absence of shock as such that is the reward. It is rather the *absence of shock (or any other aversive event) when shock is expected.*

Avoidance learning in human life An enormous amount of ordinary human activity involves avoidance, although most of the negative reinforcers we try to steer clear of are relatively mild in comparison to the intense electric shocks that rats and dogs face in the shuttle box. We stop at red lights to avoid traffic tickets, pay bills to avoid interest charges, carry umbrellas to avoid getting wet, and devise excuses to avoid having lunch with a bore. We probably perform dozens of such learned avoidance responses each day, and most of them are perfectly useful and adaptive (Schwartz, 1984).

But some avoidance learning is essentially maladaptive and is often based on more potent aversive stimuli than a boring lunch. An extreme example is phobias. As already mentioned, some people have intense fears of various situations —heights, open spaces, dogs, elevators, and so on. As a result, they will develop elaborate patterns to avoid getting into these situations. In some cases, the phobia may be caused by traumatic experiences in the past as in the case of a woman who

Avoidance learning *No doubt the infant will soon learn to avoid the flame. (Photograph by Erika Stone)*

was trapped for several hours in a swaying elevator stuck between the fortieth and forty-first floor of an office building, and never used an elevator thereafter. Such an avoidance reaction is of little future use, for elevators ordinarily function perfectly well. But the trouble is that the avoidance response is self-perpetuating. It will not extinguish even if the aversive stimulus is no longer there. The reason is that the person (or animal) will not stay in the previously dangerous situation long enough to discover whether the danger is indeed still there. The woman who avoids elevators will never find out that they are now perfectly safe, for she won't ever use them again—a rather inconvenient behavior pattern if her own office happens to be above the forty-first floor.

Is there any way to extinguish avoidance responses? (The question is of considerable practical interest because it has implications for the therapy of phobias and related conditions.) In animals, the answer is "yes." The technique is to force them to "test reality" so that they can discover that the aversive stimulus is no longer there. In a number of studies, animals were first trained to jump back and forth in a shuttle box to avoid shock. After they had learned the avoidance response, they were exposed to the stimulus that previously had signaled impending shock. They immediately tried to jump to the other side of the box, but they couldn't; their avoidance response was blocked by a floor-to-ceiling barrier that forced them to remain in the compartment. They necessarily remained and were visibly frightened. But, in fact, there was no shock. After a few such trials without shock, the avoidance reaction was extinguished. The idea is much like getting back on the horse that threw you—a good prescription for aspiring jockeys, assuming the horse won't throw them again (Baum, 1970; Mineka, 1979).

What Is Learned in Instrumental Conditioning?

Many authors believe that what is learned in instrumental conditioning is an association between an act (the operant) and its outcome (the reinforcement). But how does this association come about? This question brings us back to some of the issues we took up when we discussed classical conditioning, in which the association is between the CS and the UCS. This association is ultimately based on the animal's discovery that the UCS is contingent upon the CS. To recognize this contingency, the animal has to compare the probability that the UCS will appear when the CS is presented with the probability that it will not appear when the CS is not presented.

A similar analysis applies to instrumental conditioning. Here the relevant contingency is between an act and its outcome. If the act is lever pressing and the outcome is a food pellet, then the contingency is determined by comparing the probability of getting a pellet when the lever has been pressed and getting it when the lever has not been pressed. If the first probability is greater than the second, getting food is contingent upon lever pressing. If the two probabilities are equal, there is no contingency—lever pressing and getting pellets are independent.*

Do animals and people respond to such response-outcome contingencies? Proof that they do comes from studies that compare the effects of response-independent outcomes.

* If the second probability is greater than the first, then getting the pellet is contingent upon *not* pressing the lever. This kind of contingency is common whenever one wants the learner to refrain from doing something, for example: "I'll give you a cookie if you stop whining."

RESPONSE CONTROL IN INFANTS

One line of evidence concerns human infants. A group of two-month-old infants was provided with an opportunity to make something happen. The infants were placed in cribs above which a colorful mobile was suspended. Whenever the infants moved their heads, they closed a switch in their pillows. This activated the overhead mobile which promptly turned for a second or so and did so every time the pillow switch was closed. The infants soon learned to shake their heads about, thus making their mobiles turn. They evidently enjoyed doing so; they smiled and cooed happily at their mobiles, clearly delighted at seeing them move. A second group of infants was exposed to the same situation. There was one difference —they had no control over the mobile's movement. Their mobile turned just about as often as the mobile for the first group, but it was moved for them, not by them. After a few days, these infants no longer smiled and cooed at the mobile nor did they seem particularly interested when it turned. This suggests that what the infants liked about the mobile was not that it moved but that they made it move (Figure 4.26). This shows that the infants can distinguish between response-controlled and response-independent outcomes, which is a strong argument for the contingency approach. It also shows that infants, no less than we, prefer to exercise some control over their environments. The reason for this is by no means clear, but it appears that even a two-month-old infant wants to be master of his own fate (J. S. Watson, 1967).

HELPLESSNESS IN DOGS

The mobile-turning infants illustrate the joys of mastery. Another, highly influential series of studies demonstrates the despair when there is no mastery at all. Their focus is on *learned helplessness,* an acquired sense that one can no longer control one's environment so that one gives up trying (Seligman, 1975).

The classic experiment on learned helplessness employed two groups of dogs, *A* and *B*, who received strong electric shocks while strapped in a hammock. The dogs in group *A* were able to exert some control over the situation. They could turn the shock off whenever it began by pushing a panel that was placed close to their noses. The dogs in group *B* had no such power. For them, the shocks were inescapable. But the number and duration of these shocks were exactly the same.

4.26 Response control Infants who can make a mobile move, smile and coo at it, while those who have no control over its motion, stop smiling.

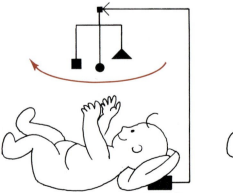
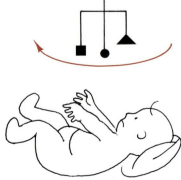

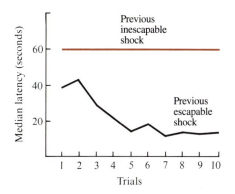

4.27 Learned helplessness The curves show the shuttle box performance of two groups of dogs. At each trial, the animals could escape a shock by jumping over the barrier; the figure shows how quickly each animal jumped. If the animal did not jump after 60 seconds, the trial was terminated. In a different situation, one group of dogs (black) had previously experienced electric shocks that they could escape by performing an instrumental response. Another group (color) received the same shocks but was unable to do anything about them. As the figure shows, the dogs that previously had been exposed to escapable shock learned to escape. In contrast, those who had previously received inescapable shocks became helpless and were unable to learn. (After Maier, Seligman, and Solomon, 1969)

For each dog in group *A* there was a corresponding animal in group *B* whose fate was "yoked" to that of the first dog. Whenever the group *A* dog was shocked, so was the group *B* dog. Whenever the group *A* dog turned off the shock, the shock was turned off for the group *B* dog. This arrangement guaranteed that the actual physical punishment meted out to both groups was precisely the same. What was different was what they could do about it. Group *A* was able to exercise some control; group *B* could only endure.

The question was how the group *B* dogs would fare when presented with a new situation that provided them with an opportunity to help themselves. To find out, both groups of dogs were presented with a standard avoidance learning task in a shuttle box (Figure 4.27). The dogs in group *A* learned just about as quickly as did the naïve dogs who had no prior experimental experience of any kind. During the first trials, they waited until the shock began and then scrambled over the hurdle; later, they jumped before their grace period was up and thus avoided shock entirely. But the dogs in group *B*, who had previously suffered inescapable shock in the hammock, behaved very differently. Initially, they behaved much like other dogs; they ran about frantically, barking, and howling. But they soon became much more passive. They lay down, whined quietly, and simply took whatever shocks were delivered. They neither avoided nor escaped; they just gave up trying. In the hammock setup they had been objectively helpless; there really was nothing they could do. But in the shuttle box, their helplessness was only subjective, for there was now a way in which they could make their lot bearable. But they never discovered it. They had learned to be helpless (Seligman and Maier, 1967).

HELPLESSNESS AND DEPRESSION

Martin Seligman, one of the discoverers of the learned helplessness effect in animals, has recently proposed that a similar mechanism underlies the development of certain kinds of depression in human patients. (For further discussion of depression, see Chapter 19.) He believes that such patients share certain features with animals who have been rendered helpless. Both fail to initiate actions but "just sit there"; both are slow to learn that something they did was successful; both lose weight and have little interest in others. To Seligman and his associates these parallels suggest that the underlying cause is the same in both cases. Like the helpless dog, the depressed patient has come to feel that his acts are of no avail. And like the dog, the depressed patient was brought to this morbid state of affairs by an initial exposure to a situation in which he was objectively helpless. While the dog received inescapable shocks in its hammock, the patient found himself powerless in the face of bereavement, business failure, or serious illness (Seligman, Klein, and Miller, 1976).

Whether learned helplessness turns out to be relevant to depression or does not, there is little doubt that it is relevant to questions about the nature of learning. It is a strong argument for the contingency approach to instrumental learning. It clearly shows that animals (much as human infants) react differently to situations in which their responses have an effect than to those in which they don't. This indicates that animals learn something about the relationship between their acts and these acts' outcomes. If they are dogs who received inescapable shocks, they learn something still more general; namely, that no such relationship exists.

BEHAVIOR THEORY AND HUMAN DISORDERS

We've already pointed out that the behavior theorists' approach to classical and instrumental conditioning has implications that go far beyond the specific laboratory phenomena they investigate. The extent to which this is true becomes clear when we consider some of the extensions and applications their work has led to.

Behavior Therapy

We'll begin by considering some applications of behavior theory to the treatment of certain mental disorders. We have previously discussed the intense, irrational fears known as phobias. A number of clinical psychologists, called *behavior therapists,* believe that the principles of classical conditioning can help us to understand how such phobias arise and may also provide the tools by which phobias can be eliminated (Wolpe and Lazarus, 1969).

FLOODING

One procedure for treating phobias follows directly from classical conditioning concepts. If the irrational fear is a CR evoked by some CS, it should be nullified by extinction. To do so, one merely has to present the CS over and over again without accompanying it with the UCS. If a patient is mortally afraid of snakes, show him snakes again and again without him suffering from any harmful effects. We've previously seen that this very procedure serves to extinguish fear and avoidance reactions: If dogs have been trained to jump back and forth in a shuttle box to avoid shock, the avoidance reaction can be extinguished by forcing the animal to remain in the now harmless compartment (Baum, 1970; Mineka, 1979).

Such forced reality testing is the main point of a therapy called *flooding,* in which the patient has to expose himself to whatever he is afraid of, sometimes for hours on end; the patient floods himself with fear in order to extinguish it (Stampfl, and Levis, 1967). In some cases, the fear-evoking conditions are real stimuli, as when a patient with claustrophobia (a fear of confined spaces) has to spend several hours in a closet. In most others, they are created in imagination. The man with a fear of dogs must imagine himself surrounded by a dozen snarling Dobermans, the woman with an obsessive fear of dirt must imagine herself immersed in a stinking cesspool.

The evidence indicates that flooding is a rather successful treatment method for phobias and related disorders. According to one study, 75 percent of a group of patients with an intense fear of wide open spaces (a rather common and incapacitating phobia) remained improved four years after treatment (Emmelkamp and Kuipers, 1979). The fact that phobias such as this can be extinguished by flooding tells us why they are extremely persistent in ordinary life. As mentioned earlier, the patient is so afraid of the objects of his phobia—whether of confined or open spaces, whether of cats or snakes—that he constantly avoids them. As a result, he can never find out that they're really perfectly safe (Rosenhan and Seligman, 1984).

DESENSITIZATION

While flooding is often quite successful, some therapists regard it as too stressful for the patient. After all, spending two or three hours in a cesspool is something one could well do without, even if the cesspool is only in one's imagination. Under the circumstances, there is reason to look for less drastic procedures.

The major alternative is ***systematic desensitization***, which by now is one of the preferred methods for dealing with phobias. In this procedure the therapist tries to eliminate the phobic's fear by ***counterconditioning.***

As an example take an irrational fear of snakes, which behavior therapists regard as a classically conditioned response. The idea is to combat the original CR, fear, by counterconditioning: connecting the stimuli that presently evoke it to a new response that is incompatible with fear and will displace it. The response that is usually picked to serve this competing role is muscular relaxation. This is a pervasive untensing of the entire musculature which is presumably incompatible with the autonomic and muscular reactions that underlie fear. The patients are first trained to achieve this deep relaxation upon command. Once they can do this, they are repeatedly exposed to various stimuli that evoke the phobia. Concurrently, they are asked to relax. According to behavior therapists, the same stimuli that initially served as a CS for fear will eventually become a CS for relaxation. As the link to relaxation becomes stronger and stronger, the fear response will presumably become gradually replaced.

There is one important qualification. In contrast to flooding, desensitization is gradual. The behavior therapist sneaks up on the phobia rather than confronting it directly in its full-blown state. The therapist doesn't start out by asking the pa-

Desensitization *(Courtesy of Henry Gleitman and Mary Bullock)*

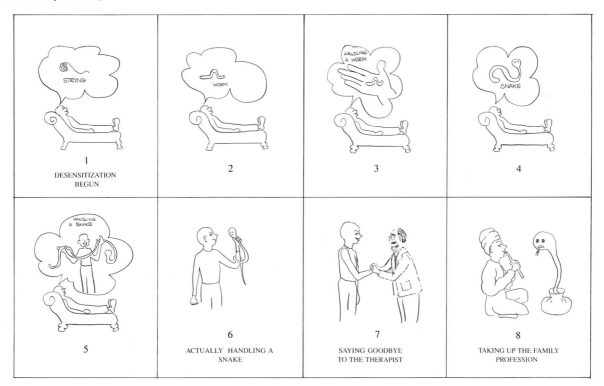

tient to fondle a rattlesnake. On the contrary, she first has the patient construct a list in which the situations that provoked his fear are arranged in order, from most frightening to least frightening. She then asks him to expose himself to these stimuli, starting with the least frightening (say, the sight of an earthworm) and gradually working up to more and more anxiety provoking stimuli. Moreover, all of this only occurs in the patient's mind. He is asked to *imagine* the fear-arousing scene as vividly as possible while in a state of deep relaxation.

OPERANT TECHNIQUES

Therapies such as desensitization and flooding are based on classical conditioning. As such they try to alter the significance of various stimulus events, as in making a patient recognize that snakes are not really threatening. Another set of behavior therapies comes from the operant laboratory and emphasizes the relations between acts and consequences. Its theme is the same as that which underlies the entire operant approach—the control of behavior through reinforcement.

Eliminating responses   Suppose a person does something that is regarded as maladaptive. A behavior therapist will tend to assume that this undesirable behavior is somehow getting reinforced. He will try to find the reinforcement and remove it, sure that once this is done extinction will necessarily follow. One method is to give so much of a reinforcer that the recipient gets sick of it; after all, a food pellet won't serve as a reinforcer for a rat which has just gorged itself.

An example of this **satiation principle** is the case of a severely disturbed patient in a mental hospital who hoarded towels. On the average, she collected about twenty-five towels in her room, frustrating all attempts of the nurses to get them back. This hoarding pattern had gone on for nine years. The treatment was a surfeit of towels. The nurses stopped taking her towels away. On the contrary, they gave her seven towels a day, without comment, and gradually increased this number to thirty. Initially, the patient was grateful; she folded the towels and stacked them neatly away. But upon accumulating over six hundred towels that spilled all over her room, she complained ever more bitterly, telling the nurses that the incessant work of folding and stacking towels was getting completely out of hand. At this point, no more towels were given, and the patient gradually divested herself of her now unwanted riches until she was finally down to a normal one or two towels a day. The towel hoarding stopped and never returned (Figure 4.28).

Strengthening desired behaviors   Elimination of undesirable behaviors is one objective of behavior modification. Another is to get patients to perform certain desirable acts. To accomplish this end, the operant behavior therapist tries to provide an appropriate reinforcer. An example is provided by **token economies** which have been set up in hospital wards, some of which house chronic patients given up as hopeless. These tokens function much as money does in our economy; they can be exchanged for desirable items within the hospital situation such as snacks, cigarettes, or watching TV. But again, like money, they must be earned by the patients, perhaps by being neatly dressed or talking to others or performing various ward chores. The overall effect seems to be salutary. While the patients are not cured, they become less apathetic and the general ward atmosphere is much improved (Ayllon and Azrin, 1968).

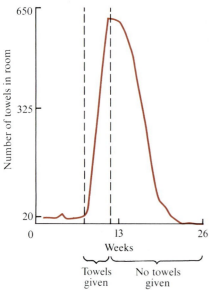

4.28   An example of behavior therapy based on operant techniques   A response, towel hoarding, was eliminated by providing the patient with an overabundance of towels. When the number of towels got up to 625, the patient started to discard them until the average number of towels in her room reached 1.5 compared to the previous average of 20. (After Ayllon, 1963)

Evaluating operant behavior modification   There is little doubt that the various reinforcement regimens we have described affect the patients: One stopped hoarding towels, others performed ward chores, and so on. While these effects fell far short of a cure, they were surely changes for the better. Even so, some worries remain.

One question concerns the relation between application and theory. Are the various behavior-modification systems really based on principles discovered in the animal laboratory? Or are they simply elaborations of common sense, dressed up in the fancy language of behavior theory? After all, many parents have long known that certain childish outbursts are best handled by being ignored. In effect, they advocated the extinction procedure developed by behavior therapists but without calling it extinction.

Another question concerns the nature of the changes that behavior modification produces. In the case of severely disturbed mental patients, these changes are on the whole beneficial. But with other groups, these gains are accompanied by certain drawbacks. An example is the use of token reinforcement in young elementary school or preschool children. These tokens—which can be exchanged for trinkets or candy—are very effective in keeping children working at such school tasks as reading or counting. But unfortunately, there is a side effect. To be sure, the children work considerably harder than they would have otherwise, but they now do so merely to earn tokens—they have lost their interest in reading or counting for their own sakes. Nursery school children who received gold stars for drawing stopped drawing when gold stars were no longer given. Drawing was no longer fun; it was work. And, at least within an operant framework, work is not its own reward (Lepper, Greene, and Nisbett, 1973). As one team of critics put it, "Token rewards may lead to token learning" (Levine and Fasnacht, 1974).

Behavior Theory and Medicine

There is considerable evidence that various bodily ills are sometimes brought on by psychological factors. These are sometimes called ***psychophysiological disorders*** (for further discussion, see Chapter 18). Examples are peptic ulcers, colitis, and hypertension. These are disorders that are based on some chronic visceral malfunction. In peptic ulcer, there is an oversecretion of gastric juices; in hypertension, there is an inability to relax the small arteries in the bloodstream. In addition, many other illnesses seem to be aggravated by psychological stress. These facts have led to the development of ***behavioral medicine,*** a new field that stands at the boundary between psychology and traditional medicine. Some important contributions to this area come from approaches derived from behavior theory.

BIOFEEDBACK AND THERAPEUTIC CHANGE

There is reason to believe that various psychophysiological disorders are based on classically or instrumentally conditioned responses. An example of a mild case is a child who has a queasy stomach on the day of an examination and is told to stay home by her solicitous parents. After a number of such experiences, she may develop a gastrointestinal escape response in similar situations that occur later on (Miller, 1978).

If conditioning is the cause of some ailments, can it be used to affect a cure? A number of investigators have tried to alleviate various disorders—such as high blood pressure and asthma—by training patients to change their own autonomic reactions, for example, by reducing their heart rates. But how can patients be taught to control such normally involuntary responses? A widely publicized approach involves *biofeedback*—a general term for any procedure that provides the individual with information about his own involuntary reactions. The patient tries to, say, slow down his heart rate, and can readily judge his success in so doing by listening to his own heart beat greatly amplified over a loudspeaker.

While the effectiveness of biofeedback has been greatly exaggerated in the media, a few procedures do seem to offer considerable promise. An example concerns patients with spinal injuries that disrupt the normal reflexive control of blood pressure. When these patients try to sit upright or stand up (with crutches), their blood pressure falls so that they become dizzy and faint. To counteract this, several patients were trained to raise their blood pressure at will. After a period of biofeedback training in which they received continuous information about their own blood pressure, three patients were able to sit or stand in an upright position without fainting, having been unable to do so in some cases for two years before this (Miller, 1978; Miller and Brucker, 1978).

SOME BIOLOGICAL CONSEQUENCES OF HELPLESSNESS

Thus far, we've looked at the medical implications of various classical or instrumental contingencies—the fact that certain visceral reactions lead to certain consequences. These contingencies can cause certain disorders (as when intestinal upsets become a way to avoid examinations); others can be used for therapeutic purposes (as in patients trained to control their blood pressure by biofeedback). But lack of contingency can have biological consequences that are no less important for medical purposes. Of particular interest are the biological consequences of learned helplessness which are produced when humans and animals discover that they have no control over stressful events in their lives.

There's an old adage that patients who "give up hope" have a poorer chance to survive than those who continue fighting. Several medical investigations suggest that there are some grounds for this belief. People who are hopeless and depressed are more likely to contract and succumb to major illness than those who try to cope. Thus, persons who suffer the loss of a loved one are more likely to die in the year after their bereavement than control subjects of the same age. Of particular interest is the role of psychological factors on cancer. There is evidence that despair and helplessness in the face of important personal losses increase the risk of cancer in subsequent years (Horne and Picard, 1979; Shekelle et al., 1981; see Figure 4.29).

What might be responsible for these relationships? Some recent studies suggest that learned helplessness impairs the so-called *immune system* of the body. This immune system produces a number of cells that fight various foreign invaders and tumors. Among these is a group called "killer cells," which deal with tumors. The killer cells recognize that the tumors are foreign and promptly dispatch them. Steven Maier and his associates have shown that the production of such killer cells is impaired when rats are put in a situation that induces learned helplessness. One group of animals was given a number of intense shocks from which they could escape by turning a treadwheel. A second group received the same shocks as the control rats but could do nothing about them. They suffered the

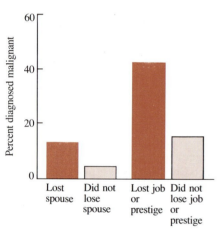

4.29 Psychological loss and lung cancer *Diagnoses were performed on over 100 patients whose X rays showed a lesion in the lungs. Some of these patients had suffered serious psychological losses in the previous 5 years; for example, loss of a spouse, parent, or sibling, retirement, loss of a job, or loss of prestige. Others had not experienced any such losses. The figure presents the percent of the cases whose lung lesions turned out to be malignant. As the figure shows, malignancy was more likely for the patients who had suffered one of the serious losses listed above (in color) than for those who had not suffered any of these losses (in black). (After Horne and Picard, 1979)*

same degree of physical stress, but unlike their counterparts in the control group, they learned that they had no control over their fate and so they became helpless. Later tests showed that animals who had been rendered helpless in this fashion produced fewer killer cells and were thus less able to stop tumor growths. This result fits in with other findings which show that learned helplessness in rats increases susceptibility to injected tumors (Visintainer, Volpicelli, and Seligman, 1982; Maier, Laudenslager, and Ryan, 1985).

Just why learned helplessness affects the immune system is still unknown. But whatever the mechanism, the fact that it does provides yet one further suggestion that learning about the contingencies (and in the case of learned helplessness, the lack of contingencies) between one's own actions and subsequent events in the world has profound effects on bodily functioning.

SOME LIMITATIONS OF BEHAVIOR THEORY

If Pavlov and Thorndike were alive today, they would surely be gratified at the success of their intellectual descendants, the behavior theorists, who built upon the foundations they had laid some eighty years ago, for behavior theory has certainly flourished. It has uncovered some basic principles of simple learning in humans and animals through the study of classical and instrumental conditioning. These principles have considerable scope and have led to important applications in such areas as behavior therapy and behavioral medicine. What began as the study of salivating dogs and lever-pressing cats has become an impressive enterprise of vastly greater generality.

Behavior theory clearly describes some important aspects of learning and behavior in humans and animals. Does this mean that it can account for all? Some advocates of behavior theory believe that it can, for they argue that ultimately all facets of human and animal behavior can be reduced to principles derived from the study of animal conditioning. This ambitious proposal has been challenged by a number of critics who have pointed to some limitations of this general approach.

The arguments of these critics are diverse, but they all represent attacks on the claim that the laws of behavior theory can be generalized across the board—that they apply to just about all learning tasks, to all associations of CS and UCS or of instrumental response and reinforcer, and to all vertebrate animals. According to the critics, such overgeneralization has led behavior theory to overestimate the intellectual capacities of certain animals and to underestimate that of many others, including ourselves.

Biological Constraints on Learning

During the last two decades, a number of investigators have become increasingly skeptical of behavior theory's claim that the laws of classical and instrumental conditioning apply equally well to all animals. In their view, there are certain built-in limitations (often called *biological constraints*) that determine what a given animal can easily learn and which sorts of learning it will find more difficult. These constraints are built into the animal's system and adapt it to the particular requirements of its own ecological niche.

The belief in such built-in constraints runs counter to one of behavior theory's basic tenets: the assumption that animals are capable of connecting just about any conditioned stimulus to any unconditioned stimulus (in classical conditioning) or of associating any instrumental response with any reinforcer (in instrumental conditioning). But as we will see, not all associations are equally easy to learn, and what is easy and what is difficult depends on the animal that has to learn them. For most animal species seem to be biologically "prepared" to form certain associations and have difficulty in forming others.

CS-UCS RELATIONS IN CLASSICAL CONDITIONING

According to strict behavior theory, the connections that are established by classical or instrumental conditioning do not depend upon the relationship between the elements that are connected. Put another way, these connections are thought to be *arbitrary.* Consider classical conditioning. A dog in Pavlov's laboratory would presumably connect the unconditioned stimulus of the food powder with just about any conditioned stimulus the experimenter might present: a tone, a light, the sound of a metronome, or what have you. Similar arbitrary connections are a continual feature of human life. As an example, take names and faces. Suppose we have two female faces and two female names, say, Joan and Carol. Which connection is more reasonable? Should it be as in Figure 4.30A? Or should it be as in Figure 4.30B?

It is obvious that both sets of pairings are equally plausible. Neither face is more Carolish or Joanlike than the other. As a result, the face-name pairing is indeed arbitrary. Much the same holds for virtually all of the sounds by which our language designates the objects in the world around us. Except for a few onomatopoeic terms like *buzz* and *hiss* the relation between the sound of a word and its meaning is completely arbitrary. The same holds for many other associations we pick up in the course of ordinary life, such as addresses, telephone numbers, and the like.

Behavior theorists believe that this arbitrariness is a basic feature of all learning. In their view, events are linked together by an associative process that acts like a universal glue which bonds just about anything to anything else. But there is some evidence to the contrary. It appears that associations between two items are more readily formed if the items somehow belong together. An important example of such a *belongingness* effect comes from classical conditioning. A number of recent studies have shown that certain conditioned stimuli are more readily related to certain unconditioned stimuli than to others. The bulk of the evidence comes from *learned taste aversions.*

It has long been known that rats are remarkably adept at avoiding foods they ate just before falling sick. This is the reason why it is very difficult to exterminate wild rats with poison: The rat takes a small bite of the poisoned food, becomes ill, generally recovers, and thereafter avoids the particular flavor. The animal has become bait shy. Similar effects are easily produced in the laboratory. The subjects (usually rats) are presented with a given flavor, such as water containing saccharin. After drinking some of this water, they are exposed to X-ray radiation—not enough to kill them, but enough to make them quite ill and nauseous. After they are recovered, they are given a choice between, say, plain water and a sac-

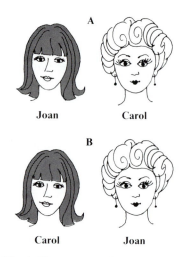

4.30 Arbitrary connections *The connection between faces and names is largely arbitrary. The names fit just as well in (A) as in (B).*

charine solution. They will now refuse to drink the saccharin even though they had much preferred this sweet-tasting drink prior to their illness.

Such learned taste aversions are usually believed to be based on classical conditioning in which the CS is a certain flavor (here, saccharin) and the UCS is being sick. The question is whether other stimuli such as colors or tones serve equally well as CS's for such taste aversions.

The test was a study in which thirsty rats were allowed to drink saccharine-flavored water. The water came from a drinking tube; whenever the rat licked the nozzle, a bright light flashed and a clicking noise sounded. Subsequently, some rats received a shock to their feet. Others were exposed to a dose of illness-producing X rays. All of the animals developed a strong aversion. When again presented with water that was sweet and was accompanied by bright flashes and clicks, they hardly touched the drinking nozzle. All rats had presumably acquired a classically conditioned aversion. The UCS was either shock or illness. The CS was a stimulus compound comprised of the flavor, the light, and the noise. But did the rats learn to avoid all of these stimulus features or only some?

To find out, the experimenters tested the rats in a new situation. They either gave them water that was saccharine-flavored but unaccompanied by either light or noise. Or they gave them plain, unflavored water that was accompanied by the light and sound cues that were present during training. The results showed that what the rats had learned to avoid depended upon the UCS. If they had been shocked (and felt pain) they refused water that was accompanied by light and noise but they had no objection to the sweet flavor. If they had been X-rayed (and became ill) the opposite was true—they avoided the saccharine flavor but were perfectly willing to drink when the water was preceded by light and noise (Table 4.3).

Table 4.3   BELONGINGNESS IN CLASSICAL CONDITIONING

In all groups: CS = saccharine taste + light + sound

TRAINING UCS:	Shock		X-ray illness	
TEST Water with:	Saccharine taste	Light + sound	Saccharine taste	Light + sound
RESULTS	No effect	Aversion	Aversion	No effect

These results indicate that rats tend to link stimuli in certain fitting ways: In rats, taste goes with illness, sights and sounds with externally induced pain. These effects may well reflect a built-in belongingness relationship. This would make good biological sense. In the world of the rat, an omnivorous creature that selects its food mainly on the basis of its flavor, taste may well be the most reliable cue that warns of impending illness. If so, a natively given bias to associate sickness with preceding tastes is likely to have survival value. In effect, the rat cannot help but ask itself, "What did I eat?" whenever it has a stomach ache (Garcia and Koelling, 1966).

If this is so, one might expect rather different results for animals who select their food on the basis of cues other than taste. An example are many species of birds that rely heavily on vision when choosing food. In one study, quail drank blue, sour water and were then poisoned. Some of the birds were later tested with

A

B

blue, unflavored water; others were tested with water that was sour but colorless. The quail developed a drastic aversion to blue water. But they drank just about as much sour water as they had prior to being poisoned. Here, the learned food aversion was evidently based on color rather than on taste (Wilcoxin, Dragoin, and Kral, 1971). It appears that the built-in belongingness relation is species-specific. Certain birds have a natively given bias to link sickness with visual cues, while rats and other mammals link it to taste. This bias *prepares* them to learn certain relations rather than others (Seligman, 1970). In both cases, the preparedness fits in with the way the animal identifies food in its native habitat.

RESPONSE-OUTCOME RELATIONS IN INSTRUMENTAL CONDITIONING

The preceding discussion has shown that the CS-UCS relation in classical conditioning is not always arbitrary. A similar nonarbitrariness characterizes many instrumental learning situations (Shettleworth, 1972).

Consider a pigeon pecking away in a Skinner box. Here surely is the very prototype of arbitrary instrumental learning. But in fact, the relation between peck and what is pecked at is far from arbitrary. One line of evidence comes from the fact that it is exceedingly hard to train pigeons to peck so as to escape or avoid electric shock (Hineline and Rachlin, 1969). This doesn't mean that shock escape or shock avoidance are inadequate reinforcers for pigeons. Far from it. The birds readily learn to fly or hop or flap their wings in order to get away from shock. What they have trouble learning is to peck to bring about the same outcome. According to Robert Bolles, this is because many animals have built-in defense reactions to danger that are specific to their species. The pigeon is no exception. Its species-specific defense reaction is speedy locomotion, preferably airborne flight. Like all other animals, the bird can learn new avoidance responses, but only to the extent that these fit in with its natively given danger reaction. Hopping, flying, and wing-flapping qualify, for they are merely modifications of the basic defense pattern. But pecking does not, and it is therefore very hard to learn as an escape or an avoidance response (Bolles, 1970).

If pigeons have so much trouble learning to peck to escape or avoid, why are they so readily trained to peck for food? The reason is that pecking is what pigeons do naturally when they consume food. In effect, they are simply performing an anticipatory eating response. That something of this sort goes on is shown by how they peck when other reinforcers are used. In one study, thirsty pigeons had to peck at a key to obtain water. Their pecks were quite different from those seen with food reinforcement; they resembled the beak movements pigeons make while drinking (Figure 4.31). In another study, key-pecking brought access to a sexually receptive mate. Now the pigeons cooed as they pressed the key. All of this means that key-pecking is not an arbitrary instrumental response. In effect, the pigeon "eats" the key when working for food, "drinks" it when working for

4.31 Key pecking for food and water (A) The pictures show a pigeon's beak movements as it pecks a key to obtain water. The movements resemble those the bird makes when it drinks. (B) These pictures show quite different beak movements made when the bird is hungry and pecks a key for food. Now the movements resemble those the animal makes when it eats. (Photographs by Bruce Moore, from Jenkins and Moore, 1973)

water, and "courts" it when working for sex. There clearly is an intimate relation between response and reinforcer (Schwartz, 1978).*

GENERALIST AND SPECIALIST

To sum up, it becomes clear that the way in which animals associate events is not arbitrary. Different species seem to come biologically prepared to acquire certain linkages rather than others. For instance, rats connect illness with taste but not with sights and sounds. Such built-in belongingnesses have the virtue of helping the animal to adapt to its particular ecological niche. But they have the drawback of making the animal into an intellectual specialist whose unusual gifts in noting certain relations are counterbalanced by its sluggishness in responding to others (Rozin and Kalat, 1971).

There is something ironic about all this. For the arbitrariness which both Pavlov and Skinner regarded as basic is something which people are more capable of than rats and pigeons. For people, a Skinner-box lever would indeed be an indifferent means to an end, as readily pressed for food as for anything else. To this extent, the box might be suitable to study people rather than the animal subjects for which it was designed (Schwartz, 1974). This is not to say that the behavior theorists' devices can begin to do justice to the human intellect. After all, a Skinner box is hardly a place in which Plato or Shakespeare would show to full advantage. But while not remotely adequate to assess our intellectual maximum, it is an apparatus that seems to fit one fact of human learning: We are generalists who can relate just about anything to anything else. *We* can learn arbitrary relations.

Many psychologists believe that this is not the end of the story. Compared to animals, we are indeed generalists who can learn arbitrary relations. But we are also specialists, with built-in predispositions to learn certain relationships very quickly. One of these species-specific predispositions is for language. That language is learned is indubitable. Eskimo children come to speak Eskimo and Chinese children speak Chinese. But the question is how it is learned. It is something that virtually all human children acquire, without fuss or effort and within the first few years of life. By the time they are four or five, they all know how to speak their native tongues, uttering sentences of considerable complexity, many of which they could never have heard before. This is not because they are taught explicitly, for most children aren't. Instead, it probably reflects a built-in tendency to fit sounds, words, and larger units into a very general framework with which the organism comes already equipped. How this process works is as yet unknown (see Chapter 15). But it seems to be the counterpart of other specializations of the learning functions found elsewhere in the animal kingdom.

---

* A number of psychologists have interpreted such findings as evidence that key-pecking in a Skinner box is a classically rather than an instrumentally conditioned response. To some extent, this may be true. One line of evidence comes from a study in which naïve pigeons were left in a box whose key lit up periodically. The pigeons received food if they did *not* peck at the key during a six-second interval. But if they did peck, the key light went out and no food was presented. Here, food reward was contingent upon not pecking. But the pigeons pecked anyway. They simply couldn't help themselves (Williams and Williams, 1969). The CS-UCS contingency (here, lit key and food) evidently outweighed the response-outcome contingency (here, not pecking and food), which may be another way of saying that the response was in part a classically conditioned CR (Schwartz and Gamzu, 1977).

Cognitive Learning

The preceding discussion showed that in many ways behavior theory had overestimated the intellectual flexibility of many animal species. For rats and pigeons are subject to biological constraints that make them unable to associate quite as arbitrarily as Pavlov and Skinner had maintained. But according to many critics, behavior theory is guilty of an even more serious error. It underestimates the capacity of many animals, especially that of the primate family to which we ourselves belong. For there seem to be instances of learning—sometimes called *cognitive learning*—whose essence seems to be rather different from that which we have taken up thus far. Consider a student who "gets the point" of a geometrical proof or a garage mechanic who figures out why an engine stalls. These examples represent manifestations of reason or intelligence of a kind that Pavlov, Thorndike, and Skinner mostly ignored. The question is whether such phenomena can be explained by the principles of behavior theory.

ANIMAL COGNITIONS

Much of the early discussion of behavior theory focused on intsrumental learning. One influential critic, Edward C. Tolman (1886–1959) argued that in instrumental learning an animal acquires various items of knowledge, or *cognitions.* These bits of knowledge are organized so that they can be utilized when needed. This is very different from asserting that the animal acquires a tendency to perform a particular response. To the *cognitive theorist,* the response an animal acquires in the course of a learning experiment is only an index that a given cognition has been gained. It is an indispensable measuring stick, but it is not the thing that is being measured. The essence of what is learned is something within an animal, a private event which will only become public when the animal acts upon its newly acquired knowledge.

Evidence that animals acquire cognitions comes from a number of experiments designed to determine whether instrumental learning can occur without the performance of the relevant response. Many behavior theorists claim that performance is an indispensable ingredient for instrumental learning. They assert that the animal "learns by doing" and in no other way. However, several studies suggest that this is not the case. Rats have been ferried from one end of a large room to another in transparent trolley cars. Later tests showed that they had learned something about the general features of the room even though they had not performed any relevant instrumental responses during their trolley-car ride (Gleitman, 1963). They had acquired what Tolman called a "cognitive map" that indicates what is where and what leads to what (Tolman, 1948).

In another study, rats were run in an enclosed *T*-maze that had a black end box on one side and a white one on the other (Figure 4.32). Both ends contained food and the animals chose indifferently between them on several trials. Subsequently, the animals were placed into each box by hand without actually running the maze. In one end box they now found food as before; in the other they were shocked. After all this, the animals were again allowed to run down the original *T*-maze. Now virtually all of them chose the side away from the end box in which they had been shocked. Clearly, the rats had learned which turn led to which box,

Edward C. Tolman (Courtesy Psychology Department, University of California, Berkeley)

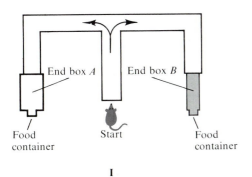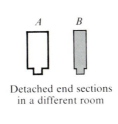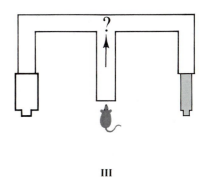

| I | II | III |

4.32 Proving that rats learn what leads to where *(I) Floor plan of a maze in the first phase of an experiment during which rats could learn that a left turn leads to end box A, a right turn to end box B. (II) The second phase of the experiment in which the two end boxes were detached from the rest of the maze and the animals were shocked in one of them, say, A. (III) In the third phase of the experiment, the animals were returned to the original situation. If they could put the two experiences together, then, having learned that a left turn led to A and that A led to shock, they should turn right—that is, away from shock. The results showed that they did. (After Tolman and Gleitman, 1949)*

but this cognition led to selective action only after the two boxes had acquired their new significance. In effect, the animals had to combine two experiences. During the first phase of the experiment, they presumably learned to associate a particular turn with a particular end box. During the second phase, they further learned that a particular end box brought shock. The results of the final test indicate that they were able to put these two experiences together—an argument against the view that all instrumental learning depends on the strengthening or weakening of particular response tendencies (Tolman and Gleitman, 1949).

Similar ***latent learning*** effects have been obtained in a number of other studies. A classic example is an experiment in which rats were run through a maze without a reward for ten days. When food was finally placed in the goal box, there was an abrupt decline in errors. Presumably the rats had learned something about the maze during the preceding days. But they did not show that they had learned until the reward was introduced. Before then, what they had learned was only latent but not yet manifest (Tolman and Honzik, 1930).

INSIGHTFUL BEHAVIOR

Köhler's studies of chimpanzees   The work on cognitions in rats showed that animals can know something without manifesting this knowledge in their actions. But it said very little about the intellectual capacities this knowledge revealed. Evidence that bore on this point came from an early study of chimpanzees, undertaken by the German psychologist Wolfgang Köhler (1887–1968) only a decade or so after Thorndike's study of cats in a puzzle box.

Köhler believed that animals can behave intelligently. To be sure, Thorndike's cats had shown little signs of understanding, but perhaps cats are not the best subjects if one wants to determine the upper reaches of animal intellect. A closer relative of man, such as a chimpanzee, might prove a better choice. Even more important, Köhler believed that Thorndike had loaded the dice in favor of blind trial and error, for the problems he had posed his cats were often impossible to solve in any other way. Thus, even an intellectual supercat could never hit on the idea of yanking the wire that pulled the door latch except by pure chance; there was no other way, for all the strings and pulleys were hidden from the animal's view. To Köhler the real question was whether animals would behave intelligently if the conditions were optimum—when all of the ingredients of the solution were visibly present.

Wolfgang Köhler (Courtesy The Warder Collection)

A   B   C   D

4.33 Tool using in chimpanzees (A)
Using a stick as a pole to jump up to a ba-
nana. (B) Using a stick as a club to beat
down a banana. (C and D) Erecting three-
and four-story structures to reach a
banana. (From Köhler, 1925)

4.34 Tool making in chimpanzees Sul-
tan making a double stick. (From Köhler,
1925)

Köhler's procedure was simple. The chimpanzee was placed in an enclosed play area. Somewhere out of its reach was a desirable lure (usually some fruit, such as a banana). To obtain it, the ape had to employ some nearby object as a tool. In this the animals were remarkably successful. They learned to use sticks as rakes to haul in bananas placed on the ground just outside the cage, but beyond the reach of their arms. Sticks were equally useful to club down fruit which was hung too high overhead. Some chimpanzees used the sticks as a pole; they stood it upright under the banana, frantically climbed up its fifteen-foot length, and grasped their reward just as the stick toppled over (a considerable intellectual as well as gymnastic feat, demonstrating the virtues of a healthy mind in a healthy body). The chimpanzees also learned to use boxes as "climb-upon-ables," dragging them under the banana and then stepping on top to claim their prizes. Eventually they even became builders, piling boxes on top of boxes and finally erecting structures that went up to four (rather shaky) stories, as Köhler spurred them on to ever-greater architectural accomplishments by progressively raising the height of the lure (Figure 4.33).

Occasionally the apes became toolmakers as well as tool-users. For example, when in need of a stick, they might break off a branch of a nearby tree. Even more impressive was the manufacture of a double stick. A particularly gifted chimpanzee called Sultan was faced with a banana far out of his reach. There were two bamboo sticks in his cage, but neither of them was long enough to rake in the lure. After many attempts to reach the banana with one stick or another, Sultan finally hit upon the solution. He pushed the thinner of the two sticks into the hollow inside of the thicker one and then drew the banana toward himself, his reach now enlarged by the length of two sticks (Figure 4.34).

Evidence for insight Köhler denied that such achievements were the result of a mechanical strengthening and weakening of response tendencies. On the contrary, the animals behaved as if they had attained some ***insight*** into the relevant relationships, as if they *saw* what led to what.

Köhler offered several lines of evidence. To begin with, when the problem was once solved, the animals usually performed smoothly and continuously thereafter as if they "knew what they were doing," in marked contrast to Thorndike's cats who went on fumbling for many trials. In further opposition to Thorndike's findings was the fact that often the insightful solution came quite suddenly, sometimes after a pause during which the chimpanzee only moved its head and eyes as if to study the situation. Once the correct response was made, further errors were rare.

The most convincing evidence for the view that the chimpanzees learned by insight rather than by blind trial and error came from tests in which the situation was changed to determine what the animals would *transfer* from the original task. This is a method that serves to define what has been learned in any given situation. Teachers use just this approach to find out what their students have understood. Consider a young child who quickly answers "7" when confronted by the symbols "$3 + 4 = ?$" Has he really grasped the notion of addition? A simple test might be to present him with another problem, "$4 + 3 = ?$" If he is now bewildered, he presumably has learned merely to give a specific answer to a specific question, but if his reply again is "7," he may be on the way to genuine arithmetic insight. Köhler used similar tests on his chimpanzees. For example, he took animals who had previously learned to use a box as a platform and presented the high lure again, but now with all boxes removed. The animals were quick to find other objects, such as a table or a small ladder, which they promptly dragged to the proper place. These were not the only substitutes. On one occasion, Sultan came over to Köhler, pulled him by the arm until he was under the banana, and then showed that in a pinch even the director of the Prussian anthropoid station would do as a climb-upon-able.

To Köhler, the main criterion for insight was wide and appropriate transfer. But is this kind of transfer really so hard to explain in behavior theory's terms? Can't one say that it is simply some form of stimulus generalization? A dog who has previously been conditioned to salivate to a tone of 1,000 hertz will also salivate when presented with 2,000 hertz. How is this different from the kind of transfer that we regard as a sign of understanding?

The answer is that in stimulus generalization, transfer is only based on perceptual similarity. A variety of stimuli are seen (or heard or felt) as more or less alike and so they are responded to in a similar fashion. But in the case of the "$2 + 4$" example, the transfer is based on something else, on a common principle, on an abstract conceptual relationship. The important thing is not that "$2 + 4$" and "$4 + 2$" (not to speak of "$1 + 5$", "$3 + 3$" and so on) look alike. The important thing is that they are alike in meaning.

ABSTRACT CONCEPTS IN ANIMALS

Learning to learn in monkeys A number of studies have shown that various primates can respond to certain abstract, conceptual aspects of a situation that transcend their perceptual characteristics. An example is **learning to learn** in monkeys. This phenomenon has been studied extensively by Harry Harlow (1905–1981). Harlow trained rhesus monkeys on a long series of different discriminations. Each discrimination involved two stimulus objects that were never used again on any further problem. Thus, in the first discrimination, the monkey

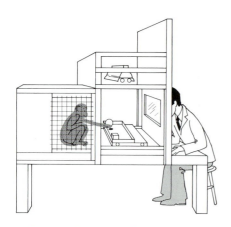

4.35 A device for studying discrimination learning in monkeys *A monkey is presented with a stimulus tray that contains two (sometimes three or more) wells. In one of the wells is a desirable food reward, such as a raisin or a grape. The wells are covered with various objects, such as the sphere and cube shown in the figure. One of these objects is designated as the correct stimulus. The animal's task is to learn which of these objects is correct, push it aside, and pick up its reward from the well below. (After Harlow, 1949)*

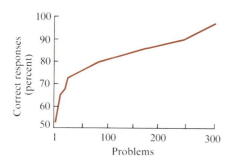

4.36 Discrimination learning sets *Monkeys were given 344 different discrimination problems, each for 6 trials. The curve shows the animals' average performance on the second trial. (After Harlow, 1949)*

might have to choose between a small red square and a large blue circle; in the second, between a white line and a yellow dot; in the third, between a green pyramid and a black hemisphere. In one such study, the animals were trained on 344 separate discrimination problems (Figure 4.35). The results were dramatic. Learning the first few discriminations was difficult, but the animals became better and better the more new problems they encountered. After 300 of them, they solved each new problem in just one trial. In Harlow's terms, the monkeys had acquired a ***learning set;*** they had learned how to learn a certain kind of problem (Figure 4.36; Harlow, 1949).

What did the animals learn during this long series of different discrimination problems that finally enabled them to solve such tasks so efficiently? At first, each monkey was prone to certain kinds of errors that it made quite systematically—choosing the right side, or alternating sides from trial to trial, or always choosing the larger of the two objects. Such errors gradually dropped out, as if the monkey realized that none of these factors was relevant to the solution. Once these error tendencies were eliminated, the animals could eventually adopt a new strategy, appropriate not just to one discrimination problem but to all of them. If you find food under some object, choose it again; if you don't, switch to the other. This "Win-stay, lose-shift" strategy obviously does not depend upon the specific stimuli employed in the task. It is based on a conceptual, not a perceptual, relationship (Harlow, 1959).

Symbol manipulation in chimpanzees   Further demonstrations of abstract concepts in animals have been obtained by David Premack who has tried to map the upper limits of the cognitive capacities in several chimpanzees, including his prize pupil, Sarah (Premack, 1976; Premack and Premack, 1983).

An example of such an abstract concept is the notion "same-different." Consider a situation in which an animal is shown three items. One serves as the sample; the other two are the alternatives. The animal's task is to choose the alternative that matches the sample. Suppose the alternatives are a triangle and a square. If so, the triangle is correct if the sample is a triangle; conversely, if the sample is a square. This procedure is called ***matching to sample*** (see Figure 4.37).

There is little doubt that animals other than primates can be taught to match if they are given enough trials to learn. Thus, pigeons can be taught to peck at a green rather than a yellow key if the sample is green, and to peck at the yellow key if the sample is yellow. But does that mean that they understand what sameness means? The question is whether they somehow understand that the relation between two yellow keys is the same as the relation between two equal tones or two identical triangles, that in all cases the two items are the same. To test whether the animal has this abstract concept of sameness, we have to determine whether there is any transfer from one matching-to-sample situation to another one in which the particular stimulus items are quite different. Take the pigeon that has learned to match green-green. Does this training facilitate learning to match red-red, or better yet, triangle-triangle? By and large, the answer seems to be no (Premack, 1978; but see also Zentall and Hogan, 1974). It can recognize that two reds are the same. But it does not recognize that this sameness is the identical relation that exists between two other equal stimulus items.

The situation is quite different in chimpanzees. Having matched to sample on only three prior problems, Sarah and a few other animals readily handled new

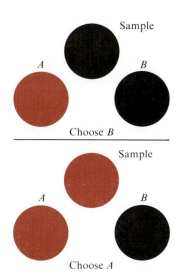

4.37 Matching to sample *The figure shows the procedure of a typical matching-to-sample experiment. The top circle in each panel represents the sample. The subject's task is to choose the one circle among the two at the bottom which matches the sample in color. In the top panel of the figure, the correct choice is B; in the bottom panel, it is A.*

(In top panel: Sample, A, B, Choose B. In bottom panel: Sample, A, B, Choose A.)

problems, performing perfectly on the very first trial. Even more impressive is the fact that Sarah learned to use two special tokens to indicate *same* and *different.* She was first shown two identical objects, such as two cups, and was then given a token whose intended meaning was *same.* Her task was to place this *same* token between the two cups. She was then presented with two different objects, such as a cup and a spoon, was given yet another token intended to mean *different,* and was required to place this *different* token between the cup and the spoon. After several such trials, she was tested with several pairs of items, some identical and some different, had to decide whether to place the *same* or the *different* token between them, and did so correctly (see Figure 4.38).

Such accomplishments show that chimpanzees can develop a way of thinking about the world that goes beyond the specific perceptual relations of the concrete moment. Like pigeons, they can of course respond to these concrete relationships, for example, the relationship between, say, red and red, circle and circle, A-flat and A-flat. But unlike pigeons, chimpanzees can also deal with some **higher-order relationships,** the relations that hold between the various concrete relationships. They can therefore recognize that the relation between red and red is identical to that between circle and circle, and for that matter between hippopotamus and hippopotamus—that in all of these the relation is *sameness.*

ACCESSING WHAT ONE KNOWS

The formation of abstract concepts is certainly one of the characteristics of what we normally call intelligence. But it is not the only one. Another criterion is whether the animal has some **access** to its own intellectual operations.

Consider a pigeon who finds its way home over large distances. That bird is a brilliant navigator. It refers to the stars, to the sun, to a number of landmarks, and somehow calculates the correct path with remarkable accuracy. But we don't therefore regard the bird as especially intelligent. The reason is that we are convinced that it doesn't really know what it is doing. Its brain constitutes a marvelous navigational computer. But the bird can't use that computer for any purpose other than that for which it was installed by evolution. It has no access to its own intellectual machinery.

In this regard, the pigeon is quite different from a human being. At least to some extent, we do have access to our own mental functioning. We think and re-

4.38 The same-different problem *(After A. Premack, 1976)*

Means *same*

Means *different*

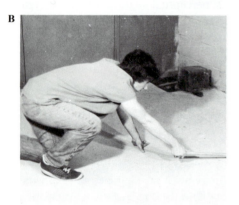

4.39 Knowing about problem solving
(A) End of brief videotaped segment showing Sarah's trainer reaching for bananas that are too high for him. (B) Two pictured alternatives. One shows the trainer stepping on a box. The other shows him reaching along the ground with a stick. Sarah tended to choose the picture that showed the correct solution; in the present case, the trainer stepping on the top of the box. (From Premack and Woodruff, 1978)

member and know that we think and remember. And we can use these and other intellectual capacities very broadly. This access to our own intellectual functions is by no means total; as we will see later on, it is especially limited in childhood (see Chapter 14). Our present point is only that this access is one of the defining features of intelligent behavior and is a characteristic of that intellectual generalist, man (Rozin, 1976a).

Some recent studies by Premack and his collaborators suggest that intellectual access is not confined to humans. They showed Sarah several videotaped scenes of a trainer struggling with different problems. In one scene, he tried to reach a banana suspended high above him. In another, he vainly stretched his arm toward a banana on the floor outside of a cage. After Sarah saw the tapes, she was shown different photographs of the trainer engaged in one of several actions. In one picture he was climbing on a box, in another he was shoving a stick under the wire mesh of the cage, and so on. Sarah's job was to pick the photograph that depicted the appropriate problem solution. Thus, if she was first shown a scene in which the trainer struggled to reach an overhead banana, she had to choose the picture of a man stepping on a box. Sarah did quite well, succeeding in 21 out of 24 trials (Figure 4.39).

Sarah's success in this task suggests that the chimpanzee's problem-solving ability goes further even than Köhler had thought. To be sure, Sarah can solve a variety of spatial problems and can do so insightfully. But her ability may go beyond this. She not only solves problems, she also seems to know something *about* problem solving. She recognizes that the trainer has a problem, what this problem is, and how it should be solved. To this extent, she has some access to her own intellectual processes.

The Generality of Behavior Theory

What is the upshot of the behavior theorists' efforts, which began with the studies of Pavlov and Thorndike some eighty years ago? There is no doubt that they uncovered some vital phenomena of human and animal behavior, for the basic principles of classical and instrumental learning are still regarded as valid, despite some qualifications that may be required by the work on biological constraints on learning. And these principles have been fruitfully extended and applied in many fields. What is debatable is the generality of these principles. Behavior theorists had claimed that their formulations could account for all of learning and all of behavior. But it now appears that this claim was premature. Behavior theory seems to have overemphasized the role of blind, arbitrary learning and to have ignored the built-in tendencies that differentiate various species. As a result, it tends to overestimate the intellectual flexibility of comparatively lower animals. And it likewise underestimates the kind of learning which many animals, especially the primates and most especially humans, are capable of.

Many of the critiques of behavior theory hinge on the fact that animals—and of course, humans—are capable of cognition. Rats learn what leads to where in a maze, while chimpanzees solve problems insightfully and can acquire certain abstract concepts. Such phenomena suggest that psychological functions concern not just what animals and humans do but also what they *know*. This runs counter to behavior theory's primary emphasis, which is on overt action. That action must be a major focus of psychology goes without saying. But it should not be the only one. Knowledge and the ways in which it is acquired—that is, cognition—are no less important as subjects of psychological inquiry. And these are the topics which we take up next.

SUMMARY

1. The simplest of all forms of learning is *habituation,* a decline in the tendency to respond to stimuli that have become familiar through repeated exposure.

2. In habituation the organism learns that it has encountered a stimulus before. In *classical conditioning,* first studied by I. P. Pavlov, it learns about the *association* between one stimulus and another. Prior to conditioning, an *unconditioned stimulus* or *UCS* (such as food) elicits an *unconditioned response* or *UCR* (such as salivation). After repeated pairings of the UCS with a *conditioned stimulus* or *CS* (such as a buzzer), this CS alone will evoke a *conditioned response* or *CR* (here again, salivation) that is often similar to the UCR.

3. The strength of conditioning is measured by the readiness with which CS elicits CR. This strength increases with the number of *reinforced trials,* that is, pairings of CS and UCS. Nonreinforced trials, during which CS is presented without the UCS, lead to *extinction,* as manifested by a decreased tendency of CS to evoke CR.

4. The CR is elicited not only by CS but also by stimuli that are similar to it. This effect, *stimulus generalization,* increases the greater the similarity between CS and the new stimulus. To train the animal to respond to CS and not to other stimuli, one stimulus (CS^+) is presented with the UCS, another (CS^-) is presented without the UCS. The more similar CS^+ is to CS^-, the more difficult this *discrimination* will be.

5. Studies on the role of the interval between CS and UCS suggest that the CS serves a signaling function since CS-UCS pairings are most effective when the CS precedes UCS by half a second or so. Further evidence for such a preparatory function comes from work on conditioned drug effects, where the CR is often the very opposite of the UCR.

6. A number of investigators have asked how the animal learns that CS is a signal for UCS. The evidence shows that CS-UCS pairings alone will not suffice; there must be trials on which the absence of CS goes along with the absence of UCS. This allows the animal to discover that UCS is *contingent* (dependent) upon CS. The discovery of this contingency may be impeded by a number of factors including *overshadowing* and *blocking.*

7. In classical conditioning, the UCS is presented regardless of whether the animal performs the CR or not. In another form of simple learning, *instrumental conditioning* (or *operant conditioning*), something analogous to the UCS, reward or *reinforcement,* is only delivered upon performance of the appropriate instrumental response.

8. An early study of instrumental conditioning was conducted by E. L. Thorndike using cats that learned to perform an arbitrary response to escape from a *puzzle box.* As Thorndike saw it, what the animals learned involved no understanding but was rather based on a gradual strengthening of the correct response and a weakening of the incorrect one. To account for this, he proposed his *law of effect,* which states that the tendency to perform a response is strengthened if it is followed by a reward (reinforcement) and weakened if it is not.

9. During the past fifty years or so, the major figure in the study of instrumental conditioning has been B. F. Skinner, who was one of the first theorists to insist on a sharp distinction between classical conditioning in which the CR is *elicited* by the CS, and instrumental (which he calls *operant*) conditioning in which the instrumental response, or *operant,* is

emitted from within. Operants are strengthened by *reinforcement,* but their acquisition may require some initial *shaping* by the method of *successive approximations.*

10. Operants can be strengthened by both *primary reinforcers* whose reinforcing power is unlearned, or by *conditioned reinforcers* whose ability to reinforce a response comes from prior pairings with primary reinforcement. A further supplement to the law of effect concerns the *delay of reinforcement:* The shorter the interval between the response and reinforcement, the stronger that response will be.

11. During *partial reinforcement* the response is reinforced only some of the time. The rule that determines the occasions on which reinforcement is given is a *schedule of reinforcement.* Responses that were originally acquired during partial reinforcement are harder to extinguish than those learned when the response was always reinforced.

12. *Positive reinforcers* are stimuli that organisms normally seek; for example, food when they are hungry. In contrast, *negative reinforcers* are *aversive stimuli* that organisms try to avoid; for example, pain. Depending on the situation, negative reinforcers can weaken or strengthen instrumental responses. In *punishment training,* the organism learns *not* to perform a response that has been followed by an aversive stimulus. In *escape* and *avoidance learning,* the animal learns to perform a response. In escape learning, this response stops some aversive stimulus that has already begun; in avoidance learning, it averts it altogether. Some of the phenomena of avoidance learning may be relevant to the understanding and possible therapy of certain maladaptive conditions in humans, such as *phobias.*

13. In instrumental conditioning, the relevant contingency is between a response and an outcome. When there is no such contingency, the organism learns that it has no *response control.* Threatening conditions in which there is no response control may engender *learned helplessness,* which often generalizes to other situations.

14. An important practical application of behavior theory is *behavior therapy,* an attempt to use the principles of conditioning to cure or alleviate various psychological disorders. Some behavior therapists stress classical conditioning and try to cure phobias and related problems by *flooding* or *desensitization.* Others use operant techniques to eliminate unwanted behaviors and to strengthen desirable ones, in some cases by the use of *token economies.* Another area of application is *behavioral medicine,* which deals with the relation between behavior and various physiological ills.

15. According to behavior theory, the connections established by classical or instrumental conditioning are essentially *arbitrary;* that is, they are independent of the relations between the elements to be connected. This view is challenged by the fact that certain CSs are more readily associated with some UCSs than with others, as shown by studies of *learned taste aversions* in rats. Similar effects occur in instrumental conditioning, for it turns out that some responses are more readily strengthened by certain reinforcers than by others.

16. Another criticism of behavior theory is that it underestimates the intellectual capacities of higher species. Early critics such as W. Köhler and E. C. Tolman argued that animals acquire *cognitions,* which represent a change in what they *know* rather than in what they *do.* These cognitions sometimes indicate an impressive ability to respond to abstract, *conceptual* relationships. Early evidence came from Köhler's studies of *insightful* learning in chimpanzees, who showed wide and appropriate transfer when later tested in novel situations. Later work showed that monkeys acquire *learning sets* and learn to learn when solving discrimination problems. Another example is provided by chimpanzees who can acquire certain *higher-order* concepts such as "same-different" and seem to have some *access* to their own cognitive operations.

PART II

Cognition

The approach to mental life we have considered thus far emphasizes action, whether natively given or modified by learning. It is an approach that always asks what organisms do and how they do it. We now turn to another approach to mental functioning that asks what organisms know and how they come to know it.

Both humans and many animals are capable of knowledge, though in our own species, knowing (or cognition *is vastly more refined. We know about the world directly around us,* perceiving *objects and events that are in our here and now, like the rose that we can see and smell. We also know about events in our past at least some of which are stored in our* memory *and can be retrieved at some later time; the rose may fade, but we can recall what it looked like when it was still in bloom. Our knowledge can be transformed and manipulated by* thinking; *we can somehow sift and analyze our experiences to emerge with new and often abstract notions, so that we can think of the faded rose petals as but one stage in a reproductive cycle which in turn reflects the procession of the seasons. Finally, we can communicate our knowledge to others by the usage of* language, *a uniquely human capacity which allows us to accumulate knowledge across the generations, each building upon the discoveries of the preceding.*

CHAPTER 5

Sensory Processes

To survive, we must know the world around us. For most objects in the world are charged with meaning. Some are food, others are mates, still others are mortal enemies. The ability to distinguish between these—say, between a log and a crocodile—is literally a matter of life and death. To make these distinctions, we have to use our senses. We must do our best to see, hear, and smell the crocodile so that we can recognize it for what it is and can do so before it sees, hears, smells, and (especially) tastes and touches us.

THE ORIGINS OF KNOWLEDGE

The study of sensory experience grows out of an ancient question: Where does human knowledge come from? Most philosophers in the past subscribed to one of two opposed positions. The *empiricists* maintained that all knowledge is acquired through experience. In contrast, the *nativists* argued that many aspects of our knowledge are based on innately given characteristics of the human mind (or, as we would now say, of the brain).

The Empiricist View

A major proponent of the empiricist position was the English philosopher John Locke (1632–1704). Locke maintained that all knowledge comes through the senses. There are no innate ideas; at birth, the human mind is a blank tablet, a *tabula rasa,* upon which experience leaves its marks.

John Locke (Courtesy National Library of Medicine)

Let us suppose the mind to be, as we say, a white paper void of all characters, without any ideas:—How comes it to be furnished? Whence comes it by that vast store which the busy and boundless fancy of man has painted on it with an almost endless variety? Whence has it all the materials of reason and knowledge? To this I answer, in one word, from *experience.* In that all our knowledge is founded; and from that it ultimately derives itself (Locke, 1690).

Locke's view fit in well with the emerging liberalism that was the dominant sentiment of the rising middle classes during the eighteenth century. The merchants and manufacturers of Western Europe had little use for the hereditary privileges of a landed aristocracy or the divine right of kings to govern (and worse, to tax) as they chose. Under the circumstances, they readily grasped at any doctrine that proclaimed the essential equality of all men. If all men enter life with a *tabula rasa,* then all distinctions among them must be due entirely to a difference in their environments.

DISTAL AND PROXIMAL STIMULI

Given the assumption that all knowledge comes through the senses, it was natural enough to ask about the kind of knowledge that the senses can give us. What is the information that the senses receive? Consider vision. We look at a tree some distance away. Light reflected from the tree's outer surface enters through the pupil of the eye, is gathered by the lens, and is cast as an image upon the photosensitive region at the rear of the eye called the **retina.** The stimuli that are involved in this visual sequence can be described in either of two ways. We can talk about the **distal stimulus,** an object or event in the world outside, such as the tree. (This is typically at some distance from the perceiver, hence the term *distal.*) We can also talk about the **proximal stimulus,** the pattern of stimulus energies that takes its origin at the distal stimulus and finally impinges on a sensory surface of the organism (hence, the term *proximal.*). In our example, this proximal stimulus would be the optical image the tree casts on the retina. As perceivers, our interest obviously centers upon the distal stimulus, the real object in the world outside. We want to know about the tree, not its retinal image. Our interest is in the tree's real size, its distance away from us, the kinds of leaves it has, and so on. But we can only learn about the distal stimulus through the proximal stimuli to which it gives rise. There is no way of really seeing the tree out there without a retinal image of the tree. The same holds for the other senses. We can only smell a rotten egg (the distal stimulus) because of hydrogen sulfide molecules suspended in the air which eddies over the sensory cells in our nasal cavities (the proximal stimulus).

If the senses are the only portals we have to the world outside, the proximal stimuli are the only messengers that are allowed to pass information through them. Such heirs of Locke as Bishop George Berkeley (1685–1753) were quick to show that this fact has enormous consequences. For one thing, the sensory information provided by the proximal stimulus seems to lack many of the qualities that presumably characterize the external object (that is, the distal stimulus) to which this information refers.

Berkeley pointed out that we cannot tell the size of the physical object from the size of its retinal image. Our tree might be a miniature plant nearby or a giant one in the distance. By the same token, we canot tell whether an object is in motion or at rest from its retinal image alone, for motion of the image may be caused by

Bishop George Berkeley *(Detail from* The Bermuda Group *by John Smibert; courtesy Yale University Art Gallery, gift of Isaac Lothrop of Plymouth, Mass.)*

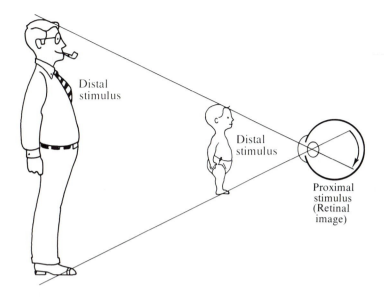

5.1   Distal and proximal stimuli   *The baby in diapers and his father are distal stimuli, real objects in the world outside. The proximal stimuli they give rise to are the images they cast on the retina. In the example, the baby is one-third the size of his father. But since the father is three times farther removed from the observer's eye than the baby, the size of the retinal image he casts is the same as the one cast by the baby.*

motion of the external object or by movements of the observer's eye. It appears that the knowledge that comes by way of the retinal image is very meager (see Figure 5.1).

SENSATIONS

Considerations of this sort led later empiricists to assume that the raw materials out of which knowledge is constructed are **sensations.** These are the primitive experiences that the senses give us and upon which we must then build. Green and brown are examples of visual sensations. An example of an auditory sensation would be a loud A-flat. An example of a gustatory (that is, taste) sensation would be a bitter taste. According to the empiricists, our perceptual experience is ultimately composed of such sensations—a mosaic of colored patches, tones of different pitch and loudness, sweets and sours, and so on.

Can this description possibly do justice to the richness of our perceptual world? The fact is that we do see trees (and innumerable other objects) and not mere patches of green and brown. While Bishop Berkeley might argue that our vision cannot inform us about depth or true size, in actual life we seem to have little difficulty in telling how far an object is away from us. (Were it otherwise, every automobile would become a wreck within minutes of leaving the showroom.) And we can in fact perceive the true size of an object. After all, even Berkeley would have had little trouble in distinguishing between a tiger in the distance and a kitten close by.

How did the empiricists reconcile these facts with their assumptions about the nature of sensation? Their answer was learning.

THE ROLE OF ASSOCIATION

The empiricists assumed that the organized character and the meaningfulness of our perceptual world are achieved by prior experience. The key to this accomplishment was held to be **association,** the process whereby one sensation is linked to another. The basic idea was very simple: If two sensations occur together often enough, eventually one of them will evoke the idea of the other. According to the

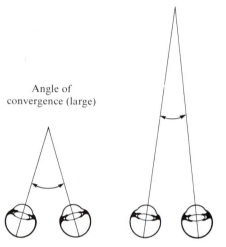

Angle of
convergence (small)

Angle of
convergence (large)

5.2 Convergence *When we look at an object, our eyes turn so as to converge upon it. The closer the object is to us, the more the eyes will have to turn, thus producing a larger angle of convergence. This angle of convergence may then provide some information about the object's distance. (After Coren, Porac, and Ward, 1978)*

Immanuel Kant *(Courtesy National Library of Medicine)*

empiricists, this associative linkage is the cement that binds the separate components of the perceptual world to each other.*

An example of how the associative principle was applied to problems of perception is Berkeley's explanation of perceived depth. In his view, the perception of distance is not directly based upon vision but rather results from associations between certain visual signs (which were later called *cues*) and sensations of touch and motor movement. Consider *convergence,* the angular motion of the two eyes as they focus upon an object. The closer the object, the more the eyes will swivel toward each other, and the larger will be the angle of convergence. As the object moves farther away, the angle of convergence becomes smaller and smaller, as the eyes approach a parallel position (see Figure 5.2). But how would we know that such and such an angle meant such and such a distance? Berkeley believed that this knowledge is provided by experience (Berkeley, 1709).

According to Berkeley, the important events date back to the crib. The infant reaches out for various objects, such as a toy. Sometimes the toy is close by; if so, a small arm movement is enough to grasp it. Sometimes the toy is farther off; the infant must then reach farther out. In both cases, the arm (and leg) movements are preceded by a particular angle of convergence. If this angle is large (toy nearby), the subsequent reaching movement will be small. If the angle is small (toy farther off), the arms will extend farther out. These states of affairs will occur over and over again until they finally forge an association between particular sensations of convergence and the memory of certain reaching movements. Eventually, the child no longer has to reach for an object to know how far it is away. She sees it, senses a given angle of convergence, and remembers a certain reaching movement. According to Berkeley, this remembered reaching movement is the basis of visually perceived distance.

Berkeley was well aware that there are cues for distance other than sensations of convergence. Some of these had been noted by the painters of the Renaissance who discovered several techniques for rendering a three-dimensional world on a two-dimensional canvas. Among them was *linear perspective*—objects appear to be farther away as they decrease in size (Figure 5.3). To Berkeley, the explanation was again a matter of prior association. Visual cues of perspective generally precede reaching or walking; eventually, the visual cue alone will produce the memory of the appropriate movement and thus the experience of depth.

The Nativist Rejoinder

The major theoretical alternative to the empiricist conception is *nativism,* which asserts that many aspects of perceptual experience are part of our natural endowment and do not depend on learning. This general position has a long ancestry with roots that go back as far as Plato. In more recent times, the more influential nativist rejoinder to empiricism came from the German philosopher Immanuel Kant (1724–1804). Kant argued that knowledge cannot come from sensory input alone; there must also be certain preexisting "categories" according to which this sensory material is ordered and organized. Examples are space, time, and causality—categories which, according to Kant, are *a priori,* built into the mind (or, as

---

* It is obvious that the notion of association is at the root of many of the theories of learning we have described in previous chapters. For instance, Pavlov's conceptions of classical conditioning are in many ways derived from the views of the early associationists.

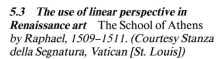

5.3   The use of linear perspective in Renaissance art   The School of Athens by Raphael, 1509–1511. (Courtesy Stanza della Segnatura, Vatican [St. Louis])

we would now say, into the nervous system). In Kant's view, there is no way in which we can see the world except in terms of these categories. It is as if we looked at the world through colored spectacles that we could never take off; if they were red, then redness would necessarily be part of everything we see. According to Kant, what experience does is to provide the sensory input that is then ordered according to the *a priori* categories. But the categories themselves, and the way in which they order the sensory information, are natively given.

Of course neither nativism nor empiricism can exist in absolute, pure form. Ultimately, the structure of our perceptual world surely depends upon both "nature" (our innate endowment) and "nurture" (learning). What is at issue is the *relative* contribution of these two factors.

PSYCHOPHYSICS

The dispute between empiricists and nativists focused attention on the role of the senses and prodded later investigators into efforts to discover just how these senses function. The question they were concerned with can be stated very simply: What is the chain of events that begins with a stimulus and leads up to reports such as "a bitter taste," a "dull pressure," or a "brightish green"? The details of this sequence are obviously very different for the different senses. Vision differs from hearing, and both differ from taste—in the stimuli that normally excite them, in their receptors, in the qualities of their sensations. Even so, we can analyze the path from stimulus to sensory experience in quite similar ways, whatever the particular sense may be.

139

In all cases, one can crudely distinguish three steps in the sequence. First, there is the proximal stimulus. Second, there is the neural chain of events that this stimulus gives rise to. The stimulus is translated (technically, **transduced**) into the only language that all neurons understand, the nerve impulse. Once converted into this form (typically by specialized receptor cells), the message is transmitted further and often is modified by other parts of the nervous system. Third, there is some sort of psychological response to the message, often in the form of a conscious, sensory experience (or sensation).

The sensory sequence can be looked at from several points of view. One concerns the **psychophysical** relations between some property of the (physical) stimulus and the (psychological) sensory experience it ultimately gives rise to, quite apart from the intervening neural steps. There are a variety of stimuli to which the human organism is sensitive. They include chemicals suspended in air or dissolved in water, temperature changes on the skin, pressure on the skin or within various parts of the body, pressure in the form of sound waves, and electromagnetic radiations within the visible spectrum. In each case, the sensory system will not respond unless the stimulus energy is above some critical level of intensity, the so-called **absolute threshold.**

Sensory Quality

The different senses obviously produce sensations of different quality. For example, the sensations of pressure, A-flat, orange, or sour clearly belong to altogether different sensory domains (technically, to different **sense modalities**). To what factor shall we ascribe these differences in experienced quality? Is it the difference in the stimuli that produce these sensations? In 1826, the German physiologist Johannes Müller (1801–1858) argued that this answer was false. To be sure, visual sensations are usually produced by light waves, but occasionally other stimuli will serve as well. Strong pressure on the eyeballs leads us to see rings or stars (to the chagrin of boxers and the delight of cartoonists). Similarly, we can produce visual sensations by electric stimulation of various parts of the nervous system. Such facts led Müller to formulate his famous **doctrine of specific nerve energies.*** According to this law, the differences in experienced quality are caused not by differences in the stimuli but by the different nervous structures which these stimuli excite, most likely in centers higher up in the brain. Thus, were we able to rewire the nervous system so as to connect the optic nerve to the auditory cortex and the auditory nerve to the visual cortex we might be able to see thunder and hear lightning.

Some of Müller's successors extended his doctrine to cover qualitative differences within a given sense modality. For example, blue, green, and red are qualitatively different even though all three are colors. To the heirs of Müller, such a qualitative difference could only mean one thing: There had to be some decisive difference in the neural processes that underlie these different sensations, perhaps at the level of the receptors, perhaps higher up. This belief ultimately led to some fundamental discoveries about the physiological basis of various sensory experiences, such as color and pitch (Boring, 1942).

* Müller used the term *energy* for what we now call *quality.*

Gustav Theodor Fechner (Courtesy National Library of Medicine)

E. H. Weber (Courtesy National Library of Medicine)

Sensory Intensity

Measuring the magnitude of a stimulus is in principle easy enough. We measure the physical stimulus energy—in pounds, in degrees centigrade, in footcandles, in decibels, or whatever. But matters become more difficult when we try to assess *psychological intensity,* the magnitude of a sensation rather than that of a stimulus.

Gustav Theodor Fechner (1801–1887), the founder of psychophysics, believed that sensations cannot be measured directly. In his view, sensations and the stimuli that produce them belong to two totally different realms—to use the terms many philosophers employ, that of the body and that of the mind. If this is so, how can one possibly describe them by reference to the same yardstick? Fechner recommended a roundabout way. He argued that while sensations can't be compared to physical stimuli, they can at least be compared to each other. A subject can compare two of his own sensations and judge whether the two are the same or are different.

Consider the sensation of visual brightness produced by a patch of light projected on a certain part of the eye. We can ask, what is the minimal amount by which the original light intensity of the patch must be increased so that the subject experiences a sensation of brightness *just* greater than the one he had before. This amount is called the ***difference threshold.*** It produces a ***just-noticeable difference,*** or ***j.n.d.*** The j.n.d. is a psychological entity, for it describes a subject's ability to discriminate. But it is expressed in the units of the physical stimulus that produced it. (In our example, this would be millilamberts, a unit of illumination.) Fechner had found an indirect means to relate sensory magnitude to the physical intensity of the stimulus.

Before proceeding we should note that the absolute threshold may be considered as a special case of a difference threshold. Here the question is how much stimulus energy must be added to a zero stimulus before the subject can tell the difference between the old stimulus ("I see nothing") and the new ("Now I see it").

THE WEBER FRACTION

To Fechner, measuring j.n.d.'s was only the means to a larger goal—the formulation of a general law relating stimulus intensity to sensory magnitude. He believed that such a law could be built upon an empirical generalization first proposed by the German physiologist E. H. Weber (1795–1878) in 1834. Weber proposed that the size of the difference threshold is a constant ratio of the standard stimulus. Suppose that we can just tell the difference between 100 and 102 candles burning in an otherwise unilluminated room. If Weber is right, we would be able to just distinguish between 200 and 204 candles, 400 and 408, and so forth. Fechner was so impressed with this relationship that he referred to it as ***Weber's law,*** a label by which we still know it. Put algebraically, Weber's law is usually written as

$$\frac{\Delta I}{I} = C$$

where ΔI is the increment in stimulus intensity (that is, the j.n.d.) to a stimulus of intensity I (that is, the standard stimulus) required to produce a just-noticeable increase, and where C is a constant. The fraction $\Delta I/I$ is often referred to as the ***Weber fraction.***

Fechner and his successors performed numerous studies to determine whether Weber's law holds for all of the sensory modalities. In a rough sort of way, the answer seems to be yes, at least for much of the normal range of stimulus intensity within each sense.* The nervous system is evidently geared to notice relative differences rather than absolute ones.

Weber's law allows us to compare the sensitivity of different sensory modalities. Suppose we want to know whether the eye is more sensitive than the ear. How can we tell? We certainly cannot compare j.n.d.'s for brightness and for loudness. To mention only one problem, the values will be in different units—millilamberts for the first, decibels for the second. The problem is avoided if we consider the Weber fractions for the two modalities. If $\Delta I/I$ is small, the discriminating power of the sense modality is great; proportionally little must be added to the standard for a difference to be observed. The opposite holds when $\Delta I/I$ is large. It turns out that we are keener in discriminating brightness than loudness; the Weber fraction for the first is 1/62, for the second it is only 1/11. Weber fractions for other sense modalities are presented in Table 5.1.

Table 5.1 REPRESENTATIVE (MIDDLE-RANGE) VALUES FOR THE WEBER FRACTION FOR THE DIFFERENT SENSES

Sensory modality	Weber fraction ($\Delta I/I$)
Vision (brightness, white light)	1/60
Kinesthesis (lifted weights)	1/50
Pain (thermally aroused on skin)	1/30
Audition (tone of middle pitch and moderate loudness)	1/10
Pressure (cutaneous pressure "spot")	1/7
Smell (odor of India rubber)	1/4
Taste (table salt)	1/3

SOURCE: Geldard, 1962.

FECHNER'S LAW

Weber's law indicated that the more intense the stimulus, the more stimulus intensity has to be increased before the subject notices a change. By making a number of further assumptions, Fechner generalized Weber's finding to express a broader relationship between sensory and physical intensity. The result was **Fechner's law** which states that the strength of a sensation grows as the logarithm of stimulus intensity,

$$S = k \log I$$

where S stands for psychological (that is, subjective) magnitude, I for stimulus intensity, and k is a constant.

* Weber's law tends to break down at the two extremes of the intensity range, especially at the lower end (for example, for visual stimuli only slightly above absolute threshold). At these intensities, the Weber fraction is larger than it is in the middle range.

This law has been challenged on several grounds which are beyond the scope of this book. For our purposes, it is sufficient to note that a logarithmic law such as Fechner's makes good biological sense. The range of stimulus intensities to which we are sensitive is enormous. We can hear sounds as weak as the ticking of a watch twenty feet away and as loud as a pneumatic drill operating right next to us. Our nervous system has to have a mechanism to compress this huge range into some manageable scope, and this is precisely what a logarithmic transformation does for us.

Detection and Decision

The goal of psychophysics is to chart the relationships between a subject's responses and various characteristics of the physical stimulus. But are these physical characteristics the only factor that determine what the subject does or says? What about her expectations or wishes? The early psychophysicists believed that such factors could be largely disregarded. But a more recent approach to psychophysical measurement insists that they cannot. This is *signal-detection theory,* a very influential way of thinking about the way people make decisions.

RESPONSE BIAS

To understand how beliefs and attitudes come into play in a psychophysical experiment, consider a study of absolute thresholds. On every trial, the harried subject is forced into a decision. Is a stimulus there or isn't it? The decision is often difficult, for at times the stimulus is so weak that the subjects may be quite uncertain of their judgment. Under the circumstances, their *response bias* will necessarily exert an effect. Such a response bias is a preference for one response over another (here "yes" or "no"), quite apart from the nature of the stimuli. Thus, some subjects will approach the task with a free-and-easy attitude, cheerfully offering "yes" judgments whenever they are in doubt. Others will take a more conservative line and will never respond with a "yes" unless they are quite certain. This will produce a difference in obtained thresholds that will necessarily be lower for the subjects who are more liberal with their "yes" responses. But this only reflects a difference in response bias, not in sensory sensitivity. Both groups of subjects can presumably hear or see or feel the stimuli equally well. They only differ in their willingness to report a stimulus when they are unsure.

SIGNAL DETECTION

Such considerations make it clear that thresholds obtained with traditional techniques reflect two factors. One is sensitivity—how well the subject can hear or see the stimulus. The other is response bias—how readily the subject is willing to say "yes, I heard" when he is not certain. How can these two factors be separated?

The early psychophysicists tried to cope with this problem by using only subjects who were highly trained observers. In absolute threshold studies, such subjects were models of conservatism; they would never say "yes" unless they were completely certain. To maintain this attitude, the experimenters threw in an occasional "catch trial" on which there was no stimulus at all (Woodworth, 1938).

Table 5.2 THE FOUR POSSIBLE OUTCOMES OF THE DETECTION EXPERIMENT

	Responds "yes"	Responds "no"
Stimulus present	Hit	Miss
Stimulus absent	False alarm	Correct negative

Table 5.3 PAYOFF MATRIX THAT WILL PRODUCE A "YES" BIAS

	Subject says "yes"	Subject says "no"
Stimulus present	+ 10¢	− 10¢
Stimulus absent	− 1¢	+ 5¢

Signal-detection theory has developed a more systematic way of dealing with response bias. To begin with, it has provided a somewhat different testing procedure, the so-called ***detection experiment,*** in which catch trials are part of the regular procedure rather than just an occasional check to keep the subjects on their toes (Green and Swets, 1966).

One version of this procedure is related to the measurement of the absolute threshold. Here the question is whether the subject can detect the presence of a stimulus. We take a fairly weak stimulus and present it on half the trials. On the other half of the trials (interspersed in random order), we present no stimulus at all. We will now look at two kinds of errors. One is a ***miss,*** not reporting a stimulus when one is presented. The other is a ***false alarm,*** reporting a stimulus when in fact none is present. By the same token, there are two different kinds of correct responses: reporting a stimulus when it is actually there (a ***hit***) and not reporting one when none is present (a ***correct negative***) (see Table 5.2).

THE PAYOFF MATRIX

The detection experiment can tell us what factors underlie response bias. One such factor is differential payoff. Suppose we (literally) pay a subject for every hit and correct negative but penalize him for every miss and false alarm according to a prescribed schedule of gains and losses called a ***payoff matrix.*** Thus the subject might gain 10 cents for every hit and 5 cents for every correct negative, while losing 10 cents for every miss and only 1 cent for every false alarm. Such a payoff matrix will lead to a bias toward "yes" judgments (Table 5.3). Suppose there are, say, fifty trials on which the subject has no sensory information on the basis of which she can decide whether the stimulus is present or not. If she consistently says "yes," she will on the average be correct on twenty-five trials (thus collecting $2.50) and wrong on the other twenty-five (thus losing $0.25) for a net gain of $2.25. In contrast, consistent "no" judgments will lead to a net loss (+ $1.25 for the correct negatives and − $2.50 for the false alarms).

If the stimulus is presented on half of the trials, the payoff bias can be calculated easily by comparing the sum of the values under the *Says "yes"* column with the sum under the *Says "no"* column. In this example, these sums are + 9¢ and − 5¢ respectively. Under the circumstances, the subject will do well to adopt a liberal criterion and give a "yes" judgment whenever she is in doubt.

Illustrations of the effect of payoff matrices abound in real life. There the differential payoff is usually reckoned in units larger than pennies. Consider a team of radiologists poring over an X ray to look for a tiny spot that indicates the start of a malignant tumor. What are the penalties for error here? If the physicians decide there is no spot when there actually is one, their miss may cost the patient's life. If they decide that they see a spot when in fact there is none, their false alarm has other costs, such as the dangers of more elaborate clinical tests, let alone those of an operation. What the physicians ultimately decide will depend, both on what their eyes tell them as they inspect the X ray and also on the relative costs of the two possible errors they may commit.

SEPARATING SENSITIVITY AND RESPONSE BIAS

The preceding discussion showed that the subject's responses are jointly determined by his sensitivity to the stimulus and his response bias. If asked whether he hears a stimulus when presented with a thunderclap, he is almost certain to say

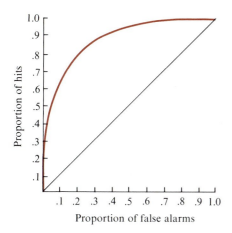

5.4 The ROC curve *The proportion of hits is plotted against the proportion of false alarms. The stimulus is kept constant but the response bias is systematically varied by asking subjects to adopt a more liberal attitude with their yeses. This bias becomes progressively larger as we move upward on the vertical axis (proportion of hits) and to the right on the horizontal axis (proportion of false alarms). Note that as the proportion of hits increases, so does the proportion of false alarms.*

"yes" even if his response bias is to say "no," for there is very little room for doubt given the intensity of the stimulus. But if the stimulus is relatively faint, he is very likely to say "no." Is there any way in which the effects of stimulus sensitivity and response bias can be disentangled? The detection procedure provides a means.

The first step is to vary response bias while keeping sensitivity constant. This can be done by changing the payoff matrix. Another way is to vary the proportion of trials on which no stimulus is presented—the fewer such trials, the greater the yes bias.

When response bias is varied in this fashion, the results are quite systematic. If we induce the subject to be more conservative, we find a reduction in the proportion of trials on which he is guilty of a false alarm. But at the same time, we also find a reduction in the proportion of hits. Similarly, upward shifts in the yes bias lead to an increase in the proportion of both hits and false alarms. These effects can be expressed graphically by plotting the two proportions against each other. The resulting function is known by the rather arcane designation of ***receiver-operating-characteristic curve,*** which is almost always abbreviated ***ROC curve*** (Figure 5.4).

The next step is to get an index of sensitivity that is uncontaminated by response bias. To do so, we obtain separate ROC curves for different levels of stimulus intensity (with each curve based on a separate detection experiment). The results are very striking. The stronger the stimulus, the more its ROC curve is bowed away from the main diagonal (Figure 5.5).

Why should this be so? To answer this question, consider a hypothetical detection experiment using a visual stimulus but a blind subject. Here the subject's sensitivity is obviously zero, so that his judgments must be based entirely upon response bias. For this blind subject, the stimulus does not exist, so that he is just as likely to obtain a hit as to strike a false alarm. In consequence, his ROC curve is necessarily the ***main diagonal.*** His yes bias can go up or down, but his proportion of hits and of false alarms will always be equal. Evidently, the main diagonal represents total insensitivity, an absolute inability to distinguish the presence of a stimulus from its absence. As sensitivity goes up, the ROC curve moves away from the diagonal. Thus, the displacement of the ROC curve from the main diagonal provides a pure measure of sensitivity for the stimulus on which the ROC curve is based; it is measured along the second diagonal (Figure 5.5).

SIGNAL DETECTION AND THE DECISION PROCESS

There is one question that we have not really considered. Why does the subject have so much trouble distinguishing between the presence of a stimulus and its absence? Signal-detection theory proposes an intriguing answer. It asserts that there really is no such thing as a zero stimulus.

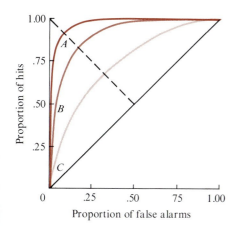

5.5 ROC curves for stimuli of different intensities *The figure shows ROC curves for three stimuli of increasing intensity (with A the strongest and C the weakest). Note that the stronger the stimulus, the more its ROC curve is displaced from the main diagonal. We can think of this diagonal as the ROC curve produced by a stimulus to which the subject is utterly insensitive. The displacement of the ROC curve from the main diagonal provides a pure index of sensitivity. It is measured along the second diagonal (broken line).*

The theory begins by assuming that psychophysical judgments are based on some underlying neural activity in the sensory system (whose exact nature is for now irrelevant) which can vary in magnitude. Let us call this hypothetical activity the *sensory process.* A sensory process can of course be produced by an actual, external stimulus (the *signal).* But signal-detection theory proposes that a sensory process will occur even when in fact no stimulus is administered. The factors responsible for this are collectively described as ***background noise.*** Take an experiment in hearing and suppose that no sound is actually presented. This does not guarantee the absence of activity in the auditory system. Some sources of stimulation come from within the subject, such as the throbbing of the pulse. In addition, there is spontaneous activity in the nervous system, with many cells firing at random intervals without any external trigger. Under the circumstances, to say that there is no stimulus only means that the experimenter did not present one. From the subject's point of view, some stimulation is always there.

We can now state the subject's task in a detection experiment in another way. He must decide whether a given sensory process should be attributed to the signal superimposed on background noise or to the background noise alone; whether what he hears is a faint tone outside or his own heartbeat (or spontaneous neural firing or whatever) within. On the average, the signal (plus background noise) produces a process of greater magnitude than does the noise alone, an average value which rises with increasing signal strength. The subject's decision problem arises because the magnitude of the two sets of sensory processes fluctuates. Occasionally, one's heartbeat sounds louder than the experimenter's stimulus tone. But the more intense the stimulus, the less likely it is that such a confusion will occur. (For a more precise account of how signal-detection theory envisages this decision process, see the Note at the end of this chapter.)

To sum up, signal-detection theorists offer a somewhat different conception of what a sensation is than did earlier psychophysicists. Fechner had no doubts that people have sensations and can report certain things about them. But according to signal-detection theorists, subjects can't simply *report* that they have a sensation. The best they can do is to *decide* that they have a sensation—that their internal sensory experience is produced by a signal rather than by noise alone. And in this decision—as indeed, in many other decisions—they can be wrong.

EXTENSIONS TO OTHER FIELDS

The general approach of signal-detection theory has applications to many areas of psychology outside of psychophysics. It is relevant whenever a person has to decide between two alternatives but can't be sure of the outcome. An example is the selection of college applicants. One error of admissions is a miss: an applicant is rejected who would have done well. Another error is a false alarm: an applicant is accepted who will be unable to graduate (for details, see Chapter 17). The important point is that in virtually all decision making some errors are inevitable and that these errors can be either misses or false alarms. There is always a trade-off between these two kinds of errors. If one wants to minimize the misses (rejected applicants who would have done perfectly well had they been accepted), one has to change the response bias toward "yes," which then inevitably increases the number of false alarms (accepted applicants who will flunk out). Conversely, if one wants to minimize the number of false alarms, one necessarily must increase the number of misses. Just which trade-off is chosen depends on the payoff matrix.

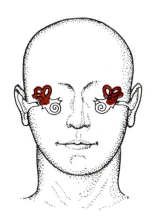

5.6 The vestibular apparatus *The location of the inner ears which are embedded in bone on both sides of the skull. The vestibules are indicated in color. The rest of the inner ear is devoted to the sense of hearing. (After Krech and Crutchfield, 1958)*

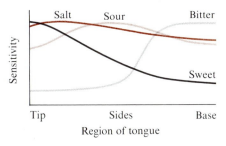

5.7 Taste sensitivity on different regions of the edge of the tongue *The figure plots the tongue's sensitivity to the four primary taste sensations: sweet, salty, sour, and bitter. Sweet is detected most readily at the tip of the tongue, bitter at its base, sour at the sides, with salty roughly equal throughout. This result is an argument for the view that these qualities are produced by different receptors that are distributed in different regions of the tongue. (After Boring, 1942)*

AN OVERVIEW OF THE SENSES

The development of psychophysical methods, coupled with various physiological techniques, gave psychology a powerful set of tools with which to study the various senses. Our primary focus will be on just one of these senses, namely vision. But we will first cast a look at several other sensory systems that provide information about various aspects of the world and about our position within it.

Kinesthesis and the Vestibular Senses

One group of senses informs the organism about its own movements and its orientation in space. Skeletal movement is sensed through **kinesthesis,** a collective term for information that comes from receptors in the muscles, tendons, and joints. Another group of receptors signals the rotation of the head. These are the receptors in the **semicircular canals,** which are located within the so-called **vestibules** of the inner ear (Figure 5.6). The three canals contain a viscuous liquid that moves when the head rotates. This motion bends hair cells that are located at one end of each canal. When bent, these hair cells give rise to nervous impulses. The sum total of the impulses from each of the canals provides information about the nature and extent of the head's rotation.

One vital function of the semicircular canal system is to provide a firm base for vision. As we walk through the world, our head moves continually. To compensate for this endless rocking, the eyes have to move accordingly. This adjustment is accomplished by a reflex system which automatically cancels each rotation of the head by an equal and opposite motion of the eyes. These eye movements are initiated by messages from the three semicircular canals which are relayed to the appropriate muscles of each eye. Thus, the visual system is effectively stable, operating as if it rested on a solid tripod.

The Sense of Taste

The sense of taste has a simple function. It acts as a gatekeeper for the organism's digestive system in that it provides information about the substances that may or may not be ingested. Its task is to keep poisons out and usher foodstuffs in. In most land-dwelling mammals, this function is performed by specialized receptor organs, the **taste buds,** which are sensitive to chemicals dissolved in water. The average person possesses about 10,000 such taste buds, located mostly in the tongue, but also in other regions of the mouth.

TASTE SENSATIONS

Most investigators believe that there are four basic taste qualities: **sour, sweet, salty,** and **bitter.** In their view, all other taste sensations are produced by a mixture of these primary qualities. Thus, grapefruit tastes sour and bitter, while lemonade tastes sweet and sour. One widely held hypothesis is that each of these primary taste qualities is associated with a different kind of taste receptor. In line with this view is the fact that the sensitivity to these qualities is not equally distributed throughout the tongue (Figure 5.7). For instance, thresholds for sweet are

147

lowest at the tip of the tongue, while those for bitter and sour are lowest at the back and the sides respectively (Bartoshuk, 1971).

What are the stimuli that produce these four basic qualities? As yet, we don't have a full answer. Consider the experience "sweet." This is produced by various sugars, but also by saccharin, a chemical compound that is structurally very different from sugar. Just what these substances have in common so that they activate the same taste receptors is still unknown.

TASTE AND SENSORY INTERACTION

The sense of taste provides several illustrations of a rather pervasive principle that holds for most (perhaps all) of the other senses and which we will here call *sensory interaction.* This principle is based on the fact that a sensory system's response to any given stimulus rarely depends on that stimulus alone. It is also affected by other stimuli that impinge, or have recently impinged, upon that system.

One kind of interaction involves the effect of simultaneously presented stimuli. Suppose two regions of the tongue were stimulated by two different solutions. For example, one might be exposed to sucrose, another to ordinary table salt. The effect will be a form of contrast. The sweet taste produced by the sucrose will make the salt taste saltier (Bartoshuk, 1971).

A second kind of sensory interaction occurs over time. Suppose one taste stimulus is presented continuously for fifteen seconds or more. The result will be *adaptation,* a phenomenon that is found in virtually all sensory systems. If a particular region of the tongue is continually stimulated with the identical taste stimulus, sensitivity to that taste will quickly decline. For example, after continuous exposure to a quinine solution, the quinine will taste less and less bitter and may finally appear to be completely tasteless. This adaptation process is reversible. If the mouth is rinsed out and left unstimulated for, say, half a minute, the original taste sensitivity will be restored in full.

Still another kind of interaction involves the relation between different sensory systems. This is especially clear in the realm of taste. The normal experience of tasting food involves many sensory experiences in addition to those provided by the taste buds; these include texture, temperature, and—most important of all—smell. When our nose is completely stuffed up by a bad cold, food appears to be without any flavor. While we can still experience the basic taste sensations, the aroma is lost and thus the food seems tasteless. If smell is gone, we can no longer distinguish between vinegar and a fine red wine or between an apple and an onion. A gourmet needs not only taste buds but also a sensitive nose.

The Skin Senses

Stimulation of the skin informs the organism of what is directly adjacent to its own body. Not surprisingly, skin sensitivity is especially acute in those parts of the body that are most relevant to exploring the world that surrounds us directly: the hands and fingers, the lips and tongue. These sensitivities are reflected in the organization of the cortical projection area for bodily sensations. As we have seen, the allocation of cortical space is quite unequal, with a heavy emphasis on such sensitive regions as face, mouth, and fingers (see Chapter 2).

How many skin senses are there? Aristotle believed that all of the sensations from the skin could be subsumed under just one rubric, that of touch. But today

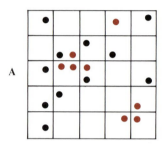

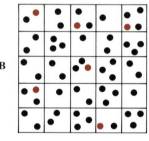

5.8 Sensitivity of different spots on the skin to warmth, cold, pressure, and pain *(A) A map of temperature sensitivity on a 1 centimeter square area of the upper arm. To determine warm spots (color), each location was gently touched with a very thin copper tip heated to 110 degrees Fahrenheit. To determine cold spots (black), the tip was cooled to 50 degrees Fahrenheit. As the map shows, the warm and cold spots do not coincide, some evidence for the view that these two temperature sensations are produced by different receptor systems. (B) A map of the sensitivity to pain and pressure on a 2.5 millimeter square area of the forearm. Pressure spots (color) were determined by a touch with a hair, pain spots (black) by a light prick with a needle. (After Boring, Langfeld, and Weld, 1939)*

we know that there are at least four different skin sensations: **pressure, warmth, cold,** and **pain.** The fact that these sensory qualities are so very different has led to the belief that they are produced by different underlying receptor systems. In support of this view is the finding that different spots on the skin are not uniformly sensitive to the stimuli which produce the various sensations. Suppose we draw a small grid on a part of a blindfolded subject's skin and then touch different squares of the grid with a hair, the tip of a warmed or cooled rod, or with a needle point. These stimuli presumably evoke sensations of pressure, warmth, cold, and pain respectively. By this means we can map the skin's sensitivity for these four sensory qualities. The results show that the four maps are not identical. Some spots are sensitive to pressure but not to warmth, others to warmth but not to pressure, and so on (Figure 5.8).

What are the receptors that correspond to these different sensations? For pressure, a number of different receptors have been discovered in the skin. Some of them are capsules made up of onionlike layers wrapped around a neuron. These capsules are easily bent by slight deformations of the skin and their bending fires the enclosed neuron. Less is known about the underlying receptor systems for temperature and pain.

Pain in particular has been the subject of much controversy. Some investigators believe that there are specialized pain receptors which are activated by tissue injury and produce an unpleasant sensation. Others hold that pain results from the overstimulation of any skin receptor. But whatever its receptor basis, there is little doubt that pain has a vital biological function. It warns the organism of potential harm. This point is vividly brought home by persons who have a congenital insensitivity to pain. On the face of it, the inability to experience this unpleasant sensation might seem to be a blessing, but nothing could be further from the truth. People who lack pain sensitivity often sustain extensive burns and bruises, especially in childhood; they never receive the first signals of danger so they don't withdraw the affected body parts. As a child, one such patient bit off the tip of her tongue while chewing food and sustained serious burns when kneeling on a hot radiator (Melzack, 1973).

The Sense of Smell

Thus far, our discussion has centered on the sensory systems that tell us about objects and events close to home: the movements and position of our own body, what we put in our mouth, and what we feel with our skin. But we clearly receive information from much farther off. We have three main receptive systems that enlarge our world by responding to stimuli at a distance: smell, hearing, and vision. Of these, smell is in many ways the most primitive.

Smell, or to use the more technical term, **olfaction,** provides information about chemicals suspended in air which excite receptors located at the top of our nasal cavity (Figure 5.9). There is still considerable debate about the nature of the chemicals that act as olfactory stimuli and the way in which they set off the olfactory receptors. Several classification schemes exist for describing all odors by reference to a number of primary smell sensations, for example, *fragrant* (rose), *spicy* (cinnamon), and *putrid* (rotten egg). But as yet, there is no agreement about the underlying principle that makes certain chemicals arouse one of these olfactory experiences rather than another.

In any case, smell is a minor sense in humans. To be sure, it can warn us of im-

5.9 The olfactory apparatus *Chemicals suspended in the air that flows through the nasal passages stimulate olfactory receptors which connect with the olfactory nerve. (After Pfaffman, 1948)*

Olfactory nerve

Nasal cavity

pending danger as when we sniff escaping gas; it greatly adds to our enjoyment of food; and it provides the basis of the perfume and deodorant industries. According to some reports, it even helps to sell cars; used cars that are given a "new car" odor are said to bring a higher price (Wenger, Jones, and Jones, 1956). Nevertheless, smell is clearly less important to us than it is to many other species. In this regard, we are similar to our primate cousins and to birds in that these animals all left the odor-impregnated ground to move up into the trees, an environment in which other senses, especially vision, became more critical. In contrast, smell is of vital importance to many ground dwellers such as dogs. For them, it furnishes a guide to food and to receptive mates, and it may give warning against certain predators. Smell often provides the sensory basis whereby members of a species (and among many mammals, individuals within a species) recognize each other.

PHEROMONES

In a number of species, olfaction has a further function: It represents a primitive form of communication. Certain animals secrete special chemical substances called **pheromones** which trigger particular reactions in other members of their own kind. Some pheromones affect reproductive behavior. In many mammals, the female secretes a chemical (often in the urine) that signals that she is sexually receptive. This arouses the male, but only if his sense of smell is functioning. If his olfactory sense is surgically destroyed, he shows no sign of sexual interest (Gleason and Reynierse, 1969). In some species, the male sends chemical return messages to the female. For example, boars apparently secrete a pheromone which renders the sow immobile so that she stands rigid during mating (Michael and Keverne, 1968).

Other pheromones signal alarm. It appears that some animals can smell danger. To be more exact, they can smell a substance secreted by members of their own species who have been frightened. Thus rats who suffer pain in an experimental chamber presumably exude a chemical which induces fear in other rats exposed to a whiff of air from that same chamber (Valenta and Rigby, 1968).

Are there pheromones in humans? There may be some vestigial remnants. One line of evidence comes from olfactory thresholds to certain musklike substances. Sexually mature women are vastly more sensitive to the smell of these compounds than are men or sexually immature girls. This sensitivity fluctuates with the menstrual cycle, reaching a peak when the level of the female hormone estrogen is at its maximum. Musklike odors characterize the sex pheromones secreted by the males of several mammalian species. An intriguing speculation is that the human female's greater sensitivity to this odor points to the existence of a human male sex pheromone. This pheromone may be in our evolutionary past. It may also be still present, though in greatly attenuated form, and in any case masked by the application of modern deodorants (Vierling and Rock, 1967).

Hearing

The sense of hearing, or **audition,** is a close relative of other receptive senses that react to mechanical pressure, such as the vestibular senses or touch. Like these, hearing is a response to pressure, but with a difference—it informs us of pressure changes in the world that may take place many meters away. In effect, then, hearing is feeling at a distance.

A

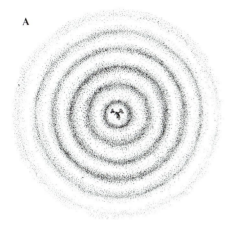

B

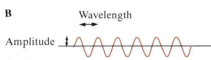

5.10 The stimulus for hearing (A) The figure depicts a momentarily frozen field of vibration in air. An insect vibrating its wings rapidly leads to waves of compression in the surrounding air. These waves travel in all directions like ripples in a pond into which a stone has been thrown. (B) The corresponding wave pattern is shown in simplified form. The amplitude of the wave is the height of each crest; the wavelength is the distance between successive crests. (From Gibson, 1966)

What is the stimulus for hearing? Outside in the world there is some physical movement which disturbs the air medium in which it occurs. This may be an animal scurrying through the underbrush or a rock dropping from a cliff or a set of vibrating vocal cords. The air particles directly adjacent to the movement are agitated, push particles that are ahead of them, and then return to their original position. Each individual air particle moves back and forth for just a tiny bit, but this is enough to set up a series of successive pressure variations in the air medium. These travel in a wave form analogous to the ripples set up by a stone thrown into a pond. When these *sound waves* hit our ears, they initiate a set of further mechanical pressure changes which ultimately trigger the auditory receptors. These initiate various further neural responses in the brain which ultimately lead to an experience of something that is heard rather than felt (which is yet another example of the operation of Müller's doctrine of specific nerve energies).

Sound waves can vary in both *amplitude* and *wavelength.* Amplitude refers to the height of a wave crest: the greater the intensity of the vibration, the higher this crest will be. Wavelength is simply the distance between successive crests. Sound waves are generally described by their *frequency,* which is the number of waves per second. Since the speed of sound is constant within any given medium, frequency is inversely proportional to wavelength (Figure 5.10).

Both amplitude and frequency are physical dimensions. Our brain translates these into the psychological dimensions of *loudness* and *pitch.* Roughly speaking, a sound will appear to be louder as its amplitude increases and will appear more high-pitched as its frequency goes up.

Amplitude and loudness The range of amplitudes to which humans can respond is enormous. Investigators have found it convenient to use a scale which compresses this unwieldy range into a more convenient form. This scale describes sound intensities in *decibels* (Table 5.4). Perceived loudness approximately doubles every time the physical intensity goes up by 10 decibels (Stevens, 1955).

Table 5.4 INTENSITY LEVELS OF VARIOUS COMMON SOUNDS

Sound	Intensity level (decibels)
Manned spacecraft launching (from 150 feet)	180
Loudest rock band on record	160
Pain threshold (approximate)	140
Loud thunder; average rock band	120
Shouting	100
Noisy automobile	80
Normal conversation	60
Quiet office	40
Whisper	20
Rustling of leaves	10
Threshold of hearing	0

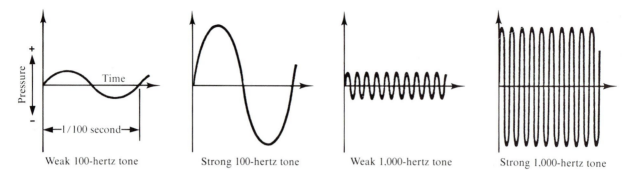

Weak 100-hertz tone   Strong 100-hertz tone   Weak 1.000-hertz tone   Strong 1.000-hertz tone

5.11 Simple wave forms vary in frequency and amplitude Simple sound waves can be graphically expressed by plotting air-pressure change over time. The result is a so-called sine curve. These curves show the sine waves for a weak and a strong 100-hertz tone (relatively low in pitch) and a strong and a weak, 1,000-hertz tone (comparatively high pitch). (After Thompson, 1973)

Frequency and pitch The frequency of a sound wave is generally measured in *hertz* (H$_z$), or waves per second (so-called after the nineteenth-century German physicist Heinrich Hertz). Table 5.5 shows the frequencies associated with some musical tones. Young adults can hear tones as low as 20 hertz and as high as 20,000 hertz, with maximal sensitivity to a middle region in between. As people get older, their sensitivity to sound declines, especially at the higher frequencies.

Simple and complex waves Thus far we have only dealt with simple wave forms. These are made up of waves that have only one frequency. Such waves are very rare in nature; they are produced by special electronic devices or by tuning forks. When such simple waves are expressed graphically, with pressure change plotted against time, they yield curves that correspond to the plot of the trigonometric sine function. Accordingly, such curves are called *sine waves* (Figure 5.11).

The sounds encountered in normal life are virtually never as simple as this. Instead, they are composed of many different waves, which differ in both frequency and amplitude. An example is this (relatively simple) *complex wave:*

This complex wave can be physically produced by the acoustic mixture of three simple tones which correspond to three sine waves, as shown below:

The point of this example is that the auditory system can analyze complex waves into their component parts. We can hear the separate notes that make up a chord; the tones are mixed, but we can unmix them. This ability has its limits. If

Table 5.5   SOUND FREQUENCIES OF SOME MUSICAL TONES

Sound	Frequency (hertz)
Top note of grand piano	4214
Top note of piccolo	3951
Top range of soprano voice	1152
Top range of alto voice	640
Middle C	256
Bottom range of baritone voice	96
Bottom range of bass voice	80
Bottom note of contra bassoon	29
Bottom note of grand piano	27
Bottom note of organ*	16

* Can be felt but not heard
SOURCE: After Geldard, 1972.

the sound is made up of a great number of unrelated waves, it is perceived as *noise,* which we can no longer analyze (Figure 5.12).

GATHERING THE PROXIMAL STIMULUS

Most of the ear is made up of various anatomical structures whose function is to gather the proximal stimulus—they conduct and amplify sound waves so that they can affect the auditory receptors (Figure 5.13). Sound waves collected by the outer ear are funneled toward a taut membrane which they cause to vibrate. This is the *eardrum* which transmits its vibrations across an air-filled cavity, the *middle ear,* to another membrane, the *oval window,* that separates the middle from the *inner ear.* This transmission is accomplished by way of a mechanical bridge built of three small bones that are collectively known as the *ossicles.* The vibrations of the eardrum move the first ossicle, which then moves the second, which in turn moves the third, which completes the chain by imparting the vibratory pattern to the oval window to which it is attached. The movements of the oval window set up waves in a fluid which fills the *cochlea,* a coiled tube in the inner ear which contains the auditory receptors.

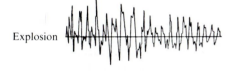

Explosion

5.12   An irregular sound wave—an explosion *As in the previous figures, pressure change is plotted against time; but now there is no more regularity, so the wave form cannot readily be analyzed into its simpler components. (From Boring, Langfeld, and Weld, 1939)*

5.13   The human ear *Air enters through the outer ear and stimulates the eardrum which sets the ossicles in the middle ear in motion. These in turn transmit their vibration to the membrane of the oval window which causes movement of the fluid in the cochlea of the inner ear. Note that the semicircular canals are anatomically parts of the inner ear. (After Lindsay and Norman, 1977)*

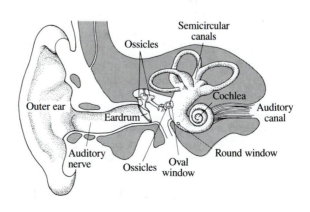

Why did nature choose such a roundabout method of sound transmission? The major reason is that the cochlear medium is a fluid which like all liquids is harder to set into motion than air. To overcome this difficulty, the physical stimulus must be amplified. This amplification is provided by various features of the middle-ear organization. One involves the relative sizes of the eardrum and of that portion of the oval window which is moved by the stapes; the first is about twenty times larger than the second. The result is the transformation of a fairly weak force that acts on the entire eardrum into a much stronger pressure that is concentrated upon the (much smaller) oval window.

TRANSDUCTION IN THE COCHLEA

Throughout most of its length the cochlea is divided into an upper and lower section by several structures including the *basilar membrane.* The auditory receptors are so-called *hair cells* which are lodged between the basilar membrane and other membranes above it. Motion of the oval window produces pressure changes in the cochlear fluid which in turn lead to vibrations of the basilar membrane. As the basilar membrane vibrates, its deformations bend the hair cells and provide the immediate stimulus for their activity (Figure 5.14).

How does the activity of the auditory receptors lead to the sensory properties of auditory experience? Much of the work in the area has focused upon the perception of *pitch,* the sensory quality that depends upon the frequency of the stimulating sound wave.

Basilar place and pitch   According to the *place theory* of pitch, first proposed by Hermann von Helmholtz (1821–1894), different parts of the basilar membrane are responsive to different sound frequencies. In Helmholtz's view, the nervous system will then interpret the excitations from different basilar places as different pitches. The stimulation of receptors at one end of the membrane will lead to the experience of a high tone, while that of receptors at the other end leads to the sensation of a low tone.

Today we know that Helmholtz was correct at least in part. The classical studies were performed by Georg von Békésy (1899–1972) whose work on auditory function won him the Nobel Prize in 1961. Some of Békésy's experiments used cochleas taken from fresh human cadavers. Békésy removed part of the cochlear wall so that he could observe the basilar membrane through a microscope when the oval window was vibrated by an electrically powered piston. He found that such stimulation led to a wavelike motion of the basilar membrane (Figure 5.15). When he varied the frequency of the vibrating stimulus, the peak of the deforma-

Hermann von Helmholtz (1821–1894)
(Courtesy National Library of Medicine)

5.14   Detailed structure of the middle ear and the cochlea   *(A) Movement of the fluid within the cochlea deforms the basilar membrane and stimulates the hair cells that serve as the auditory receptors. (After Lindsay and Norman, 1977) (B) Cross-section of the cochlea showing the basilar membrane and the hair cell receptors. (After Coren, Porac, and Ward, 1978)*

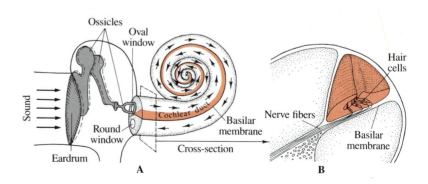

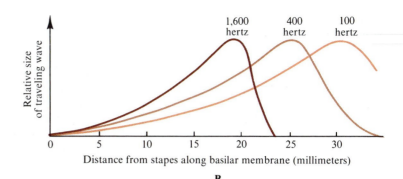

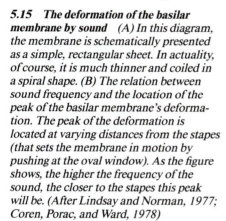

5.15 The deformation of the basilar membrane by sound *(A) In this diagram, the membrane is schematically presented as a simple, rectangular sheet. In actuality, of course, it is much thinner and coiled in a spiral shape. (B) The relation between sound frequency and the location of the peak of the basilar membrane's deformation. The peak of the deformation is located at varying distances from the stapes (that sets the membrane in motion by pushing at the oval window). As the figure shows, the higher the frequency of the sound, the closer to the stapes this peak will be. (After Lindsay and Norman, 1977; Coren, Porac, and Ward, 1978)*

Georg von Békésy (1899–1972) (Courtesy Nobel Stiftelsen)

tion produced by this wave pattern occurred in different regions of the membrane: high frequencies corresponded to regions close to the oval window, low ones to regions close to the cochlear tip (Békésy, 1957).

Sound frequency and frequency of neural firing The place theory of pitch faces a major difficulty. As the frequency of the stimulus gets lower and lower, the deformation pattern it produces gets broader and broader. At very low frequencies (say, below 50 hertz), the wave set up by the tone deforms the entire membrane just about equally so that all receptors will be equally excited. But since we can discriminate low frequencies down to about 20 hertz, the nervous system must have some means for sensing pitch in addition to basilar location.

It is generally believed that this second means for sensing pitch is related to the firing frequency of the auditory nerve. For lower frequencies, the basilar membrane vibrates at the frequency of the stimulus tone and this vibration rate is then directly translated into the appropriate number of neural impulses per second, as evidenced by gross electrical recordings taken from the auditory nerve. The impulse frequency of the auditory output is further relayed to higher centers which somehow interpret it as pitch.

A further fact leads to some complications. A neuron cannot fire more often than about 1,000 times per second (see Chapter 2). While this would suggest that the impulse-frequency mechanism does not apply to tones higher than 1,000 hertz, its potential range has been extended to tones of still higher frequency by the **volley theory.** This proposes that impulse frequencies above 1,000 per second are generated by different squads of neurons, each of which is firing at a slightly different pace. For example, consider two neurons, both responding at a uniform rate of 1,000 impulses per second. If the second neuron starts to respond half a millisecond after the first, then the combined firing rate for both of them will be 2,000 impulses per second. In principle, this may allow even higher firing rates for the auditory nerve considered as a whole. Various lines of evidence suggest that some such mechanism may operate up to frequencies of about 4,000 hertz.

It appears then that pitch perception is based upon two separate mechanisms: higher frequencies are coded by the place of excitation on the basilar membrane, lower frequencies by the frequency of the neural impulses (which may involve the volley principle or some other means of sensing the timing pattern of neural firing). It is not clear where the one mechanism leaves off and the other takes over. Place of excitation is probably relatively unimportant at frequencies below 500–1,000 hertz and has no role below 50 hertz, while impulse frequency has little or no effect for tones above 5,000 hertz. In all probability, sound frequencies in between are handled by both mechanisms (Green, 1976; Goldstein, 1984).

155

The Senses: Some Common Principles

In our discussion of the various senses, we have come across many ways in which they differ. We have also encountered a number of important phenomena that are not specific to any one sensory system but are found more generally.

First, in most sense modalities, the processing of exernal stimulus energies begins with various structures which gather and amplify these physical energies and thereby fashion a "better" proximal stimulus for the receptors to work on. An example is provided by the semicircular canals which contain a liquid that is set in motion by head rotation and then stimulates the hair cell receptors of the vestibular system.

Second, in all sense modalities, the next step involves the receptors which achieve the *transduction* of the physical stimulus energy into a neural impulse. In some sensory systems, particularly hearing and vision, the nature of this transduction process is reasonably well understood. In other systems, such as smell, it is still unknown.

Third, the processing of stimulus input does not stop at the receptor level. There are typically further neural centers at which *coding* occurs. The stimulus information is coded (so to speak, translated) into the various dimensions of sensation that we actually experience. Some of these dimensions involve intensity. In taste, we have more or less bitter; in hearing, we have more or less loud. Other dimensions involve differences in quality. In taste, we have the differences between bitter, sweet, sour, and salty; in hearing, we have differences in pitch.

Fourth, any part of a sensory system is in *interaction* with the rest of that system. This process of interaction pertains both to the immediate past and to present activity in neighboring parts of the system. We considered some examples of sensory interaction in the taste system, including the phenomena of adaptation (with continued exposure, quinine tastes less bitter) and taste contrast (sugar on one side of the tongue makes salt on the other side taste saltier).

VISION

We now turn to a detailed discussion of vision, which in humans is the distance sense *par excellence*. The organization of this account will reflect characteristics which are common to most of the senses. Specifically, we will (1) describe the eye as a structure for gathering the visual stimulus, (2) examine the transduction of light energies by the visual receptors, (3) discuss some interaction processes found in vision, and (4) consider the coding processes that are involved in experiencing a particular sensory quality—in the case of vision, color.

The Stimulus: Light

Most visual sensations have their point of origin in some external (distal) object. Occasionally, this object will be a light source which *emits* light in its own right; examples (in rather drastically descending order of emission energy) are the sun, an electric light bulb, and a glow worm. All other objects can only give off light if some light source illuminates them. They will then *reflect* some portion of the light cast upon them while absorbing the rest.

The stimulus energy we call light comes from the relatively small band of radiations to which our visual system is sensitive. These radiations travel in a wave form which is somewhat analogous to the pressure waves that are the stimulus for hearing. This radiation can vary in its *intensity,* the amount of radiant energy in unit time, which is a major determinant of perceived brightness (as in two bulbs of different wattage). It can also vary in *wavelength,* the distance between the crests of two successive waves, which is a major determinant of perceived color. The light we ordinarily encounter is made up of a mixture of different wavelengths. The range of wavelengths to which our visual system can respond is the *visible spectrum,* extending from roughly 400 ("violet") to about 750 ("red") nanometers (1 nanometer = 1 millionth of a millimeter) between successive crests.

Gathering the Stimulus: The Eye

The next stop in the journey from stimulus to visual sensation is the eye. Except for the *retina,* none of its major structures has anything to do with the transduction of the physical stimulus energy into neurological terms. Theirs is a prior function: to fashion a proper proximal stimulus for vision, a sharp retinal image, out of the light that enters from outside.

Let us briefly consider how this task is accomplished. The eye has often been compared to a camera, and in its essentials the analogy holds up well enough (Figure 5.16). Both eye and camera have a *lens* which suitably bends light rays passing through it and thus projects an image upon a light-sensitive surface behind—the film in the camera, the retina in the eye. Both have a focusing mechanism. In the eye this is accomplished by a set of muscles that changes the shape of the lens. It is flattened for objects at a distance and thickened for objects closer by, a process technically known as *accommodation.* Finally, both camera and eye have a *diaphragm* which governs the amount of entering light. In the eye this function is performed by the *iris,* a smooth, circular muscle which surrounds the pupillary opening, and which contracts or dilates under reflex control when the amount of illumination increases or decreases substantially.

The image of an object that falls upon the retina is determined by simple optical geometry. Its size will be inversely proportional to the distance of the object, while its shape will depend on its orientation. Thus, a rectangle viewed at a slant will project as a trapezoid. In addition, the image will be reversed with respect to right and left and will be upside down.

5.16 Eye and camera *As an accessory apparatus for fashioning a sharp image out of the light that enters from outside, the eye has many similarities to the camera. Both have a lens for bending light rays to project an inverted image upon a light-sensitive surface at the back. In the eye a transparent outer layer, the cornea, participates in this light-bending. The light-sensitive surface in the eye is the retina, whose most sensitive region is the fovea. Both eye and camera have a focusing device; in the eye, the lens can be thickened or flattened. Both have an adjustable iris diaphragm. And both finally are encased in black to minimize the effects of stray light; in the eye this is done by a layer of darkly pigmented tissue, the choroid coat. (Wald, 1950)*

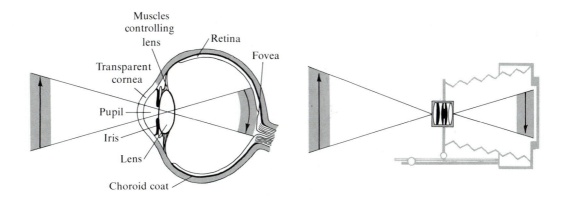

Muscles controlling lens

Retina

Fovea

Transparent cornea

Pupil

Iris

Lens

Choroid coat

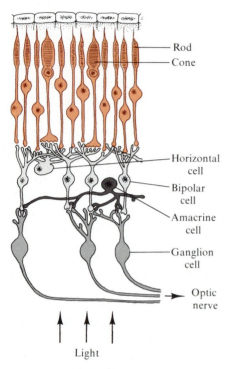

5.17 The retina *There are three main retinal layers: the rods and cones, which are the photoreceptors; the bipolar cells; and the ganglion cells whose axons make up the optic nerve. There are also two other kinds of cells, horizontal cells and amacrine cells, that allow for sideways (lateral) interaction. As shown in the diagram the retina contains an anatomical oddity. As it is constructed the photoreceptors are at the very back, the bipolar cells are in between, and the ganglion cells are at the top. As a result, light has to pass through the other layers (they are not opaque so this is possible) to reach the rods and cones whose stimulation starts the visual process. (After Coren, Porac, and Ward, 1978)*

The Visual Receptors

We have arrived at the point where the path from distal object to visual sensation crosses the frontier between optics and psychophysiology—the transformation of the physical stimulus energy into a nervous impulse. We now consider the structures which accomplish this feat: the visual receptor organs in the retina.

The retina is made up of several layers of nerve cells, one of which is the receptor layer. Microscopic inspection shows two kinds of receptor cells, whose names describe their different shapes—the *rods* and the *cones.* The cones are more plentiful in the *fovea,* a small roughly circular region at the center of the retina. While very densely packed in the fovea, the cones occur with rapidly decreasing frequency the farther out one goes toward the periphery. The opposite is true of the rods; they are completely absent from the fovea and are more frequent in the periphery. In all, there are some 120 million rods and about 6 million cones.

The receptors do not report to the brain directly, but relay their message upward by way of two intermediate neural links—the *bipolar cells* and the *ganglion cells* (Figure 5.17). The bipolar cells are stimulated by the receptors, and they, in their turn, excite the ganglion cells. The axons of these ganglion cells are collected from all over the retina, converging into a bundle of fibers that finally leaves the eyeball as the *optic nerve.* The region where these axons converge contains no receptors and thus cannot give rise to visual sensations; appropriately enough, it is called the *blind spot* (Figure 5.18).

VISUAL ACUITY

One of the most important functions of the visual sense is to enable us to tell one object from another. A minimum precondition for doing so is the ability to distinguish between separate points that are projected on the retina so that we do not see a blur. The ability to make such distinctions is called *acuity.* Under normal daylight conditions, this is greatest in the fovea, for it is there that the receptors are most closely bunched and thus provide the sharpest optical resolution. To "look at" an object means to move the eyes so that the image of that object falls upon both foveas. In peripheral vision we often see something without quite knowing what it is. To see it clearly, we swivel our eyes so that the image of the as yet unidentified something falls upon the foveal regions where our resolving power is greatest.

THE DUPLEXITY THEORY OF VISION

The fact that rods and cones differ in structure suggests that they also differ in function. Some seventy years ago, this notion led to the development of the *duplexity theory of vision,* a theory that by now has the status of established fact. The essential idea is that rods and cones handle different aspects of the visual task. The rods are the receptors for night vision; they operate at low light intensities and lead to *achromatic* (colorless) sensations. The cones serve day vision; they respond at much higher levels of illumination and are responsible for sensations of color. The biological utility of such an arrangement becomes apparent when we consider the enormous range of light intensities encountered by organisms like ourselves who transact their business during both day and night. In

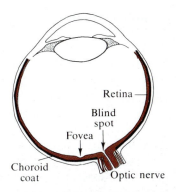

5.18 Fovea and blind spot *The fovea is the region on the retina in which the receptors are most densely packed. The blind spot is a region where there are no receptors at all, this being the point where the optic nerve leaves the eyeball. (After Cornsweet, 1970)*

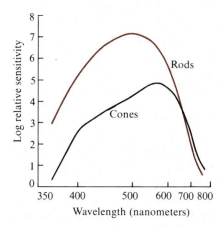

5.19 Sensitivity of rods and cones to light of different wavelengths *Sensitivity was measured by determining the threshold for different frequencies of light projected on retinal areas rich in rods or cones. Sensitivity was then computed by dividing 1 by the threshold (the lower the threshold, the greater the sensitivity). Since sensitivity varied over an enormous range, the range was compressed by using logarithmic units. Note first that the cones, overall, are less sensitive than the rods. Note also that the point of maximal sensitivity is different for the two receptor systems. The cone maximum (560 nanometers) is closer to yellow, the rod maximum (510 nanometers) closer to green. (After Cornsweet, 1970)*

humans, the ratio between the stimulus energy at absolute threshold and that transmitted by a momentary glance at the midday sun is 1 to 100,000,000,000. Evolution has evidently provided a biological division of labor, assigning two separate receptor systems to the upper and lower portions of this incredible range.

Several facts provide important evidence in support of the duplexity theory. Sensitivity to dim light is much greater in the periphery where rods are prevalent than in the center of the fovea where they are absent. This fact is familiar to sailors who know that the way to detect a faint star in the night sky is to look at it not directly, but to look off at an angle from where they think it might be. The quality of the visual sensation produced by such dim light is invariably achromatic, much like a black-and-white film.

Further evidence for the duplexity theory comes from the study of spectral sensitivity. The human eye is insensitive to light waves shorter than about 350 and longer than about 750 nanometers. What is its sensitivity to the wavelengths in between? We know that photographic film (whether chromatic or achromatic) is more responsive to some regions of the visible spectrum than to others. Is the same true for the eye?

To answer this question, we ask subjects to detect a faint test light that is projected on a retinal region which contains mostly rods. The light can be independently varied in physical intensity and in wavelength. If the light is seen, it will necessarily appear gray, since only the rods are stimulated. The question is whether these rods are more sensitive to some wavelengths than to others.

To answer this question, we determine the sensitivity for each separate wavelength. The result is the ***spectral sensitivity curve*** in which sensitivity is plotted against wavelength (Figure 5.19). Maximal sensitivity for the rods is toward the short-wave region, with a peak at about 510 nanometers.

What about the cones? We determine their spectral sensitivity by performing the same experiment, but with the test light projected on the all-cone fovea (Figure 5.19). The results show that the cones are much less sensitive than the rods. They also show that the cones' region of maximal sensitivity is toward the longer wavelengths, with a peak at about 560 nanometers (which is seen as a yellowish green). Rods and cones evidently differ in their relative sensitivity to different wavelengths. For rods, the blues are easier to detect than the yellows and reds (although of course they all appear gray); the opposite holds for the cones.

VISUAL PIGMENTS

When light hits a visual receptor, its energy somehow triggers a nervous impulse. Many of the details of how this happens are still unknown, but one thing at least is clear. The first stage of this energy conversion involves a photochemical process. We are again reminded of the camera. In a photographic plate the sensitive elements are grains of silver salt such as silver bromide. When light strikes the film, some of it is absorbed by the silver bromide molecules with the result that the silver is separated from the compound (and eventually becomes visible after several darkroom manipulations). The visual receptors contain several ***visual pigments*** which perform an analogous function for the eye. One such substance is ***rhodopsin,*** which serves as the visual pigment for the rods.

Unlike a photographic emulsion, the visual pigments constantly renew themselves. Were it otherwise, a newborn infant would open his eyes, look at the bustling world around him, and never see again—his retina would be bleached forever. The bleached pigments are somehow reconstituted to permit an unbroken succession of further retinal pictures.

Interaction in Time: Adaptation

We now turn to some phenomena which prove that the visual system (as indeed all sensory systems) is much more than the passive observer which Locke had assumed it to be. On the contrary, the visual system actively shapes and transforms the optic input; its components never function in isolation, but constantly interact.

One kind of interaction concerns the relation between what happens now and what happened just before. The general finding is simple: There will be a gradual decline in the reaction to any stimulus that persists unchanged. For example, after continued inspection of a green patch, its greenness will eventually fade away. Similar *adaptation* phenomena are found in most other sensory systems. Thus, the cold ocean water feels warmer after we have been in it for a while.

What does the organism gain by sensory adaptation? One advantage is the likelihood that stimuli which have been around for a while tend to be safe and of lesser relevance to the organism's survival; under the circumstances, it pays to give them less sensory weight. What is important is change, especially sudden change, for this may well signify food to a predator and death to its potential prey. Adaptation is the sensory system's way of pushing old news off the neurophysiological front page.

An interesting adaptation effect in vision is provided by the so-called *stabilized image.* In normal vision, the eyes constantly move. In consequence, no retinal region ever suffers prolonged exposure to the same stimulus; one moment, it will be stimulated by a dark object, the next, by a lighter one. Since every change of gaze leads to a change in the visual stimulus, there will be no visual adaptation. Even if one tries to hold one's eyes steady to fixate a stationary picture, adaptation effects will be rather minor. The fact is that we cannot truly hold our eyes motionless. Small tremors in the eye muscles lead to involuntary eye movements, and these necessarily alter the stimulus input for any given retinal region.

Several contemporary investigators have developed a technique which achieves a truly stationary retinal image. The basic idea is as clever as it is simple. Since you can't stop the eye from moving, move the stimulus along with the eye. One way to accomplish this is by means of a contact lens to which a tiny projector is attached. This projects a stimulus pattern upon the retina. The contact lens moves with every motion of the eyeball, but the projector moves with it. The result is a stabilized image. However the eye moves, so does the stimulus; thus each retinal region is continually exposed to the identical portion of the stimulus pattern (Figure 5.20). At first, the stabilized retinal image is seen very sharply, but after some seconds it fades away completely—a dramatic demonstration of the system's adaptation to unchanging stimulation. Interestingly enough, the image will reappear if the stimulus pattern is somehow altered, whether in intensity or in its retinal location (the latter by slippage of the contact lens). We can conclude that, in humans, continual involuntary eye movements serve the biologically useful purpose of keeping the visual world intact (Riggs et al., 1953).

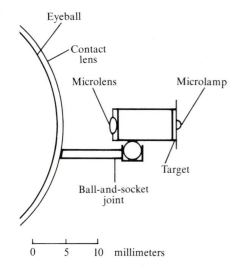

5.20 Stabilized-image device *The subject wears a contact lens on which a tiny projector is mounted. At the rear of the projector is the stimulus target which is projected onto the retina. This target will remain fixed at one point of the retina, for as the eyeball moves, so does the contact lens and its attached projector. As a result, the image on the retina remains stabilized. (After Pritchard, 1961)*

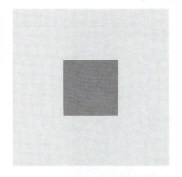

5.21 Brightness contrast *Four (objectively) identical gray squares on different backgrounds. The lighter the background, the darker the gray squares appear.*

5.22 The effect of distance between contrasting regions *(A) The white lines in the grid are physically homogeneous, but they don't appear to be—each of the "intersections" seems to contain a gray spot. The uneven appearance of the white strips is caused by contrast. Each strip is surrounded by a black square which contrasts with it and makes it look brighter. But this is not the case at the intersections which only touch upon the black squares at their corners. As a result, there is little contrast in the middle of the intersections. This accounts for the gray spots seen there. (B) The same point is made by the second grid. Here there seem to be whitish spots at the intersections. The explanation is the same. The black lines are bounded by white and thus look darker by contrast. There is less contrast operating on the regions in the middle of the intersections. As a result, they don't appear as dark as the streets, looking like whitish spots. (After Hering, 1920)*

Interaction in Space: Contrast

Adaptation effects show that sensory systems respond to change over time. If no such change occurs, the sensory response diminishes. What holds for time, holds for space as well. For here, too, the key word is *change*. In vision (as in some other senses), the response to a stimulus applied to any one region partially depends on how the neighboring regions are stimulated. The greater the difference in stimulation, the greater the sensory effect.

BRIGHTNESS CONTRAST

It has long been known that the appearance of a gray patch depends upon its background. The identical gray will look much brighter on a black background than it will on a white background. This is ***brightness contrast,*** an effect that increases the greater the intensity difference between two contrasting regions. Thus, gray appears brighter on black than on dark gray and darker against white than against light gray (Figure 5.21).

Contrast is also a function of the distance between the two contrasting regions —the smaller that difference, the greater the contrast (Figure 5.22). This phenomenon gives rise to a number of visual illusions and has been used by some contemporary artists to create some striking effects (see Figure 5.23, on p. 162).

Such contrast effects serve a vital biological function. They accentuate the edges between different objects in our visual world, and thus allow us to see them more clearly. To explain why this is so we must consider some further facts about the optics of the eye and about brightness contrast.

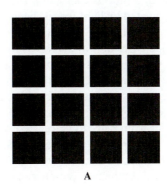
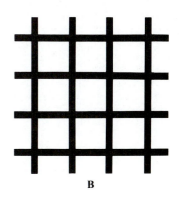

A   B

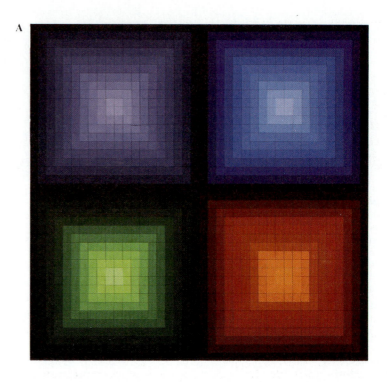

A

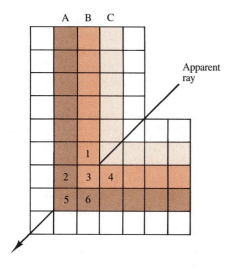

B

5.23 Contrast *(A) "Arcturus" by Victor Vasarely. The luminous rays are not in the painting itself but are created by brightness contrast. Note that the painting consists of a series of frames, which surround other frames and become progressively darker as they go from center to periphery. (© by ADAGP, Paris, 1981, and by permission of the Hirshhorn Museum and Sculpture Garden, Smithsonian Institution) (B) The figure focuses on three of the frames in the painting. Consider squares 1, 3, and 4 in frame B. Squares 1 and 4 each have an entire side next to the brighter frame C above them. As a result, they look darker because of brightness contrast. But square 3 suffers little contrast, for it only touches on the brighter frame at its corner. It therefore looks brighter than the two squares 1 and 4 that are adjacent to it. For the same reason, squares 2 and 6 in frame A will seem to be darker than square 5. Since this happens for all the squares at the corners, the observer sees four radiating luminous diagonals.*

Creating edges through contrast   In previous sections we have ignored some defects of the eye as an optical instrument. The lens and the cornea have serious optical aberrations that cause some blur of the retinal image. This blur is further aggravated by light that is dispersed as it passes through the liquid medium of the eye, scattering a diffuse haze over the entire retina. The result is a retinal image in which there are no distinct outlines but only fuzzy fringes. How then do we see the sharp edges of the world around us? The answer is that brightness contrast accentuates intensity differences between adjacent retinal areas, so much so that it sometimes creates perceived boundaries where physically there are none.

A demonstration is provided by surfaces in which the physical light intensity varies from place to place according to some prearranged function. Consider Figure 5.24A which contains strips of grays that range from very dark to very light. Within each strip, the physical light intensities are equal. But that is not how they appear. At the border between each strip and the neighboring one, there seems to

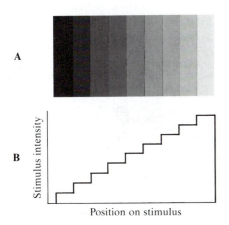

5.24   Accentuation of contours by contrast *(A) The series of gray strips is arranged in ascending brightness, from left to right. Physically, each strip is of uniform light intensity. This is graphically expressed in (B) which plots stimulus position against the physical light intensity, showing a simple series of ascending steps. But this is not what is seen, for the strips do not appear to be uniform. For each strip, the left edge (adjacent to its darker neighbor) looks brighter than the rest, while the right edge (adjacent to the lighter neighbor) looks darker. The explanation is contrast. The edges are closer to their darker or lighter neighbors, and will thus be more subject to contrast than the rest of the strip. The result is an accentuation of the contours that separate one strip from the next. (After Cornsweet, 1970; Coren, Porac, and Ward, 1978)*

be a band. A bright band is seen where the strip borders on a darker strip; a dark band is seen where the strip borders on a lighter strip. These results are summarized by Figure 5.24B in which the physical light intensities are plotted against spatial position—the strips as they really are.

These phenomena are produced by the same contrast effects we have discussed before. Contrast accentuates the difference between two adjacent regions. But this sharpening is maximal at the borders where the difference between the two contrasting regions is smallest. The bands (usually called **_Mach bands,_** after the nineteenth-century physicist Ernst Mach who discovered them) are the result.

It is generally agreed that the same process helps to overcome the optical imperfections of the eye which produce fuzzy images even though the external stimulus is outlined sharply. The contours of the retinal image are sharpened, for the visual system recreates, and even exaggerates, boundaries by the same mechanisms that generate Mach bands.

A PHYSIOLOGICAL ACCOUNT OF CONTRAST

What is the physiological mechanism that underlies spatial interaction? Today we know that the effect is based on the mutual inhibition of cells in the retina and higher up. The conclusive demonstration that this is so had to await the techniques of modern electrophysiology. But more than fifty years before this, such sensory psychologists as Ernest Mach and Ewald Hering (1834–1918) had postulated precisely such a process on the basis of what they observed in the sensory laboratory. In their view, the phenomena of contrast and Mach bands could be explained in no other way. In this regard, Mach and Hering resemble Sherrington who inferred the synapse on the basis of behavioral data alone, many decades before there was any means for providing physiological proof.

The modern physiological account of contrast effects is based on single-cell recording methods. The first step is to place a microelectrode in a cat's optic nerve so that it picks up electrical activity from only one cell. The eye of an anesthetized animal is propped open and is stimulated by spots of light of varying intensities and at different locations (Figure 5.25). We find that there is a small region of the retina whose stimulation leads to an increase in the cell's normal firing rate. The more intense the light, the greater the cell's response. But this central region is surrounded by a region in which illumination has the opposite effect. Here, illumination depresses the cell's firing rate, and this depression increases

5.25   Recording from the visual system of a cat *The experimental setup for recording neural responses from the visual system of a cat. An anaesthetized cat has one eye propped open so that visual stimulation can be directed to particular regions of the retina. A microelectrode picks up neural impulses from a single cell in the optic system, amplifies them, and displays them on an oscilloscope. (After Schiffman, 1976)*

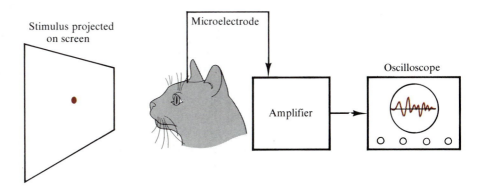

Stimulus   Oscilloscope record

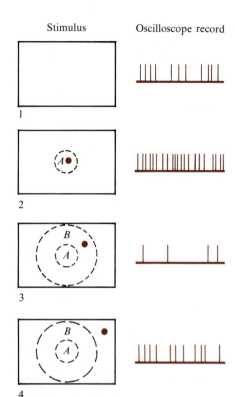

5.26 Receptive fields on the cat's visual system *Using the setup shown in Figure 5.25, stimuli are presented to various regions of the retina. The panels show the firing frequency of a particular ganglion cell. Panel 1 shows the base-level firing rate when no stimulus is presented anywhere. Panel 2 shows the effect when a stimulus is presented anywhere within an inner, central region, A, on the retina. When stimulated in A, the cell's firing rate goes up. Panel 3 shows what happens in response to a stimulus presented anywhere within the ring-shaped region, B, surrounding region A. Stimulation in B causes the cell's firing rate to go down. Panel 4, finally, shows what happens when a stimulus is presented outside of either A or B, the regions that together comprise the cell's receptive field. Now there is no significant change from the cell's normal base level. (From Kuffler, 1953)*

with increases in the light intensity (Figure 5.26). The entire area of the retina in which stimulation by light affects the cell's firing rate—whether up or down—is called the **receptive field** of that cell.

Lateral inhibition The results show that neighboring regions in the retina tend to inhibit each other. The reason is a process called **lateral inhibition** (in effect, it is inhibition exerted sideways). A simplified version of how this mechanism works is as follows: When any visual receptor is stimulated, it transmits its excitation upward to other cells that eventually relay it to the brain. But this excitation has a further effect. It also stimulates some neurons that extend sideways along the retina. These lateral cells make contact with neighboring cells whose activation they inhibit.

To see how lateral inhibition works, consider the retinal image produced by a gray patch surrounded by a lighter ring (Figure 5.27). For the sake of simplicity, we will only look at two neighboring receptor cells, *A* and *B*. *A* is stimulated by the gray patch and receives a moderate amount of light. *B* is stimulated by the lighter ring and receives much more light. Our primary interest is in the excitation which cell *A*, the one stimulated by the gray patch, relays upward to the brain. The more cell *A* is stimulated, the more excitation it will relay further, and the brighter the patch will appear to be. The important point is that the excitation from cell *A* will not be passed on unimpeded. On the contrary. Some of this excitation will be cancelled by inhibition from neighboring cells. Consider the effect of cell *B*, whose stimulation comes from the lighter ring. That cell is intensely excited. One result of this excitation is that it excites a third cell *C* whose effect is inhibitory and exerted sideways (in short, a lateral inhibitor). The effect of this lateral cell *C* is to block the excitation that *A* sends upward.

Lateral inhibition is the basis of brightness contrast. Let's go back to the three cells in Figure 5.27. The more intensely cell *B* is stimulated, the more it will excite the lateral inhibitor, cell *C*. This explains why a gray patch on a black background looks brighter than the same gray patch surrounded by white. The black background does not stimulate cell *B*, so that the lateral inhibitor *C* will not be active. But a white background will stimulate cell *B*, which excites cell *C*, which in its turn diminishes the excitation cell *A* sends upward to the brain to inform it of the apparent brightness of the gray patch. The upshot of all this is contrast. The brain gets a visual message that is an exaggeration. What is dark seems darker, what is light seems lighter.

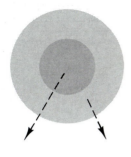

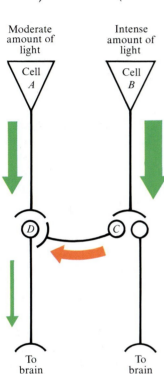

5.27 Lateral inhibition and contrast   *Two receptor cells, A and B, are stimulated by neighboring regions of a stimulus. A receives moderate stimulation; B receives an intense amount of light. A's excitation serves to stimulate the next neuron in the visual chain, cell D, which transmits the message further toward the brain. But this transmission is impeded by cell B, whose own intense excitation exerts an inhibitory effect on its neighbors. B excites a lateral cell, C, which exerts an inhibitory effect on cell D. As a result, cell D fires at a reduced rate. (Excitatory effects are shown by green arrows, inhibitory ones by red arrows.)*

Color

Despite their many differences, the sensory systems of hearing and of vision have some things in common. In both, the relevant stimulus energy is in wave form. And in both, wavelength is related to a qualitative psychological dimension—in one case pitch, in the other color. Much of the research in both domains has revolved around the question of how these sensory qualities are coded. We will here consider only one of these domains, that of color.

There is little doubt that color perception concerns sensory quality rather than intensity. The sensation red is different from green or blue in a way that cannot be described as a matter of more or less. Since Müller's formulation of the doctrine of specific nerve energies, sensory psychologists have assumed that such qualitative differences in sensation imply a difference in the neural processes that underlie these qualities. In their search for the color mechanism, they were guided largely by psychological facts, using them to infer neurological processes that could not be verified directly given the techniques of their time. As in the case of lateral inhibition, some of these inferences have ultimately been confirmed by physiological evidence, in some cases a century after they were first proposed.

CLASSIFYING THE COLOR SENSATIONS

A person with normal color vision can distinguish over seven million different color shades. What are the processes that allow him to make these distinctions? One step in answering this question is to find a classification system that will allow us to describe any one of these millions of colors by reference to a few simple dimensions. In this task we concentrate on what we see and experience, on psychology rather than physics. What we want to classify is our color sensations rather than the physical stimuli that produce them. In doing so, we cannot help but discover something about the way our mind—that is, our nervous system—functions. Whatever order we may find in the classification of our sensations is at least partially imposed by the way in which our nervous system organizes the physical stimuli that impinge upon it.

The dimensions of color   Imagine seven million or so colored paper patches, one for each of the colors we can discriminate. We can classify them according to three perceived dimensions: hue, brightness, and saturation.

Hue is a term whose meaning is close to that of the word *color* as used in everyday life. It is a property of the so-called **chromatic colors** (for example, red and blue) but not of the **achromatic colors** (that is, black, white, and all of the totally

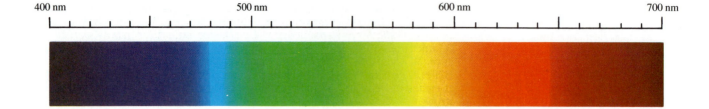

400 nm   500 nm   600 nm   700 nm

5.28 The visible spectrum and the four unique hues   *The visible spectrum consists of light waves from about 400 to 700 nanometers (1 nm = one millionth of a millimeter). White light contains all of these wavelengths. They are bent to different degrees when passed through a prism, yielding the spectrum with the hues shown in the figure. Three of the four unique hues correspond to part of the spectrum: unique blue at about 475 nm, unique green, at about 515 nm, and unique yellow, at about 580 nm. These values vary slightly from person to person. The fourth, unique red—that is, a red which has no apparent tinge of either yellow or blue—is called extraspectral because it is not represented by a single wavelength on the spectrum. It can only be produced by a mixture of wavelengths. (From Ohanian, 1984)*

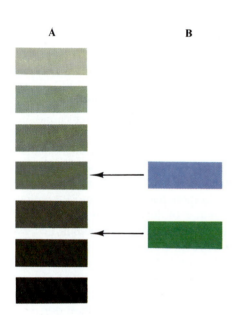

A   B

5.29 Brightness   *Colors can be arranged according to their brightness. (A) This dimension is most readily recognized when we look at a series of grays, which are totally hueless and vary in brightness only. (B) Chromatic colors can also be classified according to their brightness. The arrows indicate the brightness of the blue and dark green shown here in relation to the series of grays.*

5.30 Saturation   *The four patches A–D are identical in both hue and brightness. They only differ in saturation, which is greatest for A and decreases from A to D. The gray patch, E, on the far right matches all the other patches in brightness; it was mixed with the blue patch A in varying proportions to produce patches B, C, and D.*

neutral grays in between). Hue varies with wavelength (Figure 5.28). Thus, **unique blue** (a blue which is judged to have no trace of red or green in it), occurs on the spectrum at about 475 nanometers, **unique green** (which has no blue or yellow) at about 515 nanometers, and **unique yellow** (which has no green or red) at about 580 nanometers.

Brightness varies among both the chromatic and achromatic colors. Thus, ultramarine is darker than light blue and charcoal gray is darker than light gray (Figure 5.29). But the brightness dimension stands out most clearly if we consider achromatic colors alone. These differ in brightness only, while the chromatic colors may differ in hue (as we have seen) and in saturation (which we will discuss next). Note that white and black represent the top and bottom of the brightness dimension. Thus, white is hueless and maximally bright; black is hueless and minimally bright.

Saturation is the "purity" of a color, the extent to which it is chromatic rather than achromatic. The more gray (or black or white) is mixed with a color, the less saturation it has. Consider the various blue patches in Figure 5.30. All have the same hue (blue). All have the same brightness as a particular, achromatic gray (which is also the same gray with which the blue was mixed to produce the less saturated blue patches, *A, B, C,* and *D*). The patches only differ in one respect: the proportion of blue as opposed to that of gray. The more gray there is, the less the saturation. When the color is entirely gray, saturation is zero. This holds for all colors.

A   B   C   D   E

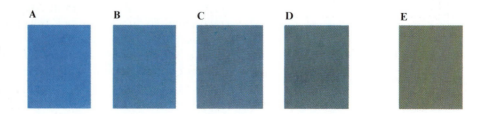

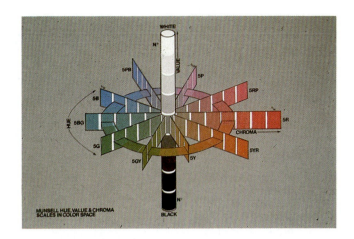

5.32   The three dimensions of color   *Brightness is represented by the central axis, going from darkest (black) to brightest (white). Hue is represented by angular position relative to the color circle. Saturation is the distance from the central vertical axis. The farther the color is from this axis, the more saturated it is. The maximal saturation that is possible varies from hue to hue; hence, the different extensions from the central axis. (Munsell Color, courtesy of Macbeth, a division of Kollmorgen Corporation)*

5.31   The color circle   *The relationship between maximally saturated hues can be expressed by arranging them in a circle according to their perceptual similarity. Note that in this version of the color circle, the spacing of the hues depends upon their perceptual properties rather than the wavelengths that give rise to them. In particular, the four unique hues are equally spaced, each 90 degrees from the next. (Hurvich, 1981)*

The color circle and the color solid   Some hues appear to be very similar to others. Suppose we only consider the color patches that look most chromatic—that is, those whose saturation is maximal. If we arrange these on the basis of their perceptual similarity, the result is a circular series, the so-called ***color circle,*** such that red is followed by orange, orange by yellow, yellow-green, green, blue-green, blue and violet, until the circle finally returns to red (Figure 5.31).

The color circle embodies the perceptual similarities among the different hues. To complete our classificatory schema, we construct the so-called ***color solid*** which incorporates the color circle with the other two dimensions of perceived color, brightness, and saturation (Figure 5.32). Each of our original seven million color patches can be fitted into a unique position in this solid (Figure 5.33). Our classificatory task is thus accomplished.

5.33   The color solid   *Every color can be placed within a so-called color solid that is based on the 3 dimensions of brightness, hue, and saturation. (A) This figure shows one view of the solid. The squashed form is due to the fact that maximal saturation of different hues occurs at different levels of brightness. Thus, maximally saturated yellow is brighter than maximally saturated blue. (B) The inside of the solid is shown by taking slices that illustrate variations in hue, brightness, and saturation. (Munsell Color, courtesy of Macbeth, a division of Kollmorgen Corporation)*

A

B

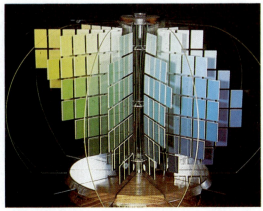

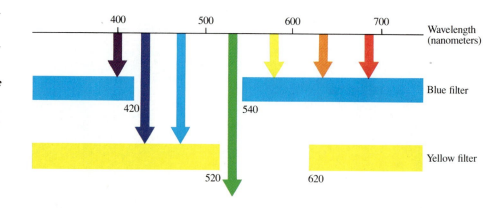

5.34 Subtractive mixture *In subtractive mixture, the light passed by two filters (or reflected by two pigments) is the band of wavelengths passed by the first minus that region which is subtracted by the second. In this example, the first filter passes light between 420 and 540 nanometers (a broad-band blue filter), the second light between 520 and 620 nanometers (a broad-band yellow filter). The only light which can pass through both is in the region between 520 and 540 nanometers, which appears green.*

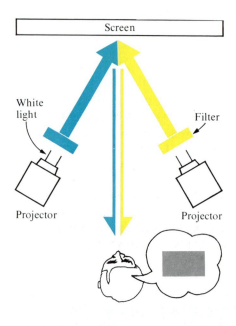

5.35 Additive mixture *In additive mixture, the light passed by two filters (or reflected by two pigments) impinges upon the same region of the retina at the same time. The figure shows two projectors throwing blue-yellow filtered light upon the same portion of the screen from which it is reflected upon the same region of the retina. In contrast to what happens in subtractive mixture, the result of adding these two colors is gray.*

COLOR MIXTURE

With rare exceptions, the objects in the world around us do not reflect a single wavelength; rather, they reflect different ones, all of which strike the same region of the retina simultaneously. Let us consider the results of some of these mixtures.

Subtractive mixture Before proceeding, we must recognize that the kind of mixture sensory psychologists are interested in is very different from the sort artists employ when they stir pigments together on a palette. Mixing pigments on a palette (or smearing crayons together on a piece of paper) is **subtractive mixture.** In subtractive mixture, one set of wavelengths is subtracted from another set. The easiest demonstration is with colored filters, such as those used in stage lighting, which allow some wavelengths to pass through them while holding others back. Take two such filters, *A* and *B*. Suppose filter *A* allows passage to all light waves between 420 and 540 nanometers but no others. The broad range of light that comes through this filter will be seen as blue. In contrast, filter *B* passes light waves between 520 and 620 nanometers but excludes all others. The band of light waves that comes through this filter will be seen as yellow (Figure 5.34).

We now ask how we see light that has to pass through *both* filters. Filter *A* (the blue filter) blocks all light above 540 nanometers, while filter *B* (the yellow filter) blocks all light below 520 nanometers. As a result, the only light waves that can pass through this double barricade are those that can slip through the narrow gap between 520 and 540 nanometers, the only interval left unblocked by *both* filters. As it happens, light in this interval is seen as green. Thus, when the mixture is subtractive, mixing blue and yellow will yield green.

Thus far we have dealt with filters which let some wavelengths through while blocking others. The same account also applies to artists' pigments. Any pigment reflects only a certain band of wavelengths while absorbing the rest. Suppose we mix pigment *A* (say, blue) to pigment *B* (say, yellow). The result is a form of subtraction. What we will see is the wavelengths reflected by the blue pigment (420 to 540 nanometers) minus the wavelengths absorbed by the yellow pigment (everything below 520 nanometers). The effect is exactly the same as if we had superimposed a blue filter over a yellow one. All that is reflected is light between 520 and 540 nanometers, which is seen as green.

Additive mixture In subtractive mixture, we alter the optic stimulus before it ever hits the eye. There is another kind of mixture that goes on in the eye itself.

5.36   Additive mixture in Pointillist art
The Harbor of Gravelines (1890) by Georges Seurat. A detail of the painting (on the left) shows the separate color daubs which, when viewed from a distance, mix additively. The pointillists employed this technique instead of mixing pigments to capture the bright appearance of colors outdoors. Pigment mixture is subtractive and darkens the resulting colors. (Courtesy Indianapolis Museum of Art, gift of Mrs. James W. Fesler in memory of Daniel W. and Elizabeth C. Marmon)

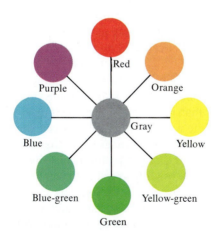

5.37   Complementary hues *Any hue will yield gray if additively mixed (in the correct proportion) with a hue on the opposite side of the color circle. Such hue pairs are complementaries. Some complementary hues are shown here linked by a line across the circle's center. Of particular importance are the two complementary pairs that contain the four unique hues: red-green and blue-yellow.*

This is ***additive mixture*** which occurs when different bands of wavelengths stimulate the same retinal region simultaneously. Such additive mixtures can be produced in the laboratory by using filtered light from two different projectors which are focused on the same spot. As a result, the light from each filtered source will be reflected back to the same retinal area (Figure 5.35).

In real life, additive mixture has many uses. One is color television, in which the additive mixture is accomplished by three different sets of photosensitive substances. Another example is provided by the Pointillist painter Georges Seurat. He used dots of different colors that are too close together to be seen separately, especially when the picture is viewed from a distance (Figure 5.36).

Complementary hues   One of the most important facts of additive color mixture is the fact that every hue has a ***complementary,*** another hue which if mixed with the first in appropriate proportions will produce the color gray. An easy way to find complementaries is by reference to the color circle. Any hue on the circumference will yield gray if mixed (additively) with the hue on the opposite side of the color circle (see Figure 5.37). Of particular interest are the complementary pairs that involve the four ***unique colors,*** red, yellow, green, and blue. Blue and yellow are complementaries which produce gray upon additive mixture; the same holds for red and green. Hues that are not complementary produce mixtures which preserve the hue of their components. Thus, the mixture of red and yellow leads to orange (which still looks like a yellowish red) while that of blue and red yields a violet (which looks like a reddish blue).

At the risk of repetition, note that all of this holds only for additive mixture. When blue and yellow are additively mixed in the right proportions the observer sees gray. This is in contrast to what happens when the mixture is subtractive, as

169

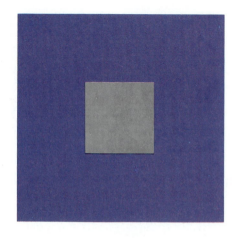
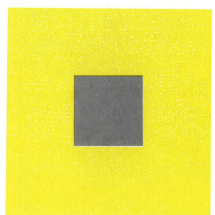

5.38 Color contrast *The gray patches on the blue and yellow backgrounds are physically identical. But they don't look that way. To begin with, there is a difference in perceived brightness: the patch on the blue looks brighter than the one on the yellow, a result of brightness contrast. There is also a difference in perceived hue, for the patch on the blue looks somewhat yellowish, while that on the yellow looks bluish. This is color contrast, a demonstration that hues tend to induce their antagonists in neighboring areas.*

in drawing a blue crayon over a yellow patch. Now the result is green. The same holds for red and green. Additive mixture of the two yields gray; subtractive mixture will produce a blackish brown.

COLOR ANTAGONISTS

The color-mixture effects we have just described suggest that blue and yellow on the one hand, and red and green on the other, are two pairs of mutually opposed antagonists which cancel each other's hue. There are some further phenomena which lead to a similar conclusion.

One effect is the chromatic counterpart of brightness contrast. In general, any region in the visual field tends to induce its color antagonist in adjoining areas. The result is ***simultaneous color contrast.*** For example, a gray patch will tend to look bluish if surrounded by yellow, yellowish if surrounded by blue, and so on (Figure 5.38).

In simultaneous contrast, the antagonistic relation involves two adjoining regions in space. In a related phenomenon, the contrast is with an immediately preceding stimulus; it is a contrast in time rather than in space. Suppose we stare at a green patch for a while and then look at a white wall. We will see a reddish spot. This is a ***negative afterimage*** (Figure 5.39). Negative afterimages have the complementary hue and the opposite brightness of the original stimulus (which is why they are called negative). Thus, fixation on a brightly lit red bulb will make us see a dark greenish shape when we subsequently look at a white screen.

Afterimages are caused by events that occur in the retina and associated visual mechanisms. This is why, when the eye moves, the afterimage moves along with it. One reason for the effect is retinal adaptation. When we fixate a white disk on a black background, the pigments in the retinal region that corresponds to the disk will be bleached more intensely than those in surrounding areas. During subsequent exposure to a homogeneous white surface, the more deeply bleached regions will respond less vigorously and will thus report a lesser sensory intensity. The result is a dark gray negative afterimage. But peripheral adaptation is probably not the whole story. In addition, there may be a ***rebound phenomenon.*** While the inspection stimulus was still present, the excited regions may well have inhibited an antagonistic process. White held back black, blue inhibited yellow, and so

5.39 Negative afterimage *Stare at the center of the figure for about a minute or two, and then look at a white piece of paper. Blink once or twice; the negative afterimage will appear within a few seconds showing the rose in its correct colors.*

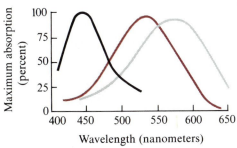

5.40   Sensitivity curves of three different cones in the primate retina   *The retina of humans and monkeys contains three different kinds of cones, each with its own photopigments which differ in their sensitivity to different regions of the spectrum. One absorbs more of the shorter wavelengths (and is thus more sensitive to light in this spectral region), a second more of the middle wavelengths, a third more of the longer ones. The resulting sensitivity curves are shown here. (After MacNichol, 1964)*

Ewald Hering *(Courtesy National Library of Medicine)*

on. When the stimulus is withdrawn, the inhibited processes rebound, like a coiled spring that is suddenly released.

COLOR RECEPTORS

What is the neurological mechanism that underlies color vision? We will consider this issue by subdividing it into two questions. (1) How are wavelengths transduced into receptor activity? (2) How is the receptor output coded into such sensory qualities as hue?

The raw material with which the visual system must begin is light of various intensities and wavelengths. Since we can discriminate among different wavelengths, there must be different receptors (that is, different types of cones) which are somehow differentially attuned to this physical dimension.

It turns out that normal human color vision depends on only three different kinds of color elements (which is why it is called ***trichromatic).*** Each of these three cone types responds to a very broad range of wavelengths in the spectrum. The main difference between these three cone elements is in their sensitivity curves. One cone type is most sensitive to wavelengths in the short-wave region of the spectrum, the second to wavelengths in the middle, and the third to the longer wavelengths (Figure 5.40).

The overlap between the three sensitivity curves is so extensive that any wavelength must necessarily stimulate each of the three receptor elements. This being so, how do we manage to discriminate wavelengths? We can because each receptor element will respond in differing degree depending upon the stimulating wavelength. If the light is from the short end of the spectrum, there will be maximal output from the cone element whose sensitivity is greater in the short-wave region. If the light is from the long end, it will elicit maximum activity from the cone element whose sensitivity is greatest in the long-wave region. As a result, each wavelength will produce a different ratio of the outputs of the three receptor types. Assuming that the nervous system can tell which receptor type is sending which message, wavelength discrimination follows.

COLOR CODING: THE OPPONENT-PROCESS THEORY

The receptor mechanisms alone cannot explain why we *see* a color the way we do, nor can they account for certain perceived relations among perceived colors. For example, some colors appear pure or primary (for example, unique blue) while others do not (for example, violet). Furthermore, these primary colors form two complementary and antagonistic pairs (red-green and blue-yellow). To explain phenomena of this kind we must assume some further mechanisms which work on the three receptor outputs and ultimately code them into the sensory qualities we know as color.

A widely accepted approach is the ***opponent-process theory*** formulated by Leo Hurvich and Dorothea Jameson which dates back to the nineteenth-century psychophysiologist, Ewald Hering. This theory asserts that there are six psychologically primary color qualities—red, green, blue, yellow, black, and white—each of which has a different neural process that corresponds to it. These six processes are not independent, but instead are organized into three opponent-process pairs: red-green, blue-yellow, and black-white. The two members of each pair are antag-

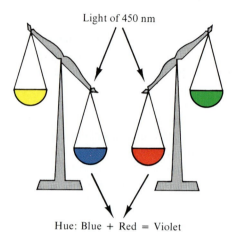

Light of 450 nm

Hue: Blue + Red = Violet

5.41 The opponent-process hue systems *The diagram shows how opponent-process theory interprets our response to light of a particular wavelength. In the example, the light is in the short-wave region of the visible spectrum, specifically, 450 nanometers. This will affect both the blue-yellow and the red-green systems. It will tip the blue-yellow balance toward blue, and the red-green balance toward red. The resulting hue will be a mixture of red and blue (that is, violet). (After Hurvich and Jameson, 1957)*

onists. Excitation of one member automatically inhibits the other (Hurvich and Jameson, 1957).

The two hue systems   According to the opponent-process theory, the experience of hue depends upon two of three opponent-process pairs—red-green and blue-yellow. (As we will see, the black-white system is not relevant to perceived hue.) Each of these opponent-process pairs can be likened to a balance scale. If one arm (say, the blue process) goes down, the other arm (its opponent, yellow) necessarily comes up. The hue we actually see depends upon the position of the two balances (Figure 5.41). If the red-green balance is tipped toward red and the blue-yellow balance toward blue (excitation of red and blue with concomitant inhibition of green and yellow), the perceived hue will be violet. This follows, because the resulting hue will be a combination of red and blue, which is seen as violet. If either of the two scales is evenly balanced, it will make no contribution to the hue experience. This will occur when neither of the two antagonists is stimulated, and also when both are stimulated equally and cancel each other out. If both hue systems are in balance, there will be no hue at all and the resulting color will be seen as achromatic (that is, without hue).

The black-white system   The brightness or darkness of a visual experience is determined by the activity of a third pair of antagonists, black and white. Every wavelength contributes to the excitation of the white system, in proportion to its intensity and the sensitivity of daylight vision to this point of the spectrum. The black process is produced by inhibition of the antagonistic white process. This is best exemplified by some phenomena of brightness contrast. A black paper placed against a dark gray background will look not black but a darker shade of gray. We can make it look pitch-black by presenting it against a brilliantly illuminated background. By doing so, we inhibit the white process within the enclosed region, which necessarily enhances the activity of its antagonist.

THE PHYSIOLOGICAL BASIS OF OPPONENT PROCESSES

When the theory was first developed, the opponent processes were only an inference, based upon the perceptual phenomena of color vision. Today there is evidence that this inference was close to the neurophysiological mark. The proof comes from single-cell recordings (in the retina or higher up) which show that some neurons behave very much as an opponent-process theory would lead one to expect.

As an example, take a study of single-cell activity in the visual pathway of the rhesus monkey, whose color vision is known to be very similar to ours. Some of its visual cells behave as though they were part of a blue-yellow system. If the retina is stimulated by blue light, these cells fire more rapidly. The opposite holds true if the same area is exposed to yellow light—the firing rate is inhibited (Figure 5.42). This is exactly what should happen if the underlying color mechanism mirrors the perceptual phenomena. Blue should have one effect and yellow the opposite. Other cells have been discovered which show a similar antagonistic pattern when stimulated by red or by green light (de Valois, 1965).

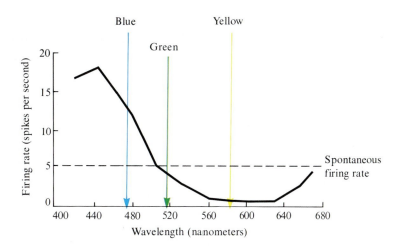

5.42   Opponent process cells in the visual system of a monkey   *The figure shows the average firing rate of "blue-yellow cells" to light of different wavelengths. These cells are excited by shorter wavelengths and inhibited by longer wavelengths, analogous to the cells in the human system that signal the sensation "blue." As the figure shows, shorter wavelengths lead to firing rates that are above the spontaneous rates obtained when there is no stimulus at all. Longer wavelengths have the opposite effect, depressing the cell's activity below the spontaneous firing rate. (Data from de Valois and de Valois, 1975)*

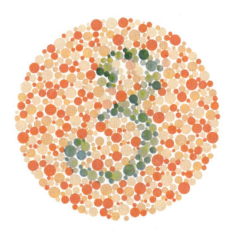

5.43   Testing for color blindness   *A plate used to test for color blindness. To pick out the number in the plate, an observer has to be able to discriminate certain hues. Persons with normal color vision can do it and will see the number 3. Persons with red-green color blindness cannot do this. (Courtesy American Optical Corporation)*

COLOR BLINDNESS

A small proportion of the total population consists of people who do not respond to color as most others do. Of these the vast majority are men, since many such conditions are inherited and sex-linked. Some form of color defect is found in 8 percent of all males as compared to only .03 percent of females.

Color deficiencies come in various forms, some of which involve a missing visual pigment, others a defective opponent process, and many involve malfunction at both levels (Hurvich, 1981). Most common is a defect in which reds are confused with greens; least common is total color blindness in which no hues can be distinguished at all. Color defects are rarely noticed in everyday life, for color-blind persons ordinarily use color names quite appropriately. They call blood red and dollar bills green, presumably on the basis of other cues such as form and brightness. To determine whether a person has a color defect he or she must be tested under special conditions in which such extraneous cues are eliminated (Figure 5.43).

How do people with color defects see colors? We may know that a particular person cannot distinguish between red and green, but that does not tell us how these colors look to him. He cannot tell us, for he cannot know what sensory quality is lacking. The question would have remained unanswerable had it not been for a subject who was red-green color blind in one eye and had normal color vision in the other. This subject (who happened to be one of the rare females with a color defect) was able to describe what she saw with the defective eye by using the color language of the normal one. With the color-blind eye she saw only grays, blues, and yellows. Red and green hues were altogether absent, as if one of the opponent-process pairs was missing (Graham and Hsia, 1954).

Let us take stock. We have looked at the way in which the different sensory systems respond to external stimuli, how they transduce the proximal stimulus and convert it into a neural impulse, how they code the incoming message into the various dimensions of our sensory experience, and how activity in any part of a sensory system interacts with the activity of other parts. All of this has led us to some understanding of how we come to see bright yellow-greens and hear high-pitched noises. But it has not yet addressed the question with which we started. How do we come to know about the objects and events outside—not just bright yellow-greens but grassy meadows, not just high-pitched noises but singing birds? That the sensory systems contribute the raw materials for such knowledge is clear enough. But how do we get from the sensory raw materials to a knowledge of the world outside? This question is traditionally dealt with under the heading of *perception,* the topic to which we turn next.

SUMMARY

1. The study of sensory processes grew out of questions about the origin of human knowledge. John Locke and other *empiricists* argued that all knowledge comes through stimuli that excite the senses. We can distinguish two kinds of stimuli. One is the *distal stimulus,* an object or event in the world outside. The other is the *proximal stimulus,* the pattern of physical stimulus energies that impinges on a given sensory surface. The only way to get information about distal stimuli outside is through the proximal stimuli these give rise to. This leads to theoretical problems, for we perceive many qualities—depth, constant size and shape—that are not given in the proximal stimulus. Empiricists try to overcome such difficulties by asserting that much of perception is built up through learning by *association.* This view has been challenged by *nativists* such as Immanuel Kant who believe that the sensory input is organized according to a number of built-in categories.

2. The path to sensory experience or *sensation* begins with a proximal stimulus. This is *transduced* into a nervous impulse by specialized receptors, is usually further modified by other parts of the nervous system, and finally leads to a sensation. One branch of sensory psychology is psychophysics, which tries to relate the characteristics of the physical stimulus to both the quality and intensity of the sensory experience.

3. Qualitative differences in sensory experience occur both between *sensory modalities* (e.g., A-flat versus red) and within them (e.g., green versus red). According to the *doctrine of specific nerve energies,* such qualitative differences are ultimately caused by differences between the nervous structures excited by the stimuli rather than by differences between the stimuli as such.

4. The founder of psychophysics, Gustav T. Fechner, studied sensory intensity by determining the ability of subjects to discriminate between stimulus intensities. Important measures of this ability are the *absolute threshold* and the *difference threshold.* The difference threshold is the change in the intensity of a given stimulus (the so-called *standard stimulus*) that is just large enough to be detected, producing a *just noticeable difference or j.n.d.* According to *Weber's law,* the j.n.d. is a constant fraction of the intensity of the standard stimulus. Fechner generalized Weber's law to express a wider relationship between sensory intensity and physical intensity. This is *Fechner's law,* which states that the strength of a sensation grows as the logarithm of stimulus intensity.

5. A way of disentangling sensory sensitivity and *response bias* is provided by *signal-detection theory.* In a typical *detection experiment,* the stimulus is presented on half of the trials, and absent on the other half. In this procedure, there can be two kinds of errors: *misses* (saying a stimulus is absent when it is present) and *false alarms* (saying it is present when it is absent). Their relative proportion is partially determined by a *payoff matrix.* When this payoff matrix is varied, the effects can be graphically expressed by an *ROC* curve. According to signal-detection theory, distinguishing between the presence of a stimulus and its absence depends on a process in which the subject has to decide whether a *sensory process* is produced by the *signal* or some *background noise.*

SUMMARY

6. Different sense modalities have different functions and mechanisms. One group of senses provides information about the body's own movements and location. Skeletal motion is sensed through *kinesthesis,* bodily orientation by the *vestibular organs* located in the *inner ears.*

7. The sense of taste acts as a gatekeeper to the digestive system. Its receptors are the *taste buds* whose stimulation generates the four basic taste qualities of *sour, sweet, salty,* and *bitter.*

8. The various *skin senses* inform the organism of what is directly adjacent to its own body. There are at least four different skin sensations: *pressure, warmth, cold,* and *pain.* Whether each of these four is produced by separate receptors is still a matter of debate, although there is no doubt that these experiences are evoked in different spots of the skin.

9. Smell or *olfaction* is the most primitive of the distance senses. In humans, it is relatively minor, but in many animals it is a vital guide to food, mates, and danger. In many species it permits a primitive form of communication based on *pheromones.*

10. The sense of hearing or *audition* informs us of pressure changes that occur at a distance. Its stimulus is a disturbance of the air which is propagated in the form of *sound waves.* These can vary in *amplitude* and *frequency,* and may be *simple* or *complex.*

11. A number of accessory structures help to conduct and amplify sound waves so that they can affect the auditory receptors. Sound waves set up vibrations in the *eardrum* which are then transmitted by the *ossicles* to the *oval window* whose movements create waves in the *cochlea* of the inner ear. Within the cochlea is the *basilar membrane,* which contains the auditory receptors that are stimulated by the membrane's deformation. According to the *place theory,* the sensory experience of pitch is based on the place of the membrane that is stimulated; each place being responsive to a particular wave frequency and generating a particular pitch sensation. According to the *frequency theory,* the stimulus for pitch is the firing frequency of the auditory nerve. Modern theorists believe that both mechanisms operate: Higher frequencies depend upon the place of the basilar membrane, while lower frequencies depend upon neural firing frequency.

12. Vision is our primary distance sense. Its stimulus is light, which can vary in *intensity* and *wavelength.* Many of the structures of the eye, such as the *lens* and the *iris,* serve mainly as accessory devices to fashion a proper proximal stimulus, the *retinal image.* Once on the retina, the light stimulus is transduced into a neural impulse by the visual receptors, the *rods* and *cones. Visual acuity* is greatest in the *fovea* where the density of the receptors (here, cones) is greatest.

13. According to the *duplexity theory of vision,* rods and cones differ in function. The rods operate at low light intensities and lead to colorless sensations. The cones function at much higher illumination levels and are responsible for sensations of color. Further evidence for the duplexity theory comes from different *spectral sensitivity curves.*

14. The first stage in the transformation of light into a neural impulse is a photochemical process that involves the breakdown of various *visual pigments* that are later resynthesized. One such pigment is *rhodopsin,* the photochemically sensitive substance contained by the rods.

15. The various components of the visual system do not operate in isolation but interact constantly. One form of interaction occurs over time, as in various forms of *adaptation.* Visual adaptation is usually counteracted by eye movements, but their effects can be nullified by the *stabilized image* procedure.

16. Interaction also occurs in space, between neighboring regions on the retina. An example is *brightness contrast.* This tends to enhance the distinction between an object and its background and also *accentuates contours.* The physiological mechanism that underlies this is *lateral inhibition,* as shown by studies of *receptive fields.*

175

17. Visual sensations have a qualitative character—they vary in color. Color sensations can be ordered by reference to three dimensions: *hue, brightness,* and *saturation.* Colors can be mixed, *subtractively* (as in mixing pigments) or *additively* (as in simultaneously stimulating the same region of the retina with two or more stimuli). The results of additive mixture studies show that every hue has a *complementary hue* which, when mixed with the first, yields gray. Two important examples are red and green, and blue and yellow. These two color pairs are color antagonists, a fact shown by the phenomena of the *negative afterimage* and *simultaneous color contrast.*

18. The first question about the mechanisms that underlie color vision concerns the way in which the different light waves are transduced into a receptor discharge. There is general agreement that this is done by the joint action of three different cone types, each of which has a somewhat different sensitivity curve.

19. A second question concerns the way the receptor message is converted into our color experience. A leading approach is the *opponent-process theory* of Hurvich and Jameson. This assumes that there are three neural systems, each of which corresponds to a pair of antagonistic sensory experiences: red-green, blue-yellow, and black-white. The first two determine perceived hue; the third determines perceived brightness. Further evidence for the opponent-process view comes from single-cell recordings of monkeys and some phenomena of *color blindness.*

NOTE: THE DECISION PROCESS AND SIGNAL-DETECTION THEORY

This chapter presented an informal account of the signal-detection approach. But how does the decision process envisaged by signal-detection theory work?

According to the theory, on any one trial, the subject has to decide whether some activity of the sensory system (that is, the **sensory process)** is produced by an actual, external stimulus (the **signal)** or by various random processes of the system (the **background noise).** How can she decide? The trouble is that the sensory process doesn't have a label that indicates its source. As a result, all the subject can use as a guide is the intensity of that sensory process.

To see how this works, consider Figure 5.44. This is a **frequency distribution** of the intensity of the hypothetical sensory process when there is no stimulus, and thus only background noise. In this frequency distribution, the intensity of the sensory process is plotted on the horizontal axis and the frequency with which that intensity occurs on the vertical. The figure shows that the intensity is sometimes smaller and sometimes larger; most of the time it hovers around a mean, or average, value that we will call M_n (the mean of the noise-only distribution).

Now consider Figure 5.45. This shows what happens when a stimulus is actually presented. Again, the intensity of the sensory process will fluctuate. But the values obtained now will in general be larger since we are dealing with trials on which there is *both* a signal and a background noise. As a result, the mean of this distribution, M_s, will be larger than M_n, the mean of the intensity values when there is noise alone.

How does the subject decide whether she heard (or saw, or felt) a stimulus or not? To see how signal-detection theory deals with this problem, consider Figure 5.46 in which the noise-alone and the signal-plus-noise distribution are plotted on the same axis. As the figure shows, the two distributions overlap. This means

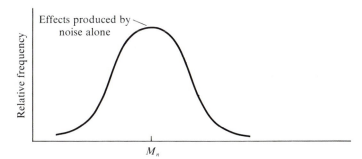

5.44 Effects produced by noise alone

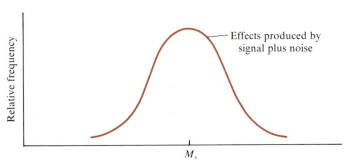

5.45 Effects produced by signal plus noise

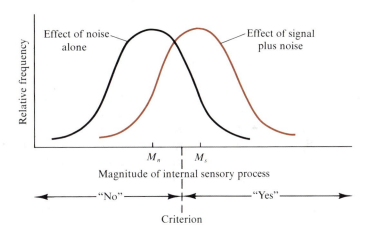

5.46 The overlap of noise-alone and signal-plus-noise distributions

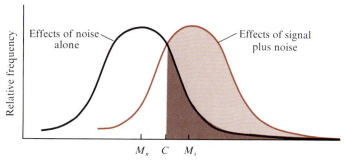

5.47 The decision process according to signal-detection theory

that on some trials, the intensity of the sensory process when there is no stimulus (noise-alone) exceeds that which is generated when a stimulus is present (signal-plus-noise).

What can the subject do now? Her task, in effect, is to decide whether a given internal experience comes from the signal-plus-noise distribution or from the noise-only distribution. According to signal-detection theory, the subject sets up a criterion and acts according to a decision rule. If the intensity of the sensory process is greater than this criterion, C, she decides that it came from the signal-plus-noise distribution and makes a "yes" judgment. If the value of the sensory process is less than C, she decides that it came from the noise-alone distribution and makes a "no" judgment.

Since the noise-alone and the signal-plus-noise distributions overlap, there is no way in which the subject can avoid errors. The nature of these errors will partially depend on the criterion. This is illustrated in Figure 5.47, p. 177. Because of the subject's decision rule, all the judgments to the left of the criterion, C, are "nos," while all the judgments to the right are "yeses." We can now read off the relative proportion of hits (saying "yes" when there was a stimulus) and false alarms (saying "yes" when there was no stimulus) from the figure. The proportion of "hits" is given by the portion of the area under the signal-plus-noise curve which falls to the right of C (and is here indicated in lighter color). The proportion of false alarms is indicated by the portion of the area under the noise-alone curve which falls to the right of the same criterion point (and is here indicated in darker color). Just where the criterion is placed depends on the subject's response bias. If she wants to minimize misses (saying "no" when a signal is actually presented), she has to shift her criterion to the left. This will decrease the number of misses, but it will also necessarily increase the number of false alarms.

CHAPTER 6

Perception

In the previous chapter, we discussed some of the simpler attributes of sensory experience, such as red, A-flat, and cold. Locke and Berkeley thought that these experiences were produced by a passive registration of the proximal stimulus energies which impinge upon the senses. But, as we have seen, the eye is more than a camera, the ear more than a microphone, for both sensory systems actively transform their stimulus inputs at the very start of their neurological journey, emphasizing differences and minimizing stimulation that remains unchanged. This active organization of the stimulus input is impressive enough when we consider the experience of simple sensory attributes, but it becomes even more dramatic when we turn to the fundamental problem traditionally associated with the term *perception:* how we come to apprehend the objects and events in the external reality around us; how we come to see, not just a brightish red, but an apple.

THE PROBLEM OF PERCEPTION

What must be explained to understand how we see the apple? Our initial reaction might be that the only problem is the perceptual meaning of the visual input, how it is interpreted as an edible fruit—which grows on trees, which keeps the doctor away, which caused the expulsion from Eden, and so on. But how objects acquire perceptual meaning is by no means the only question, or even the most basic one, for the student of perception. The fundamental issue is not why a given stimulus is seen as a particular kind of object, but rather why it is seen as any object at all. Suppose we show the apple to someone who has never seen any fruit before. He will not know its function, but he will certainly see it as some round, red thing of whose tangible existence he has no doubt—in short, he will perceive it as an object.

A

B

Going Beyond the Proximal Stimulus

Our discussion of the sensory systems thus far does not explain this basic phenomenon of object perception, the fact that we see the apple as it really is: of constant form and size, in depth, and stationary. But this reality is the reality of the distal stimulus, the actual apple in the external world. The problem is that the distal stimulus is known to us only through the proximal stimulus that it projects upon our retina, and this proximal stimulus is two-dimensional and is constantly changing. It gets smaller or larger depending upon our distance from it; it stimulates different regions of the retina; it moves across the retina as we move our eyes. How does the organism manage to perceive the constant properties of the external object despite the variations in the proximal stimulus?

The attempts to answer this question are best understood as parts of the continuing debate between the heirs of Locke, Berkeley, and Hume on the one hand, and those of Kant on the other. This controversy between empiricists and nativists will serve as an organizational framework for much of the discussion in this chapter.

Empiricism and Nativism Revisited

Most of the phenomena perception psychologists deal with involve some apparent discrepancy between what the proximal stimulus gives us and what we actually see. The question is how to resolve this discrepancy.

THE EMPIRICISTS' ANSWER

Empiricists handle the problem by asserting that the sensation produced by a particular stimulus is modified and reinterpreted in the light of what we have learned through past experience. Consider perceived size. People five feet away look just about as tall as those at a fifty-foot distance. This is not merely because we *know* them to be average-sized rather than giants or midgets. The fact is that they really *look* equally tall provided there are cues which indicate their proper distance (Figure 6.1).

How can we explain this and similar phenomena? The most influential version of the empiricists' answer was formulated by Hermann von Helmholtz in the late nineteenth century. According to Helmholtz, the perceiver has two sources of information. To begin with, there is the sensation derived from the size of the object

6.1   Perceived size and distance   *(A) The actual image of the two men in the picture—which corresponds to the size of their retinal image—is in the ratio of 3 to 1. But this is not the way they are perceived. They look roughly equal in size, but at different distances, with one about three times farther off than the other. In (B) there are no cues that indicate that one man is farther away than the other. On the contrary. The figure was constructed by cutting the more distant man out of the picture, and pasting him next to the other man, with the apparent distance from the viewer equal for the two. Now they look very different in size. (After Boring, 1964; Photograph by Jeffrey Grosscup)*

James J. Gibson   *(Courtesy E. J. Gibson)*

6.2 Texture gradient *Mudflats in Death Valley produce a higher-order pattern of stimulation that provides information about distance. (Photograph by David Muench, The Image Bank)*

on the retina. In addition, there are a number of depth cues that indicate how far away the object is. Prior learning has taught the perceiver a general rule: the farther away things are, the smaller will be the sensation derived from the retinal image. The perceiver can now infer the true size of the object, given its retinal size, its distance, and the learned rule that relates the two. As a result she adjusts her perception of size, shifting it downward if the object is seen as close by and upward if it is seen farther off. Helmholtz of course knew full well that we don't go through any *conscious* calculation of this sort when we look at objects and perceive their size. But he believed that some such process was going on anyway and he therefore called it **unconscious inference** (Helmholtz, 1909).

THE NATIVISTS' ANSWER

The nativists' reply is that the perception of size is directly given. They argue that the stimulus for the perceived size of an object is not the size of the retinal image as such. It is rather some relationship between that size and certain other attributes that pertain to depth.

A very influential modern version of this approach is that of James J. Gibson (1950, 1966, 1979). Gibson believed that such vital characteristics of an object as its size, its shape, and its distance from the observer are signaled by various **higher-order patterns of stimulation** to which the organism is innately sensitive.

As an example, let's return to size. To be sure, the size of the retinal image projected by an object must necessarily vary with its distance from the observer. But Gibson argued that this does not mean that there is no size information in the stimulus that hits the eye. One reason is that objects are usually seen against a background whose elements—leaves, pebbles, clumps of grass, or whatever—provide a texture. Since these elements are generally of about the same size, their size on the retina varies with distance and leads to **texture gradients** (see Figure 6.2). These texture gradients provide information about distance and also about the relative size of objects in the world outside. For distance has the same effect on the retinal image cast by the object as it has on the retinal image of the adjacent texture elements of its background. In both cases, the retinal size decreases with increasing distance. As a result, there is a constant ratio between the retinal size cast by an object and the retinal size of its adjacent texture elements—a higher-order stimulus relationship that remains *invariant* over changes of distance (see Figure 6.3, p. 182).

The extent to which higher-order patterns of stimulation (such as the size ratio) provide information about various attributes of the world—of which size is only one—is still a matter of considerable debate. No less controversial is the claim that the response to such higher-order patterns is part of our native endowment. To settle such issues, a number of psychologists have turned to the study of perception in early infancy. (For details, see Chapter 14, pp. 476–81.)

As we shall see, the nature-nurture controversy is still with us. Some of its skirmishes have been resolved in favor of one or the other combatant, but this doesn't mean that the conflict is over. Perception psychologists are still divided over such issues as whether visual size and form are innately given or are learned. We cannot take up these matters until we've discussed some of the phenomena in the perception of form, depth, and movement. But we should nevertheless keep them in the backs of our minds, for many of the specific questions we will take up

A   **B**

6.3 An invariant relationship that provides information about size   *(A) and (B) show a dog at different distances from the observer. The retinal size of the dog varies with distance, but the ratio between the retinal size of the dog and the retinal size of the texture elements made up of the bushes is constant. (Photographs by Jeffrey Grosscup).*

6.4 Figure and ground   *The first step in seeing a form is to segregate it from its background. The part seen as figure appears to be more cohesive and sharply delineated. The part seen as ground is perceived to be more formless and to extend behind the figure.*

6.5 Reversible figure-ground pattern
The classic example of a reversible figure-ground pattern. It can be seen as either a pair of silhouetted faces or a white vase.

are really subquestions within the great debate between the empiricists and their nativist opponents.

PERCEPTUAL ORGANIZATION

A person who looks at the world tries to organize what he sees into a coherent scene in which there are real objects (such as apples) and events (such as apples that fall from trees). To achieve this organization, he has to answer three important perceptual questions about what he sees (or hears or feels) out there: What is it? Where is it? What is it doing? To understand the ways in which the person attempts to answer these questions, we will discuss some aspects of the perception of form, of depth, and of movement.

The Perception of Form: What Is It?

FIGURE-GROUND

Before we can ask what an object is, we must first see it as a coherent whole which stands out against its background, as a tree stands out against the sky and the clouds. This segregation of *figure* and *ground* can easily be seen in two-dimensional pictures. In Figure 6.4, the bright splotch appears as the figure which seems to be cohesive and articulated. On the other hand, the darker region is normally perceived as the ground, which is relatively formless and seems to extend behind the figure.

The differentiation between figure and ground is a perceptual achievement that is accomplished by the perceptual system. It is not in the stimulus as such. This point is made very strikingly by *reversible figures* in which either of two figure-ground organizations is possible. A classic demonstration is shown in Figure 6.5 which can be seen either as a white vase on a black background or as two black profile faces on a white background. This reversibility of figure-ground patterns has fascinated various artists, especially in recent times (see Figure 6.6).

6.6 Figure-ground reversal in the visual arts *Two lovers embracing in a print by Victor Vasarely. Either lover can be seen as figure or ground. (Courtesy SPADEM, Paris/ VAGA, N.Y., 1980)*

Max Wertheimer (1880–1943) (Courtesy Omikron)

PERCEPTUAL GROUPING

Reversible figure-ground formations demonstrate that the same proximal pattern may give rise to different perceptual organizations. The same conclusion follows from the related phenomenon of perceptual *grouping.* Suppose we look at a collection of dots. We can perceive the pattern in various ways depending upon how we group the dots: as a set of rows, or columns, or diagonals, and so on. In each case, the figural organization is quite different even though the proximal stimulus pattern is always the same.

What determines how a pattern will be organized? Some factors that determine visual grouping were first described by Max Wertheimer, the founder of *Gestalt psychology,* a school of psychology that believes that organization is basic to all mental activity, that much of it is unlearned, and that it reflects the way the brain functions. Wertheimer regarded these grouping factors as the laws of *perceptual organization* (Wertheimer, 1923). A few of these are discussed below.

Proximity The closer two figures are to each other *(proximity)* the more they will tend to be grouped together perceptually. Proximity may operate in time just as it does in space. The obvious example is auditory rhythm: four drum beats with a pause between the second and third will be heard as two pairs. Similarly, these six lines generally will be perceived as three pairs of lines:

Similarity Other things equal, we tend to group figures according to their *similarity.* Thus in the figure below, we group black dots together with black dots and colored dots with colored dots. As a result, we see rows rather than columns in the left panel, and columns rather than rows in the right panel.

183

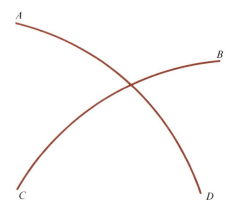

6.7 Good continuation *The line segments in the figure will generally be grouped so that the contours continue smoothly. As a result, segment A will be grouped with D, and C with B, rather than A with B and C with D.*

Good continuation Our visual system seems to "prefer" contours that continue smoothly along their original course. This principle of grouping is called ***good continuation*** (Figure 6.7). Good continuation is a powerful organizational factor that will often prevail even when pitted against prior experience (Figure 6.8). This principle is used by the military for camouflage (Figure 6.9A). It also helps to camouflage animals against their natural enemies. For example, it helps to conceal various insects from predators who tend to see parts of the insect's body as continuations of the twigs on which it stands (Figure 6.9B).

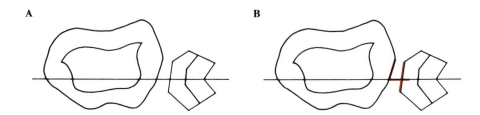

6.8 Good continuation pitted against prior experience *In (A), virtually all subjects see two complex patterns intersected by a horizontal line. Hardly anyone sees the hidden 4 contained in that figure—and shown in (B)—despite the fact that we have encountered 4's much more often than the two complex patterns which are probably completely new. (After Köhler, 1947)*

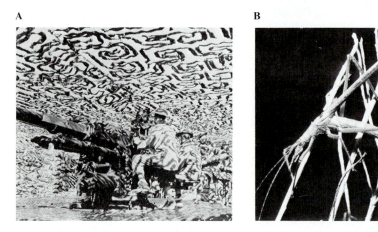

6.9 Good continuation as the basis of camouflage *(A) Here, camouflage is achieved by artificial contours that break up the outlines of the soldiers and their military installation. (Courtesy The Warder Collection) (B) Good continuation helps to conceal the insect from predators who tend to see parts of the insect's body as continuations of the twigs on which it stands. (Photograph by David C. Rentz, Bruce Coleman)*

6.10 Closure *There is a tendency to complete—or close—figures that have a gap in them, as in the incomplete triangle shown here.*

Closure We often tend to complete figures that have gaps in them. Figure 6.10 is seen as a triangle despite the fact that the sides are incomplete.

A closurelike phenomenon yields **subjective contours.** These are contours that are seen, despite the fact that they don't physically exist (Figure 6.11). Some theorists interpret subjective contours as a special case of good continuation. In their view, the contour is seen to continue along its original path, and, if necessary, jumps a gap or two to achieve the continuation (Kanizsa, 1976).

PATTERN RECOGNITION

Thus far we have considered the first steps in perceiving an object—seeing it as a figure that stands out against its background and whose parts seem to belong together. The next step is to determine *what* that object is. To do this, the organism must match the form of this figure to the form of some other figure it has previously seen and recognize it appropriately. This process is called **pattern recognition.** One of the major problems of the psychology of perception is to determine how this is accomplished.

Humans and animals can recognize a form even when all of its component parts are altered. Consider two similar triangles. It doesn't matter whether they are small, rendered as solids or as line drawings, made up of dots or dashes. The perceived form remains the same (Figure 6.12, p. 186). This phenomenon is sometimes called the **transposition of form** or **pattern.** A triangle is a triangle is a triangle, whatever the elements of which it is composed. Similar effects occur in the temporal patterning of sounds. A melody remains the same even when all of its notes are changed by transposing to another key, and the same rhythm will be heard whether played on a kettledrum or a glockenspiel.

Phenomena such as these were among the chief arguments of the Gestalt psychologists who insisted that forms are not perceived by somehow summing up all of the localized sensations that arise from individual retinal points of excitation.

6.11 Subjective contours *Subjective contours are a special completion phenomenon in which contours are seen even where none exist. In (A), we see a white triangle whose vertices lie on top of the three black circles. The three sides of this white triangle (which looks brighter than the white background) are clearly visible, even though they don't exist physically. In (B), we see the same effect with black and white reversed. Here, there is a black triangle (which looks blacker than the black background) with subjective black contours. (Kanizsa, 1976)*

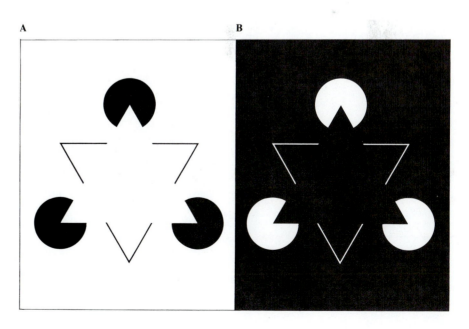

They argued instead that a form is perceptually experienced as a **Gestalt,** a whole which is different from the sum of its parts.* To recognize that a pattern is the same as one we have seen before, we must perceive certain relations among the component parts, which can remain intact despite many alterations of the parts of the figure. Just how this process of pattern recognition works is still an unsolved problem.

The Perception of Depth: Where Is It?

To know *what* a thing is, is not enough. Whether an object is a potential mate or a sabertooth tiger, the perceivers can hardly take appropriate action unless they can also locate the object in the external world. Much of the work on this problem of visual localization has concentrated on the perception of depth, a topic that has occupied philosophers and scientists for over three hundred years. They have asked: How can we possibly see the world in three dimensions when only two of these dimensions are given in the image that falls upon the eye? This question has led to a search for **depth cues,** features of the stimulus situation which indicate how far the object is from the observer or from other objects in the world.

BINOCULAR CUES

A very important cue to depth comes from the fact that we have two eyes. These look out on the world from two different positions. As a result, they obtain a somewhat different view of any solid object they converge on. This **binocular disparity** inevitably follows from the geometry of the physical situation. Obviously, the disparity becomes less pronounced the farther the object is from the observer. Beyond thirty feet the two eyes receive virtually the same image (Figure 6.13).

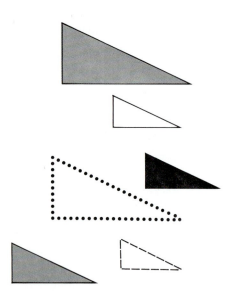

6.12 Form equivalence *The perceived forms remain the same regardless of the parts of which they are composed.*

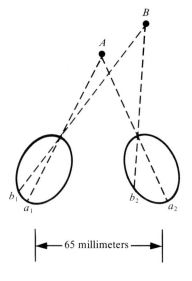

6.13 Retinal disparity *Two points, A and B, at different distances from the observer, present somewhat different retinal images. The distance between the images on one eye, a_1b_1 is different (disparate) from the distance between them on the other, a_2b_2. This disparity is a powerful cue for depth. (After Hochberg, 1978a)*

65 millimeters

* The term *Gestalt* is derived from a German word which means "form" or "entire figure."

6.14 Interposition *When one figure interrupts the contour of another figure, it provides a monocular cue for depth. This is interposition. Because of interposition, the colored rectangle in the figure is perceived to be in front of the gray one.*

Binocular disparity alone can induce perceived depth. If we draw or photograph the two different views received by each eye while looking at a nearby object and then separately present each of these views to the appropriate eye, we can obtain a striking impression of depth. To achieve this stereo effect, the two eyes must converge as they would if they were actually looking at the solid object at the given distance.

MONOCULAR CUES

Binocular disparity is a very powerful (and probably innate) determinant of perceived depth. Yet, we can perceive depth even with one eye closed. Even more important, many people who have been blind in one eye from birth see the world in three dimensions. Clearly then, there are other cues for depth perception that come from the image obtained with one eye alone—the ***monocular depth cues.***

Many of the monocular depth cues have been exploited for centuries by artists, and are therefore called ***pictorial cues.*** Examples include ***linear perspective, relative size,*** and ***interposition.*** In each case, the effect is an optical consequence of the projection of a three-dimensional world upon a flat surface. Objects that are farther away are also inevitably blocked from view by any other opaque object which obstructs their optical path to the eye (interposition; see Figure 6.14). Far-off objects necessarily produce a smaller retinal image than do nearby ones (linear perspective and relative size; Figures 6.15 and 6.16).

A very powerful set of pictorial cues is ***texture gradients,*** which we've already considered in another context (see p. 181). Such gradients are ultimately produced by perspective. Consider what meets the eye when we look at cobblestones on a road or clumps of grass in a meadow. James Gibson pointed out that the retinal projection of such objects must necessarily show a continuous change, a tex-

6.15 Linear perspective as a cue for depth *(Photograph by Dennis Brach, Black Star)*

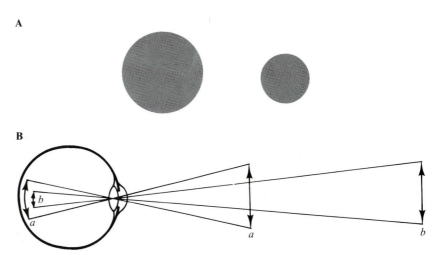

A

B

6.16 Relative size *(A) All other things equal, the larger of two otherwise identical figures will seem to be closer than the smaller one. This is a consequence of the simple geometry of vision illustrated in (B). Two equally large objects,* a *and* b, *that are at different distances from the observer, will project retinal images of different size.*

187

A

B

6.17 Texture gradients as cues for depth Uniformly textured surfaces produce texture gradients that provide information about depth: as the surface recedes, the texture density increases. (A) At a seashore, such gradients may be produced by rocks, and (B) if it is hot enough, by people (Photographs by M. Vide, Woodfin Camp, and Arthur Fellig [Weegee], Museum of Modern Art)

ture gradient, that depends upon the spatial layout of the relevant surfaces (Figure 6.17). Such texture gradients are powerful determinants of perceived depth. Discontinuities in texture gradients provide information about further spatial relationships between the various textured surfaces. Thus, the abrupt change of texture density in Figure 6.18 produces the impression of a sharp drop, a "visual cliff" (see also p. 195; J. Gibson, 1950, 1966).

A   B

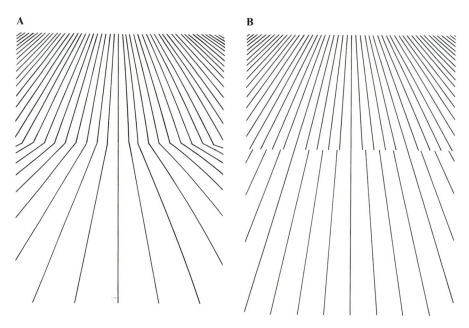

6.18 The effect of changes in texture gradients Such changes provide important information about spatial arrangements in the world. Examples are (A) an upward tilt at a corner; and (B) a sudden drop. (After Gibson, 1950)

Some recent studies have shown that the sensitivity to pictorial cues of depth begins at a rather early age. Six-month-old infants, wearing an eye patch over one eye to remove binocular cues, were shown a window frame that was in the shape of a trapezoid. In actuality, both sides of the window were equally far from the infant, but perspective cues would make the larger side appear to be nearer. To determine whether the infants reacted to perspective as adults do, the experimenters noted which side the infants reached for. Prior work had shown that babies generally reach for objects that are nearer than objects that are farther off. And indeed, the infants did reach for the side of the window that was larger, indicating that they, no less than we, react to perspective cues of depth (see Figure 6.19; Yonas, Cleaves, and Pettersen, 1978).

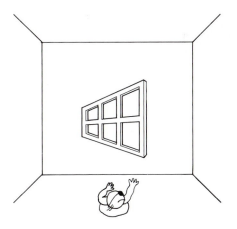

6.19   The use of pictorial cues by infants   Six-month-olds were shown a trapezoidal window frame. This frame was set up so that it was in a plane parallel to the wall right in front of the infants. This creates the illusion of being oriented at 45° to a viewer if looked at monocularly. The infants wore a patch over one eye to remove binocular depth cues. They reached for the side of the window that was larger, suggesting that they experienced the same illusion as adults and perceived the larger side as near.

MOTION PARALLAX

Thus far we have considered situations in which both the observer and the scene observed are stationary. But in real life we are constantly moving through the world we perceive. Motion provides a vital source of visual information about the spatial arrangement of the objects around us, a pattern of cues which once again follows from the optical geometry of the situation. As we move our heads or bodies from right to left, the images projected by the objects outside will necessarily move across the retina. The direction and speed of this motion is an enormously effective monocular depth cue, *motion parallax* (Helmholtz, 1909).

As we move through space, nearby objects seem to move very quickly and in a direction opposite to our own; as an example, consider the trees racing backward as one looks out of a speeding train (Figure 6.20). Objects farther away also seem to move in the opposite direction, but at a lesser velocity. These patterns of motion are a powerful factor in providing us with the experience of depth.

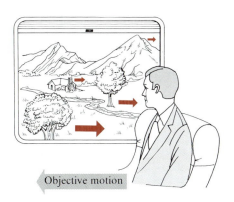

6.20   Motion parallax   When an observer moves relative to a stationary environment, the objects in that environment will be displaced (and will therefore seem to move) relative to him. (The rate of relative displacement is indicated by the thickness of the colored arrows. The thicker these arrows, the more quickly the objects seem to move. The observer's movement is indicated by a gray arrow.) (After Coren, Porac, and Ward, 1978)

The Perception of Movement: What Is It Doing?

To see a large, unfriendly Doberman in front of you is one thing; to see him bare his teeth and rush directly at you is quite another. We want to know what an object is and where it is located, but we also want to know what it is doing. Put another way, we want to perceive events as well as objects. The basic ingredient of the perception of events is the perception of movement.

ILLUSIONS OF MOVEMENT

What leads to the perception of movement? One might guess that one sees things move because they produce an image that moves across the retina. But this answer is too simple. For in fact, we sometimes perceive movement even when none occurs on the retina.

Stroboscopic movement   Suppose we briefly turn on a light in one location of the visual field, then turn it off, and after an appropriate interval (somewhere between 30 and 200 milliseconds) turn on a second light in a different location. The result is *stroboscopic movement* (sometimes called the *phi phenomenon)*. The light is seen to travel from one point to the other, even though there was no stim-

Physical events

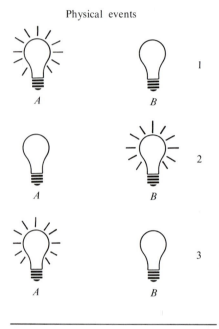

Perceptual experience

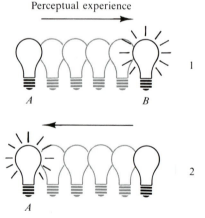

6.21 Stroboscopic movement *The sequence of optical events that produce stroboscopic movement. Light A flashes at time 1, followed by light B at time 2, then back to light A at time 3. If the time intervals are appropriately chosen, the perceptual experience will be of a light moving from left to right and back.*

ulation—let alone movement—in the intervening region (Figure 6.21). This phenomenon is perceptually overwhelming; given the right intervals, it is indistinguishable from real movement. It is an effect that has numerous technological applications, ranging from animated neon signs to motion pictures (Wertheimer, 1912). These results suggest that one stimulus for motion is relative displacement over time. Something is here at one moment and there at the next. If the time intervals are right, the nervous system interprets this as evidence that this something has moved.

Induced movement How does the perceptual system react when one of two objects is moving while the other is (physically) stationary? Consider a ball rolling on a billiard table. We see the ball as moving and the table at rest. But why not the other way around? To be sure, the ball is being displaced relative to the table edge, but so is the table edge displaced relative to the ball. One might guess that the reason is learning. Perhaps experience has taught us that balls generally move around while tables stay put. But the evidence indicates that what matters is a more general perceptual relationship between the two stimuli. The object that encloses the other tends to act as a frame which is seen as stationary. Thus, the table serves as a frame against which the ball is seen to move.

In this example, perception and physical reality coincide, for the frame provided by the table is truly stationary. What happens when the objective situation is reversed? In one study subjects were shown a luminous rectangular frame in an otherwise dark room. Inside the frame was a luminous dot. In actual fact, the rectangle moved to the right while the dot stayed in place. But the subjects saw something else. They perceived the dot as moving to the left, in the opposite direction of the frame's motion. The physical movement of the frame had induced the perceived movement of the enclosed figure (Figure 6.22).

The **induced movement** effect is familiar from everyday life as well. The moon apparently drifts through the clouds; the base of a bridge seems to float against the flow of the river current. In the second case, there may also be **induced motion of the self.** If the subject stands on the bridge which she perceives as moving, she may perceive herself to move along with it.

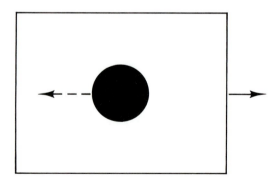

6.22 Induced movement *Subjects in an otherwise dark room see a luminous dot surrounded by a luminous frame. When the frame is moved to the right, subjects perceive the dot moving to the left, even though it is objectively stationary. (Duncker, 1929)*

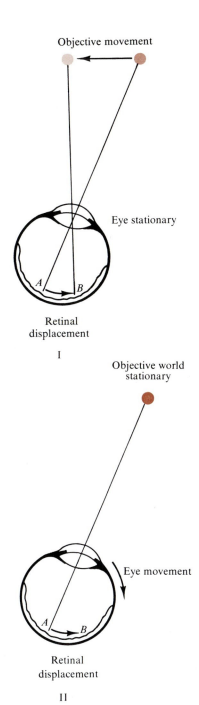

Objective movement

Eye stationary

A   *B*

Retinal
displacement

I

Objective world
stationary

Eye movement

A   *B*

Retinal
displacement

II

Thus far, we have asked why things are seen to move. A related question is why they are generally seen as stable. The issue arises because our eyes are constantly moving, so that the retinal image shifts all the time. But if so, why do we perceive the world as stationary? One interpretation follows from the fact that eye movements don't produce relative displacements. When we move our eyes as we look at a chair, the retinal image of the chair is displaced, but so is the image of the room which serves as its framework; as a result, there is no relative displacement. But this cannot be the whole story. As Helmholtz showed a century ago, movement will be seen if the eyes are moved by muscles other than their own. Close one eye and jiggle the outside corner of the other eye (gently!) with a finger. Now the world will move around, even though all relationships within the retinal image are kept intact. This shows that the perceptual system can respond to absolute displacement. But if it can do so when the eyes are pushed by a finger, why doesn't it when they are moved by the eye muscles that normally do the job?

Many students of visual perception believe that the nervous system achieves visual stability by compensating for retinal displacements which are produced by voluntary eye movements. Thus, when the brain signals the eye muscles to move, it computes the retinal displacement that such a movement would produce and then cancels out this amount in interpreting the visual input it receives. As a result, we will see a stationary point at rest, even though our eyes are moving. The brain evidently keeps track of what it told the eyes to do; say, to move 10 degrees to the right. It knows that the eye movement should produce a retinal displacement of 10 degrees in the opposite direction, and subtracts this from the visual signal (Figure 6.23).

PERCEPTUAL SELECTION: ATTENTION

We have seen that our perceptual system shapes and organizes the patchwork of different sensations into a coherent whole that has form, depth, and motion. In part, this organization arises from the fact that not all parts of the proximal stimulus pattern are given equal weight. We focus on the figure, not on the ground; we are more likely to notice shapes that are moving rather than those that are stationary. Such examples indicate that perception is selective. We don't look at all the stimuli that are there to be looked at or focus upon them all. Our ability to take in and interpret the myriad stimulations around us is finite, and so our perceptual system is forced to choose among them. The various ways by which we perceive selectively are often grouped together under the label ***attention.***

6.23   Compensation for eye movements   *When the retinal image of some object is displaced, it may be because the object has moved, because the eye has moved, or both. In panel I, there is objective movement which produces a retinal displacement, as the dot's projection shifts from point A to point B on the retina. But panel II shows that the same retinal displacement can be produced by moving the eye (in the opposite direction from that of the dot in panel I) while the object remains stationary. From the retinal point of view, the displacements in panels I and II are identical. Fortunately, our brain allows us to see motion independent of eye movements by compensating for the displacements caused by changes in eye position. In panel II, the brain would decide that there was no movement because the motion of the eye is precisely equal (and opposite) to the displacement on the retina.*

Selection by Physical Orientation

The most direct means of selecting the input is to physically orient the various sensory systems toward one set of stimuli and away from another. The organism does not passively touch, see, or hear; it actively feels, looks, and listens. It turns its head and eyes, converges and accommodates, explores the world with its hands (or paws or lips or prehensile trunk), and if it has the necessary motor endowment, pricks up its ears. These orienting adjustments of the sensory machinery are the external manifestations of attention.

EYE MOVEMENTS

In humans, the major means of physically selecting the stimulus input are movements of the eyes. Peripheral vision informs us that something is going on, say, in the upper left of our field of vision. But our peripheral acuity is not good enough to tell us what it is precisely. To find out, our eyes move so that this region falls into the fovea. A number of investigators have developed techniques for recording eye movements made when looking at pictures. The records show that the subjects glance most frequently at the regions that are visually most informative (Figure 6.24). This gaze pattern may be different for different observers, since what interests one person, may not interest another.

These results suggest that the act of looking is purposeful. People don't scan the word at random in the wistful hope that their foveas will by chance hit on some interesting bit of visual news. They pick up some information from what they've vaguely seen in the periphery and from their general notions of what the scene is about. They then move their eyes to check up on what they've seen and to refine their visual knowledge further.

INTEGRATING SUCCESSIVE GLIMPSES

On the average, our eyes move four or five times per second. Each time they move, the eyes briefly fixate at one particular region. But if so, how do we manage to get the impression of a single, stable scene? We can understand why our image seems stationary, for as we have seen there is an automatic compensation system that allows for eye movements. But why should we perceive one scene rather than a series of perceptual snapshots? Consider what happens when we look at a person's face. At one moment, the fovea receives the image of a nose; then, as the eyes move, there is the image of an eyebrow, then of an upper lip. Our perceptual system somehow manages to integate these separate images so that we manage to

A

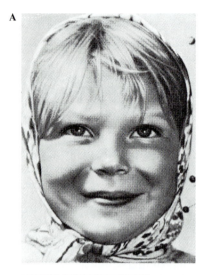

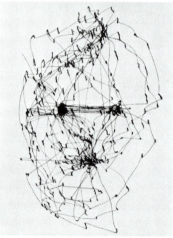

6.24 Eye-movement records when looking at pictures *Both (A) and (B) are pictures that were looked at for 3 and 10 minutes respectively. With each picture is the record of the eye movements during this period. As the records show, the bulk of the eye movements are directed toward the most visually informative regions. As a result, the eye-movement record is a crude mirror of the main contours of the picture. (From Yarbus, 1967)*

B

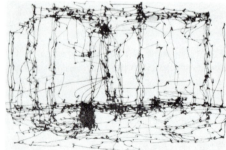

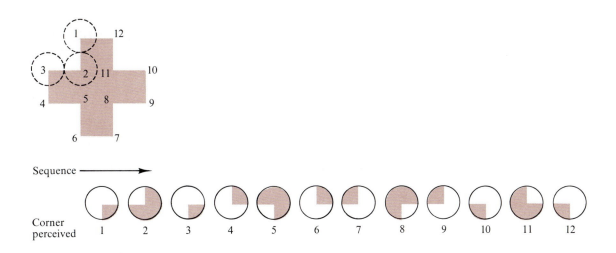

Sequence ——→

Corner perceived   1   2   3   4   5   6   7   8   9   10   11   12

6.25 Form built up by successive glimpses *Subjects look at a circular aperture. Through this aperture they receive a number of successive glimpses, each of which corresponds to a small portion of a figure (here, a cross) that is being moved around behind it. The subjects recognize the shape of the figure, even though they never saw it as a whole. The successive glimpses enable them to develop a perceptual schema of the form, in analogy to the way we integrate the separate images provided by our eye movements. (After Hochberg, 1970)*

see a face instead of an anatomical jumble of disconnected parts. What accounts for this integration?

According to Julian Hochberg, our perception of any figure is really a set of visual expectancies, a perceptual construction built up from the elements provided by different piecemeal glimpses. To test this notion, he devised a technique that provides successive glimpses artificially. Subjects are shown outline figures that are moved around behind a small aperture in a masking cardboard so that they can only see a small portion of the figure at a time. But the subjects nevertheless succeed in recognizing the shape (see Figure 6.25). Hochberg believes that much of ordinary visual perception works in a similar way. Each movement of the eyes provides a small element, which is then fitted together with other elements provided by the next point of fixation (Hochberg, 1970).

Central Selection

Eye movements and other means for changing physical orientation determine the sensory input the perceptual system receives. But this is only the first step in the selectional control of perception. From here on, central processes take over. They determine whether a particular portion of the sensory input will be dealt with further, and if so, how it will be interpreted.

SELECTIVE LISTENING

A widely used method for studying selectional attention is modeled on a phenomenon often observed in real life, the *cocktail-party effect.* During conversations at a noisy party, one tunes in on the voice of the person one is talking to. The many other voices are somehow filtered out and are consigned to a background babble. This effect has been studied experimentally by asking subjects to attend to one of two simultaneously presented verbal messages. The usual procedure is *dichotic presentation.* The subject wears two earphones and receives different messages through each of them. To guarantee selective attention, the subject is generally asked to *shadow* the to-be-attended message. This means that he has to repeat it aloud, word for word, as it comes over the appropriate earphone. Under these conditions, the irrelevant message tends to be shut out almost entirely. The subject can hear speechlike sounds, but notices little else. He is generally unable to recall the message that came by way of the unattended ear. In fact, he often does not even notice if the speaker on the unattended ear shifts into a foreign language or if the tape is suddenly played backward (Cherry, 1953).

THE FILTER THEORY OF ATTENTION

Results of this sort suggested that selective attention acts as a kind of filter. This filter is presumably interposed between the initial sensory registration and later stages of perceptual analysis. If the information is allowed through the attentional filter (that is, if it is fed into the attended ear), it can then be further analyzed—recognized, interpreted, and stored in memory. But if it does not pass through, it is simply lost. Early versions of this theory suggested that the filtering effect is all-or-none. Subjects in a dichotic listening experiment were thought to understand no part of the message that entered by way of the unattended ear (Broadbent, 1958).

This all-or-none theory turned out to be false, for there is good evidence that information which has some special significance is registered even if it is carried as part of the unattended message. The best example is the sight or sound of one's own name. No matter how intently we concentrate on the person next to us, we can't help but hear our own name in another conversation held on the other side of the room.

This everyday experience has been documented with the shadowing method. When subjects are forced to repeat a message that comes over one ear, word for word, they are almost completely oblivious of the irrelevant message that is fed into the other ear. But they do take notice when that irrelevant message contains the sound of their own name (Moray, 1959). This result suggests that the attentional filter does not block irrelevant messages completely. It only attenuates it, like a volume control that is turned down but not off. If the item is important enough (or perhaps familiar enough) then it may pass through the filter and be analyzed to some extent (Treisman, 1964).

Related evidence comes from a study in which subjects had to shadow sentences such as "They threw stones at the bank yesterday." Concurrently, the other ear was presented with either of two words: *river* or *money*. When questioned directly, the subjects couldn't recall which of the two words they had heard, if either. But some part of the meaning of these words must have come through nevertheless. The shadowed sentence contained the ambiguous word, *bank,* which can be understood as either a financial institution or as the side of a river. Which interpretation was chosen depended upon whether the unattended ear was presented with the word *money* or *river*. This shows that the subjects extracted some meaning from the unattended message even though they never knew they did (McKay, 1973).

INNATE FACTORS IN PERCEPTUAL ORGANIZATION

The common theme that runs through most of the phenomena we have just described is the same with which we began our discussion of the entire field of perception. What we perceive does not directly correspond to what the proximal stimulus gives us. Our perception is not a patchwork of separate sensations but is organized and selective. What are the factors that produce this organization? As we will see, some aspects of this organization stem from our native endowment.

Evidence for Innate Factors

How can we discover which aspects of perceptual organization (if any) are innately given? The problem has been approached in two major ways. One involves the study of very young (preferably newborn) organisms; the other asks what happens when function is restored to an organism that has been deprived of certain sensory experiences from birth.

PERCEPTUAL ORGANIZATION IN THE VERY YOUNG

Space In some organisms, important features of the perception of space are apparently built into the nervous machinery. An example is the localization of sounds in space. One investigator studied this phenomenon in a ten-minute-old baby. The newborn consistently turned his eyes in the direction of a clicking sound, thus demonstrating that some spatial coordination between eye and ear exists prior to learning (Michael Wertheimer, 1961).*

6.26 An infant on the visual cliff *The infant is placed on the center board laid across a heavy sheet of glass and his mother calls to him. If she is on the "deep" side, he pats the glass, but despite this tactual information that all is safe, he refuses to crawl across the apparent cliff. (Photograph by William Vandivert)*

A number of authors believe that some aspects of our visual depth perception are also unlearned. An early demonstration was provided by R. D. Walk and E. J. Gibson who noted that crawling infants are surprisingly (though by no means perfectly) successful in avoiding the precipices of their everyday lives (Walk and Gibson, 1961). The investigators studied infant behavior on the *visual cliff* which simulates the appearance of a steep edge but is safe enough to mollify the infants' mothers, if not the infants themselves. This device consists of a large glass table, about three feet above the floor, which is divided in half by a wooden center-board. On one side of the board, a checkerboard pattern is attached directly to the underside of the glass; on the other side, the same pattern is placed on the floor (Figure 6.26). The apparent drop-off is perceived by adults, in part because of a sudden change in texture density, in part because of motion parallax and binocular disparity. But will six-month-old infants respond to any of these cues? The babies were placed on the centerboard, and their mothers called and beckoned to them. When the mother beckoned from the shallow side, the baby usually crawled quickly to her. But only a very few infants ventured forth when called from across the apparent precipice.

An empiricist might well argue that these findings are inconclusive because the babies had six months of previous experience. Unfortunately, there is no easy way of studying visual cliff behavior in younger infants. You can't very well ask where an infant will crawl to if he cannot get up on his knees. But motor coordination matures much earlier in many species, and various very young animals show appropriate cliff-avoidance as soon as they are old enough to move around at all. Kids and lambs were tested as soon as they were able to stand. They never

* Appropriately enough for this nativist finding, the investigator was Max Wertheimer's son, the subject his newborn grandchild.

stepped onto the steep side. Chicks tested less than twenty-four hours after hatching gave the same result.

Form Innate mechanisms may also be relevant to form perception. A one-day-old chick will peck at small spheres in preference to small pyramids, even if kept in darkness from hatching to the time of the test. A prewired preference for round shapes together with the capacity to distinguish them is presumably useful to a creature whose primary foods are grain and seed (Fantz, 1957). Human form perception is less ready-made than the chick's; but even so, the visual world of a newborn infant is not a chaotic jumble of color and light. When a three-day-old infant is presented with a simple form, such as a triangle, its eyes do not move randomly. Photographs of the infant's cornea show that its eyes tend to orient toward those features of the pattern that help to define it, such as its edges and its vertices (Salapatek and Kessen, 1966; Salapatek, 1975).

Of special interest is the infant's very early tendency to look at forms that resemble a human face, in preference to others (Fantz, 1961; Freedman, 1971). This tendency is probably based on a preference for certain visual components that comprise a face, such as curved rather than straight contours (Fantz, 1970). Whatever its basis, such a built-in predisposition to look at facelike forms must have considerable survival value in an organism whose period of infantile dependence is so long and so intense.

By about three months of age, there is evidence that the infant can recognize something about the mother's face in a photograph. When presented with color slides of their mother or of a strange woman, they preferred to look at the picture of their mother. This indicates that some aspects of the familiar facial pattern were recognized even in a novel, two-dimensional form (Barrera and Maurer, 1981). (For further discussion of infant perception, see Chapter 14.)

PERCEPTION AFTER SENSORY DEPRIVATION

Another approach dates back to a question first raised by William Molyneux, a friend of John Locke's, who wondered how a man born blind would see the world were his vision suddenly restored: "Suppose a man *born* blind, and now adult, and taught by his *touch* to distinguish between a cube and a sphere. Suppose then the cube and sphere placed on a table, and the blind man to be made to see. . . . [Would he] now distinguish, and tell, which is the globe, which the cube?"

Molyneux was an empiricist and so to him (as to John Locke who quoted him approvingly) the self-evident answer was an emphatic no. "Though he has obtained the experience of how a globe, how a cube affects his touch, yet he has not yet attained the experience that what affects his touch so or so must affect his sight so or so" (Locke, 1690, p. 121).

Cases of the sort Molyneux had regarded as only imaginary do in fact occur. Persons with cataracts (an opaqueness or translucency of the lens) from birth have had them successfully removed, allowing vision—sometimes after many years of blindness. But the results are not as clear-cut as Molyneux had envisioned. In some cases, there seemed to be great difficulties in perceiving form equivalence. The patients could distinguish figure from ground and could discriminate objects on the basis of their size and color, but they had considerable trouble in distinguishing a triangle from a circle (von Senden, 1932). In other cases, there was some form recognition within a short time after the operation.

One patient was able to recognize form by using some of his previously acquired touch experience. For example, he could tell time by looking at a large wall clock in a hospital corridor without any special training. This feat was based on his prior experience with a pocket watch he had carried all his life. This watch had no glass so that he could feel the time by touching its hour and minute hands (Gregory and Wallace, 1963).

What can we conclude from these cases? The answer is, not much. One reason is that there are various postoperative disturbances, such as severe eye muscle cramp, which make proper assessment of the patient's visual abilities very difficult. Another is that different patients have different degrees of preoperative visual experience. Some cataracts may have blocked out all vision; others may have allowed the perception of some diffuse, cloudy shapes. Given all of these problems, the evidence from cataract removals must be regarded as inconclusive (Zuckerman and Rock, 1957).

The Search for the Built-in Mechanisms

All in all, there seems to be good reason to believe that some aspects of perceptual organization are innately given. But what are the mechanisms whereby the nervous system accomplishes this organization of the stimulus input? The last two or three decades have seen some steps toward an answer.

FEATURE DETECTORS

Electrophysiologists often record from single nerve cells (see Chapter 2). By such techniques they have discovered how particular cells in a sensory system respond to simple stimuli such as light of a given wavelength (see Chapter 5). More recently, they have applied the same approach using stimuli that are much more complex and relational.

Two physiologists, Nobel prize winners David Hubel and Torsten Wiesel, studied the activity of single cortical cells of cats in response to various visual stimuli. They found some cells which react to lines or edges of a particular orientation. Such a cell would be excited by a thin sliver of light slanted at, say, 45 degrees, but not otherwise, regardless of the line's specific retinal location (Figure 6.27). This cell is called a *feature detector;* it analyzes the visual stimulus to detect some fairly complex feature (such as orientation) and responds to this feature rather than to other aspects of the stimulus pattern (such as brightness or retinal location). Still other cells detect even more complex features. An example is a cell that reacts to right angles (Hubel and Wiesel, 1959).

Most psychophysiologists believe that the excitation of feature detectors leads to such perceptual experiences as movement, angular orientation, and the like. But they have no direct proof. To provide it one would have to find detector cells in (unanesthetized) human subjects and ask them to describe what they perceive while the cell is firing. Such an experiment is obviously out of the question. Nevertheless, most investigators continue to believe that what they pick up with their electrodes is somehow implicated in what we perceive.

One means of studying feature detectors from the psychological perspective is based on the phenomenon of *adaptation.* We have previously encountered adaptation effects in the case of such a relatively simple sensory quality as hue. After

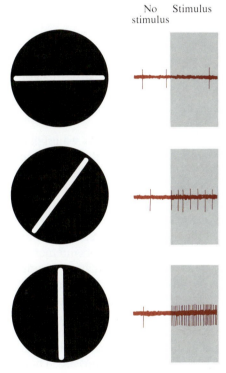

No   Stimulus
stimulus

6.27   Feature detectors in the visual system of the cat   *The response of a single cortical cell when stimulated by a slit of light in three different orientations. This cell, a simple unit, was evidently responsive to the vertical. A horizontal slit led to no response, a tilted slit led to a slight response, while a vertical slit led to a marked increase in firing. (After Hubel, 1963)*

197

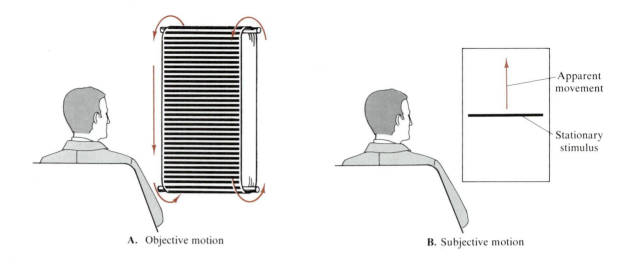

A. Objective motion   **B.** Subjective motion

6.28 Aftereffect of movement *(A) The subject first looks at a band of downward moving lines for a minute or two. (B) He then looks at a stationary horizontal line. This line will now appear to be moving upwards. This effect is probably produced by the adaptation of a movement detector that signals downward motion.*

prolonged fixation of a green patch, its apparent greenness will fade away and a neutral gray projected upon the same retinal region will look reddish (see Chapter 5). Effects of this sort laid the foundations for a theory of the opponent processes that underlie color. The same logic motivates the study of adaptation effects in more complex perceptual attributes (Anstis, 1975).

An example is the ***aftereffect of visual movement.*** If one looks at a waterfall for a while and then turns away to look at the riverbank, the bank and the trees upon it will be seen to float upward, a dramatic effect which is readily produced in the perceptual laboratory (Figure 6.28). We might expect just this result on the assumption that the direction of perceived movement is signaled by the activity of movement detectors which operate as opponent-process pairs. For example, one such pair might be composed of two kinds of movement detectors: one sensitive to upward, the other to downward movement. If these two detectors interact like the members of the color opponent-process pairs, then the stimulation of either one will automatically lead to the inhibition of the other. If one has been stimulated for a long time (say, by exposure to a downward moving pattern), it will gradually adapt. As a result, the balance will swing toward the other member of the pair (that is, the upward movement detector). This changed balance is revealed when the moving target is withdrawn and the subject looks at a stationary pattern. This (objectively stationary) pattern is now seen to move upward. The effect is analogous to the red afterimage that follows prolonged fixation of a green patch. In both cases, there is adaptation of one member of an opponent-process pair.

Is there any way to determine whether a particular feature detector in humans is located in the retina or higher up in the brain? Needless to say, we can't resort to microelectrodes. But a number of investigators used another approach. They asked subjects to look at a stimulus that moved continuously in one direction, but to do so with one eye only; the other eye was covered. Would this lead to an aftereffect of movement when the subjects were then tested with the *other* eye? If so, the motion detectors that were adapted by the moving stimulus must be located at a point beyond the retina, some region in the brain where the information from both eyes is somehow combined. The results proved that this was indeed the case. Looking at a moving stimulus with one eye led to an appropriate

6.29 Features and form *The fact that there are nerve cells that can detect such features as edges and angles does not yet explain how we come to see forms. Consider the triangle in (A). It is made up of three corners. There are probably feature detectors that can detect the presence of these corners. But the mere activation of these detectors is not enough. For they would be activated by both (B) and (C). In (B), the corners stand in the proper relationship to each other and constitute a triangle. In (C) this relationship is missing and there is no triangle form.*

adaptation effect when the test was conducted with the other eye (Mitchell, Reardon, and Muir, 1975).

FROM FEATURES TO ORGANIZED WHOLES

The organism is evidently endowed with appropriate neural devices that allow it to respond to such stimulus features as directional motion, edges, and orientation. But how does it organize these features into the organized wholes of our perceptual experience?

To take one example, how do we get from edges and orientations to the perception of a triangle? The fact that three angle detectors signal their excitement cannot by itself guarantee that we will perceive a triangle, for a triangle is not just three angles, but three angles in a particular mutual relationship (Figure 6.29). In this sense, the problem raised by the Gestalt psychologists is still with us. Such features as angles and edges and orientations are certainly broader and more relational than the discrete sensory atoms proposed by the early empiricists; but the basic issue is still the same. A whole is determined by the relations among its parts, whatever these parts may be. How do we get to this configuration?

One possibility is that the nativist solution works even at this level. Perhaps prewired systems exist which can detect complex shapes of various kinds, particularly those which have a special significance in the life of a given species. But it is inconceivable that such built-in mechanisms can account for all of the phenomena of form perception, especially in higher animals. Humans must discriminate among a multitude of patterns, and it is hardly possible that we carry specialized detectors for all of them—triangles, squares, apples, apple pies, champagne bottles, B-52s, cabbages, kings—the list is endless. But we do guess that the feature detectors are the raw materials out of which we construct the infinity of discriminable shapes by a process that somehow involves learning.

Under the circumstances, we conclude that neither extreme nativism nor extreme empiricism can wholly describe the phenomena of human form perception. The truth lies somewhere in between. At this stage, we do not know precisely where the natively given ends and experience takes over. Edges, corners, and the like may indeed be the ultimate innate units, but it is also possible that there are some higher-level units above them. For all we know, subsequent research may turn up some special cell geared to detect a more complex stimulus relationship. (For example, there might be a primitive something-like-a-face detector which would be useful in establishing the reaction to the mother at an early stage of infancy.) But it is certainly clear that at least some constellations are generated by the experience of the organism. We next turn to a discussion of what this experience can contribute.

LEARNED FACTORS IN PERCEPTUAL ORGANIZATION

Up to now, we have discussed those aspects of perceptual organization that are relatively unaffected by an observer's past or his expectations of the future. But there is little doubt that perception is often altered by just such factors. We will discuss such modifications of what we perceive under three major headings: perceptual adaptation, perceptual differentiation, and perceptual problem solving.

Perceptual Adaptation

How modifiable is perception? One question concerns the relation between different aspects of the perceptual world such as vision and bodily orientation. Can these be realigned? One of the first attempts to find out was performed by the American psychologist George Stratton (1865–1957) just before the turn of the century. He wore an optical device which inverted the entire visual scene, turning right to left and up to down for over a week. (He was thus the first man on earth whose retinal image was right side up.)

For a while, Stratton was seriously handicapped. His environment was utterly bewildering. He reached up for an object that was down; he turned left to enter a doorway that was to the right. But as time went on there was adaptation. He gradually readjusted, so that after eight days his motor coordination was perfect and his world seemed no longer strange and incongruous. When he finally removed the inverting lens system, he suffered an *aftereffect of adaptation.* Having adjusted to his upside-down existence, he had trouble returning to visual normalcy. At first, the uninverted world looked odd, and there was some difficulty in motor adjustment (Stratton, 1897).

Milder optical rearrangements produce much quicker and clear-cut effects. Examples are prisms that tilt the world in one direction or that shift the image to the right or the left. Here, the world changes its appearance very quickly. In one study, subjects wore prisms that tilted the image by 20 degrees. Two hours later some of them hardly saw the tilt. When the prisms were removed there was a strong perceptual aftereffect. Asked to adjust a luminous line in an otherwise dark room, they chose a setting of 20 degrees—in a direction opposite to the rotation imposed by the prisms (Mikaelian and Held, 1964).

Such results show that the relationship between various aspects of the perceptual world is modifiable. But how is this realignment achieved? Thus far we have only some tentative hypotheses. Some of these center on the information subjects derive from their own voluntary movements in the optically altered world. What happens if such movements are prevented? Some authors believe such active movements are an important factor in bringing perceptual adaptation about. In one study, some subjects were allowed to walk freely while wearing prisms which displaced the image to one side. Others wore the same prisms for the same period of time, but were passively transported over the same path in wheelchairs. When the prisms were removed, the subjects who had moved about on their own showed the usual aftereffect of adaptation; for them, "straight ahead" was shifted to the side opposite to the prismatic displacement. No such aftereffect was found for the subjects who had only been wheeled around. The investigators concluded that, to adapt, the subject must learn a new correlation between self-produced movements and their visual consequences (Held and Bossom, 1961).

Perceptual Differentiation

Perceptual adaptations are dramatic enough when they occur in the laboratory, but they are not an ordinary feature of everyday experience. Psychologists who want to know how learning affects perception are generally interested in other

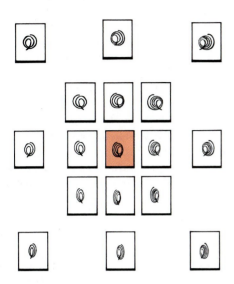

6.30 Perceptual differentiation *Subjects had to learn to differentiate between the item in the center (here shown in color) and all the other curlicues (here shown in black). In the figure, the curlicues are arranged according to such distinguishing features as number of coils, expansion or compression, coiled to right or left. Initially, all of these curlicues looked alike. With increasing experience, they became perceptually differentiated. (After Gibson and Gibson, 1955)*

questions. One of these is how we come to see differences that we did not see at first.

Common observation tells us that our perceptual world is often refined by further experience. To most of us, all gorillas look alike; to the zookeeper, each of them is utterly distinctive. The same holds for fingerprint experts, X-ray specialists, and wine tasters; they all have learned to perceive differences to which the rest of us are oblivious. This phenomenon has been called ***perceptual differentiation*** by Eleanor and James Gibson. In one of their studies subjects were shown a series of meaningless curlicues for three seconds each. Their job was to decide which of the figures was identical to one they had been shown just before. Initially, this task was quite difficult. But after a few trials, the subjects made no more errors. They had become curlicue connoisseurs, having learned what to look for in distinguishing among such patterns (Figure 6.30; Gibson and Gibson, 1955).

According to the Gibsons, perceptual differentiation is produced by a process that is akin to discrimination (see Chapter 4). The subject learns to look for those attributes of the object that distinguish it from others in its class. These distinguishing characteristics are the ***distinctive features*** to which the subject learns to attend. While doing so, the subject also learns to ignore features that are irrelevant. Thus, experienced airplane spotters can tell one plane from another by noting (often without awareness) whether it has a tapered wing or a stubby nose. According to the Gibsons, perceptual differentiation is brought about by attending to an ever more precisely delineated set of such distinguishing hallmarks. In terms of the aircraft example, the learner will gradually progress to ever finer distinctions such as "tapered with a slight upward slant" (E. J. Gibson, 1969).

Perceptual Problem Solving

There is a kind of perceptual learning that seems rather different from those we have discussed thus far. It often comes into play when we come to perceive and recognize new patterns.

Learning new patterns is a pervasive phenomenon of human life, perhaps especially so in infancy. But even as adults we sometimes manage to reorganize something we see or hear so that it looks or sounds completely new. Thus, a foreign language often sounds like gibberish before we learn to speak and understand it. Yet later on, we can no longer remember the chaotic jumble we initially heard. Similar effects are found in visual perception. Consider Figure 6.31, p. 202. First, the patches look disorganized, but after a while they take on a new appearance as we discover that they represent a dog and a horseman respectively.

A number of authors argue that such perceptual reorganizations are ***constructions*** created by the perceiver by a process that is essentially a form of problem solving (Neisser, 1967; Hochberg, 1978a; Rock, 1983). To understand how this process might operate in perception, we will discuss it in light of various approaches to pattern recognition.

FEATURE ANALYSIS

Some thirty years ago, an influential approach to pattern recognition grew out of the efforts of computer scientists to develop machines that could "read" visual

A

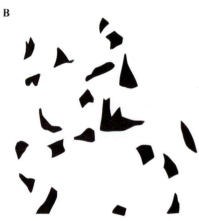

B

6.31 Perceptual reorganization *At first glance, (A) and (B) look like disorganized patches. But after looking at them for a few moments, they take on a new appearance as we see them as a dog (A) and a man on a horse (B). After they have been reorganized in this manner, it is difficult to see them as they appeared at first. (After Street, 1931)*

6.32 A feature analysis system for letter recognition *The physical stimulus "T" gives rise to a visual image. This is then analyzed for the presence or absence of various component features, such as vertical or horizontal lines, various corners, and so on. Each feature stimulates the stored letter patterns that contain it. In this example, two of the feature units stimulate the pattern "P," two the pattern "R," and four the pattern "T." As a result, the "T" is more actively excited than the "P" and "R," which leads to the decision that the letter is "T." (After Goldstein, 1984)*

forms; in particular, numerals and letters. Devices of this kind would have numerous practical applications, for example, sorting mail for the postal service, or organizing bank records.

Several attempts to design such artificial recognition systems are based on the analysis of visual features (e.g, Selfridge, 1959). Suppose we have a machine that can scan the optical image of a letter. How would it decide that this letter is, say, a *T*? What the machine might do is to start out by looking for the presence or absence of certain visual features (for example, horizontal, vertical, or diagonal bars, curves to the right or left, and so on). It could then consult a list stored in its memory which indicates the features that characterize each capital letter. By comparing the features it found in the stimulus with those on the list, it could reach the proper decision. Having done so, it would move on to the next letter, repeat the process, and so on through the text (see Figure 6.32).

As we have already seen, there is evidence that there are various neurons in the brain which can detect the presence of such features as tilts and angles. Under the circumstances, it seems reasonable that a feature-analysis model of the kind envisaged by computer scientists may underlie human pattern recognition. To be sure, the perceiver would have to learn which combination of features goes with a particular form. But once this was done, the rest would be just a matter of consulting the feature lists in one's memory and reaching the appropriate decision.

TOP-DOWN PROCESSING

The feature-analysis hypothesis just discussed regards pattern recognition as a ***bottom-up process.*** It starts with small component parts (the features) and gradu-

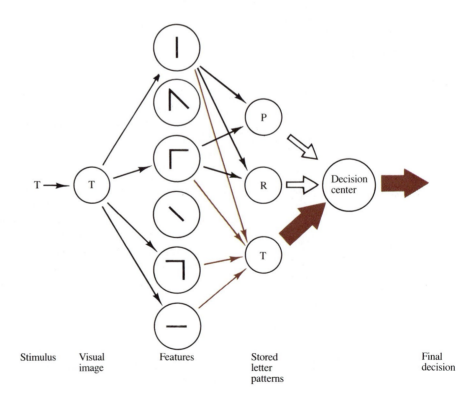

Stimulus   Visual image   Features   Stored letter patterns   Final decision

202

A

B

C

ally builds up to larger units that are, so to speak, on the top (letters, then words, then phrases, and so on). But there are reasons to believe that bottom-up processing is not enough. One of these reasons we've mentioned previously: to recognize a form one has to identify not just its features but also the relationships among them. Another problem is that there is evidence that pattern recognition often involves *top-down processes,* beginning with higher units, for it is often affected by higher-level knowledge and expectations.

One demonstration of top-down processing in perception is provided by so-called *context effects.* In many cases, this context is provided by experiences in the past (often, the immediately preceding past). A good example is provided by ambiguous figures. Consider Figure 6.33, which can be seen as either an old woman in profile or a young woman whose head is turned slightly away. In one study, subjects were first shown two fairly unambiguous versions of the figure (Figures 6.33B and C). When later presented with the ambiguous figure (Figure 6.33A), they perceived it in line with the unambiguous version they had been shown before (Leeper, 1935).

Other context effects depend on stimuli that are simultaneously present with the affected stimulus. As an example, take the two words shown in Figure 6.34 (see p. 204). The two middle "letters" of each word are physically identical, but they are usually seen as an *H* in *THE* and an *A* in *CAT.*

Similar context effects can make us hear speech sounds where in fact there are none. Something of this sort occurs in everyday life, for when people talk they sometimes cough or clear their throat so that the speech stream is interrupted. But even so, we usually hear and understand them and never notice that there were physical gaps in their actual physical utterance. In a laboratory demonstration of this phenomenon subjects listened to tape-recorded sentences in which the speech sounds were tampered with, as in the sentence:

The state governors met with their respective legislatures convening in the capital city.

In this sentence the experimenter replaced the middle *s* in the word *legislatures* with a cough-like noise. Yet, virtually none of the subjects even noticed that any speech sound was missing. They somehow restored the deleted speech sound, and "heard" the *s* that was provided by the total context (Warren, 1970).

PERCEPTUAL HYPOTHESES

Context effects demonstrate that there is some top-down processing. But this hardly means that bottom-up processing is unimportant. On the contrary. After all, if perceptual processing were only in the top-down direction, we would always see what we expect and think about—even if there were no stimulus whatever. To be sure, knowledge and expectations do help to interpret what we see and hear, but there has to be some sensory basis that confirms these interpretations.

6.33 An ambiguous figure   *(A) This is ambiguous and is just as likely to be seen as a young woman or as an old woman. (B) and (C) are essentially unambiguous, and depict the young woman and old woman respectively. If the subjects are first shown one of the unambiguous figures, they are almost sure to see the ambiguous picture in that fashion later on. (After Boring, 1930; Leeper, 1935)*

THE CAT

6.34   The effect of context on letter recognition   (After Selfridge, 1955)

As a result, perceptual processing is necessarily in both directions: from top down but also from bottom up.

This interplay of bottom-up and top-down processing is crucial to the notion that perception involves problem solving. According to this view, the perceptual system generally starts out with both a stimulus and a hypothesis. This perceptual hypothesis is then tested as the system analyzes the stimulus for some appropriate features. If these are found, the perceptual hypothesis gains plausibility and is either accepted or checked for further proof. If such features are not found, then a new hypothesis is considered, which is then tested by searching for yet other features, and so on.

Occasionally, we become consciously aware that some such process operates. This sometimes happens when we are presented with a visual display that initially makes no sense. An example is Figure 6.35. At first glance most observers don't know what to make of it. But as they continue to look at the figure, they develop hypotheses about what it might be (e.g., maybe this part is the leg of some animal, maybe the animal has a spotted hide). If they are lucky, they eventually hit on the correct hypothesis (a Dalmatian dog). When they finally see the dog, the top-down and bottom-up processes meet, and there is a perceptual insight, a visual "Aha!" Here the process of perceptual problem solving was quite conscious. But this is rare, for we usually see cars, trees, and people (and even Dalmatian dogs) without being aware that we are trying to solve any perceptual puzzles. But according to theorists who take the problem-solving approach to perception, much the same kind of thing occurs even then, though at much greater speed and outside of consciousness.

To sum up. Perceptual processing must include both bottom-up and top-down processes. Without bottom-up processing, there would be no effect of the external stimulus, and we would not perceive but only hallucinate. Without top-down processing, there would be no effect of knowledge and expectation, and we would never be able to guide and interpret what we see.

6.35   Perceptual problem solving   This is a picture of something. What? (Photograph by Ronald James)

204

THE LOGIC OF PERCEPTION

To the extent that perception involves a form of problem solving, it obeys a kind of logic. One of the laws of ordinary logic is that there can be no contradictions— a statement can't be both true and false at the same time. The perceptual system obeys a similar law. It operates to minimize perceptual contradictions and to make all parts mesh in a coherent whole. If the system detects a discrepancy, it does its best to rectify the situation (Rock, 1983).

An illustrative example comes from the study of stroboscopic motion. Subjects were briefly shown a rectangle lying upright in one location, followed by a brief exposure to a rectangle lying horizontally in another, and so on, with continued alternation of the two figures. If the intervals were appropriate, there was stroboscopic movement. But how can a figure be seen to move from one place to another, if its form is different in the two locations? The perceptual system comes up with a neat solution. The upright rectangle is seen to turn to the horizontal as it moves, and then turns upward when it moves back again (see Figure 6.36; adapted from Kolers, 1972).

In another study, the two alternating figures were a square and a circle. Again the subjects saw movement. But now the visual solution was different. The figures were seen to change smoothly from one shape to the other as they shuttled back and forth (see Figure 6.37; from Kolers and Pomerantz, 1971).

6.36   The logic of stroboscopic movement: From upright to prone   *(A) Stimulus A flashes at time 1, followed by stimulus B at time 2, and back again. (B) With appropriate time intervals, this leads to the perception of a rectangle turning from an upright to a prone position and back. (After Kolers, 1972)*

6.37   The logic of stroboscopic movement: From circle to square   *(A) Stimulus A flashes at time 1, followed by stimulus B at time 2, and back again. (B) With appropriate time intervals, this leads to the perception of a circle that changes in shape to become a square, and then changes again into a circle. (After Kolers and Pomerantz, 1971)*

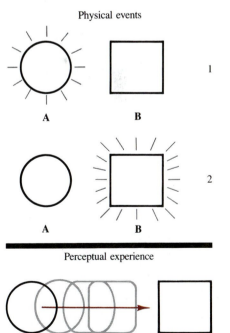

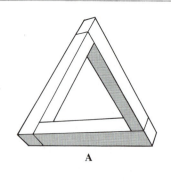

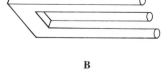

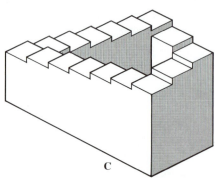

6.38 Impossible figures (A) Impossible triangle. (B) U-shape or three-pronged fork. (C) Perpetual staircase. (Penrose and Penrose, 1958)

WHEN LOGIC FAILS: IMPOSSIBLE FIGURES

We've seen that the perceptual system is very clever. With a little top-down hint, it can reconstruct imperfect speech and discover hidden Dalmatian dogs. (In a pinch, it can even square a circle.) But even the cleverest system fails when it is confronted with a problem that is in principle insoluble. In perception such problems are posed by so-called *impossible figures* in which there is no way of resolving a perceptual contradiction (Penrose and Penrose, 1958).

Take Figure 6.38A. At the left, it is a perspective drawing of three rectangular beams joined in a U-shaped form; at the right, it is a picture of three round rods. If we look at either the left or the right separately, the figure makes sense. But as our glance travels from left to right, there is a gross inconsistency, for the two halves of the figure don't add up to a whole. Consider the third horizontal line from the top. At the left, it is the bottom edge of the upper horizontal beam; at the right, it becomes the top edge of the middle rod. Now the perceptual system is stumped, for there is *no* perceptual hypothesis that can make the figure into a coherent whole.

In other examples, the impossibility takes a bit longer to appreciate. Take Figure 6.38B, which at first glance looks like a triangular, three-dimensional object. The trouble is that the perspectives are drawn differently at the different corners. If we mentally trace a path from one corner of the object to the second, then to the third, and finally try to return to the first, we find that there is no way to do so because the corners don't mate properly. The perceptual problem posed by Figure 6.38C is even more subtle. Here the inconsistency is based on yet another trick of perspective. As the figure is drawn, we can start at any place and go around the entire stair system arrangement, always climbing upwards, until we get back to the starting point.

Impossible figures underline the fact that perceptual problem solving consists of making a sensible whole out of separate parts, an integration that is often achieved over time. When we attend to any one region of an impossible figure, we are unaware that there's a problem. The difficulty comes when our attention (and our eyes) travel from one region to another, and we try to fit the two regions together. Under normal circumstances, this process of building up a mental picture of what we see out there occurs without any conscious awareness. But we become aware of it when it is somehow blocked or frustrated, as in the case of impossible figures (Hochberg, 1970).

THE PERCEPTION OF REALITY

Of what use are all the mechanisms of perceptual organization we have considered throughout this chapter, whether innately given or based on learning? The answer is simple enough: They all help us to perceive reality. To be sure, the perceptual system may occasionally lead us astray, as in illusions of depth or movement, and sometimes may leave us helpless, as in impossible figures. But these are fairly rare exceptions. By and large, the processes that lead to the perception of depth and form and movement serve toward the attainment of a larger goal—the perception of the real world outside. How is this perception of reality achieved?

The Perceptual Constancies

To see the real world is to see the properties of distal objects: their color, form, and location, their movement through space, their permanence or transience. But we have noted previously that organisms cannot gain experience about the distal stimulus directly; all information about the external world comes to us from the proximal stimulus patterns that distal objects project upon the senses. Of course the same distal object will produce different proximal stimulus patterns, but the perceptual system somehow "sees through" the different masks. It responds to the permanent features of the real object outside regardless of the illumination that falls on it and the distance and orientation from which it is viewed. The best proof is provided by the *perceptual constancies.* A crow looks black even in sunlight; an elephant looks large even at a distance; and a postcard looks rectangular even though its retinal image is a trapezoid, unless viewed directly head on. In all of these cases, we manage to transcend the vagaries of the proximal stimulus and react to certain constant attributes of the distal object such as its shape and its size.

How does the organism accomplish this feat? We will see that it does so by means of several quite different mechanisms. Some are based on simple, built-in sensory processes of the kind we discussed in the previous chapter. Others may be the result of perceptual learning.

LIGHTNESS CONSTANCY

Virtually all objects reflect a certain proportion of the light that falls upon them. The exact proportion depends upon a physical property of the object itself, its *reflectance.* Some objects have a high reflectance (snow), others a low reflectance (coal). To say that an object is perceived as light or dark is really to say that we can tell something about its reflectance. Yet, we cannot possibly see the reflectance directly; all we get from the object is the amount of light it actually reflects on any given occasion, the *luminance.* But this luminance depends not only upon the object's reflectance but also upon the *illumination* that falls upon it. A white shirt in shadow may well reflect less light than does a gray shirt in brilliant sunlight. Under the circumstances, can we ever tell that the first is lighter than the second?

The fact is that we can, at least to some extent. A swan will not suddenly seem to turn gray when a cloud hides the sun; it appears just as white, but in shadow. This effect is called *lightness constancy.* The apparent lightness of an object remains fairly constant despite rather drastic changes in the illumination that falls upon it. This phenomenon is readily demonstrated in the laboratory. Subjects are shown two gray papers of equal reflectance. One paper, *A,* receives twice the illumination of another paper, *B,* which is in shadow (Figure 6.39). But even so, the subjects judge the papers to be equally light, despite the fact that *A* reflects twice as much light as *B.*

How does lightness constancy come about? The answer seems to be that it is based on the same built-in processes that are responsible for brightness contrast (see Chapter 5). The basic idea is that illumination changes normally affect both the object in the foreground and the background against which it is seen. Con-

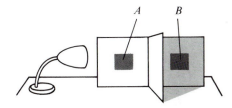

6.39 Lightness constancy Subjects are shown two identical gray papers, A and B. A is illuminated while B is in shadow. As a result, A reflects much more light than B. Even so, the two are perceived to be about equal in lightness, a manifestation of lightness constancy. (After Rock, 1975)

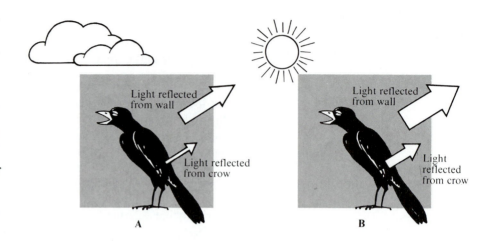

6.40 Lightness constancy and brightness contrast *In (A) the illumination on both bird and wall is moderate; in (B) it is much greater. The fact that illumination goes up increases the amount of light reflected by the bird, but it also increases the amount of light reflected by the wall that serves as its background. The two increases tend to cancel each other. Any increase in the light intensity of the background tends to inhibit the apparent lightness of the figure. This compensation effect acts in the direction of lightness constancy: The crow continues to look black even in brilliant sunshine.*

sider a black crow that stands in front of a gray garden wall (Figure 6.40). The sun is democratic, shining equally on the crow and on the garden wall. If it suddenly emerges from behind a cloud, the illumination on the crow (and hence its luminance) will go up. But the same holds for the wall. Its luminance will also increase and will cause a decline in the apparent lightness of the crow. This is just another example of brightness contrast which makes objects appear darker as the luminance of their background goes up. The result is an automatic compensation effect that works in the direction of lightness constancy.

SIZE AND SHAPE CONSTANCY

Lightness constancy is evidently due in the main to built-in mechanisms. Is the same true for other perceptual constancies, such as those for size and shape? **Size constancy** is a term which describes the fact that the perceived size of an object is the same whether it is nearby or far away. A Cadillac at a distance of 100 feet will look larger than a Volkswagen 20 feet away (a phenomenon we have described before). An analogous phenomenon is **shape constancy.** This refers to the fact that we perceive the shape of an object independent of the angle from which it is viewed. A rectangular door frame will appear rectangular even though most of the angles from which it is regarded will produce a trapezoidal retinal image (Figure 6.41).

6.41 Shape constancy *When we see a door frame at various slants from us, it appears rectangular despite the fact that its retinal image is often a trapezoid. (After Gibson, 1950)*

A nativist approach to size constancy A nativist approach such as Gibson's would try to explain size constancy by looking for some higher-order stimulus pattern that remains invariant despite changes in distance. As we saw earlier in the chapter, one such factor is the relation between the retinal size of an object and of the surrounding framework. A door does not seem to grow in size as we approach it, even though its retinal image is expanding. But one thing remains unchanged: the ratio between the size of the images projected by the door and the hallway. Does such a constant size ratio underlie size constancy effects? It probably does not, for size constancy is found even when there is no framework—nor any apparent texture gradient—that might provide the basis for a size ratio. An example is a room in which the only visible object is a luminous disk. That disk will look about equally large whether it is moved closer or further off from the subject.

An empiricist approach to size constancy An invariant size ratio is evidently unable to explain all cases of size constancy. But if so, what can? An alternative account was offered by Helmholtz who argued that we somehow take account of the object's distance and compensate for it. According to Helmholtz, the size-distance relationship is acquired through long experience. He pointed out that young children sometimes mistake objects at a considerable distance for miniatures; looking down from a tower, they see the people below as tiny dolls (Helmholtz, 1909).

Perhaps Helmholtz was right in asserting that size constancy is learned. But if so, it is certainly learned fairly quickly, for size constancy seems to be present rather early in life. Just how early is still a matter of some controversy, but it is certainly present by six months at the latest (Bower, 1966; Day and McKenzie, 1972; McKenzie, Tootell, and Day, 1980).

To test for size constancy in the first months of life, recent investigators have resorted to the **habituation method,** which is a widely used technique to determine how infants see the world. The method works as follows. The infant is presented with some visual stimulus. She looks at it for a while, but as time goes on she finally habituates: She becomes bored and looks away. She is next shown a new stimulus. The question is whether she perceives this second stimulus as different from the first. If she regards it as essentially the same, she will look at it only briefly. As far as she is concerned, it is just the same old boring stimulus again, so why should she bother with it. But if she does see a difference between the old stimulus and the new one, her original habituation will be overcome: She will inspect the new stimulus with considerable interest and for a longer time.

A recent study that employed this habituation method has shown size constancy in six-month-olds. The infants were first shown a model of a human life-sized head at a distance of 60 cm. This was a reasonably interesting stimulus, and the infants inspected it for a while. But after several trials with the same figure, they finally habituated and looked elsewhere. The critical test involved two groups. Group I was shown the same head model at a distance of 30 cm—the distal size remained the same but the retinal size was changed. Group II was shown a head model identical in form but reduced by half and presented at a distance of 30 cm—here the distal size was changed while the retinal size remained the same (see Figure 6.42). The results showed that the infants in Group II spent much more time inspecting the stimulus than did those in Group I. It appears that a de-

6.42 Size constancy in infants *(A) Six-month-old infants were exposed to a model of a human head at a distance of 60 cm until they habituated. (B) One group was then tested with the same head model at a distance of 30 cm—same distal size but altered retinal size. (C) A second group was tested with the same head model reduced to half its size but at the original distance of 30 cm—same retinal size but altered distal size. The infants in (C) spent more time looking at the model than those in (B), an indication of size constancy. (McKenzie, Tootell, and Day, 1980)*

crease in true size (with retinal image held constant) is a more effective change than a change in retinal size (with distal size held constant)—a strong indication that some measure of size constancy is present by the age of six months (McKenzie, Tootell, and Day, 1980). Such findings are certainly compatible with the view that at least some instances of size constancy are part of our native endowment, and are thus found at a very early age. But they are also compatible with the empiricist position, on the assumption that the relevant learning is acquired rather quickly.

INAPPROPRIATE COMPENSATION AND ILLUSIONS

The preceding discussion shows that we compensate for distance when perceiving size. By and large, this perceptual strategy works. It leads to size constancy, one of the ways we have for seeing the world as it really is. But occasionally, this policy backfires and produces illusions.

A well-known example is the *moon illusion.* The moon looks considerably larger at the horizon than it does when up in the sky, even though its retinal image is equal in both cases. The main reason is that the horizon looks farther away than the overhead sky. But since the perceptual system compensates for perceived distance, the horizon moon is seen as larger. To test this hypothesis, subjects viewed artificial moons through special optical devices. They experienced the standard moon illusion. In line with the size-distance hypothesis, the illusion was greater the farther off the visible horizon appeared (Kaufman and Rock, 1962; see Figure 6.43).

A number of other illusions of size may be caused by a similar effect of perceived distance upon perceived size. The Müller-Lyer illusion (Figure 6.44) and

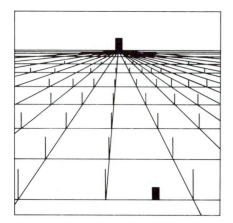

6.43   The moon illusion   *When the moon is at the horizon, depth cues such as perspective and interposition indicate that the moon is far away. As a result, the moon seems larger. When the moon is overhead, the depth cues are less prominent, so the moon appears smaller. The general principle that underlies the moon illusion is illustrated in the figure. The black rectangle resting at the horizon seems to be larger than the one in the foreground, although both are objectively identical in size. Again, the reason is apparent distance. Since the rectangle at the horizon seems farther off, it is perceived to be larger than the one that has the same retinal size but appears to be nearer. (After Rock and Kaufman, 1962)*

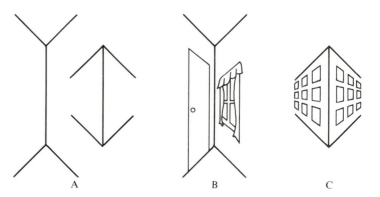

A   B   C

6.44   The Müller-Lyer illusion   *(A) In the Müller-Lyer illusion, the center line in the left figure seems longer than its counterpart on the right, though the two lengths are identical. This illusion may be another effect of misleading perspective cues. This can be seen by noting that the Müller-Lyer figure is present whenever one looks at the corners of rooms or buildings. (B) shows the interior corner of a room, in which the lines of the ceiling and floor correspond to the outward-pointing fins of the figure whose center line looks longer, presumably because it appears to be farther away. In contrast, (C) shows the outer edge of a building with receding perspective lines. Here, the perspective lines correspond to the arrow heads of the figure whose center line looks shorter, presumably because it appears to be closer by. (Coren and Girgus, 1978)*

A

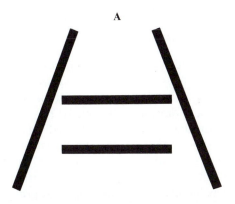

B

6.45 **The Ponzo illusion** (A) The two horizontal bars seem to be unequal, with the one on top apparently larger than the one below. In actuality, the two horizontal lines are perfectly identical. This illusion is produced by perspective cues which make the top bar appear to be farther away and thus larger, an effect similar to that which leads to the moon illusion. For a photographic version of the same illusion, see (B). (Photograph by Don Ball)

the Ponzo illusion (Figure 6.45), both named after their discoverers, are two examples. In both cases, perspective cues indicate that one part of the figure is more distant than another. This leads to a faulty compensation in which the part that seems farther away is perceived to be larger than it really is (Gregory, 1963, 1966; Coren and Girgus, 1978).

This interpretation seems to fit at least some of the size illusions. Thus, the Ponzo illusion (Figure 6.45) is considerably stronger when it is displayed as part of a photograph rather than as a line drawing. This is presumably because depth cues are generally more powerful in a photograph than a schematic line drawing (Leibowitz, Brislin, Perlmutter, and Hennessy, 1969). Other studies show that the Ponzo illusion is stronger for older than younger children. This makes sense if one assumes that older children have more experience with depth cues, especially as they appear in pictures (Coren and Girgus, 1978).

Illusions are special cases in which reality is misperceived. In ordinary life, such mistakes are rare because our perceptual systems are geared to see the world as it really is—allowing us to bypass the continual fluctuations of the proximal stimulus so that we can grasp the enduring properties of the distal reality outside.

But while illusions are fairly rare, they are exceedingly useful to those who want to understand how perception works. By studying illusions, we can learn about the mechanisms upon which our normal perception of reality is based. Some of these mechanisms are built in; illusory effects such as brightness contrast have shown the way to their discovery. Other mechanisms involve learning and past experience. The perspective illusions just discussed are a case in point. But so, of course, are many other perceptual phenomena (such as the recognition of form) which we have seen to be enormously affected by memory of the past and expectations of the future, for there is a wide region in which it is not quite clear where seeing ends and knowledge begins.

THE REPRESENTATION OF REALITY IN ART

The mechanisms of perceptual organization evolved to serve in the struggle for survival that all organisms must wage. They allow us to see reality as it actually is, so that we can perceive what is out there in the world that we must seek or must avoid. But it is part of our humanity that we have managed to turn these perceptual mechanisms to a use that goes beyond the stark necessities of sheer survival: the representation of reality in art.

The psychology of visual art is yet another illustration of the overlap between seeing and knowing that we've repeatedly encountered in our previous discussions of perceptual phenomena. We will see that an acute awareness of this overlap is found in the artists who try to represent the perceptual world on paper or on canvas.

Seeing and Knowing

Consider Figure 6.46, a mural painted in an Egyptian tomb some four thousand years ago. Why did the artist depict the various figures as he did, with eyes and shoulders in front view and the rest of the body in profile? His fellow Egyptians were surely built as we are. But if so, why didn't he draw them "correctly"?

The answer seems to be that Egyptian artists drew, not what they could see at any one moment or from any one position, but rather what they knew was the most enduring and characteristic attribute of their model. They portrayed the various parts of the human body from the vantage point that shows each form in its most characteristic manner: the front view for the eyes and shoulders, the profile for the nose and feet. The fact that these orientations are incompatible was evidently of no concern; what mattered was that all of the components were represented as the artist knew them to be (Gombrich, 1961).

On a much more humble level, the same preoccupation with representing the known may explain certain aspects of children's art. Figure 6.47 shows a boy's drawing of a town square. The square is shown from above, yet the people and houses are drawn upright all around it. But this is reasonable enough if we assume that the boy's purpose is to represent what he knows about the world. After all, people and houses are at right angles to the street on which they stand. And if so, why not let the drawing say so?

The Renaissance: Scenes through a Window Frame

The illustrations of Egyptian art (as well as the lesser masterpieces produced by children) show the enormous role of the known in the visual representation of the seen. One may argue that this simply reflects the fact that these artists never set themselves the task of mirroring nature as it appears to the eye. Does the artist copy more precisely if his purpose is to do just that?

6.46 Carved tomb relief of a government official, ca. 2350–2280 B.C. The conventions of Egyptian art required the main parts of the human body to be represented in its most characteristic view. Thus, heads are shown in profile, arms and legs from the side, but eyes are depicted in full-face view, as are the shoulders and the chest. (Courtesy The Egyptian Museum, Cairo)

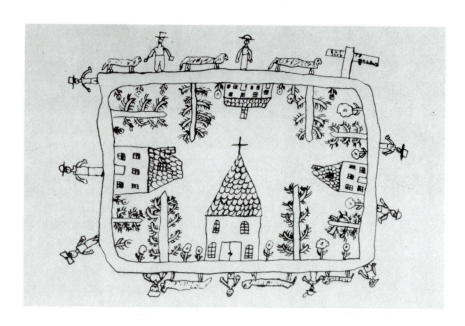

6.47 A child's drawing A Square of a Town in Connecticut *drawn by a twelve-year-old boy. (From Lewis, 1966)*

6.48 *The laws of perspective* An illustration in a 1505 treatise by Viator. (From Ivins, 1975)

The most striking examples come from the Renaissance masters who conceived the notion that a picture should look just like a real scene that is viewed through a window from one particular orientation. The painting's frame is then the frame of this window into the artist's world. One major step toward achieving this end was the discovery of the geometrical laws of perspective, the way in which all objects are foreshortened as the perspective lines converge toward a vanishing point at the horizon (Figure 6.48). This was supplemented by the systematic use of other pictorial cues for depth such as interposition.

In effect, the Renaissance masters seemed to believe that to catch visual reality, one's picture should correspond to the image the model casts on the eye also. This motivated their search for means to portray depth on a flat canvas (Figure 6.49, p. 214). The same conception also served as the starting point for such empiricists as Locke and Berkeley, whose concern was with the nature of perception. The empiricists asked how the painters' means of portraying depth—the pictorial cues—could lead to the experience of depth if the image on the eye is two-dimensional.

One may question whether these Renaissance artists really copied nature as they set out to do. The art historian E. H. Gombrich argues that they did not. In his view, "The 'Egyptian' in us can be suppressed, but he can never be quite defeated," for the artist can never create a genuine optical replica of his model, can never paint the world independently of what he knows about it.

Gombrich believes that the artist interpets his model through various visual schemas in terms of which he then renders it in pictorial form. Such schemas are like the rules whereby we read a map. A certain kind of line corresponds to a

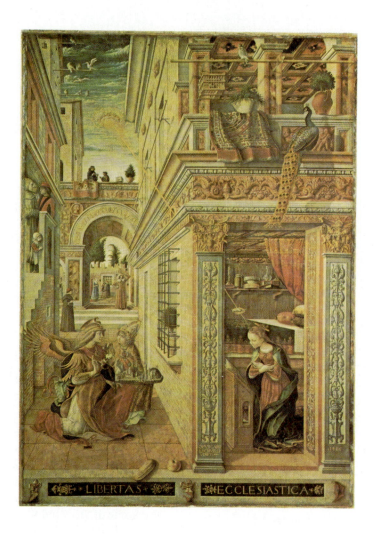

6.49 Perspective in Renaissance art
The Annunciation *by Crivelli (ca. 1430–1495). Note the loving attention to perspective detail, such as roofs and arches extending far back. (Courtesy the National Gallery, London)*

river, another to a road, and so on. The map certainly resembles the terrain in some important ways, but it is not a genuine copy.

Some evidence comes from the teaching manuals published by the artists themselves. They exhort the student to learn what a face, a hand, a foot, really are like, to study their relative proportions and their visual appearance in different bodily postures. But why bother to learn all this if you can simply draw what you see? The fact is that what you "see" is in part what you know.

The Impressionists: How a Scene Is Perceived

The Renaissance painters tried to represent a scene as it is projected on the eye (though to be sure they did very much more than that). Other schools of painting set themselves a different task. Consider the French Impressionists of the late nineteenth century. They tried to recreate certain perceptual experiences that the scene evokes in the observer, the impression it makes rather than the scene itself. One of their concerns was to render color as we see it in broad daylight. Their method was to create a seeming patchwork of different daubs of bright colors

6.50 Bend in the Epte River, near Giverny *(1888) by Claude Monet* *Monet, one of the leaders of Impressionism, was engaged in a life-long attempt to catch the fleeting sensations of light in nature. If the painting is viewed from farther back or out of foveal vision, the form becomes clearer and less impressionistic. What is lost is the brilliant shimmer of light and color. The oscillation between these two modes of appearance contributes to the total aesthetic effect. (Courtesy Philadelphia Museum of Art: The William L. Elkins Collection)*

6.51 The Races at Longchamp, Paris *(1864) by Eduard Manet* *Manet's painting captures the color, bustle, and movement of the scene, in part, by omitting details and letting the beholder fill them in. (Courtesy The Art Institute of Chicago)*

(Figure 6.50). These are clearly separate when looked at directly. But when viewed from the proper distance they change appearance, especially in the periphery where acuity is weak. The individual patches now blur together and their colors mix. But when the eyes move again and bring that area of the picture back into the fovea, the mixtures come apart and the individual patches reappear. Some authors believe that this continual alternation between mixed colors and separate dots gives these paintings their special vitality (Jameson and Hurvich, 1975).

This patchwork technique has a further effect. It enlists the beholder as an active participant in the artistic enterprise. Her active involvement starts as soon as she tries to see the picture as a whole rather than as a meaningless jumble of colored patches. This happens when the separate patches blur: when they are viewed from the periphery or from a few steps back. Now the picture suddenly snaps into focus and a whole emerges. This is both similar to and different from what happens in ordinary life. There we move our eyes to bring some part of the world to a region of greater acuity, the fovea. In the museum, we sometimes move our eyes (or our entire body) to bring a picture to a region of lesser acuity, away from the fovea. In either case, active movement leads to the perception of a figural whole (Hochberg, 1978b, 1980).

The artist often requires even more activity on the part of the beholder who is often asked to fill in various details, to complete a landscape or a facial expression for which the artist has provided only a sketchy outline. But the net result is a picture that is more rather than less lifelike because of this (Figure 6.51, p. 215).

The Moderns: How a Scene Is Conceived

The Impressionists tried to engender some of the perceptual experiences a scene evokes in the observer. Later generations went further and tried to capture not just how the scene is *perceived* but how it is *conceived;* how it is known as well as seen. Modern art provides many examples, as in Pablo Picasso's still life showing superimposed fragments of a violin (Figure 6.52). Here perception and knowledge are cunningly merged in a sophisticated return to some of the ways of Egyptian artists (Gombrich, 1961).

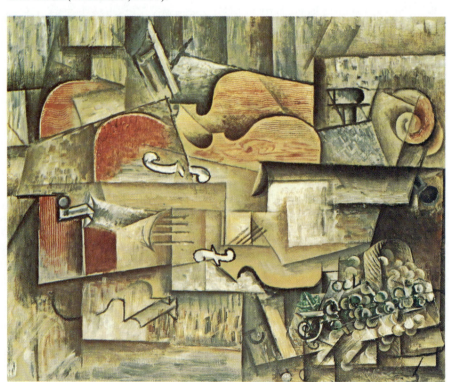

6.52 **Violin and Grapes** *by Pablo Picasso, 1912* *(Courtesy Museum of Modern Art, New York, Mrs. David M. Levy bequest)*

6.53 **Melancholy and Mystery of a Street** *by Georgio de Chirico, 1914* *(Courtesy Mr. and Mrs. Stanley R. Resor)*

Some modern artists are not satisfied to add conceptual elements to their visual representations. They want to create ambiguity by setting up visual puzzles that can't be solved. One way is to pit knowledge against visual perception, as in Picasso's faces that are seen in profile and front-face at the same time. Another is to build contradictions within the perceptual scene itself. An example is a painting by the turn-of-the century Italian Giorgio de Chirico (Figure 6.53). One reason for the disturbing quality of this picture is the fact that de Chirico used incompatible perspectives. The structure on the left converges to one horizon, that on the right to a horizon far below the other, while the wagon in the middle does not converge at all. The result is an insoluble visual problem, an eerie world which cannot be put in order.

De Chirico's streets do not look like real streets and Picasso's violins are a far cry from those one sees in a concert hall. In this regard, these modern painters appear quite different from many of their predecessors whose representations were closer to the world as it appears to the perceiver. But we have to realize that no artists, whether Renaissance masters, Impressionists, or moderns, ever try to fool the observer into thinking that he is looking at a real scene. They neither can nor want to hide the fact that their painting is a painting. It may spring to life for a moment and look like a real person or a real sunset, or it may briefly conjure up a vivid memory of what a face or a violin looks like when viewed from several angles. But whether it emphasizes the seen or the known, it is also recognized as a flat piece of canvas daubed with paint.

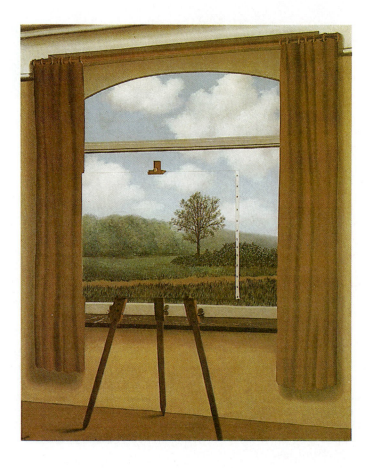

6.54 **La condition humaine I (1933)** *by* **René Magritte** *(Courtesy Collection Claude Spaak, Choisel, Seine-et-Oise).*

According to some authors, this perceptual duality is an important part of the beholder's esthetic experience as he looks at a work of representational art. In a well-known poem by Robert Browning, a duke points to his "last duchess painted on the wall,/Looking as if she were alive." The key words are *as if.* One reason why visual art leads to an esthetic experience may be because it provides us with a halfway mark between seen reality and painted appearance, because it presents a visual *as if* (Hochberg, 1980).

Some modern artists add another twist on the *as if* game by creating a deliberate confusion between the painting that depicts a scene and the scene itself. An example is a work by the modern Belgian René Magritte (Figure 6.54). In this painting within a painting, the Renaissance idea of showing the world through a picture frame is turned upside down, for now it's no longer clear what is supposed to be real and what is not.

In our discussion of visual art we have taken yet another step across the wide, shadowy region where perception and conception, seeing and knowing merge. In the next chapter we cross the boundary altogether and consider how we remember objects and events that no longer stimulate our senses.

SUMMARY

1. Most of the phenomena perception psychologists study hinge on the apparent discrepancy between what the proximal stimulus gives us and what we actually see. Attempts to resolve this discrepancy have traditionally taken either of two approaches, the *empiricist* and the *nativist.* An example is perceived size, which remains roughly constant whether the object is far off or nearby. Empiricists explain this by referring to *unconscious inference* based on a learned rule that farther objects lead to smaller retinal sensations. Nativists argue that the perception of true size is directly given and is based on some *invariant higher-order stimulus relationships,* such as certain size ratios in the retinal image. This *nature-nurture controversy* forms the background of much of the discussion in this chapter.

2. The perception of visual form depends on some prior phenomena of *perceptual organization.* One is the segregation of *figure and ground.* This is not inherent in the proximal stimulus but is imposed by the perceptual system, as shown by *reversible figure-ground patterns.* A related phenomenon is *perceptual grouping,* which depends upon such organizational factors as *proximity, similarity, good continuation,* and *closure.*

3. A crucial fact in form perception is *transposition of form.* A perceived form may remain the same even if all of its constituent parts are altered. This phenomenon is the keystone of *Gestalt psychology,* a theory which emphasizes the importance of wholes created by the relationship between their parts.

4. The visual world is seen in three dimensions even though only two of these are given in the image that falls upon the eye. This fact has led to an interest in *depth cues.* Among these are *binocular disparity* and the *monocular pictorial cues* such as *interposition* and *linear perspective.* Of special interest are various *texture gradients* which are powerful determinants of perceived depth. Even more important is *motion parallax* which depends upon the observer's movements.

5. Organizational factors play a considerable role in the perception of movement, as shown by such phenomena as *stroboscopic movement* and *induced movement* and also by the fact that the nervous system compensates for retinal displacements produced by movements of the eyes.

6. Perception is selective, for all aspects of the stimulus are not given equal weight. This selection is partially accomplished by physical orientation, as in the case of *eye movements.* It is also achieved by a central process, *selective attention,* as in *selective listening.*

7. Some of the phenomena of perceptual organization are based on built-in factors. Some evidence comes from studies of very young organisms tested on the *visual cliff* and from work on perceived relations between sights and sounds in early infancy. Less conclusive are studies of perception after *sensory deprivation,* as in cases of cataract removal in persons born blind.

8. Attempts to find the physiological mechanisms that underlie built-in perceptual organization have concentrated on *feature detectors,* both within the retina and in the brain. These are cells that respond to certain relational aspects of the stimulus, such as corners, as shown by single-cell recordings. The adaptation of such feature detectors may explain certain changes of perceptual experience after prolonged exposure to a certain kind of stimulus, as in the *aftereffect of visual movement.*

9. Perceptual organization is affected by experience. One example is *perceptual adaptation* to various optical distortions. They are based on learned realignments of several per-

ceptual systems which may occur more readily when the organism is involved in active movement.

10. Perceptual learning as it normally occurs in adulthood is probably the result of processes that are quite different from those of perceptual adaptation. According to some authors, the key is a process of *perceptual differentiation,* whereby relevant *distinctive features* in the stimulus are gradually singled out and attended to.

11. Some authors believe that learning to perceive new patterns depends on *perceptual problem solving.* According to this view, the recognition of a pattern often depends on two kinds of processes. One is *bottom-up processing,* in which the stimulus is subjected to a *feature analysis* that begins with lower-level units (such as slanted lines) to arrive at higher-level units (such as letters and words). The other is *top-down processing* that begins with higher-level units. Evidence for such top-down processing is provided by *context effects.* The two processes often operate jointly. Top-down processes provide *perceptual hypotheses* that are tested by bottom-up processes. This kind of perceptual logic sometimes fails, as in the case of *impossible figures.*

12. The ultimate function of perceptual organization is to help the organism see the outside world as it really is. An illustration is the *constancies,* in which the perceiver responds to certain permanent characteristics of the distal object despite various contextual factors —illumination, distance, and orientation—which lead to enormous variations in the proximal stimulus. In *lightness constancy,* the perceiver responds to the object's *reflectance* and tends to ignore the level of the illumination that falls upon it. This phenomenon is in large part based upon the same built-in process that yields brightness contrast. In *size and shape constancy,* the perceiver responds to the actual size and shape of the object more or less regardless of its distance and its orientation, an effect that may be based on learning in very early life. This compensation for distance leads to size constancy but sometimes produces misperceptions, as in the case of the *moon illusion.*

13. The psychology of visual art is a further illustration of the overlap between perception and thinking. The artist represents both what he sees and what he knows. *Renaissance* painters represented scenes seen through a window frame; the *Impressionists* tried to recreate certain perceptual experiences the scene evokes in the beholder; while many modern artists try to represent the scene as it is conceived and thought about.

A cartoonist's view of the problem of seeing versus knowing
(Drawing by Alain; © 1955, 1983 The New Yorker Magazine, Inc.)

CHAPTER 7

Memory

Our discussion of perception, and especially of visual perception, has emphasized the way in which psychological events are organized in space. Locke and Berkeley to the contrary, our perceptual world is not a jumbled mosaic of isolated sensory fragments, but an organized, coherent whole in which every piece relates to every other. We now turn to the subject of *memory,* in which organization plays an equally prominent part.

Memory is the way in which we record the past and later refer to it so that it may affect the present. It is hard to think of humans (or any animal that is able to learn) without this capacity. Without memory, there would be no then but only a now, no ability to utilize skills, no recall of names or recognition of faces, no reference to past days or hours or even seconds. We would be condemned to live in a narrowly circumscribed present, but this present would not even seem to be our own for there can be no sense of self without memory. Each individual wakes up every morning and never doubts that he is *he* or she is *she.* This feeling of continuous personal identity is necessarily based upon the continuity of memories which links our yesterdays to our todays.

Such considerations underline the crucial importance of memory as a psychological process. How can this process be studied?

ACQUISITION, STORAGE, AND RETRIEVAL

To begin with, we must make a few preliminary distinctions. One concerns three stages that are implied by any act of remembering. Consider a person working on a crossword puzzle who is trying to recall an eight-letter word meaning "African anteater." If she does, we can be sure that she succeeded in all three stages of the memorial process. The first is ***acquisition.*** To remember, one must first have learned; the subject must somewhere have encountered this particular item of biological exotica. During this acquisition stage, the relevant experiences presumably left some enduring record in the nervous system, the ***memory trace.*** Next comes ***storage,*** during which the information is held for later use (until the next crossword puzzle). The final stage is ***retrieval,*** the point at which one tries to remember, to dredge up this particular memory trace from among all others. Many failures to remember are failures of retrieval and not of storage. Our subject may be unable to come up with the correct answer at the time, but when she later sees the solution she realizes that she knew it all along. "Of course, Aardvark!"

Encoding

The preceding comments make it clear that there can be no remembering without prior acquisition. But just what does this acquisition consist of? The subject presumably encountered the word *aardvark* at some previous time. But to understand just what she remembered and how, we have to know more than that some such encounter took place. We must also know how the item was ***encoded.*** Taken from computer science, the term *encoding* refers to the form (that is, the code) in which an item of information is stored. In most cases, there are a number of different possible codings. The subject might have encoded the word as a sound pattern, or as a particular letter sequence, or in terms of its meaning. What she later remembers will necessarily reflect this encoding. If all she encoded was the sound and the meaning, she will probably not succeed in her crossword puzzle task, for she'll probably not know that the first two letters of the word are *Aa.*

Recall and Recognition

Another preliminary distinction concerns two means of retrieving previously encoded items of information: ***recall*** and ***recognition.*** A person who is asked to recall must produce an item or a set of items. "Where did you park your car?" or "What is the name of the boy who sat next to you in the third grade?" are examples of recall questions. The experimental psychologist often tests for the recall of materials that were learned in the laboratory; this assures that any failures in recall are not simply failures of original acquisition. Thus, a subject might have to learn a dozen unrelated adjectives which he will later be asked to recite. Recall need not be verbal. An example is the retention of a motor skill such as playing golf; here memory is best assessed by observing how the subject hits a golf ball and not by how he talks about his swing. Another example is the memory of visual patterns. This is sometimes tested by the method of reproduction in which the subject tries to draw what he has seen. (Unfortunately, such reproduction failures may only prove that he cannot draw and not that he cannot remember.)

A memory trace can also be tapped with a recognition test. A person who is shown an item must indicate whether he has encountered it before, either in general ("Did you ever see this face before?") or in a particular context ("Is this one of the girls who played on your high school field hockey team?"). In the laboratory the subject is usually asked to pick out the previously learned item from among several false alternatives. Examples are multiple-choice or true-false tests which clearly put a greater premium on recognition than do essay or short-answer fill-in examinations, which emphasize recall.

THE SENSORY REGISTERS

We usually think of memory in terms of a past that is reckoned in hours, days, or years. But memory actually comes into play as soon as the stimulus is registered on the senses. An example is a telephone number we look up and retain just long enough to complete the dialing; here the interval between acquisition and retrieval is a matter of mere seconds. Similarly, to understand speech one must still remember the beginning of a sentence by the time one hears its end. Clearly, we use memory to reach back both into the remote and the quite immediate past. Many psychologists believe that several different memory systems are involved in such acts. We will consider the three that figure in most theoretical proposals: the sensory registers, short-term memory, and long-term memory.

The first link between an organism's present and its past is forged by its *sensory registers.* These hold incoming sensory information for fractions of a second after the stimulus is withdrawn. Such registers probably exist for all the senses. The ones studied thus far are for vision and audition.

The Icon

An elegant series of studies by George Sperling dealt with some of the properties of the sensory register in vision. Sperling presented his subjects with a very brief exposure (50 milliseconds) to an array of nine letters arranged in three rows of three letters each, as shown below:

S F G
M T B
F Z N

Immediately after the array was shown, the subjects were asked to recall the letters. They reported about half of them. But Sperling believed that they saw many more letters than they were able to report. In his view, the subjects had a vivid mental picture, or *icon,* of the array immediately after the stimulus went off. But this icon fades away very rapidly. This explains why the subjects' recall scores were only 50 percent even though they started to report the letters as soon as the stimulus was withdrawn. When they began to report, the icon was still vivid. But the letters could not be named instantaneously. By the time the subject had named the fourth letter, the rest of the icon had totally faded.

To prove his point, Sperling devised a partial report procedure. He asked the subjects to recall the letters in only one of the rows in the array. This cut down on the letters that had to be named so that the report could be completed before the icon had faded. To make sure that the subject consulted his memory rather than the stimulus itself, the critical row was designated *after* the stimulus had disappeared. The subjects were informed by means of tone signals: a high tone for the first row, a medium-pitched tone for the second, and so on. In Sperling's view, the recall score on these partial reports was an adequate index of the state of the

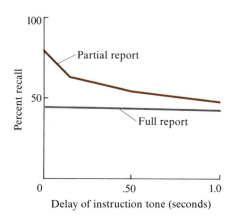

100 ┐

Partial report

50

Percent recall

Full report

0   .50   1.0

Delay of instruction tone (seconds)

7.1 The fading icon *Performance of one of Sperling's subjects when tested by the method of partial report, in which a tone indicates which row in the array is to be recalled. The colored line shows the percent recall obtained by this procedure, plotted against the interval between the presentation of the array and the sounding of the tone. As the figure shows, performance drops markedly in the first half a second or so after the array was presented. The gray line indicates performance under full report instructions. This is inferior to partial report performance with short array-tone intervals, presumably because the icon fades while the subject is still reporting. (After Sperling, 1960)*

whole icon at that point in time. His logic was similar to that used in many school tests. To test everything the student has learned in a course is very tedious; an adequate approximation can be obtained by an appropriate sample.

The results showed that when the signal was sounded immediately after the visual stimulus disappeared, recall was nearly 100 percent. But even tiny delays impaired recall seriously. If the tone was sounded 300 milliseconds later, recall dropped to about 75 percent. After one second, it was indistinguishable from the results obtained by the usual method (see Figure 7.1; Sperling, 1960).

These findings support the notion of a visual register that carries a good deal of information but for only fractions of a second. There is evidently an icon that subjects can read as if it were a printed page (which happens to turn blank within a second or less). Similar registers probably exist for most of the other senses. For example, there is some evidence for an auditory analog of the icon, a kind of mental *echo* (Crowder and Morton, 1969; Darwin, Turvey, and Crowder, 1972).

What is the physiological basis of the icon? Some investigators believe that it is the continued activity of visual receptors whose firing persists for a short period after the stimulus is withdrawn (Sakitt, 1975, 1976). If so, the icon is essentially an afterimage, much like the bright, yellowish disk we see after we look at the sun and then close our eyes (see Chapter 5). But recent evidence argues against this view. The duration of afterimages is known to depend on such factors as stimulus intensity, but the persistence of the icon as measured by partial-report performance turns out to be essentially unaffected by these factors. Under the circumstances, the best guess is that the icon is produced by processes higher up in the nervous system than those involved in receptor activity (Adelson and Jonides, 1980).

Icon and Echo as Unprocessed Information

Whatever the physiological site of the icon or echo may turn out to be, the consensus is that they represent as yet unanalyzed sensory information that is little more than a copy of what the receptors provide. But however brief their storage, it is long enough to allow the cognitive system to perform various operations upon them. One such operation is to extract features and assemble them into patterns. Another is to compare these patterns to those already stored in memory. Thus, the icon may include the visual information that corresponds to the printed letter *A*. But while still in the visual register, this information is not yet recognized as a letter, let alone a vowel, a course grade, and so on. Such recognitions are the results of further operations by means of which the incoming information is processed. This **information processing** begins with the contents of the sensory registers that represent the crude raw materials out of which the world of our knowledge is eventually fashioned.

SHORT-TERM MEMORY

When we call on memory in ordinary life, we require much more than the sensory registers can possibly give us, for we normally reach back for longer than the second or so that the icon and echo last. Remembering things like telephone numbers or people's names or where we parked the car are all cases that involve a level of processing vastly beyond anything that the sensory registers can hold. We clearly have to assume an additional memory system. But is one more enough?

Many psychologists have argued for the existence of at least two further systems beyond the sensory registers. One is *short-term memory,* which holds information for fairly short intervals, say, up to a minute. The other is *long-term memory,* in which materials are stored for much longer periods, perhaps for a lifetime.

Some Characteristics of Short-Term Memory

There is reason to believe that memory for relatively recent and remote events differs in some important ways. One pertains to the way in which these memories are consciously experienced. A second relates to the storage capacity of the two postulated memory systems.

CONSCIOUS EXPERIENCE AND SHORT-TERM MEMORY

The distinction between short-term and long-term memory appears to fit the way in which we consciously experience our remembered past. Much of our past is experienced as gone and done with. The movie seen last night, the dinner enjoyed an hour ago, are in the past tense; they are remembered but not perceived. But this is not so for events that happened just a few moments ago. We hear a melody and seem to perceive much or all of it in the present, even though the first chord has already ebbed away by the time the last note of the musical phrase reaches our ears.

THE CAPACITY OF SHORT-TERM MEMORY

The *storage capacity* of short-term memory is markedly different from that of long-term memory. The capacity of long-term memory is enormous; the size of an average college student's reading vocabulary (about 50,000 words, according to one estimate) is documentation enough. In contrast, the capacity of short-term memory is very limited, much like the loading platform that can hold only a limited fraction of what the warehouse can store.

One way to determine the capacity of short-term storage is to measure the *memory span,* the number of items an individual can recall after just one presentation. For normal adults this span is remarkably consistent. Whether the items are digits, letters, or unrelated words, whether they are presented visually or orally, the result is essentially the same—the subject can recall about seven items, give or take about two. This quantity, 7 plus or minus 2, has been called the *magic number,* a term taken from an influential paper by George Miller (Miller, 1956). According to Miller, this number represents the capacity limit of the short-term system, the number of packages that can be on the platform at any particular time. This capacity limit is sometimes regarded as the major bottleneck in passing information into the permanent memory store, for many theorists believe that it is difficult or impossible to bypass the short-term memory store with its restricted memory span.

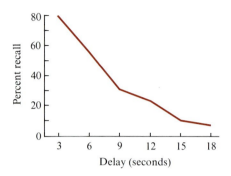

7.2 Forgetting of short-term memories
Subjects heard three consonants and then had to count backward by threes from a given number. After an interval, they were asked to recall the consonants. As the figure shows, forgetting under these conditions is quite rapid. (Peterson and Peterson, 1959)

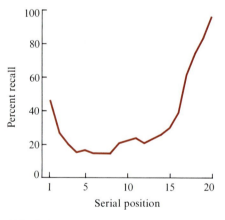

7.3 Primacy and recency effects in free recall *Subjects heard a list of twenty common words presented at a rate of one word per second. Immediately after hearing the list, the subjects were asked to write down as many of the words on the list as they could recall. The results show that the words at the beginning (primacy effect) and at the end (recency effect) were recalled more frequently than those in the middle. (After Murdock, 1962)*

The Paths from Short-Term Memory

What happens to information after it has entered short-term memory? For the vast majority of items, the answer is simple: They are forgotten, perhaps irrevocably so. While reading the morning newspaper we briefly note all kinds of extraneous matters: the coffee tastes bitter, a child is crying next door, there is a printer's error on the editorial page. But only a few moments hence these experiences are as if they had never been.

FORGETTING OF RECENT MEMORIES

The exceedingly quick forgetting of short-term memories was demonstrated by a study that required subjects to recall a set of three consonants such as *RLZ* after **retention intervals** (that is, intervals between acquisition and retrieval test) of two to twenty seconds. The trick was to find a procedure that would prevent **rehearsal.** After all, if the subject is allowed to say *RLZ* to herself over and over again during the twenty seconds after the item is presented, then her real retention interval is obviously much shorter than twenty seconds. Equally serious is the possibility that an item may be transferred from short-term to long-term storage if it is rehearsed. The solution was to fill the retention interval with a very demanding mental activity which presumably left little time for rehearsal. Immediately after the subjects heard the consonants, they were presented with a three-place number. Their task was to count backward from that number by threes (that is, 684, 681, 678, and so on) until they received the signal to recall. Under these conditions there was little or no recall after an interval of only fifteen seconds (Peterson and Peterson, 1959; see Figure 7.2).

A recent study shows that the forgetting rate may be even more rapid than this. The subjects were shown a three-consonant set that they were asked to read silently. After this, there was a period of backward counting. But for over a hundred trials, the subjects were never asked to recall the consonants; all they had to do was to count backwards. The results of an unexpected recall trial showed that under these conditions forgetting was almost complete after four seconds (Muter, 1980).

What accounts for forgetting from short-term memory? One possibility is **decay.** The memory trace may be eroded over time by some unknown physiological process, so its details become progressively less distinct. Another view is displacement. Items are somehow pushed out of short-term memory by other items, perhaps those that enter later or those already there. (In the previous study, this displacement may have been produced by the backward counting task.) The best evidence to date indicates that both factors play a role, that the packages on the loading platform rot away (decay) and also are shoved off by other packages (displacement). In either case, it is clear that they are not allowed to remain on the platform for very long (Reitman, 1974).

This rapid forgetting from short-term memory may be a blessing in disguise. Telephone companies would be in poor shape if their switchboard operators were unable to forget a number immediately after they had dialed it. Given its limited capacity, the loading platform has to be cleared very quickly to make room for new packages as they arrive (Bjork, 1970).

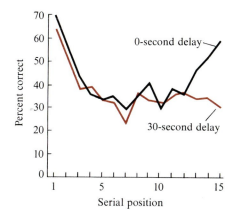

7.4 The recency effect and short-term storage *Subjects heard several fifteen-word lists. In one condition (black), free recall was tested immediately after they heard the list. In the other condition (color), the recall test was given after a thirty-second delay during which rehearsal was prevented. The long delay left the primacy effect unaffected but abolished the recency effect, indicating that this effect is based on retrieval from short-term storage. (After Glanzer and Cunitz, 1966)*

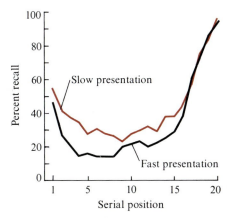

7.5 The primacy effect and long-term storage *The figure compares free-recall performance when item presentation is relatively slow (two seconds per item) and fast (one second per item). Slow presentation enhances the primacy effect but leaves the recency effect unaltered. The additional second per item presumably allowed more time for rehearsal which leads to long-term storage. (After Murdock, 1962)*

TRANSFER INTO LONG-TERM MEMORY

While most of the parcels on the loading platform disappear forever, a few find their way into long-term storage. Just why this transfer occurs will be taken up later (see pp. 232–36, 242–47). For now, our main concern is the fact that such a transfer sometimes happens, and that the recall of an item may thus indicate retrieval from either short-term or long-term storage. Is there any way of telling from which storage system the item was taken?

Most of the relevant studies utilized the method of *free recall.* The subject is presented with a list of unrelated items, such as common English words, and is asked to recall them in any order she wants to. If the items are presented only once and if their number exceeds the memory span, the subject cannot possibly produce them all. Under these circumstances, the likelihood that any one item will be recalled depends upon where in the list it was originally presented. Items that were at the beginning or at the end of the list will be produced much more often than those in the middle. The *primacy effect* describes the enhanced recall of the items presented at the beginning of the list. The *recency effect* designates the greater recall for items at the end (Figure 7.3).

It is reasonable to assume that the last few items are retrieved from short-term memory; after all, they are the ones the subject heard most recently.* In contrast, items at the beginning are probably retrieved from long-term rather than short-term storage. One reason for this supposition is that the early items have had more opportunity for rehearsal and thus for transfer into long-term memory. For example, if the first three items are "camera," "boat," and "zebra," the subject might rehearse "camera" after hearing that item; then "camera," "boat" after hearing the next; then "camera," "boat," "zebra" on hearing the third, and so on.

Supporting evidence comes from various manipulations of the primacy and recency effects. One important factor is the interval between the last item on the list and the signal to recall (assuming that some rehearsal-preventing task is interposed between them). If this interval is increased to thirty seconds, the primacy effect remains unchanged but the recency effect is completely abolished; this is just what we should expect if the last items are stored only in short-term memory from which forgetting is very rapid (Figure 7.4). Other procedures diminish the primacy effect. An example is the rate at which the items are presented. If this rate is very fast the subject has less time for rehearsal so that there will be less transfer to long-term storage. We should therefore expect a reduced primacy effect but no particular change in the recency effect, and this is exactly what happens (Figure 7.5).

RETRIEVAL FROM SHORT-TERM MEMORY

Suppose an item is still in short-term memory, having been neither forgotten nor transferred to the long-term store. How do we retrieve it? Many psychologists feel that there is no problem at all. In their view, there is no need for any kind of mental search, for the relevant memories are already in consciousness. In fact, the situation is not quite so simple. Retrieval from short-term memory is not instantaneous, but requires some mental search and comparison.

* The very last item may even have been retrieved from the sensory register.

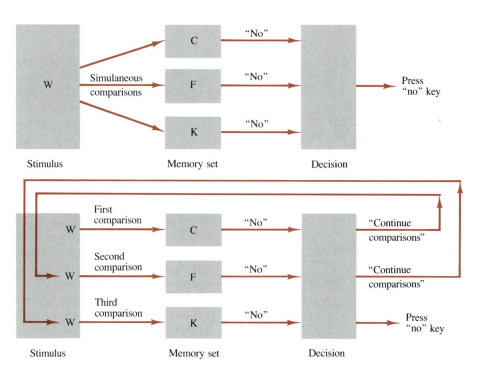

7.6 Serial and parallel search processes
A schematic representation of the steps a memory search system might go through given the task of deciding whether a given target (here, W) is or is not a member of a memory set. (A) One possibility is a parallel search. Here the search system simultaneously compares the target with each of the items in the memory set. In the example, none of the comparisons leads to a match, so the answer is "No." (B) Another possibility is a serial search. Here, the system makes one comparison after another. In the example, each of these comparisons leads to a "No," so the final decision is "No."

The evidence comes from a series of elegant experiments by Saul Sternberg. His subjects were first shown a short list of letters, the memory set, which might contain as few as one or as many as seven items. Suppose the memory set was *C, F,* and *M.* The subjects were then shown a single item (e.g., *W*) and had to indicate whether it was or was not a member of that memory set. What are the retrieval processes that allow the subject to accomplish this task? One thing is clear. To decide whether the target item was or was not presented a moment before, it must be compared with the items that are now in short-term memory. For each comparison, the memory system must decide whether the target stimulus is an adequate match for the trace. How are these comparisons conducted? One possibility is *parallel search.* This proposes that the stimulus letter *W* is simultaneously compared to each of the three items in the memory set. The second alternative is *serial search.* In serial search the comparisons occur successively. The stimulus *W* is first compared to *C,* then to *F,* and finally to *M* (Figure 7.6).

To decide between these alternatives, Sternberg measured the reaction time from the moment the target stimulus appeared until the subject made his response (pressing either a "Yes" or a "No" key). To find out whether the search process is conducted serially or in parallel, he determined how reaction time is affected by the number of items in the memory set. Suppose the process is handled in parallel. If so, then the size of the memory set should have no effect, for the various comparisons between the target and the items in memory are assumed to proceed simultaneously (Figure 7.7A).

The results should be quite different if the search is serial, for now the comparisons are assumed to occur one after the other. On the assumption that each comparison takes the same amount of time, reaction time should be a linear function of the size of the memory set (Figure 7.7B).

The results actually obtained fit the hypothesis that the search process is serial:

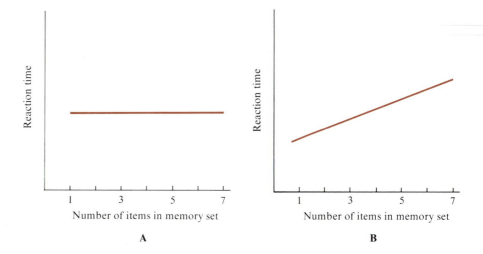

7.7 Predicted results in Sternberg's experiment *(A) If the search through short-term memory is parallel, the time to decide whether a given item is a member of the memory set should be the same regardless of the number of items. If so, the curve that relates reaction time and the size of the memory set would be a horizontal line. The height of this reaction-time function would depend on the time required for processes other than the comparison, such as the time required to recognize the target letter, the time to press the key, and so on. (B) If the search is serial, reaction time must increase with the size of the memory set, since each additional item in the set requires an additional comparison. The slope of the predicted line is the increase in reaction time added by any one comparison.*

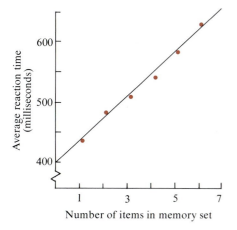

7.8 Actual results of Sternberg's study *The figure shows the actual results of one of Sternberg's experiments. The average reaction time over all trials at a given memory set size is shown by the circles. The results clearly support the prediction made by the serial search hypothesis. (After Sternberg, 1970)*

The relation between reaction time and size of memory set is best rendered by a straight line (Figure 7.8). As Sternberg sees it, the slope of this line corresponds to the time it takes to compare the target stimulus to one of the items in the memory set. This slope has generally been found to have a value of about thirty milliseconds. It appears that the search process is serial but is conducted at an exceedingly rapid rate (Sternberg, 1969).*

THE ACQUISITION OF LONG-TERM MEMORIES

The sensory registers and short-term memory provide a bridge to our very recent past. But their importance is secondary when compared to that much vaster system that holds everything else: our long-term memory. It is this memory system to which we refer when we speak, read, recognize faces, play tennis, and suddenly remember where we put the keys we couldn't find before. What can we say about the way in which such long-term memories are acquired and stored?

Most of what we know about this comes from experiments on the memorization of various verbal materials. The two major theoretical traditions are reminiscent of the opposing viewpoints we have already encountered in our study of animal learning and of perception: association and organization.

The Associationist Tradition

We are often forced to commit large bodies of verbal materials to memory. The schoolchild memorizes the multiplication tables, the actor his lines, the medical student the sundry parts of the human anatomy. The heirs of Locke and Berkeley believed that these feats are accomplished by association. By repeated joint oc-

* A number of later critics have argued that Sternberg's results don't necessarily prove that the search process he studied is serial, but a discussion of this controversy is beyond the scope of this book (e.g., Townsend, 1971; Sternberg, 1975).

currence, *4 × 4* becomes linked with *16, To be or not to be* with *that is the question,* until eventually the presentation of the one member of each associative pair is enough to evoke the other. Remembering is then simply a matter of triggering the appropriate associative connections.

Locke and Berkeley, as well as other philosophers dating back to Aristotle, believed that the associative principle was demonstrated by the train of thought. We often jump from idea to idea until we arrive at a point that seems altogether different from where we started. According to the associationists, the intervening ideas are connected through associative links. An example might be a visit to the zoo where one sees a camel. The sight of the camel evokes a mental image of an Arab, which in turn makes one think of the Middle East, which brings up the thought of oil, of oil prices, and of the possibility of gas rationing. According to the associationists, the successive constituents of this train of thought are chained together by associations which were established previously. In their view, there were some prior occasions when the relevant components were experienced together: camels and Arabs, the Middle East and oil, and so on. But this argument hinges on a hypothetical past during which the critical associations were said to have been formed. But were they really? We can't be sure. To determine the role of associations in memory, we have to do more than study how a memory is evoked in the present. We must examine how the memory was formed in the first place. To do this, one first needs an experimental technique.

EBBINGHAUS'S TECHNIQUE

The birth of an association was first studied experimentally in 1885 by the German psychologist Hermann Ebbinghaus (1850–1909), who acted as both midwife and mother, serving as the experimenter as well as his own subject. Ebbinghaus developed an experimental technique to investigate how associations are established and utilized. His procedure was to memorize unrelated verbal materials and later to test his own recall. The materials had to be carefully chosen, for Ebbinghaus wanted to study new associations uncontaminated by prior linkages. To this end he invented the ***nonsense syllable,*** two consonants with a vowel in between that do not constitute a word, such as *zup* and *rif.*

In all, Ebbinghaus constructed 2,300 such syllables, wrote each on a separate slip of paper, shuffled the slips, and then randomly drew from 7 to 36 of them to create syllable lists of various lengths. He then set himself the task of memorizing each list serially. One of his methods was ***serial anticipation.*** At a signal from a metronome, he had to recall the first item (say, *zup*). At the next beat of the metronome, that slip of paper was turned face up. This was the signal to produce the next syllable (say, *rif*) which would be exposed at the next beat, which was his signal to produce the following item, and so on through the list. This sequence was repeated over and over again until the entire list was finally mastered to some predetermined criterion, say, one errorless repetition. Remarkably enough, Ebbinghaus's experimental findings still stand up a century later, a fact that is all the more impressive considering that he used only one subject and had virtually no apparatus beyond his slips of paper and a metronome. For example, he showed the relationship between the number of trials required to learn a list and its length, and he anticipated the distinction between short-term and long-term memory by noting that a list of six or seven items is learned in only one presentation (Figure 7.9). He was also the first to plot a ***forgetting curve.*** He tested himself

Hermann Ebbinghaus *(Courtesy Historical Picture Services, Inc.)*

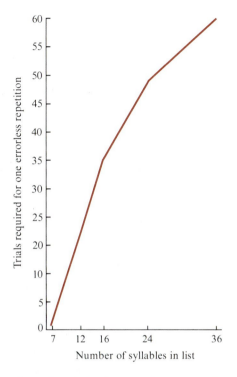

7.9 *The relation between list length and the number of trials required to learn a list of nonsense syllables* The longer the list, the more trials are required for memorization. (After Ebbinghaus, 1885)

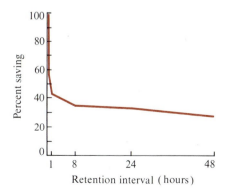

at various intervals after learning (using different lists for each interval) and then asked how much effort he had to expend in order to relearn the list to the level previously achieved. He found that there was *saving:* Relearning the list took less time (or fewer trials) than original learning. As one might expect, the saving declines as the retention interval increases. The decline is sharpest immediately after learning and becomes ever more gradual thereafter (Figure 7.10). Ebbinghaus also showed that there is much less forgetting when the lists are *overlearned,* receiving further repetitions after criterion is achieved. This fact would hardly surprise the professional actor who continues to rehearse lines long after the first errorless performance. To Ebbinghaus, it was an argument for the role of frequency in fixing the associations in memory (Ebbinghaus, 1885).

Ebbinghaus assumed that his nonsense syllables were essentially meaningless, so that any associations among them were truly virginal and must reveal the laws of associative learning in their pure form. This assumption is questionable: While *mer* is not a word (at least in English) it certainly resembles some (e.g., *mare*). One may well doubt whether there is any verbal material that is completely meaningless; associative virginity is hard to find. Contemporary workers in the field of verbal memory see no reason to restrict themselves to nonsense syllables, drawing their materials from a wide variety of additional sources, including sets of consonants (like *TQF*), words, digits, and the like.

THE INTERACTION BETWEEN ASSOCIATIONS

Associationists believe that all learning can be described as the establishment of associative bonds and all remembering as their appropriate evocation. Some of the factors that either help or hinder learning and recall are those which pertain to the particular bond in question: how often the constituent members have been paired, whether the appropriate stimulus item is presented at the moment of recall, and so on. Additional factors also enter. They involve other associations both at the time of acquisition and at the time of recall.

Learning one task will often affect the difficulty of learning another. This phenomenon is *transfer of training,* which we have already discussed in the context of animal learning studies. (Stimulus generalization is one of the simplest cases; see Chapter 4.) If learning the first task aids in learning the second, we talk of *positive transfer;* if it impedes learning the second, we call this *negative transfer.* Examples of positive transfer include learning to play the organ after having learned to play the piano or learning to read one Slavic language after having mastered another. The hope that positive transfer will occur underlies all educational systems. The ultimate aim of the teacher is that the student will be able to apply what he has learned in school to the world he encounters outside; that he will be able to read books and newspapers, not just the first-grade primer. Examples of negative transfer are also common, especially for learned patterns with a large motor com-

7.10 *Forgetting curve* The figure shows retention after various intervals since learning. Retention is here measured in percentage saving, that is, the percent decrease in the number of trials required to relearn the list after an interval of no practice. If the percentage saving is 100 percent, retention is perfect—no trials to relearn are necessary. If the percentage saving is 0 percent, there is no retention at all, for it takes just as many trials to relearn the list as it took to learn it initially. (After Ebbinghaus, 1885)

ponent. Many tennis players have trouble with the badminton swing; many Americans have experienced some harrowing moments while driving in England where traffic moves on the left.

To assess transfer, psychologists generally use two groups of subjects. The experimental group first learns task X (e.g., swinging a baseball bat) followed by task Y (e.g., swinging a golf club). The control group spends the initial period in some unrelated activity and then learns task Y. A comparison of the speed with which the two groups master task Y will indicate the transfer effect, if any (Table 7.1).

Table 7.1   TRANSFER EXPERIMENT

	Initial period	Test period
Experimental group	Learns X	Learns Y
Control group	Unrelated activity	Learns Y

Long-Term Memory and Organization

A rather different theoretical approach to long-term memory is based on the concept of *memory organization.* We have already encountered numerous instances of organization in the realm of perception; as the Gestalt psychologists pointed out, we do not see a world of unconnected colored patches, but rather we group the various elements into interrelated patterns. Many modern psychologists maintain that what is true for perception holds also for memory. As evidence they cite the fact that materials that are organized are much more easily learned and remembered than those that are not. We have little trouble remembering sentences twenty words long; the same twenty words arranged in random order offer a considerable memorial challenge. As another example, suppose a subject is asked to memorize the series

$$1\ 4\ 9\ 1\ 6\ 2\ 5\ 3\ 6\ 4\ 9\ 6\ 4\ 8\ 1$$

If she treats it as a series of fifteen unrelated digits, she will have to struggle for many trials before reaching mastery. But once she sees that the digits form a pattern

$$1\ 4\ 9\ 16\ 25\ 36\ 49\ 64\ 81$$

her task has become absurdly easy. She only has to remember the underlying relationship, "the squares of the digits from 1 to 9," and the fifteen components of the series are readily recreated.

Adherents of the organizational view argue that such examples are representative of how human memory functions generally. In their view, organization affects both acquisition and retrieval, both the form in which the memories are entered into the storehouse and the manner in which they are eventually brought back.

One recurrent theme of the organizational approach is that organization enlarges memorial capacity. To enter long-term storage, items must first pass through short-term memory. But as we have seen, the short-term loading platform has a limited capacity. It can handle only a small number of memorial packages at any one time. In view of this bottleneck, how do we manage to deposit so much material in the long-term store? The answer is organization. The capacity limit of the loading platform is on the number of packages, which generally does not exceed 7 plus or minus 2; but what these packages contain is up to us. If we can pack the input more efficiently, we may squeeze more information into the same number of memorial units. The person who interprets the series 1 4 9 . . . 8 1 as "the first nine squares" has done precisely this: he has **recoded** the inputs into larger units, sometimes called ***chunks.*** Each chunk imposes about the same load on memory as did each of the uncoded units that previously comprised it; but when eventually unpacked, it yields much more information.

Organization by phrases   Much of the job of recoding items into larger chunks has occurred in our early life. To an adult, a word is already a coherent whole, not merely a sequence of sounds. Still higher units of memorial organization are involved in the memory of sentences. The memory span for unrelated words is about seven items, but we may well recall a twenty-word sentence after only a single exposure. This fact holds even for sentences that make little sense, such as *The enemy submarine dove into the coffee pot, took fright, and silently flew away.* This dubious bit of naval intelligence consists of fourteen words, but it clearly contains fewer than fourteen memorial packages: *the enemy submarine* is essentially one unit, *took fright* is another, and so on.

One way of finding out whether higher-order units such as words and phrases have any genuine psychological reality is to consider whether their constituent parts cohere in any special manner. One investigator did this by asking subjects to learn sentences such as *The tall boy saved the dying woman.* Here there are two higher-order units: *The tall boy* and *saved the dying woman.* The demonstration that these phrases served as organizational units for memory came from an analysis of recall errors. The two phrases tended to be recalled—or forgotten—as units. A subject who recalled the words *The tall* was fairly likely to recall *boy.* If he recalled *saved,* he was likely to recall *the dying woman.* But the fact that he recalled *The tall boy* did not provide a similar guarantee that he would come up with the appropriate next word of the sentence, *saved.* It appears that the seven words of the sentence were not stored as independent items, but were rather organized as subparts of two higher-order syntactic units (Johnson, 1965; for a further discussion of syntactic issues, see Chapter 9).

Organization by semantic categories   We often organize a set of items we want to remember by pigeonholing them under several appropriate rubrics. Sometimes the categories are essentially ready-made. In a shopping list we will obviously file the items under such categories as fruits, vegetables, and meats, and we will tend to remember them in clusters that reflect these categories. This effect has been demonstrated repeatedly in the laboratory. In one study, subjects were presented with lists of items that were drawn from four different categories—animals, vegetables, professions, and first names. The order in which they were presented was random, but the way in which they were recalled was not. There was *recall clustering;* members of the same category tended to be brought up together (Bousfield, 1953).

Organization by thematic content The organization of verbal items into larger chunks such as words and sentences reflects our knowledge of the language. But the way we remember also reflects our knowledge of the world. This allows us to understand individual items of information by encoding them within an overall context that will in turn affect our later recall.

This point is made by various memory context effects. A good example is a study in which two groups of subjects were presented with a tape-recorded passage and were asked to try to understand and remember it. The passage was as follows:

> The procedure is actually quite simple. First you arrange things into different groups depending on their makeup. Of course, one pile may be sufficient depending on how much there is to do. If you have to go somewhere else due to lack of facilities that is the next step, otherwise you are pretty well set. It is important not to overdo any particular endeavor. That is, it is better to do too few things at once than too many. In the short run this may not seem important, but complications from doing too many can easily arise. A mistake can be expensive as well. The manipulation of the appropriate mechanisms should be self-explanatory, and we need not dwell on it here. At first, the whole procedure will seem complicated. Soon, however, it will become just another facet of life. It is difficult to foresee any end to the necessity for this task in the immediate future, but then one never can tell (From Bransford and Johnson, 1972, p. 722).

Both groups of subjects heard the identical passage and were treated identically in all regards but one. One group heard the passage without any further information as to what it was about. The other group was told: "The paragraph you will hear will be about washing clothes." Not surprisingly, the two groups performed very differently on both tests of comprehension and of general recall (total number of ideas in the paragraph). Once they knew the sentences were about washing, the sentences in the paragraph could be related to what the subjects already knew. This meaningful encoding helped later recall (Bransford and Johnson, 1972).

SUBJECTIVE ORGANIZATION

The preceding discussion shows that we tend to remember by using the organization that is already inherent in the material as it is understood in the light of our prior knowledge. But we sometimes go further and impose an organization of our own.

Such **subjective organizations** have a powerful effect on recall. An example is a series of studies in which subjects were presented with over fifty common English nouns, each printed on a separate index card. The subjects first had to sort the cards into different piles. They could use any category system they chose and could utilize as many rubrics as they wished. This sorting task continued over several trials until the subjects had demonstrated a stable categorization criterion by placing each card into the same pile from one trial to the next. A short time thereafter they were asked to recall as many of the words as they could.

The results showed that the larger the number of categories into which the subjects had sorted the words, the more words they remembered. According to the investigators, each of these categories represents a higher-order memorial unit into which the lower-order units (that is, the words) are packed; thus, many more words can be recalled than could be without the categorization procedure (Mandler and Pearlstone, 1966). Such organizational packaging can probably proceed still further when a hierarchy of categories is used so that higher-order categories (e.g., animal) contain subordinate ones (e.g., mammal) and so on down to the lowest level in the memorial hierarchy (e.g., raccoon). At least in principle we ought to be able to memorize a virtually endless list of items by appropriate hierarchical schemes of this sort (Mandler, 1967).

These findings underline the fact that memorial organization is generally an active process. The would-be memorizer is rarely lucky enough to have all of the material pre-chunked; he has to perform some of the chunking himself if he wants to remember successfully.

A recent experiment gives dramatic proof of the power of recoding in creating newer and larger chunks that expand our normal capacity for a particular memory task. The heroic subject was an undergraduate who devoted some 230 hours to the task of becoming a virtuoso at recalling strings of digits. In each session he heard random digits presented at a rate of one per second and then tried to recall the sequence. If his recall was correct, the sequence was increased by one digit; if it was incorrect, it was decreased by one digit. After more than twenty months of this, the subject's digit span had risen enormously: from an initial starting point of seven to a final level of almost eighty (Figure 7.11). What happened was that the subject had learned to recode the digit sequences into meaningful subparts, thus creating larger chunks. He was a long-distance runner who competed in major athletic events. This led him to express three- and four-digit groups as running times for various races (e.g., 3492 became "3 minutes 49 point 2 seconds, near world record time"), a device supplemented with ages (893 became "89 point 3, very old man") and dates (1944 was "near end of World War II"). These recoded strings of digits became chunked groups in memory. This was neatly shown by the subject's pause as he produced the digits in recall—virtually all of his pauses fell between the groups, hardly any were within (Ericsson, Chase and Faloon, 1980).

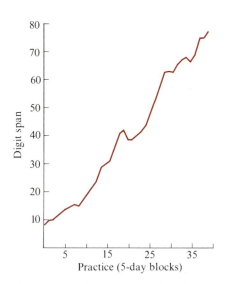

7.11 Average digit span as a function of practice *The curve shows an enormous increase in digit span after twenty months of practice during which the subject learned to recode the digit sequence into meaningful subparts. (After Ericsson, Chase, and Faloon, 1980)*

INTENTIONAL AND INCIDENTAL LEARNING

Memorial organization may help to explain another phenomenon of verbal learning: Memorization usually proceeds much more efficiently if the learner actively tries to learn. This fact is well-known from everyday experience. A similar effect is readily demonstrated in the laboratory. Two groups of subjects are exposed to the identical material, such as a tape-recorded list of words, for the same period of time. One group consists of *intentional learners* who are asked to memorize the words and who know that they will be tested later. The subjects in the other group are *incidental learners* who are forced to attend to the list (in an indirect way) by engaging in a suitable cover task; for example, they may be asked to rate how well the speakers pronounced each word. To their surprise (and occasional chagrin), they too are subsequently tested for recall of the list. The typical result is a massive superiority in the recall scores of intentional learners (Gleitman and Gillett, 1957).

What accounts for this difference? A plausible hypothesis is that the intentional learners rehearsed while the incidental learners did not. This rehearsal is an active process through which the would-be learner transforms the material. The subject who intends to learn groups items in various categories and forms higher-order chunks. As a result he will be better able to recall the material.

Evidence for this hypothesis comes from a study in which subjects were again asked to sort words into various categories. Some of the subjects were told they would be tested later (intentional learners); others were not so informed (incidental learners). When later tested for recall, the usual superiority of intentional to incidental learning did not appear; both groups did equally well. This result makes good sense once we grant that the desire to learn has only an indirect effect. It typically leads to better memorial organization which in turn is the direct cause of improved recall. Since the incidental learners necessarily organized the word list in the course of sorting the words into different categories, they suffered no disadvantage when compared to the intentional learning group (Mandler, 1967).

RETRIEVAL FROM LONG-TERM MEMORY

We have discussed some of the factors that determine how long-term memories are acquired and stored. We will now ask how they are retrieved from storage.

Retrieval Cues

The distinction between memory storage and retrieval has been noted since antiquity. St. Augustine, writing around 400 A.D., likened memory to a storehouse:

> And I enter the fields and roomy chambers of memory, where are the treasures of countless images. . . . When I am in this storehouse, I demand that what I wish should be brought forth and some things immediately appear; others require to be longer sought after, and are dragged, as it were, out of some hidden receptacle (St. Augustine, 397 A.D., p. 174).

The storehouse metaphor implies that an item may be stored and yet not found. We may know (that is, have stored) a name, a fact, an event, and still be unable to retrieve it on a particular occasion. In such a case, the memory trace is said to be presently *inaccessible.* Access to the trace may be restored by an appropriate *retrieval cue.* This point has often been demonstrated experimentally. Subjects are presented with a list of words that belong to various categories and are then tested for free recall. They may neglect to recall any word from a particular rubric. If now prompted by the category name, they readily produce several of the appropriate items (Tulving and Pearlstone, 1966).

The phenomenon of retrieving a memory that at first seemed altogether lost is well-known. The very words in which we describe our memorial functions testify to the distinction between storage and retrieval: We are *re*minded, we *re*member, we *re*collect—even our vocabulary suggests that what is now brought up was not available before. The recollection of temporarily inaccessible memories by appropriate retrieval cues is usually a rather humdrum event. We can't recall where we parked on a shopping trip, are reminded that our first stop was in a drugstore, and suddenly remember squeezing the car into a narrow space just across the street. But occasionally the effect is much more dramatic. Some persons have reported being unable to recall some of the simplest geographical features of the hometown they left years before. They finally returned for a visit, barely reached the outskirts, and suddenly all of the memories flooded back, often with a sharp pang of emotions that had been felt years before. Physical places are only one source of retrieval cues that may bring back the past. A word, a mood, a smell, a visit from a school friend not met for decades—any of these may trigger memories we thought were utterly lost.

CHANGE OF RETRIEVAL CUES

What are the characteristics of an effective retrieval cue? It is obvious that not every reminder will in fact *re*mind us, will in fact retrieve what is stored. The best guess is that success is most likely if the context at the time of retrieval approximates that during original encoding. This is sometimes called the principle of *encoding specificity* (Tulving and Osler, 1968; Tulving and Thomson, 1973).

One obvious test is to vary the physical conditions during which the subject learns and is later asked to remember. A rather dramatic illustration is provided by a study of scuba divers who had to learn a list of unrelated words either on shore or under water and who were later tested for recall in either the same or the alternate environment in which they had learned. The results showed a clear-cut context effect: what was learned in the water was best recalled in the water and similarly for what was learned on land (Godden and Baddeley, 1975; see Figure 7.12).

Similar effects can be obtained without going under water. One experimenter presented subjects with a large list of words. A day later he brought them back for an unexpected recall test that took place in either the same room or a different one that varied in size, furnishings, and so on. Recall was considerably better for subjects who were tested in the same physical environment. But the investigator found a simple way of overcoming this context effect. A different group of subjects was brought to the new room, but just prior to the recall test these subjects were asked to think about the room in which they had learned the lists—what it looked like, what it made them feel like. By doing so, they mentally recreated the old environment for themselves. On the subsequent recall test, these subjects performed no worse than those for whom there was no change of rooms. It appears that what matters is not so much that the retrieval cues physically match the conditions of acquisition; what counts is how the subject thinks about these conditions at the time he tries to recall (Smith, S.M., 1979).

THE RELATION BETWEEN ORIGINAL ENCODING AND RETRIEVAL

The preceding discussion shows that a major factor in remembering is encoding specificity: the match between the specific contexts of original encoding and of retrieval. The importance of this match has been demonstrated in numerous studies. An example is an experiment in which subjects were presented with a long list of sentences each of which included two underlined words: an adjective followed by a noun. They were told to remember these underlined words. The point of the experiment was that the meaning of the underlined nouns depended on the context provided by adjectives that preceded them (e.g., *strawberry jam* vs. *traffic jam*). The subjects were later tested with either of two test lists of adjective-noun pairs and had to indicate which of the nouns they had previously seen. In

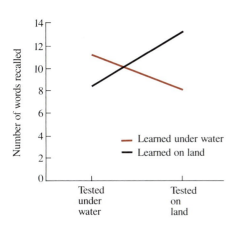

7.12   The effect of changing the retrieval situation   *Scuba divers learned a list of 36 unrelated words above water (black) or 20 feet under water (color) and were then tested above or under water. The figure shows that retention was better when the retrieval situation was the same as that in which encoding took place. (Godden and Baddeley, 1975)*

List A, the adjectives were different from those previously presented, but the new adjectives did not change the essential meanings of the nouns. Thus, a subject who had previously seen *sliced ham* and *plastic jar* might encounter *smoked ham* and *broken jar*. The situation was quite different for the adjective-noun pairs on List B. Here the new adjectives drastically changed the meaning of the noun. For example, a subject who had seen *sliced ham* and *plastic jar* might be faced with *radio ham* and *sudden jar*. The results showed that retrieval depended on how the subjects had encoded the items originally. Performance was substantially better when the subjects were tested with List A rather than List B (Light and Carter-Sobell, 1970).

Memory Search

Many investigators believe that retrieval is generally preceded by an internal process called ***memory search.*** In most cases, this process occurs without our awareness and at great speed, as when answering the question: "Which president of the United States had the first name 'George'?" But there are times when we do become aware that some such process is going on, as we consciously sift and sort among our memories until we finally recall just who it was that did what to whom on which occasion many years ago.

SEARCH STRATEGIES

In a recent study of such conscious search processes, subjects were asked to try to recall the names of their high school classmates after intervals of from four to nineteen years. Their recall accuracy was checked by consulting their high school yearbooks. The subjects came up with a fair number of names in the first few minutes of this attempt. After this, they said that they couldn't remember any more. But the experimenters asked them to keep on trying anyway. And so they did, for ten sessions of one hour each. As they continued their efforts, they surprised themselves by dredging up more and more names, until they finally recalled about a third of the names of a class of 300 (Williams and Hollan, 1982).

While going about this task, the subjects were asked to think aloud. Their comments fit the analogy to a physical search. They seemed to hunt for the sought-for names as one might search for a tangible object, inspecting one likely memory location after another. Their efforts were rarely haphazard, but seemed often based on well-formulated search strategies. For example, they mentally looked through their various classes, clubs, and teams, or scanned internal pictures to locate yet another person whom they would then try to name:

> . . . It's like I want to think of, sort of prototypical situations and then sort of examine the people that were involved in those. And things like P.E. class, where there was . . . Ah . . . Gary Booth. Umm, and Karl Brist. . . . Umm . . . I can think of things like dances. I guess then I usually think of . . . of girls . . . Like Cindy Shup, Judy Foss, and Sharon Ellis. . . . I mean it's sort of like I have a picture of the high school dance. . . . (Williams and Hollan, 1982, p. 90).

THE TIP-OF-THE-TONGUE PHENOMENON

Needless to say, search isn't always successful. Some forgotten names are never retrieved, no matter how hard we try. But occasionally, we experience a kind of halfway point, when we seem to recall something but not quite. When this occurs, we feel as if the searched-for memory is on "the tip of the tongue," but we are unable to go beyond. There is no better description of what this experience feels like than that by William James:

> Suppose we try to recall a forgotten name. The state of our consciousness is peculiar. There is a gap therein; but no mere gap. It is a gap that is intensely active. A sort of wraith of the name is in it, beckoning us in a given direction, making us at moments tingle with the sense of our closeness, and then letting us sink back without the longed-for term. If wrong names are proposed to us, this singularly definite gap acts immediately so as to negate them. They do not fit into its mold. And the gap of one word does not feel like the gap of another, all empty of content as both might seem necessarily to be when described as gaps (W. James, 1890, vol. 1, p. 251).

There is evidence that the tip-of-the-tongue experience described by James is a good reflection of how close to the mark we had actually come in our memory search, that we were really "getting warm," though unable to reach the exact spot. In one study college students were presented with the dictionary definitions of uncommon English words such as *apse, sampan,* and *cloaca.* The subjects were asked to supply the words that fit these definitions. The experimenters were concerned with those occasions on which subjects were unable to recall the target word but felt that they were on the verge of finding it (see Figure 7.13). Whenever this happened, they were asked to venture some guesses about what the target word sounded like. These guesses turned out to be closely related to the target. Given that the target word was said to be at the tip-of-the-tongue, its initial letter was guessed correctly over 50 percent of the time. Similar results were found when the subjects were asked to guess at the number of syllables. When asked to supply some other words which they thought sounded like the target, the subjects were usually in the correct phonological neighborhood. Presented with the definition "a small Chinese boat" for which the proper answer is *sampan,* subjects who said they almost remembered but not quite, supplied the following as soundalikes: *Saipan, Saim, Cheyenne,* and *sarong* (Brown and McNeill, 1966).

7.13 The tip-of-the-tongue phenomenon
This figure may provide an opportunity to demonstrate how something can be close to being retrieved from memory but not quite. (Foard, 1975)

Instructions

Here are the dictionary definitions of twelve uncommon words. Please look at each definition in turn. Try to think of the word. There are several possibilities:

1. You may be pretty sure that you know the word. Or you may be quite sure that you don't know it. In *either* case, just move on to the next definition on the list.

2. You may feel that you know the word, but can't recall it just now. In fact, it may be "on the tip of your tongue." If so, quickly do the following:

   a. Guess the letter of the first word.

   b. Try to think of one or two words that sound similar to the one you're trying to find.

Follow this procedure as you go through the whole list of definitions. Then turn to the next left-hand page for the list of the words that fit these definitions.

Definitions

1. A blood feud in which members of the family of a murdered person try to kill the murderer or members of his family
2. A protecting charm to ward off spirits
3. An old coin of Spain and South America
4. A dark, hard, glassy volcanic rock
5. A secretion from the sperm whale used in the manufacture of perfume
6. A building used for public worship by Moslems
7. An Egyptian ornament in the shape of a beetle
8. The staff of Hermes, symbol of a physician or of the medical corps
9. A sword with a short curved blade, used by the Turks and Arabs
10. A Russian sled drawn by three horses
11. A navigational instrument used in measuring altitudes
12. A narrow strip of land by which two larger bodies of land are connected

1. Vendetta
2. Amulet
3. Doubloon
4. Obsidian
5. Ambergris
6. Mosque
7. Scarab
8. Caduceus
9. Scimitar
10. Troika
11. Sextant
12. Isthmus

Retrieval and Reconstruction

The term *retrieval* implies the recovery of the same material that was originally stored. But memorial retrieval is sometimes different, for we may ***reconstruct*** the past from partial knowledge in the process of trying to remember it.

EVIDENCE FOR RECONSTRUCTION

The most influential experiments on memorial reconstruction were performed by the British psychologist Frederic Bartlett over forty years ago. Bartlett's subjects were asked to reproduce stories taken from the folklore of other cultures; thus, their content and structure were rather strange to Western ears. The reproductions showed many changes from the original. Some parts were subtracted, others were overelaborated, still others were additions that were completely new. In effect, the subjects had built a new story upon the memorial ruins of the original. This memorial reconstruction was generally more consonant with the cultural conceptions of the subjects than with the story they had actually heard. For example, certain supernatural plot elements were reinterpreted along more familiar lines.

In another variant of the same experiment, Bartlett used the method of ***serial reproduction.*** The original was presented to one subject, who reproduced it from memory for the benefit of a second, whose reproduction was shown to a third, and so on for a chain of up to ten subjects (Bartlett, 1932). With this technique (an experimental analogue of rumor transmission) each subject's memorial distortions became part of the stimulus for the next one down the line; the effect was to grossly amplify the reconstructive alteration (Figure 7.14).

Memorial reconstruction has often been noted by lawyers concerned with the accuracy of testimony. Witnesses are sometimes quite confident of various circumstances that fit their assumptions but do not fit the actual facts. An accident occurred months ago and its details have dimmed over time; as he tries to retrieve this past event the witness may fill in the gaps by an inference of which he is quite unaware.

An important factor is the way in which recall is questioned. In one study, sub-

7.14 Remembering studied by the method of serial reproduction *Ten subjects were used in the experiment. Subject 1 saw the original figure and was asked to reproduce it after half an hour. His reproduction was shown to subject 2 whose reproduction was shown to subject 3, and so on through subject 10. The figure shows the original drawing and the 10 serial reproductions, illustrating a massive reconstruction process. (After Bartlett, 1932)*

Original drawing   Reproduction 1   Reproduction 2   Reproduction 3   Reproduction 4

Reproduction 5   Reproduction 6   Reproduction 7   Reproduction 8   Reproduction 9   Reproduction 10

7.15 Remembering studied by the method of drawings done while under hypnosis *(A) Drawings done at age six (color). (B) Drawings done while subject was hypnotized and told that he was six years old (black). Note some interesting differences between the pictures, for example, the tepee, which is much more detailed in (B); the spelling of balloon; and a sense of overall design present in (B) and altogether lacking in (A). (From Orne, 1951)*

jects viewed a brief film segment of a car accident. Immediately afterward they were asked a number of questions that were in either of two forms:

"Did you see the broken headlight?"

or

"Did you see a broken headlight?"

The results showed that subjects who were questioned about *the* headlight were more likely to report having seen one than subjects who were asked about *a* headlight. This was so whether the film actually showed a broken headlight or did not. In effect, the use of the definite article, *the,* made the query a leading question, one which implied that there really was a broken headlight and that the only issue was whether the subject had noticed it. No such presupposition is made when the indefinite article, *a,* is used (Loftus and Zanni, 1975).

MEMORY, HYPNOSIS, AND THE COURTROOM

More is retained in memory storage than we can actually dig out and recall on any one occasion. This fact has led to a search for special techniques for recovering memories that have some particular importance; for example, trying to help witnesses remember what a suspect said or did. A case in point is hypnosis.

A number of U.S. law enforcement agencies have used hypnosis as a device to prompt witness recall in criminal investigations. A witness is hypnotized, told that he is back at a certain time and place, and asked to tell what he sees. On the surface, the results—in either the real world or in laboratory studies—are quite impressive. A hypnotized witness identifies an assailant as he mentally returns to the scene of the crime; a hypnotized college student is brought back to the age of six and relives his sixth birthday party with appropriately childlike glee. There is little doubt that these hypnotized people are convinced that they are actually re-experiencing these events, that what they recall really happened. But upon investigation, it often turns out that the hypnotically prodded memories are actually false. In one courtroom case, a suspect turned out to have been abroad at the time the hypnotized witness recalled having seen him during an assault (Orne, 1979). Similar points apply to the description of childhood events elicited under hypnosis. Convincing details such as the name of a first-grade teacher turn out to be quite false when later checked against available records. Some of the subjects were asked to draw a picture while mentally back at the age of six. At first glance, their drawings looked remarkably childlike. But when compared to the subjects' own childhood drawings made at that very age, it is clear that they are much more sophisticated. They represent an adult's conception of what a childish drawing is, rather than being the real thing (Figure 7.15; Orne, 1951).

How can we explain these results? It would seem that hypnosis does not have the near-magical powers often attributed to it (Barber, 1969; Orne and Hammer, 1974; Hilgard, 1977). Hypnosis does not enable us to relive our past at will (nor, for that matter, does it permit feats of agility or strength of which we would otherwise be incapable). What it does do is to make people unusually anxious to believe in and cooperate with another person, the hypnotist, and to do what he asks of them (within the bounds of certain mutually understood limitations). If he asks them to remember, they will do their very best to oblige. They will doggedly stick to the task and rummage through their minds to find any possible retrieval cue. And so of course would we all, whether hypnotized or not, providing that we wanted to remember badly enough. But what if we don't succeed? If we are not hypnotized, we will eventually concede failure. But hypnotized persons will not.

241

They try to please the hypnotist who has told them to recall and has assured them that they can. And so they do what the hypnotist asks. They produce memories—by creatively adding and reconstructing on the basis of what they already know. As we have seen, such reconstructions are a common feature in much so-called remembering. The difference in hypnosis is that the subject has little or no awareness that his reconstructions and confabulations are just that, rather than being true memories; being hypnotized, he is convinced that his fabrications are the real thing.

Some evidence comes from a study on the susceptibility to leading questions. The experimenter employed the familiar technique of showing subjects videotapes of an accident and later asking them to recall certain details, in some cases while hypnotized and in others while not. Some of the probes were leading questions, while others were more objective in phrasing. As we just saw, such leading questions lead to errors even without hypnosis. But they lead to even more errors in hypnotized subjects than in controls. When asked whether they had seen "*the* license plate . . ." (which in fact was not visible), some of the hypnotized subjects not only said yes but actually volunteered partial descriptions of the license plate number. Findings of this sort cast some serious doubts on the uncritical use of hypnosis in real-life judicial settings (Putnam, 1979).

Over and above what these findings may tell us about hypnosis, they also have some implications for what is sometimes called the tape-recorder theory of memory. According to this view, the brain contains a virtually imperishable record of all we have ever heard or seen or felt. The only trick is to find a way to turn the recorder back to some desired portion of the tape. But the evidence indicates that this suggestion is exceedingly implausible. All techniques that claim to provide such memory "playbacks"—the major example is hypnosis—have been found wanting. Under the circumstances, our best guess is that the tape-recorder theory is false. To be sure, we retain much more than we can retrieve at any given moment. But this doesn't mean we retain every bit of sensory information we encounter. Some is never entered, some is lost if not rehearsed and organized, and some is altered to fit in with incoming material (Loftus and Loftus, 1980; Neisser, 1982).

In the last chapter, we saw that perception is an active process. It depends upon incoming stimuli, but it does not provide a mere copy, for the incoming sensory information is often reshaped and transformed. A similar point applies to memory. It depends on what is stored, but a given act of remembering provides us with more than a frozen slice of the past; it often fills in gaps and reconstructs as we unwittingly try to fit our past into our present (Neisser, 1967).

STRATEGIES FOR REMEMBERING

Our previous discussion repeatedly emphasized the fact that remembering is an active process. Material isn't just entered into memory; it is encoded in different ways and is often actively searched for at the time of retrieval. Since we know that we sometimes have to recall or recognize what we have seen and heard, we have developed a whole set of techniques to help us succeed at these tasks. These include *rehearsal* and certain special tricks that go under the general name of *mnemonics*. As we will see, the success of these strategies depends on the phenomena of encoding and retrieval that we have just discussed.

Rehearsal

When presented with a list of items they will later be asked to remember, most people rehearse. As already mentioned, such rehearsal is said to affect the transfer of items from short-term to long-term storage, but just exactly what does this mean? Why does rehearsal help us to remember at a later date?

MAINTENANCE REHEARSAL

We now know that there are several kinds of rehearsal that differ in their effects. One form of rehearsal turns out to do little in the long run. This is called *maintenance rehearsal,* through which the subject merely holds the material in short-term memory for a little while. This is what we use when we try to hold on to a telephone number just long enough to complete the call. We repeat it to ourselves just long enough to finish dialing and then promptly forget it. Experimental evidence comes from an ingenious study that varied the time in which items remained in short-term memory. The subjects were presented with a fairly long list and had to report the last word on the list that began with a certain letter. Suppose the letter was *G* and that the list began with the following words:

> Daughter
> Oil
> Rifle
> Garden
> Grain
> Table
> Football
> Anchor
> Giraffe

In this situation, the subject has to hold one *G*-word in short-term memory until the next one appears which will then replace it until it is replaced in turn. Thus, *Garden* will be replaced by *Grain* which will make way for *Giraffe* and so on until the final critical word on the list is reached. This arrangement guarantees that some of the *G*-words are held longer in short-term memory than others; thus, *Grain* will stay longer than *Garden.* The question was whether this increased the chance that *Garden* would be transferred to long-term memory. To find out, the investigators gave a final—and unexpected—test after many such lists had been presented. The subjects were simply asked to report as many of the words that they had heard in all the sessions as they could. The results showed that the time an item had been in short-term memory had no effect—*Garden* was recalled just as often as was *Grain* (Craik and Watkins, 1973). The results of this and further studies suggest that maintenance rehearsal confers little or no long-term benefits (Rundus, 1977).

ELABORATIVE REHEARSAL

Pure maintenance is evidently not enough. But if so, what is? According to a widely held view, the kind of rehearsal that does establish long-term memories is *elaborative rehearsal,* a general term for the mental activities by means of which the subject organizes the items he wants to remember while they are still in short-term memory. She may group them, or recode them into fewer chunks, or relate them to each other and to other items in long-term memory—all of these are ways that help her to store the material more efficiently.

But elaborative rehearsal confers yet another and perhaps even more important advantage. By connecting the to-be-remembered items to each other or to other material already in long-term memory, the subject increases the likelihood of retrieving more of them when she is later tested. If she is asked to recall, say, a list of words, then any one that comes to mind will help to retrieve more of the others. In the ancient world, all roads led to Rome and so the traveller could always find it. Much the same is true for elaborative rehearsal. Every elaboration builds another path by which the material can later be reached; the more such paths exist, the easier retrieval will be (Craik and Tulving, 1975).

A REINTERPRETATION OF SHORT-TERM MEMORY

This general approach to the role of encoding has suggested a new interpretation of the relation between short-term and long-term memory. About twenty years ago, these two were conceived as mere memory depots in a one-way traffic flow in which information was moved from the small short-term loading platform to the much more spacious long-term store. Today, however, most theorists believe that long-term memories are formed by a more active process in which the subject's own ways of encoding the material play a major role. In their view, short-term memory should be regarded not so much as a temporary storage compartment—or loading platform—but rather as a kind of mental workbench on which various items of experience are held for a while as they are sorted, organized, and related to other items that are already in memory (Baddeley, 1976). They believe that whether the materials will be retained in memory and eventually retrieved does not depend on a simple transfer from one storage compartment to another. It rather depends on how this material is processed (that is, encoded). The more elaborate this processing, the greater the likelihood of later remembering.*

Mnemonics

The same general principles of memorial organization that make elaborative rehearsal so effective also underlie a very practical endeavor whose roots go back to ancient Greece and Rome—the development of techniques for improving one's memory, often called *mnemonics*.

MNEMONICS THROUGH VERBAL ORGANIZATION

The ancients were aware that it is much easier to remember verbal material if it is organized. They were particularly partial to the use of verse, a phonological organization of word sequences which maintains a fixed rhythm and often rhyme

---

* An earlier and related position is called the *depth of processing* hypothesis (Craik and Lockhart, 1972).

or alliteration. Without such aids, preliterate societies might never have transmitted their oral traditions intact from one generation to the next. Homeric bards could recite the entire *Iliad,* but could they have done so had it been in prose? Verse is still used as mnemonic when it seems necessary to impose some sort of order upon an otherwise arbitrary set of items (e.g., "Thirty days hath September/April, June, and November").

MNEMONICS THROUGH VISUAL IMAGERY

The methods of loci and pegs   Some of the most effective mnemonics ever devised involve the deliberate use of mental imagery. One such technique is the **method of loci** which requires the learner to visualize each of the items she wants to remember in a different spatial location (locus). In recall, each location is mentally inspected and the item that was placed there in imagination is thus retrieved. This method was first described in Roman treatises on oratory, including one by Cicero. (Training in memory was regarded as an indispensable part of the study of oratory, for public speeches were generally delivered from memory alone.) The first step is the careful selection of the different loci, which must be well-known and easily distinguishable. The second is to locate each item in its proper place. If any item is an abstract concept that is hard to visualize, it must be translated into an object that can be visualized in its stead; for example, an anchor might be a fair substitute for "navigation." To quote from one such text, written about 50 A.D.:

> The first notion is placed, as it were, in the forecourt; the second, let us say, in the atrium; the remainder . . . committed not only to bedrooms and parlours, but even to statues and the like. This done, when it is required to revive the memory, one begins from the first place to run through all, demanding what has been entrusted to them, of which one will be reminded by the image. . . . As Cicero says: "We use places as wax and images as letters" (quoted from *Institution Oratoria* by Quintillian, in Yates, 1966, p. 23).

Later authors advocated a somewhat different approach which became known as the **peg method.** The first step is the creation of a set of mental pegs, such as numerals, to which the items to be memorized could be attached. The student begins by memorizing a set of rhymes, such as *one-bun, two-shoe, three-tree,* up to perhaps twenty numbers. Once these pairs are mastered (not too hard a task considering the rhymes) they are ready to serve as mental pegs. To learn a serial list of items (e.g., *college, earthworm, top hat,* etc.) the student must form different compound images that connect each item with its cue word. The first two images might be a bun receiving a college diploma and an earthworm wriggling out of a shoe. When later asked to name an item that was in a particular position, the student must first retrieve the appropriate cue word (e.g., *bun, shoe,* etc.). This presumably triggers the compound image which carries the appropriate answer.

The underlying principles of the methods of loci and pegs are obviously quite similar. Both methods provide a scheme which allows orderly retrieval; a spatial layout for the method of loci, a well-learned system of arbitrary cues for the method of pegs. Both require a deliberate effort to relate the items that must be memorized to distinctive features of the retrieval scheme, and to do so through visual imagery. The efficacy of these mnemonic systems has been tested by several experimental studies. Subjects who recalled by the method of loci recalled up to seven times more than their counterparts who learned in rote manner. In one such study, college students had to learn lists of forty unrelated concrete nouns. Each list was presented once for about ten minutes, during which the subjects tried to visualize each of the forty objects in one of forty different locations around the college campus. Tested immediately, they recalled an average of thirty-eight of the forty items; tested one day later, they still managed to recall thirty-four (Ross and Lawrence, 1968). In another study, the subjects were instructed to connect two unrelated nouns by forming a mental picture that linked the items of each pair. Starting with lists of twenty-five pairs they gradually worked up to much longer lists, achieving recall scores of 100 percent for lists up to three hundred and 95 percent for lists of seven hundred pairs—scores that vastly exceed any level one could possibly hope to attain by the usual Ebbinghausian means (Wallace, Turner, and Perkins, 1957). It is rather sobering to realize that modern psychology had to rediscover a phenomenon that was already known to Cicero.

WHY DOES IMAGERY HELP?

Why are images such a powerful aid to memory? One of the reasons may be that they are yet another way of forming a new chunk in memory. By creating a mental image, the subject joins two unrelated items so that they form a new whole. When part of the chunk (the peg word or the imagined locus) is presented, the entire chunk is retrieved, yielding the part required for recall.

Some evidence for this view comes from studies that show that mental images will only facilitate recall if they tend to unify the items to be associated into a coherent whole. Consider a subject who has to learn a list of noun-noun pairs such as *eagle-locomotive* and is instructed to use imagery as a memorial aid. She can construct mental pictures that bring the items into some kind of unitary relationship, for example, an eagle winging to his nest with a locomotive in his beak. But she may form an image whose constituents are merely adjacent and do not interact, such as an eagle at the side of a locomotive. Several recent experiments demonstrate that unifying mental images produce much better recall than non-unifying images (Wollen, Weber, and Lowry, 1972). A similar effect is found when the test items are real pictures. If shown a drawing of a doll standing on a chair waving a flag, subjects quickly reply "chair and flag" when asked to recall the objects that were pictured with the doll. Their recall score is substantially lower if they were shown a picture of the doll, chair, and flag, drawn as separate, unrelated objects (Figure 7.16).

7.16 The effect on memory of a unitary relation between elements *Subjects shown related elements, such as a doll standing on a chair and waving a flag (A) are more likely to associate the words* doll, flag, *and* chair *than subjects who are shown the three objects next to each other but not interacting (B). (After G. Bower, 1970a)*

A

B

Rehearsal and Mnemonics as Strategies

Rehearsal and mnemonic devices are active strategies employed by the would-be memorizer. This is obvious enough for the mnemonic systems, whose invention was no mean intellectual achievement and whose utilization requires some practice and skill. But it also holds for rehearsal. Rehearsal, especially elaborative rehearsal, is just the mnemonics of everyday life. Most of us employ rehearsal techniques of one form or another, but to use them takes a certain amount of sophistication. At minimum, one has to know that such techniques help later recall. Under the circumstances, it is not surprising that young children and severely retarded adults do not rehearse when they are asked to commit something to memory. Memory is an active process. But much of this activity—rehearsal, organization during acquisition, systematic search at the time of retrieval—develops with increasing intellectual maturity. (For a further discussion, see Chapters 14 and 17.)

FORGETTING FROM LONG-TERM MEMORY

In popular usage, the word *forgetting* is employed as a blanket term that is invoked whenever memory fails. But memorial failures have different causes, as we have already seen. Some arise from faulty storage procedures (e.g., inadequate organization), while others are produced by conditions at the moment of recall (e.g., lack of appropriate retrieval cues). We now turn to the relation of memory failure to the *retention interval* that intervenes between original learning and the time of test. At least on the face of it, forgetting increases with increasing retention interval. Yesterday's lesson is fresher today than it will be tomorrow (see Figure 7.17). There are several theories designed to explain this and related phenomena, which we will now discuss.

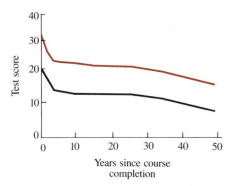

7.17 Forgetting a foreign language over time *The figure displays performance on a Spanish reading comprehension test for persons who took three or more years of high school or college Spanish, were tested from 0 to 50 years later, and had previously earned a grade of A (color) or C (black). The possible scores on this test ranged from a minimum of 0 to a maximum total of 40 points. As the figure shows, quite a bit is forgotten in the first two or three years after learning, but then performance levels off until much later in life, where aging effects probably account for the later memory loss. Of great interest is the fact that even after 50 years, the performance reflects how well the language was learned originally: On average, students who had earned an A, perform better than those who had received a C, even after half a century had passed. (After Bahrick, 1984)*

Decay

The most venerable theory of forgetting holds that memory traces gradually *decay* as time passes, like mountains that are eroded by wind and water. The erosion of memories is presumably caused by normal metabolic processes whose impact wears down the memory trace until it fades and finally disintegrates.

While this theory has considerable intuitive appeal, there is so far little direct evidence in its favor. Several studies have tried to provide an indirect test by varying body temperature. Like most chemical reactions, metabolic processes increase with increasing temperature. If these reactions are responsible for memorial decay, then forgetting should be a function of the body temperature during the retention interval. This prediction has been tested with cold-blooded animals such as the goldfish whose body takes on the temperature of its surroundings. By and large, the results have been in line with the hypothesis: the higher the temperature of the tank in which the fish is kept during the retention interval, the more forgetting takes place (Gleitman and Rozin, as reported in Gleitman, 1971).

247

But some other findings complicate this picture. There is good evidence that forgetting is determined not simply by the duration of the retention interval, but by what happens during this time. Experiments on human subjects have shown that recall is substantially worse after an interval spent awake than after an equal period while asleep (Jenkins and Dallenbach, 1924).

Such results pose difficulties for a theory that assigns all of the blame for forgetting to decay, for they show that time itself does not cause all of the loss. To explain such findings within a theory of decay, one would have to assert that the relevant metabolic processes that erode the memory trace are slowed down during sleep, an argument for which there is no evidence as yet.

Interference

A rather different theory of forgetting is *interference.* According to this view, a forgotten memory is neither lost nor damaged, but is only misplaced among a number of other memories that interfere with the recovery of the one that was sought. Seen in this light, our inability to remember the name of a high school friend is analogous to what happens when a clerk cannot find a letter he received a year ago. The letter is still somewhere in his files, but it has been hopelessly buried in a mass of other letters that he filed both before and since.

Memorial interference is easily demonstrated in the laboratory. A major example is *retroactive inhibition* in which new learning hampers recall of the old. In a typical study, a control group learns some rote material such as a list of nonsense syllables (List *A*) and is tested after a specified interval. The experimental group learns the same list as the control group and is tested after the same retention interval. But in addition it must also learn a second list (List *B*) that is interpolated during the retention interval (Table 7.2). The usual result is a marked inferiority in the performance of the experimental group; the interpolated list interferes with (inhibits) the recall of List *A*.

A similar effect is *proactive inhibition* in which interference works in a forward (proactive) direction. The usual procedure is to have an experimental group learn List *A* followed by List *B,* and then test for recall of List *B* after a suitable retention interval. The critical comparison is with a control group which learns only List *B* (Table 7.3). In general, the experimental group does worse on the recall test.

Table 7.2 RETROACTIVE INHIBITION EXPERIMENT

	Initial period	Retention interval	Test interval
Control group	Learns list *A*	————	Recalls list *A*
Experimental group	Learns list *A*	Learns list *B*	Recalls list *A*

Table 7.3 PROACTIVE INHIBITION EXPERIMENT

	Initial period		Retention interval	Test period
Control group	————	Learns list *B*	————	Recalls list *B*
Experimental group	Learns list *A*	Learns list *B*	————	Recalls list *B*

Change of Retrieval Cues

Decay theory holds that the memory trace gradually fades away with time, while interference theory asserts that the trace gets lost among other traces acquired both before and after. There is a further alternative which argues that memorial success or failure is primarily determined by the retrieval cues presented at the time of recall.

We have already seen that a change in retrieval cues disrupts remembering. But can this effect explain why forgetting increases with an increasing retention interval? To maintain the hypothesis that the critical factor is cue alteration, one must argue that such alteration becomes ever more likely with the passage of time. There are some cases for which this may be true. Certain memories may have been acquired in a particular locale; over the years the neighborhood changes as some houses are torn down and new ones are built, thus altering the physical cue situation and thereby decreasing the chance of retrieval.

This kind of interpretation may explain some of the difficulties we have in recalling the events of our childhood.* The world of the young child is utterly different from the world she occupies some ten or fifteen years later. It is a world in which tables are hopelessly out of reach, in which chairs can be climbed upon only with great effort, in which adults are giants in size and gods in ability. Whatever memories the child may store at this time are formed within this context; thus, the appropriate retrieval context is usually absent from the adult's environment. (For discussion, see Schachtel, 1947; White and Pillemer, 1979.)

The retrieval-cue hypothesis is a very plausible account of some aspects of forgetting. But it probably cannot explain them all. Forgetting increases as a function of the time since learning even when the retrieval conditions appear essentially unchanged. Some evidence comes from studies with animal subjects where all facets of the situation are under the experimenter's control. In one study, rats were trained to run an alley for food reward. Some of them were tested one day after original learning; others, after sixty-eight days. All of the physical conditions of the experiment—the location and illumination of the alley, the home cages, the animal's own weight—were kept identical throughout the entire period. Even so, there was a massive effect of the retention interval. The animals tested some two months after training were much more hesitant in the alley than they were before, as if they had forgotten what they were supposed to do (Gleitman, 1971).

In summary, we must conclude that each of the theories of forgetting proposed thus far can account for some of the aspects of the phenomenon but not all. Interference and change of retrieval cues play a major role, but neither of them can readily explain why forgetting increases with the passage of time. While the evidence for decay is by no means solid, it nevertheless seems reasonable to suppose that some such process does occur and is partially responsible for the effect of retention interval.

* Some of these difficulties undoubtedly represent failures of acquisition rather than of retrieval. There is no question that the child—especially the very young child—codes the events of her life in a rather fragmentary manner, especially during the first two or three years when language development is still at an early stage.

What is the upshot of all of this for our own attempts to remember? We cannot avoid all of the conditions that lead to forgetting. To do so, we would have to abstain from all other learning both before and after memorizing the items we want to retain, spend the retention interval asleep (preferably in a refrigerator), and refuse to take any recall test unless the retrieval situation is certified to be identical to the one in which we learned. Under the circumstances, what can we do if we want to remember? We have given the answer before. The path to recall goes through memorial organization. The clerk who must retrieve a letter cannot change the fact (if it is a fact) that some of the ink gradually fades on the paper (decay), or that he has other letters to file both before and after (proactive and retroactive interference), or that the letter he is asked for is sometimes identified by date and sometimes by name (change of retrieval cue). The best he can do is to file the letter in an organized fashion.

VARIETIES OF LONG-TERM MEMORY

We have discussed long-term memory as if it were all of a piece, one huge warehouse in which all our memories are stored, regardless of their form and content. Some recent authors have tried to make some further distinctions that may provide a clue to the way this warehouse is arranged.

Generic Memory

One important distinction is between episodic and generic memory. *Episodic memory* is the memory for particular events (episodes) of one's own life; what happened when and where, as when recalling that one ate fried chicken the other night. This contrasts with *generic memory,* which is memory for items of knowledge as such, independent of the particular occasion in which we have learned them: the capital of France, the square root of 9, and so on. In effect, generic memory is the sum total of a person's acquired knowledge—the meanings of words and symbols, facts about the world, what objects look like.

Most of the studies on memory we have described thus far are primarily about episodic memory. Consider an experiment in which subjects have to memorize a list of nouns such as *submarine, typewriter, elephant,* and so on. When the experimenter tests for later recall, his interest is in what the subjects learned at the time of the experiment, their episodic memories—that the list they were presented included *elephant* and *typewriter* but not *gazelle* and *thermometer.* This is not to say that there were not many generic memories which the subjects brought to bear on the task. After all, they all knew and understood all the words on the list. But the experimenter was not interested in these generic memories. Had he been, he would have asked questions such as, "What is an elephant?" (Tulving, 1972; Hintzman, 1978).

One of the most important components of generic memory is *semantic memory,* the memory that concerns the meanings of words and concepts (Tulving, 1972). What first comes to mind in describing semantic memory is its sheer enormity. Our entire vocabulary is in this store; every word together with its pronunciation, all of its meanings, its relations to objects in the real world, the way it is put together with other words to make phrases and sentences. How do we ever find any one bit of information in this near-infinity of verbal knowledge? One thing is certain. When we search for an item—say, a synonym for *quiet*—we don't go through all of the items in the semantic store. If we did, the hunt might last for days or weeks. The fact that we can come up with *silent* in a second or less shows that we make use of a much more efficient retrieval system. To use a library analogy, the person who takes out a book doesn't have to rummage through all of the volumes on each shelf in order to find the one he wants. He can obtain his book much faster because there is an organized system according to which the books are arranged in the stacks.

MEMORY ACTIVATION

What holds for episodic memory holds all the more for semantic memory: It is organized. How can we describe what this organization is? One way is through the study of **memory activation.** A subject is asked to think of a word that begins with a certain letter and belongs to some semantic category. Suppose she is asked for a word that is a *G-fruit.* The experimenter measures the reaction time from the presentation of the category term *fruit* and the response (say *grapes*). Shortly thereafter the subject gets tested once more. On some occasions, the same category is again called for, though with a different initial letter, as in *S-Fruit.* Now, the time to retrieve a suitable word (say, *strawberries*) is quite a bit shorter than it was the first time. What seems to have happened is that a semantic category is activated and remains that way for a while, like a section in a library that is lit up by a previous user who leaves the lights on when she departs. This part of the library will now become easier to find (Loftus, 1973).

HIERARCHICAL SEARCH

Memory activation demonstrates that in searching through semantic memory we utilize broad categories in terms of which the items are organized. Other investigators have tried to show that this search is **hierarchical.** The strategy resembles the one called for by the familiar game of Twenty Questions. The skillful player does not begin by trying to guess the final answer; she narrows the field down by progressive steps. She asks, "Is it a human being?" "Is it a man or a woman?" "Is he still alive?" "Was he born before 1000 A.D.?" Each question leads to a further branch on a decision tree that immediately eliminates all of the other twigs on the other branches. Some authors believe that retrieval from semantic memory proceeds along similar lines. According to this view, subjects, when asked to recall a particular word, search (whether consciously or not) along a decision tree whose branches correspond to semantic categories.

Some evidence comes from studies on the verification of sentences. The subjects were shown short sentences such as "A canary can fly" or "A canary is blue" and had to decide whether these sentences were true or false. To reach a decision, the subject presumably first has to retrieve the meaning of each word. How are these meanings stored? Consider the various facts that most of us know about canaries. Some properties distinguish canaries from other birds: They are yellow; they can sing. Others fit all birds: They have wings and feathers. Still others describe the superordinate category *animal* of which *birds* are a subordinate: They must eat. It is not unreasonable to suppose that the memorial dictionary is organ-

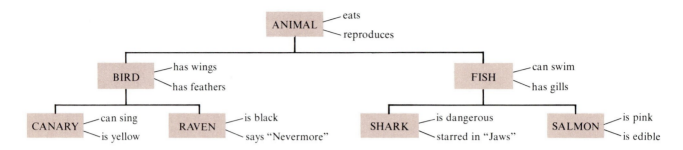

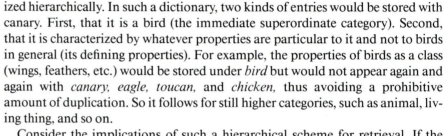

7.18   The hierarchical theory of semantic memory   *To decide whether the sentence "Ravens have feathers" is true, given the organization of the entries here pictured, one has to "look up" the information at the second level, under* bird.

ized hierarchically. In such a dictionary, two kinds of entries would be stored with canary. First, that it is a bird (the immediate superordinate category). Second, that it is characterized by whatever properties are particular to it and not to birds in general (its defining properties). For example, the properties of birds as a class (wings, feathers, etc.) would be stored under *bird* but would not appear again and again with *canary, eagle, toucan,* and *chicken,* thus avoiding a prohibitive amount of duplication. So it follows for still higher categories, such as animal, living thing, and so on.

Consider the implications of such a hierarchical scheme for retrieval. If the subject is asked a question about those characteristics of a canary that are presumably stored under *canary* ("Does a canary sing?"), the retrieval system is only required to "look up" *canary* in the memorial dictionary. Once there, the relevant entries are searched, and the answer is found. But suppose the question is about some aspect of a canary that is really a characteristic of birds as a class; for example, "Does a canary have feathers?" Now the subject must look up two words in semantic memory. He starts with *canary* but nothing is said about feathers. He now moves up one step in the hierarchy to get to *bird* and finds a relevant entry. Indeed, birds are feathered. A further step is required if the sentence refers to properties of the higher-order category *animal,* as in the question "Can a canary breathe?" Here retrieval begins with *canary,* moves up one level to *bird,* and one more level to *animal* (Figure 7.18).

To test this conception, the investigators looked at the subject's reaction times in verifying the sentences. According to the hierarchical scheme, it should take a certain amount of extra time to move up from one level of the hierarchy to the next. The results seemed to bear this out. The time required to arrive at a yes-or-no decision was shortest for sentences that required no shift in the hierarchy level, such as "A canary can sing." When the sentence required one step up, as in "A canary has wings," its verification took an additional 75 milliseconds. When the sentence called for two steps, as in "A canary can breathe," its verification took yet another 75 milliseconds (Figure 7.19). The authors reasoned that each move up in the hierarchy takes a certain amount of time; here, 75 milliseconds (Collins and Quillian, 1969). The underlying logic involves the same reaction time method we have already encountered in our discussion of serial search procedures in short-term memory retrieval.

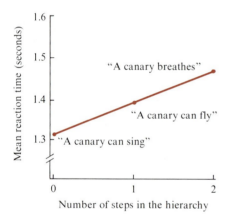

7.19   Retrieval time from semantic memory   *The figure shows the times required to decide whether certain sentences are true or false. According to a hierarchical theory of semantic memory, different sentences require stepping up 0, 1, or 2 levels in the hierarchy to retrieve the information that is necessary for a decision. The reaction times increase with each additional step. (After Collins and Quillian, 1969)*

This hierarchical scheme is very neat but, as so often, nature is much less neat than theorists would have her be. To mention only one problem, membership in many semantic categories does not seem to be all-or-none. When subjects are asked to rate various birds according to the degree to which they were "typical birds," *robins* were judged to be the most typical, *chickens* less so, and *penguins* birds by courtesy only (Rosch, 1973). While the evidence is not all in, the best guess is that these differences in typicality are reflected in verification times. Thus, subjects seem to be faster in agreeing that "*X* is a bird," if *X* is a typical bird like a canary or a robin rather than a marginal case like a penguin or an ostrich. Such effects suggest that the relation between items of information in the semantic memory is not as tidy as the hierarchical position had supposed (for further discussion, see Chapter 9).

Visual Memory

Important as words and the abstract concepts that underlie them may be, they are not all that we remember. We also seem to have memory systems that preserve some of the characteristic attributes of our senses. The idea is not just that we know that, say, people's waists are between their head and their toes. Of course we do, but that isn't all. We also seem to be able to somehow retrieve this betweenness from a mental image that has some of the characteristics of the original visual experience. As some authors (beginning with Shakespeare) have put it, we see it in "our mind's eye." While similar claims have been made for other senses —hearing with the mind's ear (composers), feeling with the mind's fingers (blind persons)—our primary concern will be with visual memory.

RATING ONE'S OWN IMAGES

The first attempt to study visual imagery goes back a hundred years ago when Sir Francis Galton (1822–1911), the founder of the field of individual differences, asked people to describe their own images and to rate them for vividness (Galton, 1883). The results showed that individuals differed widely. Some people said they could call up past scenes at will and see them with the utmost clarity. Others (including some well-known painters) denied ever having had images at all. But these differences in how people described their own experiences have surprisingly little to do with how they actually performed on tasks that seemed to call for visual memory. One study showed that there was no correlation between self-rated image vividness and performance on an objective test that measured memory for spatial designs (Di Vesta, Ingersoll, and Sunshine, 1971). Nor is there any relationship between the way subjects rate their own images and the degree to which they benefit from imagery mnemonics (Baddeley, 1976).

EIDETIC IMAGERY

Since self-judgments of imagery seemed to be of little use, psychologists turned to more sophisticated procedures. In addition to asking what the image appeared to be like, they asked what it enabled the subject to do. For example, is the image a mental picture from which we can read off information as if it were an actual visual scene outside? By and large, the answer is no. But there are some exceptions. One is *iconic memory,* which we have encountered before. It is certainly picture-like, but it is obviously not part of long-term storage since it only lasts a fraction of a second. A more pertinent phenomenon is *eidetic imagery,* which is characterized by relatively long-lasting and detailed images of visual scenes that can sometimes be scanned and "looked at" as if they had real existence outside. In one study, a group of schoolchildren was shown a picture for thirty seconds. After

7.20 Test picture for study of eidetic imagery *This picture from* Alice in Wonderland *was shown for half a minute to elementary schoolchildren, a few of whom seemed to have an eidetic image of it. (Illustration by Marjorie Torrey)*

it was taken away, the subjects were asked whether they could still see anything and, if so, to describe what they saw (Leask, Haber, and Haber, 1969). Evidence for eidetic imagery is contained in the following protocol of a ten-year-old boy, who was looking at a blank easel from which a picture from *Alice in Wonderland* had just been removed (Figure 7.20).

EXPERIMENTER: Do you see something there?
SUBJECT: I see the tree, gray tree with three limbs. I see the cat with stripes around its tail.
EXPERIMENTER: Can you count those stripes?
SUBJECT: Yes (pause). There's about 16.
EXPERIMENTER: You're counting what? Black, white or both?
SUBJECT: Both.
EXPERIMENTER: Tell me what else you see.
SUBJECT: And I can see the flowers on the bottom. There's about three stems but you can see two pairs of flowers. One on the right has green leaves, red flower on bottom with yellow on top. And I can see the girl with a green dress. She's got blond hair and a red hair band and there are some leaves in the upper left-hand corner where the tree is (Haber, 1969, p. 38).

Eidetic imagery is relatively rare. Only 5 percent or so of tested schoolchildren seemed to have it, and the proportion is almost surely smaller in adults. Nor does it seem to be an especially useful form of mental activity. Contrary to popular lore, memory experts don't generally have eidetic imagery (or photographic memory as it is sometimes popularly referred to); their skill is in organizing material in memory, rather than in storing it in picture form.

OTHER FORMS OF VISUAL MEMORY

Eidetic imagery may be a rare case of an unusually persistent sensory memory. If so, it is the one case in which visual memory corresponds to a picture in the head. But except for this, visual memory is not a simple reembodiment of stored visual sensation. Our perceptions are not like photographs, and so our visual memories can't be either. But they may nevertheless contain certain pictorial attributes that are also found in visual perception. A number of studies suggest that this is indeed the case.

Mental rotation One line of evidence comes from studies on **mental rotation.** The subjects were shown a digit or a number, either normally or in mirror-reversed form (that is, *R* or Я). But in addition, the figures were tilted so that the subject might encounter an *R* rotated by, say, 120 degrees, to yield ⅄ . Or he might be presented with the Я figure, rotated by, say, 60 degrees, as in ⅄ . The subjects' task was to press one button if the stimulus was normal, another if it was mirror-reversed.

The reaction times proved to be a regular function of how far the characters were tilted away from the upright. As the orientation of the letters changed from 0 degrees (*R*) through 60 degrees (⅄) to 180 degrees (⅄), reaction times increased. The same was true for the mirror-reversed letters. Reaction times were shortest for Я , longer for ⅄ , and the longest for ⅄ .

The authors interpret their results as evidence for a separate visual memory

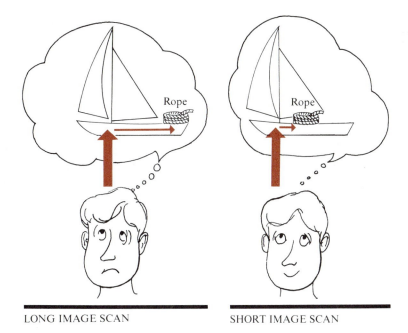

LONG IMAGE SCAN   SHORT IMAGE SCAN

7.21 Image scanning Subjects were asked to look mentally at an image of a drawing they had just seen and to decide whether it contained a particular object. They responded faster when they had to traverse a shorter distance in their mind's eye. (Kosslyn, 1973)

system. In their view, the subjects mentally rotated an image of the stimulus they were presented with until it was upright. Once they had brought it to this position, it could be compared to the visual memory of the normal and backward characters. The fact that reaction time was a function of angle shows that this mental rotation takes time; in the present case, about 30 milliseconds for every 10 degrees (Cooper and Shepard, 1973).

Image scanning Another line of evidence comes from studies on ***image scanning.*** Here the subjects were asked to conjure up an image of a drawing they had previously studied. They were asked to focus upon one end of the object they had imaged. For example, if the image was of a boat, they might be asked to take a "mental look" at the bow (Figure 7.21). After this, an object was named, say a *rope,* and the subject had to decide whether this object was present in the picture he had been shown previously. The results showed that the reaction times depended on the distance the subject had to scan along the image before the object was "found." If the subject was initially directed to focus at the boat's bow, reaction times were longer when the rope was in the stern than when it was in the boat's middle. This result would be no surprise had the subject scanned a physical object with his real eye. That the same holds when he scans an image with his mind's eye is rather remarkable (Kosslyn, 1973).

DISORDERED MEMORY

Thus far, our discussion has centered on people with normal memories. But during the last two decades, some of the most intriguing questions about human memory have been raised by studies of people with drastic defects in memory functions that are caused by certain kinds of damage to the brain (Rozin, 1976b; Cermak, 1979).

Anterograde Amnesia

Certain lesions in the human temporal cortex (specifically in the **hippocampus** and other structures near the base of the brain) produce a memory disorder called **anterograde amnesia** (anterograde, "in a forward direction"). The patient often has little trouble in remembering whatever he had learned prior to the injury; his difficulty is learning anything new thereafter. Such lesions can occur in various ways. They are found in certain chronic alcoholic patients who suffer from **Korsakoff syndrome** (named after the Russian physician who first described it). They sometimes accompany senility. In a few instances they are a tragic side effect of neurosurgery such as that undertaken to minimize seizures in severe epilepsy (see Figure 7.22).

A famous example is the case of H.M., whose hippocampal lesion was the result of surgery performed when he was twenty-nine. His memory disorder subsequent to surgery seemed to fit in well with the idea that short-term and long-term memory represent two distinct memory systems. For example, he had a normal memory span. But he seemed to be incapable of adding any new information to his long-term storage. He could not recognize anyone he had not met before the surgery, no matter how often they met afterward. He was unable to find his way to the new house his family subsequently moved into. When told that his uncle had died he was deeply moved, but then forgot all about it and repeatedly asked when this uncle would come for a visit. On each occasion he was informed once more of his uncle's death and every time his grief was as intense as before; to him, each time he was told was the first.

While H.M.'s long-term storage system apparently became almost completely closed to any new memories, his memories prior to the operation remained largely intact, especially for events that happened more than a year or so before the surgery. He could still read and write and engage in lively conversation. In many ways, his intellectual functioning was unimpaired. This is not uncommon in patients suffering damage to the hippocampus and related systems. For example, Korsakoff's original patient could still play a competent game of chess though he could not remember how any given position on the chess board came about. (Needless to say, he had learned the rules of the game previously.)

H.M. also had excellent recall for scenes from his earlier past. It is not too surprising that such memories are brought up endlessly. To quote from Brenda Milner, a psychologist who has studied H.M. over many years:

> He is also apt to tell long anecdotes from his school days, repeating them to the same person on different occasions, since he does not realize that he has told them before. These stereotyped stories which resemble the reminiscences of an elderly person, are presumably all he has with which to occupy his thoughts when he is not actively engaged in some task, so that their persistent intrusion into his conversation can be regarded as a natural consequence of the loss of memory for more recent events (Milner, 1966, pp. 115–16).

Since he still has access to his preoperative past, H.M. is aware that something is now badly amiss. Milner records some of his comments to give us an idea of what such an amnesic state is like:

| 1930s | 1940s | 1950s | 1960s | 1970s |

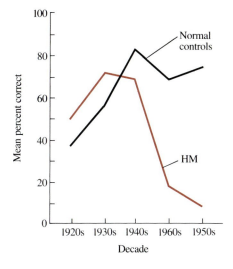

7.22   Remote and recent memory in amnesics   *(A) Sample items adapted from the "famous faces" test in which patients are asked to identify faces of individuals who reached fame in a particular decade (Albert, Butters, and Levin, 1979; Butters and Albert, 1982). One would expect that patients with anterograde amnesia would perform normally in identifying persons that were well-known prior to the onset of their disorder and more poorly with persons that became widely known after this. The figure shows three faces for each of the decades from 1930 to 1980. Their names are listed on page 258. (B) Results on the famous faces test for H.M. (color) and normal controls (black). Note that the perform-ance of H.M. was essentially equivalent to that of normals in identifying persons reaching prominence between 1920 and 1930. Like the normals, he did poorly for faces that predate 1930 when he was still a preschool child. But he performed much more poorly than the two controls on faces from the period after his operation (which was performed during the early 1950s). (Adapted from Marslen-Wilson and Teuber, 1975)*

Names of famous faces: 1930s *Marlene Dietrich, Benito Mussolini, Al Capone.* 1940s *Douglas MacArthur, Betty Grable, Joe DiMaggio.* 1950s *Mamie Eisenhower, Joe McCarthy, Adlai Stevenson.* 1960s *Nikita Khrushchev, Coretta Scott King, Golda Meir.* 1970s *Anwar Sadat, Betty Ford, Patty Hearst.*

Right now, I'm wondering. Have I done or said anything amiss? You see, at this moment everything looks clear to me, but what happened just before? That's what worries me. It's like waking from a dream; I just don't remember. [And on another occasion:] . . . Every day is alone in itself, whatever enjoyment I've had, and whatever sorrow I've had (Milner, 1966; Milner, Corkin, and Teuber, 1968).

Retrograde Amnesia

Various head injuries and brain concussions may lead to ***retrograde amnesia*** (retrograde, "in a backward direction"), in which the patient suffers a loss of memories for some period prior to the accident. Shortly after the injury, the memory loss may go back for some months or even years. As the patient recovers, the memories will come back—first, those that are farthest back in time, then those that are progressively nearer. But this recovery is generally incomplete. A few seconds or minutes just preceding the injury are typically lost forever. The driver who was hit by another car may remember approaching the intersection, but from there on, all is blank (Russell, 1959).

What accounts for the loss of memories for events preceding the cerebral injury? According to one hypothesis, it is ***trace consolidation.*** This theory asserts that newly acquired memory traces undergo a gradual change through which they become established (consolidated) ever more firmly. Some theorists believe that this effect is on storage; according to this view, newly acquired memory traces undergo a gradual change that establishes them more and more firmly. Until thus consolidated, the trace is as vulnerable as a cement mixture before it has hardened. Others believe that the effect is on retrieval; in their view, traces become more accessible some time after first encoding. An analogy is a newly acquired library book that will be difficult to find until the librarian takes the time to fill out its card for the catalogue and to file it properly (Miller and Marlin, 1979).

Current Issues in the Interpretation of Amnesia

As they were initially interpreted, the phenomena of amnesia, especially anterograde amnesia, seemed to fit a clear-cut distinction between short-term and long-term memory. H.M. and similarly afflicted patients seemed to have reasonably normal short-term functioning and could recall events prior to the point when they first suffered brain damage. This suggested that both memory stores were intact; the impairment was apparently in the ability to transfer materials from the short-term to the long-term system.

During the last fifteen years or so, this interpretation of amnesia has come into question. With further study, it has turned out that contrary to what was first thought, H.M. and other amnesics are able to acquire some long-term memories after all and manage to retain them for weeks or months. For example, they can be classically conditioned, they can learn to trace the correct path through a paper-and-pencil maze, and they can acquire certain skills like reading inverted or mirror-imaged print. Day by day, their performance gets better and better. But when they are brought back into the situation for the tenth day in a row, they continue to insist that they have never seen the conditioning apparatus or the maze

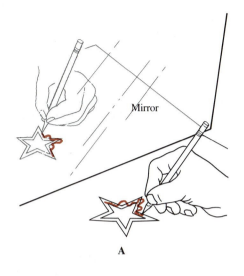

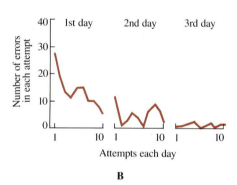

7.23 An example of what amnesics can learn (A) In mirror drawing subjects have to trace a line between two outlines of a figure while looking at their hand in a mirror. (Kolb and Whishaw, 1980) (B) Initially, this is very difficult, but after some practice subjects get very proficient at it. The same is true for amnesics. The figure shows H.M.'s improvement on this task over a period of three days. (Milner, Corkin, and Teuber, 1968)

before, and that they don't remember anything about them. Their performance continues to improve, however, and is still perfectly good when tested several weeks thereafter, although they still maintain that they remember nothing at all (Baddeley, 1982; Moscovitch, 1982).

How can we make sense of these findings? Anterograde amnesics are evidently quite competent at retaining skills such as mirror-image reading (they do just about as well as normals, despite their insistence that they don't remember anything about it; see Figure 7.23). On the other hand, they are utterly incompetent at many ordinary long-term memory tasks; for example, they don't recognize an experimenter they have met on twenty different occasions. The one kind of memory is spared; the other is not. What is the essential difference between these memories? Most students of amnesia agree that we won't understand the disorder until this question is answered. But as yet they don't agree what the answer is.

We will mention only two among a number of proposed explanations. One is that the essential difference between memory tasks the amnesic patient can and cannot perform involves the distinction between what computer scientists call **procedural** and **declarative knowledge.** Procedural knowledge is "knowing how": how to ride a bicycle, or how to read mirror writing—areas in which the amnesic's memory is relatively unaffected. In contrast, declarative knowledge is "knowing what"—areas in which the amnesic's memory is drastically impaired (Cohen and Squire, 1980).

Another alternative is that the key distinction concerns the conscious access to one's own memories. The memories may be there, but the patient doesn't know that he has them. As a result, he cannot answer questions such as "Do you remember?" or "Do you recognize?" when they pertain to events that occurred after he sustained the cerebral damage. This distinction between remembering and knowing that one remembers has been discussed by a number of authors, all of whom suggest that it may be one of the important factors of the disorder (Rozin, 1976b; Baddeley, 1982; Schacter and Tulving, 1982).

Whether either of these proposals (or one of those we did not describe) captures the essence of what the amnesic can and cannot do is still unknown. Perhaps there is no *one* distinction that does justice to the findings, for amnesia may not be a unitary disorder; not every impaired memory is necessarily impaired in the same way. In any case, there are many further questions. What is it about declarative knowledge or conscious access that makes them so vulnerable to brain damage? Why is procedural knowledge spared? As we begin to find some answers, it is likely that they will shed light not only on the amnesic disorders but on memory functions in general.

In looking back over this chapter, we are again struck by the intimate relation between the fields of perception, memory, and thinking. It is so often unclear where one topic ends and another begins. To give just one example, consider memory search. As we saw, trying to recall the names of one's high school classmates apparently involves the same thought processes that are called upon when we try to figure out how to solve a geometry problem. To the extent that this is so, it is clear that much of memory involves thinking. And as we saw previously, the same is also true of perception. For there, too, the perceiver becomes a thinker as he tries to solve perceptual problems and make sense out of ambiguous or impossible figures. In the next chapter, we will consider the topic of thinking in its own right.

SUMMARY

1. Any act of remembering implies success in each of three phases: *acquisition,* during which a *memory trace* is formed and *encoded; storage* over some time interval; and *retrieval,* which may be by *recognition* or *recall.*

2. A widely held assumption is that there are several memory systems. One is a group of *sensory registers* which hold sensory information for fractions of a second. For vision, this register seems to produce a fast-fading *icon,* as shown by studies using partial report.

3. Many psychologists believe that there are at least two further memory systems: *short-term memory (STM)* which holds material for a minute or so, and *long-term memory (LTM)* in which information is stored for much longer periods. An important difference between STM and LTM pertains to their *capacity.* That of LTM is enormous, while that of STM is only about seven items, as shown by studies of *memory span.*

4. Material in STM can be forgotten or can be transferred to LTM. Forgetting is fairly rapid as indicated by work with brief *retention intervals* filled with some activity to prevent *rehearsal.*

5. Since there is transfer from STM to LTM, the recall of an item may reflect retrieval from STM or from LTM. Studies of *free recall* with lists of unrelated items have provided a way of indicating the origin of recalled items. The *primacy effect* obtained by use of this procedure is associated mostly with retrieval from long-term storage; the *recency effect* reflects retrieval from short-term storage.

6. Retrieval from STM has been studied by *reaction time* procedures. The results suggest that this retrieval is based on a *serial* rather than on a *parallel search* process. The evidence is the relation between reaction time and the number of items in the *memory set.* Each additional item adds a constant time increment.

7. One major theoretical approach to the formation of long-term memories is *associationism.* Ebbinghaus and others developed various techniques to study how associations are formed, including memorizing serial lists of nonsense syllables. Factors that help or hinder recall include the effects of *positive* and *negative transfer.*

8. A different theoretical approach to the formation of long-term memories emphasizes *memory organization.* An example is the enlarging of memory capacity by appropriate *recoding* of material into larger *chunks.* In verbal memory, organization may be by phrases, by semantic categories, or by thematic content. The organization may be inherent in the material itself, or it may be imposed by the learner in the form of a *subjective organization.* Organizational factors may also account for the typical superiority of *intentional* over *incidental learning.* The first generally leads to memory organization, the second doesn't.

9. Recall depends partially on *trace accessibility,* which in turn depends upon the presence of proper *retrieval cues.* According to the principle of *encoding specificity,* remembering is most likely if the context at the time of retrieval is identical to that at the time of original encoding. What seems to matter is not just the physical similarity between the situation at the time of acquisition and of recall, but the way in which the subject encoded that situation.

10. Retrieval is often preceded by a process of *memory search.* In some cases, the search reaches a halfway point, where we seem to recall something but not quite and experience the *tip-of-the-tongue phenomenon.*

11. In some cases, retrieval is essentially *reconstruction,* whose nature depends in part upon the recall instructions, as shown by studies using leading questions to ask for recall. A number of recent studies suggest that hypnotized subjects will reconstruct memories to please a hypnotist. Although genuinely convinced that what they recall really happened, the hypnotized subjects often turn out to be incorrect and easily affected by leading questions.

12. Learners utilize a number of *strategies for remembering.* A common technique is *rehearsal,* which may be of two kinds. One is *maintenance rehearsal* in which material is merely held in STM and which confers little or no long-term benefits. Another is *elaborative rehearsal.* This organizes material so that it is stored more efficiently, and also connects it with other material already in long-term memory, thus creating more potential retrieval paths.

13. Special strategies for improving memory are *mnemonics.* Some mnemonic systems go back to classical times and rely on the use of *imagery,* as in the *method of loci* and the *method of pegs.* These are quite effective, in part because they force the subject to organize the material into larger units.

14. Other things equal, forgetting increases the longer the time since learning. The reason is still a matter of debate. One theory holds that traces gradually *decay.* Another argues that forgetting is caused by interference produced by other, inappropriate memories. This approach leans heavily on two forms of interference produced in the laboratory, *retroactive* and *proactive inhibition.* Still another theory asserts that forgetting is primarily caused by changes in the retrieval cues at the time of the recall.

15. A distinction is often made between two varieties of LTM, *episodic* and *generic memory.* An important component of generic memory is *semantic memory,* whose organization has been studied by various techniques for assessing memory search, including *memory activation.* Some investigators believe that this search is *hierarchical,* a claim based on results of various studies on the verification of sentences.

16. Some LTM systems seem to be essentially visual. An extreme and rather rare example is *eidetic memory.* More common are other forms of visual memory that are not a simple reembodiment of the original visual impression but still preserve some of the pictorial properties of the original. Evidence comes from studies of *mental rotation* and of *image scanning.*

17. Injury to the brain leads to certain disorders of memory. One is *anterograde amnesia,* in which the patient's ability to fix material in long-term memory is damaged. Another is *retrograde amnesia,* a loss of memories for events just prior to a head injury and which is often attributed to a disruption of *trace consolidation.* An important current issue is why patients with severe anterograde amnesia can acquire certain long-term memories (learning a maze) but not others (such as remembering that they have ever seen the maze before). According to one hypothesis, the crucial distinction is between *procedural* and *declarative knowledge;* according to another, it is between remembering and knowing that one remembers.

CHAPTER 8

Thinking

In ordinary language, the word *think* has a wide range of meanings. It may be a synonym for *remembering* (as in "I can't think of her name"), or for *attention* (as in the exhortation "Think!"), or for *belief* (as in "I think sea serpents exist"). It may also refer to a state of vague and undirected reverie as in "I'm thinking of nothing in particular." These many uses suggest that the word has become a blanket term which can cover virtually any psychological process that goes on within the individual and is essentially unobservable from without.

But thinking also has a narrower meaning which is graphically rendered in Rodin's famous statue of "The Thinker." Here, the meaning of thinking is best conveyed by such words as *to reason* or *ponder* or *reflect.* Psychologists who study thinking are mainly interested in this sense of the term. To distinguish it from the others, they refer to **directed thinking,** a set of internal activities that are aimed at the solution of a problem, whether it be the discovery of a geometric proof, of the next move in a chess game, or of the reason why the car doesn't start. In all of these activities, the various steps in the internal sequence are directed and dominated by the ultimate goal, the solution of the problem.

THE ELEMENTS OF THOUGHT

An old endeavor in the study of thinking is the search for the elements that make up thought. Some psychologists have proposed that the ultimate constituents of thought are small muscle movements, others have argued that they are mental images, yet others have felt that they are more abstract mental structures such as concepts and propositions. We will look at each of these suggestions in turn.

Thought as Motor Action

One proposal was made by J. B. Watson, a founder of behavior theory in the United States (see Chapter 4). To Watson, psychology was the science of what organisms *do*—the study of outwardly observable behavior. While this conception of the subject may be suitable to the study of such overt activities as maze running in rats and key pecking in pigeons, one might wonder how it can be extended to include thinking, for thinking is after all anything but overt; it is a very private sort of thing, known only to the thinker and easily hidden from public view.

Watson believed that at bottom there is no distinction, that thinking is a bodily activity like all other behaviors and that it involves motor reactions just as they do. He granted only one difference—the muscle movements that constitute thinking were presumed to be much smaller and thus much harder to observe than those of overt behaviors. Watson attached particular importance to the small movements of the tongue and larynx, for he regarded such *implicit speech* reactions as the basis of most human thinking. According to this view, thinking is largely a matter of silently talking to oneself (Watson, 1925).

EVIDENCE FOR THE MOTOR THEORY

Several investigators have tried to buttress Watson's theory by evidence that thinking is typically accompanied by motor activity. To measure muscle action invisible to the naked eye, they recorded the slight changes in electrical potential caused by contracting muscle fibers. By and large, the results were positive. Subjects who were trying to solve problems in logic or arithmetic showed increased motor tension, especially in the region of the speech apparatus (Jacobson, 1932). Of particular interest is a study on a group of deaf persons whose major means of communication was by sign language. When these subjects were asked to solve problems, the motor reaction was mainly found in their fingers (Max, 1937).

Such evidence suggests that thought and action are somehow related, but Watson's theory went further than that. To Watson, the motor reaction was not just a concomitant of the thought process, but was essentially equivalent to it. If so, then motor movements should be a necessary condition for thought. This has not been shown to be the case.

One line of evidence comes from several studies in which the relevant implicit speech movements were somehow interfered with. Subjects were asked to read while saying "la, la, la," to translate mentally from a foreign language while clamping their tongue between their teeth, or to find square roots while gargling. In all of these cases, the subjects were still capable of performing the required task. Even more persuasive are the results of a study in which all muscle movements were abolished by curare, a drug which paralyzes the entire skeletal musculature. One of the investigators was injected with curare; his collaborators supplied artificial respiration and other vital necessities while impatiently waiting for the paralysis to wear off so that they could hear their colleague's report. There was no interruption of consciousness. On the contrary, upon recovery the subject said that he was "clear as a bell" throughout and recalled questions that were put to him during the period of total paralysis (Smith et al., 1947).

Motor overflow (Photograph by Suzanne Szasz)

THOUGHT AS DESCENDED FROM ACTION

Watson notwithstanding, the seat of thought is evidently not in the muscles. But this is not to say that thought and action are unrelated. As we have seen, motor action often accompanies mental effort. In adults, the discovery of this relationship typically requires sophisticated gadgetry. In children, it sometimes appears without any need for magnification. A young child faced by a particularly difficult puzzle often engages in violent contortions, twisting and turning and biting his tongue. It is generally believed that this bodily effort represents a sort of motor overflow produced by the frustration of not being able to solve the problem quickly. The adult confines this overflow to wrinkling his brow and scratching his head; the child is as yet unable to control it.

In overflow reactions the bodily activity has only an indirect relation to the thinking process that goes on concurrently. Sometimes, however, the relation may be more direct. It is not unreasonable to suppose that at least some thought processes grow out of action patterns adopted at an earlier stage of life. In early childhood, trial and error is quite overt. The child who tries to reach a cookie jar acts just like one of Thorndike's cats (see Chapter 4), groping and stretching and clambering unsuccessfully until he finally pulls the right stool under the cupboard. With increasing age, he approaches new problems by *implicit trial and error* in which the response alternatives are no longer enacted in full but are rather tried out "in his head." The process of testing hypotheses thus becomes internalized, but some psychologists claim that the motor origin of these thoughts can still be discerned—a child's hands twitch just a bit in the direction of a possible tool as she considers and then discards the idea of using it. In adults, visible implicit reactions are often seen in sports. The experienced golfer precedes his swing with an anticipatory little waggle of the club and thus tries out his stroke in miniature. *Motor empathy* while watching an athletic event may be an example of a similar process. We see a pole-vaulter at the peak of his jump and go through an abbreviated version of his motor reactions, grimacing and stretching and clenching, as if we were on the field rather than in the stands.

Such considerations suggest that while thought may not be motor action, it may in part be descended from it. We will discuss this possibility more fully in a later chapter in which we take up Jean Piaget's theories of the development of directed thinking during childhood (see Chapter 14).

Thought as Mental Imagery

According to Watson's motor theory, the elements of thought are essentially peripheral—the arousal of a pattern of motor movement. Most modern psychologists disagree. In their view, thought involves phenomena that are much more central than this. An example is mental imagery.

We've previously discussed mental images as seen by the mind's eye (or heard by the mind's ear; see Chapter 7). According to Berkeley and other British empiricists, all thought is ultimately comprised of such images, which enter and exit from the stage of consciousness as the laws of association bid them. But later studies have shown that it is very unlikely that thought is the simple kaleidoscope of mental pictures (or sounds and touches) that this view claims it to be. Imagery plays an important role in thinking, but by no means an exclusive one, for much thought goes on without images. Around the turn of the century, several psychologists asked subjects to describe everything that "went through their minds" as they tried to solve various intellectual problems. The solution frequently came without a trace of imagery (and also without words). The subjects reported that when their thought was both wordless and imageless they often had a sense of certain underlying relationships, such as the experience of "this doesn't go with that" or a "feeling of *if* or *but*" (Humphrey, 1951). Mental images are evidently one of the elements of thought. But they are clearly not the only ones.

Abstract Thought

Mental images are in some ways picture-like. There are some constituents of thinking, however, that are not picture-like at all. Unlike images, they are essentially abstract and symbolic. A good example (though by no means the only one) is words.

Consider a picture of a mouse and compare it to the word *mouse.* The picture is in some ways quite different from the real animal. It *represents* a mouse rather than actually being one. But even so, the picture has many similarities to the creature that it represents, for it looks quite a bit like a real mouse. In contrast, take the word *mouse.* This word stands for the same long-tailed, big-eared, and be-whiskered creature that the picture represents. But unlike the picture, the word has no similarity to the mouse whatever. The relation between the sound "mouse" (or the written, five-letter word *mouse*) and the little long-tailed animal that it represents is entirely arbitrary and symbolic.

Many psychologists believe that the kind of thinking which utilizes mental imagery differs from the kind which underlies words and sentences much as pictures differ from words. In their view, the language-related form of thinking is more symbolic and abstract than the picture-like form that uses imagery. The attempt to describe the components of this more abstract level of thinking is relatively recent, at least for psychologists. But some of the key items of such a description are already in the vocabulary of related disciplines such as logic and linguistics. Examples are the terms *concept* and *proposition.*

CONCEPTS

The term **concept** is generally used to describe a class or category that subsumes a number (sometimes an infinite number) of individual instances. An example is *dwelling,* which includes *hut, house, tent, apartment,* and *igloo.* Other concepts designate qualities or dimensions. Examples are *length* and *age.* Still others are relational, such as *taller than.* Relational concepts don't apply to any one item in isolation. One can't be *taller than* except in relation to something else to which one's height is being compared.

PROPOSITIONS

Concepts describe classes of events or objects or relations between them. They are what we generally think about. In so doing, we tend to combine them in various ways. The British empiricists emphasized one such mental combination: the simple associative train of thought in which one idea leads to another. A more important way of relating concepts is by asserting something about them, for example, "dogs generally bite postmen." Such statements are called *propositions.* They make some assertion that relates a *subject* (the item about which an assertion is made; e.g., *dogs*) and a *predicate* (what is asserted about the subject; e.g., *generally bite postmen*) in a way that can be true or false.

That much of our thought is propositional requires little proof. The propositions we entertain may be true or false, profound or silly—what matters is that they are propositions, that they link mental elements in certain ways. In what form do such propositions exist psychologically? One possible hypothesis is that they are elaborate images. But as the philosopher Jerry Fodor has shown, this cannot be. Consider the proposition that is expressed by the sentence: "Napoleon is dead." Can this be expressed by way of a mental image? A vivid imager might conjure up an image of the emperor in an open coffin, with weeping veterans of his wars passing by to pay their last respects. But is this image equivalent to the proposition? By no means. This image implies many propositions other than the one at hand: "Napoleon was buried with his sword," "Napoleon was rather fat when he died," "Napoleon's veterans loved him," and so on. The trouble with pictures (whether real or imagined) is that one can say so many things about them. The proposition is a way of singling out the aspects of the world that one wants to make some assertion about (Fodor, 1975).

It appears that propositions cannot be based on images. But they are not equivalent to the sentences in which they are expressed either, as shown by the fact that the same proposition can be expressed in several forms. People who speak both English and German know that "The dog bites the cat" and "Der Hund beisst die Katze" mean precisely the same thing. The same holds within the same language. Consider "The dog bites the cat" and "The cat is bitten by the dog." Again, the same proposition is asserted. Something is being said (and presumably thought) about the hapless cat that does not depend upon the particular form in which this proposition is cast.

To sum up, it appears that the elements of thought are neither motor acts nor specific speech utterances. Instead, there seem to be two different thinking modes. One involves thinking in mental images which, like pictures, resemble whatever it is they represent. A second mode of thinking is more abstract and symbolic, and it involves mental structures such as concepts and propositions whose psychological nature we are just beginning to investigate. (Some of these matters were touched on in the discussion of semantic memory in Chapter 7; others will be dealt with when we take up language, in Chapter 9.)

PROBLEM SOLVING

Thus far our concern has been with what thought is. We now turn from the question of *what* to that of *how.* How does thinking operate as we try to solve the myriad of problems encountered in life, whether trying to fix a broken lawn mower, smoothing over an awkward social situation, or solving a cryptogram?

Regarded in this context, thinking is an activity. It is something an organism does. This activity is central rather than peripheral, but it is an activity nonetheless. Hobbes, Locke, and their many descendants believed that this stream of activity is produced by a chain of associated ideas, each triggered by the one before. The fundamental difficulty of this position is that thinking, like other cognitive processes, is organized.

The items in a sequence of thoughts typically do not stand in isolation but take their meaning from the overall structure in which they are embedded. A famous paper by Karl Lashley illustrates this point with examples from the psychology of language (Lashley, 1951). Uttering a sentence is not just a matter of stringing one word after another, for the selection of a word often depends not only on the immediately preceding word but upon others spoken much before or upon still others not yet uttered. In English, we say "The dog run*s*" rather than "the dog run," for verb and subject must agree with each other. This agreement rule governs our speech even when the subject comes many words after the verb, as in "Down the street run*s* the excited, barking, hungry, flea-bitten *dog.*" The fact that we produce the verb with a third-person singular *s* indicates that there is a broad mental scheme that precedes the actual utterance and determines its various parts. In effect, there was a mental plan that provided the outline according to which the specific words were produced (Miller, Galanter, and Pribram, 1960).

What holds for speech holds for many other activities, including problem solving. The problem solver goes through a sequence of internal steps. These steps are organized in a special way: They are directed toward a goal—the solution of the problem. Consider a taxi driver who is trying to decide on the best route from the city to the airport. According to a simple chain-association hypothesis, the initial stimulus ("Get me to the airport in time for a 9:15 flight") triggers various internal responses (such as "superhighway," "crosstown express," etc.) until the correct solution is finally evoked (Figure 8.1). But this interpretation cannot readily explain why the would-be solutions that come to mind, whether right or wrong, are usually relevant to the problem at hand. Nor can it explain how such potential solutions are accepted or rejected. If they were merely aroused by associative

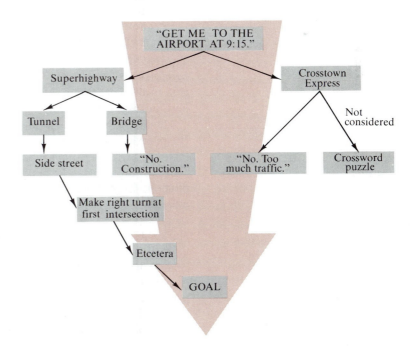

8.1 Problem solving as directed by the goal *The taxi driver's goal determines the thought processes throughout. Some would-be solutions are considered and rejected as inappropriate. Others (e.g., crossword puzzles), although associatively related, aren't even called to mind.*

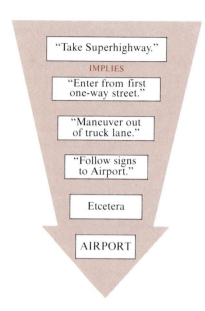

8.2 Hierarchical organization of a plan
Plans have subcomponents which have subcomponents below them, as here illustrated by the taxi driver's task.

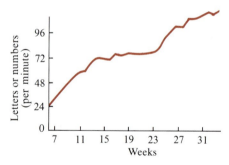

8.3 An apprentice telegrapher's learning curve *The curve plots the number of letters or digits the operator can receive per minute against weeks of practice. Note the plateau in the learning curve. The curve stays level from weeks 15 to 25 and then starts to rise again. According to Bryan and Harter, the new rise indicates the use of larger chunks. (After Bryan and Harter, 1899)*

connections, the problem solver would be adrift in a sea of irrelevancies: "crosstown express" might evoke "uptown local" or "crossword puzzle" or what have you. Instead, each mental step is determined not just by the step before but by the original problem. This sets the overall direction which dominates all of the later steps and determines how each of them is to be evaluated. The taxi driver considers the superhighway and rejects it as he recalls some road construction along the way, thinks of the crosstown express and dismisses it because of rush-hour traffic, and so on. The original problem acts like a schematic frame, waiting to be filled in by a "fitting" solution.

Hierarchical Organization and Chunking

We have encountered the notion of hierarchical organization while discussing the role of chunking in memory (see Chapter 7). A similar principle governs directed thinking. To the taxi driver, the idea "take the crosstown express" is a sort of master plan that implies various subsidiary actions: entering from the appropriate one-way street, maneuvering out of the truck lane, following the signs to the airport exit, and so on. To the experienced driver all of these substeps require no further thought, for they are a consequence of hierarchical organization which resembles that of a disciplined army. The colonel who orders his regiment to attack does not have to specify the detailed commands his second lieutenants issue to their platoons. Given the order from above, the subcommands follow (Figure 8.2).

The ability to subsume many details under a larger chunk is one of the crucial features of directed activity, including the internal activity we call thinking. As we shall see, much of the difference between master and apprentice is in the degree to which subcomponents of the activity have been chunked hierarchically. To the master, the substeps have become automatic.

DEVELOPING SKILLS

The role of chunking in directed activity is particularly clear when we study how people become proficient at various skills such as typing, driving a car, or playing golf. In all such activities, becoming skillful depends upon a qualitative change in how the task is performed.

The first experimental study in this area was done about eighty years ago by Bryan and Harter. These psychologists were trying to discover how telegraph operators master their trade. Their subjects were Western Union apprentices whose progress at sending and receiving Morse code messages was charted over a period of about forty weeks. Figure 8.3 plots one student's improvement at receiving, measured in letters per minute. What is interesting about this learning curve is its shape. Following an initial rise, the curve goes up again. According to Bryan and Harter, such plateaus are an indication that the learner gradually transforms his task. At first he merely tracks individual letters. With time, the effective units he deals with become larger and larger: first syllables and words, then several words at a time, then simple phrases, and perhaps eventually short sentences. The plateau represents the best the learner can do given a unit of a lower level (say, letters); once this lower level is completely mastered, a higher level of

A	B
YNHRE	GRAY
VDAIX	WHITE
BPOMS	PINK
FWECG	BLACK
FWECG	MAROON
YNHRE	GRAY
ZRQUT	PINK
VDAIX	WHITE
FWECG	BLACK
ZRQUT	PINK
BPOMS	MAROON
YNHRE	WHITE
VDAIX	WHITE
ZRQUT	GRAY
FWECG	BLACK
BPOMS	MAROON

8.4 The Stroop effect *The two lists, (A) and (B), are printed in four colors—black, gray, maroon, and pink. To observe the Stroop effect, name the colors (aloud) in which each of the nonsense syllables in list (A) is printed as fast as you can, continuing downward. Then do the same for list (B), calling out the colors in which each of the words of the list is printed, again going from top to bottom. This will probably be easier for list (A) than for list (B), a demonstration of the Stroop effect. This effect is usually studied using full colors, but it tends to show up even with just the four colors used here. (For a full color demonstration, see Chapter 1, p. 3.)*

organization—a larger chunk—is possible and the learning curve shoots up once more (Bryan and Harter, 1897).

Similar effects are observed in the acquisition of many other skills. To the novice, typing proceeds letter by letter; to the expert, the proper units are much larger, including familiar letter groupings, words, and occasionally phrases. Similarly, the beginning driver laboriously struggles to harmonize clutch, gas pedal, steering wheel, and brake, to the considerable terror of innocent bystanders. After a while, those movements come quite routinely and are subsumed under much higher (though perhaps equally dangerous) chunks of behavior, such as overtaking another car. An even simpler example is dressing. To the small child every article of clothing represents a major intellectual challenge; she beams with pride when she finally gets the knack of tying her shoelaces. To an adult the unit is "getting dressed" and its various components are almost completely submerged within the larger chunk. We decide to dress and before we know it we are almost fully clothed. Somehow our shoes get laced but we never notice, unless the laces break.

AUTOMATIZATION

The automatization of subcomponents in skilled activities, however, has a side effect. Once the plan is set into motion, its execution may be difficult to stop. An example is reading. When we see a billboard on a highway, we can't help but read what it says, whether we want to or not. The forms on the sign proclaim that they are letters and words; this is enough to trigger our automatized reading routines (La Berge, 1975). A striking demonstration of this phenomenon is the so-called **Stroop effect** (Stroop, 1935). Subjects are asked to name the colors in which groups of letters are printed and to do so as quickly as they can (Figure 8.4). In one case, the letter groups are unrelated consonants or vowels. In this condition, the subjects have little trouble. After a little practice, they become very proficient at rattling off the colors, "red, green . . ."

The subjects' task becomes vastly more difficult in a condition in which the letters are grouped into words, specifically color names. Diabolically enough, these are not the names of the colors in which the words are printed (see Chapter 1 and Figure 1.4).

Now the subjects respond much more slowly. They are asked to say "green, red, yellow . . ." But they can't help themselves from reading the words "yellow, black . . ." for reading is an automatized skill. As a result, there is violent response conflict. This conflict persists even after lengthy practice. One way subjects finally manage to overcome it is by learning to unfocus their eyes. By this maneuver, they can still see the colors but can no longer recognize what the letters are (Jensen, 1965).

In a modified version of the Stroop effect, subjects are shown groups of digits or letters as shown below:

MMM	666
H	3
VVVV	11111
XX	88
CCCC	7777

NAGMARA

BOLMPER

SLEVO

STIGNIH

TOLUSONI

8.5 Anagrams *Rearrange the letters on each line to form a word. (For the solution, see p. 272.)*

8.6 Concrete object problem *Assemble all six matches to form four equilateral triangles, each side of which is equal to the length of one match. (For solution, see Figure 8.19, p. 280.)*

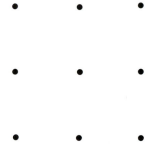

8.7 Nine-dot problem *Nine dots are arranged in a square. Connect them by drawing four continuous straight lines without lifting your pencil from the paper. (For solution, see Figure 8.16, p. 279.)*

Their job is to call out the *number* of items in each line as quickly and accurately as possible (in our example, "three, one, five, two, four"). This turns out to be surprisingly difficult when the items are digits. For here the *names* of the digits (that is, "six, three, one, eight, seven") come to mind automatically and interfere with the job of counting. In contrast, the task is much easier when the items are letters, where there is no such conflict (Windes, 1968).

THE CHUNKING PROCESS

At present we know very little about the mechanisms that underlie the chunking process. Associationists propose that the explanation involves **chaining.** In their view, many skilled acts are highly overpracticed stimulus-response chains in which the first movement provides the kinesthetic stimulus for the second, which produces the stimulus for the third, and so on. This interpretation is almost certainly false. As Karl Lashley pointed out, a trained pianist may reach a rate of six-teen successive finger strokes a second when playing an arpeggio. This speed is too high to allow time for a sensory message to reach the brain and for a motor command to come back to the fingers. We can only conclude that there is a learned neural program that allows the successive finger movements to occur without interpolated sensory monitoring (Lashley, 1951).

We may not understand precisely how this complex chunking is acquired, but there is little doubt of its importance. It is hard to imagine any organized, skilled behavior in which this process does not play a role. In Bryan and Harter's words, "The ability to take league steps in receiving telegraphic messages, in reading, in addition, in mathematical reasoning and in many other fields, plainly depends upon the acquisition of league-stepping habits . . . The learner must come to do with one stroke of attention what now requires a half a dozen, and presently, in one still more inclusive stroke, what now requires thirty-six." The expert can, if necessary, attend to the lower-level units of his skill, but for the most part these have become automatic. This acquired automatism, the submergence of lower-level units in the higher chunk, frees him to solve new problems. "Automatism is not genius, but it is the hands and feet of genius" (Bryan and Harter, 1899, p. 375).

FINDING SOLUTIONS

Psychologists have devised a large number of experimental situations for the study of human problem solving. Subjects have been asked to decipher anagrams (Figure 8.5), to manipulate various concrete objects so as to produce a desired result (Figure 8.6), or to find the solution to various geometrical problems (Figure 8.7). Considering this variety of tasks, it is hardly surprising that there are differences in the way in which they are attacked; a subject who tries to join nine dots with one continuous line will call upon a somewhat different set of mental skills than one who has to rearrange the letters *STIGNIH* into an English word. The question is whether there is a common thread that runs through all attempts at problem solving, no matter what the problem may be. Many psychologists believe that hierarchical organization is such a common feature.

The role of organization in problem solving was highlighted in a classic study by the Gestalt psychologist Karl Duncker, who asked his subjects to "think out loud" while they tried to find the solution (Duncker, 1945). One of Duncker's problems was cast in medical terms:

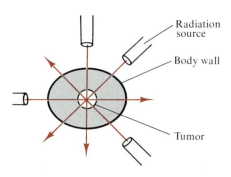

Radiation source

Body wall

Tumor

8.8   The solution to the ray-tumor problem   *Several weak rays are sent from various points outside so that they will meet at the tumor site. There the radiation of the rays will be intense, for all the effects will summate at this point. But since they are individually weak, the rays will not damage the healthy tissue that surrounds the tumor. (After Duncker, 1945)*

Suppose a patient has an inoperable stomach tumor. There are certain rays which can destroy this tumor if their intensity is large enough. At this intensity, however, the rays will also destroy the healthy tissue which surrounds the tumor (e.g., the stomach walls, the abdominal muscles, and so on). How can one destroy the tumor without damaging the healthy tissue through which the rays must travel on their way?

Duncker's subjects typically arrived at the solution in several steps. They first reformulated the problem so as to produce a general plan of attack. This in turn led to more specific would-be solutions. For example, they might look for a tissue-free path to the stomach and then propose to send the rays through the esophagus. (A good idea which unfortunately will not work—rays travel in straight lines and the esophagus is curved.) After exploring several other general approaches and their specific consequences, some subjects finally hit upon the appropriate general plan. They proposed to reduce the intensity of rays on their way through healthy tissue and then turn up this intensity when the rays reach the tumor. This broad restatement of what is needed eventually led to the correct specific means, which was to send several bundles of *weak* rays from various points outside so that they meet at the tumor where their effects will summate (Figure 8.8).

Duncker's results show that the specific would-be solutions grow out of broader solution classes, much as tactics follows from strategy on the battlefield. Figure 8.9 is a schematic representation of one subject's efforts; it is arranged in the form of a tree diagram which highlights the hierarchical nature of the underlying organization.

8.9   A summary of one subject's solution process   *One subject, given Duncker's medical problem, puzzled about it for thirty minutes. His attempted solutions are schematized in hierarchical form. (After Duncker, 1945)*

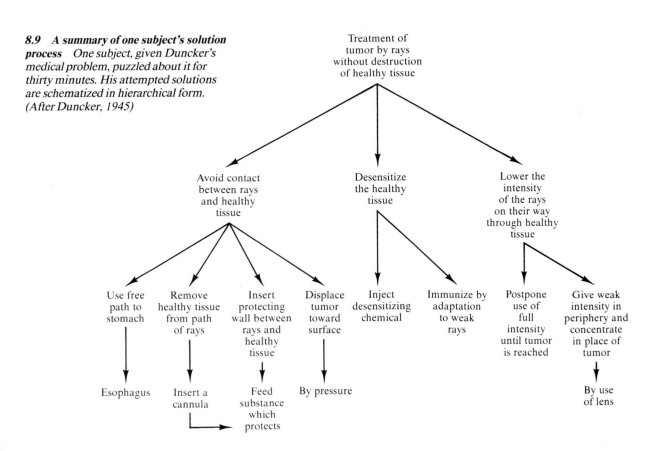

8.10   Memory for chess positions in masters, experts, and average players
(A) An actual chess position which was presented for five seconds after which the positions of the pieces had to be reconstructed. Typical performances by masters, experts, and average players are shown in (B), (C), and (D) respectively, with errors indicated by colored frames. (After Hearst, 1972)

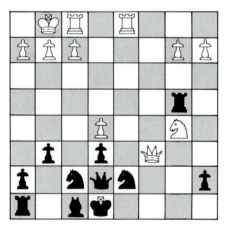

A. Actual position

MASTERS AND BEGINNERS

Some people solve certain problems better than others do. One of the reasons is simply a matter of experience; the trained mechanic is more likely to hit on the why and wherefore of automotive failure than is his young apprentice. But what exactly does experience contribute? A major factor is chunking, which plays a similar role in problem solving to that played in the execution of various skills. Experts approach a problem in different ways than beginners. They think in larger units whose components are already contained within them and thus require no further thought.

An interesting demonstration of how chunking makes the master comes from a study of chess players conducted by the Dutch psychologist Adrian de Groot whose findings have been corroborated and extended by several American investigators (de Groot, 1965; Chase and Simon, 1973). The chess world ranks its members according to a ruthlessly objective hierarchy of merit based on a simple record of who beats whom. Grandmasters are at the very top, followed by masters, experts, and so on, down to Class *D* players at the lower rungs of the chess ladder. De Groot, himself a chess master, posed various chess problems to members of each merit category (including two former world champions) and asked them to select the best move. Contrary to what might have been expected, the grandmasters and masters did not look further ahead. They considered about the same number of moves and calculated about as far into the future as the lower-ranked players. Their superiority was not in quantity, but in quality. All of them chose continuations that would have won the game, while few of the other players did. The difference is in the way the problem is organized. The chess master structures the chess position in terms of broad strategic concepts (e.g., a king-side attack with pawns) from which many of the specific moves follow naturally. Given that his chunks are larger, one would expect the chess master to grasp the position in a shorter time. Some further studies indicate that this is indeed the case. Players of different ranks were shown various chess positions for five seconds each and were then asked to reproduce them a few minutes later. Grandmasters and masters did so with hardly an error; lesser players (including mere experts) performed much more poorly (Figure 8.10). This is not because the chess

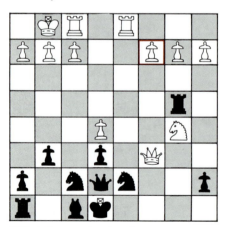

B. Typical master player's performance

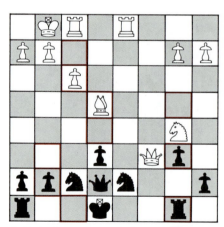

C. Typical expert player's performance

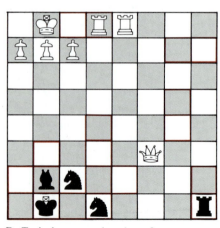

D. Typical average player's performance

masters have "better visual memory." When presented with bizarre positions that would hardly ever arise in the course of a well-played game, they recalled no better than novices. Their superiority is in the conceptual organization of chess, not in the memory for visual patterns as such.

The essence of expertise is then an organization of the relevant subcomponents, which allows fewer but vastly larger steps. Whether the field is reading or typing or musicianship, its mastery depends on the acquisition of newer and better chunkings. It is possible that somewhat similar processes underlie the cognitive growth that occurs in childhood. As infants grow into toddlers, and toddlers into children, they gradually acquire many concepts that adults take for granted, so that they eventually comprehend space, time, and causality in much the way their parents do. It may be that the way in which they achieve this has much in common with the route that beginners take in becoming masters in a particular skill. We will return to this issue in a later discussion of cognitive development (see Chapter 14).

Acquiring the appropriate chunkings is in part a matter of experience. But in part, it is also a matter of talent, for some people can see chunks where the rest of us cannot. When the mathematician Karl Friedrich Gauss was a young boy in grammar school, his teacher asked the class to add all the numbers from 1 to 10. Young Gauss got the answer almost immediately. Unlike his classmates, he did not chug through all of the tedious steps of the summation. He recognized that the series $1 + 2 + 3 \ldots + 10$ can be rewritten as a sum of 5 pairs each of which equals 11. (His reorganization of the series is rendered graphically in Figure 8.11.) Given this insight, he quickly came up with the correct answer, 55, no doubt to the considerable amazement of the teacher.

This process of reorganizing bits and pieces so that they form a unified whole is also found in artistic creation. Mozart describes it in one of his letters:

> Those ideas that please me I retain in memory, and am accustomed, as I have been told, to hum them to myself. If I continue in this way, it soon occurs to me how I may turn this or that morsel to good account, so as to make a good dish of it, that is to say agreeably to the rules of counterpoint, to the peculiarities of the various instruments, etc. All this fires my soul, and provided that I am not disturbed my subject enlarges itself and becomes methodized and refined, and the whole, though it be long, stands almost complete and finished in my mind, so that I can survey it, like a fine picture or a beautiful statue—at a glance. Nor do I hear in my imagination the parts successively, but I hear them, as it were, all at once. What a delight this is, I cannot tell. . . . What has been thus produced, I do not easily forget, and this is perhaps the best gift I have my divine maker to thank for (Quoted in Humphrey, 1951, p. 53).

Artificial Intelligence: Problem Solving by Computer

The preceding discussion has emphasized the role played by hierarchical organization in thinking. But how does this organization come about? How does the problem solver hit upon the right plan of attack and how does she recognize that it is right when she thinks of it? These questions are as yet unanswered, but there have been some promising leads.

One hopeful avenue of research comes from attempts to program computers so as to simulate certain aspects of human thinking. The impetus for this work stems from the belief, held by many psychologists, that humans and computers

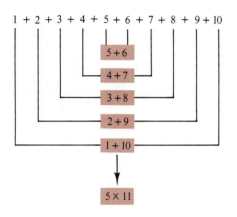

$1 + 2 + 3 + 4 + 5 + 6 + 7 + 8 + 9 + 10$

8.11 Reorganizing a series of sums
Young Gauss's solution amounts to the insight that in a series of numbers $1 + 2 \ldots + 10$, the numbers increase by one going from left to right and decrease by one going from right to left. As a result, the sum of the extreme pairs $(1 + 10)$ must equal the sum of the next-to-extreme pair $(2 + 9)$ and so on. Given this insight, it can be generalized to series of any length. Thus $1 + 2 \ldots + 1,000 = 500 (1 + 1,000)$. (After Wertheimer, 1945)

are similar in one important regard—they are both *information-processing systems.* We have already seen several examples of the information-processing approach in our discussion of memory. When we talk of items that are temporarily stored in short-term memory, recoded into fewer and more compact chunks, transferred into long-term memory, and then retrieved by various hierarchical search procedures, we are describing a system in which information is systematically converted from one form into others. There is a formal similarity between this sequence of inferred events in human memory and the actual steps of a computer program that handles the storage and retrieval of various materials (e.g., library titles, tax returns, etc.).

To be sure, the underlying physical machinery is very different. Computers use hardware made of magnetic cores and transistors, while biological systems are built of neurons. But this difference does not prohibit a similarity in their operations. Computers may be built of relays or electronic tubes or transistors, but they can be fed the identical program even so. If it doesn't matter whether the components are tubes or transistors, then—for at least some purposes—it may not matter whether they are transistors or neurons. To students of *artificial intelligence,* the important point is that both computers and human beings are information-processing systems. They therefore regard it as likely that the study of one will help in the understanding of the other.

A further advantage of computer simulation comes from the fact that machines are painfully literal. The program must be spelled out in absolutely precise detail, for the computer will balk if presented with vague or overgeneralized instructions. This limitation is a blessing in disguise. It forces the scientist to formulate his notions in completely rigorous and explicit terms.

ALGORITHMS AND HEURISTICS

Several investigators have deliberately forced their programs to be as humanlike as possible. The most prominent among these are Allen Newell and Nobel laureate Herbert Simon, who have programmed computers to play chess, to discover and prove theorems in symbolic logic, and to decipher cryptograms. They began by studying how human subjects deal with these problems, discovered their typical strategies by use of the think-aloud technique, and then incorporated these problem-solving plans into the instructions fed to their computer. Interestingly enough, the computer does fairly well if it attacks these problems as human subjects say they do (Newell and Simon, 1972).

Newell and Simon found it useful to distinguish between two major kinds of solution strategies. One is an *algorithm,* a procedure in which all of the operations required to achieve the solution are specified step by step. Examples are the various manipulations of arithmetic. An algorithm guarantees that a solution will be found in time, but this time may be very slow in coming. Consider a person working on a crossword puzzle who is trying to find a synonym for "sharp-tongued" that will fit into _c__bi_. An algorithm exists: Insert all possible alphabetic combinations into the four empty spaces and check each result in an unabridged dictionary. While this procedure is certain to produce "acerbic," it should appeal to few puzzle solvers, for it will require the inspection of nearly 460,000 possibilities.

In actual practice, crossword puzzles are solved by procedures which, though not as sure, are much less slow. These are *heuristics* which are various tricks and rules of thumb that have often worked in the past and may do so again, such as guessing at a suffix given the word's grammatical class (*ic* is a good bet for an adjective), forming hypotheses on the basis of likely letter sequences in the language (the first letter is probably an *s* or a vowel), and so on. The great majority of problems people face are solved by such heuristic procedures rather than by algorithms, for human life is short and human processing capacity is limited. Physicians reach their diagnoses by first considering a few hypotheses that seem most plausible and then testing those. If they systematically looked at every possibility, the patient would be dead before being diagnosed.

If the problem is complex enough, even high-speed computers must resort to heuristics. Consider the analysis of a chess position some ten moves ahead. The total number of possibilities (based on moves, replies, replies to replies, and so on) has been estimated at an astronomical billion billion billion. Under the circumstances, an algorithm is out of the question. (If the inspection of each possibility takes one-millionth of a second, the inspection of all of them would be completed after 1,000 billion years.) On the other hand, heuristics work reasonably well. One of Newell and Simon's programs requires the computer to search for moves that satisfy fairly immediate subgoals such as material superiority (e.g., give a pawn for a queen but not vice versa) and occupation of the center squares (which limits the opponent's mobility and enhances one's own). Such an approach resembles that of the human player. His ultimate goal is to checkmate the opponent, but he is not likely to achieve it unless he proceeds hierarchically; instead of evaluating each move in terms of the final goal, he considers it in terms of the subgoals that usually lead up to it. Chess programs that employ heuristics of this sort give a fair account of themselves. While they cannot hope to beat a master, they might hold their own against a good player on a college team (Berliner, 1977; Boden, 1977; see Figure 8.12).

Programs based on heuristics have scored similar successes in other fields. An example is a program that can prove theorems in symbolic logic (Newell, Shaw, and Simon, 1958). Its general scheme is to work backward from the desired end. The program tries to find a means to the final goal, then a means to achieve that means (which now becomes a subgoal), and so on. To accomplish this, it considers whatever state it "desires" (the goal or subgoal), and then tries to minimize the difference between this and the present state by various operations (e.g., algebraic transformations). Newell and Simon give a simplified example of how a similar strategy might be used by people faced with the ordinary problems of everyday life:

> I want to take my son to nursery school. What's the difference between what I have and what I want? One of distance. What changes distance? My automobile. My automobile won't work. What is needed to make it work? A new battery. What has new batteries? An auto repair shop. I want the repair shop to put in a new battery; but the shop doesn't know I need one. What is the difficulty? One of communication. What allows communication? A telephone . . . and so on (Newell and Simon, 1972, p. 416).

EXPERT SYSTEMS

A promising new trend in the field of artificial intelligence is the development of **expert systems.** These are problem solving programs with a very narrow scope which only deal with problems in a highly limited domain of knowledge, such as

8.12 An advice-taking chess computer *Man-versus-machine chess game played between Charles I. Kalme, an American master, and a computer that has been programmed to take advice. This computer program should eventually produce machine chess of a higher order. (Zobrist and Carlson, 1973; photograph by Mervyn Lew)*

some subfield of organic chemistry, law, or medicine. Because they are so specialized, their memory can be stocked with a considerable amount of know-how in their own area.

An example is MYCIN, a computer program designed to assist physicians in the treatment of infectious diseases. MYCIN is not just a stored table that lists drugs to combat this or the other microorganism. It can diagnose, suggest therapies, estimate their effectiveness, and will even explain how it arrived at its decisions if asked. The physician "informs" the computer of the patient's symptoms and of the results of various blood tests and bacterial cultures. The computer will then consult its memory for lists of potentially useful drugs and will then choose among them by following various decision rules (which consider the patient's age, other medications, side effects, and so on) and make a recommendation, indicating the statistical probability of success. If "asked," it will indicate how it arrived at its decision. If appropriately "instructed," it will add to or modify its rules; for example, it may note that a particular antibiotic ought not to be administered to a patient with a certain allergy (Shortliffe et al., 1973).

Thus far, MYCIN is still in an experimental stage. But in 1973 its recommendations were the same as those of human medical experts in 72 percent of the cases. Since MYCIN can be continually updated and improved, it is not unlikely that it, or some similar program, will be used in actual medical practice before long. Whether the patients will take to MYCIN's bedside manner is another question.

Is MYCIN intelligent? In a sense, it obviously isn't. Its very strengths are its weaknesses. It only "knows" about infectious diseases. If it is asked about a broken bone or a psychiatric condition it will be utterly lost. It is a highly specialized expert that may eventually become a valuable though rather limited assistant. But it is not a model of the human intellect, for it simulates only a few human mental operations. Like other expert systems that are now being developed, MYCIN is meant to be an aid to human intelligence, not a substitute.

SOME PROBLEMS OF ARTIFICIAL INTELLIGENCE

Computer simulation has added a new and exciting dimension to the study of cognitive processes. But so far at least, it still has some serious limitations as an approach to human problem solving.

Well-defined and ill-defined problems The problems which existing computer programs can handle are **well-defined.** There is a clear-cut way to decide whether a proposed solution is indeed the right one. Examples are algebraic proofs (Are the terms identical on both sides of the equation?), chess problems (Is the opposing king checkmated?), and anagrams (Is the rearranged letter sequence a word that appears in the dictionary?).

In contrast, many of the problems people face in real life are **ill-defined.** Consider an architect who is asked to design a modern college dormitory. Exactly what is a correct solution? Some proposals can obviously be rejected out of hand —for example, if there are no provisions for bathrooms—but there is no definite criterion for what is acceptable. Similarly for many other problem activities, such as completing a sonnet or organizing a lecture or planning a vacation. In all of these cases, the critical first step is to define the problem so that it can be answered and so that the answer can be evaluated. The architect begins by asking questions about the number of students who are to be housed, the facilities that must be included, the surrounding terrain, the available budget—all in an attempt to transform an ill-defined problem into a well-defined one. The progress of human knowledge is often a matter not of problem solution but of problem definition and redefinition. The alchemist looked for a way to change lead into gold; the modern physicist tries to discover the atomic structure of matter.

As of yet, computer programs do not define their own problems. People do, but so far we know little about how they accomplish this.

Loosening the program's direction   As we have seen, computers can be programmed to be purposive; they can have goals and subgoals just as we do. But "when a program is purposive, it is too purposive" (Neisser, 1963). The computer is fanatically single-minded. When set a problem, it drives toward the solution with neither pause nor conflict, never forgetting its goal nor its partial solutions achieved en route. Human thinkers may be directed, but they are never quite as directed as that. They get bored and distracted, they forget, they start to work on other problems. These human frailties may sometimes prevent the discovery of the solution, but they may occasionally help rather than hinder. Some problems—perhaps the most important ones—can only be solved by adopting a completely new approach, an altogether new set of heuristics. Faced with such problems, one might well want to loosen the direction of the thought process, or to forget a prior step which may ultimately prove to be well-forgotten.

Several recent programs have tried to avoid some of the single-mindedness of their predecessors by allowing the machine to consider all sorts of things simultaneously and to forget what it has done unless special circumstances intervene (Reitman, 1965). One of these programs can solve simple word analogies, such as "Bear is to pig as chair is to _____? (foot, table, coffee, strawberry)." It is too early to judge whether such deliberate attempts to build human imperfection into computers will produce an artificial intelligence that is more similar to its human counterpart.

Obstacles to Problem Solving

So far, we have primarily dealt with situations in which problem solvers succeed. How can we explain their all too many failures? In many cases, the solution is simply out of reach. The problem solver lacks some necessary informational prerequisites or relevant chunkings or heuristics—as when a ten-year-old is unable to solve a problem in integral calculus. But failure often occurs even when all the necessary ingredients for solution are known perfectly well, for the would-be problem solver may get stuck in a wrong approach and may not be able to get unstuck. When finally told the answer, his reaction often shows that he was blind rather than ignorant: "How stupid of me. I should have seen it all along." He was victimized by a powerful *mental set* that was inappropriate for the problem at hand.

FIXATION

A well-known study shows how mental set can make people rigid. They became *fixated* on one approach to the task, which made it hard for them to think of it in

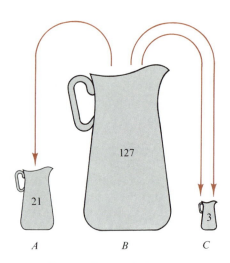

8.13   The standard method for solving the three-container problem (After Luchins, 1942)

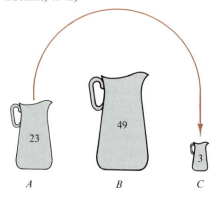

8.14   A simpler method for solving certain three-container problems (After Luchins, 1942)

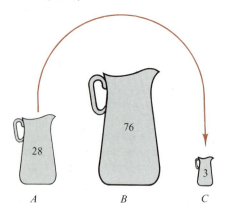

8.15   A case where only the simple method works (After Luchins, 1942)

any other way. The subjects were presented with a series of problems. They were told that they had three jars of known volume. Their job was to use these to obtain (mentally) an exact quantity of water from a well. In one problem, for example, the subjects had three containers—*A, B,* and *C*—which held 21, 127, and 3 quarts respectively. Their task was to use these three jars to obtain exactly 100 quarts. After a while, they hit upon the correct method. This was to fill jar *B* (127 quarts) completely, and then pour out enough water to fill jar *A* (21 quarts). After this, they would pour out more water from jar *B* to fill jar *C* (3 quarts), empty jar *C* and fill it again from jar *B.* The remaining water in jar *B* was the desired quantity, 100 quarts (Figure 8.13).

On the next few problems, the numerical values differed (Table 8.1). But

Table 8.1   THE THREE-CONTAINER PROBLEM

Desired quantity of water (quarts)	Volume of empty jar (quarts)		
	A	B	C
99	14	163	25
5	18	43	10
21	9	42	6
31	20	59	4

in all cases, the solution could be obtained by the same sequence of arithmetical steps, that is, B − A − 2C. Thus, $163 - 14 - 2 \times 25 = 99$; $43 - 18 - 2 \times 10 = 5$, and so on.

After five such problems, the subjects were given two critical tests. The first was a problem that required them to obtain 20 quarts, given jars whose volumes were 23, 49, and 3 quarts. Now most of the subjects showed the mechanization effect. They dutifully performed the laborious arithmetical labors they had used before, computing $49 - 23 - 2 \times 3 = 20$. They did so, even though there was a simpler method that takes only one step (Figure 8.14).

Subsequent to this was a second critical problem. The subjects were now asked to obtain 25 quarts, given jars of 28, 76, and 3 quarts. Note that here the only method that will work is the direct one; that is, $28 - 3 = 25$ (Figure 8.15). But the mechanization induced by the set was so powerful that many subjects failed to solve the problem altogether. They tried the old procedure which is inappropriate ($76 - 28 - 2 \times 3$ does not equal 25) and could not hit on an adequate alternative. The set had made them so rigid that they were blind (Luchins, 1942).

Similar effects have been demonstrated in other problem situations. In many of these there is no need to induce the misleading set by instructions or prior practice, for it is usually engendered by the perceptual arrangement of the problem situations. Examples of such perceptually induced sets are the nine-dot problem (Figure 8.16) and the horse-and-rider problem (Figure 8.17).

SET AND MOTIVATION

In fairy tales, the hero is sometimes required to solve a riddle or suffer death and, being a fairy-tale hero, he invariably succeeds. In real life, he would have a harder

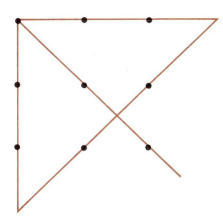

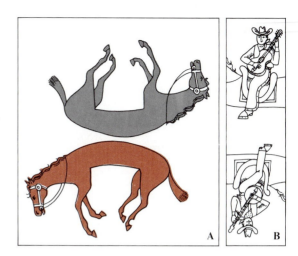

8.16   The solution of the nine-dot problem   *The problem (Figure 8.7) is solved by going outside of the square frame into which the dots are perceptually grouped. The lines have to be extended beyond the dots as shown. Most subjects fail to hit on this solution because of a perceptual set imposed by the square arrangement.*

8.17   Horse-and-rider problem   *The task is to place (B) on (A) in such a way that the riders are properly astride the horse. (After Scheerer, Goldstein, and Boring, 1941; for solution, see Figure 8.20)*

time, for problem solution, unfairly enough, becomes more difficult when the need for it is especially great. The reason stems from the relation between set and motivation. The greater the motivation toward solution, the stronger are the sets with which the problem is approached. If these sets happen to be appropriate, well and good. But if they are inappropriate, increased motivation will be a hindrance, for these sets will be that much harder to break. Since difficult problems —almost by definition—are problems that tend to engender the wrong set, their solution will be impeded as motivation becomes intense.

Evidence for these assertions comes from several experiments which show that flexibility goes down when motivation becomes intense enough. In one such study, the subjects were posed a practical problem. The problem was to mount two candles on a wall, given only the candles, a box of matches, and some thumbtacks (Figure 8.18). The solution is to empty one of the boxes, tack it to the wall, and then place the candles upon it. The difficulty is caused by *functional fixedness.* This is a set to think of objects in terms of their normal function: a box is to put things in and not on top of. The tendency to maintain this set (that is, functional fixedness) was enhanced by motivation. Subjects who expected no particular reward solved the problem more quickly than subjects who were told that they might win a $20 reward (Glucksberg, 1962).

Restructuring

The solution of a difficult problem often involves a dramatic shift in the way in which the problem is viewed. This shift may be very sudden and is then experienced as a flash of insight, a sense of "aha" that occurs when the misleading set is finally broken. Restructuring is especially clear in problems which impose a false perceptual set. To solve the nine-dot problem, the subject has to move out of the

8.18   Functional fixedness   *(A) The problem is to mount two candles on the wall, given the objects shown. (B) To solve the problem, one has to think of a new function for the box. (After Glucksberg, 1962; photograph by Ed Boswell)*

279

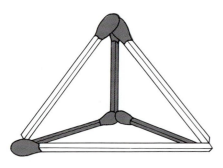

8.19 Solution of the matchstick problem *To arrange six matches (see Figure 8.6) into four equilateral triangles, the matches have to be assembled into a three-dimensional pyramid. Most subjects implicitly assume the matches must lie flat. (After Scheerer, 1963)*

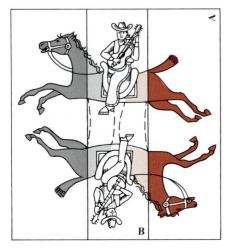

8.20 Solution of the horse-and-rider problem *To solve the horse-and-rider puzzle (see Figure 8.17) requires a change of perceptual set. (A) must be rotated 90 degrees so that the two old nags are in the vertical position. One can now see that the head of each (vertical) can join (horizontally) with the hindquarters of the other. The final step is to slide (B) over the middle of (A) and the problem is solved. (After Scheerer, Goldstein, and Boring, 1941)*

square frame imposed by the dots (see Figure 8.7). In a similar vein, the match problem requires working in three dimensions rather than two (Figure 8.19), while the horse-and-rider problem can only be solved by a 90-degree rotation of the drawing which recombines the fore- and hindquarters of the misshapen horses to form two new animals entirely (Figure 8.20).

Gestalt psychologists have proposed that this kind of perceptual restructuring lies at the heart of most problem solving in both animals and humans (see Chapter 4). So far, little is known about the mechanisms that underlie the restructuring effect, but there can be little doubt that it is a central phenomenon in the psychology of thinking.

CREATIVE THINKING

The creative thinker is one who generates a problem solution that is both new and appropriate. At the top of the pyramid are such giants as Archimedes, Descartes, and Newton, whose creations define whole chapters of intellectual history. On another level are the anonymous copywriters who develop new advertising slogans for spray deodorants. But whether great or humble, these real-life achievements are quite similar to those of the problem solver in the psychological laboratory. They represent a conceptual reorganization of what was there before.

According to the creators' own accounts, the critical insights typically occur at unexpected times and places. There is usually a period of intense preparation during which the thinker is totally immersed in the problem and approaches it from all possible angles. But illumination tends not to come then. Quite the contrary. After the initial onslaught fails, there is usually a period of retreat during which the problem is temporarily shelved. Rest or some other activity intervenes, and then suddenly the solution arrives, not at the writer's desk or the composer's piano, but elsewhere entirely—while walking in the woods (Helmholtz), or riding in a carriage (Beethoven, Darwin), or stepping onto a bus (the great mathematician Poincaré), or, in the most celebrated case of all, while sitting in a bathtub (Archimedes; Figure 8.21).

Such effects have sometimes been attributed to a process of **incubation** (Wallas, 1926). According to this view, a thinker does not ignore the unsolved problem altogether when she turns away from it in baffled frustration; she continues to work on it, but does so "unconsciously." This hypothesis adds little to our understanding, for it merely substitutes one mystery for another. Unless we know the why

8.21 Archimedes in his bathtub *A sixteenth-century engraving celebrating a great example of creative restructuring. The Greek scientist Archimedes (287–212 B.C.) tried to determine whether the king's crown was made of solid gold or had been adulterated with silver. Archimedes knew the weight of gold and silver per unit volume but did not know how to measure the volume of a complicated object such as a crown. One day, in his bath, he noticed how the water level rose as he immersed his body. Here was the solution: the crown's volume is determined by the water it displaces. Carried away by his sudden insight, he jumped out of his bath and ran naked through the streets of Syracuse, shouting "Eureka! I have found it!" (Engraving by Walter H. Ryff, courtesy Burndy Library)*

and wherefore of unconscious thought (whatever that may be), we know no more than we did before. A possible answer relates to mental set. To find the solution, the problem solver must shake off one or more false sets. These become ever more constricting the longer she stays at the task, all the more so since her motivation is very intense. Leaving the problem for a while may very well break the set which is less likely to be reinstated when the retrieval cues have been drastically altered, as in the woods or in the bathtub. Once the false set is dropped, the true solution has a chance to emerge.

RESTRUCTURING AND HUMOR

At least on the face of it, there is a certain similarity between insightful problem solution and humor. A joke does not strike us as funny unless we "get the point." (The "shaggy dog" story is a special case. Its point is that, contrary to our expectation, there is no point.) Conversely, insights often have a comic aspect, especially when one recognizes how absurdly simple the solution actually is.

Several writers suggest that the essential similarity lies in the fact that both insight and humor involve a dramatic shift from one cognitive organization to another (e.g., Suls, 1972; Figure 8.22). The joke teller creates one expectation during the early stage of the narrative, and then betrays it when he comes to the punch line. There is surprise followed by the realization that the unexpected ending makes some sense after all.

As an example consider the story about three men, a doctor, a lawyer, and an engineer, all of whom are to be executed on a guillotine. As they step up to the scaffold, each is given a choice of lying face up or face down. The doctor is the first and decides that death would come more quickly if he were to lie face up. The blade drops, and then stops just a foot above the doctor's body. There is much amazement and then the prisoner is released. Next is the lawyer. He is sure that legal precedent would lead to his own release if the blade were to stop for him as it had for the doctor, so he too lies face up. Again the blade stops short, and again the prisoner is released. It's now the engineer's turn. He decides his best bet is to go with whatever worked before. As he lies on his back, he too can see the blade directly overhead. But then, just before the blade descends, he turns to the executioner and says, "Say—I think I see what your problem is."

The story is set up to lead to the expectation of another ending, perhaps a third failure whose mechanical nature the engineer might then explain. The actual ending is unexpected and incongruous, but it makes sense even so—the engineer can't help but solve an engineering problem, even if it kills him. But incongruity as such is not enough, for without a viable cognitive alternative into which the ending fits, there will be no humor. If the engineer had asked the executioner to lend him a handkerchief, there would have been no joke at all, only puzzlement.

In other cases, the cognitive structure of the joke is more subtle. As an example consider the story about a mountain climber who slipped over a precipice and barely hung on to a long rope with a thousand-foot drop gaping underneath. There was no one with him, and he knew he couldn't hold on much longer. In his fear and despair, he looked up to the heavens and shouted: "Is there anyone up there who can help me?" There was a long pause and then a deep voice was heard from above: "You will be saved if you show your faith by letting go of the rope." The mountain climber looked down at the deep abyss beneath him, and then looked up again and cried: "Is there anyone *else* up there who can help me?"

Here, the joke sets up a puzzle—what will the mountain climber do now? His

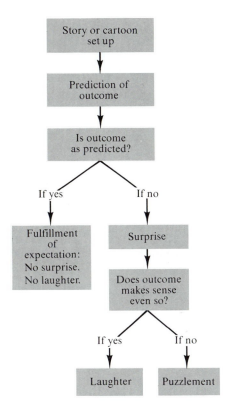

8.22 A cognitive analysis of the appreciation of humor *The joke or cartoon sets up an expectation. The experience of humor will arise (1) if this expectation is not fulfilled and (2) if the outcome nevertheless makes sense. (After Suls, 1972)*

8.23 Humor in a cartoon

(Drawing by Charles Addams; © 1940; 1968 The New Yorker Magazine, Inc.)

response is unexpected. He both has faith and doesn't. Not content with hearing from one deity, he wants to hear from yet another, trying to get a better bargain. A similar relation between humor and puzzles is apparent in many cartoons. For example, when a viewer first sees the famous skiing cartoon of Charles Addams, he tries to figure out what is going on. The solution is incongruous, but it fits, and is therefore funny (see Figure 8.23).

Surprise and reinterpretation are probably not the only cognitive factors required for humor to occur. Another ingredient is the comparison of the two cognitive structures that are juxtaposed. The critical element can be seen in *both* contexts. This simultaneous membership of an item in two radically different cognitive contexts seems to be a crucial aspect of humor. Thus, one of Oscar Wilde's dowagers, on interviewing a potential son-in-law, asks:

> LADY BRACKNELL: . . . Now to minor matters. Are your parents living?
> JACK: I have lost both my parents.
> LADY BRACKNELL: Both? . . . That seems like carelessness.
>
> (Wilde, *The Importance of Being Earnest,* Act 1)

The humor derives from the sudden jolt caused by the second meaning of "lost" which is then contrasted with the first.

While cognitive restructuring is an important and perhaps a necessary condition for the production of humor, it is clearly not a sufficient one. A whole variety of emotional and motivational factors are also involved. Thus humor can serve as a relatively harmless outlet for aggressive or sexual wishes that can't be indulged directly, as in sarcastic wit and "dirty jokes." A further condition is that the new and unexpected meaning (the point of the joke) has to be emotionally acceptable to the listener. Jokes about Hitler's extermination camps are not funny to anyone. This point holds even for the so-called "sick joke." We can (barely) accept, "Yes, yes, Mrs. Lincoln, but how did you like the play?" because 1865 is over a hundred years in the past. An equivalent line about Mrs. John F. Kennedy would be unspeakable.

SPATIAL THINKING

Thus far, we have discussed problem solving as if all problems were essentially alike. In some ways, they may well be; for example, they may all be susceptible to sets that obstruct their solution. But it's likely that they also differ in some important ways. One difference is in the kinds of thinking that different problems tend to elicit.

Our present interest is in *spatial thinking,* the kind that we use when we want to determine a shortcut between two locations, or when we mentally try to rearrange the furniture in the living room.

Spatial Problem Solving and Imagery

How do people solve spatial problems? One way is by means of mental images. Such images have a picture-like quality that can be an important aid in various thinking tasks. By consulting a mental picture, the traveller can read off shortcuts as he might from an actual map, and the decorator who wants to modify his furniture placement can save wear-and-tear on his back muscles by rearranging his images before moving the actual armchairs and sofas. Evidence for the picture-like aspects of images comes from various laboratory studies. We've already seen that images can be scanned and rotated (see Chapter 7). Further demonstrations come from studies on mental maps.

MENTAL MAPS THAT ARE PICTURE-LIKE

Most people have a general conception of the spatial layout of their environment. According to some investigators, part of this geographical knowledge is based on mental maps that have picture-like qualities. In one study, students were asked to estimate the distance between various locations on their university campus—for example, between their dormitory and the gymnasium, or between the student union and the library. It turned out that the subjects were quite accurate in their estimates. But even more interesting was the time it took to provide these estimates. The longer the distance, the longer the estimation time. It was as if the subjects measured distances with a mental ruler on a mental map, much as one might measure the length of a wall with a small ruler. The longer the wall, the more often the ruler would have to be moved from point to point, and the more time the process would take (Jonides and Baum, 1978).

MENTAL MAPS THAT ARE CONCEPTUAL

Some kinds of spatial thinking may refer to picture-like images, but others involve processes that are much more abstract and conceptual. In one study, subjects were asked to indicate the relative locations of two cities. One of the pairs

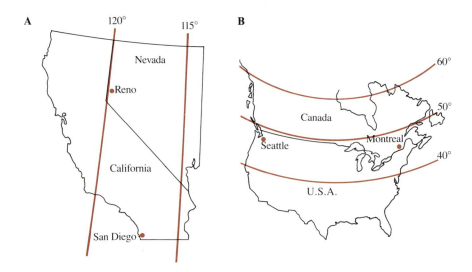

8.24 Conceptual mental maps *Subjects tend to judge San Diego to be west of Reno and Montreal to be north of Seattle. But these judgments are in error. (A) A map of California and Nevada with colored lines of longitude (angular distance from an arbitrary reference point in Greenwich, England) which shows that in fact San Diego is east of Reno. (B) A map of the U.S. and southern Canada with colored lines of latitude (angular distance from the equator) which shows that Seattle is slightly north of Montreal. (Stevens and Coupe, 1978)*

was San Diego, California, and Reno, Nevada. The subjects judged San Diego to be west of Reno, although it actually is farther east. Another pair was Montreal, Canada, and Seattle, Washington. Here the subjects judged Montreal to be farther north, although its actual direction is south of Seattle. These results suggest that the subjects didn't base their answers on picture-like mental maps resembling the real maps shown in Figure 8.24. If they had, they would have said that Reno is west of San Diego. But in fact, they (falsely) asserted the very opposite.

How can we explain the subjects' errors? The most plausible explanation is that their judgments were affected by what they knew about the relative locations of the states or countries that contain the cities about which they were asked (e.g., Nevada is east of California and Canada is north of the U.S.). But this knowledge was symbolic and conceptual rather than picture-like. What the subjects knew about San Diego and Reno can be summarized by the three propositions shown below:

> California is west of Nevada.
> San Diego is in California.
> Reno is in Nevada.

This way of representing spatial knowledge could easily lead to error, for it might suggest that the east-west relation that holds for the states also holds for all the cities within them. This would be true if the larger geographical units (California and Nevada) were conceptual categories such as *bird.* (If we know that owls and robins are birds, it automatically follows that they both have wings, beaks, and feathers.) Of course, states and countries are not at all equivalent to conceptual categories such as *bird:* Reno is not *a* Nevada but is *in* Nevada. But even so, most of us often store spatial information in such a rough-and-ready conceptual way. (One hopes that airplane navigators are an exception.) To the extent that we do store some geographical information under category rubrics, our spatial knowledge cannot be exclusively—or even largely—picture-like (Stevens and Coupe, 1978).

Is Spatial Knowledge Visual?

The preceding discussion shows that in many cases, our mental maps are quite inaccurate, in part because they become affected by various items of conceptual knowledge. But accurate or not, are these maps necessarily visual?

The answer is no, for a remarkable degree of spatial knowledge is found in persons born blind. In a recent study, the subject was Kelli, a two-and-a-half-year-old girl who had been blind since birth. Kelli was brought into an unfamiliar playroom in which there were four major landmarks. One was her mother (M), another was a stack of pillows (P), a third was a basket full of toys (B), and the fourth was a table (T), as shown in Figure 8.25. Initially, Kelli was given experience with three paths; she was walked from M to P and back, from M to T and back, and from M to B and back. The question was, what would she do if now confronted with a choice between paths she had never taken? Did her experience provide her with some sort of mental map (although needless to say, not a *visual* map) by means of which she could derive the angle of a new path? The test was a series of trials on which she was either taken to T (the table), P (the pillows), or B (the toy basket), and then asked to take one of the paths she had not previously traversed. For example, if at T, she might be told "Go to the toy basket," if at B, "Go to the pillows." As it turned out, she did remarkably well. In fact, her performance was not much worse that that of sighted adults who were given the same test when they were blindfolded.

It's clear that spatial knowledge is not necessarily visual. Kelli obtained information about space through sensory channels other than vision—largely by exploring with her hands. But the way in which she put that information together was ultimately much the same as that used by persons whose information comes through the eyes (Landau, Spelke, and Gleitman, 1984).

REASONING AND DECISION MAKING

How do people reason? For many years, the assumption was that the processes they use are intimately related to the formal laws of logic. Thus, George Boole, a famous nineteenth-century mathematician, entitled his treatise on the laws of logic "An Investigation into the Laws of Thought," with little doubt that the laws that governed the one would also govern the other (Henle, 1962). Today, this belief is no longer held as widely. For by now, there is ample evidence that people are very prone to errors of reasoning. As a result, some psychologists have argued that the laws of logic have more to say about how people *should* think than about how they really do think, for in their view humans are not quite as rational as one would like to believe.

Deductive Reasoning

Logicians have developed various systems to determine—that is, deduce—whether certain conclusions are true or false given some initial assertions and cer-

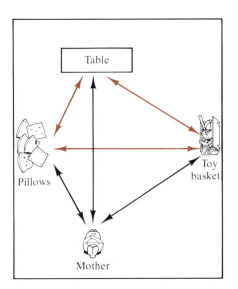

8.25 Cognitive maps *This figure shows the room layout for the spatial inference experiment with a blind girl, Kelli. The room was 8 × 10 feet. Black arrows show routes on which Kelli was trained, and colored arrows show routes on which Kelli was tested. (After Landau, Gleitman, and Spelke, 1981)*

8.26 Syllogistic argument *Insisting upon the execution of the Cheshire Cat, the King of Hearts argued that "anything that had a head could be beheaded . . ."* (*Lewis Carroll,* Alice's Adventure in Wonderland, *p. 69*)

tain basic operations (such as affirmation, negation, and so on). An early example is the analysis of **syllogisms,** an enterprise that goes back to Aristotle. Each syllogism contains two premises and a conclusion. The question is whether the conclusion logically follows from the premises (see Figure 8.26). A few examples of such syllogisms (some valid, others invalid), are:

> All A are B.
> All B are C.
> Therefore: All A are C. (valid)

> All A are B.
> Some B are C.
> Therefore: Some A are C. (invalid)

Or, stated in more concrete terms:

> All American Eagles are patriots.
> All patriots are redblooded.
> Therefore: All American Eagles are redblooded. (valid)

To give another example:

> All heavenly angels are accomplished harp players.
> Some accomplished harp players are members of the American musicians' union.
> Therefore: Some heavenly angels are members of the American musicians' union. (invalid)*

Until the nineteenth century, most philosophers were convinced that the ability to evaluate syllogisms of this kind was an essential aspect of human rationality. Under the circumstances, it was a bit disheartening when experimental psychologists demonstrated that subjects make a considerable number of errors on syllogism tasks.

According to an early hypothesis, one of the reasons for these errors is that terms such as *some* or *all* produce a psychological atmosphere of "someness" or "allness." This **atmosphere effect** leads to a tendency to affirm a conclusion that contains an *all* if both premises contain *all;* similarly for *some* (Woodworth and Sells, 1935). That this doesn't always work, is shown by considering the syllogism:

> Some X are Y.
> Some Z are Y.
> Therefore: Some X are Z.

whose invalid nature is readily appreciated by casting it in a more concrete form:

> Some psychoanalysts are males.
> Some giraffes are males.
> Therefore: Some psychoanalysts are giraffes.

Another cause of errors is the subjects' tendency to perform inappropriate logical transformations. They hear the statement "All A are B" and somehow inter-

---

* Note that the validity of the syllogisms only depends on whether the conclusion follows *logically* from the premises. The empirical plausibility of the conclusion (e.g., that the angels of heaven are unionized) has nothing to do with the matter.

pret it as if it were symmetrical. As a result, they convert it to: "All A are B and all B are A." Such invalid conversions will then of course lead to invalid judgments (Revlin and Leirer, 1980).

Yet more difficulty is caused by the fact that many subjects don't interpret the task as a strictly logical one in which the content of the individual sentences doesn't really matter. In solving logical problems one is supposed to assume that the individual sentences that comprise the premises are "true"; what has to be evaluated is only the relationship among these sentences. But the subjects frequently lose sight of this. Instead of evaluating the conclusions on logical grounds, they judge them in terms of the empirical truth of the individual sentences. As an example, take the syllogism:

> All unicorns are Republicans.
> Harry Truman was a unicorn.
> Therefore: Harry Truman was a Republican.

Needless to say both premises are absurd and the conclusion is (empirically) false. But this doesn't change the fact that the syllogism is perfectly valid. Since the subject is asked to evaluate the logical validity of the syllogism, he ought to answer "true." But to do so, he has to accept the conventions of formal reasoning in which premises can be temporarily accepted "for the sake of argument." This undoubtedly requires some special training, of a kind that generally comes with formal schooling.

Inductive Reasoning

In deductive reasoning, we typically go from the general to the particular. We apply some general rule or rules ("All men are mortal") and ask how it applies to a particular case ("John Smith is mortal"). In *inductive reasoning,* this process is reversed. Here we go from the particular to the general. We consider a number of different instances and try to determine—that is, *induce*—what general rule covers them all.

Induction is at the very heart of the scientific enterprise, for the object of science is to determine what different events have in common. To do so, scientists formulate various *hypotheses*—tentative assumptions about what constitutes the general rule from which the individual observations can be derived. Hypotheses are developed by laymen as well as scientists. All of us try to see some general pattern in the world around us, as in trying to explain the behavior of a moody daughter or a troublesome automobile. The hypotheses we come up with may not be particularly profound ("She's a teen-ager" or "It's a lemon"), but profound or not they are attempts to comprehend an individual case by subsuming it under a more general statement.

What do people do to determine whether their hypotheses are correct? A number of investigators have concluded that there is a powerful *confirmation bias.* By and large, people seek evidence that will confirm their hypotheses, but they only rarely set out to see whether their hypotheses are false.

An illustration is provided by a study in which subjects were presented with the three numbers "2–4–6" and were told that they were an example of a series that conforms to a general rule which the subjects were asked to discover. To do this, they had to generate three-number series of their own. Every time they produced

"There it comes again."

such a series, the experimenter would tell them whether it did or not fit the rule. The subjects always indicated why they chose a particular series, and after a number of trials they announced their hypothesis. This continued until the subject succeeded or finally gave up.

The rule the experimenter had in mind was exceedingly simple: "Any three numbers in increasing order of magnitude." It was so simple in fact that the subjects took quite a while before they discovered what it was. But the real issue was how they went about their task. All of them soon developed one or another hypothesis. But whenever they did, they almost always generated a series that fit this hypothesis—to confirm it. They very rarely generated a series that was not consistent with their current hypothesis, and would *dis*confirm it.

For example, one subject began with the notion that the rule was: "You start with any number and then add 2 each time." She came up with four successive series: "8–10–12," "14–16–18," "20–22–24," and "1–3–5" and was told each time that they conformed to the experimenter's rule. She then announced her hypothesis, was informed that it was false, and developed a new hypothesis: "The middle number is the average of the other two." To test this hypothesis she first offered "2–6–10" and then "1–50–99." After learning that each of these conformed to the correct rule, she announced her new hypothesis, and was again told that it was false. She continued to formulate new hypotheses, for example, "the difference between the first and second number is equal to the difference between the second and third." She again tested the hypothesis by looking for confirmations, generating the series "3–10–17" and "0–3–6," was again told that each of them conformed to the rule, and again discovered that this hypothesis too was incorrect. Eventually, she did hit on the correct hypothesis. But what is interesting is that she hardly ever tested any of her hypotheses by generating a sequence that was *in*consistent with them. For example, she never tried a sequence such as "2–4–5," a quick way to show that the "add 2" hypothesis was wrong (Wason, 1960, 1968; Wason and Johnson-Laird, 1972).

The confirmation bias shown in the 2–4–6 experiment is a very pervasive phenomenon. It is not restricted to the psychologist's laboratory, for it is also found in the real-world behavior of scientists and engineers. They too tend to seek confirmations of their hypotheses and are disinclined to seek evidence that contradicts them. When Galileo provided visible proof that Jupiter has moons that rotate around it, some of his critics were so incensed at this challenge to their geocentric views of the universe that they refused even to *look* through his telescope (Mitroff, 1974; Mahoney, 1976).

There is little doubt that the confirmation bias can be a genuine obstacle to understanding, for in many ways, disconfirmations are more helpful in the search for truth than are confirmations. *One* disconfirmation shows that a hypothesis is false, but countless confirmations cannot really prove that it is true. (For another demonstration of the confirmation bias, see Figures 8.27 and 8.28; Wason and Johnson-Laird, 1972.)

What accounts for the confirmation bias? A plausible guess is that humans have a powerful tendency to seek order in the universe. We try to understand what we see and hear, and impose some organization upon it. The organization may not be valid, but it is better than none at all, for without some such organization we would be overwhelmed by an overload of information. But this benefit also has a corresponding cost, for our confirmation bias often condemns us to remain locked within our false beliefs and prejudices (Howard, 1983). Our ten-

8.27 A demonstration of the confirmation bias *The figure shows four cards laid out on a table. Each of the cards has a letter on one side and a number on the other. Your job is to test the following hypothesis: "If a card has a vowel on one side, it has an even number on the other side." To test this hypothesis, you have to flip over some card or cards, but you must flip only that card (or those cards) that are required to test the hypothesis—no more and no less. Indicate the cards you decide to flip. (For solution, see Figure 8.28, p. 290.)*

dency to come up with plausible hypotheses often serves us well. But we would be better off if we would be more ready to consider their falsity and would heed Oliver Cromwell's advice to a group of clergymen: "I beseech you, in the bowels of Christ, think it possible you may be mistaken."

Decision Making

Deductive reasoning is about certainties: If certain premises are true, then certain conclusions will follow. There are no exceptions. If it is true that John Smith is a man and that all men are mortal, then it inevitably follows that John Smith is mortal. The situation is very different in inductive reasoning, in which we try to find (that is, induce) a general rule when given a number of individual instances. Once this rule is induced, we will then try to apply it to new instances. But in contrast to deductions, inductions can never be certain but only probable. This even holds for Mr. Smith's mortality. For in actual fact, the proposition "All men are mortal" is only an induction. To be sure, this induction is based on all of human history in which every single man that ever lived was ultimately observed to die. That John Smith will be an exception is therefore exceedingly unlikely—in fact, astronomically improbable. But death (or for that matter, taxes) is not an *utter* certainty in the sense in which deductively arrived truths always are.

In ordinary life, we are usually concerned with probabilities that are much less clear-cut, and evaluating these probabilities is often crucial. Baseball batters have to estimate the likelihood that a pitcher will throw a fast ball; brokers must judge the probability that a certain stock will rise; patients who contemplate elective surgery must do their best to weigh the relevant medical risks. How do people form the relevant probability estimates? And how do they utilize them to decide whether to swing at the pitch, to buy the stock, or to undergo surgery? These questions are the province of an area of psychology (and other social sciences) called *decision making.**

AVAILABILITY

Technically, the probability that a particular event will happen is defined by a ratio: the frequency of that event (for example, the number of times a coin falls "heads") divided by the total number of observations (the number of times the coin is tossed). But in actual practice we often don't know these frequencies. And even if we do, we often don't use them properly. Instead, we make use of various *heuristics,* which are rules of thumb that help us estimate likelihoods. But these heuristics sometimes lead to serious errors (Tversky and Kahneman, 1973, 1974).

One such rule of thumb has been called the *availability heuristic.* The idea is that we often estimate the frequency of certain events by considering how many such events readily come to mind (are available to memory). One study involved guesses of how often certain letters appear in different positions in English words. As an example, take the letter *R.* Considering all the words in the language, does it occur more frequently in the first position or in the third position of all the

---

* For a discussion of the relation between these probability estimates and the costs associated with different kinds of errors, see Chapters 5 and 17.

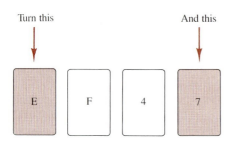

8.28   Solution to problem posed in Figure 8.27   *The solution is to turn over two cards: The one with the "E" and the one with the "7."*

Most subjects flip the "E" card in a perfectly reasonable attempt to confirm that the hypothesis is true (if it is, the other must contain an even number). But they generally make two errors.

One is an error of commission which is flipping over the "4" as well as the "E." This is presumably done to check whether the other side contained a vowel. But this is quite irrelevant to the hypothesis, which only asserts that if there is a vowel on one side, then there will be an even number on the other. The hypothesis makes no predictions at all if one side contains a consonant (or for that matter, a blank, or a dollar sign).

A second error is one of omission. Virtually all subjects fail to flip over the "7" card. Note that this card provides a potential disproof of the hypothesis. If it is turned over and the other side is seen to contain a vowel, the hypothesis ("if vowel, then even number") is disconfirmed. The fact that the vast majority of the subjects did not hit on this method at all is yet another demonstration of the confirmation bias. Interestingly enough, this same error was also made by a few professional logicians, to their considerable embarrassment. (Wason and Johnson-Laird, 1972)

words in the language? Over two-thirds of the subjects said that it is more common in the first than the third position. In actuality the reverse is true. The reason for the errors is availability. The subjects made their judgments by trying to think of words in which *R* is the first letter (e.g., *r*ed, *r*ose, *r*ound) and of words in which it is the third (e.g., er*r*ing, bo*r*ing, ca*r*t, st*r*ong). They then compared the number they managed to generate in each category. But this method leads to a wrong estimate because our memorial dictionary (as well as Webster's) is organized according to the first rather than to the third letter in each word. As a result, words that start with an *R* are much more easily retrieved (that is, more available) than those whose third letter is an *R*. As a result, their frequency is seriously overestimated (Tversky and Kahneman, 1973).

The availability heuristic can have serious practical consequences. What are the chances that the stock market will go up tomorrow or that a certain psychiatric patient will commit suicide? The stockbrokers and psychiatrists who have to decide on a particular course of action must base their choice on their estimate of these probabilities. But this estimate is likely to be affected by the availability heuristic. The stockbroker who remembers a few vivid days on which the market went up may overestimate the chances of an upswing; the psychiatrist who remembers one particular patient who unexpectedly slashed his wrists may underestimate the likelihood of eventual recovery.

Another example is the assessment of a politician's chances in an election. The people who surround him generally tend to overestimate how well he will do. In part, this may be caused by wishful thinking; but in part, it may be another manifestation of the availability heuristic. Evidence comes from interviews of the reporters who covered the election campaign of Senator George McGovern, the unsuccessful Democratic candidate for President in 1972 (Figure 8.29). Senator McGovern lost by a landslide, yet on the night of the election these highly experienced reporters believed that the election would be much closer. The reporters were affected by the enthusiastic crowds of McGovern supporters they had been exposed to. Of course, they knew these were a biased sample, but they couldn't help but be affected anyway. The wildly cheering crowds were much more vivid than the pale statistics of the polls they read. This led to an increased availability to memory, which then colored the reporters' estimates of McGovern's national support (Nisbett and Ross, 1980).

THE CONJUNCTION FALLACY

The availability heuristic can produce still another error in decision making. It may lead to an overestimate of the likelihood of the ***conjunction*** (that is, joint occurrence) of two independent events. A basic law of probability is that the probability that two independent events will occur is given by the product of their separate probabilities. If the probability of a coin coming up "heads" is .5, then the probability that it will come up heads twice in a row is .5 × .5 or .25. Subjects may or may not know this formal expression of conjunct probability, but one would guess that virtually all of them know that the conjunction is less probable than each probability taken alone. But some recent evidence suggests that they don't always act as if they do.

Consider the following studies conducted in 1982. A number of students were asked to estimate the probability of the events described in either of the following two statements:

(1) A massive flood somewhere in North America in 1983, in which more than 1,000 people drown.

or (2) An earthquake in California sometime in 1983, causing a flood in which more than 1,000 people drown.

In a related study using professional analysts employed by industry, universities, and research institutes, the subjects were asked to estimate the probability of the events described in either of these two statements:

(3) A complete suspension of diplomatic relations between the U.S.A. and the Soviet Union, sometime in 1983.

or (4) A Russian invasion of Poland, and a complete suspension of diplomatic relations between the U.S.A. and the Soviet Union, sometime in 1983.

Note that the events described in (2) are *necessarily* less probable than those in (1); by the same token (4) has to be less probable than (3). This follows from the nature of conjunctions. "Earthquake *and* flood in California" must be *less* probable than "flood anywhere in North America"; similarly for "invasion *and* suspension of relations" compared to "suspension of relations" alone. But the subjects evidently felt otherwise. They committed the **conjunction fallacy**—taking a conjunction to be more likely than one (or both) of the two events regarded alone. They judged (2) to be more probable than (1), and (4) to be more probable than (3).

What explains the conjunction fallacy? One guess is that it is yet another manifestation of the availability heuristic. The added item (earthquake, and invasion of Poland) provides a vivid scenario that links the two conjoined events in a cause-and-effect relationship. The scenarios are plausible enough, for an earthquake in California makes a flood more likely, and an invasion of Poland may well produce a diplomatic rupture. But this doesn't change the fact that a flood alone is more likely than one caused by an invasion (Tversky and Kahneman, 1983).

8.29 The availability heuristic as a cause of political misjudgment *The photo shows Senator McGovern surrounded by enthusiastic crowds of supporters during his unsuccessful presidential campaign in 1972. Reporters who covered his campaign mistakenly believed that the election outcome would be much closer than it was. (Photograph courtesy of AP/Wide World Photos)*

Are People Really Irrational?

The preceding discussion has considered a large body of evidence that throws a rather poor light on human rationality. People make many errors in deductive reasoning; they often misunderstand or misconvert the premises and so come up with an incorrect conclusion. They make errors in inductive reasoning; they are primarily concerned with demonstrating that their hypotheses are correct and don't try to discover whether they are wrong. They are also very prone to error when they have to make decisions in the face of uncertainty; they use a number of heuristics that may lead to mistakes in estimating the probability of events. Intellectually, we evidently have much to feel modest about. But if so, how could humanity possibly have achieved what it has in mathematics, philosophy, and science?

To begin with, despite our many errors, it seems rather likely that some aspects of rational thinking are part and parcel of our mental apparatus, in much the sense in which the fundamental operations of arithmetic (addition, subtraction, multiplication, and division) are built into a pocket calculator. But the calculator will not yield correct results if its owner punches in the wrong numbers or inadvertently presses the key for addition instead of the one for subtraction. In the same way, the capacity for logical thinking may very well be part of our makeup, even though we don't always make use of it or use it incorrectly. But the fact that this capacity is there allows for the possibility of its use if certain other factors are present. But what are these other factors?

One depends on human history. There is little doubt that most of our great intellectual achievements are at bottom collective. They depend on countless prior generations, each of which bequeathed some bits of new knowledge and some new ways of gaining yet further knowledge, to the generation that followed it. Because of them, we possess an immense arsenal of intellectual tools, including various techniques of formal thinking. Our mental machinery has some limited capacity for deductive and inductive reasoning, but this capacity is not finely honed until experience makes it so—the individual's own and that of his ancestors before him.

Of course, this is not all. For even if we have the necessary intellectual tools, we may not use them. We may know statistics and still fall prey to the availability heuristic; we may be trained in science and still be subject to the confirmation bias. But here, too, we are helped by the fact that much of human thought is a collective enterprise. An individual scientist may very well be biased toward confirmation and may not be inclined to look for evidence that falsifies her hypothesis. But there are other scientists who will not have the same compunction. Many of them will not entertain the same hypothesis, and so they will be only too glad to do what's necessary to falsify *hers.* The collective upshot is likely to be a victory for rationality.

This is not to say that reason will always win out in the end. It surely does not. Many of the errors of thought we've discussed are still with us after millennia of human history, and they are found whether we're alone or in groups. But this doesn't prove that we are not rational beings. At worst our rationality is bounded —by habit, circumstance, and by the fact that our processing capacity is limited (Simon, 1956).

Some of the leading investigators in this area have drawn an analogy between errors of thought and perceptual illusions (Tversky and Kahneman, 1983). If the analogy holds, there is yet further hope for human rationality. Both kinds of errors are distortions: in the one, we misjudge truth or probability; in the other, we misperceive the world of concrete reality. But the fact that there are perceptual illusions does not mean that by and large we don't see reality as it actually is. Perceptual illusions are an exception and not the rule, for by and large our perceptual machinery generally does a fine job of informing us about the world. It may be that errors of thought have a similar status—that they are special distortions of patterns of thought that ordinarily work and serve us perfectly well.

If we take the analogy between errors of thought and perceptual illusions seriously, there is a further consequence. Some of the perceptual illusions have helped us understand the processes whereby we see without error. The classical case is brightness contrast, which is crucial in the understanding of many perceptual and psychophysiological phenomena (see Chapter 5). It remains to be seen whether the study of errors of thought will have an analogous effect in helping psychologists understand the processes of ordinary thinking in which we do tolerably well. After all, in ordinary life, we don't manage all that badly. We usually find our way from place to place, devise sensible courses of action, and have beliefs about daily-life phenomena which are generally formed on fairly good evidence. Perhaps the *special* cases in which we go wrong may help us understand the *general* machinery of thinking by means of which we often go right.

A BACKWARD LOOK AT PERCEPTION, MEMORY, AND THINKING

In looking back over the three domains of cognition—perception, memory, and thinking—we can only repeat a theme we have struck before. There are no clear boundaries that demark these three domains. In describing perception, we often cross over the border into memory. For the way we perceive familiar objects—let alone such ambiguous figures as the young woman–old woman picture—is based in part on how we perceived them in the past. But perception also shades into thinking. We look at the moon at the horizon, decide that it must be larger than it first appears since it looks farther off, and promptly perceive it in line with this (presumably unconscious) inference. Nor is it clear where memory leaves off and thinking begins. Much of remembering seems like problem solving. We try to recall to whom we lent a certain book, conclude that it has to be Joe, for we know no one else who is interested in the book's topic, and then suddenly have a vivid recollection of the particular occasion on which he borrowed it (and the way he swore that he'd return it right away). But if remembering is sometimes much like thinking, thinking can hardly proceed without reference to the storehouse of generic memory. Whatever we think about—which route to take on a vacation trip, how to fill out a tax form—requires retrieval of items from various memory systems.

All of this shows that there are no exact boundaries between perception, memory, and thinking. These areas are not sharply separated intellectual domains, with neat lines of demarcation between them. They are simply designations for somewhat different aspects of the general process of cognition. We will now turn to the one aspect of cognition that we have thus far discussed only in passing—language. It, too, is intertwined with the other domains of cognition, but unlike perception, memory, and thinking, which are found in many animals, language is unique to human beings.

SUMMARY

1. A classical issue in the study of thinking concerns the *elements* that make up thought. J. B. Watson's *motor theory* proposed that thinking consists of very small muscle movements, especially those of *implicit speech*. Today this view is largely rejected because while thinking is often accompanied by bodily activity, it is not equivalent to it and can proceed even during paralysis.

2. Another hypothesis held that all thought is necessarily composed of *mental images*. While there is good evidence that some thinking has the picture-like quality of imagery, most psychologists doubt that all thinking is of this kind. They feel that there is another, more abstract and symbolic form of thinking which involves mental structures such as *concepts* and *propositions*.

3. Considered as an activity, thinking is *directed.* In problem solving, all steps are considered as they fit into the overall structure set up by the task. This structure is typically *hierarchical,* with goals, subordinate subgoals, and so on. This hierarchical structure is not unique to problem solving but may be a general characteristic of any directed activity.

4. Increasing competence at any directed activity goes together with an increase in the degree to which the subcomponents of this activity have become chunked and *automatized.* In learning to send and receive Morse code, as in the attainment of many skills, learning curves exhibit *plateaus,* followed by a later rise, suggesting the acquisition of progressively larger units. Similar chunking seems to occur in many forms of mental activity, including problem solving, and differentiates masters and beginners in many endeavors such as mental calculation, musical composition, and playing chess.

5. An influential approach to problem solving comes from work on *artificial intelligence,* which tries to simulate certain aspects of human thinking. A number of solution strategies have been incorporated into several computer programs, including *algorithms* and *heuristics.* Some further extensions have provisions for loosening the computer's single-mindedness in the hope that certain imperfections may produce an artificial intelligence more similar to our own. Still other extensions feature the use of *expert systems.*

6. Problem solving is not always successful. One reason may be a strong, interfering *mental set* which makes the subject *rigid,* and which is especially hard to overcome under conditions of intense motivation.

7. The solution of certain problems often involves a radical *restructuring* in which a misleading set is overcome. Such restructurings may be an important feature of much of *creative thinking.* Accounts by prominent writers, composers, and scientists suggest that restructuring often occurs after a period of *incubation.* Restructuring may also play a role in *humor,* which often occurs when an unexpected cognitive organization turns out to make sense after all.

8. While the solution of *spatial problems* often depends on mental imagery, it is sometimes based on a more abstract, conceptual form of thinking. Evidence comes from studies which indicate that geographical knowledge is often organized in a conceptual rather than picture-like form. Further evidence shows that spatial thinking need not be visual, as indicated by studies on *cognitive maps* in persons born blind.

9. Studies of *deductive reasoning* show that people are prone to various errors in thinking. Errors of reasoning in dealing with *syllogisms* are caused by a number of factors, including the *atmosphere effect,* the tendency to perform inappropriate logical transformations, and the confusion of empirical and logical truth.

10. In deductive reasoning, the thinker tries to deduce a particular consequence from a general rule or rules. In *inductive reasoning,* the direction is reversed, for here the thinker tries to induce a general rule from particular instances. An initial, tentatively held induction is a *hypothesis.* A number of studies have pointed to a powerful *confirmation bias* that makes subjects seek evidence which will confirm their hypothesis rather than look for evidence that would show their hypothesis to be false.

11. *Decision making* involves the estimation of probabilities and the utilization of these estimates in deciding on a course of action. Some recent studies have shown that such estimates are often in serious error. One reason may be the *availability heuristic:* estimating the frequency of an event by how readily an example of such an event comes to mind. Another reason for error is the *conjunction fallacy:* overestimating the joint occurrence of two independent events. The study of these and other ways in which our thinking can go wrong may ultimately help us understand the general machinery of thinking by means of which we often go right.

CHAPTER 9

Language

By Lila R. Gleitman and Henry Gleitman

When we consider the social forms and physical artifacts of human societies, we are struck by the diversity of cultures in different times and places. Some humans walk on foot, others travel on camels, and still others ride rockets to the moon. But in all communities and all times, humans are alike in having languages. This essential connection, between *having language* and *being human,* is one reason why those interested in the nature of human minds have always been particularly intrigued with language.

To philosophers such as Descartes, language was that function which most clearly distinguished between beasts and humans, and was "the sole sign and only certain mark of thought hidden and wrapped up in the body." Descartes held that humans were utterly distinct from the other animals because all humans have language, while no other animals have anything of the sort. But this claim comes up against an immediate objection: There are about 5,500 languages now in use on earth. Obviously, these are different from one another, for the users of one cannot understand the users of another. In what sense, then, can we speak of "language in general" rather than about French or English or Hindi? The answer is that human languages are at bottom much more alike than they seem at first glance to be. For example, all languages convey thought by the same *means:* They all use sounds, words, and sentences to organize ideas. In contrast, animal communications often have something like sounds or words (for instance, a cat can purr happily and hiss angrily), but they never have complicated sentences (such as *I'm going to stop purring and start hissing unless you give me that catnip immediately).*

Another similarity is in the *ideas* human languages can express. When the

Adam Gives Names to the Animals *The recognition that language is distinctively human goes back to antiquity. An example is the biblical tale illustrated in this medieval wall painting which shows Adam assigning names to the animals. According to some ancient legends, this act established Adam's intellectual superiority over all creation, including even the angels. In one such tale the angels were unable to call the animals by name, but Adam could: " 'Oh Lord of the world! The proper name for this animal is ox, for this one horse, for this one lion, for this one camel!' And so he called all in turn by name, suiting the name to the peculiarity of the animal." (Ginzberg, 1909, vol. 1, p. 62; photograph courtesy Ferentillo, S. Pietro)*

United Nations ambassador from France makes a speech at the UN, numerous translators immediately whisper its equivalent in English, Russian, Arabic, and so on, to the listening ambassadors from other countries. The fact that the French speech can readily be translated suggests that, by and large, the same things that can be said in French can be said in English and Russian as well. This is true despite the fact that the Russian and English listeners may disagree with what the Frenchman is saying. But the translation will allow them to *know* that they disagree, so that they are in a position to stomp out of the room in a rage, or make a counterspeech—which will also be translatable.

Thus all human languages are much alike in the ideas they can express as well as in the means used for expression. In this chapter, we use English as our main example of a human language. But it is important to keep in mind that what we say about English generally goes for all the other human languages as well. Evidently there is a special kind of vocal communication system characteristic of all human cultures, despite considerable differences in the sounds of words and the ways the words are sequenced in sentences (for instance, German often puts the verb at the end of the sentence, while English more often puts it in the middle of the sentence).

MAJOR PROPERTIES OF HUMAN LANGUAGE

We now take up two major properties shared by all human languages: The use of language is characterized by **novelty**, for we create new sentences constantly, rather than just repeating those we might have heard before. But despite this creativity, language use conforms to principles of **structure** which control the forms of words and sentences that we say.

Language Use Is Creative

At first glance, language use might seem to be merely a complicated habit, a set of acts by ear and mouth that have been learned by memorization and practice. According to this view, the explanation of talking is simple: Each of the memorized speech acts is simply performed whenever the appropriate circumstances arise. Our mothers said *That's a rabbit* when they saw a rabbit. Having observed this, we now say *That's a rabbit* when we see a rabbit. But this position of language as habit is hard to maintain, for speakers of the language can and will utter and understand a great many sentences that they have never uttered or heard before. To see this point, it is only necessary to realize that, in addition to *That's a rabbit,* each of us can also say and understand:

> *That's a rabbit over there.*
> *A rabbit is what I see over there.*
> *Obviously, that's a rabbit.*
> *How clearly I recall that the word for that animal is rabbit.*
> *Well bless my soul, if that isn't a rabbit!*

And so on, with hundreds of other examples. A little child who has memorized all these sentences must be industrious indeed. And he must also be lucky to have a mother who is so talkative as to say all these rabbit sentences while the child is around listening. But the situation is really incredibly more complicated than this, for surely we learn to talk about objects and creatures other than rabbits, including aardvarks and Afghans, apples and armies, and proceeding all the way to zebras and Zyzzogetons.

Furthermore, the sheer number of English sentences also rules out habit as the explanation for language use. A good estimate of the number of reasonably short (20 words or fewer) English sentences is 10^{30}. Considering the fact that there are only 3×10^9 seconds in a century, a learner memorizing a new sentence every second would have learned only a minute fraction of them in the course of a lifetime. But the fact is that we can all say and understand most of them (Postal, 1968).

In sum, we effortlessly create and interpret new sentences on the spot. Only a very few such as *How are you?, What's new?,* and *Have a nice day* are said and heard with any frequency. All the rest are at least partly new—new to the person who says them and new to his listeners as well. Thus, memorization and habit formation cannot explain how we learn and use language (in Chapter 15, we will discover how language learning actually takes place in the young child). To express all the thoughts, we combine a limited—though large—number of words into sentences. Thus language is a system that allows us to reach a limitless end from limited means: Our stock of memorized, meaningful words is finite, but we nevertheless have the capacity to speak of an infinite number of new thoughts and events. We can do so because our language system allows us to combine the old words in novel ways.

Language Is Structured

While language use is creative in the sense that we can and do invent new sentences all the time, it is also restricted (or ***constrained***): There are unlimited numbers of strings of English words which—accidents aside—we would never utter. For example, we do not sometimes say *Is rabbit a that* or *A rabbit that's* even though these are fairly comprehensible ways to say *That's a rabbit.* Speakers construct their utterances in accordance with certain abstract principles of language structure. These principles are not the so-called "rules of grammar" that many of us learned painfully at school in the fourth grade (and forgot thankfully in the fifth grade), such as "Never say ain't" or "A sentence cannot end with a preposition." These are recipes or *prescriptive rules* for speaking and writing handed down from certain authorities about how they think we *ought* to speak, and very often they do not conform to the facts about natural talking and understanding. Most of us are quite comfortable ending sentences with a preposition (as in the sentence *Who did you give the dog to?*) or even two prepositions (as in the sentences *What are you up to?* and *Who did the short-stop make a force out on?*). Sometimes it sounds quite odd not to do so, as Winston Churchill pointed out by spoofing this "rule" in the sentence *This is the kind of language up with which I will not put.*

The *structural principles* we will be concerned with in this chapter are those that every normal speaker honors without effort, without special thought, and without formal training in school—for example, the principle by which we invariably say *the rabbit* rather than *rabbit the.* It is these regularities that are fundamental to understanding language as a universal human skill. In fact, most human cultures outside of America and Western Europe do not have prescriptions for "proper" speech at all. Even so, we pause here to ask how and why the prescriptive rules sometimes arise.

PRESCRIPTIVE RULES OF GRAMMAR

In some cultures, a particular dialect of the language is elevated for professional, literary, and other formal purposes, and called the prescribed or *standard dialect.* This is the case for English, which has marvelously many dialects depending on the geographical area (regional dialects) and ethnic and social grouping (class dialects). A standard form is useful for the joint intercommunications of these many groups. It is often argued, however, that the standard dialect is somehow better than others (Bernstein, 1967), a claim that is very hard to defend on objective grounds.

Consider certain inner-city Black dialects of American English. These are often called *substandard* rather than merely *nonstandard* and attacked as "illogical" (Bereiter and Engelmann, 1966). One reason given is that speakers of these dialects often omit the present tense copula (the verb *be*), yielding such sentences as *He a fool* or *We bad* rather than the standard *He is a fool* and *We are bad.* But which style is the more logical? Many prestigious languages of the world, including Russian, Hungarian, and Arabic, are like Black English in omitting the present tense of the copula, but never are called illogical. This suggests that the Black American dialects are frowned upon as a matter of convention or even prejudice, and not because they are poorer vehicles for expressing meaning or thinking logically.

To see this point clearly, it is important to notice how superficial the dialect difference really is. In standard English, we can often contract the copula: We can say *He's a fool* rather than *He is a fool.* Black English can omit the copula exactly

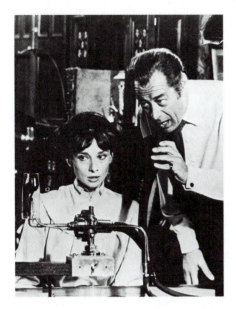

The power of an "H" *In a scene from the film version of* My Fair Lady, *the cockney flower girl, Eliza (Audrey Hepburn), is taught by Henry Higgins (Rex Harrison) how to pronounce an "H." She thus becomes a lady. (Courtesy The Museum of Modern Art/Film Stills Archive)*

where standard English can contract it. But there are positions in which the standard dialect does not allow contraction: It sounds very strange to say *I wonder who he's* to mean *I wonder who he is.* This same subtle detail is true of Black English. In that dialect, one cannot omit the copula and say *I wonder who he,* but rather—just like in standard English—one must say *I wonder who he is* (or *be*) (Labov, 1970a). Thus, both dialects include precise rules about use of the copula, rules honored very exactly and without formal instruction by their users. Hence, whether or not one chooses to use a certain dialectical form, one cannot easily say that this choice is based on whether the dialect is objectively more systematic or more logical than some other dialect. The two forms are a little different from each other, to be sure, but there seems no way to defend the view that one is superior.

Such objective considerations do not stop each dialect group from disdaining the speech of the next group. Long before the English language was born, the ancient Athenians were laughing at the "rude vowels" of Ionian farmers. More recently, Henry Higgins changed the "H" of Eliza Doolittle, whereupon she was welcomed into the British upper classes and called "My Fair Lady." Such social prejudices can scarcely by justified by claiming one style of speech is more logical or beautiful (after all, what is so beautiful about an "H"?). Still, speaking the standard dialect, just like wearing the right clothes to a cocktail party, may be a requirement for some coveted job or social status. Scientific study demonstrates, however, that each language and dialect is as complex and as meaningful as the next (Labov, 1970b). Every human community uses one (or more) of these complex systems we call a *language,* and each of these languages includes an abstract set of structural principles that govern usage.

THE STRUCTURE OF LANGUAGE

All human languages are organized as a hierarchy of structures. At the bottom of the hierarchy, each language consists of little snippets of sound; and at the other end, of sentences and conversations. We begin by describing the basic building blocks: the 50 or so phonemes, the 50,000 or so morphemes, and the hundreds of thousands of words (see Figure 9.1).

9.1 The hierarchy of linguistic structures *Every sentence is composed of phrases, which are composed of morphemes (simple units of meaning such as* strange *and the plural* -s*), which in turn are composed of phonemes (the units of speech sound, such as* p *and* ə*). The phonemes are described by symbols from the phonetic alphabet because English spelling is not always true to the sounds of words.*

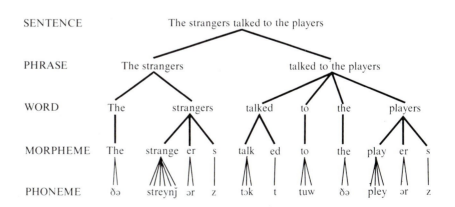

299

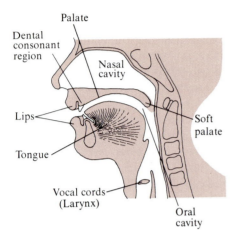

9.2 The human vocal tract *Speech is produced by the air flow from the lungs which passes through the larynx (popularly called the voice box) containing the vocal cords and from there through the oral and nasal cavities which together make up the vocal tract. Different vowels are created by movements of the lips and tongue which change the size and shape of the vocal cavity. Consonants are produced by various articulatory movements which temporarily obstruct the air flow through the vocal tract. For some consonants the air flow is stopped completely. Examples are* p, *where the stoppage is produced by bringing both lips together; and* t *where it is produced by bringing the tip of the tongue to the back of the upper teeth. Some other consonants are created by blocking the air flow only partially, for example* th *(as in* thick), *produced by bringing the tip of the tongue close to the upper teeth but without actually touching. (After Lieberman, 1975)*

Phonemes

To speak, we move the various parts of the vocal apparatus from one position to another in a rapid sequence while expelling a column of air up from the lungs and out through the mouth. Each of these movements shapes the column of air from the lungs differently, and thus produces a distinctive speech sound. Many of these differences among speech sounds are ignored by the listener. Consider the word *bus* which can be pronounced with more or less of a hiss in the *s.* This difference is irrelevant to the listener, who interprets what was heard to mean 'a large vehicle' in either case. But some sound distinctions do matter, for they signal differences in meaning. Thus neither *butt* nor *fuss* will be taken to mean 'a large vehicle.' This suggests that the distinction between *s, f,* and *t* sounds is relevant to speech perception, while the difference in hiss magnitude is not relevant. The distinctions that are perceived to matter are called **phonemes.** They are the perceptual units of which speech events are composed (see Figure 9.2).

To get a rough idea of how phonemes are defined, consider the words *din, dun,* and *den.* Each of these begins with a sound that is different from those that begin *kin, bun,* and *pen,* but is more or less the same as the sound that ends *hid, mud,* and *bed.* The common element is the phoneme that we designate by the symbol *d.*

UNDERSTANDING UNFAMILIAR SPEECH

Because of the construction of the human speech apparatus, children can learn to pronounce a couple of hundred different speech sounds clearly and reliably. But each language restricts itself to using only some of them. English uses about forty.* Other languages select differently from among the possible phonemes. For instance, German uses certain gutteral sounds that are never heard in English, and French uses some vowels that are different from the English ones. Once children have learned the sounds used in their native tongue, they usually become quite rigid in their phonemic ways: It becomes difficult for them to utter or perceive any others. This is one reason why foreign speech often sounds like a vague and undifferentiated muddle, rather than like a sequence of separable sounds.

Another difficulty in understanding unfamiliar speech—even in one's own language—has to do with the sheer rate at which the speech sounds are produced in sequence; adults can understand speech at the rate of 250 words per minute (Foulke and Sticht, 1969), which converts to about 16 phonemes per second. There are no gaps or silences that mark off one speech unit from the next. This holds not only for the successive phonemes, but for the words and phrases as well. All these units run into each other, so that it is often difficult to tell where one ends and the other starts. Thus when one person speaks of a *grey tabby,* her listener may hear *a great abbey.* Children are notorious in making such segmentation errors. For example, asked to tell what he had learned on the first day of school, one child responded *We learned "Aplejal"* (presumably, *I pledge al . . .*).

---

* The English alphabet provides only twenty-six symbols (letters) to write these forty phonemes, so it often uses the same symbol for more than one. Thus, the letter *O* stands for two different sounds in *hot* and *cold,* an "ah" sound and an "oh" sound. This fact contributes to the difficulty of learning how to read English.

COMBINING PHONEMES

As speakers of a language, we have learned the phonemes that constitute its sound elements. But we have learned something further as well—the way these phonemes can be combined into words. Some of these choices are a matter of historical accident—for instance, English happens to have a word *pledge,* composed phonemically of the sounds p-l-e-j, but as we just discussed, it does not happen to have a word *aplejal,* composed of the sounds a-p-l-e-j-a-l. But some of the facts about how phonemes combine in words are systematic, rather than accidental choices.

To see this point, consider the task of an advertising executive who tries to find a name for a new breakfast food. She will have to find some sequence of phonemes that has not already been used to mean something else. Will any new arrangement of phonemes do? The answer is no. To begin with, some, such as *gogrps* or *fpibs,* would be hard to pronounce. But even among phoneme sequences that can be pronounced, some seem somehow un-Englishlike. Consider the following possibilities: *Pritos, Glitos,* and *Tlitos.* They can all be pronounced, but one seems wrong: *Tlitos.* English speakers sense intuitively that English words never start with *tl,* even though this sequence is perfectly acceptable in the middle of a word (as in *motley* or *battling*). So the new breakfast food will be marketed as tasty, crunchy *Pritos* or *Glitos.* Either of these two names will do, but *Tlitos* is out of the question. The restriction against *tl*-beginnings is not a restriction on what human tongues and ears can do. For instance, one Northwest Indian language is named *Tlingit,* obviously by people who are perfectly willing to have words begin with *tl.* This shows that the restriction is a structural principle of English specifically. Few of us are conscious of this principle, but we have learned it and similar principles exceedingly well, for we honor them in our actual language use.

Morphemes and Words

At the next level of the linguistic hierarchy (see Figure 9.1), fixed sequences of phonemes are joined into morphemes. The ***morphemes*** are the smallest language units that carry bits of meaning. They are approximately the units we usually call roots, stems, prefixes, and suffixes. One morpheme can constitute a whole word, but very often words are sequences of morphemes, as we will describe further below.

COMBINING MORPHEMES INTO WORDS

Like phonemes, the morphemes of a language can be combined only in certain ways. Some words consist of a single morpheme, such as *strange,* meaning 'alien' or 'odd.' But many morphemes cannot stand alone and must be joined with others to make up a complex word. Examples are *er* (meaning 'one who') and *s* (meaning 'more than one'). When these are joined within the complex word *strangers (strange + er + s),* the meaning becomes correspondingly complex ('alien + person + plural'). Each of these morphemes has a fixed position within

English words. Thus *er* has to follow the root *strange* and must in turn be followed by *s;* other orders (such as *erstranges* or *strangeser*) are not allowed.

The average English speaker knows about 50,000 morphemes along with their meanings and the positions they can occupy within a word. If we count vocabulary in terms of whole words rather than morphemes, each adult has a vocabulary of several hundred thousand, for then the items *strange, stranger, strangers, strangest,* etc., would all be counted separately. Our memory for all these words is really quite amazing, considering the fact that some words may not be encountered for years and yet are recollected quite effortlessly. Such words as *strangler, yodel, backache, wormy,* and *abrasive* occur less than once per million words (Thorndike and Lorge, 1944), but we do not forget them. Each is stored forever in the brain, against the day when we want to "mean" them.

THE MEANINGS OF WORDS

The question "What do words mean?" is one of the knottiest in the whole realm of language. The subfield that deals with this question, **semantics,** has thus far been able to give only a few rather tentative answers. As so often, the first step is to eliminate some of the answers that appear to be false. (For recent general discussions, see J. D. Fodor, 1977; J. A. Fodor, 1981; E. E. Smith and Medin, 1981.)

Meaning as reference   One of the oldest approaches to the topic equates word and phrase meaning with **reference.** According to this position, the meaning of a word or phrase is whatever it refers to in the real world. Thus this view asserts that words and certain phrases are essentially names or labels. Proper names such as *Chris Evert Lloyd, Australia,* and *The Eiffel Tower* are surely labels for a particular person, place, and object. The reference theory of meaning holds that expressions such as *tennis player, continent,* and *building* function in a similar manner. According to this view, the only difference between such expressions and true proper names is that the former are more general: *tennis player* refers to various male and female players and to champions as well as hackers, while *Chris Evert Lloyd* refers to one player and to no one else.

The reference theory of meaning runs into several difficulties. One is that some words or phrases are perfectly meaningful even though it is hard to know exactly what they refer to. Some of these are abstract expressions such as *justice, infinity,* and *historical inevitability.* One cannot point to a real "infinity" somewhere out there in the world. Others are imaginary, such as *unicorn* and *the crown prince of South Dakota,* which presumably have no real-world referents at all.

Further problems arise from the fact that words or phrases that have the same referent are not substitutable for each other in all sentences. As an example, consider the following phrases:

> *Franklin D. Roosevelt*
> *Eleanor Roosevelt's husband*
> *the most eminent citizen from Hyde Park, N.Y.*
> *the most famous victim of polio*

There is no doubt that all of these expressions have one and only one referent: the man who was the thirty-second president of the United States, Franklin D. Roosevelt. But do they really all mean the same thing, as the reference theory of meaning asserts? If they do, we should be able to use them interchangeably in a sentence without affecting its meaning. But this clearly is not the case. Consider the sentence:

When I grow up, I want to be the most eminent citizen from Hyde Park, N.Y.

A person might very well say and mean this, without committing herself to a host of other desires such as:

When I grow up, I want to be Franklin D. Roosevelt.
When I grow up, I want to be Eleanor Roosevelt's husband.
When I grow up, I want to be the most famous victim of polio.

The fact is that all these expressions mean different things, so that one can truly want some of them and not others. But this shows that—though words often refer to real things and persons in the world—there must be more to the meaning of a word or phrase than all the things it refers to. In short, *meaning* is not the same thing as *reference*.

Meaning as image   A variant of the reference theory argues that meanings are mental images. According to this theory, the meaning of a word or phrase is a mental image of whatever the word or phrase refers to. Thus the meaning of *triangle* is a mental picture of a triangle. On closer analysis, this theory faces some of the same difficulties that beset the reference theory.

One problem was pointed out three centuries ago by the philosopher Bishop Berkeley (1710). The meaning of a word is necessarily more general and abstract than any mental image can possibly be. Suppose we conjure up a mental image of a triangle. If this imagined triangle is essentially equivalent to a visual experience, it has to have some particular triangular shape (say, a right triangle) and probably also has to have a specific size (say, an altitude of three inches). But if so, how can we possibly recognize a ten-inch isosceles triangle as a triangle when we come across it? To do so, we presumably have to say, "The exact shape and length of the triangle in my head are irrelevant. What matters is whether the external object is similar to the image in the appropriate regards. So long as it is a closed, two-dimensional figure with three straight sides whose angles add up to 180 degrees, it is a triangle all the same." But given this mental statement, who needs the mental image? Its work—in recognizing triangles—is entirely done by the statement.

The definitional theory of meaning   The preceding arguments show that the meaning of a word is neither just the thing it refers to nor a mental picture of that thing. But then what can word meaning be?

One proposal tries to analyze word meaning into a set of necessary subcomponents. This approach starts out with the fact that there are various meaning relationships among different words and phrases. Some words are similar in meaning *(wicked-evil),* others are opposites *(wicked-good),* and still others seem virtually unrelated *(wicked-ultramarine).* According to one proposal, these relationships can be explained by assuming that words are bundles of semantic features (J. J. Katz and J. A. Fodor, 1963; J. J. Katz, 1972) which, taken together, add up to the word's full meaning. As an example, take the word *bachelor.* This word clearly has something in common with *uncle, brother, gander,* and *stallion.* As speakers of English, we know that all of these words carry the notion 'male.' This point is forcefully made by considering various sentences that most English speakers will regard as odd (or, to use the technical term, **anomalous**). Thus the

Can a white rose be red?   *The Queen had ordered the gardeners to plant a red rose bush but they planted a white one by mistake. They're now trying to repair their error by painting the white roses red. On the definitional theory of meaning, this seems reasonable enough. For the expressions* red rose bush *and* white rose bush *differ by only a single feature—red versus white. But if so, why are they so terrified that the Queen will discover what they did? (From Lewis Carroll,* Alice in Wonderland, *1971, p. 62)*

sentence *My _____ is pregnant* sounds very peculiar if the missing word is any of the members of the bachelor-related group listed below:

$$
My \quad \left\{ \begin{array}{l} \textit{uncle} \\ \textit{brother} \\ \textit{gander} \\ \textit{stallion} \\ \textit{bachelor} \end{array} \right\} \quad \textit{is pregnant.}
$$

Demonstrations of this sort suggest that words like *stallion* and *bachelor* are not simple in meaning, but rather are composed of a number of meaning atoms —the semantic features. Further demonstrations with anomalous sentences show that *bachelor* contains additional features such as 'unmarried' and 'adult.' This explains why the following sentences are also odd in meaning:

> *My sister is married to a bachelor.*
> *I met a two-year-old bachelor yesterday.*

The ultimate aim of this kind of analysis is to describe the meanings of words as packages which bundle together a limited set of primitive semantic attributes or *features.* For *bachelor,* these might be 'never married,' 'human,' 'adult,' and 'male'; for *stallion,* they would include 'adult,' 'male,' and 'horse.' Words like *stallion* and *bachelor* will be perceived to be related because when an individual looks up the features for each of these words in her mental dictionary (or **lexicon**), she will find that the meaning atom 'male' is listed for both of them. Taken together, the semantic features constitute a definition of a word—much like the definitions in a standard dictionary. According to this theory, we carry such definitions in our head as the meanings of words.

The prototype theory of meaning   The definitional theory faces a problem, for some members of a meaning category appear to exemplify that category better than others do. Thus a German shepherd seems to be a more doglike *dog* than a Pekinese, and an armchair seems to be a better example of the concept of *furniture* than a reading lamp. This seems to be at odds with the analysis we have described thus far, whose aim was to specify the necessary and sufficient attributes that *define* a concept. When a dictionary says that a bachelor is "an adult human male who has never been married," it claims to have said it all. Whatever fits under the umbrella of this definitional feature list is a bachelor. Whatever does not, is not. But if so, how can one bachelor be more bachelorlike (or one dog more doglike) than another?

The question is whether the meaning categories described by words are really as all-or-none as the definitional theory would have it. Several investigators have made a strong case for an alternative view, called the **theory of prototypes** (Rosch, 1973; Rosch and Mervis, 1975; Smith and Medin, 1981).

The facts that the prototype theory tries to account for can be easily illustrated. Close your eyes and try to imagine a bird. It is pretty safe to guess that you just imagined something like a robin or sparrow, not a buzzard, ostrich, or goose. There is something quintessentially *birdy* about a robin, while a goose does not seem such a good example of a bird. The definitional theory would have considerable trouble explaining why this is so. According to this theory, some feature or features associated with the concept *bird* (such as 'has feathers,' 'lays eggs,' 'flies,' 'chirps') are both necessary and sufficient to pick out all birds and only birds. But

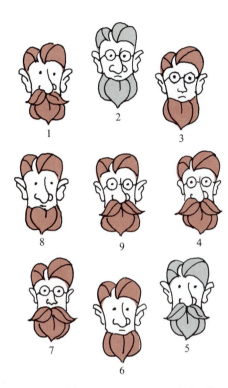

9.3 The Smith brothers and their family resemblance *The Smith brothers are related through family resemblance, though no two brothers share all features. The one who has the greatest number of the family attributes is the most prototypical. In the example, it is Brother 9, who has all the family features: brown hair, large ears, large nose, moustache, and eyeglasses. (Courtesy Sharon Armstrong)*

if geese and robins are both said to be birds because they share these necessary and sufficient features, what makes the robin more birdy than the goose?

According to the prototype theory, the answer is that the meaning of many words is described as a whole set of features, no one of which is individually either necessary or sufficient. The concept is then held together by what some philosophers call a ***family resemblance structure*** (Wittgenstein, 1953). Consider the way in which members of a family resemble each other. Joe may look like his father to the extent that he has his eyes. His sister Sue may look like her father to the extent that she has his nose. But Joe and Sue may have no feature in common (he has his grandfather's nose and she has Aunt Fanny's eyes), and so the two of them do not look alike at all. But even so, the two are physically related through a family resemblance, for each has some resemblance to their father (see Figure 9.3).

In sum, a family resemblance structure is like a collection of attributes. Probably no single member of the family will have them all. Nor will any two members of a family have the same ones (except for identical twins). But all will have at least some. Some individuals will have many of the family features. They are often called the "real Johnsons" or "prototypical Smiths." They are the best exemplars of the family resemblance structure because they have, say, the most Johnson-attributes and the least Jones-attributes. Other family members are marginal. They have only the nose or the little freckle behind the left ear, but nothing else.

Many investigators believe that what holds for the Smiths and the Johnsons may hold for many word concepts, such as *bird,* as well. For in fact, there is little doubt that, except for professional biologists, most people don't really know the features that all birds have in common (and which could thus serve as a definition for *bird*). Thus, contrary to our first guess, not all birds fly (ostriches don't fly). And not everything that lays eggs is a bird (giant tortoises lay eggs). Not all birds chirp (crows do not chirp, they caw), and some chirpers (crickets) are not birds. What are we left with from our list of defining features? Nothing but a pile of feathers! But feathers alone do not make something a bird. Hats have feathers too. And, after all, if one plucked all the feathers out of a robin, it would be a mutilated robin, but it would still be a bird for all that. (You think this unfair? What would *you* call it? A hippopotamus?)

According to prototype theorists, birdyness is largely a matter of the total number of bird features a given creature exhibits. No one of these features is necessary and none is sufficient, but animals that have few (such as penguins and ostriches) will be judged to be poor members of the bird family, while those that have many (such as robins) will seem to be exemplary members. According to the theory, these judgments are based on a comparison with an internal ***prototype*** of the concept. Such prototypes represent mental averages of all the various examples of the concept the person has encountered. In the case of birds, people in our culture have presumably seen far more robins than penguins. As a result, something that resembles a robin will be stored in their memory system and will then be associated with the word *bird.* When the person later sees a new object, he will judge it to be a bird to the extent that it resembles the prototype in some way. A sparrow resembles it in many ways and so is judged to be "a good bird"; a penguin resembles it just a little and hence is "a marginal bird"; a rowboat resembles it not at all and hence is judged to be no bird.

Evidence for the prototype view comes from the fact that when people are asked to come up with typical examples of some category, they generally produce

"*Attention, everyone! I'd like to introduce the newest member of our family.*"

instances that are close to the presumed prototype (e.g., *robin* rather than *ostrich*). A related result concerns the time required to verify category membership. Subjects respond more quickly to the sentence *A robin is a bird* than to *An ostrich is a bird* (Rosch et al., 1976; for a related discussion, see Chapter 7, pp. 251–53).

Combining definitional and prototype descriptions   It appears that both the definitional and the prototype approaches to word meaning have something to offer. The prototype view helps us to understand why robins are better birds than ostriches. But the definitional theory explains why an ostrich is nevertheless recognized as a bird, while an airplane (which has wings, flies, etc.) is not. Perhaps we can combine both views of meaning rather than choosing between them.

Consider the word *grandmother.* This word designates people who are 'mothers of a parent.' Thus *grandmother* clearly has a set of necessary and sufficient attributes that neatly define it. The definitional theory seems just right for words like this. But now reconsider. Everyone knows that a grandmother is a person who bakes cookies, is old and gray, and has a kindly twinkle in her eye. When we say that someone is *grandmotherly,* we are referring to such prototypical attributes of grandmothers, not to geneology. But some grandmothers lack these typical properties. Zsa Zsa Gabor is a mother of a parent, but she is hardly gray or twinkly. And we all know some kindly lady who is gray and twinkly but never had a child; she may be grandmotherly, but she is not a grandmother.

The most plausible assumption is that people have two partly independent mental representations for the meaning of a word. They know about prototypical attributes that are good symptoms of being a grandmother, such as being old and gray. They probably store a list (or perhaps a picture) of such attributes (or prototypical features) as a handy way of picking out likely grandmother candidates. But they also store defining grandmother features (e.g., 'mother of a parent'). These definitional features determine grandmother limits, and tell one how to use the prototype appropriately (Armstrong, Gleitman, and Gleitman, 1983).

Combining the two approaches allows us to deal with the disparate phenomena of meaning which we have been discussing. The prototype description enables us to understand why people are surprised to hear that Elizabeth Taylor is a grandmother. The definitional description enables us to laugh at the little boy who bought his grandmother a birthday card whose legend read "You have been just like a grandmother to me" (Landau, 1982).

THE ORGANIZATION OF THE MENTAL LEXICON

One might suppose that the words we know are stored in our brains in much the way they are in Webster's dictionary—perhaps in alphabetical order. But the precision and rapidity with which we produce and understand utterances suggests that the words (along with their meanings) must be stored in a more efficient and flexible manner in the mental lexicon. Current evidence suggests that the mental lexicon is organized more like the filing system in a university library, where books can be found according to several kinds of classification: by the title, by the author, or the topic, and so forth. There may even be a special shelf for "new acquisitions" or "frequently asked for books." Similarly, words in the mental lexicon can be found (or **accessed**) in a number of different ways.

Word frequency A number of methods have been developed to study **lexical access**—recognizing and understanding a word. A common procedure is to show the subject sequences of letters on a computer screen. For instance, he may be shown *nard* on one trial and then *bird* on the next. His job is to decide as quickly and accurately as he can whether what he sees is really an English word. The experimenter is interested in the reaction time to the real English words. The nonwords, like *nard,* are only included to keep the subject honest—without them, the subject might simply push the "yes" button and never look at the words. This method has unearthed some of the principles according to which words are organized together in the mental lexicon.

One finding concerns word frequency. The frequency with which a word occurs in the language (which presumably affects how often and how recently the subject is likely to have encountered this word) affects performance in a lexical access task. The more frequently the word is used, the more quickly it is accessed (Foss, 1969). It appears that our lexicon is organized so that the most common words are stored in a way that places them at the mental forefront and makes them the most readily accessible for speech and understanding. This is similar to the university library, in which the most frequently requested books will be on a nearby shelf where they are easiest to reach.

Word meaning Another principle that determines how words are filed and organized in the lexicon is their meaning. In one study, subjects were presented with two strings of letters, with one string printed above the other. Three examples are:

doctor	*doctor*	*doctor*
nurse	*butter*	*nard*

The subject's job was to press a "yes" button if *both* letter sequences were real words (that is, for *doctor-nurse* and *doctor-butter*), and the "no" button" if both were not (that is, for *doctor-nard*). The results showed that the reaction time was shorter when the two real words were related in meaning (as in *doctor-nurse*),

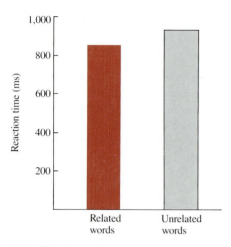

9.4 Word meaning and lexical access
*The figure shows reaction times on a
lexical access task. The subjects were
shown two strings of letters and had to
press a "yes" button if both were real
words and a "no" button if one or both
were not. On some trials they saw two real
words that were related in meaning (e.g.,
bread-butter), while on others they saw
two real words that were unrelated (e.g.,
bread-doctor). Reaction times were
shorter when the two words were
meaningfully related (color) than when
they were not (black). This suggests that the
system according to which words are filed
in the lexicon includes their semantic
relatedness. (Data from Meyer and
Schvaneveldt, 1971)*

rather than being unrelated (as in *doctor-butter*). It appears that seeing the word
doctor readied or "activated" related words such as *nurse* but had no such facili-
tating effect on unrelated words such as *butter* (see Figure 9.4). This suggests that
one of the bases according to which words are stored and filed is their semantic relatedness (Meyer and Schvaneveldt, 1971).

Sound similarity Yet another principle according to which words are filed in the
lexicon is the way they sound. Anyone who has ever punned or rhymed knows
that it is fairly easy to come up with words that sound alike, even if they are quite
different in their meaning, word frequency, or grammatical classification. One
does not have to run through one's whole vocabulary to find a word that sounds
like *red,* for *bed* and *said* and even *instead* will rapidly occur to us.

Further evidence of a mental filing system that uses sound similarity comes
from the tip-of-the-tongue phenomenon we have discussed in a previous chapter
(see Chapter 7). When thinking of a word they can't recall, people sometimes
have a feeling that they are just on the verge of finding it, even though they are
unable to reach the exact spot. In fact, when asked to guess what the word sounds
like, they often come up with words that are very similar in sound. Thus, when
unsuccessfully trying to recall the word *sampan,* they supply sound-alikes such as
Siam, salmon, and *sarong,* suggesting that words that are similar in sound are
somehow stored together in the mental lexicon (Brown and McNeill, 1966).

Grammatical category There is yet another group of properties that determines
how words are filed and organized in the mental lexicon: their **grammatical category.** This determines how they can be used when they are combined with other
words in a phrase or sentence. Some words describe persons and things (usually
nouns such as *man* and *tree*), others describe properties (usually adjectives such
as *red* or *crazy*), and still others describe activities and states of mind (usually
verbs such as *kick* and *know*). It appears that words which belong to these different grammatical categories are stored in different ways. Thus, if asked to add to a
list of words such as *house, man, tree,* we will tend to come up with more nouns
such as *apple* and *cat,* for a list of nouns will activate yet more nouns. Similarly,
lists of verbs will lead us to think of still more verbs, and so on.

Open-class and closed-class morphemes The mental lexicon maintains an even
more overarching classification: the distinction between members of the open
class and of the closed class. The **open class** consists of all the nouns, adjectives,
and verbs taken together. These are the words that carry the major meanings in
sentences. The **closed class** consists of all the "little" words and morphemes
whose function is grammatical: articles such as *the* and *that,* connectives such as
and and *who,* prepositions such as *of* and *to,* and various suffixes such as *s, -er, -
ed,* and so on. The closed class has many fewer members than the open class. In
addition, it rarely admits new members or loses old ones over historical time
(hence, the class is virtually "closed"). In contrast, the composition of the open
class changes rapidly. For example, the language allows us to invent new nouns
readily to name new cultural artifacts: *software, break-dancer,* and so forth. As we
will see later, these two broad word classes seem to be organized quite differently
in the mental lexicon and each class functions differently in comprehension and
speech.

Sentences

It is clear that the system of words in a language is very rich and allows us to express an enormous variety of meanings with great precision and rapidity. Nevertheless, as we discussed earlier, we could not memorize a new word for each of the hundreds of millions of thoughts that we want to, and do, express in language. Thus, to express all the thoughts, we combine a limited—though large—number of words into sentences. We may remark either *The lion kicked the gnu* or *The gnu kicked the lion;* both these sequences of words are meaningful, but there is a difference in the meaning that is of some importance—at least to the lion and the gnu. The term **syntax** (from the Greek, "arranging together") is the general name for the system that arranges words together into phrases and sentences. This topic has been investigated extensively by the American linguist, Noam Chomsky, and his colleagues, and much of the subsequent discussion is based on their work (Chomsky, 1957, 1965, 1975, 1980).

PHRASE STRUCTURE

Just as a morpheme is an organized grouping of phonemes, and a word is an organized grouping of morphemes, so a **phrase** is an organized grouping of words. The phrases are the basic building blocks of which sentences are composed. Consider, for example, the sentence

The French bottle smells.

This sentence is **ambiguous:** It can be understood two ways depending on how the words are grouped into phrases; either

(The French bottle) (smells)

or

(The French) (bottle) (smells).

Thus, by the choice of phrasing, the word *bottle* comes out a noun in one interpretation, in which case the sentence is telling us something about French bottles, and *bottle* comes out a verb in another interpretation, in which case the sentence is telling us what the French put into bottles—namely, smells (that is, perfumes).

The phrase is thus the unit that organizes words into meaningful groupings within the sentence. Just as for phoneme sequences and morpheme sequences, some phrase sequences, like those just considered, are acceptable, while others are outlawed, for example:

(The French) (smells) (bottle).

The meaning of a sentence depends not only on the phrases it contains, but also on the way these are put together. But the principles whereby phrase combinations yield meaning are by no means simple. Consider the sentence *The boy hit the ball* which, grouped into phrases, becomes *(The boy) (hit) (the ball).* If we now switch the first noun phrase (that is, *the boy*) with the second (that is, *the ball*), the result is *(The ball) (hit) (the boy),* which obviously means something else.

How phrase structure affects meaning
On being asked what a Mock Turtle is, the Queen tells Alice "It's the thing Mock Turtle Soup is made from." Needless to say, this is a misanalysis of the phrase mock turtle soup. *It ought to be organized as* (mock) (turtle soup)—*a soup that is not really made out of turtles (and is in fact usually made out of veal). Instead, the queen analyzes the phrase as* (mock turtle) soup—*a soup made of mock turtles. (Lewis Carroll,* Alice in Wonderland, *1971, p. 73)*

This example shows that there are some cases when meaning is drastically affected by switching the position of the first and second noun phrases in the sentence. But this isn't always true. Consider again *(The boy) (hit) (the ball)* and the further sentence *(The ball) (is what) (the boy) (hit).* In the new sentence, *ball* comes before *boy* rather than after it, and yet much of the meaning is kept intact.

How can we explain the fact that some arrangements of phrases mean very different things, while other arrangements have much the same meaning? Many linguists believe that the reason is that each sentence in a language is mentally represented in two different ways. Both of these mental descriptions are phrase structures, but they are organized quite differently. One is the **surface phrase structure** of a sentence. This is the organization that describes the sequence of phrases in a sentence as it is actually spoken or read. Thus all three of our example sentences have different surface structures, for each is a different sequence of spoken or written English phrases. The second kind of mental organization of a sentence is its **underlying phrase structure.** This underlying structure pertains to sentence meaning. Two sentences may be very different in their surface structure but much alike in the underlying structure, as in *The boy hit the ball* and *What the boy hit was the ball,* which sound quite different (that is, they differ in surface structure) and mean much the same thing (that is, they are much alike in their underlying structure).

Surface phrase structure   Consider again the simple sentence *The boy hit the ball.* This sentence seems to be naturally organized into two main phrases. One is a so-called **noun phrase** *(the boy).* The other is a **verb phrase** *(hit the ball).* Modern linguists use a special notation to convey this partitioning of sentences into their natural parts. It is a **tree diagram,** so called because of its branching appearance, and similar to those we have encountered in the discussion of hierarchical plans in directed thinking (see Chapter 8):

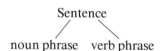

The tree-diagram notation is a useful way of showing that sentences can be thought of as a hierarchy of structures. Each sentence can be broken down into phrases, which in turn can be broken down into subphrases, which in their turn can be broken down into words, and they into morphemes, and finally into phonemes. The descending branches of the tree correspond to the smaller and smaller units of sentence structure. Figure 9.5 shows the surface phrase structure of the example sentence *The boy hit the ball.* Figure 9.6 shows the surface phrase structure of *The ball was hit by the boy,* which is in the so-called **passive** form. Clearly the two figures look very different, for their surface phrase structures differ, despite the fact that they mean about the same thing.

Even schoolchildren with virtually no formal training can analyze sentences into the phrase-sized pieces of Figures 9.5 and 9.6, which suggests that this analysis is not unnatural (Braine and Hardy, 1982; Read and Schreiber, 1982). Further evidence comes from various laboratory studies. One investigator asked whether recall is helped if the subject is able to think of the item in phrase-sized units. To find out, he asked subjects to memorize strings of nonsense words. One kind of string had almost no structure at all: *The yig wur vum rix hum in jag miv.* The sec-

Noam Chomsky

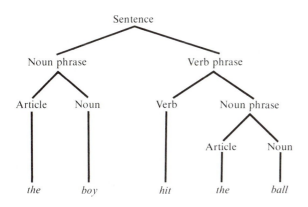

9.5 The surface structure of the sentence The boy hit the ball. *This surface-structure tree is called a phrase-structure description, for it shows how the sentence can be analyzed into phrase units. Notice particularly that there are two noun phrases in this sentence: one noun phrase* (the ball) *is part of the verb phrase* (hit the ball); *the other noun phrase* (the boy) *is not part of the verb phrase. A description of this kind also shows the word class types (e.g.,* article, noun, verb) *of which each phrase consists. Finally, it shows the words of the sentence. Reading these (the bottom row in the tree) from left to right, we get the actual sequence of words in the sentence being described. Thus (in its bottom row) a surface-structure tree describes the actual words that speakers say and listeners hear.*

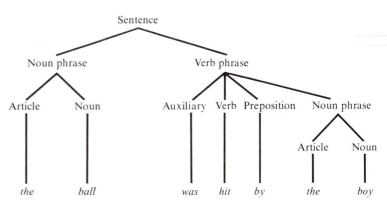

9.6 The surface structure of the sentence The ball was hit by the boy. *Notice that the surface phrase descriptions in Figures 9.5 and 9.6 look quite different: The words in the bottom row are arranged in different ways. Thus the two surface-structure trees succeed in describing the fact that the active sentence and the passive sentence sound quite different (even though, to be sure, they have quite a few words in common).*

ond kind was identical to the first, except that English suffixes such as *s, ly,* and so on, were added to some of the nonsense syllables, resulting in sequences such as *The yigs wur vumly rixing hum in jagest miv.*

On the face of it, the second sequence should be harder to memorize than the first, for it is longer. But in fact, the opposite was true. The English suffixes allowed the subject to organize the sequence of items in terms of a phrase structure, so that it was easier to memorize (Epstein, 1961). Compare

(The dogs) (were sadly serenading Naomi) (in mellowest tone)

and

(The yigs) (wur vumly rixing hum)   (in jagest miv).

This is of course the method that Lewis Carroll used in the poem *Jabberwocky* to make such nonsense as " *'Twas brillig and the slithy tove"* appear to be meaningful. The mere existence of language structure gives the illusion of meaningfulness. In the nonsense-syllable experiment, the subjects were able to learn the suffixed versions more easily than the unsuffixed versions because the suffixes gave clues for performing a phrase analysis: The phrase unit seems to be an efficient package for storing language-like information.

Underlying phrase structure Underlying phrase structure, or the structure of sentence meaning, has two aspects: proposition and attitude. The **proposition** is the basic thought that a sentence expresses, what it is about. Therefore, the proposition is the same in all the different sentences below, for they are all about the idea of boy-hitting-ball.

(1) *The boy hit the ball.*
(2) *The boy did not hit the ball.*
(3) *Did the boy hit the ball?*
(4) *The ball was hit by the boy.*

311

To the extent that all these sentences contain the same proposition, they are related in meaning. But they are clearly not identical in meaning. What differs for the four sentences is the stance or **attitude** the speaker (or writer) is adopting toward the proposition. Namely, the first sentence asserts the truth of the proposition about boy hitting ball; the second sentence denies it; the third sentence questions it; and the fourth sentence again asserts it, but shifts the main focus of attention from *the boy* onto *the ball.*

The whole logic of the sentence meaning, its underlying structure, is the proposition and attitudes taken together. Again, phrase-structure trees describe these underlying forms. This is because the meaning of the sentence (as well as its outward surface form) is still naturally organized as phrase-sized units. A word group (or phrase) such as *the boy* acts as a coherent whole in the meaning of sentences.

Figures 9.7, 9.8, and 9.9 are tree diagrams of the underlying phrase structure of three related sentences. One is in the active form: *The boy hit the ball.* Another is passive: *The ball was hit by the boy.* A third is negative-passive: *The ball was not hit by the boy.* These figures are a compact way of describing the two aspects of sentence meaning. To begin with, they graphically show that all three sentences are related in meaning, for all contain the same proposition organized mentally in the same way (the part of the diagram that is shaded in color). But these diagrams also show the ways these sentences differ in meaning. Each has a different list of attitudes it expresses toward the proposition—focus, assertion, negation.

There are many convincing demonstrations that what people remember primarily is the underlying structure rather than the surface structure. This is not surprising, for we usually care about what somebody meant to say to us, not the exact way it was phrased. One investigator asked adult subjects to listen to stories. Afterward, she presented some isolated sentences and asked if these exact ones had appeared in the stories heard earlier (Sachs, 1967). For instance, a sentence in the original story might be:

(1) *He sent a letter about it to Galileo.*

The later test sentences were

(2) *Galileo sent a letter about it to him.*
(3) *A letter about it was sent to Galileo by him.*

Neither (2) nor (3) had ever appeared in the original story. While the subjects generally knew that (2) was not in the story, they often believed that (3) was. This is because the underlying structures of (1) and (3) contain the same proposition *(He sent a letter about it to Galileo).* In contrast, (2) contains a different proposition *(Galileo sent a letter about it to him).* In short, people remember the plot, but they often forget its exact presentation. They are more likely to recall propositions—meaningful ideas—than the surface shapes of sentences. Sometimes, they even forget which ideas were packaged into which sentences, remembering only the gist of whole conversations (Bransford and Franks, 1971).

SENTENCE RELATIONS

The dual-structure theory of syntax which we have just discussed makes it possible to describe in a quite precise way how sentences are related to each other in meaning.

9.7   Underlying structure of The boy hit the ball.   *Notice that the actual English sentence* The boy hit the ball *looks exactly like the proposition* The boy hit the ball *as it appears in this underlying structure. But as the diagram shows, the real sentence is something more than the proposition: It is an assertion of the truth of the proposition. In informal wording, when a person says, "The boy hit the ball," he really means, "I assert that it is true that the boy hit the ball." The tree diagram here describes both aspects of the thought: its proposition and the attitude about it. (Since our discussion focuses on phrases particularly, we leave out here, and in the succeeding figures, some details such as word-class names—e.g., noun, article.)*

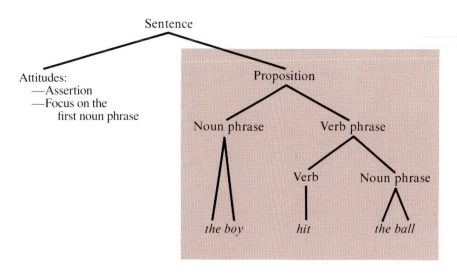

9.8   Underlying structure of the passive sentence The ball was hit by the boy.   *The similarity of meaning of this sentence to the one shown in Figure 9.7 is that both have the same proposition. The difference is that their list of attitudes is partly different.*

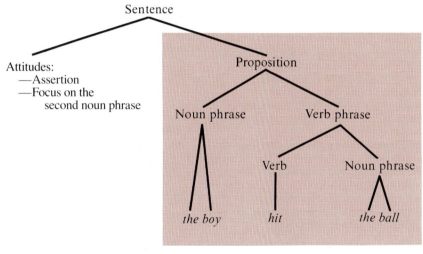

9.9   Underlying structure of the negative-passive sentence The ball was not hit by the boy.   *Notice that again the proposition is shown identically to the way it appeared in Figures 9.7 and 9.8. This makes clear that the sentence is related to the previous two sentences: It has the same proposition. But it does not mean the same thing: It denies the truth of the proposition, rather than asserting the truth of the proposition. Notice particularly, from this example, that a sentence can express many of the attitudes at once. It is possible to switch focus onto the second noun phrase of a proposition (i.e., to say a passive sentence) and also express denial (i.e., to say "not").*

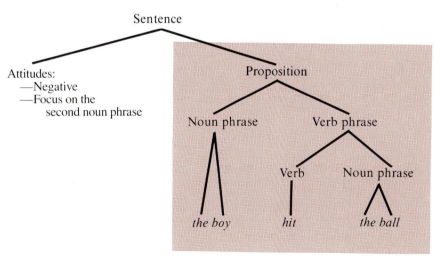

313

Paraphrases and opposites   As we have already seen, whenever two sentences have the same proposition in their underlying structure, they are related in meaning. But the precise nature of this relation depends on the sentence attitudes as well. If the only difference between two sentences is in the focus from which the action is regarded, as in the active versus the passive form, then the two sentences are **paraphrases**—their meanings are essentially equivalent (see Figure 9.10). Thus

(1) *Wellington defeated Napoleon*

and

(2) *Napoleon was defeated by Wellington*

say the same thing in different words.

Some differences in sentence attitude, on the other hand, alter the meaning radically, as in the case of assertion versus denial. The sentence

(3) *Wellington did not defeat Napoleon*

obviously does not mean the same as sentence (1), but is its opposite. This is not to say, however, that (1) and (3) are unrelated in meaning, for they both take a stand (to be sure, an opposing stand) on the same proposition. They are related in a different way than sentence (1) is related to

(4) *Wellington ate hard-boiled eggs.*

A negative sentence attitude describes how (3) differs from (1), but a propositional difference describes how (4) differs from (1).

Ambiguity   Some of the preceding examples described sentences that differ in their surface structures but have the same proposition in their underlying structure. These turn out to be paraphrases, opposites, and so forth. What happens

9.10   An analogy between linguistic paraphrase and perceptual constancy
Linguistic paraphrase is in some ways similar to perceptual constancies of the kind we discussed in Chapter 6. For in both cases, we interpret superficially different patterns of stimulation as roughly equivalent. (A) Shape constancy. *When we look at a tabletop, the image that actually falls on our eye is a trapezoid whose exact shape depends on our orientation to the table. But shape constancy allows us to perceive the unchanging rectangular shape that gives rise to these images. (B)* Paraphrase. *The ear literally hears a variety of surface sentences, but the linguistic system interprets them all as containing the same proposition.*

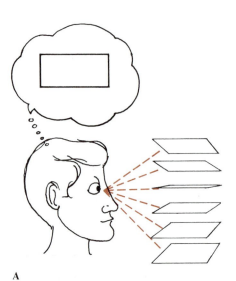

A

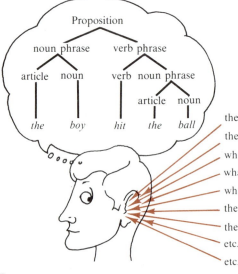

B

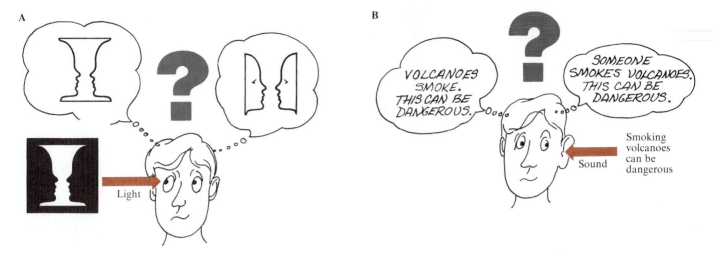

9.11 An analogy between linguistic and perceptual ambiguity *Linguistic ambiguities are in some ways quite similar to perceptual ambiguities of the kind we encountered in Chapter 6. For in both cases, a stimulus can be interpreted in either of two different ways. (A) Ambiguity in visual perception.* The same figure can be seen as either two profiles or a vase. *(B) Ambiguity in sentence perception.* The same sentence can refer to volcanoes that smoke or to volcanoes that are smoked.

when the conditions are reversed, when the two sentences have the same surface structure but contain different propositions in their underlying structures? In this case, we will have two sentences that look for all the world as if they were a single sentence—on the surface they surely are, for they consist of the identical string of words. But this single word string has two meanings, depending on its two possible underlying structures. As a result, it is **ambiguous,** a single form that can be interpreted in two ways (see Figure 9.11).

As examples, consider *Visiting relatives can be boring* and *Smoking volcanoes can be dangerous.* Each of these sentences has more than one meaning. The first can mean either that going to visit relatives can be boring, or that relatives who come and visit can be boring. The more interesting case is the second example, because sheer sanity suggests it can mean only one thing—that a volcano with smoke billowing out of it is potentially dangerous since it might erupt (Figure 9.12A). But another interpretation comes to mind. One can envision a deranged giant smoking away on a volcano, with effects the surgeon-general would regard as dangerous to his health (Figure 9.12B).

9.12 Ambiguity of underlying structure

A
SURFACE: Smoking volcanoes can be dangerous

B
SURFACE: Smoking volcanoes can be dangerous

UNDERLYING PROPOSITIONS:
Volcanoes smoke This can be dangerous

UNDERLYING PROPOSITIONS:
Someone smokes volcanoes This can be dangerous

315

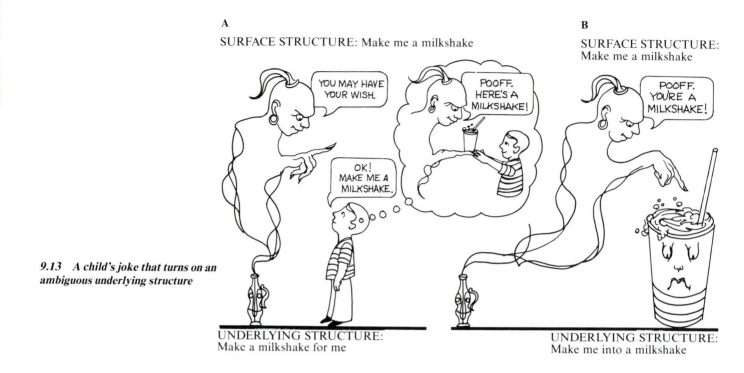

A
SURFACE STRUCTURE: Make me a milkshake

B
SURFACE STRUCTURE:
Make me a milkshake

YOU MAY HAVE YOUR WISH.

POOFF. HERE'S A MILKSHAKE!

OK! MAKE ME A MILKSHAKE.

POOFF. YOU'RE A MILKSHAKE!

9.13 A child's joke that turns on an ambiguous underlying structure

UNDERLYING STRUCTURE:
Make a milkshake for me

UNDERLYING STRUCTURE:
Make me into a milkshake

How does a single physical event (the actual sequence of words, *smoking-volcanoes-can-be-dangerous)* lead to two different ideas in the listener's mind? The answer is that the surface sequence *smoking volcanoes* goes back to two different underlying propositions: *volcanoes smoke* (as in Figure 9.12A) or *someone smokes volcanoes* (as in Figure 9.12B).

In sum, the identical sequence of words can come from different underlying structures. When listeners hear the sequence, they attempt to understand it by constructing its surface structure and underlying structure representations. In this instance, there was more than one choice for what the underlying structure might have been. Here, our listeners construct both these possible underlying propositions, and thus come up with two possible meanings.

Underlying structure ambiguity, as in the smoking volcano example, is appreciated even by young school-age children, and is the basis for much of their verbal humor—such as it is. As an example consider:

We're going to have our grandmother for Thanksgiving dinner.

Oh, we're *going to have turkey.*

A similar example is shown in Figure 9.13.

But there are several other kinds of ambiguity as well. One is ***surface structure ambiguity,*** which arises when the surface sentence can be marked off into phrases in several ways (Figure 9.14). The sentence *Harvey saw a man eating fish* can be marked off into phrases either as *(man) (eating fish)* or as *(man eating) (fish).* Of course, the sentence can be pronounced so as to eliminate the ambiguity; but in verbal humor, pronunciation will be carefully neutral to maintain the ambiguity.

9.14   A child's joke that turns on an ambiguous surface structure

Harvey saw ((a man) (eating fish))   Harvey saw ((a man-eating) (fish))

A further kind of ambiguity arises when we don't know how to segment words from each other, as in our earlier examples of *grey tabbies* and *great abbeys.* Finally, there is ***word meaning ambiguity.*** This occurs whenever words have double meanings. Thus, *Someone stepped on his trunk* will give rise to different mental pictures, depending on whether *his* refers to a traveller with a suitcase or a kneeling elephant. As may have been noticed, word meaning ambiguity accounts for yet a third interpretation of the smoking volcano sentence. To say *volcanoes smoke* could also mean *volcanoes puff on pipes or cigarettes* (Shultz and Horibe, 1974; Hirsh-Pasek, Gleitman, and Gleitman, 1978).

THE MEANING OF PROPOSITIONS

The dual theory of syntax has described many relationships among sentences. At bottom, the claim has been that a particular proposition is represented in a uniform way in the mental underlying structure (as in Figures 9.7, 9.8, and 9.9). It is in terms of this uniform representation that propositions are recognizably the same despite their surface disguises (as in Figures 9.5 and 9.6). What has been left aside in our discussion so far is what sense the comprehender makes of the particular proposition itself.

A simple proposition is most easily thought about as a sort of miniature drama in which the verb is the action and the nouns are the performers, each playing a different role. For example, in the proposition about *boy-hitting-ball* shown in Figure 9.15, the *boy* is the "doer" of the action, the *ball* is the "done-to," and *hit* is the action itself. The job of a listener is much like that of a playgoer (Healy and Miller, 1970). First, she must recover the plot of the story, regardless of the many ways that it might have been staged. This is analogous to the listener's recovery of the underlying structure which renders this plot (the proposition) in a uniform way. But then the playgoer must determine which actors are portraying the various roles in this drama (the *boy* who did it, the *ball* it got done to) and what happened between them *(hitting).* This is a matter of interpreting the propositional structure itself.

If the mental representation of the proposition is like the diagram of Figure 9.15, the listener could identify the characters and the action by inspecting the

317

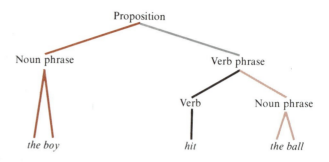

9.15 The underlying proposition in *The boy hit the ball,* **The ball was hit by the boy,** *and so on* *This reproduces the shaded areas of Figures 9.7, 9.8, and 9.9. The emphasis here is on the propositional aspect of sentence meaning. Here, the doer is shown in brown, the done-to in light brown, and the action in black. Thus the basic plot line of the proposition is recoverable from its underlying structure representation.*

subparts of the diagram. The doer of the action is the one who appears as this part of the tree:

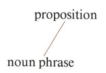

Looking at this part of the tree in Figure 9.15 (brown), we see that *the boy* was the doer. The done-to is whoever appears as this part of the tree:

Looking at this part of the tree in Figure 9.15 (light brown), we find that *the ball* was the done-to. But what was the action? Whatever occupies this place in the tree in Figure 9.15 (black):

This part of the tree refers to the action, so *hit* is what happened.

Thus we can begin to explain how the listener reconstructs the logical meaning of propositions from varying (surface) forms of sentences: He reconstructs a uniform (underlying) representation of the proposition, and then analyzes that proposition into doer, done-to, and action.

COMPLEX SENTENCES

In our discussion of syntax, we have given examples of how sentences are mentally organized. But all of our attention has been centered on very simple sentences—those that contain only a single proposition. Yet it is easy to see that some sentences contain more than one proposition (and thus convey more than one propositional thought). For example, the sentence

(1) *John visited Chicago and John ate pizza.*

consists of two propositions combined within a single sentence. But when multiple propositions occur within a single sentence, their structure is rarely as simple as in the example just given. Consider, then, a rather more normal way of expressing this same idea:

(2) *John visited Chicago and he ate pizza.*

Notice that the word *John* is not mentioned twice in (2) but nevertheless, just as in (1), *John* can be understood to be the doer of the second proposition *(John ate pizza)* as well as the first *(John visited Chicago).* This is because the listener can interpret the pronoun *he* as "standing for" John. Thus the structure of complex sentences is in reality more intricate than in the easier cases of syntactic structure discussed earlier: It can include more than one proposition in a sentence, and it can include the use and comprehension of pronouns that stand for other nouns.

Why do speakers bother to join more than one proposition within a sentence, use pronouns rather than nouns, etc., rather than speaking in very simple sentences? Part of the answer has to do with connecting propositional thoughts together in a logical way. As one example, consider the sentence

(3) *John visited Chicago and ate pizza.*

Here, even a pronoun representing the second instance of *John* is omitted. But does this make the sentence harder to understand? On the contrary, omitting one of the propositional elements (the second instance of *John*) paradoxically makes the logic of the sentence easier to understand! For in fact sentence (1) is rather ambiguous, because it could conceivably have been about two different people, both named John, rather than a single individual. A related problem occurs in sentence (2); the "he" in (2) could have referred to someone other than John (perhaps someone else—Jim or Joe or Harry—ate pizza when John visited Chicago). In contrast, (3) must concern only one John, the one who visited Chicago and the same one who ate pizza. Thus there is a real communicative advantage to combining one's propositional ideas into complex sentences. In this case, the structure of sentence (3) tells us unambiguously that we are referring to the selfsame John in asserting two different propositions.

The examples just mentioned hardly begin to do justice to the real intricacy of our everyday language use, in which we efficiently combine propositions in complicated ways to convey the nuances of our thought. To get the flavor of how complex even the most homely everyday language use really is, consider the following sentence (which appeared as the opening sentence in a Letter to the Editor of the magazine, *TV Guide*):

> *How Ann Salisbury can suggest that Pam Lauber's anger at not receiving her fair share of acclaim for* Mork and Mindy's *success derives from a fragile ego escapes me.*

Despite the very complex syntactic structure, users of English can extract the set of propositions, each with a doer, action, and done-to, in this sentence, and understand it perfectly well. Moreover, the yoking of these propositional thoughts together in the sentence is the most efficient way for the writer to convey his interacting opinions and beliefs about Salisbury, Lauber, "Mork and Mindy," and himself. In our discussion of far more simple example sentences, we have only scratched the surface of these marvelous human capacities to weave a subtly connected story through the use of elaborate sentences. Such capacities are shared by even the most ordinary speakers of a language (Gleitman and Wanner, 1982).

319

THE ORGANIZATION AND USE OF LANGUAGE

We have discussed the system of language that all normal humans share, and found that it is organized into structures at many different levels—from phonemes at the bottom of the hierarchy, to sentences at the top. Now we ask how humans use all this knowledge for the two main communicative functions of language: understanding (or *comprehending* utterances), and speaking (or *producing* utterances).

Comprehension

How do listeners understand the sentences they encounter? All they hear are sequences of words that occur one after another. But these sequences are only the surface forms of the sentences. To understand what the sentences mean, the listeners must somehow recover their underlying structure. How can they do this? After all, few listeners are lucky enough to encounter utterances such as *Focus on the done-to: John saw Mary.* Instead, they hear: *Mary was seen by John.* How do they reconstruct the underlying logic from the surface forms?

In some ways, the problem of the listener is similar to that of the visual perceiver who has to determine the real shape of an object given its retinal image. This retinal shape changes with the object's orientation to the observer. But the observer can nevertheless perceive the object's actual shape, for he has a number of cues, such as perspective, that tell him about the orientation from which the object was viewed. Given these cues, the observer can now reconstruct the actual shape of the object perceptually (see Figure 9.10, and Chapter 7 for discussion).

Something analogous happens with language. Here, the underlying structures give rise to various surface forms. But these forms still bear telltale traces of the underlying structures to which they are related. These telltale traces are generally the appearance of certain closed-class words, such as *by* or *who.* An example is the presence of a pattern such as *is verb-en by* (as in *is taken by, is given by,* and so on). This particular pattern is a good hint that we are dealing with a passive surface structure and that the focus of the underlying structure therefore is on the done-to. Similarly, as we shall see, other closed-class words, such as *who* and *or,* are a good clue that there is more than one proposition in the sentence being heard.

THE SENTENCE ANALYZING MACHINERY

Just how are these clues utilized to reconstruct the underlying structure from the surface form? According to several psycholinguists, the *Sentence Analyzing Machinery* (let us call him—or her—SAM) operates in terms of several general strategies, three of which are discussed below. Depending on how easy or hard the sentence is to comprehend by use of these strategies, the sentence will be correspondingly easy or hard for subjects to understand. (For general descriptions of sentence comprehension, see Frazier and J. D. Fodor, 1978; Wanner and Maratsos, 1978; Marcus, 1980.)

SAM moves through the sentence from left to right   SAM starts with the first word of the sentence, looking up its meaning in the mental lexicon, and analyzing the role it plays in the sentence. He then proceeds to the second word, the third word, and so forth, until he gets to the end of the sentence. Of course, SAM must consider all the possible meanings and categorizations of the words he finds, because he doesn't know which will be correct for a particular sentence. This means that if a word has two or more meanings (such as *trunk,* which can be an elephant's nose or a large suitcase) or can belong to two word categories (such as *dance,* which can be either a verb or a noun), SAM will consider both or all of the possibilities in analyzing the sentence.

SAM searches for simple sentences   SAM's assumption, in starting this analysis, is that he is going to encounter a simple, complete sentence consisting of a noun phrase, followed by a verb, usually followed by another noun phrase, and that these phrases stand for the doer, the action, and the done-to—in that order.*

SAM searches for clue words that signal complexities   SAM is well aware that some of the sentences he will hear are not simple, but will contain more than one proposition. But when this is so, SAM assumes that there will be a clue about the complexity in the surface structure: a closed-class word, such as *and* or *who,* will appear to inform him that he has arrived at a new proposition.

Sometimes one or more of the three strategies just described will fail for SAM. In that case, he must double back over the sentence and make some new guesses, which apply to rarer sentences. Several psychologists have shown that subjects will take unusually long to understand certain sentences, or err in their interpretation, whenever the usual three comprehension strategies fail. Presumably, it is these subjects' mental "SAMs"—which are being forced to revise their favorite guesses—who are having trouble in these cases. Let us consider some particular sentence types that cause trouble for SAM.

ACTIVE VERSUS PASSIVE SENTENCES

The strategy of tentatively casting the first noun phrase in the role of the doer and the second in that of the done-to is quite useful, for in ordinary speech the active form of sentences (e.g., *John hits Fred*) is much more frequent than the passive form *(Fred is hit by John).* But infrequent or not, passive sentences do occur. Here, SAM's doer-first strategy necessarily fails, for in passive sentences the done-to comes *before* the doer. Now SAM has to correct himself. He recognizes his error when he gets far enough along in the left-to-right procedure to arrive at the words *is* and *by,* which occur in passive sentences. Having found these clues, he will revise his first guess and reassign the first noun phrase as done-to (and the second noun phrase as doer).

Evidence comes from studies of reaction time. The first-noun-did-it strategy necessarily implies that it will take a bit longer to understand a passive sentence

---

* This discussion is limited to so-called **transitive verbs** such as *hit* or *embrace,* which have to be followed by a second noun phrase that represents the done-to (*John embraces Mary* sounds natural; *John embraces* sounds incomplete). This is in contrast with so-called **intransitive verbs,** which cannot be followed by a done-to (*John vanishes* sounds fine; *John vanishes Mary* is exceedingly odd).

A

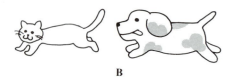

B

9.16   Deciding who is doer and who is done-to   Subjects were presented with sentences such as The cat chases the dog *and* The dog is chased by the cat. *They were then shown either (A) or (B) and had to decide whether the sentence described the picture. Reaction times were faster for active than for passive sentences. (Slobin, 1966)*

than its corresponding active form, for revising the first guess will take some extra time. To show that this is so, one investigator had subjects listen to sentences such as *The dog is chasing the cat* and *The cat is chased by the dog.* Immediately after hearing the sentence, the subjects were shown one of two pictures—a dog chasing a cat or a cat chasing a dog. Their job was to decide whether the sentence did or did not describe the picture. Both children and adult subjects reached the decision faster when the sentence was in the active rather than the passive form (Slobin, 1966; see Figure 9.16).

TWO-PROPOSITION SENTENCES

SAM is expecting a single proposition when he encounters a sentence, but sometimes the sentence contains more than one. Consider the following sentence:

(1)   *The princess kissed the frog and the king knighted the frog.*

This sentence contains two cases of doer–action–done-to. Here the fact that there are two propositions is directly apparent. SAM analyzes the first proposition by his usual strategy, finding *the princess, kissed,* and *the frog* as doer, action, and done-to. Then SAM encounters the closed-class word *and.* This clue tells SAM that there is a second proposition in this sentence, which he comprehends by going through his usual procedure all over again: extracting *the king, knighted,* and *the frog* as the second doer, action, and done-to. In this simple case, the extra proposition is easy for SAM to detect and analyze, using his usual strategies: working left to right, finding doer, action, and done-to in that order, finding a closed-class clue to a second proposition, and then going through the same procedure again. Because sentence (1) fits in with SAM's preferred strategies, then, it is quite easy to understand.

TWO-PROPOSITION SENTENCES THAT OMIT A PROPOSITIONAL ROLE

There are many sentences whose extra proposition is deformed and hidden in surface structure. One major problem is that one of the propositional roles (doer or done-to) may be omitted. To see this point, compare the following two sentences:

(1)   *The princess kissed the frog and the king knighted the frog.*
(2)   *The princess kissed the frog whom the king knighted.*

Both of these sentences contain a clue word *(and* or *whom)* that informs SAM that he is encountering a second proposition. And both sentences mean similar things, for each consists of the two propositions *The princess kissed the frog* and *The king knighted the frog.* But in sentence (2), the done-to of the second proposition *(the frog)* is omitted from the surface structure in everyday speech. SAM can reconstruct this missing propositional role when he finds that this proposition ends (right after the verb *knighted*) without expressing the done-to, but this reconstruction requires an active effort on his part. The job is easier in sentence (1), where *the frog* appears again in the surface structure. SAM's inventors have found that human subjects presented with sentences such as (2) find that its comprehension requires more effort than sentences such as (1), suggesting that our mental comprehension system is organized much like that of the hypothetical SAM (Wanner and Maratsos, 1978).

SENTENCES LACKING CLOSED-CLASS CLUES

As if SAM weren't having enough trouble already, it turns out that sentences used by ordinary people can omit the closed-class clues (such as *whom*) that usually inform SAM that he is encountering a second proposition within a single sentence. For example, one might say the following:

(3) *The princess kissed the frog the king knighted,*

omitting the *whom* that appeared in sentence 2 (repeated below for comparison):

(2) *The princess kissed the frog whom the king knighted.*

Since the *whom* is an important clue for SAM, we should expect that sentences lacking it, such as sentence (3), would take slightly longer to comprehend, and would lead to more errors in comprehension than sentence (2). This prediction, too, has been confirmed in comprehension tests with normal adult subjects (Bever, 1970).

PUSHING SAM BEYOND HIS CAPACITIES: A LINGUISTIC ILLUSION

Taking together all the factors that SAM must consider during the process of comprehension, the analysis of sentences so as to recover their propositional content is a very complex job. Yet, humans usually manage to do it very well, and without much effort or conscious attention. But there are cases where SAM fails. When all or most of SAM's favored strategies are wrong for a particular sentence, the burden becomes too great for him to handle. Thus we should expect SAM to throw up his hands—if he has hands—and cry "Uncle!" if a sentence presented to him:

a. fails to present its propositional roles in the order of doer, action, done-to;
b. omits one of the propositional elements; and
c. omits the closed-class clue words.

Here is such a sentence:

(1) *The horse raced past the barn fell.*

Almost no English listener (or reader) understands this sentence. Almost all believe it to be ungrammatical. They believe it has one too many verbs. Nevertheless, there are good reasons to believe that this sentence is both grammatical and meaningful (see Figure 9.17). Almost all listeners acknowledge it to be so once they have compared it to a related sentence; the trick is to notice that it is just a short form of:

(2) *The horse, who was raced past the barn, fell.*

Notice, in contrast, that speakers will never acknowledge a truly ungrammatical sentence such as

(3) *House the is red.*

to be grammatical even if an experimenter asks them to compare it to

(4) *The house is red.*

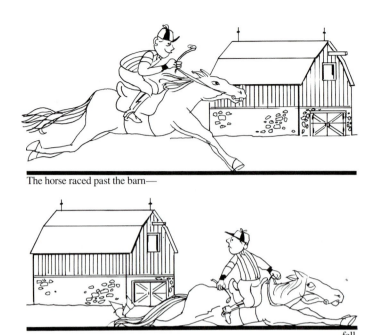

The horse raced past the barn—

—fell.

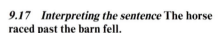

9.17   Interpreting the sentence The horse raced past the barn fell.

Thus (1) is understood—at least in retrospect—by speakers to partake of the regularities observable in (2), and therefore to be grammatical, while (3) is never understood—even in retrospect—to partake of the regularities observable in (4). That is, (3) is forever perceived to be ungrammatical, but (1) is ultimately perceived to be difficult—but grammatical.

Since (1) is a real case of a grammatical and meaningful sentence, we must explain just what makes it so hard to understand. The answer is that none of the usual strategies of SAM work well for this sentence. For one thing, rather than consisting of two separate cases of doer, action, done-to, in that order, as in our previous kissing-frog example *(The princess kissed the frog and the king knighted the frog),* sentence (1) inserts the second proposition *(the horse was raced past the barn)* right in the middle of the first—after its doer, but before its action. Moreover, like sentence (2), it is the kind of sentence that omits a propositional role: *the horse* is omitted from the second proposition, which appears in the surface structure simply as *raced past the barn.* A third problem is that it is a passive sentence, which again reverses the preferred order of doer and done-to *(The horse was raced past the barn,* rather than *Someone raced the horse past the barn).* In addition, the clue word for the passive *(was)* is omitted, and the clue word for the extra proposition *(who)* is also omitted. No wonder that SAM registers "TILT" and fails to comprehend.

According to the inventor of this especially difficult sentence, SAM has gone haywire here primarily because he doggedly uses his favorite strategies even when they make trouble. Thus SAM sets out to comprehend this sentence in his usual fashion. Arriving at the first word, he first seeks a doer, and finds *the horse.* Now falsely assuming that the next word is in the same proposition as *the horse*—because no clue word was found to tell him otherwise—SAM proceeds to seek an action and assumes that the next word *(raced)* is the action. Then he finds a completing phrase (a place-phrase, rather than a done-to, in this case), *past the barn,* and considers that he has finished his job and understood: SAM falsely believes he has heard and understood the active sentence *The horse raced past the barn.*

But now to SAM's horror, the sentence fails to come to an end. He hears (or reads) the extra word *fell,* and can think of nothing to do with it. Therefore SAM registers "TILT," believing that the sentence is ungrammatical and meaningless (Bever, 1970).

As we have just shown, sentence (1) gives the illusion of ungrammaticality and incomprehensibility because of the way SAM works. SAM has a variety of favorite tricks and strategies that work to make sense of almost all meaningful sentences. But the rare grammatical and meaningful sentences that cannot be analyzed by using these tricks are close to impossible for SAM to understand.

Summarizing our discussion of sentence understanding, we have seen that the comprehension machinery in the head (SAM) is very complex and can deal with many difficult sentences (though, to be sure, it occasionally fails). The reconstruction of the underlying meaning of thousands of sentences is carried out daily by all of us in the natural course of conversation, usually without great difficulty and without our even noticing that we are performing these impressive computational feats at all. Thus the facts of comprehension are one important instance of the intricacy of language knowledge that somehow is embodied in the brains of all normal human adults.

Speech Production

So far we have considered how sentences are understood. But language users speak as well as listen. (In fact, many of them seem to listen only rarely.) How do they plan out the words of their sentences? How do they speak?

SPEECH AS AN ORGANIZED PLAN

Presumably, the speaker has some general idea in mind that she wants to express before she starts to talk. She may know that she wants to talk about the weather, or politics, or yesterday's ball game, and so she decides roughly what to say. She now has to extract the right words from her stored lexicon and organize them into a sequence that will properly convey her thought. Modern theorists agree that she does so by formulating a mental (though usually not conscious) plan that directs her utterances. This plan deals with the entire sentence from the first word to the last. What comes at the close of a sentence is generally in mind before the speaker has uttered the first few words, for the overall mental plan contains the end as well as the beginning.

One line of evidence comes from the use of pronouns. In English, pronouns must agree with their antecedents in number and gender. Thus we do not say *I saw John and you saw her too* (*her* is the wrong gender) or *I saw John and you saw them too* (*them* is the wrong number, plural rather than singular). In some cases, the pronoun is uttered before the noun that it stands for. An example is *When he arrived home, John fed the dog.* Here the pronoun *he* occurs before *John.* This means that the speaker already had *John* in mind when she decided on the pronoun *he,* which came three words earlier in the sentence. If she did not, she couldn't have decided on the proper pronoun (after all, she might have said *she* or *they*). This shows that in some ways the sentence was planned as a whole; the noun must have been mentally chosen before the pronoun was, despite the fact that the pronoun was uttered first (Lashley, 1951).

SPEECH ERRORS

How are speech plans formulated? Some important evidence comes from work on speech errors. What comes out of our mouths is not always what we planned to say; bits and pieces of words get scrambled up and interchanged in various "slips of the tongue." These slips can lead to amusing results (though rarely for the person who produced them), as in the case of a nineteenth-century dean of Oxford University, Reverend Spooner, whose many speech errors gave rise to the term *spoonerism* (Potter, 1980). When introducing the queen, who had come to visit Oxford, Dr. Spooner announced her as "our queer old dean" rather than "our dear old queen." When escorting her to dinner, he remarked "Let me sew you to another sheet" instead of "Let me show you to another seat."

Errors of this kind are by no means random. Some are made all the time, but other kinds of errors never occur. The systematic pattern of these errors shows us the ways in which speech plans go wrong. And this in turn gives clues to how speech plans are mentally organized (Fromkin, 1973; Garrett, 1975).

Speech errors often involve a transposition in which parts of morphemes are interchanged as in "*d*ear old *q*ueen" and "*q*ueer old *d*ean." Another example (this too by Dr. Spooner) is *Work is the curse of the drinking classes* in which the interchange is between the morphemes *work* and *drink*. It turns out that such interchanges occur only when the morphemes belong to the open class, whose function is lexical—the many content words such as *queen, dean, run, black,* and so on. No such interchanges are observed between morphemes of the closed class—items such as *a, the, of, -ing,* and so on, whose function is to provide the syntactic structure of the sentence. Consider the speech error *The older men prefer to tend younger women.* Here the two open-class morphemes *prefer* and *tend* are transposed, for the speaker presumably meant to say *The older men tend to prefer younger women.* The closed-class morphemes are not transposed in this way. One never hears errors in which, say, *to* and *the* exchange their position. Thus, *To older men tend the prefer younger women* will never occur even "by mistake." It appears that there is method—even to errors—in natural speech.

In the preceding example, the exchange was between two morphemes that are whole words: *tend* and *prefer*. But transpositions often involve morphemes that are parts of words. Consider *McGovern favors pushing busters,* when what the speaker meant to say was *McGovern favors busting pushers.* Here parts of the word are exchanged (the morphemes *push* and *bust*) while others stay in place (the morphemes *-ing* and *-ers*), so that we end up with *pushing* and *busters.* But note that we have the same distinction between open- and closed-class items that we saw before. *Push* and *bust* belong to the open class and are exchanged. In contrast, the morphemes *-ing,* and *-ers* belong to the closed class and stay put (see Garrett, 1975).

Findings of this sort suggest that the mental plan for uttering a sentence involves at least two steps. An early step is to fashion the syntactic structure of the utterance. The materials for this structure are the closed-class morphemes (*a, the, in, -s, -ing, -ed,* and so on) which are chosen and arranged in sequence. The next step involves the open-class content morphemes. These content morphemes are now inserted into their places within the framework provided by the closed-class items.

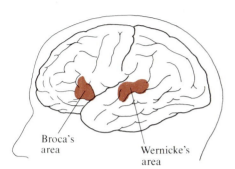

9.18 Language areas of the brain *Certain areas of the cerebral cortex (in most right-handers, in the left hemisphere) are devoted to language functions. Damage to these areas produces various kinds of aphasia. The figure shows the location of two of the most important of these language regions—Broca's area and Wernicke's area. For details, see the accompanying text and Chapter 2.*

SPEECH FAILURES IN APHASIA

Speech errors point to an important distinction between the role of closed- and open-class morphemes. A similar distinction emerges in the catastrophic disturbances of speech that follow brain damage. As we saw in a previous chapter, certain lesions of the brain produce disturbances of speech and comprehension known as ***aphasia*** (see Figure 9.18). In aphasia, the patient can move his mouth and tongue, can see and hear, but is impaired in his ability to speak and/or comprehend speech (see Chapter 2).

Some of these patients suffer from ***Broca's aphasia,*** which is produced by lesions in a region of the brain called Broca's area. These patients generally can speak only with great effort (and some cannot speak at all). One of their major problems is that they tend to omit almost all of the closed-class items. They have less trouble with the open-class content words, many of which they can use quite properly. When asked to describe a picture of a dog chasing a cat, one such patient said: "Dog . . . chase, . . er, cat . . . dog cat." The appropriate content words *(dog, cat, chase)* are there; what's missing is the closed-class items.

The absence of closed-class items in Broca's aphasia has several consequences. One is a serious difficulty in expressing propositional relationships. (Imagine trying to express the logic of *The dog who chased the cat was bitten by the cat's fleas* without the morphemes *-ed, by, -ed, -s,* and so on.) Another consequence is that the patient's speech is extremely slow and full of hesitations. In normal speech, the closed-class items provide a framework into which the open-class items are inserted. This framework seems to provide a kind of mental glue for the open-class items. Without it, the speech plan is seriously disrupted and the open-class items have to be groped for, one by one. Often, even their correct sequencing seems to disintegrate.

Another group of patients suffer from ***Wernicke's aphasia*** (produced by lesions in a region called Wernicke's area). The speech of these patients is fluent and rapid. This is partly because they—unlike Broca's aphasics—have no problem with closed-class items, and they can therefore readily construct the speech plan framework that is built out of these items. Their trouble is with the open-class vocabulary. In this, they are extremely deficient; they utter only a few and very general content words, often without making much sense in doing so. A typical sentence uttered by such a patient is *And then they went and did it with them and they did it and got the supermarket and that all over there.*

These differences between Broca's and Wernicke's aphasics provide further evidence for the different roles that closed- and open-class items play in language. The distinction between these two aspects of the mental lexicon seems to be reflected in a difference in how the two morpheme classes are organized in the brain, so that one can be compromised by a lesion while the other is left intact (Bradley, Garrett, and Zurif, 1979; Marin, Saffron, and Schwartz, 1976).

Relations between Speaking and Comprehending

Up to now, we have emphasized somewhat different aspects of comprehending and speaking. But it is worth noting that the two processes have much in common—which they should, for the same person seems to be equipped to utter just about the same things he can comprehend. One common factor concerns the distinction between open- and closed-class words. We have just discussed the difference in the role these two play in speech production. But the same distinction was already made when we discussed comprehension. We saw that the open-class words were extracted by SAM to recover the propositional roles of doer, action, and done-to. The closed-class words were used differently, to direct quite general procedures that SAM should follow. For example, the word *whom* in one of our example sentences told SAM that he had arrived at a new proposition within the overall sentence. In a similar fashion, SAM seems to use such closed-class words as *a* and *the* as clues to the fact that a noun phrase is about to begin (i.e., we say *a rabbit,* not *rabbit a*).

In sum, in both speech and comprehension the language user's task is to construct and apprehend the propositional content of what he says or hears—what the sentence is about. To convey or understand these ideas, he primarily uses the open-class morphemes. But he can only execute this task successfully and efficiently if he attends to the grammatical organization of the sentence. And this is chiefly carried by the rigid frame built of the closed-class morphemes.

LANGUAGE AS AN INTERPERSONAL HUMAN ENDEAVOR

We have so far given an overview of properties of language knowledge in a single human mind. But there is something bloodless about descriptions of language as the property of an individual. For language is at bottom a social process in which the thoughts of one mind are conveyed into another. To accomplish these social ends, speakers must know not only the phonemes, words, and sentences of their language, but ***principles of conversation*** as well. These pertain to how language is used appropriately under varying circumstances.

Suppose, for example, that one sees a lion in the parlor and wants to tell a companion about this. It is not enough that both parties speak English. One has to estimate the listener's mental state, capacities, motivations, and relations to oneself in order to speak appropriately. If the companion is a sharpshooter with a revolver, one might say:

Quick, shoot! There is a lion in the parlor.

But if the companion is an artist, one might say:

Quick, draw! Lion of a gorgeous shade of ochre in the parlor.

To a biologist, one might say:

Quick, look! Member of the genus Felis leo *in the parlor.*

And to an enemy,

Lovely morning, isn't it? See you later.

Clearly, what one says about a situation is not just a description of that situation, but depends upon one's knowledge, beliefs, and wishes about the listener. To communicate successfully, then, one must build a mental picture of "the other" to whom speech is addressed (Austin, 1962; E. Clark and H. Clark, 1977).

The same problem arises for the listener, of course. To determine the sense of what one has heard, one must make an estimate of the speaker and the circumstances of her utterances. Suppose, for example, someone said, *Can you pass me the salt?* To know how to respond appropriately, one must ask oneself (implicitly, of course), *Does this speaker think my arms are broken?* (in which case the answer should be *Yes, I can* or *No, I can't,* depending on whether one's arms *are* in fact broken). But if one is hale and hearty, the normal supposition would be, *The speaker must know that I can, physically, pass the salt. Therefore she is not asking me whether I* can *pass it, but rather this is a polite way of requesting me* to *pass it.* And now the answer might be, *Sure. Here you are,* accompanied by the action of passing the salt (Searle, 1969).

In sum, the actual speech acts that pass between people are merely hints about the thoughts that are being conveyed. Talking would take just about forever if one literally had to say all, only, and exactly what one meant. Rather, the communicating pair takes the utterance and its context as the basis for making a series of complicated inferences about the meaning and intent of the conversation. A listener who fails to make these inferences is taken as an incompetent at best and a bore at worst. A person who blandly answers *Yes* when you say *Could you tell me the time?* has failed to obey the principles of conversation that make communication possible (Grice, 1968).

LANGUAGE AS A HUMAN CAPACITY

We have considered some of the characteristics and structures of human language, and some of the mechanisms by means of which speakers produce words and sentences and listeners understand them. Many modern investigators believe —as did Descartes—that the ability to form these linguistic structures and to utilize these mechanisms for speaking and understanding are peculiarly human capacities. In line with this view is the fact that the speech areas of the human brain have no parallel in the brains of animals. Further evidence comes from studies of human language development in the child, for the pattern of this development seems to be remarkably uniform and just about universal. If children are reared under more or less normal circumstances, language emerges in all of them much in the same way—first they babble, then they speak in one-word sentences, then in sentences of two-words, then they move on to more complex sentence forms. This also holds for mentally handicapped children. Even children with IQ's below 50, who begin to speak only at age four or five years, show an orderly acquisition of language, constrained by the same structural principles that guide language learning by normals. These handicapped children do not usually progress anywhere as far as normals; but to the extent that they do learn to talk, their speech is much like that of young children of normal intelligence (Lenneberg, 1967; Lackner, 1976; Fowler, 1986; for more details on language development, see Chapter 15).

Such results suggest that language is a heavily pre-programmed skill that depends on our human biological endowment. What happens when this endowment is no longer human? To answer this question, we will look at attempts to teach language to our closest animal relative, the chimpanzee.

9.19 Chimpanzees signing (A) Washoe making the sign for "bird." (Courtesy Roger Fouts) (B) Nim, a young chimpanzee studied by another research group, making the sign for "hug." (Terrace, 1979; photograph courtesy Herbert Terrace)

Language in Chimpanzees

A number of early studies asked whether chimpanzees could learn to speak. Two investigators raised a young chimpanzee, Viki, in their home and patiently tried to get her to utter human sounds, initially manipulating her lips to produce *Mama.* Their efforts failed. After six years of such heroic labors, Viki's total speech output consisted of only three words: *Mama, Papa,* and *cup* (Hayes, 1952).

Such results show that chimpanzees can't talk, but this doesn't necessarily mean they are unable to acquire language. Several investigators reasoned that Viki's failure was a mere consequence of her inability to articulate human speech sounds. To overcome this obstacle, they employed various visual languages. Some were artificial visual systems based on colored plastic chips or signs on a computer screen (Premack, 1976; Rumbaugh, 1977). Other studies adapted items from American Sign Language, or ASL, a manual language used by deaf persons (Gardner and Gardner, 1969, 1975, 1978; Terrace et al., 1979; see Chapter 15 for a discussion of sign language). While the interpretation of these studies is a matter of controversy, there is no doubt that chimpanzees taught by these visual means give a much better account of themselves than Viki (see Figure 9.19).

VOCABULARY

Chimpanzees can learn a substantial number of visual "words," whether these are ASL signs or artificial tokens. Consider Washoe, a chimpanzee introduced to signs at eleven months of age by Allen and Beatrice Gardner. Washoe was raised in an environment not too different from that of a human child, with scheduled meals and naps, baths, and diapers. She was taught some ASL signs by having her hands physically molded into the desired position; others were acquired by imitation (Fouts, 1972). After four years, she had learned about 130 signs, including signs for objects *(banana, hand),* actions *(bite, tickle),* and action modifiers *(enough, more).* Although the rate of the chimpanzee's learning cannot compare to the accomplishments of a human child who—without molding the lips or other formal teaching and drilling sessions—acquires a vocabulary of about 3,000 words in the first four years of life, Washoe's accomplishments are greater than most of us would have expected from a "dumb" animal.

PROPOSITIONAL THOUGHT

As we have seen, human language is more than a disjointed collection of words. It expresses propositional meaning such as the relation among doer, action, and done-to. Are chimpanzees capable of any such propositional thought? We know that they have mental representations of various objects and events in the world, for as we just saw, they can be taught words for them. But do they have anything like a notion of this-does-something-to-that?

One line of evidence comes from David Premack's (1976) studies on the concept of causation in chimpanzees. Premack showed his animals pairs of objects. In each pair the second object was the same as the first but had undergone some change. One pair consisted of a whole apple and an apple that was cut in pieces;

A

B

9.20   A test for propositional thought in chimpanzees   (A) A chimpanzee is shown a whole apple and two halves of an apple. Its task is to place one of three alternatives between them: a pencil, a bowl of water, or a knife. (B) The animal chooses the knife, the instrument which produced the change from the uncut to the cut state. In other trials, when the animals were shown a blank piece of paper and a scribbled-upon piece of paper, they would generally put the pencil in the middle. When shown a dry sponge and a wet sponge, they chose the bowl of water. (Premack, 1976; photographs courtesy David Premack)

another pair was a dry towel and a wet towel; a third was an unmarked piece of paper and a piece of paper covered with pencil marks. The chimpanzee's task was to place one of several alternatives between the objects—a knife, a bowl of water, or a pencil. The question was whether the animals would choose the item that caused the change (see Figure 9.20). Premack's star pupil, Sarah, performed correctly on 77 percent of the trials, far more than would be expected by chance. Perhaps these animals have some primitive notions of the relation between certain objects, acts, and outcomes—knives cut up things, water wets them, and pencils mark them. To the extent that the apes have these concepts, they have the germs of propositional thought.

SYNTAX

We have shown that human beings organize their thoughts into complex, hierarchically organized sentences in order to speak and understand; this speech is characterized in terms of a set of abstract structural principles. Can chimpanzees do anything of this sort? Can they organize their signs for *Mama, tickle,* and *Washoe* so as to say either *Mama tickles Washoe* or *Washoe tickles Mama?* The Gardners believe that Washoe has some such ability. As evidence, they refer to apparently novel sequences of signs produced by Washoe on her own. For instance, she once signed *listen eat* on hearing an alarm clock that signals mealtime, and she signed *water bird* upon seeing a duck.

A number of critics feel that such observations prove little or nothing. They are anecdotes that can be interpreted in several ways. Take the sequence *water bird.* On the face of it, its use seems like a remarkable achievement—a chimpanzoid equivalent of a compound noun that presumably means something like *bird that lives in water.* But is this interpretation justified? Or did Washoe merely produce an accidental succession of two signs: *water* (perhaps water was seen just before) and *bird* (because of the duck)? It is hard to believe that she really understood the significance of the order (in English) in which the two words are uttered: a *water-bird* is a bird that lives in water, but *bird-water* is water for a bird. Since all we have is an anecdote, we cannot be sure.

There are other confusing issues as well. Washoe and other signing chimpanzees often produce repetitive sequences such as *me banana you banana me you give.* According to some critics, several investigators eliminate such repetitions from their reports of what the animals "say," much as a court stenographer ignores coughs and hmm's when taking a verbatim report. If so, the result can be misleading. For one thing, this sort of random repetition is not at all characteristic of early childhood speech. More important, eliminating the repetitions may create an unjustified impression of meaningfulness. If our example sequence is rendered as, say, *me banana you give,* the result makes a bit more sense (it might mean *You give me a banana*). But is this sense the chimpanzee's, or is it the experimenter's? (see Seidenberg and Pettito, 1979; and for a strenuous rebuttal, see Van Cantfort, 1982).

Current evidence, then, is that chimpanzees can learn words and show some propositional thought. But there is little satisfactory evidence that they can sequence their words into a syntactic structure to express these propositions, or that they can understand these structures if they are signed to the animal. Moreover, even if the chimpanzees can deal with simple two- and three-word sequences, there is no evidence at all of hierarchical structure at many levels of complexity—phonemes, morphemes, phrases, sentences. By now, it ought to be clear to the reader that these levels of organization are not just frills or niceties in the human use of language. The comprehension of speech—whether dogs chase cats or vice versa, for example—depends crucially on the apprehension of the syntactic structures, which may be complex indeed. And as even the speech errors of normals—and Broca's aphasics—have shown us, the process of producing a meaningful sentence to convey one's ideas is highly organized, delicate, and intricately fashioned; if this process breaks down, it is difficult or impossible for humans to say things and mean things at all. Thus, since chimpanzees lack the ability to acquire the organizing principles that make communication by language possible, they cannot be said to be "linguistic beasts."

To sum up, language learning and use seem to be capacities that humans are naturally equipped for. Chimpanzees' abilities in this regard are surely greater than that of any other nonhuman animal, but they are titanically less than our own. The chimpanzees' small successes (mainly, learning a stock of vocabulary items) make sense on the assumption that language is a biologically pre-programmed activity, for it should not be too surprising that the animal biologically closest to us shows some rudiments of this capacity. Whether these rudiments are enough to warrant the title *language* of course depends on one's definition of the term. We can choose to say that trained chimpanzees use language. But in doing so, we have changed the technical meaning of the term so as to exclude from consideration the usual learning, speech, and comprehension machinery. Worse, we have even changed the ordinary, common-sense meaning of the term *language*. For one thing is certain: If any of our children learned or used language the way Washoe or Sarah does, we would be terror-stricken and rush them to the nearest neurologist.

In this chapter, we have looked at what language is, and how it is used by humans to convey their thoughts to one another. However much we may differ in our cultural background and in our individual interests, talents, and thoughtfulness, we are all endowed with the capacity to learn and use a human language. And while the linguistic accomplishments of college-educated chimpanzees are remarkable, they are remarkable only for chimpanzees. For the evidence suggests that even the most talented and best-trained chimpanzees do not use language as we do—naturally, fluently, and in accordance with structural principles that allow us to form and understand an infinite number of sentences.

No one has put this crucial distinction between man and the animals more eloquently than Descartes who, three centuries ago, directed philosophers' attention to the topic of human language:

> Now all men, the most stupid and the most foolish, those even who are deprived of the organs of speech, make use of signs, whereas the brutes never do anything of the kind; which may be taken for the true distinction between man and brute (Descartes, 1649; in Eaton, 1927).

SUMMARY

1. Among the most important properties of language are that it is *creative* and highly *organized*. The creative aspect of language allows us to utter and understand an unlimited

SUMMARY

number of sentences we have never heard before. This potential infinity is produced by organizing principles of sound, meaning, and grammar which permit ever-new sentences to be spoken and understood. These are *structural* principles that every speaker of a language necessarily obeys. These must be distinguished from so-called *prescriptive rules* that describe how certain authorities say people *ought* to speak rather than how they *do* speak.

2. Every language is organized as a hierarchy of structures, going from *sentence,* down to *phrases,* to *words,* to *morphemes,* with *phonemes* at the bottom level. Each level of the hierarchy is governed by its own system of principles, such as those that specify which phonemes can and cannot go together in a given language.

3. The field of *semantics* is concerned with the meaning of words. There is wide agreement on what meaning is not: It is not the same as *reference* and it is not a *mental image.* Two current approaches are the *definitional theory* and the *prototype theory.* While neither seems to be an adequate description of word meaning when taken alone, the combination of the two looks promising.

4. There is a distinction between *closed-class* morphemes (such as *a, the,* and *-ed*) and *open-class* morphemes (such as *house, red,* and *eat*). The first are primarily relevant to syntactic organization, the second to lexical meaning. Clues to the organization of the *mental lexicon* come from *lexical access studies.* These suggest that the characteristics according to which words are stored in the lexicon include sound, grammatical category, similarity of meaning, and frequency of use.

5. *Syntax* is a system for organizing words and phrases into sentences. Sentences are mentally represented in two different ways. One is the *surface phrase structure,* the sequence of phrases as it is actually spoken or read. The second is the *underlying phrase structure,* which more directly pertains to sentence meaning. A convenient way to describe both the surface and the underlying phrase structures is by means of *tree diagrams.*

6. Underlying phrase structure has two aspects: *proposition* and *attitude.* Many sentences that differ greatly in their surface structure, such as sentences in *active* and *passive* form, have very similar underlying structures, sharing the same proposition and differing only in the speaker's attitude to it. A number of studies indicate that listeners attend to and remember the underlying structure rather than its surface manifestation.

7. The difference between surface and underlying structure is highlighted by various relationships between surface sentences. Some sentences are *paraphrases:* They are essentially the same in meaning (in underlying structure) but have different surface structures. Other sentences exhibit *ambiguity:* They consist of one surface structure that can go back to two different underlying structures.

8. The meaning of propositions can be described as a set of relationships exhibited in their underlying phrase structure. In English, the *doer* is described by the first noun phrase in the underlying structure, the *action* by the verb, and the *done-to* by the noun phrase that is contained in the verb phrase.

9. The listener's task in comprehension is to reconstruct the underlying structure from clues in the surface structure. To accomplish this, listeners utilize various strategies, including a left-to-right analyzing procedure in which it is initially assumed that each sentence contains a simple proposition that consists of a noun phrase (the doer), then a verb (the action), usually followed by another noun phrase (the done-to), in that order. This strategy leads to faster comprehension for active than for passive sentences.

10. Complex sentences contain more than one proposition. In many such sentences, one or more propositions are deformed and hidden in the surface structure. To comprehend complex sentences, the listener employs further strategies—she looks for certain clue words such as *and* or *who,* and tries to reconstruct missing propositional roles. In the absence of closed-class clues, comprehension is more difficult. When all of the usual sentence

333

comprehension strategies are inappropriate for a particular sentence, comprehension is rarely achieved.

11. *Speech production* is often studied by examining *speech errors.* These suggest that the process begins with the construction of a syntactic framework built out of closed-class morphemes. After this, open-class morphemes are chosen and inserted. Studies of *aphasia* suggest a similar conclusion. Patient's with *Broca's aphasia* have considerable difficulty with closed-class items, while those with *Wernicke's aphasia* have difficulty with the open-class items.

12. In addition to the procedures for forming and combining language sounds, morphemes, and words, there are *principles* of conversation that govern the way in which language is used as a vehicle to convey the thoughts of one mind to that of another.

13. There have been several attempts to teach language to chimpanzees. The techniques include the use of a modified form of sign language and several artificial visual systems. The results suggest that chimpanzees can acquire a respectable vocabulary and are capable of some rudiments of propositional thought. There is as yet no evidence, however, that they can learn syntactic principles. To this extent, the results are in line with the view that language is characteristic of humans only.

PART III

Social Behavior

In the preceding chapters, we have asked what organisms do, what they want, and what they know. But thus far we have raised these questions in a somewhat limited context, for we have considered the organism as an isolated individual, abstracted from the social world in which it lives. For some psychological questions this approach may be perfectly valid. Robinson Crusoe's visual system was surely no different on his lonely island than back home in London. But many other aspects of behavior are impossible to describe by considering a single organism alone, without reference to its fellows. Consider a male parrot feeding a female in a courtship ritual, a monkey mother clasping her infant closer at a stranger's approach, two stags locking antlers during the rutting season, or the front runner of a band of wild hunting dogs cutting off a fleeing zebra's escape— all of these activities are social by definition. Courtship, sex, parental care, competition, and cooperation are not merely actions. They are interactions in which each participant's behavior is affected by the behavior of the others.

Social interactions are vital in the lives of most animals; after all, successful reproduction (that is, sex and parental care) is what species survival is all about. In humans, the role of social factors is even more powerful than in animals, for our world is fashioned not only by our contemporaries but by generations preceding whose vast cultural heritage structures the very fabric of our lives. Most of our motives are social for they concern other people—the desire to be loved, to be accepted, to be esteemed, perhaps to excel, and in some cases, unhappily, to inflict pain and hurt. The all-importance of social factors extends even to motives that, on the face of it, seem to involve only the isolated organism, motives such as hunger, thirst, and temperature maintenance. These motives as such may pertain primarily to the individual, but the ways in which they are satisfied are enormously affected by the social context in which we live. We eat food that is raised by a complex agricultural technology based on millennia of human discovery, and we eat it, delicately, with knife and fork, according to the etiquette of a long-dead king. Even the isolated Robinson Crusoe was no exception. In Defoe's tale, Crusoe's survival depended upon a few items of valuable debris he managed to salvage from his sunken ship. Thus his existence was not truly solitary; he was still bound to a world of others—by a few nails, a hammer, and a plank or two. Robinson Crusoe was on an island, but even he was not an island entire to itself.

In the following chapters we will discuss these social factors in some detail, as they bear on our actions, motives, thoughts, and knowledge.

CHAPTER 10

The Biological Basis of Social Behavior

A classic question posed by philosophers is, "What is the basic social nature of man?" Are greed, competition, and hate (or, for that matter, charity, cooperation, and love) unalterable components of the human makeup, or can they be instilled or nullified by proper training? To answer these questions, we will have to consider not just humankind but some of its animal cousins as well.

THE SOCIAL NATURE OF HUMANS AND ANIMALS

Are human beings so built that social interaction is an intrinsic part of their makeup? Or are they essentially solitary creatures who turn to others only because they need them for their own selfish purposes? The English social philosopher Thomas Hobbes (1588–1679) argued for the second of these alternatives. In his view, man is a self-centered brute who, left to his own devices, will seek his own gain regardless of the cost to others. Except for the civilizing constraints imposed by society, men would inevitably be in an eternal "war of all against all." According to Hobbes, this frightening "state of nature" is approximated during times of anarchy and civil war. These were conditions Hobbes knew all too well, for he lived during a time of violent upheavals in England when Stuart royalists battled Cromwell's Puritans, when commoners beheaded their king in a public square, and when pillage, burning, and looting were commonplace. In such a state of nature, man's life is a sorry lot. There are "no Arts; no Letters; no Society; and which is worst of all, continuall fear, and danger of violent death; And the life

Thomas Hobbes *(After a painting by William Dobson; courtesy The Granger Collection)*

335

of man solitary, poore, nasty, brutish, and short" (Hobbes, 1651, p. 186). Hobbes argued that under the circumstances, men had no choice but to protect themselves against their own ugly natures. They did so by entering into a "social contract" to form a collective commonwealth, the State.

Hobbes's psychological starting points are simple enough: Man is by nature asocial and destructively rapacious. Society is a means to chain the brute within. Only when curbed by social fetters does man go beyond his animal nature, does he become truly human. Given this position, the various social motives that bind us to others (that is, love, loyalty) presumably are imposed through culture and convention. They are learned, for they could not possibly be part of our intrinsic makeup.

Natural Selection and Evolution: Charles Darwin

During the nineteenth century, Hobbes's doctrine of inherent human aggression and depravity was garbed in the mantle of science. The Industrial Revolution seemed to give ample proof that life is indeed a Hobbesian battle of each against all, whether in the marketplace, in the sweatshops, or in the far-off colonies. Ruthless competition among men was regarded as just one facet of a more general struggle for existence that is waged among all living things. This harsh view of nature had gained great impetus at the start of the nineteenth century when Thomas Malthus announced his famous law of population growth. According to Malthus, human and animal populations grow by geometrical progression (for example, 1, 2, 4, 8, 16, . . .) while the food supply grows arithmetically (for example, 1, 2, 3, 4, 5, . . .). As a result, there is inevitable scarcity and a continual battle for survival.

When Charles Darwin (1809–1882) read Malthus's essay, he finally found the explanatory principle he had been seeking to account for the evolution of living things. He, as others before him, believed that all present-day plants, animals, and even humans, were descended from prior forms. The evidence came from various sources, such as fossil records that showed the gradual transformation from long-extinct species to those now living. But what had produced these changes? Within each species there are individual variations; some horses are faster, others are slower. Many of these variations are part of the animal's hereditary makeup and thus are bequeathed to its descendants. But will an individual animal have descendants? That depends on how it fares in the struggle for existence. As a matter of fact, most organisms don't live long enough to reproduce. Only a few seedlings grow up to be trees; only a few tadpoles achieve froghood. But certain characteristics may make survival a bit more likely. The faster horse is more likely to escape predatory cats than its slower fellow, and it is thus more likely to leave offspring. This process of *natural selection* does not guarantee survival and reproduction; it only increases their likelihood. In consequence, evolutionary change is very gradual and proceeds over eons (Darwin, 1872a).

Charles Darwin   *(Courtesy The American Museum of Natural History)*

INHERITED PREDISPOSITIONS TO BEHAVIOR

The inherited characteristics that increase the chance for biological survival (that is, reproduction) may concern bodily structures, such as the horse's hooves. But Darwin and his successors pointed out that natural selection may also involve behavior. Squirrels bury nuts and beavers construct dams; these behavior patterns are characteristic of the species and depend on the animals' **genes,** the basic units of heredity. Whether these genes are selected for or not depends upon the **adaptive value** (that is, the biological survival value) of the behavior they give rise to. A squirrel who has a genetic predisposition to bury nuts in autumn is presumably more likely to survive the winter than one who doesn't. As a result, it is more likely to have offspring who will inherit the nut-burying gene (or genes). The end product is an increase in the number of nut-burying squirrels.

Granted that behavior can be shaped by evolution, what kind of behavior is most likely to evolve? And, most important to us, what kind of built-in predispositions are most likely to characterize humankind? Many nineteenth-century thinkers answered in Hobbesian terms. They reasoned that man is an animal and that in the bitter struggle for existence all animals are shameless egoists by sheer necessity. At bottom, they are all solitary and selfish, and man is no exception. To the extent that humans act sociably and on occasion even unselfishly—mating, rearing children, living and working with others—they have learned to do so in order to satisfy some self-centered motive such as lust or hunger.

On the face of it, this Hobbesian view seems to fit evolutionary doctrine. But on closer examination, Darwinian theory does not imply anything of the sort. It holds that there is "survival of the fittest," but "fittest" only means most likely to survive and to have offspring; it says nothing about being solitary or selfish. Darwin himself supposed that certain predispositions toward cooperation might well be adaptive and would thus be selected for. We now know that something of this sort is true, for animals as well as human beings. As we shall see, there is considerable evidence that, Hobbes to the contrary, humans and animals are by nature social rather than asocial and that much of their social behavior grows out of natively given predispositions rather than running counter to them.

Konrad Lorenz   *(Photograph by Nina Leen)*

Niko Tinbergen   *(Photograph by Nina Leen)*

Instinctive Social Patterns and Ethology

Most systematic studies of built-in social behavior have been conducted within the domain of **ethology,** a branch of biology that studies animal behavior under natural conditions. Led by the Europeans Konrad Lorenz and Niko Tinbergen, both Nobel Prize winners, ethologists have analyzed many behavior patterns that are characteristic of a particular species and seem to be primarily built-in or instinctive. Many of these instinctive, **species-specific** behavior patterns are social; they dictate the way in which creatures interact with others of their own kind. Some involve a positive bond between certain members of the same species— courtship, copulation, care of the young. Others concern reactions of antagonism and strife—the struggle for social dominance, competition for a mate, and dispute over territory.

SPECIES-SPECIFIC BEHAVIOR: A CASE STUDY

An example of species-specific social patterns is provided by the three-spined stickleback, an innocuous little fish that is common in North European fresh waters. In early spring, both sexes become ready to mate. But how will they get together and meet at the right time? This synchronization is achieved by an intricately tuned system of built-in reactions. Each member of the pair acts in turn,

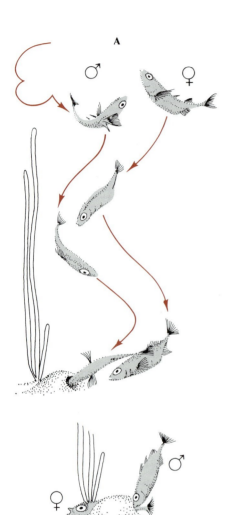

10.1   The mating ritual of the three-spined stickleback   (A) The figure illustrates the steps in the male and female stickleback's pre-programmed mating pattern. The female appears, which triggers the male's zigzag dance, which leads her to swim toward him, and so on until fertilization. Each step in this reaction chain is a fixed-action pattern which serves as a releasing stimulus for a fixed-action pattern by the mate. (After Tinbergen, 1951) (B) Three-spined stickleback. (Courtesy Animals Animals/Oxford Scientific Films)

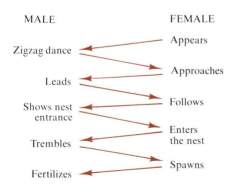

and its action provides the stimulus for the other to take the next step in the sequence.

The mating cycle begins as the male stickleback stakes out a territory for himself from which he chases all intruders. He then builds a small nest at the water bottom—a small depression in the sand covered with a bridge of weeds. His belly now turns bright red, an unmistakable advertisement: "Mature male, ready and anxious to mate." Sooner or later, a female stickleback will enter his territory. As she does, she displays her egg-swollen abdomen by adopting a head-up posture. This triggers the male's next response, a back-and-forth, zigzag dance which prompts her to swim toward him. This stimulus makes the male turn round and swim toward the nest. She now follows and this prompts him to poke his head into the nest opening. Having "shown" her the nest, he withdraws, and she enters it with her entire body. At this point, the male starts to quiver and prods her rhythmically at her tail base. This is her stimulus to lay the eggs, after which she quickly leaves the nest. The male now enters, releases his sperm and thus fertilizes the eggs (Figure 10.1).

FIXED-ACTION PATTERNS

Stereotyped, species-specific movements such as the female stickleback's head-up posture or the male's zigzag dance are called *fixed-action patterns.* According to ethologists, these fixed-action patterns are just as much a part of the animal's genetic makeup as are its bodily structures.

Ethologists believe that fixed-action patterns are largely elicited by genetically pre-programmed *releasing stimuli.* For example, newly hatched herring gull chicks beg for food by pecking at the tips of their parents' beaks. The parent will then regurgitate some food from its crop and feed it to the young. But what is the critical stimulus that elicits the begging response? To answer the question, Tinbergen offered newly hatched gull chicks various cardboard models of gull heads and observed which of these they pecked at the most. The most successful model was one that was long and thin and had a red patch at its tip. These are the very characteristics of an adult herring gull's beak, but the newly hatched chicks had never encountered a parent's beak previously. Evolution has evidently done a good job in pre-programming the chick to respond to certain critical stimulus features so as to recognize the parent's beak at first sight.

Among the most important of all releasing stimuli are those which are produced by an animal's own behavior. Such response-produced stimuli are called *displays.* They produce an appropriate reaction in another animal of the same species and are thus the basis of a primitive, built-in communication system. The stickleback's zigzag dance is an example of such a display, as is the gull chick's begging peck. One elicits an approach movement in the egg-carrying female; the other leads to feeding by the parent (Tinbergen, 1951).

THE BIOLOGICAL SOURCES OF AGGRESSION

The preceding discussion provided a general introduction to built-in social patterns. The stickleback's mating behavior shows many facets of its social nature: the aggression between competitors, the attraction between male and female, the provision for future generations. We will begin our examination of these social processes by considering the biological basis of aggression.

Human aggression is clearly a fact. The question is, "What are its causes?" Some presumably are events in the immediate present, such as threats and frustrations that provoke anger and hostility. Others stem from the individual's own past and prior learning. Our present concern is with sources that lie in our inherent makeup, the biological roots of aggression that derive from our evolutionary past. To uncover these, we have to study animals as well as humans, for the biological sources of human aggression are often obscured by cultural factors and tradition.

Conflict between Species: Predation and Defense

Most psychobiologists restrict use of the term *aggression* to conflict between members of the same species. When an owl kills a mouse, it has slaughtered for food rather than murdered in hatred. As Lorenz points out, the predator about to pounce upon his prey does not look angry; the dog who is on the verge of catching a rabbit never growls nor does it have its ears laid back (Lorenz, 1966). Neurological evidence leads to a similar conclusion. Rat-stalking (predatory attack) and arched-back hissing (aggression or self-defense) are elicited by the stimulation of two different areas of a cat's hypothalamus (Wasman and Flynn, 1962). Predatory attack is an outgrowth of the hunger motive and not of aggression; the hypothalamic site whose stimulation gives rise to rat-stalking also elicits eating (Hutchinson and Renfrew, 1966).

Somewhat closer to true aggression is the counterattack lodged by a prey animal against a predatory enemy. Flocks of birds sometimes *mob* an intruding cat or hawk. A colony of lovebird parrots will fly upon a would-be attacker in a body, flapping their wings furiously and uttering loud, shrill squeaks. In the face of this commotion, the predator often withdraws to look for a less troublesome meal (Dilger, 1962). Defense reactions may also occur when a hunted animal is finally

10.2 Aggressive fighting *Male rats generally fight in fairly stereotyped ways, including a "boxing position" (A) that often escalates into a leaping, biting attack (B). (From Barnett, 1963)*

cut off from retreat. Even normally reticent creatures may then become desperate fighters, as in the case of the proverbial cornered rat.

Aside from these defense behaviors, aggression is the exception rather than the rule among members of different species. In an aquarium filled with tropical fish, like attacks like but leaves unlike alone. Vicious fights between unrelated species such as tigers and pythons have been photographed for wildlife films, but they are rare; the animals involved are either half-starved or they are goaded into the unnatural contest by having their escape route blocked (Lorenz, 1966).

Conflict between Like and Like

There is probably no group among the animal kingdom that has foresworn aggression altogether; fighting has been observed in virtually all species. Fish chase and nip each other; lizards lunge and push; birds attack with wing, beak, and claw; sheep and cows butt heads; deer lock antlers; rats adopt a boxing stance and eye each other warily, until one finally pounces upon the other and begins a furious wrestling match, with much kicking and leaping and occasionally serious bites (Figure 10.2).

Among vertebrates, the male is generally the more aggressive sex. In some mammals, this difference in combativeness is apparent even in childhood play. Young male rhesus monkeys, for instance, engage in more vigorous rough-and-tumble tusslings than do their sisters (Harlow, 1962). A related result concerns the effect of **testosterone,** a male sex hormone. High testosterone levels in the bloodstream accompany increased aggressiveness in males; the reverse holds for decreased levels. This generalization seems to hold over a wide range of species including fish, lizards, turtles, birds, rats and mice, monkeys, and human males (Davis, 1964).

SECURING RESOURCES

What do animals fight about? Their struggles are about scarce **resources**—something valuable in their world that is in short supply. Such a resource may be a food source or a water hole; very often it is a mate. To secure a modicum of such resources many animals stake out a claim to a particular region which they will then defend as their exclusive preserve, their private **territory.**

We have already encountered one example of this territorial pattern in the male stickleback, who selects a few square feet which he then guards jealously against all other stickleback males. Another example is provided by male songbirds. In the spring, they endlessly patrol their little empires and furiously repel all male intruders who violate their borders. Contrary to the poet's fancy, the male bird who bursts into full-throated song is not giving vent to inexpressible joy, pouring out his "full heart in profuse strains of unpremeditated art." His message is more prosaic. It is a warning to male trespassers and an invitation to unattached females: "Have territory, will share."

A biological benefit of territoriality is that it secures an adequate supply of resources for the next generation. The stickleback male who chases his rivals away will probably leave more offspring than the one who doesn't, for his progeny will have a better start in life. Once his claim is staked out he can entice the female, offering his territory as a kind of dowry.

LIMITING AGGRESSION

A certain amount of aggression may be biologically adaptive. For example, a more aggressive songbird will conquer a larger or more desirable territory and bequeath this advantage to his progeny. As a result, we would expect some selection for aggressiveness. But this only holds up to a point. Aggressiveness may confer some benefits, but it also has its costs. Combat is dangerous and can lead to death or serious injury. In addition, it distracts the animal from other vital pursuits. The male who is continually fighting with his sexual rivals will have little time (let alone energy) left to mate with the female even after his competitors have fled. Under the circumstances, natural selection strikes a compromise; there is aggression, but it is kept firmly in hand. Many animals have evolved built-in codes for conflict that set limits to the violence they do to their own kind.

Territoriality One means of minimizing actual combat is territoriality. While this is an aspect of aggression, it also serves to hold it in bounds. Good fences make good neighbors, at least in the sense that they keep the antagonists out of each other's hair (or fins or feathers).

The mechanism whereby territoriality limits combat is rather simple. Once a territory is established, its owner has a kind of home-court advantage in further disputes. On his home ground, he is courageous; if he ventures beyond it, he becomes timid and is readily repulsed. As a result, there are few actual conflicts other than occasional border skirmishes. This phenomenon is utilized by circus trainers who make sure that they are the first to enter the training ring; the animals come in later. As a result, the ring becomes the trainer's territory and even the big cats are more readily cowed (Hediger, 1968).

Bluffs and ritual fighting The limitation on violence appears in other ways as well. Many conflicts are settled by blustering diplomacy before they erupt into actual war. For example, male chimpanzees try to intimidate each other by staring, raising an arm, shaking some branches, or uttering fearsome shouts. This approach is found throughout the entire animal kingdom: Whenever possible, try to get your way by threat and bluff rather than by actual fighting. This holds even

Aggressive encounter between bristle worms (Photograph by Lennart Nilsson)

A

B

10.3   Threat displays   *(A) Some species threaten by making themselves appear larger and more impressive, as when lizards expand a throat skin fold. (Courtesy Animals Animals/J. H. Robinson) (B) Other species threaten by displaying their weapons, as when baboons bare their teeth. (Photograph by Irven DeVore/Anthro-Photo)*

10.4   Ritualized fighting   *Two South African wildebeest males in a harmless ritualized dual along an invisible but clearly defined mutual border between their territories. (Photographs by Lennard Lee Rue III, Photo Researchers)*

for creatures as large as elephants or as fierce as tigers. Both these and other species have **threat displays,** which often represent a compromise between an expression of fierce vehemence and one of submission (Figure 10.3).

Of course, fighting sometimes occurs in spite of these mechanisms. When it does, it is often conducted in a ritualized manner, as though it were some kind of tournament with rigid rules of fair play. The combatants behave as if under an internal compulsion not to inflict serious damage (Figure 10.4). For example, male

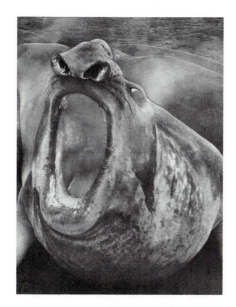

Bull seal threatens in order to defend his harem against an intruding male (Photograph by George Holton, Photo Researchers)

antelopes rarely gore each other with their horns, only engaging in head-pushing contests. This is not because they can't use their horns as weapons: when attacked by lions, they certainly do.

Wolves have an even more complex dueling code. They snap and bite at each other until one "admits defeat" by adopting a special submissive posture, such as begging like a puppy or rolling on his back (Figure 10.5). This is an ***appeasement signal*** that is functionally equivalent to our white flag of surrender. Unlike some human warriors, the victorious wolf is without rancor. He generally accepts the loser's submission, and all fighting stops. According to Lorenz, the appeasement signal is a built-in device that is very adaptive in an animal whose natural weapons are so lethal that the species might very well kill itself off if it didn't have some sort of arms control (Lorenz, 1966).

Dominance hierarchies Potential combatants can be kept at peace by still subtler means. Animals that live in groups often develop a fairly stable social order based on ***dominance hierarchies*** in which struggle is kept at a minimum. This is especially clear among primates such as baboons. The dominant individual has usually achieved his status in one or more prior aggressive encounters, after which his status is settled and he no longer has to confirm it, at least for a while. Lower-ranking baboons generally step aside to let the "alpha-male" pass, and they nervously scatter if he merely stares at them. The result is lessened aggression—everyone "knows his place." Whatever fighting occurs is mainly among the younger males who have yet to determine who outranks whom (Rowell, 1966).

Rank has considerable privileges. The alpha-male has first choice of sleeping site, enjoys easier access to food, and has priority in mating (see Figure 10.6). Such perquisites undoubtedly make life more pleasant for the alpha than for his less fortunate fellows. But these personal benefits are relatively minor compared to the long-run evolutionary consequences of high rank, for in terms of genetic survival, the higher-ranked animal is more "fit." Since he has much greater access to the females, he will presumably leave more offspring (e.g., Seyfarth, 1978).

10.5 Appeasement signals in wolves *Wolves adopt submissive postures by begging like a puppy or rolling on their back. (Courtesy I. Eibl-Eibesfeldt)*

10.6 Dominance hierarchies *The dominant male baboon with a harem of females and young. (Courtesy of Bruce Coleman)*

In the early days of ethology, the primary emphasis was on dominance relations among male primates. To be sure, their aggressive encounters were quite obvious as they fought and strutted and bellowed. Many authors took this as evidence that the social order among most primates (and by implication, our own) was ultimately based on the political struggles among males. But more recent work shows that this conclusion is off the mark. In many primate societies, females compete no less than males and develop hierarchies that in some species are more permanent than those of males. Moreover, female rank has important long-term consequences, for mothers tend to bequeath their social rank to both sons and daughters (Hrdy and Williams, 1983).

TERRITORIALITY IN HUMANS

Is any of this relevant to human behavior? At least on the surface there are parallels which have led some writers to suppose that concepts such as territoriality, dominance hierarchy, and the like, apply to humans as well as to animals. There are certainly some aspects of human behavior that resemble territoriality. Even within the home, different members of a family have their private preserves—their own rooms or corners, their places at the dinner table, and so on. Other territorial claims are more temporary, such as a seat in a railroad car, whose possession we mark with a coat, a book, or a briefcase if we have to leave for a while.

A related phenomenon is *personal space,* the physical region all around us whose intrusion we guard against. On many New York subways, passengers sit on long benches. Except during rush hour, they will carefully choose their seats so as to leave the greatest possible distance between themselves and their nearest neighbor (Figure 10.7).

In one study, personal space was deliberately violated. Experimenters went to a

10.7 Personal space (A) Relatively even spacing in herring gulls. (Courtesy Animals Animals/Leonard Lee Rue III) (B) A number of ethologists believe that the maintenance of personal space in humans is a related phenomenon. (Photograph by Wallace Litwin)

A

B

library and casually sat next to a person studying there, even though a more distant chair was available. After some fidgeting, the victim tried to move away. If this was impossible, books and rulers were neatly arranged so as to create a physical boundary (Felipe and Sommer, 1966). A desire to maintain some minimum personal space is probably nearly universal, but the physical dimensions seem to depend upon the particular culture. In North America, acquaintances stand about two or three feet apart during a conversation; if one moves closer, the other feels crowded or pushed into an unwanted intimacy. For Latin Americans, the acceptable distance is said to be much less. Under the circumstances, misunderstanding is almost inevitable. The North American regards the Latin American as overly intrusive; the Latin American in turn feels that the North American is unfriendly and cold (Hall, 1959).

Interestingly enough, men and women seem to have a somewhat different definition of personal space. Evidence came from another study using the library intrusion technique. The intruders could be either male or female. Sometimes they sat down face-to-face with the victim. If so, the male victims often felt crowded and defended their privacy with barriers of books and notes. In contrast, women were relatively unconcerned with face-to-face intrusions. The situation was reversed when the intruder sat down at the side of the victim. Now the men were relatively unaffected, but the women felt uncomfortable and often erected a physical barrier. It appears that, at least in our culture, men tend to define their personal space as the region directly in front of them, while women are more likely to regard it as the zone adjacent to them (Fisher and Byrne, 1975).

How seriously should we take such parallels between humans and animals? There is no doubt that many people—though not all—care deeply about private ownership, whether of things, of real estate, or more subtle private preserves. The question is whether this concern stems from the same evolutionary roots as does the territoriality of the songbird, whether humans really respond to a built-in "territorial imperative" that, according to some writers, is part of our genetic ancestry and cannot be disobeyed (Ardrey, 1966).

The best guess is that while the overt behaviors may sometimes be similar, the underlying mechanisms are not. Territoriality in robins is universal and innately based; but in humans it is enormously affected by learning. For example, there are some societies in which private ownership is relatively unimportant, which certainly suggests that cultural factors play a vital role.

THE BIOLOGICAL BASIS OF LOVE: THE MALE-FEMALE BOND

The preceding discussion has made it clear that there is some biological foundation for strife and conflict. The tendencies toward destruction are kept in bounds by a set of counteracting tendencies such as territoriality and ritualized fighting. As we shall see, they are also controlled and modified by learning, especially during childhood in humans, and their expression is greatly affected by situational factors (see Chapters 11 and 16).

But over and above these various inhibiting checks on aggression, there is a positive force that is just as basic and deeply rooted in the biological makeup of animals and humans. The poets call it love. Scientists use the more prosaic term

10.8 Grooming in chimpanzees *(Courtesy Animals Animals/Miriam Austerman)*

10.9 Advertising one's sex *A male peacock of a white-feathered species displaying to a female. (Photograph by Peter Jackson, Bruce Coleman)*

bonding, the tendency to affiliate with others of one's own kind. Such attractive forces are most obvious in the various facets of the reproductive cycle—between mate and mate, between child and parent. But positive bonds occur even outside of mating and child care. An example is ***grooming*** in monkeys and apes, who sit in pairs while the groomer meticulously picks lice and vermin out of the groomee's fur (Figure 10.8). The animals evidently like to groom and be groomed over and above considerations of personal hygiene; it is their way of "relating to one another." A comparable human practice may be small talk, in which we exchange no real information but simply talk for the sake of talking to the other person. Other people are part of our universe and we need them and want their company. Much the same is probably true for most animals.

Sexual Behavior in Animals

In some very primitive organisms, reproduction is asexual; thus, amoebas multiply by a process of simple division. But the vast majority of animal species reproduce sexually. Sexual reproduction may or may not be more enjoyable than the asexual varieties, but its biological advantage goes beyond mere pleasure—it assures a greater degree of genetic variability. An amoeba who splits into two has created two replicas of its former self. Here natural selection has no differences to choose between; the second amoeba can be neither better nor worse in its adaptation to the environment than the first, for the two are genetically identical. Things are quite different in sexual reproduction in which specialized cells, ***sperm*** and ***ovum,*** must join to create a new individual. This procedure amounts to a kind of genetic roulette. To begin with, each parent donates only half of the genetic material; and, within some limits, it is a matter of chance that determines which genes are contained in any one sperm or ovum. Chance enters again to determine which sperm will join with which ovum. As a result there must be differences among the offspring. Now natural selection can come into play, perhaps favoring the offspring with the sharper teeth or the one with the more frightening aggressive display, and thus enhancing the survival of the gene that produced these attributes.

For sexual reproduction to occur, sperm and ovum must meet in the appointed manner, at the proper time, and in the proper place. The resulting fertilized egg, or ***zygote,*** requires a favorable environment in which it can develop as an embryo. Many structures have evolved to accomplish these ends and so have many behavior patterns.

SEXUAL CHOICE

Advertising one's sex   Many animals have structures whose primary purpose is to display their owner's sex; for example, the comb and wattle of the rooster or the magnificent tail feathers of the male peacock (see Figure 10.9). These structures are often crucial for appropriate mating behavior. In one species of woodpecker, the male has a moustache of black feathers while the female does not. An unkind ethologist trapped a female and attached a moustache. When she later flew back to her nest, her mate attacked her mercilessly, presumably under the impression that he was warding off an intruding male (Etkin, 1964).

10.10 Courtship rituals in birds *The courtship ceremonials of the great crested grebe, a European water fowl, are quite elaborate. (A) A head-shaking ritual in which both birds face each other, display their head feathers, and solemnly shake their heads from side to side. (B) An acquatic ballet in which the male swims toward the female with his head submerged and then suddenly shoots high out of the water just in front of her. (C) A mutual gift exchange in which both partners dive to the bottom and then emerge simultaneously to present each other with gifts of water weeds. (After Etkin, 1964)*

In humans, structural displays of sex differences are less pronounced, but they are present nonetheless. A possible example is the enlarged female breast whose adipose tissue does not really increase the infant's milk supply. According to some ethologists, it evolved as we became erect and lost our reliance upon smell, a sense which provides the primary information about sex and sexual readiness in many mammals. Under the circumstances, there had to be other ways of displaying one's sex. The prominent breasts of the female may be one such announcement among hairless, "naked apes" (Morris, 1967).

Announcing one's intention In many animals, sexual display involves various species-specific behavior patterns. Some are mainly a means to exhibit the structural sex differences, as in the male peacock spreading its tail feathers. Others are more complex **courtship rituals.** Penguins bow deeply to each other while rocking from side to side, and certain gulls complete an elaborate aquatic ballet by exchanging gifts of seaweed (Figure 10.10).

In many animals, courtship involves alternating bouts of approach and withdrawal, of coy retreat and seductive flirtation. What accounts for these apparent oscillations between yes and no? There is an underlying conflict between attraction and fear; neither animal can really be sure that the other is not hostile. Each must therefore inform the other that its intentions are not aggressive. This is especially true of the male who in many species performs various appeasement rituals

Male terns court by feeding the female *(Photograph by J. Fott, Bruce Coleman)*

that allay the female's fears. The appeasement gestures are often derived from the animal's infancy. Thus, many birds woo their intended mates by offering bits of food, as parents do to their fledglings. In effect, the courting animal announces that its feelings are gentle, as those of a parent to its young. In many cases, the rituals are only vestigial remnants of the parent-infant feeding patterns. Courting finches only touch each others beaks–they "bill."

Indicating one's species Courtship patterns have a further function. They not only increase the likelihood that boy meets girl, but they virtually guarantee that the two will be of the same species. This is because the courtship rituals are so highly species-specific, as in the case of the gift-exchanging gulls. Differences between the courtship patterns of related species are found at all levels of the animal kingdom. An elegant example is provided by fireflies. These are beetles whose males fly around emitting light flashes until a female flashes back. Different species of fireflies have their own characteristic codes, using different flashing rates and rhythms. The important fact is that both sexes respond only to the flash pattern of their own kind. As a result, there are no attempts to mate between different species. Certain fireflies use this flash system to provide themselves with food as well as love. The females answer both their own males and the males of other species. For the latter, they mimic the appropriate flash patterns and then eat the would-be suitors when they arrive (Smith, 1977).

The effect of these species-specific courtship codes is that they maintain the integrity of the species. Contrary to popular view, different species can interbreed if they are related closely enough. They do not do so under natural conditions, but they are occasionally mated in captivity. The offspring of such "unnatural" unions are often infertile; an example is the mule, a result of crossing a horse with a donkey. But in other cases, fertile offspring may ensue. Different courtship patterns are a way of preserving what evolution has wrought by keeping populations in **reproductive isolation,** thus maintaining them as separate species, each adapted to its own ecological niche.

Who makes the choice? The preceding discussions have centered on the various factors that bring male and female together. But, interestingly enough, the two don't have an equal voice in the ultimate decision. In most species, the female finally decides whether or not to mate. The biological reason is simple—the female shoulders the major cost of reproduction. If she is a bird, she supplies not only the ovum but also the food supply for the developing embryo. If she is a mammal, she carries the embryo within her body and later provides it with milk. In either case, her biological burden is vastly greater than the male's. If a doe's offspring fails to survive, she has lost a whole breeding season. In comparison, the stag's loss is minimal—a few minutes of his time and some easily replaced sperm cells. Under the circumstances, natural selection would favor the female who is particularly choosy about picking the best possible male; that is, the male whose genetic contribution will best ensure their offsprings' survival. From the male's point of view, the female seems coy or "plays hard to get." But in fact this is not just play-acting for, to the female, reproduction is a serious business with heavy biological costs.

There are a few interesting exceptions. One example is the sea horse, whose young are carried in a brood pouch by the male. In this animal, the male exhibits

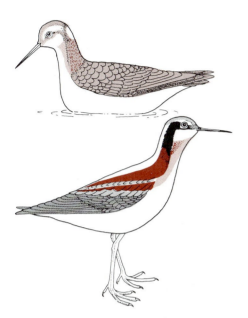

10.11 Plumage pattern in the male and female phalarope *The phalarope male hatches and feeds the chicks. Since he carries a larger share of the biological cost of reproduction, he is more coy and choosy than the female. As the drawing indicates schematically, the female phalarope (bottom) is larger and more colorfully plumaged than the male (top). (After Hohn, 1969)*

greater sexual caution and discrimination than the female. A similar effect is found in the phalarope, an arctic seabird whose eggs are hatched and whose chicks are fed by the male (Figure 10.11). Here a greater part of the biological burden falls on the male, and we should expect a corresponding increase in his sexual choosiness. This is just what happens. Among the phalaropes, the female does the wooing. She is brightly plumaged, and aggressively pursues the dull-colored, coyly careful male (Williams, 1966).

REPRODUCTION AND TIMING

Once male and female have met, the next step is to arrange for the union of their respective sperm and ovum. Terrestrial animals have evolved a variety of sexual mechanics to accomplish this end. In general, the male introduces his sperm cells into the genital tract of the female, where the ovum is fertilized. The problem is synchronization. The sperm has to encounter a ready ovum, and the fertilized egg can develop only if it is provided with the appropriate conditions. Under these circumstances, timing is of the essence. In birds and mammals, the timing mechanism depends on a complex feedback system between brain centers and hormones.

Hormonal cycles Except for the primates, mammals mate only when the female is in heat, or *estrus.* For example, the female rat goes through a fifteen-hour estrus period every five days. At all other times, she will resolutely reject any male's advances. If he nuzzles her or tries to mount, she will kick and bite. But during estrus, the female responds quite differently to the male's approach. She first retreats in small hops, then stops to look back, and wiggles her ears provocatively (McClintock and Adler, 1978). Eventually, she stands still, her back arched upward, her tail held to the side, in all respects a willing sexual partner.

What accounts for the difference between the female's behavior during estrus and at other times? The crucial fact is a simple matter of reproductive biology. The time of estrus is precisely the time when the female's ova are ripe for fertilization. Evolution has obviously provided a behavioral arrangement that is exactly tuned to reproductive success.

The mechanism is an interlocking system of hormonal and neurological controls which involves the pituitary gland, the hypothalamus, and the ovaries. In effect, there are three phases: (1) During the first, follicles in the ovary mature under the influence of pituitary secretions. The follicles produce the female sex hormone *estrogen.* As the concentration of estrogen in the bloodstream rises, the hypothalamus responds by directing the pituitary to change its secretions. In consequence, follicle growth is accelerated until the follicle ruptures and releases the mature ovum. (2) This triggers the second phase during which the animal is in estrus. Estrogen production climbs to a steep maximum and stimulates certain structures in the hypothalamus which make the animal sexually receptive. (3) The third phase is dominated by the action of another female sex hormone, *progesterone,* which is produced by the ruptured follicle. Its secretion leads to a thickening of the uterus lining, a first step in preparing the uterus to receive the embryo. If the ovum is fertilized, there are further steps in building an appropriate womb. If it is not, the thickened uterus walls are reabsorbed and another cycle begins. In humans and some primates, too much extra tissue is laid on to be

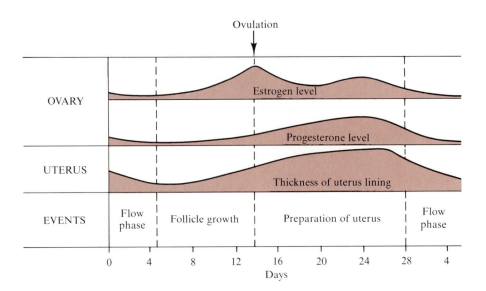

10.12   The main stages of the human menstrual cycle   *The figure shows estrogen and progesterone levels and thickness of the uterus lining during the human menstrual cycle. The cycle begins with the growth of a follicle, continues through ovulation and a maximum estrogen level, is followed by a phase during which the uterus becomes prepared to receive the embryo, and ends with a flow phase during which the thickened uterus lining is sloughed off. (After Keeton, 1980)*

easily reabsorbed; the thickened uterus lining is therefore sloughed off as **menstrual flow** (Figure 10.12).

Hormones and behavior   Some hormonal changes affect behavior dramatically. When male rats are castrated, they soon lose all sexual interest and capacity, as do female rats without ovaries. But sexual behavior is quickly restored by injections of testosterone or estrogen respectively.

Many investigators believe that behavioral effects of hormone levels are caused by cells in the hypothalamus which can sense the concentration of sex hormones in the bloodstream. These "hormone receptors" are increasingly aroused with increasing hormone concentration, and they trigger sexual appetite and behavior. This hypothesis has been tested by injecting minute quantities of various hormones into several regions of the hypothalamus. The total amounts were negligible and could hardly affect the overall hormone concentration in the blood. Will the hypothalamic sexual control system be fooled by the local administration of the hormone, as is its thermostatic counterpart when it is locally cooled or heated (see Chapter 3)? It evidently is. A spayed female cat will go into estrus when estrogen is implanted in her hypothalamus (Harris and Michael, 1964). Analogous effects have been obtained with **androgens** (that is, male hormones) administered to castrated male rats (Davidson, 1969).

Hormones affect behavior, but the relation can also work the other way around. What an animal does and what it sees and feels will often have drastic effects on its hormonal secretions. An example is the effect of copulation on progesterone secretion in female rats. Some progesterone is secreted during the normal cycle, but not enough to permit the implantation of the fertilized egg in the uterus. Yet more progesterone is released as a reflex response to sexual stimulation. In rats, the male evidently has two reproductive functions. He supplies the sperm, but he also supplies the necessary stimulation which triggers the extra progesterone secretion without which there can be no pregnancy. This is shown by the fact that when the male rat ejaculates too quickly, no pregnancy results. There has been too little stimulation to set off the female's hormonal reflex (Adler, 1969).

Human Sexuality

The major difference between animal and human sexuality concerns the flexibility of sexual behavior. When does it occur, how, and with whom? Compared to animals, we are much less automatic in our sexual activities, much more varied, much more affected by prior experience. Human sexuality is remarkably plastic and can be variously shaped by experience, especially early experience, and by cultural patterns (see Chapters 12 and 16). This flexibility is evidently part of an evolutionary trend, for the sexual behavior of lower mammals such as rats and cats is much more stereotyped than that of primates. Virgin male and female rats who have never even seen another rat since weaning copulate quite competently on their very first encounter, if the female is in estrus. Sexual behavior in primates is another matter. Here experience plays a larger role. Inexperienced chimpanzees of either sex fumble clumsily at first until they gradually learn what to rats comes naturally, either by trial and error, or by appropriate instruction from a more sophisticated partner (Nissen, 1953).

EMANCIPATION FROM HORMONAL CONTROL

The difference between animal and human sexual behavior is especially marked when we consider the effects of hormones. In rats and cats, sexual behavior is highly dependent upon hormone levels; castrated males and spayed females stop copulating a few months after the removal of their gonads (Figure 10.13). In humans, on the other hand, sexual activity may persist for years, even decades, after castration or ovariectomy, provided that the operation was performed after puberty (see Chapter 16; Bermant and Davidson, 1974).

The liberation from hormonal control is especially clear in human females. To be sure, women are subject to a physiological cycle, but this has relatively little impact on sexual behavior, at least when compared to the profound effects seen in animals. The female rat or cat is chained to an estrus cycle that commands her to be receptive during one period and prevents her from being so at all other times. There are no such fetters on the human female, who is capable of sexual behavior at any time during her cycle, and also capable of refusing.

Although we are evidently not the vassals of our hormones that most animals are, this is not to say that hormonal factors have no effect. Androgen injections into men with abnormally low hormone levels will generally increase their sex drive. An important demonstration of this concerns the effects of androgen administration on male homosexuals. The androgen-injected homosexual becomes more sexually active; but, contrary to a common misconception, his renewed sexual vigor is toward homosexual partners just as before (Kinsey, Pomeroy, and Martin, 1948).

Another demonstration of hormonal effects comes from studies of the menstrual cycle. While women can respond sexually at virtually all points of their cycle, there are still some variations within that period. Sexual desire and activity tend to be highest during the middle of the cycle, when ovulation occurs (Hamburg, Moos, and Yalom, 1968). These effects are not very pronounced; they probably represent a small remnant of the old animal estrus cycle, buried under layers of evolutionary change.

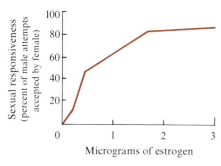

10.13 Estrogen and sexual behavior
The effect of estrogen injections on the sexual responsiveness of female rats was measured by the number of male attempts at mounting that were accepted by the female. The females' ovaries had been removed, so they could not produce estrogen themselves. The hormone was injected daily in the doses shown above. Sexual behavior was measured eight days after hormone treatment began. (After Bermant and Davidson, 1974)

EVOLUTION AND THE MALE-FEMALE PAIR-BOND

In most species of animals, the male and female part company after copulation and may well never meet again. But in some species the partners remain together. In many cases, their arrangement is polygamous and the resulting family typically consists of one male, a number of females, and their various offspring. But in a sizable number of species, the mating pattern may be essentially monogamous, with the sexual partnership leading to a special, relatively permanent tie.

In humans, the bond between man and woman has been celebrated in literature since Adam and Eve. What accounts for the origin of this special tie that bonds two individuals together?

The sexual hypothesis According to one account, the human **pair-bond** is ultimately based on sexuality and is related to the abolition of the estrus period. About a million years ago, our primitive ancestors were hunter-gatherers, adopting a mode of existence that required a larger and much more complex social structure than any found among primates up to then. The males—stronger and faster than the females, and unencumbered by pregnancy—formed into hunting bands that pursued big game with spears and axes. The women stayed at the home site, took care of the infants, and gathered whatever edibles were available nearby. But what led the men to return from their far-ranging hunting trips to share their kill with the women and children back home? Some authors believe that one inducement was sex, an inducement all the stronger once there was no estrus period limiting sexual activity to a few days every month.

There is an intriguing speculation that goes along with the hypothesis that the human pair-bond is based on sexuality. It has to do with anatomy. When our ancestors adopted a fully erect position there were various anatomical side effects. One consequence was a forward shift in the vaginal opening. This allowed the possibility of a face-to-face position during sexual intercourse. Animals mount from the rear. Humans of course can do so too; in fact, they can employ any one of countless other positions. But interestingly enough, their preferred position is face-to-face. This preference is not unique to our culture; it is found in virtually all other cultures that have been studied in this regard, from Greenland Eskimos to Pacific Islanders. In part, the reason is that in this position the woman's clitoris receives more stimulation. But another reason is that the face-to-face position allows each partner to perceive the other's unique humanity, to see and feel who the partner is, so that sexual intercourse is not just copulation, not just a reproductive act, but is—making love (Morris, 1967).

The reproductive hypothesis Many modern theorists doubt that sex is the primary cement that underlies the human pair-bond. One of their arguments is that sex as such can't account for pair-bonding in many animal species. An example is provided by certain primates such as gibbons (see Figure 10.14). Among gibbons, copulation is a relatively rare event, but they remain monogamously attached even so. What holds the pair together? The best guess is their infants. Newborn primates are virtually helpless. If a gibbon father stays with his mate to protect his young, the infants are more likely to live into adulthood and then bequeath their genes to the next generation—including whatever genes there are that lead to pair-bonding.

10.14   Gibbon monogamous pair-bond *(Photograph by Ylla, Photo Researchers)*

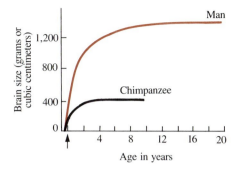

What holds for gibbons holds even more for humans. Human babies are delivered when their brain is less developed than that of any other primate (see Figure 10.15). As a result, their initial helplessness at birth is considerably greater than that of any ape's or monkey's and lasts for a much longer period. To give only one example, an infant chimpanzee can cling to its mother while she moves about, but a human baby must be cradled. As a result, the mother is necessarily "tied down" and cannot efficiently gather food and protect herself or her infant. This being so, she necessarily needs help, and this help is generally provided by the infant's father, who thus acts to assure himself of his own genetic survival. Whether the resulting family structure is based on monogamy or polygamy depends on a variety of cultural and economic (and perhaps biological) factors whose discussion is beyond the scope of this book. But whatever its nature, the family structure seems to be one of the bases of human pair-bonding (for discussion, see Ford and Beach, 1951; Daly and Wilson, 1978; Hrdy, 1981; Passingham, 1982).

10.15   Growth of the brain in humans and chimpanzees   *The figure plots brain growth in humans (color) and chimpanzees (black), from conception to maturity, with birth indicated by the arrow. The figures for humans are for brain weight, for chimpanzees they are for cranial capacity. The figure indicates that in humans the brain continues to grow at about the same rate it did in the fetus for some two years after birth. In chimpanzees, the growth rate is slowed down considerably right after birth. As a result, humans have a much longer period of infantile dependence than any other animal. This in turn may well be the basic biological reason for the male-female pair-bond. (After Passingham, 1982)*

THE BIOLOGICAL BASIS OF LOVE: THE PARENT-CHILD BOND

There is another bond of love whose biological foundations are no less basic than those of the male-female tie—the relation between mother and child (and in many animals, the relation between father and child as well). In birds and mammals some kind of parental attachment is almost ubiquitous. In contrast to most fish and reptiles that lay eggs by the hundreds and then abandon them, birds and mammals invest in quality rather than quantity. They have fewer offspring, but they then see to it that most of their brood survives into maturity. They feed them, clean them, shelter them, and protect them during some initial period of dependency. While under this parental umbrella, the young animal can grow and become prepared for the world into which it must soon enter and can acquire some of the skills that will help it survive in that world. As already mentioned, this period of initial dependency is longest in animals that live by their wits, such as monkeys and apes, and is longest of all in humans.

The Infant's Attachment to the Mother

In most birds and mammals, the young become strongly attached to their mother. Ducklings follow the mother duck, lambs the mother ewe, and infant monkeys cling tightly to the mother monkey's belly. In each case, separation leads to considerable stress; the young animals give piteous distress calls, and quack, bleat, and keen continuously until the mother returns. The biological function of this attachment is a simple matter of personal survival. This holds for humans as well as animals. For there is little doubt that in our early evolutionary history, a motherless infant would probably have died an early death—of exposure, starvation, or predation. There are very few orphanages in nature.

The mechanisms that lead to this attachment will be discussed in a later section (see Chapter 16). For now, we will only say that while some theorists believe that the main factor is the child's discovery that the mother's presence leads to the alleviation of hunger, thirst, and pain, there is strong evidence that the attachment

Chimpanzee mother and her one-year-old son   (Photograph by Tom McHugh, Photo Researchers)

is more basic than that. For the distress shown by the young—whether birds, monkeys, or humans—when they are separated from their mother, occurs even when they are perfectly well-fed and housed. It appears that the infant's attachment to its mother is based on more than the satisfaction of the major bodily needs. The infant evidently comes predisposed to seek social stimulation, which is rewarding in and of itself.

The Mother's Attachment to the Infant

For the infant, the function of the mother-child bond is simple personal survival. For the mother, the biological function is again a matter of survival, but for her, the survival is genetic rather than personal, for unless her young survive into adulthood, the parents' genes will perish. But what are the mechanisms that produce the parents' attachment? After all, robins and gibbons don't know about evolution or genetic survival (and if they did, they probably wouldn't care). They behave like proper parents; they care for their young and protect them. But they surely don't do this because they know that their failure to act in this way would lead to genetic extinction. The real reason must lie elsewhere. One possibility is that there are some built-in predispositions toward parental behavior. If such predispositions do exist, they would then be favored by natural selection.

There is good evidence that the young of many animal species have a set of built-in responses that elicit caretaking from the parents. To give only one example, many baby birds open their mouths as wide as they can as soon as the parent arrives at the nest. This "gaping" response is their means of begging for food (see Figure 10.16). Some species of birds have special anatomical signs that help to elicit a proper parental reaction. An example is the Cedar Waxwing, whose bright red mouth lining evidently provides a further signal to the parent: I'm young, hungry, and a Cedar Waxwing!

Child care in humans is obviously more complex and flexible than it is in Cedar Waxwings, but it too has biological foundations. The mother-child relation grows out of a number of built-in reaction patterns, of child to mother and mother to child. The human infant begins life with a few relevant reflex patterns, including some that help him find the mother's nipple and suck at it once it is

10.16 Gaping in young birds *(A) The gaping response of the young yellow warbler serves as a built-in signal that elicits the parents' feeding behavior. (Photograph by Robert J. Erwin, Photo Researchers) (B) Cuckoos are parasites who lay their eggs in other birds' nests. The figure shows a young cuckoo being fed by its unwitting foster parent, a reed warbler. Since the cuckoo fledgling is much larger than its nest mates (some of whom it often pushes out of the nest), its gaping mouth cavity is wider and therefore provides an even more powerful stimulus in eliciting feeding. (Courtesy of Ian Wyllie, Monks Wood Experiment Station)*

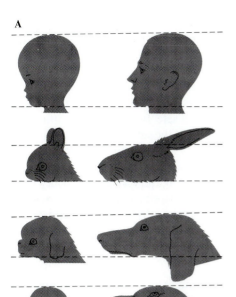

10.17   The stimulus features of "babyness"   *"Cute" characteristics of the "baby schema" are common to humans and a number of animals. (A) These include a rounded head shape, protruding forehead, and large eyes below the middle of the head. (After Lorenz, 1943) These properties, as well as a rounded body shape and large head-to-body ratio, produce cuteness in a lap dog (B). (Photograph by Wallace Litwin)*

found. He also has an essentially innate signal system through which he tells the mother that he is in distress: he cries. Analogous ***distress calls*** are found in many animals, for when the young chirp, bleat, mew, or cry, the mother immediately runs to their aid and comforts them.

According to ethologists, evolution has further equipped the infant with a set of stimulus features that function as innate releasers of parental, and especially maternal, feelings. The cues that define "babyness" include a large, protruding forehead, large eyes, an upturned nose, chubby cheeks, and so on. Endowed with these distinctive properties, the baby looks "cute" and "cuddly," something to be picked up, fussed over, and taken care of. The case is similar for the young of various animals who share aspects of the same "baby schema." Various commercial enterprises are devoted to the deliberate manufacture of cuteness. Dolls and Walt Disney creatures are designed to be babied by children, while certain lap dogs are especially bred to be babied by adults (Figure 10.17).

Nature has provided the infant with yet another trick to disarm even the stoniest of parental hearts: the smile. In some fashion, smiling may begin within the first month; it is often considered a built-in signal by which humans tell each other, "I wish you well. Be good to me." There is reason to believe that it is innate. Infants who are born blind smile under conditions that also produce smiling in sighted children, as when they hear their mother's voice. They obviously could not have learned this response by imitation.

SELF-SACRIFICE AND ALTRUISM

Many animals go to considerable lengths to defend their offspring. Various birds have evolved characteristic ways of feigning injury such as drooping one wing

10.18 A misleading display *In feigning injury, the killdeer, a small American bird, runs and flies erratically from predators that approach its nest, often flopping about as if it had a broken wing. (Photograph by Wayne Lankinen, Bruce Coleman)*

10.19 Alarm call *Ground squirrels give alarm calls when they sense a nearby predator. Such alarm calls are more likely to be given by females rather than males. The females usually have close relatives living nearby. As a result, their alarm call is more likely to benefit genetically related rather than unrelated individuals, which suggests that it is based on kin selection. (Photograph by Georg D. Lepp, Bio-Tec Images)*

and paddling around in circles to draw a predator away from their nests (see Figure 10.18). On the face of it, such acts appear heroically unselfish, for the parents court the danger that the predator will seize them. But here again we come up with the difference between personal and genetic survival. For what seems unselfish from the vantage of the individual looks different from a biological point of view (Wilson, 1975). The mother bird who does not divert a potential attacker may very well live longer because she has played it safe. But from an evolutionary perspective what counts is not her own survival but the survival of her genes. And these are more likely to perish if she flies off to safety; while she hides in the bushes, the marauding cat will eat her chicks. As a result, she will have fewer offspring to whom she can pass on her genes, including the very gene or genes that underlie her maternal indifference. Those of her offspring that do survive will in turn have fewer offspring, and so on, until her genetic attributes will disappear.

Altruism in Animals

Seen in this light, parental self-sacrifice can be understood in evolutionary terms. Can a similar analysis be applied to unselfish acts that benefit individuals who are not one's own children? Such apparently altruistic acts are found in various animal species.* A case in point is the warning signal given off by many species at the approach of a predator (see Figure 10.19). When a robin sees a hawk overhead, it gives an alarm call, a special cry that alerts all members of the flock and impels them to seek cover. This alarm call is based on a built-in, inherited tendency and is essentially unlearned. All robins emit this cry when in danger, and they do so even if raised in complete isolation from their fellows. There is no doubt that this alarm benefits all robins who hear it. They crouch low and hide, so their chances of escape are enhanced. But what does it gain the bird who sounds the alarm? Doesn't it place him in greater danger by increasing the likelihood that the hawk will detect *him?* Why does the robin play the hero instead of quietly stealing away and leaving his fellows to their fate?

There are several possible factors, each of which may play a role.

ENLIGHTENED SELF-INTEREST

One possibility is that this act of avian heroism is not as unselfish as it seems, for it may well increase the warner's own chance of personal survival in the long run. If a particular robin spies a hawk and remains quiet, there is a greater chance that some bird in the flock will be captured, most likely another bird. But what about tomorrow? A hawk who has seized a prey in a particular location will probably return to the very same place in search of another meal. And this meal may be the very same robin who originally minded his own business and stayed uninvolved (Trivers, 1971).

KIN SELECTION

There is another alternative. Let us assume that our heroic robin is unlucky, is seized by the hawk, and dies a martyr's death. While this act may have caused the

---

* In modern biological usage, the term *altruism* is reserved for cases in which the good deed benefits neither the doers nor their own offspring.

robin to perish as an individual, it may well have served to preserve some of that bird's genes. This may be true even if none of the birds in the flock are the hero's own offspring. They may be relatives who carry some his genes, brothers and sisters who share half the same genes, or nieces and nephews who share one-fourth. If so, the alarm call may have saved several relatives who carry the alarm-calling gene and who will pass it on to future generations of robins. From an evolutionary point of view, the alarm call had survival value—if not for the alarm caller or its direct offspring, then for the alarm-calling gene (J. M. Smith, 1964).

According to this view, altruistic behavior will evolve if it promotes the survival of the individual's kin. This *kin-selection* hypothesis predicts that unselfish behavior should be more common among relatives than unrelated individuals. There is some evidence that this is indeed the case. Certain deer snort loudly when alarmed, which alerts other deer that are nearby. Groups of does tend to be related; bucks who disperse when they get old enough are less likely to be related. The kin-selection hypothesis would then predict that does should be more likely to give the alarm snort than bucks. This is indeed what happens. Similar results have been obtained for various other species (Barash, 1982).

RECIPROCAL ALTRUISM

There is yet another possible mechanism that leads to biologically unselfish acts. Some animals—and we may well be among them—may have a built-in Golden Rule: Do unto others, as you would want them to do to you (or to your genes). If an individual helps another, and that other later reciprocates, the ultimate upshot is a benefit to both. For example, male baboons sometimes help each other in aggressive encounters, and the one who received help on one occasion is more likely to come to the other's assistance later on.

A built-in predisposition toward reciprocity may well be one of the biological foundations of altruism in some animals (and perhaps ourselves as well). If the original unselfish act doesn't exact too great a cost—in energy expended or in danger incurred—then its eventual reciprocation will yield a net benefit to both parties. A tendency toward reciprocal altruism of this kind, however, presupposes relatively stable groups in which individuals recognize one another. It also presupposes some safeguards against "cheating," accepting help without reciprocating. One such safeguard might be a link between a disposition toward altruism and a disposition to punish cheaters (Trivers, 1971).

Altruism in Humans

Can human altruism be understood in similar, biological terms? According to Edward Wilson, the founder of *sociobiology,* the answer is yes, at least to some extent. While Wilson emphasizes the enormous variations among human social systems, he still notes certain common themes, which he regards as grounded in our genetic heritage. One example is the great human capacity for loyalty to a group and the heroic self-sacrifices this can inspire. Examples are soldiers on suicide missions or religious martyrs burning at the stake. Wilson suspects that such heroic acts are rooted in one built-in element—the hero's ability to subordinate himself to a group. The genes that underlie this capacity enable the individual to risk death in battle or in martyrdom. Wilson suggests that by doing so the individual helps to ensure the survival of the group (and thus of his own genes since the group probably includes his own kin). As with the robin, the individual hero may die, but his genes will survive (Wilson, 1975).

This sociobiological analysis is highly controversial. Some of its critics argue that human social behavior depends crucially on culture. To understand human self-sacrifice, we have to understand it in its own social terms (Blurton-Jones, 1976). The ancient Romans fell on their swords when defeated not to save their brothers' genes but to save their honor; the early Christians defied death because of a religious belief rather than to maintain a particular gene pool. We cannot comprehend the ancient Romans without considering their concept of honor, nor can we explain the martyrdom of the early Christians without reference to their belief in a hereafter. This is not to say that in unravelling the cultural contexts of these acts we have explained them fully. We surely have not. After all, not all defeated Romans fell on their swords, nor did all early Christians choose martyrdom. There is much about human altruism that is still a mystery. But any attempt to solve this mystery must include some reference to the cultural conditions in which such human acts occur. Our human genetic makeup is relevant, but this relevance is probably indirect. Our genes allow us to have a culture, they make us sociable, they give us the capacity for language, they endow us with the enormous gift for learning on which culture rests. But they don't explain the products of culture directly. And according to Wilson's critics, one such product is altruism, as we normally encounter it.

COMMUNICATING MOTIVES

The preceding discussion has given ample testimony that animals exist within a social framework in much the same way as humans do. What one creature does often has a crucial effect on the behavior of another of its own kind. As we have seen among animals, the major means for exerting such social influences is signaling display. What is the origin of this largely built-in mode of communication?

Expressive Movements: Animal Display

Displays represent a simple mode of communication whereby animals inform each other of what they are most likely to do in the immediate future. The crab waves its claws and the wolf bares its fangs; these threat displays may save both sender and receiver from bodily harm if the message is heeded. In effect, displays communicate the animal's present motive state—its readiness to fight or to mate, its need for food, or parental attention, and so forth. For this reason, displays are sometimes said to "express" the animal's inner state and are therefore described as *expressive movements.* In humans, such built-in social displays are relegated to a lesser place. After all, we have the much richer communication system provided by human language. But even so, we still possess a sizable repertory of built-in social displays that tell others about our feelings and needs.

DECIPHERING THE MESSAGE

How do ethologists determine what message is conveyed by a given display? If the sender is an animal, we cannot ask it directly. We can, however, infer the message by noting the correlation between a given display and the animal's behavior just before and after its occurrence. For example, if a certain posture is generally followed by attack, then it is often called a threat display (see Figure 10.20); if it is usually followed by mating, it is probably a courtship signal, and so on.

In actual fact, displays often convey not one motive, but several conflicting ones. This is especially true of threat displays which occur when the animal is torn between the tendency to attack and the tendency to flee. If there were only aggression or only fear, there would be no conflict and the animal would either attack or run away without hesitation. Because it is in conflict, it does neither, at least for a while. Instead, it threatens. Some evidence for this view comes from the fact that threat displays are most frequent in situations in which attack and flight tendencies are nearly equal; for example, at territory boundaries (Hinde, 1970).

There is reason to believe that displays do not mirror the animal's inner motives directly. In such cases, the meanings of the message are not given by the display alone; to decipher the message, the recipient must also note the context in which it occurs. One investigator studied a special call uttered by a flycatching bird, the Eastern phoebe. This call is given in a wide variety of circumstances which undoubtedly involve very different motive states. But there is a common factor: Whenever the bird gives this call, it is likely to change its present locomotion. The call apparently indicates some conflict between two opposing motor patterns. Should it continue to fly straight ahead or veer off to one side, should it keep on flying or stop on a perch? The motives that underly this locomotor hesitancy may be aggression and fear ("Do I dare attack him?"), sex and fear ("Will she reject me if I approach her?"), or food begging and fear ("Will my father peck at me if I ask to be fed?"). Which of these motives is actually involved can be de-

10.20 Threat displays *Threats may be bluffs, but they are often valid signals of an animal's impending action. In (A) a male bison gives a threat signal by lifting its tail, and (B) promptly acts upon it. (Photographs by David G. Allen)*

A

B

termined only by noting the context in which the message is given (W. J. Smith, 1977).

THE EVOLUTIONARY ORIGIN OF DISPLAYS

What is the origin of social displays? One answer dates back to Charles Darwin, who suggested that various gestures which seem to convey an emotional state have evolved from preparatory movements for an action the animal is about to take. Darwin gives the example of an angry dog's snarl. The lips are retracted from the sharp canines which are now ready for action (Figure 10.21). Analogous *intention movements* are seen in the threat postures of many species. For example, herring gulls threaten by pointing their beaks downward (preparatory to striking) and slightly raising their wings from their bodies (preparatory to beating another herring gull with them).

While some displays may represent preparatory movements of the sort that Darwin envisaged, many do not. They rather seem to have no function apart from communication. An example is provided by certain species of birds who lower their tail feathers as part of a threat display. In effect, they are announcing that they are about to fly at an antagonist with beak and claw. But the lowered tail feathers are not appropriate as the first preparatory movement for a takeoff. A bird that is about to take flight must first raise its tail feathers and then lower them (Figure 10.22). The display is out of sequence for proper takeoff and is therefore useless as a preparatory motion. Thus, whatever its evolutionary origin, the lowering of the tail feathers is now a signal and nothing more.

Phenomena of this sort can tell us something about the function that a display movement serves now. But how can we do more than idly speculate about its evolutionary history? Displays leave no fossils, so there is no direct method for reconstructing their biological past. One approach is to compare built-in displays in related species. By noting their similarities and differences, the ethologist tries to infer the evolutionary steps in their history, much as a comparative anatomist charts the family tree of fins, wings, and forelegs.

An example of how this *comparative method* has been applied to species-specific behaviors is a study of an odd courtship ritual in a predatory insect, the dancing fly (Kessel, 1955). At mating time, the male dancing fly secretes a little ball of silk which he brings to the female. She plays with this silk ball while the male mounts her and copulates.

How did this ritual arise? The courtship patterns in a number of related species give a clue. Most flies of related species manage with a minimum of precopulatory fuss; the trouble is that the female may decide to eat the male rather than mate with him. However, if she is already eating a small prey animal, the male is safe. Some species have evolved a behavior pattern that capitalizes on this fact. The male catches a small insect and brings it to the female for her to eat while he mates with her. In still other species, the male first wraps the prey in a large silk balloon. This increases his margin of safety, for the female is kept busy unwrapping her present. The dancing fly's ritual is probably the last step in this evolutionary sequence. The male dancing fly wastes no time or energy in catching a prey animal, but simply brings an empty ball of silk, all wrapping and no present. Copulation can now proceed unimpeded since the female is safely occupied—perhaps the first creature in evolutionary history to realize that it is the thought and not the gift that matters (Figure 10.23).

10.21 Emotional expressions as intention movements *The drawing is taken from Darwin's own work,* The Expression of the Emotions in Man and Animals, *and shows a dog's snarl. Darwin regarded this as a kind of preparation for the aggressive action the animal is about to take—the dog is now ready to bite. (Darwin, 1872b)*

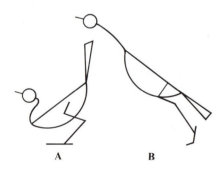

A   B

10.22 Displays that are not preparatory movements *The figure shows two phases of a bird's take-off leap as it is about to fly. (A) It crouches and raises its tail, and then (B) reverses these movements and springs off. Many aggressive displays of birds resemble (B) rather than (A), a strong argument that such displays evolved as signals in their own right. (After Hinde, 1974)*

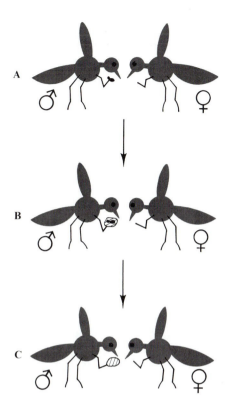

10.23 The evolution of courtship in dancing flies *(A) In some species, the male catches a prey animal and gives it to the female to eat during copulation; this keeps her busy so she is less likely to eat him. (B) In other species, the male first wraps the prey in a balloon of secreted silk. This keeps the female even busier since she has to unwrap the prey. (C) Finally, in the dancing fly, the male gives the female a ball of silk without anything in it. (After Klopfer, 1974)*

The Expression of Emotions in Humans

The study of animal display systems may have considerable relevance to the understanding of human emotions. For now, we will look at the way in which these emotions are expressed overtly.

THE UNIVERSALITY OF EMOTIONAL EXPRESSIONS

We obviously have a sizable repertory of emotional expressions, most of them conveyed by the face. We smile, laugh, weep, frown, snarl, and grit our teeth. Are any of these expressive patterns our human equivalent of displays? If so, they should be universal to all humans and innately determined (Ekman, 1973; Ekman and Oster, 1979; Fridlund, Ekman and Oster, 1983).

In one study, American actors posed in photographs to convey such emotions as fear, anger, and happiness. These pictures were then shown to members of different cultures, both literate (Swedes, Japanese, Kenyans) and preliterate (members of an isolated New Guinea tribe barely advanced beyond Stone-Age culture). When asked to identify the portrayed emotion, all groups came up with quite similar judgments. The results were much the same when the procedure was reversed. The New Guinea tribesmen were asked to portray the emotions appropriate to various simple situations such as happiness at the return of a friend, grief at the death of a child, and anger at the start of a fight. Photographs of their performances were then shown to American college students who readily picked out the emotions the tribesmen had tried to convey (Figure 10.24).

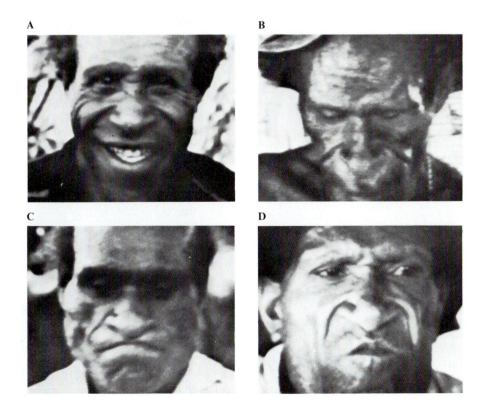

10.24 Attempts to portray emotion by New Guinea tribesmen *Acting out emotions appropriate to various situations: (A) "Your friend has come and you are happy" (B) "Your child has died" (C) "You are angry and about to fight" (D) "You see a dead pig that has been lying there for a long time." (© Paul Ekman, 1971)*

361

These results indicate that there may be some emotional expressions that are common to all humans. This conclusion fits observations of children born blind. As already noted, these children cry, smile, and laugh under essentially the same conditions that elicit these reactions in sighted children. In fact, much the same is true even of children born both blind and deaf. It would be hard to argue that these children had *learned* the emotional expressions considering that their sensory avenues of both sight and sound had been blocked off from birth (see Figure 10.25).

At least in part, such built-in expressions may serve a similar function as do animal displays. They act as social signals by which we communicate our inner states to others, a way of saying what we are likely to do next.

THE ROLE OF CULTURE

These findings do not imply that smiling and other emotional expressions are unaffected by cultural conventions. According to some accounts, Melanese chieftains frown fiercely when greeting each other at a festive occasion, and Samurai mothers are said to have smiled upon hearing that their sons had fallen in battle (Klineberg, 1940). But such facts do not disprove the claim that facial expressions are built-in social signals; they only show that such signals can be artificially masked and modified later on. The Japanese child is taught to maintain an outward smile of politeness whatever she may feel inside. Her smile has come under voluntary control at least in part. It can be held back artificially and can be produced artificially. How and when such artifice comes into play, however, depends on the culture.

Some evidence for this view comes from studies in which American and Japanese subjects were presented with a harrowing documentary film of a primitive puberty rite. As they watched the film, their facial expressions were recorded with a hidden camera. The results showed that when alone, the facial reactions of the Japanese and American subjects were virtually identical. But the results were quite different when the subject watched the film in the company of a white-coated experimenter. Now the Japanese looked more polite and smiled more than the Americans (Ekman, 1977; see Figure 10.26).

10.25   The smile in children born blind   (A) Smiling in a child born blind. (Courtesy The Lighthouse, N.Y.C.) (B) Smiling in a child born both blind and deaf. (Courtesy I. Eibl-Eibesfeldt)

10.26   Spontaneous facial expressions (A) A Japanese and (B) an American student watched a film that depicted a rather grueling scene. The figure shows their expressions when they were alone. Under these conditions, their facial expressions were virtually identical. But when they watched in the presence of another person, the Japanese masked his expression of unpleasant emotions more than the American did. (From Ekman and Friesen, 1975)

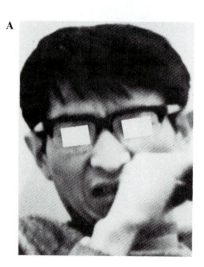

The Difference between Display and Language

How are display repertories different from the communication achieved by human language? There is an obvious similarity. In both cases, the behavior of one organism affects that of its fellows. But the differences between these two communication systems far outweigh the similarities.

CREATING NEW MESSAGES

One obvious difference is in the complexity and flexibility of the two communicative systems. Consider the relative size of the two "vocabularies." Most mammals have some twenty to forty distinguishable display signals. This contrasts with an estimated vocabulary size of at least 50,000 words for the average human adult. The contrast is even sharper when we compare the way in which these vocabulary items are combined. Human language is based on a ***productive*** principle. Given the rules for putting words together (syntax), the speaker can construct any number of new messages he has never heard before (see Chapter 9). Not so for animal displays. The display system is rigid. Each stickleback, robin, and rhesus monkey sends only messages that were sent by previous sticklebacks, robins, and rhesus monkeys. There is no room for originality in the language of display.

One reason is that in animal display systems there is no provision for rearrangements of parts so as to make a new whole. Consider the messages of the jackdaw. This bird has two distinct calls that beckon others to fly with it—a high-pitched call that sounds like *kia,* uttered when the jackdaw migrates southward in the fall, and a lower-pitched call that sounds like *kiaw* uttered when the bird returns home in the spring. Yet another jackdaw call is *zick-zick-zick* which occurs during courtship. There is also an angry, *rattle*like sound, emitted when the jackdaw is about to attack an enemy (Lorenz, 1952). These various calls are useful in helping the jackdaw communicate with its fellows, but they should not be considered as the analogues of words in a language. If they were, the jackdaw should be able to shuffle the individual calls around to create new and ever more complex messages. They might produce a sentence in Jackdawese: *"Kia, rattle-rattle; Kiaw, zick-zick-zick."* Freely translated, this sentence might read, "Let us fly south to fight the enemy and then fly home to make love." No jackdaw—or indeed, any animal but man—has ever achieved such a linguistic feat.

THE CONTENT OF THE MESSAGES

Thus far, we have looked at the difference in the ways display and true language systems express their messages. But there is also a difference in the content of these messages. Displays are ways of telling a fellow creature what one is about to do. In effect, they are statements about the sender's interpersonal motives at a given time and place. If this is indeed what displays are about we can understand why the relative poverty of the system is no barrier to communication. There is no need for a large vocabulary or a productive combinatorial system, because there is a limit on the number of things an animal wants to do to (or with) another of its own kind: flee, attack, feed or be fed by, copulate, and a few others.

In contrast, human language must describe precisely the world outside and is thus virtually unlimited in its topics. For this, a productive system is absolutely

(Photograph by Benny Ortiz)

363

crucial. The variety of possible events and relationships in the world is infinite, and only a system that is capable of an infinite number of utterances can do justice to this variety.

Some evidence for a fundamental difference in the content of the messages of display and of human language comes from our own experience. We obviously don't use our display systems to tell others about the external world. We don't smile, blush, or embrace so as to inform each other about the Pythagorean theorem or the leak in the upstairs toilet. But conversely, we sometimes feel "at a loss for words" to express emotion and motive (the proper content of display messages). Such matters are often difficult to put into words, or at least words seem inadequate when we finally manage to do so. "I love you" is hard to say and, even if said, is somehow not enough. "I'm very sorry" is pallid as an expression of grief or consolation. In these situations, the more primitive display system is more appropriate because the signal to be sent concerns interpersonal feelings. The beloved is touched, the bereaved is cradled, and these "simple" gestures seem somehow right. Nothing more is gained by speech, because what matters has already been displayed.

ETHOLOGY AND HUMAN NATURE

Over three hundred years have passed since Hobbes described the "war of all against all," which he regarded as the natural state of all mankind. We are still far from having anything that even resembles a definite description of our basic social nature. But at least we know that some of Hobbes's solutions are false or oversimplified. Humans are not built so as to be solitary. Other people are a necessary aspect of our lives, and a tendency to interact with others is built into us at the very outset. What holds for humans holds for most animals as well. The stickleback is pre-programmed to deal with other sticklebacks, the robin with other robins, the baboon with other baboons. Some of these interactions are peaceful, while others are quarrelsome; what matters is that there is always some intercourse between like and like. This social intercourse is an essential aspect of each creature's existence, as shown by an elaborate repertory of built-in social reactions that govern reproduction, care of offspring, and intraspecies competition at virtually all levels of the animal kingdom. No man is an island; neither is any other animal.

SUMMARY

1. Are humans inherently asocial and self-centered? Thomas Hobbes believed that they are. An alternative position, championed by Charles Darwin among others, is that both humans and animals have built-in social dispositions. The study of such innate bases of social reactions has largely focused on animal behavior and has been undertaken by *ethologists.*

2. Most animals exhibit various stereotyped behaviors that are specific to their species, such as the mating pattern of the stickleback. Many of these reactions are *displays,* which serve as communicative signals.

3. One realm of social behavior that has important biological roots is *aggression,* a term generally reserved for conflict between members of the same species. To secure a supply of

resources for themselves and their descendants, many animals (usually the males) stake out a *territory* which they then defend. Various methods have evolved to keep aggression within bounds, including *territoriality* which separates potential combatants in space and *dominance hierarchies* which separate them in social status. Further limitations on aggression include *ritualized fighting,* as well as *threat* and *appeasement displays.*

4. While there are certain parallels between aggression among animals and among humans—for example, *territoriality* and *personal space*—there is reason to suppose that most of the underlying mechanisms are different, in that human aggression depends in great part upon learning and culture.

5. Built-in predispositions figure heavily in various aspects of sexual reproduction. Various displays advertise the animal's sex, its readiness to mate, and its species. Examples are *courtship rituals* which are highly species-specific and tend to prevent animals from interbreeding with members of other species.

6. Sexual behavior is partially controlled by several sex hormones. In mammalian animals, the male hormone, *testosterone,* or the female hormone, *estrogen,* stimulate cells in the hypothalamus which trigger sexual activity. Female animals only mate when they are in *estrus,* the time during which the ovum is ready for fertilization. The female's *estrus cycle* depends on the interplay of estrogen, which stimulates the development of the ovum and makes the animal sexually receptive, and *progesterone,* another female hormone, which prepares the uterus to receive the embryo.

7. In humans, sexual behavior is less dependent upon hormonal conditions. Thus, human females are capable of sexual behavior at any time in their cycle. Some authors believe that the human male-female *pair-bond* grew out of sexual partnerships and is related to the abolition of the estrus period. Others argue that the evolutionary origin of this bond has more to do with the establishment of a family as a better means for taking care of the young.

8. In birds and mammals, innate factors are an important determinant of another bond, that between parents and children. Parental reactions are elicited, at least in part, by various stimulus releasers produced by the young, such as *distress calls* and the human infant's smile.

9. Some inherited behavior patterns, such as the *alarm calls* of certain birds, seem to be biologically unselfish since they don't directly contribute to the survival of the individual or his offspring. Their survival value often depends on *kin selection,* for such acts may save a number of relatives who carry the "altruist's" genes. Another mechanism that may lead to biologically unselfish acts is *reciprocal altruism.* Some authors have tried to explain human altruism in similar, *sociobiological* terms, an attempt that is highly controversial.

10. The key to most animal social behavior is communication by means of displays. Attempts to explain the evolutionary origin of such displays go back to Darwin who proposed that emotional expressions are a preparation for certain actions. Such *intention movements* underlie only some displays. Many others have evolved to serve a signal function but nothing more.

11. Displays are found in humans as well as animals. The major example is *emotional expression.* Many facial expressions seem to be partially based on built-in predispositions; one demonstration is smiling in children born blind. But such facial expressions are also affected by cultural conventions and can be voluntarily inhibited or "faked."

12. While both display repertoires and human language are communications systems, they differ in some important regards. Display systems have a much smaller vocabulary, have no system for rearranging the individual signals to create new "sentences," and only convey something about the sender's present intentions. Human languages have a large vocabulary, have some syntactic system that can rearrange words to form an infinite number of sentences, and can convey messages about just about anything in the world.

CHAPTER 11

Social Psychology

In the preceding chapter, we considered the built-in bases of social behavior. Toward that end, we turned to the animal kingdom and looked at social interactions among sticklebacks and robins, wolves and baboons. None of these animals lives in isolation from their fellows, and so their interactions tell us something about the biological foundations upon which all social life rests, whether in animals or in ourselves. Both animals and humans compete in aggressive encounters, court and mate, provide for their young, and have a repertoire of built-in expressive displays. But these similarities aside, there are of course enormous differences. While the social behavior of animals is relatively rigid and inflexible, that of humans is much more affected by learning—based on their own experience as well as that of previous generations. And our social interactions are vastly more complex than that of any other animal.

In part, this is simply because human social behavior occurs within an intricate network of cultural patterns. Unlike wolves or baboons, we attend school, vote, buy stock, go to church, and join protest demonstrations. These and countless other actions only make sense because of a whole set of social institutions around which much of our life is organized. But in addition, there are cognitive factors. For most of our social interactions depend on how we understand the situation in which they occur.

As an example, take the herring gull which pecks at its neighbor if it comes too close. This is sometimes regarded as analogous to our desire to maintain our "personal distance," and in some ways it may be (see Chapter 10). But the differences are no less striking than the similarities. Consider personal distance in a railroad car. Suppose you are all alone in the car and a stranger approaches and sits down next to you. Your reaction depends upon your interpretation of his action. Is it an attempt to start a conversation, an unwelcome intrusion, a sexual invitation? Or is it simply a response to the fact that all other seats in the car happen

Solomon E. Asch *(Courtesy Swarthmore College)*

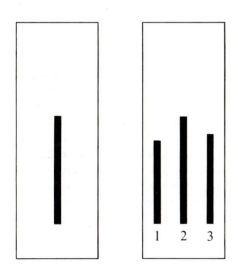

11.1   The stimulus cards in Asch's social pressure experiment   *The cards are drawn to scale. In the actual experiment, they were generally placed on the ledge of a blackboard, separated by forty inches. (Asch, 1956)*

to be covered with soot? The point is that humans don't respond to other people's actions automatically; they respond to those actions as they interpret them. The herring gull has no such subtle problems; any other gull that invades his personal space has to be repelled and that's that.

The purpose of this chapter is to give some sense of the complexity of social behavior in humans. We will organize our account around a central question that is one of the major concerns of modern social psychology: How does an individual interpret social events and how does this interpretation affect his or her actions?

BELIEF AND SOCIAL REALITY

An individual's response to a social situation depends upon what he understands it to be. Romeo killed himself in front of Juliet's tomb because he believed that Juliet was dead; had he known that she was only drugged, the play would have had a happy ending. This simple point forms the basis for much of modern social psychology. But many modern social psychologists make an important further assertion: The way in which we interpret such social events is in principle no different from the way in which we interpret and try to comprehend any event, whether social or not. Seen in this light, many facets of social psychology are simply an aspect of the psychology of thinking and cognition in general.

The Interpersonal Nature of Belief

Much of what we know, we know because of others. The primary medium of this cognitive interdependence is, of course, human language which allows us to share our discoveries and to pass them on to the next generation. As a result, we look at the world not just through our own eyes but also through the eyes of others. To some extent, we all realize that this is so; for example, we are quite aware that our ideas about many foreign lands and cultures are based on what we have heard or read. But the shared aspects of human knowledge go deeper than this, for our very notion of physical reality is at least in part a matter of mutual agreement. This point is made very dramatically in a classic study performed by Solomon Asch (Asch, 1956).

In Asch's experiment, nine or ten subjects are brought together in a laboratory room and shown pairs of cards placed a few feet in front of them. On one card is a black line, say, 8 inches long. On the other card are three lines of varying lengths, say 6¼, 8, and 6¾ inches (Figure 11.1). The subjects are asked to make a simple perceptual judgment. They have to indicate which of the three lines on the one card is equal in length to the one line on the other card. Then the experimenter tells the subjects that this procedure is only a minor prelude to another study and casually asks them, in the interest of saving time, to indicate their judgments aloud by calling them out in turn (the three comparison lines are designated by the numbers 1, 2, and 3 printed underneath them). This procedure continues for a dozen or so pairs of cards.

Considering the sizable differences among the stimuli, the task is absurdly simple except for one thing: There is only one "real" subject. All of the others are the experimenter's secret confederates. They have arranged their seating order so that

A   B   C

*11.2   The subject in a social pressure
experiment   (A) The true subject (center)
listens to the instructions. (B) On hearing
the unanimous verdict of the others, he
leans forward to look at the cards more
carefully. (C) After twelve such trials, on all
of which he remained independent, he
explains that "he has to call them as he sees
them." (Photographs by William
Vandivert)*

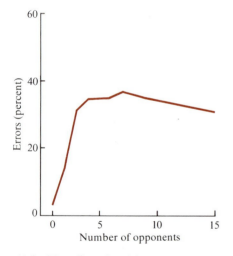

*11.3   The effect of social pressure   The
extent to which the subject yielded against
the size of the group pitted against him is
demonstrated by this figure. In this
situation, the effect of group size seems to
reach a maximum at three, though other
studies (such as Gerard, Wilhelmy, and
Connolley, 1968) have found that
conformity continues to rise beyond this
point as the number of opponents
increases. (After Asch, 1955)*

most of them will call out their judgments before the real subject's turn comes
around. After the first few trials, they unanimously render false judgments on
most of the ones thereafter. For example, the confederates might declare that a
6¼-inch line equals an 8-inch line, and so on, for a dozen more trials. What does
the real subject do now? (See Figure 11.2.)

Asch found that the chances were less than one in four that the real subject
would be fully independent and would stick to his guns on all trials on which the
group disagreed with him (Figure 11.3). Most of them yielded to the group on at
least some occasions, in fine disregard of the evidence of their senses—a result
with rather uncomfortable implications for the democratic process. When interviewed after the experiment, most of the yielding subjects made it clear that the
group didn't really affect how they *saw* the lines. No matter what everyone else
said, the 8-inch line still looked bigger than the 6¼-inch line. But the subjects
wondered whether they were right, became worried about their vision and sanity,
and were exceedingly embarrassed at expressing their deviance in public (Asch,
1952, 1956; Asch and Gleitman, 1953).

But the really important question is not why some subjects outwardly complied with the group while others stood their ground. For our present purposes,
there is an even more important result of Asch's study that pertains to how the
subjects *felt*. In this regard, most of them were alike. Some yielded and some were
independent; but, assuming they did not suspect a trick (and few of them did),
they were generally very much disturbed. Why all the furor?

The answer is that Asch's procedure had violated a basic premise of the subjects' existence: However people may differ, they all share the same physical reality. Under the circumstances, it is small wonder that Asch's subjects were deeply
alarmed by a discrepancy they had never previously encountered. (Needless to
say, the whole experiment was carefully explained to them immediately thereafter.) There is an old movie, *Gaslight*, in which the villainous husband of a
wealthy heiress cleverly stage-manages various physical occurrences, such as in-
explicably flickering gaslights, which he then denies having seen. His object is to
have his wife doubt her own sanity so he can gain control of her fortune. Both
Asch and the movie make the same point. Our belief in physical reality is tied up
with our assumption that it is shared by others.

What accounts for this assumption of a socially shared reality? To answer this
question we must first ask what we mean when we say that an object is "real."
One criterion is that the various senses provide *consistent* information. Macbeth
sees a dagger but cannot touch it and therefore regards it as "a dagger of the mind,
a false creation proceeding from the heat-oppressed brain." Another criterion is
consistency across time. Real objects provide what one philosopher called a "per-

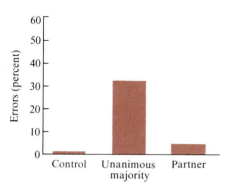

11.4 The effect of social pressure when the subject has a partner *The figure shows the errors when there is no social pressure, when there is a unanimous majority (here, of eight), and when the subject has a partner. It is clear that the amount of yielding drops markedly when the subject is no longer alone. (Data from Asch, 1958)*

manent possibility of a sensation." You may look away from a tree, but it is still there when your gaze returns to it a moment later (J.S. Mill, 1865). At least in adults, the general notion of a fixed reality that is "out there" and independent of our momentary point of view is a rock-bottom concept which is accepted without question. If it is challenged, we become deeply disturbed.

A similar consistency principle may account for the fact that our reality is shared with others. If reality is initially defined by agreement among different perceptions and memories within one person, it may well be that this definition is eventually expanded to include agreement among different persons. The belief that others see, feel, and hear pretty much as we do will then become a cognitive axiom of our everyday existence. When this axiom is violated, as it is in Asch's experiment, a vital prop is knocked out from under us, a prop so basic that we never even knew that it was there.

How many people have to share our perception of the world if we are to maintain our faith in its reality? We can tolerate (or ignore) some disagreement with others if we are not completely devoid of social support. In a pinch, one lone supporter is enough. In a variation of Asch's experiment, one of the experimenter's confederates acted as the real subject's ally; all other confederates gave unanimous false judgments while the one ally's judgments were true. Under these conditions, the real subject yielded very rarely and was not particularly upset. The moral is simple: One person who believes as we do can sustain us against all others. Two against all is a valiant band; one against all is all too often regarded as a crackpot (Figure 11.4).

Social Comparison

The Asch study shows what happens when the clear evidence of one's own senses is contradicted by the verdict of a unanimous group. But suppose that our own perception does not provide a clear-cut answer. This would happen for example if the lines differed by only a small amount. If left to our own devices, we would try to obtain some further sensory evidence. We must look at the lines once more but from a different angle, or try to measure them with a ruler. But if we can't do that, it is only reasonable to listen to what others say. Their judgment can then be used in lieu of further information provided by our own eyes or hands. If the others should now disagree with us, we might well change our own answer on their say-so. Several studies have shown that this is precisely what occurs in an Asch-type experiment in which the discrimination is fairly difficult. There is more yielding and very little emotional disturbance (Crutchfield, 1955).

This general line of reasoning may explain why people seek the opinion of others whenever they are confronted by a situation which they do not fully comprehend. To evaluate the situation, they need more information. If they cannot get it first hand, they will try to compare their own reactions to those of others (Festinger, 1954). The need for *social comparison* is especially pronounced when the evaluations pertain to social issues, such as the qualifications of a political candidate or the pros and cons of fluoridating the water supply.

REFERENCE GROUPS

Whose opinion will we seek out if we ourselves are unsure? Not everyone serves equally well. If we have to judge which of two very similar tones is of higher pitch,

369

we are more likely to ask a musician than a friend whom we know to be tone deaf. But to whom do we turn when we want to evaluate what to do or to think about social matters? Here the tendency is to refer to persons who share some common sentiments and social assumptions and who will then represent our *reference group.* The adolescent who is in doubt about what to wear to a dance wants to know what his friends think; his parents' views on this matter (and many others) have little effect.

GROUP SUPPORT

A widely quoted demonstration of the social comparison process is provided in a study by Stanley Schachter (1959). Schachter's subjects were told that the experiment for which they volunteered was about the effects of electric shock on human physiology. Some subjects were made to feel extremely apprehensive by being informed that the shocks they were to receive "will be quite painful but, of course, . . . will do no permanent damage." Others were assured that the shocks would produce only a mild tingle and would not be painful at all. Not surprisingly, the first group of subjects was much more frightened than the second, as shown by subsequent questioning.

In actual fact, no shocks were ever administered. The key part of the experiment occurred just prior to an initial ten-minute delay while the subjects were waiting (so they thought) for the equipment to be set up. The experimenter explained that the subject could wait in one of several rooms outside of the laboratory. As an afterthought, he added that some people might prefer to wait alone while others might like to spend the ten minutes in the company of other subjects who were also waiting to participate in the same experiment. The results were clear-cut. The more frightened subjects were much more likely to choose the company of others than were subjects who had been reassured that the shocks would be of little consequence.

Fear evidently leads to a desire to be with others, but why? According to Schachter, one reason is social comparison. The fearful subject is unsure whether his own emotional reactions are really appropriate. One way of evaluating his own feelings is to talk to others who are about to suffer a similar fate. To paraphrase Schachter's own summary, misery loves company—especially if it is miserable company.

Cognitive Consistency and Beliefs

The preceding discussion has shown that people try to make sense of the world they encounter. But how? In effect, they do this by looking for some consistency among their own experiences and memories, and then turning to other people for comparison and confirmation. If all checks out, then well and good. But what if there is some inconsistency? The Asch study showed what happened when there is a serious inconsistency between one's own experiences (and the beliefs based on them) and those reported by others. But suppose the inconsistency is among the person's own experiences, beliefs, or actions? Many social psychologists believe that this will trigger some general tendency to restore cognitive consistency —to reinterpret the situation so as to minimize whatever inconsistency may be there. According to Leon Festinger, this is because any perceived inconsistency among various aspects of knowledge, feelings, and behavior sets up an unpleasant

internal state—***cognitive dissonance***—which people try to reduce whenever possible (Festinger, 1957).

Suppose you read a newspaper headline, "Citizens of Moscow Denounce Communism at Mass Rally." At first you are puzzled by this new bit of information, for it doesn't fit in with what you already know and believe. Is it a joke? You look at the date and find out that it is not April 1. Was there another revolution in Russia? You haven't read a paper for a week, but surely someone would have told you. The whole business makes no sense. Unless . . . You suddenly find the reinterpretation that sets your cognitive world aright—it was Moscow, *Idaho.*

Cognitive dissonance is not always reduced so easily. An example is provided by a study of a sect that was awaiting the end of the world. The founder of the sect announced that she had received a message from the "Guardians" of outer space. On a certain day, there would be an enormous flood. Only the true believers were to be saved and would be picked up at midnight of the appointed day in flying saucers. (Technology has advanced considerably since the days of Noah's Ark.) On doomsday, the members of the sect huddled together, awaiting the predicted cataclysm. The arrival time of the flying saucers came and went; tension mounted as the hours went by. Finally, the leader of the sect received another message: To reward the faith of the faithful, the world was saved. Joy broke out, and the believers became more faithful than ever (Festinger, Riecken, and Schachter, 1956).

Given the failure of a clear-cut prophecy, one might have expected the very opposite. A disconfirmation of a predicted event should presumably lead one to abandon the beliefs that produced the prediction. But cognitive dissonance theory says otherwise. By abandoning the belief that there are Guardians, the person who had once held this belief would have to accept a painful dissonance between her present skepticism and her past beliefs and actions. Her prior faith would now appear extremely foolish. Some members of the sect had gone to such lengths as giving up their jobs or spending their savings; such acts would lose all meaning in retrospect without the belief in the Guardians. Under the circumstances, the dissonance was intolerable. It was reduced by a belief in the new message which bolstered the original belief. Since other members of the sect stood fast along with them, their conviction was strengthened all the more. They could now think of themselves, not as fools, but as loyal, steadfast members of a courageous little band whose faith had saved the earth.

ATTITUDES

Thus far, we have focused on the way people interpret the social situation in which they find themselves and how these interpretations determine what they think and believe. What we have not dealt with as yet is the fact that in the social realm, many beliefs are accompanied by strong feelings. Take the conviction that abortion is murder—a far cry from the many beliefs we hold that are completely unencumbered by emotion, such as our nonchalant assurance that the sum of the angles of a triangle is 180 degrees. Emotionally tinged social views of the former kind are generally called ***attitudes.*** Since various people often have different attitudes, they tend to interpret many social situations differently; the same crowd may look like a group of peaceful demonstrators to one observer and like a rioting mob to another.

As modern social psychologists use the term, an attitude is a rather stable mental position held toward some idea, or object, or person. Examples are attitudes toward nuclear power, the legalization of marijuana, school integration, or packaged breakfast foods. Every attitude is a combination of beliefs, feelings, and evaluations, and some predisposition to act accordingly. Thus, people who differ in their attitudes toward nuclear power will probably have different beliefs on the subject (e.g., "nuclear power plants are—or are not—unsafe"), will evaluate it differently (from extreme *pro* to extreme *con*), and these differences will make them more likely to take some actions rather than others (e.g., to support or protest the construction of a new nuclear plant).

Attitudes and Behavior

Attitudes can be measured in a number of ways. The most widely used methods involve some form of self-report. For example, the subject might be given an ***attitude questionnaire*** with items that relate to the matter at hand. Thus, in a questionnaire on energy policy and a cluster of related issues, subjects might be given a statement such as: "The current gasoline shortage is not a real one; it is being caused by the big oil companies so that they can raise prices." They would then be asked to select a number between, say, $+10$ and -10 to indicate the extent of their agreement or disagreement. The sum of a person's responses to a number of statements that all tap the same concerns may then provide a quantitative expression of that person's attitude.

Do attitudes as measured by self-report predict what people actually do? The question has led to controversy, for some earlier reports suggested that the relationship is much weaker than one might have thought. During the thirties when there was considerable prejudice against Orientals, Richard LaPiere traveled through the country with a Chinese couple and stopped at over fifty hotels and motels and at nearly two hundred restaurants. All but one hotel gave them accommodations, and no restaurant refused them service. Later on the very same establishments received a letter that asked whether they would house or serve Chinese persons. Ninety-two percent of the replies were "No" (LaPiere, 1934). It appeared that there was a major inconsistency between people's attitudes as verbally expressed and their actual behavior.

What explains this inconsistency? One factor is the role of the situation. Situational pressures are sometimes strong enough to override other considerations: just about everybody stops at a red light, regardless of whether they are bold or shy (see Chapter 18). The same holds true for attitudes. LaPiere's Chinese couple consisted of two young students who were attractive and well-groomed and who were accompanied by a white professor. Here, the situational pressures might have made refusal sufficiently difficult and embarrassing to override the ethnic prejudice.

Another factor is how specifically the attitude is defined. One study analyzed the relation between general attitudes to environmentalism and a particular act: volunteering for various activities of the Sierra Club. They found no relation. But when they tested the attitudes toward the Sierra Club as such, they found a substantial correlation between attitude and action; those who stated strongly positive views were much more likely to volunteer (Weigel, Vernon, and Tognacci, 1974). Still, there is some evidence that even some rather generally defined attitudes can predict behavior under at least some circumstances. In a study conducted in England, the investigators first assessed attitudes toward the Irish in various households. They then sent letters to these same households, but these letters had the wrong address. In half the cases, the addressee had an English name; in the other half, the name was clearly Irish. Although there was a return address, the question was whether or not the letter would be returned. If the addressee's name was Irish, the result depended upon the recipient's attitudes. Those who had previously expressed pro-Irish sentiments were more likely to return the letters than those who held unfavorable views (Howitt and McCabe, 1978).

Attitude Change

While attitudes have a certain resilience, their stability is threatened at every turn; especially in modern mass society, our attitudes and beliefs are under continual assault. Hundreds of commercials urge us to buy one product rather than another, political candidates clamor for our vote, and any number of organizations exhort us to fight for (or against) arms control, or legalized abortion, or environmental protection, and so on and so on. When we add these mass-produced appeals to the numerous private attempts at persuasion undertaken by our friends and relatives (let alone our would-be lovers), it is hardly surprising that attitudes sometimes do change. Social psychologists have spent a great deal of effort in trying to understand how such attitude changes come about.

PERSUASIVE COMMUNICATIONS

A number of investigators have studied the effectiveness of so-called *persuasive communications.* These are messages that openly try to persuade us—to stop smoking, endorse the ERA, favor capital punishment, or whatever. There have been numerous studies to isolate the factors that determine whether the message has the desired effect. By and large, the results of such studies have not been especially surprising. One factor is the credibility of the source. Does the speaker seem to know what she is talking about? Can we assume that she has nothing to gain from persuading us? If the answer to both questions is yes, we're more likely to

Trying to persuade the voters *When Grover S. Cleveland ran for president in 1884, he was accused of being the father of an illegitimate child and therefore as being morally unfit for office. Cleveland admitted the charge but won the election anyway.*

believe her (Hovland and Weiss, 1952; Walster, Aronson, and Abrahams, 1966). Another factor concerns the message itself. If the position it advocates is too far removed from that held by the listener, persuasion is less likely (Freedman, 1964; Eagly and Telaak, 1972).

COGNITIVE DISSONANCE AND ATTITUDE CHANGE

We've already seen that attitudes can affect behavior. But the relation can also go the other way. For in some situations, what an individual does will lead to a change in his attitude. According to some social psychologists, this effect is produced by a tendency to reduce cognitive dissonance analogous to that which we've considered in the context of a change in beliefs.

Justification of effort Suppose there is some inconsistency between a person's attitudes and his behavior. Suppose further that the behavior is something he has already done. How can he reconcile the inconsistency now? He can't change his behavior, for that's past and done with. All he can do is to readjust his present attitude.

Dissonance theorists point to a number of studies that demonstrate attitude changes that preserve some harmony between past acts and present attitudes. Some of these studies concern the retrospective justification of effort. People often make considerable sacrifices to attain a goal—backbreaking exertion to scale a mountain, years and years of study to become a cardiologist. Was it worth it? According to dissonance theory, the goal will be esteemed more highly the harder it was to reach. If it were not, there would be cognitive dissonance. Support comes from common observation of the effects of harsh initiation rites, such as fraternity hazing or the rigors of Marine bootcamp. After the ordeal is passed, the initiates seem to value their newly found membership all the more. Similar ef-

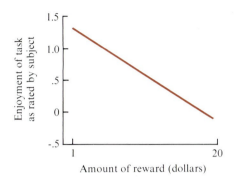

11.5 The effect of forced compliance on attitude *After being paid either $1 or $20 to tell someone that a boring task they had just performed was very interesting, subjects were asked to rate their own true attitude. As the figure shows, subjects who were only paid $1 gave a much higher rating than those paid $20. (After Festinger and Carlsmith, 1959)*

fects have been obtained in the laboratory. Subjects admitted to a discussion group after going through a fairly harsh screening test put a higher value on their new membership (Aronson and Mills, 1959; Gerard and Mathewson, 1966).

Forced compliance   A related result is the effect of ***forced compliance.*** The basic idea is simple. Suppose someone agrees to give a speech in support of a view that is contrary to his own position, as in the case of a bartender arguing for prohibition. Will his public act change his private views? The answer seems to depend upon why he agreed to make the speech in the first place. If he was bribed by an enormous sum, there will be little effect. As he looks back upon his public denunciation of alcohol, he knows why he did what he did; $500 in cold cash is justification enough. But suppose he gave the speech with lesser urging and received only a trifling sum. If we later ask what he thinks about prohibition, we will find that he has begun to believe in his own speech. According to Festinger, the reason is cognitive dissonance. If the bartender asks himself why he took a public stand so contrary to his own attitudes, he can find no adequate justification; the few dollars he received are not enough. To reduce the dissonance, the compliant bartender does the only thing he can: He decides that what he said wasn't really all that different from what he believes.

A number of studies have demonstrated such forced compliance effects in the laboratory. In a classic experiment, subjects were asked to perform several extremely boring tasks, such as packing spools into a tray and then unpacking and turning one screw after another for a quarter turn. When they were finished, they were induced to tell another subject (who was about to engage in the same activities) that the tasks were really very interesting. They were paid either $1 or $20 for lying in this way. When later asked how enjoyable they had found the tasks, the well-paid subjects said that they were boring, while the poorly paid subjects said that they were fairly interesting. This result is rather remarkable. One might have guessed that the well-paid liar would have been more persuaded by his own arguments than the poorly paid one. But contrary to this initial intuition—and in line with dissonance theory—the exact opposite was the case (Figure 11.5).

Protecting the self-picture   Justification of effort and the effect of forced compliance seem to be ways of reducing dissonance. But just what is this dissonance that is here reduced? In the early days of dissonance theory, dissonance was regarded as largely equivalent to logical inconsistency, like the inconsistency between the belief that the earth moves around the sun and the belief that it is at the center of the solar system. There is little doubt that cognitions are often adjusted to become consistent in just this sense. A person who hears the mumbled sentence *The woman shaved himself* is likely to hear it as *The man shaved himself* or *The woman shaved herself,* so that noun and pronoun will agree. The question is whether all cases of dissonance reduction boil down to an analogous tendency to keep cognitions logically consistent. A number of authors believe that some noncognitive, emotional factors often also play a role. One such factor is an effort to maintain a favorable picture of ourselves (Aronson, 1969).

Consider the justification of effort. People who have made a great sacrifice to attain some goal will value it more than those who achieved the goal with little effort. One reason could be a tendency toward logical consistency: the worth of the goal has to match its cost, just as the noun must fit with the pronoun. But another reason might be a desire to maintain a favorable self-picture. An individual who goes through a difficult initiation rite to join a club, and later discovers that the club is really rather dull, might well feel like a fool. To avoid this, she adjusts her attitude to fit her own acts and overvalues her group membership.

A similar point applies to the effect of forced compliance. A subject who has argued for a position he himself doesn't hold will change his attitude to fit his arguments (assuming he wasn't paid too much for presenting them). The critical factor may again be an attempt to maintain a favorable self-picture. We prefer to think of ourselves as good and moral. But can we do so if we have just persuaded someone of a view we do not hold ourselves? If we can manage to change our own views just a bit (which is easier if we weren't paid too much for lying), we can salve our conscience. Some evidence for this interpretation comes from a study in which subjects were paid to write an essay that gave arguments in favor of a position they themselves were opposed to (the legalization of marijuana). Writing this essay only led to a change in the (poorly paid) subjects' own views if they believed their essay would be shown to people who had *not* made up their minds on the issue. What mattered is that the subjects thought that they would affect another person's views. If so, they might well feel responsible and experience moral qualms. But these qualms could be allayed if they changed their attitude in the direction of the views in their essays (Nel, Helmreich, and Aronson, 1969).*

Attitude Stability

We've seen that attitudes can be changed—by certain forms of persuasion (if the source is credible and trustworthy and if the message is appropriate) and by tendencies toward cognitive consistency (especially with regard to acts we've already performed). But on balance, the overall picture is one of attitude stability rather than of attitude change. Attitudes can be altered, but it takes some doing. By and large, there seems to be a tendency to hold on to the attitudes one already has.

Why should this be so? One reason is cognitive consistency, which on the whole is a force to keep things as they are. As an example, take the general public's evaluation of televised presidential debates. Such confrontations may have an effect on those who are still undecided, but they seem to do little to shake the faith of those who are already committed. In the 1976 presidential debates between Gerald Ford and Jimmy Carter, the judgment of "who did the better job" depended largely on who did the judging. Those initially in favor of Carter were sure that he had won the debate; those originally in favor of Ford were no less certain that their candidate was the winner (Freedman, Sears, and Carlsmith, 1981).

Another reason for attitude stability is that people generally stay in the same social and economic environment. Their family, their friends and fellow workers, their social and economic situations tend to remain much the same over the years. Top-level executives know other top executives, and trade union members know other union members. On any one day, they may read or hear a speech that advocates a position contrary to their own, and they may even be affected. But on that evening and the day after, they will go back to the same old setting and will encounter the same old views that they had held before. Under the circumstances, it is hardly surprising that attitude stability is more common than atti-

---

* Seen in this light, dissonance reduction is essentially equivalent to what Sigmund Freud called "rationalization" (see Chapter 12).

tude change. To be sure, there are striking events that may transform our attitudes completely—not just our own, but also those of everyone around us. An example is the news of the attack on Pearl Harbor on December 7, 1941. Without a doubt, this led to an instant and radical change in Americans' attitudes toward Japan. But by their very nature, such events—and the extreme changes in attitudes they produce—are rare.

PERCEIVING OTHERS

Thus far our discussion of how people interpret the social world has focused upon the way in which they try to harmonize various events with their beliefs and attitudes. A similar approach has been applied to find out how we form impressions of other people and how we try to understand why they do what they do.

Forming Impressions

In the course of ordinary life we encounter many other people. The vast majority of them play the role of anonymous extras in each of our private dramas, especially in the big cities where we briefly cross the paths of countless strangers of whom we will never know anything. But a sizable number of other persons do impinge upon our lives, as bit players (a traffic cop of whom we ask directions), supporting cast (a casual acquaintance), and starring leads (friends, lovers, bosses, enemies). These we cannot help but evaluate and try to understand as they, in their turn, evaluate and try to understand us. Much of the plot of our own dramas (and of theirs) depends upon the outcome of these mutual social attempts at understanding. How are they achieved?

Perceiving the characteristics of another person is in some ways analogous to perceiving certain stable attributes of a physical object, such as its shape or size. In our previous discussion of visual perception, we saw that to do this the observer must extract certain invariant properties from the stimulus pattern (see Chapter 6). He must abstract the crucial relationships within the stimulus input so that he can see the form of the object, say, a catlike shape. He must also disregard various features of the stimulus pattern that tend to obscure the stable characteristics of the object; examples are illumination, distance, and angle of regard. By doing all this, the observer attains perceptual constancy and can answer such life-and-death questions as whether he is dealing with a kitten nearby or a tiger far away. He has managed to perceive the real, distal stimulus through the masking surface manifestations of the ever-changing proximal stimulus.

Something analogous occurs when we perceive—or rather, infer—such attributes of a person as his violent temper or warmth, and so on. In effect, we are making a judgment as to what the person is "really" like, a judgment independent of the particular moment and occasion. His personal attributes (often called *traits)* are inferred invariant properties that seem to characterize his behavior in different situations. When we say that a person is irascible, we don't mean that he will utter an impolite expletive when someone deliberately steps on his toe. We mean that he will generally be short-tempered over a wide range of circumstances. To put it another way, the attempt to understand what another person is like boils down to an effort to note the *consistencies* in what he does over time and under different circumstances (see Chapter 18).

The question is how this consistency is abstracted from the few bits of behavior of the other person that are all we can actually observe. Several authors have dealt with different facets of this question, using much the same analogy to visual perception as the one here presented (Heider, 1958).*

IMPRESSIONS OF OTHERS AS PATTERNS

The most fundamental fact of form perception is that perceived form depends upon the *relations* among the elements of which the form is composed; it is a Gestalt which does not depend upon these elements in isolation. Thus, a triangle can be composed of dots or crosses and remain the same triangle (see Chapter 6). According to Solomon Asch, a similar principle describes our conceptions of other people. In his view, these conceptions of others are not a simple aggregate of the attributes we perceive them to have. Instead, they form an organized whole whose elements are interpreted in relation to the overall pattern (Asch, 1952).

To test his hypothesis, Asch performed several experiments on how people form impressions of others. His technique was to give subjects a list of attributes which they were told described the same person. Their task was to write a short sketch of the person so characterized and to rate this person on a checklist of antonyms (generous/ungenerous, good-natured/irritable). In one study, some subjects were given a list of seven traits: *intelligent, skillful, industrious, warm, determined, practical, cautious.* Other subjects received the same list except that *cold* was substituted for *warm.* The resulting sketches were quite different. The "warm person" was seen as "driven by the desire to accomplish something that would be of benefit" while the "cold person" was described as "snobbish . . . calculating and unsympathetic." The checklist results were in the same direction. The person described as warm was seen as generous, happy, and good-natured. The "cold person" was characterized by the appropriate antonyms (Asch, 1946). It appears that the warm/cold trait acted as a focus around which the total impression of the person was organized. To use Asch's term, it was a **central trait** that determined the perception of the whole.

Some other findings give further credence to the patterning hypothesis. One group received a list in which *warm* was embedded in a rather unflattering context: obedient, weak, shallow, *warm,* unambitious, vain. Given this backdrop, the attribute *warm* acquired a different and less favorable meaning. It was seen as "a dog-like affection . . . passive and without strength." (For some methodological criticisms, see Wishner, 1960.)

Some recent investigators have tried to understand this patterning process by appealing to some concepts in modern theories of memory and thinking. Their idea is that our perception of others is based upon schemas and prototypes. A **schema** is a set of organized expectations about the way in which different behaviors of people hang together; a **prototype** is a mental concept of the typical way that a person would act. Schemas and prototypes necessarily govern the way we interpret what people do. If we believe that someone is outgoing and gregarious,

---

* A similar analogy holds for language. Speakers and listeners perceive the common **underlying structure** in sentences that differ in their **surface structure,** recognizing that *The dog bites the cat* is more or less equivalent to *The cat is bitten by the dog* (Gleitman, 1985; see Chapter 9).

we will also expect her to be relatively talkative. In this regard, our perception of people is analogous to the way in which we perceive forms. If we think that a form is a triangle, we expect it to have three angles. If we believe that a person is a "strong-and-silent man," we expect him to be heroic (Cantor and Mischel, 1978).

FIRST IMPRESSIONS

New items of information are often incorporated into patterns of organization that are already there. A familiar example is the effect of mental set. If subjects expect to be shown the name of an animal, then a very brief presentation of D-CK will be seen as DUCK rather than as DOCK (see Chapter 8). Our everyday experience suggests that a similar phenomenon occurs in person perception. Our first impression of someone often determines how we interpret what we find out about him later on.

This point was illustrated by Asch in another version of his experiment with personal trait lists. One group of subjects was told to describe their impressions of a person who is *intelligent, industrious, impulsive, critical, stubborn,* and *envious.* Another group received the same traits in reverse order. The results suggest that it pays to put one's best foot forward. If the list began on a positive note, it set up a favorable evaluative tone that seemed to overpower the later negative attributes; the opposite effect occurred when the unfavorable traits came first (Asch, 1946). Similar ***primacy effects*** have been obtained by other investigators, but their explanation is still a matter of debate. According to Asch, the later attributes take on different shades of meaning depending upon the context provided by the traits encountered earlier in the sequence.

Primacy effects can be considerable, but they can of course be overcome just as mental set can be broken. We sometimes do change our minds and come to respect or even love a person whom we detested on first meeting. The primacy effect only means that such alterations in judgment encounter a certain inertia. In old Hollywood movies, the fact that the hero and heroine took an instant dislike to each other was a tip-off to the audience that they would clinch by the final frame. But in real life, first impressions generally make more of a difference. If nothing else, they often preclude the chance of a later reevaluation.

Attribution

As previously pointed out, the attempt to understand what another person is like is really an attempt to find the pattern, the consistency, in what he does. An important step is to infer what *caused* his behavior, for the meaning of any given act depends upon its cause. Consider a football player who bumps an opponent in the course of a game. If the bumping occurred while a play was in progress, not much is revealed about the bumper's personality; he was behaving according to the rules of the game. But if the bump occurred some seconds after the official blew his whistle and the play was over, the situation is different. Now the act is more revealing, suggesting a grudge or a nasty disposition. The bumpee will conclude that the bumper's action was *internally caused* and he will self-righteously become a bumper in his turn.

In such examples, the observer has to decide to which of several possible causes the behavior of the person should be attributed. An influential approach, often called *attribution theory,* takes the study of how such decisions are reached as its special concern (Heider, 1958; Jones et al., 1971; Jones and Nisbett, 1972; Kelley and Michela, 1980). To answer the question "Why did he bump me?" one considers the conditions under which bumping is known to occur. Does it generally occur in circumstances just like now? Would most other people do the same under similar circumstances? If the answer is yes, the behavior will be attributed to essentially external causes, such as the social pressures of team play. But if the answer is no, the act will be attributed to an internal disposition of the actor. He is a dirty player who took a "cheap shot."

SITUATIONS VERSUS DISPOSITIONS

These everyday observations are supported by several laboratory investigations which show that people consider *situational factors* when trying to infer the *dispositional qualities* of a person on the basis of that person's actions. Here, "dispositional quality" refers to any underlying attribute that characterizes a particular individual and makes him more disposed than others to engage in the particular act we've just observed. Examples of such dispositional qualities are the presence or absence of some ability (e.g., falling because one is clumsy) or of some motive or personality pattern (e.g., not tipping a waiter because one is stingy). In one study, subjects were asked to rate the personality traits of job applicants on the basis of a (specially prepared) taped job interview. When the applicant described himself in terms that fit the position's requirements, the subjects had little confidence that they learned what the job-seeker was really like. But when the applicant's self-description was discrepant from what the job called for, the subjects usually took him at his word (Jones, Davis, and Gergen, 1961). A waiter who smiles at a guest tells us less about himself than one who is surly.

But while we take account of situational factors in judging the behavior of others, we do so less than we really should. There seems to be a powerful bias to attribute behavior to dispositional qualities in the person while underrating the role of the external situation. The person on welfare is often judged to be lazy (a dispositional attribute) when he is really unable to find work (a situational attribute). Similarly for our interpretation of public affairs. We look for heroes or scapegoats and tend to praise or blame political leaders for acts they had little control over.

Our perception of others is evidently often off the mark. To put this in terms of our previous perceptual analogy, it appears that there is imperfect "person constancy." Our visual system does an excellent job at discounting illumination, distance, and orientation, thus yielding the perceptual constancies of brightness, size, and shape. But social perception is nowhere as accurate as this. We are too prone to view acts as caused by something within an actor, so that all too often, the question "Why did it happen?" becomes "Whose fault was it?"

ACTORS VERSUS OBSERVERS

The tendency to underrate the importance of situational factors only occurs when we try to understand the behavior of others. The results are quite different when we ourselves are the actor rather than the observer. When we now try to explain our own acts, the cause seems less in us and more in the external situation. Someone trips and we think he's careless or clumsy. But when we ourselves trip, we say the floor is slippery. This is the ***actor-observer difference*** in attribution—situational when we ourselves are the actor, dispositional when we are the observer (Jones and Nisbett, 1972).

The actor-observer difference has been repeatedly demonstrated in the laboratory. An example is a study which showed that subjects were quite willing to describe their friends by choosing between various pairs on a personality questionnaire (e.g., lenient vs. firm, cautious vs. bold). But when asked to characterize themselves by means of the same adjective pairs, they were much more careful about the use of dispositional terms and often checked the noncommittal alternative "it depends on the situation" (Nisbett et al., 1973).

What explains this actor-observer difference in attribution? One explanation may simply be that we know ourselves better than we know anyone else. Let's say that on one evening we undertip a waiter in a restaurant. Should we make the dispositional attribution that we're stingy? Others who have never seen us in a similar situation might well conclude that we are. But we ourselves will disagree. We have observed ourselves in many restaurants and know that we normally tip properly. But if this is so, our recent act says nothing about our personal characteristics; rather, it must be caused by the situation—perhaps the waiter was rude, or we suddenly discovered that we didn't bring enough cash. Our attribution is different when we see someone else do the very same thing. We'll interpret his action dispositionally and conclude that *he* is stingy. After all, we haven't seen him in remotely as many restaurant situations as we've seen ourselves. So the one act of his that we did see weighs more heavily and can't be discounted. Some evidence in line with this hypothesis comes from a study which shows that the tendency to make dispositional attributions is somewhat less when the person we're describing is a close friend than a mere acquaintance (Nisbett et al., 1973).

There is another factor that contributes to the difference between actors and observers—the two have different perspectives. To the observer, what stands out perceptually is the actor and his actions. The situation that calls out these actions is seen much less clearly; in part, because the stimuli to which the actor responds are not as readily visible from the observer's vantage point. The reverse holds for the actor. He is not focused on his own behavior. One reason is that he can hardly see his own actions (some, such as his own facial expressions are literally invisible to him). What he attends to is the situation around him—the place, the people, and how he interprets them all. If we assume that whatever serves as the main center of attention is more likely to be seen as the cause of whatever happens, then the differences in attribution follow: dispositional for the observer, situational for the actor (Heider, 1958).

Perceiving Others While Being Seen

The means whereby we interpret the social world are in many ways analogous to those that underlie the perception of our physical environment. In both cases, we try to abstract some intrinsic characteristic of an object from the welter of distorting stimulus features in which it appears: to perceive the real size of a distal object independent of its distance, to infer the real feelings or motives of a person independent of her role, even when that person happens to be our own self.

But this analogy to visual perception can be pushed too far, for social perception is more complex. It is a two-way process in which all participants are potential stimuli as well as observers, are capable of being seen as well as of seeing. And most important, each participant knows this and knows that the others know it too. As a result, perceiving people is in one sense very different from perceiving a physical object like a rock. The rock doesn't know that we are looking at it, and it surely isn't trying to make a particular impression. People are considerably more troublesome than this.

SELF-PRESENTATION

In contrast to rocks, people are constantly working at *impression management,* a term coined by the sociologist Erving Goffman (1959). As Goffman sees it, much of social interaction is akin to a theatrical performance in which the actors are "putting on a front." Some "play hard to get," others wear elaborately contrived "casual looks," still others try to appear "above it all." Many of these impressions go along with social or professional roles. The medical student soon discovers that there is more to becoming a doctor than acquiring certain medical skills. He must also learn how to look like a doctor, how to instill confidence, how to develop a proper "bedside manner." The audience for whom such productions are staged often includes the actors themselves. The would-be-healer gradually comes to believe his own role, as one patient after another greets him as "Doctor" and treats his pronouncements with reverential awe.

Goffman points out that many of these social performances are jointly produced. To begin with, the actor is often supported by a team. The doctor's image is maintained not only by his own behavior but by that of various aides and nurses as well. Further support comes from the audience itself. We often go to considerable lengths to preserve another person's self-presentation, to allow her to "save face." If we want to break off an encounter at a cocktail party, we pretend that we are going to the bar for another drink. The other person knows that we have no intention of returning, and we know that he knows, but this doesn't matter. Both participants tactfully play along. This kind of tact can reach consummate heights as in the case of the legendary English butler who accidentally surprised a lady in her bath and hurriedly mumbled, "I beg your pardon, Sir."

Impression management *The advertising industry spares no effort to tell us that we can be who we want to be by wearing the appropriate clothes, makeup, eyeglasses, and so on and so on. (Courtesy Country Set)*

KEYS

There is yet another dimension to social perception that adds to its already awesome complexity. A particular pattern of social interaction can have different meanings depending upon how it is *keyed,* to use Goffman's term (1974). A *key* is a signal (analogous to keys in musical notation) that indicates the sense in which some act or utterance should be taken. Consider a nude model at an art class. The situation is keyed to make nudity nonsexual. To preserve this key, both model and art students will avoid each other's eyes. The model is looked at, but as a sort of statue, as an anatomical specimen, not as a person who could be a potential sexual partner.

Our ability to see social interaction in terms of the appropriate key is reminiscent of some effects of context in linguistic communication. A well-known example is the use of certain questions as implied imperatives (Searle, 1969). "Do you have a cigarette?" is not a question about possession. It is very different from questions like "Do you have a two-car garage?" or "Do you have a hippopotamus?" It is a polite way of asking for a cigarette, and there are only two possible answers. One is "No. I'm sorry" and the other is the offer of a cigarette. The reply "Yes" without any accompanying action is either a joke or a rude refusal (see Chapter 9).

Attraction

Thus far, our concern has been with how people perceive each other—what they think the other one is really like. But we don't just think about people; we also have feelings about them. Some we like, others we dislike, a few we love, while the vast majority of our fellow humans leaves us indifferent. What explains these positive and negative reactions? Our primary concern will be with liking.

Could we ever hope to discover what it is that determines who will become friends or even lovers? On the face of it, it seems hard to believe. For we've all been exposed to the romantic notions of our culture; we've all read and seen scores of novels and movies that show millionaires befriending tramps, princes marrying showgirls, and Beauty enamored by the Beast—each teaching the lesson that friendship and most especially love are not ruled by reason. But as we will see, the factors that determine much of the attraction that humans have for each other are not all that obscure. In fact, many of them are rather obvious, but on reflection this ought not to have surprised us. For the fact is that when Beauty finally marries the Beast, he turns out to be a prince after all.

PROXIMITY

What are the factors that make people like—let alone love—one another. Some of them are surprisingly simple. One of the most important factors is sheer physical *proximity.* By now, dozens of studies have documented the fact that if you want to predict who makes friends with whom, the main thing to ask is who is nearby. Students who live next to each other in a dormitory, or sit next to each other in classes, develop stronger relations than those who live only a bit farther away; similarly, members of a bomber crew become much more friendly to fellow crewmen who work right next to them than to others only a few feet away (Berscheid and Walster, 1978).

What holds for friendship also holds for mate selection. The statistics are rather impressive. For example, there is evidence that more than half of the couples who took out marriage licenses in Columbus, Ohio, during the summer of 1949 were persons who lived within sixteen blocks of each other when they went out on their first date (Clarke, 1952). Much the same holds for the probability that an engagement will ultimately lead to marriage; the farther apart the two live, the greater the chance that the engagement will be broken off (Berscheid and Walster, 1978).

Why should physical proximity be so important? One answer is that you can't like someone you've never met, and the chances of meeting that someone are much greater if he is nearby. But this doesn't explain why the interaction leads to like rather than dislike.

One reason may be the effect of *familiarity.* There is a good deal of evidence that people tend to like what's more familiar. This seems to hold for just about any stimulus, whether it's a nonsense syllable, or a word in a foreign language, or a melody, or the name of a commercial product—the more often it is seen or

"There's really not much to tell. I just grew up and married the girl next door."

(Drawing by Saxon; 1970 The New Yorker Magazine, Inc.)

11.6 Familiarity and liking The figure shows two versions of a rather well-known lady. Which do you like better—the one on the right or the one on the left? (Courtesy Documentation Photographique de la Réunion des Musées Nationaux) (Please turn to page 386.)

heard, the better it will be liked (Zajonc, 1968; Brickman and D'Amato, 1975; Stang and Crandall, 1977). The same process probably plays an important role in determining what we feel about other people. The hero of a well-known musical comedy explains his affection for the heroine by singing "I've grown accustomed to her face." In a more prosaic vein, the laboratory provides evidence that photographs of strangers' faces are judged to be more likable the more often they have been seen (Jorgensen and Cervone, 1978). Another study applied this general idea to the comparison of faces and their mirror images. Which will be better liked? If familiarity is the critical variable, then our friends should prefer a photograph of our face to one of its mirror image, since they've seen the first much more often than the second. But we ourselves should prefer the mirror image, which for us is by far the more familiar. The results were as predicted by the familiarity hypothesis (Mita, Dermer, and Knight, 1977; see Figure 11.6).

SIMILARITY

Do people like others who are similar to themselves, or do they prefer those who are very different? To put it differently, which bit of folk wisdom is more nearly correct: "Birds of a feather flock together" or—perhaps by analogy with magnets —"Opposites attract." It appears that birds have more to teach us in this matter than magnets do, for the evidence suggests that, in general, people tend to like those who are *similar* to themselves.

In one study, students were assigned to dormitory rooms on the basis of their response to various attitude questionnaires. In some cases, the roommates were chosen to be quite similar in general outlook; in others, they were quite dissimilar. The results showed that roommates who were selected to be similar liked each other and became friends. The reverse was true of roommates who were dissimilar (Newcomb, 1961). The same point is made by a comparison of the personality characteristics of happily and unhappily married couples. The similarity between husband and wife was greater in happy than in unhappy marriages (Dymond, 1954; see Figure 11.7).

A related fact concerns various characteristics of engaged couples. A widely cited study found that couples in the United States were similar in race, ethnic origin, social and educational level, family background, income, religion, and also in a number of social patterns such as their degree of gregariousness, and their drinking and smoking habits (Burgess and Wallin, 1943). The authors interpreted

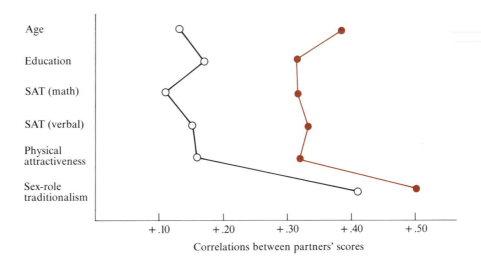

11.7 Homogamy *The figure shows the similarity on a variety of attributes of over 200 couples, followed over a two-year period. After two years, about half of the couples (shown in black) had broken up; the other half (shown in color) were still dating, were engaged, or were married. All the correlations are positive, but the correlations are greater for the couples that stayed together than for those that broke apart. (Data from Hill, Rubin, and Peplau, 1976)*

these findings as evidence for ***homogamy***—an overwhelming tendency of like to marry like.

Is homogamy really produced by the effect of similarity on mutual liking? It may be a mere byproduct of proximity, of the fact that "few of us ever have an opportunity to meet, interact with, become attracted to, and marry, a person markedly dissimilar from ourselves" (Berscheid and Walster, 1978, p. 87). But whether similarity is a cause of the attraction, or is a side effect of some other factors that led to it initially, the end product is the same: like pairs with like, and no heiress ever marries the butler except in the movies. We're not really surprised to discover that when a princess kisses a frog he turns into a prince. What would really be surprising is to see the frog turn into a *peasant*.

PHYSICAL ATTRACTIVENESS

There's little doubt that for a given time and culture there is considerable agreement as to how ***physically attractive*** a given man or woman is. Nor is there any doubt that this factor is overwhelming in determining attraction—or at least initial attraction—to members of the opposite sex. The vast sums of money spent on cosmetics, fashion, diets, and various forms of plastic surgery are one kind of testimony; our everyday experience is another. Under the circumstances, one may wonder whether there is any need to document the point experimentally, but such documentation does exist. In one study, college freshmen were randomly paired at a dance and later asked how much they liked their partner and whether they wanted to go out again with him or her at some future time. The primary factor that determined each person's desirability as a future date was his or her physical attractiveness (Walster, Aronson, Abrahams, and Rottman, 1966).

The halo effect and physical attractiveness Good looks are an obvious asset in attracting a romantic partner. But physically attractive people have further advantages. They benefit from a ***halo effect,*** the tendency to assume that people who have one positive characteristic must have other ones as well. A large number of studies show that physically attractive people are judged to be of

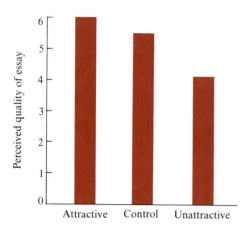

11.8 *Physical attractiveness and the halo effect* *The figure shows ratings of essays that were said to have been written by a woman whose photograph was attached to the essay and who was either attractive or relatively unattractive. (Data from Landy and Sigall, 1974)*

Revisiting Figure 11.6 *The familiarity-leads-to-liking hypothesis would predict a preference for the right panel—a re-touched photograph of the Mona Lisa (see p. 384). The panel on the left is a mirror image of that photograph, which is presumably the less familiar of the two.*

higher social status, tend to be overvalued on personality characteristics, are unlikely to be considered maladjusted, and have a better chance to be recommended for a job after an initial interview (Berscheid and Walster, 1978; Wrightsman and Deaux, 1981). As if this weren't enough, physically attractive people are also judged to be morally better than the rest of us. In one study, college women were shown photographs of children who were said to have misbehaved. In general, the more attractive children received the benefit of the doubt, while the less attractive ones were described as being deviant and maladjusted (Dion, 1972). In an adult variant on the same theme, mock juries handed out stiffer sentences to unattractive "defendants" than to attractive ones (Landy and Aronson, 1969; see Figure 11.8). It is as if people operate on the implicit assumption that what's beautiful is necessarily good (Dion, Berscheid, and Walster, 1972).

The simple idea that beauty equals goodness (or any other positive attribute) is clearly an error. But even so, it has some slight basis in fact. For it turns out that there is a moderate correlation between good looks and a number of other desirable attributes. Attractive children have higher self-esteem than unattractive ones, and by the time they reach college age, they are generally less shy, more assertive, and more socially adept. On reflection, there's little mystery to this. Attractive children are more favored by others, and so they develop greater self-confidence. As they get older, they have more dates and more sexual experience, resulting in greater social skill (Baron and Byrne, 1981).

Matching for attractiveness Physical attractiveness is clearly a very desirable quality. But if we all set our sights on only those who occupy the very top of this dimension, the world would soon be depopulated—there are simply not enough movie queens and matinee idols to go around. One would therefore assume that people will behave in a more sensible fashion. They may desire the most attractive of all possible mates, but they also have a fairly reasonable perception of their own social desirability (which is determined in part by their own physical attractiveness). In consequence, they seek partners of roughly comparable social assets; while aiming to get a partner who is most desirable, they also try to avoid rejection. This is the so-called *matching hypothesis* which predicts a strong correlation between the physical attractiveness of the two partners (Berscheid et al., 1971). This matching hypothesis is well supported by observations from everyday life ("They make such a fine couple!") and has been repeatedly documented in various empirical investigations. In one study, dating couples were observed in bars, theater lobbies, and at various social events, and were rated for physical attractiveness. There was a remarkable similarity in the rated attractiveness of the partners (Silverman, 1971).

What underlies physical attractiveness? Our discussion has assumed that physical attractiveness is a given and that people pretty much agree on who is and who is not attractive. But why should this be? Why should one set of particular features, one set of bodily proportions, represent the apex of attractiveness for so many members of the population of our time and culture? The plain fact is that we really don't know.

It would be much easier to come up with an explanation if it turned out that the standards of physical attractiveness were essentially the same across different times and places. But the facts say otherwise. To be sure, some similarities do

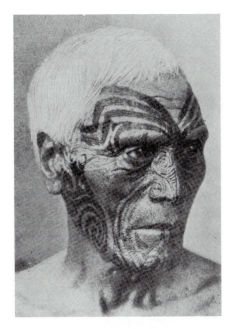

11.9 Tattooed Maori chieftain in 1907 *Among the Maori of New Zealand, tattooing was a highly ritualized part of their culture. Many males and females had ornamental tattoos etched on their faces and on various parts of their bodies, sometimes including the genitals.*

exist. Signs of ill health and deformity (which might suggest a poor genetic bet) are considered unattractive in all cultures. The same holds for signs of advancing age, which generally signal lower fertility (especially in females). In addition, all cultures want males to look male and females to look female, though the specific cues that weigh in this judgment (and that are considered attractive) vary widely. But beyond that, the differences far outweigh the similarities.

Consider the kind of female body build preferred by males. Are plump women more attractive than slim ones? You will probably agree with enthusiasm if you happen to be a Chukchi of Northeast Siberia or a Thonga of Mozambique. But your views will be very different if you are a Dobuan from New Guinea to whom corpulence is disgusting. While men in many cultures are especially attracted to women with wide hips and a broad pelvis (presumably an advantage for child-bearing), men in one or two of the cultures on which data exist strongly dislike women with these bodily characteristics (Ford and Beach, 1951).

What holds for body build, holds even more for facial features. Different cultures seem to have different conceptions of facial beauty. What's more, some of them have permanent means of facial adornment that at least some members of our own culture would probably find rather repellent. Some peoples have developed complex systems for sculpting decorative patterns of scar tissue; others have created elaborate schemes of tattooing the face and body of both men and women (Figure 11.9). Some of these practices seem quite odd from our own perspective. An example is a custom of the Ainu (indigenous inhabitants of Japan who are now largely assimilated) who used to tattoo elaborate moustaches on their young girls' faces, without which they would not be considered attractive and could not possibly hope to attract a husband (see Figure 11.10).

It's clear that there are considerable variations in what constitutes attractiveness. One culture's sex goddess may very well be another's lonely heart. What conclusions can we draw from all this? Our best guess is that the phenomenon of heterosexual attraction as such, the fact that men are attracted to women and women to men, is largely based on built-in factors. Some of the bodily character-

11.10 Tattooed moustaches among Ainu women *An Ainu family around 1910.*

istics that differentiate the sexes, such as the female's breasts, may have evolved to serve precisely such a function (see Chapter 10). But the phenomenon of differential attraction, the fact that some men and women are more attractive than others, cannot be explained without some appeal to learning. The Ainu male must surely learn that tattooed moustaches are a sign of physical beauty—while to us, and probably most other peoples, they assuredly are not.

(Photograph by Inge Morath © 1964 Magnum Photos)

PERCEIVING ONESELF

We have discussed some of the ways in which we see various qualities in others. What about the ways in which we see such qualities in ourselves? We all have a conception about our own selves, what we are really like and why we do what we do: "I am a certain kind of person with such and such capacities, beliefs, and attitudes." But before we can deal with this matter, there is a prior question. What is this *I* about which such assertions are made?

The Self-Concept

All of us have a sense of "I," of "me" and "mine." But how does that notion arise? One factor is the recognition that one's own body is fundamentally different from all other objects in the universe. How is this discovery made? One way is through vision. Unlike all other objects, the child's own body does not change in retinal size as she moves through the world. A similar discovery can come through touch. As the infant explores the world with mouth and fingers, she will surely note that some things feel quite different from all others. When they are touched, they "touch back." This feeling of "double touch" occurs whenever the child touches a part of her own body, but not otherwise; it provides yet another means for differentiating one's own body from the outside. Still further sources of the bodily self-concept are the numerous sensations that arise from within. There are feelings of muscular movement and strain, of visceral aches and pleasures. All of these sensations eventually become linked as part of a more general concept—one's own body. This in turn becomes the foundation upon which our complex self-concept is built.

The bodily self may be the foundation on which all further aspects of the self are built. But there is at least one other element—some reference to other people. There is little doubt that there can be no full-fledged "I" without a "you" or "they"; for a crucial component of the self-concept is social. According to many authors, the child begins to see herself through the eyes of the important figures in her world and thus acquires the idea that she is a person—albeit at first a very little person—just as they are (Mead, 1934). As the social interactions become more complex, more and more details are added to the self picture. In effect, the child sees herself through the mirror of the opinions and expectations of those others—mother, father, siblings, friends—who matter to her. Her later behavior cannot help but be shaped by this early "looking-glass self" (Cooley, 1902). Examples of such effects include the roles in which society casts children from the moment of birth: black, white, male, female, and so on. (For further discussion of the development of the self-concept, see Chapters 12, 14, and 16).

Self-Perception and Attribution

The preceding discussion has sketched some of the hypotheses about the ways in which we come to know ourselves—as a body bounded in space, as a person who is much like other persons. How do we find out what kind of person we really are? In part, as we have seen, we find out from others. But isn't there a more direct method? Can't we discover who we are and what we feel simply by observing ourselves?

According to some authors, the answer is no. In their view, our conceptions of self are attained through an attribution process no different in kind from that which allows us to form conceptions of other people. Advocates of this *self-perception theory* maintain that, contrary to common-sense belief, we do not know our own selves directly (Bem, 1972). In their view, self-knowledge can only be achieved indirectly, through the same attempts to find consistencies, discount irrelevancies, and interpret observations that help us to understand other people.

One line of evidence concerns the relation between attitude and behavior. Common sense argues that attitudes cause behavior, that our own actions stem from our feelings and our beliefs. To some extent, this is undoubtedly true. The pro-segregationist is unlikely to join a civil rights demonstration. But under some circumstances, the cause-and-effect relation is reversed. Sometimes our feelings or beliefs are the *result* of our actions.

A simple example is our liking for people. Naturally enough, we are more prone to do favors for the people we like than for those we do not. But occasionally there is a reverse effect. This is the basis of Benjamin Franklin's cynical advice on how to win someone's good graces: Get that person to do you a small favor, such as lending you a book, and he will end up beholden to *you.*

Whether Franklin's advice was ever followed by any of his revolutionary colleagues is unknown, but his suggestion was recently tested in a study in which subjects were made to act either kindly or harshly to someone else. The subjects had to supervise two "learners" in a learning task. They were told to compliment one of the learners whenever he made a right response. In contrast, they had to criticize the other learner harshly for any error. After the session was over, the subjects were asked to rate the learners' personalities. Benjamin Franklin would have been pleased to know that the subjects had a more favorable judgment of the learner they had praised than the one to whom they had issued reproofs (Schopler and Compere, 1971). The subjects were presumably unable to attribute their own acts entirely to the instructions imposed by the experimenter. Under the circumstances, they had to find some additional reasons within themselves: "I couldn't have been that unpleasant unless I disliked him."

A similar effect involves the "foot-in-the-door" technique, originally perfected by traveling salesmen. In one study, suburban homeowners were asked to comply with an innocuous request, to put a 3-inch square sign in their window advocating auto safety. Two weeks later, another experimenter came to visit those homeowners who agreed to display the small sign. This time they were asked to grant a much greater request, to permit the installation of an enormous billboard on their front lawns, proclaiming "Drive Carefully" in huge letters while obstructing most of the house. The results showed that agreement depended upon prior agreement. Once having complied with the first, small request, the subjects were much more likely to give in to the greater one (Freedman and Fraser, 1966).

One interpretation of this and similar findings is a change in self-perception

Commitment by doing The competent political organizer gets volunteers involved in some activity, even if that activity is not especially useful at the time. The important thing is to get the person committed, and the best means to accomplish this is through some form of action. (© Gilles Peress, Magnum Photos)

389

(Snyder and Cunningham, 1975). Having agreed to put up the small sign, the subjects now thought of themselves as active citizens involved in a public issue. Since no one forced them to put up the sign, they attributed their action to their own convictions. Given that they now thought of themselves as active, convinced, and involved, they were ready to play the part on a larger scale. Fortunately for their less involved neighbors, the billboard was in fact never installed—after all, the request was only part of an experiment. But in real life we may not be let off so easily. The foot-in-the-door approach is a common device for persuading the initially uncommitted; it can be used to sell encyclopedias or political convictions. Extremist political movements generally do not demand violent actions from newcomers. They begin with small requests like signing a petition or giving a distinctive salute. But these may lead to a changed self-perception that ultimately may ready the person for more drastic acts.*

This line of argument may have some bearing on our understanding of how social systems function. The social world casts people in different roles that prescribe particular sets of behaviors; representatives of labor and management will obviously take different positions at the bargaining table. But the roles determine attitudes as well as behavior. If one has to act like a union representative, one starts to feel like one. The same holds for the corporation executive. This point has been verified in a study of factory workers both before and after they had become union stewards or were promoted to foreman (Lieberman, 1956).

In short, our attitudes are affected by what we do and are expected to do. To some extent at least, the role makes the man or the woman. If one is appointed a judge, one begins to feel judicious.

EMOTION: PERCEIVING ONE'S OWN INNER STATE

We have seen that there is evidence that we come to know our own attitudes by a process of self-attribution. A similar process may be involved in the production of the subjective experience of emotion. We say that we feel love, joy, grief, or anger. But are we always sure exactly which emotion we experience? In one of Gilbert and Sullivan's operettas a character notes that the uninitiated may mistake love for indigestion. The point may be valid for most of us. We often have to interpret our own internal states, have to decide whether the knot in our stomach is fear (say, of an examination) or is impatient anticipation (say, of a lover's meeting). According to some psychologists, such interpretative processes are involved whenever we experience an emotion (Schachter and Singer, 1962; Mandler, 1975; 1984). To put their views in perspective, we will begin with a discussion of some earlier theories of emotion.

The James-Lange Theory

The topic of emotion has perplexed generations of investigators. Psychologists and biologists have had reasonable success in uncovering some of the objective,

---

* These phenomena are very reminiscent of the effects of forced compliance and justification of past effort we discussed previously in the context of dissonance reduction. Under the circumstances, it may not be surprising that some authors have suggested that such effects are best explained by self-perception theory rather than by a tendency to reduce cognitive dissonance. The resulting controversy between adherents of the dissonance position and of the self-perception approach is beyond the scope of this book (Bem, 1967, 1972).

bodily manifestations of emotional states; examples are the physiological concomitants of fear and rage (see Chapter 3) and emotional expressions such as the smile (see Chapter 10). But what can we say about the way our emotions are experienced subjectively, how they feel "inside"?

Many nineteenth-century psychologists tried to catalogue various emotional experiences, much as they had classified the different sensations provided by the senses (such as red, sour, A-flat). But their efforts were not too successful. There were simply too many emotional experiences that people reported, and the classification schemes that were proposed did not seem to do justice to the richness of these subjective feelings. In addition, there were disagreements about the precise meanings of emotional terms. How does sadness differ from dolor or weariness or dejection? Different people reported different shades of meaning, and there was little hope of agreement so long as the description was confined to the subjective experience alone (which is private by definition).

A different approach to the problem was proposed by William James. To James, the crucial facet of emotion was that it is an aspect of what a person *does*. In fear, we run; in grief, we weep. The common-sense interpretation is that the behavior is caused by the emotion. James stood common sense on its head and maintained that the causal relation is reversed; we are afraid *because* we run:

> Common-sense says, we lose our fortune, are sorry and weep; we meet a bear, are frightened and run; we are insulted by a rival, are angry and strike. The hypothesis here . . . is that we feel sorry because we cry, angry because we strike, afraid because we tremble. . . Without the bodily states following on the perception, the latter would be purely cognitive in form, pale, colorless, destitute of emotional warmth. We might then see the bear, and judge it best to run, receive the insult and deem it right to strike, but we should not actually *feel* afraid or angry (James, 1890, v. II, p. 449).

These phrases are the core of what is now known as the ***James-Lange theory of emotions.*** (Carl Lange was a contemporary of James and offered a similar account.) In effect, the theory asserts that the subjective experience of emotion is neither more nor less than the awareness of our own bodily changes in the presence of certain arousing stimuli. These bodily changes might be produced by skeletal movements (running) or visceral reactions (pounding heartbeat), though later adherents of James's theory emphasized the visceral responses and the activity of the autonomic nervous system that underlies them (Figure 11.11).

11.11   The sequence of events as conceived by the James-Lange theory of emotions   *According to the James-Lange theory, the subjectively experienced emotion is simply our awareness of our own response to the anger- or fear-arousing situation. We see a dangerous object (an attacking dinosaur will do as well as any other), this triggers a bodily response (running, pounding heart), and the awareness of this response is the emotion (here, fear).*

e.g., attacking dinosaur

e.g., pounding heart

FEAR

STIMULUS SITUATION   RESPONSE   SUBJECTIVE EMOTION

OBJECTIONS TO THE JAMES-LANGE THEORY

The James-Lange theory has been the focus of considerable controversy. One of the major criticisms was raised by Walter Cannon, the pioneer in the study of autonomic functioning (see Chapter 3). Cannon pointed out that sympathetic reactions to arousing stimuli are pretty much the same, while our emotional experiences vary widely. Thus, if subjective emotions are really nothing but the awareness of our own visceral responses, how can we possibly tell the difference between them when we are unable to distinguish among these visceral reactions? One of Cannon's examples was the relation between fear and rage. He argued that these two emotions are accompanied by pretty much the same sympathetic discharge. But if so, the James-Lange theory must have a flaw since we are certainly able to distinguish between these two emotional experiences (Cannon, 1927).

A different objection concerns the effect of autonomic arousal. In several early studies, this was accomplished by injecting subjects with adrenalin. This triggered sympathetic activation with all its consequences—palpitations, tremor, and sweaty palms. According to the James-Lange theory, these are among the internally produced stimuli that give rise to the intense emotions of fear and rage. But in fact the subjects did not experience these emotions. Some simply reported the physical symptoms. Others said they felt "as if" they were angry or afraid, a kind of "cold emotion" that they knew was not the real thing (Landis and Hunt, 1932). These findings seemed to constitute a further argument against the James-Lange theory. The visceral reactions are evidently not a sufficient condition for the emotional experience.

The Cognitive Theory of Emotion

Schachter and Singer formulated a different account which emphasized the role of cognitive factors. They argued that autonomic arousal and other bodily reactions provide only the raw materials for an emotional experience, a state of undifferentiated excitement and nothing more (Schachter and Singer, 1962). This excitement is shaped into a specific emotional experience by an attribution process. A person's heart beats rapidly and her hands are trembling—is it fear, rage, joyful anticipation, or a touch of the flu? If the individual has just been insulted, she will interpret her internal reactions as anger and feel and act accordingly. If she is confronted by William James's bear, she will attribute her visceral excitement to the bear and experience fear. If she is at home in bed, she will probably assume that she is sick. In short, according to Schachter and Singer, emotional experience is produced, not by autonomic arousal as such, but rather by the interpretation of this arousal in the light of the total situation as the subject sees it (Schachter and Singer, 1962; see Figure 11.12).

To test this conception, subjects were injected with a drug they thought was a vitamin supplement but which was really adrenalin. Some subjects were informed of the drug's real effects, such as increase in heart rate, flushing, tremor, and so on. Other subjects were misinformed. They were told that the drug might have some side effects, such as numbness or itching, but they were not informed

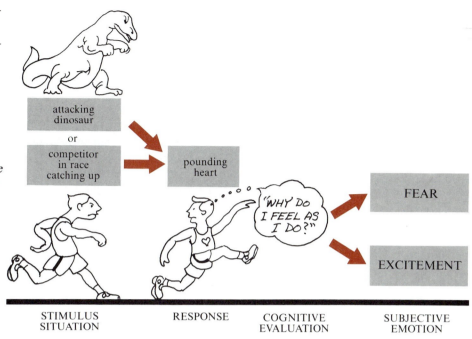

11.12 The sequence of events as conceived by Schachter and Singer's cognitive evaluation theory of emotions *According to Schachter and Singer, subjectively experienced emotion is the result of an evaluation process in which the subject interprets his own bodily reactions in the light of the total situation. Any number of external stimuli (ranging from attacking dinosaurs to competition in a race) may lead to the same general bodily reaction pattern—running and increased heart rate. The subjective emotion depends upon what the subject attributes these bodily responses to. If he attributes them to a danger signal (the dinosaur) he will feel fear. If he attributes them to the race, he will feel excitement.*

STIMULUS SITUATION   RESPONSE   COGNITIVE EVALUATION   SUBJECTIVE EMOTION

of its actual bodily consequences. After the drug had been administered, the subjects sat in an anteroom while waiting for what they thought was a test of vision. In actual fact, the main experiment was conducted in this waiting room with a confederate posing as another subject while the experimenter watched through a one-way screen. One condition was set up to produce anger. The confederate was sullen and irritable and eventually stalked out of the room. Another condition provided a context for euphoria. The confederate was ebullient and frivolous. He threw paper planes, played with a hula hoop, and tried to engage the subject in an improvised basketball game with paper wads. Following their stay in the waiting room, the subjects were asked to rate their emotional feelings (Schachter and Singer, 1962).

The critical question was whether the prior information about the drug's effects had influenced the subject's emotional reaction. Schachter and Singer reasoned that those subjects who had been correctly informed about the physiological consequences of the injection would show less of an emotional response than those who had been misinformed. The informed subjects could attribute their tremors and palpitations to the drug rather than to the external situation. In contrast, the misinformed subjects had to assume that their internal reactions were caused by something outside—the elation of the euphoric confederate or the sullenness of the angry one. Given this external attribution, their emotional state would be in line with the environmental context—euphoric or angry as the case might be. The results were as predicted. The misinformed subjects in the euphoria condition were more joyful than their correctly informed counterparts. They said that they were in a happier mood, and they were more likely to join in the confederate's mad antics. Analogous results were obtained in the anger condition.

A

B

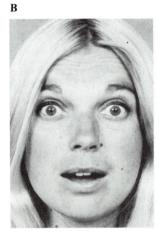

C

D

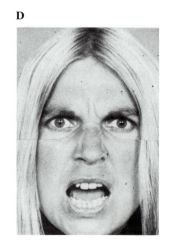

E

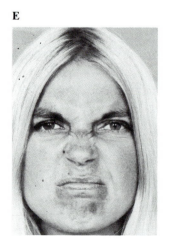

F

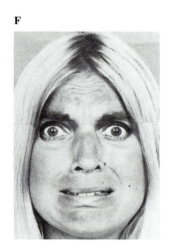

A Compromise Approach

Schachter and Singer's conception has come in for some criticism. One point at issue is their contention that visceral arousal can lead to any and all emotional experiences, depending on the person's interpretation of the situation. Some later studies suggest that emotional experience is not quite as flexible as this. In particular, injections of epinephrine may be more likely to lead to negative emotional experiences (e.g., fear and anger) than to positive ones (e.g., euphoria), regardless of the social context in which they occur (Marshall and Zimbardo, 1979; Maslach, 1979).

The issue is by no means settled, but a plausible possibility is that emotion is best described by a position that stands midway between the James-Lange and Schachter-Singer theories. The first asserts that emotional experience is entirely determined by the sensory feedback from our bodily state. The second claims that this bodily state only provides the raw material of emotional arousal and that the nature of the emotional experience depends entirely on the way we interpret the situation. As so often, the truth is probably in between.

As we saw, the Schachter-Singer approach starts out with the assumption (taken from Cannon's critique of the James-Lange theory) that all human emotions have the same bodily underpinning. But this assumption can be questioned. Some investigators claim that there are differences in the autonomic patterns that accompany such different emotions as anger, fear, and disgust (e.g., Ax, 1953; Funkenstein, 1956; Ekman, Levenson and Friesen, 1983). Others focus on the facial expressions that accompany different emotions (see Chapter 10). If these authors are right, there may be several distinct bodily reactions that underlie several different "fundamental emotions" (although this point is still under debate; see Mandler, 1984). If so, the autonomic raw materials may not allow themselves to be shaped into virtually any emotional experience as Schachter and Singer had supposed.

But this doesn't mean that cognitive factors play no role in emotional experience. Even if we grant that there are several fundamental, biologically based emotions, their number is surely rather small. Investigators of facial expression suppose that there are six: happiness, surprise, sadness, anger, disgust, and fear (Ekman and Oster, 1979; Ekman, 1985; see Figure 11.13). Other authors offer different lists, none of which contains more than, say, ten basic emotions. But we surely can distinguish between many more emotional experiences than this—for example, between sadness, resignation, regret, grief, and despair, and between happiness, jubilation, rapture, and serene delight. But how can we do this if we possess at most ten different fundamental emotions? The best guess is that these further distinctions are made by just the kind of interpretive process that Schachter and Singer had described. If so, there is a two-stage process. A situation arouses the bodily states corresponding to one of a few fundamental emotions. This produces an emotional experience whose exact nature is then further shaped by the situation as the person interprets it to be.

The role of such cognitive factors is suggested by studies in which subjects misinterpret their internal sensations in matters of romance. In one experiment, male subjects were allowed to listen to an amplification of their own heartbeats while looking at slides of nude females (Valins, 1966). These amplified heartbeats were in fact rigged by the experimenter; they were sometimes faster and sometimes slower than the subject's own. The subject's task was both pleasant and simple. He had to rate the attractiveness of each nude. The results showed that the subjects based their judgments not only upon what they saw but also on what they heard—or thought they heard. If their heartbeat was rapid, they were more likely to judge the nude as especially attractive. She had to be, for she made their heart race. It appears that in erotic situations we listen to our heart in a more than figurative sense.

Emotion and the Theater

There is a certain emotional experience that is in some ways quite unlike those we encounter in everyday life—the emotion we feel when watching a play or a movie. Is it a real emotion? Sometimes it seems to be. Some plays or movies can obviously move us to tears. As children, we weep at Lassie's illness; as adults, at Juliet's death. In retrospect, we may insist that while watching the play or the movie, we were "really in it" and had come to accept the characters' joys and sorrows as though they were real. But did we truly? Consider a great performance of *Oedipus Rex,* climaxed by that awesome scene in which Oedipus blinds himself. We may say that while watching the play we believed that what happened on stage was reality. In fact, we did no such thing. If we had, we would have experienced horror instead of tragic awe; we would have rushed for help, perhaps shouting, "Is there an ophthalmologist in the house?" In fact, we never believe that the stage Oedipus is real; at best, we are willing to suspend our *dis*belief, as the poet Coleridge put it so aptly. But in the fringes of our consciousness there is always the feeling that we are sitting in a comfortable theater armchair. We may suspend disbelief, but this does not mean that we believe.

The emotion we experience in the theater cannot be identical to the one we feel in the real world. But then, what is it? Let us assume that when we witness certain events that befall others in real life—a tearful reunion, a fistfight, a death scene—we experience real emotions. When analogous events occur on stage or on the screen, they trigger a similar arousal. But the cognitive context is quite different, for we still know that we are sitting in a darkened theater hall. The experience is analogous to the "cold fear" produced by injecting adrenalin, an "as if" emotion that occurs in subjects who cannot attribute their arousal to any external cause.

The special esthetic flavor of the theatrical experience probably depends upon

Emotion and the actor A scene from Shakespeare's King Lear *in which the old king, half-crazed with impotent fury, screams at the world during a raging storm. Lear was surely in a state of vehement frenzy. But was the actor who portrayed him? (Paul Scofield and Alec McCowen in a Royal Shakespeare production; photograph by Zoë Dominic)*

395

just this "as if." But this quality requires a delicate balance between disbelief and belief, between too little arousal and too much. On the one hand, there must be some sense of "being in it," or the experience will be cold and dispassionate, like that of the bored usher who has seen the same show over and over again. On the other hand, too much arousal will also defeat the esthetic goal, for the "as if" feeling will then be lost altogether. A theatrically naïve audience may believe that what happens on stage is the real thing, as in children's theater where the four- and five-year-olds shout fearful warnings at Snow White when the evil old witch approaches. Their seven-year-old cousins are less naïve, and thus more capable of enjoying a genuine dramatic experience. They feel aroused and excited, but they can reassure their younger friends with an air of theater-wise sophistication, "Don't worry. It's not really real."

When a performance threatens to become too real, sophisticated adults may protect themselves by laughing nervously and thus breaking the spell altogether. This reaction to the loss of "psychical distance" (Bullough, 1912) is sometimes seen in in-the-round theaters, where the audience surrounds the playing area and those in the front row can almost touch the actors. If the play is a blood-and-guts melodrama, in-the-round staging may become too close for comfort. Suppose there is a well-acted scene in which a man almost murders his wife with an ax. The members of the audience directly adjacent to the two actors are very likely to avert their heads. The scene has become too real and the emotion too genuine. The audience responds by breaking contact.

The "as if" experience may be an important ingredient in the emotion the actor feels as he plays his part. Many dramatic critics have asked the question, "What does the actor feel when he portrays the jealousy of an Othello or the rage of a Lear?" According to some schools of acting (such as the famous Actors' Studio of New York, which teaches "method" acting), the actor's job is to bring emotional reality to his role. In practice, the actor accomplishes this by vividly recalling some emotion-filled fragments of his own life that are appropriate to his present role and scene. The result is often a sense of genuine dramatic truth, felt by both actor and audience. But admirable as this may be, is it real in the sense in which everyday emotion is real? Again, the answer is almost surely no. No sane actor who ever played Othello really wanted to strangle the actress who portrayed Desdemona. Yet, there is nevertheless this "as if" experience, a state of arousal perceived and interpreted against a cognitive context that includes both the situation of the character and that of the actor who plays that character (Gleitman, 1983).

The "as if" experience may be an important ingredient in the appreciation of several art forms. In theater, it is the simultaneous awareness of events that may move us deeply and are yet known to be unreal. In the visual arts, it is the simultaneous awareness of a scene or object that looks real and lifelike but is nonetheless seen to be a flat, painted canvas (see Chapter 6).

Children at a Punch-and-Judy show
One child, upset over the fate of one of the puppets, is reassured by her older brother. (Photograph by Suzanne Szasz)

BLIND OBEDIENCE

Thus far, our main focus has been on the way in which the individual interprets social situations and events. To the extent that she acts in accordance with her interpretation (which may or may not be correct), her behavior is often described as

Obedience *The commandant of a concentration camp in Germany stands amid some of his prisoners who were burned or shot as the American army approached the camp during the last days of World War II. Most Nazis who held such positions insisted that they were "just following orders." (Courtesy United Press International)*

rational. But there are various behavior patterns that at first sight seem not to be rational in this sense. They usually involve actions that people perform as members of a group and which they would rarely commit alone. Can social psychology contribute to our understanding of such actions? We will begin by considering blind obedience to orders that violate one's own conscience, actions in which the individual subordinates her own rationality to the presumed rationality of some authority.

A certain degree of obedience is a necessary ingredient of living in a society. In any society, no matter how primitive, some individuals have authority over others, at least within a limited sphere. Obedience is particularly relevant as societies get more complex, where the spheres within which authority can be exerted become much more differentiated. Teachers assign homework, doctors order intravenous feedings, and policemen stop automobiles. The pupils, nurses, and motorists generally obey. Their obedience is based on an implicit recognition that the persons who issued the orders were operating within their legitimate domain of authority. If this domain is overstepped, obedience is unlikely. Policemen can't order motorists to recite lists of irregular French verbs or to take two aspirins and go to bed.

Some tendency to obey authority is a vital cement that holds society together; without it, there would be chaos. But the atrocities of this century—the slaughter of the Armenians, the Nazi death camps, the Cambodian massacres—give terrible proof that this disposition to obedience can also become a corrosive poison that destroys our sense of humanity. Some of these atrocities could not have been committed without the obedience of tens or hundreds of thousands and the acquiescence of many more. How could such obedience have come about? Attempts to answer this question have focused on either of two factors. One concerns the personality structure of the blindly obedient individual; the other emphasizes the social situation in which the obedient person finds himself.

Obedience and Personality Structure

What makes people obey and thus participate in any of the unspeakable acts of which history tells us? One interpretation is that some personalities are more prone to obey than others, that the crucial determinant is *within* the person rather than in the situation.

An influential version of the person-centered hypothesis was presented in the decade after World War II by a research group at the University of California at Berkeley. These investigators believed they had discovered a personality type that was predisposed toward totalitarian dogma and might thus be more ready to obey unquestioningly (Adorno, Frenkel-Brunswik, Levinson, and Sanford, 1950). Their evidence came from the responses of American subjects in clinical interviews and on various attitude tests. According to the investigators, some of the subjects could be aptly described as ***authoritarian personalities.*** Such persons were prejudiced against various minority groups and also held certain sentiments about authority, including submission to those above, harshness to those below, and a general belief in the importance of power and dominance. These authoritarian attitudes were indicated by a tendency to agree emphatically with such statements on the attitude scales as, "Obedience and respect for authority are the most important virtues children should learn," "Most of our social problems would be solved if we could somehow get rid of the immoral, the crooked and fee-ble-minded people," and "People can be divided into two distinct classes: the weak and the strong."

The Berkeley investigators believed that this constellation of attitudes was an expression of underlying personality patterns formed in childhood. They found that people who scored high on minority prejudice and authoritarianism de-scribed their childhoods as dominated by a stern and harshly punitive father who insisted on absolute obedience. According to the investigators, the children thus reared had little choice but to suppress their hostility toward the all-powerful fa-ther. They couldn't even allow themselves to become aware of this hostility and had to push it out of consciousness. On the contrary, they developed what psy-choanalysts call a "reaction formation"; they went to the opposite extreme and adopted obedience and submission to authority as exalted virtues (see Chapter 12). But their hostility was not submerged entirely; it found new outlets and was directed at safer targets, such as minority groups. In addition, they glorified toughness and put a kind of taboo on tenderness. The hostility that these persons were unable to accept in themselves was instead perceived as outside of them-selves. (In psychoanalytic terms, this hostility was "projected.") As a result, they saw the outside world as populated by a horde of dangerous enemies who had to be crushed before they themselves would be crushed by these "enemies"— blacks, Hispanics, Orientals, Jews, foreigners, Bolsheviks, and so on.

The Berkeley studies have been the target of considerable criticism (Christie and Jahoda, 1954). Some critiques focused on the way in which the items were worded, others on the fact that the information about the subjects' childhoods was mainly based upon the subjects' own recollections. But while the original claims of the Berkeley group may have been too extravagant, their studies did focus on an important set of relationships between political and social attitudes (Brown, 1965). Minority prejudice probably does tend to go together with au-thoritarian sentiments, and these in turn are often accompanied by certain ways of remembering and idealizing one's parents and a belief in stern childhood disci-pline. But whether this constellation of attitudes is caused by childhood experi-ences and emotions is still debatable. There is evidence that authoritarianism is more pronounced among persons of lower socioeconomic status, of lower educa-tion, and of lower intelligence (Christie, 1954). As one writer put it, "Authoritari-anism may be the world-view of the uneducated in western industrialized societies" (Brown, 1965, p. 523).

Obedience and the Situation

Can the person-centered hypothesis explain the atrocities of recent times? Were those who obeyed the order to massacre countless innocents sick minds or abnor-mal personalities, completely different from the rest of us? Some of them proba-bly were (Dicks, 1972). But the frightening fact is that many of these men seemed to be cast in a much more ordinary mold; what is horrifying about them is what they did and not who they were. An example is a convicted war criminal who had personally murdered dozens of persons. He obtained his position as a guard so as to get ahead in the world. According to the psychiatric interview, he was a rather average man who "could have lived his life is quieter days unnoticed, a respect-able craftsman and probably harming nobody" (Dicks, 1972, p. 141). In a well-

known account of the trial of Adolf Eichmann, the man who supervised the deportation of six million Jews to the Nazi gas chambers, the author comments on this grotesque "banality of evil": "The trouble with Eichmann was precisely that so many were like him, and that the many were neither perverted nor sadistic, that they were, and still are, terribly and terrifyingly normal" (Arendt, 1965, p. 276).

It appears that obedience to inhuman orders is in part a function of the total situation in which a person finds himself. Under some social systems—Hitler's Germany, Stalin's Russia—the conditions for compliance or tacit acceptance are so powerful that an outsider might well pause to wonder whether "there but for the grace of God go I."

THE MILGRAM STUDY

The importance of situational factors in producing obedience is highlighted by the results of one of the best-known experiments of modern social psychology, a study conducted by Stanley Milgram (1963). Milgram's subjects were drawn from a broad spectrum of socioeconomic and educational levels; they were recruited by a local newspaper ad offering $4.50 per hour to persons willing to participate in a study of memory. Milgram's subjects arrived at the laboratory where a white-coated experimenter told them that the study in which they were to take part concerned the effect of punishment on human learning.

The subjects were run in pairs and drew lots to determine who would be the "teacher" and who the "learner." The task of the learner was to master a list of paired associates. The task of the teacher was to present the stimuli, record the learner's answers, and—most important—to administer punishment whenever the learner responded incorrectly. The learner was conducted to a cubicle where the experimenter strapped him in a chair, to "prevent excess movement," and attached the shock electrodes to his wrist—all in full view of the teacher. After the learner was securely strapped in place, the teacher was brought back to the main experimental room and seated in front of an imposing-looking shock generator. The generator had 30 lever switches with labeled shock intensities, ranging from 15 volts to 450 volts in 15-volt increments. Below each of the levers there were also verbal descriptions ranging from "Slight Shock" to "Danger: Severe Shock." The labels below the last two levers were even more ominous; they were devoid of any verbal designation and were simply marked "XXX" (Figure 11.14).

The teacher presented the items that had to be memorized. He was instructed to move on to the next item on the list whenever the learner responded correctly but to administer a shock whenever an error was made. He was told to increase the level of punishment with each succeeding error, beginning with 15 volts and going up by one step for each error thereafter until 450 volts was reached. To get an idea what the learner experienced, the teacher first submitted to a sample shock of 45 volts, the third of the 30-step punishment series, which gave an unpleasant jolt. During the experiment, all communications between teacher and

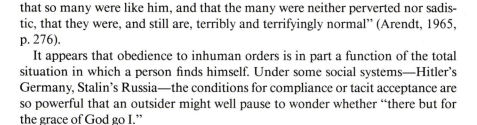

11.14 The obedience experiment   *(A) The "shock generator" used in the experiment. (B) The learner is strapped into his chair and electrodes are attached to his wrist. (C) The teacher receives a sample shock. (D) The teacher breaks off the experiment. (Copyright 1965 by Stanley Milgram. From the film* Obedience, *distributed by the New York University Film Library)*

learner were conducted over an intercom, since the learner was out of sight, strapped to a chair in the experimental cubicle.

Needless to say, the shock generator never delivered any shocks (except for the initial sample) and the lot drawing was rigged so that the learner was always a confederate, played by a mild-mannered, middle-aged actor. The point of the experiment was simply to determine how far the subjects would go in obeying the experimenter's instructions. Since the learner made a fair number of errors, the shock level of the prescribed punishment kept on rising. By the time 120 volts was reached, the victim shouted that the shocks were becoming too painful. At 150 volts he demanded that he be let out of the experiment. At 180 volts, he cried out that he could no longer stand the pain. At 300 volts, he screamed that he would give no further answers and insisted that he be freed. On the next few shocks there were agonized screams. After 330 volts, there was silence.

The learner's responses were of course predetermined. But the real subjects—the teachers—did not know that, so they had to decide what to do. When the victim cried out in pain or refused to go on, the subjects usually turned to the experimenter for instructions. In response, the experimenter told the subjects that the experiment had to go on, indicated that he took full responsibility, and pointed out that "the shocks may be painful but there is no permanent tissue damage."

How far do subjects go in obeying the experimenter? When the study was described to several groups of judges, including a group of forty psychiatrists, all predicted considerable defiance. In their view, only a pathological fringe of at most 2 percent of the subjects would go to the maximum shock intensity. But these predictions were far off the mark. In fact, about 65 percent of Milgram's subjects continued to obey the experimenter to the bitter end. This proportion was unaffected even when the learner mentioned that he suffered from a mild heart condition. This isn't to say that the obedient subjects had no moral qualms. Quite the contrary. Many of them were seriously upset. They bit their lips, twisted their hands, sweated profusely—and obeyed even so.

Is there a parallel between obedience in these artificial laboratory situations and obedience in the all-too-real nightmares of Nazi Germany or Cambodia? In some ways, there is no comparison, given the enormous disparities in scope and degree. But Milgram believes that some of the underlying psychological processes may be the same in both cases.

BEING ANOTHER PERSON'S AGENT

In Milgram's view, one of the crucial factors is a personal history in which there is a continual stress on obedience to legitimate authority, first within the family, then in the school, and still later within the institutional settings of the adult world. The good child does what he is told; the good employee may raise a question but will accept the boss's final decision; the good soldier is not even allowed to question why. As a result, all of us are well practiced in adopting the attitude of an agent who performs an action that is initiated by someone else. The responsibility belongs to that someone else, and not to us.

This feeling of being another person's agent was repeatedly encountered in Milgram's obedient subjects. When interviewed after the experiment, they said they felt they had no choice, that the responsibility was not theirs but the experimenter's. Very similar statements were made by the Nazi guards and by Adolf Eichmann.

11.15   Obedient subject pressing the learner's hand upon the shock electrode   *(Copyright 1965 by Stanley Milgram. From the film* Obedience, *distributed by the New York University Film Library)*

The sense of not being personally responsible is enhanced by any factor that minimizes the awareness of one's own personal identity. An example is a military uniform, which tends to make its wearer feel anonymous; if he pulls the trigger, he does so as a faceless agent of his government and not of his own volition. Cloaked in anonymity, he becomes *deindividuated* (see pp. 407–8) and can perform acts he would not normally engage in. According to one writer, tribal masks serve a similar function in certain primitive cultures. They announce that the wearer is not "personally involved" (Redl, 1973).

Another way of reducing the sense of personal responsibility is by increasing the psychological distance between one's own actions and their end result. This phenomenon has been observed in Milgram's laboratory. In one variation, two teachers were used. One was a confederate who was responsible for administering the shocks; the real subject was engaged in a subsidiary task. In this new role, the subject was still essential to the smooth functioning of the experimental procedure. If he stopped, the victim would receive no further shocks. But he felt much further removed from the ultimate consequence of the procedure, like a minor cog in a bureaucractic machine. Under these conditions, over 90 percent of the subjects went all the way.

In another experimental manipulation, Migram tried to decrease the psychological distance between what the subject did and its effect upon the victim. Rather than being out of sight in an experimental cubicle, the victim was seated next to the subject who had to administer the shock in a brutally direct manner. He had to press the victim's hand upon a shock electrode, holding it down by force if necessary (Figure 11.15). Compliance dropped considerably, in analogy to the fact that it is easier to drop bombs on an unseen enemy than to plunge a knife into his body when he looks you in the eye. But even so, 30 percent of the subjects reacted with perfect obedience.

COGNITIVE REINTERPRETATIONS

To cope with the moral dilemma posed by compliance with immoral orders, the obedient person develops an elaborate set of cognitive devices to reinterpret the situation and his own part in it. One of the most common approaches is to put on psychic blinders and try to shut out the awareness that the victim is a living, suffering fellow being. According to one of Milgram's subjects, "You really begin to forget that there's a guy out there, even though you can hear him. For a long time I just concentrated on pressing the switches and reading the words" (Milgram, 1974, p. 38). This *dehumanization* of the victim is a counterpart to the obedient person's self-picture as an agent of another's will, someone "who has a job to do" and who does it whether he likes it or not. The obedient person sees himself as an instrument; by the same token, he sees the victim as an object. In his eyes, both have become dehumanized (Bernard, Ottenberg, and Redl, 1965).

The dehumanization of the opponent is a common theme in war and mass atrocity. Victims are rarely described as people, but only as bodies, objects, numbers. The process of dehumanization is propped up by euphemisms and bureaucratic jargon. The Nazis used terms such as "final solution" (the mass murder of six million persons) and "special treatment" (death by gassing); the nuclear age contributed "fallout problem" and "preemptive attack"; the Vietnam War gave us "free-fire zone" and "body count"—all dry, official phrases that are admirably suited to keep all thoughts of blood and human suffering at a reasonably safe distance.

Dehumanizing the victim *As Joseph Goebbels, Hitler's infamous minister of propaganda, put it, "I keep on hearing voices that assert that Jews are also humans. To this I can only reply that bedbugs are also animals, but extremely disagreeable ones." (From a radio broadcast heard in 1938 in Germany; photograph courtesy Photoworld)*

By dehumanizing the victim, moral qualms are pushed into the background. But for all but the most brutalized, these qualms can't be banished forever. To justify continued obedience, such queasy feelings may be suppressed by reference to some higher, overriding moral ideology. In Milgram's study, the subjects convinced themselves that science had to be served regardless of the victim's cries; in Nazi Germany, the goal was to cleanse humanity by ridding it of Gypsy and Jewish "vermin." In a related kind of self-justification, the fault is projected on the victims; they are considered to be subhuman, dirty, evil, and only have themselves to blame. In part, this cognitive reorientation may stem from a primitive belief that by and large the world is "just"; if someone is punished, there is probably a good reason. This general conception has been tested in several laboratory experiments. The results suggest that persons who suffer some misfortune are judged to have deserved it (Lerner, 1971). An extreme example of the same phenomenon was reported when the British forced a group of German civilians to march through a nearby Nazi death camp in the days just after the war. One of the civilians was overheard to remark, "What terrible criminals these prisoners must have been to get such punishment" (Cohn, in Dicks, 1972, p. 262).

The cognitive reorientation by which a person no longer feels responsible for his own acts is not achieved in an instant. Usually, inculcation is by gradual steps. The initial act of obedience is relatively mild and does not seriously clash with the person's own moral outlook. Escalation is gradual so that each step seems only slightly different from the one before. This of course was the pattern in Milgram's study. A similar program of progressive escalation was evidently used in the indoctrination of death-camp guards. The same is true for the military training of soldiers everywhere. Draftees go through "basic training," in part to learn various military skills, but much more important, to acquire the habit of instant obedience. Raw recruits are rarely asked to point their guns at another person and shoot. It's not only that they don't know how; most of them probably *wouldn't* do it.

CROWD BEHAVIOR

The obedient person may perform acts that he would never engage in as a private individual, but we have seen that we can nevertheless explain some aspects of his behavior by asking how he interprets the situation in which he is placed. A similar point applies to the behavior of crowds in riots or panics. On the face of it, their behavior appears irrational. But is it as irrational as it seems? Upon closer inspection, here too, cognitive factors play a vital role.

There is little doubt that under some circumstances people in crowds behave differently from the way they do when alone. They occasionally express aggression at a level of bestial violence that would be inconceivable if they acted in isolation. A gruesome example was the lynch mob of the American South. These mobs murdered some two thousand persons, mostly blacks, in the first fifty years of this century, often after hideous tortures. On other occasions, crowds may become frantically fearful. An example is the panic that may sweep a tightly packed theater auditorium when someone shouts "Fire." The resulting stampede will often claim many more victims than the fire as such. One such case occurred when a fire broke out in a Chicago theater in 1903. There were 602 victims. Many

of them died because they blocked the exits or jammed the stairways in their frightened rush to escape; they were smothered or trampled to death by the surging mass of those behind them. Others jumped to their deaths off the packed fire escapes or were pushed off by the fear-frenzied crowd. When the firemen later disentangled their bodies, "the heel prints on the dead faces mutely testified to the cruel fact that human animals stricken by terror are as mad and ruthless as stampeding cattle" (Foy and Harlow, 1928, quoted in Brown, 1965, p. 715).

What does the crowd do to the individual to make him act so differently from his everyday self? According to one view, it transforms him completely until his behavior is no longer describable by the usual laws that apply to individual functioning. He becomes wild, stupid, and irrational as he gives vent to primitive impulses that are normally suppressed. The foremost exponent of this position was Gustav Le Bon (1841–1931), a French journalist of conservative political leanings whose disdain for the masses was reflected in his theory of crowd behavior. According to Le Bon, persons in a crowd become alike. They infect each other with whatever emotion they may feel. This emotion rises to an ever-higher pitch as more and more crowd members are affected. In consequence, fear becomes panic and hostility turns into murderous rage. In the grip of such intense passions, the crowd members become creatures of impulse rather than reason. As Le Bon put it,

> By the mere fact that he forms part of an organized crowd, a man descends several rungs in the ladder of civilization; in a crowd, he is a barbarian—that is, a creature acting by instinct. . . . [He can be] induced to commit acts contrary to his most obvious interest and best known habits. An individual in a crowd is a grain of sand amid other grains of sand, which the wind stirs up at will (Le Bon, 1895).

The Panicky Crowd

Is crowd behavior really as irrational as Le Bon held it to be? The example of panic described above testifies to the fact that people in groups sometimes act in ways that have disastrous consequences which none of them foresaw or desired. This shows that crowd behavior can be profoundly maladaptive, but does it prove that the individual members of the crowd acted irrationally? Several social psychologists have argued that it does not (Brown, 1965). They point out that in certain situations, such as fires in crowded auditoriums, the optimum solution for all participants (that is, escape for all) can only come about if they all trust one another to behave cooperatively (that is, not to run for the exits). If this trust is lacking, each individual will do the next best thing given her motives and her expectations of what others will do. She will run to the exit because she is sure that everyone else will do the same, hoping that if she runs quickly enough she will get there before them. The trouble is that all others make the same assumption that she does, and so they all arrive more or less together, jam the exit, and perish.

According to this cognitive interpretation, intense fear as such will not produce crowd panic, contrary to Le Bon's assertion. What matters are people's beliefs about escape routes. If they think that the routes for escape (the theater exits) are open and readily accessible, they will not stampede. Nor will panic develop if all escape routes are thought to be completely blocked, as in a mine collapse or a submarine explosion. Such disasters may lead to terror or apathetic collapse; but there will be none of the chaos that characterizes a panicky crowd. For panic to occur, the exits from danger must be seen to be limited or closing. In that case, each individual may well think that he can escape only if he rushes ahead of the others. If everyone thinks this way, panic may ensue (Smelser, 1963).

THE PRISONER'S DILEMMA

Roger Brown believes that some facets of escape panic can be understood in terms of a problem taken from the mathematical theory of games (Brown, 1965). It is generally known as the ***prisoner's dilemma*** (Luce and Raiffa, 1957). Consider the hypothetical problem of two men arrested on suspicion of bank robbery. The district attorney needs a confession to guarantee conviction. He hits on a diabolical plan. He talks to each prisoner separately and offers each a simple choice—confess or stay silent. But he tells each man that the consequences will depend, not just on what he does, but also on his partner's choice. If both confess, he will recommend an intermediate sentence of, say, eight years in prison for each. If neither confesses, he will be unable to prosecute them for robbery but he will charge them with a lesser crime such as illegal possession of a gun and both will get one year in jail. But suppose one confesses and the other does not? In this case the two men will be dealt with very differently. The one who confesses will be treated with extra leniency for turning state's evidence; he will receive a suspended sentence and won't go to jail at all. But the one who remains silent will feel the full force of the law. The D.A. will recommend the maximum penalty of twenty years.

As the situation is set up, there are four possible combinations of what the prisoners may do. Both may remain silent; Prisoner A may confess while B does not;

B may confess while A does not; both may confess. Each of the four sets of decisions has a different consequence or **payoff** for each of the two prisoners. The four sets of decisions and the payoffs associated with each yield a so-called **payoff matrix** as shown in Table 11.1.

Table 11.1   PAYOFF MATRIX FOR THE PRISONER'S DILEMMA

		Prisoner B:	
		Stays silent	Confesses
Prisoner A:	Stays silent	1 year for *A* 1 year for *B*	20 years for *A* No jail for *B*
	Confesses	No jail for *A* 20 years for *B*	8 years for *A* 8 years for *B*

Given this payoff matrix, what can the prisoners do? If both remain silent, the consequence is reasonably good for each of them. But how can either be sure that his partner won't double-cross him? If A remains silent while B tells all, B is even better off than he would be if both kept quiet; he stays out of jail entirely, while poor, silent A gets twenty years. Can A take the chance that B will not confess? Conversely, can B take this chance on A? The best bet is that they will *both* confess. The D.A. will get his conviction, and both men will get eight years.

In a sense, the prisoners' behavior is maladaptive, for the outcome is far from optimal for each. But this doesn't mean that either of the two men behaved irrationally. On the contrary. Paradoxically enough, each picked the most rational course of action considering that he couldn't be sure how his partner would decide. Each individual acted as rationally as possible; the ironic upshot was an unsatisfactory outcome for each. In the best of all possible worlds they would have been able to trust each other, would have remained silent, and been in jail for a much shorter period.

THE PRISONER'S DILEMMA AND PANIC

The underlying logic of the prisoner's dilemma applies to various social interactions whose payoff matrix is formally analogous. Brown has shown how it pertains to panic. Here there are more than two participants, but the essential ingredients are much the same. Each individual in the burning auditorium has two choices—she can wait her turn to get to the exit or she can rush ahead. What are the probable outcomes? As in the case of the prisoners, they partially depend upon what others in the auditorium (especially those nearby) will do. If the individual rushes to the exit and everyone else does too, they will all probably suffer severe injuries and run some risk of death. If she takes her turn and others decorously do the same, the outcome is better; they will probably all escape, though they may suffer some minor injuries. The best outcome for the individual is produced if she ruthlessly pushes herself ahead of the others while the others continue to file out slowly. In this case *she* will surely escape without a blister, but the chances for the others to escape are lessened. Suppose the situation is reversed so that the individual waits her turn while everyone near her runs ahead? Now the others may very well get out without injury while she herself may die. These sets of decisions and their associated outcomes represent just another version of the prisoner's dilemma, which are shown in the payoff matrix of Table 11.2.

Table 11.2   PAYOFF MATRIX FOR AN INDIVIDUAL *(I)* AND OTHERS *(O)* IN A BURNING AUDITORIUM

		Others (O):	
		Take turns	Rush ahead
Individual (I):	Takes turn	Minor injuries for *I* Minor injuries for *O*	Increased chance of death for *I* No injuries for *O*
	Rushes ahead	No injuries for *I* Increased chance of death for *O*	Severe injuries for *I* Severe injuries for *O*

Given the payoff matrix of Table 11.2, most persons will probably opt to rush ahead rather than wait their turn. As in the case of the two prisoners, this solution is grossly maladaptive, but from the point of view of each separate individual it is, sadly enough, quite rational. We again face the peculiar irony of the prisoner's dilemma. As Brown notes, "This irony about escape behavior . . . is always worked over by newspaper editorialists after panic occurs. 'If only everyone had stayed calm and taken his turn, then . . .'" (Brown, 1965, p. 741).

Brown's model of panic applies only if certain qualifications are met. As already noted, the danger must seem serious enough and the escape routes must appear to be inadequate. Another factor is the strength of certain social inhibitions. Most of us have been socialized to act with some modicum of respect for others; pushing ahead is socially disapproved and would therefore contribute a negative value to the relevant cells in the payoff matrix. The weight of this factor depends on the situation. If the fire seems minor enough, the embarrassment at behaving discourteously (or acting like a coward) might outweigh the fear of being the last to escape. If so, the payoff matrix will not be that of the prisoner's dilemma, and no panic will ensue.

The Hostile Crowd

The preceding discussion has shown that there is a plausible explanation for crowd panic, based on the laws of individual behavior. There is thus no need to appeal to some new principles of "mob psychology" according to which men are transformed into savage beasts as Le Bon had claimed. Can the same be said about the behavior of violent crowds whose frenzy is turned either against defenseless victims (as in lynchings or pogroms) or against another group that fights back (as in many riots)? Can such hostile group acts also be understood by reference to the laws of individual behavior?

Most modern social psychologists believe that the answer is yes. Of course, the specific explanation must be different from that which handles panic. In panic, the members of the group are essentially all competing with one another. If there is a fire or a run on the bank, their governing philosophy is to "Let the Devil Take the Hindmost"; in consequence, he often takes them all. In lynching or rioting mobs, there is no such within-group competition. On the contrary, the members

A lynching in the South, 1882   *(Courtesy The Bettmann Archive)*

of the crowd are united against others outside of their group. We will consider one example taken from a shameful page of American history—the lynching of blacks in the rural South.

THE MOTIVES FOR LYNCHING

What motives impelled the lynchers, who often tortured and mutilated their victims and finally burnt them alive? There is little doubt that one major purpose was to maintain the unequal status of blacks. While lynching has an early history that goes back to the frontier days of the West, blacks did not become its primary victims until some time after the Civil War. From then on, lynching became a bloody instrument to maintain social and economic control over the newly freed slaves, to keep them "in their place." It was a response to threatening signs of defiance and assertion; the mere suspicion of an attack on a white person was often grounds enough. The horrible fate of the victim would then serve as a warning to other blacks. It is probably no accident that lynchings were comparatively uncommon in Southern counties run on the plantation system in which blacks worked as tenant farmers and wage hands. Here the caste system was so sharply drawn that whites saw little threat. Lynchings were more prevalent in poor rural communities in which blacks were a minority who often competed economically with lower-class whites (Brown, 1954).

Many authors believe that an additional motive for lynching was displaced aggression (see Chapter 12). The life of the poor white in the rural South was filled with many social and economic frustrations. Frustration often begets aggression. But toward whom should this aggression be directed? The black was an all too convenient target.

OVERCOMING SOCIAL PROHIBITIONS

However intense the individual mob member's hatred, it would probably not suffice to make him kill and torture were he alone. There are various social restraints on violence, some based on fear of retribution, others on internalized moral qualms. The presence of others somehow weakens these restraints. The question is how.

One factor is anonymity. According to many social psychologists, this tends to produce a state of *deindividuation*—a weakened sense of personal identity in which self-awareness is submerged in the collective goals of a group. Deindividu-

11.16   The apparent homogeneity of a crowd   *(Right) A long-shot view of a crowd of students surrounding Nelson Rockefeller during a 1964 campaign address. (Left) An enlargement of a part of the photograph shows that the crowd is not as homogeneous as it may appear at first. Some members of the crowd look at Rockefeller, others look away, and so on. (Milgram and Toch, 1969; Wide World Photos)*

ation disinhibits impulsive actions that are normally under restraint. But just what the impulses are that are disinhibited by deindividuation depends on the group and the situation. In a carnival, the (masked) revelers may join in wild orgies; in a rioting lynch mob, the group members will kill and torture (Festinger, Pepitone and Newcomb, 1952; Diener, 1979).

Another factor is the perception of unanimity. This enhances each crowd member's belief in the righteousness of his actions. More important, it produces a sense of *diffusion of responsibility.* There is a diminished fear of retribution. When there are dozens of participants, it becomes harder to determine what each of them actually did. The same applies to the person's own sense of guilt, which becomes diluted by the fact that there are so many others. (A similar diffusion effect occurs in a firing squad whose members know that only some of the rifles are loaded with real bullets while the rest contain blanks.)

Yet another effect of the appearance of unanimity is that it leads to *pluralistic ignorance* among the waverers in the crowd. In actuality, the crowd is not as homogeneous as it seems (few crowds are; see Figure 11.16). But the waverers don't know that. They hear only the vociferous clamors for violence, assume that they are alone in their opposition, and therefore go along, in ignorance of the fact that there are others who feel as they do.

The Apathetic Crowd

Diffusion of responsibility helps to allay moral misgivings in a crowd bent on violence; everyone feels that if all join in, none can be blamed. A similar effect may explain why city dwellers sometimes ignore a stranger's cry for help. The classic example is the tragic case of Kitty Genovese who was attacked and murdered on an early morning in 1964 on a street corner in Queens, New York. The assault lasted over half an hour, during which time she screamed and struggled while her assailant stabbed her repeatedly until she finally died. It later developed that thirty-eight of her neighbors had watched the episode from their windows. But none of them came to her aid; no one even called the police (Rosenthal, 1964). Why this appalling inactivity?

To answer this question we must first ask how the individual interprets the situation he confronts. Consider the passerby who sees a man lying unconscious on a city street. How can he tell whether the man is ill or is merely drunk? A similar confusion troubled some of the witnesses to the Genovese slaying. They later reported that they weren't quite sure what was going on. Perhaps it was a joke, a drunken bout, or a lovers' quarrel; were it any of these, intervention might have proven very embarrassing. One reason for failure to act in an emergency is that the emergency is not recognized as such.

But suppose the emergency *is* recognized, as it probably was by many of those who watched Kitty Genovese die. To understand why they failed to act even so, we have to realize that they were all in an implicit crowd situation. Like the passerby on the city street, they knew that many others watched the same scene. As a result, they felt a diffusion of responsibility. The witness or the passerby may want to help, but he also has self-centered motives that hold him back. Some of the witnesses of the Genovese murder later explained that they didn't want to get involved, that they were afraid of the assailant, or that they were apprehensive about dealing with the police. The conflict between the desire to help and to mind one's own business was finally resolved in favor of inaction through the knowledge that others witnessed the same event. Everyone assumed that someone else would do something or had already done it (such as calling the police); as a result, no one did anything.

(Photograph by Susan Shapiro)

Responsibility diffusion has essentially the same effect in the violent crowd and in the implicit crowd situation produced by the city dweller's cry for help. In both cases it tips the scale against personal morality. In the violent crowd, it leads all mob members to join in a hideous act of *commission*—the lynching. In the crowd of onlookers, it makes all witnesses perform an unfeeling act of *omission* —the failure to help.

This general line of thinking has been tested in several experiments on **bystander intervention.** In one study, subjects were asked to participate in what they thought was a group discussion about college life with either one, three, or five other persons. The subjects were placed in individual cubicles and took turns in talking to each other over an intercom system. In actuality, there was only one subject; all the other discussants were tape recordings. The discussion began as one of the (tape-recorded) confederates described some of his personal problems, which included a tendency toward epileptic seizures in times of stress. When he began to speak again during the second round of talking, he feigned a seizure and gasped for help. The question was whether the subjects would leave their own cubicles to assist the stricken victim (usually, by asking the experimenter's help). The results were in accord with the diffusion of responsibility hypothesis. The larger the size of the group that the subject thought he was in, the less likely he was to come to the victim's assistance (Darley and Latané, 1968).

Some further studies have shown that the effect of other bystanders depends on what the subject thinks about their competence in the situation. In one experiment, the subject was convinced that the only other person who knew about the emergency was in another building, too far to help. The result was that the subject responded as quickly as he would have if he had been alone; under the circumstances, there was no one to whom he could pass the buck (Bickman, 1971). Conversely, the subject will tend to do nothing if he believes that another bystander is

409

better qualified to handle the problem. Thus subjects in a variation of the epileptic-seizure experiment were less likely to intervene if they thought that one of the other members in the discussion group was a medical student (Schwartz and Clausen, 1970).

In the preceding pages, we asked how the individual interprets the social world, how he tries to render it meaningful and consistent, how he perceives the motives and acts of others and of his own self. We also discussed several phenomena that at first glance seemed incompatible with a cognitive approach, including blind obedience to inhuman commands and various crowd reactions. But on closer inspection, we saw that some of the same cognitive factors still apply. To understand obedience, one has to ask how the individual reinterprets what the authority commands him to do; to comprehend panic, one must consider the crowd members' assumptions about the behavior of others around them.

Phenomena of this kind make it clear that human social behavior is exceedingly more complex than the social behaviors we see in animals. Like wolves and baboons, we mate and court, care for our offspring, and compete for a higher place in dominance hierarchies. But the ways in which we execute these social maneuvers involve subtleties that are beyond the ken of even the most socially adroit baboon. Baboons recognize each other; they know who is an alpha and who is not. But they never wonder whether another chimpanzee acts like an alpha because of his disposition or the situation in which he finds himself. Baboons are untroubled by attribution errors, or cognitive inconsistency, or diffusion of responsibility, or the difficulties of impression management. Like ourselves, they are social animals. But their social interactions occur at a vastly more primitive level than ours.

To a large extent, this difference is simply a matter of a different level of cognitive functioning. Humans have language and can manipulate abstract concepts in ways that are impossible for even the smartest chimpanzee, let alone a baboon. Humans have a built-in cognitive equipment that is vastly more powerful than that of any other animal, and they continually augment its power by learning from experience. This experience is not just limited to their own personal past, but includes that of prior generations. For humans inherit more than their parents' genes. They also inherit an intricate web of shared knowledge that is called culture. To understand what is truly human about social behavior, we must understand how the built-in biological patterns laid down in our genes are shaped and modified by social experience as we grow up to become members of the society in which we are born.

One of the major figures in modern intellectual history who asked how this process occurs was the founder of psychoanalysis, Sigmund Freud, whose ideas are the topic to which we now turn.

SUMMARY

1. Social behavior depends in part on how people interpret situations they encounter. The processes that lead to such interpretations are in many ways similar to those that underlie cognitive processes in general.

2. Our conception of what is real is heavily affected by confirmation from others, as shown by Asch's study on the effects of group pressure and by the need for *social comparison,* especially in ambiguous situations.

3. To make sense of the world, people look for *cognitive consistency.* According to *dissonance theory,* they will do what they can to reduce any inconsistency (dissonance) they perceive by reinterpreting information to fit in with their *beliefs, attitudes,* and actions.

4. The interpretation of the situations people encounter is affected by their *attitudes,* which tend to vary from one person to another. Attitudes are rather stable mental positions held toward some idea, object, or person, which combine beliefs, feelings, and predispositions to action.

5. Social psychologists have studied a number of approaches to changing attitudes. These include *persuasive communications* and *reducing cognitive dissonance.* There is some evidence that the dissonance reduction effects observed in justification of effort or forced compliance studies are a way to protect the individual's *self-picture* rather than a means to remove logical inconsistency.

6. While these various means for changing attitudes have some effect, attitudes tend to remain rather stable, in part because of cognitive consistency, which on the whole is a force for keeping things as they are.

7. The way we perceive others is in some ways similar to the way we perceive inanimate objects or events. *Impressions of others* can be regarded as Gestalt patterns whose elements are interpreted in terms of the whole, thus accounting for related phenomena such as *primacy effects* in impression formation.

8. *Attribution theory* tries to explain how we infer the causes of another person's behavior by attributing them either to *situational factors* or *dispositional qualities.* In judging others, we tend to underestimate the role of the first and to overestimate that of the second. This attribution bias is reversed when we ourselves are the actor rather than the observer. Reasons for the *actor-observer difference* include the fact that we know ourselves better than anyone else and that actors and observers have different perspectives.

9. Our perception of people is further complicated by the fact that they know they are being perceived which may create attempts at *impression management.* Further complications arise because social communications are often *keyed* to provide the context in which the message should be taken.

10. Social psychologists have studied some of the factors that attract people to each other. These include *physical proximity, familiarity, similarity,* and *physical attractiveness.*

11. According to *self-perception theory,* similar attribution processes determine how we perceive our own selves. An example is Schachter and Singer's revision of the *James-Lange theory of emotions.* This revision argues that the emotion we feel is an interpretation of our own autonomic arousal in the light of the situation to which we attribute it.

12. Some social behaviors seem irrational. An example is *blind obedience.* This has sometimes been ascribed to factors within the person, as in studies on the *authoritarian personality.* But situational factors may be even more important, as shown by Milgram's obedience studies. His findings suggest that obedience is partially caused by *depersonalization* and *cognitive reinterpretation.*

13. Another kind of apparent irrationality characterizes the *behavior of crowds,* as in *panics.* Such social behavior may not be as irrational as it appears. The *prisoner's dilemma* shows that under certain conditions there can be collective irrationality even though all of the participants behave rationally as individuals.

14. Other forms of apparently irrational crowd behavior are violent *group hostility* and *apathy.* In violent crowds there is *deindividuation,* a weakened sense of personal identity produced by anonymity. But part of the explanation lies in the way in which the individual members of the group interpret the situation. An important factor is *diffusion of responsibility,* which applies to both sins of commission (as in rioting mobs) and sins of omission (as in *bystander apathy*).

CHAPTER 12

The Individual and Society: The Contributions of Sigmund Freud

In the last chapter we looked at the subtle patterns of human social perceptions and social acts. Much of this subtlety reflects the effects of human culture. All men and women are born into some culture, whether they are Polynesian islanders, or African bushmen, or Scandinavian villagers. This culture represents a complex network of basic beliefs and attitudes, a whole set of do's and don'ts, in terms of which all social interactions are conducted, interpreted, and judged. This culture necessarily channels and modifies many of the built-in social patterns that are part of our biological makeup. To understand human social nature, we must ask how people transmit their culture from one generation to the next. A major figure who asked this question was the founder of psychoanalysis, Sigmund Freud (1856–1939), whose views were to revolutionize all subsequent accounts of what humans are really like.

THE ORIGINS OF PSYCHOANALYTIC THOUGHT

Freud's basic conception holds that man is divided against himself. This view is in many ways a reflection of the nineteenth-century conflict between two major intellectual movements. The dominant view was a faith in reason, formulated by several generations of European thinkers, from such men of the French Enlight-

Sigmund Freud *(Courtesy National Library of Medicine)*

The Dream of Reason Produces Monsters
An engraving by Francisco Goya (1799) which suggests that the same mind that is capable of reason also produces unknown terrors. (Courtesy National Library of Medicine)

enment as Voltaire to such heirs of Locke in England as John Stuart Mill. These men preached that reason will ultimately lead to human happiness, that evil and misery are always caused by ignorance and superstition, and that education and understanding will eventually create a world of peace and contentment for all. Their creed of reason found justification in the accomplishments of nineteenth-century science and technology which promised ever-increasing progress in all spheres of human endeavor.

But this faith was not shared by all. The followers of the Romantic movement sounded another note. They championed feeling over reason, instinct over intellect. At first, these sentiments were in an optimistic vein. Philosophers like Rousseau and poets like Byron and Shelley insisted that man is intrinsically good and should therefore always follow the dictates of the heart. But as the century wore on, as wars of liberation failed and as revolutions only brought disappointment, the mood of Romanticism turned grim and despairing. The heroes of Dostoevsky's novels gain comfort from neither heart nor intellect. They may be brilliant and well-educated but they still become murderers without knowing why, victims of dark forces that well up from some mysterious depths inside. As the century ended, the grounds for optimism became fewer and fewer. Reason had promised much but had delivered little, a failure that was ultimately climaxed by the mad slaughter of World War I.

Freud's intellectual contribution was an attempt to understand the forces of human irrationality through reason and science. The son of a lower middle-class Jewish wool merchant, he studied medicine and began his career as a physiologist and neurologist. His training imbued him with an unshakable faith in the power of rationality as expressed through the methods of science. But when he later dealt with psychiatric patients, he found himself face to face with irrationality magnified manifold; his patients' symptoms were bizarre and incomprehensible by any ordinary criterion. His attempt to decipher these symptoms and the underlying disorder that produced them led to a new conception, not only of psychopathology, but of human nature in general.

In some ways, Freud can be regarded as a modern Hobbesian. Hobbes had insisted that at bottom men are savage brutes whose natural impulses would inevitably lead to murder, rape, and pillage if left unchecked (see Chapter 10). To curb this beast within, they had formed a social contract in some distant past and subordinated themselves to a larger social unit, the state. Like Hobbes, Freud regarded the basic human instincts as a "seething cauldron" of pleasure seeking that blindly seeks gratification regardless of the consequences. This savage, selfish human nature had to be tamed by civilization.

Unlike Hobbes, Freud did not believe that the subjugation of the brute in man was a onetime event in human political history. It occurs in every lifetime, for the social contract is renewed in the childhood of every generation. Another difference concerns the nature of the taming process. According to Hobbes, men's baser instincts are curbed by *external* social sanctions; they want to rob their neighbors but don't do so because they are afraid of the king's men. According to Freud, the restraints of society are incorporated internally during the first few years of childhood. The first curbs on behavior are based on a simple (and quite Hobbesian) fear of direct social consequences—of a scolding or spanking. But eventually the child inhibits his misdeeds because he feels that "they are bad," and not just because he fears that he will be caught and punished. At this point, the taming force of society has become internalized. The king's men are now within us, internalized embodiments of society's dictates whose weapons—the pangs of conscience—are no less powerful for being mental.

According to Freud, the taming process is never fully complete. The forbidden impulses cannot be ruled out of existence. They may be denied for a while, but eventually they will reassert themselves, often through new and devious channels, leading to yet further repressive measures which will probably fail in their turn as well. As a result, there is constant conflict between the demands of instinct and of society, but this war goes on underground, within the individual and usually without his or her own knowledge. As a result, man is divided against himself, and his unconscious conflicts express themselves in thoughts and deeds that appear irrational.

Hysteria and Hypnosis

When Freud began his medical practice, many of his patients suffered from a disorder called *hysteria.* The symptoms of hysteria presented an apparently helter-skelter catalogue of physical and mental complaints—total or partial blindness or deafness, paralysis or anesthesia of various parts of the body, uncontrollable trembling or convulsive attacks, distortions, and gaps in memory. Except for these symptoms, the patients were in no sense "insane"; they were generally lucid and did not have to be institutionalized. Was there any underlying pattern that could make sense of this confusing array of complaints?

The first clue came with the recognition that hysterical symptoms are *psychogenic,* the results of some unknown psychological cause rather than the product of organic damage to the nervous system. This discovery was made by Jean Charcot (1825–1893), a French neurologist, who noticed that many of the bodily symptoms of hysteria make no anatomical sense. For example, some patients suffered from anesthesia of the hand but lost no feeling above the wrist. This *glove anesthesia* could not possibly be caused by any nerve injury, since it is known that an injury to any one of the relevant nerve trunks must affect a por-

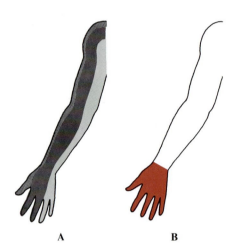

12.1 Glove anesthesia *(A) Areas of the skin of arms and hands that supply sensory information to different nerves. (B) A typical region of anesthesia in a hysterical patient. Anatomically, the anesthesia makes no sense. If there were nerve injury (in the spinal cord) the anesthesia would extend the length of the arm, as in (A).*

A   B

Charcot demonstrating hypnosis (Courtesy National Library of Medicine)

tion of the arm above the wrist (Figure 12.1). This rules out a simple organic interpretation and suggests that glove anesthesia has some psychological basis. While such findings showed that the hysterical symptoms are somehow psychological, this does not mean that they are therefore unreal. The patients weren't simply faking; their symptoms were real enough to them and often caused considerable suffering.

Charcot and other French psychiatrists of the period tried to relate hysteria to **hypnosis.** This is a temporary, trancelike state which can be induced in normal people but which may produce effects that resemble hysterical symptoms. The hypnotized person is exceedingly **suggestible.** If told that he cannot move his arm, he will act as if paralyzed. Similarly for suggestions of blindness, deafness, or anesthesia. If the trance is deep enough, the hypnotist can induce hallucinations in which the subject "sees" or "hears" imaginary objects. There are also effects on memory. If the subject is asked to forget everything that happened during the trance he generally complies. During this period of **posthypnotic amnesia** he will respond to suggestions planted during the trance. He might, for example, take off his shoes when the hypnotist gives the previously arranged signal. Such characteristics of the hypnotized state, especially those that involve paralysis and sensory deficit, buttressed the suspicion that hypnosis and hysteria were somehow related.

One of Charcot's contemporaries, Hippolyte Bernheim, thought that the link between the two phenomena is suggestion. In his view, the hysterical symptom was caused by suggestion, usually produced under conditions of intense emotional stress. If so, couldn't one fight fire with fire and remove the suggested symptom by a countersuggestion made during hypnosis? Bernheim and his colleagues tried to do just that. There were occasional successes, but in many cases the symptom proved obdurate. Sometimes the hysterical symptoms disappeared upon direct posthypnotic suggestion but were then replaced by others; a patient might regain the use of her legs but lose her sight.

In collaboration with another physician, Josef Breuer (1842–1925), Freud took an important further step. Both men came to believe that removing hysterical symptoms by suggestion is essentially futile; it was an attempt to erase a symptom without dealing with its underlying cause, like trying to cure measles by painting the spots. Their own efforts were based on the notion that hysterical symptoms are a disguised means of keeping certain emotionally charged memories under mental lock and key. When such memories are finally recovered, there is **catharsis,** an explosive release of previously dammed up emotions that has therapeutic effects.

Initially Breuer and Freud probed for these memories while the patients were in a hypnotic trance. One of Breuer's cases was Anna O., a twenty-one-year-old girl who was a walking collection of assorted symptoms: various paralyses, hysterical squints, coughs, occasional disorders of speech, and so on. When hypnotized, she was able to recall certain crucial events in her past that seemed to be at the root of this or the other symptom. Many of these events dated back to a particularly traumatic period during which she nursed her dying father. An example is a nervous cough which she traced to an occasion at her father's bedside. She heard the sound of dance music coming from a neighbor's house, felt the wish to be there, and was immediately struck by guilt and self-reproach. She covered up her feelings with a nervous cough, and thereafter coughed uncontrollably whenever she heard rhythmic music. The symptom disappeared when the forgotten episode was remembered (Freud and Breuer, 1895).

A commemorative stamp issued in honor of Anna O. *In the annals of psychoanalysis, Anna O. figures only as a famous case history. But in real life, Anna—or to use her true name, Bertha Pappenheim—was much more than that. After she recovered from her various disorders, she became a distinguished pioneer in the field of social work, as well as a militant and effective champion of women's rights in Eastern Europe. (Courtesy the Ministry of Post, Bonn, West Germany)*

Resistance and Repression

Eventually Freud abandoned hypnosis altogether, in part because not all patients were readily hypnotized. He found that crucial memories could be recovered even in the normal, waking state through the method of *free association.* The patients are told to say anything that enters their mind, no matter how trivial and unrelated it might seem, or how embarrassing, disagreeable, or indiscreet. Since all ideas are presumably related by an associative network, the emotionally charged "forgotten" memories should be evoked sooner or later. At first, this procedure seemed to work and yielded results similar to those obtained through hypnotic probes. But a new difficulty arose, for it became clear that the patients did not really comply with Freud's request. There was a *resistance* of which the patient was often unaware:

> The patient attempts to escape . . . by every possible means. First he says nothing comes into his head, then that so much comes into his head that he can't grasp any of it. Then we observe that . . . he is giving in to his critical objections, first to this, then to that; he betrays it by the long pauses which occur in his talk. At last he admits that he really cannot say something, he is ashamed to. . . . Or else, he has thought of something but it concerns someone else and not himself. . . . Or else, what he has just thought of is really too unimportant, too stupid and too absurd. . . . So it goes on, with untold variations, to which one continually replies that telling everything really means telling everything (Freud, 1917a, p. 289).

Freud noticed that the intensity of resistance was often an important clue to what was really important. When a patient seemed to struggle especially hard to change a topic, to break off a train of thought, she was probably close to the recovery of an emotionally charged memory. Eventually it would come, often to the patient's great surprise. But if this was so, and if the recovery of these memories helped the patient to get better (as both Freud and his patients believed), why then did the patients resist the retrieval of these memories and thus obstruct their own cure? Freud concluded that the observed phenomenon of resistance was the overt manifestation of some powerful force that opposed the recovery of the critical memories into consciousness. Certain experiences in the patient's life—certain acts, impulses, thoughts, or memories—were pushed out of consciousness, were *repressed,* and the same repressive forces that led to their original expulsion were mobilized to oppose their reentry into consciousness during the psychiatric session.

What are the ideas whose recollection is so vehemently resisted, which have to be repressed and kept out of mental sight? According to Freud, they are always connected with some wish or impulse that the person is unable to face without suffering intense anxiety. Repression is a defense; the unacceptable wish and various thoughts associated with it are pushed out of consciousness to ward off intolerable pain. The repressed wishes are invariably linked to the basic biological urges, especially the sexual ones, whose full expression is forbidden by society.

Freud also concluded that the critical repressions date back to early life, when the instinctual urges of the child first clash with the restraints imposed by society as embodied in his parents. As evidence he cited his clinical observations. In patient after patient, the eventual recovery of a repressed memory merely led to further resistance, which ultimately gave way to reveal a repressed memory earlier on, and so on back to the early years of childhood.

Freud believed that the repressed material is not really eradicated but remains in the *unconscious.* This is a metaphorical expression which only means that the repressed ideas still exert a powerful effect. Again and again, they push up from below, like a jack-in-the-box, fueled by the biological urges that gave rise to them in the first place, or triggered by associations in the here and now. As these repressed ideas well up again, they also bring back anxiety and are therefore pushed down once more. The result is a never-ending unconscious conflict. This conflict often leads to a compromise in which the rejected wishes are expressed, but in a censored form. According to Freud, many symptoms of psychopathology represent conflict solutions of this kind. An example is a patient who repeatedly pulls off her blouse with one hand and pulls it back on with the other. Freud would probably argue that this is a dramatized sexual fantasy in which the patient plays two roles—a lover who is trying to undress her and that part of herself that tries to resist.

The task Freud set for himself was the analysis (as he called it, the ***psychoanalysis***) of these conflicts, the discovery of their origins, of their effects in the present, of their removal or alleviation. But he soon came to believe that the same mechanisms which produce the symptoms of psychopathology also operate in normal persons, that his discoveries were not just a contribution to psychiatry, but were a foundation for a general theory of human personality.

UNCONSCIOUS CONFLICT

Our sketch of Freud's theory of the nature and development of human personality will concentrate on those aspects that seem to represent the highlights of a complex theoretical formulation that was continually revised and modified during the course of Freud's long career. In this description, we will separate two aspects of Freudian theory. We will begin with the conception of the mechanisms of unconscious conflict. We will then deal with Freud's theory of the origins of these conflicts in the individual's life history, and of their relation to the development of sex identity and morality.

The Antagonists of Inner Conflict

Freud's theories concern the forces whose antagonism produces unconscious conflict and the effects produced when they clash. But, who fights whom in unconscious conflict?

When conflict is external, the antagonists are easily identified: David and Goliath, St. George and the Dragon, and so on. But what are the warring forces when the conflict is inside of the individual? In essence, they are different behavior tendencies, such as Anna O's sexually tinged desire to be at a dance and her conflicting reactions of guilt at leaving a dying father. One of the tasks Freud set himself was to classify the tendencies that participate in such conflicts, to see which of them are usually arrayed together and fight on the same side. The result was a threefold classification of conflicting tendencies within the individual, which he

Inner conflicts as envisaged by Plato The Greek philosopher Plato anticipated Freud's tripartite division of the mind by over two thousand years. In one of his Dialogues, *he likened the soul to a chariot with two horses that often pull in opposed directions. The chariot's drive is Reason, the two horses are Spirit (our nobler emotions) and Appetite. This Renaissance medallion depicts Plato's image of the internal conflict.*

regarded as three more or less distinct subsystems of the human personality: the *id*, the *ego*, and the *superego*. In some of Freud's writings, there is a tendency to treat these three systems as if they were three separate persons that inhabit the mind. But this is only a metaphor that must not be taken literally; *id, eg,* and *superego* are just names for three sets of very different reaction patterns. They are not persons in their own right (Freud, 1923).

THE ID

The *id* is the most primitive portion of the personality, from which the other two are derived. It contains all of the basic biological urges: to eat, drink, eliminate, be comfortably warm and, most of all, to gain sexual pleasure.* The id's sole law is the *pleasure principle*—satisfaction now and not later, regardless of circumstances and whatever the cost.

The id's blind strivings for pleasure know no distinction between self and world, between fantasy and reality, between wishing and having. Its insistent urges spill out into reflex motor action, like emptying the bladder when it is full. If that doesn't work, the clamoring for pleasure leads to primitive thoughts of gratification, fantasies of wish fulfillment that cannot be distinguished from reality.

THE EGO

At birth, the infant is all id. But the id's shrill clamors are soon met by the harsh facts of external reality. Some gratifications come only after a delay. The breast or the bottle are not always present; the infant has to cry to get them.

The confrontations between hot desire and cold reality lead to a whole set of new reactions that are meant to reconcile the two. Sometimes the reconciliation is by appropriate action (saying "please"), sometimes by self-imposed delay (going to the bathroom), sometimes by suppression of a forbidden impulse (not touching one's genitals). These various reactions become organized into a new subsystem of the personality—the *ego.* The ego is derived from the id and is essentially still in its service. But unlike the id, the ego obeys the *reality principle.* It tries to satisfy the id (that is, to gain pleasure), but it does so pragmatically, in accordance with the real world and its real demands. As time proceeds, the opposition between need and reality leads to the emergence of more and more skills, all directed to the same end, as well as a whole system of thought and memories that grows up concurrently. Eventually, this entire system becomes capable of looking at itself and now deserves the name Freud gave it, ego or self. Until this point, there was no "I" but only a mass of undifferentiated strivings (appropriately named after the Latin impersonal pronoun *id,* literally "it").

THE SUPEREGO

The id is not the ego's only master. As the child grows older, a new reaction pattern develops from within the ego that acts as a kind of judge that decides whether the ego has been "good" or "bad." This new mental agency is the *superego* which

---

* These urges are sometimes called instincts, but that is a misnomer caused by an unfortunate translation of Freud's original term.

represents the internalized rules and admonitions of the parents, and through them, of society. Initially, the ego only had to worry about external reality. It might inhibit some id-inspired action, but only to avert some future trouble: You don't steal cookies because you might be caught. But a little later, the forbidden act is suppressed even when there can never be any real punishment. This change occurs because the child starts to act and think as if he himself were the parent who administers praise and reproof. A three-year-old is often seen to slap his own hand as he is about to play with mud or commit some other heinous deed; he sometimes mutters some self-righteous pronouncement like "Dirty. Bad." This is the beginning of the superego, the ego's second master, which praises and punishes just as the parents did. If the ego lives up to the superego's dictates, the reward is pride. But if one of the superego's rules is broken, the superego metes out punishment just as the parents scolded or spanked or withdrew their love. There is then self-reproach and a feeling of guilt.

The formation of the superego puts the ego in a difficult position, for its two masters often issue conflicting commands. The promptings of the id are all too often in forbidden directions; if the ego gives in, the superego will punish it. What's worse is that both masters are essentially infantile. We have seen that the id's demands are blind and unreasoning, but the superego's strictures are also rooted in childish irrationality. The superego was formed when the child's cognitive abilities were still quite primitive. At that time, it could only internalize what it understood then—blind do's and don'ts. As a result, the superego is essentially irrational; Freud regarded it as largely unconscious. It issues absolute imperatives that are not accessible to reason. If the ego obeys, it must throttle various urges of the id, even if those are merely expressed in a thought or a memory. To accomplish this feat, the ego must resort to repression.

In summary, Freud's threefold division of the personality is just a way of saying that our thoughts and actions are determined by the interplay of three major factors: our biological drives, the various ways through which we have learned to satisfy these drives and master the external world, and the commands and prohibitions of society. Freud's contribution is his insistence that the conflicts among these three forces are inside the individual, that they are derived from childhood experiences, and that they are waged without the individual's conscious awareness.

The Nature of Unconscious Conflict

We now turn to Freud's formulation (here drastically simplified) of the rules by which these inner wars are waged. In rough outline, the conflict begins when id-derived urges and various associated memories are pushed underground, are repressed. But the forbidden urges refuse to stay down. They find substitute outlets whose further consequence is a host of additional defenses that are erected to reinforce the original repression, hold off the id-derived flood, and allow the ego to maintain its self-regard (S. Freud, 1917a, 1926; A. Freud 1946).

REPRESSION AND ANXIETY

What underlies repression? Freud believed that the crucial factor here is intense *anxiety,* an emotional state akin to fear (see Chapter 3). According to Freud, various forbidden acts become associated with anxiety as the child is scolded or disciplined for performing them. The parents may resort to physical punishment or they may merely register their disapproval with a frown or reprimand; in either case, the child is threatened with the loss of their love and becomes anxious. The next time he is about to, say, finger his penis or pinch his baby brother, he will feel a twinge of anxiety, an internal signal that his parents may leave him, and that he will be abandoned and alone.

Since anxiety is intensely unpleasant, the child will do everything he can in order to remove it or to ward it off. If the cause is an external stimulus, the child's reaction is clear. He runs away and thus removes himself from the fear-inducing object. But how can he cope with a danger that comes from within? As before, he will flee from whatever evokes fear or anxiety. But now the flight is from something inside himself. To get rid of anxiety, the child must suppress that which triggers it—the forbidden act.

Freud's concept of repression applies to the thought no less than the deed. We can understand that a four-year-old boy who is punished for kicking his baby brother will refrain from such warlike acts in the future. But why does the boy stop *thinking* about them and why does he fail to remember the crucial incident, as Freud maintains? One answer is that thinking about an act is rather similar to performing it. This is especially so given the young child's limited cognitive abilities. He has not as yet fully mastered the distinction between thought and action. Nor does he know that his father can't really "read his mind," that his thoughts are private and thus immune from parental prosecution. The inhibition therefore applies not just to overt action, but to related thoughts, memories, and wishes.

SUPPLEMENTARY MECHANISMS OF DEFENSE

Repression can be regarded as the primary, initial ***mechanism of defense*** that protects the individual against anxiety. But repression is often incomplete. Often enough the thoughts and urges that were pushed underground refuse to stay buried and surge up again. But as they do, so does the anxiety to which they are associated. As a result, various further mechanisms of defense are brought into play to reinforce the original dam against the forbidden impulses.

Displacement   One such supplementary defense mechanism is ***displacement.*** When a geyser is dammed up, its waters usually penetrate other cracks and fissures and eventually gush up elsewhere. According to Freud, the same holds for repressed urges, which tend to find new and often disguised outlets. An example is ***displaced aggression*** that develops when fear of retaliation blocks the normal direction of discharge. The child who is reprimanded by her parent turns on her playmate or vents her anger on the innocent household cat. According to many social psychologists, the same mechanism underlies the persecution of minority groups. They become convenient scapegoats for aggressive impulses fueled by social and economic unrest.

Reaction formation   In displacement, the forbidden impulse is rechanneled into a safer course. Certain other mechanisms of defense are attempts to supplement the original repression by blocking off the impulse altogether. An example is ***reaction formation*** in which the repressed wish is warded off by its diametrical opposite. The young girl who jealously hated her sister and was punished for hos-

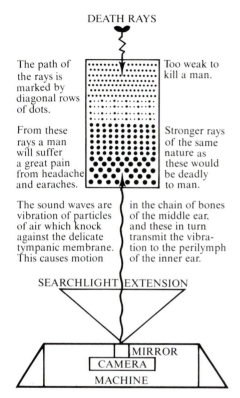

DEATH RAYS

The path of the rays is marked by diagonal rows of dots.

Too weak to kill a man.

From these rays a man will suffer a great pain from headache and earaches.

Stronger rays of the same nature as these would be deadly to man.

The sound waves are vibration of particles of air which knock against the delicate tympanic membrane. This causes motion

in the chain of bones of the middle ear, and these in turn transmit the vibration to the perilymph of the inner ear.

SEARCHLIGHT EXTENSION

MIRROR
CAMERA
MACHINE

12.2 An influencing machine   *This diagram was drawn by a paranoid patient and depicts a mysterious "machine" by which he insists his "enemies" have influenced his thoughts and actions since his birth. By means of this influencing machine, they read and control his feelings, induce all kinds of evil sexual and other forbidden desires, and can cause him to suffer pain, illness, or even death. This delusion is an extreme manifestation of the mechanism of projection. The patient denies that his evil thoughts and desires are really his, but instead imputes them to outside agents who force these thoughts and feelings on him by mechanical means. (After Masserman, 1946)*

tile acts may turn her feelings into the very opposite; she now showers her sister with an exaggerated love and tenderness, a desperate bulwark against aggressive wishes that she cannot accept. But the repressed hostility can still be detected underneath the loving exterior; her love is overly solicitous and stifling and the sister probably feels smothered by it.

Rationalization   In reaction formation, there is an attempt (albeit not too successful) to keep the forbidden wishes at bay. Some other mechanisms represent a different line of defense; the repressed thoughts break through but they are reinterpreted and are not recognized for what they are. One example of this is **rationalization** in which the person interprets some of his own feelings or actions in more acceptable terms. The cruel father beats his child mercilessly but is sure that he does so "for the child's own good." Countless atrocities have been committed under the same guise of altruism; heretics have been tortured to save their immortal souls and cities have been razed to protect the world against barbarism. Rationalization is also employed at a more everyday level, as a defense not only against repressed wishes but against any thought that would make the individual feel unworthy and anxious. An example is the sour-grapes phenomenon. The jilted lover tells his friends that he never really cared for his lost love; eventually he believes it himself.

Projection   Another example of a defense mechanism in which cognitive reorganization plays a major role is **projection.** Here the forbidden urges well up and are recognized as such. But the person does not realize that these wishes are his own; instead, he attributes them to others. "I desire you" becomes "You desire me," "I hate you" becomes "You hate me"—desperate defenses against repressed sexual or hostile wishes that can no longer be banished from consciousness (Freud, 1911).

An extreme form of projection is characteristic of **paranoid schizophrenia,** a disorder in which the patient loses contact with reality and is generally institutionalized (see Chapter 19). The paranoid schizophrenic often suffers from delusions of persecution, accusing various people—his wife, the doctor, the grocer next door, the Pope—of conspiring against him. His own feelings of rage terrify him, and he therefore imputes them to people in the outside world. But his projected rage recoils and makes things even worse. If all those people really hate him, how can he help but hate them all the more? His feelings of rage are now intensified, which leads to an increase in the hostility he projects outside, and so on, in a vicious cycle (Figure 12.2).

Unconscious Conflict in Normal Life

Freud arrived at his theory of unconscious conflict by studying the behavior of disturbed individuals, usually hysterics. But he soon concluded that the same clash of unconscious forces that results in neurotic symptoms is also found in the life of normal persons. Their inner conflicts are under control, with less resulting anxiety and no crippling effects, but they are present nonetheless. We will consider two areas to which Freud appealed for evidence: lapses of memory and slips of the tongue in everyday life, and the content of dreams.

ERRORS OF SPEECH AND MEMORY

Freud drew attention to what he called the psychopathology of everyday life, in which we momentarily forget a name that might call up embarrassing memories or in which we suffer a slip of the tongue that unwittingly reveals an underlying motive (Freud, 1901). Shakespeare's Portia is obliged by her father's will to be impartial among her several suitors and to select her husband essentially by lot. Before the final choice is made, she tells her favorite suitor:

> One half of me is yours, the other half yours—
> Mine own I would say . . .
>
> *(The Merchant of Venice,* Act III, Scene ii)

She thus commits a "Freudian slip" nearly three hundred years before Freud was born. Suppressed intentions sometimes emerge to make us become "absent-minded" about things we don't really want to do. Freud cites the example of a friend who wrote a letter which he forgot to send off for several days. He finally mailed it, but it was returned by the post office, for there was no address. He addressed it and sent if off again only to have it returned once more because there was no stamp.

This is not to say (though psychoanalytic writers often seem to say it) that all slips of the tongue, all mislayings of objects, and all lapses of memory are *motivated* in Freud's sense. The host who cannot call up a guest's name when he has to introduce him to another guest is unlikely to have some hidden reason for keeping that name out of his consciousness. The name is probably blocked because of simple, and quite unmotivated, memory interference (see Chapter 7).

THE THEORY OF DREAMS

One of Freud's most influential works was his theory of dreams (Freud, 1900). He argued that dreams have a meaning which can be deciphered if one looks deeply enough. In his view, the dream concerns the dreamer's past and present, and it arises from unknown regions within. He saw the dream as somewhat analogous to a hysterical symptom. On the surface, they both appear meaningless and bizarre, but they become comprehensible when understood as veiled expressions of an unconscious clash between competing motives.

Freud began with the assumption that at bottom every dream is an attempt at **wish fulfillment.** While awake, a wish is usually not acted upon right away, for there are considerations of both reality (the ego) and morality (the superego) that must be taken into account: "Is it possible?" and "Is it allowed?" But during sleep these restraining forces are drastically weakened and the wish then leads to immediate thoughts and images of gratification. In some cases the wish fulfillment is simple and direct. Starving explorers dream of sumptuous meals; men stranded in the desert dream of cool mountain streams. According to a Hungarian proverb quoted by Freud, "Pigs dream of acorns and geese dream of maize."

Simple wish-fulfillment dreams are comparatively rare. What about the others, the strange and illogical nightly narratives that are far more usual? Freud argued that the same principle of attempted wish fulfillment could explain these as well. But here a new process comes into play. The underlying wish touches upon some forbidden matters that are associated with anxiety. As a result, various mechanisms of defense are invoked. The wish cannot be expressed directly; it is **censored** and is only allowed to surface in symbolic disguise. The dreamer never experiences the underlying **latent dream** that represents his own hidden wishes and concerns. What he does experience is the carefully laundered version that emerges after the defense mechanisms have done their work—the **manifest dream.** The end product is reminiscent of hysterical symptoms and various pathologies of everyday life. It represents a compromise between forbidden urges and the repressive forces that hold them down. The underlying impulse is censored, but it surreptitiously emerges in a veiled disguise.

Fragments of the same day's events *(day residues)* are often interwoven with disguised urges to produce the manifest dream. An example is a dream reported during World War I by a middle-aged woman whose son was in the army. Here, the underlying sexual wish is readily discernible and the censorship is expressed by gaps in the stream of events. She dreamed of volunteering for some unspecified patriotic service for the benefit of the troops:

> She approached a staff surgeon with her request, and he understood her meaning after she said only a few words. The actual wording of her speech in the dream was: "I and many women and girls in Vienna are ready to . . ." At this point in the dream her words turned into a mumble ". . . for the troops—officers and other ranks without distinction." . . . There followed an awkward silence of some minutes. The staff surgeon then put his arm around her waist and said: "Suppose, madam, it actually came to . . . (mumble)" . . . She replied: "Good gracious, I'm an old woman and I might never come to that. . . . It must never happen that an elderly woman . . . (mumble) . . . a mere boy. That would be terrible." "I understand perfectly," replied the staff surgeon. Some of the officers, and among them one who had been a suitor of hers in her youth, laughed out loud (Freud, 1917b, p. 137).

In other dreams, the disguise is achieved by more elaborate means. The underlying wish finds expression in various displaced forms. There is **symbolism** in

Dreams and symbolism *The 1927 German silent film* The Secrets of a Soul *by Georg Pabst tried to depict a case history in psychoanalytic terms. Its subject was a middle-aged man suffering from impotence. The film portrays several of the patient's dreams. In this one, he tries to plant a tree, a symbol for impregnating his wife. (Courtesy The Museum of Modern Art/Film Stills Archive)*

which one thing stands for another. Some symbols are widely shared because certain physical, functional, or linguistic similarities are perceived by most people (for example, screwdriver and box for penis and vagina). But there is no simple cipher that can be generally applied. After all, many physical objects are either long and pointed or round and hollow; a pat equation with male and female genitals will be of little use. Most symbolic relationships depend upon the dreamer's own life experience and can only be interpreted by noting his free associations to the dream.

Origins of Unconscious Conflict

Freud believed that the unconscious conflicts he uncovered—in dreams, in memory lapses, in neurotic symptoms—always referred to certain critical events in the individual's early life. His observations of his patients convinced him that these crucial events are remarkably similar from person to person. He concluded that all human beings go through a largely similar sequence of significant emotional events in their early lives, that some of the most important of these involve sexual urges, and that it is this childhood past that shapes their present (Freud, 1905).

STAGES OF PSYCHOSEXUAL DEVELOPMENT

Freud's theory of psychosexual development emphasizes different stages, each of which is built upon the achievements of those before. (In this regard it resembles Jean Piaget's theory of cognitive growth, which we will take up in Chapter 14.) In Freud's view, the child starts life as a bundle of pleasure-seeking tendencies. Pleasure is obtained by the stimulation of certain zones of the body that are particularly sensitive to touch: the mouth, the anus, and the genitals. Freud called these regions *erogenous zones,* for he believed that the various pleasures associated with each of them have a common element which is sexual.* As the child develops, the relative importance of the zones shifts. Initially, most of the pleasure seeking is through the mouth (the *oral stage*). With the advent of toilet concerns, the emphasis shifts to the anus (the *anal stage*). Still later, there is an increased interest in the pleasure that can be obtained from stimulating the genitals (the *phallic stage*). The culmination of *psychosexual development* is attained in adult sexuality when pleasure involves not just one's own gratification but also the social and bodily satisfaction brought to another person (the *genital stage*).

OBSTACLES TO SMOOTH PROGRESSION

How does the child move from one stage to the next? In part, it is a matter of physical maturation. For example, bowel control is simply impossible at birth, for the infant lacks the necessary neuromuscular readiness. But there is another element. As the child's bodily maturation proceeds, there is an inevitable change in what the parents allow, prohibit, or demand. Initially, the child nurses, then he is weaned. Initially, he is diapered, then he is toilet trained. Each change automat-

---

* One of his arguments for regarding oral and anal stimulation in infancy as ultimately sexual was the fact that such stimulation sometimes precedes (or replaces) sexual intercourse in adulthood.

ically produces some frustration and conflict as former ways of gaining pleasure are denied. Under the circumstances, many of the dynamics of conflict we have previously discussed come into play.

One possible mode of response to frustration during development is reaction formation. Consider toilet training. The child's urge is to relax his sphincter whenever there is pressure in his bowels. Given his parents' clearly expressed disapproval, this urge leads to anxiety. One means of dealing with the conflict is to do the exact opposite of what he really wants—to inhibit the bowels rather than to relax them. This reaction formation may broaden and become manifest in more symbolic social terms. As a result, the child may become compulsively clean and orderly ("I must not soil myself").

Freud believed that there are several other long-term consequences of this reaction formation during toilet training. One is obstinacy. The child asserts himself by holding back when on his potty ("You can't make me if I don't want to"), a stubbornness which may become a more generalized "no." Another consequence may be stinginess. According to Freud, this is a general form of withholding, a refusal to part with what is one's own (that is, one's feces). This refusal generalizes so that the child becomes obsessed with property rights and jealously hoards his possessions. According to Freud, this childhood reaction formation may lay the foundation of an adult personality in which compulsive neatness, stubbornness, and stinginess go together (Abraham, 1927; Freud, 1940).

THE OEDIPUS COMPLEX

We now turn to that aspect of the theory of psychosexual development that Freud himself regarded as the most important—the family triangle of love and jealousy and fear that is at the root of internalized morality and out of which grows the child's identification with the parent of the same sex. This is the *Oedipus complex,* named after the mythical king of Thebes who unknowingly committed the two most awful crimes—killing his father and marrying his mother. According to

Oedipus Rex   From a 1955 production directed by Tyrone Guthrie with Douglas Campbell in the title role, at Stratford, Ontario. (Courtesy Billy Rose Theatre Collection, The New York Public Library at Lincoln Center, Astor, Lenox and Tilden Collections)

Freud, an analogous family drama is reenacted in the childhood of all men and women. Since he came to believe that the sequence of steps is somewhat different in the two sexes, we will take them up separately. We will start with his theory of how genital sexuality emerges in males (Freud, 1905).

First act: Love and hate At about three or four years of age, the **phallic stage** begins. The young boy becomes increasingly interested in his penis, which becomes a source of both pride and pleasure. He masturbates and this brings satisfaction, but it is not enough. His erotic urges seek an external object. The inevitable choice is his mother (or some mother substitute). After all, he has already become attached to her through the various gratifications she provided during the oral stage. It seems only logical to direct his phallic urges to this source of all other pleasure. In some cases, this tendency is intensified by the mother herself who takes a special interest in her "little man." (An analogous pattern is seen in fathers who very often are especially fond of their daughters.) The little boy wants to be near his mother, wants to touch and caress her. In addition, he perhaps has some vaguely erotic fantasies about her when he touches his penis. He has found his first sexual partner.

But there is an obstacle—the boy's father. The little boy wants to have his mother all to himself, as a comforter as well as an erotic partner, but this sexual utopia is out of the question. His father is a rival and he is bigger. The little boy wants his father to go away and not come back—in short, to die. This is not to say that the child's wish for his father's death is in any sense the same as a murderous wish in an adult, for the boy has as little conception of death as he has of adult sexuality. As Freud remarks, all of this may not be much when compared to the tragic acts of Oedipus, but it is enough. The family drama is played in the small arena of the nursery, but the basic pattern is the same: a love of mother and a jealousy of father.

Second act: Fear and renunciation At this point, a new element enters into the family drama. The little boy begins to fear the father he is jealous of. What brings this fear about? Freud suggests several causes. To begin with, the parents have by now probably discovered and condemned their son's masturbational practices. They may have done so quite severely; in Freud's day there were often threats of dire consequences. As a result, the pleasurable sensations from the penis and their associated thoughts become connected with anxiety. In addition, there is the son's jealous hate of his father which ultimately recoils back upon him. The little boy is sure that the father knows of his son's hostility and that the father will surely answer hate with hate.

With childish logic the little boy suspects that his punishment may be all too horribly appropriate to his crime. The same organ by which he sinned will be the one that is made to suffer. The result is **castration anxiety** which is aggravated by whatever threats the parents may have issued when they saw him masturbate. As a result, the boy tries to push the hostile feelings underground, but they refuse to stay buried. They return and the only defense that is left is projection: "I hate father" becomes "Father hates me." This can only increase the boy's fear, which increases his hate, which is again pushed down, comes back up, and leads to yet further projection. This process spirals upward, until the father is finally seen as an overwhelming ogre who threatens to castrate his son.

Freud at age sixteen with his mother, Amalie Nathanson Freud *Freud was his mother's first-born and her favorite, a fact that may have affected his theory of the human family drama. As he put it, "A man who has been the indisputable favorite of his mother keeps for life the feeling of a conqueror, that confidence of success that often induces real success." (E. Jones, 1953, p. 5, photograph courtesy Mary Evans Picture Library)*

Third act: Renunciation and final victory As the vicious cycle continues, the little boy's anxiety eventually becomes unbearable. At this point, he throws in the towel, renounces his mother as an erotic object, and more or less renounces genital pleasures, at least for a while. Instead, he ***identifies*** with his father. He concludes that by becoming like him, he will eventually enjoy an erotic partnership of the kind his father enjoys now, if not with his mother, then at least with someone much like her.

According to Freud, the renunciation of the Oedipal problem is accomplished by the repression of all the urges, feelings, and memories of the family drama. One lasting residue is the superego, the internalized voice of the father admonishing his son from within.

Freud believed that once the tumult of the Oedipal conflict dies down, there is a period of comparative sexual quiet which lasts from about five to twelve years of age. This is the ***latency period*** during which phallic sexuality lies dormant; boys play only with boys, devote themselves to athletics, and want to have nothing to do with the opposite sex. All of this changes at puberty. The hormone levels rise, the sex organs mature rapidly, and the repressed sex impulses can no longer be denied. But as these urges come out of their closet, parts of the Oedipal family skeleton come out as well, dragging along many of the fears and conflicts that had been comfortably hidden away for all these years.

According to Freud, this is one of the reasons why adolescence is so often a period of deep emotional turbulence. The boy is now physically mature and he is strongly attracted to the opposite sex, but this very attraction frightens him and he doesn't know why. Sexual contact with women arouses the unconscious wishes and fears that pertain to mother and father. In healthy individuals, the Oedipus complex has been resolved well enough so that these fears can be overcome without generating still further defenses. The boy can eventually accept himself as a man and achieve ***genital sexuality,*** in which he loves a woman as herself rather than as some shadowy substitute for his mother, and in which his love involves giving as well as taking.

THE ELECTRA COMPLEX

We have traced Freud's account of the male psychosexual odyssey to adult sexuality. What about the female? In Freud's view, she goes through essentially identical oral and anal phases as does the male. And in many ways, the development of her phallic interests (Freud used the same term for both sexes) is symmetrical to the male's. As he focuses his erotic interests on the mother, so she focuses hers upon the father. As he resents and eventually comes to fear the father, so she the mother. In short, there is a female version of the Oedipus complex (sometimes called the ***Electra complex*** after the Greek tragic heroine who goaded her brother into slaying their mother). But there is a theoretical difficulty. How does the little girl get to desire her father in the first place? Her first attachment was to the mother. According to Freud, this initial attachment was ultimately sexual. But if so, what accounts for the little girl's switch of sex objects?

To answer this question, Freud elaborated a far-fetched scheme that is widely regarded as one of the weakest aspects of his whole theory. The shift of attachments begins as the little girl discovers that she does not have a penis. According to Freud, she regards this lack as a catastrophe and develops ***penis envy.*** Her little

Electra In Eugene O'Neill's tragedy, Mourning Becomes Electra, *the Electra myth is set in the period of the American Civil War. Like the Greek plays from which it derives, O'Neill's tragedy focuses on the murderous hatred a daughter may bear her mother. From the 1947 film based on the play, with Rosalind Russell, Katina Paxinov, and Raymond Massey. (Courtesy The Museum of Modern Art/Film Stills Archive)*

brother might fear that he *will* be castrated; she believes that she already *is,* and feels unworthy. One consequence is that she withdraws her love from the mother, whom she regards as equally unworthy. The little girl wants a penis, but how can she get one? She turns to her father who does have the desirable organ and who she believes can help her obtain a penis substitute—a child. (Why *child* equals *penis* requires even more far-fetched arguments.) At this point, she directs her affections toward the father. From here on, the rest of the process unfolds more or less analogously to its counterpart in the boy: love of father, jealousy of mother, increasing fear of mother, eventual repression of the entire complex, and identification with the mother (Freud, 1925, 1933).

This theory of psychosexual development has been widely attacked on both scientific and political grounds. For example, why does the girl want a penis? (And if she does, why does she blame her mother for the lack of it?) That she envies her little brother's social role in a culture in which men have more power and status is not surprising (of this more later, see Chapter 16). But there is no evidence she really envies the particular male organ as such rather than the role and status which maleness confers in many cultures.

We conclude that Freud's theory of female psychosexual development is inadequate. Freud began with the basic premise that the *initial* attachment to one's mother is sexual. Given this belief, he was forced to find an explanation for the eventual shift in the girl's sexual choice. But this first premise is very suspect, for filial and sexual attachments probably do not stem from the same biological source. In consequence, there is no need to postulate any intrinsic difference in the pattern of psychosexual development of males and females. By and large, males choose females and females choose males, mostly because of built-in tendencies that are probably reinforced by cultural factors. Under the circumstances, the development is symmetrical. Whether Freud was right about the basic family triangle is still an open question. But if he was right, the drama unfolds in the same way regardless of whether the starring role is played by a boy or a girl.

THE EXPANDED FAMILY DRAMA

The family drama often has a cast that is larger than three. As a result, the basic loves and jealousies and fears may be more complex. There may be some erotic feeling between brother and sister; there may also be *sibling rivalry.* The legends of mankind are ample testimony to the enduring grudges of the child who thinks he has been less favored: Esau and Jacob, Cinderella and her stepsisters. In each case, we have the jealous child's fantasy of ultimate ascendance over his hated rivals: Jacob gets his father's blessing and Cinderella wins the prince.

According to Freud, the patterns of infantile love, fear, and hate developed in the early family constellation lay the groundwork for everything that follows. In his view, the essentials of the adult personality are determined during these first five or six years. Unless drastic events intervene, all persons are destined to reenact their own childhood drama over and over again for the rest of their lives—the dialogue may be more sophisticated, but the underlying plot is always the same.

A REEXAMINATION OF FREUDIAN THEORY

Thus far, we have presented Freud's views with a minimum of critical comment. We now shift our perspective to consider some of his assertions in the light of present-day thought and evidence.

Testing Freud's Theories

By what criteria can one determine whether Freud's assertions are in fact correct? Freud's own criterion was the evidence from the couch. He considered the patient's free associations, his resistances, his slips of the tongue, his dreams, and then tried to weave them into a coherent pattern that somehow made sense of all the parts. But can one really draw conclusions from this kind of clinical evidence alone? Clinical practitioners cannot be totally objective no matter how hard they try. As they listen to a patient, they are more likely to hear and remember those themes that fit in with their own views than those that do not. (This point is especially pertinent to Freud who never took notes during psychoanalytic sessions.) Would a clinician with different biases have remembered the same themes?

The issue goes deeper than objective reportage. Even if the analyst could be an utterly objective observer, he cannot possibly avoid affecting that which he observes. His own theoretical preconceptions are inevitably noticed by his patients, whose dreams and free associations will very likely be colored by them. The trouble is that there is no way of disentangling the effect of the analyst (and of his theories) upon the patient's mental productions (which we want to use as evidence for or against these theories).

Conceptual Difficulties

Yet another problem is conceptual. Scientific theories lead to certain predictions; if these fail, the theory is refuted. But are Freud's assertions theories in this sense?

What specific predictions do they lead to? Consider the hypothetical case of a boy raised by a harsh, rejecting mother and a weak, alcoholic father. What will the boy be like as an adult? Will he seek dominating women who will degrade him as his mother did? Will he try to find a warm, comforting wife upon whom he can become dependent and thus make up for the mothering he never had as a child? There is no way of predicting on psychoanalytic grounds. Each outcome makes perfectly good sense—*after* it has occurred.

Another problem with many psychoanalytic arguments is that the analyst's theory often determines whether a patient's statement should or should not be accepted at face value. Suppose a woman insists that she hates her mother. The analyst will probably believe her. But if she swears that she loves her mother, the analyst may conclude that she, like Shakespeare's lady, "doth protest too much." He may then interpret her protestations of love as meaning the exact opposite, as reflecting a reaction formation against her "real" feelings of hate. The trouble with this kind of two-way reasoning is that it becomes difficult to find any sort of disproof.

Such considerations suggest that if we want to test Freud's assertions, we must look for more objective evidence and must be more rigorous in the way in which we interpret it. We will begin by considering some work that bears on Freud's theories of unconscious conflict.

The Evidence for Repression and Defense

According to Freud, human beings are impelled by inner conflicts, of which they are mostly unaware. Unacceptable impulses are kept out of consciousness by elaborate devices of internal censorship: the mechanisms of defense, headed by repression. This notion of repressive forces is the cornerstone of psychoanalytic thought. What does modern psychology have to say about this notion? Our primary concern will be with cases that involve memory and are thus akin to what Freud called repression.

CLINICAL EVIDENCE

A recent study tried to provide some objective evidence for a repressionlike effect during psychoanalytic sessions. During such sessions (as of course, in ordinary life) patients sometimes have a momentary lapse of memory. They say, "I just had a thought, but it slipped my mind." Eventually they think of what they had wanted to say, often within the same session. Are these memory lapses related to the patient's emotional preoccupations? Freud would certainly have guessed that they are, that they occur when the patient is thinking (or is about to think) of something that is especially charged with emotion.

In a test of this hypothesis, several hundred tape-recorded psychoanalytic sessions were examined for instances of such momentary forgetting. When did such lapses occur? The investigator examined the topics the patient talked about just before and just after the memory lapse. He then compared these topics with those dealt with during control intervals (taken from other sessions in which there were no lapses). The results indicate that the lapses did not occur at random; they were much more likely during periods when the patient dealt with a crucial emotional theme (Luborsky, 1973; Luborsky, Sackheim, and Christoph, 1979).

LABORATORY STUDIES OF ANXIETY AND RECALL

There have been many efforts to produce repression and related effects in the laboratory (see Eriksen and Pierce, 1968). But this task is far from easy. According to psychoanalytic theory, motivated forgetting is a defense against anxiety. One would therefore expect that materials that are associated with anxiety will be recalled less readily than neutral items. But how can the experimenter be sure that the critical material is really anxiety-provoking for the subject?

To cope with this problem, several investigators have pre-selected their items to fit each subject's own pattern of anxieties. One way of doing this is by an initial word-association test. The subject is given a list of words; she has to reply to each with the first word that comes to mind. If her reaction to any one stimulus word is unusually slow or if it is accompanied by increased heart rate or a marked galvanic skin response, that word is presumably emotion-arousing for her. Using this method, one experimenter selected a set of neutral and emotional words for each subject (Jacobs, 1955). When these were later used as the responses in a paired-associate task, the subject had more trouble in producing the emotional than the neutral items. One way of explaining the result is to assume that as the emotionally loaded word was about to be retrieved from memory, it triggered anxiety which blocked further efforts at retrieval.

Seen in this light, repression may turn out to be a special case of retrieval failure. We have previously seen that recall is enormously dependent upon the presence of an appropriate retrieval cue. We forget the street names of the city we grew up in, but most of them come back when we revisit the city after many years. The same may hold for memories that Freud said are repressed. Perhaps they are not really held back by some imperious censor; perhaps they are rather misfiled under a hard-to-reach rubric and cannot be retrieved for this reason. One might want to add some further assumptions about the role of anxiety in maintaining this state of affairs. Perhaps anxiety blocks refiling; perhaps it impedes the use of appropriate retrieval cues (Erdelyi and Goldberg, 1979.)

LABORATORY EVIDENCE FOR PERCEPTUAL DEFENSE

A somewhat similar process may operate in recognition as well as in recall. This effect is often called *perceptual defense.* An example is provided by a study in which subjects were shown a series of nonsense syllables at very brief exposures. The task was to report the syllables which they saw. Some of the syllables were anxiety-arousing; they had previously been paired with a painful electric shock. These syllables were recognized less readily than neutral items—as if the subject "tried not to see" the syllable that reminded him of pain (Lazarus and McCleary, 1951). But at another level, the subject did seem to recognize the item. The investigators measured the subjects' autonomic arousal by obtaining their galvanic skin response as each of the items was presented. The critical, shock-associated syllables evoked a larger GSR than did the control syllables, despite the fact that the subject did not recognize them. The authors concluded that the anxiety-provoking items were recognized "subconsciously," a process of subterranean recognition which they called *subception.* Subception triggered anxiety (as indicated by the GSR), which blocked conscious recognition (as indicated by the subjects' verbal report).

The subception hypothesis has drawn various criticisms. What does it mean to see a stimulus at one level and not to see it at another? One possible interpretation is that the verbal report and the GSR measure the recognition of two different aspects of the same stimulus. When paired with shock, a syllable such as XAT becomes conditioned to autonomic fear reactions. But this connection may hold not just for the full-fledged syllable but also for its component parts, such as one or two of the individual letters, X, A, or T. These components would not suffice for recognition of the whole syllable (as indexed by the verbal report), but they might well elicit the fear response (as measured by the GSR). According to this interpretation, perceiving something is not an all-or-none affair, but a process that occurs in stages: a shape, a human figure, a woman . . . oh, it's mother! If anxiety is evoked at an early stage, further recognition processes are impeded and the later stages may never emerge (Erdelyi, 1974).*

REPRESSORS AND SENSITIZERS

The preceding discussion suggests that repressionlike phenomena can occur under laboratory conditions. But further studies indicate that these effects are not found in everyone. Some individuals are **repressors.** When presented with materials that arouse anxiety, they tend not to recall or recognize them. But other persons seem to lack this convenient ability to shut the door on their own anxieties. They are **sensitizers** who are unable to overlook or to forget that which worries them; in fact, they pay special attention to it. Interestingly enough, the repressors seem to have some of the personality characteristics (to be sure, in a milder form) of hysterics. For example, they are more likely to complain about various minor bodily ills (Byrne, 1964). According to Freud and other analysts, hysterics adopt repression as their major defense mechanism. In other neuroses, other defense mechanisms such as reaction formation play a larger role (see Chapter 19).

Problems of Freud's Dream Theory

The preceding discussion suggests that unconscious conflict and defense are probably genuine phenomena. To this extent, Freud's general position has been upheld. But the verdict has been less favorable on some of his more specific assertions. An example is his theory of dreams.

Stated in the most general terms, Freud's theory asserts that dreams tend to reflect the current emotional preoccupations of the dreamer, including those of which he is unaware, often portrayed in a condensed and symbolic form. This is probably quite true. Thus, patients who await major surgery reveal their fears in what they dream about during the two or three nights before the operation. Their fears are rarely expressed directly; few, if any, of their dreams are about scalpels or operating rooms. The reference is indirect, in condensed and symbolized form, as in dreams about falling from tall ladders or standing on a high, swaying bridge, or about a decrepit machine that needs repair (Breger, Hunter, and Lane, 1971).

* Such a stage analysis avoids some of the logical problems that are posed by Freud's repression concept. According to Freud, threatening items are excluded from consciousness. But in order to know which items are to be excluded, we must first recognize them. This leads to a paradox. We have to recognize an item in order to determine whether it is an item we must not recognize. By assuming that there are several stages of recognition this problem is circumvented.

The Nightmare *This painting by Henry Fuseli (painted in 1783 and said to have decorated Freud's office) highlights what seems to be one of the difficulties of Freud's dream theory. If all dreams are wish fulfillments, what accounts for nightmares? According to Freud, they are often dreams in which the latent dream is not sufficiently disguised. The forbidden wish is partially recognized, anxiety breaks through, and the sleeper suffers a nightmare. (Courtesy The Detroit Institute of Arts)*

Such evidence indicates that dreams do express whatever motives are currently most important. But Freud's theory went much further than this. As we saw, he believed that the manifest dream is a censored and disguised version of the latent dream that lies underneath and represents a wish fulfillment. This conception of dreams has been much criticized. To begin with, there is considerable doubt that all (or even many) dreams are attempts at wish fulfillments, whether disguised or open. In one study, subjects were made extremely thirsty before they went to sleep. Since thirst is hardly a forbidden urge, there is no reason to suppose an internal censorship. However, none of the subjects reported dreams of drinking. Since they were so thirsty, why didn't they gratify themselves in their dreams (Dement and Wolpert, 1958)?

Another problem is the fact that the same urge is sometimes freely expressed in dreams, but heavily disguised on other occasions. Tonight, the sleeper dreams of unabashed sexual intercourse; tomorrow night, she dreams of riding a team of wild horses. For sake of argument, let us agree that riding is a symbol for intercourse. But why should the censor disguise tomorrow what is so freely allowed tonight?

One investigator, C. S. Hall, has come up with a plausible suggestion (Hall, 1953). According to Hall, the dream symbol does not *disguise* an underlying idea; on the contrary, it *expresses* it. In Hall's view, the dream is a rather concrete mental shorthand that embodies a feeling or emotion. Riding a horse, plowing a field, planting a seed—all of these may be concrete renditions of the idea of sexual intercourse. But they are not meant to hide this idea. Their function is much the same as the cartoonist's picture of Uncle Sam or John Bull. These are representations of the United States and of England, but they are certainly not meant as disguises for them. During sleep, more specifically during REM sleep (see

433

Chapter 3), we are incapable of the extreme complexity and abstractness of waking mental life. We are thus reduced to a more concrete and archaic form of thinking. The wishes and fears of our waking life are still present at night, and we dream about them. But the way in which these are now expressed tends to be more primitive, a concrete pictorialization that combines fragments of various waking concerns and serves as a kind of symbolic cartoon.

Biology or Culture?

While many psychologists agree with Freud's thesis that there is unconscious conflict, they are more skeptical of his particular assertions of what these conflicts are. One of their major quarrels is with Freud's insistence that the pattern of these conflicts is biologically based and will therefore be found in essentially the same form in all men and all women.

THE EMPHASIS ON SOCIAL FACTORS

Since Freud believed that the key to emotional development is in biology, he assumed that its progression followed a universal course. In his view, all humans pass through oral, anal, and phallic stages and suffer the conflicts appropriate to each stage. This conception has been challenged by various clinical practitioners, many of whom used Freud's own psychoanalytic methods. These critics felt that Freud had overemphasized biological factors at the expense of social ones. This point was first raised by one of Freud's own students, Alfred Adler (1870–1937). It was later taken up by several like-minded authors who are often grouped together under the loose label *neo-Freudians,* including Erich Fromm (1900–1980), Karen Horney (1885–1952), and H. S. Sullivan (1892–1949).

According to the neo-Freudians, human development cannot be properly understood by focusing on the particular anatomical regions—mouth, anus, genitals—through which the child tries to gratify his instinctual desires. In their view, the important question is how humans relate, or try to relate, to others—whether by dominating, or submitting, or becoming dependent, or whatever. Their description of our inner conflicts is therefore in social terms. For example, if they see a mother who toilet trains her child very severely, they are likely to interpret her behavior as part of an overall pattern whereby she tries to push the child to early achievement; the specific frustrations of the anal stage as such are of lesser concern to them. Similarly for the sexual sphere. According to Freud, the neurotic conflict centers on the repression of erotic impulses. According to the neo-Freudian critics, the real difficulty is in the area of interpersonal relationships. Neurosis often leads to sexual symptoms, not because sex is a powerful biological motive that is pushed underground, but rather because it is one of the most sensitive barometers of interpersonal attitudes. The man who can only relate to other people by competing with them may well be unable to find sexual pleasure in his marriage bed; but the sexual malfunction is an *effect* of his neurotic social pattern rather than its *cause.*

The same emphasis on social factors highlights the neo-Freudian explanation for how these conflicts arise in the first place. In contrast to Freud, it denies that these conflicts are biologically pre-ordained; they rather depend upon the specific cultural conditions in which the child is reared. According to the neo-Freudians, the conflicts that Freud observed may have characterized *his* patients, but this does not mean that these same patterns will be found in persons who live at other times and in other places.

THE REJECTION OF CULTURAL ABSOLUTISM

One set of relevant findings came from another discipline, ***cultural anthropology,*** which concerns itself with the practices and beliefs of different peoples throughout the world. There are evidently considerable variations in these patterns, with accompanying variations in the kind of person who is typical in each setting. Personality characteristics that are typical in our culture are by no means universal, a result that was beautifully tuned to the antibiological bias of the neo-Freudians.

A well-known example concerns cultural variations in the roles that different societies assign to the two sexes. An influential study by the American anthropologist Margaret Mead, "Sex and Temperament," compared the personality traits of men and women in three New Guinea tribes that lived within a hundred-mile radius. Among the Arapesh, both men and women were mild, cooperative, and, so to speak, "maternal" in their attitudes to each other and especially to children. Among the neighboring Mundugomor, both sexes were ferociously aggressive and quarrelsome. In yet another tribe, the Tchambuli, the usual sex roles were reversed. The women were the hale and hardy breadwinners who fished and went to market unadorned. While the women managed the worldly affairs, the men gossiped and pranced about, adjusted elaborate hairdos, carved and painted, and practiced intricate dance steps (Mead, 1935, 1937). The neo-Freudians took such findings as a strong argument against the cultural absolutism which regards the patterns of modern Western society as the built-in givens of human nature.

Several anthropologists have criticized Mead's account as an oversimplification. They point out that there are probably some universal sex roles after all; for example, warfare is generally conducted by the men, even among the Tchambuli. They argue that some of the difference between male and female aggressiveness may very well be due to biological factors, for aggression is in part under hormonal control; as androgen levels rise, both human and animal males become more aggressive (see Chapter 10). What culture does is to determine how this aggression is to be channeled and against whom, whether it is to be valued, and how much of it is allowed.

Margaret Mead *(Courtesy The American Museum of Natural History)*

Critiques of Freud's Theories of Development

It's rather ironic that Freud, whose views of childhood development had such a powerful influence on Western thought, never himself studied children. His theories of early development were mostly based on his adult patients' recollections, dreams, and free associations. Under the circumstances, it was essential to gather evidence on actual childhood behavior.

Today the study of human development is a flourishing enterprise. We will describe it in some detail in Chapters 13, 14, 15, and 16. For now our concern is with evidence that bears directly on Freud's theories of childhood psychosexual development. While some of Freud's broader concepts are still of considerable influence, the verdict has not been too favorable on his more specific hypotheses. (For an overview, see Zigler and Child, 1972.)

CHILD-REARING PRACTICES

An example concerns the effects of toilet training. Some mothers begin training when the infant is as young as five months; others wait until the child is two years old. There are some slight indications that starting later makes the whole process simpler and may minimize certain childhood disorders of elimination, such as bed-wetting (Brazelton, 1962). But what about the more interesting long-term effects that Freud had in mind when he described the childhood reaction formations that in his view produce obstinacy and stinginess in the adult?

On the whole, the verdict is negative. There is little if any evidence that shows any long-term effects from toilet-training practices, either in our own or other cultures (Orlansky, 1949). For example, there seems to be no relationship between the severity of toilet training in different cultures and the degree of hoarding or economic competition (Cohen, 1953). There is thus little evidence for Freud's claim that the toilet is a prep school for becoming a banker or a captain of industry.

CULTURAL DIFFERENCES AND THE OEDIPUS COMPLEX

The most influential of Freud's assertions about early childhood concerns sexuality and the Oedipus complex. Our major source of information in this area comes from studies of other cultures. On the whole, the evidence was welcome grist to the neo-Freudian mill: The Oedipus conflict is not universal but depends upon cultural variations in the family constellation.

This point was first raised some fifty years ago by the English anthropologist Bronislaw Malinowski on the basis of his observations of the Trobriand Islanders of the Western Pacific (Malinowski, 1927). The family pattern of the Trobriand Islanders is quite different from our own. Among the Trobrianders, the biological father is not the head of the household. He spends time with his children and plays with them, but he exerts no authority. This role is reserved for the mother's brother who acts as a disciplinarian. The Trobriand Islanders thus separate the roles that in Freud's Vienna were played by one and the same person.

According to Freud, this different family pattern should make no difference. There should still be an Oedipus complex in which the father is the hated villain for, after all, it is he who is the little boy's sexual rival. But this did not turn out to be the case. Malinowski saw no signs of friction between sons and fathers, though he did observe a fair amount of hostility directed at the maternal uncle. The same held for dreams and folk tales. The Trobriand Islanders believe that there are prophetic dreams of death; these generally involve the death of the maternal uncle. Similarly there are no myths about evil fathers or stepfathers; again, the villain is typically the mother's brother. If we accept Freud's notion that dreams (and myths) involve unconscious wishes and preoccupations, we are forced to conclude that the Trobriand boy hates his uncle, not his father. In sum, the child has fears and fantasies about the authoritarian figure in his life, the man who bosses him around. This is the father in Freud's Austria, but the uncle on the Trobriand Islands. His fears are not about his mother's lover as such, for the Trobriand boy does not hate the father who plays this role.

THE HOME ATMOSPHERE

The cross-cultural findings show that while the emotional relations between the child and members of the family may exert long-lasting effects, the specific factors that enter into the equation are not those that Freud had made so much of. The same holds true for our own culture. The results of many studies suggest that parents influence their children, not so much by this or the other specific practice (say, early toilet training), but rather by the general social atmosphere in which the child is raised. The parents communicate their attitudes about the child, about the world, about the role they expect the child to fill. These attitudes have an important effect on the child at each stage of his development. A given child-rearing practice may be less important than the attitude with which it is carried out. (For a further discussion of this and other topics of social development, see Chapter 16.)

PSYCHOANALYTIC INTERPRETATION OF CULTURE, MYTH, AND LITERATURE

Thus far, our primary focus has been on Freud's theories of human personality, both from his own perspective and from that of his critics. But in Freud's hands, psychoanalysis had become a world view with still broader implications. He and his followers tried to extend its scope to shed light, not only on human nature, but on humanity's important accomplishments: its civilization, its religions, its myths, its works of art. Partially because of these extensions, Freud's views had an enormous impact not only within psychiatry and psychology, but also on fields outside, such as anthropology and literature.

The Origin of Society and the Incest Taboo

One extension of psychoanalytic thinking is provided by Freud's speculations about the origin of human society. In his view, the Oedipus complex is a universal human experience and society is at bottom an outgrowth of this basic struggle between parents and children. He supposed that early humans lived in "primal hordes" dominated by one strong male who was the father of all the young and who had exclusive sexual rights to all the females. The sons who rebelled were killed, castrated, or expelled from the group. Eventually, the exiled sons banded together and defeated and killed their father. But after the patricide, they quarreled among themselves, each trying to achieve the father's primal eminence. They finally decided to form a sexual social contract whose basic law was the *incest taboo.* The war of all against all was averted and brothers could live in harmony, for no mating was allowed within the family (Freud, 1913a).

Modern anthropologists regard this account as a quasi-Hobbesian fairy tale, for they doubt that there were ever any primal hordes under one male's exclusive dominion. But they share Freud's interest in the incest taboo, which is certainly one of the very few universal thou-shalt-nots; it is found in all human societies. Its origin is unknown, though there are some plausible speculations. It is clear that the taboo is not based on an aversion. After all, the taboo is sometimes violated, especially among those who are regarded as semidivine and thus exempt from mortal laws, such as Egyptian pharaohs and their sisters. Another argument against the view that the taboo is based on an aversion is the fact that there are no taboos against acts that no one wants to perform anyway (there is no taboo against sleeping with crocodiles).

What then can account for the taboo? The best guess is that those groups who developed it had a better chance to survive and prosper than those who did not. The prohibition against incest avoids the deleterious genetic effects of in-breeding. If parents are closely related, there is a good chance that they will bequeath to their offspring the same harmful recessive gene. Another advantage is social and economic. If there is a prohibition against incest, the children of one family are necessarily forced to select their mates from among the sons and daughters of another family. This tends to create an enlarged network of emotional ties; as a result the small band expands to a larger tribe. Such tribes have a selective advantage over smaller ones. They can hunt and gather more efficiently and, upon confrontation, they can defeat the smaller group in warfare. As the group survived, so did its taboo (Aberle et al., 1963).

Some recent studies have pointed to another factor that counteracts incest: being reared together in childhood. In Israeli kibbutzim, boys and girls are brought up from birth in groups of the same age. What happens when they become adolescents and adults? Since they are unrelated, there are no prohibitions against sexual contact. But by all accounts this does not seem to occur even so. Raising boys and girls together from infancy apparently blocks the sexual attraction that would otherwise arise. This mechanism would tend to prevent incest between brothers and sisters, but it might not work perfectly at all times. Cultural taboos would then serve as a further bulwark against any tendency toward inbreeding (Spiro, 1958; Shepher, 1971).

These lines of argument are certainly far from the historical speculations Freud proposed. But social scientists still find much of interest in Freud's description if it is taken as a kind of metaphor. Their views of culture have been much affected by many aspects of Freud's theories, such as his emphasis on the family as the medium through which society transmits its rules and prohibitions, and as the cornerstone upon which all further social organization is built.

Psychoanalytic Theory of Myths

Freud and his students contended that as dreams are a window into the individual's unconscious, so myths, legends, and fairy tales allow us a glimpse into those hidden concerns that are shared by whole groups of men, if not all of humanity. Indeed, psychoanalysts found an ample supply of Oedipal themes. There are numerous ogres, dragons, and various monsters whom the hero must slay if he wants to reach the fair maid. The part of the villain is often taken by a cruel stepparent, a fairly transparent symbol of Oedipal hostilities.

As an example of a psychoanalytic interpretation of a fairy tale, consider Snow White and the seven dwarfs (J. F. Brown, 1940). Snow White is a child princess who is persecuted by her stepmother, the wicked queen. The queen is envious of Snow White's beauty and tries to have her killed. The child escapes and lives with seven dwarfs who work in an underground mine. The queen finally discovers

Snow White and persuades her to eat part of a poisoned apple. Snow White falls as if dead. The dwarfs place her in a beautiful coffin in which she lies motionless for seven years. At this point, a handsome prince appears, opens the casket with his sword, awakens Snow White from her long sleep, and the two live happily ever after.

According to psychoanalytic authors, this fairy tale is a veiled allegory of the Oedipal sequence. The wicked queen is the mother on whom the child projects her own hate and sexual jealousy. The Oedipal conflict is temporarily resolved as the child's erotic urges go underground and remain dormant for the seven years of the latency period, symbolized both by Snow White's long sleep and by the seven dwarfs. At the end of this period, her sexuality is reawakened in adult form by the young prince. (The meaning of the sword is left as an exercise for the reader.)

Is this interpretation valid? It is hard to know by what ground rules validity can be judged. There are undoubtedly many alternative (and perhaps more plausible) interpretations of this and many other legends that psychoanalysts have tried to squeeze into their scheme. Death and resurrection are old themes in mythology which probably refer to many important natural cycles such as the daily succession of darkness and light and the yearly alternation of winter's desolation and spring's green rebirth. Myths may also embody dim folk memories of long-past wars, dynastic conflicts, previously held religions, and various catastrophes. The psychoanalytic view may throw some further light on a fascinating aspect of our cultural heritage, but it is just one light among many others.

Psychoanalysis and Literature

Freud's approach to the interpretation of works of art and literature was very similar to the way in which he tried to understand the hidden meaning of dreams and myths. The artistic production reflects the artist's own inner conflicts and has impact upon others because it strikes the same unconscious chords in them. Perhaps the most famous example of psychoanalytic literary interpretations is Freud's analysis of *Hamlet,* later elaborated by his student Ernest Jones (Jones, 1954). The central puzzle of the play is Hamlet's indecisiveness. He waits until the end of the fifth act before he finally avenges his father's death upon his hated uncle, a delay that causes his own death as well as the death of virtually everyone else in the play, innocent as well as guilty. To Freud and Jones, the clue to Hamlet's inaction is the Oedipus complex. Hamlet is paralyzed because he must kill a man who did precisely what he himself unconsciously wants to do, kill his father and marry his mother. According to Freud and Jones, the play grips the audience because it stirs the same latent conflicts in them.

Shakespearean scholars are by no means agreed on the virtues of this interpretation, though some find it interesting. But the issue goes further than that. Suppose we accept the interpretation that Freud and Jones offer. Is this *the* key to Hamlet, which is then shorn of all its mysteries, like a completed crossword puzzle that is discarded once it is solved? The truth is that there is no one key, there is no one meaning of *Hamlet,* for a work of art is necessarily ambiguous. As with myths and legends, this or the other interpretation may help to illuminate them, but it does not explain them away. *Hamlet* may be about Oedipal conflicts, but many hack novels have the same theme. What makes the one a great literary treasure while the others are forgotten almost immediately?

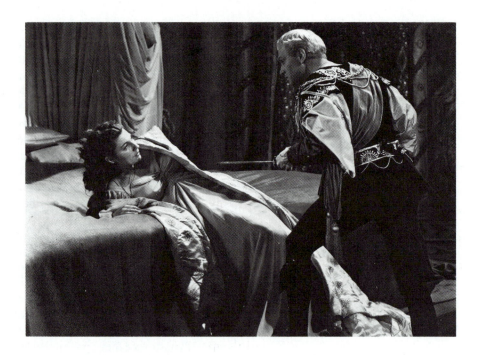

Hamlet confronting his mother in her bedroom *A scene from Laurence Olivier's 1948 film* Hamlet. *Olivier's conception of the role of Hamlet was seriously affected by Ernest Jones's psychoanalytic interpretation of the play. His casting of a young attractive actress, Eileen Herlie, for the part of Hamlet's mother helped to underscore the Oedipus theme. (Courtesy Universal Pictures)*

These points argue against the overenthusiastic application of psychoanalytic interpretation to literary works. But for good or ill (probably for both), Freud's impact on literature and literary criticism has been enormous. Most literary critics today have at least a passing acquaintance with Freud's basic works, and many major authors have been consciously affected by him. By now, his insights have become part of our culture and Freudian lore (often vulgarized) has become a staple of our popular literature, our stage, and our screen.

FREUD'S CONTRIBUTIONS IN RETROSPECT

We have seen that many of Freud's beliefs have not been confirmed. There are good grounds to doubt Freud's essentially Hobbesian view of human nature. There is little evidence for his general theory of psychosexual development, even less for his male-centered conception of feminine psychology, and there is a good reason to believe that he overemphasized biological givens at the expense of cultural factors. We have also seen that Freud can be criticized not just for what he asserted but for the way in which he tried to prove his claims. By now, there is general agreement that the psychoanalytic couch is not a source of objective fact, and that many of Freud's theoretical proposals are a bit vague and metaphorical, so that it is not clear how one can decide whether they are right or wrong.

All in all, this a formidable set of criticisms. But even so, many psychologists would maintain that, wrong as he probably was in any number of particulars, Sigmund Freud must nevertheless be regarded as one of the giants of psychology, one of the few our field has known thus far. There are at least two reasons.

The first concerns one major conception of Freud's that still stands, however much it may have to be modified and reinterpreted—the notion that there is internal conflict of which we are often unaware. Freud was not the first to recognize that we are often torn in opposite directions and that we frequently deceive ourselves about what we want (Ellenberger, 1970). But he was the first for whom this insight was the cornerstone of an entire point of view. Whether his own therapeutic procedure, psychoanalysis, is an appropriate tool to make the unknown known and thus to restore a measure of free choice to the emotionally crippled victims of inner conflict is still debatable (see Chapter 20). But whether his therapy works or not, Freud's contribution remains. He saw that we do not know ourselves, that we are not masters of our own souls. By pointing out how ignorant we are, he set a task for later investigators who may ultimately succeed, so that we may then be able to follow Socrates's deceptively simple prescription for a good life, "Know thyself."

The other major reason why Freud has a lasting place among the greats of intellectual history is the sheer scope of his theoretical conception. His was a view of human nature that was virtually all-embracing. It tried to encompass both rational thought and emotional urges. It conceived of neurotic ailments as a consequence of the same psychological forces that operate in everyday life. It saw humans as biological organisms as well as social beings, as creatures whose present is rooted in their past and who are simultaneously children and adults. The range of psychological phenomena that Freud tried to comprehend within his theory is staggering—neurotic symptoms, personality patterns, social groupings, family relations, humor, slips of the tongue, dreams, artistic productions, aspects of religious thought. Freud's theory has many faults, but this long list highlights some of its virtues. It dealt with matters of genuine human significance; it concerned both human beings and their works; it was an account that was about humanity as a whole. To this extent Freud provided a goal for posterity. He showed us the kinds of questions that we have to answer before we can claim to have a full theory of human personality.

The discussion of Freud's work provides an appropriate halfway mark for our treatment of social behavior. We began by considering the biological foundations of social interactions in man and beast. We saw that neither exist as isolated beings but that they are social through and through. They compete, they mate, and they care for their young. These biological roots of social life are quite apparent in animals. But in humans, they are often hidden in a mass of cognitive complexity, for in us, the blood-and-guts passions of aggression, sex, and parental concern are overlaid by layers of reason and thought. One of Freud's contributions was his insistence that thought is not as cool and dispassionate as it might first appear, but is inextricably intertwined with feeling and emotion.

To unravel the tangled threads of human thought and feeling, Freud turned to development. For in his view, one way of shedding light on the puzzling complexity of adult thought and action was to consider its childhood origins. Freud was not alone in this conviction, for the belief that the child is father to the man was widely held by many thinkers, both before, during, and subsequent to Freud's own time. This general view led to an ever-increasing interest in the phenomena of childhood development, whose study is by now the subject of one of psychology's important subdisciplines.

In the next three chapters, we will consider development as a topic in its own right. We will look at what scientists in various fields have discovered about the way in which humans develop, as physical organisms, as thinking individuals, and as social beings.

SUMMARY

1. Sigmund Freud asserted that all persons experience *unconscious conflicts* originating in childhood. His theories grew out of studies of *hysteria*, a *psychogenic* mental disorder whose symptoms are similar to some effects observed in *hypnosis*. Freud proposed that hysterical symptoms are a means of keeping *repressed* thoughts or wishes unconscious. He believed that the symptoms would be eliminated once the repressed materials were recovered, and devised a procedure, *psychoanalysis*, directed toward this end.

2. Freud distinguished three subsystems of the human personality. One is the *id*, a blind striving toward biological satisfaction that follows the *pleasure principle*. The second is the *ego*, a system of reactions that tries to reconcile the id-derived needs with the actualities of the world, in accordance with the *reality principle*. A third is the *superego*, which represents the internalized rules of the parents and punishes deviations by feelings of guilt.

3. Internal conflict is initially prompted by *anxiety*, which becomes associated with forbidden thoughts and wishes, usually in childhood. To ward off this anxiety, the child resorts to *repression*, and pushes the forbidden materials out of consciousness. Repression is the initial, primary *mechanism of defense* against anxiety. But the repressed materials generally surface again, together with their associated anxiety. To push these thoughts and wishes down again, further, supplementary defense mechanisms come into play, including *displacement, reaction formation, rationalization,* and *projection.*

4. Freud tried to apply his theory of unconscious conflict to many areas of everyday life. An example is his theory of dreams. To Freud, all dreams are attempts at wish fulfillment. Since many of these wishes prompt anxiety, their full expression is *censored*. As a result, the underlying *latent dream* is transformed into the *manifest dream* in which the forbidden urges emerge in a disguised, sometimes *symbolic* form.

5. Freud believed that most adult unconscious conflicts are ultimately sexual in nature and refer back to events during childhood *psychosexual development.* This passes through three main stages that are characterized by the *erogenous zones* through which gratification is obtained: *oral, anal,* and *phallic.* At each stage, socialization thwarts some of these gratifications, as in weaning and toilet training.

6. During the phallic stage, the male child develops the *Oedipus complex.* He directs his sexual urges toward his mother, hates his father as a rival, and comes to dread him as he suffers increasing *castration anxiety.* He finally renounces his sexual urges, identifies with his father, and represses all relevant memories, which then become the nucleus of the superego. At adolescence, repressed sexual urges surface, are redirected toward adult partners, and the person generally achieves *genital sexuality.* In female children, the *Electra complex* develops, with love toward father and rivalry toward mother.

7. Attempts to find evidence for repression and unconscious conflict outside of the psychoanalytic session have met with some moderate success, for example in work on *motivated forgetting* and *subception.* The verdict on Freud's more specific hypotheses about the nature of such conflicts is less favorable. An important challenge comes from the *neoFreudians*, who emphasize social and cultural factors rather than biological ones and from *cultural anthropology* which has shown that personality patterns typical of our own culture are not universal.

8. Some critics of Freud's theories of emotional development have studied child rearing and found little evidence for long-lasting effects of toilet-training practices, or for a universal Oedipus complex, independent of culture.

9. Psychoanalytic thinking extends to fields beyond psychiatry and psychology. Its extensions include Freud's theory of the origin of society and psychoanalytic interpretations of myths and literature.

PART IV

Development

How do psychologists try to explain the phenomena they describe? Thus far, we've primarily dealt with two main approaches. One is concerned with mechanism—it tries to understand how something works. A second approach focuses on function—it tries to explain what something is good for. But there is yet another approach to explanation in psychology which focuses on development. This approach deals with questions of history—it asks how a given state of affairs came into being.

In the next three chapters, our concern will be with this developmental perspective on psychological phenomena. We will ask how various psychological processes arise in the organism's history—how we come to see and remember, speak and think, feel and act as we now do; how it is that we are no longer children, but for better or worse have become adults in mind as well as body.

CHAPTER 13

General Issues in Development

Attempts to understand the processes that underlie human development are relatively recent. They grew out of an increasing interest in childhood that has several roots—some practical and humanitarian, others scientific.

CHANGING CONCEPTIONS OF CHILDHOOD

In contrast to their modern descendants, parents a few centuries ago were relatively untroubled by issues regarding the nature of childhood. Children entered adult life much earlier than they do today. By five or six, they began to work—on their parents' farm or in their workshop, or a bit later as apprentices to some tradesman, or as pages to some lord if they were of noble birth. Much the same was true of their pastimes. Yesterday's children joined in the same games and festivities as the adults of their time, sang the same songs, and danced the same dances. Nor for that matter were they distinguished from adults by dress. During medieval times and beyond, once children were out of swaddling clothes, they wore much the same clothes as did adults of their own class. Facts of this kind have led some historians to argue that the very concept of childhood—at least after the age of five or so—is a relatively modern invention (Ariès, 1962).

The situation changed drastically in the succeeding periods. In the eighteenth and nineteenth centuries, the old certainties began to disintegrate. Western society had become more flexible, and there were many more avenues to the future, especially for children of the rising middle classes. But just how should the parents teach their young to help them make the best of the new opportunities? They had little in the way of an organized system of beliefs that might guide them—religion had lost much of its former hold, and the rigid social patterns of the past

The changing views of children In the past, children were treated as miniature adults. As such, they dressed as did the adults of their time and class as shown in a painting of the royal children by Velás-quez. (Las Meninas *by Diego Rodríquez de Silva y Velásquez, courtesy El Prado)*

had been replaced in the aftermath of several revolutions. Nor did the parents have wise uncles or grandmothers living nearby who could advise them, for the extended family—the cousins and aunts and grandparents who made up one's kinfolk in former days—had gradually scattered as people moved from region to region in search of better economic opportunities. Now the parents had to confront the many questions about child rearing and education whose answers former generations had regarded as self-evident.

But just what should be done to help children develop properly? Philosophers and educators were by no means agreed. Some felt that rearing should be strict, while others believed that it should be gentle; some argued that children should be required to learn as much and as quickly as they possibly could, while others insisted that the child had to go at his own pace. How could one possibly decide between these divergent views? Eventually, various practical-minded persons decided that issues of this sort might be decided by the methods of science. An example is Cora Hillis, an Iowa housewife who launched a campaign in 1906 to persuade the Iowa legislature that if research could improve hogs and corn, why not the rearing of children. Her campaign was one of the factors that eventually led to the establishment of various agencies devoted to scientific research in all areas of relevance to the physical and mental health of children.

THE CONCEPT OF DEVELOPMENT AS PROGRESSIVE CHANGE

Practical and humane concerns were among the factors that led to an increasing interest in the study of child development. But in the long run, another impetus proved to be even more important: an increasing interest in all forms of historical change.

To many philosophers at the beginning of the nineteenth century, human development was only one facet of a general pattern of progressive change that revealed itself in many different aspects of the world. They lived at a time of dramatic upheavals—the French Revolution, which ushered in a period of continued political unrest, and the Industrial Revolution, which transformed the social and economic structure of Europe and North America. These massive changes suggested that human history is more than a mere chronicle of battles and successive dynasties, but that it also reveals an underlying pattern of social development toward greater "progress" (Bury, 1932). Given this intellectual background, many scientists became interested in development wherever they saw it: in the history of the planet as it changed from a molten rock and formed continents and oceans; in the history of life as it evolved from simple earlier forms to yield myriad species of plants and animals. The crowning step of this intellectual movement was Darwin's formulation of evolutionary theory with the publication of the *Origin of Species* in 1859 (see Chapter 10).

The Graham Children by **William Hogarth**   *(Courtesy The Tate Gallery)*

Development in the Embryo

Our primary interest here is in yet another kind of development studied by scientists of the time: the history of an individual organism as it develops from a single egg and assumes the complex shape and function of its adult form. The study of how this embryological history unfolds is one of the important starting points of modern developmental psychology.

THE THEORY OF RECAPITULATION

Darwin had shown that the key to the mysteries of the plant and animal kingdoms was in the history of their various species. Some fragments of this history are preserved in the fossil record that showed the remains of prior forms, now long extinct. Several of Darwin's contemporaries felt that this same evolutionary history is also reflected in the early life history of any given individual organism, which shows similar remnants of its ancestral past while still in embryonic form. As an example they cited the human embryo, which initially has gill slits (like a fish), then later develops a three-chambered heart (like a reptile), and still later sports a tail (like many mammals). In their view, such facts argued for the so-called *recapitulation theory:* the idea that in his own early history, each individual goes through the evolutionary history of the species of which he is a member.

As we will see, recapitulation theory turned out to be quite wrong, but it was very influential even so. Among other things, it led to some of the first investigations of child development. The idea was simple enough. If our embryonic development shows traces of our animal history, might not the same hold true for our early childhood? Perhaps the child's early mental processes mirror the thought patterns of early, primitive Man which were presumably similar to those found in "uncivilized savages" (the usual term applied by nineteenth-century writers to the natives who were unfortunate enough to live in their colonies). In line with this idea, a number of psychologists and biologists of the period kept "baby diaries" or sent questionnaires to parents in the hope that they might reconstruct the mental history of the human species by such means. They interpreted the results in line with recapitulation theory. For instance, they saw parallels between the dolls of children and the totems and fetishes of some illiterate tribes, or between the drawings of children and those of American Indians or Ugandan tribesmen (Sully, 1910). As one theorist put it: "There is a sort of natural recurrence of the child mind to the typical activities of primitive people; witness the hut which the boy likes to build in the yard, playing hunt, with bows, arrows, spears and so on" (Dewey, quoted in Gould, 1977, p. 154).*

DIFFERENTIATION

Recapitulation theory was soon refuted (although its supporters, especially in areas outside of biology, were slow to abandon it). One argument was that the simple sequence predicted by recapitulation theory occurred but rarely. Many

---

* Psychoanalysis was also influenced by recapitulation theory. Thus Freud subscribed to the notion of a "racial unconscious," which contains relics of emotional conflicts suffered by long-dead forebears. The major example is the *Oedipus Complex,* which he traced to ancestral memories of murderous rebellions against tyrannical fathers ruling over "primal hordes" hundreds of millennia before.

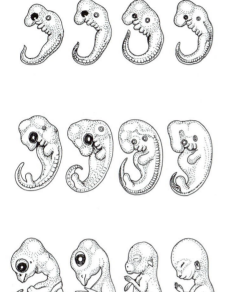

Tortoise   Chick   Rabbit   Human

13.1 Differentiation during embryonic development *The figure shows three stages in the embryonic development of four different vertebrates—tortoise, chick, rabbit, and human. At the first stage, all of the embryos are very similar to each other. As development proceeds, they diverge more and more. By the third stage, each embryo has taken on some of the distinctive characteristics of its own species. (From Keeton, 1980. Redrawn from Romanes, 1901)*

features seen in the embryo of a given animal are never found in the adults of any of its possible ancestors. An example is the placenta of mammalian embryos, which represents a special adaptation of embryonic life and is found nowhere outside of the womb. Nor is there any reason to suppose that members of various preliterate societies think like young children, or that they are primitive in the sense the recapitulationists held them to be.

Recapitulation theory was in error, but what was to take its place? An important suggestion came from the work of the German biologist Karl Ernst von Baer (1792–1876), who argued that the crucial fact of embryological development is that it reveals a gradual process of *differentiation*—a progressive change from the more general to the more particular, from the simpler to the more complex. In embryonic development anatomical differentiation is directly apparent. Initially there is one cell, then several cell layers, then the crude beginnings of the major organ systems, until the different organs and their component parts gradually take shape. This—rather than recapitulation—is the reason why embryos of very different species are very similar when they are very young and utterly dissimilar at later stages (see Figure 13.1). Initially, the embryo only manifests the very general body plan characteristic of a broad class of animals. Thus a very young chick embryo looks much like the embryo of any other vertebrate animal at a similar stage of its development. The embryonic structures that will eventually become wings are quite similar to those structures of a very young human embryo that will eventually become human arms. As embryonic development proceeds, special features begin to emerge and the chick embryo begins to look like a bird, then like some kind of fowl, and still later like a chicken (Gould, 1977).

Differentiation and Behavior

Von Baer's differentiation principle was initially regarded as a description of anatomical development and nothing else. But a number of psychologists suggested that a similar differentiation principle also applies to the development of behavior. Consider the development of grasping movements in human infants. When reaching for a small block, they initially can barely touch it; later they manage to curl their entire hand around the block; still later, they oppose the thumb to all four fingers. By the time they are one year old, they can victoriously coordinate hand, thumb, and one or two fingers to pick up the block with an elegant pincer movement (although such ultimate triumphs of manual differentiation as picking up a tea cup while holding the little finger extended will probably have to wait until they are old enough to read a book on etiquette) (Halverson, 1931; see Figure 13.2).

Developmental psychologists have tried to apply the differentiation concept to a wide variety of areas. An example is the development of emotions. Some early workers concluded that newborns have only one emotion, a sort of generalized excitement, which soon becomes differentiated into excitement, delight, and distress, until it reaches a gamut of specific emotions by the age of two (Bridges, 1932).* Another example is perceptual differentiation. Children (and also adults)

---

* More recent studies indicate that the sound patterns produced when young babies cry fall into several different groups. Some are cries of rage, others of pain, still others of frustration, and so on, which suggests that the emotions in early infancy are rather more differentiated than had been supposed at first (Wolff, 1969).

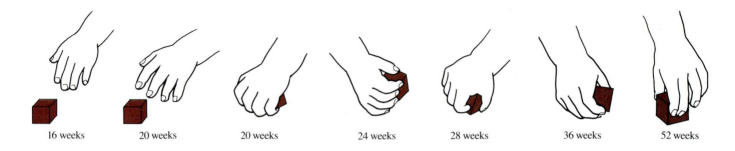

| 16 weeks | 20 weeks | 20 weeks | 24 weeks | 28 weeks | 36 weeks | 52 weeks |

20 weeks

24 weeks

28 weeks

52 weeks

13.2   The development of manual skills   *The diagram shows the progressive differentiation in the infant's use of the hand when holding an object. At 16 weeks of age, he reaches for the object but can't hold on to it. At 20 weeks, he grasps it using the hand as a whole, with no differentiated use of the fingers. Between 24 and 36 weeks, the fingers and thumb become differentiated in use, but the four fingers operate more or less as a whole. By 52 weeks of age, hand, thumb, and fingers are successfully differentiated to produce precise and effective pincer movements. (Adapted from Liebert, Polous, and Strauss, 1974) Photos illustrate the same point at 20, 24, 28, and 52 weeks going from top to bottom. (Photographs by Jeffrey Grosscup)*

come to perceive differences that they had not seen before. Experienced tea tasters taste subtle differences that are imperceptible to those of less educated palates, while children learning to read come to notice some of the characteristic features that distinguish the various letters from each other (Gibson, Gibson, Pick, and Osser, 1962).

Can we regard the differentiation principle as a general law of behavioral development? It is a matter of some dispute. The problem is that the term *differentiation* may not mean the same thing when used to describe different areas of psychological development. Differentiation of motor patterns is probably based on different processes than is the differentiation of emotional expressions, whose underlying causes may in turn be very different from that of perceptual differentiation. In short, the statement that "development proceeds from the general to the specific" is not an explanation, it is only a rough and ready generalization that crudely describes the sequence of events in human and animal development. The real task is to determine just what is differentiated in different aspects of development and to discover how and why this differentiation occurs. But to accomplish this, we have to study each aspect of development in its own right.

SOME CHARACTERISTICS OF DEVELOPMENT

In this chapter our primary concern is with some general points that apply to all aspects of human development, whether it is *motor development,* the progressive attainment of various motor skills, *cognitive development,* the growth of the child's intellectual functioning, or *social development,* which deals with changes in the way the child deals with others.

We will begin by discussing the fact that development involves physical and mental growth, and that this growth generally occurs through an orderly progression. Throughout this chapter, most of our illustrations will focus on the individual's physical and motor development.

Development as Growth

One of the most obvious characteristics of all development is growth (see Figure 13.3). Organisms "grow up" as they change from a fertilized egg to a fetus, and after birth, they continue to grow in many different dimensions ranging from sheer physical size to mental complexity.

GROWTH BEFORE BIRTH

Each human existence begins at conception when a sperm and egg cell unite to form the fertilized egg. This egg divides and redivides repeatedly and produces a cellular mass that attaches itself to the wall of the uterus. Two weeks after conception, the mass of cells (now called an ***embryo***) begins to differentiate into separate cell layers. From now until birth, growth and development proceed at a rapid pace (see Figure 13.4). At one month after conception, the embryo is a fifth of an inch long and looks like a little worm that hardly resembles a human. At two

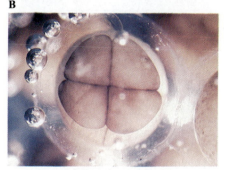

13.3 The beginnings of embryonic growth *Electron micrographs of frog egg showing the first stages of anatomical differentiation in the embryo. (A) Unfertilized egg. (B) Eight-cell stage. (From Carolina Biological Supply Company)*

13.4 Early stages of human prenatal development *(A) Six-week-old embryo, shown in its amniotic sac. It is three-fifths of an inch long, and its eyes, ears, and limbs are beginning to take shape but are still at a comparatively early stage of differentiation. For example, the hands have not yet differentiated into separate fingers. (B) Seven-week-old embryo, now nearly an inch long. Differentiation is further along as witness the presence of fingers. (C) Three-month-old fetus, three inches long. By now the fetus's features are recognizably human. Fingers and toes are fully formed, and there are external ears and eyelids. (D) Four-month-old fetus pushing against amniotic sac. The fetus is more than six inches long, with all organs formed. (From Nilsson, 1974)*

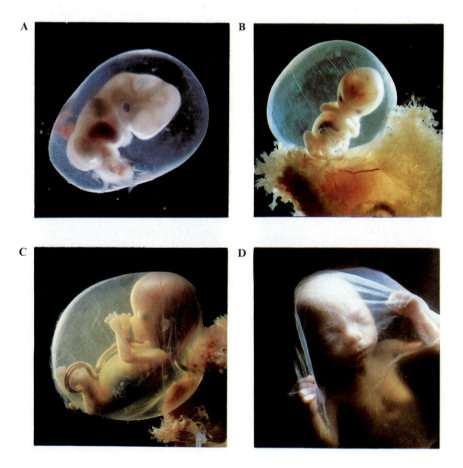

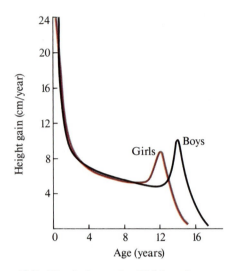

13.5　Physical growth　*Heights of British boys (black) and girls (color) from birth until 19 years of age. Physical growth continues for almost 20 years after birth with a special spurt at adolescence. (From Tanner, 1970)*

months after conception the mass of cells is about one inch in length and is now called a ***fetus.*** Just one month later, the fetus has grown to about three inches in length and has begun to look like a miniature baby with some functioning organ systems and a number of early reflexes, including sucking movements when the lips are touched. In another four months (that is, seven months after conception), the fetus has grown to sixteen inches, has a fully developed reflex pattern, can cry, breathe, swallow, and has a good chance of survival if it should be delivered prematurely at this time.

These stages of our prenatal life attest to the massive changes in sheer size and structural complexity that take place over this period. In addition to these gross gains, however, there are also many subtler ones that have far-reaching effects. Some of the most important of these concern the developing nervous system. In

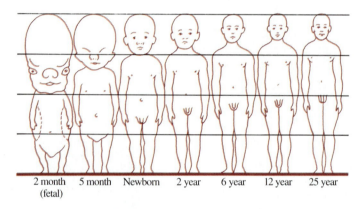

13.6　Change in body proportions as a function of age　*(From Liebert, Polous, and Strauss, 1974)*

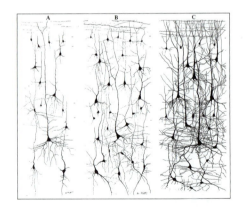

13.7　Growth of neural interconnections　*Sections of the human cortex in (A) a newborn, (B) a three-month-old, and (C) a fifteen-month-old. (Conel, 1939, 1947, 1955)*

the later stages of prenatal growth, the neurons begin to mature, and their axons and dendrites form increasingly complex branches and interconnections with other nerve cells (Schacher, S., 1978).

GROWTH AFTER BIRTH

Physical growth continues for almost two decades after birth, with a special spurt at adolescence (see Figure 13.5). As development progresses, parts of the body that grew at a disproportionate rate before birth (particularly the head and brain) start to grow at a more leisurely rate so that the bodily proportions become more and more adult (see Figure 13.6).

The growth of the child's body is accompanied by the no less striking growth of her mind—in the way she perceives, thinks, speaks and understands, and reacts to others. The details of these accomplishments will be discussed in later sections. For now we only note that some of these feats are probably based on the continuation of events that began before birth. Of particular importance is the growth of neural interconnections beginning in fetal life and continuing long into infancy, as illustrated in Figure 13.7, which shows sections of the human cortex in a newborn, a three-month-old, and a fifteen-month-old child (Conel, 1939, 1947,

Capacity for learning *Learning from culture is not accomplished overnight. A twenty-four-month-old boy is trying to master the intricacies of dressing. (Photograph courtesy of Kathy Hirsh-Passek)*

1955). This increasing neural complexity may well be one of the reasons for the increase in the child's mental capacities as development proceeds.

THE SLOW RATE OF HUMAN GROWTH AND ITS EFFECTS

Nine months after conception, the fetus is presumably ready to enter the outer world. But is it really ready? Left to its own devices, it obviously is not. It is singularly helpless and inept, more so by far than the young of most other mammals. To be sure, a newborn calf has to suckle and follow its mother, but it can walk at birth, and it can pretty well manage on its own after a fairly short period. But in humans (and to a lesser extent, in monkeys and apes), a considerable degree of development continues far beyond birth. For example, in most mammals the newborn's brain is just about fully formed. Not so in primates, and most especially not so in Man. The human newborn has achieved only 23 percent of her adult cranial capacity at birth, and is still only at 75 percent of this final value when she is about two and a half years old (Catel, 1953, cited in Gould, 1977; for a further illustration, see Figure 10.15).

What holds for brain growth also holds for other aspects of physical development. At birth, the bones of the skull are not yet joined together and certain wrist bones are still made of cartilage. All in all, the human newborn is further removed from adulthood than is the newborn of most other species. In a way, we are all born premature.

A number of authors believe that this retarded rate of development is what most distinctively makes us human, for the inevitable result is a long, protracted period of dependency. In some ways, this is quite inconvenient—for child and parent alike. But in many others, there are great benefits. For such a long period of dependency is tailor-made for a creature whose major specialization is its capacity for learning, and whose basic invention is ***culture***—the ways of coping with the world which each generation hands on to the next. As there is so much to learn, the young have much to gain by being forced to stay a while with those who teach them.

THE NEWBORN'S EQUIPMENT

What does a newborn bring into the world to serve as a foundation for further psychological development? In this chapter, we will only ask about her motor and sensory capacities.

The infant's response capacities Initially infants have little control of their motor apparatus. Newborns can do very little—they thrash around in an uncoordinated manner and can't even hold up their heads. By four months of age they'll be able to sit up with support and reach for visible objects (which they often miss). But what do they do in the meantime?

Part of the answer is that newborns start life with a neurological survival kit that will see them through their first period of helplessness: a set of early reflexes.

Some reflexes of early infancy have to do with clinging to the person who supports her. An example is the ***grasp reflex***—when an object touches the infant's palm, she closes her fist tightly around it. If the object is lifted up, the infant hangs on and is lifted up along with it, supporting her whole weight for a minute or more. This and some related reflexes are sometimes regarded as a primitive heri-

A

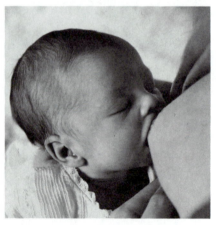

B

13.8 Some reflexes of newborns
(A) The grasping reflex, which is elicited by stimulation of the palm. (Courtesy Monkmeyer) (B) The sucking reflex. Initiated when an appropriate object is inserted three to four centimeters into the mouth. (Photograph by Jackie Curtis, Photo Researchers)

tage from our primate ancestors, whose infants cling to their mothers' furry bodies (see Figure 13.8A).

Other infantile responses pertain to feeding. An example is the ***rooting reflex.*** When the cheek is lightly touched, the baby's head turns toward the source of stimulation, her mouth opens, and her head continues to turn until the stimulus (usually a finger or nipple) is in her mouth. When this point is reached, sucking begins (see Figure 13.8B).

Many infantile reflexes disappear after a few months. In some cases, the reflex is eventually replaced by a more directed response. Thus infants stop reflexive grasping when they are about three or four months old, but this doesn't mean that they will never again grasp objects in their hands. Of course they will. But when they do (at about five months of age), they'll do so because they want to—their grasp has become voluntary rather than reflexive. Such voluntary actions could not be performed (however clumsily) before various parts of the cerebral cortex had matured sufficiently to make them possible. But until this point, the infantile reflexes had to serve as a temporary substitute.

The infant's sensory capacities   While newborns' motor capacities are initially very limited, their sensory channels function rather nicely from the very start. Evidence comes from changes in their rates of breathing, of sucking, and of similar indices in response to stimulation. Newborns hear very well; they can discriminate between tones of different pitch and loudness and have some tendency to respond preferentially to a soft human (especially, female) voice than to other sounds (Freedman, 1971). They can see; while somewhat short-sighted and unable to focus on objects farther off than about four feet, they can readily discriminate brightness and color and can follow a moving stimulus with their eyes. In addition, they are sensitive to touch, smell, and taste (Kessen, Haith, and Salapatek, 1970).

All in all, infants seem to come rather well equipped to *sense* the world they enter. But do they come pre-equipped to *interpret* what it is they see, hear, or touch? This is a disputed issue to which we will return in a later section (see Chapter 14). For now we merely note that the young infant is quite competent to receive sensory inputs. Whether he has some built-in knowledge of what these inputs might signify (as nativists would argue) or has to acquire this knowledge by relating various sensory inputs to each other (as empiricists would have it) is another matter.

Development as Orderly Progression

In prenatal growth some events necessarily come before others. The embryo consists of primitive tissue layers before it develops organs; the skeleton is made of cartilage before it becomes bone. Developmental psychologists point out that similar patterns of orderly progression characterize development after birth.

A good example is motor development. There is a regular sequence of achievements that begins with the ability to hold the head erect, followed by the ability to roll over, then to creep, crawl, sit up, stand up, take a step or two, and finally to walk, first shakily and then with increasing confidence. The average ages of these accomplishments are shown in Figure 13.9. As the figure shows, there is a good deal of variability in the age at which a given baby masters each skill. But a few

2 days

1 month

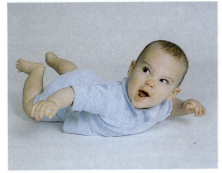

5 months

9½ months

FETAL POSITION
0 month

CHIN UP
1 month

CHEST UP
2 months

REACH AND MISS
3 months

SIT WITH SUPPORT
4 months

SIT ON LAP
GRASP OBJECT
5 months

SIT ON HIGH CHAIR
GRASP DANGLING OBJECT
6 months

SIT ALONE
7 months

STAND WITH HELP
8 months

CREEP
10 months

WALK WHEN LED
11 months

PULL TO STAND
BY FURNITURE
12 months

CLIMB STAIR STEPS
13 months

STAND ALONE
14 months

WALK ALONE
15 months

13.9 The development of locomotion *The average age at which babies master locomotor skills, from holding their chins up to walking alone. (From Hetherington and Parke, 1979)*

months more or less make little difference for later development. What matters is that each step in the sequence comes before the next. No baby walks before it can crawl.

Somewhat similar progressions are found in aspects of intellectual development. An example is the acquisition of language (see Chapter 15). Here too there is an orderly sequence. Initially the baby coos, then he babbles, then he utters the first word or two, then he develops a small, first vocabulary but is limited to one-word sentences, then he increases his vocabulary and utters two-word sentences, after which both vocabulary and sentence complexity increase until they finally reach adult levels. Table 13.1 gives a rough idea of the ages at which these achievements occur. As with motor development, there is a good deal of variability among different infants. Some may begin to talk by ten months, others as late as

12 months

15 months

twenty, but age of initial language onset is no predictor of later linguistic competence. The important point is that linguistic development follows the same general progression for all children.

Developmental psychologists have mapped various other sequences in which important cognitive and social skills are acquired in the course of childhood. Some of them have tried to show that these various sequences are interrelated and indicate a succession of general stages of development. We will turn to these matters in the next two chapters. For now, we only want to underline the main point—development generally proceeds by an orderly sequence of steps, and this holds for the growth of our minds as well as our bodies.

Table 13.1   CHARACTERISTIC LINGUISTIC ACHIEVEMENTS IN THE FIRST 30 MONTHS

Age	Linguistic achievement
3 months	cooing
4 months	babbling
10 months	first word
18 months	about 20 words; one-word utterances
24 months	about 250 words; two-word utterances
30 months	about 500 words; three-plus utterances

SOURCE: From Lenneberg, 1967, pp. 128–30.

THE INTERACTION OF HEREDITY AND ENVIRONMENT

What causes the many changes that constitute development? This question has led to a long debate that echoes the nature-nurture controversy we have discussed in several previous sections. There are those who feel that what we become after birth is largely a matter of environment and learning. Conversely, there are those who believe that the main course of human development is largely predetermined by our own hereditary biological nature—an unfolding of potentialities that were there all the time.

The theoretical tug-of-war between these two views runs through virtually all areas of developmental psychology. Take motor development. Are walking and grasping learned (at least in part), or does their emergence reflect a consequence of a program of maturation that merely obeys a set of genetic instructions built into the fertilized cell? Similar questions can be raised about cognitive and social development. As the child develops, she grows in the way she comes to perceive, to remember, to think, speak, and to interact with others. Are these changes primarily caused by the way the child is molded by the environment (nurture) or by her biological makeup (nature)?

It is hardly surprising that virtually everyone agrees that the answer cannot be all-or-none, for surely neither nature nor nurture can act alone. However important the role of environment and learning, it will have no effect without the genetic potential—there's no way in which you can train a cat to compose sonatas. By the same token, genetic potential cannot express itself without some appropriate environment—Isaac Newton would not have rewritten the laws of the

Prodigies and built-in talent   One argument for a genetic component in certain mental abilities is the occasional appearance of prodigies who display their extraordinary talents at a very early age. The outstanding example is Wolfgang Amadeus Mozart (1756–1791). At 3, he picked out chords on the harpsichord; at 4, he played pieces from memory; at 5, he composed sonatas; and at 6, he gave concerts before most of the sovereigns of Germany. (The painting, which shows Mozart at a concert with his father and sister is by Louis Carmontelle, Chantilly, Musee Conde, courtesy of Giraudon/Art Resource)

physical universe if he had been kept in a black, soundproof box from birth to adulthood. Such hypothetical examples may demonstrate that both heredity and environment are required (did anyone ever doubt it?) and that the two must act in concert. But they say little about the role of each and the way they exert their effects.

The joint action of genetic potential and the environment in which that potential is expressed is often described by the statement that "heredity and environment interact." In the following sections we will try to give some indications of how this interaction might work.

Heredity

We begin by considering the mechanisms that underlie the transmission of genetic relationships from one generation to the next.

THE CHROMOSOMES

Each organism starts life with a genetic blueprint, a set of instructions that steers its development from fertilized cell to mature animal or plant. The genetic commands are contained in the *chromosomes* in the cell's nucleus. In organisms that reproduce sexually, the chromosomes come in corresponding pairs, with one member of each pair contributed by each parent.

With one exception, all cells in the human body have twenty-three chromosome pairs, for a total of forty-six chromosomes (see Figure 13.10). The exceptions are certain cells in the father's testes and the mother's ovaries that divide in two by a special form of cell division call *meiosis* in which each of the two halves acquires one member of each chromosome pair. The results of meiosis are the *sperm* and *egg cells.*** Every human existence begins when one sperm cell joins up with one egg cell and pairs up each of its twenty-three chromosomes to one of the twenty-three chromosomes contributed by its partner.

An important consequence of meiosis is that it leads to considerable genetic variability. Each sperm cell of a given male is produced by a kind of genetic lottery—while it receives one member of each of the individual's chromosome pairs, which of the two it receives is a matter of chance. Similarly for the female's egg cells. This indicates that the number of potential combinations of human sperm and egg cell is enormous. It is a humbling number—in the neighborhood of ten million million—that suggests that all in all, any one of us represents a singularly improbable event.

Sex determination The genetic commands that determine whether a given organism will be a male or a female are inscribed in a pair of so-called sex-chromosomes. In males, the two members of that pair are different: one is an *X-chromosome;* the other is somewhat smaller and is called a *Y-chromosome.* In females, both members of the pair are X-chromosomes. Which sex the child will

13.10   The human chromosome pairs
The figure shows the 23 pairs of chromosomes in a human male. The twenty-third pair determines the individual's sex. In males, one member of each pair is an X-chromosome, the other a Y-chromosome. In females, both are X-chromosomes. (Photograph courtesy of M. M. Grumbach)

---

* To appreciate the biological benefits of this halving process, consider what would happen if sperm and egg cells had the same number of chromosomes as all other cells of the body. When uniting at conception, they would pool their 46 chromosomes so that the cells of the next generation would have 92, those of the next would have 184, and so on, until the number of chromosomes in each cell would exceed the total number of atoms in the universe.

be depends entirely on the father. For while every egg cell contains one X-chromosome, sperm cells either contain an X-chromosome or a Y-chromosome. Depending upon which of the two kinds joins up with the egg cell, the resulting fertilized egg may contain an XX pair (a female) or an XY pair (a male).

THE GENES

Every chromosome stores thousands of genetic commands, each of which is biologically engraved in a *gene,* the unit of hereditary transmission. The genes dictate much of the course of the organism's development—they determine whether it will grow up to be a man or a mouse, an earthworm or a bald-headed eagle.

Dominant and recessive genes   Any given gene is located at a particular place on a given chromosome. Since chromosomes come in pairs, both members of each pair have corresponding loci at which there are genes that carry instructions about the same characteristic (for example, eye color). These two related genes—one contributed by each parent—may or may not be identical. Consider eye color. If both of the genes for eye color are identical (blue-blue or brown-brown), the result is simple: The eye color will follow suit. But suppose they are different. Now the overt expression of the genetic blueprint depends upon still other relationships between the two members of the gene pair. In humans, the brown-eyed gene is *dominant;* it will exert its effect regardless of whether the other member of the gene pair calls for brown or blue eyes. In contrast, the blue-eyed gene is *recessive.* This recessive blue-eyed gene will lead to blue eyes only if there is an identical (that is, blue-eyed) gene on the corresponding locus of the paired chromosome.

There are many other human traits that are (largely) based on a single gene pair, such as dark hair, dimples, and thick lips (dominant); and baldness, red hair, and straight nose (recessive). Some are more deleterious, and many of those are recessive. Examples range from mild conditions such as susceptibility to poison ivy and red-green color blindness, to hemophilia (in which the blood does not clot so that a person may bleed to death from a minor injury). Since these and most other damaging genetic characteristics are recessive, their expression is relatively rare. There will be no overt effect unless both parents transmit the recessive gene. This fact may partially account for the widespread cultural prohibition against incest. The offspring of close relatives run a much greater risk of serious genetic defects (let alone susceptibility to poison ivy).

Phenotype vs. genotype   The phenomenon of gene dominance illustrates a crucial distinction in the study of heredity. On the one hand, there is the overt appearance of an organism—its visible structure and behavior. This is the *phenotype,* the characteristic we actually observe in a given individual. But this phenotype is by no means equivalent to the organism's genetic blueprint, its *genotype.* As we have seen, two people who have brown eyes may well have different genotypes for eye color; one may be brown-brown, the other brown-blue (see Figure 13.11). Nonetheless, the phenotypes are the same, for if a blue-eyed gene is present it will be masked by its brown-eyed counterpart.

Polygenic inheritance   Most of the preceding discussion concerns hereditary traits that are for the most part produced by the action of one gene pair. Such

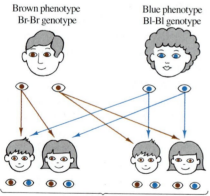

Brown phenotype
Br-Br genotype

Blue phenotype
Bl-Bl genotype

Brown phenotype
Br-Bl genotype

13.11   Phenotype and genotype in the transmission of eye color   *Eye color of the children of a brown-eyed and a blue-eyed parent if the brown-eyed parent's genotype is brown-brown. All of the children's eyes (phenotypes) will be brown, although their genotypes will be brown-blue. In the figure, genotypes are indicated by a pair of schematic eye-color genes under each face.*

characteristics are usually all-or-none: brown-eyed or blue-eyed, dimples or no dimples. But what can we say about attributes that vary continuously, such as height? Such traits are clearly not all-or-none in nature. The answer is *polygenic inheritance,* in which the inheritance of the trait is controlled not by one but by many gene pairs. Take height. Some gene pairs pull toward increased stature, others toward lesser stature, and the individual's ultimate genetic potential for height (for now, ignoring environmental effects) is then determined by the combined action of all the height-controlling gene pairs.

THE INHERITANCE OF BEHAVIOR

So far, our examples have concerned the inheritance of bodily attributes, but there is ample evidence that many behavioral characteristics are also affected by hereditary makeup. Basset hounds are relatively lethargic, German shepherds are relatively excitable, and the offspring of their cross-matings have temperaments in between (James, 1941). Some behavioral tendencies seem to be determined by a single gene. An example is the response to intense, high-pitched noises in mice. Some mice are relatively unaffected by such stimuli, while others react with violent epileptic seizures. Breeding experiments have shown that this proneness to seizures is carried by a single recessive gene (Collins and Fuller, 1968).

Phenylketonuria An illustration of a human psychological characteristic that is determined by a single gene is a severe form of mental retardation, *phenylketonuria* or *PKU.* In the United States, about one baby in every fifteen thousand is born with this defect. PKU is caused by a deficiency in an enzyme that allows the body to transform *phenylalanine,* an amino acid (a building block of proteins) into another amino acid. When this enzyme is missing, phenylalanine is converted into a toxic agent that accumulates in the infant's bloodstream and damages his developing nervous system. Analyses of the incidence of PKU among the siblings of afflicted children and among others in their family trees indicate that this disorder is produced by a single recessive gene.

Although PKU is of genetic origin, it can be treated by appropriate environmental intervention. The trick is a special diet that contains very little phenylalanine. If this diet is introduced at an early enough age, retardation can be minimized, or even eliminated.

This result demonstrates the fallacy of the popular belief that what is inborn is necessarily unchangeable. The genes lay down certain biochemical instructions that determine the development of a particular organ system. If we understand the genetic command clearly enough, we may eventually find ways to circumvent it. In the case of PKU, we are already on the way to doing so (McClearn and De-Fries, 1973).

Methods of studying human inheritance How can we determine whether a human behavioral attribute has a genetic basis? In the case of characteristics based on the action of a single-gene pair, such as PKU, we can consult the family tree. But what about traits that have a polygenic basis? If we were dealing with animals, we could perform breeding experiments. but outside of science fiction novels, such studies cannot be performed on humans, who generally insist on choosing their own mates. Under the circumstances, how can we proceed?

One method is the study of twins. There are two kinds of twins—*identical* and

13.12 Identical twins *Photographs of a pair of identical twins taken at ages 18 months, 5, 15, and 50 years. (Photographs courtesy of Franklin A. Bryan)*

fraternal. Identical twins originate from a single fertilized egg that splits into two identical replicas, which then develop into two genetically identical individuals (see Figure 13.12). In contrast, fraternal twins arise when each of two eggs in the female reproductive tract is fertilized by a different sperm cell. As a result, the genetic similarity between fraternal twins is no greater than that between ordinary siblings.

Identical twins are of considerable interest. If identical twins turn out to be more similar on a certain trait than are fraternal twins, one can conclude that this trait is in part genetically determined, assuming—and this assumption can be questioned—that the twins' environments are no more similar if they are identical than if they are fraternal. Greater similarities between identical than fraternal twins have in fact been found for a number of psychological characteristics, including performance on intelligence tests and some personality traits (Scarr and Kidd, 1983). On the face of it, this seems to be good evidence for a genetic component in the determination of these traits. (For a more detailed discussion of these issues, see Chapters 17 and 18.)

Environments at Different Points of Development

Thus far, our focus has been on the genetic blueprint that dictates the course of the organism's development. What about the environment? How does this interact with the genetic instructions to produce, first the newborn, and eventually, the mature organism? The first thing to realize is that what is meant by *environment* changes as development proceeds. We will begin by considering physical growth during early embryonic development.

EMBRYONIC DEVELOPMENT AND THE CELL ENVIRONMENT

The embryo has various tissues that will ultimately become its inner organs, muscles, skin, and nervous system. How does any given cell in the embryo know how to fulfill its proper destiny—to become part of a mouth, or of a spinal cord, or whatever? After all, every cell of the organism has the same genes, so that they all presumably get the same genetic instructions. But if so, how do they manage to develop differently?

Part of the answer is that the fate of any given cell is partially determined by the cells that are adjacent to it and form its physical environment. Evidence comes from studies of salamander embryos. At an early stage of their development, they have an outer layer of tissue whose cells can turn into skin or teeth. They will become teeth if they make contact with certain other cells in the mouth region that belong to an inner layer of the embryo. Proof comes from studies in which parts of the flank of a salamander embryo were cut out and then transplanted into the embryo's mouth region. Had those cells stayed where there were, they would have eventually developed into the skin of the flank region. Having been brought into a different cell environment, however, they became teeth.

Such findings show that the environment matters even in early embryonic development when the genetic forces are presumably at the height of their strength. But there is a further result that highlights the role of the cell's genetic constitution. In another study, the experimenters took a part of the flank of a frog embryo and transplanted it into the same mouth region of a salamander embryo they had used previously. The outcome has something to offer to both sides of the nature-nurture controversy. The transplanted cells became part of a mouth—in strict obedience to their new environment. But they became horny jaws rather than teeth—the mouth appendages of a frog rather than of a salamander—in appropriate homage to their genetic heritage. The cells could become the skin of a frog's sides or the horny jaw of its mouth, depending on the environment, but they could never escape their essential froghood (Spemann, 1967).

Studies such as these tell us that both heredity and environment are effective from the very start of life. The two interact to determine the further course of development.

EMBRYONIC DEVELOPMENT AND THE HORMONAL ENVIRONMENT

In an early stage of embryonic development, the environment consists of other cells. Somewhat later, development is affected by another kind of environment that we have discussed previously in another context—the internal environment that consists of the organism's own body fluids, especially its bloodstream (see Chapter 3). In mammalian embryos this is intimately linked up with the mother's blood supply. Various hormones that circulate within the embryo's blood or that of its mother will have a vital effect on the future course of development. An example is the development of sexual structures and behavior.

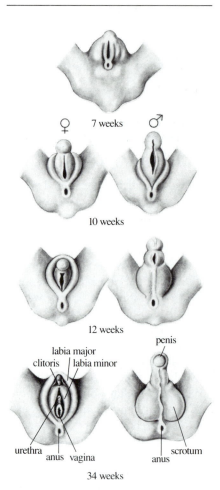

♀ 7 weeks ♂

10 weeks

12 weeks

penis

labia major
clitoris | labia minor

urethra
anus vagina

scrotum
anus

34 weeks

**13.13   The development of external
genitals in the human fetus**   *At 7 weeks,
the genitalia of human male and female
fetuses are virtually indistinguishable.
Some differentiation is seen at 10 weeks,
and becomes increasingly more pronounced in the weeks thereafter. At 34
weeks, the distinctive characteristics of the
different genitalia are fully apparent.
(From Keeton, 1980)*

What determines whether an individual is biologically male or female? One
might guess that the answer is just a matter of genetics—you are male if you are
chromosomally XY, and female if you are XX. But the actual story is more complicated than that.

At around six weeks of age, the human embryo has primordial gonads and
some external grooves and swellings that as yet give no indication of the baby's
sex. A week or so later, the chromosomes initiate the differentiation of ovaries
and testes, but the external genital apparatus still gives no clue as to whether its
owner is male or female (see Figure 13.13). Now it is up to the hormones. In a genetic male, the XY chromosome pair leads to the formation of testes. Once
formed, these produce ***androgen,*** the male sex hormone. The presence of this hormone in the bloodstream leads to the differentiation of the external genitals, and
now the fetus is on the way to becoming a little boy.

The pattern is different for females. The XX chromosome pair will lead to the
formation of ovaries, but the formation of the female's external genitals does not
depend on hormones except indirectly. As long as no androgen circulates in the
bloodstream, the fetus will develop the appropriate female organs. In mammals,
the basic developmental plan evidently calls for the building of a female, and it
will run its course in that direction if left undisturbed. It would seem that biologically—if not biblically—speaking, Adam is created after Eve (Money and Ehrhardt, 1972; Money, 1980).

The role of hormones in determining genital structure is dramatized by certain
abnormal cases of human development. Some concern genetically male embryos
who have a so-called androgen insensitivity. Their embryonic testes may secrete
an adequate amount of the hormone, but their tissues do not respond to it. As a
result, such individuals may be born with external genitals that look essentially
like a girl's, and they may well be diagnosed and raised as such despite the fact
that they are genetically males (that is, have an XY chromosome pair). The con-
verse effect occurs in genetic females who are exposed to androgen at around two
to three months after conception. (One cause is a malfunction of the embryo's
adrenal glands which releases a hormone that is the functional equivalent of androgen.) The result is a masculinization of the embryo. The external genitals become similar to males, so that in extreme cases the child may be born with a penis
and a (empty) scrotum—chromosomally a female, but in many other respects a
male.

We will return to this topic in a later section, where we will consider the psychological effects of these embryonic hormonal malfunctions and look at
methods for dealing with such cases when they occur (see Chapter 16). For now,
our primary point is to reiterate that development depends on an interaction between genetic makeup and environmental conditions. The chromosome pairs
define an individual's genetic sex. But the way in which that sex is actually shaped
depends upon the organism's internal environment—the presence or absence of
male hormones in its bloodstream.

THE ENVIRONMENT AFTER BIRTH

After birth, the crucial environmental events that affect development are those in
the surrounding physical and social world. But here, too, what is important in
one period of the individual's life has a lesser effect in another. The point is obvi-

ous in the case of social development. Who could doubt that the relevant social environment of a six-month-old baby is totally different from that of a teen-ager, even if both should be exposed to the identical sights and sounds?

The same point applies to the cognitive realm. We will later discuss theories of how children come to understand the world around them. But no one can doubt that this world is different at three months and at three years if for no other reason than that the babbles heard in early infancy are not heard as language until two years later. Under the circumstances, it is clear that what we call "environment" is not the same at different ages. Imagine a three-month-old who hears an older sibling's loud (and no doubt well-intentioned) shout "Surprise!" as the parents put some new toy in the baby's crib.* In all likelihood, the baby would cry in fear, for all *he* heard was a loud noise. At three years of age, the same shout would probably produce joyous squeals of anticipation, for now the sound has meaning and that meaning is vastly more important than its auditory intensity.

CRITICAL PERIODS

The preceding discussion underlines a fact that everyone has always known—that what is important at one stage in life may not be so at some later point. But various developmental theorists have expanded this idea to make a much stronger claim. They argue that there are certain *critical periods* in development during which certain important events will have an impact that they would not have (or would have to a much lesser extent) at earlier or later times.

The hypothesis of critical periods was derived from embryological development. Take the differentiation of organ tissue. We've previously seen that at a very early stage, parts of an embryo's outer tissue may become skin or teeth, depending upon the cells they are adjacent to. If transplanted at this time, they will take the shape appropriate to their new surroundings. But at a later point in time, this plasticity is gone. Skin and teeth have become unalterably differentiated; if the teeth are transplanted from mouth to flank and vice versa, then a skin flap will form in the mouth and the flank will sport teeth—proof positive that a critical period has been passed (Spemann, 1967).

Many developmental psychologists believe that similar critical periods exist after birth or hatching. An example is the attachment of the young of many species to their mother, an attachment that typically can only be formed at an early age (see Chapter 16). Another example is bird song. There are many species of birds whose males learn the characteristic song of their species as young fledglings. To learn the song, they must be exposed to it during a critical period in their first year of life (see Chapter 15). If the exposure comes after this period has passed, the experience has no effect and the birds will never sing normally (Marler, 1970).

Whether such critical periods exist in human development is still an open question. One possibility concerns the acquisition of language, a topic which we will take up later in some detail (see Chapter 15).

---

* Though some younger siblings argue that *nothing* an older sibling ever does could possibly be well intentioned. (Personal communication from the author's younger brother, G. Gleitman, 1985.)

The Organism Helps to Shape Its Own Environment

In discussions of the roles of heredity and environment, the environment is sometimes caricatured as something that impinges on an essentially passive organism that patiently allows itself to be shaped and molded. Most modern developmental psychologists reject this view of the child as a piece of human clay that is simply molded by environmental forces. Instead of regarding the child as a passive object, they see her as an active agent whose own acts can refashion the world she lives in. They don't doubt that the environment may affect the child, but they argue that the environment is often partly of the child's own making. The environment may shape the child, who will then reshape her environment, which in its turn will then shape the child yet further.

This back-and-forth interaction between organism and environment begins at the very start of life. As we saw, the differentiation of the external genitals depends on the presence or absence of male hormones in the embryo's bloodstream. But this internal environment is in turn created by the embryo's own gonads, which are either testes or ovaries depending upon its genetic makeup. Here the environment is actually shaped by the organism's own hereditary makeup. Organisms are affected by their environment—both internal and external. But they themselves help to shape the environment, which then in turn shapes *them.*

Similar effects are found in early childhood. Consider the treatment of male and female infants. They are different anatomically, and on the average, they also seem to differ in some psychological respects. For now, our concern is with the role of the environment in promoting such differences. Our culture has different expectations for boys and girls and so it treats them differently. Once the parents recognize an infant's sex, they will treat this infant in line with these expectations and create environments that differ accordingly—little girls are dressed in pink rather than blue, are presented with dolls rather than toy trucks, and are treated more gently by both parents from babyhood on.

Some early differences in the way male and female infants are treated have been documented experimentally. Mothers of young infants were asked to participate as subjects in an experiment on "how children play." The mothers were introduced to a six-month-old baby, little "Joey" or "Janie," and asked to play with him or her for a few minutes. In fact, the six-month-old was a "baby actor" who was dressed up as a boy or a girl regardless of its actual sex. The results showed that the subjects' behavior depended on whether they thought they were playing with "Joey" or "Janie." To "Joey" they offered toys such as a hammer or a rattle, while "Janie" was invariably presented with a doll. In addition, there were differences in the way "Joey" and "Janie" were physically handled. In dealing with "Joey," they often tended to bounce "him" about, thus stimulating the whole body. In contrast, their response to "Janie" was gentler and less vigorous (Smith and Lloyd, 1978).

These findings give further proof—if proof is needed—that male and female infants are treated differently from the very start of life (see Figure 13.14). In effect, they live in different environments. But these different environments are themselves a product of the differences in the children's biological makeup. Heredity and environment are not independent, for a given genetic structure often leads to a given environment.

13.14 Organisms affect and are affected by their environment *Once parents and others recognize an infant's sex, they will create different environments for him or her. Notice the difference in the cards sent to parents in the sixties and seventies congratulating them on the birth of a son or daughter. Currently, such announcements are considerably less sexist in tone. (Courtesy Hallmark)*

Environment and Maturation

As noted earlier, development is orderly and progressive. Infants sit up before they can walk, and babble before they can talk. What accounts for this well-nigh inevitable schedule of early developmental achievements?

A number of developmental psychologists believe that many of these achievements (especially of motor and sensory development) are produced by *maturation*—an inevitable unfolding of behavior patterns that is genetically programmed into the species and is independent of specific environmental conditions. They believe that this sequence of behavioral milestones is analogous to the ordered progression that characterizes physical growth. The particular rate of this behavioral schedule may vary somewhat from one baby to the next, but the steps in that schedule are essentially the same for all—crawling precedes walking, and uncoordinated reaching precedes precise grasping. Maturation theorists believe that these achievements result primarily from the growth and development of the infant's brain and musculature and that they have little to do with experience.

MATURATION AND PRACTICE

The orderliness of early development argues that it is heavily based on maturational processes. How are such processes affected by practice?

A number of investigators focused on motor development by comparing infant-rearing practices in different cultures. In some societies—for example, the Hopi and Navaho Indians—the infant is swaddled and bound to a cradle or carrying board, with his activity severely inhibited for much of the first year of life (see Figure 13.15). Despite some initial reports to the contrary (Dennis, 1940), the bulk of the evidence suggests that such early restrictions do have a retarding effect on later motor milestones (e.g., among the Mayan Indians; Brazelton, 1972), while systematic practice in various motor activities leads to some acceleration (e.g., in certain Kenyan communities; Super, 1976).

Do these studies prove that the maturation concept should be discarded? Not really. For the effects of immobilization or special practice are relatively slight—the onset of walking may occur a bit earlier or later, but the child's ultimate performance is pretty much the same in either case. The important developmental achievement is to walk at all, and this is very probably based on maturation.

In line with this conclusion are studies using twins, one of whom was trained in such basic motor activities as walking or climbing stairs. The results showed that while practice may help, it doesn't have long-run effects. If a twin practiced before he was "ready," he did indeed surpass his untrained twin. But the gains were short-lived. For once the other twin was given similar practice after reaching the appropriate maturational point, he quickly caught up with his specially educated twin and attained the same level of locomotor proficiency (Gesell and Thompson, 1929; McGraw, 1935).

All in all, it looks as if certain activities that are basic to the species—sitting, walking, climbing—occur as a function of maturation. They can be modified somewhat by experience, but they will emerge—more or less on schedule—regardless of specific practice.

13.15   Learning, maturation, and walking   *An Indian child strapped into a cradle. (Photograph by Michal Heron, Woodfin Camp)*

463

SPECIFIC VS. NON-SPECIFIC EXPERIENCE

In animals Various achievements of early development such as walking seem to depend on maturation. But that does not mean that the organism's environment has no effect. What is relatively unimportant is *specific* experience—such as training in how to walk. But there is a good deal of evidence that certain *general* kinds of experience exert important effects on a number of sensory and motor patterns. For example, animals reared in total darkness in early life will not develop certain structures of the visual system that allow them to see properly when they are later exposed to light (Gottlieb, 1976b). Further studies show that just as sensory deprivation retards maturation, sensory "enrichment" helps it along. One investigator manipulated the sensory environment of rat pups from birth until they were eight days old. One group of pups was simply left in their cages. The other received an unusual amount of sensory stimulation—they were handled and stroked, heard noises and saw flashing lights, and were subjected to wide variations of temperature. At the end of the eight-day period, the animals' brains were examined. In the cortex of the animals whose sensory environment had been enriched (who had experienced a wide range of stimulation), there were many more neural branchings and interconnections. This may well be the biological basis on which later behavioral development depends (Schapiro and Vukovich, 1976).

The organism's genetic instructions dictate the maturation of many of its early achievements. But these dictates will not be obeyed without a proper environment in which maturation can take place.

In humans Do the results of sensory deprivation studies in animals have any implications for human development? A number of investigators believe that something analogous happens to human children raised in institutions under conditions of serious deprivation. In one such setting, there was very little stimulation during the first year of life; the infants only came in contact with other persons when they were fed. Nor was there much in the way of physical stimulation. The infants had few toys and saw little of the world around them because their cots were draped with sheets that obstructed their view. They spent most of their time lying on their cots and wore deep hollows into their mattresses. Follow-up studies showed serious adverse effects. At the age of three they were markedly retarded in physical development, toilet training, speech, and the ability to feed and dress themselves (Spitz, 1945). According to some investigators, the consequences of early deprivation continue into the school years. When observed at age ten to fourteen, children raised under similar conditions of early deprivation were markedly lower in social and intellectual attainments than age mates in a control group (Goldfarb, 1955).

These results have not gone unquestioned. To begin with, there is some question whether the difference between the institutionally reared and the control children can really be ascribed to the conditions of early deprivation since the two groups may not have been equivalent to begin with. Consider the effects of early compared to later adoption. One investigator looked at the intelligence-test scores of children whose early life was spent in an orphanage but who were eventually adopted. He found that children adopted before the age of two reached normal levels when later tested at the age of sixteen. Those adopted later had lower scores. This result may have been produced by the deleterious effect of early deprivation. But there is also the possibility that the two groups were different to begin with; perhaps the brighter children were adopted at an earlier age or were placed in better homes (Dennis, 1973).

Such considerations make it clear that the reported effects of early experience are still open to several interpretations. But even if such effects are genuine, it is by no means clear that they are necessarily irreversible. Nor is it clear what the relevant environmental deprivations are that produce them. Is it a general lack of sensory stimulation, analogous to the kind that led to an atrophy of neural structures in rats reared in the dark? Is it a more specific deprivation, such as lack of social interactions or inadequate contact with human language? We will discuss these and related questions in more detail in later sections (see Chapters 15 and 16). For now, we only note that these issues are still far from settled.

We saw that psychological development generally involves growth and differentiation and that these proceed in an orderly progression. This comes about through the interaction of both heredity and environment. To understand this interaction, we have to realize that what is meant by environment changes as development proceeds, beginning at conception and continuing after birth. And this environment is itself shaped by the organism from the very start of life. In the next two chapters we will see how these general characteristics describe cognitive and social development.

SUMMARY

1. The study of development has several historical roots. One grew out of the changing conception of childhood and the accompanying concern with finding better ways of child rearing and education. Another impetus came from an increasing interest in all forms of historical change, especially those that concerned the evolution of the species, and the growth of the individual organism from conception to adulthood.

2. Initially, it was widely believed that the individual's embryological development recapitulates the evolutionary history of the species of which he is a member. This *recapitulation theory* was abandoned when it was recognized that embryological development is better understood as a progressive process of anatomical *differentiation*. According to many theorists, the differentiation principle also applies to the development of behavior. An example is the development of grasping during the infant's first year.

3. Development can be considered as a process of *growth.* After conception, the fertilized egg divides, redivides, and differentiates. In the process, it becomes an *embryo,* and then, two months later, a *fetus.* At birth, the infant comes equipped with a set of early reflexes and good sensory capacities. Compared to animals, human newborns are further removed from adulthood than are the newborns of most other species. This leads to a long period of postnatal growth and dependency which may be one of the factors that led to the development of human culture.

4. A general characteristic of development is that it is *progressive.* An example is *motor development* in which such steps as creeping, crawling, and walking occur in much the same sequence for all babies.

5. The changes that constitute development are produced by the interaction of genetic endowment and environmental factors.

6. In humans, the genetic commands are contained in twenty-three pairs of *chromosomes.* One of these pairs determines the sex of the organism. If female, it is an *XX* pair; if male, an *XY* pair. Every chromosome contains thousands of *genes,* some *dominant* and some *recessive.* The genes determine an individual's *genotype,* but this is not equivalent to its *phenotype* which corresponds to its visible structure and behavior. While some of the individual's genetically based characteristics are determined by a single gene, many others are determined by *polygenic inheritance.*

7. Genes affect behavior as well as structure. An example of a psychological characteristic determined by a single gene is *phenylketonuria* or *PKU,* a severe form of mental retardation which can be controlled by an appropriate diet in early infancy.

8. To study psychological characteristics that have a polygenic basis, psychologists often compare the performance of *identical* and *fraternal twins.* If the identical twins are more similar on some trait than are fraternal twins of the same sex, this is usually regarded as evidence for a genetic component in the determination of that trait.

9. What is meant by the term *environment* changes as development proceeds. In early embryonic development the environment of a given cell is the other cells with which it makes contact. Somewhat later, the embryonic environment includes hormonal conditions. An example is the formation of external genitals, which differentiate into those of a male in the presence of androgen, but become those of a female when androgen is absent. Similar effects occur after birth, since the same physical environment exerts different effects at different ages. Another example which shows that environment can exert radically different effects at different ages is provided by *critical periods,* as in the development of bird song.

10. In may ways, the environment is shaped by the organism. An example is the different ways in which male and female human infants are treated from the very start of life.

11. Some aspects of the orderly progression of development are determined by *maturation,* which is genetically pre-programmed and is independent of specific environmental conditions. An example is walking. This and other early sensory and motor achievements seem to be relatively unaffected by specific practice. On the other hand, more general kinds of experience, such as sensory deprivation and sensory enrichment, seem to exert important effects in animals as well as humans.

CHAPTER 14

Cognitive Development: Thought

Thus far, our discussion of development has focused on physical growth and changes in motor behavior. But the child grows in mind as well as body—in what she knows, how she comes to know it, how she thinks about it, and in the fact that she can tell it to others (sometimes interminably so). This intellectual growth that accompanies the progress from infancy to adulthood is generally called *cognitive development.*

A useful analogy to cognitive development may be the transformation of beginners into masters in many fields of endeavor, as they become expert typists, or chess champions, or musical virtuosos. As we saw previously, masters and novices differ in the kind of conceptual organization they bring to their tasks (see Chapter 8). Masters no longer ply their trade as they once did as apprentices—they type by words and phrases rather than by letters, see chess positions as constellations rather than as the locations of individual pieces, and play whole musical passages rather than separate notes. Many psychologists believe that analogous qualitative changes accompany the cognitive development all humans undergo as they grow up. For compared to the child, all adults are masters. Adults live in a world that contains real objects that exist independently of the observer, a world that is ordered according to such basic conceptual categories as space, time, number, and causality, and a world that can be conceived of abstractly. These conceptual categories are the basic foundations upon which all further intellectual activity rests—they are so basic in fact, that we have come to take them for granted. We hardly even notice that we have them, but they are the categories that make us masters at the trade we are all engaged in: understanding the world.

According to many investigators, these same conceptual categories are far

Apprentices and masters *All children are apprentices at knowing, even those who eventually become the greatest masters of all. (Left: photograph by Nina Leen, Life; right: Albert Einstein, photograph by Ernst Haas, Magnum)*

from self-evident in childhood. Young children may not think about space and time and causality the way adults do, and for this reason they are unable to solve many problems whose solution we find self-evident in later life. Students of cognitive development have tried to chart the paths by which the child comes to understand what adults take for granted.

Jean Piaget *(Photograph by Yves DeBraine, Black Star)*

PIAGET'S THEORY OF COGNITIVE DEVELOPMENT

We will organize our discussion of the child's mental growth around the work of the Swiss psychologist Jean Piaget (1896–1980). Piaget's conceptions have aroused considerable controversy, but there is hardly a developmental psychologist who has not been greatly affected by them.

Piaget believed that mental growth involves major qualitative changes. This hypothesis is relatively recent. According to the eighteenth-century empiricists, the child's mental machinery is fundamentally the same as the adult's, the only difference being that the child has fewer associations. Nativists also minimized the distinction between the child's mind and the adult's, for they viewed the basic categories of time, space, number, and causality as given *a priori,* being part of the native equipment that all humans have at birth. Thus both empiricists and nativists regarded the child as much like an adult; the first saw him as an adult-in-training, the second as an adult-in-miniature. In contrast, Piaget and many other developmental psychologists usually look for qualitative differences and try to chart the orderly progression of human intellect as the child grows into an adult.

Piaget's original training was as a biologist, which may be one of the reasons why his conception of intellectual development bears many resemblances to the way an embryologist thinks of the development of anatomical structures. The human fetus doesn't just get larger between, say, two and seven months; its whole structure changes drastically. Piaget argued that mental development is characterized by similar qualitative changes. He proposed that there are four main stages of intellectual growth, whose overall thrust is toward an increasing emancipation from the here-and-now of the immediate, concrete present, to a conception of the world in increasingly symbolic and abstract terms. These stages are the period of *sensory-motor intelligence* (from birth to about two years), the *preoperational period* (two to seven years), the period of *concrete operations* (seven to eleven years), and the period of *formal operations* (eleven years and on). The age ranges are very approximate and successive stages are often thought to overlap and blend into each other.

Sensory-Motor Intelligence

According to Piaget, at first there is nothing but a succession of transient, unconnected sensory impressions and motor reactions, for mental life during the first few months contains neither past nor future, no distinction between stable objects and fleeting events, and no differentiation between the *me* and the *not me*. The critical achievement of the first two years is the development of these distinctions.

OBJECT PERMANENCE

A

B

14.1 Object permanence (A) A six-month-old looks intently at a toy. (B) But when the toy is hidden, the infant does not search for it. According to Piaget, this is because the infant does not as yet have the concept of object permanence. (Photographs by George Zimbel, Monkmeyer)

Consider an infant holding a rattle. To an adult, the rattle is an object, a *thing,* of whose existence he has no doubt, whether he looks at it or briefly looks away. The adult is sure of its existence, for he is certain that he will see it once more when he looks at it again.* But does the rattle exist as a thing in the same sense to the infant? Or, to use Piaget's term, does the infant have the notion of *object permanence?*

According to Piaget, there is little object permanence in the first few months of life. The infant may look at a new toy with evident delight, but if it disappears from view, he shows little concern (see Figure 14.1). It seems as if what's out of sight is also out of mind and does not really exist for the infant. Piaget described one such incident when his daughter was seven months old:

> . . . Jacqueline tries to catch a celluloid duck on top of her quilt. She almost catches it, shakes herself, and the duck slides down beside her. It falls very close to her hand but behind a fold in the sheet. Jacqueline's eyes have followed the movement, she has even followed it with her outstretched hand, but as soon as the duck has disappeared —nothing more (Piaget, 1951, pp. 36–37).

Needless to say, infants eventually come to live in a world whose objects do not capriciously appear and disappear with the movement of their eyes. At about ten months of age, they start to search for toys that have been hidden or that have

* This view is essentially the same as that held by many empiricist philosophers who tried to explain what people mean when they say that external objects exist even when no one is looking at them. Their interpretation was that such objects exist as "permanent possibilities of sensation" (J.S. Mill, 1865, Chapter 11). Helmholtz put this same view more concretely: "We notice that we can get various images of the table in front of us by simply changing our position . . . and that the table may vanish from sight and then be there again at any moment we like, simply by turning our eyes. . . . We explain the table as having existence independent of our observation, because at *any moment we like,* simply by assuming the proper position with respect to it, we can observe it" (Helmholtz, 1909, p. 31).

fallen out of their cribs. According to Piaget, the notion that objects exist on their own, and continue to exist even if they are not seen or heard or felt, is a major accomplishment of the sensory-motor period. This notion emerges as the infant gradually interrelates his various sensory experiences and motor reactions. Eventually he coordinates the sensory spaces provided by the different modalities—of vision, hearing, touch, and bodily movement—into one real space in which all of the world's objects—himself included—exist.

SENSORY-MOTOR SCHEMAS

Directed action The newborn starts life with a rather limited repertoire of built-in reactions, such as gross bodily movements in response to distress, sucking and swallowing reflexes, and after a few days, certain orienting responses such as head and eye movements. These recurrent action patterns are the first mental elements—or, to use Piaget's term, *schemas*—through which the infant organizes the world that impinges upon her. At first, these various schemas operate in isolation. A one-month-old infant can grasp a rattle and can also suck it or look at it. But she will perform these actions only if the stimulus object is directly applied to the relevant sensory surface. She will suck the rattle if it touches her mouth and will grasp it if it's pressed into her palm. But she is as yet unable to grasp whatever she's sucking or to look at whatever she's grasping. The coordination of all these patterns takes time and is not complete until she is about five months of age. By then, looking, reaching, grasping, and sucking have all merged into one unified exploratory schema (Piaget, 1952).

Imitation As adults, we often consider imitation as a mental activity of a lower order and have little regard for those who merely "ape" what others do. And compared to creative invention, imitation is indeed of baser coin. But upon reflection, it represents no mean intellectual achievement, especially when it first appears in infancy. To imitate, an infant must have some grasp of the relation between his own movements and those produced by others. This expansion of sensory-motor schemas does not begin until the child is about nine months old. The resulting growth in the capacity for imitation is a vital prerequisite for many further aspects of intellectual development including the acquisition of language (see Chapter 15) and the adoption of various social roles (see Chapter 16).

During the first few months, infants are capable only of what Piaget calls *pseudo-imitation*. If the mother does something the baby has done just a moment before (such as saying "ba-ba"), he is likely to resume this activity. This phenomenon probably represents an extension of a *circular reaction*. Such reactions are a pervasive feature of early infancy—the child scratches at an object and then gropes at it, scratches and gropes again, repeating the sequence over and over. Similarly for early babbling, in which one "ba-ba" leads to another "ba-ba," and then to yet another, and so on. The sensory feedback from each behavior sequence seems to prime its own immediate recurrence. In pseudo-imitation, the cycle is reactivated from the outside: The infant treats the mother's "ba-ba" as if it were a "ba-ba" of his own.

With increasing age, imitation becomes more genuine. From about four months on, infants can imitate actions that they themselves did not perform just

Playing pat-a-cake *Imitating an adult playing pat-a-cake is easy because the infant can see her own hands do just what the parent's hands do. (Photograph by Suzanne Szasz)*

moments previously. But they can only do so if their parents' actions lead to sights and sounds that are similar to those the infants encounter when they perform that same action themselves. Examples are squeezing a pillow or hitting a toy. In each case, what the infant sees when she watches her parent's hands is very similar to what she sees when her own hands go through the same motions. The problem becomes much more difficult when imitation requires movements that are invisible to the imitator. Consider a child who tries to imitate someone sticking out his tongue. Not being a frog, the child cannot see her own tongue. Under the circumstances, she can only copy her elders if she has some rather well-developed mental picture of her own facial anatomy, and of the correspondence of her own anatomy to the anatomy of others. By eight or nine months of age, the infant's sensory-motor schemas are sufficiently well-developed to allow imitations of this kind.*

Imitation may be difficult even in adulthood. To be sure, adults have no trouble copying simple movements like closing the eyes or sticking out the tongue. But when they try to imitate complex movement patterns like a dance step or a golf swing, their initial attempts are only crude approximations. Successful imitation requires a well-developed comprehension of what the model is doing, together with a schema that allows the translation of a desired perceptual outcome into motor patterns that bring this about. Were it otherwise, we could all become dancers, actors, or bullfighters just by watching the experts perform.

In short, imitation is an active process that requires the development of increasingly differentiated sensory-motor schemas, a process that starts in early infancy but continues into adulthood. Imitation is only easy when the appropriate schemas are already formed.

BEGINNINGS OF REPRESENTATIONAL THOUGHT

The last phase of the sensory-motor period (about eighteen to twenty-four months) marks a momentous change in intellectual development. Children begin to conceive of objects and events that are not immediately present by representing (that is re-presenting) some prior experience with these to themselves. Such *representations* may be internalized actions, images, or words. But in all cases, they function as symbols that stand for whatever they may signify but are not equivalent to it.

One demonstration of this change is the achievement of full object permanence. At eighteen months or so, children actively search for absent toys and are surprised (and sometimes outraged) if they don't find them under the sofa cover where they saw the experimenter hide them; it is reasonable to infer that they have some internal representation of the sought-for-object. Even more persuasive are examples of *deferred imitation* in which children imitate actions that occurred some time past, such as a playmate's temper tantrum observed a day ago. A related phenomenon is make-believe play, which is often based on deferred imitation.

---

* Several recent studies show that some modicum of facial imitation (including tongue protrusion) is found in infants as young as two weeks of age. Whether this is imitation in Piaget's sense, or some primitive, reflexive precursor, is still a matter of debate (e.g., Bower, 1976; Meltzoff and Moore, 1977; Jacobson and Kagan, 1979).

THE EMERGING SEPARATION OF SELF AND WORLD
AS SEEN BY PIAGET AND FREUD

There is an interesting similarity between Piaget's conceptions of early cognitive development and some of Freud's views of the way the ego develops during the child's first years (see Chapter 12). Both Freud and Piaget believed that initially the young infant does not distinguish between himself and the world outside, let alone between himself and others. They both assert that these distinctions are achieved through the infant's active intercourse with his environment. The difference is one of emphasis. Freud's emphasis was on wishes and emotions, and so he concentrated upon the emerging distinction between desire and goal attainment, on the child's growing awareness that he or she has to do something to make a wish come true (see Chapter 12). In contrast, Piaget was primarily concerned with the nature of thought, and so he focused on the way in which the infant comes to recognize the separation between the self and the physical world outside.

The Preoperational Period

Given the tools of representational thought, the two-year-old has taken a gigantic step. A year ago, he could interact with the environment only through direct sensory or motor contact; now he can carry the whole world in his head. But while his mental world now contains stable objects and events that can be represented internally, it is still a far cry from the world of adults. The two-year-old has overcome the initial chaos of separate sensations and motor impressions, but only to exchange it for a chaos of ideas (that is, representations) that he is as yet unable to relate in any coherent way. The achievement of the next five years is the emergence of a reasonably well-ordered world of ideas. According to Piaget, this requires higher-order schemas that he calls *operations,* which allow the internal manipulation of ideas according to a stable set of rules. In his view, genuine operations do not appear until about seven or so, hence the term *preoperational* for the period from two to seven years.

FAILURE OF CONSERVATION

Conservation of quantity and number   A revealing example of preoperational thought is the young child's failure to **conserve quantity.** One of Piaget's experimental procedures uses two identical glasses, A and B, which stand side by side and are filled with the same amount of some colored liquid such as orangeade. A child is asked whether there is more orangeade in the one glass or in the other, and the experimenter obligingly adds a drop here and pours a drop there until his subject is completely satisfied that there is "the same to drink in this glass as in that." Four-year-olds can easily make this judgment.

The next step involves a new glass, C, which is much taller but also narrower than A and B (see Figure 14.2). While the child is watching, the experimenter pours the entire contents of glass A into glass C. He now points to B and C, and asks, "Is there more orangeade in this glass or in that?" For an adult, the question

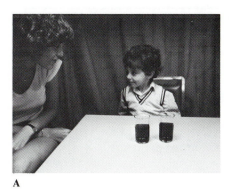

A

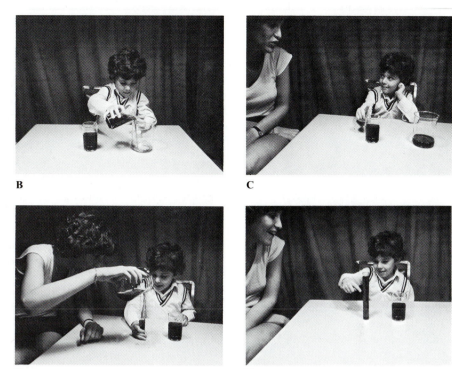

B **C**

D **E**

14.2   Conservation of liquid quantity
(A) Bobby, aged five years and one month, is asked by the experimenter, "Do we both have the same amount of juice to drink?" Bobby says: "Yep." (B) Bobby pours his juice into a large beaker. (C) When asked, "Do I have as much to drink as you?" Bobby answers, "You have more." (D) The experimenter pours the juice from the beaker into a new, thin glass. (E) Bobby is now asked, "Now do we both have the same amount of juice to drink or does one of us have more?" Bobby points to the thin glass and answers, "You have more." (Photographs by Ed Boswell)

is almost too simple to merit an answer. The amounts are obviously identical, since A was completely emptied into C, and A and B were set to equality at the outset. But four- or five-year-olds don't see this. They insist that there is more orangeade in C. When asked for their reason, they explain that the liquid comes to a much higher level in C. They seem to think that the orangeade has somehow increased in quantity as it was transferred from one glass to another. They are too impressed by the visible changes in appearance that accompany each transfer (the changing liquid levels) and do not yet realize that there is an underlying reality (the quantity of liquid) that remains constant throughout.

By the time children are about seven years old, they respond much like adults. They hardly look at the two glasses, for their judgment needs little empirical support. "It's the same. It seems as if there's less because it's wider, but it's the same." The experimenter may continue with further glasses of different sizes and shapes, but the judgment remains what it was: "It's still the same because it always comes from the same glass." To justify their answer, the children point to the fact that one can always pour the liquid back into the original glass (that is, A), and thus obtain the same levels. They have obviously understood that the various transformations in the liquid's appearance are *reversible.* For every transformation that changes the way the liquid looks, there is another that restores its original appearance. Given this insight, children at this age recognize that there is an underlying attribute of reality, the quantity of liquid that remains constant (is *conserved*), throughout the various perceptual changes.

Comparable results are obtained with malleable solids like clay or plasticene. The child is first shown two equal balls of plasticene, one of which is then rolled

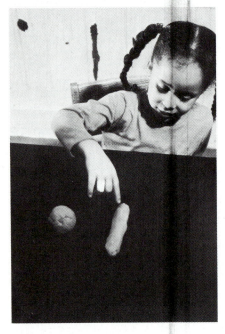

14.3   Conservation of mass quantity
Jennifer, aged four years and four months, is shown two clay balls which she adjusts until she is satisfied that there is the same amount of clay in both. The experimenter takes one of the balls and rolls it into a "hot dog." When now asked which is more, Jennifer points to the hot dog. (Photograph by Ed Boswell)

into a sausage (see Figure 14.3). Until about age seven, children deny that there is the same amount of plasticene in both ball and sausage. Some say that the sausage contains more because it is longer, others insist that it contains less because it is thinner.

A related phenomenon is **conservation of number.** The child is first shown a row of six evenly spaced bottles, each of which has a glass standing next to it. The child agrees that there are as many bottles as there are glasses. The experimenter now rearranges the six glasses by setting them out into a much longer row while leaving the six bottles as they were. Here the turning point comes a bit earlier, at about five or six. Up to that age, children generally assert that there are more glasses (or disks, or checkers, or whatever) because "they're more spread out" (see Figure 14.4). From about six on, there is conservation; the child has no doubt that there are just as many bottles in the tightly spaced row as there are glasses in the spread-out line. In all these conservation tasks, the older child's explanation emphasizes reversibility—the plasticene sausage can be remolded into a ball, and the long line of glasses can be reassembled into a compact row.

Attending to several factors simultaneously   Why are preschool children unable to appreciate that the amount of a substance remains unaffected by changes of shape or that the number of objects in a given set does not vary with changes in the spatial arrangement? According to Piaget, part of the problem is the child's inability to attend to all of the relevant dimensions simultaneously. Consider conservation of liquid quantity. To conserve, the children must first comprehend that there are two relevant factors: the height of the liquid column and the width. They must then appreciate that an *increase* in the column's height is accompanied by a *decrease* in its width. Initially, they center their attention only on the height and do not realize that the change in height is compensated for by a corresponding change in width. Later on, say at five, they may well attend to width on one occasion and to height on another (with corresponding changes in judgment), but they cannot attend to both dimensions at the same time. To attend to both dimensions concurrently and to relate them properly requires a higher-order schema that reorganizes initially discrete perceptual experiences into one conceptual unit.

In Piaget's view, this reorganization occurs when the child focuses on the transformations from one experience into another, rather than on the individual transformations by themselves. The child sees that these transformations are ef-

14.4   Conservation of number   *(A) The experimenter points to two rows of "cookies," one hers, the other Bobby's. She asks, "Do I have as many cookies as you?" Bobby says, "Yes." (B) One row of "cookies" is spread out and the experimenter asks, "Now do we still have the same?" Bobby says no and points to the row he says has more. (Photographs by Ed Boswell)*

A

B

fected by various reversible overt actions, such as pouring the contents of one glass into another. The overt action eventually becomes internalized as a reversible operation so that the child can mentally pour the liquid back and forth or remold the plasticene. The result is conservation of quantity (Piaget, 1952).

In summary, the preoperational child is the prisoner of his own immediate perceptual experience and tends to take appearance for reality. When a seven-year-old watches a magician, she can easily distinguish between her perception and her knowledge. She *perceives* that the rabbits come out of the hat, but she *knows* that they couldn't possibly do so. Her four-year-old brother has no such sophistication. He is delighted to see rabbits anytime and anywhere, and if they want to come out of a hat, why shouldn't they?

EGOCENTRISM

The inability of preoperational children to consider two physical dimensions simultaneously has a counterpart in their approach to the social world. They cannot understand another person's point of view, for they are as yet unable to recognize that different points of view exist. This characteristic of preoperational thought is often called *egocentrism.* As Piaget uses the term, it does not imply selfishness. It is not that children seek to benefit at the expense of others; it is rather that they haven't fully grasped that there are other selves.

An interesting demonstration of egocentrism involves a literal interpretation of "point of view." If two adults stand at opposite corners of a building, each knows that the other sees a different wall. But according to Piaget, preoperational children don't understand this. In one study, children were shown a three-dimensional model of a mountain scene. While the children viewed the scene from one position, a small doll was placed at various other locations around the model. The child's job was to decide what the doll saw from *its* vantage point (see Figure 14.5). To answer, the child had to choose one of several drawings that depicted different views of the mountain scene. Up to four years of age, the children didn't even understand the question. From four to seven years old, their response was fairly consistent—they chose the drawing that showed what they saw, regardless of where the doll was placed (Piaget and Inhelder, 1956).

Concrete and Formal Operations

Seven-year-olds have acquired mental operations that allow them to abstract some of the essential attributes of reality such as number and substance. But according to Piaget, these operations are primarily applicable to the relations between concrete events (hence the term *concrete operations*). They do not really suffice when these relations must be considered entirely in the abstract. Eight- or nine-year-olds can perform various simple manipulations on specific numbers they are presented with, but they generally fail to understand that certain results will hold for any number whatsoever. They may realize that 4 is an even number and 4 + 1 is odd, and similarly for 6 and 6 + 1, 8 and 8 + 1, and so on, but they are by no means sure that the addition of 1 to any even number must always produce a number that is odd. According to Piaget, the comprehension of such highly abstract and formal relationships requires *formal operations,* operations of a higher order which emerge at about eleven or twelve years of age. Given formal

14.5   The three-mountain test of egocentrism   The child is asked to indicate what the doll sees. The results suggest that the child thinks the doll sees the scene just as she does, including the little house which is of course obstructed from the doll's vantage point. (After Piaget and Inhelder, 1967)

operations, the child's thought can embrace the possible as well as the real. He can now entertain hypothetical possibilities, can deal with what *might be* no less than what *is*.

An illustration of the role of formal operations comes from a study in which children had to discover what makes a pendulum go fast or go slow. They were shown how to construct a pendulum by hanging some object from a string. They were also shown how to vary the length of the string, the weight of the suspended object, and the initial force that set the pendulum in motion. Children between seven and eleven typically varied several factors at a time. They might compare a heavy weight suspended from a long string with a light weight suspended from a short string, and would then conclude that a pendulum swings faster the shorter its length and the lighter its weight. Needless to say, their reasoning was faulty, for the way to determine whether a given factor (e.g., weight) has an effect is to hold all others (e.g., length) constant. Children below about eleven cannot do this, for they can operate only on the concretely given. They are unable to consider potential cause-and-effect relationships, which must first be deliberately excluded and then tested for later on. In contrast, older children can plan and execute an appropriate series of tests. Their mental operations proceed on a more formal plane so that they can grasp the notion of "other things being equal" (Inhelder and Piaget, 1958).

The period of formal operations is the last important milestone in the child's intellectual progression that Piaget and his co-workers have described in some detail. Their account of the developmental steps that led up to this point has been enormously influential and is a major achievement in psychology's attempt to understand human intelligence. But this does not mean that it has gone unchallenged. We will now consider some efforts to look at Piaget's description of human cognitive development with a more critical eye.

PERCEPTION AND MOTOR ACTION IN INFANCY

Piaget's account of human intellectual growth has been seriously criticized on several grounds. One important challenge concerns his views on what is given at the very start of life.

A number of modern developmental psychologists contend that Piaget—who in this regard was much like the early British empiricists—had seriously underestimated the infant's native endowment. These critics deny that the infant's mind is the mere jumble of unrelated sensory impressions and motor reactions that Piaget had declared it to be, for they believe that some of the major categories by which adults organize the world—such as the concepts of space, time, objects, and causality—have primitive precursors in early life. They have buttressed their position by systematic studies of perception and action in very young infants.

The Gibsonian Approach to Perception

A very influential alternative to Piaget's view of cognitive development in infancy grows out of the perceptual theories of James and Eleanor Gibson (Gibson, E.J., 1969, 1984; Gibson, J.J., 1950, 1966, 1979; see Chapter 6, pp. 181, 201).

14.6 Texture gradient *The retinal size of texture elements (in this case, sunflowers) decreases with distance and provides information about depth. (Photograph by Grant Heilman)*

The Gibsons deny that the perception of objects and events is built out of piecemeal impressions provided by the different senses—the sights and sounds and feelings that have to be coordinated through experience to yield the cognitive world of adulthood. According to the Gibsons, we don't have to depend on a long history of learning to relate, say, retinal size to cues of depth (as the empiricists argued). Nor do we have to wait for the development of cognitive representations (as Piaget maintained). For in their view, the objects and events out in the environment give rise to various patterns of *higher-order stimulation* that provide the organism with information about the true nature of these objects and events, such as texture gradients which give information about depth (see Figure 14.6; also see Chapter 6). As they see it, such vital characteristics of an object as its size, its shape, its distance, and its motion in space are signaled directly by these higher-order stimulus patterns to which the organism is innately sensitive.

One line of argument for this nativistic position is an appeal to evolution. The world in which we live is three-dimensional and contains solid objects whose size and shape stay the same regardless of the position from which we look at them. This is a fact today, but it was surely also true for eons before humans ever came upon the scene. Under the circumstances, it may not be unreasonable to suppose that such all-important truths might have been built into the perceptual apparatus of the species during the millions of years of its evolution rather than being acquired through learning during the few months or years of an individual's early personal history (Shephard, 1982; Gibson, 1984).

Evolutionary arguments of this sort give some plausibility to the idea that the response to higher-order patterns of stimulation is part of our built-in endowment. But they don't provide genuine evidence. A first step in this direction is to look at perception in early infancy.

Links between Eye and Ear

Some recent findings concern the way in which the infant links sights, sounds, and touches. Normally, such sensory impressions provide information that refers to the same object or event outside. A cup breaks, and we see it shatter and also hear the crash. As adults, we don't ordinarily experience these visual and auditory messages separately; they both seem to refer to the same event—the breaking cup. But according to Piaget (and the British empiricists before him), the infant is initially quite unaware that these auditory and visual experiences are in some way related. For Piaget believed that, at first, the various senses are utterly separate doorways to the real world and that they become interconnected only after a period of learning and mental growth.

A number of investigators suggest that at least some intersensory relations may be present at the very outset. Evidence comes from the fact that very young infants are remarkably sensitive to various correspondences between sights and sound. When shown films of a speaker's face in which the voice is sometimes synchronized and sometimes not, infants as young as three months will spend more time looking at the voice-synchronized face (Dodd, 1979). This phenomenon is not limited to speech. In one series of studies, four-month-olds were shown two films side by side. One featured a game of peek-a-boo, the other showed a hand that repeatedly struck various percussion instruments with a baton. Simultaneously, the infants heard either the peek-a-boo or the percussion sound track.

477

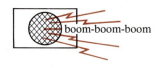

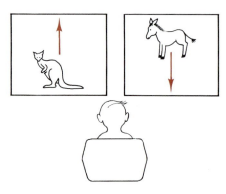

14.7 Intersensory relations in infancy
Four-month-olds are shown two films side by side, which show a toy kangaroo and a toy donkey bouncing up and down once every 2 seconds, but not in synchrony with each other. A loudspeaker broadcasts a gong booming once every 2 seconds, in synchrony with either the kangaroo or the donkey. The infant looks at the animal that bounces in time with the gong. (Spelke, 1981)

The results were clear-cut—the infants spent almost twice as much time looking at the film that was appropriate to the sound track than at the film in which the sound did not match the sight (Spelke, 1976, 1981; see Figure 14.7).

Analogous links between touch and vision have been reported in twenty-nine-day-old infants (Meltzoff and Borton, 1979). And some intersensory correspondence seems to exist even in newborns; when presented with a click to either the right or the left, they move their eyes to the appropriate side (Wertheimer, 1961; Harris, 1983).

Links between Eye and Hand

Some correspondence between the different senses evidently appears at a very early age. A similar correspondence has been shown between sensory input and motor action.

By about five months of age, infants reach out toward objects and with a bit of luck manage to grasp them, however clumsily. This motor achievement obviously depends on some coordination between muscular action and visual experience. How is this coordination attained?

Piaget believed that, except for simple reflexes, there is at first no connection between the infant's motor acts and any of her sensory impressions. In his view, the relevant sensory-motor integration is gradually developed as the infant watches her own hand approaching some object. The sight of her own hand and arm movements eventually creates a mental schema that relates the visual world to motor action and provides the basis for visually guided reaching (Piaget, 1954).

REACHING IN NEWBORNS AND YOUNG INFANTS

Some recent evidence suggests that, contrary to Piaget, a certain amount of coherence between sight and directed movement is present at the very start of life. In one study, newborns were strapped to a special chair that supported their head and trunk but allowed free movement to the arms. A small colored ball of yarn was suspended from above, and moved back and forth in front of the infant's eyes. The infants thrashed their arms and legs, and at first glance, their limbs seemed to move in a hopelessly random fashion. But on closer analysis, a pattern emerged. On some occasions, the infants looked at the ball; on others, they did not. It turned out that their arm movements were (somewhat) better aimed at the ball when they looked at it than when they did not. This result suggests that there is some initial linkage between eye and hand that is part of our native endowment (Von Hofsten, 1982).

Needless to say, the newborn still has a very long way to go before he is ready to grasp and manipulate objects. For until he is about five months old, his efforts at reaching and grasping objects are very clumsy and relatively unsuccessful. But even then, his knowledge is greater than it might seem at first. One study looked at how infants from two to five months react when they try to reach for objects with both hands. Until the end of that period, the infants don't succeed in grasping reached-for objects. But the investigators showed that the infants were not as ignorant about reaching as they might appear; they knew that they had to adjust their grip to the size of the object they were presented with. If it was a small ball, their hands came together at the midline of the body. But if the ball was ten times larger and could only be grasped when the two hands were separated, the infants rarely joined their hands but instead kept them farther apart. In both cases, the infants' arms generally failed to reach out for the ball, so the hands missed their goal and the ball remained ungrasped. But the fact that there was some appropriate anticipation of a successful two-handed grasp gave yet further demonstration that vision affects motor movement even before the child can execute that movement properly. Here, as so often, later developmental achievements have precursors earlier in life (Bruner and Koslowski, 1972).

CATCHING A MOVING OBJECT

A series of further experiments asked how infants between four and eight months catch moving objects. The infants sat on a baby chair and were presented with a small, colored "wobbler" with yellow and black eyes which was attached to a rod that moved back and forth in front of the infant at speeds from six to twelve feet per second. The infants were intrigued and often reached for the wobbler. The important fact is that such reachings were fairly successful—the infants often managed to touch the wobbler as it passed by, and sometimes even caught it in their hands (if caught, the wobbler stopped moving).

How did the infants determine how to aim their arm in reaching for the moving wobbler? To catch a moving object, the infant had to judge the object's trajectory to tell where it would be by the time his arm had shot out to meet it, like an artillery gunner who aims ahead of where his moving target is at the moment he fires. Even at four months of age, the infants' aim was remarkably accurate (see Figure 14.8). This again suggests a built-in foundation, since infants of that age probably get little practice in catching fast-moving objects outside of the laboratory. But again, this is only a beginning. While four-month-olds aim well enough, their arms and hands aren't steady as they progress toward the goal, and they don't quite know how to adjust their hand to hold onto the object once they touch it. By the time they are eight months old they do much better, and they catch the wobbler on half of their attempts, at speeds of twelve feet per second. This may not seem like much when compared to the feats of a baseball catcher coping with balls that travel over ten times faster, but it's a start (Von Hofsten and Lindhagen, 1979; Von Hofsten, 1980, 1983).

14.8 Reaching and catching in infancy
A seven-month-old at various stages in the act of catching an object moving at the rate of 45 cm per second. (Photographs courtesy of Claus von Hofsten)

A

B

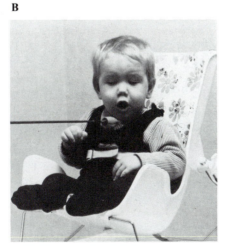

C

The Perception of Objects

The preceding discussion suggests that there are early and perhaps built-in correspondences between the different sensory channels and between sensory input and motor reaction. Other evidence bears on an even more fundamental Piagetian (and empiricist) claim: the view that infants begin life with no conception that the world outside consists of real objects that exist independently of whether they are touched or seen.

One series of studies hinged on the perceptual effect of *occlusion.* Consider Figure 14.9A, which shows an object that partially obscures (occludes) the view of an object behind it. When adults encounter this sight, they will surely perceive it as a tree behind a gate. They are completely certain that when the gate is opened so that the partial occlusion is removed, they will see a whole tree (Figure 14.9B) and would be utterly astounded if the opened gate revealed a tree with gaps in it (Figure 14.9C). This ability to perceive partly hidden objects as they really are is continually called upon in our everyday life, for most of the things we see are partly concealed by others in front of them. But even so, we perceive a world of complete objects rather than disjointed fragments.

What accounts for the adult's ability to perceive partly hidden objects? To some extent, it is surely a matter of learning. We know that trees have no gaps in them, and that even if they do, they can't stand unsupported in mid-air. But does this mean that Piaget is correct and that the infant starts life with no idea at all that there are external objects outside? Some authors believe it does not. In their view, the infant comes pre-equipped with some primitive concept of a physical world that contains unitary objects whose parts are connected and stay connected regardless of whether the object is partially hidden. Their evidence comes from experiments which show that under some conditions four-month-old infants seem to perceive occluded objects in much the manner that adults do. Most of these experiments employed the *habituation procedure* (Figure 14.10).

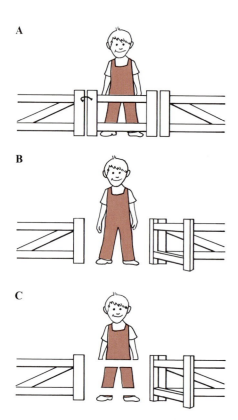

14.9   The perceptual effect of occlusion *(A) A child occluded by a gate is perceived as a whole person behind a gate, so that he will look like (B) when the gate is opened, rather than being perceived as (C) a child with gaps in his body.*

14.10   The habituation method   *(A) A four-month-old's face, looking at a small slowly rotating pyramid in front of him (the pyramid can be seen in the mirror that is behind the infant and above his head). (B) Habituation: The infant becomes increasingly bored and looks away. (C) Dishabituation: The infant sees a new object (the rotating cube shown in the mirror) and looks again. This dishabituation effect provides evidence that the infant perceives a difference between the first and the second stimulus (that is, the pyramid and the cube). (Photographs courtesy of Phillip Kellman)*

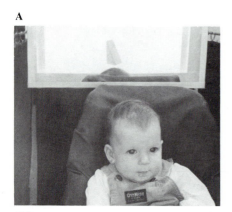

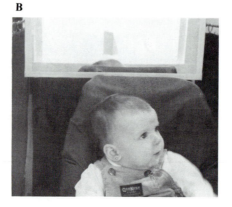

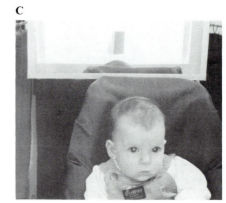

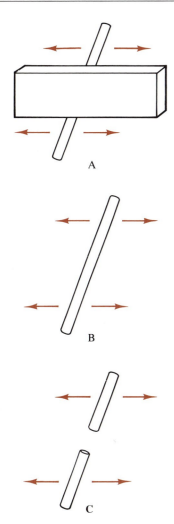

14.11 Object perception in the four-month-old *Infants looked at a rod that moved back and forth behind an occluding block as shown in (A). After they became habituated to this display and stopped looking at it, they were shown two new displays, neither of which was occluded. (B) was an unbroken rod that moved back and forth. (C) was made of two aligned rod pieces that moved back and forth together. The infants spent much more time looking at (C) than at (B). (After Kellman and Spelke, 1983)*

In one such study, the infants were shown a rod that moved back and forth behind a solid block that occluded the rod's central portion (Figure 14.11A). This display was kept in view until the infants became bored (that is, ***habituated***), and stopped looking at it. The question was whether the infant perceived a complete, unitary rod, despite the fact that this rod was partially hidden. To find out, the experimenters presented the infants with two new and unoccluded displays. One was an unbroken rod that moved back and forth (Figure 14.11B). The other consisted of two aligned rod pieces, that moved back and forth in unison (Figure 14.11C). If the infants saw the original display as a complete rod that moved behind the block, they would presumably regard the broken rod as a novel stimulus. If so, they would keep on looking at it for a longer time than at the (now unobstructed) complete rod. This is just what happened. The fact that the top and bottom of the rod in the original display were seen to move together behind the block apparently led to the perception that they were connected. This suggests that some notion of a real physical object exists even at four months of age (Kellman and Spelke, 1983).

Such results do not really prove that some foundation for object perception is built in. After all, the subjects in these studies had already lived four months, and some learning may well have occurred during this period. But the results make such a built-in basis far more plausible than had been previously supposed (Spelke, 1982, 1983). All in all, there is reason to believe that, Piaget and the empiricists to the contrary, infants come remarkably pre-equipped to see the world as it really is.

THE PRESCHOOLER AND THE STAGE CONCEPT

The preceding discussion showed why many critics feel that Piaget has underestimated the infant's native endowments in its cognitive development. If these critics are right, the starting point of mental growth is higher than that which Piaget assumed it to be. But what about the process of development from then on? As Piaget described it, cognitive development goes through several distinct ***stages*** that are in some ways analogous to the stages found in embryological development. This stage notion of development has been the subject of considerable debate. No one doubts that there is mental growth, that the child changes in the way she thinks as she gets older. But is this growth best described as a progression through successive stages?

The Meaning of Mental Stage

What do we mean by *stage?* There is one sense of the term that is essentially empty. Suppose someone announces that "Johnny is going through the thumb-sucking stage." This is just a cumbersome way of saying that Johnny is currently sucking his thumb, for it asserts nothing further. The same is true for a whole host of similar statements, such as "Jane is in the no-saying stage," or "Joey is in the covering-the-wall-with-crayons stage," which respectively inform us that Jane generally says "no" and that Joey crayons the wall, regrettable facts we already knew and to which nothing more is added by calling them stages.

When Piaget used the term *stage* he tried to say considerably more than this. In effect, he took the embryological analogy seriously. In this context, a developmental stage has two characteristics. One is that development at a given stage is more or less *consistent.* That is, the characteristics of a given embryological stage hold pretty much across the board—the development of the gastrointestinal tract is more or less on a par with the development of the circulatory system, and so on. A second characteristic is that embryological stages tend to be *discrete* rather than continuous. There is a qualitative difference between a tadpole and a frog; to be sure, the change from one to the other takes a while, but by the time the creature is a frog, its tadpole days are emphatically over. As Piaget is generally interpreted, his claim was that the same two characteristics—consistency and discreteness—apply to cognitive development. A number of critics have questioned whether they really do. For the most part, these critics have focused on the preschooler's abilities.

The Question of Consistency

How consistently do children behave in various intellectual tasks at any given time in their development? According to a strict interpretation of Piaget's stage theory, children who succeed in tests of conservation should also perform well on other indices of the same stage (that is, the stage of concrete operations), such as taking another person's social or visual point of view. But in fact, the correspondence between these different indices is fairly low; a child may be able to conserve mass or number and fail on tests of point of view. Unlike an embryo, the child does not seem to obey one single developmental clock that synchronizes all aspects of his mental growth. While this result does not constitute a decisive disproof of the Piagetian view, it is not exactly what a simple stage theory might lead one to expect (Gelman and Baillargeon, 1983).*

The Question of Discreteness

How discrete are developmental stages? As Piaget's account is often understood, many cognitive capacities that mark one period of development are totally absent at prior periods. Consider conservation of mass or number. According to a simple discrete-stage hypothesis, these should be totally absent at an early age, say, five years old and younger. They are then thought to emerge, virtually full blown, when the curtain finally opens on the next act of the developmental drama, the period of concrete operations. A number of modern investigators disagree, for they deny that cognitive development is essentially all-or-none. As these critics see it, various cognitive achievements such as conservation have primitive precursors that appear several years earlier than the Piagetian calendar would predict (Gelman, 1978; Gelman and Baillargeon, 1983).

* The issue of what is meant (or what should be meant) by a developmental stage has led to a considerable amount of rather technical discussion that is beyond the scope of this book. (For some examples, see Flavell and Wohlwill, 1969; Wohlwill, 1973; Brainerd, 1978; and Flavell, 1982). One problem is caused by the fact that Piaget's theory seems to have some escape clauses because he admits that there are some "slippages" in the process of development. To give only one example, Piaget attributes the fact that children may show conservation on one task but not on another to such factors as differences in task difficulty which mask the actual developmental stage the child is in (Piaget, 1954).

EGOCENTRISM REVISITED

One area of reevaluation concerns the concept of egocentrism. According to Piaget, young preschool children are unable to appreciate the difference between another's point of view and their own. But recent studies show that a modicum of this ability is found in children between two and four.

One study used a picture-showing task. Children from one to three years of age were asked to show a photograph to their mother who was seated opposite them. At two and a half and three years of age, all children turned the picture so that it faced the mother. But this implies that they had some conception of the difference between one person's angle of regard and another's. If they had been totally egocentric, they should have shown their mothers the back of the picture while continuing to look at it from the front (Lempers, Flavell, and Flavell, 1977; see also Figure 14.12).

A SECOND LOOK AT CONSERVATION

Another phenomenon whose reexamination suggests that preschoolers are less inept than Piaget supposed is conservation, especially conservation of number. We have previously described the standard Piagetian finding: When preschoolers are asked to compare two rows that contain the same number of, say, toy soldiers, they often say that the longer row contains more soldiers, in an apparent confusion of length and number. But recent studies show that children as young as three have surprising precursors of number conservation if the test conditions are suitably arranged.

In one procedure, the children were shown two toy plates, each with a row of toy mice attached with velcro. One plate might have two mice, while the other had three. One plate was designated the "winner," the other the "loser." Each plate was then covered by a can and shuffled around while the children were instructed to keep track of the winner—a small-fry version of the venerable shell game. After each trial, the plates were uncovered, and the children received a prize if they could correctly identify the winner and the loser. After several such trials, the real test was conducted. The experimenter surreptitiously substituted a new plate for the original winner. In one case, the new plate contained the same number of mice as the original, but the row was made longer or shorter. In the

14.12 A simplified test of egocentrism
Poor performance on Piaget's test of egocentrism may have resulted from the fact that the spatial layout of his three-mountain task is unduly complicated. In a later study, three- and four-month-olds were shown various three-dimensional displays such as (A) and (B), as well as a three-mountain scene (C). Grover, a doll, was shown to drive a toy car around each layout. When he stopped the car, the child was asked to turn an identical display on another table until "you are looking at it the same way Grover is." The children did quite well with all displays except (C), the three-mountain scene. This one probably caused trouble because the children couldn't distinguish the mountains as readily as they could distinguish the toy objects in (A) and (B). (Borke, 1975; photograph courtesy of H. Borke)

A

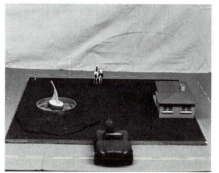

B

C

14.13 Gelman's mouse-plate test
(A) The experimenter points to the plate that has two mice and says it is the "winner" while three-year-old Carly watches. (B) After the experimenter covers the plates and rearranges the plates by a sleight-of-hand trick, (C) Carly points to the correct "winner" and then looks at the experimenter with surprise and says, "Hey—they're spreaded out!" (Photographs courtesy of Hilary Schmidt)

other case, the row length stayed unchanged, but a mouse was added or subtracted. The results showed that spatial arrangement made little difference. But changes in number had dramatic consequences even at three and four years of age. The children were surprised, asked where the missing mouse was, and searched for it (Gelman, 1972; see Figure 14.13).

It appears that three- and four-year-olds have a better understanding of number than Piaget had supposed. They can evidently distinguish, at least to some extent, between the number of items that compose a set and the way these items are spatially arranged. As an indignant four-year-old put it to the experimenter on confronting a lengthened row of mice on the winner plate:

CHILD: What you did!
EXP.:   What happened?
CHILD: Look at that!
EXP.:   What?
CHILD: Spreaded it out!
EXP: I did?
CHILD: Yep.
EXP.:   How do you know that plate wins a prize?
CHILD: Cause it has five.

(Gelman and Gallistel, 1978, p. 168)

Such findings suggest that the number concepts of later periods are built upon foundations established much earlier. One such foundation is counting. Some initial rudiments of this skill appear as early as two and a half. At this age, children may not yet know the conventional number terms. But nevertheless they may have grasped some aspect of what the counting process is all about. For example, some children employ an idiosyncratic number series. Thus one two-year-old consistently used "one, two, six."

EXP.:   How many on this [three-item] plate?
CHILD: One, two, six!
EXP.:   You want to do that again?
CHILD: Ya, one, two, six!
EXP.:   Oh! Is that how many were at the beginning of the game?
CHILD: Ya.

(Gelman and Gallistel, 1978, p. 91)

Other two-year-olds had still other private number series. What is important is that they use these series consistently. At first glance we may be puzzled by the two-year-old who looks at three toy animals and triumphantly announces that there are nineteen. But the grounds for his triumph are much clearer when we realize that he employs the idiosyncratic series "one, thirteen, nineteen." In due time, he will use more conventional tags. But he has already grasped some of the essential concepts that underlie the counting process. He realizes that each of these number tags has to be applied to each object in the set on a one-to-one basis, that the tags must always be used in the same order, and that the last number applied is the number of items in the set. And this realization is the foundation on which counting rests (Gallistel and Gelman, 1978).

Phenomena of this kind argue against the notion that cognitive development proceeds by sudden, dramatic leaps. The achievements of the concrete-operational period do not come out of the blue. If we look carefully enough, we see that they have preludes in much earlier childhood years. It may well be true that there are stages of intellectual growth that have to be passed in an ordered sequence. But there are no neat demarcations between stages and no sharp transitions. The stages of cognitive development are not as all-or-none as the changes from tadpole to frog (let alone from frog to prince).

Sequence or Stages?

What can we conclude about Piaget's stages of mental development? The evidence as a whole suggests that the child's mental growth does not proceed as neatly as a simple stage theory might lead one to expect. Most developmental psychologists would agree that there is a well-ordered *sequence* of mental steps, but many have come to doubt that this sequence of steps is best described as a succession of mental stages, analogous to those found in embryological development (Flavell, 1982).

Does this mean that Piaget's cognitive milestones have no psychological reality? Not really. The cognitive sequence may not be as neat as one might have wished, but there is little doubt that some such sequence exists. Consider the difference between seven-year-olds and preschoolers. Despite all the precursors of concrete operations at four or even earlier, there is no question that seven- and eight-year-olds have something preschoolers lack—the ability to apply their insights to a much wider range of problems (Fodor, 1972). Three-year-olds can tell the difference between two and three mice regardless of how they are spaced on the table. But they haven't fully grasped the underlying idea—that number and spatial arrangements are in principle independent and that this is so for all numbers and all spatial arrangements. As a result, they fail—and will continue to fail until they are six or seven years old—the standard Piagetian test for conservation of number in which they have to recognize that two rows of, say, nine buttons contain the same number of buttons, regardless of how the rows are expanded or compressed. This task baffles the preschool child, who finds the number in each row too large to count and gets confused. Seven-year-olds have no such problems. They can count higher, but that's not the issue. They know that there is no need to count, that the number of buttons in each row has to be identical, regardless of the way they are arranged. As a result, they can conserve number in general.

What holds for conservation of number holds for many other intellectual achievements that are generally associated with the first school years. Most of them have precursors, often at much earlier ages than Piaget led us to suppose. But these preschool abilities usually represent isolated pockets of knowledge that can't be applied very widely. The seven- or eight-year-old's understanding of physical, numerical, and social reality is considerably more general, so much so that it seems qualitatively different from what went on before. By simplifying the task in various ways, experimenters can induce preschoolers to perform more creditably. But the interesting fact remains that by the time the child is seven or eight years old, no such simplification is necessary. A seven- or eight-year-old conserves with barely a glance at the containers in which the liquid is sloshed around. He *knows* that the liquid quantity is unaffected no matter how the containers are shaped.

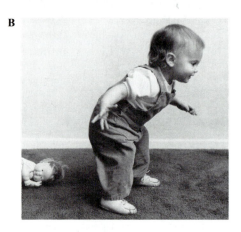

14.14 Development as maturation? *(A) A butterfly emerging from its crysalis and (B) walking are largely matters of maturation. (C) Is the cognitive growth that underlies an eight-year-old's success in a Piagetian conservation task to be understood in similar terms? (Photographs by Photo Researchers, Suzanne Szasz, and Mimi Forsyth, Monkmeyer)*

THE CAUSES OF COGNITIVE GROWTH

Thus far, our primary concern has been with description. We looked at cognitive growth and saw that there is some question of how it might be best described (e.g., stage or sequence). We now turn to attempts at explanation. Children grow in the way they think and remember and talk. The question is why. To date, there is no satisfactory answer. Trying to explain cognitive development has turned out to be even more difficult than trying to describe it. As so often in the field of cognition, the attempts to come up with an adequate explanation have fluctuated between the two poles of the nature-nurture controversy.

The Nativist Approach: Maturation

Some investigators are inclined toward a nativist interpretation. There is of course no doubt that native endowment must play some role in cognitive development. The human infant begins life with a potential that is quite different from that of his near and distant cousins in the rest of the animal kingdom, and no amount of training and nurturing can ever erase these differences in the equipment with which the varying species begin. Worms won't fly, playtypuses won't form higher-order chunkings, and polar bears won't conserve liquid quantity, no matter what environments they are reared in. Our native equipment is thus a necessary precondition for all development. But can this endowment explain the orderly progression of cognitive development?

Some theorists believe that it can. They believe that development is largely driven by some form of physical *maturation,* a pre-programmed growth process based on changes in underlying neural structures that are relatively independent of environmental conditions. Maturation is obviously an important factor in motor development—for example, flying in sparrows and walking in humans. These are behavior patterns that are characteristic of all adult members of the species. They emerge as the organism matures, but their development is relatively unaffected by environmental changes (except those extreme enough to cripple or kill).

Could cognitive development be a matter of maturation (in part or whole), in the sense in which walking is (Figure 14.14)? A number of authors suspect that it might be. In their view, there is something inexorable about cognitive development, especially up to age seven or eight (Wohlwill, 1973). This view is buttressed by the fact that, at least in broad outline, mental growth seems rather similar in children of different cultures and nationalities. While children of different cultures master intellectual tasks such as conservation at somewhat different ages, they usually pass these landmarks in the same order. Thus Arab, Indian, Somali, and British children show the same progression from nonconservation of quantity to conservation (Hyde, 1959). This is reminiscent of physical maturation. Different butterflies may emerge from their chrysalis at slightly different times, but none is a butterfly first and a chrysalis second. The timing of the transitions may well be affected by environmental conditions: in humans, by culture; in butterflies, by temperature. But according to the maturational hypothesis, the order of the stages is predetermined by the genetic code.

The Empiricist Approach: Specific Learning

The simplest alternative to a maturation-centered approach is one that emphasizes learning by exposure to the environment. The most extreme version of this view is that of the empiricists who followed in the footsteps of John Locke (see Chapter 5). To them, the human mind starts out as a blank wax tablet, a *tabula rasa,* upon which experience gradually leaves its mark. But can such a radical empiricist position explain the systematic sequence of cognitive development that Piaget and other investigators have chronicled?

Piaget argued that simple learning theories of the kind espoused by the early empiricists—and by their modern heirs such as Pavlov and Skinner—will not do. According to such theories, learning is the acquisition of relatively specific patterns that in principle could be mastered at any age. But this is precisely what Piaget denied. According to Piaget, four-year-olds cannot possibly be taught how to use a measuring cup correctly, no matter how attractive the reinforcements or how many the number of trials. He argued that four-year-olds lack the prerequisite concepts of number and quantity (which they cannot attain before the concrete-operational level), so that any attempt to teach them is as fruitless as trying to build the third story of a house without a second story underneath it. This view has obvious relevance to educational policy. If Piaget is right, then there is little point in efforts to teach children this or that aspect of the curriculum before they are "ready" for it; in fact, such premature instruction may actually do some harm by turning the children against the subject.

In an attempt to test this claim, several investigators have tried to determine whether children can be trained to reach certain cognitive landmarks such as conservation ahead of schedule. The results are a bit ambiguous. Until recently, most investigators concluded that specific training has little impact. In some cases, conservation was speeded up by special coaching, but later checks revealed that the children had not really understood the underlying principles and quickly reverted to their previous, nonconserving ways (e.g., Smedslund, 1961). Some recent studies have shown more substantial effects. In some cases, these were brought about by mere observation; for example, six-year-old nonconservers who watched conservers perform showed subsequent conservation of mass or number (Botvin and Murray, 1975; Murray, 1978). But the best guess is that the children already had most of the necessary conceptual ingredients at the time they were "trained." If so, then training (or watching another child) did not really teach conservation; it only helped to uncover what was already there (Gold, 1978; Gelman and Baillargeon, 1983).

Related findings come from a study conducted in a Mexican village whose inhabitants made pottery and whose children helped and participated in this activity from early on. When tested for conservation of mass, these children turned out to be more advanced than their North American counterparts (or those studied by Piaget in Switzerland). Having spent much of their lives working at a potter's wheel, they were more likely to know that the amount of clay is the same whether it is rolled into a ball or stretched into a long, thin sausage (Price-Williams, Gordon, and Ramirez, 1969). But these effects of pottery making were relatively specific. They led to an advance on tests of conservation of mass but to little else. (For further discussion, see Glick, 1975; Greenfield, 1976; Steinberg and Dunn, 1976; Price-Williams, 1981.)

All in all, there is little doubt that environment must play *some* role in cognitive development. To acquire liquid conservation, one presumably has to live in a world in which liquids exist. If a frozen planet like Jupiter had inhabitants whose cognitive potential was like our own, their young would never know that when water is poured from a wide jar into a tall, thin beaker the amount of water stays unchanged (at least not until they achieved the Jovian equivalent of formal operations, so that they could entertain the notion of a liquid state as a hypothetical possibility). But this is not to say that the environment shapes human (or Jovian) children in the simple, passive way proposed by an extreme empiricist position.

Piaget's Approach: Assimilation and Accommodation

Piaget's own view was that neither maturation nor specific learning can by themselves account for cognitive development. As he saw it, development involves a constant interchange between the organism and its environment. To be sure, the child can only interpret external events in terms of the mental schemas she has at the time; in Piaget's phrase, the environment is **assimilated** to the schema. But the schemas change as the child continues to interact with the world around her; they **accommodate** to the environment. Without active involvement with the outer world, there will be no such accommodation and hence no mental growth.

As an example of assimilation and accommodation, consider the infant's sucking response (Figure 14.15). Initially, this is directed only at the nipple. But with time, the infant starts to suck other objects such as her rattle. Piaget would say that by doing this she has assimilated the rattle into the sucking schema; it is now understood and dealt with as a "suckable." But the process does not stop there. After all, rattles are not the same as nipples; while both may be suckable, they are not suckable in quite the same way. This necessarily leads to new discriminations. As a result, the sucking schema adjusts (that is, accommodates) to the new object to which it is applied.

Piaget's conception of these two opposite processes, assimilation and accommodation, may be a useful way of emphasizing the fact that organism and environment interact in producing mental growth. But is it an explanation? Many psychologists argue that it is not, for Piaget offered no mechanism whereby schemas are changed through accommodation. Lacking such a mechanism, we do not really understand why children go from one stage of thought into another.

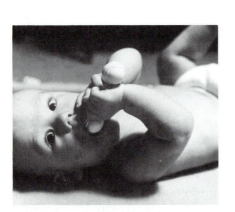

14.15 Assimilation and accommodation *The four-month-old has assimilated the rattle into her sucking schema and has accommodated the schema so that it now includes the rattle as a suckable object. (Photograph by Lew Merrim, Monkmeyer)*

The Information-Processing Approach: Chunking and Strategies

The preceding discussion has shown that while there has been some progress in describing cognitive development, we are still far from explaining why it occurs. Some grounds for hope come from recent attempts to apply the information-processing approach to cognitive development. According to this approach, all cognitive activities are ways of handling—that is, **processing**—information. Whenever a person perceives, remembers, or thinks, he has to acquire, retrieve, or transform information (see Chapters 6, 7, and 8). If adults think differently (and with greater success) than children, this is presumably due to the fact that they process information differently.

THE CHILD AS NOVICE

In a previous section, we saw that in the course of acquiring skills as in becoming a typist or a telegraph operator, the performance of the learner changes qualitatively. He has presumably formed various higher-order *chunks,* so that he no longer responds to individual letters but to letter groupings and words (see Chapter 8). It may be that much of cognitive development can be understood as a similar process that all human beings go through as they go from infancy to adulthood.

This view assumes that the difference between child and adult is in large part a matter of expertise—the adult has had the time to develop many conceptual chunkings that the child still lacks. But suppose we found some task on which the child is the expert and the adult the novice? One investigator studied memory for chess positions in adults and ten-year-olds. Experts generally do much better than novices because they can draw on more and larger chunks (see Chapter 8, pp. 272–73). But the study had a novel twist because here the children were the experts (they were recruited from local chess clubs), while the adults were the novices. Now that the tables were turned, what mattered was specific mastery rather than overall level of cognitive development. The children recalled many more chess positions than did the adults (Chi, 1978).

According to some authors, such findings suggest that intellectual growth is largely produced by the acquisition of more and more knowledge. In their view, some of this knowledge is in the form of cognitive capital goods—tools for acquiring new knowledge. These are strategies for learning and thinking that become increasingly efficient and more widely applicable as the child gets older. As a result, he can become an expert in many areas.

MEMORY AND COGNITIVE DEVELOPMENT

A number of investigators have studied the child's growing expertise by focusing on the development of memory. There is little doubt that on many conventional tests of recall, younger children do worse than older ones. Take memory span—the number of items a subject can reproduce after just one presentation. For digits, this is roughly equal to the child's age until she is about five: one digit at eighteen months, three at three-and-a-half years, and four at four-and-a-half, compared to a digit span of seven or eight in adulthood (see Figure 14.16).

Maturation and memory capacity What has happened during development that makes us so much better at remembering than young children are? Several theorists (sometimes called neo-Piagetians) believe the immature learner has a limited memory capacity that gradually increases as she gets older. Their hypothesis is that this increase is produced by maturation. Initially, the child's mind is like a small computer with limited storage and processing capacity. As her brain grows, so does her memory capacity. This in turn allows her to develop a whole set of cognitive skills that she could never have acquired previously (Pascal-Leone, 1970, 1978; Case, 1978).

On the face of it, this neo-Piagetian hypothesis has a certain plausibility. It fits in with the finding that there is a continual increase in the neural interconnec-

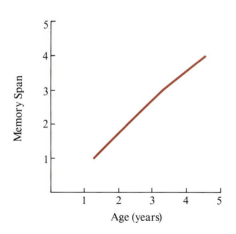

14.16 Memory span in young children (*After Case, 1978*)

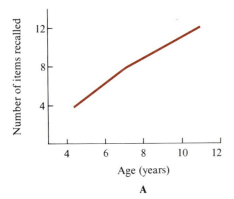

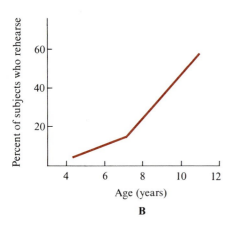

14.17 Strategies for memorizing in children *(A) Nursery-school children, first-graders, and fifth-graders were shown a number of pictures and were asked to try to remember. The figure shows recall as a function of age. (B) While the subjects watched the stimuli, the experimenters observed them for signs of rehearsal— naming the pictures, moving the lips while watching, and so on. The figure shows the proportion of all children who rehearsed. In the older children, there was quite a bit of rehearsal, but there was very little for the first-graders and virtually none for the nursery-school children. Absence of rehearsal has also been found for retarded subjects. (Data from Appel et al., 1972)*

tions of the cortex that lasts into the school years, suggesting that maturation is a factor in cognitive development (see Chapter 13). But even so, the evidence indicates that maturational processes are at best only part of the story. For it appears that the young child's poor performance at memory tasks is largely caused by the fact that he knows so little and has very limited strategies for remembering the little that he does know (Flavell and Wellman, 1977; Brown, Bransford, Ferrara, and Campione, 1983).

Strategies for remembering When an adult is presented with a series of items and told to repeat them a moment later, she does her best to "keep them in mind." She rehearses, perhaps by repeating the items mentally, perhaps by organizing them in various ways. But the very young child doesn't do this, for he hasn't yet learned how. Some first precursors of rehearsal are found at age three. In one study, three-year-olds watched while an experimenter placed a toy dog under one of two containers. The experimenter told the children that he'd leave the room for a little while, but that they should tell him where the dog was hidden as soon as he came back. During the interval, some children kept on looking at the hiding place and nodding "yes"; others steadfastly maintained their eye on the wrong container while shaking their head "no"; yet others kept their hand tightly grasping the correct container. They had found a way of building a bridge between past and present by performing an overt action—keeping the toy dog in their mind by marking its location with their body. Piaget, who believed that all mental activity is ultimately an outgrowth of overt action, might well have been pleased at this outcome (Wellman, Ritter, and Flavell, 1975).

Keeping one's hand on the to-be-remembered object may be a forerunner of rehearsal, but it's still a far cry from the real thing. Genuine rehearsal does not occur spontaneously until around age five or six. One experiment used subjects of five, seven, and ten years of age. The stimuli were pictures of seven common objects (e.g., a pipe, a flag, an owl, etc.), and the experimenter slowly pointed at three of them in turn. The children's job was to point at the three pictures in the same order after a fifteen-second interval. During this interval their eyes were covered (by a specially designed space helmet) so they couldn't bridge the interval by looking at the pictures, or by surreptitiously pointing at them. Not surprisingly, the older children did better on the recall test than the younger ones (Figure 14.17). Was this because they had greater memory capacity? The main cause lay elsewhere. One of the experimenters was a trained lip reader who observed that almost all of the ten-year-olds were silently mouthing the words—that is, rehearsing—compared to only 10 percent of the five-year-olds. The older children remembered more than the younger ones, not because they had more "memory space," but because they had used it better (Flavell, Beach, and Chinsky, 1966).

With increasing age, the strategies used for remembering become more efficient. As children grow older, they are more likely to supplement rote repetition by various forms of active rehearsal in which the items are grouped and organized. This trend has educational implications, for it also appears in the schoolroom. There students have to "study"—that is, read, understand, and remember. To do this, they use various means—they underline, take notes, write outlines. As one might expect, tenth-graders are more adept at using these techniques than fifth- and seventh-graders—they are more likely to copy relevant topic sentences, and occasionally they may invent their own way of summarizing what they've read (Brown, Bransford, Ferrara, and Campione, 1983).

METACOGNITION

When young nonrehearsers are taught to rehearse, they will then recall as well as their age-mates who rehearsed on their own. But there is one problem. When later presented with another memory task, many of these subjects will abandon the rehearsal method they have just been taught. This is especially likely if the new task is somewhat different from the old. A child might be taught to remember a set of names by reciting it aloud, but he won't apply the same principle to a shopping list. What is evidently lacking is a "master plan" for dealing with memory tasks in general, a strategy for using strategies (Flavell, 1970, 1977).

Normal adults adopt this higher-order strategy as a matter of course whenever they try to learn. They know that remembering telephone numbers, or traffic directions, or the names of the twelve cranial nerves are at bottom similar memory tasks. They also know that trying to commit them to memory requires certain mental activities—perhaps rehearsal, or rhythmic and semantic grouping, all of which are lower-order strategies that are subsumed under the general memory master plan. But young children lack this general insight. They don't recognize what all memory tasks have in common. As a result, they don't realize that what helps in mastering one will also help in mastering the other. The adult's strategy of using strategies is an instance of a class of higher-order cognitive processes that go under the general label of ***metacognition.*** Human adults can reflect on the cognitive operations whereby they gain knowledge. They know, and they also know a good deal about *what* they know and *how* they come to know it. But in children, metacognition is less well developed. Take memory. An adult has a fairly realistic idea of what he might or might not recall. When briefly shown pictures of four common objects, he will predict that he could recall them correctly after one presentation; when shown ten such pictures, he will predict that he could not. First- and second-graders are much less realistic about what they can and cannot do (Yussen and Levy, 1975).

Metacognition is not limited to memory. Older children and adults manifest it in perception so that they can do more than perceive—they can recognize the role of perspective, know the difference between reality and illusion, and become artists and art connoisseurs (Flavell, Flavell, and Green, 1983). They manifest it in language, so that they can do more than talk and understand—they can play with language, as in puns or poems, recognize that some sentences are ill-formed, and become poets or linguists (Gleitman, Gleitman, and Shipley, 1972). They also manifest metacognition in thinking and problem solving. Of course we think and solve problems, but we can do more—we can use general strategies for reaching solutions, know when we need more information, can recognize a paradox, and may become scientists or logicians. It may well be that metacognitive processes of this kind are one of the distinguishing hallmarks of adult human intelligence (Gleitman, 1985).

Whatever the area of metacognition, the general finding is that it develops with age. One study was on comprehension. Six-, seven-, and eight-year-olds were shown a magic trick and were given "instructions" as to how to perform it. The children's job was to indicate whether these instructions were clear and to make suggestions about how they might be improved. In actual fact, the "instructions" were hopelessly inadequate. To give an example, the experimenter put a plate on an empty cup and wrapped a penny in a piece of paper. She then placed the

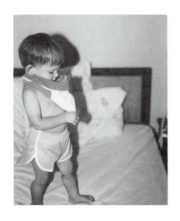

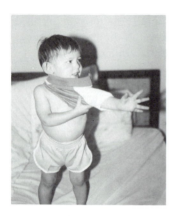

From apprentice to master At two, getting the right body part through the right hole of a shirt is still a major problem. Only a few years later, dressing has become an automatized skill. (Photographs courtesy of Kathy Hirsh-Passek)

wrapped penny on the plate and apparently pushed it through the plate into the cup below where it landed with a clink. Her "explanation" of how to do the trick would have puzzled Houdini:

> . . . Here's the trick. When you wrap the penny you only pretend to wrap it. It really falls in your lap like this. (The experimenter demonstrates.)

Most of the younger children seemed to be completely oblivious to the fact that the "instructions" had nothing to do with the task at hand. They said they understood, didn't ask for further information, and blithely tried to perform the trick on their own. There was something altogether inadequate about their metacognition of their own comprehension. They didn't know that they didn't understand (Markman, 1979).

THE DEVELOPMENT OF COGNITIVE MASTERY

How does any of this help us to explain why cognitive development occurs? From an information-processing point of view, what happens is that the child acquires ever more knowledge—about the world, about his own cognitive functioning, and about ways in which he can add to his knowledge and understanding. As his knowledge expands, so do his strategies (and later on, his strategies for using strategies) for remembering and thinking. These strategies eventually become so automatized that they allow him to circumvent the limited capacity of his cognitive system (Case, 1974; Shatz, 1978).

Seen in this light, the cognitive attainments that Piaget regarded as a symptom of concrete (let alone, formal) operations may be analogous to the higher-order chunkings of the master telegrapher, pianist, or chess player. These masters don't have to plod through a message letter by letter, or look at each chess piece individually—as a result, they can take giant mental steps. The ability to conserve number and quantity confers a similar advantage. The child who can truly conserve sees that there are certain underlying invariant qualities that remain intact despite all sorts of apparent deformations. As a result, she can disregard various superficial differences; she doesn't have to count the items in each row, or worry about the shape of the two jars. Her cognitive task has been simplified, for one concept can now subsume many individual instances.

Can this general approach explain why cognitive development occurs in a certain orderly sequence? It might, again by analogy with chunking in the development of skills. The apprentice telegraph operator goes through successive stages of mastery: letters, then letter sequences, then familiar words. This is presumably because each successive chunking level is based on lower levels in the hierarchy. The fact that all apprentice telegraph operators go through similar stages suggests two things: first, that they can all learn by hierarchical chunking, and second, that they were all exposed to the same linguistic world in which they encountered the same letter clusters (in English, combinations such as *th* or *ly* but not *sb*).

It may be that the developing child is in the same situation as the apprentice telegrapher. Like the telegrapher, the child is presumably capable of learning by chunking (although at a more primitive level to start with). And, again like the telegrapher, the child is faced with a world of complex relations whose mastery probably requires a step-by-step progression in which higher-order concepts (such as conservation of number) are based on lower-order ones (like object permanence). The near-universal, orderly sequence of cognitive development is sometimes taken as evidence for a maturation-centered approach. Maturation may indeed play a role in determining this sequence, but this orderly progression may also reflect the fact that all children live in the same physical world. It doesn't matter whether they live in a high-rise apartment or a teepee; in both environments the quantity of a liquid is unchanged by its container. The principles that eight-year-olds understand and that four-year-olds do not concern the basic dimensions of space, time, number, mass, and causality. These principles describe certain invariant properties of the world in which all children live. And as such, they might be learned by some process of hierarchical chunking.

Seen from this perspective, cognitive development is produced by the progressive acquisition of ever more complex conceptual chunkings. As a result, the child gradually progresses from being a complete novice to becoming an all-around expert—in other words, an adult.

SUMMARY

1. All humans go through a process of *cognitive development.* According to Jean Piaget, they do so by passing through the same sequence of *developmental stages.*

2. In Piaget's account, the first stage is the period of *sensory-motor intelligence,* which lasts until about two years of age. During this period, the infant develops the concept of *object permanence,* builds up *coordinated sensory-motor schemas,* becomes capable of genuine *imitation,* and acquires increasingly complex mental *representations.*

3. The next period lasts till about five or six. It is the *preoperational period* during which children are capable of representational thought but lack mental operations that order and organize these thoughts. Characteristic deficits include an inability to *conserve* number and quantity; and *egocentrism,* an inability to take another person's perspective, which is related to a very concrete approach to moral judgment.

4. At about six or seven, children have begun to acquire a system of mental operations that allows them to manipulate their representations with consequent success in conservation tasks and similar tests. But until they are about eleven, they are still in the period of *concrete operations* which lacks an element of abstractness. After eleven, they enter the period of *formal operations.* As a result, they can consider hypothetical possibilities and become capable of scientific thought.

5. Piaget's views of cognitive development have come in for some serious criticisms. Some concern his views of the infant's native endowment. According to James Gibson and Eleanor Gibson, many aspects of the perception of objects and events are built into the perceptual system from the very start. Evidence comes from studies of infant perception, such as intersensory relations, early correspondence between sight and reaching movements, and appropriate reactions to perceptual occlusion in early infancy. Other criticisms suggest that Piaget underestimated the preschoolers' abilities and overestimated their egocentrism.

6. Trying to explain cognitive growth has turned out to be even more difficult and controversial than trying to describe it. The nativist approach assumes that development is largely driven by *maturation.* Empiricists assume that the answer is *specific learning.* Piaget himself rejected both empiricist and nativist extremes, arguing that development involves a constant interchange between organism and environment as the environment is *assimilated* to the child's current schema and the schema in turn *accommodates* to aspects of the environment. A current approach sees cognitive development as a change in *information processing* and argues that increased mental growth is based in part on the acquisition of better and larger *chunks* and of various *strategies* for thinking and remembering.

CHAPTER 15

Cognitive Development: Language

BY LILA R. GLEITMAN AND HENRY GLEITMAN

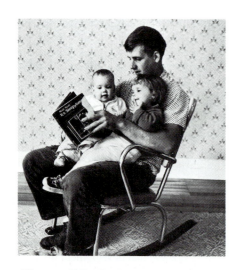

(Photograph by Ken Heyman)

Thus far, our discussion of cognitive development has focused on the way the child perceives, remembers, and thinks. But there is another aspect of the child's cognitive growth that we have barely touched upon as yet: the development of language. Whatever their talent, their motivation, or their station in life, normal human children learn their native tongue to a high level of proficiency during the preschool years. This holds for British upper-class children reared by nannies and sent to the poshest nursery schools, as well as children reared in poverty on the streets of New York and in the deserts of North Africa. How do children accomplish this feat?

There is little doubt that language learning depends on a rich innate endowment (which matures over developmental time). That the potential for language is "built in" to humans and to no other organisms is easy to see. All the children in the house but none of the pet dogs and cats acquire language. This is so even though, in many ways, the infants, cats, and dogs all share the same environment. This even holds for the "baby talk" that mothers use when speaking to their young children. Dog owners often employ a very similar mode of speaking to their pet dogs (Hirsh-Pasek and Treiman, 1982). But despite this similarity in environment, even the cleverest dogs learn only to respond to a few words such as *Blackie, out,* and *biscuit,* while the children learn just about everything there is to learn about language.

It is just as obvious that language is learned from the environment as that the capacity to learn it is built in. For after all, children raised in Greece by Greek speakers learn Greek, while children raised in France by French speakers learn French. In our discussion of language learning, we shall try to understand which components of language are pre-programmed and thus emerge in a maturationally driven sequence, and which are learned and thus depend crucially on specific environmental exposure. As we shall see, here as in so many other aspects of development, built-in factors and environment continually interact. The end result of this interaction is the marvelous speech and comprehension capacity of the adult.

THE PROBLEM OF LANGUAGE LEARNING

Language seems to pose awesome problems for the mere babes who must learn it. It is not even obvious which sounds are relevant and which can be ignored. The infant listening to adults is exposed to an enormous jumble of sounds. Some of these sounds constitute speech, but others are coughs, hums, whistles, and even animal imitations ("and the big cow said 'Mooooooooo' "). How does the learner ever sort this jumble of noise to discover which of the sounds she hears are speech sounds and which are not?

Let's suppose the infant has somehow managed to solve this task, and knows which sounds are relevant to language. How does she relate these sounds to meanings? Here matters become even more complicated. One problem is that the same speech events seem to refer to different things at different times. Thus the caregiver may say "dog" when the child sees a Great Dane, but also when the child sees the very different looking Boston terrier or even a fluffy stuffed toy. Symmetrically, sometimes the child will hear different speech signals when she observes a single thing, for the mother may refer to the pet in the house as "Spot," "the dog," "that animal," or even as "that housewrecker." And oftentimes, when the child is attending closely to the dog, the mother will be saying something quite irrelevant, such as "Time for your nap, honey." Under the circumstances, how does the child ever discover that "dog" means 'dog' while "nap" refers to sleeping?

It is clear that the young language learner is confronted with a confusing welter of sounds and information about the world. But she somehow makes sense out of all this jumble even so. If she is a learner of English, she extracts the general fact that the sound "see" means 'gaze with the eyes;' if she is a learner of Spanish, she extracts the different fact that the same sound "see" (as in "Si!") means 'yes.' The question is how.

IS LANGUAGE LEARNING THE ACQUISITION OF A SKILL?

The first hypothesis that comes to mind to explain language learning is that it is acquired in much the way in which humans learn any skill whatever, such as knitting or hitting a tennis ball. If so, the laws of simple learning studied by behavior theorists might help to provide the framework for an answer. In fact, behavior theorists such as Skinner have tried to account for language learning in just this way (Skinner, 1957). But it turns out that this approach won't work. To be sure, *something* about language must be directly learned from the environ-

495

ment—for example, that "see" means 'yes' or 'gaze with the eyes.' But even this rather simple and specific example of learning is hard to describe by such familiar learning mechanisms as imitation, correction, and reinforcement. Let us see why this is so.

Language Learning and Imitation

Is language learning based on *imitation?* The answer is no. It is true that young children say "dog" and not "perro" or "chien" if they are exposed to English, and this certainly looks like imitation. But the real trick in word learning and use is creative: The word *dog* must apply to new dogs that language learners see. What served as a name for the neighborhood poodle and the pet bulldog must apply to the birthday terrier as well. Since language learners soon come to call new dogs "dog," we must acknowledge that the process of word learning involves much more than imitation. Moreover, young children are very selective in which words they will imitate. Consider such closed-class words as *the* and *of.* These are among the most common words that young children hear. Yet they never say them until they are well on the road to advanced language knowledge.

What goes for words goes for sentences as well. Young children say sentences they have never heard and thus have had no opportunity to imitate. For instance, a mother may say to her child "I love you, Jane." But in response the child may very well say "I hate you, Mommy" or "I'm going to crayon a face on this wall." These sentences are clear, though unwelcome, creative language acts of Jane's. They could not possibly have been learned by imitation.

Language Learning and Correction

Another popular hypothesis about language learning is that it is based on explicit *correction* or *reinforcement* by parents. According to this view, grammatical mistakes are immediately pointed out to the young learner, who subsequently avoids them. But in fact, this hypothesis is false. In actual practice, mistakes in grammar and pronunciation generally go unremarked, as in the following exchange:

> 2-year-old: Mama isn't boy, he a girl.
> Mother: That's right.

The situation is quite different if the child makes an error of fact. In that case, the mother often does provide a correction:

> 2-year-old: And Walt Disney comes on Tuesday.
> Mother: No, he does not.

(Brown and Hanlon, 1970, p. 49)

These findings are perfectly reasonable. Parents are out to create socialized and rational beings, not little grammarians, and so they correct the rules of conduct, not the "rules of grammar." Another reason for the parents' usual tolerance is less obvious. Correction (negative reinforcement) doesn't work, as is shown by the following interchange:

Child: Nobody don't like me.
Mother: No, say "Nobody likes me."
Child: Nobody don't like me.
Mother: No, say "Nobody likes me."
Child: Nobody don't like me.
          [seven more repetitions of this same interchange]
Mother: No, now listen carefully: "Nobody likes me."
Child: Oh! Nobody don't likes me.

(McNeill, 1966, p. 69)

Such examples make it clear that children don't acquire their language by imitation, reinforcement, or correction. They do not come to the task of language learning as little robots who can only notice and copy whatever they hear, whenever they hear it. But then how do they ever learn to speak and comprehend?

THE NORMAL COURSE OF LANGUAGE LEARNING

As a first step in understanding language acquisition, we will discuss the child's progress in the early years of life, beginning with the infant who neither speaks nor understands.

The Social Origins of Speech Production

Children begin to vocalize from the first moments of life. They cry, they coo, and at about four months of age they begin to babble. They make sounds such as "ga" and "bagoo" that sound very much like real words—except that, insofar as anyone can tell, these babbles have no real or intended meaning. To be sure, such cries often signal some emotional state such as joy or fretfulness and will cause the caregiver to respond. But this is not why children coo and babble. This is shown by the fact that even deaf infants, who cannot hear their own or others' vocalizations, also coo and babble. Apparently, it is simply natural for infants to vocalize. But in the hearing child, these "gagas" and "googoos" soon take on a social quality. By six months or so, children are more likely to babble and coo when an adult vocalizes to them (Collis, 1975; de Villiers and de Villiers, 1978).

Though true speech is absent in the first year of life, prelinguistic children have their own ways of making contact with the minds, emotions, and social behaviors of others. Quite early in life, babies begin to exchange looks, caresses, and touches with caregivers. Several investigators have suggested that these gestures are precursors and organizers of the language development to follow. The idea is that the gesture-and-babble interaction helps children to become linguistically socialized; to realize, for instance, that each participant in a conversation "takes a turn," and responds to the other (Bruner, 1974/1975; Sinclair, 1970, 1973).

A further important function of preverbal communication is to allow babies and adults to make reference to the same things, events, and scenes in view (Bruner, 1974/1975). Parents and infants begin to establish a mutuality of reference as they both gaze at the same object, wave it about, and point to it. Even if the child learner is blind, similar coattentive methods, such as mutual touching of objects, are developed between the mother and the young child (Urwin, 1983).

Social origins of speech (Top: *Photograph by George Zimbel, Monkmeyer.* Bottom: *Photograph by Michael Hardy, Woodfin Camp)*

True speech begins just when mutual gesturing of this kind becomes increasingly focused and precise. The relationship between mutual gesturing and the onset of meaningful speech makes a lot of sense, for as the parent and child mutually touch and wave, the parent naturally accompanies the interaction by naming and talking about objects and situations. Surely, the mother's naming of items as she and the child play with them and wave them about helps the child discover which sounds in English mean 'Eleanor' or 'Joey,' which mean 'see,' and which mean 'rabbit.'

Thus language knowledge is essentially social and interpersonal from the beginning. Though the capacity to learn it is built into the individual brain of the child, specific knowledge of a particular language requires social interactions between more than one person at a time. To speak to another, one has to have an idea—no matter how primitive—that the other lives in the same, mutually perceived, world (Bates, 1976).

Discovering the Forms of Language

Infants' first attempts to speak are rather unimpressive. But careful analysis shows that they know more about language than they seem to at first glance. For at a very early age, they make some perceptual distinctions about the sounds they hear that are crucial to later language learning.

THE RUDIMENTS OF PHONEME DISCRIMINATION

We have previously seen that all languages of the world are built out of a few basic sound distinctions (see Chapter 9). Each language uses some forty or so basic sounds *(phonemes)* out of which all the words in that language are constructed. But these linguistic sound atoms vary from language to language. Thus in English, there is a crucial difference between the sounds "l" and "r" (as in *lob* vs. *rob*). Though physically these sounds are quite similar, each of them falls within a different phoneme in English. As a result, English speakers can readily pronounce both sounds and notice the difference between them. In contrast, this difference has no linguistic significance in Japanese, and so Japanese speakers can neither perceive this distinction nor make this distinction in their speech. For the Japanese, "l" and "r" sounds fall within a single phoneme. (Of course the Japanese make various other sound distinctions that English speakers cannot make or hear.) How does an infant learn which sound distinctions are the phonemes of *his* language?

The answer seems to be that initially infants can respond to just about all sound distinctions made in any language. They discover the phonemes of their language by learning to *ignore* the distinctions that don't matter in their language. Their first step in understanding, say, Japanese, is to learn not to become speakers of all the other 5,500 languages spoken on earth.

Evidence for this view comes from studies which show that two-month-old babies can distinguish between the sounds "ba" and "pa." The experimenters used a version of the habituation method (see pp. 480–81). The babies were given a pacifier. Whenever they sucked on the pacifier, the syllable "ba" was broadcast

A

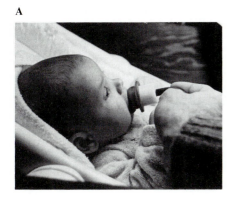

B

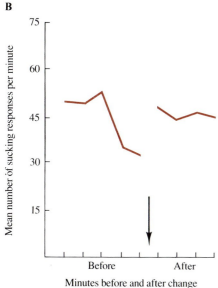

15.1 **Sucking rate and speech perception in the infant** *(A) An infant sucks to hear "pa" or "ba." (Photograph courtesy of Philip Morse, University of Wisconsin) (B) The graph shows the sucking rate of four-month-olds to "pa" or "ba." The infants soon become habituated, and the sucking rate drops. When a new stimulus is substituted ("ba" for "pa" and "pa" for "ba"), the infant dishabituates and sucks quickly once again. Similar results have been obtained for one-month-olds. The point of the shift is indicated by the arrow. (From Eimas, Siqueland, Jusczyk, and Vigorito, 1971)*

over a loudspeaker. The infants quickly learned that their sucking led to the sound, and they began sucking faster and faster, since they evidently enjoyed hearing this vocalization. After a while, the babies habituated to the "ba" sound and their sucking rate diminished. At this point, the experimenters changed the speech sound from "ba" to "pa." Now the babies started to suck again at a rapid rate. They had presumably become dishabituated. This result indicates that they could discriminate between the sounds "ba" and "pa" (see Figure 15.1; Eimas, Siqueland, Jusczyk, and Vigorito, 1971).

One may argue that the "ba"–"pa" effect is based on prior learning since the subjects in this experiment had already reached the ripe old age of two months when tested. (Younger neonates are hard to test with this procedure because when given the pacifier, they contentedly go to sleep rather than sucking industriously.) To show that speech sound discriminations of this sort are built in rather than learned, the experimenters tested Japanese babies with the sounds "la" and "ra," which their adult Japanese parents cannot distinguish from each other. But the babies could and did show the increased sucking rate when the loudspeaker switched from "la" to "ra." It appears that young infants are naturally predisposed to attend to speech sounds that will eventually form the phoneme building blocks of their language. It is not that American (or Japanese) children have to acquire the discrimination "la"–"ra." This much is built in, allowing babies to learn either English or Japanese. Later stages of learning will be a matter of ignoring some of these distinctions—just the ones that never affect meaning in the particular language the child is being exposed to.

THE RUDIMENTS OF THE SENTENCE UNIT: "MOTHERESE"

In Chapter 9, we saw that a crucial characteristic of all human language is that it includes *syntax*—general principles that allow us to combine a finite stock of words into an infinite number of sentences. To discover what these principles are, the infant must first recognize what a sentence is—where one ends and the next one begins. How does he master this task?

One cue that helps the infant is a special way of speaking that is almost universally employed by adults when they talk to babies. This special speech style has come to be called, somewhat whimsically, *Motherese* (Newport, 1977). Of course, "Motherese" is something of a misnomer, for this style of speaking is adopted by fathers as well as mothers and by strangers as well as relatives when they are talking to an infant. It is characterized by a special tone of voice, with high pitch, slow rate of talking, and exaggerated intonations. (Just hold a baby and talk to him; you will discover that you irresistibly use Motherese, and that you will feel quite awkward if you try to sound the way you do when you talk to adults.) This way of talking may be especially informative to the young learner. One reason is that it is slower and more distinct than the rapid-fire mumblings of adult-to-adult speech. This facilitates picking out the words and the phrases that the child must acquire.

There is good evidence that infants prefer Motherese to adult-to-adult speech, even though they as yet understand neither. One investigator conditioned four-month-old babies to turn their heads to the left or right so they could listen to speech sounds that came out of two loudspeakers. When the baby turned his head toward the loudspeaker on the right, he heard Motherese (produced not by his own, but by another child's mother). When he turned to the left, he heard adult-to-adult talk. The infants soon began to turn their heads to the right, indicating a preference for Motherese despite the unfamiliarity of the speaker's voice (Fernald, 1984; Fernald and Simon, 1984).

This remarkable coadjustment between adult and child—the caregiver finding it irresistible to speak in a special way to infants, and the infants finding that style of speech bewitching to listen to—is a first hint of how our species is biologically adapted for the task of learning language. Indeed, such early observers as Charles Darwin (1877) had already noticed these protolinguistic interactions between mothers and their infants, and he called Motherese "the sweet music of the species."

The tones of Motherese and the responsive cooing of the infant surely are among the behavioral patterns related to the affective bonding between caregiver and child. But Motherese has more specific uses in language learning as well. Motherese has acoustic properties that make it useful for learning to recognize the phrases and sentence units in speech. Both in adult speech and in Motherese there are certain sound cues that mark off the boundaries between phrases and sentences. These include changes of pitch: The pitch tends to start high at the beginnings of sentences and to go down at their ends. Another characteristic is the presence of pauses (brief periods of silence) that often occur at the boundaries between sentences. But these cues (and their co-occurrence) are much more reliable and clear in the exaggerated style of Motherese than in the speech adults use to each other. As a result, the Motherese style may help the infant to recognize sentence units and their phrase components (Gleitman and Wanner, 1982, 1984).

Evidence comes from a recent experiment in which the investigators asked whether seven-month-olds prefer to hear speech in which these two cues (pitch fall and silent interval) occur together to speech in which they do not. To find out, they inserted extra-long pauses (one second in length) in recorded Motherese. The pause was inserted either at the end of sentences in that speech (where a fall in pitch naturally occurred) or some arbitrary distance earlier (three words from the end of the sentence, a place where the pitch usually did *not* fall). A loudspeaker on the child's left broadcast the speech in which the pauses co-occurred with the fall in pitch; a loudspeaker on the right broadcast the speech in which the pause was placed elsewhere. The infants showed a marked preference for the speech that came from the left in which the fall in pitch and the pause coincided (as shown by the fact that they turned their heads toward this rather than toward the other loudspeaker). This could hardly be because the infants preferred pauses at the end of sentences—for they presumably didn't know as yet what sentences are. What they preferred was speech in which a pause went along with a fall in pitch. A pause in the middle of sentences, where the pitch was still high, evidently sounded less natural (Hirsh-Pasek, Kemler-Nelson, Jusczyk, Wright, and Druss, forthcoming).

This preference for the coincidence of falling pitch and pause will be useful for the babies in later language learning. For they eventually must learn what is a sentence and what is not, and this coincidence will provide an important clue. It may well be that infants are specially tuned by nature to notice just those aspects of the sound stream that will be important to language learning—and that their caregivers are specially tuned by nature to make these properties available by exaggerating them in Motherese. (For discussions of the relation between language and speech perception, see Liberman, 1970; Liberman and Pisoni, 1977).

The One-Word Speaker

When and how does the child learn words? Children begin to understand a few words that their caregivers are saying as early as five to eight months of age. For example, some six-month-olds will regularly glance up at the ceiling light in response to hearing their mother say "light." Actual talking begins sometime between about ten and twenty months of age. Almost invariably, children's first utterances are one word long. Some first words refer to simple interaction with adults, such as *hi* and *peekaboo.* Others are names, such as *Mama* and *Fido.* Most of the rest are simple nouns, such as *duck* and *spoon,* adjectives such as *hot* and *big,* and action verbs such as *give* and *push.* And lest one think that child rearing is all pleasure, one of the first words is almost always a resounding *No.* The early vocabulary tends to concern things that can be moved around and manipulated or that move by themselves in the child's environment. For example, children are less likely to talk about ceilings than about rolling balls. And this early vocabulary refers more often to attributes and actions children can perceive in the outside world, such as shape or movement, than to internal states and feelings, such as pain or ideas (Nelson, 1973; Huttenlocher, 1974).

Missing totally are certain closed-class words and suffixes, such as *the, and, can, be,* and *-ed* (see Chapter 9). These are among the items the child hears most frequently from adults, but they are never uttered by the beginning learner even so. There are two reasons for why these closed-class items are late to appear. One has to do with how hard they are to perceive. As we saw before, infants are especially interested in such properties of the sound wave as high pitch. But the closed-class words usually occur with low pitch; in general they are not stressed in speech. A second reason is that an important function of the closed-class items is to help in sentence analysis (see Chapter 9). But since the young children say only one word at a time, they presumably have little need to utter items whose central function is to organize groups of words into sentence form.

WORD MEANING AT THE ONE-WORD STAGE

It is hard to find out precisely what young children mean by the words they say. To be sure, we hear the tots say "rabbit" and "ball" but what exactly do these words mean to their young users? One reason for our relative ignorance about these earliest word meanings is that the same scene or event can often be described in many ways, depending on the particular words chosen. The very same creature can be described as *Peter, the rabbit, the animal, the creature with a tail,* and so forth. Therefore, even if a young child says "rabbit" on seeing a rabbit, he may mean 'tail' or 'animal' or 'white' or even 'runs by' for all we know.

The same problem that makes it hard for investigators to find out exactly what the children mean ought to make it hard for the children themselves to discover these meanings. Even if the helpful mother points out a rabbit to her child, saying "rabbit," the child still has a big job to do. He has to make up his mind whether the utterance "rabbit" means a particular animal (in which case "rabbit" is a name, such as 'Peter Rabbit'), anything that falls within the animal kingdom (in which case "rabbit" means 'animal'), anything within a particular species (so "rabbit" means 'rabbit'), or even some property, part, or action of a rabbit (in which case "rabbit" means 'white' or 'tail' or 'hops'; see Figure 15.2, p. 502).

501

A

B

15.2 Symmetrical problems for child learners and investigators of child language *(A) The child's helpful mother points out a rabbit, saying "rabbit." The child sees a rabbit—but also sees an animal, an ear, and the ground beneath the rabbit. Which one does the mother mean by the word* rabbit? *(B) The mother's (and the investigator's) problem in understanding young children's speech is much the same. The child may say "rabbit" when she observes a rabbit, but for all the mother knows the child may have made an error in learning, and thus may mean something different by this word.*

Because such problems for the learner are real, beginners often ***undergeneralize*** the meaning of a word: They may know that the word *house* refers to small toy buildings but not that it also refers to large real buildings. And they may ***overgeneralize*** the meanings of other words. They may think that the word *Daddy* refers to any man, not just their own father. These overgeneralizations and undergeneralizations are common for the first seventy-five or so words the child utters, but very rare thereafter (Rescorla, 1980). At later stages of learning, the child is almost always exactly on the mark in using words to refer to the right things in the world. We shall return in later discussion to how the child manages to be right overwhelmingly often despite the real problem of rabbits, rabbit parts, and the like. But for now it is important to realize that even the young overgeneralizer is surprisingly correct in what he has learned. Though he just about always observes the ground whenever he observes a rabbit (and hears the word *rabbit*)—because rabbits can't fly or swim, and thus are always found near the ground—still, he virtually never mistakenly learns that "rabbit" means 'ground' (or that "ground" means 'rabbit'). His only error is to make the category a bit too broad or narrow at first.

Developmental psychologists have made a number of attempts to learn something about the child's earliest word meanings, despite all the difficulties of interpretation that arise. Some investigators take a ***functional*** approach. They believe that children use words to classify things together that act alike in their world—a ball is that which one throws and bounces in the playground (Nelson, 1973). Others argue for a ***featural*** approach. These investigators believe that children use words to designate things that look alike in at least some regards, things that share certain perceptual features. Thus "ball" may be overgeneralized to anything that is round, including faces, balls, and the moon (Clark, 1973). Still others believe that early word meanings are based on ***prototypes.*** In their view, children call things "ball" to the extent that they resemble a particular ball which serves as the model (prototype) for the entire concept. Thus only things like the large red balls the child has seen may be called "ball," so the concept is undergeneralized. It may not apply to small green balls (Anglin, 1975; J. de Villiers, 1980; Keil and Batterman, 1984). And yet others believe that the child's word meanings are about the same as those of adults (Carey, 1978, 1982). All of these views probably have some truth to them. Different aspects of vocabulary may be acquired differently and children's word learning is probably different at different developmental moments.

PROPOSITIONAL MEANING AT THE ONE-WORD STAGE

There is another question about children's first words: Are these little foreshortened sentence attempts? That is, do children have a proposition and attitude in mind when they say "Doggie!" as a dog runs by? To listening adults, it does seem as though children have in mind a comment, request, question, or command. Thus adults are inclined to interpret "Eat" as "The duck is eating" when the child says it as he watches a duck eat, but as "Eat this cookie!" if it is said as the child forces a cookie into a stuffed duck's beak. Many investigators of child language believe young children have propositional ideas in mind even when they are speaking only one word at a time.

One basis for this belief is that one-word speakers seem to fill out their—one-word—speech with accompanying gestures (Greenfield and Smith, 1976). A child may say "rabbit" and also reach toward a rabbit at the same time, so the meaning 'Give me that rabbit' or 'I want that rabbit' comes across to the watching-listening adult. Still, it is unclear whether these toddlers comprehend syntactic distinctions—for instance, that specific arrangements of words contribute to meaning. That is, one-word speakers may not realize that "Kiss the doggie" and "The doggie kisses" would mean different things in English (Bloom, 1970, 1973; Huttenlocher, 1974; Gleitman, Shipley, and Smith, 1978; Sachs and Truswell, 1978).

The Two-Word (Telegraphic) Speaker

A similar pattern of early language development is found in children all over the world who learn different languages under different conditions of child rearing; they all show about the same developmental timeframe (Lenneberg, 1967; Bowerman, 1973; Slobin, 1973). In each language community, children speak no intelligible words until ten to twenty months of age. Then for some period of time, most children will say only one word at a time, as we have just seen.

Many drastic changes take place beginning at about the second birthday. The child's vocabulary begins to spurt, rising to many hundreds of words. Soon, she begins to put words together into primitive sentences, and then we are aware most poignantly that another human mind is among us.

Though we can recognize propositional ideas in these first sentences, these hardly sound like adult speech. Generally, each rudimentary "sentence" is only two words long, and each of its component words comes from the open class. The closed-class words and suffixes are still largely missing from the learner's speech, and so her sentences sound like the short ones we often use in telegrams and

A

B

C

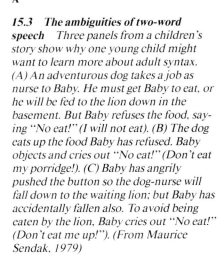

15.3 The ambiguities of two-word speech *Three panels from a children's story show why one young child might want to learn more about adult syntax. (A) An adventurous dog takes a job as nurse to Baby. He must get Baby to eat, or he will be fed to the lion down in the basement. But Baby refuses the food, saying "No eat!" (I will not eat). (B) The dog eats up the food Baby has refused. Baby objects and cries out "No eat!" (Don't eat my porridge!). (C) Baby has angrily pushed the button so the dog-nurse will fall down to the waiting lion; but Baby has accidentally fallen also. To avoid being eaten by the lion, Baby cries out "No eat!" (Don't eat me up!"). (From Maurice Sendak, 1979)*

newspaper headlines: "Throw ball," "Daddy shoe," "No eat" (R. Brown and Bellugi, 1964).

These first sentences show some organization, however, despite their simplicity. From the earliest moments of "telegraphic" two-word speech, the words seem to be serially ordered according to the propositional roles they assume in the simplest (active declarative) sentences—doer, action, done-to. The child who says "Throw ball" usually does not say "Ball throw" to mean the same thing (Braine, 1963, 1976; R. Brown, 1973; de Villiers and de Villiers, 1973). With rare exceptions, the word order for two-word English speakers is the right one for the simplest sentences in English (and the word order for French speakers is right for French, etc.). Thus English-speaking children put the doer of the action first, and so will say "Mommy throw!" if they want the mother to throw the ball; and they put the done-to last, and so will say "Throw ball!" in approximately the same circumstances—and so mothers of two-year-olds are probably right in feeling a bit miffed if their child says "Throw Mommy!" The two-year-olds' correct use of word order tells us that these children now know something about English syntax, as well as knowing something about meaning: They know about doers of actions and that these come first in simple sentences, about actions which come next, and about done-to's which come last. Apparently it is only problems in memory and information handling that limit their sentences to two words for some period of time. (In fact, since the two-word sentence now expresses propositions so well, one might wonder why children bother to learn anything further; see Figure 15.3 for a demonstration of why two-word speech is not sufficient for precise human communication.)

The idea that two-word speakers "know" full underlying propositions (even though they don't fully express them) is bolstered by studies of children's responses to language from adults. One experiment showed that two-word speakers appreciate well-formed adult sentences even though they cannot yet speak them. They obey more frequently if the mother says "Throw me the ball!" (using the mother's own normal speech forms) than if she says "Throw ball!" (mimicking the child's own normal speech; Shipley, Smith, and Gleitman, 1969). In sum, there is good evidence that two-year-olds understand much of how propositional thought is expressed in sentences. But their earliest sentences fail to display this knowledge fully because the problems of memory and information handling make the task too hard.*

Later Stages of Language Learning

By two-and-a-half years or so, children progress beyond the two-word stage. Their utterances now become longer (Figure 15.4). They can say little sentences that contain all three terms of a basic proposition, and closed-class words have begun to appear. Their utterances are still short and simple, but—at least initially —they are quite correct as far as they go. Soon, however, a new phenomenon appears. Children start to make various kinds of errors in their word formation and in their syntax. Does this mean that they are *un*learning English?

OVERGENERALIZATION AGAIN

An example concerns the *-ed* suffix which represents 'pastness.' At the age of two and three, children use correct regular forms of the past tense (as in *walked* or *talked*), as well as correct irregular ones (such as *ran, came,* and *ate*). But at the age of four and five, these same children often say "runned," "comed," and "eated" (Ervin, 1964; Cazden, 1968; R. Brown, 1973; Kuczaj, 1977). And they resist correction even when they hear their parents use the correct form, as in the following exchange:

Child:	My teacher holded the baby rabbits and we patted them.
Mother:	Did you say your teacher held the baby rabbits?
Child:	Yes.
Mother:	What did you say she did?
Child:	She holded the baby rabbits and we patted them.
Mother:	Did you say she held them tightly?
Child:	No, she holded them loosely.

(Bellugi, 1971)

What has happened to this child who in earlier years said "held" but who now doggedly keeps saying "holded"? The answer seems to be that the child is now seeking general rules that operate over the whole vocabulary or set of sentence structures. If some words choose to be exceptions to these rules, so much the worse for these words. Thus the child now overgeneralizes the use of certain structures though, as we saw earlier, she no longer overgeneralizes the meanings of individual words.

A further example is plural formation. The general rule is to add -*s,* so the little learner says "foots" and "mouses." Another example is the use of nouns as verbs. The child has heard "John bats the ball," where *bat* means 'hit with a bat,' so he

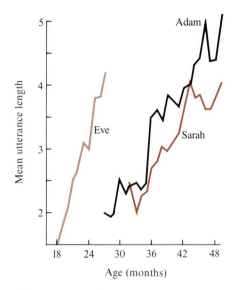

15.4   The growth of utterance length   *The mean utterance length in three children between 1½ and 4 years of age. The utterance length is measured in morphemes, so that the word* dolls *counts as two* (doll + s). *Note the variations among the children, who were all within the normal range. (After Brown, Cazden, and Bellugi-Klima, 1969)*

---

* The hypothesis that children appreciate the three terms of a proposition though information-processing limitations restrict their spoken sentences to two words fits in with an intriguing observation of the way sound patterns are learned at the same age. P. de Villiers (1978) noticed that at the age of two his child was unable to put the sounds "s" and "p" together, so he said "poon" instead of "spoon." A few months later, he could and did say "spoon." But in a complicated situation he fell back to his earlier ways; he said "table-poon" instead of "table-spoon." Here too there is evidence that the child may have certain knowledge but may be unable to exhibit it all when the task situation is complex.

invents "John *broomed* Mary" to mean 'John hit Mary with a broom' (Clark, 1982). A more complicated case is the invention of so-called **causative verbs** (Bowerman, 1982). Children apparently notice that there are many ways to express causation in English. Given a sentence like "The ship sank," one can express the causal agent in this affair by saying "John made the ship sink," "John caused the ship to sink," or "John sank the ship." So since children know sentences like "She eats," they make an analogy from *sink* and say "Don't eat the baby" to mean 'Don't cause her to eat' (don't feed her).

THE DEVELOPMENT OF WORD MEANING

We have already discussed some of the difficulties children must confront as they try to discover which word stands for which meaning. But even so, they seem to experience very little difficulty. Five-year-olds have a vocabulary of about 5,000 to 10,000 words, whereas at one year of age they had a vocabulary of only 10 words or so. Simple computation shows that they must have learned an average of 5 to 7 words a day—every day, every week, every month—starting from about twelve months of age (Carey, 1978). It is likely that none of us adults could do as well.

Syntactic clues to word meaning   Part of the explanation for this remarkably rapid learning may come from the quite regular ways in which mothers talk to their children, for syntax often contains useful hints about what a word could mean. Let's return to the problem of learning which word means 'ear' and which means 'rabbit' (see p. 502 and Figure 15.2). It turns out that when mothers refer to the whole rabbit, they use simple sentences ("This is a rabbit") and often point to the rabbit at the same time. But when they want to refer to the ear, they first refer to the whole rabbit, and then use such words as *his* in referring to the part: "This is a rabbit; these are his ears" (Shipley, Kuhn, and Madden, 1983).

Are the very young learners attentive to such clues in the *structure* of sentences in order to discover the *meanings* of words? In one study, infants of only one-and-a-half years of age were presented with nonsense words such as *zup,* which were used to refer to an unusual looking doll. To some of the children, the investigators said "This is a zup," while displaying the new doll. To others, they said "This is Zup." Notice that the word *a* in "a zup" implies to adults that there is a whole class of zups, while "zup" alone implies that this is a name for a single individual. Did these toddlers draw the same implication? Indeed they did, for the children introduced to "a zup" were happy to apply this word to new dolls that they were then shown ("Those are zups too"). In contrast, the children introduced to "Zup" refused to call any other new doll "zup." Thus, remarkably enough, mere toddlers use the syntax in which a word appears as clues to what it could mean (Katz, Baker, and MacNamara, 1974; see also Brown, 1957; Landau and Gleitman, 1985).

Conceptual clues to word meaning   Syntactic clues are useful to the learner. But much of the child's word learning is explained by how she is disposed to carve up **(categorize)** the world that she observes. Some ways of conceptualizing and organizing experience are natural to the child, while others are less natural (Rosch, 1973; Keil, 1979; Fodor, 1983). Thus the child can learn easily if she assumes that each word represents some "natural" organization of experience. One indication

15.5 The meaning of "look"
(A) A blindfolded, sighted three-year-old tilts her head upward in response to "Look up!," for to her the word look *means 'perceive by eye.' (B) A congenitally blind three-year-old raises her arms upward in response to "Look up!," for to her the word* look *means 'perceive by hand.'*
Drawings by Robert Thacker

of this is the fact that young children acquire the "basic-level" words (e.g., *dog*) before the superordinates *(animal)* or subordinates *(Chihuahua)* (Rosch, 1978; see Chapter 9). One might think this is just because the basic-level words are used most frequently to children. But this does not seem to be the explanation. In some homes, the words *Spot* or *Rex* (specific names) are used much more often than *dog* (a basic-level term), for obvious reasons. And it is true that in this case the young learner will soon utter "Spot" and not "dog." But she has first learned it as a basic-level term all the same. This is shown by the fact that she will then utter "Spot" to refer to the neighbor's dog as well as her own. She overgeneralizes *Spot* just enough to convert it from a specific name to the basic level of categorization—evidently, the most natural level for carving up experience (Mervis and Crisafi, 1978; Shipley and Kuhn, 1983).

Another series of studies indicates just how rich and subtle the child's word learning actually is. The young learners take their relatively sparse information about the world and use it to build up meanings that are important to their own perceptual and conceptual life. One example comes from studies of blind children (Landau and Gleitman, 1985). Blind children as young as two-and-a-half years use words like *look* and *see*. This is surprising, for these words seem to refer directly to the experience of vision. Indeed, a young sighted listener, even if her vision is blocked by a blindfold, will tilt her covered eyes upward when asked to "Look up!" This suggests that to the sighted child, looking *must* refer to vision (Figure 15.5A). But a congenitally blind child, when also told to "Look up!," shows that she too has a sensible interpretation of *look,* though a somewhat different one. Keeping her head immobile, the blind youngster reaches upward and searches the space above her body with her hands (Figure 15.5B). Thus each of these children understands *look* differently. But the meanings resemble each other even so. Both children realize that *look* has something to do with perceiving the world by use of the sense organs. The children arrive at meaningful interpretations of words even though their information about the world is often quite different.

LANGUAGE LEARNING AND LANGUAGE CHANGE

Our discussion of language learning has shown that children are not merely learners of the language. In the process of extracting language principles, they overgeneralize and become active and creative contributors to the learning process. In so doing, they arrange the language to their fancy as they acquire it. As a result, the children of the world can change their language whether their parents like it or not. And in fact, they not only can but do. The evolution of different languages is partially produced by children's failure to learn what is "hard," thus transforming the language into an easier one.

Languages change with the passage of time. Once Latin was spoken in Rome, but now the language spoken there has changed so that it would be unintelligible to the ancient Romans; this new language is called Italian. Latin was also spoken in other parts of Europe, including Spain, France, and Romania. There it has also evolved and changed, and has new forms (Spanish, French, and Romanian). One source of these changes has to do with the pre-existing language of the native populations who learned Latin from the invading Roman armies. But another source

The biblical account of the origin of different languages *According to the bible, all men once spoke a common language. But they built a tall structure, the Tower of Babel, and tried to reach the heavens. To punish them for their pride and folly, God made them unable to understand each other, each group speaking a different language. (*Tower of Babel *by Jan Brueghel, the elder, 1568–1625, Courtesy of Pinacoteca)*

of change is in the "errors" children make as they learn the language (Kiparsky, 1968).

As an example of what is going on here, let us reconsider the formation of the English past tense by adding *-ed.* Clearly, this "rule" fails very often. In fact, for the most frequently used verbs of English, it works less than 25 percent of the time (consider such common irregular pasts as *broke, saw, went, ate, brought, took,* etc.). Still, children learn the rule; poor as it is, there is no better one in English that works more often. Children apply the rule correctly to the common verbs that require it, but as we have seen, they apply it to the other "irregular" verbs as well. Over the passage of the next five or ten years of life, children will memorize the irregular forms for most common verbs. But what about the uncommon ones? The child must be excused if she fails to remember that a word she hears once every two or three years (e.g., *wring,* meaning 'squeeze' and its past tense *wrung*) has a particular irregular ending. If she forgets, she will go with the regular rule and say "wringed." If such a process is at work in English, through the imperfect learning of its speakers, we would expect the rarer irregular words to undergo regularization, but the commonest irregular words (heard often, so their special forms are easily memorized) to stay irregular over the passing generations. This turns out to be true. While only relatively few of the most common English verbs have the regular *-ed* ending today, fully 98 percent of a sample of uncommon English verbs follow the regular rule. So English moves inexorably, over time, toward the general use of *-ed* as the mark of pastness. The rare verbs gradually lose their special forms.

Thus in many ways, language becomes what language learning makes it. Humans constantly seek general principles to order their behavior, rather than learning things one at a time. Hence, as any parent can tell you, we hear creative, highly patterned inventions from the small child, for example, "holded" rather than "held." Naively, we take such innovations to be errors or inelegancies which, if left uncorrected, will alter our language to its detriment. One is free, of course, to look down one's nose at this kind of language creativity and call it childish, slangy, barbaric, or ignorant. Even so, one must accept the facts: No matter how dearly we love old plurals such as *hooves* (hoofs) and *celli* (cellos), these are doomed by the organizational aspects of human minds. No matter that some authorities forbid *leg* ("I legged it out") and *foot* ("I foot the bill") to be verbs rather than nouns. The learners over many generations have decided that any body part can become a verb. We already have *elbow* ("I elbowed him out of the way"), *finger, arm, shoulder, nose, eye,* etc., as established verbs in English, and *leg* and *foot* will achieve similar respectability with the passage of time (Clark and Clark, 1977).

The reason for these regularizing changes is that learners seek to acquire their native tongue "on the cheap." They want everything that they have gone to the trouble of memorizing to extend to hundreds or thousands of new cases, to minimize the rote labor. The effect of this central fact about learning is that irregular variations and prohibitions are lost with the passage of linguistic time (Bloomfield, 1933).

Given these phenomena of learning, one might well expect new languages such as modern English to have became more regular than old languages such as ancient Greek. But in fact, they are not. Modern languages have not evolved to be neater, more regular, or more principled than older ones. The reason is that language learning by children is not the only factor that influences language change.

There are other influences that work in the direction of irregularity. One such factor has to do with **rhetoric**—the desire for elegant variation and alternative forms in poetry and oratory. A more important factor is **language mixture**—the influence of foreign speakers, whose native language usages impose themselves on their adopted language. Though each of the original languages (say, English and Spanish as they intermix on the streets of New York and Los Angeles today) may have some simple and regular form, the two regularities are different from each other. The end product of mixing them is two forms—in short, a new irregularity.

Roughly, language learning tends to level old irregularities (by overgeneralization of single rules), while language mixing (by speakers of different languages or different dialects) tends to create new irregularities. Hence, the language moves in two directions at once. As one author has put it, the overall effect is that the more language changes, the more it stays the same (Slobin, 1977).

In sum, it is somewhat misleading to consider "the language" as a body of cultural knowledge and skills that the child willy-nilly must acquire from observation and practice through traditional mechanisms of learning. Compare learning language to learning arithmetic. Each child must learn that $2 + 2 = 4$, and if the child guesses "5" or "3" during the learning period, this does not affect arithmetic at all. The child must *discover* the absolute truth—the answer is "4" today, was "4" before he was born, and will be "4" forever more. The case is quite different for language. For example, before we were born, *disinterested* meant 'open-minded' or 'objective' (while *uninterested* meant 'not interested' or 'bored'). But the learners tended to interpret *dis-* as meaning 'not'—as it does in many words —and so today *disinterested* and *uninterested* are becoming synonymous, both meaning 'not interested.' Children by their learning *cannot* change the numerical sums, but they *can* change the language. Thus the fairest view of language learning is that it represents a mutual accommodation between what the child observes out there in the speech of others, and his procedures and biases as to how to organize such observational data. So children partly "learn their language" from adults, but languages also "learn to be" what suits the mental requirements of their young users.

LANGUAGE LEARNING IN CHANGED ENVIRONMENTS

Thus far, our focus has been on language development as it proceeds normally. Under these conditions, language seems to emerge in much the same way in virtually all children. They progress from babbling to one-word speech, advance to the two-word telegraphic stage, and eventually graduate to complex sentence forms and meanings. The fact that this progression is so uniform and so universal has led many psycholinguists to the view that children are somehow biologically pre-programmed to acquire language. Further evidence for this view stems from studies of language development under certain unusual conditions, when children grow up in environments that are radically different from those in which language development usually proceeds. Which aspects of the early environment are essential for language learning? One line of evidence comes from reports of children who grew up in the wild or under conditions of virtual social isolation.

Wild Children

There are some remarkable examples of children who wandered (or were abandoned) in the forest, and who survived, reared by bears or wolves. Some of these cases have been discussed by the psycholinguist Roger Brown (1958). In 1920, some Indian villagers discovered a wolf mother in her den together with four cubs. Two were baby wolves, but the other two were human children, subsequently named Kamala and Amala. No one knows how they got there and why the wolf adopted them. Brown tells us what these children were like:

> Kamala was about eight years old and Amala was only one and one-half. They were thoroughly wolfish in appearance and behavior: Hard callus had developed on their knees and palms from going on all fours. Their teeth were sharp edged. They moved their nostrils sniffing food. Eating and drinking were accomplished by lowering their mouths to the plate. They ate raw meat . . . At night they prowled and sometimes howled. They shunned other children but followed the dog and cat. They slept rolled up together on the floor . . . Amala died within a year but Kamala lived to be eighteen . . . In time, Kamala learned to walk erect, to wear clothing, and even to speak a few words (Brown, 1958, p. 100).

The outcome was much the same for the thirty or so other wild children about whom we have reports. When found, they were all shockingly animal-like. None of them could be rehabilitated so as to use language at all normally, though some, including Kamala, learned to speak a few words (Figure 15.6).

Initially, such cases were regarded as crucial to the nature-nurture controversy.

 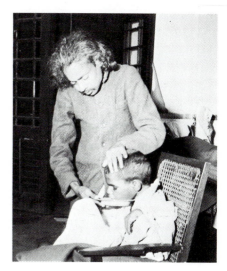

15.6 A modern wild boy Ramu, a young boy discovered in India in 1976, appears to have been reared by wolves. He was deformed, apparently from lying in cramped positions, as in a den. He could not walk, and drank by lapping with his tongue. His favorite food was raw meat, which he seemed to be able to smell at a distance. After he was found, he lived at the home for destitute children run by Mother Theresa in Lucknow, Uttar Pradesh. He learned to bathe and dress himself, but never learned to speak. He continued to prefer raw meat, and would often sneak out to prey upon fowl in the neighbor's chicken coop. Ramu died at the age of about 10 in February, 1985. (New York Times, Feb. 24, 1985; photographs courtesy Wide World Photos)

Quite a few authors believed that the knowledge and behavior of these children provide an index of what is innately given. But as Brown points out, the findings can be interpreted to fit either a nativist or an environmentalist bias. Nativists can claim that the children were retarded in the first place (for physically or mentally abnormal children are those most likely to be abandoned).* They may also argue that the children were damaged during their time in the forest, nutritionally (by eating a carnivore diet) or psychologically (by living in a predatory society). Environmentalists will take a different tack. They will admire the plasticity of these children, which enabled them to adapt to the ways of wolves and then to recover partly, in gait and a little primitive speech. All we can say for sure is that having a wolf or a bear for a mother is not conducive to learning a human language.

Isolated Children

Kamala and Amala were removed from all human society. Some other children have been raised by humans, but under conditions that were almost unimaginably inhumane, for their parents were either vicious or deranged. Sometimes, such parents will deprive a baby of all human contact. "Isabelle" was hidden away, apparently from early infancy, and given only the minimal attention necessary to sustain her life. Apparently no one spoke to her (in fact, her mother was deaf and did not speak). Isabelle was six years old when discovered. Of course she had no language, and her cognitive development was below that of a normal two-year-old. But within a year, this girl learned to speak. Her tested intelligence was normal, and she took her place in an ordinary school (Davis, 1947; Brown, 1958). Thus Isabelle at seven years, with one year of language practice, spoke about as well as her peers in the second grade, all of whom had had seven years of practice.

---

* The mythical Greek king Oedipus was said to have been abandoned as an infant in the wild to die because of a prophesy that he would kill his father (a prophesy that eventually came true). But the myth also notes that Oedipus was club-footed.

Rehabilitation from isolation is not always so successful. A child, "Genie," discovered in California about twenty years ago, was fourteen years old when found. Since about twenty months, apparently, she had lived tied to a chair, was frequently beaten, and never spoken to—but sometimes barked at, for her father said she was no more than a dog. Afterwards, she was taught by psychologists and linguists (Fromkin et al., 1974). But Genie did not become a normal language user. She says many words, and puts them together into meaningful propositions as young children do, such as "No more take wax" and "Another house have dog." Thus she has learned certain basics of language. Indeed, her semantic sophistication—what she means by what she says—is far beyond young children. Yet, even after many years of instruction, Genie did not learn the closed-class words, pronouns, auxiliary verbs, and so on, that appear in mature English sentences, nor did she combine propositions together in elaborate sentences (Curtiss, 1977).

Why did Genie not progress to full language learning while Isabelle did? The best guess is that the crucial factor is the age at which language learning began. Genie was discovered after she had reached puberty while Isabelle was only six. As we shall see later, there is some reason to believe there is a *critical period* for language learning. If the person has passed this period, language learning proceeds with greater difficulty.

Language without Sound

The work on wild and isolated children argues that a necessary condition for learning language is some contact with other humans. If one's early life is spent entirely among animals, the effects are irreversible. If it is spent among people who do not talk to one, language may still be acquired later on if the crucial learning period has not been passed as yet. Our next question concerns the more specific factors of the learner's human environment. What aspects of this environment are essential for language to emerge?

It has sometimes been suggested that an important ingredient is exposure to language sounds. According to this view, language is intrinsically related to the way we organize what we hear. If so, language cannot develop in the absence of sound.

This hypothesis is false. For there is one group of humans that is totally cut off from the auditory-vocal language—the deaf, who cannot hear it. Yet this doesn't mean that they have no language. Most deaf people eventually learn to read and write the language of the surrounding community of persons who can hear. But they usually learn it as a second language; the result is that they are generally less expert at this than are their hearing peers (E. Gibson, Shurcliff, and Yonas, 1970). But most deaf persons also have a first language, a *manual system.* A widely used system of this kind is *American Sign Language* or *ASL.* If their parents are also deaf, deaf children pick up the manual system from the adults around them, through informal interaction rather than by explicit instruction, just as we learn our spoken language (Newport and Ashbrook, 1977). Apparently infants are responsive to gestures of the hand and body much in the same way that they are responsive to the gestures of tongue and mouth that underlie spoken language.

Is the manual system a genuine language? Evidence comes from comparing it to the structure and development of spoken languages. ASL has hand shapes and

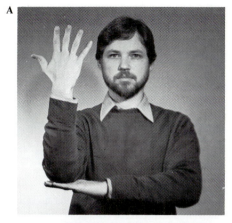

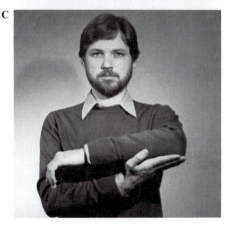

positions of which each word is composed, much like the tongue and lip shapes that allow us to fashion the sounds of spoken language (see Figure 15.7; Stokoe, Casterline, and Croneberg, 1955; Stokoe, 1960). It has morphemes as well as devices for building complex words out of simple ones, and it has grammatical principles for combining such words into sentences that are similar to those of English. Finally, babies who acquire this communication system go through the same steps as hearing children who are learning English. They first gesture one word at a time, then two, and so on. Eventually they come to use the full complement of ASL words and structures, including the ASL equivalent of closed-class items (a number of modifiers of the signs that have effects similar to those English achieves by the use of -ed, plural s, and the like). It is hard to avoid the conclusion that ASL and similar manual systems have the status of human languages (Supalla and Newport, 1978; Klima, Bellugi et al., 1979; Newport, 1984).

It appears that language does not depend on the auditory-vocal channel. When the usual modes of communication are denied to humans of normal mentality, they come up with an alternative that reproduces the same contents and structures as other language systems. It seems that language is an irrepressible trait: Deny it to the mouth and it will dart out through the fingers.

Language without a Model

The evidence we have reviewed shows that language emerges despite many environmental deprivations. Still, each case seemed to have one requirement—some adults who knew a language and could impart it to the young. But this must leave us puzzled about how language originated in the first place. Is it a cultural artifact (like the internal combustion machine or the game of chess) rather than a basic property of human minds, an invention that happened to take place in prehistoric times? Our bias has been the opposite, for we have argued that humans are biologically predisposed to communicate. But our case would have been much better if Kamala and Amala had invented a language of their own, down there in the wolf's den. Why didn't they? There are many ways to write off or ignore this case—maybe they were too busy learning to be good wolves, and maybe a human language is of no special use for learning to devour raw chickens. Is there a better test?

It certainly would be interesting if we could find a case of mentally normal humans, living in a socially human (not wolf) way but not taught any language. The easy method would be to maroon some spare infants on a desert island (while providing them with life's necessities). If they invented a language, we

15.7 Some common signs in ASL (A) *The sign for* tree. *One difference between ASL and spoken language is that many of the signed words physically resemble their meanings. This is so for* tree, *in which the upright forearm stands for the trunk and the outstretched fingers for the branches. But in many cases, such a resemblance is not present. Consider (B) which is the modern sign for* help, *whose relation to its meaning seems as arbitrary as that between most spoken words and their meanings. Even so, such a relation was once present, as shown in (C), a nineteenth-century sign for* help. *At that time, the sign was not arbitrary; it consisted of a gesture by the right hand to support the left elbow, as if helping an elderly person cross a street. (B) grew out of (C) by a progressive series of simplifications in which signs tend to move to the body's midline and use shorter, fewer, and more stylized movements. All that remains of (C) is an upward motion of the right palm. (Frishberg, 1975; photographs of and by Ted Supalla)*

513

would have strong evidence for a human urge to communicate. People have dreamed of this "ultimate language learning experiment" from earliest times, and this is of course why Kamala, Genie, and Isabelle so intrigued psychologists. The trouble is that these cases are so contaminated by brutish mistreatment that they cannot be interpreted easily.

We will instead consider an experiment that the ancients claim to have performed and will then turn to a modern study that reproduces some of its theoretically important properties. Herodotus, an ancient Greek historian, reports a tale told to him when he visited Egypt in about 460 B.C.:

> [The Egyptian king] Psammeticus . . . made an attempt to discover what men were most ancient [of mankind] . . . He took two children of the common sort, and gave them over to a herdsman to bring up at his folds, strictly charging him to let no one utter a word in their presence, but to keep them in a sequestered cottage . . . see that they got their fill of milk, and in all other respects look after them. His object herein was to know, after the first indistinct babblings of infancy were over, what word they would first articulate. The herdsman obeyed his orders for two years, and at the end of that time . . . the children ran up to him with outstretched arms, and distinctly said *becos* . . . Psammeticus . . . learnt that *becos* was the Phrygian word for bread. In consideration of this circumstance the Egyptians admitted the greater antiquity of the Phrygians (Modern Library Edition, 1942, pp. 116–17).

Feldman, Goldin-Meadow, and Gleitman (1978) found six children who were in a situation similar in many ways to that created by King Psammeticus. These children were deaf, so they had not learned spoken language. Their parents, who could hear, had decided not to allow the children to learn a manual language. This is because they shared the belief (held by some groups of educators) that deaf children can achieve an adequate knowledge of spoken language by special training in lip reading and vocalization. The investigators looked at these children before they had acquired any knowledge of English, for a number of prior studies had shown that under these circumstances deaf children will spontaneously begin to gesture to others (Tervoort, 1961; Fant, 1972). This informal gesturing pattern, called **home sign,** is initially a rough-and-ready pantomime, like the earliest communication systems of the deaf. The question was which aspects of communication these youngsters would come up with as they developed. Unlike Herodotus, the investigators did not expect this self-made language to be Egyptian or Phrygian. But they expected it to have some of the properties of human language, because even though these children were totally isolated from language experience, they were human nevertheless. And unlike Kamala, Genie, and Isabelle, these children had not been socially mistreated. They were living with loving parents, in normal homes.

The results showed that the children invented something much like language, using hand gestures rather than sounds produced by moving the mouth. This finding was all the more surprising since the investigators found that the parents, true to their word, were doing very little complicated gesturing of their own (though, to be sure, they waved and pointed to their deaf children in simple ways). The development of this self-made language showed many parallels to the course of learning in hearing children. The deaf children all began by simple pointing to express their thoughts and desires. They gestured one sign at a time in the period when hearing learners speak one word at a time. They pointed to ducks and bouncing balls rather than to sofas and ceilings: that is, their "vocabu-

A

B

15.8 Self-made signs in a deaf boy never exposed to sign language *A two-sign sequence. (A) The first sign means "eat" or "food." Immediately before, the boy had pointed to a grape. (B) The second sign means "give." The total sequence presumably means "give me the food." (Goldin-Meadow, 1981; drawing courtesy Noel Yovovich)*

laries" too looked like those of the children who learn spoken language from their parents. The children then began to invent pantomimic gestures; for example, flapping their arms to express *bird* and fluttering their fingers to express *snow* (Figure 15.8). Eventually, the children began putting the pointings and panto-mimes together into two- and three-word sentences. This was in the same developmental period during which hearing children (exposed to a spoken language) begin to say two- and three-word sentences.

In sum, the early stages of a self-made first language in these deaf children without adult models looked remarkably similar to the early stages of a first language acquired by hearing children with parents "teaching them how." In later years, the deaf children went on to say longer and longer sentences in their home-made language. But in these deprived circumstances, certain further developments that are found in four- and five-year-olds did not appear. By now these are familiar. They are the closed-class words (or gestures to take their place) and complex methods for putting propositions together into single sentences. We previously saw that children in normal circumstances first learn the **basics** of language, including open-class words and simple sentences, and then the **elaborations,** in terms of closed-class words and complex sentences. Radically deprived children such as Genie never learn the elaborations, but only a few basics. The deaf children without a language model do very much better, but there are still some elaborations that they do not invent in their deprived situation (Goldin-Meadow, 1982).

The home-sign study provides us with a fairly pure case of a group of children who were isolated from language but not society. The results showed that something like language emerged even so. This finding suggests that language is a deep-seated property of the human mind—at least in its basics if not in its elaborations. Whatever the environmental circumstances (brutish mistreatment being the exception), children evolve a communication system that is uniquely human. This fits with evidence we discussed earlier—for example, the finding that language changes whenever, through historical accident, it contains properties that are not useful to the communicative needs of its learners. We thus have no need to ask further, with Psammeticus, about the origins of human language. Our best guess is that as human nature originated in evolutionary history, language necessarily and inevitably made its appearance too.

LANGUAGE LEARNING AND CRITICAL PERIODS

Language learning is much easier in children than in adults. This and related facts are often regarded as evidence that there is a **critical period** for language learning. There is thought to be an especially sensitive period ending in the early school years, but with the whole critical period extending roughly to puberty. According to this hypothesis, some characteristics of the brain change as the critical period draws to its close, so that later learning (both of the first language and of other ones) becomes more difficult (Lenneberg, 1967).

Critical periods seem to govern the acquisition of a number of important behavior patterns in many animals. One example is the attachment of the infant to his mother, which generally can only be formed in early childhood (see Chapter 16). Another example is bird song. Male birds of many species have a song that is

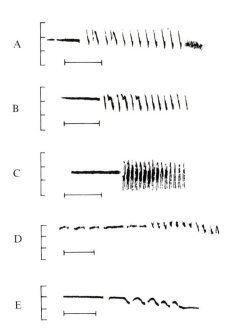

15.9   Critical period in the development of bird song   *(A) A graphic presentation of the song of an adult, male white-crowned sparrow. The figure, a so-called sound spectrogram, plots the frequency region of the bird's vocal output over time. Frequency is indicated by the vertical axis, in steps of 2,000 hertz. The horizontal time marker indicates ½ second. The figure shows that the normal song begins with a whistle or two, continues with a series of trills, and ends with a vibrato. (B) The song of a bird raised in acoustic isolation but exposed to four minutes of normal song between the ages of 35 and 56 days. His adult song was almost normal. (C) The song of an isolated bird exposed to normal song between days 50 and 71. The adult song of this bird has some crude similarities to normal white-crowned sparrow song. There is a whistle followed by trills, but the details are very different. (D) and (E) show the songs of birds whose exposure to normal song occurred very early in life (days 3 to 7) or very late (after 300 days of age) respectively. Birds trained at either of these times produced songs indistinguishable from those of birds with no training at all. (After Marler, 1970)*

characteristic of their own kind. They learn this song by listening to adult males of their own species. But this exposure will only be effective if it occurs at a certain period in the bird's life. This has been extensively documented for the white-crowned sparrow. To learn the white-crowned sparrow song in all its glory (complete with special trills and grace notes), the baby birds must hear an adult's song sometime between the seventh and sixtieth day of their life. The next forty days are a marginal period. If the fledgling is exposed to an adult male's song during that period but not before, he will acquire only some limited basics of the sparrow song, without the full elaborations heard in normal adults (see Figure 15.9). If the exposure comes still later, it has no effect at all. The bird will never sing normally (Marler, 1970).

Related evidence for a critical period in language learning comes from various sources. Taken alone, none of these is particularly convincing. But considered as a whole, they seem to make a rather good case.

First Language Learning

The most direct test of the hypothesis involves first language learning. Can one learn to speak (or sign) after childhood has passed? We have already discussed the case of children in the wild, but their circumstances were clearly too brutish to allow rehabilitation of any kind. But consider Isabelle who was deprived of exposure to language until six and Genie whose isolation lasted until age fourteen. As we saw, Isabelle became a normal speaker while Genie's speech never progressed beyond the most primitive basics. It is tempting to suppose that when Isabelle was discovered she was still in the heart of the critical period and so could still develop into a normal language user. But Genie had entered puberty and was thus at the critical period's margin. This may be why she was able to learn the language basics and never acquired its elaborations. This may be analogous to the performance of young birds whose first exposure to the adult song comes in the marginal period; they learn the song basics but not its elaborations (Goldin-Meadow, 1982).

Second Language Learning

Cases like Isabelle and Genie are (fortunately) rare, so we have little information about first language learning in the years after childhood. In contrast, we know quite a bit about second language learning. Whether learning a second language is comparable to learning the first is debatable, but it probably taps some of the same capacities. In any case, there is little doubt that adults and children differ in their ability to learn a second language. Children pick up a foreign language very rapidly and soon speak it just like natives. This is much less common in adults. Consider immigrants who acquire the language of their new home. Many of them continue to speak this language with an accent and may have occasional lapses on subtle points of grammar, even after thirty or forty years in the new language community. The general impression is that the cutting line is puberty. If immigration occurred before then, there will probably be no accent; if afterward, an accent is very likely. Once again we have a suggestion of a critical period. If this period is passed, language learning is more difficult, at least for the language elaborations.

Deaf youngsters signing *(Courtesy of New York School for the Deaf)*

Learning American Sign Language

One of the most striking lines of evidence on the relation between age and language learning comes from work on American Sign Language. Deaf children born to signing parents acquire ASL just like hearing children acquire English or French, and in the same time period. They are exposed to ASL from the beginning of life. But as we have seen for the case of the deaf isolates, many deaf children—those who have hearing parents—are not exposed to ASL. They invent home sign, but this is different in many ways from ASL which, like English, is much more formal and elaborate. Usually, these deaf isolates will eventually come into contact with deaf signers of ASL, and then they will learn it. But the age when they make this first contact varies widely. Some are exposed to ASL in the early school years. Others may be in their teens, or even older. Such persons learn ASL as a *first* language (leaving aside the informal home sign), but at a much later time than first languages are usually learned.

Does it matter whether ASL is learned as an infant, as a school child, or as a young adult, assuming the total exposure time to the language is equated? To find out, some investigators tested a number of congenitally deaf persons who had been exposed to ASL for an equal period of time, say, ten years. Some of the persons who were tested had learned ASL by watching their parents use it since they were born; thus their ten-year exposure covered the ages from zero to ten years. Others were children of hearing parents who were initially isolated from the deaf community. Of these, some began to learn ASL at ten years of age and used it until tested at the age of twenty. Still others were first exposed to ASL at twenty years of age and used it until tested at the age of thirty.

The findings were dramatic. All of these users were quite fluent in ASL, but even so there was an effect of age of first exposure. Those who learned it from birth used all the elaborations of ASL, including various signed equivalents of the closed class. But those whose first exposure to ASL came after about age seven showed subtle deficits in their use of the closed class. Those whose exposure began in adolescence or adulthood had much greater deficits, with use of the closed class that was sporadic, irregular, and often incorrect (Newport and Supalla, forthcoming).

It appears that young children show sensitivities to language that are a requirement for achieving native fluency. When exposure is late, there are significant deficits in learning that can be observed even after many years of practice and use. These findings thus provide quite convincing evidence for a "sensitive" if not "critical" period for language learning. Of course, such studies might be even more compelling if conducted with spoken languages rather than with the signed language that is so unfamiliar to most of us. But as we have stated earlier, it is impossible to find such a test population in a human community without going to children who, like Kamala, Isabelle, and Genie, were deprived of much more than exposure to language.

Recovery from Aphasia

Further support for the critical-period hypothesis comes from studies of aphasia. We have seen that damage to certain regions of the left cerebral hemisphere leads to marked disturbances of language functions, called aphasia (see Chapters 2 and

517

9). Do aphasia patients ever recover? The answer depends on the patient's age. If the damage to the brain was suffered in adulthood, recovery will rarely be complete. The outlook is much better if the injury occurred in early childhood. If so, language use is often regained entirely. This means that children can relearn language even after they have lost most of it, while adults cannot, which certainly fits in with the hypothesis that there is a critical period for language learning (Lenneberg, 1967).

Is the Critical Period Specific to Language?

The notion of a critical period seems fairly plausible. What is less clear is whether such a critical period is specific to language. One can take a broader view, which simply asserts that children are better at picking up any and all complex skills, of which language is only one. As of now, we have insufficient evidence to choose between the narrow and the broad conceptions of the critical period. It may be specific to language alone. Or it may be nonspecific—so much so, perhaps, that to assert that such a period exists amounts to little more than the statement that you can't teach an old dog (or an old language learner) new tricks. (For discussions that emphasize the relations between cognitive stage and language stage, see MacNamara, 1972; Cromer, 1976; Gleitman, 1981.)

THE NECESSARY CONDITIONS FOR LANGUAGE LEARNING

We are still far from a satisfactory theory of language learning. But when we consider the whole range of the evidence, we find much value in Descartes's claim (Chapter 9) that language is an inevitable part of human nature. There is reason to believe that human children come equipped with a species-specific urge to communicate in certain uniquely human ways. They come prepared to notice the differences in sound that will be crucial for later speech perception, and they have the tendency to interpret simple words in terms of basic-level categories that will be invaluable for acquiring word meanings. A similar biological predisposition enables children to acquire language basics—a simple system for arranging words to form propositions. If they are not exposed to any language model, they will invent a set of basics for themselves, as in the case of the isolated deaf children.

As children grow older, they learn more and more elaborations, such as closed-class words and principles for combining propositions. But this progression from basics to elaborations is not universal. If exposure to a language does not take place during some critical period, many elaborations will never appear, as in Genie's case. As for nonhuman populations—even including the college-educated chimpanzees that were discussed in Chapter 9—they do not come close to learning even the basics of a human language.

To sum up, children find it easy to acquire language because they are predisposed to organize language inputs in certain ways. They assume that language must contain meaningful words lawfully arranged into propositions. Such rock-bottom assumptions are guiding principles that make language learning possible.

Then these assumptions interact with the specific information given in the environment, with the outcome that children acquire the language of their community—with each generation doctoring a few grammatical irregularities in what they hear, adding some useful new words and structures, and discarding a few old ones that no longer serve their communicative purposes. Armed with strong biases about what language is, taken together with their experiences in the world around them, children mold a communication system that allows them to express all their myriad human thoughts and to understand the thoughts of others in their linguistic community.

THE GROWTH OF THE MIND

We have seen that cognitive development can be regarded from two radically opposed theoretical vantage points. One extreme position holds that the child changes because of what he learns from his environment. He begins as a novice, for he knows nothing about the world, and he ends as an expert through his growing interactions with that world. The other extreme position maintains that the change in children over developmental time is a function of the maturation of their nervous system, that they become progressively less childish because their brains become more and more like those of adults.

Modern developmental psychologists—and in this as in so many other regards, Piaget was a ground-breaking pioneer—reject both of these extremes, for they find that neither of them can account for the complex facts of how human infants turn into human adults. This holds for the development of thought as well as the development of language. Human infants are not like bees or birds, who can acquire little beyond what nature built into their brains. But no more are they like learning robots or recording devices, who will simply copy everything to which they are exposed. Rather, cognitive development involves the interaction of innate capacities and biases with the kaleidoscopic information in the world outside. Thus far, we know only fragments of how this internally given and externally given information come together to yield the competent and knowledgeable adult. Perhaps the central challenge in the field of cognitive development is to understand the interactive position so as to learn why, though infants are wise indeed, they are not wise in the same ways that adults are wise.

SUMMARY

1. There is little doubt that *language learning* depends on both genetic endowment and the environment. While language is learned, it is not learned in the way in which a skill such as knitting is acquired. Thus certain principles of simple learning such as *imitation, reinforcement,* and *correction* cannot account for language learning in human children.

2. The normal course of early language development involves a number of steps. Infants vocalize from birth on and their vocalizations, together with their responses to the vocalizations of others, soon take on a social quality. The infants are pre-equipped to produce and respond to language sounds of all kinds, but learn to ignore sound distinctions that do not matter in their own language. They also seem predisposed to respond to *Motherese*—a

special way that adults speak to babies—which emphasizes sound cues that help the infant to recognize the *sentence* as a speech unit.

3. Initially, children talk in *one-word utterances.* At about two years, they become *telegraphic* speakers and utter *two-word sentences.* In the process of learning word meaning and some of the principles of syntax, they often *overgeneralize.* Some phenomena of *language change* can probably be traced to such overgeneralizations that occur in the process of language acquisition.

4. There has been considerable interest in how language acquisition proceeds in radically altered environments, as in the case of *wild children* reared by animals, *isolated children* raised in human company but under monstrous conditions, and *deaf children who have no language model* because they are raised by nonsigners. The results indicate that children isolated from language but not from human society learn at least language basics, including deaf children without a language model who may invent an elementary language system. Deaf children with signing parents learn a manual language as elaborate as spoken language. These facts have been interpreted as evidence for a biologically pre-programmed language learning capacity.

5. Several phenomena suggest that there is a *critical period* for language learning in humans, analogous to that which characterizes the development of bird song in certain sparrows. Evidence comes from studies of first language learning in isolated children and deaf learners of *American Sign Language,* of second language learning, and of recovery from aphasia.

CHAPTER 16

Social Development

In the preceding chapters we discussed physical and cognitive development: the ways in which we progress from embryos to full-grown adults, from crawling infants to energetic tricyclists, from babbling babes to sophisticated eight-year-olds who understand all about liquid conservation. But children don't just grow in size and thought; they also develop in their relations to other people. To find out how they do this is the task of psychologists who study the field of *social development.*

SOME GENERAL CHARACTERISTICS OF SOCIAL DEVELOPMENT

Physical, cognitive, and social development pertain to different aspects of the human journey from birth to maturity. But even so, they share important general characteristics. In all three, we see an ever-increasing enlargement of the developing individual's universe. And in all three, attempts have been made to discover stages of this developmental progress.

Social Development as the Widening of Social Scope

In biological development, the infant enlarges her physical horizons. As she grows in sheer size and strength, she develops the ability to move freely within her environment and becomes emancipated from her initial limitations in physical space. Cognitive development leads to an analogous expansion of horizons, but now of the mental rather than the physical world as the growing child comes to transcend the immediate here-and-now to live in a world of ever more abstract ideas.

In social development, there is a similar pattern of continued expansion. In the first months of life, the baby's social world is limited to just one person, usually the mother. In time, her social horizons become enlarged to include both parents, then the rest of the family, then young peers in the nursery and in school. As adolescence sets in, friends of the opposite sex assume more and more importance, sexuality begins in earnest, and the individual soon becomes a parent in her own right and starts the reproductive cycle all over again. But the expansion of the child's social world goes yet further. As she grows older, she comes to understand the system of social rules through which she is linked, not just to her own family circle, but to a larger social universe. A major concern of this chapter is to chart the course of this social expansion through which babes in arms grow into citizens of the world.

Stages of Social Development

In previous chapters, we saw that physical and cognitive development are marked by a fairly regular and orderly progression. Is the same true of social development? There have been no attempts to chart the course of social growth in anything like the painstaking detail that Piaget devoted—whether successfully or not—to the description of the stages of cognitive development. The proposals that come closest are those of Sigmund Freud, although these are more in the nature of interesting speculations than of a scientific theory. We have previously presented Freud's theory of how humans come to be members of society (see Chapter 12). His description of the stages of this process is in line with the main theme of this chapter—social development involves an ever-increasing enlargement of the child's social horizons. To Freud, the infant's development begins with the oral stage, when he is little more than a mouth that becomes attached to the one person who provides the necessary nipple. With the onset of toilet training during the anal stage, the child's social universe expands as he encounters one of the first demands society imposes upon him. The phallic stage enlarges the cast of characters—his relations no longer involve the mother alone, but concern an entire family. A still further expansion occurs during the genital stage, when emotional relationships become genuinely reciprocal and each partner cares about the other's feelings.

As we saw in a previous chapter, Freud's theory of how this social expansion comes about has been challenged on many grounds. According to many critics, Freud exaggerated the importance of infantile sexuality, was in error in his belief in a universal rivalry between fathers and sons, daughters and mothers, and underemphasized the role of cultural factors. Furthermore, Freud never collected the relevant factual evidence in favor of his developmental theory, which was built entirely upon his patients' recollections of their childhood experiences (for details, see Chapter 12).

Given all this, it is not surprising that there are few psychologists (or even psychoanalysts) left who accept Freud's theory of social development in anything like its original form. But even so, some of the issues he addressed are still with us. Are our first bonds to other persons forged by a crude form of self-interest so that the child becomes attached to the mother—and eventually to others—because she satisfies his creature needs? Is early childhood experience all-important in determining later personality? Freud's answers to both questions were an emphatic "Yes." Today, these positions are in serious dispute, but that does not detract from Freud's importance. For in science, to ask the right question is almost as important as supplying the answer, and many of the problems that modern investigators of social development are concerned with are ultimately derived from the questions that Freud began to raise a hundred years ago.

ATTACHMENT

Social development begins with the first human bond that is sometimes said to lay the foundations for all later relationships with others: the infant's **attachment** to the person who takes care of him.* The infant wants to be near his mother, and if unhappy, he is comforted by her sight, her sound, and her touch. In this regard, human children have much in common with the young of many other species. Rhesus infants cling to their mother's body, chicks follow the hen, and lambs run after the ewe. As the young grow older, they venture farther away from the mother, gaining courage for ever more distant explorations. But for quite a while, the mother continues to provide a secure home base, a place to run back to should unmanageable threats be encountered.

Attachment (Photograph by Suzanne Szasz)

The Roots of Attachment

What accounts for the infant's attachment to the mother (or to some other person), an attachment so powerful that the mere threat of the loved one's departure can lead to panic? Until fairly recently, most theorists believed that the love for the mother is a secondary consequence of her association with basic creature satisfactions such as the alleviation of hunger, thirst, and pain. The most influential version of this approach was probably that of Sigmund Freud, who believed that the infant's upset at the mother's absence is based on the crass fear that his bodily needs would now go unsatisfied. The British psychiatrist John Bowlby has called this the "cupboard theory" of mother love; it boils down to the view that the first love object is the breast or the bottle (Bowlby, 1969, 1973). In effect, Freud's theory is just another expression of the Hobbesian doctrine that humans are at bottom self-centered brutes whose only concern is to fill their stomach and satisfy their lust. According to this view, any apparent tendency to care for others—as in the love between man and woman, child and mother, and so on—will inevitably turn out to be just another manifestation of their self-directed strivings when it is examined carefully enough (see Chapter 10).

IS THE NEED FOR THE MOTHER PRIMARY?

The cupboard theory of the infant's tie to his mother has been criticized on several grounds. One problem is the fact that babies often show great interest in

---

* Since the caregiver is typically the child's mother (and almost always was in earlier eras), we will from here on refer to the child's caregiver by the traditional term *mother,* despite the fact that the actual caregiver may well be another person, such as the father or a babysitter.

523

A

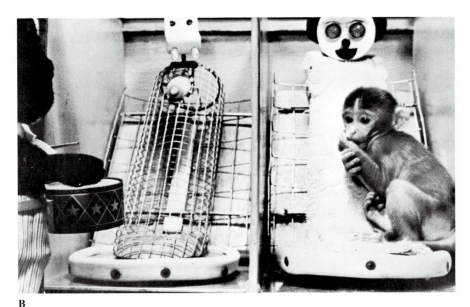

B

16.1 The need for contact comfort *(A) Harry Harlow with an infant rhesus monkey and a terry-cloth mother (which here, atypically, has a bottle). (Photograph by Nina Leen) (B) A baby rhesus, frightened of a mechanical toy animal, clings to its terry-cloth mother for contact. (Courtesy Harry Harlow, University of Wisconsin Primate Laboratory)*

16.2 Contact comfort in humans *(Photograph by Mimi Forsyth, Monkmeyer)*

other people, even those who have never fed them or satisfied their other bodily needs. They seem to enjoy seeing others smile or playing peek-a-boo. Does anyone seriously propose that infants want someone to play peek-a-boo with them because this game has previously been associated with food? It seems much more reasonable to assume that the infant comes predisposed to seek social satisfaction, which is rewarding in and of itself.

Another demonstration that love of mother goes beyond bodily needs comes from the work of Harry Harlow (1905–1981). Harlow raised newborn rhesus monkeys without their mothers. Each young monkey lived alone in a cage that contained two stationary figures. One of these models was built of wire; the other was made of soft terry cloth. The wire figure was equipped with a nipple that yielded milk, but no similar provision was made for the terry-cloth model. Even so, the monkey infants spent much more time on the terry-cloth "mother" than on the wire figure. The terry-cloth figure could be clung to and could provide what Harlow called "contact comfort" (Figure 16.1). This was especially clear when the infants were frightened. When placed in an unfamiliar room or faced with a mechanical toy that approached with clanking noises, they invariably rushed to the terry-cloth mother and clung to her tightly. The infants never sought similar solace from the wire mothers, who were their source of food and nothing more (Harlow, 1958).

These results are in complete opposition to the cupboard theory. The monkey infant evidently loves its mother (whether real or terry cloth), not because she feeds it, but because she feels so "comforting." Some of the characteristics of the figure toward whom the monkey can direct its attachment are evidently pre-programmed. In monkeys, these evidently include the way the figure feels to the touch. Whether touch is equally important to human infants is as yet unclear, but very likely it plays some role. Frightened young humans run to their mothers and hug them closely just as rhesus infants do (Figure 16.2). Children also like stuffed, cuddly toys such as teddy bears, whom they hold tightly when they feel apprehensive. Perhaps Linus's security blanket is a kind of terry-cloth mother. It may or it may not be; but contrary to the cupboard theory, it is emphatically not a substitute tablecloth.

BOWLBY'S THEORY OF ATTACHMENT

What is the alternative to the cupboard theory? According to John Bowlby, attachment results from the fact that the young of most mammals and birds have a built-in fear of the unknown and unfamiliar. As a result they do everything they can to stay close to some object that has become familiar to them—they become attached. But while familiarity is an important factor it is not the only one, for there seems to be an innate bias to become attached to things that have certain stimulus properties rather than others—as in the case of infant monkeys who prefer soft, furry terry cloth to hard wire. In the real world, the most likely object of attachment will be the mother. She has been around throughout the infant's short life and has therefore become familiar. And she obviously has the appropriate stimulus properties for the young of her species: if she is a duck, she quacks; if she is a rhesus monkey, she is furry.

Why do infants have the built-in fear of the unfamiliar, which Bowlby regards as the basic cause of attachment? According to Bowlby, this fear has a simple survival value. Infants who lack it would stray away from their mother and are thus more likely to get lost and perish. In particular, they might well fall victim to predators, for beasts of prey tend to attack weak animals that are separated from their fellows.

Needless to say, infants don't know enough about the world to fear specific predators. But Bowlby argues that the built-in fear is initially quite unspecific. He conjectures that the fear aroused by the mother's absence is analogous to what psychiatrists call *free-floating anxiety.* This is a state in which the patient is desperately afraid but doesn't know what he is afraid of; he therefore becomes all the more afraid. Given this anxiety, even mild external threats become enormous to the child; the increased need for reassurance may lead to wild clinging and "childish" dependency, as in the dark or during a thunderstorm. This may occur even when the threat comes from the parents themselves. A child who is severely punished by his parents often becomes even more clinging and dependent than before. The parents caused the fear, but they are the ones who are approached for reassurance. This is analogous to the dog who licks the hand that whipped him. The whipping led to fear and pain, but whom can the dog approach for solace but his master?

IMPRINTING

According to Bowlby, the fear of the unfamiliar produces an attachment to a familiar object. In the real world, this object is generally the mother. But it needn't be. Harlow's studies have already shown us that the focus of filial devotion is not rigidly predetermined by the genes, as witness the love borne for the terry-cloth mother.

A similar point is made by *imprinting* in birds, which has been studied extensively by the European ethologist Konrad Lorenz. Imprinting is a kind of learning that occurs very early in life and provides the basis for the chick's attachment to its mother. When a newly hatched duckling is first exposed to a moving stimu-

Separation anxiety *(Photograph by Tana Hoban/DPI)*

16.3 imprinting in ducklings
Imprinted ducklings following Konrad Lorenz. (Courtesy Nina Leen)

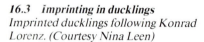

16.4 Imprinting and the critical period *The curve shows the relation between imprinting and the age at which a duckling was exposed to a male moving model. The imprinting score represents the percentage of trials on which the duckling followed the model on a later test. (From Hess, 1958)*

lus, it will approach and follow this stimulus as soon as it is able to walk (at about twelve hours after hatching). If the duckling follows the object for about ten minutes, an attachment is formed; the bird is imprinted. In nature, the moving stimulus is the duckling's mother and all is well. But in the laboratory, it need not be. The duckling may be exposed to a moving duck on wheels, or to a rectangle sliding back and forth behind a glass window, or even to Konrad Lorenz's booted legs. In each case, the result is the same. The duckling becomes imprinted on the wooden duck or on the rectangle or on Lorenz; it follows one of these objects as if it were its mother, uttering piteous distress calls whenever it is not nearby (Figure 16.3). The real mother may quack enticingly so as to woo her lost offspring back, but to no avail; the imprinted duckling continues to follow the wooden duck or the moving rectangle or Lorenz (Hess, 1959, 1973).

Imprinting occurs most readily during a critical period which in ducklings lasts for two days with a maximum sensitivity at about fifteen hours after hatching (Hess, 1959). Subsequent to this period, imprinting is difficult to achieve. According to one interpretation, this is because by then the young bird has become thoroughly afraid of all new objects. When exposed to the wooden duck, it flees instead of following. Having lived for two or three days, it has learned something about what is familiar, and it can therefore appreciate—and fear—what is strange (Figure 16.4).

Phenomena analogous to imprinting have been observed in various mammals. Harlow's terry-cloth mothers are one example. Others are provided by attachments between members of different species. Lambs raised with a dog accompany it everywhere and bleat continuously upon separation, and one- or two-month-old puppies readily approach and follow people (Cairns and Johnson, 1965). Older animals do not bestow their affections so generously. Puppies who first meet humans when they are four months or older are generally quite wary; they can be tamed, but they tend to remain timid and unresponsive to people (Scott, 1963).

Whether the underlying mechanisms that produce attachments in birds and mammals (let alone ourselves) are actually the same is still an open question. But at least on the surface there are some striking similarities. A lasting attachment is formed during a particular—and perhaps, critical—period in the animal's youth, such that proximity to the attachment figure provides comfort and security, while separation from it leads to distress. The attachment seems to be important—and according to some authors, is crucial—to the animal's subsequent development. Given these similarities, it is reasonable to suppose that studies of the development of attachment in subhuman mammals and birds may have some bearing for our understanding of analogous phenomena in human childhood.

Separation and Loss

The attachment to the mother has a corollary: A separation from her evokes distress. During the first few months of life, the infant will accept a substitute, perhaps because there is as yet no clear-cut conception of the mother that differentiates her from all other persons. But from somewhere between six and eight months of age, the infant comes to know who his mother is; he now cries and fusses when he sees her leave (Figure 16.5). The age at which children begin to register this protest against separation is pretty much the same across such diverse cultures as African Bushmen in Botswana, U.S. city dwellers, Indians in a Guatemalan village, and members of an Israeli kibbutz (Kagan, 1976).

LONG SEPARATION AND PERMANENT LOSS

To the child, seeing the mother leave is bad enough, but it's even worse if she doesn't return shortly. Lengthy separations can have serious effects. Infants of seven months or older who are placed in a hospital for a short stay fret and protest and seem negative and frightened. After returning home, they remain anxious for a while, as if terrified of another separation. They continually cling to their mother, scream when left alone by her, are unusually afraid of strangers, and may even become suspicious of such familiar persons as fathers and siblings (Schaffer and Callender, 1959). Such phenomena are yet another argument against the cupboard theory of attachment. Children in hospitals are presumably well-fed and diapered and have all of their bodily needs taken care of. If that is all the child wants, why the intense depression at the mother's absence?

Similar effects are often seen in older children. One study dealt with two- and three-year-olds who were placed in a residential nursery for some weeks. During the first few days, they cried frequently and desperately clung to some favorite toy they had brought along. After a while their crying abated, but not their distress. They became apathetic and hostile and lost previously acquired bowel control (Heinicke and Westheimer, 1966).

As children get older, they become increasingly secure in the knowledge that the mother will be there when needed; they can therefore accept increasingly long separations. According to some psychologists, this emotional knowledge provides a basic trust which then serves as the foundation for further attachments and allows the child to become independent, to become an adult (Erikson, 1963).

However firm our trust, eventually all of us must face the grim reality of irrevo-

A

B

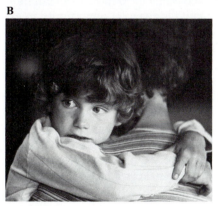

16.5 Fear of strangers *(A) An eight-month-old's response to a stranger's attempt to communicate. (From Bower, 1977; photo by Jennifer G. Wishart) (B) Even at age four, some fear of strangers remains. (Photograph by Suzanne Szasz)*

16.6 Grief in apes and humans *Two orphans, a young chimpanzee after losing his mother and an orphaned nineteenth-century boy. (Photograph by Jane von Lawick-Goodall, left; courtesy Barnardo Photo Library, right)*

cable separation (Figure 16.6). According to some authors, the grief experienced by adults at a loved one's death is in many ways akin to the separation anxiety of a child away from her mother. The first symptoms of grief are often crying, as in the mother-separated infants. Following this—again similar to the separated infants—the symptoms are those of hopeless despair: numb apathy, withdrawal, and profound depression (Bowlby, 1973). Similar effects are sometimes seen in ape and monkey mothers whose infants have died. They refuse to abandon the dead body, and carry it with them until it is only skin and skeleton.

ASSESSING ATTACHMENT

The reaction to separation provides a means for assessing the kind of attachment a particular infant has to his mother. A widely used procedure is the so-called "Strange Situation" devised by Mary Ainsworth and her colleagues for children of about one year of age (Figure 16.7). The child is first introduced to an unfamiliar room that contains many toys, and the child is given an opportunity to explore and play while the mother is present. After a while, a stranger enters, talks to the mother and then approaches the child. The next step is a brief separation—the mother goes out of the room, and leaves the child alone with the stranger. A reunion follows—the mother comes back and the stranger leaves (Ainsworth and Bell, 1970; Ainsworth, Blehar, Waters, and Wall, 1978).

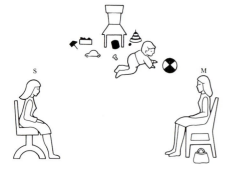

16.7 A diagrammatic sketch of the "Strange Situation" M *indicates the mother, and* S *the stranger. (Adapted from Ainsworth, Blehar, Waters, and Wall, 1978, p. 34)*

The quality of attachment The behavior of one-year-olds falls into several broad categories. One group (over two-thirds of the children in one of Ainsworth's studies) is described as "securely attached." As long as the mother is present, these children explore, play with the toys, and even make wary overtures to the stranger. They show some distress when the mother leaves, but greet her return with great enthusiasm. The remaining children show various behavior patterns that Ainsworth and her colleagues regard as signs of "insecure attachment." Some appear to be very anxious; they don't explore even in the mother's presence, become intensely upset and panicky when she leaves, and act emotionally ambivalent during the reunion, running to her to be picked up and then angrily struggling to get down. Others are distant and aloof from the very outset; they show little distress when the mother leaves and ignore her when she returns.

Attachment   *(Photograph by Sybil Shelton, Monkmeyer)*

There is some reason to believe that these behavior patterns reflect fairly stable characteristics, at least for the first few years of life. In one study, children who were rated as securely attached when observed in the Strange Situation at fifteen months of age were judged to be more outgoing, popular, and well-adjusted in nursery school at age three and a half (Waters, Wippman, and Sroufe, 1979).

The role of the father   Ainsworth's general approach has provided a means for studying various other aspects of early social development. An example is the infant's relation to the father. Thus far, we've concentrated entirely on the child's attachment to the mother. Is the father left out in the cold? To find out, one investigator used the Strange Situation with fathers as well as mothers and found signs of distress when the father left and some clinging and touching when he returned. It appears that the emotional life of the child is not exclusively wrapped up in the mother. But the mother seems to be more important, at least at an early age. There was more distress at the mother's departure than at the father's and more enthusiasm at her return (Kotelchuk, 1976).

These results suggest that the attachment to the father is less powerful than that to the mother. The best guess is that this disparity reflects the fact that for the vast majority of children in our society, the bulk of the caregiving is performed by the mother. In one study, infants had a little microphone attached to them which activated a recorder whenever anyone "talked" to them (or cooed or made other noises). During the first three months of their offspring's life, the fathers, on the average, spent less than one minute per day in such interactions. Under the circumstances, it may not be so surprising that, by and large, infants are more attached to their mothers, who spend very much more time in contact with them. What is surprising, given this extremely limited degree of interaction, is the fact that the attachment to the father is as strong as it is (Rebelsky and Hanks, 1971).

How Crucial Is Early Experience?

Theoretical details aside, Freud made two major claims about human social development. One was that the initial human social relationship is ultimately based on the gratification of basic creature needs. The other held that what happens in early childhood determines all future development. As we saw, there is good reason to believe that Freud's first claim is false, for it appears that humans—no less than ducks, lambs, and monkeys—are built to be social beings from the very outset. What can we say about his second claim? Here, there is still a great deal of controversy.

We will begin by describing some of the evidence that seems to be in line with Freud's belief in the all-important role of early experience.

THE ABSENCE OF ATTACHMENT

What happens when the initial attachment of the child to the mother is not allowed to form? The effects are apparently drastic.

Motherless monkeys   We previously considered Harlow's studies on rhesus monkeys raised with substitute mothers made of terry cloth. Some later studies

529

A   B

16.8 Motherless monkeys
*(A) A monkey reared in isolation,
huddling in terror in a corner of its cage.
(B) An isolated monkey biting himself at
the approach of a stranger. (Courtesy
Harry Harlow, University of Wisconsin
Primate Laboratory)*

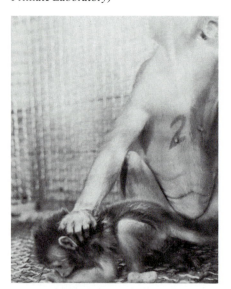

16.9 Motherless monkeys as mothers
*Female monkeys raised in isolation may
become mothers by artificial impregnation.
They usually ignore their infants.
Sometimes, as shown here, they abuse
them. (Courtesy Harry Harlow, University
of Wisconsin Primate Laboratory)*

asked what happens when monkey infants are reared without any contact at all. The infants were isolated for periods that ranged from three months to one year. During this time, they lived in an empty steel chamber and saw no living creature, not even a human hand.

After their period of solitary confinement, the animals' reactions were observed in various test situations. A three-month isolation had comparatively little effect. But longer periods led to dramatic disturbances. The animals huddled in a corner of the cage, clasped themselves, and rocked back and forth. When they were brought together with normally reared age-mates, the results were pathetic. There was none of the active chasing and playful romping that is characteristic of monkeys at that age. Whenever the normals took an aggressive lunge at them, the monkeys reared in isolation were unable to fight back. They withdrew, huddled, rocked—and bit *themselves* (Figure 16.8).

This social inadequacy persisted into adolescence and adulthood. One manifestation was a remarkable incompetence in sexual and parental matters. Formerly isolated males were utterly inept in the business of reproduction: As Harlow put it, "Isolates may grasp other monkeys of either sex by the head and throat aimlessly, a semi-erotic exercise without amorous achievements." Formerly isolated females resisted the sexual overtures of normal males. Some were eventually impregnated, in many cases by artificial means. When these motherless monkeys became monkey mothers themselves, they seemed to have no trace of love for their offspring. In a few cases, there was horrible abuse. The mothers crushed the infant's head to the floor, chewed off its toes or fingers, or bit it to death (Figure 16.9). Early social deprivation had evidently played havoc with the animals' subsequent social and emotional development (Suomi and Harlow, 1971, Harlow and Harlow, 1972; Harlow and Novak, 1973).

Humans reared in institutions Can we generalize from infant monkeys to human children? There is reason to suspect that there are some important similarities. After all, the monkey is related to *Homo sapiens,* however distantly; and like humans, monkeys go through a long period of development before they attain adulthood. In any case, it appears that human infants reared under conditions of comparative social isolation (although needless to say, not as drastic as that imposed on the monkeys) suffer somewhat analogous deficits.

The evidence comes from studies of infants reared in institutions. In many cases, they received perfectly adequate nutrition and bodily care; the problem was that there was very little social stimulation. In one institution the infants were kept in separate cubicles for the first eight months or so as a precaution against infectious disease. Their brief contacts with adults were restricted to the times when they were fed or diapered. Feeding took place in the crib with a propped-up bottle. There was little social give and take, little talk, little play, and little chance that the busy attendant would respond to any one baby's cry (Goldfarb, 1955; Provence and Lipton, 1962).

When these infants were compared to others who were raised normally, there were no differences for the first three or four months. Thereafter, the two groups diverged markedly. The institutionalized infants showed serious impairments in their social development. Some were insatiable in their incessant demands for individual love and attention. But the majority went in the opposite direction and became extremely apathetic in their reactions to people. They rarely tried to approach adults, either to hug and caress them or to get reassurance when in distress. A few others were reminiscent of Harlow's monkeys; they sat in a corner of their cribs, withdrawn and expressionless, and rocked their bodies.

It appears that many of these early deficits persist into later life. A number of studies have shown that in a fair number of cases—although by no means all—there are a number of intellectual deficits, for example in language and in abstract thinking, which persist into adolescence and beyond. There are also various long-term effects in the social and emotional sphere: heightened aggression, delinquency, and indifference to others (Yarrow, 1961).

The parallels to Harlow's monkeys are striking. As with monkeys, social deprivation in early life (although not at the very outset) led to serious disruption of subsequent social development.

ARE THE EFFECTS OF EARLY SOCIAL DEPRIVATION REVERSIBLE?

It's clear that early social deprivation has serious and unfortunate effects. But is that because the experience occurred early in life? And is the effect of that early experience irreversible? According to Freud—and many others—the answer to both questions is yes. To Freud there was no question that "the events of [the child's] first years are of paramount importance for his whole subsequent life." In effect, this position is in some ways analogous to the Calvinist doctrine of predestination. According to John Calvin, each person is predestined to be blessed or damned before he is ever born. To Freud, the die is cast by the age of five or six.

On the face of it, Freud's position fits the facts of maternal deprivation we've just described. It also fits in with the work of ethologists on imprinting. As we saw, this is established during a critical period in the bird's early life (analogous to the critical periods found for the acquisition of bird song and human language) and is often said to be essentially irreversible. All this argues for the proposition that there is a critical period for the establishment of social attachment and affection and that what happens then has effects that are virtually irreversible.

A

B

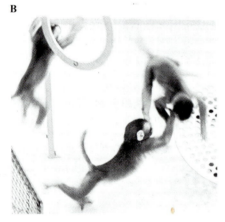

16.10 Therapy to undo the effects of early isolation *(A) A young, would-be therapist tenaciously clings to an unwilling isolate. (B) Some weeks later, there are strong signs of recovery as both patient and therapist engage in vigorous play. (Courtesy Harry Harlow, University of Wisconsin Primate Laboratory)*

Undoing the past in animals Some further evidence suggests that the dead hand of the past is not quite as rigid as Freud had supposed. For one thing, many of the effects of early isolation in monkeys turn out to be reversible. In one study, young rhesus monkeys were rehabilitated for social life after six months of isolation. They were placed together with monkey "therapists." These therapists were carefully chosen. They were normally reared and were three months *younger* than their patients. They were thus too young to display aggression but old enough to seek and initiate social contact. At first, the previously isolated monkeys withdrew and huddled in a corner. But they hadn't counted on the persistence of their little therapists who followed them and clung to them. After a while, the isolates clung back, and within a few weeks patients and therapists were vigorously playing with each other (Figure 16.10). Six months later, the patients seemed to be completely recovered. A later study showed that this kind of therapy worked even for monkeys isolated for an entire year (Suomi, Harlow, and McKinney, 1972; Novak and Harlow, 1975).*

A related finding concerns formerly isolated females who later became mothers. As we saw, these motherless females were total failures at the business of mothering. But while they ignored, rejected, or abused their first-borns, they were perfectly maternal to their second offspring—so much so, that they were virtually indistinguishable from normal rhesus monkeys. What could account for this discrepancy? One guess is that the first-borns served as "therapists" who helped their mothers become accustomed to another animal, especially an infant. This helped the mothers later, when dealing with a new offspring. The therapy was evidently not sufficient to protect the little therapists themselves, but that may only show that psychiatrists shouldn't treat their own mothers (Seay, Alexander, and Harlow 1964).

Undoing the past in humans With some luck and appropriate intervention, the past can evidently be overcome in animals, at least to some extent. Is the same true for humans?

The evidence is by no means clear-cut, but the results of one study give some grounds for optimism. The subjects were children at an overcrowded orphanage. There were few staff members and little individual attention. After about one and a half years, some of the children were transferred out of the orphanage to an institution for the mentally retarded. Ironically, this institution provided the necessary means for emotional and intellectual rehabilitation. There was a richer and more stimulating environment, but most important, there were many more adult caregivers. Each of the transferred children was "adopted" by one adult who became especially attached to the child. This new emotional relationship led to improvements in many spheres of behavior. While the intelligence-test scores of the children who remained in the orphanage dropped during the succeeding years, those of the transferred children rose considerably. Similarly for their social adjustment. When they reached their thirties, the transferred subjects had reached an educational and occupational level that was about average for the country at the time. In contrast, half of the subjects who remained behind never finished the third grade (Skeels, 1966).

---

* Related results have been obtained in various studies on birds, which suggest that imprinting is not quite as rigid and irreversible as it was once believed to be (Bateson, 1979).

ARE THERE ANY LONG-TERM EFFECTS OF EARLY MATERNAL SEPARATION?

The long-term effects of maternal deprivation can perhaps be overcome, but what about the effects of early maternal separation? A number of authors believe that such early separations may lead to lasting psychological damage. Thus John Bowlby asserts that any disturbance of the initial attachment of the child to the mother will render the person more emotionally insecure in later life. In his view, separation is psychologically dangerous, for the continuity of the child's relationship to the first attachment figure is a necessary element for the child's ultimate mental health (Bowlby, 1973). This position has had various social consequences. It has made many women uneasy about becoming working mothers and leaving their children with another person or in a day-care center. It has also affected legal policies in cases of child placement, with a bias in favor of keeping children in homes (in which they had presumably formed attachments) despite evidence of neglect or abuse (Maccoby, 1980). But a number of studies indicate that the long-term consequences of maternal separation are by no means irreversible.

One group of investigators studied children who were placed in adoptive homes when they were between six and eighteen months of age. Most of these infants had foster mothers to whom they had become attached, and upon separation they showed various degrees of distress. If separation has the traumatic effect it is sometimes said to have, one would expect that the children's ultimate adjustment should depend upon the magnitude of their emotional disturbance at the time of the adoption. But when tested at the age of ten, they showed no signs of such a relationship. The best guess is that the child's adjustment at age ten does not depend on the quality of her emotional life at age one or two, but rather on what happened in all the years in between (Yarrow and Goodwin, 1973; Yarrow et al., 1973).

Further findings throw doubt on the view that the attachment relationship has to be continuous, or that the attachment between mother and child is necessarily weakened when there are several caregivers. An example comes from a study that compared children reared entirely at home with children enrolled in a day-care program. The children in the day-care center were no less attached to their mothers than were children raised entirely at home. Nor were there any differences in tests for social and intellectual development (Kagan, Kearsley, and Zelazo, 1978). Much the same holds for comparisons of mothers who work with those who don't. The bulk of the evidence suggests that maternal employment does not usually have detrimental effects (Hoffman, 1974).

REASSESSING THE ROLE OF EARLY EXPERIENCE

In light of all this, we must evidently reassess our views on the all-importance of early social experience. That experience certainly provides a vital foundation upon which further social relationships are built. But experiences in infancy or childhood do not affect adult behavior directly. What happens instead is that each step in a sequence of social developments paves the way for the next. In monkeys, the mother's presence during the first six months allays the infants' fears of approaching other monkeys. As a result, they can play with their age-mates and enter the social apprenticeship of childhood and adolescence. In interacting with their peers, they gradually acquire the social skills of adult monkeyhood; they can chase and be chased, can cope with aggression, and if necessary inhibit their own. These skills allow both sexes to mate when they reach maturity and also enable them to respond appropriately to their own offspring. Each stage is a preparation for the next: The mother-infant tie enables the infant to enjoy peer regulations that ultimately lead to mating, and so on. Given this step-by-step progression, the motherless infants can be redeemed by introducing them to the subsequent peer stage by an unusual and special means—the unthreatening young therapists.

Something of a similar nature probably holds for human social development as well. The early years are crucial in the sense that certain social patterns are much more likely to be acquired then, such as the capacity to form attachments to other people. These early attachments are a likely prerequisite for the formation of later ones. The child who has never been loved by his parents will be frightened by his peers and probably hampered in his further social development. But while the earlier attachments (to mother and father) lay the foundation for later ones (to friends, lovers, and one's own children), the two are nevertheless quite different. As a result, there may be ways—as with Harlow's monkey therapists—of acquiring the social tools for dealing with one's later life that circumvent the handicaps of one's early childhood. For while the past affects the present, it does not predetermine it.

To sum up. The easiest way of getting to the second floor of a house is by way of the first floor. But in a pinch one can always bring a ladder and climb in through a window.

CHILDHOOD SOCIALIZATION

The infant's attachment to her caregiver marks her entrance into the social world. This is the starting point of *socialization,* the process by which the child acquires the patterns of thought and behavior that are characteristic of the society in which she is born. But socialization doesn't begin in earnest until somewhat later in childhood, when the individual starts to learn what she must and musn't do as a member of her society. Our primary focus will be on the first agent of this socialization process: the child's family, which instills the first do's and don'ts of social life.

Cultural Values and Child Rearing

Some of the goals of socialization are pretty much the same all over the world and probably were so throughout human history. The child may be an African bushman or a New York city dweller; in either case, he'll have to develop some control over his own bodily functions (for example, toilet training) and over his own impulses (for example, aggression). For wherever he lives, he'll have to learn that he has to live with others and that those others may have wants that take precedence over his own. As a result, there have to be some important similarities in the way all children are brought up.

But there are some important differences as well. Some of these simply reflect differences in the dominant values of the culture of which the parents are a part.

Socialization   Most authors agree that parents exert some effect on the personality development of their children. What is at issue is what effects they have and how they achieve them.

This is hardly surprising. The child is socialized to become a member of a *particular* society, whether it be a band of nomad herdsmen, a medieval village, or a tribe of Polynesian fishermen. Each of these societies will inevitably try to instill different characteristics in its young members-to-be. This point is especially clear when we consider the economy on which the society is based. Cultures that make their living through agriculture or animal husbandry tend to stress compliance, conformity, and responsibility as they raise their children. These attributes fit the adult role that the child must eventually assume—the patient, cooperative life of a farmer who must plough his soil or milk his cows at specified times so as to protect and augment an accumulated food supply. In contrast, hunting and fishing societies emphasize self-reliance and initiative—reasonable values for people who have to wrest their food from nature in day-to-day individual encounters (Barry, Child, and Bacon, 1959).

In our own culture, some differences in child rearing are associated with the parents' social class. Several comparisons of the ways in which middle-class and working-class parents rear their children point to one major difference: Working-class parents tend to stress the importance of controls from the outside, while middle-class parents try to instill control from within. When asked what parents should emphasize in raising their children, working-class parents mention "obedience," while middle-class parents are more likely to say "self-control." This makes sense if we consider the world the parents live and work in. By and large, members of the working class are in occupations in which their work is closely supervised—a boss or a foreman tells them what to do and they do it. In contrast, the work of middle-class persons is only loosely supervised, if at all, and it may be entirely self-directed. Thus parents try to make their children behave at home as they themselves do in the working place—the one is required to become obedient and to follow orders, the other to become his own boss and to learn how to control himself. A further result fits in neatly: The more closely supervised the father is at work, the more likely he is to use physical punishment—external control in one of its more extreme versions (Kohn, 1969; Hess, 1970).

Theories of Socialization

We've asked about the goals of socialization. But what about the means whereby these goals are achieved? Different theories emphasize different mechanisms that bring this about. Some stress the role of reward and the fear of punishment. Others point to the importance of imitation. Still others argue for the importance of the child's growing understanding of what she is supposed to do and why.

SOCIALIZATION AND REINFORCEMENT

Freud believed that the socialization process is essentially one of taming. The seething instinctual urges of the id are blocked and rechanneled and the parental do's and don'ts are ultimately internalized. Some aspects of this position are similar to those of operant behavior theory (see Chapter 4). Both views share one basic tenet: The child is socialized by a calculus of pain and pleasure. She will continue to do (or wish or think or remember) whatever previously brought her gratification and will refrain from whatever led to punishment and anxiety.

SOCIAL LEARNING THEORY

Many psychologists believe that a theory exclusively based on classical and instrumental conditioning cannot possibly do justice to the socialization process. For we are animals with a culture, which makes us altogether unlike any of the animals studied in the learning laboratory. Thorndike's cats had to discover how to get out of the puzzle box by themselves (see Chapter 4). No other cat told them how to do it; no other cat could. But in the course of a lifetime, human beings learn a multitude of problem solutions that were discovered by those who came before them. They do not have to invent spoken language or the alphabet; they do not have to discover fire or the wheel or even how to eat baby food with a spoon. Other people show them.

Modeling A group of psychologists who are sometimes called *social learning theorists* regard *observational learning* as one of the most powerful mechanisms of socialization. The child observes another person who serves as a *model* and then proceeds to imitate what the model does and thus learns how to do something he didn't know before (Figure 16.11). The child sees an adult hammer a nail into a board and tries to duplicate the same feat (with any luck, not on the new dining room table). Many cultures explicitly use such imitative patterns as a way of inducting the child into adult ways. In one Central American society, young girls are presented with miniature replicas of a water jar, a broom, and a grinding stone. They observe how their mothers use the real objects and through constant imitation acquire the relevant skills themselves (Bandura and Walters, 1963).

How does a person learn a new response by imitation? There is little doubt that imitative learning is not a species of classical or instrumental conditioning. As social learning theorists point out, imitation may occur even though the observer

16.11 Learning by imitation *Skills as diverse as hunting and performing a traditional tea ceremony are learned by imitating an accomplished model. (*Left: *photograph by N. R. Farbman,* Life. Right: *photograph by Michal Heron, Woodfin Camp)*

does not copy the model's actions at the time that he sees them (learning without performance) and even though he neither receives a reward himself nor sees the model receive one (learning without reinforcement).

Imitation and performance Imitation may involve a response one already knows. In this case, what is learned by watching others is whether a response should or should not be performed. Consider a foreign visitor who is invited to a feast on some South Sea island. At the end of the meal, her hosts belch thunderously and then look at her. She pauses, gulps, and finally belches too. She obviously didn't learn how to belch by watching her hosts. But she learned that it was acceptable (in fact, demanded) that she do so now. In this example, a previously learned but generally inhibited response is disinhibited by observational learning. A similar effect is the inhibition of responses by imitation. When others lower their voices, we generally do the same. Such imitative effects sometimes occur without awareness, as when we start to whisper to a person with laryngitis.

Social learning theorists have conducted a number of experiments which show that the performance of an observed act depends in part upon the characteristics of the model. Not surprisingly, subjects are more likely to imitate people they like, respect, and regard as competent (Lefkowitz, Blake, and Mouton, 1955). Whether they will imitate something the model does will also depend upon the consequences that seem to befall the model. In a widely cited study, several groups of nursery-school children were shown a film that featured an adult and a large plastic "Bobo doll." The adult walked over to the doll and ordered it out of the way. When the doll did not comply, the adult punched it, hit it with a mallet, and kicked it around the room, punctuating her attacks with suitable phrases such as "Right on the nose, boom, boom," and "Sockeroo, stay down." One group saw the film up to this point but no further. Another group saw a final segment in which villainy was shown to come to a bad end. A second adult arrived on the scene, called the aggressor a big, bad bully, spanked her, and threatened further spankings if she should ever do such a bad thing again. After seeing the films, all children were brought into a room that contained various toys, including a Bobo doll. They were left alone but were watched through a one-way screen. The children who never saw the villain's comeuppance imitated the model's aggressive acts and the Bobo doll came in for a hard time (Figure 16.12). In contrast, those children who had seen the model's punishment behaved much more pacifically (Bandura, 1965).

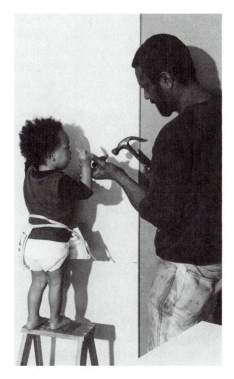

Modeling in real life (Photograph by Frostie, Woodfin Camp)

16.12 Copying a model Children watch an adult strike an inflated rubber doll with a mallet and promptly strike it too. (From Bandura, Ross, and Ross, 1963)

A

B

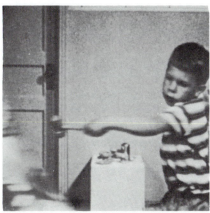

C

COGNITIVE DEVELOPMENTAL THEORY

Psychologists who emphasize social learning are clearly at odds with those theorists who argue that socialization is a process whereby the child is passively molded, whether through the taming of instinctual urges (Freud), through classical conditioning (Pavlov), or instrumental learning (Skinner). The social learning approach focuses on processes like observational learning that operate much less blindly than the mechanisms in which Freud, Pavlov, and Skinner put their trust. But there is yet another point of view which argues that social learning has not gone far enough in its opposition to blind molding. This is the ***cognitive approach*** to socialization, which emphasizes the role of understanding in interpersonal conduct and thought.

Cognitive theorists believe that there are many situations in which the child behaves neither as a creature impelled by irrational forces, nor as a puppet controlled by schedules of reward and punishment, nor as a sheep that follows an adult leader. For the child has some understanding of her own actions; she not only knows that some things are "bad" and others "good" but has some sense of why. Initially her understanding is quite dim, but as her mental development unfolds, so does her rational comprehension of how one does (or should) relate to others. As a result, much of social development is a consequence of cognitive development.

Imitation through understanding To illustrate the cognitive theory of socialization, let's go back to the topic of imitation. Cognitive theorists argue that understanding plays a crucial role, both in learning by imitation and in performing a response one has learned by watching others. There's little doubt that imitative learning involves considerable cognitive complexity (see Chapter 14). One of the requirements seems to be a realization of the correspondence between one's own body and that of the model's. Consider a boy who imitates his father hitching up his trousers. In order to do so, he has to relate his own clothes and body to those of his father: my trouser belt is to my hands as his trouser belt is to his hands, and so on. In effect, the imitator takes the model's role. But he can do so only if the model's behavior fits into what Piaget would have called a well-developed cognitive "schema" (Piaget, 1951; Aronfreed, 1969). Under the circumstances, it is hardly surprising that children imitate more accurately as they get older, for their ability to utilize what they see the model do presumably increases with their cognitive development (Yando, Seitz, and Zigler, 1978).

The desire for competence Another difference concerns the motive for imitation. Here, as in other areas of the child's behavior, cognitive theorists stress that the child wants to be an active agent rather than a passive object. She wants to master her universe and come to do things on her own, rather than being passively molded or blindly led. When she imitates an adult model, she is not primarily interested in getting cookies or receiving praise. A no less important reason for copying her elders is that she wants to be able to do some of the many things the all-powerful adults are capable of. For eventually, she wants to be all-powerful too. In this sense, imitation is its own reward. The child wants to attain some sense of her own competence. Once she can copy an adult's action, she wants to be observed in her own turn, to be an actor and not just a passive watcher, and so she clamors eagerly: "Watch *me* do it! Watch!"

Given this view of what the child wants, her imitation of adult models no longer seems blind and irrational. The novice climber who follows a guide is in no way like a sheep that runs after a leader; he follows because he know that the guide will bring him safely up and down the mountain slope. The child who imitates is no less rational, for he proceeds from the perfectly reasonable premise that, by and large, adults know more than he (Kohlberg, 1969).

Patterns of Child Rearing

Thus far, we have looked at socialization from the standpoint of the child who is being socialized, and we have considered how he learns the lessons that society tries to teach him—whether by reinforcement, or modeling, or understanding, or all three. We now shift our focus to those that serve as society's first teachers: the child's parents. Do different ways in which they rear children produce differences in the children's behavior? If so, how lasting are the effects?

FEEDING AND TOILET TRAINING

To answer questions of this sort, one must first decide which particular aspects of the parents' behavior one wants to focus on. Until thirty years ago, developmental psychologists interested in these general issues were heavily influenced by psychoanalytic theories. As a result, they concerned themselves with aspects of child rearing that Freud and his followers had made so much of. They asked about the effects of different practices associated with feeding, weaning, and toilet training. Does breast feeding produce happier (or unhappier) infants? What about early weaning or early toilet training? As it turned out, the answer is that these (and many other) child-rearing particulars have little or no effect (Orlansky, 1949; Zigler and Child, 1969; Zigler, Lamb, and Child, 1982).

CHILD-REARING STYLES

In recent years, developmental psychologists have taken a different approach. Instead of concentrating on specific child-rearing practices, they have turned their attention to the general home atmosphere in which the child is raised (Baumrind, 1967, 1971; Maccoby and Martin, 1983).

Different kinds of parents In a number of studies, parents were asked to describe the way they dealt with their children and were also observed with them in various situations. Several patterns of child rearing emerged. One is the so-called *autocratic* pattern in which the parents control the child strictly, and often quite sternly. The rules they set down are essentially edicts whose infraction leads to severe (and frequently physical) punishment. Nor do they attempt to explain these rules to the child, who has to accept them as a simple manifestation of parental power: "It's because I say so, that's why."

At the opposite extreme is the *permissive* pattern in which children encounter few don'ts and even fewer do's. The parents try not to assert their authority, impose few restrictions and controls, tend not to have set time schedules (for, say, bedtime or watching TV), and rarely use punishment. They also make few demands on the children—such as putting toys away, or doing schoolwork, or helping with chores.

539

Autocratic parents brandish parental power; permissive parents abdicate it. But there is a third pattern that is in some ways in between. It is called **authoritative-reciprocal** because the parents exercise their power but also accept the reciprocal obligation to respond to the child's point of view and his reasonable demands. Unlike the permissive parents, they govern; but unlike the autocratic ones, they try to govern with the consent of the governed.

Parents whose pattern is authoritative-reciprocal set rules of conduct for their children and enforce them when they have to. They are fairly demanding, assign duties, expect their children to behave maturely and "act their age," and spend a good deal of time in teaching their children how to perform appropriately. But they also encourage the child's independence, and allow a good deal of verbal give-and-take.

Different kinds of children   Are there any differences between children that are raised in these three different styles? One investigator observed preschoolers in various settings. She found that children raised autocratically were more withdrawn, lacked independence, and were more angry and defiant (especially the boys). Interestingly enough, children at the opposite end of the spectrum had similar characteristics. Thus children whose parents were permissive were not particularly independent and (if boys) they were more prone to anger. In addition, they seemed very immature and lacked social responsibility. In contrast, the children raised in the authoritative-reciprocal mode were more independent, competent, and socially responsible. Here, as so often, there seems to be a happy medium.

There is evidence that the parental pattern when the child was three or four is related to the way the child behaves in later years. When observed at the age of eight or nine, children whose parents had been judged to be either autocratic or permissive five years earlier seemed to be relatively low in intellectual self-reliance and originality. Once again, the children raised in the authoritative-reciprocal style fared best. They were more self-reliant when faced by intellectual challenges, strove for achievement, and were socially more self-confident and at ease (Baumrind, 1977).

"They never pushed me. If I wanted to retrieve, shake hands, or roll over, it was entirely up to me."

The Child's Effect on the Parents

Thus far, we have discussed socialization as something that is done *to* the child. But in recent years, developmental psychologists have become increasingly insistent that socialization is a two-way street. For the child is more than a lump of psychological clay that is shaped by various social agencies. In actual fact, he actively participates in his own rearing. His own behavior affects that of the parent, whose behavior then in turn affects him. To the extent that this is true, the parents don't just socialize the child. They are also socialized by him (Bell, 1968; Bell and Harper, 1977).

One of the main reasons why socialization works in both directions is that infants differ from the very day they are born. For example, there are differences in *temperament* that probably have a built-in, genetic basis (see Chapter 18). One infant may be relatively placid and passive; another may be more active and assertive. These differences persist over at least the first two years of life and may last much beyond. The mother will respond quite differently to these two infants. If we later study the correlation between what the mother did and how the child behaves, we will find a correlation. But in this case, the order of cause and effect is the reverse of the one that is actually expected. A difference in the child led to a difference in the way his parents treated him (Thomas, Chess and Birch, 1970; Osofsky and Danzger, 1974; Olweus, 1980).

Such reversed cause-and-effect relations can never be ignored as possible (although probably only partial) explanations of correlations between the way a child was reared and his personality. As an example consider the effect of physical punishment. As already mentioned, there is some evidence which suggests that parents who resort to physical punishment have children who tend to be more aggressive than average (Feshbach, 1970; Parke and Slaby, 1983). If this relationship is genuine, how should we interpret it? One possibility is that the parents provide a model for their child who learns to do to others what his parents have done unto him. But there is an alternative. Some children may be more aggressive to begin with, and they are the ones who are more likely to be spanked. The relation may be even more complex. The more aggressive child will probably be punished more severely; this will lead to more aggression in the child, which will then provoke yet further parental countermeasures.

The best guess is that all these cause-and-effect relationships exist side by side. The parents' behavior affects the child, but the child's behavior also affects the parents—a continual, interactive pattern in which the characteristics of all parties in the family act as both cause and effect.

THE DEVELOPMENT OF MORALITY

Initially, the child's social world is largely confined to the family. His first lessons in social behavior are taught in the limited family context: pick up your toys, don't push your baby brother, and so on—circumscribed commands and prohibitions that apply to a very narrow social setting. But his social sphere soon grows to include young peers: at home, in day-care centers, in preschool settings, still later in the schools. These peers become increasingly important and their approval is then sought as eagerly (if not more eagerly) than that of his parents. Eventually the child's social universe expands still further as he acquires rules of social thought and action that are vastly broader than the simple commands and prohibitions of his toddler years. For these rules pertain not just to the persons he meets face-to-face but to countless others he has never met and probably never will meet. Among the most important of these rules are those of moral conduct.

Not Doing Wrong

All societies have prohibitions that its members must learn to obey despite various temptations to the contrary. It's easy enough to set up external sanctions that enforce the prohibitions from the outside. Children rarely steal from the cookie jar when their parents are present. The trick is to make them resist temptation when they are not being watched. The person who does not steal or cheat because he thinks that he will be caught is not moral; he's merely prudent. One aim of socialization is to instill moral values that are ***internalized,*** so that the individual will shun transgressions because he feels that they are wrong and not because he is afraid of being punished.

THE ROLE OF PUNISHMENT

What leads to the internalization of right and wrong? According to Freud the primary agent of internalization is the superego, a component of the personality that controls various forbidden impulses by administering self-punishment in the form of guilt and anxiety (see Chapter 12). The child kicks his little brother, and the parents punish him. As a result, the forbidden act (or, for that matter, the mere thought of that act) becomes associated with anxiety. As a result, the child will feel a pang of anxiety the next time he starts to attack his younger brother. To stop this painful feeling, he must stop that which triggered it: the thought, let alone the execution, of the forbidden behavior. The sum total of all such internalized inhibitions is the ***superego,*** a remnant of our childhood that remains with us for the rest of our lives and makes sure that we commit no wrong. The external authorities that once punished our transgressions have long stopped watching the cookie jar. But they no longer have to because they now inhabit our minds, where we can no longer hide from them.

INTERNALIZING PROHIBITIONS

This general view of the inhibition of forbidden acts makes certain predictions about the relation between child rearing and moral behavior. If the superego is a remnant of punishment administered during childhood, one would expect that the internalization of prohibition is most pronounced in children whose parents relied on sheer power in raising them—whether this power was exercised by the use of physical punishment, or deprivation of privileges, or threats of withdrawal of love and of abandonment.

This prediction turns out to be false. For a number of studies suggest that prohibitions are *less* internalized in children whose parents primarily relied on power in its various forms than in children whose parents took pains to explain just why a misdeed was wrong and why the child ought to behave differently. The children of power-asserting (autocratic) parents were more likely to cheat for a prize when they thought no one was looking, and they were less likely to feel guilt about their misdeeds or to confess them when confronted (Hoffman, 1970).

A recent proposal tries to deduce these and other phenomena of socialization from the so-called principle of *minimal sufficiency*. This states that a child will internalize a certain way of acting if there is just enough pressure to get him to behave in this new way, but not enough so that he feels he was forced to do so. This principle seems to fit a number of experimental findings. An example is a study in which children were prohibited from playing with a particularly attractive toy. For some children, the prohibition was backed with a mild threat (e.g., "I will be a little bit annoyed with you"); for others, the threat was severe (e.g., "I will be very upset and very angry with you"). When later tested in a rather different situation in which they thought they were unobserved, the mildly threatened children resisted temptation more than the severely threatened ones. The punishment led to internalization, but it did so only if it was *not* the most memorable part of the child's experience.

The same principle may help account for some of the effects of child rearing we've discussed in a prior section. We saw that the children of authoritative-reciprocal parents are more likely to internalize their parents' standards than the children of autocratic or permissive parents. This is in accord with the minimal sufficiency hypothesis. Autocratic parents supply too much force to induce their children to behave in the appropriate way, so their children become outwardly compliant but will not change their inner attitudes. Permissive parents apply no force at all, so their children never change their behavior in the first place—they won't even comply outwardly, let alone internalize. But authoritative-reciprocal parents somehow manage to strike the proper balance. They apply a force just strong enough to get their children to change their behavior, but mild enough so that the children come to believe that they performed the moral act of their own free will (Lepper, 1983).*

Doing Good

Thus far, our discussion of moral action has dealt with the inhibition of forbidden acts. But moral action pertains to do's no less than to don'ts, to doing good as well as to not committing evil. How does the child develop the capacity for positive moral actions that call for some personal sacrifice and *altruism*—to do something for others even at some cost to herself?

Thus far, we are still far from an answer. A number of studies show that even very young children try to help and comfort others, and occasionally share with them (e.g., Staub, 1970; Rheingold, Hay, and West, 1976). The question is why. According to a Hobbesian view of human nature, such apparently unselfish acts are much more egoistic than they appear to be on the surface. Perhaps the child only gives to others in order to reap some ultimate benefit for himself, such as avoiding censure and obtaining social approval. There is some evidence that this hypothesis is false, for in fact children who tend to help others are more popular

---

* This is reminiscent of the effects of forced compliance on attitudes. As we saw in Chapter 11, subjects who are pressured into performing some action that runs counter to their own attitudes, will tend to change this attitude if the pressure (the threat or the bribe) is relatively small, but will not change the attitude if the pressure is large (Festinger and Carlsmith, 1959; Aronson and Carlsmith, 1963).

A

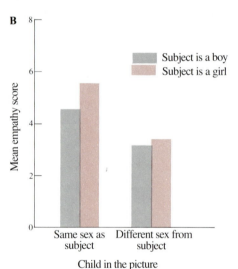

B

16.13 **It is easier to empathize with those who are similar** (A) Six- and seven-year-olds were presented with sequences of pictures such as this. After looking at each sequence, the child was asked "How do you feel?" Empathy was scored as a feeling that corresponded to that of the child in the picture (here, anger). (Courtesy of Norma Feshbach) (B) The children's empathy scores (the maximum score was 8). As the figure shows, the boys (in black) felt greater empathy when the child in the picture was a boy than when it was a girl; girls felt more empathy when it was a girl than when it was a boy. (Adapted from Feshbach and Roe, 1968)

and self-confident than children who are less inclined to do so. This suggests that altruism is more likely when one's own needs for social approval are already satisfied. But if so, its main motivation is probably not the desire to gain yet further social approval (Hoffman, 1975a).

EMPATHY

Such findings argue against the Hobbesian position that humans are by nature self-centered. A further argument comes from studies of **empathy** in very young infants. Empathy is a direct emotional response to another person's emotions; we see a patient writhe in pain in a hospital bed and we ourselves experience distress (Aronfreed, 1968). Some precursors to such empathic reactions are found in the first two days of life. On hearing a newborn's cry, one-day-old infants cry too and their hearts beat faster (Simner, 1971; Sagi and Hoffman, 1976).

What accounts for such empathic reactions at this tender age? According to one hypothesis, the reason is classical conditioning. In this view, the response of crying becomes conditioned to the sound of crying. Initially, crying was evoked by some pain or discomfort. But soon the sound of the infant's own crying became a conditioned stimulus for further crying. Since another baby's cry resembles the infant's own, it will elicit his own cry as a conditioned response (in addition to various other distress reactions, such as increased heart rate). An alternative hypothesis is that some empathic reactions are innately given, a position that is by no means implausible given the facts on built-in alarm and distress reactions in many animals (see Chapter 10). As yet it is too early to choose between these two views. But whichever turns out to be correct, it is clear that some forerunner of what may later become a feeling for others is found at the very start of life. No man is an island, not even as a newborn.

The newborn's response to another baby's cry is just the first step in the development of empathic feelings for others. Initially, there is probably no clear separation between "self" and "other," and the infant may not really know that he is reacting to *another* child's distress. Genuine empathy, in which one feels for another while yet perfectly aware that this other is not oneself, probably doesn't come much before the end of the first year. At about two years of age, children can put it in words: "Her eyes are crying—her sad" or "Janie crying, want mommy" (Bretherton, McNew, and Beeghly-Smith, 1981; see Figure 16.13).

FROM EMPATHIC DISTRESS TO UNSELFISH ACTION

The mere fact that one feels empathy doesn't mean that one will do anything about it. For to help one's fellows, one has to do more than just feel for them. One also has to act on this feeling. And one has to know how.

Consider a two-year-old girl who sees an adult in pain—say, an uncle who has cut his finger with a knife. In all likelihood, she will feel empathy and become distressed herself. But what will she do? A number of anecdotes suggest that she will give her uncle whatever *she* finds most comforting herself—for example, her favorite doll. While appreciating her kindly sentiments, the uncle would probably have preferred a band-aid or a stiff drink. But the child is as yet too young to take his perspective and doesn't realize that his needs are not the same as hers (Hoffman, 1976, 1977).

As we develop, we become increasingly able to tell what other people are likely to feel in a given situation and how to help if help is needed. But even that is not enough to ensure that we will act unselfishly. For helping is only one means of getting rid of the empathic distress that is caused by the sight of another person's pain. There is an easier but more callous method: one can simply look away. This often occurs in the big city, with its many beggars and derelicts and victims of violence, where empathy may seem a luxury one can no longer afford. It may also occur in war or other situations where people "harden their hearts" to become immune to the sufferings of others, in part because they come to believe that these others are not really "human" after all (see Chapter 11).

Such arguments indicate that while empathy is a likely precursor of altruism, it does not guarantee it. In fact, there may be some circumstances in which empathy will interfere with appropriate helpful action. An interesting finding concerns a group of nurses who worked in a ward for severely ill persons. Those nurses who seemed to experience the greatest degree of empathy for their patients were the least effective. The reason was simple. They couldn't bear their patients' pain, and so they tried to have as little contact with them as possible (Stotland, Mathews, Sherman, Hansson and Richardson, 1978).

Moral Reasoning

Thus far, our focus has been on the development of moral behavior. What about the development of moral thought? What happens to the child's conception of right and wrong as he grows up? Much of the research on this topic has been strongly influenced by Piaget's cognitive developmental approach.

PIAGET AND THE CHILD'S CONCEPTION OF MORALITY

As we saw in our discussion of cognitive development, Piaget believed that children before age five or six are relatively egocentric, being unable to see the world from any perspective other than their own (see Chapter 14). According to Piaget, this same egocentric pattern is revealed when the child has to make a moral judgment. Our adult conceptions of crime and punishment place great emphasis upon the perpetrator's intention and carefully distinguish between accident and design. But this distinction requires an ability to take account of another person's motives. Young children cannot readily do this, anymore than they can take account of width in a liquid conservation task while attending to height. In consequence, they tend to consider only the extent of the injury produced by the deed, regardless of the motive. In one of Piaget's studies, children had to judge which of two boys was the naughtier. John accidentally tripped, fell against a cupboard, and smashed fifteen cups. In contrast, Henry only broke one cup, which he knocked to the floor while climbing the cupboard to steal some forbidden jam. Younger children generally judged John to be the greater villain who should be punished more severely; after all, he had broken fifteen cups! Older children were much more likely to consider intent (Piaget, 1932).*

* Whether the situation is as clear-cut as Piaget believed is debatable. After all, we saw that even very young children have some primitive empathic notion of another person's joy or distress, which indicates that the child's egocentrism is by no means complete. In fact, there is evidence that if the judgment task is made somewhat easier, then intentions are considered even by six-year-olds (e.g., Feldman, Klosson, Parsons, Rholes, and Ruble, 1976).

KOHLBERG'S STAGES OF MORAL REASONING

Piaget's account of moral development is the basis of a more elaborate stage theory devised by Lawrence Kohlberg, who has tried to extend it to adolescence and adulthood. Kohlberg's basic method is to confront subjects with a number of stories that pose a moral dilemma. An example is a story about a man whose wife will die unless treated with a very expensive drug that costs $2,000. The husband scraped together all the money he could, but it was not enough. The pharmacist refused to give him the drug and to let him pay the balance later. In desperation, the husband broke into the pharmacy and stole the drug. The subjects were asked whether the husband's act was right or wrong and why (Kohlberg, 1969).

Stages of moral reasoning   Kohlberg analyzed the subjects' answers and concluded that moral reasoning proceeds through a series of successive stages. Roughly speaking, there is a progression from a primitive morality guided by personal fear of punishment or desire for gain ("If you let your wife die, you'll get in trouble"), through stages in which right or wrong are defined by convention, by what people will say ("Your family will think you're an inhuman husband if you don't"), to the highest stage in which there are internalized moral principles that have become one's own ("If you didn't steal the drug, you wouldn't be blamed and you would have lived up to the outside rule of the law, but you wouldn't have lived up to your own standards of conscience"). As one might expect, there is a rough correlation between Kohlberg's levels and age. But even in adulthood only a small proportion of the subjects give answers that correspond to Kohlberg's highest level. Given that Kohlberg considers this as the level that characterized such moral giants as Mahatma Gandhi and Dr. Martin Luther King, the failure of most of his subjects (and no doubt, most of us) to attain it is perhaps not too surprising (Figure 16.14; Table 16.1).

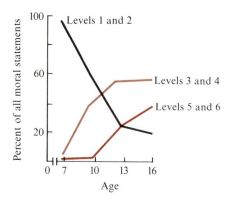

16.14   Level of moral reasoning as a function of age   *With increasing age, the level of moral reasoning changes. In this figure, the percent of all moral judgments made by children at various ages falls into one of three general categories defined by Kohlberg. At seven, virtually all moral judgments are in terms of avoiding punishment or gaining reward (Kohlberg's levels 1 and 2). At ten, about half the judgments are based on criteria of social approval and disapproval or of a—rigid— code of laws (Kohlberg's levels 3 and 4). From thirteen on, some of the children refer to more abstract rules—a generally agreed-upon social contract or a set of abstract ethical principles (Kohlberg's levels 5 and 6). (After Kohlberg, 1963)*

Table 16.1   KOHLBERG'S STAGES OF MORAL REASONING

Stage of moral reasoning	Moral behavior is that which:
Preconventional morality	
Level 1	Avoids punishment
Level 2	Gains reward
Conventional morality	
Level 3	Gains approval and avoids disapproval of others
Level 4	Is defined by rigid codes of "law and order"
Postconventional morality	
Level 5	Is defined by a "social contract" generally agreed upon for the public good
Level 6	Is based on abstract ethical principles that determine one's own moral code

SOURCE: Adapted from Kohlberg, 1967.

Moral reasoning and moral conduct   Are Kohlberg's stages of moral development related to ethical conduct? To some extent they may be. Thus a number of studies found that delinquents were at a lower stage of moral reasoning than nondelinquents of the same age and IQ. Other studies suggest that individuals at higher, principled levels of moral reasoning are less likely to cheat in an ambiguous situation in which they are unobserved and are more likely to maintain their position against the pressure of other people's views. But taken as a whole, the evidence suggests that the relation between moral reasoning and moral conduct is quite weak (Kurtines and Greif, 1974; Blasi, 1980). The trouble is that Kohlberg's stages do not specifically pertain to conduct. They concern an individual's ability to *describe* certain moral principles, but they don't tell us much about the individual's actual behavior, which may or may not be ruled by the principles he described.

Kohlberg has shown that the ability to describe and reason about such moral principles roughly increases with age and mental development. But this is not particularly surprising. After all, the same holds for the ability to describe and to reason about various other rules of mental life—for example, those that pertain to space, to causality, or to language. Seen in this light, Kohlberg's stages may have less to do with the development of morality than with the development of something we might call "meta-morality" (in analogy to the metacognitive processes we've described in a previous section): the ability to reflect on moral rules, regardless of whether one lives by them (see Chapters 8 and 14).

THE DEVELOPMENT OF SEX ROLES

Thus far, our emphasis has been on social development considered as growth and expansion. But social development is more than that. Like physical and cognitive development, it involves growth, but this growth is not just a matter of increasing size. It is also accompanied by increasing differentiation. For as the child gets older, she becomes increasingly aware of the fact that people differ from each other and from herself. In so doing, she also gains a clearer conception of her own self and of her own personality—what she is really like, in her own eyes and in those of others.

Seen in this light, social development goes hand-in-hand with the development of a sense of personal identity. One of the most important examples of this is sexual identity—of being male or female and all that goes with it.

Biologically, sexual identity seems simple enough. It may refer to XX vs. XY chromosome pairs or to the external genitals. But what does it mean psychologically? It refers to three issues. One is **gender identity**—our inner sense of whether we are male or female. A second is **gender role**—a whole host of external behavior patterns that a given culture deems appropriate for each sex. A third is **sexual orientation**—the choice of a sexual partner, which is by and large—though of course not always—directed toward the opposite sex. Gender identity, gender role, and sexual orientation are among the most important determinants of a person's social existence.* How do they come about?

* It has become customary to distinguish between *sex* and *gender*. The term *sex* is generally reserved for aspects of the male-female difference that pertain to reproductive functions (for example, ovaries versus testes, vagina versus penis) or to designate erotic feelings, inclinations, or practices (for example, heterosexual, homosexual). The term *gender* refers to social or psychological aspects of being seen as a man or woman or regarding oneself to be so. It is one thing to be a male, it is another to be a man. The same holds for being female and being a woman (Stoller, 1968).

Gender Roles

Gender roles pervade all facets of social life. The induction into one or the other of these roles begins with the very first question that is asked when a human being enters the world: "Is it a boy or a girl?" As soon as the answer is supplied, the process of *sex-typing* begins and the infant is started along one of two quite different social paths. Some of the patterns of sex-typing have probably changed in the wake of the women's movement of the sixties and seventies, but many differences in child rearing persist.

GENDER-ROLE STEREOTYPES

The stereotype is simple enough: The infant is dressed in either pink or blue; the child plays with either dolls or trucks; the adult woman's place is in the home, while the man's is in the marketplace—or the buffalo hunting grounds, or whatever. Society not only has different expectations of what the two sexes should *do;* it also has different conceptions of what they should *be.* In our own culture, the male has been expected to be more aggressive and tough, more restrained emotionally, and more interested in things than in people. The contrasting expectations for females are greater submissiveness, greater emotional expressiveness, and an interest in people rather than in things.

There is no doubt that these gender-role stereotypes have a considerable effect on the way we perceive people, even newborns and very young infants. As we have previously mentioned, when adults are shown a fully clothed infant and told that it is a "boy" or a "girl" (regardless of what its actual sex may be), their reaction depends on how the infant was labeled. They offer toy trucks to "boys" and dolls to "girls," bounce the "boys" vigorously, and treat the "girls" more gently (see Chapter 13; Frisch, 1977; Smith and Lloyd, 1978).

The children soon behave as the adults expect them to. Starting at about age one and a half, they begin to show sex-typed differences. By three years of age, they prefer different toys and play with peers of their own sex (Huston, 1983). As they grow older, they become increasingly aware of male and female stereotypes. In one study, both male and female children had to decide whether certain characteristics were more likely in a man or a woman. Over 90 percent of a group of U.S. eleven-year-olds thought that the adjectives *weak, emotional, appreciative, gentle, soft-hearted, affected, talkative, fickle,* and *mild* probably described a woman, and that the adjectives *strong, aggressive, disorderly, cruel, coarse, adventurous, independent, ambitious,* and *dominant* probably described a man. Boys and girls had just about the same sex stereotypes (Best, Williams, Cloud, Davis, Robertson, Edwards, Giles, and Fowles, 1977).

There is little doubt that many of these gender-role stereotypes are reinforced by parents and peers. When young children play with toys that are judged to be inappropriate—as when a boy plays with a doll house—their parents are likely to express disapproval. This is especially so for fathers, who vehemently object to any such behaviors in their sons. By and large, girls are allowed more latitude in such matters. A girl can be a tomboy and get away with it; a boy who is a sissy is laughed at (Langlois and Downs, 1980).

Social learning of sex roles (Photograph by Suzanne Arms, Jereboam)

In later life, deviations from these stereotypes may bring internal turmoil. A well-known example is the drive for achievement in women. At least until fairly recently, women who strove for success in the "man's world" found themselves in a hopeless conflict; they lost if they failed, but they also lost if they succeeded. In one study, college men and women were asked to complete stories, given a few opening lines that featured either a hero or a heroine: "After the first term, John (Anne) finds himself (herself) at the top of his (her) medical school class." In writing about a male protagonist, men foresaw a bright and happy future. Women were less sanguine about the prospects of the heroine. About 65 percent of them wrote stories that featured a fear of success. Some described Anne's future life as friendless, lonely, and unfulfilled. Others solved the problem by having her withdraw from any direct competition with men: "Anne will deliberately lower her academic standing the next term, while she does all she subtly can to help Carl . . . His grades come up and Anne soon drops out of med school. They marry, and he goes on in school while she raises their family" (Horner, 1970, p. 60). Society has apparently changed somewhat in the succeeding fifteen years, however, since such fear-of-success stories in women are much less common today. (For discussion, see Zuckerman and Wheeler, 1975; Spence and Helmreich, 1983.)

Constitutional Factors and Sex Differences

What accounts for the difference in current gender roles? We will consider both constitutional and social factors in an attempt to understand how biology and society conspire to make boys into men and girls into women.

Which of the differences between the sexes are based on constitutional differences? Apart from the obvious anatomical and physiological differences that pertain to reproduction, there are of course differences in average size, strength, and physical endurance. But what about *psychological* differences? There is no doubt that such differences do exist and that some of them fit cultural stereotypes. The question is whether any of these differences—in aggression, independence, emotional expressiveness, social sensitivity, and so on—are biologically given, whether they accompany the sexual anatomy the way menstruation goes along with a female XX chromosome pair.

Before proceeding, note two preliminary cautions. The first is that any psychological difference between the sexes is one of averages. The *average* three-year-old girl seems to be more dependent than her male counterpart; she is more likely to ask for help, to cling, and to seek affection (Emmerich, 1966). But this doesn't mean that the two groups don't overlap. For there are certainly many three-year-old girls who are *less* dependent than many three-year-old boys. After all, the same holds true even for many physical differences. There is no doubt that men are, on the average, taller than women. But it is equally clear that a considerable number of women are taller than many men.

A second caution concerns interpretation. Suppose we obtain a difference. What accounts for it? It might be a difference in biological predispositions. But it may also reflect the society in which the children are raised. In our society—as in-

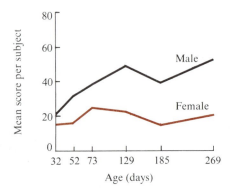

16.15   The development of rough-and-tumble play in male and female rhesus monkeys   *Roughhouse play in two male and two female rhesus monkeys during the first year of life. The scores are based on both frequency and vigor of this activity, in which monkeys wrestle, roll, or sham bite—all presumably in play, since no one ever gets hurt. Roughhouse play is considerably more pronounced in males than in females, a difference that increases during the first year of life. (After Harlow, 1962)*

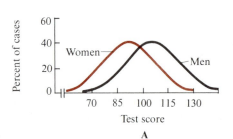

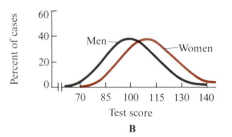

deed, in many others—boys are encouraged to be independent, to be "little men," beginning at a very early age, and the obtained difference in dependency may simply reflect this cultural fact. Here, as in so many other areas, nature and nurture are difficult to disentangle.

AGGRESSION

If there is one sex difference that might well be constitutional in origin, at least in part, it is aggression. Males tend to be more active and assertive than females. This difference is apparent from the very outset; male infants are more irritable and physically active than female infants. At two or three, boys are much more likely to engage in rough-and-tumble play and mock fighting than are girls (a difference also seen in apes and monkeys; see Figure 16.15). By four or five, they are more ready to exchange verbal insults and to repel aggression by counterattack. The difference continues into adulthood. While acts of physical violence are relatively rare among both sexes, they are very much more common among men than women; thus among adolescents, arrests for violent crimes occur five times more often among males than females (Johnson, 1979). A similar pattern of results holds in different social classes and in such widely different cultural settings as Ethiopia, India, Kenya, Mexico, Okinawa, and Switzerland (Whiting and Whiting, 1975; Maccoby and Jacklin, 1974, 1980; Parke and Slaby, 1983).

The fact that this sex difference in aggression is found so early in life, is observed in so many different cultures, and is also seen in our primate relatives, suggests a constitutional origin—all the more so given the fact that aggressiveness is enhanced by the administration of the male sex hormone (see Chapter 10).

PATTERN OF INTELLECTUAL APTITUDES

There is another psychological difference between the sexes that is often said to be based on biological givens—a different pattern of intellectual aptitudes. On the average, women do better on tests of verbal rather than spatial or mathematical ability, while the reverse holds for men (see Figure 16.16). In part, this may simply reflect a difference in the way boys and girls are brought up. But various lines of evidence suggest that social factors are only part of the story. An example is a recent study of SAT scores in 40,000 male and female adolescents. The investigators found the usual sex difference even when they limited their comparison

16.16   Sex differences in cognitive ability   *Characteristic performance curves of men and women on tests of spatial-mathematical and verbal ability. Men are generally superior on the first, women on the second. (A) Results on a spatial-mathematical test which included questions such as, "How many times between three and four o'clock do the hands of a clock make a straight line?" The curve plots the percentage of subjects who receive a particular score (with men in black, women in color). As the figure shows, the men perform better than the women, though the two curves overlap considerably. (B) Results on a vocabulary test asking for synonyms. Here, the women (again in color) do better than the men (again in black), though here, too, there is a great deal of overlap. (Data from Very, 1967. To make the figures comparable, the test scores were adjusted by a method called normalization, as if they were based on two tests which had the same mean and variance.)*

to boys and girls who had taken the same high school math courses and had expressed the same degree of interest in mathematics (Benbow and Stanley, 1983).

Facts of this sort have led to a search for a constitutional basis of the verbal-spatial difference. According to one hypothesis, there is a recessive gene located on the X chromosome that contributes to spatial ability. If boys have it, its effect will always be manifested since males have only one X chromosome. But if girls have it, there is a 50:50 chance that its effect will be canceled by a dominant gene on the other X chromosome. The upshot would be a greater average genetic potential for the acquisition of spatial skills in men than in women. This hypothesis has recently been questioned on various grounds. One problem concerns the correlation between the spatial skills of sons and those of their mothers, as compared with the correlation between spatial skills of sons and fathers. The sex-linked gene hypothesis would predict that the son-mother correlation is higher than the son-father correlation. This is because the presence or absence of the sex-linked gene depends entirely on the X chromosome, which the son received from his mother. But the actual correlations don't fit these predictions (Scarr and Kidd, 1983; for some relevant pros and cons, see Boles, 1980, and Harris, 1978).

Some recent findings suggest that the sex difference in spatial-verbal abilities may be related to maturation rates. Late-maturing children tend to do better on spatial tests than early-maturing ones, but they have no particular advantage on verbal tests. An intriguing hypothesis is that these effects are related to the different functions of the two cerebral hemispheres. As we've previously seen, the right hemisphere is specialized for spatial tasks, the left for language (see Chapter 2). By making the assumption that the right hemisphere matures more slowly than the left, and that neurological maturation comes to an effective end at the time of puberty, we can account for most of the evidence. The usual male-female difference in cognitive orientation follows from the fact that girls generally reach puberty before boys. If so, their right (spatial) hemisphere is stopped at an earlier point of neurological organization (Waber, 1977, 1979).

THE ADAPTIVE VALUE OF BUILT-IN SEX DIFFERENCES

Most modern biologists would probably argue that built-in characteristics have some survival value or they would have been bred out of the species by natural selection. But what is the biological value of sex differences in aggression and spatial ability, if we grant that they are indeed of constitutional origin? One guess is that these attributes, coupled with the greater strength of the male, went along with the basic division of labor that characterized our primitive ancestors. The women were gatherers who stayed near home and cared for the children while the men hunted big game miles away from the campsite. Strength, aggressiveness, and the ability to think in spatial terms must have been useful traits to the males, who had to track down and face dangerous animals, had to find their way back home, and were probably often forced to defend their home territory against marauding fellow men. In addition, strength and aggressiveness were probably of advantage in sexual competition among males. One would guess that this built-in pattern of sexual differentiation was incorporated into our ancestors' social institutions, which led to the exaggeration of whatever differences were there initially. The origin of sex roles may well lie in such beginnings. For our ancestors this general arrangement made sense; the sex-role distinction was grounded in their way of keeping themselves alive. The irony is that these differences are still with us more than a half million years later. Our modern economy puts little special premium on strength or physical courage, but we nevertheless continue to adhere to sex-role patterns that have by now outlived their usefulness.

Social Factors and Sex Differences

While some psychological sex differences may have biological roots, even more important is the way in which boys and girls are socialized. We will begin our discussion by taking a second look at the two characteristics for which there is some evidence of a biologically based sex difference: aggression and the discrepancy between spatial and verbal aptitudes. We'll see that even here there is some reasonable evidence that social effects augment and interact with whatever constitutional difference may have been there to start with.

ARE CONSTITUTIONALLY GIVEN DIFFERENCES REALLY CONSTITUTIONAL?

There may well be a greater initial predisposition toward aggression in boys than in girls, but cultural pressures serve to magnify whatever sex differences exist at the outset. Parents will generally allow (and even foster) a degree of aggressiveness in a boy that they would not countenance in a girl. Thus fathers often encourage their sons to fight back when another boy attacks them (Sears, Maccoby, and Levin, 1957). The result of such differential training is that the initial built-in bias toward a sex difference in behavior is considerably exaggerated.

Similar considerations may apply to the discrepancy between spatial and verbal aptitudes. In our society, girls are expected to do better in English than in math. This belief is shared by teachers, parents, and pupils, who all help to make it come true. As a result, even the girl who does have the appropriate genetic potential may do worse on spatial and mathematical tests than her ability warrants.

FEAR OF FAILURE

In recent years, a number of investigators have become interested in another difference between male and female schoolchildren: their reactions to failure. It turns out that, at least in our society, boys and girls tend to respond differently to failure. If boys are told they have done poorly on a school test (or on some appropriate laboratory task), they tend to attribute their failure to something that can be remedied—such as not having tried hard enough. But the girls' reaction is quite different. They are more likely to see their failure as a sign that they are not competent and never will be. As a result, they often lower their expectations and eventually give up altogether (Crandall, 1969; Dweck, Goetz, and Strauss, 1980).

According to Carol Dweck and her associates, this tendency to regard failure as insurmountable may be related to the phenomenon of learned helplessness. When rats are forced to endure a number of inescapable shocks, they become incapable of learning to escape or avoid in later situations. They have learned that they have no control over their environment, and so they become helpless (Seligman and Maier, 1967; see Chapters 3, 4, and 19). Dweck suggests that something similar may happen to schoolchildren after a series of repeated failures. If they come to believe that there is nothing that they can do about their failure, they may become helpless when faced with similar tasks (Dweck and Elliott, 1983).

Can this approach help us to understand why girls and boys have a different reaction to failure? It might, if it were true that girls encounter more failures in school (or at home) than do boys. But at least on the face of it, what actually happens is quite the reverse. In elementary school, girls consistently receive higher grades than boys. They are also better liked by teachers, who praise them more and criticize them less than they do boys. But if so, why should the girls regard failure as insurmountable? According to Dweck, the reason is that boys and girls are criticized for different things. Boys are generally reproved for their conduct. They are too loud or sloppy or don't work hard enough. But when they do receive praise, it tends to be about the intellectual quality of their work. In contrast, girls generally earn praise for conduct. They are well behaved and neat and hard working. On the other hand, when they do receive criticism, it almost always pertains to their intellectual, work-related performance. As a result, boys come to discount criticism and don't see it as an indicator of a lack of ability, while praise gives them confidence of further successes. The opposite holds for girls. They tend to discount praise, while criticism makes them fear further failures (Dweck, Davidson, Nelson, and Enna, 1978; Dweck, Goetz, and Strauss, 1980; Dweck and Licht, 1980).

Why are teachers (and other adults) more likely to scold boys rather than girls? The answer is simple. Boys are much more likely to misbehave than girls. Unlike most of the girls, the boys are often loud and rowdy and get into fights. In other words, they are more aggressive. Seen in this light, Dweck's general hypothesis is an interesting example of the way in which constitutional and social factors combine to produce a difference between the sexes. A sex difference based on constitution—aggression—leads to different behavior patterns, which in turn trigger differences in the way teachers and other adults treat the boys and girls in school situations. This in its turn leads to a difference in the reaction to failure, which may ultimately affect later achievement goals. Note that this differential susceptibility to learned helplessness can be attributed neither to nature nor to nurture, but can only be understood as an interaction between the two (Dweck and Elliott, 1983).

SEX REASSIGNMENT IN CHILDHOOD

The most dramatic examples of the effect of social factors in the determination of gender identity and gender role come from studies of children who at birth were declared to be of one sex but who were later reassigned to the other. This sometimes occurs if the newborn is a *hermaphrodite,* with reproductive organs that are anatomically ambiguous so that they are not exclusively male or female. In such cases, parents and physicians sometimes decide to reverse the initial sex assignment. Corrective surgery is undertaken, the sex is officially reassigned, and the child is raised accordingly. The results suggest that if the reassignment occurs early enough—according to some investigators, up to eighteen months, according to others, up to three or four years—the child adjusts to a remarkable degree. It becomes a he or a she, in part because this is how other people now regard it (Money and Ehrhardt, 1972).

The effects of reassignment The reports of parents leave no doubt that the child is seen very differently before and after the reassignment. One case involved a child that was genetically male. It had a male's XY chromosome pair and testes.

But the external genitals were otherwise more similar to a female's than to a male's. At birth the child was pronounced a boy, but the decision was reversed seventeen months later, at which time there was corrective surgery. According to the parents, there was an immediate change in the way the child was now treated. Even her three-year-old brother reacted differently and showed a "marked tendency to treat her much more gently. Whereas before he was just as likely to stick his foot out to trip her as he went by, he now wants to hold her hand to make sure she doesn't fall" (Money and Ehrhardt, 1972, p. 124).

Even more startling is the case of two normally born male identical twins, one of whom suffered a surgical accident at the age of seven months—his penis was amputated flush with the abdominal wall. After lengthy medical consultation, the parents decided upon sex reassignment. In cases of this sort, there is considerable plastic surgery to construct female genitals. There is also endocrine treatment to produce pubertal growth and femininization. The end result is a person who looks exactly like a female and can enjoy female sexual functions (the remnant of the penis becomes the clitoris). Since she lacks ovaries, she obviously cannot have children and is told that as an adult she can become a mother by adopting a baby.

Following sex reassignment and surgery, the two twins were treated very differently. The girl was dressed in frilly blouses and her hair was allowed to grow long. She was encouraged to be neat and to help her mother with the housekeeping. She was also reproved for being too rough and noisy, qualities that were regarded as perfectly natural in the boy. By the time they were four and a half, the twins behaved very differently and in accordance with their gender roles. The girl was neat and tidy, helped with the housework, played with dolls, and spent hours admiring herself in a new dress or curling her hair. The boy was sloppy, always forgot to wash his face, played with toy cars in a toy garage, and said that he wanted to be a fireman when he grew up. These differences are all the more impressive considering that the twins are identical. Genetically, they are both males—an excellent demonstration that gender identity is not a simple function of one's chromosomes (Money and Ehrhardt, 1972).

Constitutional factors in early reassignment   Results such as these point to the importance of social factors in determining one's sense of being male or female and of what being male and female means. But needless to say, constitutional factors also enter. In the case of the genetically male identical twin who was turned into a female, the male genetic blueprint had some effect. For example, the child was unusually active physically when compared to normal girls of that age. Related results come from a study of girls who were exposed to an abnormally high level of male hormone in the womb because of some malfunction during their mother's pregnancy. At birth, many of these girls were hermaphrodites, with ambiguous external genitals. After appropriate surgery, all was well and they were raised as females. But follow-up studies showed that the excess androgen during pregnancy had some long-term psychological effects. When compared to a control group, the androgenized girls were much more likely to be "tomboys" during childhood. They chose trucks over dolls, loved to participate in energetic team sports, preferred functional slacks to feminine dresses, and had little interest in jewelry or perfume. As adolescents, they looked forward to a future in which marriage and maternity were subordinated to a career. Interestingly enough, this masculinization of interests did not apply to the choice of a sex partner (a point that is relevant to the interpretation of homosexuality, of which more below). While the androgenized girls embarked upon their sex life at a later age than the controls, their sexual fantasies were about men and not about women (Money and Ehrhardt, 1972; Money, 1980).

It is generally believed that these psychological effects are produced by the prenatal masculinization of some system in the brain (probably the hypothalamus). This masculinization is presumably triggered by the excess androgen during the mother's pregnancy. This hypothesis fits in with the results of prenatal hormone administration in animals. For example, prenatally androgenized female monkeys act somewhat like human "tomboy" girls. Unlike normal monkey females, they engage in rough-and-tumble play with mutual chasing and mock fighting. Since monkeys have no culture that tells them about the appropriate female role, these effects are presumably based on constitutional changes that occurred during the prenatal period (Goy, 1968).

A critical period for gender identity?   Until fairly recently, most practitioners felt that sex reassignment is virtually impossible after at most four or five years of age. This in turn led to the belief that there is a critical period for the establishment of gender identity (e.g., Money and Ehrhardt, 1972). But this view has been called into question by the discovery of a number of male children in three rural villages in the Dominican Republic with a rare genetic disorder. In the fetal stage, they are relatively insensitive to the effects of androgen. As a result, their external genitals at birth look much like a female's and so they often are thought to be girls and raised as such. But puberty with its sudden upsurge in male hormone levels brings a dramatic change. The so-called girls develop male genitals, their voice deepens, and their torso becomes muscular. If sex reassignment after age four or five is really as difficult or traumatic as it has been said to be, there ought to be a psychological catastrophe. But in fact, the great majority of these adolescents come to adopt their new male identity with relatively little difficulty. They change their name and take up male occupations. While they are initially anxious about sexual relationships, they ultimately seem to be fairly successful. Thus fifteen out of sixteen such subjects eventually married or lived in common-law relationships (Imperato-McGinley, Guerrero, Gautier, and Peterson, 1974; Imperato-McGinley, Peterson, Gautier, and Sturla, 1979).

It's hard to know how this surprising finding should be interpreted. The successful change in gender identity may be a result of the massive increase in androgen at puberty. It may also reflect the role of social factors, for these changes are by now accepted by the community and are common enough so that the villagers have coined a name for individuals with this condition: *machihembra* (first woman, then man). In any case, the phenomenon is an argument against the view that gender identity is essentially unchangeable after the age of five.

Theories of Sex Typing

Social factors are evidently of great importance in fashioning our sense of being men or women and they shape our behavior accordingly. But exactly how do these social factors exert their effects? Each of the three main theories of socialization—psychoanalysis, social learning theory, and the cognitive developmental approach—has tried to come up with an answer (see Figure 16.17, p. 556).

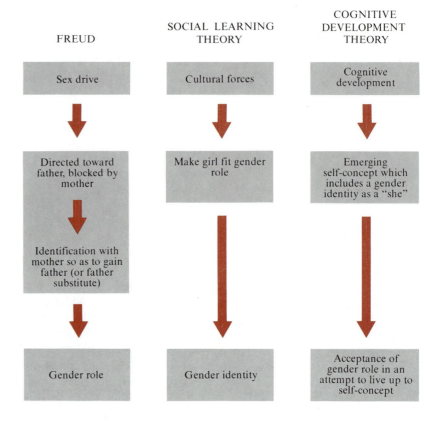

FREUD	SOCIAL LEARNING THEORY	COGNITIVE DEVELOPMENT THEORY
Sex drive	Cultural forces	Cognitive development
Directed toward father, blocked by mother	Make girl fit gender role	Emerging self-concept which includes a gender identity as a "she"
Identification with mother so as to gain father (or father substitute)		
Gender role	Gender identity	Acceptance of gender role in an attempt to live up to self-concept

16.17 Three theories of sex typing *The figure summarizes the three major theories of sex typing (for females).*

PSYCHOANALYTIC THEORY

According to Freud, the basic mechanism is ***identification.*** The child models himself or herself on the same-sex parent in an effort to become like him or her. In Freud's view, identification is the end product of the Oedipus conflict, which reaches its culmination at about age five or six. The little boy is unable to cope with the mounting anxieties aroused by his sexual longing for the mother and his resentment of the father. He therefore represses both incestuous love and patricidal hate. But his renunciation of the mother is only for the time being. He identifies with the all-powerful father in an effort to propitiate him (if I am like him, he won't want to hurt me), and also in the hope that he will thereby gain the mother's sexual love in some blissful future (if I am like him, she will love me). By means of this identification process, which Freud thought to be largely unconscious, the boy incorporates many aspects of the father's personality, including those that pertain to sex role. By a roughly analogous process the little girl comes to identify with her mother (see Chapter 12).

SOCIAL LEARNING THEORY

A very different position is held by social learning theorists, who argue that gender role and gender identity do not arise from the sex drive. In their view, children behave in sex-appropriate ways for the simplest of possible reasons: They are rewarded if they do so and are punished if they don't. For the most part, they

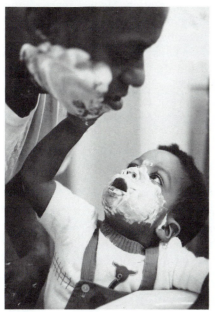

Male and female models (Top: *photograph by Suzanne Szasz.* Bottom: *photograph by Burk Uzzle, Woodfin Camp*)

learn what each sex is supposed to do by *imitation.* But whom shall they imitate? They quickly discover that they must choose a model (usually the parent) of their own sex. The girl imitates her mother and is rewarded for rocking the baby (for the time being a doll may have to do), for prettying herself up, for becoming mother's little helper. The boy who imitates these maternal acts will be ridiculed and called a sissy. He will do better by imitating his father who rewards him for doing boylike things (Mischel, 1970).

According to this view, the sex drive has little to do with the matter and anatomy enters only indirectly. The penis and vagina are relevant only in determining whether the child is a boy or a girl in the parents' eyes. From this point on, differential rewards and punishments do the rest.

Why do parents push their sons and daughters into different social molds? A social learning theorist would probably reply that the parents' behavior (as well as that of peers, teachers, and so on) is also shaped by various reinforcers, all of which act to maintain a particular social structure. In effect, the socialization of children is simply an apprenticeship into the roles they will adopt as adults.

COGNITIVE DEVELOPMENTAL THEORY

Yet another proposal has been offered by Lawrence Kohlberg who regards sex typing in the context of cognitive development. Kohlberg's emphasis is on the child's emerging awareness of his or her gender identity, the sense of being male or female (Kohlberg, 1966).

Kohlberg points out that the concept of gender is quite vague until the child is age five or six. The four-year-old has only a shadowy notion of what the categories "male" and "female" mean. He has no real comprehension of how these categories pertain to genital anatomy, no matter how diligently his parents may have tried to enlighten him in this regard. When presented with dolls that have either male or female genitals and varying hair length, and asked to tell which are the boys and which the girls, preschoolers generally decide on the basis of hair length (McConaghy, 1979).

More important is the fact that the four-year-olds don't really understand that gender is one of the permanent and (for all intents and purposes) unchangeable attributes of the self. Children develop a sense of gender identity by about age three. But it takes them another two years or so to achieve the concept of *gender constancy*—the recognition that being male and female is irrevocable. When shown a picture of a girl, four-year-olds say that she could be a boy if she wanted to, or if she wore a boy's haircut or wore a boy's clothes. But in Kohlberg's view, the problem is not with gender as such. For the majority of four-year-olds also say that a cat could be a dog if it wanted to, or if its whiskers were cut off. This suggests that the lack of gender constancy is just another reflection of the preschooler's failure to comprehend the underlying constancies of the universe. After all, children at this stage of cognitive development do not conserve liquid quantity, mass, or number (see Chapter 14).

According to Kohlberg, the child's identification with the parent of the same sex *follows* the acquisition of gender identity. Once they recognize that they are boys or girls, they will try to live up to their sense of gender identity, to act in a manner that befits their own self-concept. They will now look for appropriate models—and the most readily available ones are their mothers and fathers—that can show them how to get better and better at being a male or a female.

James Morris, who at the age of 46 had a transsexual operation and became Jan Morris (Courtesy United Press International, top; photograph by Henry Grossman, bottom)

SEXUAL FEELING, GENDER ROLE, AND GENDER IDENTITY

The approaches to sex typing we have just discussed—psychoanalytic theory, social learning theory, and cognitive developmental theory—differ in many particulars. But details aside, the real difference lies in their emphases. According to Freud, the roots of sex typing consist of sexual orientation—they grow out of the child's erotic feelings and the direction in which they are aimed. To social learning theorists, the critical factor is gender role. Their emphasis is on the cultural forces that impinge upon the individual and shape his or her behavior by suitable rewards and punishments until it fits into the appropriate social mold. According to Kohlberg and other cognitive developmental theorists, the emphasis is on gender identity, an individual's self-concept as a he or a she.

According to a common-sense view, gender identity, gender role, and sexual feeling and orientation are essentially equivalent as definitions of maleness and femaleness. And indeed they are for most of us. The great majority of human beings are male and female in all three of these senses. The person who regards himself as a man is also regarded as such by others, and he will choose women as his sexual partners. But as we have repeatedly pointed out, the three facets of sex and gender are in principle independent. Consider James Morris, a man whose sex was surgically altered in adulthood from male to female. Prior to the operation, he had all the external trappings of a male gender role. Among other things, he was a member of Sir Hilary's expedition to climb Mt. Everest. He also had the appropriate credentials of a masculine sexual orientation. He was married and had fathered three children. What was discordant was his sense of gender identity. From early childhood on, he felt that he was really a woman who was somehow trapped in the body of a man (Morris, 1974). Thus sexual orientation, gender role, and gender identity are not really one and the same, despite the fact that they generally go together. What we need is a theory that describes their interrelations. Thus far, we have only the barest beginnings of an answer, for until recently the subject of human sexuality was a forbidden topic, shrouded by superstition and taboo.

Sexual Orientation

The majority of men and women are ***heterosexual.*** They seek a partner of the opposite sex. But for a significant minority, the sexual orientation is otherwise; their erotic and romantic feelings are directed primarily or exclusively toward members of their own sex; they are ***homosexual.*** What are the factors that determine which sexual orientation is adopted?

THE INCIDENCE OF HOMOSEXUALITY

According to a survey made in the 1940s that is still regarded as the most reliable study of sexual patterns among American males, 4 percent of American males are exclusively homosexual during their lifetime (Kinsey, Pomeroy, and Martin, 1948). The comparable incidence of exclusive homosexuality among women

seems to be lower—about 2 percent (Kinsey, Pomeroy, Martin, and Gebhard, 1953). It is clear that a substantial number of men and women are erotically oriented toward a partner of their own sex despite the fact that our society sharply stigmatizes such behavior. This cultural taboo is by no means universal. According to one cross-cultural survey, two-thirds of the societies studied regarded homosexuality as normal and acceptable, at least for some persons or for some age groups (Ford and Beach, 1951). In certain historical periods the practice was glorified and extolled, as in classical Greece where Pericles, the great Athenian statesman, was regarded as rather odd because he was *not* attracted to beautiful boys.

Homosexuality is yet another illustration of the fact that sexual orientation, gender identity, and gender role are in principle independent. Most male homosexuals think of themselves as men and are so regarded by others; the analogous point holds for female homosexuals (Marmor, 1975).

HOMOSEXUALITY: DISEASE OR DIFFERENT LIFE STYLE?

Is homosexuality an illness that requires a cure if any can be found? Or is it simply a different form of sexual expression that happens to be disapproved of in this culture at this time? Few issues in the area of human sexuality have been debated more hotly than this.

According to one psychiatric view, homosexuality is pathological, based on incapacitating fears of the opposite sex and "incompatible with life" (Bieber, 1965). The primary evidence for this view comes from a widely cited study of 106 male homosexuals under psychiatric treatment. Their therapists described them as more deeply disturbed and unhappy than a group of heterosexual patients with whom they were compared. But this study suffers from several flaws. One concerns the sample of homosexuals upon which the conclusions were based. This sample is biased since it included only persons who sought psychiatric help. Such people are almost certain to be more disturbed than the population at large and are not representative of the many homosexuals who never enter a psychiatrist's office.

In an effort to meet these objections, several investigators have compared nonpatient homosexuals to nonpatient heterosexuals of equal age, educational level, and intelligence. The results of such studies show that the differences between homosexuals and heterosexuals are much less than had been supposed. Some investigators found no difference whatever (Hooker, 1957; Thompson, McCandless, and Strickland, 1971). Others found that homosexuals (especially male homosexuals) were somewhat more likely to lack confidence, to suffer from low self-esteem, and to clown at their own expense (Saghir and Robins, 1973). But such differences are probably best explained by the fact that homosexuals in our society are members of a rejected minority group. Self-hatred and protective clowning are common characteristics in any persecuted minority (Hooker, 1965).

In any case, the real issue is not whether homosexuals as a group are as happy or well-adjusted as heterosexuals are as a group. Given the stigma attached to their orientation, it would be surprising if they were. The question is whether homosexuality as such necessarily implies personal disturbance and neurosis. The answer seems to be no. Under the circumstances, there is no reason to maintain that homosexuality is a psychological disorder. In 1974, this view became part of the official position of the American Psychiatric Association, which voted that "homosexuality by itself does not necessarily constitute a psychiatric disorder" (Marmor, 1975, p. 1,510).*

To be sure, some homosexuals may want to change their sexual orientation, and if they do, a therapist might try to help them. But this undertaking is by no means easy, especially for persons who have been exclusively homosexual. Freud himself was doubtful that it could be done. Later psychoanalysts were more optimistic, but they rarely reported lasting changes in more than about one-third of the cases treated.

The safest conclusion seems to be that sexual orientation—both heterosexual and homosexual—is a fairly stable condition. It can be changed in some cases but not easily. Nor do most homosexuals *wish* for such a change. Homosexuality is not a disease nor a personality disturbance. But neither is it a simple matter of personal choice that can be done or undone more or less at will.

WHAT CAUSES HOMOSEXUALITY?

What leads to homosexuality? So far there is no clear answer. It may well be that this question simply represents the other side of the question, "what leads to heterosexuality?" This second question is rarely asked because we take the heterosexual preference for granted. Yet if we did know how to explain the origin of heterosexuality, we would probably be much closer to an understanding of how homosexuality comes about as well.

Genes and hormones   One approach has looked to biology. Some authors have argued that there is a genetic predisposition. An early study showed that the correlation between homosexual tendencies in pairs of twins is much greater if the twins are identical (formed from the same egg and thus possessed of the same genetic makeup) than if they are fraternal (formed from two different eggs and thus no more alike than any two ordinary siblings). This result is impressive, but its significance has been undermined by some later discrepant findings (Kallman, 1952; Rainer, Mesnikoff, Kolb, and Carr, 1960).

Other investigators have concentrated upon sex hormones on the simple assumption that male heterosexuality is correlated with male hormone levels in the bloodstream. But the results are very inconsistent. Some authors found that androgen levels tend to be lower in male homosexuals than in heterosexuals, while others obtained no such difference (e.g., Kolodny, Masters, Hendryx, and Toro, 1971; Brodie, Gartrell, Doering, and Rhue, 1974). In any case, male hormone levels are a very implausible candidate as the cause of male homosexuality. For, as already mentioned, the administration of androgen to male homosexuals enhances their sexual vigor but does not change its direction—the renewed interest is still toward homosexual partners (see Chapter 10; Kinsey, Pomeroy, and Martin, 1948). Male homosexuality is evidently not caused by an insufficiency of male hormones. It seems reasonable to assume that an analogous statement ap-

---

* The current diagnostic manual of the American Psychiatric Association makes this position more precise. It distinguishes between two kinds of homosexuality. One is *ego-syntonic homosexuality,* which the individual accepts, does not want to change, and which causes him or her no distress. The other is *ego-dystonic homosexuality,* which the individual does not accept, wants very much to alter, and which causes him or her considerable distress (DSM-III, 1980).

plies to female homosexuals. (For a more recent discussion of the relation between homosexual orientation and neuroendocrine effects, see Gladue, Green, and Hellman, 1984.)

Childhood experience A different approach stresses the role of childhood experience. The most famous example is Freud's theory of homosexuality. According to Freud, homosexuality is a response to fears aroused during the Oedipal conflict. The little boy is too terrified to compete with his father for his mother's affections and his terror generalizes to other women. He therefore tries to propitiate the father by identifying with the mother instead (after all, father loves *her*).

There is very little evidence to support Freud's theory. In a recent study, about 1,000 male and female homosexuals provided various items of information about their life histories. There was some difference in how homosexuals and heterosexuals viewed their parents. Compared to heterosexual controls, homosexuals had a less satisfactory relation with their parents, especially with those of their own sex. But on closer analysis, these familial relationships did not have much of an effect on the development of sexual orientation. If homosexual men don't get along too well with their father (although in fact, many of them do), this is probably because the fathers can't accept various aspects of their sons' sexual orientation. If so, the unsatisfactory father-son relationship is a result of the son's sexual orientation, not its cause. Something of the same sort applies to the mother-daughter relationship in female homosexuals. Such findings give little support to the psychoanalytic framework with its emphasis on the crucial role of the early family constellation (Bell, Weinberg, and Hammersmith, 1981).

THE ACQUISITION OF A SEXUAL ORIENTATION

How then can we explain the origin of homosexuality, or of sexual orientation generally? Thus far, we have no answer, but we at least know that some of the simple answers that have been suggested are likely to be false. Homosexuality is not produced by a particular family pattern, or by early homosexual experiences, or by current hormone levels. What is clear is that whether someone is homosexual or heterosexual is a fundamental aspect of his or her being, that goes back as far as he or she can remember. The majority of homosexual men and women have had homosexual dreams, fantasies, and romantic attachments prior to adolescence. Many of them say that "I've been that way all my life" (Saghir and Robins, 1973).

Do learning and environment play any role? Perhaps they do, but if so, whatever is learned must occur quite early. In addition, it must be established by a learning mechanism—perhaps akin to imprinting—that is hard to reverse, for as we have seen, the homosexual orientation (and no doubt, the heterosexual orientation) is very difficult to change. There may be a critical period during which the developing child's sexual orientation becomes imprinted on this or the other kind of sex object. It's also likely that there is a built-in predisposition that can bias sexual orientation in one direction or the other. In the majority of cases, this built-in bias is presumably for heterosexual objects. Perhaps those children who eventually become homosexuals have a different initial bias and are thus more likely to be affected if they encounter environmental conditions that might tip their sexual orientation toward members of their own sex.

DEVELOPMENT AFTER CHILDHOOD

Thus far, our primary focus in describing human development has been on infancy and childhood. This emphasis reflects the orientation of the major figures in the history of the field. Thus Piaget tried to describe the growth of the mind until the achievement of formal operations at about age eleven. Freud was even more narrowly focused on childhood; to him, the most important events of social development took place before the age of five or six. Both Freud and Piaget, in common with most developmental psychologists, understood the term *development* in much the sense in which it is generally used by biology: the processes by which the newly formed organism changes until it reaches maturity.

In recent years, a number of authors have argued that this interpretation of the term *development* is too narrow. In their view, there is no reason to assume that human personality stops developing after childhood is passed, for humans continue to change as they pass through the life cycle. The problems faced by an adolescent boy are not the same as those of a young man about to get married and become a father, let alone of a middle-aged man at the peak of his career, or a seventy-year-old. This being so, it seems reasonable to chart the course of psychological development after puberty is reached in the hope that one can find some psychological milestones in adult development analogous to those that students of child development have tried to describe for earlier ages (Baltes, Reese, and Lipsitt, 1980).

Table 16.2   ERIKSON'S EIGHT AGES OF MAN

Approximate age	*Developmental task of that stage*	*Psychosocial crisis of that stage*
0–1½ years	Attachment to mother, which lays foundations for later trust in others	Trust versus mistrust
1½–3 years	Gaining some basic control of self and environment (e.g., toilet training, exploration)	Autonomy versus shame and doubt
3–6 years	Becoming purposeful and directive	Initiative versus guilt
6 years–puberty	Developing social, physical, and school skills	Competence versus inferiority
Adolescence	Making transition from childhood to adulthood; developing a sense of identity	Identify versus role confusion
Early adulthood	Establishing intimate bonds of love and friendship	Intimacy versus isolation
Middle age	Fulfilling life goals that involve family, career, and society; developing concerns that embrace future generations	Productivity versus stagnation
Later years	Looking back over one's life and accepting its meaning	Integrity versus despair

SOURCE: Based on Erikson, 1963.

Erik Erikson *(Photograph by Jon Erikson)*

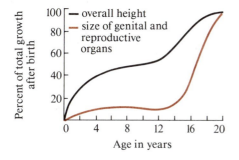

16.18 The growth spurt at adolescence *The figure shows the percentage of total growth after birth attained between the ages of 0 and 20 years for overall height (black) and size of genital and reproductive organs (in color) averaged for males and females. (After Tanner, 1970)*

What are the stages of development after childhood? Most later investigators have been strongly affected by proposals of the psychoanalyst Erik Erikson. According to Erikson, all human beings pass through a series of major crises as they go through the life cycle. At each stage, there is a critical confrontation between the self the individual has achieved thus far and the various demands posed by his or her social and personal setting. In all, Erikson sets out "eight ages of man," of which the first few occur in early childhood and roughly correspond to Freud's oral, anal, and phallic stages. These are followed by adolescence, early adulthood, middle age, and the final years (Erikson, 1963; see Table 16.2).

Erikson's developmental scheme has influenced many investigators of adult development. We will continue to refer to his organization as we briefly discuss some issues in the study of adolescence and adulthood.

Adolescence

The term **adolescence** is derived from the Latin for "growing up." It is a period of transition in which the individual changes from a state of childhood to that of an adult. There are biological changes: a physical growth spurt, a change in bodily proportions, and the attainment of sexual maturity (see Figure 16.18). Biological maturing ultimately leads to social and economic changes: from dependence on one's family to ever-increasing independence. And of course there are the numerous psychological changes that accompany the process of growing up. These include the progressive maturing of sexual attitudes and behavior that will ultimately allow the adolescent to start his or her own family, and the acquisition of various skills that will eventually enable him or her to become a fully functioning member of adult society. In effect, adolescence is simply a protracted version of what in birds is a rather abrupt procedure—when the fledglings are forced to fly out of the nest and to make their own way.

THE NATURE OF THE TRANSITION

Compared to other animals, humans attain sexual maturity rather late in their development. This is just another facet of an important difference between ourselves and our animal cousins—a lengthened period of immaturity and dependence that provides more time for each generation to learn from the one before. When is this period over?

Biology has set a lower limit at roughly age fifteen for girls and seventeen for boys when physical growth is more or less complete. But the point that marks the beginning of adulthood is decreed by social conditions as well as biology. As an example, a study of colonial New England families shows that the age at which sons become autonomous from their parents changed over the course of four generations. The sons of the first settlers stayed on their parents' farm until their late twenties before they married and became economically independent. As farm land became scarcer and other opportunities opened in the surrounding villages and towns, the sons left home much earlier, learned a trade, married, and became autonomous at a younger age (Greven, 1970). But with the onset of mass education in the mid-nineteenth century, this pattern was reversed again. Instead of leaving to become an apprentice or take a job, more and more youths continued to live with their families and remained in school through their late teens. This allowed them to acquire the skills required for membership in a complex,

A

B

Initiation rites *These rites signify induction into adulthood, as in (A) a bar mitzvah or (B) a West African ceremony featuring a frightening ghost figure that tests the boys' courage just prior to their ritual circumcision. (Top: photograph by Van Bucher, Photo Researchers. Bottom: photograph by Arthur Tress, Photo Researchers)*

technological society, but it postponed their social and economic independence and their full entry into the adult world (Elder, 1980).

Culture evidently has an important say in the when and how of the transition period. It also sets up special occasions that mark the end of that period or highlight certain points along the way. A number of human societies have ***initiation rites*** that signify induction into adulthood. In some preliterate cultures, these are violent, prolonged, and painful, especially in certain puberty rites for boys that involve ceremonial beatings and circumcision. According to some anthropologists, such initiation rites are especially severe in cultures that try to emphasize the dramatic distinction between the roles of children and adults, as well as between those of men and women. In our own society, the transition to full adulthood is much more gradual, with milestones that refer not just to biological changes but also to various educational and vocational attainments. It is therefore not too surprising that we have not one initiation rite but many (none of which would ever be regarded as especially severe): confirmations and bar (or bas) mitzvahs, "sweet sixteen" parties, high school and college graduations, and so on. Each of them represents just one more step on a protracted road to adulthood (Burton and Whiting, 1961; Muuss, 1970).

Cultural factors also determine the time at which other bench marks of development are reached. An example is the age at which virginity is lost, which has steadily decreased in our own society during the past few decades, reflecting a change in sexual mores for both men and women. This change is undoubtedly caused by many factors, not the least of which is the existence of increasingly effective methods of birth control which allow the separation of the emotional and recreational functions of sexuality from its reproductive ones.

IS ADOLESCENCE ALWAYS TURBULENT?

There is a traditional view of adolescence which holds that it is inevitably a period of great emotional stress. This notion goes back to the romantic movement of the early nineteenth century, when major writers such as Goethe wrote influential works that featured youths in desperate conflict with a cynical, adult world that drove them to despair, suicide, or violent rebellion. This position was later endorsed by a number of psychological theorists, including Sigmund Freud and many of his followers. To Freud, adolescence was necessarily a period of conflict, since this is the time when the sex urges repressed during the closing phase of the Oedipal conflict can no longer be denied and clash violently with the unconscious prohibitions previously set up. Further conflicts center on struggles with the older generation, especially the same-sex parent, that were repressed in childhood but now come to the fore (see Chapter 12).

This traditional view of adolescence has been seriously challenged by several modern writers who argue that the turbulence of the period is by no means inevitable. Whether there is marked emotional disturbance depends on the way the culture handles the transition. Some evidence for this view comes from studies of preliterate cultures in which the shift from childhood to adulthood is very gradual. Among the Arapesh of New Guinea, the young increasingly participate in adult activities as they get older. The child begins by tilling her parents' garden and eventually tills her own. Given the relatively simple social and economic structure of Arapesh life, the change is not very drastic. Correspondingly, there seems to be no psychological crisis among the Arapesh during adolescence (Mead, 1939).

Adolescence Adolescence may be a period of moodiness and alienation, but it often is not. (Left: *photograph by Alex Webb, Magnum.* Right: *photograph courtesy of Leo de Wys*)

However enviable, the gentle adolescent transition of the Arapesh is difficult to achieve in our modern industrial society. It's hard to see how a five-year-old can help his father at his job if that job happens to be computer programming. Accordingly, one might expect a fair level of disturbance during adolescence in our own society. And indeed, such emotional disturbance is a theme often sounded by the mass media and much modern literature (for example, J. D. Salinger's *Catcher in the Rye*). But in fact, a number of studies suggest that such turbulence is by no means universal among modern American adolescents. Several investigators find that for many adolescents "development . . . is slow, gradual, and unremarkable" (Josselson, 1980, p. 189). What probably matters is the particular social and psychological setting, which surely differs from individual to individual in a complex society such as ours.

TRYING TO FIND A PERSONAL IDENTITY

It appears that adolescence is not necessarily a time of troubles. But even so, it does pose a number of serious problems as the adolescent has to prepare to become an autonomous individual in his or her own right. A number of writers have tried to understand some characteristic adolescent behavior patterns in light of this ultimate goal.

Establishing a separate world Unlike fledglings, adolescents in our society remain in the nest for quite a while after they can fly (or perhaps more precisely, get their driver's license). This probably makes it all the more essential for them to establish some elements of a separation between themselves and the world of their parents. As one means to this end, many adolescents adopt all kinds of external trappings of what's "now" and what's "in," such as distinctive tastes in dance steps, clothing, and idiom (Figure 16.19, p. 566). These often change with bewildering rapidity as yesterday's adolescent fads diffuse into the broader social world and become today's adult fashions (as witness men's hair styles). When this happens, new adolescent fads spring up to maintain the differentiation (Douvan and Adelson, 1958).

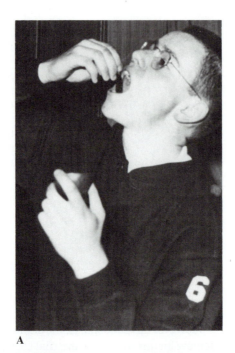

16.19 *Adolescent fads* *New adolescent fads spring up to maintain the differentiation between adolescents' own world and that of the adults around them. They then disappear rather quickly to be replaced by yet newer fads. The photos show some such fads prominent in recent years. (A) thirties—swallowing goldfish, (B) fifties—jamming into phone booths, seventies—streaking, and (D) eighties— punk hair styles. (Photographs courtesy of AP/Wide World Photos)*

A

B

C

D

The identity crisis of adolescence According to Erikson, the separation from the adult's sphere is only one manifestation of what adolescents are really trying to achieve. Their major goal throughout this period is to discover who and what they really are as they go through what he calls an ***identity crisis.*** In our complex culture, there are many social roles, and adolescence is a time to try them on to see which one fits best—which vocation, which ideology, which group membership. The adolescent's primary question is, "Who am I?" and to answer it, he strikes a succession of postures, in part for the benefit of others, who then serve as a mirror in which he can see himself. Each role, each human relationship, each world view is first temporarily adopted on an all-or-none basis with no room for compromise. Each is at first a costume. When the adolescent finds that some costume fits, it becomes the clothes of his adult identity. Most adolescents eventually succeed, but the process of identity seeking has its difficulties:

> . . . The danger of this stage is role confusion . . . . To keep themselves together they temporarily overidentify, to the point of apparent loss of identity, with the heroes of cliques and crowds. This initiates the stage of "falling in love," which is by no means entirely, or even primarily, a sexual matter . . . . To a considerable extent adolescent love is an attempt to arrive at a definition of one's identity by projecting a diffuse ego image on another and by seeing it thus reflected and gradually clarified. This is why so much of young love is conversation . . ." (Erikson, 1963, p. 262).

Adulthood

Erikson describes a number of further stages of personality development. In young adulthood, the healthy individual has to achieve the capacity for closeness and intimacy through love, or else suffer a sense of isolation that will permit only shallow human relationships. In early middle age, she has to develop a sense of personal creativity that extends beyond her own self. This includes a concern for others, for her work, for the community of which she is a part. And toward the end of life, there is a final crisis during which each person has to come to terms with his or her own life and accept it for what it was, with a sense of integrity rather than of despair. Erikson eloquently sums up this final reckoning: "It is the acceptance of one's own and only life cycle as something that had to be and that, by necessity, permitted of no substitutes . . . healthy children will not fear life if their elders have integrity enough not to fear death" (Erikson, 1963, pp. 268–69).

RECENT ATTEMPTS TO FIND COMMON STAGES

Erikson's developmental scheme is a literary and moving account of the human odyssey through life, but in what sense is it a true description? Are the crises he listed *the* crises through which all of us must pass, and are their characteristics what he described them to be? A number of modern investigators have studied adults at various stages of their life to find out what, if any, patterns are common to a given time of life. By and large, most of them have described a number of developmental periods that resemble some of Erikson's "ages of man" (Gould, 1978; Levinson, 1978). Others have tried to find similarities between youthful patterns and adult fulfillment when the same person is interviewed some thirty years later (Vaillant, 1977).

A stage of adult development that has received considerable attention from both Erikson and later authors is the so-called "mid-life transition," in which the individual reappraises what she has done with her life thus far and may reevaluate her marriage and her career. It is a period when the individual begins to see physical changes that show that the summer of life is over and its autumn has begun, a recognition that may occur earlier in women than in men (in part, because of the psychological impact of menopause). There is a shift in the way one thinks about time, from "How long have I lived?" to "How much time do I have left?" Some investigators point out that the middle-aged person is in the middle in more than one sense as she observes her children grow up and her own parents age and die:

The ages of man   (Photograph by Nina Leen, Life)

It is as if there are two mirrors before me, each held at a partial angle. I see part of myself in my mother who is growing old, and part of her in me. In the other mirror I see part of myself in my daughter . . . . (Neugarten and Datan, quoted in Colarusso and Nemiroff, 1981, p. 124).

HOW UNIVERSAL ARE THE STAGES OF ADULT DEVELOPMENT?

There is enough consistency in the results obtained by various investigators of adult development to suggest that the stages and transitions they describe apply fairly widely to people in our time and place. But are they universal? When we considered various stage theories of child development, we asked whether these stages occur in all cultures. The same question can be asked about adult development. Is there a mid-life transition among the Arapesh? Does a Kwakiutl man of fifty go through an agonizing reappraisal of what he's done with his life to date? If the answer is no, then we have to ask ourselves what the various stages described by Erikson and other students of the adult life-span really are.

Thus far, there is little concrete evidence one way or the other, so we can only guess. Certain adult milestones are clearly biological. In all cultures, humans reach puberty, mate, have children, begin to age, go through female menopause or male climacteric, age still further, and finally die. But the kind of crises that confront persons at different points of the life cycle surely depend on the society in which they live.

An example of the effect of social conditions on adult crises is the transition into old age. Over a century ago in the U.S., different generations often lived close together as part of an extended family system. There was much less segregation by age than there is now; children, parents, and grandparents frequently lived under the same roof or close to each other in the same neighborhood. In times of economic hardship, older people contributed to the family's resources even when they were too old to work—by caring for the children of working mothers, helping with the housekeeping, and so on. Older people—especially women—had yet another function: they were often sought out for advice on matters of child rearing and homekeeping. But today, the elderly have no such recognized family role. They usually live apart, are effectively segregated from the rest of society, are excluded from the work force, and have lost their role as esteemed advisers. Given these changes, it follows that the transition into old age today is quite different from what it was 150 years ago. People still age as they did then—although the proportion of persons who live into their seventies has increased radically—but they view aging differently (Hareven, 1978).

Facts of this sort suggest that various aspects of the stages proposed by students of adult development may be quite specific to our society and can therefore not be said to be universal. But if so, can we say anything about the life cycle that goes beyond the narrow specifics of our own time and social condition? Perhaps the best suggestion comes from a recent lecture by Erikson in which he tried to define adulthood:

> . . . In youth you find out what you *care to do* and who you *care to be* . . . . In young adulthood you learn whom you *care to be with.* . . . In adulthood, however, you learn what and whom you can *take care of.* . . (Erikson, 1974, p. 124).

Seen in this light, the later phases of the life cycle can perhaps be regarded as the culmination of the progressive expansion of the social world that character-

(Photograph by Eve Arnold, Magnum)

izes the entire course of social development from early infancy on. In a way, it is a final expansion in which our concern turns from ourselves to others and from our own present to their future (and in some cases, the future of all mankind).

This may or may not be a good description of what genuine adulthood *is*. But it seems like an admirable prescription for what it *ought* to be.

SUMMARY

1. Social development can be regarded as a widening of social scope. An early attempt to chart the stages of social development was Freud's theory of psychosexual development.

2. The infant's *socialization* begins with the first human bond he forms—his *attachment* to his mother (or other caregiver). Studies of infant humans and monkeys indicate that this attachment is not caused by the fact that the mother feeds them, but rather because she feels so "comforting." A separation from the mother generally leads to *separation anxiety,* a fact which has led some theorists to propose that the infant's attachment grows out of a (perhaps built-in) fear of being away from a familiar object.

3. Experiments on *imprinting* in birds suggest that the attachment to the mother-object can only be formed during a *critical period* in early life. If the early attachment is not formed, later social development may be seriously impaired, as shown by studies of motherless monkeys and institution-reared children. Studies of motherless monkeys and adopted children suggest that this impairment is not necessarily irrevocable.

4. The process of *socialization* continues with child rearing by the parents. Some important differences in the way children are reared depend on the dominant values of the culture of which the parents are a part. Modern attempts to explain the mechanisms that underlie socialization include *social learning theory* which emphasizes *modeling,* and *cognitive developmental theory* which emphasizes the role of understanding as opposed to imitation.

5. The evidence indicates that different models of weaning or toilet training have little or no long-term effects. What seems to matter instead is the general home atmosphere, as shown by the effects of *autocratic, permissive,* and *authoritative-reciprocal* patterns of child rearing. On the other hand, how the parents treat the child is partially determined by the child's own characteristics, as suggested by studies on infant *temperament.*

6. One aspect of moral conduct concerns the *internalization* of prohibitions. According to some theorists, punishment is more likely to lead to such internalization if the threatened punishment fits the principle of *minimal sufficiency.* Another aspect of moral conduct involves altruistic acts. Studies of *empathy* suggest that some precursors of altruism may be present in early infancy.

7. The study of *moral reasoning* has been strongly affected by Piaget's cognitive developmental approach. An important example is Kohlberg's analysis of progressive stages in moral reasoning.

8. Socialization plays a role in determining various senses of being male or female, including *gender identity, gender role,* and *sexual orientation.*

9. Certain psychological differences between the sexes may be based on biological differences. One is *aggression,* which tends to be more pronounced in men. Another is a tendency for males to perform better on spatial rather than verbal tests of mental ability, with the opposite pattern characteristic of females. Such biologically based differences—if any —are undoubtedly magnified by socially imposed sex roles. The importance of such roles is illustrated by the effects of *sex reassignment* in childhood.

10. Each of the three main theories of socialization—psychoanalysis, social learning theory, and cognitive developmental theory—tries to explain how social factors shape our sense of being male or female. Psychoanalysis asserts that the basic mechanism is *identification.* Social learning theory proposes that it is *imitation* of the parent of the same sex. Cognitive developmental theorists believe that identification comes after the child acquires gender identity which presupposes an understanding of *gender constancy.* Some of these theoretical differences grow out of differences of emphasis: Psychoanalysis focuses on sexual orientation, social learning theory concentrates on gender role, and cognitive developmental theory is most interested in gender identity.

11. In the past, some psychiatrists regarded homosexuality as a psychological disorder, but the presently dominant view is that it is not. Its causes are still unclear. Constitutional factors probably play a role, but some aspects of early childhood learning may also be relevant. Whatever its causes, this sexual orientation (no less than heterosexuality) is a fairly stable condition that can be changed only with difficulty, if at all.

12. Development continues after childhood is past. Some theorists, notably Erik Erikson, have tried to map later stages of development. One such stage is *adolescence,* which marks the transition into adulthood.

PART V

Individual Differences

People are different. They vary in bodily characteristics such as height, weight, strength, and hair color. They also vary along many psychological dimensions. They may be proud or humble, adventurous or timid, gregarious or withdrawn, intelligent or dull—the list of psychological distinctions is very large. Thus far such individual differences have not been our main concern. Our emphasis has been on attempts to find general psychological laws that apply to all persons, whether in physiological function, perception, memory, learning, or social behavior. To be sure, we have occasionally dealt with individual differences, as in the discussions of handedness, color blindness, variations in imagery, and differences in the need for achievement. But our focus was not on these differences as such; it was rather on what they could tell us about people in general— on how color blindness could help to explain the underlying mechanisms of color vision or how variations in child rearing might help us understand some aspects of socialization. In effect, our concern was with the nature of humankind, not with particular men and women.

We now change our emphasis and will consider individual differences as a topic in its own right. We will first deal with the measurement of psychological attributes, specifically intelligence and personality traits. We will then turn to the discussion of psychopathology and attempts to treat it, a field in which the fact that people are in some ways different—sometimes all too different—is starkly clear.

CHAPTER 17

Intelligence: Its Nature and Measurement

In twentieth-century industrialized society, especially in the United States, the description of individual differences is a flourishing enterprise that has produced a multitude of psychological tests to assess various personal characteristics, especially those that pertain to intellectual aptitude. This effort is a relatively recent phenomenon, for until the turn of the century most psychologists preferred to study the "generalized human mind" without worrying about the fact that different minds are not identical.

As we will see, the interest in individual differences grew in part from an effort to apply evolutionary ideas to humanity itself. But even more important was the social climate of the times, which provided a fertile soil for such concerns. The study of individual differences makes little sense in a society in which each person's adult role is fully determined by the social circumstances of his or her birth. In a caste society there is no need for vocational counselors or personnel managers. In such a society farmers beget farmers, soldiers beget soldiers, and princes beget princes; there is no point in administering mental tests to assist in educational selection or job placement. The interest in human differences arises only if such differences matter, if there is a social system that will accommodate them.

In a complex, industrialized society like our own, with its many different socioeconomic niches and some mobility across them, we have the precondition for a systematic assessment of human characteristics. Such a society will try to find a means, however imperfect, for selecting the proper person to occupy the proper niche.

Mental tests were meant to supply this means. They were devised as an instrument to help in educational and occupational selection, for use in various forms

Francis Galton *(1822–1911), a pioneer in the study of individual differences (Courtesy National Library of Medicine)*

of personal guidance and diagnosis. As such, they are often regarded as one of the major contributions of psychology to the world of practical affairs. However, for this very reason, the discussion of test results and applications necessarily touches upon social and political issues that go beyond the usual confines of scientific discourse. Under the circumstances, it is hardly surprising that some of the questions raised by testing, especially intelligence testing, are often debated in an emotionally charged atmosphere. Should a student be denied admission to a college because of his or her scholastic aptitude test score? Are such tests fair to disadvantaged ethnic or racial groups? Are scores on such tests determined by heredity, by environment, by both? This chapter will not be able to provide definitive answers to all of these questions. Some involve value judgments about social and political matters; others hinge on as yet unresolved issues of fact. Our primary purpose is to provide a background against which such questions have to be evaluated.

MENTAL TESTS

Mental tests come in different varieties. Some are tests of **achievement;** they measure what an individual can do *now,* his present knowledge and competence in a given area—how well he understands computer language or how well he can draw. Other tests are tests of **aptitude;** they predict what an individual will be able to do *later,* given the proper training and the right motivation. An example is a test of mechanical aptitude, which tries to determine the likelihood that an individual will do well as an engineer after an appropriate training period. **Intelligence tests** are sometimes considered as tests of a very general cognitive aptitude, including the ability to benefit from schooling. Still another kind of test is a **test of personality,** which tries to assess an individual's characteristic behavior dispositions—whether she is generally outgoing or withdrawn, placid or moody, and so on.

   We will begin our discussion by considering the nature of mental tests in general, regardless of what in particular they try to measure. We must begin by realizing that mental tests are in many ways different from tests used in medicine and the physical sciences. To be sure, there is a similarity on the face of it. A high score on a psychological test, such as a mechanical aptitude test, suggests a better than average ability for work in engineering; a certain reaction on chemical tests used by obstetricians indicates pregnancy. But there are some important differences as well. For one thing, the relation between the test result and what it signifies is much more tenuous in psychology than in the physical or biological sciences. To begin with, there is a difference in predictive accuracy. A high mechanical aptitude test score makes it more likely that the individual will succeed in engineering, while a certain chemical reaction on the obstetrician's test makes pregnancy a virtual certainty. More important yet is the fact that for most medical tests we have a much better understanding of why the test result signifies what it does. When a physician diagnoses the heart's condition from an electrocardiogram, the inference is fairly direct, for the test provides a graphic record of the heartbeat. Mental testers are usually in a less fortunate situation, for they can point to few theoretical links between their tests and what these tests try to measure. To understand the reasoning that underlies the construction and use of mental tests, we will have to take a detour and look at the general problem of variability and of its measurement.

The Study of Variation

The study of how individuals vary from each other grew up in close association with the development of statistical methods. Until the nineteenth century, the term *statistics* meant little more than the systematic collection of various state records (*state*-istics) such as birth and death rates or the physical measurements of army recruits. In poring over such figures, the Belgian scientist Adolphe Quetelet (1796–1874) saw that many of them fell into a pattern. From this, he determined the ***frequency distribution*** of various sets of observations, that is, the frequency with which individual cases are distributed over different intervals along some measure. For example, he plotted the frequency distribution of the chest expansion of Scottish soldiers, noting the number of cases that fell into various intervals, from 33 to 33.9 inches, 34 to 34.9 inches, and so on (Table 17.1).

VARIABILITY

Two facts are immediately apparent. The scores tend to cluster around a central value. One of the most common measures of this central tendency is the ***mean,*** or average, which is obtained by summing all of the values and dividing by the total number of cases. But the clustering tendency is by no means perfect, for there is variability around the average. All Scottish soldiers are not alike, whether in their chest sizes or anything else. An important measure of variability in a distribution is the ***variance (V).*** This is computed by taking the difference between each score and the mean, squaring this difference, and then taking the average of these squared differences. For many purposes, a more useful measure of variability is the ***standard deviation (SD)*** which is simply the square root of the variance.*

Quetelet's main contribution was the realization that, when put on a graph, the frequency distributions of various human physical attributes have a characteristic bell-shaped form. This symmetrical curve approximates the so-called ***normal curve*** which had already been studied by mathematicians in connection with games of chance. The normal curve describes the probability of obtaining certain combinations of chance events. Suppose, for example, that someone has the patience to throw six coins for over a hundred trials. How often will the coins fall to yield six heads, or five, four, three, two, one, or none? The expected distribution is shown in Figure 17.1, which also indicates what happened when a dedicated statistician actually performed the experiment. As more and more coins are thrown on any one trial, the expected distribution will approach the normal curve (Figure 17.2, p. 574).

According to Quetelet, the variability found in many human characteristics can be explained in similar terms. He believed that nature aims at an ideal value —whether of height, weight, or chest size—but that it generally misses the mark, sometimes falling short and sometimes overshooting. The actual value of an at-

Table 17.1   QUETELET'S DISTRIBUTIONS OF CHEST MEASURES OF SCOTTISH SOLDIERS

Measures of the chest in inches	Number of men per 1,000
33	4
34	31
35	141
36	322
37	732
38	1,305
39	1,867
40	1,882
41	1,628
42	1,148
43	645
44	160
45	87
46	38
47	7
48	2

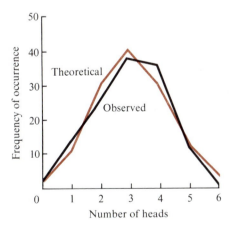

17.1   Theoretical and observed distribution of number of heads in 128 throws of six coins   *(After Anastasi, 1958)*

---

* For a fuller description of these and other statistical matters which will be referred to in this chapter, see the Appendix, "Statistics: The Collection, Organization, and Interpretation of Data."

17.2 The normal curve (A) The probability of the number of heads that will occur in a given number of coin tosses. (B) When the number of coins tossed approaches infinity, the resulting distribution is the normal curve. The fact that this curve describes the distribution of many physical and mental attributes suggests that these attributes are affected by a multitude of independent factors, some pulling one way and some another.

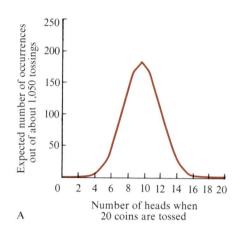

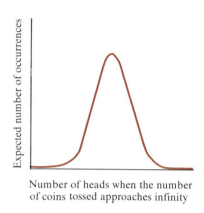

A — Number of heads when 20 coins are tossed

B — Number of heads when the number of coins tossed approaches infinity

tribute such as height depends upon a host of factors, some of which lead to an increase, others to a decrease. But each of these factors is independent and their operation is determined by chance. Thus nature is in effect throwing a multitude of coins to determine any one person's height. Each head adds, say, a millimeter to the average, and each tail subtracts one. The result is a frequency distribution of heights that approximates a normal curve.

VARIABILITY AND DARWIN

After Darwin published his *Origin of Species,* variability within a species was suddenly considered in a new perspective. Darwin showed that it provides the raw material on which natural selection can work. Suppose that the average finch on a particular island has a fairly long and narrow beak. There is some variability; a few finches have beaks that are shorter and wider. These few would be able to crack certain hard seeds that the other finches could not open. If these hard seeds suddenly become the primary foodstuffs in the habitat, the short-beaked finches might find themselves at a reproductive advantage. They would outlive and thus outbreed their long-beaked comrades and eventually a new species might be born (or more precisely, hatched). Seen in this light, variability is far from being an error of nature that missed the ideal mark as Quetelet had thought. On the contrary, it is the very stuff of which evolution is made (Figure 17.3).

17.3 Darwin's finches In 1835 Charles Darwin visited the Galapagos Islands in the Pacific Ocean and observed a number of different species of finches. They eventually provided an important stimulus to his theory of natural selection, as he supposed that "one species had been taken and modified for different ends." The figure shows two of these finches. One has a rather narrow beak and is a woodpecker-like bird that lives in trees and feeds on insects. The other is a large-beaked seed-eater. (After Lack, 1953)

CORRELATION

Could this line of reasoning be applied to variations in human characteristics? It might, if these characteristics could be shown to be hereditary, at least in part. This assumption seemed reasonable enough for physical attributes of the kind that Quetelet had tabulated, but is it appropriate for mental characteristics such as intellectual ability? A half-cousin of Darwin's, Francis Galton (1822–1911) spent much of his life trying to prove that it is. Most of the subsequent work in the area rests on the statistical methods he and his followers developed to test his assertions.

An important part of Galton's program called for the assessment of the similarity among relatives. The trouble is that such relationships are not perfect. Children tend to be like their parents, but only to some extent. The problem was to

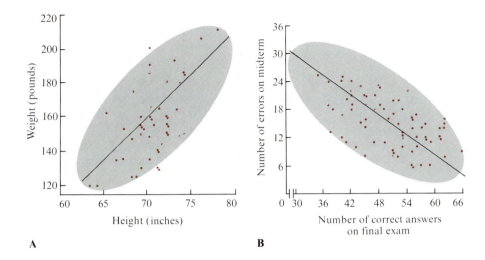

A   B

17.4   Correlation   *(A) A scatter diagram
of the heights and weights of 50 male
undergraduates. Note that the points fall
within an ellipse which indicates the
variation around the line of best fit. The
correlation for these data was +.70. (B) A
scatter diagram of the test performances of
70 students in an introductory psychology
course. The diagram plots number of
errors in a midterm against number of
correct answers on the final. The correlation was −.53. If errors (or correct
answers) had been plotted on both exams,
the correlation would of course have been
positive.*

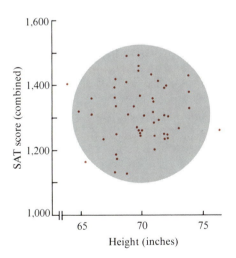

17.5   A correlation of zero   *A scatter
diagram of the scholastic aptitude scores
and the heights of 50 undergraduate
males. Not surprisingly, there was no relation as shown by the fact that the points
fall within a circle. The actual correlation
was +.05, which for all essential purposes is
equivalent to zero.*

find some measure of this relationship. Put more generally, the question was how
one could determine whether a variation along one characteristic could be accounted for by variation along another. The two characteristics might be the
height of a father and that of his son. They might also be characteristics within the
same individual such as a person's height and the same person's weight.

Take as an example an individual's weight. How is this related to his height?
The first step is to construct a ***scatter diagram*** in which one axis represents weight
and the other height. Each person will be represented by one point corresponding
to his position along the weight and height axes (see Figure 17.4A). Inspection of
the scatter diagram reveals that the two variables are related, for they covary: that
is, as height goes up, so does weight. But this covariation, or ***correlation,*** is far
from perfect. We can draw a ***line of best fit*** through the points in the scatter diagram, which allows us to make the best prediction of a person's weight given his
height. But this prediction is relatively crude, for there is considerable variability
around the line of best fit.

Galton and his students developed a mathematical expression that summarizes both the direction and the strength of the relationship between the two
measures. This is the ***correlation coefficient*** which varies between + 1.00 and
− 1.00 and is symbolized by the letter *r*. The plus or minus sign of the correlation
coefficient indicates the direction of the relationship. In the case of height and
weight this direction is positive: as height increases so does weight (17.4A). With
other measures, the direction is negative: as the score on one measure increases,
the score on the other declines (Figure 17.4B).

The strength of the correlation is expressed by its absolute value (that is, its
value regardless of sign). A correlation of *r* = .00 indicates no relation whatsoever. An example might be the relation between a man's collar size and his yearly
income. If we plot the scatter diagram, the points will be arranged in a circle.
There is no way of predicting income from collar size, so there is no single line of
best fit (Figure 17.5)

As the absolute value of *r* increases, the dots on the scatter diagram form an ellipse around the line of best fit. As the correlation goes up, the ellipse gets thinner
and thinner. The thinner the ellipse, the less error there is as we try to predict the
value of one variable (say, weight) when given the value of the other (say, height).

575

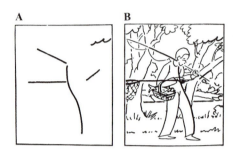

17.6 *A test of art aptitude* *The person tested is presented with (A). Using the lines in this card as a start, he has to make a completed drawing. (B) A completed sample. The test score is based on ratings by an experienced art teacher. These scores correlated quite well (.66) with grades in a special art course for high-school seniors. (Cronbach, 1970a. Test item from the Horn Art Aptitude Inventory, 1953; courtesy Stoelting Co., Chicago)*

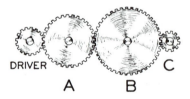

17.7 *A test of mechanical comprehension* *One of the items asks, "Which gear will make the most turns in a minute?" (From the Bennett Test of Mechanical Comprehension; courtesy The Psychological Corporation)*

When the absolute value of r reaches 1.00 (whether $+ 1.00$ or $- 1.00$), the ellipse finally becomes a straight line. There is no more variation at all around the line of best fit; the correlation is perfect and prediction is error-free. However, such perfect correlations are virtually never encountered in actual practice; even in the physical sciences there is bound to be some error of measurement.

While correlations are a useful index of the degree to which two variables are related, they have a limitation. The fact that two variables are correlated says nothing about the underlying causal relationship between them. Sometimes, there is none at all. Examples are correlations that are produced by some third factor. The number of umbrellas one sees on a given day is surely correlated with the number of people who wear raincoats. A Martian observing the human scene might conclude that umbrella-carrying causes raincoat-wearing or vice versa; our own earthly wisdom tells us that both are caused by the rain.

Evaluating Mental Tests

While the correlation techniques developed by Galton and his students were initially meant to investigate the extent to which relatives resemble each other, they were soon extended to other problems. One important application was to mental testing, for which they provided the underlying statistical methodology.

A mental test is meant to be an objective yardstick to assess some psychological trait or capacity on which people differ (for example, artistic and mechanical aptitude; see Figures 17.6 and 17.7). But how can one tell that a given test actually accomplishes this objective?

RELIABILITY

One important criterion of the adequacy of a test is its *reliability,* the consistency with which it measures what it measures. Consider a spring balance. If the spring is in good condition, the scale will give virtually identical readings when the same object is repeatedly weighed. But if the spring is gradually losing its elasticity, repeated weighings will give different values. If it does this, we throw away the scale. It is unreliable.

The same logic underlies test reliability. One way of assessing this is by administering the same test twice to the same group of subjects. The correlation between test and retest scores will then be an index of the test's reliability.

One trouble with the *test-retest method* is that the performance on the retest may be affected by what the subject learned the first time around. For example, some people may look up the answers to questions they missed. To avoid this problem, testers sometimes develop *alternative forms* of a test; if the two alternate forms are exactly equivalent, reliability can be assessed by using one form on one occasion and another on a second. Since any two halves of a single test can be considered "alternate forms," reliability is often measured by the *split-half technique* (correlating subjects' scores on, say, all of the odd items with their scores on all of the even items). If both halves correlate highly, we consider the test reliable; if they don't, we regard it as unreliable.

Most standard psychological tests now in use have *reliability coefficients* (that is, test-retest or split-half correlations) in the .90s or in the high .80s. Tests with lower reliability are of little practical use.

High reliability alone does not guarantee that a test is a good measuring rod. Even more critical is a test's *validity,* which is most simply defined as the extent to which it measures what it is supposed to measure.

Again consider the spring scale. If the spring is made of good steel, the scale may be highly reliable. But suppose someone decides to use this scale to measure *length.* This bizarre step will produce an instrument of high reliability but virtually no validity. It measures some attribute very precisely and consistently but that attribute is not length. As a test of length, the scale is invalid.

In the case of the scale, we can readily define the physical attribute that it is meant to measure and this lets us assess validity. But how can we define the psychological attribute which a mental test tries to assess?

Predictive validity   One approach is to consider the test as a ***predictor*** of future performance. If a test claims to measure scholastic aptitude, a score on that test should predict later school or college performance. The same holds for tests of vocational aptitude, which ought to predict how persons later succeed on the job. One index of a test's validity is the success with which it makes such predictions. This is usually measured by the correlation between the test score and some appropriate ***criterion.*** For scholastic aptitude, a common criterion is the grade-point average the student later attains. For vocational aptitude, it is some measure of later job proficiency. For example, aptitude tests for salespersons might be validated against their sales records.

Validity coefficients (that is, the correlations between test scores and criteria) for scholastic aptitude are generally in the neighborhood of .50 or .60, which means that the prediction is far from perfect. This is hardly surprising. For one thing, the tests probably don't provide a perfect index of one's "capacity" (ignoring for the time being just what this capacity might be). But even if they did, we would not expect validity coefficients of 1.00, for we all know that school grades depend on many factors in addition to ability (for example, motivation).

An important fact about validity coefficients is that their magnitude depends upon the ***range of ability*** within the group in which they are determined. As this range is narrowed, the correlation between test score and criterion declines. This relationship holds for all correlation coefficients. Consider the correlation between height and weight. If we choose to narrow the range by excluding jockeys and basketball players, the height-weight correlation will be reduced. If we narrow the range more drastically by, say, looking only at persons between 5′7′′ and 5′8′′, the correlation will become virtually insignificant.

The same phenomenon occurs in the field of testing. Scholastic aptitude tests do a reasonably good job in predicting high school and college grades. However, they tend to be less useful in predicting how a student will perform in graduate or professional school. The reason is that the postgraduates are already preselected. They have survived many years of schooling and are thus screened for academic ability, at least to some extent. As a result, the range of scholastic aptitude within this group is necessarily less than that found within the population at large. Since the differences in scholastic aptitude within this preselected group are relatively small, they are of less value in predicting future academic performance (Figure 17.8). But this does not mean that the test has no bearing on the prediction of fu-

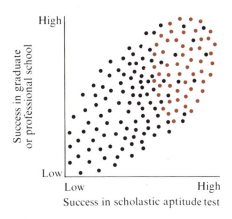

17.8   The effect of preselection upon correlation   *Hypothetical data which show the relation between some scholastic aptitude test taken in high school and success in graduate or professional school. When we look at the records of those who actually entered postgraduate schools (color), we find little if any relation to aptitude scores in high school. If there had been no preselection—that is, if every high school student eventually ended up in graduate or professional school—the resulting scatter diagram would include all dots (both black and color) and would indicate a sizable correlation. (After Cronbach, 1970a)*

ture performance. It may not be able to predict success in graduate or professional school for those who are already admitted. But it can be used for the larger, unselected population. For example, it may help a vocational guidance counselor in advising a high school student who is considering, say, a career in medicine (Cronbach, 1970b).

Construct validity Predictive validity is not the only way of assessing whether a test measures what it claims to measure. Another approach is to establish that the test has **construct validity** (Cronbach and Meehl, 1955). This is the extent to which the performance on the test fits into a theoretical scheme—or construct—about the attribute the test tries to measure. For example, suppose someone tries to develop a test to assess behavioral tendencies toward depression (see Chapter 19). The validity of such a test would not be established by correlating it with any *one* factor, such as feelings of helplessness. Instead, the investigator would try to relate the test to a whole network of hypotheses about depression. To the extent that the results do indeed fit into this larger pattern, they confer construct validity on the test. In terms of the medical analogy we used before, present-day chemical tests of pregnancy have both construct and predictive validity. They have construct validity because modern medical science knows enough about the hormonal changes during pregnancy to understand why the chemical reacts as it does. They also have predictive validity, for they correlate almost perfectly with the highly visible manifestations of pregnancy which appear a short time later.

STANDARDIZATION

To evaluate a test, we need one further item of information in addition to its reliability and validity. We have to know something about the group on which the test was **standardized.** A person's test score by itself provides little information. It can, however, be interpreted by comparing it with the scores obtained by other people. These other scores provide the **norms** against which an individual's test scores are evaluated. To obtain these norms, the test is first administered to a large sample of the population on which the test is to be used. This initial group is the **standardization sample.**

A crucial requirement in using tests is the comparability between the subjects who are tested and the standardization sample that yields the norms. If these two are drawn from different populations, the test scores may not be interpretable. Consider a scholastic aptitude test standardized on ten-year-olds in 1920. Its norms will surely not apply today to ten-year-olds whose schooling undoubtedly differs in many ways. There will be no way of evaluating a particular test score, for the comparison is with ten-year-olds today rather than sixty years ago.

A similar issue crops up when tests are administered to persons whose cultural backgrounds are different from that of the standardization sample. This problem is by no means hypothetical; examples are the cultural differences between ethnic and racial groups and between rural and urban dwellers. Some test items clearly discriminate in favor of one group or another. When urban schoolchildren were asked questions like "What is the largest river in the United States?" or "How can banks afford to pay interest on the money you deposit?" they did considerably better than rural schoolchildren of the same age. The difference was reversed for questions like "Name a vegetable that grows above ground" or "Why does seasoned wood burn more easily than green wood?" (Shimberg, 1929).

Using Tests for Selection

Suppose we have a test of good reliability and reasonable validity. How is it used? One important application in our society is as a selection device. A well-known example is an aptitude test for pilot training developed by the Army Air Force during World War II. A large number of separate subtests were constructed for this purpose, including tests of motor coordination, reaction time, perceptual skills, and general intellectual ability. These subtests were administered to over 185,000 men who went through pilot training. The initial question was how each of these subtests correlated with the criterion—success or failure in training. The scores of each subtest were then weighted to produce a composite score that gave the best estimate of the criterion. The use of this composite pilot aptitude test score led to an appreciable improvement in trainee selection. Without the test, the failure rate was 24 percent. By using the test, the failure rate was cut to 10 percent. This was accomplished by setting a ***cutoff score*** on the test below which no applicant was accepted (Flanagan, 1947).

Given a reasonable validity coefficient, the use of tests evidently helps to reduce the number of selection errors. The overall number of such errors declines as the validity coefficient of the test increases. But some errors will always be present, for validity coefficients are never at 1.00; in fact, most vocational aptitude testers count themselves lucky if they manage to obtain validity correlations of .40 or .50.

The important point is that selection errors are of two kinds. On the one hand, there are "false accepts," persons who are accepted but who will fail. On the other hand, there are "false rejects," people who are rejected but who would have performed adequately. What determines which of the two kinds of errors will predominate? The answer depends upon the choice of the cutoff score. Suppose we decide to use a very stringent cutoff point. The result will be a marked reduction in the number of false accepts; but there is a price, an increased frequency of false rejects. We can reduce the number of false rejects by picking a lower cutoff score; but again there is a trade-off, a concomitant increase in the number of false accepts (Figure 17.9).

What cutoff score is the appropriate one? The answer hinges on the costs and benefits the selector assigns to each of the four possible outcomes: false accepts,

17.9   Selection errors and cutoff scores   Applicants to pilot training are selected on the basis of an aptitude test. The line of best fit indicates the prediction of trainee performance from aptitude test score; the ellipse shows the variation around this line. The choice of a cutoff aptitude score, below which no applicant is accepted, determines the nature of selection errors. (A) A high cutoff score will increase the proportion of false rejects relative to false accepts. (B) A low cutoff score has the reverse effect.

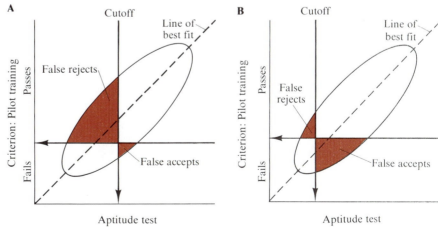

false rejects, correct accepts (accepted applicants who succeed), and correct rejects (rejected applicants who would not have succeeded). These costs and benefits yield a *payoff matrix* similar to some we have already encountered (see Chapters 5 and 11).

Just what these costs and benefits are depends upon a number of social, economic, and institutional values. Let us consider only the selection errors. Which is the more harmful? It obviously depends. In selecting combat pilots, there is a premium on avoiding false accepts. Pilot training is extremely costly. A trainee who doesn't make the grade represents a serious loss: in instruction time, in tying up expensive equipment, and—in case of really extreme failure—in life and limb. From the point of view of the Air Force, a false reject is much less serious. A rejected applicant who would in fact have succeeded as a pilot is still perfectly useful as a member of the ground crew. Under the circumstances, a high cutoff score makes good sense. In other selection situations, however, the payoff matrix may be very different. Suppose that there is a serious shortage in a particular occupation, say, engineering. If the number of applicants to engineering schools is relatively low, the schools would be well advised to set a lower cutoff point on an engineering aptitude test. Given the increased need for engineers and the reduced pool of applicants, there are good reasons to minimize false rejects. Graduating a few additional engineers may now be worth the price of a larger number of student dropouts.

The payoff matrix that underlies a selection procedure obviously varies with the situation. It also varies according to one's perspective. The best example is the contrast between the institution that does the selecting and the applicant (see Chapter 5). A college with a large number of applicants might well decide to reduce the number of false accepts. But many applicants will see things very differently, especially if they have applied only to this one school. From their point of view, the worst error is to be falsely rejected (Table 17.2). This is not to say that the payoff matrices of selector and potential selectee are always different. Occasionally they are in harmony. In picking combat pilots, the Air Force wants to minimize the number of false accepts. But so do the applicants. When poor job performance may mean a fiery death, a high cutoff score is in the best interest of both parties.*

To conclude, the use of tests in selection involves several factors. To begin with, there is the question of how well the test predicts performance, whether in school or on the job. To answer this question we need to know the test's reliability and validity. But since prediction is necessarily imperfect, we have the further question of where to set the cutoff point. And this decision cannot be settled on the basis of the test alone. It is inextricably tied up with all kinds of value judgments that determine the payoff matrix for the possible outcomes.

---

* There is a formal similarity between the selection problem just discussed and the decision subjects have to make in a detection experiment. In a detection study, a subject can make two kinds of errors: "false alarms" (reporting a stimulus when in fact there is none) and "misses" (failing to report a stimulus when in fact there is one). False alarms are analogous to false accepts, while misses are analogous to false rejects. In both the selection problem and the detection experiment, the choice between yea and nay is partially determined by a cutoff value, which in turn depends on a payoff matrix (see Chapter 5, pp. 143–46).

Table 17.2 TWO PAYOFF MATRICES FOR ACCEPTING COLLEGE APPLICANTS (IN ARBITRARY UNITS)

A. From the perspective of the college

		Performance in college	
		Passes	Fails
Decision	Accept	*Correct accept:* Delighted + 5	*False accept:* Waste of resources, lowers general intellectual level, etc. − 5
	Reject	*False reject:* Too bad, but not really serious, for there are more applicants than openings − 1	*Correct reject:* Satisfaction in having decided correctly + 1

B. From the perspective of the applicant

		Performance in college	
		Passes	Fails
Decision	Accept	*Correct accept:* Delighted + 5	*False accept:* A wasted year but not completely since something was gained away − 1
	Reject	*False reject:* A calamity − 10	*Correct reject:* Ok, if really so + 1

INTELLIGENCE TESTING

What is ***intelligence?*** In a crude sense, of course, we all have some notion of what the term refers to. The dictionary is full of adjectives that distinguish levels of intellectual functioning such as *bright* and *dull, quick-witted* and *slow.* Intelligence tests try to get at some attribute (or attributes) that roughly corresponds to such distinctions. But the test constructors did not begin with a precise conception of what it was they wanted to test. There was no consensus as to a definition of intelligence, and those definitions that were offered were usually so broad and all-inclusive as to be of little use. Intelligence was said to be a capacity, but what is it a capacity for? Is it for learning, for transfer, for abstract thinking, or judgment, comprehension, reason, or perhaps all of these? There was no agreement. Edward Thorndike suggested a first approximation according to which intelligence was to be defined "as the quality of mind . . . in respect to which Aristotle, Plato, Thucydides, and the like, differed most from Athenian idiots of their day." While this seemed sensible enough, it hardly went beyond the intuitive notions people had long before psychologists appeared on the scene (Heim, 1954).

Measuring Intelligence

Given the difficulty in defining intelligence, devising tests for this hard-to-define attribute was an undertaking of a rather different sort from constructing a specialized aptitude test for prospective pilots. The pilot aptitude test has a rather clear-cut validity criterion. But what is the best validity criterion for intelligence tests? Since the nature of intelligence is unclear, we can't be sure of what the appropriate validity criterion might be.

But our theoretical ignorance notwithstanding, we do have intelligence tests, and many of them. They were developed to fulfill certain practical needs. We may not understand exactly what it is that they assess, but the test consumers—schools, armies, industries—want them even so. The fact is that for many practical purposes these tests work quite well.

TESTING INTELLIGENCE IN CHILDREN

The pioneering step was taken by a French psychologist, Alfred Binet (1857–1911). As so often in the field of individual differences, the impetus came from the world of practical affairs. By the turn of the century, compulsory elementary education was the rule among the industrialized nations. Large numbers of schoolchildren had to be dealt with and some of them seemed mentally retarded. If they were indeed retarded, it appeared best to send them to special schools. But mere backwardness was not deemed sufficient to justify this action; perhaps a child's prior education had been poor, or perhaps the child suffered from some illness. In 1904, the French minister of public instruction appointed a special committee, including Binet, and asked it to look into this matter. The committee concluded that there was a need for an objective diagnostic instrument to assess each child's intellectual state. Much of what we now know about the measurement of intelligence comes from Binet's efforts to satisfy this need.

Intelligence as a general cognitive capacity   Binet and his collaborator, Théodore Simon, started with the premise that intelligence is a rather general attribute that manifests itself in many spheres of cognitive functioning. This view led them to construct a test that ranged over many areas. It included tasks that varied in both content and difficulty—copying a drawing, repeating a string of digits, recognizing coins and making change, explaining absurdities. The child's performance on all these subtests yielded a composite score. Later studies showed that

Alfred Binet   *(Courtesy National Library of Medicine)*

this composite measure correlated with the child's school grades and with the teacher's evaluations of the child's intelligence.

Binet and other intelligence testers have sometimes been criticized on the ground that some—perhaps all—of their test items depend upon prior knowledge. One obviously cannot define a word without having seen or heard it, nor can one make change for a franc without exposure to arithmetic and French currency. But Binet did not regard this as a drawback. He felt that there is no such thing as pure, disembodied intelligence which develops independently of environmental input. In constructing his tests he tried to use only items whose content was in principle familiar to all of the children that he tested. He believed that once this condition is met, the test score makes sense. Each child has had some contact with a common culture; one assesses the children's underlying capacity by noting what they have picked up from this environment and how they can put it together in different ways.

The intelligence quotient, IQ Binet made another assumption about intelligence. He believed that it develops with age until maturity is reached. Here too his ideas fit our intuitive notions. We know that an average group of six-year-olds is no intellectual match for an average group of eight-year-olds. It's not just that they know less; they're not as smart. This conception provided the basis for the test's scoring system.

Binet and Simon first gave the test to a standardization sample composed of children of varying ages whose test performance provided the norms. Binet and Simon noted which items were passed by the average six-year-old, and so on. (Items that were passed by younger but not by older children were excluded.)

The resulting classification of the test items generated a ladder of tasks in which each rung corresponds to a number of subtests that were successfully passed by the average child of a given age. Testing a child's intelligence was thus tantamount to a determination of how high the child could ascend this ladder before the tasks finally became too difficult. The rung she attained indicated her **mental age** (usually abbreviated MA). If she successfully coped with all items passed by the average eight-year-old and failed all those passed by the average nine-year-old, her MA was said to be eight years. Appropriate scoring adjustments were made when the performance pattern did not work out quite as neatly; for example, if a child passed all items at the seven-year-old level, 75 percent of those at the eight-year-old level, 25 percent of those at the nine-year-old level, and none beyond. Table 17.3 (p. 584) presents representative test items for the Stanford-Binet, a widely used American adaptation of the Binet-Simon test.

The MA assesses an absolute level of cognitive capacity. To determine whether a child is "bright" or "dull" one has to compare her MA with her chronological age (CA). To the extent that her MA exceeds her CA, we regard the child as "bright" or advanced; the opposite is true if the MA is below the CA. But a particular lag or advance clearly has different import depending upon the child's age. A six-year-old with an MA of three is obviously more retarded than a ten-year-old with an MA of seven. To cope with this difficulty, a German psychologist, William Stern (1871–1938), proposed the use of a ratio measure, the **intelligence quotient** or **IQ.** This is computed by dividing the MA by the CA. The resulting quotient is multiplied by 100 to get rid of decimal points. Thus,

$$IQ = \frac{MA}{CA} \times 100$$

Table 17.3 REPRESENTATIVE TASKS FROM THE STANFORD-BINET

Age	Task
2½	Points to toy object that "goes on your feet" Names *chair, flag* Can repeat two digits
4	"In daytime it is light, after night it is . . .?" "Why do we have houses?"
6	"What is the difference between a bird and a dog?" "An inch is short, a mile is . . .?" "Give me _____ blocks" (up to ten)
9	"Tell me a number that rhymes with *tree.*" "If I buy 4 cents worth of candy and give the store keeper 10 cents, how much money will I get back?" Repeats four digits in reversed order
12	Defines *skill, muzzle* "The streams are dry _____ there has been little rain." ". . . 'In an old graveyard in Spain, they have discovered a small skull which they believe to be that of Christopher Columbus when he was about ten years old.' . . . What is foolish about that?" Repeats 5 digits in reversed order

SOURCE: Modified from Terman and Merrill, 1972.

By definition, an IQ of 100 indicates average intelligence; it means that the child's MA is equivalent to his CA and thus to the average score attained by his age-mates in the standardization sample. By the same token, an IQ greater than 100 indicates that the child is above average; an IQ of less than 100 that he is below average.

Stern's quotient measure has various drawbacks. The major problem is that the top rung of Binet's mental age ladder was sixteen (in some later revisions of the Stanford-Binet, the ceiling was higher). In some ways, this makes good sense, for intelligence does not grow forever, any more than height does. But since CAs keep on rising beyond the MA ceiling, the IQ (defined as a quotient) cannot help but decline. Consider the IQ of an adult. If her CA is 48 and her MA is 16, the use of the standard computation results in an IQ of 33 ($16/48 \times 100 = 33$), a score that indicates severe mental retardation—an obvious absurdity.

Eventually a new approach was adopted. In the last analysis, an intelligence score indicates how an individual stands in relation to an appropriate comparison sample—his own age-mates. The intelligence quotient expresses this comparison as a ratio, but there are more direct measures of getting at the same thing. One example is an individual's **percentile rank;** that is, the proportion of persons in his comparison group whose score is below his. A more commonly used measure that provides the same information is the **deviation IQ.** We will not go into the details of how this measure is arrived at; suffice it to say that an IQ of 100 indicates a score equal to the average of the comparison sample (and thus a percentile rank of 50); that for most standard tests, IQs of 85 and 115 indicate percentile ranks of about 16 and 84, IQs of 70 and 130 percentile ranks of 2 and 98.

TESTING INTELLIGENCE IN ADULTS

Although the Binet scales were originally meant for children, demands soon arose for the diagnosis of adults' intelligence. One reason was that the Binet scale had not been standardized on an adult population so that there were no appropriate norms. Such considerations led David Wechsler to construct an intelligence test for adults—the Wechsler Adult Intelligence Scale (Wechsler, 1958).

Performance versus verbal tests   One of Wechsler's objections to the Binet scales was that they were too heavily loaded with items that require verbal skills. Wechsler argued that there are intellectual abilities that are not predominantly verbal (a view that has found later confirmation in studies of hemispheric function; see Chapter 2).

To cope with this, Wechsler divided his test into a verbal and a performance subtest. The verbal test includes items that assess general information, vocabulary, comprehension, and arithmetic. The performance test includes tasks that require the subject to assemble the cut-up parts of a familiar object so as to form the appropriate whole, to complete an incomplete drawing, or to rearrange a series of pictures so that they are in the proper sequence and tell a story (Figure 17.10).

COMPREHENSION	INFORMATION
1. Why should we obey traffic laws and speed limits?	1. Who wrote *Huckleberry Finn?*
2. Why are antitrust laws necessary?	2. Where is Finland?
3. Why should we lock the doors and take the keys to our car when leaving the car parked?	3. At what temperature does paper burn?
4. What does this saying mean: "Kill two birds with one stone."	4. What is entomology?

ARITHMETIC	
1. How many 15¢ stamps can you buy for a dollar?	3. A man bought a used stereo system for ¾ of what it cost new. He paid $225 for it. How much did it cost new?
2. How many hours will it take a cyclist to travel 60 miles if he is going 12 miles an hour?	4. Six men can finish a job in ten days. How many men will be needed to finish the job in two and a half days?

A. Verbal tests

B. Picture completion

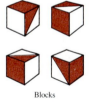

Blocks   Pattern

C. Block design

17.10   Test items similar to some in the Wechsler Adult Intelligence Scale   *(A) Verbal tests. These include tests of information, comprehension, and arithmetic. (B) Picture completion. The task is to note the missing part. (C) Object assembly. The task is to arrange the cut-up pieces to form a familiar object. (D) Block design. The materials consist of four blocks, which are all red on some sides, all white on other sides, and half red and half white on the rest of the sides. The subject is shown a pattern and has to arrange the four blocks to produce this design. (Courtesy The Psychological Corporation)*

D. Object assembly

585

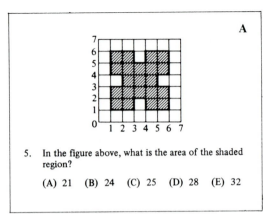

5. In the figure above, what is the area of the shaded region?

(A) 21 (B) 24 (C) 25 (D) 28 (E) 32

25. LINGUISTICS : LANGUAGE ::
(A) statistics : sociology
(B) ceramics : clay
(C) gymnastics : health
(D) dynamics : motion
(E) economics : warfare

17.11 Two items from the Scholastic Aptitude Test (SAT) *(Courtesy of The College Entrance Examination Board and the Educational Testing Service)*

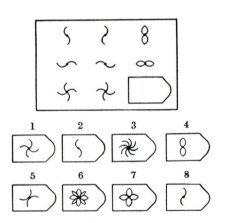

17.12 An example item from the Raven Progressive Matrices Test *The task is to select the alternative that fits into the empty slot above. (Courtesy The Psychological Corporation)*

Group tests   Both the Binet and the Wechsler scales are administered individually. This has the advantage of permitting a more careful evaluation of the person who is tested. But there is the obvious drawback that individual testing is a lengthy and expensive business. If the object is to assess a large number of persons —army recruits, potential employees in large industrial organizations, myriads of children in a city's schools, college applicants—the cost of administering tests individually becomes prohibitive.

Such economic facts of life led to the development of group tests of intelligence, usually of the paper-and-pencil multiple-choice format. Some examples are the Scholastic Aptitude Test (SAT) taken by many college applicants, and the Graduate Record Examination, a more difficult version of the SAT designed for applicants to graduate schools (Figure 17.11). A test that emphasizes abstract, nonverbal intellectual ability is the Progressive Matrices Test (Figure 17.12).

An Area of Application: Mental Deficiency

Binet's original purpose was to design an instrument for the diagnosis of mental retardation. How well did he and his followers succeed? On the whole, the tests seem to perform their diagnostic function rather well; they certainly provide one of the main bases for classification. The usual line of demarcation for retardation is an IQ of about 70 or below. Thus defined, 3 percent of the population of the United States would be regarded as retarded (Cytryn and Lourie, 1975). But the test performance criterion is by no means the only one. Equally important is social and cultural competence, the ability to learn and to cope with the demands of society, to take care of oneself, to earn a living. This competence obviously depends in part upon the nature of the society in which a person lives. A complex technological culture like ours puts a higher premium on various intellectual skills than an agrarian society. Someone classified as mildly retarded in the twentieth-century United States probably would have managed perfectly well in, say, feudal Europe.

CLASSIFYING RETARDATION

A widely used classification system distinguishes several degrees of mental deficiency: "mild" (IQ of 52 to 67), "moderate" (IQ of 36 to 51), "severe" (IQ of 20 to 35), and "profound" (IQ below 20). The more severe the retardation, the less frequently it occurs in the population: in 100 retarded persons, one would expect that the degree of retardation would be "mild" in 90, "moderate" in 6, "severe" in 3, and "profound" in 1 (Robinson and Robinson, 1970).

Table 17.4 presents a description of the general level of intellectual functioning in each of the categories at various ages. The table shows that mentally retarded persons do not have to be excluded from useful participation in society. This is especially true for those whose degree of retardation is mild, and they account for almost 90 percent of all the cases. If provided with appropriate education and training, such persons can ultimately achieve an acceptable level of adjustment in adult life (Tyler, 1965).

Table 17.4 CHARACTERISTICS OF THE MENTALLY RETARDED

Degree of retardation	IQ range	Level of functioning at school age (6–20 years)	Level of functioning in adulthood (21 years and over)
Mild	52–67	Can learn academic skills up to approximately sixth-grade level by late teens; can be guided toward social conformity.	Can usually achieve social and vocational skills adequate to maintain self-support, but may need guidance and assistance when under unusual social or economic stress.
Moderate	36–51	Can profit from training in social and occupational skills; unlikely to progress beyond second-grade level in academic subjects; may learn to travel alone in familiar places.	May achieve self-maintenance in unskilled or semiskilled work under sheltered conditions; needs supervision and guidance when under mild social or economic stress.
Severe	20–35	Can talk or learn to communicate; can be trained in elemental health habits; profits from systematic habit training.	May contribute partially to self-maintenance under complete supervision; can develop self-protection skills at a minimum useful level in controlled environment.
Profound	below 20	Some motor development present; may respond to minimal or limited training in self-help.	Some motor and speech development; may achieve very limited self-care; needs nursing care.

SOURCE: Adapted from Mental Retardation Activities of the U.S. Department of Health, Education, and Welfare. Washington, D.C.: United States Government Printing Office, 1963, p.2.

THE CAUSES OF RETARDATION

Retardation is not a condition that has one single cause. It is a symptom that can reflect any number of underlying conditions, many of which are as yet unknown. Some forms of retardation are produced by certain known genetic disorders or by aberrations in the chromosome structure (see p. 457). Others are produced by brain damage suffered in the womb, during delivery, or after birth. Still others may reflect the composite effect of hundreds of genes. And yet others may be the result of impoverished environmental conditions, especially during early life.

A number of investigators have tried to order this hodgepodge of known and unknown causal factors by arguing that cases of mental retardation can be classified into two main types—those that are produced by one factor and those that are produced by many. According to this hypothesis, **unifactor** forms correspond to the more severe varieties of retardation; these are thought to result from a major pathology, such as a gene defect, chromosomal aberration, or brain damage. In contrast, mild retardation is believed to be a **multifactor** phenomenon. According to this view, mild retardation simply represents the lower portion of the distribution of intelligence. Seen in this light, intelligence in normals as well as mild retardates is produced by the joint action of numerous separate factors, some genetic and some environmental. Their composite effect determines the degree of intelligence. Adherents to this view believe that the lower end of the distribution consists of those unlucky cases for whom the large majority of causal factors fell in the wrong direction (Zigler, 1967).

THE NATURE OF INTELLIGENCE

We have seen that there is no consensus on a definition of intelligence and thus no clear-cut validity criterion for a test that claims to measure it. But even so, many psychologists would agree that such instruments as the Stanford-Binet and the Wechsler tests do distinguish people in ways that have a rough correspondence with our initial, intuitive conceptions of the term *intelligence.* There is no doubt that with appropriate modifications, either scale would easily differentiate between Aristotle and the Athenian village idiot. Can we get any further than this?

The Psychometric Approach

According to one group of investigators, the starting point for further inquiries into the nature of intelligence is just the fact that intelligence tests do make some distinctions between people that fit out initial sense of what intelligence is about. They believe that we can refine our knowledge of the nature of intelligence by a careful further study of these distinctions. This line of reasoning underlies the **psychometric approach** to the study of intelligence. In effect, it amounts to a bootstrap operation. One looks at the results the measuring instrument provides in order to find out what the instrument really measures.

THE STRUCTURE OF MENTAL ABILITIES

When we use the term *intelligence,* we imply that it is a unitary ability. But is it really? In principle, one could imagine several kinds of mental ability that are quite unrelated. Perhaps different intellectual tasks draw on distinctly different cognitive gifts. It may also be that the truth is in between. Perhaps human intellectual abilities are composed of both general and more particular capacities. How can we decide among these alternatives?

All we have to go on are people's scores on various tests. These scores presumably reflect some underlying abilities—perhaps one, perhaps several. But these underlying capacities are not observable directly; they can only be inferred. Students of psychometrics have tried to perform this inference by looking at the intercorrelations among different tests.

To get an intuitive idea of this general approach, consider a man who looks at a lake and sees what appear to be serpentlike parts:

He can entertain various hypotheses. One is that all visible parts belong to one huge sea monster (a hypothesis that is analogous to the assumption that there is a unitary intellectual ability):

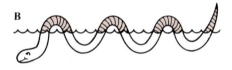

He might also assume that there are several such beasts (analogous to separate mental abilities):

Or finally, he might believe that there are as many sea animals as there are visible parts (analogous to the hypothesis that every test measures a totally different ability):

How can he choose among these alternatives, given that he has no way of peering below the waters? His best bet is to wait and watch how the serpentine parts change over time and space. If he does this, he can find out which parts go together. If all parts move jointly (B), the most reasonable interpretation is that they all belong to one huge sea monster. (For the purposes of our example, we will assume sea serpents are severely arthritic and are unable to move their body portions separately.) If the first part goes with the second, while the third goes with the fourth (C), there are presumably two smaller creatures. If all parts move separately (D), the best bet is that there are as many sea serpents as there are visible parts. In effect, our sea-serpent watcher has studied a correlation pattern on the basis of which he can infer the invisible structure (or structures) under the sea.

Spearman and the concept of "general intelligence" The psychometric equivalent of the joint movements of sea-serpent portions is the correlation pattern among different tests of mental abilities. As an example, consider the correlations among four subtests of the Wechsler Adult Scale: Information *(I),* comprehension *(C),* arithmetic *(A),* and vocabulary *(V).* These intercorrelations are all quite high. The correlation between *I* and *C* is .70, that between *I* and *A* is .66, and so on. These results can be presented in the form of a **correlation matrix,** in which the intercorrelations can be read off directly (Table 17.5).

Table 17.5 CORRELATION MATRIX OF FOUR SUBTESTS ON THE WECHSLER ADULT SCALE

	I	*C*	*A*	*V*
I (Information)	—	.70	.66	.81
C (Comprehension)		—	.49	.73
A (Arithmetic)			—	.59
V (Vocabulary)				—

SOURCE: From Wechsler, 1958.
NOTE: The matrix shows the correlation of each subtest with each of the other three. Note that the left-to-right diagonal (which is here indicated by the dashes) can't have any entries because it is made up of the cells that describe the correlation of each subtest with itself. The cells below the dashes are left blank because they would be redundant.

An inspection of this correlation matrix suggests that there is a common factor that runs through all four of these subtests. The positive correlations indicate that people with a greater fund of information are also people who are likely to get higher scores in comprehension, who are probably better at arithmetic, and who generally have a larger vocabulary. Given the fact that all of these measures are correlated, it is plausible to assume that they share something in common, that they all measure the same underlying attribute. This was exactly the conclusion reached by the English psychologist Charles Spearman (1863–1945), who developed the first version of **factor analysis,** a statistical technique by which one can "extract" this common factor that all of the various tests share. In his view, this factor was best described as **general intelligence,** or **g,** a mental attribute that is called upon in any intellectual task a person has to perform.

Spearman pointed out that this *g*-factor alone cannot explain the intercorrelations among mental tests. If test performance were determined by *g* and only *g,* then the correlations between any two subtests should be perfect except for errors of measurement. But in fact the intercorrelations fall far short of this. To explain why this is so, Spearman proposed that any test taps not only *g* but also some other ability, *s,* that is completely specific to the particular test used. Thus performance on an arithmetic subtest depends in part on *g* and in part on numerical skills *(s)* that are specific to that subtest. Since people vary along both general intelligence, *g,* and these different specific factors, the *s*'s, the intercorrelations among different tests cannot be perfect (Spearman, 1927).

Group-factor theories Spearman's theory of intelligence is sometimes described as "monarchic." As he saw it, there is one and only one underlying factor, *g,* that reigns supreme over all intellectual functions. But his position was soon challenged by other investigators who argued that the intercorrelations among test scores are better explained by a set of underlying mental abilities than by one overarching *g*-factor. Spearman called this **group-factor theory** an "oligarchic" conception of intelligence, since it viewed intelligence as just the composite of separate abilities without a sovereign capacity that enters into each. As an illustration of the kind of evidence that led to the multiple-factor theory, consider the hypothetical (and idealized) correlation matrix in Table 17.6 among four tests: digit span *(D),* paired-associate learning *(P),* vocabulary *(V),* and comprehension *(C).*

Table 17.6   HYPOTHETICAL CORRELATION MATRIX BETWEEN FOUR TESTS

	D	*P*	*V*	*C*
D (Digit span)	—	.65	.40	.25
P (Paired associates)		—	.35	.30
V (Vocabulary)			—	.75
C (Comprehension)				—

In looking over the matrix, we see that all of the tests are positively correlated; this of course is the phenomenon that led Spearman to insist on *g.* But we also see that some of the tests form clusters. Scores on *D* tend to go more with those on *P* than with the scores on the other tests; the same holds for *V* and *C.* An adherent of the oligarchic view would interpret this pattern by postulating two underlying factors: The first is an ability tapped mostly by tests *D* and *P,* while the second enters primarily into tests *V* and *C.* To identify these two abilities, we look at the tests that enter into each and try to determine what they have in common. A reasonable guess is that the first factor (digit span and paired-associate learning) corresponds to a capacity for rote memory, while the second (vocabulary and comprehension) pertains to verbal ability.

Needless to say, this illustration is a drastic oversimplification. In actual practice, group-factor analysts operate on correlation matrices that are based on many tests deliberately selected to be as varied as possible. L. L. Thurstone (1887–1955), who originated most of the concepts and techniques that underlie group-factor theory, started with a set of 56 tests, yielding a matrix of 1,540 intercorrelations. Thurstone invented powerful new statistical techniques to extract the underlying factors, which he called "primary mental abilities." Some of the more important of these are spatial, numerical, verbal, and reasoning abilities.

Later investigators have come up with increasingly refined ways of classifying the mental abilities that underlie test performance. One of the most influential re-

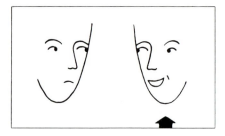

1 I'm glad you're feeling a little better.

2 You make the funniest faces!

3 Didn't I tell you she'd say "No"?

17.13 Testing for social intelligence An item on one of Guilford's tests of social intelligence. The task is to decide what the person marked by the arrow is most probably saying to the other. (The answer is number 3). Thus far, there is relatively little evidence concerning the validity of this and similar tests of social intelligence. (From Guilford, 1967)

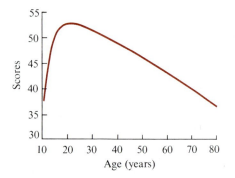

17.14 Mental test scores as related to age The scores are based on comparisons of different age groups. They are expressed in units that allow comparisons of different tests and are based on averaged results of three different studies. (After Jones and Kaplan, 1945)

cent attempts was undertaken by J. P. Guilford, who proposed an ambitious three-dimensional classification of intellectual functions containing 120 factors in all. But Guilford's proposal amounts to more than just a new way of slicing up the intellectual pie. His scheme is based on a theory of how intellectual tasks can be classified: by the kind of operation the thinker is asked to perform (e.g., evaluation, memory), by the materials on which she has to operate (e.g., visual figures, verbal meanings), and by the end result that is asked for (e.g., relations, implications). An attractive aspect of Guilford's approach is an unusually broad conception of what intelligence is. Some of his factors pertain to a kind of social intelligence, including the ability to infer another person's state of mind or to predict her probable behavior (Figure 17.13). Another example is a set of factors probably related to creativity, an attribute largely ignored in traditional tests of intelligence.

But despite these virtues, Guilford's system has not gone unchallenged. One major objection is that he has gone to the opposite extreme from Spearman. Where Spearman had one sole monarch, Guilford has a veritable parliament—as he sees it, there are 120 separate and distinct factors. Guilford's critics contend that this carries the fractionation of human abilities too far, that 120 separate fragments are too narrow and specific to predict human behavior in any actual situation (Vernon, 1964).

INTELLIGENCE AND AGE

Factor analysts tried to get some insight into the nature of intelligence by studying how scores on various subtests correlate with one another. Another psychometric approach is to relate test performance to other attributes on which people vary. An obvious candidate is age, which after all was the basis on which the first intelligence tests were standardized. But Binet used only the age range of three to sixteen years. Numerous later studies have asked about the development of intelligence throughout the entire life-span. Their procedure was straightforward. The same test was administered to different age groups matched by sex and socioeconomic level. Figure 17.14 presents a composite curve based on several investigations. The figure should hearten the young and bring gloom to all who are past twenty: There is a sharp increase in mental ability between ten and twenty, and an accelerating decline thereafter.

Later investigators (perhaps prompted by the fact that they were over thirty) concluded that the situation could not be as bleak as that. They argued that the steep decline in intelligence could have resulted from an artifact, a byproduct of an irrelevant factor: On the average, the older age groups had a lower level of education. Such a difference might have been present even if the groups were matched by years of schooling, for curricula have probably improved over time. One way of getting around this difficulty is through a *longitudinal* study in which the same persons are tested at different ages. The results of such longitudinal studies show a continued *rise* on tests for verbal meaning, for reasoning, and for educational aptitude until about fifty. After this, there is a moderate decline (Figure 17.15).

Further studies have shown that the age curves are different depending upon the particular ability that is tested. Many facets of verbal intelligence show no decline until seventy. Tests of vocabulary are even more encouraging to those of later years; they show no drop even at eighty-five (Blum, Jarvik, and Clark,

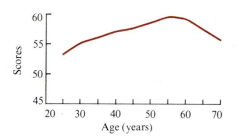

17.15 Mental test scores as related to age when studied by a variation of the longitudinal method *The scores, which cover a fifty-year age range, were obtained over a seven-year period from several adult populations, the youngest of which was twenty at the beginning of the study and the oldest in their sixties. (After Schaie and Strother, 1968)*

1970). In contrast, nonverbal abilities that are tapped by such tests as the Progressive Matrices decline earlier, usually around forty (Green, 1969). The most pronounced drops are found for tests that depend on quick recall, especially when there is no memory organization that can aid in retrieval (see Chapter 7). An example is the word fluency test, in which the subject has two minutes to write down as many words as he can think of which start with a particular letter. Such mental calisthenics are best left to the young; declines in word fluency are very steep and are seen as early as thirty (Schaie and Strother, 1968).

Some authors believe that the different age curves found for different subtests of intelligence scales reflect an important distinction between two underlying intellectual abilities (Cattell, 1963). One is *fluid intelligence,* which is the ability to deal with essentially new problems. The other is *crystallized intelligence,* which is the repertoire of information, cognitive skills, and strategies acquired by application of fluid intelligence to various fields. According to the theory, fluid intelligence declines with age, beginning in middle adulthood or earlier. But crystallized intelligence does not drop off. On the contrary, it will continue to grow until old age if the person is in an intellectually stimulating environment. From the point of view of actual functioning in middle age and beyond, the drop in the one ability may be more than compensated for by the increase in the other.* The older person has "appropriated the collective intelligence of the culture for his own use" (Horn and Cattell, 1967). By so doing, he has not only amassed a store of knowledge larger than the one he had when he was younger, but he has also developed better ways of organizing this knowledge, of approaching problems, and of filing new information away for later use.

These cognitive achievements are similar to those we discussed in Chapter 8 in which we considered the distinction between "masters" and "apprentices." The masters have chunked and organized the material at a different level than the apprentices. On balance, then, the slight loss in fluid intelligence can be tolerated if made up for by an increase in crystallized intelligence.

The Information-Processing Approach

What has the psychometric approach taught us about intelligence? We know that the instruments devised by Binet and his successors can diagnose the extreme form of intellectual deficit we call mental retardation; they can also predict school success, at least as defined in a middle-class, twentieth-century industrial world. We have considered the hypothesis that these instruments measure an underlying set of abilities, of which some are more and some less general. Finally, these tests show marked changes in performance over age—an initial sharp improvement followed by a moderate decline on some subtests in later years.

Many of these results are of considerable practical importance. Since tests are used in diagnosis, guidance, and selection, they often have an important impact on individual lives. But has any of this helped us to understand the processes that underlie more or less intelligent behavior? Does it explain why individuals fail (or succeed) on a particular problem? The psychometric approach provides tools whereby we can compare how people perform relative to each other; their relative

* Some of these issues are still a matter of debate (e.g., Horn and Donaldson, 1976; Baltes and Schaie, 1976).

standing gives us a measure of a presumed attribute we call intelligence. But it provides little insight into the mechanisms that lead to problem solution or to failure. It tells us that some people are better and others worse at the various mental tasks that intelligence tests pose, but it doesn't tell us why.

A number of psychologists believe that the answer will come from an analysis of the relevant cognitive operations that intelligence tests call for. The basic idea is to link differences in test performance to differences in the way individuals process information as they perceive, attend, learn, remember, and think. This general approach to the analysis of individual differences in mental abilities is reminiscent of similar attempts in the study of various aspects of cognition and cognitive development (see Chapters 7, 8, and 14).

SIMPLE COGNITIVE CORRELATES

Some investigators have adopted the so-called *cognitive correlates* approach (Pellegrino and Glaser, 1979). They concentrate on relatively simple cognitive operations and try to correlate differences in the way these are carried out with differences in intelligence-test performance. In the main, they have concentrated on processes that involve memory.

An example is looking up well-known items in long-term memory. When we hear the word *mouse* and recognize it, we presumably make contact with some memory file that includes all sorts of information about small, bewhiskered, long-tailed rodents that go by that name. The same memory file is presumably accessed when we see the word *mouse* in print and also when we see a picture of a mouse. Many cognitive psychologists believe that this process of accessing well-established memories is a fundamental step in many mental tasks. To speak and understand, we must look up words in a mental dictionary; to read, we must look up the letters. According to some investigators, differences in the speed with which people perform this memory look-up operation may be one of the factors that underlie differences in intelligence-test performance (Hunt, Lunneborg, and Lewis, 1975; Hunt, 1976). Each individual look-up will only take a few milliseconds. But those milliseconds will soon add up in tasks that involve thousands of such look-up operations, for example, reading or arithmetic.

To test this hypothesis, a number of investigators used an experimental situation designed to measure the speed with which letter names are retrieved from long-term memory. Subjects are presented with pairs of letters that sometimes differ in their name *(A and B)*, and sometimes in their type case *(A and a)*, and they must then decide whether the two letters are the same or different. In one condition, the judgment "same" means that the letters are physically identical. (By this criterion *A* and *a* are different.) In another condition, the judgment "same" means that the letters have the same name. (By this criterion, *A* and *a* are the same.) To measure the speed with which a letter name is looked up, two reaction times are compared: that for judging name identity (N) and that for judging physical identity (P). Look-up time is obtained by subtracting P from N. The idea is that both tasks require the subjects to identify the physical forms of the letters. In physical identification that is all the subject has to do. But in name identification he has to perform the further step of looking up the letter name in memory (see Figure 17.16; Posner, Boies, Eichelman, and Taylor, 1969).

There is some indication that memory look-up times assessed by such methods are shorter in persons who do well on conventional tests of verbal intelligence

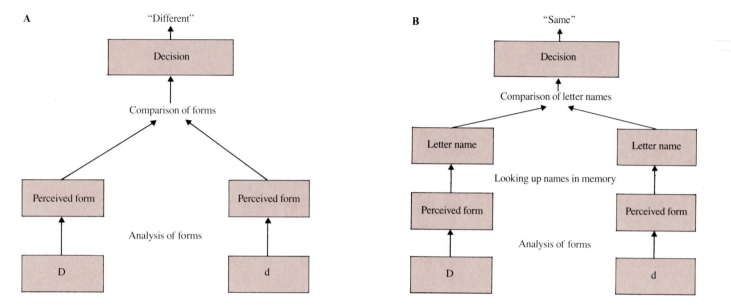

A
"Different"

Decision

Comparison of forms

Perceived form   Perceived form

Analysis of forms

D   d

B
"Same"

Decision

Comparison of letter names

Letter name   Letter name

Looking up names in memory

Perceived form   Perceived form

Analysis of forms

D   d

17.16 A schematic representation of the steps required to judge the physical identity and name identity of letters In (A) the subject has to judge whether two letter stimuli, D and d, are physically identical. This requires a form analysis of each stimulus, followed by a comparison of the analyzed forms and a decision. In (B), the subject must decide whether the names of the two letters are the same. This also requires an analysis of the two forms, followed by retrieval from the memory store, and a comparison of the names for a same-different decision. Since task B requires an additional step, it will take more time than does task A. The time required for this extra step—the memory look-up time—is the difference between the reaction times for tasks A and B.

than in those who do more poorly (Hunt, Lunneborg, and Lewis, 1975). The difference is especially marked when the comparison is between normal subjects and groups at the lower extremes of the population, such as mentally retarded or brain-damaged persons (Hunt, 1978). But to a lesser extent, such differences also have been obtained within normal populations; for example, between college students with high and low scores on tests of verbal intelligence (Hunt, Lunneborg, and Lewis, 1975) or on tests of reading comprehension (Jackson and McClelland, 1975, 1979).

COMPLEX COGNITIVE COMPONENTS

Simple cognitive operations such as memory look-up may be correlated with intelligence-test performance, but a number of investigators doubt that studying these operations will go very far in helping us to understand what intelligence really is. Intelligence may depend on the smooth operation of certain simple, rock-bottom cognitive processes, but it is not equivalent to them. Consider the performance of a ballet dancer. She can't dance if she can't walk and run and jump, but dancing is more than walking, running, and jumping. It involves the intricate organization of various higher-level motor actions such as pirouettes, combinations of ballet steps, and so on. These cannot be performed without the lower-level operations (that is, walking, running, and jumping), but this doesn't mean that the two levels are identical. Much the same may be true for intelligence. To reason about a problem in arithmetic, one has to recognize the numbers (e.g., *1* means "one") and one may have to retrieve the multiplication table (e.g., $2 \times 3 = 6$). But recognizing numbers and retrieving from the multiplication table are not the same as reasoning with arithmetic.

Such considerations led to attempts to study some of the higher-level rather than the lower-level cognitive processes that underlie intelligence. In attempts to discover what some of these higher-level processes are, several investigators turned to items in standard intelligence tests. Their object was to find the

595

cognitive components such tasks call for, most of which would presumably be higher-level processes rather than more elementary operations such as memory look-up (Sternberg, 1977).

One such undertaking was Robert Sternberg's analysis of ***analogical reasoning.*** Analogy problems are a staple of many intelligence tests, and they are often regarded as a particularly good measure of Spearman's *g*-factor. Below are several examples:

> *Hand* is to *foot* as *finger* is to (*arm, leg, thumb, toe*).
> *Pistol* is to *bow* as *bullet* is to (*gun, sword, arrow, blade*).

Or, to give a somewhat more difficult item:

> *Washington* is to *one* as *Lincoln* is to (*five, ten, twenty*).

Sternberg's interpretation of how such problems are solved has the step-by-step quality of a computer program (in this it resembles other information-processing approaches to thinking and problem solving; see Chapter 8). He believes that the problem is solved in separate stages (which he calls components). The first step is the identification of some potentially relevant attributes of each term (e.g., both Washington and Lincoln were presidents; Washington was the first and Lincoln the sixteenth president). After this, the subject tries to infer some possible relations between the first and second terms of the analogy (e.g., Washington was the first president, and his portrait is on the one-dollar bill), and then she tries to map possible relations between the first and third terms (both Washington and Lincoln were presidents and both appear as portraits on U.S. currency). The last step is to decide which of the alternatives offered is the appropriate term to complete the analogy. To accomplish this, the subject takes the various relations he inferred for the *Washington–one* pair and tries to apply them to create an appropriate match for *Lincoln.* One such relation is *president–the first.* This doesn't fit, for Lincoln was the sixteenth president, not the fifth, tenth, or twentieth. But there is another relation that is appropriate—*portrait of Washington–one-dollar bill.* This works, for Lincoln's portrait is on the five-dollar bill and "five" is one of the options. At this point, everything matches up, the subject makes his choice, and the analogy is solved (Sternberg, 1977).

Will an analysis of complex cognitive task components help us to understand what intelligence really is? To answer this question, we would have to know whether the components isolated by Sternberg (and by other investigators using different intellectual tasks) have some reasonable level of generality. Do the same components underlie performance on different intellectual tasks? Or do we have to postulate separate components for every kind of test item used in intelligence tests? A considerable amount of current research is directed at these issues, but thus far, it is too early to decide.

STRATEGIES AND INTELLECTUAL FUNCTIONING

Concepts derived from information processing have provided still another approach to the study of individual differences in intellectual functioning. This approach asks whether subjects use various flexible mental ***strategies*** for solving problems, for learning, and for remembering. We have previously discussed such cognitive strategies in the context of cognitive development (see Chapter 14). As we saw, a normal adult can master tasks (such as memorizing a sixteen-place

17.17   Washington is to One as Lincoln is to Five.

number) that are generally beyond the reach of a normal six-year-old. One reason is that the adult uses a well-developed repertoire of strategies for solving problems, for learning, and for remembering. When asked to memorize unrelated items, she rehearses and tries to organize the material by imposing some kind of structure upon it, by rhythmic grouping, syntactic order, or semantic categories.

The utilization of such cognitive strategies may account for some of the intellectual differences between adults. Much of the evidence comes from studies on the use of strategies for remembering (see Chapter 7). Such strategies, if they exist at all, are much more primitive in retarded individuals, who attack memory tasks with little or no resort to organization. Mentally retarded persons are less likely to rehearse, to group the items in a list, or to use mnemonic aids such as meaningful connections between items, or to show category clustering (A. Brown, 1974). Similar results have been found in young children (Flavell, 1970; Flavell and Wellman, 1976; see Chapter 14).

Is there any way of teaching retardates some of the strategies for problem solving and remembering that they so grossly lack? This question has important implications; if the answer is yes, then some aspects of retardation may be remediable. The results of several investigations provide a glimmer of hope. There is evidence that retarded subjects can be trained to rehearse; for example, by being required to repeat the items cumulatively and aloud (A. Brown et al., 1973). This induced rehearsal procedure leads to recall performance virtually identical to that of normal adults.

These results would be extremely encouraging except for one discordant note. According to many investigators, the newly acquired strategies are often abandoned shortly after they are taught. Furthermore, they tend not to be generalized to tasks other than the one in which they were acquired. An example is training in the use of semantic categories, which shows little transfer to new lists with different verbal materials (Bilsky, Evans, and Gilbert, 1972). Other investigators take a more optimistic view. They cite evidence that retardates can retain a rehearsal strategy over a six-month interval (Brown, Campione, and Murphy, 1974).

Strategies for using strategies   How is it that retarded persons and young children are generally so narrow in their use of the strategies they are taught? If retardates learn to remember a set of names by rehearsing them aloud, why don't they apply the same principle to a shopping list? According to several writers, what is lacking is a "master plan" for dealing with memory tasks in general, a strategy for using strategies (Flavell, 1970). Normal adults adopt this higher-order strategy as a matter of course whenever they try to learn. They know that remembering telephone numbers, or traffic directions, or the names of the twelve cranial nerves, are at bottom similar memory tasks. They also know that trying to learn them means using some aids to learning—the lower-order strategies of rehearsal, rhythmic and semantic grouping, or whatever. Both young children and retardates lack this general insight. They don't recognize what all memory tasks have in common and what they all require for their mastery. Young children will get it in time; retardates may never attain it.

The Lack of a Process Theory

As we look back, it is clear that we are still far from an understanding of the processes that underlie differences in intellectual performance. To put it another way, we have taken only a few tentative steps toward the construct validation of intelligence tests. Psychologists concerned with the study of cognitive processes have provided us with some promising leads, including the notion of cognitive components and the role of various strategies that young children and mentally retarded persons lack. But these are only guideposts for the future. Thus far, we have no general theory of intelligence. We may be able to measure intelligence, but as of yet we don't know what it really is.

HEREDITY, ENVIRONMENT, AND IQ

While it is far from clear just what intelligence tests really measure, this state of affairs has not deterred psychologists—nor indeed, the general public—from making intelligence-test performance one of the major foci of the nature-nurture controversy, debating it with a stormy passion rarely found in any other area of the discipline.

The vehemence of the debate is understandable considering that mental testing is a field in which the concerns of the scientist impinge drastically upon those of the practical world. In our society, those who are well off tend to do better on intelligence tests than those who are disadvantaged. The same holds for their children. What accounts for this difference? There is some tendency for social groups to be biased in favor of different answers to this question. This bias was especially marked some sixty years ago when the prevailing social climate was much more conservative. Then—and to a lesser extent even now—advantaged groups were more likely to believe that intelligence is largely inherited. This assertion was certainly comforting to those who benefited from the status quo since it suggested they got what they "deserved."

In contrast, spokesmen for the disadvantaged took a different view. To begin with, they often disparaged the tests themselves, arguing that the tests are not fair to their own subculture. In addition, they argued that intellectual aptitudes are much more determined by nurture than nature. In their view, differences in intelligence, especially those between different ethnic and racial groups, are determined predominantly by environmental factors such as early home background and schooling. Seen in this light, the children of the poor obtain lower test scores, not because they inherit deficient genes, but rather because they inherit poverty.

These contrasting views lead to different prescriptions for social policy. An example of the impact of a hereditarian bias is the rationale behind the United States immigration policy between the two World Wars. The Immigration Act of 1924 set definite quotas to minimize the influx of what were thought to be biologically "weaker stocks," specifically those from Southern and Eastern Europe. To prove the genetic intellectual inferiority of these immigrants, a congressional committee pointed to their army intelligence-test scores, which were indeed substantially below those attained by Americans of Northern European ancestry.

In actual fact, the differences were primarily related to the length of time that the immigrants had been in the United States prior to the test; their average test scores rose with every year and became indistinguishable from native-born Americans after twenty years of residence in the United States. This result undermines the hypothesis of a hereditary difference in intelligence between, say, Northern and Eastern Europeans. But the congressional proponents of differential immigration quotas did not analyze the results so closely. They had their own reasons for restricting immigration, such as fears of competition from cheap labor. The theory that the excluded groups were innately inferior provided a convenient justification for their policies (Kamin, 1974).

A more contemporary example of the relation between psychological theory and social policy is the argument over the value of compensatory education programs for preschool children from disadvantaged backgrounds. Such programs have been said to be failures because they often do not lead to improvement in later scholastic performance. The question is why. A highly controversial paper by Arthur Jensen suggests that heredity may be a significant contributing factor. According to Jensen, the fact that the average intelligence-test score of American blacks is lower than that of whites may be due in part to genetic differences between these groups. Given this hereditarian position, Jensen argues that environmental alterations such as compensatory education programs can at best mitigate the group difference; they cannot abolish it (Jensen, 1969). Jensen's thesis has been vehemently debated on many counts, some of which we will discuss below. For now, we will only note that the failure of a given compensatory program (assuming that it was really a failure) does not prove the hereditarians' claim. Perhaps the preschool experience that was provided was not of the right sort; perhaps it was inadequate to counteract the overwhelming effects of ghetto life* (J. McV. Hunt, 1961).

Our emphasis thus far has been on the social and political aspects of the nature-nurture issue in intelligence, the considerations that bias people to take one or another side of the issue. But while it is interesting to know what people prefer to believe about the world, our primary concern is with what that world is really like. What is the evidence about the contributions of heredity and environment in producing differences *within* groups (for instance, among American whites) and *between* groups (for instance, between American whites and blacks)?

Genetics and Intelligence

Before turning to the relationship between intelligence-test performance and genetic endowment, let us review a few points about the transmission of genetic characteristics discussed in a previous chapter (see Chapter 13, pp. 455–58).

PHENOTYPE VERSUS GENOTYPE

A key distinction in any discussion of hereditary transmission is that between *phenotype* and *genotype.* The phenotype corresponds to the overt appearance of the organism—its visible structure and behavior. But this phenotype is by no means equivalent to the organism's *genotype,* which describes the set of relevant *genes.* Each genetic instruction is carried by two corresponding genes, one from

---

* By now, there is a growing consensus that Jensen and others underestimated the effectiveness of preschool education on school performance in later years (Zigler and Seitz, 1982). Such preschool experiences may or may not raise intelligence-test scores, but they seem to have a positive effect on school performance in later years. Thus, low-income children who have participated in preschool programs seem to perform more acceptably in later grades (from fourth to twelfth) than children who did not, as measured by not being held back in grade, not dropping out of school, and so on (Lazar and Darlington, 1978; Darlington, Royce, Snipper, Murray, and Lazar, 1980).

each parent. If one member of a gene pair is ***dominant*** while the other is ***recessive,*** the first will mask the effect of the other, thus producing a difference between phenotypic expression and the underlying genotype. Another way in which a genotype may be kept from overt expression is by the interaction between genotype and environment. This interaction is especially important during the early stages in the organism's development since a particular genetic command can only be executed if certain physical characteristics (oxygen concentration, hormone levels, temperature) both within and outside of the developing body are within a certain range.

As an example, consider the dark markings on the paws, tail, and eartips of a Siamese cat. These markings are not present at birth, but they appear gradually as the kitten matures. The genealogical records kept by cat breeders leave no doubt that these markings in the mature animal are determined by heredity. But this does not mean that they emerge independently of the environment. The dark markings will only appear if the kitten's extremities are kept at their normal temperature, which happens to be lower than that of the rest of the animal's body. If the extremities are deliberately warmed during early kittenhood by such devices as leggings and tail- and earmuffs, they will not turn darker—in apparent defiance of the creature's genotype (Ilyin and Ilyin, 1930).

This example underlines the fact that genes do not operate in a vacuum. They are instructions to a developing organism, instructions that will be followed only within a given range of environmental conditions. It therefore makes no sense to talk of heredity alone or environment alone, for there is no trait that does not depend upon both. There can be no organism without a genotype, and this genotype cannot ever express itself independently of the environment.

GENETIC CONTRIBUTIONS TO INTELLIGENCE

How can we find out whether human intelligence (at least as measured by intelligence-test performance) has a genetic basis? To do so, we have to infer the underlying genotypes from the observable phenotypic behavior. One strategy is to examine the similarities between relatives, an approach that dates back to Francis Galton. Galton found that eminence (which he measured by reputation) runs in families; eminent men were more likely to have eminent relatives than the average person (Galton, 1869). Similar results have been repeatedly obtained with intelligence-test scores. For example, the correlation between the IQs of children and parents, or between the IQs of siblings, runs in the neighborhood of .50 (Erlenmeyer-Kimling and Jarvik, 1963). From Galton's perspective, such findings document the inheritance of mental ability. But the environmentalist has a ready reply. Consider eminence. The relatives of an eminent person obviously share his or her social, educational, and financial advantages. As a result, there is a similarity of environmental background, as well as an overlapping set of genes. The same argument applies to the interpretation of the correlations between the IQs of close relatives.

A similar problem arises in another connection. As we've previously seen, IQs tend to be fairly stable; the ten-year-old with an IQ of 130 will probably get a roughly similar score at age fifteen. Supporters of the genetic theory of intelligence have often argued that this constancy of the IQ shows that intelligence tests measure an inborn capacity, "native intelligence," which is an essentially unalterable characteristic of an individual and is genetically based. This argument has been used as a justification of such educational practices as early assignment to one or another school track. But IQ constancy is no proof that intelligence is fixed or inborn. To the extent that this constancy occurs, it only demonstrates that a child tends to maintain his relative standing among his age-mates over time. This may be because of a genetically given attribute that remains unchanged with age. But it may also be because the child's environmental advantages stay pretty much the same as time goes on. If a child is born in a slum, the odds are pretty good that she will still be there at twelve; the same holds if she is born in a palace. Once again, the evidence is inconclusive.

During the last fifty years, psychologists have developed a variety of research designs that were meant to disentangle hereditary and environmental factors. We will consider two main attempts to accomplish this end: (1) the study of twins and (2) the study of adopted children.

Twin studies   **Identical twins** originate from a single fertilized egg that splits into two exact replicas which then develop into two genetically identical individuals. In contrast, **fraternal twins** arise from two different fertilized eggs. Each of two eggs in the female reproductive tract is fertilized by a different sperm cell. Under the circumstances, the genetic similarity between fraternal twins is no greater than that between ordinary siblings. Since this is so, a comparison between identical twins and fraternal twins of the same sex is of considerable interest, if one is willing to assume that the twins' environments are no more similar if they are identical than if they are fraternal. Given this premise, it follows that if identical twins turn out to be more similar on some trait than fraternals, one can conclude that this trait is in part genetically determined.

The relevant comparisons have been performed in over a dozen studies. In each case, the essential result was the same. The correlation between the IQs of identical twins was substantially larger than that between the IQs of fraternal twins. Considering only twins in the United States, the average correlation is .89 for identicals, and .63 for fraternals (Jencks et al., 1972, p. 292). A summary of these and related findings is presented in Figure 17.18.

On the face of it, this pattern of results seems like clear-cut evidence for a genetic component in the determination of IQ. But during recent years, a number

17.18 Correlations between intelligence-test performance of children and other members of the family with whom they live *The figure is a summary of a large number of studies of correlations between intelligence-test performance of children and other members of the family with whom or by whom they were reared. Every point represents the correlation obtained in an individual U.S. study. The vertical slashes indicate the averages for the studies in each condition, weighted according to the number of cases.*

The results point to a genetic contribution to intelligence-test performance. The correlations between identical twins are higher than those between fraternal twins, siblings, and children with natural parents. The lowest correlations are those between unrelated children reared together and between children and unrelated adoptive parents. (The format of presentation is that of Erlenmeyer-Kimling and Jarvik, 1963; but the data included in the figure are limited to studies performed in the U.S. as summarized by Jencks et al., 1972)

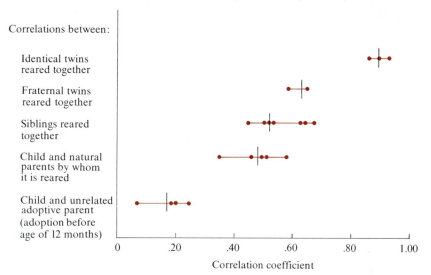

of criticisms have been leveled at these and related studies. One argument bears on the assumption that the similarity in the environments of identical and fraternal twins is essentially equal. But is it really? Since identical twins look alike, there may be a tendency to treat them the same way. Ultimately, parents and teachers may develop the same expectations for them. In contrast, fraternal twins are no more or less similar in appearance than ordinary siblings and may thus evoke a more differentiated reaction from others. If this is so, the comparison of the IQ correlations between identical and fraternal twins is not as neat a test of the nature-nurture issue as it seemed at first (Anastasi, 1971; Kamin, 1974).

A recent study was designed to meet this criticism. Over three hundred twins were classified as identical or fraternal according to two criteria. One was by a comparison of twelve blood-type characteristics. This is as objective a method for assessing genotype identity as is now available. To be judged identical, both members of a twin pair must correspond on all of the twelve indices. Another criterion involved the subjects' own belief in whether they are identical or fraternal. This belief is presumably based on how similar the twins think they are and how similarly they feel that they are treated. In a sizable number of twins this subjective judgment did not correspond to the biological facts as revealed by the blood tests. Which of the two ways of classifying a twin is a better predictor of the similarity in intelligence-test scores? The results suggest that the primary determinant is the true genotype. When the classification was by blood tests, there was the usual effect; identical twins scored more similarly than did fraternals. But when the classification was based on the twins' own judgments, this effect was markedly reduced. This result suggests that the greater intellectual similarity of identical as compared to fraternal twins is not an artifact of different environments. The best guess is that the effect occurs because intelligence-test performance is in part genetically determined (Scarr and Carter-Saltzman, 1979).

Adopted children   Another line of evidence comes from studies of adopted children. One study was based on two hundred children who were adopted immediately after birth (Horn, Loehlin, and Wellerman, 1975). When these children were later tested, the correlation between their IQs and those of their *biological* mothers (whom they had never seen) was greater than the corresponding correlation with the IQs of their *adoptive* mothers (.32 versus .15). Other investigators have shown that this pattern persists into adolescence. When the adopted child is tested at age fourteen, the correlation between his IQ and that of the biological mother's education is greater than that between the child's IQ and the educational level of the adoptive mother (.31 versus .04; Skodak and Skeels, 1949).

These results seem like strong evidence for the genetic view, but they have not remained unchallenged. One criticism concerns **selective placement.** Adoption agencies generally try to place infants in homes that are similar in social and educational backgrounds to those of their biological parents. This leads to a problem. To the extent that IQ is determined by the environment and that the adoption agency is successful in matching those environments, there is an inevitable—and quite spurious—correlation between the IQs of the children and those of their biological parents (Kamin, 1974). This environmentalist argument is plausible except for one thing: it does not readily explain why there is a smaller correlation between the children and the adoptive parents.

There may be a way of circumventing this problem. The trick is to estimate the degree of selective placement directly; one way of doing this is to compute the correlation between the biological and adoptive parents' IQs. (If placement were random, this correlation should be zero.) Given this estimate, one can statistically correct for selective placement. When this was done using data from a recent study, the corrected correlations between the IQs of children and their biological parents was .30, while the corresponding correlation with the IQs of the adoptive mother was .10 (Horn et al., 1975). In light of this, one may well question the environmentalists' reinterpretation of the results of the adoption studies.

ENVIRONMENTAL CONTRIBUTIONS TO INTELLIGENCE

There is evidently a genetic component in the determination of intelligence-test performance. But heredity alone does not account for all of the variance in intellectual performance. Environmental factors also play a role.

Enriched and impoverished environments Evidence for environmental effects comes from several sources. One is the comparison of mean IQs of whole populations following some significant change in cultural life or of educational practices. An example is a community in East Tennessee that was quite isolated from the United States mainstream in 1930 but became less and less so during the following decade with the introduction of schools, roads, and radios. Between 1930 and 1940, the average IQ of individuals in this community rose by 10 points, from 82 to 92 (Wheeler, 1942).

Enriching the environment is evidently beneficial. Impoverishing it has the opposite effect. Evidence comes from children who worked on canalboats in England during the 1920s and hardly attended school at all (Gordon, 1923), or who lived in remote regions of the Kentucky mountains (Asher, 1935). These are poor environments for the development of the intellectual skills tapped by intelligence tests. If so, exposure to such an environment should have a cumulative effect; the longer the child has been in it, the more depressed his IQ should be. This is precisely the result that was obtained. There was a sizable *negative* correlation between IQ and age. The older the child, the longer he had been in the impoverished environment, and thus the lower his IQ.

More adoption studies Further evidence comes from adoption studies. We have previously seen that they show the importance of genetic factors. But they also document the contribution of environment. One group of investigators studied the mean IQ of adopted children, most of whom were placed in foster homes before they were three months old (Skodak and Skeels, 1945, 1947, 1949). At age four, their mean IQ was 112; at age 13 it was 117. The authors argue that these values are considerably higher than the mean IQ that would have been predicted for this group of children, given the fact that the occupational and educational level of the biological parents was known to be below average. Since the adopting parents were above average on these indices as well as on IQ, it seemed only natural to assume that the home background they provided led to an increase in the IQs of their adopted children.

HERITABILITY

The evidence as a whole dictates the conclusion that both genetic and environmental factors play a role in determining IQ variations within groups. On this

603

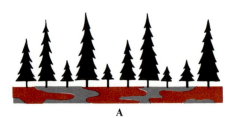

A

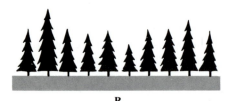

B

17.19 Heritability *Consider the group of evergreen trees shown in (A). They vary in height, and the degree to which they vary from each other is measured by the variance. What produces this variance? Some is presumably caused by genetic factors. To determine how much, we equate environmental conditions—the soil, water, light, and so on (here indicated by different shadings of the ground). We now take a group of seedlings randomly chosen from (A), plant them in this equated environment, and patiently wait until they reach maturity (see B). We note that the size variation in (B) is less than that in (A). This reduction in the variance reflects the fact that environmental conditions are equal for (B), so that one important source of variation has been removed. The remaining variance in (B) is entirely produced by genetic factors. We can now determine the heritability of height for (A). It is the variance in (B) (that is, the variation attributable to genetic factors), divided by the variance in (A) (that is, the total variation in the population).*

point there is wide agreement. What is at issue is the relative weight exerted by each of these factors.

Just what is meant by the relative importance of heredity and environment in determining the variation of any given trait? To answer this question, we must refer to a technical expression developed by geneticists, the ***heritability ratio (H)***. This is the proportion of the variance of the phenotypic expression of a trait in a given population that is attributable to genetic variation among the individuals within that population* (Figure 17.19).

To get a feeling for what *H* means, suppose that all children born in the U.S. (within a given racial-ethnic group) are raised in completely identical environments. When this environmentally equalized group is later tested, there will still be variations in IQ. These will be entirely attributable to genetic variation, for environment is no longer a factor. Under these conditions, *H* would necessarily equal 1.00.

There are some widely held misconceptions about the nature of heritability. Perhaps the worst is the notion that the heritability ratio applies to individuals. In popular discussions it is sometimes said that 80 percent—or 70 percent or 40 percent, depending on the value of *H* the author accepts—of a person's intelligence is determined by heredity, the rest by environment. This is sheer nonsense. Heritability is a concept that applies only to trait variations within a particular population at a particular point in time; it does not apply to individuals. For any given person, both heredity and environment are equally important in determining whatever he or she is. As an example, consider height, for which heritability is about .90. This means that if genotype variation were eliminated (in other words, if all subjects were derived from the same fertilized egg) the remaining variance would be only 10 percent of what it is in the normal population. But it does not mean that a man whose height is six feet can thank heredity for sixty-five of his inches and credit environment with the remaining seven.

Group Differences

Thus far, we have focused on IQ differences *within* groups and have considered the nature-nurture debate as it pertained to these. But the real fury of the controversy rages over another issue—the differences in average IQ that are found between groups, such as different socioeconomic classes or racial-ethnic groups.

Numerous studies have shown that the average score of American blacks is about 15 IQ points below the average of the white population (Loehlin, Lindzey, and Spuhler, 1975). The fact that there is such a difference is not in dispute. What is at issue is what this difference means and how it comes about.

Before proceeding, we should emphasize that the differences are between *averages*. There is considerable overlap between the two distributions. From 15 to 25

---

* The idea is that the total variance of the trait (V_T)—be it height, weight, or IQ—can be considered as the sum of several constituents: the variance produced by genetic differences (V_G), the variance produced by different environments (V_E), and some others. The heritability ratio, *H*, is then given by

$$H = \frac{V_G}{V_T}$$

The actual value of *H* for IQ (in industrialized populations like ours) is still a matter of debate, though most experts would probably agree that it falls within the range of .4 to .8.

percent of the blacks score higher than half of the whites (Shuey, 1966). Clearly the numerical IQ variations *within* either group are much greater than those between groups.

ARE THE TESTS "CULTURE FAIR"?

Some psychologists have tried to deal with the between-group difference by explaining it away. They have suggested that it is primarily an artifact of a cultural bias built into the tests themselves (Sarason, 1973). According to this view, the intelligence tests now in use were designed to assess the cognitive skills of the white middle class. When these tests are administered to another group with different customs, values, and even dialects—such as inner-city black children—there cannot help but be a cultural bias which makes the yardstick no longer applicable. This point is obvious when the test item calls for verbal information, as in vocabulary or analogy tests. If different subgroups have different degrees of exposure to the relevant information, any difference in test scores becomes uninterpretable. We have already noted evidence for some such effects when discussing the test results obtained with rural and urban children; it is very likely that a similar point applies to comparisons between children from white suburbs and black ghettos. Further problems stem from different motivations in the test-taking situation and to different attitudes toward the tester. Yet another complication is posed by different degrees of language comprehension. According to some linguists, many American blacks speak a dialect of English—black English—the syntax, phonology, and lexicon of which differ in some important ways from standard English (e.g., Labov, 1970b; see Chapter 9). Since intelligence tests are usually administered in standard English, the black children who take them are under a linguistic handicap.

Such considerations suggest that some component of the black-white test score difference is attributable to cultural bias, either in the tests themselves, in their administration, or both. The question is whether this accounts for all of the difference. There are reasons to believe that it does not. The evidence comes from studies in which one or another possible source of cultural bias has been eliminated or at least minimized. An example is an attempt to test American blacks in black English. To this end, the Stanford-Binet was translated into black English and was then administered orally to black children by black examiners (Quay, 1971). The performance of these children was virtually identical to that of a group that was tested with the regular version. The dialect difference is evidently not the crucial variable.

BETWEEN-GROUP DIFFERENCE: HEREDITY OR ENVIRONMENT?

The between-group difference in average IQ is evidently not just an artifact. But what accounts for it? In the thirty years before 1965, the consensus among social scientists in the United States was that the effect resulted from the massively inferior environmental conditions that were (and in many ways, still are) the lot of most blacks—systematic discrimination, poorer living conditions, lower life expectancies, inadequate diets and housing, and inferior schooling. But the issue was reopened in the sixties and early seventies, by among others, Arthur Jensen, who felt that the hypothesis of a genetic contribution to the between-group difference had been dismissed prematurely (Jensen, 1969, 1973).

As currently conceived, human racial groups (some authors prefer the term *racial-ethnic* groups) are populations whose members are more likely to interbreed than to mate with outsiders. This restriction on the gene flow between different subgroups may be imposed by geographical barriers, such as oceans or mountains, or by social taboos, such as prohibitions on intermarriage. The restrictions are not complete, but if they last long enough, they may result in a population that differs from other groups in the statistical frequency of various genes. That this is the case for genes that determine such characteristics as eye and skin color, pattern of hair growth, various blood groups, and so on, is undeniable. But does the same hold for behavioral traits like intelligence-test performance? More specifically, is the difference in average black and white IQs partially attributable to different frequencies of IQ-determining genes in the two populations?

Within-group heritability   One of Jensen's arguments was based on the finding that IQ has a substantial within-group heritability. Jensen suggested that, given this fact, it was plausible to suppose that the between-group difference (that is, the difference between the black and white averages) could be interpreted in similar terms. A number of critics disagreed. They countered by saying that the fact that within-group heritability is high does not imply that between-group differences are genetically determined (Layzer, 1972).

One writer gave an example of two samples of seed, randomly drawn from a bag that contains several genetically different varieties. One sample is placed in barren soil and the other in soil that is extremely fertile. When the plants are fully grown they will differ in height. There will be within-group differences as measured by the variance within each of the two samples. There will also be a between-group difference as indicated by a difference in the average height of the plants in the two samples. The within-group difference can be attributed to genetic variation; the samples were drawn from a genetically mixed bag so that there is high within-group heritability. But the between-group variation must be primarily of environmental origin since the two sets of seeds were planted in soils of different fertility (Lewontin, 1976; see Figure 17.20).

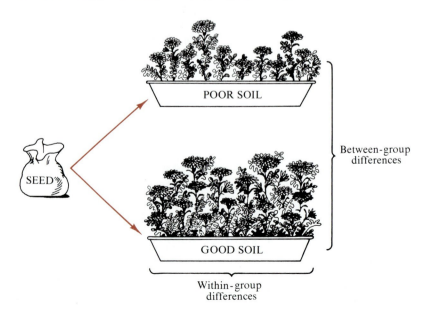

17.20   Between-group and within-group differences   *Between-group differences may be caused by very different factors than within-group differences. Here, the between-group difference reflects an environmental factor (soil) while the difference within each group reflects genetic variation (seed).*

The moral is simple: Differences within and between groups may be produced by very different causal factors. This holds for plants and the heights they attain at maturity. And it may also apply to human racial-ethnic groups and IQ.

Matching for environment If the black-white difference in IQs is really a result of environmental factors, that difference should disappear if one compares black and white groups who are equated in these regards. It is reasonable to suppose that the relevant factors include socioeconomic variables like parents' education, income, occupational level, and so on. A number of studies have tried to match black and white children on indices of this kind and then compared the IQ averages of the two matched groups. The general result was that the black-white difference was markedly reduced (Loehlin, Lindzey, and Spuhler, 1975).

On the face of it, such results seem like vindications of the environmentalists' view: equate the soil and the two sets of seeds will grow up much alike. But hereditarians will emphasize another finding. While equalizing socioeconomic variables diminishes the black-white difference, it does not abolish it. In their view, this residual difference makes the genetic hypothesis all the more plausible. Environmentalists reply that the environments of the black and white children were not truly matched, despite the social scientists' very best efforts. For matching parental education, income, and occupational level is not enough. The very fact that one child is black and the other white means that they grow up in different environments, since our society is riddled with racial discrimination that will hit the one child but not the other.

A somewhat better approximation to an equalized environment is found in a study of the illegitimate offspring of United States servicemen stationed in Germany after World War II. The investigators compared two groups of such children whose white, German mothers were roughly similar in socioeconomic background. One group of children was fathered by black soldiers and the other by white ones. When the children were tested with a German version of the Wechsler scale, the main finding was that both groups had about the same average IQ. This result seems to contradict the genetic interpretation of the black-white difference, for the children received half of their genes from a black father. To maintain the genetic hypothesis, one would have to postulate a special kind of mating selection—whatever the reasons, the choice of mates might have been such that black fathers and white fathers had about the same average IQ. This possibility cannot be ruled out, but it does not seem very plausible (Loehlin, Lindzey, and Spuhler, 1975).

The effect of environmental change Some investigators have taken another tack. Instead of trying to match environments, they have tried to see what happens when the environment is changed. In particular they looked at the effects of migration from the South to the (relatively) more benign North during the thirties and forties. They found that migration led to a moderate increase in the IQ of black children; the longer their stay in the North (and in Northern schools), the greater this increase (Lee, 1951).

A more drastic environmental change is interracial adoption. One group of investigators studied ninety-nine black children who were adopted at an early age by white middle-class parents, most of whom were college-educated (Scarr and Weinberg, 1976). The mean IQ of these children was 110. This value exceeds the national average for black children by about 25 IQ points. Some of this increase may well have been an artifact of selective placement by the adoption agency, but a part of it may represent a genuine environmental effect. (For further discussion, see Scarr and Carter-Saltzman, 1982.)

SOME TENTATIVE CONCLUSIONS

How can we summarize? Perhaps the fairest thing to say is that there is not a single study whose results or interpretations cannot be challenged, nor is there a single argument (whether genetic or environmental) for which there is no counterargument. Under the circumstances, no conclusion can be anything but tentative. Even so, the weight of the evidence seems to tilt toward the environmentalist side, especially when one's intuitions about the effects of three hundred years of slavery and racist oppression are thrown into the balance.

But suppose that the genetic interpretation is correct after all. Suppose that some significant fraction of the black-white IQ difference is in fact determined by the genes. What then? What effects should this have on our thinking about social issues and socioeconomic policy? In our view, relatively little. There are several reasons for this.

First, the genetic interpretation does not imply that environmental intervention—in home or school—will have no effect. There is no one who denies that environmental factors are responsible for some proportion of the between-group variance. There are thus no grounds for abandoning appropriate educational efforts for improving cognitive skills (and presumably raising IQs). The trouble is that thus far we have only the skimpiest ideas about the kinds of environmental changes that would do the trick.

Second, what about the portion of the variance that, according to the hereditarians, is determined by the genotype? Is that unchangeable? Some participants on both sides of the controversy seem to feel that, almost by definition, environmentally determined traits are alterable while genetically determined ones are fixed. But this is far from true. Some environmentally produced effects are almost impossible to change, including some that are acquired through certain forms of learning. Examples are the long-lasting effects of imprinting (see Chapter 16) and the difficulty most adults have in shedding the phonological system of their mother tongue when trying to speak another language without an accent (see Chapter 9). Nor is it true that genetically determined traits are necessarily unchangeable. The widely cited counterexample is PKU, an inherited form of mental retardation which, as we have seen, can be treated by an appropriate diet (see Chapter 13). Conceivably, other approaches may be found to alter the effects of some of the genes that underlie the distribution of IQs.

Third, there are reasons to believe that the black-white IQ difference, regardless of what causes it, is not a major factor in producing the economic inequality between whites and blacks. To be sure, IQ is correlated with adult income, but according to at least some writers, this correlation accounts for only 12 percent of the total variance in individual incomes in the United States (Jencks et al., 1972). Given this relatively low value, the emphasis on IQ in discussions of social inequality may well be misplaced.

We should make a final point (which has been stressed by Jensen no less than by his environmentalist critics). In a democratic society the emphasis is on *individuals* and their own abilities and attributes. A given individual's subgroup may have a greater or smaller average gene frequency for this or the other trait, but this has no bearing on how this particular person should be judged. When people are assessed according to the average characteristics of the group to which they belong, rather than according to the characteristics that they themselves possess, one of the most essential premises of a democratic society is violated.

SUMMARY

1. Many physical and psychological characteristics vary from one individual to another. This pattern of variation is often displayed by *frequency distributions.* The scores in a frequency distribution tend to cluster around a central tendency, often measured by the *mean.* The *variability* around this central tendency is indicated by the *variance,* or its square root, the *standard deviation.* The graphed frequency distributions of many physical and psychological characteristics have a shape approximating that of the *normal curve,* which describes the probability of obtaining certain combinations of chance events.

2. The extent to which two characteristics vary together, is measured by the *correlation coefficient,* or *r.* Perfect correlation is indicated by an *r* of +1.00 or −1.00; zero correlation by an *r* of .00.

3. An important application of the correlation technique was the development of mental testing. A *mental test* is meant to be an objective yardstick to assess some psychological trait or capacity about which people differ. One criterion of a test's adequacy is its *reliability,* the consistency with which it measures what it measures, as given by *test-retest* correlations and similar indices. An even more important criterion is the test's *validity,* the extent to which it measures what it is supposed to measure. *Predictive validity* is assessed by determining the correlation between the test and an appropriate *criterion. Construct validity* is the extent to which performance on a test fits into some relevant theoretical scheme.

4. Tests with good reliability and reasonable predictive validity may be useful as a selection device. But since validity coefficients are less than 1.00, there are inevitable selection errors, some of which are "false accepts" while others are "false rejects." The relative proportion of these two errors depends on the choice of a *cutoff point* below which no applicant is selected. The choice of this cutoff value depends on the selector's *payoff matrix.*

5. Binet, the originator of intelligence tests, was primarily interested in assessing children. His tests measured *mental age,* or *MA.* The relative standing of a child relative to her age-mates was determined by comparing her MA with her *chronological age,* or *CA.* A widely used measure of this relative position is the *intelligence quotient,* or *IQ,* which equals MA/CA × 100. Modern testers prefer another measure, the *deviation IQ.* This is based on a comparison between an individual's score and that of her age-mates and can be used with adults.

6. Intelligence tests can be used to diagnose several levels of *mental retardation,* varying from mild to profound. According to one hypothesis, the more severe forms of retardation are caused by one factor such as major brain pathology, while the milder forms are produced by the joint effect of many factors.

7. Investigators using the *psychometric approach* try to discover something about the underlying nature of intelligence by studying the pattern of results provided by intelligence tests themselves. One issue is the *structure of mental abilities.* To determine whether intelligence is one unitary ability or is composed of several unrelated abilities, investigators have looked at the correlations between different subtests. *Factor analysis* of these correlations led to a number of competing theories of mental structure, including *Spearman's theory of general intelligence, or g,* and *group factor theory.*

609

8. Another psychometric issue is the relation between intelligence-test performance and age, which suggests a distinction between *fluid intelligence* which declines with age and *crystallized intelligence* which does not drop off.

9. The *information-processing approach* tries to understand individual differences in intellectual performance as differences in the operations of remembering, problem solving, and thinking, as studied by cognitive psychology. One line of inquiry tries to relate intelligence-test performance to simple *cognitive correlates,* such as memory look-up times. Another tries to understand the more complex *cognitive components* of the tasks posed by standard intelligence tests, as exemplified in studies of *analogical reasoning.* Yet another line of inquiry tries to relate intellectual differences to success or failure in the acquisition and use of various *cognitive strategies.*

10. Intelligence-test performance has become one of the major foci of the nature-nurture controversy, fueled in great part by various social and political forces. The factual questions concern the relative contributions of heredity and environment in producing differences within and between groups in contemporary America.

11. Human intelligence-test performance seems to be determined by both environmental and genetic factors, though the issue is not regarded as fully settled by all psychologists. Evidence for the role of genetic factors comes from the fact that the correlation between IQs of *identical twins* are higher than those for *fraternal twins.* Further evidence for a hereditary contribution comes from *adopted children* whose IQs correlate more highly with those of their biological than their adoptive parents. Evidence for environmental effects is provided by increases and decreases in the mean IQ of populations whose cultural or educational level has been raised or lowered. A similar point is made by adoption studies that show IQ increases in adopted children after being placed in superior foster homes.

12. The relative weight of genetic and environmental factors in determining the variation of a given characteristic is given by the *heritability ratio,* or *H.* The value of *H* depends in part upon the given population, for *H* only describes the degree to which the variability within this population can be attributed to genetic variance.

13. In recent years, much interest (and polemic) has focused on IQ differences *between* different racial-ethnic groups. The mean IQ of American blacks is about 15 points lower than that of American whites. Some authors have argued that this is in part a consequence of a genetic difference between the two groups. Environmentalists reply that the difference is markedly reduced by various environmental changes such as interracial adoption. A similar point is made by the fact that the mean IQs of illegitimate children of white German mothers fathered by U.S. soldiers after World War II are just about the same whether the fathers were black or white.

CHAPTER 18

Personality Assessment

In the preceding chapter, our focus was on differences in cognitive ability. But people also differ in nonintellectual attributes. They differ in their predominant desires, in their characteristic feelings, and in their typical modes of expressing these needs and feelings. All of these distinctions fall under the general heading of ***personality differences.*** The specific attributes that define these distinctions (for example, energetic versus lazy) are called ***personality traits.***

The fact that personality differences exist is hardly a recent discovery. In the fourth century B.C., the Greek philosopher Theophrastus (ca. 370–287 B.C.) wrote a series of sketches, "The Characters," that featured such diverse types as the Coward, the Flatterer, the Boor, and so on. At least some of his types are as recognizable today as they were in ancient Greece:

> The Garrulous man is one that will sit down close beside somebody he does not know, and begin talk with a eulogy of his own life, and then relate a dream he had the night before, and after that tell dish by dish what he had for supper. As he warms to his work he will remark that we are by no means the men we were, and the price of wheat has gone down, and there's a ship of strangers in town. . . . Next he will surmise that the crops would be all the better for some more rain, and tell him what he is going to grow on his farm next year, adding that it is difficult to make both ends meet . . . and "I vomited yesterday" and "What day is it today?" . . . And if you let him go on he will never stop (Edmonds, *The Characters of Theophrastus,* 1929, pp. 48–49).

There is an implicit assumption that underlies Theophrastus's sketches, and that assumption is shared by subsequent authors who have written about personality, even to the present. The personality patterns they ascribed to their characters were presumed to be essentially consistent from time to time and from situation to situation. The hero was generally heroic, the villain villainous, and the garrulous man kept on talking regardless of who listened (or rather, tried not

Theophrastus *(Courtesy Villa Albani, Rome)*

611

to listen). Some of the traits by which modern students of personality describe people are more subtle than those that Theophrastus wrote about, but for many investigators the key assumption of this *trait theory* still exists. They presume that these traits characterize a person's behavior in a variety of situations. This is just another way of saying that knowledge of an individual's personality traits will permit us to predict what he is likely to do, even in situations in which we have never observed him (Allport, 1937). Personality tests were devised in an attempt to supply the information that makes such predictions possible.

METHODS OF ASSESSMENT

Psychologists have developed several approaches to the problem of describing and assessing different personalities. We will discuss two of the major ones: those that are structured and objective ("paper-and-pencil tests") and those that are relatively unstructured ("projective techniques").

Structured Personality Tests

As in the case of intelligence measurement, the impetus for the development of personality tests came from the world of practical affairs. But the parallel is even closer than that, for both kinds of tests began as instruments to determine certain undesirable conditions. Binet's test was originally designed to identify mentally retarded children. The first personality test had a parallel diagnostic aim. It was meant to identify emotionally disturbed United States Army recruits during World War I. This test was an "adjustment inventory" consisting of a list of questions that dealt with various symptoms or problem areas (for instance, "Do you daydream frequently?" and "Do you wet your bed?"). If the subject reported many such symptoms, he was singled out for further psychiatric examination (Cronbach, 1970a).

The parallel between tests of intelligence and those of personality ends when we turn to the question of how these tests are validated. Binet and his successors had various criteria of validity: teachers' evaluations, academic performance, and, perhaps most important, chronological age. It turns out that validity criteria are much harder to come by in the field of personality measurement.

THE MMPI: CRITERION GROUPS FROM THE CLINIC

To provide an objective validity criterion, some later investigators turned to the diagnostic categories developed in clinical practice. Their object was to construct a test that could assess a person's similarity to this or the other psychiatric criterion group—hysterics, depressed patients, schizophrenics, and so on. The best-known test of this sort is the *Minnesota Multiphasic Personality Inventory,* or *MMPI,* which first appeared in 1940 and is still one of the most widely used personality tests on the current scene, especially in clinical practice. It was called multiphasic because it was developed to assess a number of psychiatric patterns simultaneously.

Constructing the MMPI The authors of the MMPI began by compiling a large set of test items taken from previously published inventories, from psychiatric examination forms, and from their own clinical hunches. These items were then administered to several patient groups with different diagnoses as well as to a group of normal subjects. The next step was to eliminate all items that did not discriminate between the patients and the normal controls and to retain those items that did. The end result was the MMPI in substantially its present form—an inventory of 550 items, the responses to which can be analyzed by reference to ten major scales. The score on each of these scales indicates how the subject's answers compare with those of the relevant criterion group (Table 18.1).

Table 18.1   SOME MMPI SCALES WITH REPRESENTATIVE EXAMPLE ITEMS*

Scale	Criterion group	Example items
Depression	Patients with intense unhappiness and feelings of hopelessness	"I often feel that life is not worth the trouble."
Paranoia	Patients with unusual degree of suspiciousness, together with feelings of persecution and delusions of grandeur	"Several people are following me everywhere."
Schizophrenia	Patients with a diagnosis of schizophrenia, characterized by bizarre or highly unusual thoughts or behavior, by withdrawal, and in many cases by delusions and hallucinations	"I seem to hear things that other people cannot hear."
Psychopathic deviance	Patients with marked difficulties in social adjustment, with histories of delinquency and other asocial behaviors	"I often was in trouble in school, although I do not understand for what reasons."

* In the example items here shown, the response appropriate to the scale is "True." For many other items, the reverse is true. Thus, answering "False" to the item "I liked school" would contribute to the person's score on the psychopathic deviance scale.

Using the MMPI   In actual practice, interpreting an MMPI record is a complicated business. Clinicians don't merely look at the absolute scores obtained on any one scale. Instead, they consider the various scale values in relation to each other. This is most easily done by inspecting **score profiles** which present the scores on every scale in graphic form (Figure 18.1). An example is the interpreta-

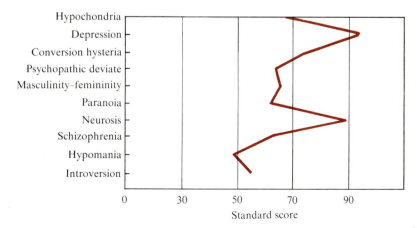

18.1   MMPI profile   *The profile is of an adult male seeking help in a community health center. The scales are those described in Table 18.1. The scores are based on the performance of the standardization group. Scores above 70 will occur in about 2.5 percent of the cases; scores above 80 in about .1 percent. The profile strongly suggests considerable depression and neurotic anxiety. (After Lanyon and Goodstein, 1971)*

613

tion of scores on the so-called depression scale. This consists of items which differentiated a group of patients diagnosed to be in a depressive state from normal persons. But a high score on this scale alone tells little more than that the patient is very unhappy. If we want to know more about the nature of this disturbance, we have to look at the profile as a whole (Meehl, 1956).

Validity scales One trouble with self-administered personality inventories is that the subjects can easily misrepresent themselves. To cope with this and related problems, the originators of the MMPI added a set of further items that make up several so-called validity scales. One is a simple lying scale. It contains items like "I gossip a little at times" and "Once in a while I laugh at a dirty joke." The assumption is that a person who denies a large number of such statements is either a saint (and few of those take personality tests) or is lying. Another validity scale consists of a number of bizarre statements like "There are persons who are trying to steal my thoughts and ideas" and "My soul sometimes leaves my body." To be sure, some of these statements are accepted by severely disturbed psychiatric patients, but even they endorse only a small proportion of them. As a result, we can be reasonably sure that a person who checks an unusually large number of such items is either careless, or has misunderstood the instructions, or is trying to fake psychiatric illness. If the score on these and similar validity scales is too high, the test record is discarded as invalid.

THE CPI: CRITERION GROUPS FROM NORMAL LIFE

While the MMPI can be employed to test normal subjects, it has some limitations when used in this way. The main problem is that the criterion groups that defined the scales were composed of psychiatric patients. This prompted the development of several new inventories constructed according to the same logic that led to the MMPI, but with normal rather than with pathological criterion groups. One of the best known of these is the ***California Psychological Inventory, or CPI.*** The CPI is especially aimed at high school and college students. It tests for various personality traits such as dominance, sociability, responsibility, sense of well-being, and so on.

As an example of how scales for these and other traits were derived, consider *dominance.* High school and college students were asked to name the most and the least dominant persons within their social circles. The persons who comprised these two extremes were then used as the criterion groups that defined the dominance-submission dimension. From here on, the procedure paralleled that which led to the construction of the MMPI. A large set of items (many of them taken from the MMPI) was administered to both groups, and those items that differentiated between the groups were kept to make up the dominance scale. Other traits were defined in a similar manner and several validity scales were added to assess the subjects' test-taking attitudes (Gough, 1957).

THE VALIDITY OF PERSONALITY INVENTORIES

The originators of the MMPI, the CPI, and other personality inventories based on criterion groups, took considerable pains to provide their instruments with a solid, empirical foundation. To evaluate the success of their efforts, we must look at the validity of these tests.

Predictive validity   The usual way to assess validity is to determine the degree to which a test can predict some real-world events. There is evidence that personality tests do indeed have some predictive power. For instance, among college women during the fifties and sixties, the sociability scale of the CPI correlated with how often the subject went out on dates and whether she joined a sorority. Other scales correlate with how subjects are rated by their peers (Hase and Goldberg, 1967).

The trouble is that while personality inventories can predict, their efficiency in doing so is quite low. The correlations between test scores and validity criteria are generally in the neighborhood of +.30. This contrasts poorly with the validation coefficients of intelligence tests (usually assessed by correlating IQ and academic performance), which are about +.50. The contrast is even sharper if we compare the usefulness of these personality tests with the predictive efficiency of common-sense measures such as relevant past behavior in related situations. The result is simple. The best predictor of future performance (for example, psychiatric breakdown, delinquency) is past performance. A dramatic and widely cited example is provided by a study which showed that the thickness of a mental patient's file folder correlates +.61 with the probability of his rehospitalization following his release (Lasky et al., 1959).

Construct validation   The low validity coefficients of personality inventories may not be grounds for as much chagrin as one might assume at first. One line of defense is an attack on the criterion measures. Consider peer ratings, dating frequency, and sorority joining as criterion measures of sociability. Could peer ratings be in error? Is sorority joining really an appropriate criterion? There are surely some reasons why a very sociable college woman might not want to become a sorority sister.

Arguments of this sort suggest that the best index for evaluating a test is not necessarily given by its correlation with *one* criterion measure. To be sure, this correlation (that is, the predictive validity) may sometimes be all that counts, as when the primary concern is pragmatic forecasting. An example is aptitude tests for pilot training. Here, the object is not to discover what pilot aptitude really is; all we want to do is to minimize the number of training failures and airplane crashes (see Chapter 17). But our interest in assessing personality is not so narrowly practical. What most personality tests try to get at is some hypothesized psychological entities, such as traits, that are presumed to underlie overt behavior. In effect, the trait—whether sociability, or psychopathic deviance, or whatever—is a theoretical concept devised by the psychologist in an effort to make sense, not just of one set of observations, but of many. To validate such a construct, one has to devise and test hypotheses about the relation between the underlying trait and various behavioral effects. This is **construct validation,** an approach we have discussed previously, in the context of intelligence testing (see Chapter 17).

Construct validation is often built upon a set of diverse relationships between the test scores and rather different behavioral manifestations. An example is provided by the psychopathic deviance scale (Pd) of the MMPI, a scale originally based upon those items that differentiated a group of delinquents from other groups (see Table 18.1). Not too surprisingly, normal (that is, nondelinquent) high school students who are regarded as "least responsible" by their classmates have much higher Pd scores than students rated as "most responsible." A related fact is that high Pd scores are characteristic of school dropouts. Another set of findings shows that high Pd scorers tend to be relatively aggressive. For example, nurses with high Pd scores are judged to be "not shy" and "unafraid of mental patients," while persons with low Pd scores are considered "good-natured." Rather further afield is the fact that high Pd scores are also characteristic of professional actors. Still more remote is the finding that hunters who have "carelessly" shot someone in a hunting accident have higher Pd scores than other hunters. On the face of it, many of these findings seem unrelated, but they do fit together if understood as different manifestations of the same underlying personality trait, psychopathic deviance. In its extreme form, this trait is characterized by shallow social and emotional ties, a disregard of social mores and conventions, a failure to consider potential dangers and to worry about the consequences of one's own actions—in short, an attitude that says, "I just don't give a damn" (Cronbach and Meehl, 1955).

The various correlations just described are all fairly small. None of these effects —being rated "irresponsible," having hunting accidents, and so on—correlate strongly enough with the Pd scale to provide a decent single criterion for predictive validity. But when they are considered together, they fit into a network of relationships that does seem to give some validity to the underlying construct. Seen in this light, the fact that the individual correlations are not very strong is not surprising. "If they were, we would find the same person dropping out of school, being ill-natured, becoming a Broadway actor and shooting a fellow hunter. . . . Personality structure, even if perfectly measured, represents only a disposition rather than a determining force" (Cronbach, 1970a, p. 555). How that disposition will manifest itself depends upon the particular circumstances the person is in.

Unstructured Personality Tests

The 1940s and 1950s saw the increasing popularity of a new approach to personality assessment, an approach which is an offshoot of psychoanalytic thought—the use of *projective techniques.* These techniques present the subject with a relatively unstructured task, such as making up a story to fit a picture or describing what one sees in an inkblot. In part, this approach was a protest against the highly structured paper-and-pencil tests of personality discussed above. Exponents of the projective approach granted that the MMPI and similar tests contained various safeguards to assure that the subject would not lie to the test administrator. But they pointed out that these tests give no guarantee that the subjects would not lie to themselves. Following Freud, they were convinced that the deeper layers of any individual's personality contain repressed wishes, unconscious conflicts, and various hidden defense maneuvers that are not accessible by ordinary means. But how can one penetrate below the surface to find out what the subject does not know himself?

The trick was to find a technique that could circumvent the subject's own defenses against threatening impulses and ideas. The basic idea is that when structuring unstructured materials the subject cannot help but unveil some deeper facets of his personality makeup. The test materials are thus considered as a kind of screen upon which the subject "projects" his inner feelings, wishes, conflicts, and ideas.

The number and variety of projective techniques invented during the past fifty years is remarkable. Some require the subject to give word associations or to complete sentences; others to draw a person or to copy designs; yet others ask subjects to state "three wishes." We will consider only the two that are used most widely—the Rorschach inkblot technique and the Thematic Apperception Test.

THE RORSCHACH INKBLOTS

Hermann Rorschach, a Swiss psychologist, used the perception of unstructured forms as a diagnostic tool. That unstructured forms can be perceived in many different ways was well known before Rorschach's inkblots became part of every clinical psychologist's tool kit. An illustration is provided by Prince Hamlet:

HAMLET: Do you see yonder cloud that's almost in the shape of a camel?
POLONIUS: By the mass, and 'tis like a camel, indeed.
HAMLET: Methinks it is like a weasel.
POLONIUS: It is backed like a weasel.
HAMLET: Or like a whale?
POLONIUS: Very like a whale.

(*Hamlet,* Act III, scene ii)

In 1921, Rorschach published an "experimental study of form perception." This study used ten symmetrical inkblots, some colored and some black and white, that he had presented to various groups of psychiatric patients. When the patients were asked what they saw in the inkblots, their responses seemed to differ depending upon the diagnostic group to which they belonged. Rorschach regarded these findings as tentative, but he nevertheless used them to devise a system for scoring and interpretation (Zubin, Eron, and Shumer, 1965).

Administration and scoring   An example of a card similar to those employed by Rorschach is shown in Figure 18.2. The subject is presented with each of ten cards, one at a time, and is asked to tell what she sees, what the blots might be. After all ten of the cards have been presented, the examiner queries the subject

18.2   An inkblot of the type used in the Rorschach test   *Because familiarity with the cards makes it difficult to evaluate a person's first reaction, most psychologists prefer not to print the actual inkblots used in the test. Five of the actual cards are in black and white, five others are colored.*

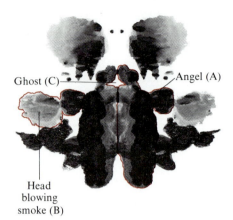

Ghost (C)

Angel (A)

Head
blowing
smoke (B)

**18.3   Sample responses and scoring on a
Rorschach-type inkblot**   (A) *"Two angels
with wings, flying among clouds."* Where
are they? *"The whole thing? Here are the
angels; here are their wings. The rest is
clouds."* What makes them look like that?
*"Their shape. The shaded parts are
clouds."* Scoring: Location—Whole;
Determinants—Human movement, shading. (B) *"A man's head blowing smoke."*
Scoring: Location—Large detail;
Determinants—Human movement,
shading. (C) *"A ghost in a shroud. In
white."* Scoring: Location—Small detail;
Determinant—White space.

about each response to find out which part of the blot was used and which of its
attributes determined its nature.

The scoring is according to three categories: location, determinants, and content. *Location* concerns the portion of the blot that is used in the response. Is it
the whole blot, a large detail, or a small detail? *Determinants* are the attributes of
the stimulus that are the basis of the response, such as form, shading, or color.
Also classed as a determinant is movement, a scoring category which is used
whenever the subject describes a person, animal, or object that is said to be in motion. The final scoring category, *content,* refers to what the subject sees, rather
than where or how he sees it. Among the major content categories are human figures or parts of human figures, animals or parts of animals, inanimate objects,
plants, blood, X rays, and so on (Figure 18.3).

Interpretation   Rorschach experts insist that the interpretation of a Rorschach
record cannot be performed in a simple cookbook fashion, for it demands the in-
terrelation of all of its various features in all their complexity. In their view, interpretation is a subtle art which requires much talent and even more experience.
Nevertheless, we can at least sketch a few of the major hypotheses about certain
Rorschach signs. For example, using the entire inkblot is said to indicate integrative, conceptual thinking, whereas the use of a high proportion of small details
suggests compulsive rigidity. A relatively frequent use of the white space (which
then serves as figure rather than as ground) is supposed to be a sign of rebellious-
ness and negativism. Responses that describe humans in movement are said to
indicate imagination and a rich inner life; responses that are dominated by color
suggest emotionality and impulsivity.

Traditional approaches to Rorschach interpretation hold that content is less
important for diagnosis than the formal categories of location and determinants.
But even so, most interpreters use content to some extent. That knives and mutilated bodies are generally regarded as indicators of hostility is not surprising.

Assessing the validity of Rorschach interpretation is a difficult task. We will
consider this issue together with similar ones raised by the other major projective
technique in current use, the *Thematic Apperception Test,* or *TAT* developed by
Henry Murray and his associates (Morgan and Murray, 1935).

THE THEMATIC APPERCEPTION TEST (TAT)

To Rorschach, content was a secondary concern. To the originators of the TAT, it
was the primary focus, for their emphasis was on a person's major motives and
preoccupations, defenses, conflicts, and ways of interpreting the world.

Administration   The TAT test materials are a number of pictures of various
scenes (Figure 18.4). The subject is asked to tell a story about each picture, to describe what is happening, what led up to the scene, and what the outcome will be.

Interpretation   In clinical practice, TAT interpretation is usually a rather free-
wheeling affair. Each story suggests a hypothesis which is then checked and elaborated (or discarded) by looking at later stories. The desired end product is a
picture of the person's major motives and conflicts, pieced together by interpreting the TAT stories in the light of all previously available information, of which
the case history is probably the most important.

18.4   A picture of the type used in the TAT

An illustration of this impressionistic and global approach to TAT interpretation is provided by the case of Morris, a twenty-six-year-old securities salesman, one of whose conflicts centered upon his sex life. He was puzzled why sex was relatively unimportant to him, and he had at least as many homosexual as heterosexual experiences. Condensations of two of his TAT stories are presented below:

> *Picture of a naked man . . . in the act of climbing a rope up or down:* The man is a eunuch in Ethiopia . . . and there this man Ahab, as he was called by the Arabs, lived for 20 years as servant in the sheik's harem. Surprisingly, instead of developing the usual lackadaisical castrated attitude that comes to eunuchs . . . this Ahab was constantly tormented by the presence of all the women and his complete inability to do anything about it . . . he decided he must escape . . . threw a rope out of the window . . . and let himself down. . . . Fate was against him. He got to the bottom: four of the servants of the Arab chief were there, ready to grab him. . . . He died in the most unique way the chief could think up . . . in a room with a couple of colonies of red ants.

> *Picture of a young man standing with downcast head buried in his arm. Behind him is the figure of a woman lying in bed:* "Jesus, what a shape! Positively indecent! . . ." His first thought was that the man was "going to the bathroom to make sure he doesn't catch anything!" He then said that the scene was in Hawaii, where a man and a girl were "sitting and drinking on a terrace." After "six drinks, they stagger upstairs and land on the bed"; a couple of minutes later, the man goes to the bathroom to throw up. (Janis, Mahl, Kagan, and Holt, 1969, pp. 700–701)

In both these stories heterosexual love comes to an unhappy end. The same holds true for two other stories in this person's TAT record that contained heterosexual themes. There is also the fact that each of these four stories was set in such distant places as Ethiopia and Hawaii. To the TAT interpreter this meant that Morris was unable to imagine any heterosexual involvement in the here and now. In contrast, homosexual themes occurred in contemporaneous settings close to home. A related fact concerns another TAT picture which shows a male embracing a female. But in Morris's story, the sexes are misperceived. The male is seen as a mother, the female as the mother's weak and pudgy son who has to lean on her. This confusion of sexual identity goes together with the theme of castration that is quite explicit in one of the two stories summarized here. According to the TAT interpreter, this theme is linked to Morris's life history. His father deserted the family when Morris was only eight, a fact which may have contributed to Morris's unsure sense of being a heterosexual male (Janis et al., 1969).

Interpretations of this sort are very beguiling. They suggest facets of an individual's personality which might never have been revealed otherwise. But are these facets actually there? To what extent can we trust the projective tester's interpretations? Are these interpretations equally astute when the tester does not have the benefit of hindsight, when she does not know the salient facts of the subject's life history?

THE VALIDITY OF PROJECTIVE TECHNIQUES

By now, there are probably seven thousand published articles that are explicitly devoted to the Rorschach and the TAT. Considering all of this effort, the upshot has been disappointing. According to some experts, these techniques have some limited validity; according to others, they have none.

Validity and the Rorschach Individual Rorschach indices—especially those that don't refer to content—show little or no relation to external validity criteria. In one study of psychiatric patients, over thirty different measures from the Rorschach records (for instance, the number of responses using the whole inkblot) were studied to see whether there was any relation to later diagnosis. There was none. Similar results apply to nonpsychiatric populations. For example, a preponderance of human movement responses is said to indicate creativity, but a group of eminent artists were no different from ordinary persons in this regard (Zubin, Eron, and Shumer, 1965).

Studies of this kind have sometimes been criticized as too "atomistic," for they compare individual indices one by one in various criterion groups. Wouldn't it be better to use the test as a whole, and to allow the judge to read the entire record verbatim (or even to administer the test) and then predict the criterion on the basis of this overall, "global" knowledge? One study that meets these conditions used twelve eminent Rorschach experts who tried to assess various aspects of the personalities of various patients on the basis of their complete Rorschach records. The external criterion was the pooled judgment of a number of psychiatrists who read each patient's case history, obtained in six or so interviews of several hours each. The mean correlation between the Rorschach experts' predictions and the psychiatrists' judgments was +.21 (Little and Shneidman, 1959).

Global assessment on the basis of the verbatim record evidently has some modest validity. Some authors believe that this is because some important information is provided by the specific content of the subject's responses (Zubin, 1954). This fits in with other evidence that shows moderate relationships between Rorschach content and external criteria. For example, hostile Rorschach content (knives) correlates with hostility as rated by judges (Zubin, Eron, and Shumer, 1965). Thus, contrary to traditional Rorschach lore, *what* subjects see in the inkblots seems to be more revealing than *how* they see it.

Validity and the TAT If content is the crucial variable, then one should have high hopes for the validity of the TAT, which aims for little else but thematic content. But in fact, the TAT has fared no better than the Rorschach in those validity studies that assessed its ability to predict psychiatric diagnosis. In one case study, the TAT was administered to over a hundred male veterans, some in mental hospitals and others in college. There was no difference between normals and patients, let alone between different psychiatric groups (Eron, 1950).

While such results indicate that the TAT may have drawbacks as a diagnostic tool for psychiatric classification, the test does seem to have some validity for more limited purposes. A number of studies have shown that the TAT may be a fair indicator of the presence of certain motives, though probably not of all. One group of investigators worked with subjects who had not eaten for various periods of time. When presented with TAT-like pictures, some of which suggested food or eating, hungry subjects came up with more stories whose plots concerned hunger or food-seeking than a control group of sated subjects (Atkinson and McClelland, 1948). Related findings have been obtained with various other motives including aggression, sexual arousal, the need for achievement, and so on. The success of these efforts represents a kind of construct validation of the TAT as an assessment device for at least some motives.

Projective techniques and incremental validity Given the verdict of these various validation studies, many projective experts have become convinced that

18.5   Projective techniques for use with children   *Special projective techniques have been developed for use with children. An example is the Children's Apperception Test, CAT, that consists of ten pictures in which all characters are animals. (Courtesy Leopold Bellak)*

their devices are not really tests at all, but instead are important adjuncts to a clinical interview (Zubin, Eron, and Shumer, 1965). Rorschach and TAT scores make little sense to a practitioner who has not administered the tests personally or at least read the verbatim records. They are also hard to interpret without a knowledge of the subject's background and life history. but proponents of these techniques argue that when they are used as part of the total clinical evaluation, they help to provide a richer understanding of the person (Figure 18.5).

We have seen that when the Rorschach or TAT are used in this manner, they do indeed have some modest predictive validity for diagnosis. But according to some critics, predictive validity is not enough; the real issue is whether these tests have ***incremental validity*** (Meehl, 1959). The question is how much additional (that is, incremental) information these techniques provide over and above that which is contained in case histories and similar data that have to be gathered anyway. To give and score a Rorschach and/or a TAT is very time-consuming; since this is so, these tests ought to provide a reasonable increment in information. But the available evidence suggests otherwise. Several studies have shown that when clinical psychologists were asked to make inferences about a subject's personal characteristics, they were just as accurate with only the case history to go on as they were when provided with additional data in the form of the Rorschach or TAT records (Kostlan, 1954; Winch and More, 1956.)

TRAITS VERSUS SITUATIONS

The preceding discussion has shown that personality tests are not particularly accurate probes into the human psyche. What accounts for this state of affairs? One possibility is that the fault lies with the tests themselves, that the tests have somehow failed to uncover those traits (or inner motives, conflicts, or whatever) that characterize the difference between one human personality and another. But there is another possibility that is more disquieting. Perhaps the tests do so poorly because that which they are trying to measure—a set of stable personality traits—isn't really there. To put it another way, perhaps Theophrastus was wrong, and there is no real consistency in the way people behave at different times and on different occasions.

The Difficulties with Trait Theory

The concept of stable personality traits was seriously challenged by Walter Mischel, whose survey of the research literature led him to conclude that people behave much less consistently than a trait theory would predict (Mischel, 1968). A classic study concerns honesty in children (Hartshorne and May, 1928). Grade-school children were given the opportunity to lie, cheat, or steal in a wide variety of settings: in athletic events, in the classroom, at home, alone, or with peers. The important finding was that the child who was dishonest in one situation (cheating on a test) was not necessarily dishonest in another setting (an athletic contest). There was some consistency, but it was rather unimpressive; a later reanalysis of the results came up with an average intercorrelation of +.30 (Burton, 1963). The correlations were greater the greater the similarity between the two situations in which honesty was assessed. Honesty in one classroom situation was more consistent with honesty in another classroom situation than with honesty assessed at home.

Mischel argued that a similar lack of cross-situational consistency is found for many other behavior patterns. Examples are aggression, dependency, rigidity, and reactions to authority. The intercorrelations among different measures of what seems to be the same trait are often low and sometimes nonexistent. In Mischel's view, the fact that personality tests have relatively low validities is just another demonstration of the same phenomenon. A personality test taps behavior in one situation while the validity criterion of that test assesses behavior in another context. Since cross-situational consistency tends to be low, so are validity coefficients.

If this view is right, the underlying consistency of the personalities of our friends and acquaintances (as well as our own) is more or less illusory. But if so, how can one explain the fact that most people have held this particular illusion since Theophrastus's time and no doubt much before? Mischel's answer was that personality traits are largely mental constructions devised by the observer who watches another person's actions and tries to make sense out of them. To do so, the observer *attributes* the act to some inner, stable characteristic of the actor (see Chapter 11 for a discussion of this attribution process).

SITUATIONISM

The failure to find behavioral consistency has been taken as an argument against the importance of personality characteristics in determining what a person will do. But if these are not relevant, what is? One answer is **situationism,** the notion that human behavior is largely determined by the characteristics of the situation

In some situations most people behave the same way (Photograph by Hiroji Kubota, Magnum Photos)

In other situations, most people behave differently A major task of personality psychologists is to discover whether they behave consistently across different situations. (Photograph by Elliott Erwitt, Magnum Photos)

rather than by those of the person. That this is so for some situations is indubitable. Given a red light, most drivers stop; given a green light, most go—regardless of whether they are friendly or unfriendly, stingy or generous, dominant or submissive, and so on. Situations of this sort produce predictable reactions in virtually all of us. But according to situationism, the same principle applies to much or nearly all of human behavior. Consider the enormous effect of social roles which often define what an actor must do with little regard to who the actor is (see Chapter 11). To predict how someone will act in a courtroom, there is little point in asking whether he is sociable or extravagant with money or whether he gets along with his father. What we really want to know is the role that he or she will play—judge, prosecutor, defense attorney, or defendant. Seen in this light, what we do depends not on who we are, but on the situation in which we find ourselves.

This is not to say that situationists deny the existence of individual differences. They certainly agree that various demographic and socioeconomic factors are powerful determinants of human behavior. Examples are age and sex, marital status, ethnic background, occupation, and income. Nor do they dispute the important effect of differences in ability, especially cognitive ability. As they see it, all of these factors determine the kinds of situations a person is likely to encounter or to have encountered (and thus learned from). But in their view, it is these situations, rather than personality traits, that determine what people actually do.

In Defense of Traits

The emphasis on situations provided a useful corrective to those who sought to explain everything people do as a manifestation of their own inner nature. But if pushed to the extreme, this position becomes just as questionable as the one it had tried to correct. For in this form it can be interpreted as asserting that personality does not exist at all. Whether any psychologist has actually gone to this extreme is doubtful; certainly Mischel never did (Mischel, 1973, 1979). But the very possibility that someone might climb all the way out on this particular theoretical limb was enough to produce a spirited counterreaction against Mischel's attack on the trait concept.

CONSISTENCY OVER TIME

The reaction to the situationist position took several forms. Many authors felt that there is considerable personal consistency over time (Block, 1971, 1977). Proof comes from a number of longitudinal studies that show a fair degree of behavioral consistency over sizable stretches of the life span. Thus in one study, dependability in males as judged in high school correlated quite well with ratings of the same attribute made by different judges some ten or more years later ($r=+.55$; Block, 1971). In another study, male adults between seventeen and eighty-five years of age were given the same personality inventory at six- and twelve-year intervals. The correlations between their scores on the first and second administration of the inventory (on traits such as dominance, sociability, and emotional stability) ranged from $+.59$ to $+.87$ (Costa, McCrae, and Arenberg, 1980).

CONSISTENCY ACROSS SITUATIONS

Consistency over time there might be, but what about consistency across situations, which was the major focus of Mischel's critique? According to Seymour Epstein, this cross-situational consistency is much higher than Mischel had supposed.

In Epstein's view, studies that seem to show low cross-situational consistency usually employ only a small sample of behaviors. As a result, the assessment of the relevant trait is necessarily unreliable. But if so, the correlation between two (unreliable) measures of this trait cannot help but be low or nonexistent. Consider the correlation between college grades in calculus and physics. This correlation is likely to be fairly high if it is between the two final grades, but it will surely be much diminished if it is between the grades on just *one* quiz in each of the two courses. Now chance factors will play a much larger role, and the correlation will decline correspondingly. Epstein argues that the same point holds for personality traits and cross-situational consistency. To determine whether people behave consistently from one situation to another, the behavior in each situation (e.g., cheating in class and cheating on the athletic field) must be measured not just once, but on a number of different occasions.

To buttress his position, Epstein observed subjects' moods, behavior, and various physiological indices on about thirty days. He found that correlations from one day to any other day were very low. He then compared correlations based on the average score on any two days, then on any three days, and so on. As the number of observations increased, the correlations rose from about .30 to .80 (Epstein, 1979, 1980).

Epstein interprets these findings as evidence for cross-situational consistency. But Mischel and his collaborators reply that they are essentially demonstrations of consistency in time and not across situations, though this is still a matter of considerable debate (Mischel and Peake, 1983; Epstein, 1983).

CONSISTENCY OF UNDERLYING SOURCE

A different argument was sounded by critics who insisted that behavioral inconsistency is often more apparent than real. They argued that on closer examination, two reactions that are superficially quite dissimilar may turn out to be a manifestation of the same underlying source. An example is aggression. In males, this is fairly consistent between childhood and adolescence, but it takes different overt forms at different ages. Young boys pummel each other with their fists; young men rarely do more than shout in anger (Kagan and Moss, 1962). Another example concerns the distinction between the attributes *happy/outgoing* and *somber/reserved.* When different judges were asked to assess this trait in persons first studied at age six and then again at age fifteen, their ratings were quite similar, yielding correlations of about +.60. This consistency disappeared, however, when the judges were asked to rate overt behavior only. The five-year-old who is reserved and somber shows this by a low level of physical vitality. At ten, the same underlying attribute manifests itself as cautiousness and emotional vulnerability. Still later, during adolescence, this basic pattern goes together with a sense of inferiority (Bronson, 1966). Here, as in many other facets of the behavior of organisms, a superficial difference may disguise a deeper sameness.

Aggression in boys and men *The same trait is often (though not always) expressed differently at different ages. (Left: Photograph by Robert Smith, Black Star. Right: Photograph courtesy of Leo de Wys)*

THE INTERACTION BETWEEN PERSON AND SITUATION

Yet another group of commentators felt that the debate between situationists and trait theorists had harped on the wrong distinction. As originally formulated, the question was whether an individual's actions are better predicted by the situation or by his or her own personal characteristics. But there is a third alternative: The critical factor may be the ***interaction*** between person and situation.

The term *interaction* is used here in a technical sense. To explain what is meant by interaction in this context, let us consider a hypothetical experiment in which we study the reactions of several pairs of individuals to two different situations. The response will be anxiety as indicated by the galvanic skin response (GSR); the two situations are waiting to take a test and being threatened with electric shock. Let's call the subjects Jane and Carol, Mary and Claire, and let us assume that the GSR scale runs from 0 (no anxiety) to 12 (maximal anxiety). Two extreme outcomes are displayed in Tables 18.2 and 18.3.

Table 18.2 AN EFFECT OF SITUATION

		Situation		Average for each person
		Test	Shock	
Person	Jane	3	9	6
	Carol	3	9	6
Average for situation		3	9	

Table 18.3 AN EFFECT OF INDIVIDUAL DIFFERENCES

		Situation		Average for each person
		Test	Shock	
Person	Mary	3	3	3
	Claire	9	9	9
Average for situation		6	6	

The pattern of results shown in Tables 18.2 and 18.3 is diametrically opposed. Table 18.2 depicts a powerful effect of the situation. For these two subjects, Jane and Carol, shock is evidently much more frightening than the test. But there is no effect of individual differences since Jane and Carol behave identically. In Table 18.3 we see the reverse. Here, there is a massive effect of individual differences;

Claire is evidently much more fearful than is Mary. But in this second example, the situations are essentially equivalent in the fear they provoke.

These two illustrations fit the extreme positions that ascribe all behavior either to the situation or to personality differences. Needless to say, there are much more plausible intermediate outcomes in which both factors play a role. But our concern is with another alternative, which has quite different theoretical implications. Consider the pattern of results shown by yet another pair of subjects as indicated in Table 18.4.

Table 18.4   AN INTERACTION EFFECT

		Situation		Average for each person
		Test	Shock	
Person	Anne	3	9	6
	Donna	9	3	6
Average for situation		6	6	6

What is important about the results of Table 18.4 is that they do not exhibit effects of the situations as such nor of the individual differences as such. When we look at average GSRs, Anne and Donna prove equally fearful. The same holds for the difference between the situations; *on the average,* the test and the threatened shock produce equal GSRs. But there is a new twist that is obscured by the averages. The two situations produce radically different effects in the two persons. Anne is evidently much more afraid of the shock than of the test, while the opposite holds for Donna. In statistical language, a relationship of this kind, in which the effect of one variable (fear-evoking situation) depends upon another variable (individual differences) is called an *interaction.*

The test-shock experiment here described is a highly simplified version of a large number of studies that have actually been carried out. An example is a study in which subjects were asked to describe their usual reaction to various threats (Endler and Hunt, 1969). Some of these perils involved loss of self-esteem (failing an examination), others physical danger (being on a high ledge on a mountaintop), still others a threat whose nature was still unclear (getting a police summons). The results showed that both individual differences and situations affected behavior to some extent. Some people seemed more generally fearful than others, and some situations ("being approached by cars racing abreast") evoked more fear than others ("sitting in a restaurant").

What is more interesting is that the bulk of these effects were produced by the person-by-situation interaction. Put in other words, people tend to be frightened (or angered or reassured) by different things. A simple situationism is evidently untenable; the man who is terrified of heights may well be a passionate scuba diver. But this finding also undercuts the usefulness of general traits such as "anxiety." To predict behavior better, such traits should be qualified; for example, "anxiety in an interpersonal setting," "anxiousness when facing physical danger," "anxiety in the face of the unknown." By this utilization of the person-by-situation interaction, the notion of stable personality differences can be maintained. But there is a price, for the process of qualification may be endless.

Consider interpersonal anxiety. It probably depends on whether the situation involves members of the same or the opposite sex. If it does, should we subdivide the trait still further? The end result can only be an enormous proliferation of ever more finely drawn traits.

Person Constancy

In the light of all this, what can we say about the assumption that there is an underlying unity in how any one individual acts and thinks and feels, a basic consistency that we now call personality? The evidence indicates that this assumption—which goes back to Theophrastus—still stands. To be sure, behavioral consistency may be obscured by the demands of the situation. In addition, it is generally too subtle to be captured by a few simple trait descriptions; a list of highly qualified mini-traits is often the best we can do. But there is no reason to discard our intuitive belief in something like "person constancy," a phenomenon analogous to "object constancy" in perception (see Chapter 6). A chair is perceived as a stable object whose size remains the same whether we are near to it or far away and whose shape stays unchanged regardless of our visual orientation. These constancies are not illusions; they reflect a genuine stability in the external world. The constancy of personality is not as sturdy as that of chairs, but it has some reality even so. For while the evidence on cross-situational consistency is debatable, most psychologists agree that there is much more consistency over time—that people remain more or less what they are as time goes on.

To be sure, this person constancy is far from perfect. We change from day to day; we're grouchy on Monday because of a headache, and cheery on Tuesday because of a sunny sky. We also change from year to year—with age, experience, and various shifts of fortune. A number of psychologists suspect that we tend to underestimate the degree to which such changes occur. In observing others, we form a notion of their personality. In observing ourselves, we form a so-called *self-concept*—a set of ideas about who we ourselves are. But our perception of the personality of others, as well as our own self-concept, are at bottom mental constructions and as such they are subject to error. One such error is the tendency to see more uniformity and coherence than is actually there, to exaggerate person constancy in others and in ourselves (Mischel, 1973; Nisbett and Wilson, 1977; Kihlstrom and Cantor, 1984).

Person constancy may not be perfect, but at some level it must surely exist. For the fact that people differ from each other and are essentially unique seems like a basic fact of our existence. An extreme version of situationism (which few if any psychologists ever maintained) might argue that this uniqueness is an illusion—that we act as we do because of the situations in which we find ourselves, regardless of who we are. But this runs contrary to much of our own experience. People gossip about each other and tell tales of what X did to Y. Are they merely describing situations? They grieve when a loved one dies; why all the tears if all they lost is a set of habitual reactions to situations?

Person constancy is a fact. Jane remains Jane whether she is at home or at the office, whether it is today or yesterday or the day after tomorrow. And at some level she is different from Carol and Margaret and four billion other humans alive today, for her personality—just like theirs—is unique.

THE SEARCH FOR A TAXONOMY

To the extent that person constancy exists, one of Theophrastus's basic assumptions is upheld. But on reflection, his character sketches—and the modern trait theory of personality—imply something over and above person constancy. Trait theorists assume not only that a particular person will behave consistently, but that this person can be categorized along with others whose behavior is in some ways equivalent. But what are the categories along which people should be grouped together? Theophrastus picked a few attributes that were easy to caricature—loquaciousness, boorishness, stinginess, and so on. But are these the proper traits by which personality should be classified?

In a way, much the same question is faced during the early stage of any science. At this point, a major task is the development of a useful *taxonomy,* or classification system. Consider the early biologists. They recognized that the various creatures differ in a multitude of ways—their size and color, the absence or presence of a skeleton, the number and kind of appendages, and so on. The biologists had to decide which of these distinctions provide the most useful classification categories. Exactly the same issue faces the psychologist who studies personality differences. The dictionary lists eighteen thousand trait names (Allport and Odbert, 1936). But without some kind of taxonomy how can we decide by which of these many traits to classify people?

We have seen that personality inventories rarely generate validity coefficients much above +.30. In part, this reflects various shortcomings of the tests. In part, it reflects the fact that personal differences are often obscured by the demands of the situation. But in part, it probably also reflects our failure to find the proper classification scheme that tells us which personality traits to assess.

Classification by Factor Analysis

One major approach to the development of a taxonomy of personality traits used the methods of factor analysis employed in the study of intelligence-test performance (see Chapter 17). By studying the intercorrelations of various subtests, investigators had discovered *group factors* such as verbal intelligence, spatial intelligence, and so on. Could something similar be done by an inspection of the subcomponents of personality inventories?

FACTOR ANALYZING TRAIT TERMS

One of the earliest approaches to the development of a taxonomy of personality grew out of an examination of the language we use to describe personality attri-

An early taxonomy of personality A medieval illustration of one of the earliest attempts to classify human personality, Hippocrates's four temperaments: sanguine (cheerful and active), melancholic (gloomy), choleric (angry and violent), and phlegmatic (calm and passive). According to Hippocrates, these temperaments reflected an excess of one of four bodily humors; thus sanguine persons were thought to have relatively more blood. Today the humor theory is a mere historical curiosity, but some aspects of Hippocrates's classification are still with us. (Courtesy the Bettmann Archive)

butes. Advocates of this procedure argue that the adjectives used to describe people embody the accumulated observations of many previous generations. A systematic sifting of dictionary trait words may then give clues about individual differences whose description has been important enough to survive the test of time. This line of reasoning led to the development of a widely used personality inventory by Raymond Cattell (1957). Cattell's starting point was a set of 4,500 terms taken from the 18,000 trait words in the unabridged dictionary (Allport and Odbert, 1936). This list was drastically reduced by throwing out difficult or uncommon words and eliminating synonyms. Finally, 171 trait names were left. A group of judges was then asked to rate subjects by using these terms. Their ratings were subsequently factor analyzed by using methods similar to those employed in the study of intelligence-test performance—that is, by finding out which test items correlated highly with one another while correlating little or not at all with others. The resulting item clusters were then inspected to see what they had in common, yielding what Cattell thought were some 15 to 20 primary factors of personality.

Later work by Cattell and others reduced this number to a smaller set. Such efforts have led to several contending lists of basic personality factors. An example is a model featuring five major dimensions of personality: extraversion, agreeableness, conscientiousness, emotional stability, and culturedness. This model is hierarchical in the sense that various lower-level traits (for example, tidy/careless, persevering/fickle) are seen as manifestations of higher-order factors (here, conscientiousness) (see Table 18.5; Norman, 1963).

Table 18.5   FACTOR DESIGNATIONS FOR TWENTY TRAIT-RATING SCALES

Factor names	Scale dimensions
Extraversion	Talkative/Silent Frank, open/Secretive Adventurous/Cautious Sociable/Reclusive
Agreeableness	Good-natured/Irritable Not jealous/Jealous Mild, gentle/Headstrong Cooperative/Negativistic
Conscientiousness	Fussy, tidy/Careless Responsible/Undependable Scrupulous/Unscrupulous Persevering/Quitting, fickle
Emotional stability	Poised/Nervous, tense Calm/Anxious Composed/Excitable Not hypochondriacal/Hypochondriacal
Culture	Artistically sensitive/Artistically insensitive Intellectual/Unreflective, narrow Polished, refined/Crude, boorish Imaginative/Simple, direct

SOURCE: Adapted from Norman, 1963.

THE RELATION BETWEEN TRAIT TERMS AND LANGUAGE

A number of psychologists have built upon Cattell's belief that personality measurement must be grounded upon the trait words of the language. Their work involves a further linguistic analysis of the trait words. One question is whether a given word has many synonyms or near-synonyms. If so, it probably concerns a dimension of individual differences which the speakers of a language regard as important. After all, why else would they want to talk about it with so many different nuances of meaning (Goldberg, 1981a)? Another question concerns the generality of the trait word. If it is found in many languages, it presumably describes a rather basic attribute of human behavior (Goldberg, 1981b).

Still another question pertains to the separation of descriptive and evaluative aspects of trait words. Consider the terms *thrifty* and *extravagant.* They differ in the behavior they describe—unlikely to spend money versus likely to do so. But they also differ in the evaluation they place on these behaviors: the first is good, the second is bad. To separate the descriptive and evaluative aspects, one has to find a pair of words in which these relations are reversed, such as *stingy* and *generous* (Peabody, 1967). If subjects are rated on all four of these adjectives, we can separately determine the extent to which the judge believes that the subject will spend his money and the extent to which she likes or dislikes him for doing so. Such procedures may help to eliminate some of the defects in traditional testing procedures (Goldberg, 1975).

NEUROTICISM AND EXTRAVERSION/INTROVERSION

Another factor-analytic approach to the classification of personality traits is that of Hans Eysenck, who tried to encompass personality differences in a space defined by only two dimensions—neuroticism and extraversion-introversion. *Neuroticism* is equivalent to emotional instability and maladjustment. It is assessed by affirmative answers to questions like "Do you ever feel 'just miserable' for no good reason at all?" And "Do you often feel disgruntled?" *Extraversion-introversion* are terms that refer to the main direction of a person's energies, toward the outer world of material objects and other people or toward the inner world of one's own thoughts and feelings. The extravert is sociable, impulsive, and enjoys new experiences, while the introvert tends to be more solitary, cautious, and slow to change. Extraversion is indicated by affirmative answers to questions such as "Do you like to have many social engagements?" and "Would you rate yourself as a happy-go-lucky individual?"

As Eysenck sees it, neuroticism and extraversion-introversion are independent dimensions. To be sure, both introverts and many neurotics have something in common; they are both unsociable and withdrawn. But, in Eysenck's view, their lack of sociability has different roots. The healthy introverts are not afraid of social activities; they simply do not like them. In contrast, neurotically shy persons keep to themselves because of fear; they want to be with others but are afraid of joining them (Figure 18.6).

TEST FACTORS AND LABORATORY PHENOMENA

Can we be sure that the factors extracted by these statistical methods are the "real" dimensions of personality? Unfortunately, the answer has to be no. To

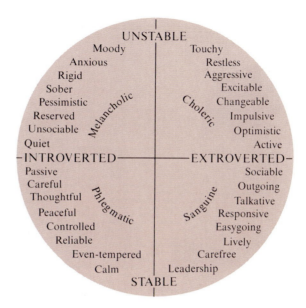

18.6 Eysenck's two-dimensional classification of personality *Two dimensions of personality—neuroticism (emotional instability) and extraversion-introversion—define a space into which various trait terms may be fitted. Eysenck points out that the four quadrants of this space seem to fit Hippocrates's temperaments. Introverted and stable—phlegmatic; introverted and unstable—melancholic; extraverted and stable—sanguine; extraverted and unstable—choleric. (Eysenck and Rachman, 1965)*

begin with, factor analysts disagree with each other on too many points; they often come up with different classification systems to order the same set of data. Even more important is the fact that the end product of the analysis has to depend on what is fed into it. The factors describe the coherence among a certain set of items; if some items are added and others subtracted, the pattern of coherence (and thus the factors) will usually be different. In short, factor analysis is a technique that helps us understand how subparts of a test hang together. It is not a magic shortcut toward a taxonomy of personality traits.

Some of these objections can be partially met by formulating and testing some theoretical notions about the nature of the dimensions extracted through factor analysis. Eysenck and his associates have tried to provide this kind of construct validation for extraversion-introversion by relating it to many psychological phenomena outside of the personality domain.

As Eysenck sees it, introversion corresponds to a higher level of central nervous system arousal than does extraversion; in effect, introverts are thought to be more awake than extraverts (see Chapter 3). As a result, they are less distractible and better able to attend to the task at hand. For example, they do better at signal-detection tasks (Harkins and Green, 1975) and perform a monotonous tapping task with fewer involuntary rest pauses than persons with high extraversion scores (Eysenck, 1967). A related finding is that they are more reactive to external stimuli than extraverts; according to Eysenck, this is one of the reasons why they shy away from the world while extraverts embrace it enthusiastically. For example, introverts have lower pain tolerance (Lynn and Eysenck, 1961). On the other hand, people with high extraversion scores tend to seek out sensations; they enjoy taking off on trips without preplanned routes and say that they might like to try parachute jumping (Farley and Farley, 1967). They need external stimulation more than do the naturally aroused introverts. It's not surprising that volunteer firemen and salvage divers score higher on a scale that measures this tendency to seek sensation than does a matched control group of college students (Zuckerman, 1978, 1979).

Whether Eysenck's formulations will stand the test of time is a matter of debate. For example, it is still unclear whether the extraversion-introversion dimen-

Some people seek sensations whether on land, in the air, or under water (Photographs from left to right by Everett C. Johnson, Leo de Wys; Wilhelm Ostgathe, Leo de Wys; Flip Schulke, Black Star)

Others prefer a more quiet existence (Photograph by Don Rutledge, Black Star)

sion is really independent of neuroticism (Carrigan, 1960). In addition, some of the laboratory effects are not as sturdy as one might have hoped (for example, Purohit, 1966). But whatever the ultimate verdict on Eysenck's specific hypotheses, future investigators will probably accept his more general thesis that a taxonomy of personality differences can only be successful if it makes contact with the rest of psychological and biological fact.

Classification through Biology

Other approaches to the development of a taxonomy of personality also try to build it within the framework of the more established biological sciences. We will consider two different lines of attack. One tries to relate personality differences to body build; the other focuses on the contribution of heredity.

PERSONALITY AND BODY BUILD

The notion that personality is somehow related to bodily physique probably goes back to antiquity. Shakespeare must have echoed the views of his contemporaries (and of the Roman writer, Plutarch, from whom he took several of his plots) when he linked Cassius's "lean and hungry look" with the fact that "he thinks too much." Is there any evidence to support this belief in a substantial correlation between temperament (that is, basic and presumably built-in personality characteristics) and physique? A number of investigators have thought that there is, and that it provides an appropriate starting point for a taxonomy of personality.

Physique and temperament The most widely known exponent of this position is William Sheldon, who classified body types (or ***somatotypes***). According to Sheldon, a person's somatotype can be described in terms of three components: ***endomorphy, mesomorphy,*** and ***ectomorphy.*** A person who is high in endomorphy and low in the other two components is soft and round; one who is high in only mesomorphy is hard, rectangular, and well muscled; one who is high in ectomorphy alone is thin, of delicate build, and lightly muscled. Needless to say, such ex-

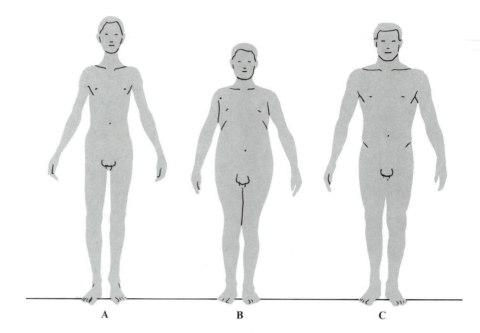

18.7 Sheldon's dimensions of physique *Three extreme somatotypes: (A) ectomorph; (B) endomorph; (C) mesomorph.*

tremes are rare; in actuality most people have intermediate somatotypes, although one component usually predominates (Figure 18.7). Somatotypes are determined by a combination of judges' ratings (based on nude photographs) and various physical measurements (Sheldon, 1940).

The next step was to decide on the personality traits to which these somatotypes might be related. Three clusters of traits were chosen. One is *viscerotonia,* which includes a love of food and comfort, relaxed tolerance, sociability, and a need for affection. A second is *somatotonia,* which is characterized by a desire for power and dominance, a zest for physical activity and adventure, and a relative indifference to other people. Finally, there is *cerebrotonia,* which includes self-consciousness, overreactiveness, and a preference for privacy. Sheldon's hypotheses about the relations of these temperaments and body build are implicit in the names he gave each cluster. The names indicate the body regions which he believed to be most relevant for these personality attributes. Thus endomorphy should go along with viscerotonia, mesomorphy with somatotonia, and ectomorphy with cerebrotonia.

Testing the relations between physique and temperament To test these hypotheses, Sheldon studied two hundred young men over a five-year period and then determined their somatotypes. The direction of the relationships were exactly as he had predicted. What is more, the correlations were huge, with an average of about +.80 (Sheldon, 1942). There was only one trouble. The results were too good to be true, for correlations of this size are unheard of in personality research. Several critics soon pointed out a basic flaw in the procedure. The same person—Sheldon himself, who presumably believed his own theory—had rated both the temperaments and the somatotypes. Under the circumstances, it is not surprising that his ratings of temperament were contaminated by his observation of the subjects' physiques (Humphreys, 1957).

Sheldon and other investigators tried to meet this criticism by having physique and temperament assessed by different judges. The resulting correlations were in

633

line with Sheldon's hypotheses but very much lower than those he had originally reported, with an average of +.26 (Child, 1950).

A more impressive set of findings concerns juvenile delinquency. Here is a behavior pattern that presumably involves some of the characteristics of somatotonia: physical action, aggressiveness, and a disregard of what others think or want. One would therefore expect a relationship with mesomorphy, and this is just what the data show. When five hundred male delinquents were compared to five hundred matched nondelinquents, about 60 percent of the delinquents were found to be predominantly mesomorphic, compared to 30 percent of the nondelinquent group (Glueck and Glueck, 1956). A similar relationship seems to characterize female delinquents (Epps and Parnell, 1952).

All in all, there is little doubt that Sheldon's initial claims were overstated. But even so, there seems to be a core of truth to his (and other writers') assertion that physique and temperament are related. The underlying factors may turn out to be somewhat different from those that Sheldon had proposed. For instance, several authors believe that the critical dimensions for body type are skeletal height and width and that the proportion of fat to muscle makes no difference. The result is a two-dimensional classification that ignores endomorphy. It apparently yields a better fit to the facts (Rees and Eysenck, 1945).

Accounting for the relation between physique and temperament What explains the relation between body build and personality, if it indeed exists? One possibility is that certain physiques foster some behavior patterns rather than others. If a boy wants to bully his peers, he had better have the musculature with which to back it up. If he has, he is more likely to succeed (and thus be reinforced) than if he hasn't; the end product is an association between physical action and mesomorphy. Another possibility is that the relation between physique and temperament is a byproduct of popular stereotypes. Such stereotypes are very prevalent; they are already found in five-year-olds (Lerner and Korn, 1972). If a chubby boy learns that others think of him as easygoing and compliant, he may come to see himself the same way and behave accordingly. This hypothesis does not explain how the stereotype arose in the first place, but it does suggest how it is perpetuated.

In sum, there probably is a relation between body build and personality attributes. This relationship is relatively weak and its origins are still a matter of speculation. It is of considerable interest all the same, for it may provide a clue about the way in which some personality differences develop from childhood origins. But thus far at least, the correlations between physique and temperament are too small and too poorly understood to provide the basis of a viable taxonomy of personality differences.

PERSONALITY AND GENETICS

In principle, there are several other ways in which biology might provide some clues for the development of a classification system. One promising approach centers on certain consistencies of behavior beginning in infancy. This holds for attributes like sociability and activity level, which seem to be remarkably stable from early childhood to adolescence (Kagan and Moss, 1962). Such consistencies have been observed beginning from the first weeks of life. An example comes from a study of 141 children, observed for about a decade following birth.

Donald exhibited an extremely high activity level almost from birth. At three months . . . he wriggled and moved about a great deal while asleep in his crib. At six months he "swam like a fish" while being bathed. At twelve months he still squirmed constantly while he was being dressed or washed. . . . At two years he was "constantly in motion, jumping and climbing." At three, he would "climb like a monkey and run like an unleashed puppy." . . . By the time he was seven, Donald was encountering difficulty in school because he was unable to sit still long enough to learn anything (Thomas, Chess, and Birch, 1970, p. 104).

Consistencies of this sort suggest the operation of genetic factors. One line of evidence comes from the same methods used to study hereditary effects in the determination of intelligence: the comparison of twins. In general, identical twins have proved to be more alike than fraternal twins on various personality attributes. Examples are extraversion-introversion, emotionality, and activity level (Buss and Plomin, 1975). These results argue for some contribution of heredity to personality makeup. But, as one might have expected, the proportion of the variance accounted for by genetic factors is considerably lower for personality than for intelligence.

Still, such facts might provide the basis of the long-sought taxonomy. The idea is simple: Those traits that are especially heritable are presumably more basic and should therefore serve as the primary categories for classification. But which traits are the basic ones? For a while it seemed as if extraversion-introversion was one, since it seemed to have higher heritabilities than all the rest (Loehlin, 1969). But later research argues otherwise.

In one study, 850 twins of high school age took a standard personality test, the California Psychological Inventory. As expected, the scores of the identical twins were more alike than those of the fraternal twins. The trouble was that this difference was just about the same on each of the test's eighteen scales. This suggests that all of these traits are about equally heritable (Loehlin and Nichols, 1976). This result is surprising; perhaps it reflects something about the test rather than the nature of the underlying attributes. But, at least for the time being, it rules out any classification scheme based on the belief that some traits are more heritable than others.

Is a Classification System Possible?

In addition to those we've discussed, there have been several other approaches to a taxonomy of personality differences. One is based on the similarity to various forms of mental illness. For example, normal persons might be classified by how closely their behavior resembles that found in mania, depression, or schizophrenia. Some of the early interpretations of normals' responses to the MMPI or the Rorschach were essentially in this vein. A very different taxonomy might be based on certain crucial events in childhood; Freud's theory of fixation at various stages of psychosexual development is a famous example. No doubt there are many other possibilities as well.

Have any of them worked? Some have, to a limited extent. But the kind of taxonomy on which a science can really build, the kind that biologists have known for centuries, is not yet in sight.

SUMMARY

1. *Personality traits* are attributes that define distinctions in the predominant desires and feelings and the typical modes of expressing these, which are characteristic of different persons. The underlying assumption of *trait theory* is that such traits are fundamentally consistent over time and situations.

2. One approach to personality assessment is by *objective personality inventories.* An example is the *Minnesota Multiphasic Personality Inventory, or MMPI.* It assesses traits by means of a number of different *scales,* each of which measures the extent to which a person's answers approximate those of a particular psychiatric *criterion group.* In actual practice, MMPI records are interpreted by inspecting the person's *score profile,* including his response to various *validity scales.* A number of other personality inventories such as the *California Psychological Inventory, or CPI,* were constructed in an analogous manner but using normal rather than pathological criterion groups.

3. The validity of personality inventories has been evaluated by using indices of *predictive validity.* The results show that while these tests predict, they predict not too well, for their *validity coefficients* are relatively low. When the evaluation is based on *construct validity,* the results look more promising.

4. A very different way of assessing personality is by means of *projective techniques.* Two prominent examples are the *Rorschach inkblot test* and the *Thematic Apperception Test, or TAT.* While these tests are often used in clinical practice, they have been criticized because of their relatively low predictive validity and even lower *incremental validity* coefficients.

5. The concept of stable personality traits has been seriously challenged by the claim that people behave much less consistently than a trait theory would predict. One alternative view is *situationism,* which claims that human behavior is largely determined by the situation in which the individual finds himself. While most investigators have concluded that there is strong evidence for *behavioral consistency over time,* there is still disagreement over the degree to which there is *behavioral consistency across situations.* Some authors argue that the failure to find cross-situational consistency is caused by assessments that are based on too few observations. Others argue that many inconsistencies in behavior are apparent rather than real. Many commentators argue that behavioral consistencies will show up best if one looks at the *interaction* between person and situation.

6. A major problem of modern personality theory is the absence of an established *taxonomy* for personality traits. One attempt to develop such a taxonomy depends on *factor analysis* and has led to a number of contending lists of basic personality factors. An example is Eysenck's scheme which is based on two dimensions—*neuroticism* and *extraversion-introversion.*

7. Other investigators have tried to build a taxonomy by relating personality traits to bodily physique. The major example is Sheldon's classification of *somatotypes* according to the dimensions of *endomorphy, mesomorphy,* and *ectomorphy.* Sheldon asserted that these dimensions of body type go together with three clusters of personality traits, *viscerotonia, somatotonia,* and *cerebrotonia.* The evidence indicates that the correlations between somatotype and personality are very much smaller than Sheldon had claimed initially, though some modest relation between physique and temperament may well be present.

8. Another approach centers on genetic factors. The existence of inherited dispositions which affect personality is suggested by consistencies in temperament, from early infancy through adulthood. Further evidence comes from studies that show that the scores on many personality inventories are more similar for identical than for fraternal twins.

CHAPTER 19

Psychopathology

In the preceding chapter, we considered differences in human personality traits. We now turn to conditions in which such differences go beyond the range of normal functioning and take on the appearance of psychological disorder. The study of such disorders is the province of ***psychopathology*** or, as it is sometimes called, ***abnormal psychology.*** There is considerable debate about how the subject matter of abnormal psychology is to be defined. Is it simply a problem of statistical deviance, of behavior that is markedly different from the norm? Or should we take the term *psychopathology* more literally and regard its manifestations as something akin to illness? But if these manifestations are illnesses, of what kind are they? Are they caused by some bodily disorder, such as a defect in brain function or a biochemical imbalance? Or are they better conceived of as *mental* illnesses whose origin is psychological, such as a learned defense against anxiety?

As we shall see, there is no one answer to these questions. The reason is that the various conditions that are generally subsumed under the rubric of psychopathology are a very mixed lot. For some, the term *illness* seems quite appropriate; for others, this is not so clear. In any case, there is little doubt that many of the conditions that come to the attention of the psychopathologist—the psychiatrist, the clinical psychologist, or other mental-health specialists—often cause considerable anguish and may seriously impair the afflicted person's functioning. Two examples will suffice here.

The first is a case of an ***obsessive-compulsive disorder*** (formerly called an ***obsessive neurosis;*** plural, ***neuroses***): "A farmer developed obsessive thoughts of hitting his three-year-old son over the head with a hammer. The father was completely unable to explain his 'horrible thoughts.' He stated that he loved his son very much and thought he must be going insane to harbor such thoughts" (Coleman, 1972, p. 233). In neurosis, the patient has not lost contact with reality. He can generally hold on to a job, maintain a household, and so on, no matter how miserable he may feel. The situation is different in a ***psychosis*** (plural, ***psychoses***), a broad category that includes some of the most severe mental disorders.* In psychoses, the patient's thoughts and deeds no longer meet the demands of reality. An example is a thirty-two-year-old woman with bizarre delusions and a diagnosis of schizophrenia:

> DR.: When did you come here?
> PT.: 1416, you remember, doctor . . .
> DR.: Do you know why you are here?
> PT.: Well in 1951 I changed into two men. President Truman was judge at my trial. I was convicted and hung . . .
> DR.: Can you tell me the name of this place?
> PT.: I have not been a drinker for 16 years. I am taking a mental rest after a "carter" assignment or "quill." You know, a "penwrap." I had contracts with Warner Brothers Studios and Eugene broke phonograph records but Mike protested. . . . I am made of flesh and blood—see, doctor (pulling up her dress) (Coleman, 1972, pp. 280–81).

We will begin our discussion of psychopathology by considering some of the historical roots of our conceptions of what "madness" is and how it should be dealt with.

DIFFERENT CONCEPTIONS OF MADNESS

Mental disorders existed for many millennia before psychiatrists appeared on the scene. Early mythological and religious writings are proof enough. The Greek hero, Ajax, slew a flock of sheep which he mistook for his enemies; King Saul of Judea alternated between bouts of murderous frenzy and suicidal depressions; and the Babylonian King Nebuchadnezzar walked on all fours in the belief that he was a wolf. Such phenomena were evidently not isolated instances. According to the Bible, young David feigned madness while seeking refuge from his enemies at the court of a Philistine king. This king had obviously encountered insanity before and upbraided his servants, "Do I lack madmen, that you have brought this fellow to play the madman in my presence?"

Insanity as Demonic Possession

What leads to mental disorder? One of the earliest theories held that the afflicted person was possessed by evil spirits. It followed that the cure for the malady was to drive the devils out. If the patient was lucky, the exorcism procedures were fairly mild; the unruly demons were calmed by music or were chased away by

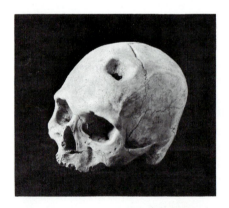

19.1 Trephining *A trephined prehistoric skull found in Peru. The patient apparently survived the operation for a while, for there is some evidence of bone healing. (Courtesy The American Museum of Natural History)*

---

* Modern psychiatrists have abandoned the distinction between neurosis and psychosis, and have largely dropped these terms from the current official diagnostic catalogue of their profession (the third edition of the *Diagnostic and Statistical Manual of Mental Disorders,* or *DSM-III*). But we will nevertheless use these two terms in the present account, at least in an informal way. To avoid them altogether is difficult, given the fact that they have become part of common parlance. The same holds for a number of other terms that are no longer used in official diagnosis; for example, *sociopath, hysteria,* and some others.

An early example of mental disorder
King Nebuchadnezzar as depicted by William Blake (1795). (Courtesy the Tate Gallery, London)

19.2 Witch hunts in sixteenth-century Europe *A witch about to be burned at the stake. (Courtesy the Bettmann Archive)*

prayers and religious rites. More often the techniques were less benign. One approach was to provide a physical escape hatch for the devils. According to some anthropologists, this may explain why Stone Age men sometimes cut large holes into their fellows' skulls; many such *trephined* skulls have been found, often with signs that the patient managed to survive the operation (Figure 19.1). The plausibility of this hypothesis is enhanced by the fact that trephining is still performed by some preliterate tribes, and for much the same reasons (Stewart, 1957). Yet another idea was to make things as uncomfortable for the devil as possible so as to induce him to escape. Accordingly, the patient was chained, immersed in boiling hot or ice-cold baths, was starved, flogged, or tortured. That such procedures usually drove the patient into worse and worse derangement is hardly surprising.

According to some medical historians, the demonological approach to mental disorder reached its culmination during the witch hunts of the sixteenth and seventeenth centuries (Zilboorg and Henry, 1941). This was a period marked by a host of social, political, and religious upheavals, of wars, famines, and pestilence, all of which triggered a search for scapegoats whose punishment might alleviate these ills. Persons accused of witchcraft were doomed to this role; according to most theological authorities of the times they had become possessed by striking a bargain with the devil, which gave them power to cause effects ranging from plagues and floods to sexual impotence and the souring of milk (Figure 19.2).

Since such people were clearly a menace to society, no measures were too stern to deal with them. As a result, there was an unrelenting series of witch hunts that involved most of Europe and whose bonfires claimed about 500,000 lives (Harris, 1974). Some of these unfortunates were undoubtedly deranged in one way or another; many were senile, some suffered from various delusions, from hysteria, or mania, and so on. Some may have experienced hallucinations under the influence of LSD-like drugs, taken either wittingly or by accident. Such hallucinogenic substances are now known to occur in grains that have been invaded by a certain fungus; it is quite possible that the girls whose visions sparked the Salem witchcraft trials had eaten bread made of such hallucinogenic rye (Caporael, 1976). But many of those accused of witchcraft seem not to have suffered from any mental disorder. Some may have participated in various local cults derived from pagan origins which orthodox Christianity condemned as a form of Satanism. Others probably fell prey to some neighbor's avarice, since a considerable proportion of a condemned person's property was awarded to his or her accuser (Kors and Peters, 1972).

Insanity as a Disease

The demonological theory of mental disorder is a thing of the past. Even in its heyday there was an alternative conception which attributed such conditions to natural causes. The difficulty was in specifying these causes. The great physicians of antiquity assumed that the key to mental derangement was an imbalance between the main body fluids or *humors,* a position that dominated medical thought until a few centuries ago. Later writers proposed different hypotheses. Some felt that the cause of mental disorder was an imbalance of nervous energy produced by overexcitement; others believed that such conditions depended upon the condition of the blood vessels of the brain (Mora, 1975).

HOSPITALS THAT WERE PRISONS

The belief that mental disorders have natural causes does not, however, automatically lead to a more humane treatment of the afflicted. It might if a ready cure were available but, until recently, there was little hope of that. As a result, the "madmen" were treated with little sympathy, for they seemed to have no common bond with sane humanity, and there was little likelihood that they ever would have. They were seen as a nuisance at best and a menace at worst. In either case, the interests of society seemed best served by "putting them away."

To this end, a number of special hospitals were established throughout Europe. But until the beginning of the nineteenth century (and in some cases, much later still), most of these were hospitals in name only. Their real function was to serve as a place of confinement in which all kinds of social undesirables were segregated from the rest of humankind—criminals, idlers, old people, epileptics, incurables of all sorts, and the mentally disturbed (Rosen, 1966). After they had been in the "hospital" for a few years, it became hard to distinguish among them. Their treatment was barbaric. One author describes conditions in the major mental hospital for Parisian women at the end of the eighteenth century: "Madwomen seized by fits of violence are chained like dogs at their cell doors, and separated from keepers and visitors alike by a long corridor protected by an iron grille; through this grille is passed their food and the straw on which they sleep; by means of rakes, part of the filth that surrounds them is cleaned out" (Foucault, 1965, p. 72).

To most of their contemporaries, this treatment seemed only natural; after all, the so-called madmen were like dangerous animals and had to be caged. But since such animals are interesting to watch, some of the hospitals took on another function—they became a zoo. At London's Bethlehem hospital (whose name was slurred until it was popularly known as Bedlam), the patients were exhibited to

19.3 The mentally disturbed on exhibit *(A) An eighteenth-century engraving by Hogarth of a tour of Bedlam. (Courtesy Philadelphia Museum of Art) (B) An admission ticket to view the insane.*

anyone curious enough to pay the required penny per visit. In 1814, there were 96,000 such visits (Figure 19.3).

A number of reformers gradually succeeded in eliminating the worst of these practices. Historians have given much of the credit to the French physician, Phillipe Pinel (1745–1826), who was put in charge of the Parisian hospital system in 1793 when the Revolution was at its height. Pinel wanted to remove the inmates' chains and fetters, but the government gave its permission only grudgingly (Figure 19.4). A high functionary argued with Pinel, "Citizen, are you mad yourself that you want to unchain these animals?" (Zilboorg and Henry, 1941, p. 322).

19.4 Pinel ordering the removal of the inmates' fetters *From a nineteenth-century painting by Charles Muller. (Courtesy the Bettmann Archive)*

Within a few decades, Pinel's efforts were followed by similar reforms elsewhere, primarily in England and the United States. This is not to say that all forms of physical restraint were abolished. Far from it. Patients considered violent were often put in straitjackets, wrapped in wet sheets, strapped to special confinement chairs, and held by various belts, straps, and locked gloves. The extent to which such devices were used depended upon the hospital's resources. Many of these hospitals were crowded by "pauper lunatics," who had the double misfortune of being both mentally disordered and poor. Their care was paid for by the community, whose taxpayers had even less patience for "budgetary frills" than their modern counterparts today. The result was serious overcrowding, far too few attendants, and a consequent resort to physical restraint. The policy of nonrestraint was regarded as an ideal, but this ideal was difficult to attain for any but the well-to-do (Hunter and Macalpine, 1974).

MENTAL DISORDER AS AN ORGANIC ILLNESS

Pinel and other reformers sounded one main theme: Madness is a disease. By this assertion, they transformed the inmates from prisoners to patients for whom a cure had to be found. To find such a cure, one first had to discover the cause of the disease (or rather, diseases, since it was already known that there were several varieties of mental disorder). Today, almost two hundred years after Pinel, we are still searching for the causes of most of them.

At least initially, the notion of mental disorder as an illness implied a bodily cause, most likely some disease of the brain. Proponents of this **somatogenic** hypothesis (from *soma,* "body") could point to such relevant discoveries as the effects of cerebral strokes in impairing speech (see Chapter 2). But the somatogenic position gained its greatest impetus at the end of the nineteenth century from the discovery of the organic cause of a once widely prevalent psychosis, **general paresis.** This psychosis is characterized by a general decline in physical and psychological functions, culminating in marked personality aberrations which may include childish delusions ("I am the Prince of Wales") or wild hypochondriacal depressions ("My heart has stopped beating"). Without treatment, there is increasing deterioration, progressive paralysis, and death within a few years (Dale, 1975).

By the end of the nineteenth century, the conviction had grown that general paresis has its roots in a syphilitic infection contracted many years prior to the appearance of overt symptoms. In some untreated syphilitics (according to recent estimates, perhaps 5 percent), the infection seems to be cured, but the spirochete that caused it remains, invading and damaging the nervous system. Experimental proof came in 1897. Several paretic patients were inoculated with matter taken from syphilitic sores, but none of them developed any of the earlier symptoms of syphilis.* This was a clear sign that they had contracted the disease previously. Once the cause of the disease was known, the discovery of its cure and prevention was just a matter of time. The preferred modern treatment is with penicillin. Its effectiveness is unquestioned. While general paresis at one time accounted for

* Modern medical and scientific practitioners are considerably more sensitive than our forebears to the ethical issues raised by this and similar studies. Today such a procedure would require the patients' informed consent.

more than 10 percent of all admissions to mental hospitals, today it accounts for less than 1 percent (Dale, 1975).

The conquest of general paresis reinforced the beliefs of somatogenicists that ultimately all mental disorders would be traced to some organic cause. They could point to some successes. Several psychoses had been explained as brain malfunctions. In the case of senile patients, the cause is atrophy of cortical cells; in the case of chronic alcoholics, the cause is a change in cerebral structures brought on by the dietary deficits that often accompany alcoholism. The question was whether this view could account for all mental disorders.

MENTAL DISORDER AS A PSYCHOLOGICAL ILLNESS

The achievements of the somatogenic approach were very impressive, but by the end of the nineteenth century it became clear that it could not include the full spectrum of mental disorders. One of the main stumbling blocks was neurosis, especially in the form of hysteria (which is now called a **conversion disorder,** see p. 670).

The story of hysteria is part of the background that led to psychoanalytic theory. For now, we will only reiterate the key discoveries. Hysteria featured a variety of symptoms that seemed to be organic but really were not; for example, paralyzed limbs that moved perfectly well during hypnosis. This suggested that hysteria is a **psychogenic** disorder; that is, a disorder whose origin is psychological rather than organic. A number of cases studied by French hypnotists of the nineteenth century seemed to have their origins in traumatic incidents. A patient trapped in a derailed railroad car developed hysterical paralysis of his legs; the legs were actually in perfect physical condition but the patient's belief that they were crushed ultimately produced his hysterical symptoms. Freud's theories were cast in a similar psychogenic mold, but they were much more elaborate, focusing on repressed sexual fantasies in early childhood that threatened to break into consciousness and could only be held back by drastic defense maneuvers, of which the somatic symptom was one (see Chapter 12).

Exactly what produced the hysteria is not our present concern. The important point is that by the turn of the century most theorists had become convinced that the disorder was psychogenic. This was another way of saying that there are illnesses that have mental *causes* as well as mental *symptoms.*

EVALUATING THE SOMATOGENIC-PSYCHOGENIC DISTINCTION

The distinction between somatogenic and psychogenic disorders is sometimes criticized as artificial. The argument is that all behavior is ultimately based on organic processes in the nervous system. But if so, what remains of the distinction? Doesn't it then simply boil down to the difference between conditions whose organic basis has already been discovered and those for which it is as yet unknown?

The answer is no. There is no doubt that all psychological processes—whether in psychosis, neurosis, or normalcy—have a neurophysiological underpinning. But this doesn't necessarily mean that the proper scientific explanation of all psychological phenomena is necessarily at this neurophysiological level. As an example, consider two persons who can speak and see but who are unable to read. One of the two has a certain combination of brain lesions that disconnect the regions that control vision from those that handle language functions (see Chapter 2,

p. 47). The other person can't read because she was never taught. One can maintain that in a way both conditions are organically caused. In one case, the organic basis is the set of brain lesions; in the other, it consists of the failure to establish the various neurological changes that are brought about by learning to read. But it is perfectly obvious that while the organic account is a useful explanation in the one case, it provides no illumination in the other. This is not just because we don't yet know much of anything about the neurological basis of learning. Even if we did, to explain why someone is illiterate in terms of, say, a specification of millions of synaptic connections that were or were not formed is a much more cumbersome account than the simple statement that she can't read because she never learned.

The same analysis applies to the distinction between somatogenic and psychogenic disorders. To say that a disorder is somatogenic is to claim that the most direct explanation of the malfunction is at the organic level, as in the case of the syphilitic infection in general paresis. To say that the disorder is psychogenic is to assert that the most direct explanation of what ails the patient is at the psychological level, such as a learned mode of coping with anxiety in hysteria. This is not to deny that all psychological events are ultimately based on some underlying neurological processes. Of course they are, but for many purposes this fact is of little relevance.

THE PATHOLOGY MODEL

Whatever their views about the somatogenic or psychogenic origins of mental disorders, most psychiatrists agreed on one thing—these conditions are illnesses. They are called *mental* illnesses because their primary symptoms are psychological, but they are illnesses all the same, in some ways analogous to such nonpsychiatric illnesses as tuberculosis and diabetes. Given this assumption, it was only logical to propose that one should try to understand (and treat) such diseases according to the same broad set of rules by means of which we try to understand disease in general.

Just what are these rules? We will here class them together under a very general category that we'll call the ***pathology model.*** (Different practitioners subscribe to different subcategories of this model, of which more below.) According to the pathology model, various overt symptoms are produced by an underlying cause—the disease or pathology. The main object of the would-be healer is to remove the underlying pathology. After this is done, the symptoms will presumably disappear. As here used, the term *pathology model* makes no particular assumption about the kind of pathology that underlies a particular mental disorder. It might be somatogenic or psychogenic or perhaps a little of both.

Subcategories of the Pathology Model

There are a number of different approaches to psychopathology, which can be regarded as subcategories of the pathology model. We will briefly present a few of these. As we will see, some of these models are probably more appropriate to some forms of mental disorder than to others.

THE MEDICAL MODEL

Some authors endorse the ***medical model,*** which is a particular version of the pathology model which makes certain further assumptions. To begin with, it assumes that the underlying pathology is organic. Its practitioners therefore employ various forms of somatic therapy such as drugs. In addition, it takes for granted that the would-be healers are members of the medical profession (Siegler and Osmond, 1974).

THE PSYCHOANALYTIC MODEL

Adherents of the ***psychoanalytic model*** follow the general conception of psychopathology developed by Sigmund Freud and other psychoanalysts. In their view, the symptoms of mental disorder are produced by psychogenic causes. The underlying pathology is a constellation of unconscious conflicts and various defenses against anxiety, often rooted in early childhood experience. Treatment is by some form of psychotherapy based on psychoanalytic principles, which allows the patient to gain insight into his own inner conflicts and thus removes the root of the pathology.

THE LEARNING MODEL

The ***learning model*** tends to view mental disorders as the result of some form of maladaptive learning. According to some practitioners (usually called ***behavior therapists***), these faulty learning patterns are best described and treated by the laws of classical and instrumental conditioning. According to others (often called ***cognitive therapists***), they are more properly regarded as faulty modes of thinking that can be dealt with by changing the way in which the patient thinks about himself and his situation.

Mental Disorder as Pathology

To get a better understanding of how mental disorder is viewed from the perspective of the general pathology model—in principle, regardless of subcategory—we must first ask what is meant by disease in general. A moment's reflection tells us that the concept of disease is both a scientific and an evaluative notion. To say that measles and rickets are diseases is to say something about the kinds of causes that produce such conditions—infections, dietary insufficiencies, and so on. But it also says that such conditions are undesirable. They produce pain and disability, and sometimes they lead to death. Speaking most generally, they are conditions that interfere with the organism's proper functioning as a biological system.

The extension of the disease concept to the psychological realm is based on certain parallels between the effects of psychopathology and those of nonpsychiatric, organic disorders. Where ordinary organic illnesses are often associated with physical pain, many mental disorders are accompanied by psychological distress in the form of anxiety or depression. (Some may lead to death, as in the case of suicidal depression.) But the most important criterion is the interference with proper psychological functioning. The mentally disordered person may be unable to form or maintain gratifying relationships with others. Or she may be unable to work effectively. Or she may be unable to relax and play. According to advocates of the pathology model of mental disorder, the inability to function properly in these psychological areas is the behavioral analogue of the malfunctions in such biological domains as respiration, circulation, digestion, and so on, that characterize ordinary organic illnesses.

Some special questions arise from the fact that the terms *psychopathology* and *abnormal psychology* are often used interchangeably. Does this mean that psychopathology necessarily involves behavior that deviates from some statistical norm? Advocates of the pathology model would answer no. They would concede that in actual practice mental disorder often involves aberrations from what people usually do in a given situation; the disordered person may hear voices, suffer from severe mood swings, or behave in ways that are clearly bizarre. It was surely for reasons of this sort that the term *abnormal* has become a near-synonym for *psychopathological.* But within the framework of the pathology model, deviation from a statistical norm is not what defines psychopathology. Consider the Black Death which wiped out half of the population in the fourteenth century. At that time, having the plague may well have been statistically normal. But this did not change the plague's status as a disease. The same applies to behavior. Certain behavior patterns may be pathological no matter how common they are.

Classifying Mental Disorders

The ways in which we decide what is and what is not a mental disorder are by no means settled. But no less controversial is the issue of classifying these disorders. How do we decide whether two patients have the same disorder or two different ones?

To answer this question, practitioners have tried to set up classificatory schemes for mental disorders analogous to the diagnostic systems in other branches of medicine. Here, as elsewhere in science, the purpose of a taxonomy is to bring some order into what at first seem a host of diverse phenomena. If the taxonomy is valid, then conditions that have been grouped together will turn out to have the same cause, and better yet, the same cure.

As in other branches of medicine, the diagnostic process begins with a consideration of the overt **symptoms.** In nonpsychiatric disorders, these might be such complaints as fever or chest pains. Examples of symptoms in psychopathology would be anxiety or a profound sense of worthlessness. The trouble is that an individual symptom is rarely enough for diagnosis; fever occurs in a multitude of organic illnesses, and anxiety is found in many different mental disorders. As a result, the diagnostician often looks for a pattern of symptoms that tend to go together, a so-called **syndrome.** An example of such a syndrome in psychopathology is a set of symptoms that includes disorganization of thinking, withdrawal from others, and hallucinations. This syndrome is characteristic of schizophrenia.

By groupings of this kind, psychiatrists have set up a taxonomy of mental disorders. The list covers an enormous range that includes mental deficiency, senile deterioration, schizophrenia, affective disorders such as mania and depression, various conditions that were once covered under the general heading of neuroses (for example, phobias, obsessive-compulsive disorders, and conversion dis-

Emil Kraepelin (1855–1925) The major figure in psychiatric classification, Kraepelin distinguished between two groups of severe mental disorders, schizophrenia and manic-depressive psychosis (now called bipolar affective disorder). (Courtesy Historical Pictures Service)

orders), psychophysiological disorders such as hypertension produced by emotional stress, personality disorders such as antisocial personality, alcoholism and drug addiction, and various forms of sexual deviation.

The most recent taxonomy used by psychiatrists is embodied in the new diagnostic manual of their profession, DSM-III (1980). This departs from its predecessors in a number of ways. The most important is a greater stress on the description of disorders rather than on theories about their underlying cause. As a result, a number of disorders that had formerly been grouped together because of a—psychoanalytically inspired—belief that they are ultimately alike, are now classified under different headings (for example, various conditions that had been regarded as subcategories of neurosis; see pp. 665–71 below). One consequence of the adoption of this new manual has been a considerable increase in diagnostic reliability (Eysenck, Wakefield, and Friedman, 1983).

Explaining Disorder: Diathesis, Stress, and Pathology

Adherents of the pathology model believe that all—or at least many—mental disorders will ultimately prove to result from underlying causes, some organic and others psychological, that mirror the pathological processes found in other diseases. But since many of these pathologies are still unknown, how can we evaluate the assertion that they are actually there? One approach is to analyze a disease that is already well understood. This can then provide a standard against which the claims of the model's advocates can be judged. Our illustrative example will be an organic illness, diabetes.

The first step in the analysis of this, as of other medical disorders, is to look at the overt symptoms. In diabetes, these include declining strength, a marked increase in the quantity of urine passed, enormous thirst, and, in many cases, voracious appetite. The next step is to look for the underlying physiological pathology of which this syndrome is a manifestation. This pathology was discovered to be a disorder of carbohydrate metabolism which is produced by an insufficient secretion of insulin (see Chapter 3). These pathological conditions represent the immediate cause of the symptoms. But a full understanding of the disease requires a further step, an inquiry into the more remote causes that led to the present pathology.

When the causal chain is traced backward, two general factors emerge. One is a predisposition (technically called a *diathesis*) toward the illness. The other is a set of environmental conditions which *stress* the system and precipitate the defective insulin mechanism; for example, obesity. In diabetes, the diathesis is based on genetic factors that create a marked susceptibility to the disease, which is then triggered by precipitating stress.

The treatment follows from the analysis of the cause-and-effect relations. Since the diabetic's pancreas does not secrete enough insulin, this substance must be supplied from the outside. Further control of the faulty metabolism is then imposed by an appropriate diet (Dolger and Seeman, 1985).

The preceding discussion illustrates the so-called *diathesis-stress* conception which has proved helpful in the understanding of many organic as well as mental disorders. Many of these conditions result from the interaction of a diathesis that makes the individual potentially vulnerable to a particular disorder, and some form of environmental stress that transforms the potentiality into actuality. Just

SYMPTOMS:

| Declining strength | Unusual amount of urine | Intense thirst | Voracious appetite |

Disorder of carbohydrate metabolism

IMMEDIATE CAUSE:
THE PHYSIOLOGICAL
PATHOLOGY

Insufficient secretion of insulin

REMOTE CAUSES:

Diathesis (hereditary predisposition)

Precipitating stress (e.g., obesity)

19.5 The pathology model as applied to diabetes

what the diathesis is that creates the vulnerability depends on the particular disorder. In many cases, as in diabetes, it is based on genetic constitution. In others, it may be produced by various social and psychological factors, such as chronic feelings of worthlessness.

Figure 19.5 provides a schematic summary of our discussion of diabetes, a nonpsychiatric ailment. The figure gives us an idea of what the analysis of a disease looks like when the disease is reasonably well understood. This is the framework we will use when we ask whether a particular mental disorder is an illness, and if so, in what sense. How such disorders are treated will be taken up in the next chapter.

SCHIZOPHRENIA

One of the most serious conditions in the whole field of psychopathology is *schizophrenia* (from the Greek *schizo,* "split" and *phrene,* "mind").* The term was coined in 1911 by the Swiss psychiatrist, Eugen Bleuler (1857–1939) to designate what he regarded as the main attribute of this disorder—a fragmentation of mental functions (Bleuler, 1911).

Schizophrenia is quite prevalent. According to one estimate, about one in a hundred Americans will need treatment for this disorder at some period during his or her lifetime, typically between the ages of fifteen and forty. At any one time, about four hundred thousand persons are hospitalized with this condition, accounting for about half of all of the beds in the country's mental hospitals. The total cost to society, including the indirect costs of time lost from employment and so on, has been estimated at around $14 billion a year (Babigian, 1975). The total cost in human anguish to patients and their families is incalculable.

Many investigators believe that schizophrenia is a disease, in the straightfor-

Eugen Bleuler   (Courtesy National Library of Medicine)

* This etymological derivation is responsible for a widespread confusion between schizophrenia, which is a psychosis, and *multiple (or split) personality,* which may be regarded as a rare kind of neurosis. While both fall under the general rubric of psychopathology, the two conditions have little in common.

ward, somatogenic, sense of the term. To evaluate this position, we will discuss the disorder within the same framework we used when we considered the interpretation of the organic disease, diabetes—the symptom pattern, the underlying pathology, the less immediate causes such as genetic predisposition, and the precipitating factors.

The Symptoms

The fragmentation of mental life characteristic of schizophrenia can be seen in disorders of cognition, of motivation and emotion, and of social relationships. Few patients who are diagnosed as schizophrenics show all of these signs. How many symptoms must be present, and in what degree, to justify this diagnosis depends upon the clinician's judgment. Under the circumstances, it is not surprising that diagnostic agreement is far from perfect.

DISORDERS OF COGNITION

Disturbance of thought   A key symptom is a pervasive thought disturbance. The schizophrenic doesn't "think straight"; he can't maintain one unified guiding thought, but rather skips from one idea to the next. An example is a fragment of a letter written by one of Bleuler's patients:

> I am writing on paper. The pen I am using is from a factory called "Perry & Co." This factory is in England. I assume this. Behind the name of Perry Co., the city of London is inscribed; but not the city. The city of London is in England. I know this from my school-days. Then, I always liked geography. My last teacher in that subject was Professor August A. He was a man with black eyes. I also like black eyes. There are also blue and gray eyes and other sorts too. I have heard it said that snakes have green eyes. All people have eyes. There are some, too, who are blind. These blind people are led about by a boy (Bleuler, 1950, p. 17).

This kind of simple idea-hopping sometimes leads to an endless cataloguing of associated items:

> I wish you, therefore, a very happy, pleasant, healthy, blessed and fruit-crop-rich year; and also many good wine-harvest years thereafter, as well as good potato-crop years; as well as fine potato years, and sauerkraut years, and sprouts years, and cucumber years, and nut years; a good egg-year, and also a good cheese year (Bleuler, 1950, p. 28).

Disturbance of attention   Such examples show that the schizophrenic may have difficulty in suppressing irrelevant ideas that come from within. Similar problems arise with irrelevant stimuli that assail her from without. We have seen that in ordinary perception one focuses on some aspects of the world while de-emphasizing others. We somehow filter out the irrelevant stimuli so that we can follow a conversation without being continually distracted by other people's voices or radiator clankings or whatever (see Chapter 6). But schizophrenics seem to be less efficient in attending selectively. They hear (and see and feel) too much, perhaps because they can't exclude what is extraneous. Some patients (only mildly disordered or recovered) describe what this feels like:

During the last while back I have noticed that noises all seem louder to me than they were before. It's as if someone turned up the volume. . . . I notice it most with background noises. . . . Now they seem to be just as loud and sometimes louder than the main noises that are going on. . . . it makes it difficult to keep your mind on something when there's so much going on that you can't help listening to (McGhie and Chapman, 1961, p. 105).

LOSING CONTACT

A common facet of schizophrenia is a withdrawal from contact with other people. In some patients this withdrawal begins quite early; they have had few friends and little or no contact with the opposite sex. What brings on this withdrawal is still unknown. One possibility is that it is a defense against the overstimulation to which they are exposed because of their inability to filter out the irrelevant. Another possibility is that it grows out of pathological family relations during childhood and adolescence.

Whatever the reason that led up to it, the schizophrenic's withdrawal from social contacts has drastic consequences. The individual starts to live in a private world of his own, a condition which becomes increasingly worse. The withdrawal from others provides fewer and fewer opportunities for *social-reality testing* in which one's own ideas are checked against those of others and corrected when necessary. As a result, the schizophrenic's ideas become ever more idiosyncratic, until the patient may have trouble communicating with others even if he wants to; they may very well rebuff him because they can't understand him and think he's "weird." The result is further withdrawal, which leads to further idiosyncracy, still further withdrawal, and so on. The final consequence of this vicious cycle is a condition in which the patient can no longer distinguish between his own thoughts and fantasies and external reality. He has lost contact.

Once this state is reached, it becomes extremely difficult to understand what a patient is trying to say. To begin with, there is the basic thought disturbance in which irrelevant ideas crowd each other out in fast succession. But, in addition, there is a whole set of private fantasies, personal symbolisms, and special words invented by the patient himself *(neologisms).* As an example, consider a patient's answer to the question "Who is the doctor in charge of your ward?"

A body just like yours, sir. They can make you black or white. I say good morning, but he just comes through there. At first it was a colony. They said it was heaven. These buildings were not solid at the time, and I am positive this is the same place. They have others just like it. People die, and all the microbes talk over there, and *prestigitis* you know is sending you from here to another world. . . . I was sent by the government to the United States to Washington to some star, and they had a pretty nice country there. Now you have a body like a young man who says he is of the prestigitis (White, 1932, p. 228).

ELABORATING THE PRIVATE WORLD

The private world of some schizophrenics is organized in elaborate detail. They have strange beliefs, and may see and hear things that aren't there.

Delusions   Once having initiated the break with the social world, many schizophrenics develop **ideas of reference.** They begin to believe that external events are specially related to them, personally. The patient observes some strangers talking and concludes that they are talking about *her;* she sees people walk by and decides that they are following *her;* she hears a radio commercial and is sure that it contains a specially disguised message aimed at *her.* Eventually, these ideas become systematized in the form of false beliefs or **delusions.** Such delusions are especially common in a subcategory called **paranoid schizophrenia.**

An example of paranoid schizophrenia is a delusion of persecution. The patient is sure that *they*—the Communists or the FBI or the Jews or the members of the American Medical Association or whoever—are spying on him and plotting against him. This delusion gradually expands as the patient gathers further evidence which convinces him that his wife and children, the ward psychiatrist, and the man in the bed near the door, are all part of the conspiracy.

Hallucinations Delusions result from misinterpretations of real events. In contrast, **hallucinations** are perceived experiences that occur in the absence of actual sensory stimulation. This phenomenon is fairly common in schizophrenia. The patient "hears" voices, or, less commonly, "sees" various persons or objects. The voices may be of God, the devil, relatives, or neighbors. If the patient can make out what they say, she hears that they are talking about her, sometimes threateningly and sometimes obscenely.

The best guess is that such hallucinations reflect an inability to distinguish between one's own memory images and perceptual experiences that originate from without. Some evidence for this view comes from a study in which hallucinating patients were asked to press a key whenever they heard one of their voices. At the same time, the investigator recorded muscular activity in the patient's larynx. The results showed that the patients generally experienced auditory hallucinations when their larynx became especially active. It appears that the patients were talking to themselves and then interpreted their own inner speech as originating from outside. They "heard themselves talk" and thought they heard voices (McGuigan, 1966).

DISORDERS OF MOTIVATION AND EMOTION

Thus far our focus has been on the schizophrenic's thoughts. When we look at his motives and feelings, we find similar evidence of disruption and fragmentation. In the early phase of the disorder, there is often a marked emotional oversensitivity in which the slightest rejection may trigger an extreme response. As time goes on, this sensitivity declines. In many patients it dips below normal until there is virtual indifference to their own fate or that of others. This apathy is especially pronounced in long-term schizophrenics, who stare vacantly, their faces expressionless, and answer questions in a flat and toneless voice.

In some cases, emotional reaction is preserved but the emotion is strikingly inappropriate to the situation. A patient may break into happy laughter at the news of a brother's death "because she was so pleased at receiving letters with black borders"; another becomes enraged when someone says hello (Bleuler, 1950).

DISORDERS OF BEHAVIOR

Given the disruptions in the schizophrenics' thoughts, motives, and feelings, it is hardly surprising that there are often concomitant disorders in how they act.

19.6 Patient with a diagnosis of catatonic schizophrenia who spent virtually all waking hours in this crouched position (Photograph by Bill Bridges, Globe Photos)

Some patients develop bizarre mannerisms. They may grimace, or make odd, repetitive gestures, or continually imitate the movements of people around them. Other patients—in a subcategory called **catatonic schizophrenia**—remain virtually motionless for long periods of time. They may be standing or sitting, or they may adopt some unusual posture which they often maintain for hours on end (Figure 19.6). While in this state, the patient seems to be completely oblivious to everything around him. In actual fact, this is not the case. When questioned later, the patient shows excellent recall of conversations that were carried on in front of him while he was immobile.

According to some theorists, the patient's immobility is a secondary reaction to the basic disturbance of thought and attention. The schizophrenic is overstimulated as it is, but this stimulation becomes even greater when she is in motion. So she stops moving, in sheer self-defense. As one patient put it, "I did not want to move, because if I did everything changed around me and upset me horribly so I remained still to hold on to a sense of permanence" (quoted in Broen, 1968, p. 138).

The Search for the Underlying Pathology

We have described the various symptoms that define schizophrenia. As in diabetes or in any other organic disease, the next step is to look for the underlying malfunction from which these symptoms spring. But since schizophrenia is not an ordinary (so to speak, orthodox) disease, in as much as its main symptoms are behavioral, any attempt to discover its pathology has to involve two steps. To begin with, one has to specify the underlying **psychological malfunction** of which the symptoms are a manifestation. This done, then—if there is reason to suspect that the disorder is somatogenic—one searches for the organic pathology of which this psychological malfunction is an expression.

WHAT IS THE PSYCHOLOGICAL DEFICIT?

A widely held view is that the schizophrenic's primary trouble is cognitive. The details of the proposed explanations vary, but most of them agree that the patient's major deficit is an inability to keep things in proper focus. Normal people focus in both space and time. They perceive objects without being distracted by extraneous stimuli; they execute plans without interference by irrelevant responses. Not so the schizophrenic who has considerable difficulty in holding onto one line of thought or action and is forever lured off the main path (Shakow, 1977).

Given this deficit, the patient's many disturbances of language and thought follow. His speech is marked by one tangent after another; sometimes the sheer sound of a word is enough to trigger a series of rhyming associations, as in "How are you today by the bay as a gay, doctor?" (Davison and Neale, 1982, p. 399). His inability to disregard irrelevant attributes leads to strange conceptualizations in which incongruous items are grouped together. One patient explained that Jesus, cigar boxes, and sex are all identical. This was because all three are encircled—the head of Jesus by a halo, a cigar box by the tax band, and a woman by a man's sexually interested glance (Von Domarus, 1944).

It is tempting to believe that the other main symptoms of schizophrenia—social withdrawal and emotional inappropriateness—are consequences of the primary cognitive disturbance, though whether this is actually so is still unknown. Social withdrawal, at least initially, may be a defense against overstimulation. The relative absence or inappropriateness of emotional feeling may reflect yet another aspect of the fragmentation of the schizophrenic's mental life. Certain other symptoms, such as delusions and hallucinations, may be further consequences of the basic thought disturbance. Bleuler believed that these symptoms are the elaborations of the private world of a person who has lost contact with other people and can no longer distinguish between his private fantasies and external reality.

WHAT IS THE ORGANIC PATHOLOGY?

Many investigators are convinced that the psychological deficit that underlies schizophrenia is an expression of an organic pathology. This belief persists despite the fact that we still don't know just what this organic pathology is. Under the circumstances, what accounts for this belief?

Cross-cultural arguments for an organic basis One argument is the pattern of results obtained by cross-cultural studies. It turns out that there is a remarkable similarity in what different peoples consider insane. One investigator studied Eskimo villagers on an Arctic island and a group of Yorubas, a tribe in West Africa. Both groups had a word for "being crazy." Among the Yorubas, a person is called *were* if he hears voices where there are none, laughs when there is nothing to laugh at, talks all the time or not at all, picks up sticks and leaves for no reason except to put them in a pile, tears off his clothes, defecates in public, or suddenly attacks others with a weapon. This pattern of bizarre symptoms would probably lead to a diagnosis of schizophrenia in a Western society.

Similar patterns of behavior characterize people that the Eskimos consider "crazy" (their word happens to be *nuthkavihak*). Interestingly enough, the prevalence of such conditions is roughly comparable to that found in Western societies. Among samples collected in Canadian and Swedish villages, the rate of schizophrenia was 5.6 per 1,000. Among the Yorubas, 6.8 per 1,000 were described as *were* by local village headmen; among the Eskimos, 4.4 per 1,000 were regarded as *nuthkavihak* by neighbors or friends (Murphy, 1976).

On the face of it, these results suggest that schizophrenia has an organic basis, at least in part. A psychogenic theory would emphasize factors in the social environment, most likely some aspect of the way the patient was treated as a child. Since different cultures differ widely in their child-rearing practices, we would expect rather different rates of incidence. The fact that a disorder that resembles schizophrenia is found in many different cultures, and occurs with about the same rate of incidence in all of them, suggests that some of the causal factors lie elsewhere.

Biological arguments Another line of evidence that is sometimes used to buttress a somatogenic interpretation of schizophrenia is the therapeutic effect of a group of drugs called **phenothiazines.** The effect of these drugs seems to be fairly specific to schizophrenia. They lead to a marked alleviation of primary schizophrenic symptoms, that is, thought disorder, social withdrawal, and hallucinations. On the other hand, they have little or no effect on nonschizophrenic symptoms such as anxiety, depression, and guilt (Klein and Davis, 1969). Some

653

authors regard these results as an argument for an organic basis of the disorder, reasoning by analogy to the effects of drugs on many ordinary diseases, as in the case of insulin and diabetes. Whether this line of reasoning is valid is debatable; the fact that an organic treatment alleviates—or even cures—a disorder does not really prove that the disorder has an organic cause.

Perhaps the strongest argument of all comes from genetic studies. Their results have convinced most investigators that schizophrenia has an important hereditary component. But how would such a genetic factor exert its influence? The most reasonable hypothesis is that it does so by some modification of normal neurological functioning. We will present the details of the genetic evidence in a later section; for now, we only note that such a genetic factor exists and that it—together with the cross-cultural evidence and the effects of antischizophrenic drugs—is an argument for a somatogenic theory of schizophrenia.

Malfunctioning neurotransmitters Most recent investigators believe that the underlying organic pathology is some malfunction of neurotransmitters, the substances whose secretion by one neuron may either trigger or inhibit an impulse in another neuron on the other side of the synapse. A likely candidate is ***dopamine.*** This is one of the ***catecholamines,*** transmitters liberated by neurons which have an arousing function in various parts of the brain (see Chapter 2). According to the dopamine hypothesis, many neurons in the schizophrenic's brain have become oversensitive to dopamine. One line of evidence comes from the effect of the group of drugs called ***phenothiazines.*** As mentioned before, phenothiazines are known to block dopamine at the synapse (Figure 19.7). This dopamine blockade is more pronounced in some phenothiazine drugs than in others. As predicted by the dopamine hypothesis, the stronger the blockade, the more therapeutic the drug (Snyder, 1976).

If a decrease of dopamine activity makes schizophrenics better, an increase should presumably make them worse. This is indeed the case. One group of investigators injected small doses of a drug that increases dopamine activity into the veins of schizophrenics who were in a comparatively mild state. Within a minute, the patients' symptoms became wild and extreme. One started to shred a pad of paper, announcing that he had been sending and receiving messages from ancient Egypt. Others became catatonic (Davis, 1974). Related effects are seen in normals who take overdoses of amphetamines. These are stimulants which enhance dopamine activity. If taken often enough and in large enough doses, they produce a temporary ***amphetamine psychosis*** that is in many ways quite similar to paranoid schizophrenia (Angrist et al., 1974). As the dopamine hypothesis would predict, phenothiazines that block dopamine activity at the synapse will also reduce the psychotic symptoms that follow amphetamine overuse.

Why should an oversensitivity to dopamine produce the psychotic reactions characteristic of schizophrenia? One possibility is that a hyperreactive dopamine system is equivalent to chronic overstimulation. When dopamine-releasing neurons in the limbic system of the brain are destroyed, the animals ignore sensory stimuli (Ungerstedt and Ljungberg, 1974). Perhaps the opposite is true when dopamine tracts are overreactive. This may cause an inability to ignore anything, whether sensory messages from the outside or irrelevant thoughts from the inside, leading to that jangling, screaming cognitive overload which some schizophrenics describe in retrospective accounts of their condition (Carlson, 1977).

Despite some intriguing evidence in its favor, as yet the dopamine hypothesis is

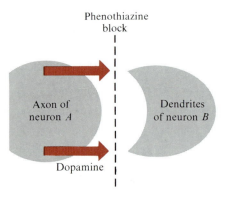

19.7   The dopamine-block hypothesis of phenothiazine action

still what its name implies—a hypothesis. Not all investigators subscribe to it; for example, some authors believe that the transmitter malfunctioning lies elsewhere, specifically in an insufficiency of *norephinephrine* (Stein and Wise, 1971). But whatever the final verdict on issues of detail, it is very likely that our eventual understanding of schizophrenia will include some reference to a biochemical defect.

More Remote Causes of Schizophrenia

We have considered several analyses of the basic pathology in schizophrenia, including hypotheses about the underlying psychological deficit and some guesses about organic malfunctions. These hypotheses about pathological processes—at either the psychological or the physiological level—are about the *immediate causes* of the disorder. The next question concerns causes that are less immediate and further back in time. As we have seen in our discussion of diabetes, any attempt to understand a disease involves both a consideration of its immediate causes (a metabolic malfunction brought on by insulin insufficiency) and a search for causes that are more remote (genetic factors, environmental effects) that might suggest a possible diathesis-stress interpretation. We will follow the same approach in our discussion of schizophrenia.

HEREDITARY PREDISPOSITION

Evidence for a genetic factor   Does schizophrenia have a hereditary basis? This question has been studied by the same means used to assess the role of heredity in other human traits such as intelligence. The basic approach is to consider family resemblance. In schizophrenia, as in intelligence, this resemblance is considerable. For example, the likelihood that a person who has a schizophrenic sibling is schizophrenic himself or will eventually become so is about 8 percent; this compares to a 1 percent risk of schizophrenia in the general population (Rosenthal, 1970). But again, as in the area of intelligence, such family resemblances don't settle anything about the nature-nurture issue, for they can be interpreted either way. For more conclusive evidence we have to turn to the familiar methodological standbys that are used to disentangle the contributions of heredity and environment—studies of twins and of adopted children. A widely used method focuses on twins, one of whom is schizophrenic. The question is whether the schizophrenic's twin is schizophrenic as well. The probability of this event, technically called *concordance,* is 44 percent if the twins are identical, compared to only 9 percent if they are fraternal and of the same sex (averaged over eleven studies; Rosenthal, 1970). Further evidence comes from adoption studies. Children born to schizophrenic mothers and placed in foster homes within a week or so after birth, are much more likely to become schizophrenic than persons in a matched control group of adoptees born to normal mothers (Heston, 1966).

The specificity of the genetic factor   There is evidently an inherited predisposition to schizophrenia. But how specific is this predisposition? Is it specific for schizophrenia only? Or is it a more general susceptibility that renders its possessor liable to other mental disorders as well?

The evidence suggests that there is some specificity. For example, schizophrenia and bipolar affective disorder (see p. 659) are genetically distinct (Rosenthal, 1970). But the genetic effect seems to have a more general side. Adoptees born of schizophrenic mothers are almost three times more likely than those born to normal mothers to exhibit serious social or psychological problems in later life, quite apart from schizophrenia. Some have police records for assault or other impulsive, antisocial acts; others are alcoholics; still others are emotionally unstable (Heston and Denney, 1968).

One interpretation of these results is that the underlying diathesis toward schizophrenia is determined by many genes. The greater the number of pathological genes carried by an individual, the greater his chance of becoming schizophrenic. If this number is smaller, it tends to predispose the person to lesser psychological malfunctions. These probably have to be within a schizophrenia-related spectrum, which includes some of the characteristics found in schizophrenia proper, such as looseness of thought, withdrawal, and so on. But the schizophrenic genes would presumably have no effect on the likelihood of developing disorders outside this spectrum, such as bipolar affective disorder or conversion disorders.

ENVIRONMENTAL STRESS

The preceding discussion indicates that schizophrenia has a genetic basis. But there is no doubt that environment also plays a role. One line of evidence comes from identical twins. Their concordance for schizophrenia is considerable, but is much less than 100 percent. Since identical twins have the same genotype, there must be some nongenetic factors that also have a say in the determination of who becomes schizophrenic and who does not.

What are these nongenetic factors? As yet, there is no consensus. We will consider a few lines of evidence that relate to various potentially stress-producing situations. Some involve the person's social class and economic condition; others concern his family. According to many modern investigators, these and other stress-producing environmental factors may bring out the latent pathology in a person with a genetic predisposition toward schizophrenia and will eventually precipitate the actual disorder, much as obesity or continued emotional stress precipitates diabetes. The stronger the diathesis, the less stress would presumably be required to convert the predisposition into actuality (Meehl, 1962; Gottesman and Shields, 1982).

Social class In searching for environmental causes, sociologically minded investigators have focused upon social class. They have found a sizable relationship. The proportion of schizophrenics is much higher at the bottom of the socioeconomic hierarchy than it is at the top. According to one study, the ratio is 9 to 1 (Hollingshead and Redlich, 1958). The prevalence of schizophrenia is highest in the poorest and most dilapidated areas of the city and diminishes progressively as one moves outward toward the higher status regions (Figure 19.8). This general relation between social class and schizophrenia has been found in city after city, from New York, Omaha, New Haven, and Milwaukee in the United States to Oslo, Helsinki, London, and Taiwan abroad (Kohn, 1968).

Some critics argue that this finding is an artifact. Incidence rates of schizophrenia are usually based on admissions to mental hospitals, and lower-class psy-

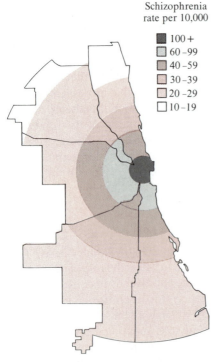

Schizophrenia
rate per 10,000

■ 100+
▨ 60–99
▨ 40–59
▨ 30–39
□ 20–29
□ 10–19

19.8 *The prevalence of schizophrenia in different regions of a city* A map of Chicago (1922–1934) represented by a series of concentric zones. The center zone is the business and amusement area, which is without residents except for some transients and vagabonds. Surrounding this center is a slum region inhabited largely by unskilled laborers. Further out are more stable regions: a zone largely populated by skilled workers, followed by zones of middle- and upper-middle-class apartment dwellers and, furthest out, the upper-middle-class commuters. The map shows clearly that the incidence of schizophrenia increases the closer one gets to the city's center. (After Faris and Dunham, 1939)

chotics may be more likely to be hospitalized in such institutions than are psychotics from higher strata. To get around this problem, some investigators studied a representative sample of all persons in a community—whether inside a hospital or not—and had psychiatrically trained interviewers rate their mental health. The same general result was found; the poor are more likely to become schizophrenic than the rich.

One interpretation of this result is that poverty, inferior status, and low occupational rank lead to increased environmental stresses which sooner or later convert a genetic susceptibility toward schizophrenia into the actual disorder. According to this view, given the predisposition, one becomes a schizophrenic because one is at the lowest rung of the social ladder. But there is a theoretical alternative, for the causal direction may be reversed. Perhaps one falls to the bottom of the ladder because one is a schizophrenic. The evidence to date suggests that both factors play a role. If so, schizophrenia is an effect of lower socioeconomic status as well as a cause, although the issue is by no means settled (Kohn, 1968).

Pathology in the family A different emphasis pervades the work of more psychoanalytically oriented investigators. True to their general outlook, they have concentrated upon the schizophrenic's family. They paint a gloomy picture. As they describe them, schizophrenics' mothers are rejecting, cold, dominating, and prudish, while their fathers are detached, humorless, weak, and passive (Arieti, 1959). Later studies concentrated on the relationships within the family. In general, they found a high degree of instability. Many schizophrenics come from homes in which a parent was lost early in the patient's life through death or divorce. In homes with both parents, there is often serious discord. In many such families the children become directly involved in the marital schism, with each parent trying to undercut the other in continual attempts to enlist the child as an ally (Lidz et al., 1957).

Later critics argued that this family portrait of the schizophrenics is inaccurate. The descriptions of the parents were often sketched by the same psychiatrists who treated the children and who were probably guilty of partisanship, as they saw the parents through the patients' eyes (Hill, 1955). When these and other procedural flaws are eliminated, the schizophrenic's family doesn't appear to be quite as pathological as it did at first. But enough signs of pathology remain even so. Objective studies in which the families of schizophrenic patients are observed in discussions of various topics (such as "When should teenagers begin dating?") have shown more within-family conflicts than normal controls (Fontana, 1966).

Communication in the family Several authors feel that one source of the patient's difficulties is a confused pattern of communication within the family. Compared to normals, the members of the patient's family are less likely to give each other clear and unambiguous signals, a possible prelude to the patient's own communicative difficulties (Wynne and Singer, 1963a and b). Of particular interest is the continual employment of self-contradictory communications. A parent may tell a child one thing while simultaneously conveying the message that what is really meant is the very opposite. The child is in a ***double bind;*** she is damned if she does and damned if she doesn't. According to some writers, schizophrenia is the residue of a long exposure to such double-bind situations. An example is provided by a young schizophrenic who was visited by his mother:

He was glad to see her and impulsively put his arms around her shoulders whereupon she stiffened. He withdrew his arm and she asked, "Don't you love me any more?" He then blushed and she said, "Dear, you must not be so easily embarrassed and afraid of your feelings." The patient was able to stay with her only a few minutes more and following her departure he assaulted an aide (Bateson et al., 1956, p. 258).

As the authors see it, the patient was placed in an impossible dilemma: To secure his mother's love, he had to show his own affection; but if he did so, he would lose her love.

The double-bind hypothesis is intriguing, but it can claim little in the way of empirical support. Some parents no doubt put their children into double-bind situations and some may do so more frequently than others. But there is no evidence that double-binding parents are more likely to have schizophrenic offspring than anyone else (Ringuette and Kennedy, 1966).

Disentangling cause and effect Schizophrenics evidently come from a less benign family background than normal children. But this does not prove that the familial environment is a *cause* of the patient's disorder. It may also be an effect; after all, having a schizophrenic in the family is probably quite disturbing. Several studies of mother-child interactions suggest that something of this sort does play a role (Mishler and Waxler, 1968). The investigators studied mothers who had both a schizophrenic and a healthy daughter. When observed with their schizophrenic daughters, the mothers seemed aloof and unresponsive. But when seen with their healthy daughters, the mothers behaved more normally. Their unresponsiveness may then not be a general characteristic of their personality (and thus perhaps a *cause* of the child's disorder) but rather a reaction to the schizophrenic daughter (and thus an *effect* of the child's disorder upon the mother's behavior).

All in all, there is evidently a relation between schizophrenia and various psychological characteristics of the family. This relationship is probably caused by three contributing factors. One is genetic; both the parents and their schizophrenic offspring may share some pathological genes. A second factor is environmental; the parents' psychopathology may precipitate the disorder of the child. A third factor involves the reversed causal relation; having a schizophrenic child may produce psychopathological reactions in the rest of the family.

The Pathology Model and Schizophrenia

We have considered schizophrenia under the same headings that are used to analyze nonpsychiatric illnesses—the symptom patterns, the underlying pathology, the role of more remote causes such as genetic predisposition, and precipitating factors. What can we conclude? To guide our evaluation, we will refer to a schematic diagram of the main factors in the schizophrenic disorder that is analogous to the one we used to analyze diabetes (Figure 19.9).

It appears that the main symptoms of schizophrenia can be regarded as the manifestations of an underlying psychological deficit, perhaps a defect in the ability to focus in space and time. The best guess is that this psychological malfunction reflects an underlying organic pathology whose exact nature is still unknown. Many investigators suspect that it is a biochemical defect, most likely one that involves some neurotransmitter system. The pathology that represents

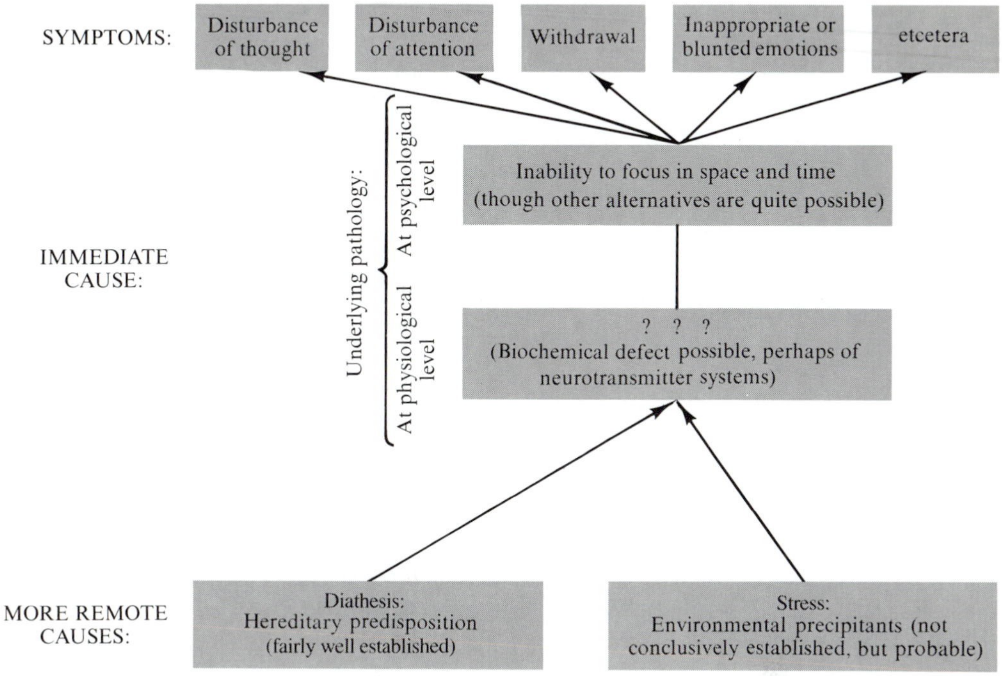

19.9 The pathology model as applied to schizophrenia *The diagram shows that the causal analysis by which nonbehavioral disorders such as diabetes are described (see pp. 647–48) can be applied to mental disorders such as schizophrenia. The basic logic applies regardless of whether the disorder ultimately turns out to be in part somatogenic or not.*

SYMPTOMS:

| Disturbance of thought | Disturbance of attention | Withdrawal | Inappropriate or blunted emotions | etcetera |

Underlying pathology:

At psychological level

Inability to focus in space and time (though other alternatives are quite possible)

IMMEDIATE CAUSE:

At physiological level

? ? ?
(Biochemical defect possible, perhaps of neurotransmitter systems)

MORE REMOTE CAUSES:

Diathesis: Hereditary predisposition (fairly well established)

Stress: Environmental precipitants (not conclusively established, but probable)

the immediate cause of the disorder is in turn produced by more remote causes. One is a hereditary diathesis. Another is a set of environmental stresses, including socioeconomic and familial pressures, which trigger the pathological process in persons with the initial diathesis.

A final word. Schizophrenia, like most other disorders, varies in severity. In describing it, we have necessarily concentrated on the most clear-cut examples, and these tend to be quite severe. But this should not blind us to the fact that there are some schizophrenics whose affliction is relatively mild and who may be able to function reasonably well in the ordinary world. There are also cases in which the symptoms are present mostly during acute psychotic episodes; at other times, the patient may be nearly symptom free. Total disability is relatively rare (Bernheim and Lewine, 1979).

AFFECTIVE DISORDERS

While schizophrenia can be regarded as essentially a disorder of thought, in another group of disorders the dominant disturbance is one of *mood.* These are the **affective disorders,** which are characterized by two emotional extremes—the vehement energy of **mania,** the despair and lethargy of **depression,** or both. (The term *affective* is a synonym for emotional feeling.)

The Symptom Patterns

An initial distinction is that between bipolar and unipolar disorders. In one variety of the condition, **bipolar affective disorder** (formerly called **manic-depressive** *psychosis),* the patient swings from one emotional extreme to the other, sometimes with intermittent periods of normalcy, and experiences both manic and depressive episodes that may be as short as one or two days and as long as several months or more. Bipolar disorders occur in about one percent of the population. Much more frequent are cases that are ***unipolar;*** in these, the mood extremes are of one kind only. Patients who suffer from only manic episodes are very rare. The vast majority of the unipolar depressions consists of people who suffer from deep depressions. According to one estimate, this condition may afflict about 10 percent of all persons at one time in their lives (Weissman and Myers, 1978).

MANIA

In their milder form, manic states are often hard to distinguish from normal high spirits. The person seems to have shifted into some form of mental high gear; she is more lively and infectiously merry, is extremely talkative and always on the go, is charming, utterly self-confident, and indefatigable. It is hard to see that something is wrong unless one notices that she jumps from one plan to another, seems unable to sit still for a moment, and quickly shifts from unbounded elation to intense irritation if she meets even the smallest frustration. These pathological signs become greatly intensified as the manic episode becomes more severe *(acute mania).* Now the motor is racing and all brakes are off. There is an endless stream of talk that runs from one topic to another and knows no inhibitions of social or personal (or for that matter, sexual) propriety. Patients are incessantly busy. They rarely sleep, burst into shouts of song, smash furniture out of sheer overabundance of energy, do exercises, conceive grandiose plans for rebuilding the hospital or redirecting the nation's foreign policy or making millions in the stock market —a ceaseless torrent of activity that continues unabated over many days and sleepless nights and will eventually sap the patients' health (and that of those around them) if they are not sedated.

An example of a manic episode is described in an autobiography by Clifford Beers, a man who lived through three years of a severe bipolar disorder, recovered, and went on to become a crusader for mental hospital reform. Beers started to write letters about everything that was happening to him. He soon ran out of stationery so he obtained large rolls of wrapping paper which he cut into one-foot strips and pasted together into long rolls, writing letters that were twenty to thirty feet long, and continuing to write at the rate of twelve feet per hour. He eventually tried to take charge of the hospital, was put in a small cell, and soon tried his hand at inventions. He decided to overcome the force of gravity. He tore a carpet into strips and used the makeshift ropes to suspend his bed (with himself in it) off the floor. "So epoch-making did this discovery appear to me that I noted the exact position of the bed so that a wondering posterity might ever afterward view and revere the exact spot on the earth's surface whence one of man's greatest thoughts had winged its way to immortality" (quoted in White and Watt, 1973).

DEPRESSION

In many ways, depression is the polar opposite of mania. The patient's mood is utterly dejected, his outlook is hopeless; he has lost his interest in other people and regards himself as completely worthless. In many cases, both thought and action slow down to a crawl:

Depression (Photograph by Rhoda Sydney, Leo de Wys)

The patient appears dejected and cheerless; everything he says and does is with effort. . . . He speaks only in response to questions and even then answers in a word, not a sentence. . . . He speaks in such a low tone that one finds oneself moving close to him and speaking more loudly as if he were the one who could not hear. He says that everything is hopeless, that he is a disgrace to his family; he recalls that when he was a boy he took a paper from the newsstand and did not pay for it (Cohen, 1975, p. 1,019).

In severe cases, there may be delusions or even hallucinations. Most are variations on the same theme of personal worthlessness: "I must weep myself to death. I cannot live. I cannot die. I have failed so. It would be better if I had not been born. . . . I am the most inferior person in the world. . . . I am subhuman" (Beck, 1967, p. 38).

In addition there are various physical symptoms. There is a loss of appetite, weakness, fatigue, poor bowel functioning, disturbance of sleep, and little if any interest in sex. It is as if both bodily and psychic batteries have run down completely.

Depression and suicide Given the depressive's bottomless despair, it is not surprising that suicide is a very real risk. Probably no patient in real life has described his preoccupation with death, suicide, and dissolution as eloquently as that greatest depressive in all of English literature, Prince Hamlet:

> O that this too too sullied flesh would melt,
> Thaw, and resolve itself into a dew,
> Or that the Everlasting had not fixed
> His canon 'gainst self-slaughter. O God, God,
> How weary, stale, flat, and unprofitable
> Seem to me all the uses of this world!
> Fie on 't, ah fie, 'tis an unweeded garden
> That grows to seed.
>
> (*Hamlet*, Act I, Scene ii)

Like Hamlet, many depressives think of suicide. Some attempt the act, and more than a few succeed. The suicide rate among depressives is high; according to some estimates, it is about twenty-five times greater than that found in the population as a whole. But contrary to what one might expect, the risk of suicide is relatively low while the patient is still in the trough of the depressive phase. At that point his gloom is deepest, but so too is his apathy. The risk increases as the patient comes out of his depression. Suicide rates are greatest during weekend leaves from the hospital and shortly after discharge (Beck, 1967). Then the patient's mood may still be black, but he has regained some of his energy and ability to act. He has recovered just enough to do the one thing that will prevent all further recovery.

Organic Factors

What produces the mood extremes that are characteristic of affective disorders? According to one view, some of these conditions—especially the bipolar variety —are ***endogenous,*** that is, produced by some internal, organic pathology.

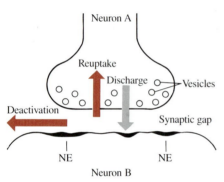

**19.10 A schematic presentation of two
ways in which a drug may increase the
available supply of a neurotransmitter** A
*neurotransmitter, norephinephrine (NE),
is discharged by Neuron A into the
synaptic gap and diffuses across the gap to
stimulate Neuron B. The more NE
accumulates at the membrane of Neuron
B, the more that neuron will fire. The
amount of NE at the synapse is diminished
in several ways. One is* **reuptake,** *a process
in which NE is pumped back into Neuron A.
Another is* **deactivation,** *a process whereby
certain enzymes (such as monoamine
oxidase or MAO) break down the
neurotransmitter and render it ineffective.
Tricyclics and monoamine oxidase
inhibitors are antidepressants that increase
the amount of available NE (and serotonin) at the synaptic junction but that
accomplish this in different ways.
Tricyclics do so by interfering with neurotransmitter uptake; monoamine oxidase
inhibitors do so by preventing MAO from
breaking the transmitters down.*

GENETIC COMPONENTS

The belief that such an organic pathology exists is based on several considerations. As in schizophrenia, there is the rather specific therapeutic effect of certain
drugs (described below). And again, as in schizophrenia, there is good reason to
suppose that at least some forms of the disorder have an important hereditary
component. This is almost certainly true for the bipolar condition. The average
concordance for identical twins one of whom suffers from bipolar affective disorder is 67 percent, while the comparable figure for fraternal twins is 16 percent
(based on Slater and Cowie, 1971). The evidence suggests that the genetic factor is
much weaker in unipolar cases.

BIOCHEMICAL HYPOTHESES

The genetic evidence is a strong argument for the view that there is some biological factor that underlies bipolar affective disorders. This view is further bolstered
by the fact that in bipolars, the switch from one mood to the other is generally
quite divorced from external circumstances. The most plausible interpretation is
that there is some internal, biological switch.

According to one hypothesis, the disorder is based on a biochemical defect that
involves the supply of some neurotransmitter at certain critical sites of the brain.
When there is an oversupply, there is mania; when there is a shortage, there is depression. Some investigators believe that this transmitter is **norepinephrine;**
others feel that it is **serotonin,** a biochemical relative of norepinephrine; still
others suspect that both substances are involved (Schildkraut, 1965).

Evidence for the role of these neurotransmitters comes from the analysis of
various byproducts of the breakdown of these substances in the spinal fluid or
urine. If the level of these byproducts is low, one would surmise that there is a correspondingly low supply of the neurotransmitters from which they were derived.
These byproduct levels were in fact lower in depressed patients than in controls.
Further evidence comes from studies of norepinephrine levels in bipolar patients.
These were below average when the patients were depressed and increased when
the patients became manic (Davison and Neale, 1982).

Of greatest interest is the effect of two kinds of **antidepressant** drugs: the **monoamine oxidase (MAO) inhibitors** and the **tricyclics.** Both of these kinds of drugs
have some success in relieving depression, and both increase the amount of norepinephrine and serotonin available for synaptic transmission. (The mechanisms
whereby they accomplish this mission are different; for details, see Figure 19.10).

Evidence of this kind lends considerable plausibility to the hypothesis that
some malfunction of one or another neurotransmitter is implicated in affective
disorders. While the details of the mechanism are still very much a matter of dispute, most investigators agree that at least some forms of affective disorders have
an important organic component (Shopsin, Wilk, Sathananthan, Gershon, and
Davis, 1974).

Psychogenic Factors

The organic pathology—whatever it may turn out to be—might account for the
extremes of some patients' moods, the fact that they are speeded up or slowed

down in virtually all respects. But can it explain *what* the patient thinks or does, the manic's glow of overweening self-satisfaction and the depressive's hopeless despair and self-loathing? How does an inadequate supply of norepinephrine or serotonin lead to the belief that one is "the most inferior person in the world?"

MOOD OR COGNITION?

What comes first, mood or cognition? The question is again one of cause and effect. Theorists who regard the disorder as primarily somatogenic believe that what the patient thinks *follows* from her mood. If a transmitter insufficiency (or some other biochemical state) makes her feel sluggish and gloomy, she looks for reasons to explain her own mood. Eventually she will find them: the world is no good, nor is she. The end result is that her cognitions match her feelings. (For an analogous approach to the nature of emotional feelings in normals, see Chapter 11.)

Does this approach really do justice to the phenomenon? Theorists who believe in a psychogenic interpretation think not. They grant that affective disorders—especially those that are bipolar—may involve a constitutional predisposition toward mood excess, but they insist that psychological factors play a vital role. In their view, the patient's belief that he and the world are no good comes first and his depression comes second—as an *effect* of these cognitions rather than as their cause.

One such view has been proposed by Aaron Beck, who feels that the patient's condition ultimately can be traced to a number of intensely negative beliefs about himself and the world around him: that he is utterly worthless, that his future is bleak, and that whatever happens around him is sure to turn out to be for the worst (Beck, 1967).

LEARNED HELPLESSNESS AND DEPRESSION

Where Beck's cognitive theory grew out of clinical observations of depressed patients, a related cognitive account, proposed by M.E.P. Seligman, had its source in studies of animal learning (Seligman, 1975). The initial findings that led to Seligman's approach concerned **learned helplessness,** first observed in the animal laboratory (see Chapter 4).

When normal dogs are placed in a shuttle box in which they have to jump from one compartment to another in order to escape an electric shock, they learn to do so with little difficulty. This is in contrast with a second group of dogs who have first been exposed to a series of painful shocks about which they could do absolutely nothing. When this second group was later placed in the shuttle box, their performance was drastically different from that of normal dogs. Unlike normal animals, they did not run around frantically looking for some means of escape. Nor did they ever find the correct response—jumping over the hurdle. Instead, they simply gave up: they lay down, whimpered, and passively accepted their fate. They had learned to become helpless (Seligman, Maier, and Solomon, 1971).

Seligman argues that learned helplessness in animals is in many ways similar to at least some forms of human depression. Like the helpless dogs, depressed patients have given up. They just sit there, passively, unable to take any initiative that might help them cope. Some further similarities concern the effects of certain antidepressant drugs (see Chapter 20). These drugs alleviate the symptoms of many depressive patients. They have a similar effect on animals rendered helpless: the helplessness disappears and the animals behave much like normals (Porsolt, LePichon, and Jalfre, 1977).

In an attempt to buttress the analogy, Seligman and his collaborators have tried to demonstrate something akin to learned helplessness in human laboratory subjects. In one such study, subjects were exposed to loud, unpleasant noises through earphones. One group of subjects was able to escape the noises by performing a simple response; a second group received the same number of noises as the first but was unable to do anything about them. When later tested in a variety of situations, the subjects pretreated with inescapable noise behaved somewhat like the dogs who had received inescapable shock. They became impaired in their ability to solve rather simple problems, such as anagram puzzles, that posed little difficulty for the control subjects. Seligman argues that this manipulation had induced a temporary sense of helplessness, a feeling that there was no point in trying, since one's actions would have no effect. This analogy is supported by a further finding. Subjects who were already depressed before the experiment started, performed poorly on the anagram puzzles whether they experienced inescapable noise or not. These subjects presumably required no special technique to render them helpless. They were already helpless—and hence depressed—before the experiment began (Klein and Seligman, 1976; Miller and Seligman, 1975; see Figure 19.11).

Seligman believes that the parallels between learned helplessness in animals and in humans point to a common factor that may help to explain depression. Both the dogs who suffered inescapable shock and the humans who experienced inescapable noises developed an expectation that their own acts would be of no avail. As a result, both became unable to initiate responses, or to recognize that something they do has a desirable effect. Something similar may happen in human depression. The precipitating factor may be some personal catastrophe—rejection, bankruptcy, physical disease, the death of a loved one. This leads to a generalized sense of impotence: a belief that there is nothing one can do to shape one's destiny, that one is a passive victim with no control over events—that one is helpless.

Whether learned helplessness theory can adequately account for the phenomena of depression, is still a matter of debate (Abramson, Seligman, and Teasdale, 1978; Costello, 1978; Depue and Monroe, 1978). But whatever the outcome of this debate, the parallels that Seligman has pointed to will have to be considered by any future theory of the disorder.

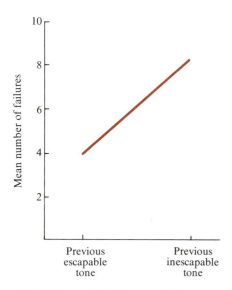

19.11 Learned helplessness in laboratory subjects *College students were previously exposed to escapable or inescapable loud tones. If the tones had been inescapable, the subjects' ability to solve anagrams was impaired. The authors regard this as a human analogue to learned helplessness in animals. (After Hiroto and Seligman, 1975)*

THE DEPRESSIVE'S SELF-HATRED

There is one facet of depression that does not follow from any of the theoretical positions we have described thus far—the depressive's violent self-hatred. Hopelessness, helplessness, or a shortage of certain neurotransmitters might well lead him to feel that the world is a terrible place, but why does he blame himself? One possible explanation involves the patient's upbringing. Several authors have suggested that the parents of depressives made unusually strict demands upon them when they were children, insisting on high achievement and a rigid code of morality, with severe punishments for failure to live up to these standards (Gibson, Cohen, and Cohen, 1959). Reared in this manner, the child might well develop a marked tendency toward self-blame, setting off torrents of self-directed abuse in times of misfortune. The idea seems plausible enough, but the evidence is still unclear, for many of the investigations whose results seem to support it can be criticized for failure to control age, social class, and similar factors.

Affective Disorders and the Diathesis-Stress Conception

Affective disorders are often preceded by some stressful event—marital difficulties, difficulties at work, serious physical illness, or a death in the family. But it's clear that environmental stress cannot be the whole story. After all, there are many people who suffer major setbacks and serious losses but who don't fall into a depressive collapse. There is evidently a diathesis—some people are more prone to affective disorders than others. This diathesis may be based on biological factors—such as an insufficiency of available norepinephrine or serotonin. But the predisposition may well be psychological in nature—such as a negative view of oneself and the world or a generalized sense of helplessness. In either case, the diathesis makes the individual more vulnerable to later stress.

ANXIETY DISORDERS

In affective disorders, as we have seen, it is still unclear whether the underlying pathology is best regarded as somatogenic or psychogenic or as both. There is much more agreement about a number of other disorders in which both the main symptoms and the underlying pathology are primarily mental. These are the *anxiety disorders.* In these conditions the primary symptom is either anxiety or defenses that ward off anxiety. While such symptoms often cause serious distress and impair the person's functioning, they generally do not render him incapable of coping with external reality. He is a neurotic, not a psychotic.*

Phobias

In some neuroses, the primary symptom is a *phobia,* an intense and irrational fear of some object or situation. During the nineteenth century, some of these irrational fears were catalogued and assigned high-sounding Greek or Latin names. Examples are fear of high places (acrophobia), or open places (agoraphobia), or enclosed places (claustrophobia), or of crowds (ocholophobia), or germs (mysophobia), or cats (ailurophobia)—the list is potentially endless. The crucial point in the definition is that the fear must be *irrational,* that there really is no danger or that the danger is exaggerated out of all proportion. An African villager who lives at the outskirts of the jungle and is worried about leopards has an understandable fear; a San Francisco apartment dweller with a similar fear has a phobia. In many

---

* In the psychiatric classification system prior to DSM-III, anxiety disorders were listed under the general rubric *neurosis* because of the belief that these conditions, along with a number of others such as conversion disorders and dissociative states, could all be understood as the manifestations of unconscious defenses against anxiety. Since DSM-III tries to classify conditions by observable symptoms rather than by their inferred causes, these various disorders are now listed separately.

665

A   B

Phobias *An artist's conception of (A) the fear of dirt, and (B) the fear of open spaces. (Paintings by Vassos)*

cases, this irrationality is quite apparent to the sufferer, who knows that the fear is groundless but continues to be afraid all the same.

In phobia, the irrational fear exerts an enormous effect on every aspect of the sufferer's life, for he is always preoccupied with his phobia. On the face of it, it is not entirely clear why this should be so. Why can't the phobic simply avoid the situations that frighten him? If he is afraid of leopards and snakes, he should stay away from the zoo; if he is terrified of heights, he should refrain from visits to the top of the Sears Tower. Some phobias may be minor enough to be handled this easily, but most cannot. In many cases this is because the phobia tends to expand. The fear of leopards becomes a fear of the part of the city where the zoo is located, of all cats and catlike things, or of all spotted objects, and so on. Other phobias may be more wide-ranging to begin with. An example is *agoraphobia* (from a Greek word meaning "fear of the marketplace") which is sometimes described as a fear of open spaces, but really amounts to a fear of being alone and away from the safety of one's own home.

THE CONDITIONING ACCOUNT OF PHOBIAS

What is the mechanism that underlies phobias? One notion goes back to John Locke who believed that such fears are produced by a chance association of ideas, as when a child is told stories about goblins that come by night and is forever after terrified of the dark (Locke, 1690). Several modern authors express much the same idea in the language of conditioning theory. In their view, phobias result from classical conditioning; the conditioned stimulus is the feared object (e.g., cats) and the response is the autonomic upheaval (increased heart rate, cold sweat, and so on) characteristic of fear (Wolpe, 1958).

A number of phobias may indeed develop in just this fashion. Examples include fear of dogs after dog bites, fear of heights after a fall down a flight of stairs, and fear of cars or driving after a serious automobile accident (Marks, 1969). Conditioning theorists can readily explain why phobias acquired in this manner expand and spread to new stimuli. The fear response is initially conditioned to a particular stimulus. If this stimulus subsequently occurs in a new context, the fear will be evoked and thus conditioned to a whole set of new stimuli. An example is a woman who developed a fear of anesthetic masks after experiencing a terrifying sensation of suffocation while being anesthetized. This same sense of suffocation reoccurred later when she was in a stuffy, crowded elevator. This in turn led to a dread of elevators, whether empty or crowded. The phobia generalized to any and all situations in which she could not leave at will, even playing cards (Wolpe, 1958, p. 98).

THE PSYCHOANALYTIC ACCOUNT OF PHOBIAS

According to some writers, many phobias cannot be explained quite as simply as the classical conditioning account would have it. The point is that phobias sometimes have a twisted sort of function. The patient gets some devious benefit from his fear, a fact which is hard to explain if classical conditioning is all that is involved. Psychoanalysts believe that one such benefit is *displacement.* The patient is afraid of something that he cannot face consciously. As a protective measure, he displaces his fear to a conceptually related object, but without recognizing the relationship. Thus a husband's phobia about knives may be a displaced fear of his own impulse to stab his wife.

According to the displacement hypothesis, phobias (or at least some phobias) are a defense in which a patient trades a greater fear for a lesser one. If this were true, then removing the phobia (for example, the fear of knives) should lead to the substitution of other symptoms that protect the patient from the hidden, greater fear that he cannot confront. But in fact, such *symptom substitution* does not seem to occur. By now, there are several behavior therapies that try to extinguish the link between the phobic object (the knives) and the fear (see Chapter 20). Such therapies have been quite successful in removing the phobia without further repercussions from substitute symptoms, a result that casts some doubt on the displacement hypothesis and the psychoanalytic account of phobias from which it is derived.

Generalized Anxiety Disorders

In phobias, anxiety is focused on a particular object or situation; in *generalized anxiety disorders* (an older term is *anxiety neurosis),* it is all-pervasive, or, as it is sometimes called, free-floating. The patient is constantly tense and worried, feels inadequate, is oversensitive, can't concentrate or make decisions, and suffers from insomnia. This state of affairs is generally accompanied by any number of physiological concomitants—rapid heart rate, irregular breathing, excessive sweating, frequent urination, and chronic diarrhea.

According to one interpretation, generalized anxiety disorders show what happens when there are no defenses against anxiety or when those defenses are too weak and collapse, so that unacceptable impulses are able to break into consciousness and to precipitate anxiety reactions.

Conditioning theorists offer another account. In their view, a generalized anxiety condition is much like a phobia. The difference is that anxiety is conditioned to a very broad range of stimuli so that avoidance is virtually impossible (Wolpe, 1958). The trouble is that the stimuli to which anxiety is said to be conditioned are not easily specified. Since this is so, the conditioning interpretation of this disorder is hard to evaluate.

667

Obsessive-Compulsive Disorders

In phobias, anxiety is aroused by external objects or situations. In contrast, anxiety in *obsessive-compulsive disorders* is produced by internal events—persistent thoughts or wishes that intrude into consciousness and cannot be stopped. An example of such an *obsession* is a mother who has recurrent thoughts of strangling her children. To ward off the anxiety produced by such obsessions, the patient often feels compelled to perform a variety of ritualistic acts. Such *compulsions* are attempts to counteract the anxiety-producing impulse that underlies the obsessive thought; in Freud's terms, a way of *undoing* what should not have been done. Examples of such compulsions are ritualistic cleaning, handwashing, and incessant counting. The mother with uncontrollable thoughts of committing infanticide might feel compelled to count her children over and over again, as if to check that they are all there, that she hasn't done away with any. The obsessive-compulsive patient is aware that his behavior is irrational but he can't help himself even so. Lady Macbeth knew that "what's done cannot be undone," but she nevertheless continued to wash the invisible blood off her hands.

Minor and momentary obsessional thoughts or compulsions are commonplace. After all, most people have had the occasional feeling that they ought to check whether the door is locked even when they are perfectly sure that it is. But in obsessive-compulsive disorders, such thoughts and acts are the patient's major preoccupation and are crippling:

Compulsive hand washing in literature *A scene from the Old Vic's 1956 production of* Macbeth *with Coral Browne. It shows Lady Macbeth walking in her sleep and scrubbing imaginary blood off her hands, as she relives the night in which she and her husband murdered the king. (Courtesy of the Performing Arts Research Center, The New York Public Library)*

> A man in his 30's, fearing lest he push a stranger off the subway platform in the path of an oncoming train, was compelled to keep his arms and hands glued rigidly to his sides. . . . [He] was on one occasion obsessed with the idea that, despite his stringent precautions, he had, after all, inadvertently knocked someone off the subway platform. He struggled with himself for weeks to dispel what he rationally knew was a foolish notion but was at length compelled to call the transport authority to reassure himself that there had not in fact been any such accident. The same patient was for a time preoccupied with the concern that, when he walked on the streets, he was dislodging manhole covers so that strangers passing by would fall into the sewer and be injured. Whenever he passed a manhole in the company of friends, he would be compelled to count his companions to make sure that none was missing (Nemiah, 1975b, p. 1,245).

Anxiety Disorders and the Pathology Model

Anxiety disorders (as well as many other conditions) were until recently considered as subclasses of a larger category, the neuroses. Their symptoms vary widely and so they are now grouped separately for diagnostic purposes. But are they nevertheless similar in sharing a common underlying pathology?

ANXIETY AS A POSSIBLE UNDERLYING CAUSE

Many modern practitioners follow Freud in believing that there is a pathology that underlies all of these conditions, but that it is behavioral (that is, mental) rather than organic. In their view, the symptoms of these disorders are primarily a defense against some intolerable anxiety. This view fits some of these conditions rather well. For example, compulsive acts can be understood as responses that block an anxiety-related obsessive thought, even if only temporarily. But in other disorders, the role of the symptom in defending the patient against anxiety is a matter of debate, which is one reason why the term *neurosis* is no longer in standard use as an overarching category.

Suppose a person has a crippling phobia about water that makes it hard for him to drink, wash, and so on. A psychoanalyst would argue that this water phobia is only the visible part of the disorder. To understand this symptom, we have to dig deeper and find out what he is "really" afraid of, what water stands for in his private symbolism. But a behavior theorist would probably take a different tack. He would argue that the patient's trouble is a conditioned fear of water, no more and no less, and that there are no hidden conflicts of which this fear of water is a devious manifestation. In his view, the symptom *is* the disease, and it is the removal of this symptom toward which treatment—or as he would call it, ***behavior therapy***—should be directed. Having rejected the distinction between symptom and underlying pathology as applied to these kinds of disorders, some behavior therapists go the rest of the way: They reject the entire pathology model that insists on this distinction.

Is the pathology model really inapplicable to anxiety disorders? The question is primarily relevant to issues that concern psychotherapy (see Chapter 20). For now, we merely point out that cases in which a symptom *is* the pathology are not unheard of in ordinary, organic medical practice. An example is a broken bone that is visible to the naked eye. Here symptom and pathology seem to be one and the same, so that to heal the one is equivalent to healing the other. But this in itself does not seem to be an adequate reason for abandoning the pathology model as a general conceptual framework.

MORE REMOTE CAUSES

Whatever their theoretical differences, most psychopathologists agree that anxiety disorders are largely based on learning. The reactions against anxiety may represent the immediate cause of the symptoms, but they in turn are based on learned experience farther back in the individual's life.

In many cases, the disorder can be traced to a stressful event in the just-preceding past, some traumatic episode that led to a phobia, or a marital breakup that initiated an anxiety attack. Oddly enough, there is usually a lag of a few days between the trauma and the onset of the symptoms. During this lag, the individual thinks about the stressful event and relives the fearful emotions, which keep on increasing and finally erupt into the full symptom pattern.

Upon investigation, it turns out that in many cases the stress alone was not the sole cause; the patient had some prior adjustment problems. In effect, the trauma served to reevoke some earlier reactions to anxiety acquired in a more distant past. An example is psychiatric breakdown during combat. Soldiers who collapse under relatively minor stress are more likely to have a history of prior psychiatric difficulties, signs of serious maladjustment in childhood, and so on (Slater, 1943).

CONVERSIONS AND DISSOCIATIVE DISORDERS

The defense reactions set up in many of the anxiety disorders are cumbersome and never work completely. Thus patients with obsessive-compulsive patterns are always encumbered with guilt and vacillation. But there is another group of disorders in which the person seems to do a better job at managing anxiety. Some are **conversion disorders** in which the patient "converts" a psychological conflict into an apparent bodily symptom. Others are **dissociative disorders** in which a whole set of mental processes is split off from the rest of the individual's consciousness. Freud believed that these are conditions in which the primary defense seems to be repression. In both disorders, the individual pushes all anxiety-evoking materials out of consciousness. This allows him to deny that there is anything to be anxious about. Patients with these conditions are virtuosos at refusing to take responsibility for their own unacceptable behavior. Some forbidden impulse may break through or some forbidden act may get performed, but the patient saves the situation—he simply insists that it really wasn't his fault.

Conversion Disorders

One way of escaping responsibility is by being sick. This is the path chosen by persons with a **conversion disorder,** or to use an earlier term, **conversion hysteria.** According to Freud, these individuals resolve some intolerable conflict by developing a hysterical bodily ailment, such as paralysis of a limb (see Chapter 12).* The soldier who is terrified of going into battle but cannot face the idea of being a coward may become hysterically paralyzed. This allows him to give in to his impulse of refusing to march. But it also lets him do so without guilt or shame—he is not marching because he *cannot* march.

Dissociative Disorders

Another way in which a person can deny responsibility for some acts (or thoughts or wishes) is by insisting that they were never committed, or at least not by him. This approach is characteristic of **dissociative reactions.** In these disorders, a whole set of mental events—acts, thoughts, feelings, memories—is shoved out of ordinary consciousness. One example is psychogenic **amnesia** in which the individual is unable to remember some period of his life, or sometimes all events prior to the onset of the amnesia, including his own identity. In other cases, the dissociation involves a **fugue state,** in which the individual wanders away from home, and then, days, weeks, or even years thereafter, suddenly realizes that he is in a strange place, doesn't know how he got there, and has total amnesia for the entire period.

Still more drastic are cases of **multiple personality.** Here the dissociation is so massive that it results in two or more separate personalities. The second—and sometimes third or fourth—personality is built upon a nucleus of memories that already had some prior separate status. An example is a shy and inhibited person who has had fantasies of being carefree and outgoing from childhood on. These memories eventually take on the characteristics of a separate self. Once formed, the new self may appear quite suddenly, as in the famous case of Eve White:

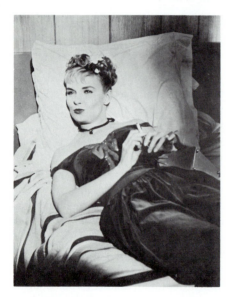

A movie recreation of a case of multiple personality Joanne Woodward in The Three Faces of Eve *portraying Eve White (above) and Eve Black (below) (Courtesy the Museum of Modern Art/Film Stills Archive)*

* The term "conversion" was coined by Freud who believed that the repressed energies that power the patient's unconscious conflict are converted into a somatic symptom much as a steam engine converts thermal energy into mechanical energy. Until recently, this condition was called *conversion hysteria.* The authors of DSM-III dropped the term *hysteria* because of its erroneous implication that it is a disorder found only in women. (The term *hysteria* is derived from the Greek *hystera,* meaning *womb.*)

After a tense moment of silence, her hands dropped. There was a quick, reckless smile and, in a bright voice that sparkled, she said, "Hi there, Doc." . . . There was in the newcomer a childishly daredevil air, an erotically mischievous glance, a face marvelously free from the habitual signs of care, seriousness, and underlying distress, so long familiar in her predecessor. This new and apparently carefree girl spoke casually of Eve White and her problems, always using *she* or *her* in every reference, always respecting the strict bounds of a separate identity. When asked her own name she immediately replied, "Oh, I'm Eve Black" (Thigpen and Cleckley, 1957, as described in Coleman, 1972, p. 246).

Factors That Underlie Conversions and Dissociative Conditions

The cause of conversion and dissociative symptoms is still obscure. Freud believed that such symptoms are a defense against anxiety. Conditioning theorists hold a similar position, translated into their own conceptual framework. But this anxiety hypothesis only accounts for the patient's motives. It may explain why he wants not to see or not to walk or to develop an alternate personality; it does not explain how he accomplishes these feats, especially the wholesale alterations of consciousness that characterize dissociations.

Some authors suggest that such phenomena may represent an unusual form of self-dramatization in which the person acts *as if* she were blind or *as if* she were Eve Black without any consciousness that any playacting is going on (Ziegler, Imboden, and Rodgers, 1963; Sarbin and Allen, 1968). According to this view, the patient is like an actor who becomes so involved in his role that he is no longer aware that he is on stage. In actuality, of course, no actor ever completely forgets that he is playing a part; if he did, he would be unable to leave the stage when the play calls for his exit. But by the same token, no patient is ever completely paralyzed or blind and so on; his "paralyzed" leg still responds to reflex stimulation and will probably serve quite well in emergencies such as a fire.

Much the same kind of as-if behavior characterizes a deeply hypnotized patient who is given a suggestion, say, not to see a chair in the middle of the room. When asked whether she sees it, she answers no; but when she walks across the room, she somehow never bumps into it; she manages to circle around it, as if to see it so as not to see it. The important point is that the patient, the hypnotized person, and—to a lesser extent—the deeply involved actor, are not aware of what they are aware of.

Whether dissociations and conversion reactions are a defense against anxiety or an unconscious kind of playacting, most investigators suspect that they have roots in earlier patterns of behavior that set the stage for the full-blown disorder under later conditions of stress. An example is provided by cases of multiple personality who often seem to have histories of severe abuse in childhood (Bliss, 1980).

PSYCHOPHYSIOLOGICAL DISORDERS

Thus far, our concern has been with psychopathological conditions whose primary symptoms are psychological. But certain other conditions can lead to genuine organic damage. For example, peptic ulcer or asthma may be produced by

PSYCHOPATHOLOGY · Ch. 19

organic causes, as in the case of an asthmatic allergic reaction. Yet they may also be produced (or aggravated) by emotional factors. If so, they are called *psychophysiological conditions* (or, to use an older term, *psychosomatic disorders*).* But whether their origin is organic or mental makes no difference to the victim; they are equally real in either case.

In this regard, the symptoms of a psychophysiological condition are quite different from the somatic complaints of a patient with a conversion disorder. That patient's paralysis of the legs will probably disappear shortly after his underlying conflict is resolved; after all, his locomotor machinery is still intact. But the patient with a psychophysiological ulcer (or asthma, or high blood pressure) has a disorder that often plays for keeps. His ulcer will bleed and hurt just as much as an ulcer caused by a gastric disease, and if it perforates his stomach wall he will suffer the same case of peritonitis and, if he dies, his death will be no less final.

Essential Hypertension

We will consider one psychophysiological disorder in some detail—*essential hypertension.* This is a chronic elevation of blood pressure that can lead to serious disability and premature death. While some cases of hypertension result from various organic pathologies, essential hypertension is at least partially psychogenic (Lipowski, 1975; Harrell, 1980).

THE EFFECT OF CONTINUED AUTONOMIC AROUSAL

Blood pressure is the pressure exerted by the blood as the heart pumps it through the body's arteries. One way in which this pressure can rise is by the constriction of the arteries. This occurs in fight-or-flight emergencies, as when a zebra suddenly sees a hungry lion (see Chapter 3). The sympathetic branch of the autonomic nervous system is aroused and, among other things, this leads to the contraction of the muscles of the arterial walls. The effect is much like squeezing on a water hose. There is an immediate increase in the force of the liquid spurting out. As a result, the skeletal muscle, and the heart muscles themselves, get blood more quickly—a vital necessity in life-or-death situations which call for sudden, violent exertions.

Such extraordinary measures are all very well for zebras trying to get away from lions. The emergency really does call for increased muscular effort; when it is over, the muscles inform the nervous system that they no longer need the same supply of food. When this happens, the circulatory system soon returns to normal. The situation is quite different for us today. We rarely encounter emergencies that call for violent muscular effort. But our lives are filled with any number of fear- and anger-producing situations. An unfair grade, a neighbor's snub, a near-miss on the superhighway—all these trigger the sympathetic emergency reaction, even though a sudden spurt of muscular energy is of no avail. But our autonomic nervous system doesn't know that. And so we are put on an emergency basis, some of us more than others, but all to some extent. As a result, our blood pressure goes up, again and again, in the daily stress of living. Since the emer-

* In DSM-III, they are listed under "psychological factors affecting physical conditions."

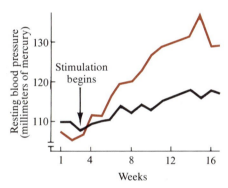

19.12 Chronic autonomic arousal and hypertension *A group of rats was exposed to continued electrical stimulation of the hypothalamic defense area. The electric stimulation was mild; it merely produced alerting reactions such as sniffing. But the stimulation was chronic, with one stimulus every minute for 12 hours every day over the better part of a four-month period. The figure shows the average resting blood pressure of the rats in this group (color) compared to the blood pressure of a control group that suffered no hypothalamic stimulation (black). The toll exacted by the continued defense reaction is shown by the difference between the two groups after four months. (After Folkow and Rubenstein, 1966)*

gency does not lead to any extra muscular effort, the autonomic nervous system never gets the proper message that signals the end of the emergency. As a result, the blood pressure remains up for a while after the incident has passed.

In some people, continued autonomic overactivity eventually takes its toll—the elevated blood pressure no longer comes down to normal. One reason is a gradual thickening of the arterial muscle walls. This, together with an increased sensitivity to stimulation, makes these muscles overreact to normal neural impulses. As a result, they are in an almost continual state of constriction. The more constricted they are, the thicker and more sensitive they get. The ultimate effect of this vicious cycle is *hypertension,* a condition that afflicts twenty-three million Americans and represents a major public-health problem. Among its relatively minor symptoms are headaches and dizziness. If serious and prolonged, the disorder leads to lesions in the arteries that supply the kidneys, the brain, and the heart. The final results include kidney failure, cerebral stroke, coronary disease, and heart attacks (Lipowski, 1975).

HYPERTENSION AND EMOTIONAL STRESS

Hypertension is evidently a residue of continued sympathetic arousal. Thus, we would expect its incidence to go up with increasing emotional stress. This is indeed the case. For example, there was a marked increase in the rate of hypertension among the inhabitants of Leningrad during the siege and bombardment of that city during World War II (Henry and Cassel, 1969). Similar effects are produced by socioeconomic stress. Hypertension is much more common among blacks than whites in the United States; and it is especially prevalent in metropolitan regions marked by high population density, poverty, and crime (Lipowski, 1975). Still other studies show that hypertension is more prevalent among persons whose occupations impose unusual emotional stress. An example is provided by air-traffic controllers, especially those who work in airports in which traffic density is high (Cobb and Rose, 1973).

In all of these cases, the critical element is not environmental stress as such, but rather the individual's reaction to it. What the besieged citizen of Leningrad, the unemployed inner-city black, and the overburdened air-traffic controller have in common is unremitting sympathetic arousal; they are continually afraid or angry or harassed and eventually their bodies pay the price in the form of hypertension (Figure 19.12).

The Diathesis-Stress Concept and Psychophysiological Disorders

Emotional stress can lead to hypertension but it can also lead to various other psychophysiological disorders such as peptic ulcers. Is there any way to predict which disorder stress will produce in any one person? What determines whether "she will eat her heart out" or "whether she'll tie her stomach into knots?" The answer is diathesis and stress.

There is reason to believe that the susceptibility to a given psychophysiological disorder depends on a preexisting somatic diathesis that may be of genetic origin. Given enough emotional stress, the body will cave in at its most vulnerable point.

Some evidence for this view comes from studies which show that elevated

673

blood pressure tends to run in families, in mice as well as men. In humans, a blood-pressure correlation between children and parents is seen as early as infancy. The best guess is that there is a genetic factor which is partially responsible for the initial blood-pressure elevation. This may bias the individual to respond to stress with his arterial muscles rather than with his lungs or stomach. If the stress is prolonged enough, the individual will become a hypertensive rather than an asthmatic or an ulcer patient (Henry and Cassel, 1969).

A somewhat similar account applies to psychogenic peptic ulcer. This is a lesion in the lining of the stomach or duodenum whose immediate physiological cause is an oversecretion of gastric acid; in effect, the stomach or duodenum digests itself. A number of studies have shown that in some individuals, emotional stress leads to gastric oversecretion and ultimately to ulcer formation (Wolf, 1971). Similar results have been reported for various animals (Sawrey, Conger, and Turrell, 1956).

Once again the question is why certain individuals respond to tension in this way. And again the answer is that one of the factors is an initial diathesis. One group of investigators measured gastric secretion levels in army recruits just prior to the stressful months of basic training. After several months some of these men developed ulcers. Everyone who did had very high gastric secretion levels before he entered basic training (Weiner et al., 1957).

A CATEGORIZING REVIEW

We have looked at a number of different mental disorders. The pathology model provides a convenient framework to review the way in which these disorders are generally considered today. This review is summarized in Table 19.1, which classifies disorders by the nature of their main symptoms and of their presumed underlying pathology (which in many cases is still controversial). Either the main symptoms or the pathology or both, can be organic. But they can also be mental, that is, defined by behavioral rather than by organic attributes.

Table 19.1   A CLASSIFICATION OF MENTAL DISORDERS

		Symptoms	
		Primarily organic	Primarily mental
Presumed underlying pathology	Primarily organic	Diabetes Measles Rickets	General Paresis Schizophrenia* Bipolar affective disorders*
	Primarily mental	Psycho-physiological disorders	Anxiety disorders Dissociative disorders

* Whether the underlying pathology of these disorders is primarily organic or psychogenic is still a matter of some debate.

A

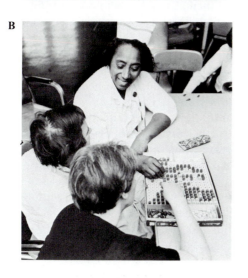

B

THE SOCIOLOGICAL CRITIQUE OF THE PATHOLOGY MODEL

Thus far, our focus has been on the psychological and biological aspects of mental disorder. But psychopathological conditions can also be looked at from a sociological perspective which emphasizes how disordered people are viewed and dealt with by society. This sociological approach has led to several influential attacks on the pathology model.

What Society Does to Those It Calls Mad

The sociological critique of the pathology model is among other things a form of social protest. One of its recurrent themes is that mentally disordered persons are treated as outcasts, even today. Social historians point out that this has been their role since before medieval times. During the late Middle Ages, many European towns placed their "madmen" into special boats, "ships of fools," that dumped their deranged human cargo on far-off foreign shores. Later, the madmen were caged like beasts. Although their fate has improved considerably in modern times, even today they are still largely exiles from the rest of the world.

Some critics of the way in which mental disorder is dealt with in modern society accuse psychiatrists of acting more like jailors than like physicians. Many mentally disordered people are relegated to mental hospitals whose function is custodial rather than therapeutic. Such hospitals are similar to prisons in that they are "total institutions" with round-the-clock control by attendants who train and regiment the inmates in virtually all aspects of daily life (Goffman, 1961). There is little time or money left for psychiatric treatment. This is partially due to extreme understaffing. For instance, in 1969, the ratio of patients to psychiatrists in the mental hospitals of Pennsylvania was so large that the average patient could expect to see a psychiatrist for no more than a fifteen-minute interview every ten days (Kittrie, 1971). The inevitable consequence is boredom, apathy, and despair. The best the patient can do is to learn to play the part of the "good mental patient" as the attendants and psychiatrists want her to; if she does, she may gain various little favors such as coffee, cigarettes, and access to TV or a sunlit dayroom (Figure 19.13).

Until fairly recently, the inmates of such institutions had few legal rights, especially if they were committed. In 1949, only 10 percent of the admissions to mental hospitals in the United States were voluntary. Today, this proportion is much higher, but involuntary institutionalizations are still more common than voluntary ones. Like many other social ills, involuntary institutionalization befalls the

19.13 The condition of mental patients (A) As recently as 1946 and 1947, the conditions in many state mental hospitals led Albert Deutsch to entitle a book on the subject The Shame of the States. (From Deutsch, 1948; courtesy the Lucy Kroll Agency) (B) Conditions have improved considerably, but in many cases the mental hospital is still more of a custodial than a therapeutic institution, and the patient's life there is often empty and barren. (Photographs by Ken Heyman)

poor more often than the well-to-do. The mental patient whose family can keep him at home or put him in a private hospital is less likely to be legally committed (Kittrie, 1971). A number of recent patients' rights campaigns have led to the establishment of more stringent safeguards on commitment procedures. But while such measures have curbed some abuses, they have not changed the fact that mentally disturbed people are still more or less banished and live under a social stigma that is hard to remove. In retrospect, it is ironic that some of the first mental asylums in Europe were set up in former leper houses that had become empty. Leprosy had disappeared, so now the "madman" took over the part of the pariah which the leper had played in former times (Foucault, 1965).

Whom Does Society Call Mad?

The treatment society metes out to mentally disordered persons is grim even with enlightened attitudes. The sociological critics of the pathology model ask who the people are who are treated in this way. To the mental health practitioner, the answer is obvious: Those who demonstrate mental illness by a variety of signs and symptoms. The sociological critics reply that in many ways the causal chain works in reverse; sometimes the label creates the symptoms. The fact that a person is called mentally ill makes others see and treat him differently. Eventually, the labeled individual may change his own self-perception; then he and others will behave so as to make the label fit more and more.

To the extent that this is true, it is a demonstration of a self-fulfilling prophecy. This sometimes has paradoxical effects. To the hospital authorities—attendants, nurses, psychiatrists—the very fact that a person is an inmate is virtual proof that there must be something wrong with her. If a mental patient proclaims her sanity, this is merely evidence that she is even more deranged than anyone had suspected; she doesn't even "have insight." The patient has a better chance of getting discharged if she first admits that she is sick. She can then announce that she is getting better; now the authorities will tend to look at her more kindly, for she is obviously "responding to treatment" (Goffman, 1961).

Are those whom society calls mad merely those of whom society disapproves? The film One Flew over the Cuckoo's Nest *with Jack Nicholson dramatizes this question. (Courtesy the Museum of Modern Art/Film Stills Archives)*

MENTAL ILLNESS AS A MYTH

Some critics maintain that the key to mental disorder is the label; without this, there would be no disorder at all. A prominent exponent of this position is psychiatrist Thomas Szasz. According to Szasz, mental illness is a myth (Szasz, 1974). He and other critics charge that it is merely a term by which we designate people whose behavior deviates from the norms of their society but does not fall into any of the recognized categories of nonconformity. They are neither criminals, nor prostitutes, nor heretics, nor revolutionaries, and so on. To account for their deviance, only one explanation is left—they are mentally ill (Scheff, 1966). Seen in this light, mental disorder is not a condition that is inherent in the individual; instead, it depends upon how the individual is seen by others. According to this position, madness (like beauty) is in the eye of the beholder.

THE EVIDENCE ON THE ROLE OF LABELING

Cross-cultural comparisons   What evidence supports the labeling theory? One line of argument comes from the study of different cultures. There is no doubt that what is deviant in one culture is not necessarily deviant in another. The Kwakiutl Indian who burns valuable blankets at a special ceremony to shame his rivals is honored by his fellow chiefs; the Los Angeles executive who decides to dynamite his speedboat and swimming pool to prove that he can afford to do so is quietly sent off to a private sanitarium. To labeling theorists this suggests that what is meant by *mental disorder* is relative to the culture and is therefore essentially arbitrary.

This point does not follow. Even if it were true that all mental disorders are culturally determined, this would not prove that these disorders are caused by labeling. Such a result might support the notion that the disorders are psychogenic and are somehow caused by the cultural pattern. But this is quite different from the statement that the disorder does not really exist except as a label attached by others.

In any case, there is good evidence that shows that there is less cultural relativism in psychiatric matters than is sometimes supposed. To be sure, some kinds of disorders may be more prevalent in a given culture. An example is conversion disorder, which appears to be much less common today than it was in the nineteenth century; according to some authors this is because of a less restrictive family atmosphere and more permissive child rearing, especially in the sexual sphere (Chodoff, 1954). But the fact that some disorders may be culturally determined does not prove that all disorders are. The best evidence suggests that schizophrenia and bipolar affective disorders are found throughout the world. As we have seen, the symptom patterns of schizophrenia have been observed among Greenland Eskimoes and West African villagers, as well as among ourselves.

Being sane in insane places   Proponents of labeling theory often appeal to the results of a study by David Rosenhan to support their position. Rosenhan arranged to have himself and seven other normal persons admitted as patients to various psychiatric hospitals across the country. Each pseudopatient came to the hospital admissions office with the same complaint—he or she heard voices that

677

said "empty," "hollow," or "thud." They employed a pseudonym and sometimes misrepresented their professions, but in all other respects they reported their own life histories and their true present circumstances. All pseudopatients were admitted to the psychiatric ward, all but one with the diagnosis of schizophrenia. Once on the ward, the pseudopatients' behavior was completely normal. They said that they no longer heard voices and that they felt perfectly fine.

There was not a single case in which a hospital staff member detected the deception. The fact that pseudopatients behaved quite normally did not help, for whatever they did was generally interpreted in line with the original diagnosis. For example, all of the pseudopatients took extensive notes. At first, they did so surreptitiously, but they soon found out that there was no need for circumspection. The note-taking was seen as just one further manifestation of the disorder. A typical nurse's report read, "Patient engaged in writing behavior." No one ever asked what was written and why; presumably it was an aspect of being schizophrenic.

Once labeled in this way, the pseudopatients suffered much the same neglect that was the lot of the other patients. They felt depersonalized and powerless. They received many pills (which they flushed down the toilet), but had little access to members of the professional staff. Their average daily contact with psychiatrists, psychologists, residents, and physicians combined was 6.8 minutes.

Prior to the study, all of the pseudopatients had agreed that they would try to get discharged without outside help by convincing the hospital staff that they were sane, but without admitting the original deception. They found that it was easier to get in than out. On the average, it took nineteen days; in one case, it took fifty-two. When they were finally discharged, it was with the diagnosis "Schizophrenia, in remission." In lay terms, this means that there are no symptoms, at least for now. The validity of the original diagnosis was never questioned (Rosenhan, 1973).

The Rosenhan findings paint an unflattering picture of conditions in mental hospitals and add legitimate fuel to social protests and cries for reform. They also show that a diagnostic label may reinforce a preexisting conception of what a patient is like. But do they really show that the distinction between sane and insane depends *only* upon the label and that mental illness is a myth?

The answer is no. Consider the situation from the psychiatrist's point of view. A patient had auditory hallucinations on entering the hospital. This symptom promptly disappears. What are the psychiatrists to do? The idea of deception never occurs to them. (After all, who would be paranoid enough to suspect that it was all part of a psychological experiment?) Under the circumstances, they must conclude that the patient is or was suffering from some psychotic disorder, probably schizophrenia, and should be kept under further observation. The fact that the patient's later acts are interpreted in terms of the original diagnosis is now quite understandable. He did hear voices a few days ago, so his present sanity is probably more apparent than real. Seen in this light, the psychiatrists' acts don't seem all that irrational (Wishner, 1974).

MENTAL ILLNESS AS MENTAL REBIRTH

A rather different approach to mental disorder, and especially to schizophrenia, is associated with the Scottish psychiatrist, R. D. Laing. Laing does not believe that

The romantic view of mental disorder
The idea that madness makes a person better, or purer, or confers a deeper understanding of the world, has a long history in Western thought. One example is Cervantes's Don Quixote who tilted with windmills but was more kindly and noble than the sane people around him. (Picasso's Don Quichotte, *1955. Courtesy of the Musée Municipal, St. Denis-Seine)*

schizophrenia is a *dis*order. On the contrary, he regards it as in some ways preferable to what we ordinarily call normality. His thesis is as old as Western literature: The sane are mad, and the mad are sane. He argues that what we call normality is a web of hypocrisies and contradictions which stunt our potential for self-awareness and genuine love: "By the time the new human being is fifteen or so, we are left with a being like ourselves, a half-crazed creature more or less adjusted to a mad world. This is normality in our present age" (Laing, 1967, p. 58).

In Laing's view, schizophrenia is not a *mal*function, is not a reflection of a pathology. It is rather a kind of "voyage of self-discovery," at least for some patients, which represents an attempt to heal the wounds a sick society has inflicted on them. Laing therefore believes that schizophrenics don't need therapy in any of the traditional forms that psychiatry has to offer. They may, however, need compassionate understanding as well as guidance on the journey into their own inner life.

Quite apart from Laing's views about treatment there is another issue: his belief that schizophrenia is not a pathological condition but an attempt at a mental rebirth. This suggests that schizophrenia is in some ways a desirable state. But schizophrenics do not seem to think that it is. Those who recover sufficiently to tell us about their experience in retrospect leave little doubt that they felt in desperate straits—they did not think of themselves as intrepid Marco Polos exploring some inner space.

Some critics have likened Laing's view of schizophrenia to the romanticizing of tuberculosis in a prior era. Many nineteenth-century plays and operas featured ethereal, consumptive heroines who were spiritually purified by their suffering and proclaimed their undying love for the hero while gently expiring at the end of Act V. But in fact, tuberculosis is not a romantic condition; it is a slow, insidious, ugly killer, now fortunately robbed of its horror because physicians learned to understand it as an illness and then went about the unromantic business of finding its cure (Siegler and Osmond, 1974). Much the same is true for schizophrenia. No amount of romantic prose can change the fact that it is a scourge. Perhaps the next few decades will lead to its elimination through the discovery of a definite cure.

Social Deviance

It is rather ironic that the sociological critics of the pathology model have concentrated most of their fire on a mental disorder which the pathology model handles reasonably well, namely schizophrenia. A similar critique might have found more appropriate targets had it been directed at certain other diagnostic categories that also huddle under the psychiatric umbrella. The psychiatric classification system includes a number of human conditions that are certainly deviant and usually undesirable, such as antisocial personality, alcoholism, drug addiction, and various sexual deviations. But it is by no means clear that all of these are really mental disorders. Nor is it clear that the pathology model is the most appropriate framework within which they should be viewed.

Society calls some forms of deviance criminal while calling others mad, and it has set up institutions to deal with each—the judicial system for the first and the mental health system for the second. In actual fact, the two classifications overlap

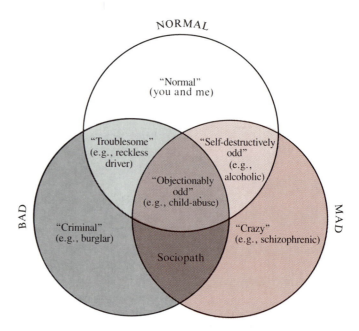

19.14   The three labels, BAD, MAD, and NORMAL, and some labels for their areas of overlap   *(After Stone, 1975)*

and both shade off into normality. Figure 19.14 is an attempt to provide a graphic description of how the terms "normal," "bad," and "mad" are usually applied. Some kinds of persons can be classified unambiguously: you and I (definitely "normal," or at least, so we hope), a professional criminal ("bad"), and a severe case of schizophrenia ("mad"). But there are also areas of overlap. Some people occupy a gray area between normality and lawlessness. An example might be a person who is a habitual reckless driver. Others are on the boundary between mental disorder and normality. An example would be a man with a serious drinking problem. Still others are in the region of overlap between criminality and mental disorder. They are somehow both "mad" and "bad" at the same time. Our present concern is with one such group of individuals, the so-called ***antisocial personalities,*** or, as they have also been called, ***sociopaths.****

THE SOCIOPATH

The clinical picture   The sociopath is an individual who gets into continual trouble with others and with society. He is grossly selfish, callous, impulsive, and irresponsible. His—or, somewhat less frequently, her—difficulties generally start with truancy from school, runaway episodes, and a "wild adolescence" marked by belligerence and precocious sexual experience and promiscuity (Robins, 1966). Later on there are various minor scrapes that often escalate into increasingly serious legal and social offenses. But the distinguishing characteristics of sociopathy go deeper than this. One feature is the lack of any genuine feeling of love or loyalty for any person or any group. Another characteristic is that there is relatively little guilt or anxiety. As a result, the sociopath is a creature of the present whose primary object is to gratify the impulses he feels now, with little concern about the future and even less remorse about the past.

---

* *An earlier designation was* **psychopath.** *Some versions of this term are still in current use. An example is the MMPI scale which attempts to measure* psychopathic deviance.

All of this is another way of saying that sociopaths are not truly socialized. They are not pack animals; they are genuine loners. They are often quite adept at the outward skills of social living; they are frequently charming and of greater than average intelligence. In these regards, sociopaths are quite different from ordinary criminals and delinquents. These too are in conflict with established society, but unlike sociopaths, they generally have a society of their own, such as a juvenile gang or a crime syndicate, whose code they try to honor and to which they have some sense of loyalty.

Another contrast is that between sociopaths and neurotics. Most neurotics are overcontrolled. They are guilt-ridden, anxious, and unable to express their impulses except in devious, roundabout ways. The sociopath on the other hand is undercontrolled and readily yields to the fleeting impulse of the moment (McCord and McCord, 1964). An illustration is the case of a forty-four-year-old man:

> [Roger] was reared in a well-to-do family, the only child of a doting mother. In the past ten years, Roger squandered a substantial inheritance and was beginning to "fall on hard times." Handsome, well-educated and suave in manner, he had always been skillful·in charming and exploiting others, especially women. Faced with economic adversity, Roger allied himself with a group of stock promoters involved in selling essentially worthless shares of "sure-bet" Canadian mining stock. This led to other "shady deals"; and in time Roger became a full-fledged "love swindler" who intrigued, lived off, and "borrowed" thousands of dollars from a succession of wealthy and "lonely" mistresses (Millon, 1969, p. 434).

Some possible causes of sociopathy   What accounts for the inadequate socialization that characterizes sociopaths? A number of investigators have focused on the sociopath's lack of concern about the future consequences of his actions. Sociopaths are comparatively fearless. This is especially true when the danger is far off. One investigator told sociopaths and normals that they would receive a shock at the end of a ten-minute period. The subjects' apprehensiveness was assessed by their galvanic skin response (GSR). As the time grew closer, the control subjects grew increasingly nervous. In contrast, the sociopaths showed little anticipatory fear (Lippert and Senter, 1966). If future pain had just as little import when the sociopath was young, his inadequate socialization becomes partially comprehensible. Whoever tried to teach him the don'ts of childhood had no effective deterrents (Figure 19.15).

The strange fearlessness of sociopaths has been observed by several writers who have noted their "extraordinary poise," their "smooth sense of physical being," and their "relative serenity" under conditions that would produce agitation in most of us (Cleckley, 1964). How does this difference between sociopaths and normals come about? Several investigators believe that there is a difference in some underlying physiological functions. One line of evidence concerns the EEG (electrical recordings from the brain; see Chapter 3). It appears that a fairly high proportion of sociopaths have abnormal EEGs which resemble those of children. One possible interpretation is that this cortical immaturity of sociopaths is the physiological counterpart of their essential childishness—their desire for instant gratification and their belligerent tantrums when thwarted.

Another hypothesis is that the sociopath is cortically underaroused, as if he were not fully awake under normal conditions (see Chapter 3). Proponents of this hypothesis argue that because of this underarousal, sociopaths actively seek stim-

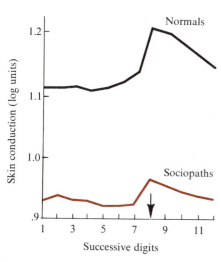

19.15   Anticipation of electric shock in normals and sociopaths   *Normals and sociopaths were repeatedly presented with a series of 12 consecutive digits from 1 to 12. Whenever the digit 8 appeared, the subjects suffered an electric shock. To determine whether there were any differences in anticipatory anxiety prior to the advent of shock, the galvanic skin response (GSR) was measured. The results are shown in units of log conductance (a measure of GSR activity) for each of the 12 digits in the series. The sociopaths showed a much lower base-response level. In addition, they showed less anticipatory reaction to the digits just prior to the critical digit. (After Hare, 1965)*

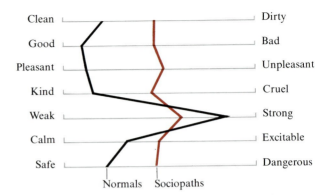

19.16 Sociopaths' perceptions of their fathers *Sociopaths and normals were asked to describe the concept "my father" by reference to a series of bipolar adjectives (such as good-bad, weak-strong). The figure shows that sociopaths evaluated their fathers much more negatively than normal controls. (After Marks, 1966)*

ulation—they court thrills and danger to rouse themselves to some optimal level of stimulation, much as the rest of us might pinch our arms to keep ourselves from dozing off (Hare, 1970).

Such physiological differences suggest that there may be a constitutional predisposition toward sociopathy. This predisposition may well be genetic, as shown by the fact that identical twins have higher concordance rates on sociopathy than fraternal twins. Early environment also plays a role. There is considerable evidence that sociopaths are more likely to have a sociopathic or alcoholic father than are normals (Figure 19.16). An additional factor is discipline; inconsistent discipline in childhood or no discipline at all correlates with sociopathy in adulthood (Robins, 1966).

Sociopathy and the pathology model By now, we are starting to get some understanding of how sociopathy might come about. But does that justify our calling it a mental disorder? Put another way, does this mean that the pathology model applies to this condition? There is some doubt whether it really does. In what sense is sociopathy a mental disorder? To be sure, the sociopath often comes to grief, but so do ordinary criminals and for the same reason: they get caught. Why should we call the one mad and the other bad? Why should one be the province of the mental-health system while the other is the business of the courts?

The question is especially pertinent given the fact that many modern psychiatrists and psychologists are pessimistic about the possibility of therapy for sociopaths. An additional difficulty is caused by problems of differential diagnosis, for in actual practice it is by no means easy to distinguish criminals and sociopaths. Under the circumstances, it is not obvious what is gained by classifying sociopathy as a psychiatric condition. To be sure, there is some evidence that the sociopath is a distinctive kind of person with a particular set of factors that make him so. But then so is the ordinary criminal. It is also true that sociopathy is an undesirable condition—if not for the sociopath himself, then for those around him. But so again is ordinary criminality.

Some Contributions of Labeling Theory

Sociopathy is only one of the questionable categories in the psychiatric catalogue. Similar questions can be raised about drug addiction or alcoholism or a number of other deviant patterns. Are these really mental disorders in the sense in which schizophrenia and obsessive-compulsive disorders are? By stretching the meaning of the term so wide as to include virtually all forms of human behavior that cause personal unhappiness, psychopathologists court the danger of proving their critics right after all. When defined so broadly, mental illness may indeed become the myth that Szasz has claimed it to be.

The imperialism of modern psychopathology that makes it try to subsume ever more conditions is not the fault of an overambitious psychiatric establishment. Instead, it is the product of a society that insists on quick and simple solutions. We think that by designating a given human or social problem a *mental disorder* we have somehow taken a stride toward its solution. But we've really done nothing of the sort. For calling a problem—alcoholism, sexual exhibitionism, drug addiction, or whatever—a psychiatric disorder does not necessarily make it so. Nor does it mean that we therefore know what to do about it.

Critics like Thomas Szasz and R. D. Laing may have overstated their cases against the pathology model, but they have nevertheless performed several vital functions. One comes from their insistence on the social role of labeling. This provides a constant reminder that terms such as *schizophrenia* are not merely diagnostic categories. In many cases, they are also applied as stigmatizing labels that impede the patient's path to recovery and make his eventual return to the community difficult and frightening (Bernheim and Lewine, 1979). These critics of the pathology model have also served as watchdogs against various forms of psychiatric tyranny. In this capacity, they have pointed to certain abuses that grow out of civil commitment procedures and they have raised public concern about the far from optimum conditions that still prevail in many mental hospitals.

As we have seen, Szasz and Laing are primarily interested in patients diagnosed as schizophrenics. But their humane concerns apply with even greater force to several other groups. Examples are patients who are said to suffer from **senile dementia** and related problems of aging. While many such patients in mental hospitals have trouble in remembering recent events and experience disorientation, their main difficulties often lie elsewhere. As one writer put it in describing a 1966 court decision:

> The superintendent of St. Elizabeth's at the time testified that "only 50 percent of the patients . . . require hospitalization in a mental institution" and that "for many older patients, the primary need was found to be for physical rather than psychiatric care." . . . Nor was this need well met at the hospital. The court recognized that long-term hospitalization debilitates patients, and that the last thing an aged person needs is the depersonalization of a large institution, further isolation, loss of dignity, and boredom" (Stone, 1975, p. 172).

Less frequent now, but fairly common a few decades ago, is the institutionalization of another group of persons who have even less business in a mental hospital but who were put there nevertheless. These were deaf people who do not speak. Today we know that the deaf can communicate perfectly well by means of sign language if they are in the company of other deaf people. In fact, if there is no such community, they sometimes invent a sign system of their own (see Chapter 15). But until recently, they were regarded as mutes and "dummies," as people who were retarded or mentally disordered, and who were therefore often placed in special institutions. Once there, their fate was even worse than in the outside world; their inability to speak was seen as further proof that they were mentally defective. Given the label, they were treated accordingly. One report tells of a deaf child who was in a mental institution for five years before he was finally recognized for what he was and released (Vernon and Brown, 1964; Sullivan and Vernon, 1979).

THE SCOPE OF PSYCHOPATHOLOGY

We have seen that an enormous range of conditions are encompassed within psychiatric classification schemes. Most of these conditions cause personal distress and some impair social functioning. But what else do they have in common? Some are somatogenic disorders, while others seem to be psychogenic. Still others are in a murky borderland between criminality and psychopathology, or between normality and psychopathology. Still others may simply be deviant behavior patterns that our own society doesn't approve of. But since they are all categories of the same psychiatric classification scheme, they must have something in common. What exactly is it?

There is really only one answer. What all of these conditions share is that they are all dumped into the lap of the same group of mental-health professionals who are then told, "They are your responsibility. You take care of them. If at all possible, you cure or treat or rehabilitate them. If you can't, then confine them. But whatever you do or don't do, they are yours." In a way this is very similar to what our ancestors did when they threw criminals, ne'er-do-wells, seniles, psychotics, neurotics, and political dissenters into the same asylum dungeons.

Under the circumstances, we must not expect to find one set of principles that accounts for all conditions that psychopathologists deal with. There may be some principles that underlie schizophrenia, some others that underlie anxiety disorders, still others for drug addiction, and so on. But these principles may very well be quite different. For the simple fact is that the field of psychopathology is not a scientifically coherent enterprise. Its coherence comes from a social need that asks that a certain set of problems be taken care of. But these problems are very heterogeneous and so the same conceptual and curative models will almost surely not apply to all.

SUMMARY

1. The field of *psychopathology,* which is sometimes called *abnormal psychology,* deals with a wide assortment of behavioral conditions that generally cause considerable anguish and seriously impair the person's functioning. Examples are cases of *neurosis,* in which contact with reality is maintained, and *psychosis,* in which it often is not.

2. In certain periods of history, mental disorder was seen as a form of demonic possession. In others, as in our own, it was regarded as a form of illness. Some of these disorders are *somatogenic,* being the result of a bodily malfunction. An example is *general paresis,* which was discovered to result from a syphilitic infection contracted years before. Other mental disorders are thought to be *psychogenic,* resulting from psychological rather than organic causes, a view which seemed to apply to many cases of neurosis, especially *hysteria* (now called a *conversion disorder*).

3. A very general conception of the cause of mental disorder is the *pathology model,* which states that mental disorder is analogous to nonpsychiatric disease. A given disorder has various *symptoms* which often form a pattern or *syndrome;* these are the bases for diagnosis and classification. The symptom patterns are thought to result from some underlying and relatively immediate cause, the *pathology.* Many disorders seem well described by the *diathesis-stress* conception, which sees the pathology as jointly produced by various predispositions (diathesis) and precipitating triggers (stress). As here formulated, the pathology model is largely descriptive and makes no assertion about the nature of the symptoms, their psychogenic or somatogenic causes, or the appropriate mode of treatment. Three subcategories of the general pathology model are the *medical model,* the *psychoanalytic model,* and the *learning model.*

4. One of the most serious conditions in the realm of psychopathology is *schizophrenia.* Its main symptoms are disorders of thought and attention, social withdrawal, disruption of emotional responding, and in many cases, the construction of a private world accompanied by *delusions* and *hallucinations.*

5. One question about the pathology of schizophrenia is how best to characterize the schizophrenic's underlying psychological malfunction. Many authors believe that it is fundamentally a disorder of thought, based on an inability to focus mentally in space and time. A different question concerns the cause of this psychological deficit. This is widely believed to be an expression of an organic pathology. Evidence comes from studies which show that the incidence of what appears to be schizophrenia is roughly the same in different cultures, from genetic studies which show that it has a substantial hereditary component, and from the fact that a certain class of drugs, the *phenothiazines,* have a specific therapeutic effect on schizophrenic symptoms.

6. Exactly what the underlying organic pathology of schizophrenia is—assuming that there is one—is still unknown. According to one hypothesis, the critical malfunction is an oversensitivity to *dopamine,* a neurotransmitter that has an arousing function in the brain. Supporting evidence derives from the therapeutic effect of the phenothiazines, which are known to block dopamine at neuron synapses.

7. More remote causes of schizophrenia include a genetic factor. The evidence is provided by *concordance* studies of identical and fraternal twins and by studies of children of schizophrenic mothers adopted shortly after birth. But this genetic factor is only a predisposition; its conversion into the actual schizophrenic disorder depends on some precipitating environmental stress. Some investigators believe that the critical environmental factors include socioeconomic class. Others emphasize various pathological interactions within the family, including confusing patterns of communication such as the *double bind.*

8. In another group of conditions, *affective disorders,* the dominant disturbance is one of mood, as in the frenzied energy of *mania* or the despair and lethargy of *depression.* Affective disorders are often periodic, and may be *bipolar,* with recurrent swings from one emotional extreme to the other, or *unipolar,* in which the mood extreme is of one kind only, generally depression. According to one view, affective disorders, especially the bipolar ones, are produced by an organic pathology, a belief bolstered by evidence that such conditions have a genetic component. One hypothesis has it that there is a defect in the supply of certain neurotransmitters, in particular, *norepinephrine, serotonin,* or both. Other investigators stress the role of psychogenic factors, such as cognitive outlook. An influential example of a psychogenic approach is the *learned helplessness* theory of depression.

9. In another group of conditions, *anxiety disorders* (including *phobia, generalized anxiety disorder,* and *obsessive-compulsive disorders*), both the main symptoms and the underlying pathology are primarily psychological. The same holds for *conversion disorders* and *dissociative disorders* including cases of *multiple personality.* Many practitioners believe that the symptoms of all these conditions are either anxiety or various learned reactions to ward off anxiety.

10. In *psychophysiological conditions,* psychogenic causes have genuinely organic consequences. An example is *essential hypertension.* Hypertension is evidently a residue of continual sympathetic arousal brought about by chronic emotional stress.

11. A contemporary critique of the pathology model takes a *sociological perspective,* emphasizing the fact that those whom society calls "mad" are socially *deviant.* This position has led to *labeling theory,* a view which finds some—controversial—support from studies of *pseudopatients.* An extreme version of labeling theory was proposed by Szasz who holds that mental illness is a myth. A related conception is Laing's, who goes further and regards certain disorders such as schizophrenia as voyages of mental rediscovery. The evidence suggests that while labeling may make a patient's condition worse, it has little bearing on how it arose in the first place, nor does it undermine the view that many mental disorders reflect genuine pathologies.

12. The problem of defining psychopathology is especially acute for conditions such as *sociopathy* in which the deviance overlaps mental disorder and criminality. The causes of sociopathy are still unknown; hypotheses include cortical immaturity, a chronic state of underarousal that leads to attempts to seek continued stimulation, and a genetic predisposition.

13. Labeling theory has made some important contributions by pointing to various abuses in psychiatric commitment procedures. It has also called attention to many questionable categories in the psychiatric catalogue whose status as mental disorders is highly debatable, including drug addiction, alcoholism, and *senile dementia.*

CHAPTER 20

Treatment of Psychopathology

What can be done about mental disorders? There is no scarcity of proposed remedies, each with its adherents. Some rely on biological interventions such as drugs. Others approach the condition at the psychological level; the classical example is psychoanalysis. Unfortunately, the proven accomplishments are thus far relatively modest. In a way, this is hardly surprising. Considering that we know so little about the causes of the various mental disorders, can we expect to know much more about their cures?

SOMATIC THERAPIES

One approach to treatment is through various manipulations of the body. Such **somatic therapies** constitute medicine's classical attack on any disease. Thus, once mental disorder was cast as an illness, it was only natural to try to heal it with the traditional tools of the physician's trade. But in fact, until fairly recently, most such attempts were unsuccessful. In some cases, the would-be cures were worse than the disease. We already mentioned a very early example: trephining, the removal of sections of the skull, a prehistoric practice that persisted into medieval times. Other early procedures involved a relentless succession of bloodlettings and purgatives, all in the hope of restoring a proper harmony among the bodily humors. Later developments were hardly milder. For example, Benjamin Rush (1745–1813), one of the signers of the Declaration of Independence and the acknowledged father of American psychiatry, dunked patients into hot or cold water and kept them under just short of drowning, or twirled them on special devices at speeds that often led to unconsciousness (Figure 20.1). Such methods were said to reestablish the balance between bodily and mental functions. They

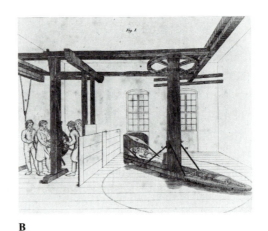

A   B   C

20.1   Early methods for treating mental disorder   *(A) A crib for violent patients. (Courtesy Historical Pictures Service) (B) A centrifugal-force bed. (Courtesy National Library of Medicine) (C) A swinging device. (Courtesy Culver Pictures)*

almost certainly had no such salutary effects, although they were probably welcomed by hospital attendants since such methods undoubtedly terrified the inmates and thus helped to "keep order" (Mora, 1975).

Drug Therapies

The bleak outlook for somatic therapy did not appreciably brighten until the beginning of this century. The first step was the conquest of general paresis, a progressive deterioration of physical and psychological functioning, by an attack on the syphilitic infection that caused it (see Chapter 19). But the major breakthrough has come only during the last thirty years or so with the discovery of a number of drugs that seem to control, or at least to alleviate, schizophrenia and affective disorders.

MAJOR PSYCHIATRIC DRUGS

Antipsychotic drugs   In the last chapter, we saw that one of the arguments for a biochemical theory of schizophrenia is the effectiveness of drugs such as ***chlorpromazine*** which belong to a family called the ***phenothiazines.*** Chlorpromazine and its pharmacological relatives tend to reduce many of the major symptoms of schizophrenia, such as thought disorder, withdrawal, and hallucinations. These drugs block synaptic receptors in pathways of the brain that are sensitive to ***dopamine,*** and it is this blockade that is thought to produce the therapeutic effects.

The impact of the phenothiazines and related antipsychotic drugs (together with that of drugs aimed at affective disorders) upon psychiatric practice has been enormous. In 1955, there were 560,000 patients in the mental hospitals of the United States; about half of these were schizophrenics. Based on the rate at which that population had increased prior to 1955, a reasonable projection for 1970 was about 738,000. But the actual figure in 1970 was 340,000—less than half of that estimate. One reason for this was the psychiatric revolution produced by the new drugs that appeared during the mid-fifties. These drugs made it possible to discharge schizophrenic patients more quickly than ever before, with average hospi-

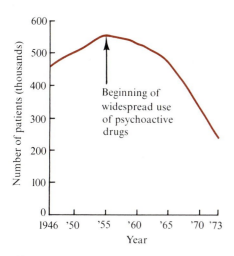

20.2   Number of residents in state and local government mental hospitals between 1946 and 1973 in the United States   *(Based on data from U.S. Public Health Service)*

tal stays of about two months. The result was a drastic reduction in the total hospital population (Figure 20.2).*

It has sometimes been argued that drugs like chlorpromazine are not really antischizophrenic agents at all, but merely fancy sedatives that quiet patients down. This position does not square with the facts. While chlorpromazine and other phenothiazines alleviate schizophrenic symptoms, such powerful sedatives as phenobarbital have no such effect. Furthermore, the antischizophrenic drugs seem to improve the behavior both of patients who are highly agitated and of those who are apathetic and withdrawn; they calm the frenzy of the first and help bring the second out of their stupor. Still other evidence suggests that the phenothiazines have a *specific drug effect.* They work on the symptoms that characterize schizophrenia but not on symptoms that are not specific to that disorder. For example, they help to clear up the patient's disordered thought but have little effect on depression or anxiety. It is thus hardly surprising that chlorpromazine and other phenothiazines do not calm down normals or patients with anxiety disorders (Davis and Cole, 1975).

Antidepressants   Shortly after the introduction of the antischizophrenic agents, two major groups of drugs were found that acted as *antidepressants: monoamine oxidase (MAO) inhibitors* and *tricyclics.* Of these, the tricyclics are the most widely used; they tend to be more effective and have fewer adverse side effects. The therapeutic effectiveness of such antidepressants seems to be due to the fact that they increase the amount of norepinephrine and serotonin available for synaptic transmission. These drugs can be very effective in counteracting depression, but not all of them work for all patients. It appears that different patients have somewhat different biochemical deficits, and thus require different antidepressant medication. Some recent studies suggest that there may be "biological markers" (for example, blood tests) that may help to match the proper antidepressant drug to the particular patient (Maugh, 1981).

Just as the phenothiazines are not mere sedatives, so the MAO inhibitors and the tricyclics are more than mere stimulants, for they seem to have a specific effect on depression. Evidence comes from the fact that these drugs do not produce euphoria in normals; they evidently have little effect on mood if there is no depression to begin with (Cole and Davis, 1975).

Lithium   A fairly recent development is the use of lithium salts such as *lithium carbonate* in the treatment of mania. Most manic patients show remarkable improvement within five or ten days after starting lithium therapy. There is some further evidence that the drug can forestall depressive episodes in bipolar affective disorders (see Chapter 19). Just what accounts for these effects is largely unknown. According to one hypothesis, lithium limits the availability of norepinephrine, an effect opposite to that of the antidepressant drugs. This would explain its role in counteracting mania but sheds no light on how it forestalls depression in bipolar patients (Fieve, 1975; Berger, 1978).

---

* Another factor was a change in social policy, prompted in part by economic considerations, which stressed discharge rather than long-term hospitalization.

How can we assess the effectiveness of a drug? We will consider how this is done in detail, for some of the issues raised by drug evaluation methods are not limited to tests of drug therapy. In principle, they apply to the evaluation of any therapeutic procedure whatever, including psychotherapy.

Suppose we want to find out whether a given drug, say, chlorpromazine, has the curative effects its advocates claim. The most obvious approach is to administer the drug to a group of schizophrenic patients for some period and then make a before-and-after assessment. In fact, many of the clinical studies reported in the literature are of just this kind. But a little reflection shows that this procedure is not adequate.

Controlling for spontaneous improvement   One problem with the simple before-and-after test is that it ignores the possibility that the patient's condition would have cleared up without treatment, whether permanently or just for a while. Such spontaneous improvements occur in many disorders. To control for this factor one has to compare two groups of patients drawn from the same population. One group would receive the drug for, say, six weeks; a control group would not. Both groups would be judged at the start and the end of the study (and perhaps during periods in between). Initially, they ought to be equivalent. The question is whether they will be judged to be different when the six weeks are up.

Controlling for placebo effects   Suppose that after six weeks the patients who were given chlorpromazine seem to be less disoriented and withdrawn than the untreated controls. The fact that the untreated control group improved less or not at all rules out the possibility that this change for the better was produced by spontaneous improvement. So can we now conclude that the lessening of schizophrenic symptoms was caused by the drug as such? The answer is no, for we have not controlled for the possibility that the result is a so-called ***placebo effect.***

In medicine, the term *placebo* refers to some inert (that is, medically neutral) substance that is administered to a patient who believes that this substance has certain therapeutic powers, although it actually has none. Numerous studies have shown that, given this belief, a sizable proportion of patients suffering from many disorders will show some kind of improvement after ingesting what are actually sugar pills or receiving injections of harmless salt solutions. Such placebo effects probably account for many of the cures of ancient physicians whose medications included such items as crocodile dung, swine teeth, and moss scraped from the skull of a man who died a violent death (Shapiro, 1971).

Given the power of the placebo effect, how can we be sure that the improvement in the drug-treated group of our example is caused by the properties of the drug itself? Perhaps a sugar pill—or a bit of crocodile dung—would have done as well. To rule out this possibility, we must administer a placebo to the control patients. They will thus no longer be "untreated." On the contrary, they will receive the same attention, will be told the same thing, and will be given the same number of pills at the same time as the patients in the true drug group. There will be only one difference between the two groups: the control patients will swallow pills that, unbeknownst to them, contain only inert materials. As a result of this stratagem, we achieve simultaneous control for two factors—spontaneous improve-

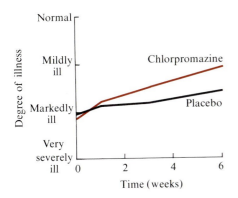

Normal
Mildly ill
Chlorpromazine
Markedly ill
Placebo
Very severely ill

Degree of illness

0   2   4   6
Time (weeks)

20.3   Severity of illness over a six-week period during which patients were treated with either chlorpromazine or a placebo

ment and placebo effects. Now that these two factors are controlled, a difference in the way the two groups appear after treatment can finally be attributed to the effect of the drug itself. Figure 20.3 shows the results of such a study, comparing the effects of chlorpromazine and a placebo control after one, three, and six weeks of treatment. As the figure shows, chlorpromazine is clearly superior. But as the figure also shows, some slight improvement is found in the placebo group as well, thus highlighting the need for such a control in the evaluation of drug effectiveness.

What explains placebo effects? Some of them may be the result of **endorphins,** chemicals produced by the brain itself which act like opiates and reduce pain (see Chapter 2). Evidence for this view comes from a study in which pain was reduced by a placebo medication which the patients believed was a pain reliever. But this relief stopped as soon as the patients received a dose of a drug that is known to counteract the effects of any opiate (Levine, Gordon, and Fields, 1979).

Controlling for the doctor's expectations   By definition, a placebo control implies that all of the patients in the group think that they are being treated with the real drug. But to guarantee this desired state of ignorance, the doctors—and the nurses and attendants—must also be kept in the dark about who is getting a placebo and who the real drug, for the true information may affect their ratings of the patients' progress. If they believe in the drug's effectiveness, they may exaggerate signs of improvement in members of the drug-treated group.

The staff members' knowledge may also have a more indirect effect. They may unwittingly communicate it to the patients, perhaps by observing the drug-treated ones more closely or by being less concerned if a placebo-treated patient fails to take her morning pill. By such signals, the patients may find out whether the doctors expect them to get better or not. If so, there is no genuine placebo control. To guard against such confounding effects of expectation, modern drug evaluators use the **double-blind technique** in which neither the staff members nor the patients know who is assigned to which group. The only ones who know are the investigators who run the study.

LIMITATIONS OF DRUG THERAPY

The preceding discussion may have suggested that present-day psychiatric drugs are an unqualified boon which provide a definitive cure for schizophrenia or affective disorders. At least as yet, this is not the case. To begin with, these drugs can have side effects. For example, phenothiazines may produce various disruptions of autonomic functioning that range from chronic dryness of the mouth to blurred vision, difficulty in urination, and cardiac irregularities. In addition, there are sometimes disturbances of posture and involuntary movement, with symptoms such as tremors, a shuffling gait, and a curiously inexpressive, mask-like face. Individuals react differently to the drugs. For some, the side effects are great, for others only minimal.

These side effects can be regarded simply as a kind of cost exacted by the use of the drugs. But how great are the drugs' benefits? Critics of drug therapy contend that currently the beneficial results of drug therapy are still rather limited. This is especially so for the antischizophrenic drugs. To be sure, the phenothiazines have made it possible to discharge schizophrenic patients much sooner than in predrug days. But this doesn't mean that these patients are fully cured. For one thing, they

Some adverse effects of deinstitutionalization *Some of the homeless in American cities may be persons discharged from mental hospitals who are unable to make an adjustment to the world outside. (Photograph by Herlinde Koelbl, Leo de Wys)*

have to stay on a ***maintenance dose*** of the drug outside of the hospital, which they often prefer not to do, given the drug's unpleasant side effects. If they discontinue taking the drug, they may relapse. Discontinued maintenance medication is most likely to produce relapse in discharged patients facing special stress, such as a family situation in which there is intense emotion and hostility (Vaughn and Leff, 1976).

But even with a maintenance dose, there is no guarantee that the discharged patients will become normal members of the community. This is especially unlikely for patients whose social adjustment was poor before they developed psychotic symptoms. Such patients will probably make only a marginal adjustment to the external world. The picture is brighter for drug therapy of the affective disorders, especially in the case of lithium treatment. But even here patients must usually be kept on a maintenance dose and the cure is not always complete.

Despite these limitations, modern drug therapies do represent a major step forward. They have restored some patients to normal functioning and have allowed those who would otherwise have spent much of their lives in hospital wards to manage, however imperfectly, in a family or community setting. No less important is the fact that these drugs—especially the phenothiazines—have completely changed the atmosphere in mental hospitals. Until a few decades ago, straitjackets were common, as were feces-smeared and shriek-filled wards; today, such things are comparatively rare because the drugs do diminish the more violent symptoms of many mental ailments. As a result, the mental hospital can function as a therapeutic center. It can provide important social and psychological services, including psychotherapy, all of which would have been unthinkable in the "snake-pit" settings of former times.

Other Somatic Therapies

PSYCHOSURGERY

Until the advent of the major psychiatric drugs, psychiatrists relied on several other somatic therapies, all of which involved more drastic assaults on the nervous system. Some of these consisted of brain surgery. An example is ***prefrontal lobotomy,*** in which the neurological connections between the thalamus and the frontal lobes are severed, in whole or in part. This operation was meant to liberate the patient's thoughts from the pathological influence of his emotions, on the dubious neurological assumption that thought and emotion are localized in the frontal lobes and the thalamus respectively.

Evaluation studies of these surgical procedures have come up with largely ambiguous results (Robbin, 1958). Furthermore, there is a serious possibility that such operations produce some impairment of higher intellectual functions, such as foresight and the ability to sustain attention. Therefore these procedures are now used only rarely in the United States. Irreversible damage to the brain is a stiff price to pay, whatever the therapeutic benefits. If one can't even be sure that such benefits exist, the price appears exorbitant (Maher, 1966).

CONVULSIVE TREATMENTS

Other attempts at somatic therapy involve the deliberate production of massive convulsive seizures. This procedure was an outgrowth of an assumption that was

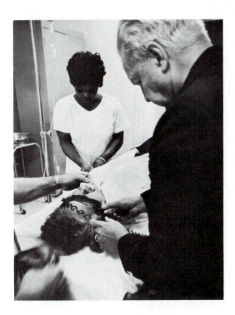

20.4 Patient about to undergo electro-convulsive shock treatment *(Photograph by Paul Fusco, Magnum Photos)*

later found to be in error; it appeared that people with epilepsy rarely suffered from schizophrenia. This suggested that convulsions somehow counteract the psychotic process. If so, perhaps one could treat schizophrenia by inducing convulsions deliberately. Originally, this was accomplished by injecting the patient with high doses of certain drugs, such as insulin.

Today, the most widely used form of the convulsive method is ***electroconvulsive shock treatment,*** or ***ECT.*** A current of moderate intensity is passed between two electrodes attached to each side of the patient's forehead; it is applied for about half a second. The result is immediate loss of consciousness, followed by a convulsive seizure similar to that seen in epilepsy (Figure 20.4). When this treatment first came into use, patients sometimes suffered serious bruises or bone fractures while thrashing about during their convulsions. To prevent this, modern practitioners usually administer muscle relaxants prior to the treatment (Redlich and Freedman, 1966).

While ECT was originally meant as a treatment of schizophrenia, appropriate evaluation studies soon showed that its area of primary effectiveness is depression. Here, its efficacy is considerable. It may well be more effective than any MAO inhibitor or tricyclic, and it works for a sizable proportion of patients who don't respond to any antidepressant drug. In addition, it seems to act more quickly than the drugs usually do (Cole and Davis, 1975).

Despite these advantages, physicians tend to use ECT only reluctantly. The main reason is the possibility of brain damage. After all, a current intensity great enough to set off convulsion may well be sufficient to injure nervous tissue; the danger is all the greater since ECT is usually administered to the patient repeatedly. In addition there are various side effects (which may well be a result of tissue injury)—amnesia for the events preceding the treatment and a memory impairment that may last for months or even longer. Under the circumstances, ECT is generally used only after drug therapy has failed or when there seems to be a serious chance of suicide. In the latter case, the fast-acting quality of ECT treatment may be an overriding advantage (Kalinowsky, 1975). This has prompted several attempts to minimize possible tissue damage. One recent technique is to apply the current flow to just one cerebral hemisphere (typically, the nondominant one), a procedure that seems to lessen memory impairments and other side effects (Coleman, Butcher, and Carson, 1984).

What accounts for the therapeutic effect of ECT? The plain fact is that we just don't know. The early notion that the effect is related to epilepsy turned out to be false. But what other theory is there? One interpretation is that ECT increases the availability of norepinephrine and serotonin in the brain. But this is little more than a speculation. As so often in medicine, ECT is used because it works, even though we don't understand the reasons. In some ways, its effect is reminiscent of what happens when we kick a recalcitrant TV set; the kick may help, but we certainly don't know why.

PSYCHOTHERAPY

Biological manipulation represents one approach to the treatment of psychopathology. But as we have already seen, there is another approach to the treatment of such disorders that forgoes all ministrations to the patient's body. Instead, it relies on psychological means alone. Such attempts to treat mental dis-

An early attempt at psychotherapy *The biblical King Saul was subject to severe bouts of rage and depression but was apparently calmed by listening to young David playing the harp. (Rembrandt's* David Playing the Harp Before Saul, The Hague, Mauritshuis, courtesy Giraudon/ Art Resource)

turbance by psychological rather than somatic methods can be grouped under the general label ***psychotherapy.***

There are many different schools of psychotherapy. According to one author, there were thirty-six such systems in 1959 (Harper, 1959). The chances are that this number has doubled in the interim. One difference among the schools is in their theories about the nature of psychopathology. These range from a Freudian emphasis on unconscious conflicts rooted in childhood to a humanistic concern for free will and the need to imbue life with coherent meaning to models of mental disorder based on conditioning theories of animal avoidance learning. No less different are the techniques of therapy which are often dictated by these different theories of psychopathology.

We will distinguish among four subtypes of psychotherapy conducted with individual patients: (1) orthodox psychoanalysis, (2) modern offshoots of psychoanalysis, (3) behavior therapy, and (4) humanistic approaches to psychotherapy.* Our discussion will emphasize attempts to treat the disorders that were once grouped together under the general label of neurosis, especially the anxiety disorders and various borderline conditions.

---

* Many practitioners use the term *psychotherapy* to describe only a subset of the full range of psychological treatments. The problem is that these subsets are different for different writers. Freudian psychoanalysts speak of psychotherapy when they want to describe briefer, and in their view, more diluted versions of psychoanalysis. Conversely, behavior therapists use the term to embrace virtually all forms of psychological treatment that try to help patients gain insight into their own inner thoughts and wishes rather than deal with the undesirable behavior patterns by themselves. The result of these divergent usages is considerable terminological confusion. The usage here adopted treats the term as a simple nonevaluative category label that embraces all forms of psychological treatment and makes no further statements about their methods, theories, or therapeutic effectiveness (White and Watt, 1973).

Classical Psychoanalysis

Classical psychoanalysis is the method Freud developed at the start of this century. According to some writers, this technique is the ancestor of virtually all forms of modern psychotherapy, whether they acknowledge this heritage or not (London, 1964).

As we have previously seen, Freud's basic assumption was that the neurotic's ills stem from unconscious defenses against unacceptable urges that date back to early childhood. The neurotic has drawn a mental blanket over his head and is unable to see either the outer or the inner world as it really is. His symptoms are an indirect manifestation of his unconscious conflicts (see Chapter 12). To overcome his neurosis, the patient must drop the blanket, must achieve access to his buried thoughts and wishes, and gain insight into why he buried them. By so doing, he will master the internal conflicts that crippled him for so long. Once these are resolved, his symptoms will presumably wither away by themselves. In effect, Freud's prescription for the neuroses is the victory of reason over passion: "Where id was, there shall ego be."

THE RECOVERY OF UNCONSCIOUS MEMORIES

Free association   The origin of psychoanalytic technique dates back to Freud's attempts to treat hysteria by helping the patient recover some emotionally charged memories (see Chapter 12). Initially, Freud and his then collaborator, Josef Breuer, probed for these memories while their patients were hypnotized. Later on it became clear that such memories could be dug up even in the normal waking state by the method of ***free association.*** The patient was asked to say whatever came into his mind, and sooner or later the relevant memory was likely to emerge. Various forms of ***resistance,*** usually unconscious, by which the patient tried to derail a given train of thought—by changing the topic, forgetting what he was about to say, and so on—often gave important clues that the patient was about to remember something he had previously tried to forget.

In popularized movie or TV versions, this dredging up of forgotten memories is often presented as the essence of psychoanalysis. The distraught heroine finally remembers a childhood scene in which she was spanked for a little sister's misdeed, suddenly a weight lifts from her shoulders, she rises from the couch reborn, is ready to face life and love serenely, and will live happily—or at least unneurotically—ever after. But as Freud described it, what actually happens is much less dramatic. The discovery of the patient's unconscious conflicts comes bit by bit, as a memory surfaces here, a dream or a slip of the tongue suggests a meaning there, and as the analyst offers an occasional interpretation of the resistances that crop up in a given session. To help the patient see how all of these strands of her mental life are woven together is one of the analyst's main tasks.

Interpretation   How does one decide whether a particular interpretation is correct? According to Freud, the best test is the patient's reaction. If she genuinely accepts it, perhaps with a sense of "Aha!" the interpretation is probably right. But many psychoanalysts contend that an interpretation is not necessarily wrong even if the patient rejects it; her "No" may simply be a sign of resistance and the very vehemence of her denial a hint that the analyst's assertion is really true.

695

Given this "Heads, I win; tails, you lose" style of argument, how can we possibly decide?

Freud felt that there was a way. In his view, psychoanalysis is a bit like solving a jigsaw puzzle. By the time the puzzle is completed, each piece can fit into one and only one place. In a similar way, one can judge the correctness of an interpretation by noting how it fits into the overall picture (Fenichel, 1945). This analogy is interesting but not altogether convincing. Is it really true that the dreams, memories, and thoughts of a patient will make sense in one and only one arrangement?

EMOTIONAL INSIGHT

Psychoanalysts want their patients to attain insight into the motives of which they were formerly unaware, but they don't want that insight to be merely intellectual. The patient must regain access, not just to various repressed thoughts and memories, but also and more importantly, to the feelings that go along with them. Freud was emphatic that recollections without emotions have little therapeutic effect. Genuine self-discovery is only achieved when the patient rids himself of the repressive forces that had kept the insights from him, and this typically requires a good deal of emotional involvement. Without this involvement, the psychoanalytic process is an intellectual exercise rather than a therapy (Freud, 1913b).

Catharsis What would produce the necessary emotional involvement? Originally, Freud put his faith in the **catharsis** that accompanied the recovery of certain long-lost memories. When these surfaced, a host of associated emotions followed in their wake and were explosively discharged in fits of sobbing or in bursts of sharp anger. Such an emotional release is generally experienced as a kind of relief. It turned out, however, that dramatic reactions of this kind were fairly rare. Moreover, even when they did occur, their benefits proved rather short-lived; after a while, the symptoms reappeared. If emotions are a necessary ingredient of analytic therapy, they have to be evoked by another means.

It is worth noting that it is by no means clear why catharsis should be therapeutic (or whether it always is). But right or wrong, the notion that catharsis helps goes back to antiquity. The Greeks used the term to describe both the purging of the body (by an emetic or strong laxative) and the purification of the emotions (by watching a deeply moving event, as in a tragedy on stage). In effect, they drew an analogy between indigestible foods and troubling, unexpressed emotions. They evidently believed that both ought to be expelled, as if voiding and vomiting were to the body as weeping is to the soul.

Transferences As Freud saw it, that means is the **transference** relationship between patient and analyst (see Chapter 12). The patient starts to respond to the analyst in increasingly personal terms. He reacts to him as he had reacted to the major figures in his own life, and he will therefore love or hate the analyst as he had loved or hated his mother, father, siblings and, more recently, his lovers and friends. All of these feelings are transferred to the analyst, as a kind of emotional reliving of the unresolved problems of the patient's childhood.

Freud argued that this transference relation can be a powerful therapeutic tool.

It lets the analyst hold up a mirror to the patient, to show him how he really feels and acts toward the important people in his life. As an example, take a person who expresses violent anger at the psychiatrist, and then is immediately seized by a feeling of total terror. What is going on? A psychoanalytic interpretation is that the patient had equated the analyst with his own tyrannical father. Having transgressed against him, he could not help but expect some awful retribution. But needless to say, the analyst will not retaliate. Instead, he may say something mildly reassuring, such as "That was hard to get out, wasn't it?" After that he will probably interpret the patient's outburst and subsequent fear and will point out the discrepancy between the actual present and the long-dead past.

Through many such experiences, the patient's anxieties are gradually extinguished. The analyst's role in all of this is to serve as a temporary stand-in for the significant characters in the patient's early family drama. But he won't let himself be drawn into the play. He will let the patient say the same old lines and go through the same old motions, but he won't respond to them as the patient's father (or mother, brother, or whoever) did. The analyst's job is to let the patient see what he is really doing, what is really happening on his private stage. The effect is a gradual process of emotional reeducation.

Modern Versions of Psychoanalysis

A sizable number of present-day psychotherapists still use techniques that bear Freud's imprint. Although some practice psychoanalysis just as Freud did, this is becoming less frequent. The majority of practitioners have modified Freud's theories and procedures in various ways. Many of them subscribe to *neo*-Freudian views; their emphasis is on interpersonal and cultural factors rather than on psychosexual development, and on the patient's problems in the present rather than on the origin of these problems in his early past (see Chapter 12). But like Freud, they believe that the key to neurosis is unconscious conflict, and that therapy requires emotional insight into these unconscious processes.

These variations on Freud's theoretical themes are accompanied by corresponding alterations of therapeutic technique. In classical analysis, sessions are scheduled for five times per week, and may continue for five or more years. This obviously restricts psychoanalysis to the affluent few, and whether it is all that beneficial even to them is debatable. According to some critics, a five-times-a-week, five-years-or-more analysis can easily become a patient's last-ditch defense against getting well; she escapes from her real problems in the present by hiding in a never-ending stream of free associations about her past. In effect, she has become couch-ridden.

To counter this trend, many psychoanalytically oriented therapists are adopting a schedule of fewer sessions per week. They believe that this helps to keep the sessions from becoming routine and intellectualized (Alexander and French, 1946). Others have tried to condense the whole process into a few months or one year, sometimes by defining therapeutic goals in advance or setting definite time limits (Malan, 1963). One casualty of these modifications is that venerable instrument of Freudian orthodoxy, the psychoanalytic couch. Many practitioners have dispensed with it in favor of the simpler face-to-face interview. One reason is

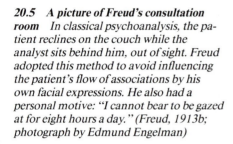

20.5   A picture of Freud's consultation room   *In classical psychoanalysis, the patient reclines on the couch while the analyst sits behind him, out of sight. Freud adopted this method to avoid influencing the patient's flow of associations by his own facial expressions. He also had a personal motive: "I cannot bear to be gazed at for eight hours a day." (Freud, 1913b; photograph by Edmund Engelman)*

that a prone position encourages a feeling of dependency on the all-powerful analyst from which the patient may be hard to wean (Figure 20.5).

Yet other modifications concern the relation between what goes on in the therapist's office and what happens in the outer world. Freud believed that the crucial theater of operations is the analysis itself. He argued that it is there that the patient is shown how he reacts to the analyst, how that reaction mirrors his childhood responses to his mother or father, and how these childish patterns have been endlessly repeated in his dealings with the important figures in his later life. Once the patient gains emotional insight into these transference patterns, the beneficial results will automatically generalize to the interpersonal relations of his real-life world. But many modern therapists prefer to help the generalization along by encouraging external activities that they regard as healthy. They point out that the transference relation is an enormously valuable sort of rehearsal of how to relate to others. But they believe that this rehearsal must be followed by actual performance and that the therapist has some responsibility to help bring this performance about (Alexander and French, 1946).

Behavior Therapy

Not all psychotherapists use techniques that are as directly affected by psychoanalytic thinking as those we have just described. The last two or three decades have seen the emergence of two major movements. Both are reactions against psychoanalysis, but for reasons that are diametrically opposed. The first is ***behavior therapy,*** which maintains that the theoretical notions underlying psychoanalysis are vague and untestable, while its therapeutic effectiveness is a matter of doubt. The other group consists of various ***humanistic therapies,*** which regard psychoanalysis as too mechanistic and too atomistic in its approach. Freud, who had a fine sense of irony, would have been wryly amused to find himself in the middle of this two-front war in which one side accuses him of being too scientific and the other of not being scientific enough.

Behavior therapists hold that neurosis is caused by maladaptive learning and that its remedy is a form of reeducation. Taken by itself, this view is hardly original. What makes it different is that the behavior therapists take the emphasis on learning and relearning much more seriously than anyone had before them. They see themselves as applied scientists whose techniques for reeducating troubled people are adapted from principles of learning and conditioning discovered in the laboratories of Pavlov, Thorndike, and Skinner (see Chapter 4).

Like the learning theorists to whom they trace their descent, behavior therapists have a basically tough-minded and pragmatic outlook. They emphasize overt, observable behavior rather than hypothetical underlying causes, such as unconscious thoughts and wishes, which they regard as hard to define and even harder to observe. Their concern is with what a person does, especially if it causes him distress. If so, the behavior therapists want to modify such behaviors—to get the agoraphobic over his fear of open places, to help the compulsive overcome his hand-washing rituals that threaten to rub his skin away. To accomplish these ends, behavior therapists resort to various techniques for learning and unlearning —extinction of fear responses, conditioning of incompatible reactions, or whatever. But their treatment does not include any attempt to have the patient gain insight into the origin of these neurotic symptoms. As these therapists see it, such insights into the past have no therapeutic effect, even if they happen to be valid. What is wrong is the patient's behavior in the here and now, and it is this that has to be righted.

Before turning to details, there is a broader question. The principles of learning on which behavior therapeutic techniques are based are themselves derived from studies of animals. Can we be sure that the same principles apply to human beings? Behavior therapists are not seriously troubled by this issue since most of them believe that the same laws of learning apply to rats as to humans. But suppose that the laws do not apply equally across the species (as much recent evidence does in fact suggest; see Chapter 4). Behavior therapists might argue that this is irrelevant to their purposes. The main difference in the ways rats and people learn concerns complex cognitive relationships, as in playing chess or writing poetry. But according to most behavior therapists, the essence of neurotic behavior is not in its cognitive complexity. There is something irrational, and unthinking, about neurotic acts. So it may just be that the laws that account for conditioning in dogs, rats, and pigeons apply to just those aspects of human behavior that seem most impervious to human reason—aspects of behavior of which neurosis is one example.

THERAPIES BASED ON CLASSICAL CONDITIONING

Our primary focus will be on behavior therapies that are based on concepts drawn from classical conditioning. (Techniques derived from operant conditioning were discussed in a previous section; see Chapter 4.) The major target of these therapists is unrealistic fear or anxiety, as in the case of a morbid dread of heights. Their basic hypothesis is that this fear is a classically conditioned response that is evoked by various eliciting stimuli such as looking down a flight of stairs or being on a rooftop (see Chapters 4 and 19). Exactly how the original conditioning took

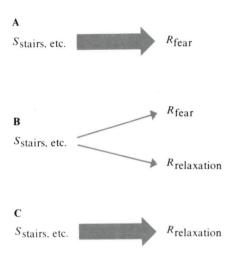

20.6 Behavior therapy through counterconditioning *(A) The state of affairs in phobia. Various stimuli such as flights of stairs arouse the response of fear. (B) These stimuli are conditioned to the response of relaxation. As this connection becomes stronger, the connection between the stimulus and the fear response is weakened. (C) The state of affairs when counterconditioning is complete. The relaxation response has completely displaced the old fear response.*

place is not our present concern. It may have been produced by a single traumatic incident or by a series of cumulative experiences. The present issue is how this connection between stimulus and fear can be broken, regardless of how it was originally forged.

Systematic desensitization The most widely used behavior therapeutic technique for unlearning such fears is **systematic desensitization,** a procedure developed by the psychiatrist Joseph Wolpe. The basic idea is to fight the original conditioning by **counterconditioning,** to connect the stimuli that now evoke fear to a new response that is incompatible with fear and will therefore displace it (Wolpe, 1958). The competing response is usually **muscular relaxation,** a pervasive untensing of the body's musculature that is presumably incompatible with the autonomic and muscular reactions that underlie the fear response. This relaxation has to be learned. The usual method is to focus the patient's full attention on each of his major muscle groups in turn by asking him to first tense and then untense them. After several training sessions, the patient can achieve this state of relaxation whenever the therapist asks him to. Once this point is reached, the goal is to condition the relaxation to such fear-evoking stimuli as stairs and rooftops (Figure 20.6).

To establish the desired link between relaxation and the fear-evoking stimuli, one must somehow bring these stimuli into the behavior therapist's office. But how can this be done? Some phobics are afraid of heights, others of enclosed places, or snakes, or meeting strangers; there is no practicable way of physically presenting most of these stimuli in a clinic room. Wolpe hit on a simple alternative. He asked the patients to *imagine* these situations as vividly as possible while in deep relaxation. It turned out that such imagined encounters had enough reality for most patients to evoke a reasonable amount of anxiety (Wolpe and Lazarus, 1966).

There is another problem. The presumption is that as the link between the relaxation response and the feared stimuli gets stronger and stronger, the old fear will gradually be displaced and the phobia will be overcome. But unfortunately, things are not quite so simple. The trouble is that just as muscular relaxation competes with fear, fear competes with muscular relaxation. Since this is so, how can one get the phobic person to perform the relaxation response in the first place when the fear-evoking stimuli are around, even if only in imagination.

Wolpe's answer is a deliberate policy of gradualism. The therapist sneaks up on the fear response, step by step. The therapist first asks the patient to construct an **anxiety hierarchy** in which feared situations are arranged from least to most anxiety-provoking. The patient then starts out by imagining the first scene in the hierarchy (for instance, being on the first floor of the Empire State Building). He imagines this scene while in a state of deep relaxation. He will stay with this scene —imagining it and relaxing—until he no longer feels any qualm. After this, the next scene is imagined and thoroughly counterconditioned, and so on, until the patient finally can imagine the most frightening situation of all (leaning over the railing of the observation tower above the 102nd floor) and still be able to relax.

According to Wolpe and his followers, this procedure of taking the sting out of imagined horrors carries over almost completely into the actual world. But other investigators argue that the transfer into real life is less than Wolpe claims and often lags behind the desensitization of the images. A plausible guess is that the shift from image to reality is not automatic but requires some active participation on the part of the patient (Davison, 1968). Toward this end, many patients are given "homework assignments" that force them to expose themselves actively to progressively more fear-evoking situations in the real world.

While the desensitization method is most directly applicable to simple phobias, many behavior therapists believe that it is useful whenever anxiety is a major factor in the disorder and when the stimuli that trigger this anxiety are known. Examples are sexual disturbances such as impotence and frigidity (Brady, 1972).

Flooding In recent years, some behavior therapists have experimented with a technique that is the very opposite of desensitization. Instead of having the patient inch his way up an anxiety hierarchy, they ask him to imagine the most fear-evoking situations from the very start. The woman with a fear of dogs must imagine herself surrounded by half a dozen snarling Dobermans; the man who is plagued by an obsessive fear of contamination that he tries to allay by endless washing rituals must imagine himself immersed in a stinking sewer. The patients are told to lose themselves in these scenes and to experience them with full emotion, an approach rather reminiscent of the cathartic method of Freud's early years. The result is that they are *flooded* with anxiety. The idea is to extinguish the conditioned link between the stimulus and the fear response. According to some theorists, this is most readily achieved if the fear response is actually evoked. Putting it another way, the trick is to have the patient become so terrified that he can see how silly his terror really is.

The proponents of this flooding procedure argue that it is considerably more efficient than desensitization, with marked improvement after fewer sessions (Stamfl and Levis, 1967). Other behavior therapists are more skeptical. They admit that the flooding technique often works as well as desensitization, but they feel that it is potentially dangerous. In the view of such critics, flooding can be much like throwing a child into a swimming pool to get him over his fear of water. It's fine if it works, but if it doesn't, the child's fear will be greater than ever before.

Aversive therapy Another behavior therapy technique, **aversive therapy,** tries to attach negative feelings to stimulus situations that are initially very attractive so that the patient will no longer want to approach them. The object of this endeavor is to eliminate behavior patterns that both patient and therapist regard as undesirable. Examples are overeating, excessive drinking, or engaging in certain sexual deviations such as exhibitionism.

The basic procedure of aversion therapy is very simple. One pairs the stimulus that one wants to render unpleasant with some obnoxious unconditioned stimulus. An example is aversion therapy for excessive drinking. The patient takes a sip of alcohol while under the effect of a nausea-producing drug. He tastes the liquor while he desperately wants to vomit.

Whether aversive therapy works is debatable. No one doubts that it works in the therapist's office; the question is whether it is effective outside when the shocking device is no longer attached or the nausea-producing drugs are no longer administered. The evidence on this point is as yet meager (Rachman and Teasdale, 1969).

COGNITIVE THERAPY

Desensitization, flooding, and aversion treatments focus on behaviors that are more or less overt and try to modify them by techniques based on the principles of simple learning. In desensitization and flooding, the emphasis is on some external stimulus (such as heights) that is connected with anxiety, a connection the therapy tries to sever. In aversion treatment, it is on some overt response (such as excessive drinking), a response the therapy tries to eliminate. But what treatment is appropriate when the patient's problems cannot be so readily described by referring to fear-evoking stimuli or to overt, undesirable responses? There are many patients whose difficulties stem from anxiety that is triggered by their own thoughts and feelings. An example is the obsessive-compulsive whose own obsessional thoughts lead to an intense panic that can be relieved only by ever more frantic compulsive rituals. Here the critical features of the disorder derive from covert rather than overt sources: thoughts and feelings that go on "within the patient's head." How does behavior therapy handle cases such as these?

A number of therapists deal with such problems by a frontal attack on the way the patient thinks. They try to replace the patient's irrational beliefs and attitudes that caused his emotional stress by a more appropriate mode of thinking that is better in accord with reality. This general form of therapy goes under various labels; we will call all such approaches *cognitive therapy* (see Beck, 1976).

On the face of it, the goal of cognitive therapy seems similar to the psychoanalytic quest for emotional insight. But cognitive therapists see themselves as more closely allied to behavior therapy. While they make little use of conditioning principles and concentrate on what the patients think rather than on what they do overtly, their techniques share many of the characteristics of behavior therapy. They are extremely *directive.* They are primarily concerned with the patient in the here and now rather than with his history, and they focus on beliefs that affect what the patient actually does.

The basic technique of cognitive therapists is to confront the patients with the contradictions inherent in their neurotic beliefs. To accomplish this end, the therapist adopts an active, dominant role throughout the proceedings, and often gives the patient "homework assignments." Albert Ellis, one of the founders of this general approach (he calls his own method *rational-emotive psychotherapy),* asks his patients to discover the illogical phrases or sentences they say to themselves in various anxiety-provoking situations. Once these irrational conceptions are ferreted out, the patients have to tell themselves repeatedly that they are false (Ellis, 1962). The way this treatment deals with irrational thoughts indicates its close affinity to behavior therapy. A fear-evoking thought is regarded as a form of behavior: the response of saying an illogical sentence to oneself.

THERAPY AS SOCIAL EDUCATION

Most of the therapeutic techniques we have discussed thus far have goals that are essentially negative—to eliminate irrational fears, suppress unwanted behaviors, and root out illogical beliefs. These goals are certainly admirable but do they go far enough? There is no doubt that, say, agoraphobia or compulsive drinking are millstones around a person's neck. But what happens after they are removed? Is the therapist's task to help the patient find new and more appropriate behavior patterns to take the place of the unhealthy ones he has finally managed to shuck off?

Many therapists feel that the answer is yes. They point out that the neurotic's fears had kept him from learning all kinds of interpersonal skills that are by no means easy to acquire: how to conduct an initial approach to the opposite sex, how to assert oneself without being overly aggressive, and so on. These skills have to be learned and practiced in the real world, but the patient can get a modest start in the therapist's office.

A number of techniques have been developed to help the therapist conduct this tutorial course in interpersonal relations. One technique employs *graded task assignments,* in which the patient is asked to take progressively larger steps in the real-life social interactions that give him trouble. We have already discussed an application of this step-by-step approach in the treatment of phobias. Another example is training in assertiveness, which would progress from tasks like maintaining eye contact with other people, to asking directions from a stranger, to complaining to a waiter about an overdone steak (Lazarus, 1971). Another technique is *modeling* in which the therapist shows the patient some effective ways of handling a particular situation. Yet another is *role-playing* in which the patient and therapist act out some scenes, such as a marital confrontation, that are likely to take place at some future time.

An illustration of the use of role-playing is provided by a patient who was unable to make a genuinely affectionate statement to his wife:

> [The therapist] says "Tom, do you really care for me?" Tom says "I would say to her that I do, but she'd complain." Therapist: "Don't tell me what you *would* do. I'm Jane. Talk to me. Tom, do you really care for me?" Tom (turning away, looking slightly disgusted): "Yes." Therapist (still as Jane): "You don't say it like you mean it." Tom: "Yeah, that's what she says, and I usually . . ." Therapist (interrupting): "You're again telling me *about* what you'd say. I'm Jane. Tom, you don't say it like you mean it." Tom: "It's very hard for me to answer her when she says that." Therapist: "How do you feel when she says it?" Tom: "Angry, pushed." Therapist: "OK, I'm Jane. Tell me how you feel." Tom: "Jane, when you do that it really turns me off. Maybe if you didn't ask me so often I'd be able to say it spontaneously without feeling like a puppet . . . (then, in a tone that indicates he is now talking to the therapist as therapist) Gee, I wonder what would happen if I really said that to her" (Wachtel, 1977, pp. 234–35).

Humanistic Therapies

A number of practitioners charge that behavior therapy (and to a lesser extent, psychoanalysis) describes human beings too atomistically, explains them too mechanistically, and treats them too manipulatively. These *humanistic therapists* try to deal with the individual at a more global level, not as a bundle of conditioned fear responses to be extinguished, nor as a collection of warring, unconscious strivings to be resolved, but rather as a whole person, who must be "encountered and understood" in his own "living, suffering actuality."

One example of a humanistically oriented approach is *client-centered therapy.* This psychotherapeutic system was initially developed by the psychologist Carl Rogers during the early 1940s. One of its main premises is that the process of personality development is akin to growth. Rogers followed theorists like Abraham

Carl Rogers (*Photograph by Nozizwe S.*)

Maslow (1908–1970) in believing that all persons have a native impulse toward the full realization of their human potentialities (Maslow, 1968). In this sense, he holds that human nature is inherently good. But, alas, such self-actualization is fairly rare, for personality growth is often stunted. There are many people who dislike themselves, are out of touch with their own feelings, and are unable to reach out to others as genuine fellow beings. Rogers's remedy is to provide the appropriate psychological soil in which personal growth can resume; this soil is the therapeutic relationship.

Rogers believes that therapy should be essentially democratic. The Rogerian therapist does not act as an omniscient authority who sagely interprets what the patient says or dreams (as does a psychoanalyst) or who tells him what to do for his own good (as does a behavior therapist). Instead, he tries to help the patient— whom he calls a client—help himself.

Rogers initially tried to achieve this client-centered quality by a variety of **nondirective techniques** (Rogers, 1942). He would never advise or interpret directly, but would only try to clarify what the client really felt, by echoing or restating what the client himself seemed to say or feel.

In later formulations, Rogers decided that there is no way of being truly nondirective. Despite one's best intentions one can't help but convey some evaluation with even the blandest nod. But more important, Rogers came to believe that the main contribution of the therapist does not lie in any particular approach or technique; it is rather to supply the one crucial condition of successful therapy, *himself* or *herself,* as a genuinely involved, participating fellow person. The Rogerian therapist's main job is to let the client know that she understands how the world looks through *his* eyes; that she can empathize with his wishes and feelings; and, most important of all, that she accepts and values him as a human being. In Rogers's view, this awareness that another person unconditionally accepts and esteems him, ultimately helps the client to accept and esteem himself (Rogers, 1961). Perhaps this is just a modern restatement of the old idea that love can redeem us all.*

Some Common Themes

Our emphasis thus far has been on the differences among the various therapeutic schools. But despite all of their divergences, some underlying common themes run through their beliefs and practices.

EMOTIONAL DEFUSING

All psychotherapies aim at some kind of emotional reeducation. They try to help the patient rid himself of various intense and unrealistic fears. To this end, these fears, and other strong emotions such as anger, are evoked during the therapeutic session. Since this happens in the presence of an accepting, noncondemning therapist, the fear is weakened.

---

* Rogers's humanistic approach has often been attacked by behavior therapists who regard him as "antiscientific." Under the circumstances, it is somewhat ironic that Rogers was one of the pioneers of psychotherapy evaluation, the first major figure in the field of psychotherapy who looked for evidence that his techniques were actually having some effect.

INTERPERSONAL LEARNING

All major schools stress the importance of interpersonal learning and follow Freud in believing that the therapeutic relationship is an important tool in bringing this about. This relationship shows the patient how she generally reacts to others and also provides a vehicle through which she can discover and rehearse new and better ways for doing so.

INSIGHT

Most psychotherapists try to help their patients achieve greater self-knowledge, though different therapeutic schools differ in what kind of self-knowledge they try to bring about. For psychoanalysts, the crucial emotional insights the patient must acquire refer to his own past; for Rogerians, they concern one's feelings in the present; for behavior therapists, the relevant self-understanding is the correct identification of the stimuli to which fear has been conditioned.

THERAPY AS A STEP-BY-STEP PROCESS

There is general agreement that therapy is a gradual affair and that this is so regardless of whether the therapy emphasizes cognitive insight, feelings, or behaviors. There are few sudden flashes of insight or emotional understanding which change a patient overnight. Instead, each newfound insight and freshly acquired skill must be laboriously applied in one life situation after another before the patient can call it her own.

THERAPY AS A SOCIALLY ACCEPTED PRACTICE

Most psychotherapists operate within a social context that gives them the status of officially designated healers for emotional ills. As a result, the stage is set for a number of nonspecific gains of psychotherapy. One is an intimate, confiding relation with another person. This alone may be a boon to some persons who have no close bonds to anyone and for whom psychotherapy may amount to what one author calls "the purchase of friendship" (Schofield, 1964). Another nonspecific gain is the hope that one will get better. This may lead the patient to think better of himself, which may lead to small successes in the outside world, which may fuel further hope, and increase the chances of yet other successes.

Psychotherapy—the purchase of friendship? (© 1950, 1952 United Feature Syndicate Inc.)

EVALUATING THERAPEUTIC OUTCOME

We have just surveyed what different kinds of therapists do. We now ask whether what they do does any good. This question often arouses important protests from therapists and patients alike. For many of them feel utterly certain that they help or have been helped; they therefore see no point in questioning what to them is obvious. But their testimonials alone are not convincing. For one thing, both patients and therapists have a serious stake in believing that psychotherapy works. If it doesn't, the patient has wasted his money and the therapist has wasted his time.

Under the circumstances, neither may be the most objective judge in assessing whether there was a significant change. But even granting that change occurred, what caused this change? Was it produced by the therapeutic situation, or would it have come about in any case? And, assuming that the therapy did play a role, was the improvement caused by the therapy as such or was it produced by non-specific, placebolike factors such as hope, expectations of cure, and the decision to "turn a new leaf"?

These questions are very similar to those encountered in the evaluation of drug therapies. It is therefore not surprising that investigations that try to determine whether psychotherapy works use rather similar research plans.

Does Psychotherapy Work?

Much of the impetus for discussions of psychotherapeutic outcomes came from a sharp attack on the efficacy of psychoanalysis and similar "insight therapies" launched by the British psychologist Hans Eysenck (Eysenck, 1961). Eysenck surveyed some two dozen articles that reported the number of neurotic patients who improved or failed to improve after psychotherapy. Overall, about 60 percent improved, a result that might be considered fairly encouraging. But Eysenck argued that there was really nothing to cheer about. According to Eysenck's analysis, the spontaneous recovery rate in neurotics who received *no* treatment was, if anything, even higher—about 70 percent. If so, psychotherapy apparently has no curative effects.

More recent reviews suggest that Eysenck's appraisal was unduly harsh. In particular, he apparently overestimated the rate of spontaneous improvement. On the basis of more recent data, this rate seems to be closer to 40 percent. While the difference between this figure and 60 percent (the average improvement rate in neurotics who receive psychotherapy) is not exactly staggering, it is at least in the right direction and thus constitutes what one author calls "some modest evidence that psychotherapy 'works' " (Bergin, 1971, p. 229). Still more recent analyses provide an even more optimistic picture (Smith and Glass, 1977; Landman and Dawes, 1982).

The preceding comments applied to averages. When we look at individuals, we find that while psychotherapy may have an effect, this effect is not always for the better. A certain proportion of patients seem to get worse. Evidence comes from an inspection of the variability of post-treatment test scores (for example, self-rating). After psychotherapy, the scores on such tests are more spread out than the scores of an untreated control group. This suggests that while some patients are improving, some others—fortunately a smaller number—become worse than they were to start with. The cause of this so-called *deterioration effect* is still unclear. One hypothesis is that psychotherapy sometimes disturbs an unstable neurotic equilibrium without supplying an appropriate substitute (Bergin, 1967).

Comparing Different Therapies

In some ways the question "Does psychotherapy work?" is a rather peculiar one. Suppose the same question were asked about ordinary (that is, nonpsychiatric) medical practice, for example: "Does medical treatment work?"

On the face of it, that last question sounds absurd, for it doesn't specify either the treatment or the disease for which it is recommended. But at an earlier stage of medical practice, this very general question might not have been so inappropriate. The great French playwright Molière asked it repeatedly in the sixteenth century, when he lampooned the physicians of his time. His caustic comments might have been justified at the time, but today of course they are entirely off the mark. Today, the only question that makes sense is: "Does such and such a procedure work for such and such a condition?"

By now, the field of psychotherapy is ready for such more specific questions. The general question Eysenck had raised (much as Molière had raised it about medicine) can be answered in the affirmative. Psychotherapy evidently works, but we now have to find out "*What* treatment, by *whom,* is most effective for *this* individual with *that* specific problem, and under *which* set of circumstances? (Paul, 1967a, p. 111).

A STUDY OF THERAPEUTIC OUTCOME

Comparisons of improvement across different studies (of the kind just described) have certain limitations. Different studies are often not strictly comparable. The patient groups may differ in age, socioeconomic background, and severity of disorder, and different therapists may use different criteria to assess improvement. As a result, it is often difficult to make specific comparisons that would allow us to distinguish between genuine effects of treatment and placebo effects, or to decide whether different forms of therapy produce different results. To accomplish these aims, the investigator has to adopt more systematic and controlled procedures.

An example is an elegant study by Gordon Paul which has set a model for much of the subsequent research in the area. We will describe it in some detail because it highlights the methodological issues that any investigation of the effectiveness of psychotherapy has to face (Paul, 1966).

Paul's "patients" were ninety-six undergraduates who suffered from rather severe anxiety when they had to talk in front of others. This disability was especially distressing since they were currently enrolled in a required course in public speaking. All of these students had accepted an offer of free treatment and were randomly assigned to one of several groups:

Insight therapy The subjects in this group received five sessions of insight-oriented psychotherapy. The therapists tried to reduce the subjects' stage fright and related anxieties by helping them to understand their own fears and the way these related to other problem areas in their lives.

Desensitization therapy The subjects in this group received five sessions of systematic desensitization, in which a hierarchy of speech-related anxieties was progressively worked through.

Placebo control This group was run to control for placebo effects. The subjects were seen for five sessions during which they took what they thought was a potent tranquilizer (it actually was a bicarbonate capsule) and performed a boring discrimination task. They were told that this task was ordinarily very stressful but would not be so for them because of the "tranquilizer." If repeated often enough, this experience would then inoculate them against anxiety-provoking situations in ordinary life. Needless to say, all of this was a ruse, but the subjects accepted it and believed that the treatment would help them. As a result they did for Paul what a sugar-pill group does for a pharmacologist—they controlled for placebo effects.

No-treatment control   A final group was the usual no-treatment control. This group received the identical before-and-after tests that were administered to the other three groups. The subjects were drawn from the same population that had volunteered for treatment. They were told that they could not be accommodated just then but were promised treatment some time in the future (a promise that was kept).

All subjects were assessed before and after the first three groups received their five treatment sessions. The assessments included both objective and subjective indices. The subjects were observed while speaking in front of a class and were rated for behavioral signs of anxiety, such as trembling hands and quivering voice. Additional objective measures included physiological indices, such as sweating and pulse rate. The subjects also rated their own anxiety on several questionnaires.

The results showed that the two groups that received treatment improved significantly as compared to the no-treatment control. But the same was true of the placebo control: They also improved, despite the fact that all they had been given was faith and bicarbonate of soda. This finding is a clear demonstration of a placebo effect in psychotherapy. People get better because they believe they will and because someone pays special attention to them.

The critical question was whether there was some specific effect of psychotherapy over and beyond the placebo. To answer this question, Paul compared the improvements observed in the two real treatment groups with those found for subjects in the placebo control. The results were clear-cut. Desensitization produced considerably more improvement than the placebo treatment, but insight treatment did not (Table 20.1). These effects were still present on a follow-up two years later in which all subjects were again questioned about their speech anxiety. Relative to the statements they had made two years earlier, improvement was shown by 85 percent of the desensitization subjects and by 50 percent of both the insight and placebo subjects (Paul, 1967b).

Table 20.1   PSYCHOTHERAPY FOR PERFORMANCE ANXIETY

Group	Percentage of cases "significantly improved"		
	Self-report of anxiety	Objective behavior	Physiological indices
Desensitization	100	100	87
Insight	53	60	53
Placebo control	47	73	47
No-treatment control	7	24	28

SOURCE: Data from Paul, 1966.

THERAPY OUTCOME FOR SERIOUS CONDITIONS

Paul's results show that desensitization is a more effective means of combating stage fright and related anxieties than are insight therapies. But what is the story on more serious conditions? To answer this question a group of investigators selected about a hundred clinic outpatients whose psychiatric complaints were of moderate severity. The complaints included anxiety attacks, depression, obsessive thoughts, and so on. One-third of these patients was treated by behavior therapy (which usually included a heavy dose of desensitization), another third by traditional insight therapy, and a final third was assigned to an untreated control group that received therapy later on. Both treatment groups improved more than the untreated control, with a slight edge in favor of behavior therapy. An interesting finding concerns the match between patients and therapies. Insight-oriented therapy only helped patients who were relatively young, had more education, and were financially better off. In contrast, behavior therapy was effective for a wider patient spectrum, but was slightly more helpful for older, less educated, and financially worse-off persons (Sloane et al., 1975).

It appears that psychotherapy works, but not too dramatically. It works to a modest extent. It is too early to tell whether one particular therapeutic method is better than the others. But one thing at least seems clear. The very fact that behavior therapy comes off quite well when compared to other methods—sometimes just as well, sometimes even better—suggests that emotional insight is not always a necessary ingredient for therapeutic success. What seems to matter is much simpler. The patient learns. He extinguishes anxieties and he acquires new ways of thinking, feeling, and behaving.

Will these new learned patterns help the patient when he leaves the therapist's office? The answer depends on the similarity between what he learned there, during therapy, and the situation he has to face outside. The more similar the two, the greater the transfer. It is probably for these reasons that behavior therapy is sometimes found to be more effective than other therapeutic methods. Behavior therapists often give their patients "homework" and ask them to apply their therapeutic lessons in their own, real world.

Some psychoanalytically oriented therapists have cautioned that the behavior therapists' emphasis on symptoms may backfire. In their view, when therapy concentrates on symptoms (as does behavior therapy) the symptom may subside but at a cost—there will be *symptom substitution* because the underlying conflict is still there. The facts suggest, however, that this is not the case. When symptoms get better during behavior therapy, they are not replaced by other symptoms. If anything, the reverse is true: As particular symptoms disappear, the patient starts to improve in other areas as well (Sloane et al., 1975).

EXTENSIONS OF PSYCHOTHERAPY

In Freud's time, psychotherapy was still considered a somewhat arcane art, practiced by a few initiates and limited to a selected group of well-educated adult patients. Since then, psychotherapy has been broadened and extended to cover

709

increasingly more terrain. One set of extensions widened the patient population to include children, retarded persons, various kinds of sociopaths, and psychotics (Figure 20.7). Another extension was a shift from the original one-therapist, one-patient formula to various modes of *group therapy* that feature all conceivable permutations: one therapist and several patients, several therapists and several patients, several patients and no therapist, and so on. Some practitioners went beyond treating patients in groups to defining the group itself as the patient. Examples are *family therapists* whose primary interest is in the "pathological" interaction patterns within the family, rather than the individual family members as such. An even broader sociocultural perspective led other therapists to an interest in community mental health, to questions of prevention, and to problems of social reform. But perhaps most drastic of all has been a change in treatment goals. At first the goal was cure or alleviation of distress. Now some therapists aim at broader and more diffuse objectives, such as happiness or the discovery of "meaning" in life.

20.7 Play therapy, an extension of psychotherapy adapted for children *In play therapy, the therapist tries to help the child understand his feelings about his parents and other family members through play with various toys. (Photograph by Sybil Shelton, Monkmeyer Press)*

Group Therapy

One of the fastest growing movements in the mental health field is treatment in groups. One reason is economic. The per-patient cost of therapy can be much less when patients are treated in groups rather than individually. Another reason is scarcity of personnel. There simply aren't enough trained therapists for all the people who want their services; seeing clients in groups is one way of making the supply fit the demand. But the appeal of group therapy may have some deeper reasons as well. For instance, the new therapeutic groups seem to fill a void, at least temporarily, left by the weakening of family and religious ties in modern urbanized society.

SHARED-PROBLEM GROUPS

One approach is to organize a group of people all of whom have the same problem: They may all be alcoholics, or drug addicts, or ex-convicts. The members meet, share relevant advice and information, help newcomers along, exhort and support each other in their resolve to overcome their handicaps. The classic example is *Alcoholics Anonymous,* which provides the alcoholic with a sense that he is not alone and helps him weather crises without suffering a relapse. In such we-are-all-in-the-same-boat groups, the primary aim of the group is to *manage* the problem that all members share. No specific therapy is provided for emotional problems that are unique to any one individual.

THERAPY GROUPS

The rules of the game are very different in groups explicitly organized for the purpose of *group therapy.* Here, a group of selected patients, usually around ten, are treated together under the guidance of a trained therapist. Economic considerations aside, this form of therapy may have some advantages that individual treatment lacks. According to its proponents, in group therapy the therapist does not really treat the members of the group; instead, he helps them to treat each other. The specific techniques of the therapist may vary from psychoanalytically oriented insight therapy to various forms of behavior therapy to Rogerian client-

A

B

20.8   The extension of psychotherapy to groups   *(A)A structured group therapy session. (Courtesy the National Institutes of Mental Health) (B) Systematic desensitization conducted for a group. The therapist is Arnold Lazarus, a major figure in the development of various behavioral and cognitive therapies. (© Van Bucher, Photo Researchers)*

centered approaches. But whatever techniques the therapist favors, the treatment of each group member really begins as he realizes that he is not all that different from the others. He learns that there are other people who are painfully shy, who have hostile fantasies about their parents, or whatever. Further benefits come from a sense of group belongingness, of support, and of encouragement. But most important of all is the fact that the group provides a ready-made laboratory in interpersonal relations. The patient can discover just what he does that rubs others the wrong way, how he can relate to certain kinds of people more effectively, and so on (Sadock, 1975).

It is hard to evaluate the effectiveness of group psychotherapy for emotional disorders. One major problem in assessing effectiveness is that in group therapy, all group members are considered to be informal co-therapists. Since this is so, who they are and how they relate to each other may well be expected to affect the outcome. This factor is very hard to control, which makes outcome evaluation difficult. Still, the available evidence suggests that group therapy does lead to some moderate improvement (Figure 20.8).

The Expansion of Therapeutic Goals

Group methods and other extensions made psychotherapy available to a much larger number of people. But did all of them really need it? The answer depends on what one believes the goals of therapy to be.

To Freud, the matter was simple. Most of the neurotics he saw were incapable of any kind of healthy life. They were crippled by terrorizing phobias or all-consuming compulsions and were thus unable to work and love. Freud wanted to cure these pathologies so that his patients could once again deal with their everyday existence. But he never regarded this cure as equivalent to happiness or fulfillment or the discovery of a meaning in life. These the patients had to find for themselves, and they might very well fail to do so even when no longer saddled with their neuroses.

Later therapists broadened the treatment goals. This is especially true of humanistic therapists such as Rogers. To be sure, Rogerian therapists try to remove or alleviate their clients' distress. But their ambitions go further. They aim at more than a cure (the goal of psychoanalysts, at least in their early days) and at more than the modification of unwanted behavior patterns (the goal of behavior

711

therapists). Their ultimate object is to help their clients to "grow" and to "realize their human potentialities." But with this expansion of the therapeutic goal, there is a concomitant widening of the group to which the therapeutic enterprise may be said to apply. Now therapy can be appropriate for just about anyone, regardless of whether he suffers some form of psychopathology or does not (Orne, 1975). After all, who among us can claim to have achieved his full potential?

Rogers's emphasis on growth represents one expansion of the goals of therapy. We will discuss some related extensions of therapeutic aims by considering a further offshoot of the humanistic movement—existential therapy.

EXISTENTIAL THERAPY

Rogers's approach to therapy is distinctively American in its optimistic faith in an almost limitless human capacity for growth and self-improvement. Another humanistic approach to therapy originates in Europe and takes a more somber view. This is *existential therapy,* a movement that echoes some of the major themes sounded by a group of philosophers called *existentialists.* Existential therapists are primarily concerned with what they regard as the major emotional sickness of our times, an inability to endow life with meaning. In their view, this condition is a byproduct of the rootless, restless anonymity of twentieth-century Western life; it is especially prevalent in modern Europe, in the wake of the despair that followed two bloody world wars and the Nazi terror. It is marked by a sense that one is alienated, lost, and dehumanized; that one is nothing but a cog in a huge, impersonal machine; and that one's existence is meaningless. According to existential therapists, this feeling that everything is pointless is a common facet of many modern emotional disorders. It is this, rather than the specific symptoms of neurosis—the phobias, the obsessions, and the like—that they want to rectify.

In essense, existential therapists try to help people achieve a personal outlook that gives meaning to their lives. How to they do this? It turns out that most existential therapists have no distinctive technique. Some use the couch and ask the patient to free-associate, while others sit face to face and have lengthy philosophical discussions. What is distinctive about them is their underlying attitude. They try to make their patients aware of the importance of free choice. They insist that people are persons and not objects, that human acts spring from within rather than being imposed from without, that there are always choices—even in jail, even in a concentration camp—and that what one is is ultimately what one chooses to do. The therapist's job is to help the patient realize that the responsibility for finding and for making her life's choices is hers and hers alone. If and when the patient accepts this responsibility, she will no longer be plagued by the vacuum of her own existence but will begin to feel "authentic."

Like practitioners of most other schools, existential therapists stress the role of the therapeutic relationship in affecting the changes they want to bring about. In their view, the key element of this relationship is what they call the *encounter,* in which two individuals meet as genuine persons of whose independent human existence neither has any doubt. According to existential therapists, the experience derived from this encounter will ultimately transfer to the way in which the patient sees himself and others (May, 1958).

In the past, the task that existential therapists set themselves was generally held to be the province of clergymen. It was priests and parsons and rabbis who tried to help people find some meaning in their existence. They did so within a relig-

SUMMARY

ious framework that defined the spiritual dimension of human life. As religious values have eroded, other social institutions have stepped in and have tried to take the clergy's place. One of these is modern humanistic psychotherapy, especially the existentialist school. It is no accident that an influential book by a prominent existential therapist bears the title *The Doctor and the Soul* (Frankl, 1966).

No one would dispute that the spiritual goals of existential therapy are admirable. To help people find some meaning to their existence is surely a worthwhile task. The question is whether success at this task can be properly evaluated as we have tried to evaluate that of other therapies. The trouble is that the goals of existential therapy are so broad that we don't know how to judge whether they have been achieved.

A CENTURY OF PSYCHOTHERAPY

Where does all of this leave us? What can we say today about psychological treatments of mental disorders, now that almost a hundred years have passed since Freud and Breuer conducted their classic studies of hysteria?

To begin with, there is little doubt that psychotherapy produces some nonspecific benefits. It helps people by providing someone in whom they can confide, who can give them advice about troubling matters, who listens to them, and instills new hope and the expectation that they will get better. The critic will reply that such gains merely reflect placebo effects and similar factors. In this view, the benefits are not produced by any specific psychotherapeutic technique, but might just as easily have been provided by a wise uncle or an understanding family doctor. Perhaps so, but the point may not be relevant. For wise uncles are in short supply today. The extended family in which uncles, nieces, and grandparents lived in close proximity is largely a thing of the past. The same holds for the family doctor who has vanished from the scene, together with his bedside manner. All of this suggests that psychotherapy has come to fill a social vacuum. Some of its effects may well be placebolike, but until a definitive treatment comes along a placebo may be better than nothing. And for the present, the psychotherapeutic professions seem to be the officially designated dispensers of such placebos.

This is not to say that there are no genuine specific psychotherapeutic effects. As we have seen, there is reasonable evidence for a positive effect—improvement, though rarely complete cure. The specific ingredients that bring these effects about have not been identified with certainty but they probably include emotional defusing, interpersonal learning, and some insight—all acquired within the therapeutic situation and somehow transferred to the patient's life beyond.

SUMMARY

1. One major form of treatment of mental disorder is by *somatic therapies.* Of these, *drug therapies* seem to be the most promising. Psychiatric drugs in current use include the *phenothiazines* such as *chlorpromazine,* which seem to reduce the major symptoms of schizophrenia, *antidepressants* such as *MAO inhibitors* and *tricyclics,* and *lithium carbonate* for the treatment of mania.

713

2. The effectiveness of drug treatment—as indeed of all therapies—requires careful evaluation procedures that control for *spontaneous improvement* and *placebo effects,* and that also guard against both the physicians' and the patients' expectations by use of *double-blind techniques.* Such studies have demonstrated genuine effects of certain psychiatric drugs, some of which are quite specific to a particular disorder. But thus far these drugs have not produced complete cures, especially in schizophrenia. Without a *maintenance dose,* a discharged patient may relapse; even with it, his adjustment may be only marginal.

3. Other somatic therapies include *prefrontal lobotomy,* a procedure now widely suspect, and *electroconvulsive shock treatment* or *ECT,* which is sometimes used in cases of severe depression.

4. Another approach to mental disorder, *psychotherapy,* relies on psychological means alone. It derives from *classical psychoanalysis.* Psychoanalysts try to help their patients to recover repressed memories and wishes so that they can overcome crippling internal conflicts. Their tools are *free association* and the *interpretation* of the patient's *resistance.* The goal is emotional rather than mere intellectual insight, an achievement made possible by an analysis of the *transference* relationship between analyst and patient.

5. Many modern psychoanalysts practice modified variants of Freud's technique. They generally place greater emphasis on interpersonal and social problems in the present than on psychosexual matters in the past. They also tend to take a more active role in helping the patient extend the therapeutic experience to the world outside.

6. A different approach is taken by *behavior therapists* whose concern is with unwanted, overt behaviors rather than with hypothetical underlying causes. Many of the behavior therapists' techniques are derived from the principles of classical and instrumental conditioning. An example is *systematic desensitization,* which tries to *countercondition* irrational fears by a policy of gradualism. Another is *flooding,* which attempts to extinguish the patient's fear by evoking the fear response in full force. Yet another is *aversive therapy* in which undesired behavior patterns are coupled with unpleasant stimuli.

7. Some recent offshoots of behavior therapy share its concrete and *directive* orientation but not its emphasis on conditioning. One example is *cognitive therapy,* which tries to change the way the patient thinks about his situation. Others include various attempts to advance the patient's social education, using techniques such as *graded task assignments, modeling,* and *role-playing.*

8. Another group of practitioners, the *humanistic therapists,* charge that both behavior therapy and psychoanalysis are too mechanistic and manipulative and that they fail to deal with their patients as "whole persons." An example of such a humanistic approach is Rogers's *client-centered therapy,* which is largely *nondirective,* and is based on the idea that therapy is a personal growth process.

9. Evaluation studies suggest that psychoanalysis and other insight therapies such as Rogers's have a modest effect: On the average, they produce improvement in about 60 percent of the patients in contrast to a 40 percent spontaneous recovery rate. Comparing the effectiveness of different therapies is enormously difficult. Such evidence as there is suggests that desensitization is more effective than insight therapy for certain phobias, especially milder ones. The story on more serious conditions is still unknown.

10. The last few decades have seen an enormous extension of psychotherapy. One extension was of method. An example is *group therapy,* in which patients are treated in groups rather than individually. Another extension concerns the therapeutic goals. The original purpose was to cure a pathology. As time went on, the goal was broadened to include personal growth and the discovery of meaning in life. This last is the special concern of *existential therapists,* who try to help their patients recognize the importance of personal responsibility and free choice.

Epilogue

We have come to the end of our journey. We have traveled through the sprawling fields of psychology, a loosely federated intellectual empire that stretches from the domains of the biological sciences on one border to those of the social sciences on the other. We have considered some aspects of human and animal action: how it is based on certain biological underpinnings, how it is directed and purposive, how it is modified and shaped through various forms of learning. We have looked at some problems in the psychology of knowledge: how it is acquired, interpreted, stored, retrieved, thought about, and communicated to others. We have asked about the sources of social interaction: how some are based on our ancestral, biological past; how some grow out of our childhood rearing; and how still others depend upon the conditions of the social present. We finally took up how people differ from each other: in intelligence, in personality, and occasionally in ways that are so extreme and so disabling that they are considered pathological. We have gone from one end of psychology to another. What have we learned?

In looking back over our journey, there is little doubt that we have encountered many more questions than answers. To be sure, more is known today about mind and behavior than was known in the days of, say, Thorndike and Köhler, let alone those of Descartes, Locke, and Kant. But this does not change the fact that what we know today is just a tiny clearing in a vast jungle of ignorance.

What can we say? We can point at what we know and congratulate ourselves. Or we can consider what we do not know and bemoan our ignorance. Perhaps a wiser course is one recommended by Sigmund Freud on thinking about some aspects of human intellectual history (Freud, 1917).

Freud suggested a parallel between the psychological growth of each human child and the intellectual progress of humanity as a whole. As he saw it, the infant is initially possessed by an all-prevading sense of his own power and importance. He cries and his parents come to change or feed or rock him and so he feels that he is the cause of whatever happens around him, the sole center of a world that revolves around him alone. But this happy delusion of his own omnipotence cannot last forever. Eventually the growing infant discovers that he is not the hub of the universe. This recognition may come as a cruel blow, but he will ultimately be the better for it. For the child cannot become strong and capable without some awareness that he is not so as yet, without first accepting the fact that he can't have his way just by wishing. His first achievements will be slight—as he lifts his own cup or a bit later says his first word—but they are real enough and will lay the foundations for his later mastery of his environment.

Freud thought that a similar theme underlies the growth of humankind's awareness of the world in which we live. On two crucial occasions in our history, we had to give up some cherished beliefs in our own power and importance. With Copernicus, we had to cede our place in the center of the physical universe: the sun doesn't circle us, but we the sun. With Darwin, we had to perform a similar abdication in the biological sphere: we are not specially created but are descended from other animals. Each of these intellectual revolutions ran into vehement opposition; in large part because each represented a gigantic blow to humanity's self-love and pride. They made us face our own ignorance and insignificance. But however painful it may have been initially, each recognition of our weakness ultimately helped us gain more strength, each confession of ignorance eventually led to deeper understanding. The Copernican revolution forced us to admit our minute place in the celestial scheme of things, but this admission was the first step in a journey of ever-increasing physical horizons, a journey which in our own time brought human beings to the moon. The Darwinian revolution made us aware that we are just one biological species among millions, the product of the same evolutionary process that brought forth sea urchins and penguins as well as us. But this awareness opened the way for continually expanding explorations of the biological universe, explorations that have already given us much greater control of our own bodily condition and of the fragile environment in which humans and other species exist.

In this century we have had to suffer yet another blow to our self-pride. We learned that we are not sure of what goes on in our own minds. Modern psychology, for all its accomplishments, has made it utterly clear that thus far we know even less about our own mental processes and behavior than we know about the physical and biological world around us. Here, too, we have to confess that we are weak and ignorant. We can only hope that this confession will have some of the effects of our previous ones, that here again strength will grow out of weakness and knowledge out of folly and ignorance. If so, we may finally understand why we think and do what we think and do, so that we may ultimately master our inner selves as we have learned to master the world around us.

We can only hope. There are few goals in science that are worthier than this.

APPENDIX

Statistics: The Collection, Organization, and Interpretation of Data

By Neil A. Macmillan

A large body of psychological knowledge has been summarized in this book, and a good part of the discussion was devoted to the ways in which this knowledge was obtained. But there are certain methodological issues that were dealt with only in passing. These concern *statistical methods,* the ways in which investigators gather, organize, and interpret collections of numerical data.

Suppose some investigators want to find out whether three-year-old boys are more aggressive than three-year-old girls. To answer this question is a very big job. To start with, the investigators will have to come up with some appropriate measure of aggression. They will then have to select the subjects. The investigators presumably want to say something about three-year-olds in general, not just the particular three-year-olds in their study. To make sure that this can be done, they have to select their subjects appropriately. Even more important, their groups of boys and girls must be as comparable as possible, so that one can be reasonably sure that any differences between the two groups is attributable to the difference in sex rather than to other factors (such as intellectual development, social class, and so on).

The investigators are now ready to collect their data. But having collected them, they will have to find some way of organizing these data in a meaningful way. Suppose the study used two groups of, say, 50 boys and 50 girls, each observed on 10 separate occasions. This means that the investigators will end up with at least 1,000 separate numerical entries (say, number of aggressive acts for each child on each occasion), 500 for the boys and 500 for the girls. Something has to be done to reduce this mass of numbers into some manageable, summarized form. This is usually accomplished by some process of averaging scores.

The next step involves statistical interpretation. Suppose the investigators find that the average aggression score is greater for the boys than for the girls (it probably will be). Can they be sure that the difference between the groups is large enough not to be dismissed as a fluke, a chance event? For it is just about certain that the data contain *variability.* The children in each group will not perform equally; furthermore, the same child may very well behave differently on one occasion than another. As a result, the scores in the two groups will almost surely overlap; that is, some girls will get a higher aggression score than some boys. Could it be that the difference *between* the groups (that is, the difference between the two averages) is an accidental chance product of the variability that is seen to hold *within* the two groups? One of the key functions of statistical methods is to deal with questions of this sort, to help us draw useful and general conclusions about organisms despite the unavoidable variability in their behavior.

The preceding example indicates the main tasks to which statistical methods have been applied. In this appendix, we will sketch the logic that underlies these methods as psychologists use them.

DESCRIBING THE DATA

The data with which statistics deals are numerical, so a preliminary step in statistical analysis is the reduction of the actual results of a study to numbers. Much of the power of statistics results from the fact that numbers (unlike responses to a questionnaire, videotapes of social interactions, or lists of words recalled by a subject in a memory experiment) can be manipulated with the rules of arithmetic. As a result, scientists prefer to use response measures that are in numerical form. Consider our hypothetical study of aggression and sex. The investigators who watched the subjects might rate their aggression in various situations (from, say, "extremely aggressive" to "extremely docile") or they might count the number of aggressive acts (say, hitting or insulting another child), and so on. This operation of assigning numbers to observed events (usually, a subject's responses) is called *scaling.*

There are several types of scales that will concern us. They differ by the arithmetical operations that can be performed upon them.

Categorical and Ordinal Scales

Sometimes the scores assigned to individuals are merely *categorical* (also called *nominal.*) For example, when respondents to a poll are asked to name the television channel they watch most frequently, they might respond "4," "2," or "13." These numbers serve only to group the responses into categories. They can obviously not be subjected to any arithmetic operations.

Ordinal numbers convey more information, in that their relative magnitude is meaningful—not arbitrary, as in the case of categorical scales. If individuals are asked to list the ten people they most admire, the number 1 can be assigned to the most admired person, 2 to the runner-up, and so on. The smaller the number assigned, the more the person is admired. Notice that no such statement can be made of television channels: Channel 4 is not more anything than channel 2, just different from it.

Scores which are ordinally scaled cannot, however, be added or subtracted. The first two persons on the most-admired list differ in admirability by 1; so do the last two. Yet the individual who has done the ranking may admire the first person far more than the other nine, all of whom might be very similar in admirability; in other words, given an ordinal scale, differences of 1 are not necessarily equal psychologically. Imagine a child who, given this task, lists his mother first, followed by the starting lineup of the Chicago Cubs baseball team. In this example, the difference of 8 between person 2 and person 10 probably represents a smaller difference in judged admirability than the difference of 1 obtained between persons 1 and 2 (at least so the mother hopes).

Interval Scales

Scales in which equal differences between scores, or intervals, *can* be treated as equal units are called *interval scales.* Reaction time is a common psychological variable which is usually treated as an interval scale. In some memory experiments, a subject must respond as quickly as possible to each of several words, some of which he has seen earlier in the experiment; the task is to indicate whether each word has appeared before by pressing one of two buttons. An unknown, but possibly constant, part of the reaction time is simply the time required to press the response button; the rest is the time required for the decision-making process:

$$\text{reaction time} = \text{decision time} + \text{button-press time} \qquad (1)$$

Suppose a subject requires an average of 2 seconds to respond to nouns, 3 seconds for verbs, and 4 seconds for adjectives. The difference in decision time between nouns and verbs ($3 - 2 = 1$ second) is the same as the difference in decision time between verbs and adjectives ($4 - 3 = 1$ second). We can make this statement—which in turn suggests various hypotheses about the factors that underlie such differences—precisely because reaction time can be regarded as an interval scale.

Ratio Scales

Scores based on an interval scale allow subtraction and addition. But they do not necessarily allow multiplication and division. Consider the centigrade scale of temperature. There is no doubt that the difference between 10 and 20 degrees centigrade is equal to that between 30 and 40 degrees centigrade. But can one say that 20 degrees centigrade is *twice* as high a temperature as 10 degrees centigrade? The answer is no, for the centigrade scale of temperature is only an interval scale. It is not a *ratio scale* which allows statements such as 10 feet is 1/5 as long as 50 feet, or 15 pounds is 3 times as heavy as 5 pounds. To make such statements one needs a true zero point. Such a ratio scale with a zero point does exist for temperature—the Kelvin absolute temperature scale, whose zero point is about -273 degrees centigrade.

Some psychological variables can be described by a ratio scale. This is true of various forms of sensory intensity—brightness, loudness, and so on. For example, it makes sense to say that the rock music emanating from your neighbor's apartment is four times as loud as your roommate singing in the shower. But there are many psychological variables which cannot be so readily described in ratio terms. Let's go back to reaction time. This cannot be considered a ratio scale for the decision process. In our previous example we saw that the reaction time for adjectives was 4 seconds, while that for nouns was 2 seconds. But we cannot say that the 4-second response represents twice as much *decision* time as the 2-second response, because of the unknown time required to press the response button. Since this time is unknown, we have no zero point.

The fact that very few variables are ratio scaled does not, of course, prevent people from describing ordinal- or interval-scaled variables in ratio terms. A claim by an advertiser that drug *A* is "twice as effective" as drug *B* may mean that *A* works twice as fast, or for twice the time, or is successful on twice as many people, or requires only half the dose. A potential consumer needs to know the advertiser's meaning of "effective" to evaluate the claim. Similarly, a 4-second reaction time in the word-recognition experiment is certainly twice as long as a 2-second reaction time; there is no harm in saying so, as long as it is understood that we are not talking about the decision time but rather about the total reaction time.

COLLECTING THE DATA

The kinds of scales we have just discussed concern the ways in which psychological variables are described in numerical terms. The point of most psychological investigations is to see how such variables are related to various factors that may produce them. Psychologists—and most other scientists—employ three major methodological tools to achieve this end: the experiment, the observational study, and the case study.

The Experiment

An *experiment* is a study in which the experimenter deliberately manipulates one or more variables to determine the effect of this manipulation on another variable. As an example, consider an experiment conducted to determine whether visual imagery aids memory. Participants in the experiment listen to a list of words, which they are instructed to memorize; later they are asked to recall as many words as possible. Two groups of subjects are chosen. One is the *experimental group;* this is the group to which the experimenter's manipulation is applied. It consists of subjects who are instructed to form visual images that connect each word to the preceding word. Other subjects form the *control group,* a group to which the experimenter's manipulation is not applied. These control subjects are not given imagery instructions. Many experiments have more than one experimental group (in this example, different groups might be told to do their visual

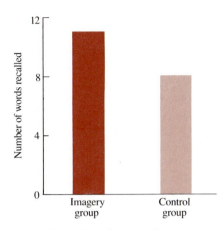

12

Number of words recalled

8

4

0

Imagery
group

Control
group

A.1 The results of an experiment on memorizing *Subjects in the imagery group, who formed visual images of the words they were to memorize, recalled an average of 11 words. Subjects in the control group, who received no special instructions, recalled an average of 8 words.*

imagining in different ways), or more than one control group (here, a second control group might be instructed to rehearse by repeating each word over and over).

Like many other experiments, this one can be thought of as a situation in which the experimenter varies something (here the instructions given to the subjects) and observes the effect of this variation on certain responses of the subjects (the number of words they correctly recall). The variable which is manipulated by the experimenter (imagery instructions) is called the ***independent variable.*** The subject's response (number of words recalled) is called the ***dependent variable,*** since the investigator wants to know whether it is dependent upon his manipulation of the independent variable. Speaking loosely, independent variables are sometimes regarded as causes, dependent variables as effects.

The results of our experiment are graphically presented in Figure A.1. The values of the independent variable are indicated on the horizontal, or *x*-axis, and the values of the dependent variable on the vertical, or *y*-axis. The figure displays the average number of items recalled for subjects who used visual imagery in memorizing and for those who did not. We will have more to say about this experiment presently.

Observational Studies

Much psychological research departs from the experimental method in that investigators do not produce the effects directly, but only observe them. They do not so much design the experiment as discover it. Such an investigation is called an ***observational study.*** Consider the question "What is the effect of prenatal malnutrition on IQ?" This question can only be answered by locating children whose mothers were malnourished during pregnancy and measuring their IQs; to deliberately provide pregnant women with inadequate diets is obviously worse than unethical. But even though the investigators do not manipulate the mother's diet (or indeed, anything else), some of the methodological terms used before can still be applied. We can consider the mother's diet as the independent variable, and the child's IQ as the dependent variable. A group analogous to the experimental group would consist of children whose mothers were malnourished during pregnancy. An analogue to the control group is a group of children whose mothers' diet was adequate.

Observational studies like this one are sometimes called "experiments of nature." Because nature does not always provide exactly those control groups which the investigator might have wished for, observational studies can be difficult to interpret. For example, children whose mothers were malnourished during pregnancy are often born into environments which might also be expected to have negative effects on IQ. Women whose diet is inadequate during pregnancy are likely to be poor; they are therefore less likely to provide some of the physical advantages (like good food and health care) and educational advantages (like books and nursery schools) which may well be helpful in developing intelligence.

The Case Study

In many areas of psychology, conclusions are based on only one person who is studied intensively. Such an investigation is called a ***case study.*** Individuals who

A5

display unusual psychological or physiological characteristics, such as rare forms of color blindness, exceptionally good or poor memory, or brain injuries, can sometimes provide information about normal vision, memory, or brain function that would be difficult or impossible to obtain from normal individuals. Take the patient known as H.M., who suffered severe amnesia after brain surgery (see Chapter 7). Before the operation his memory was normal; afterward he could remember virtually nothing about events that occurred after the operation. This patient has been extensively studied because of his unusual memory disorder. Since his amnesia is apparently the result of the destruction of a particular structure in the brain, the hippocampus, a comparison of H.M.'s performance with that of normal individuals allows us to make inferences about the role of the hippocampus in normal memory.

Some of the most famous case studies in psychology are those described by Sigmund Freud, whose extensive psychoanalytic interviews of his patients led him to develop theories of dreams, defense mechanisms, and other psychological processes (see Chapter 12).

SELECTING THE SUBJECTS

How does one select the subjects for a psychological study? To answer this question, we have to consider the difference between a population and a sample.

Sample and Population

Psychologists—again like other scientists—usually want to make statements about a larger group of persons (or animals) than the particular subjects they happen to use in their study. They want their conclusions to apply to a given *population:* all members of a given group—say, all three-year-old boys, all schizophrenic patients, all U.S. voters, and in some cases, all humans. But they obviously can't study all members of the population. As a result, they have to select a *sample,* that is, a subset of the population they are interested in. Their hope is that the results found in the sample can be generalized to the population from which the sample is drawn.

It is important to realize that generalizations from a given sample to a particular population can only be made if the sample is representative (that is, typical) of the population to which one wants to generalize. Suppose one does a study on memory by using college students. Can one generalize the results to adults in general? Strictly speaking one cannot, for college students are on the average younger than the population at large and are more accustomed to memorizing things. Under the circumstances, the safest course may be to restrict one's generalizations to the population of college students.

Most experimenters would probably argue that college students don't differ too greatly from the general population (at least in memory skills), so that results obtained with them do apply in general, at least approximately. But there are many cases in which inadequate sampling leads to gross blunders. The classic example is a 1936 poll which predicted that Franklin D. Roosevelt would lose the presidential election. In fact, he won by a landslide. This massive error was produced by a ***biased sample***—all persons polled were selected from telephone directories. But in 1936 having a telephone was much more likely among persons of higher than of lower socioeconomic status. As a result, the sample was not representative of the voting population as a whole. Since socioeconomic level affected voting preference, the poll predicted falsely.

Random and Stratified Samples

To ensure that one can generalize from sample to population, investigators use a ***random sample.*** This is a sample in which every member of the population has an equal chance of being picked—as in a jury drawn by lot from all the voters of a given district (if none are disqualified or excuse themselves). The random sampling procedure applies with special force to the assignment of subjects in an experiment. Here every effort has to be made to assign subjects randomly to the various experimental or control groups.

For some purposes, even a random sample may not be good enough. While every member of the population has an equal chance of being selected, the sample may still turn out to be atypical by chance alone. This danger of chance error becomes less and less the greater the size of the sample. But if one is forced to use a small sample (and one often is because of lack of time or money), other sampling procedures may be necessary. Suppose we want to take a poll to determine the attitudes of American voters toward legalized abortion. We can expect peoples' attitudes to differ depending on (at least) their age, sex, and religion. If the sample is fairly small, it is important that each subgroup of the population be (randomly) sampled in proportion to its size. This procedure is called ***stratified sampling,*** and is common in studying psychological traits or attitudes which vary greatly among different subgroups of the population.

Sampling Responses

The distinction between sample and population does not only apply to subjects. It also applies to the subjects' responses. Consider the investigators who studied aggressive behavior in 50 three-year-old boys. Each of these boys was observed on 10 occasions. Those 10 occasions can be regarded as a sample of all such occasions, just as the 50 boys can be regarded as a sample of all three-year-old boys (or at least of all middle-class U.S. boys). The investigators will surely want to generalize from this sample of occasions to the population of all such occasions. To make sure that such a generalization is warranted, one has to see to it that the occasions are not atypical—that the child isn't especially tired, or sick, and so on.

ORGANIZING THE DATA: DESCRIPTIVE STATISTICS

We have considered the ways in which psychologists describe the data provided by their subjects by assigning numbers to them (scaling) and the ways in which they collect these data in the first place (experiments, observational studies, case studies). Our next task is to see how these data are organized.

The Frequency Distribution

Suppose we have designed and performed an experiment such as the imagery study described previously. The data will not automatically arrange themselves in the form shown in Figure A.1. Instead, investigators will first be faced with a list of numbers, the scores (number of words recalled correctly) for each subject in a given group. For example, if there were 10 subjects in the control group, their scores (in words correct) might have been

$$8, 11, 6, 7, 5, 9, 5, 9, 9, 11$$

A first step in organizing the data is to list all the possible scores and the frequency with which they occurred, as shown in Table A.1. Such an arrangement is called a *frequency distribution.*

Table A.1   FREQUENCY DISTRIBUTION

Score	Frequency
11	2
10	0
9	3
8	1
7	1
6	1
5	2

The frequency distribution can be expressed graphically. A common means for doing this is a *histogram* which depicts the frequency distribution by a series of contiguous rectangles (Figure A.2). The values of the dependent variable (here, number of words recalled) are shown by the location of each rectangle on the horizontal or x-axis. The frequency of each score is shown on the vertical or y-axis, that is, by the height of each rectangle. This is simple enough for our example, but in practice graphic presentation often requires a further step. The number of possible values the dependent variable can assume is often very large. As a result, exactly equal values rarely occur, as when reaction times are measured to the nearest millisecond (thousandth of a second). To get around this, the scores are generally grouped by intervals for purposes of graphic display. The histogram might then plot the frequency of all reaction times between, say, 200 and 225 milliseconds, between 226 and 250 milliseconds, and so on.

A.2 Histogram In a histogram, a frequency distribution is graphically represented by a series of rectangles. The location of each rectangle on the x-axis indicates a score value, while its height shows how often that score value occurred.

Measures of Central Tendency

A frequency distribution is a more concise description of the result of the experiment than the raw list of scores from which it was derived, but for many purposes we may want a description that is even more concise. We often wish to summarize an entire distribution by a single, central score; such a score is called a *measure of central tendency.* Three measures of central tendency are commonly used to express this central point of a distribution: the mode, the median, and the mean.

The *mode* is simply the score that occurs most frequently. In our example, the mode is 9. More subjects (to be exact, 3) recalled 9 words than recalled any other number of words.

The **median** is the point that divides the distribution into two equal halves, when the scores are arranged in increasing order. To find the median in our example, we first list the scores:

$$5, 5, 6, 7, 8, 9, 9, 9, 11, 11$$
$$\uparrow$$

Since there are 10 scores, the median lies between the fifth and sixth scores, that is, between 8 and 9, as indicated by the arrow. Any score between 8 and 9 would divide the distribution into two equal halves, but it is conventional to choose the number in the center of the interval between them, that is, 8.5. When there is an odd number of scores this problem does not arise.

The third measure of central tendency, the **mean (M),** is the familiar arithmetic average. If N stands for the number of scores, then

$$M = \frac{\text{sum of scores}}{N}$$

$$= \frac{5 + 5 + 6 + 7 + 8 + 9 + 9 + 9 + 11 + 11}{10} = \frac{80}{10} = 8.0$$

Of these three measures, the mode is the least helpful, because the modes of two samples from the same population can differ greatly even if the samples have very similar distributions. If one of the 3 subjects who recalled 9 words recalled only 5 instead, the mode would have been 5 rather than 9. But the mode does have its uses. For example, in certain elections, the candidate with the most votes —the modal candidate—wins.

The median and the mean differ most in the degree to which they are affected by extreme scores. If the highest score in our sample were changed from 11 to 111, the median would be unaffected, whereas the mean would jump from 8.0 to 18.0. Most people would find the median (which remains 8.5) a more compelling "average" than the mean in such a situation, since most of the scores in the distribution are close to the median, but are not close to the mean (18.0).

Distributions with extreme values at one end are said to be **skewed.** A classic example is income, since there are only a few high incomes but many low ones. Suppose we sample 10 individuals from a neighborhood, and find their yearly incomes (in thousands of dollars) to be:

$$5, 5, 5, 5, 10, 10, 10, 20, 20, 1,000$$

The median income for this sample is 10 ($10,000), since both the fifth and sixth scores are 10, and this value reflects the income of the typical individual. The mean income for this sample, however, is $(5 + 5 + 5 + 5 + 10 + 10 + 10 + 20 + 20 + 1,000)/10 = 109$, or $109,000. A politician who wants to demonstrate that his neighborhood has prospered might—quite honestly—use these data to claim that the average (mean) income is $109,000. If, on the other hand, he wished to plead for financial aid, he might say—with equal honesty—that the average (median) income is only $10,000. There is no single "correct" way to find an "average" in this situation, but it is obviously important to know which average (that is, which measure of central tendency) is being used.

When deviations in either direction from the mean are equally frequent, the distribution is said to be **symmetric.** In such distributions, the mean and the median are equal. Many psychological variables have symmetric distributions, but for variables with skewed distributions, like income, measures of central tendency must be chosen with care.

Measures of Variability

In reducing an entire frequency distribution to an average score, we have discarded a lot of very useful information. Suppose we (or the National Weather Service) measure the temperature every day for a year in various cities, and construct a frequency distribution for each city. The mean of this distribution tells us something about the city's climate. That it does not tell us everything is shown by the fact that the mean temperature in both San Francisco and Albuquerque is 56 degrees Fahrenheit. But the climates of the two cities nonetheless differ considerably, as indicated in Table A.2.

Table A.2   TEMPERATURE DATA FOR TWO CITIES (DEGREES FAHRENHEIT)

City	Lowest month	Mean	Highest month	Range
Albuquerque, New Mexico	35	56	77	42
San Francisco, California	48	56	63	15

The weather displays much more variability in the course of a year in Albuquerque than in San Francisco. A simple measure of variability is the **range,** the highest score minus the lowest. The range of temperatures in San Francisco is 15, while in Albuquerque it is 42.

A shortcoming of the range as a measure of variability is that it reflects the values of only two scores in the entire sample. As an example, consider the following distributions of ages in two college classes:

Distribution *A:* 19, 19, 19, 19, 19, 20, 25
Distribution *B:* 17, 17, 17, 20, 23, 23, 23

Each distribution has a mean of 20. Intuitively, distribution *A* has less variability, since all scores but one are very close to the mean. Yet the range of scores is the same (6) in both distributions. The problem arises because the range is determined by only two of the seven scores in each distribution.

A better measure of variability would incorporate every score in the distribution rather than just two scores. One might think that the variability could be measured by the average difference between the various scores and the mean, that is, by:

$$\frac{\text{sum of (score} - M)}{N}$$

This hypothetical measure is unworkable, however, because some of the scores are greater than the mean and some are smaller, so that the numerator is a sum of both positive and negative terms. (In fact, it turns out that the sum of the positive terms equals the sum of the negative terms, so that the expression shown above always equals zero.) The solution to this problem is simply to square all the terms in the numerator, thus making them all positive.* The resulting measure of variability is called the *variance (V):*

$$V = \frac{\text{sum of (score} - M)^2}{N} \tag{2}$$

The calculation of the variance for the control group in the memorization experiment is shown in Table A.3. As the table shows, the variance is obtained by subtracting the mean (*M,* which equals 8) from each score, squaring each result, adding all the squared terms, and dividing the resulting sum by the total number of scores (*N,* which equals 10), yielding a value of 4.4.

Table A.3 CALCULATING VARIANCE

Score	Score − mean	(Score − mean)²
8	$8 - 8 = \ \ 0$	$0^2 = 0$
11	$11 - 8 = \ \ 3$	$3^2 = 9$
6	$6 - 8 = -2$	$(-2)^2 = 4$
7	$7 - 8 = -1$	$(-1)^2 = 1$
5	$5 - 8 = -3$	$(-3)^2 = 9$
9	$9 - 8 = \ \ 1$	$1^2 = 1$
5	$5 - 8 = -3$	$(-3)^2 = 9$
9	$9 - 8 = \ \ 1$	$1^2 = 1$
9	$9 - 8 = \ \ 1$	$1^2 = 1$
11	$11 - 8 = \ \ 3$	$3^2 = 9$

Because deviations from the mean are squared, the variance is expressed in units different from the scores themselves. If our dependent variable were a distance, measured in centimeters, the variance would be expressed in square centimeters. As we will see in the next section, it is convenient to have a measure of variability which can be added to or subtracted from the mean; such a measure ought to be expressed in the same units as the original scores. To accomplish this end, we employ another measure of variability, the *standard deviation,* or *SD.* The standard deviation is derived from the variance (*V*); it is obtained by taking the square root of the variance. Thus

$$SD = \sqrt{V}$$

In our example, *SD* is about 2.1, the square root of the variance which is 4.4.

---

* An alternative solution would be to sum the absolute value of (score − *M*), that is, consider only the magnitude of this difference for each score, not the sign. The resulting statistic, called the *average deviation,* is little used, however, primarily because absolute values are not too easily dealt with in certain mathematical terms that underlie statistical theory. As a result, statisticians prefer to transform negative into positive numbers by squaring them.

Converting Scores to Compare Them

Suppose a person takes two tests. One measures her memory span—how many digits she can remember after one presentation. The other test measures her running ability—how fast she can run 100 yards. It turns out that she can remember 8 digits and runs 100 yards in 17 seconds. Is there any way to decide whether she can remember digits better (or worse or equally well) than she can run 100 years? On the face of it, the question seems absurd; it seems to be like comparing apples and oranges. But in fact, there is a way, for we can ask where each of these two scores is located on the two frequency distributions of other persons (presumably women of the same age) who are given the same two tasks.

PERCENTILE RANKS

One way of doing this is by transforming each of the two scores into **percentile ranks.** The percentile rank of a score indicates the percentage of all scores that lie below that given score. Let's assume that 8 digits is the 78th percentile, which means that 78 percent of the relevant comparison group remembers fewer digits. Let's further assume that a score of 17 seconds in the 100-yard dash is the 53rd percentile of the same comparison group. We can now answer the question with which we started. Our subject can remember digits better than she can run 100 yards. By converting into percentile ranks we have rendered incompatible scores compatible, allowing us to compare the two.

STANDARD SCORES

For many statistical purposes there is an even better method of comparing scores or of interpreting the meaning of individual scores. This is to express them by reference to the mean and standard deviation of the frequency distribution of which they are part, by converting them into **standard scores** (often called **z-scores**).

Suppose you take a test that measures aptitude for accounting and are told your score is 36. In itself, this number cannot help you decide whether to pursue or avoid a career in accounting. To interpret your score you need to know both the average score and how variable the scores are. If the mean is 30, you know you are above average, but how far above average is 6 points? This might be an extreme score, or one attained by many, depending on the variability of the distribution.

Let us suppose that the standard deviation of the distribution is 3. Your score of 36 is therefore 2 standard deviations (6 points) above the mean (30). A score which is expressed this way, as so many standard deviations from the mean, is called a standard score, or z-score. The formula for calculating a z-score is:

$$z = \frac{(\text{score} - M)}{SD} \tag{3}$$

Your aptitude of 36 has a z-score of $(36 - 30)/3 = 2$; that is, your score is 2 standard deviations above the mean.

The use of z-scores allows one to compare scores from different distributions. Still unsure whether to become an accountant, you take a screen test to help you decide whether to be an actor. Here your score is 60. This is a larger number than the 36 you scored on the earlier test, but it may not reveal much acting aptitude. Suppose the mean score on the screen test is 80, the standard deviation 20; then your z-score is $(60 - 80)/20 = -1$. In acting aptitude, you are 1 standard deviation below the mean (that is, $z = -1$); in accounting aptitude, 2 standard deviations above (that is, $z = +2$). The use of z-scores makes your relative abilities clear.

Notice that scores below the mean have negative z-scores, as in the last example. A z-score of 0 corresponds to a score which equals the mean.

Percentile rank and a z-score give similar information, but one cannot be converted into the other unless we know more about the distribution than just its mean and standard deviation. In many cases this information is available, as we shall now see.

The Normal Distribution

Frequency histograms can have a wide variety of shapes, but many variables of psychological interest have a *normal distribution* (often called *normal curve*), which is a symmetric distribution of the shape shown in Figure A.3. The graph is smooth, unlike the histogram in Figure A.2, because it approximates the distribution of scores from a very large sample. The normal curve is bell-shaped, with most of its scores near the mean; the farther a score is from the mean, the less likely it is to occur. Among the many variables whose distributions are approximately normal are IQ, scholastic aptitude test scores (SAT), and women's heights (see Table A.4).*

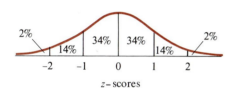

A.3 Normal distribution *Values taken from any normally distributed variable (such as those presented in Table A.4) can be converted to z-scores by the formula z = (score − mean)/(standard deviation). The figure shows graphically the proportions that fall between various values of z.*

Table A.4   NORMALLY DISTRIBUTED VARIABLES

			z-scores				
Variable	Mean	Standard deviation	−2	−1	0	1	2
IQ	100	15	70	85	100	115	130
SAT	500	100	300	400	500	600	700
Height (women)	160 cm	5 cm	150	155	160	165	170

* Men's heights are also normally distributed, but the distribution of the heights of all adults is not. Such a distribution would have two peaks, one for the modal height of each sex, and would thus be shaped quite differently from the normal curve. Distributions with two modes are called *bimodal.*

These three variables, IQ, SAT score, and height, obviously cannot literally have the "same" distribution, since their means and standard deviations are different (Table A.4 gives plausible values for them). In what sense, then, can they all be said to be normal? The answer is that the distribution of z-scores for all these variables is the same. For example, an IQ of 115 is 15 points, or 1 standard deviation, above the IQ mean of 100; a height of 165 centimeters is 5 centimeters, or 1 standard deviation, above the height mean of 160 centimeters. Both scores, therefore, have z-scores of 1. Furthermore, the percentage of heights between 160 and 165 centimeters is the same as the percentage of IQ scores between 100 and 115, that is, it is 34 percent. This is the percentage of scores which lie between the mean and one standard deviation above the mean for any normally distributed variable.

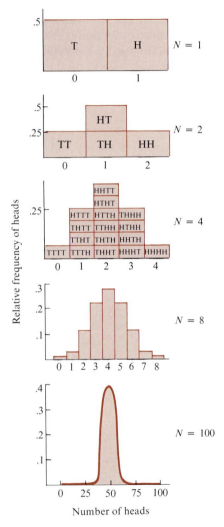

T = Tail
H = Head

A.4 Histograms showing expected number of heads in tossing a fair coin N times *In successive panels, N = 1, 2, 4, and 8. The bottom panel illustrates the case when N = 100 and shows a smoothed curve.*

THE PERCENTILE RANK OF A *z*-SCORE

When a variable is known to have a normal distribution, a *z*-score can be converted directly into a percentile rank. A *z*-score of 1 has a percentile rank of 84, that is, 34 percent of the scores lie between the mean and $z = 1$, and (because the distribution is symmetric) 50 percent of the scores lie below the mean. A *z*-score of -1 corresponds, in a normal distribution, to a percentile rank of 16: only 16 percent of the scores are lower. These relationships are illustrated in Figure A.3 and Table A.4.

HOW THE NORMAL CURVE ARISES

Why should variables such as height or IQ scores—and many others—form distributions that have this particular shape? Mathematicians have shown that whenever a given variable is the sum of many smaller variables, its distribution will be close to that of the normal curve. An example is height. Height can be thought of as the sum of the contributions of the many genes (and some environmental factors) which influence this trait; it therefore satisfies the general condition.

The basic idea is that the many different factors that influence a given measure (such as the genes for height) operate independently. A given gene will pull height up or push it down; the direction in which it exerts its effort is a matter of chance. If the chances are equal either way, then a good analogy to this situation is a person who tosses a coin repeatedly and counts the number of times the coin comes up heads. In this analogy, a head corresponds to a gene that tends to increase height, a tail to a gene that tends to diminish it. The more often the genetic coin falls heads, the taller the person will be.

What will the distribution of the variable "number of heads" be? Clearly, it depends on the number of tosses. If the coin is tossed only once, then there will be either 0 heads or 1 head, and these are equally likely. The resulting distribution is shown in the top panel of Figure A.4.

If the number of tosses (which we will call *N*) is 2, then 0, 1, or 2 heads can arise. However, not all these outcomes are equally likely: 0 heads come up only if the sequence tail-tail (*TT*) occurs; 2 heads only if head-head (*HH*) occurs; but 1 head results from either *HT* or *TH*. The distribution of heads for $N = 2$ is shown in the second panel of Figure A.4. The area above 1 head has been subdivided into two equal parts, one for each possible sequence containing a single head.*

As *N* increases, the distribution of the number of heads looks more and more like the normal distribution, as the subsequent panels of Figure A.4 show. When *N* becomes as large as the number of factors that determine height, the distribution of the number of heads is virtually identical to the normal distribution. Similar arguments justify the assumption of normality for many psychological variables.

---

* The distribution of the number of heads is called the ***binomial distribution,*** because of its relation to the binomial theorem: the number of head-tail sequences which can lead to k heads is the $(k + 1)$st coefficient of $(a + b)^N$.

DESCRIBING THE RELATION BETWEEN TWO VARIABLES: CORRELATION

The basic problem facing psychological investigators is to account for observed differences in some variable they are interested in. Why, for example, do some people display better memory than others? The experimental approach to the problem, described earlier, is to ask whether changes in an independent variable produce systematic changes in the dependent variable. In the memory experiment, we asked whether subjects using visual imagery as an aid to memorizing would recall more words on the average than those who did not. In an observational study, however, our approach must be different, for in such a study we do not manipulate the variables. What is often done here is to observe the relationship between two—sometimes more—variables as they occur naturally, in the hope that differences in one variable can be attributed to differences in a second.

Positive and Negative Correlation

Imagine that a taxicab company wants to identify drivers who will earn relatively large amounts of money (for themselves and, of course, for the company). The company's officers make the plausible guess that one relevant factor is the driver's knowledge of the local geography, so they devise an appropriate test of street names, routes from place to place, and so on, and administer the test to each driver. The question is whether this test score is related to the driver's job performance as measured by his weekly earnings. To decide, one has to find out whether the test score and the earnings are *correlated*—that is, whether they tend to vary together.

In the taxicab example, the two variables will probably be *positively correlated* —as one variable (test score) increases, the other (earnings) will generally increase too. But other variables may be *negatively correlated*—when one increases, the other will tend to decrease. An example is a phenomenon called Zipf's law, which states that words that occur frequently in a language tend to be relatively short. The two variables word length and word frequency are negatively correlated, since one variable tends to increase as the other decreases.

Correlational data are often displayed in a *scatter plot* (or scatter diagram), in which values of one variable are shown on the horizontal axis and variables of the other on the vertical axis. Figure A.5*A* is a scatter plot of word frequency versus word length for the words in this sentence.* Each word is represented by a single point. An example is provided by the word *plot,* which is 4 letters long and occurs with a frequency of 37 times per million words of English text (and is represented by the circled dot). The points on the graph display a tendency to decrease on one variable as they increase on the other, although the relation is by no means perfect. It is helpful to draw a straight line through the various points in a scatter plot which comes as close as possible to all of them (Figure A.5*B*). The line is called a *line of best fit,* and it indicates the general trend of the data. Here, the line slopes downward because the correlation between the variables is negative.

---

* There is no point for the "word" A.5*A* in this sentence. The frequencies of the other words are taken from H. Kucera and W. N. Francis, *Computational Analysis of Present-Day American English* (Providence, R. I.: Brown University Press, 1967).

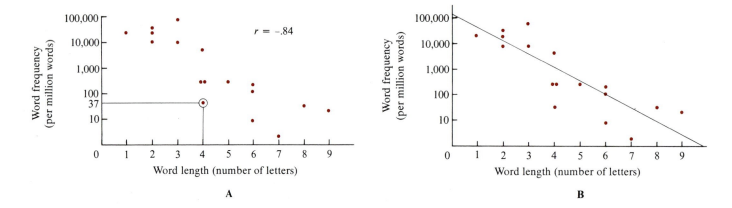

A.5   Scatter plot of a negative correlation between word length and word frequency

The three panels of Figure A.6 are scatter plots showing the relation between other pairs of variables. In Figure A.6*A* hypothetical data from the taxicab example show that there is a positive correlation between test score and earnings (since the line of best fit slopes upward), but that test score is not a perfect predictor of on-the-job performance (since the points are fairly widely scattered around the line). Points above the line represent individuals who earn more than their test score would lead one to predict, points below the line individuals who earn less.

The examples in Figures A.5 and A.6*A* each illustrate moderate correlations; panels *B* and *C* of Figure A.6 are extreme cases. Figure A.6*B* shows data from a hypothetical experiment conducted in a fourth-grade class to illustrate the relation between metric and English units of length. The heights of five children are measured twice, once in inches and once in centimeters; each point on the scatter plot gives the two height measurements for one child. All the points in the figure fall on the line of best fit, because height in centimeters always equals 2.54 times height in inches. The two variables, height in centimeters and height in inches, are perfectly correlated—one can be perfectly predicted from the other. Once you know your height in inches, there is no information to be gained by measuring yourself with a meterstick.

Figure A.6*C* presents a relation between IQ and shoe size. These variables are unrelated to each other; people with large shoes have neither a higher nor a lower IQ than people with small ones. The line of best fit is therefore horizontal, because the best guess of an individual's IQ is the same no matter what his or her shoe size—it is the mean IQ of the population.

The Correlation Coefficient

Correlations are often described by a ***correlation coefficient,*** denoted ***r,*** a number that can vary from $+1.00$ to -1.00 which expresses the strength and the direction of the correlation. For positive correlations, r is positive; for negative correlations, it is negative; for variables which are completely uncorrelated, $r = 0$. The largest positive value r can have is $+1.00$, which represents a perfect correlation (as in Figure A.6*B*); the largest possible negative value is -1.00, which is also a perfect correlation. The closer the points in a scatter plot come to falling on the line of best fit, the nearer r will be to $+1.00$ or -1.00, and the more confident we

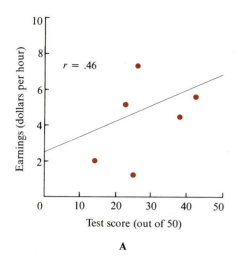

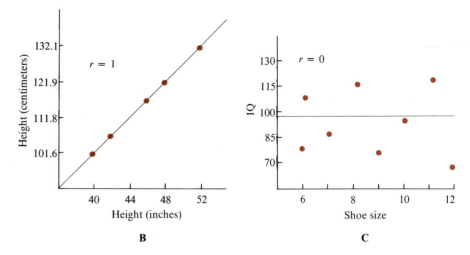

A

B

C

A.6 Scatter plots of various correlations *(A) The scatter plot and line of best fit show a positive correlation between a taxi-driving test and earnings. (B) A perfect positive correlation. The line of best fit passes through all the points. (C) A correlation of zero. The line of best fit is horizontal.*

can be in predicting scores on one variable from scores on the other. The values of r for the scatter plots in Figures A.5 and A.6A are given on the figures.

The method for calculating r between two variables, X and Y, is shown in Table A.5. The formula is

$$r = \frac{\text{sum } (z_x z_y)}{N} \tag{4}$$

The variable z_x is the z-score corresponding to X; z_y is the z-score corresponding to Y. To find r, each X and Y score must first be converted to a z-score by subtracting the mean and then dividing by the standard deviation. Then the product of z_x and z_y is found for each pair of scores. The average of these products (the sum of the products divided by N, the number of pairs of scores) is the correlation coefficient r.

Figure A.7 illustrates why this procedure yields positive values of r for posi-

A.7 Correlation coefficients *(A) Two positively correlated variables. Most of the points lie in the upper right and lower left quadrants, where $z_x z_y$ is positive, so r is positive. (B) Two negatively correlated variables. Most of the points lie in the upper left and lower right quadrants, where $z_x z_y$ is negative, so r is negative.*

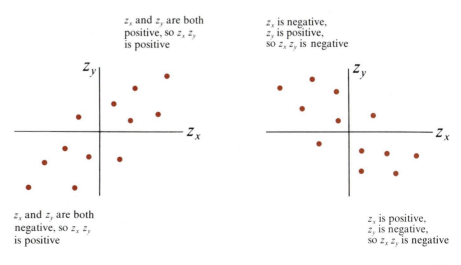

Table A.5 CALCULATION OF THE CORRELATION COEFFICIENT

1. Data (from Figure A.6A).

Test score (X)	Earnings (Y)
45	6
25	2
15	3
40	5
25	6
30	8

2. Find the mean and standard deviation for X and Y.

For X, mean = 30, standard deviation = 10
For Y, mean = 5, standard deviation = 2

3. Convert each X and each Y to a z-score, using $z = \dfrac{(\text{score} - M)}{SD}$

X	Y	z-score for X (z_x)	z-score for Y (z_y)	$z_x z_y$
45	6	1.5	0.5	0.75
25	2	−0.5	−1.5	0.75
15	3	−1.5	−1.0	1.50
40	5	1.0	0.0	0.00
25	6	−0.5	0.5	−0.25
30	8	0.0	1.5	0.00
				2.75

4. Find the product $z_x z_y$ for each pair of scores.

5. $r = \dfrac{\text{sum}(z_x z_y)}{N} = \dfrac{2.75}{6} = .46$

tively related variables and negative values of r for negatively related variables. For positively correlated variables, most points are either above or below the mean on both variables. If they are above the mean, both z_x and z_y will be positive; if they are below, both z_x and z_y will be negative. (This follows from the definition of a z-score.) In either case the product $z_x z_y$ will be positive, so r will be positive. For negatively correlated variables, most points which are above the mean on one variable are below the mean on the other—either z_x is positive and z_y is negative, or vice versa. The product $z_x z_y$ is therefore negative, and so is r.

Interpreting and Misinterpreting Correlations

It is tempting, but false, to assume that if two variables are correlated, one is the cause of the other. There is a positive correlation between years of education and annual income in the population of North American adults; many people, including some educators, argue from these data that students should stay in school as long as possible in order to increase their eventual earning power. The difficulty with this reasoning is not the existence of counterexamples (such as Andrew

Carnegie, the American industrialist and millionaire who never finished high school), which merely show that the correlation is less than 1.00. It is rather that it is difficult to infer causality from this correlation because both variables are correlated with yet a third variable. Years of schooling and income as an adult are not only correlated with each other, they are also correlated with a third variable —the parents' income. Given this fact, can we make any assertions about what causes adult income? Perhaps income is determined by one's education (it probably is, in part). But perhaps the relationship between income and education is a spurious byproduct of the parents' income. Perhaps this third factor partially determines both one's education and one's income, and there is no real causal connection between the two.

Another demonstration of the fact that correlation is not equivalent to causation occurs while waiting for a bus or a subway whose schedule is unknown. There is a negative correlation between the number of minutes a rider will have to wait for the next subway and the number of people waiting when the rider enters the station: the more people who are waiting, the sooner the subway will arrive. This negative correlation is fairly substantial, but even so, one would hardly try to cut down one's waiting time by arriving at the station with fifty friends. Here, the third, causal variable (time since the last train or bus left) is fairly obvious.* But even when it is harder to imagine just what the third variable might be, it is still possible that such a third variable exists and is responsible for the correlation. As a result, correlations can never provide solid evidence of a causal link.

INTERPRETING DATA: INFERENTIAL STATISTICS

We have seen that a psychologist collecting data encounters variability. In memory experiments, for example, different individuals recall different numbers of items, and the same person is likely to perform differently when tested twice. An investigator wishes to draw general conclusions from data in spite of this variability, or to discover the factors that are responsible for it.

Accounting for Variability

As an example of how variability may be explained, consider a person shooting a pistol at a target. Although he always aims at the bull's eye, the shots scatter around it (Figure A.8A). Assuming that the mean is the bull's eye, the variance of these shots is the average squared deviation of the shots from the center; suppose this variance is 100.

Now we set about explaining the variance. If the shooting was done outdoors, the wind may have increased the spread; moving the shooter to an indoor shooting range produces the tighter grouping shown in Figure A.8B. The new variance is 80, a reduction of 20 percent—this means that the wind accounts for 20 percent of the original variance. Some of the variance may result from the unsteady hand of the shooter, so we now mount the gun. This yields a variance of 50 (Fig-

* I thank Barry Schwartz for this example.

ure A.8*C*), a reduction of 50 percent, so 50 percent of the variance can be attributed to the shaky hand of the shooter. To find out how much of the variance can be accounted for by both the wind and the shaking, we mount the gun *and* move it indoors; now we may find a variance of only 30 (Figure A.8*D*). This means we have explained 70 percent of the variance, leaving 30 percent unaccounted for.* Not all changes in the situation will reduce the variance. For example, if we find that providing the shooter with earmuffs leaves the variance unchanged, we know that none of the original variance was due to the noise of the pistol.

VARIANCE AND EXPERIMENTS

Figure A.9 shows how this approach can be applied to the experiment on visual imagery described earlier (see page A5). Figure A.9*A* shows the distribution of scores for all 20 subjects in the experiment lumped together; the total variance of this overall distribution is 6.25. But as we saw, 10 of these subjects had been instructed to use visual imagery in memorizing, whereas another 10 control subjects were given no special instructions. How much of the overall variance can be accounted for by the difference in these instructions? In Figure A.9*B*, the distributions are no longer lumped together. They are instead presented as two separate histograms; the subjects who received imagery instructions are shown in color while those who did not are indicated in gray. As the figure shows, there is less variability within either the imagery group or the control group than in the overall distribution that lumped both kinds of subjects together. While the var-

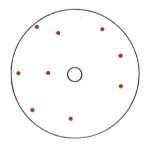

A. Outdoors, no mount. Variance = 100.

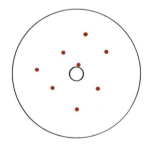

C. Outdoors, mount. Variance = 50.

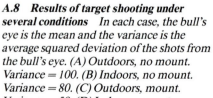

A.8 Results of target shooting under several conditions   *In each case, the bull's eye is the mean and the variance is the average squared deviation of the shots from the bull's eye. (A) Outdoors, no mount. Variance = 100. (B) Indoors, no mount. Variance = 80. (C) Outdoors, mount. Variance = 50. (D) Indoors, mount. Variance = 30.*

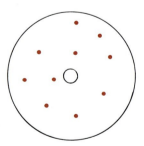

B. Indoors, no mount. Variance = 80.

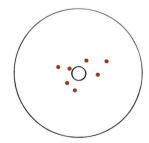

D. Indoors, mount. Variance = 30.

* I am grateful to Paul Rozin for suggesting this example.

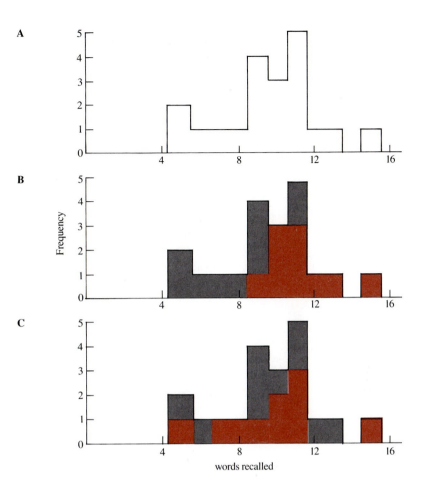

A.9   Accounting for variance in an experiment on memorizing   *(A) The distribution of number of words recalled is shown for all 20 subjects lumped together; the variance of this distribution is 6.25. (B) The distributions of the experimental and control groups are displayed separately. The number of words recalled by the group that received imagery instructions is shown in color; the number recalled by the control group that received no special instructions is shown in gray. Within each of these groups, the variance is about 4.00. (C) The distribution of number of words recalled is plotted separately for men and women regardless of how they were instructed. Color indicates the number of words recalled by women, gray the number recalled by men. The variance is 6.25.*

iance in the overall distribution is 6.25, the variance within the two subgroups averages to only 4.0. We conclude that the difference between the instructions the subjects were given accounted for 36 percent of the variance, and that 64 percent ($4 \div 6.25$) still remains unexplained.

Figure A.9*C* shows a situation in which an independent variable (in this case, sex) accounts for little or none of the variance. In this figure, the subjects' scores are again presented as two separate histograms; one for the scores of the men (regardless of whether they were instructed to use imagery or not), and the other for the scores of the women (again, regardless of the instructions they received). The men's scores are shown in gray; the women's, in color. Now the variance of the two subgroups (that is, men vs. women) averages to 6.25, a value identical to that found for the overall distribution. We conclude that the subject's sex accounts for none of the overall variance in memorizing performance.

VARIANCE AND CORRELATION

The technique of explaining the variance in one variable by attributing it to the effect of another variable can also be applied to correlational studies. Here, the values of one variable are explained (that is, accounted for) when the values of the other variable are known. Recall the taxicab example. In it a correlation of .46

was found between taxi drivers' earnings and their scores on a screening test. Since the correlation is neither perfect nor zero, some but not all of the variance in job performance can be explained by the aptitude test scores. The greater the magnitude of the correlation coefficient, r, the more variance is accounted for. The rule is that the proportion of variance which is explained equals r^2: If $r = .46$, one variable accounts for $(.46)^2 = .21$ of the variance of the other. (Just why this proportion is r^2 is beyond the scope of this discussion.) To put this another way, suppose all the cab drivers were identical on the one variable, their performance on the geographical text. This means that the variance on that variable would be zero. As a result, the variability on the second variable, earnings, would be reduced. The formula tells us by how much. The original variance on earnings can be determined from the data in Table A.5. It is 4. Its correlation with the geography test is .46. Since the effect of this variable, the geography test, is completely controlled, the variability on earnings will be $4 - (.46)^2 \times 4 = 3.16$. The drop in the variance from 4 to 3.16 is a reduction of 21 percent. The aptitude test does help us to predict taxicab earnings, for it accounts for 21 percent of the variance. But a good deal of the variance, 79 percent, is still unexplained.

Hypothesis Testing

Much behavioral research attempts to answer two-alternative questions. Does the amount of food a person eats depend on the effort required to eat it? Can people learn while they are sleeping? Is drug X more effective than aspirin? Each of these questions suggests an experiment, and the procedures described in the previous section could be used to discover how much of the variance in the dependent variable could be accounted for by the independent variable. But how can the results of such experiments lead to simple yes-or-no answers to the questions that inspired them?

TESTING HYPOTHESES ABOUT SINGLE SCORES

We will begin by testing a hypothesis about single scores. Consider the problem in interpreting a lie-detector test. In such a test, a person is asked a series of questions and various measures of physiological arousal are taken as he answers. An answer that is accompanied by an unusually high degree of arousal is taken as possible evidence that the person is lying. The question is how high is "unusually high?"

To answer this question we will first rephrase it. Can we reject the hypothesis that the given score came from the distribution of responses the same individual gave to neutral questions? (An example is "Is your name Fred?") Suppose the average arousal score to such control questions is 50, that the standard deviation of these neutral responses is 10, and that the arousal scores are normally distributed. We now look at the arousal score to the critical item. Let us say that this is 60. How likely is it that this score is from a sample drawn by chance from the population of responses to neutral questions? To find out, we convert it to a z-score, by computing its distance from the mean and dividing it by the standard deviation. The resulting z-score is $(60 - 50)/10$ or 1. Since the distribution is normal, Figure A.3 tells us that 16 percent of this person's arousal scores would be as high or higher than this. Under the circumstances we don't feel justified in rejecting the hypothesis that the score in question comes from the distribution of neutral responses. Put another way, we don't feel justified in accusing the person of lying. Our feelings might be different if the score were 70 or above. For now the z-score is $(70 - 50)/10$, or 2 standard deviations above the mean of the neutral distribution. The chances that a score this high or higher is from a sample drawn from the population of neutral responses is only 2 in a 100. We might now feel more comfortable in rejecting the hypothesis that this score is simply a chance event. We are more likely to assume that it is drawn from another distribution—in short, that the person is lying.

In this example we had to decide between two hypotheses. We look at a given score (or a set of scores) obtained under a particular experimental condition (in this case, a loaded question). One hypothesis is that the experimental condition has no effect, that the score is merely a reflection of the ordinary variability around the mean of a control condition (in this case, neutral questions). This is the so-called **null hypothesis,** the hypothesis that there really is no effect. The **alternative hypothesis** is that the null hypothesis is false, that the score is far enough away from the control mean so that we can assume that the same experimental condition has some effect. To decide between these two hypotheses, the data are expressed as a z-score, which in the context of hypothesis testing is called a **critical ratio.** Behavioral scientists generally accept a critical ratio of 2 as a cutting point. If this ratio is 2 or greater, they generally reject the null hypothesis and assume there is an effect of the experimental condition. (Such critical ratios of 2 or more are said to be **statistically significant,** which is just another way of saying that the null hypothesis can be rejected.) Critical ratios of less than 2 are considered too small to allow the rejection of the null hypothesis.

This general procedure is not foolproof. It is certainly possible for a subject in the lie-detection example to have an arousal score of 70 (a critical ratio of 2) or higher even though he is telling the truth. According to Figure A.3, this will happen about 2 percent of the time, and the person administering the test will erroneously "detect" a lie. Raising the cutoff value to the critical ratio of 3 or 4 would make such errors less common, but would not eliminate them entirely; furthermore, such a high critical value might mean failure to discover any lies the subject does utter. One of the important consequences of the variability in psychological data can be seen here: the investigator who has to decide between two interpretations of the data (the null hypothesis and the alternative hypothesis) cannot be correct all the time.

TESTING HYPOTHESES ABOUT MEANS

In the preceding discussion, our concern was with hypotheses about single scores. We now turn to the more commonly encountered problems in which the hypotheses involve means.

In many experiments, the investigator compares two or more groups—subjects tested with or without a drug, with or without imagery instructions, and so on. Suppose we get a difference between the two groups. How do we decide whether the difference is genuine rather than a mere chance fluctuation?

Let us return to the experiment in which memory for words was tested with and without instructions to imagine the items visually. To simplify the exposition, we will here consider a modified version of the experiment in which the same subjects serve in both the imagery and the nonimagery conditions. Each subject memorizes a list of 20 words without instructions, then memorizes a second list of 20 words under instructions to visualize. What we want to know is whether the subjects show any improvement with imagery instructions. There is no separate control group in this experiment, but, because a subject's score in the imagery condition can be compared with his score in the uninstructed condition, each subject provides his own control.

Table A.6 gives data for the 10 subjects in the experiment. For each subject, the table lists the number of words recalled without imagery instructions, the number recalled with such instructions, and the improvement (the difference between the two scores). The mean improvement overall is 3 words, from a mean of 8 words recalled without imagery to a mean of 11 words with imagery. But note that this does not hold for all subjects. For example, for Fred and Hortense, the "improvement" is negative—they both do better without imagery instructions. The question is whether we can conclude that there is an imagery facilitation effect overall. Put in other words, is the difference between the two conditions statistically significant?

Table A.6   NUMBER OF ITEMS RECALLED WITH AND WITHOUT IMAGERY INSTRUCTION, FOR 10 SUBJECTS

Subject	Score with imagery	Score without imagery	Improvement
Alphonse	11	5	6
Betsy	15	9	6
Cheryl	11	5	6
Davis	9	9	0
Earl	13	6	7
Fred	10	11	−1
Germaine	11	8	3
Hortense	10	11	−1
Imogene	8	7	1
Jerry	12	9	3
Mean	11	8	3

$$\text{Variance of improvement scores} = \frac{\text{sum of (score} - 3)^2}{10} = 8.8$$

$$\text{Standard deviation of improvement scores} = \sqrt{8.8} = 2.97$$

To show how this question is answered, we will follow much the same logic as that used in the analysis of the lie-detection problem. We have a mean—the average difference score of 10 subjects. What we must realize is that this mean—3—is really a sample based on the one experiment with 10 subjects we have just run. Suppose we had run the experiment again, with another set of 10 subjects—not just once, but many times. Each such repetition of the experiment would yield its own mean. And each of these means would constitute another sample. But what is the population to which these samples refer? It is the set of all of these means— the average differences between imagery and nonimagery instructions obtained in each of the many repetitions of the experiment we might possibly perform. And the mean of these means—a kind of grand mean—is the mean of the population. Any conclusions we want to draw from our experiment are really assertions about this population mean. If we say that the difference we found is statistically significant, we are asserting that the population mean is a difference score which is greater than zero (and in the same direction as in the sample). Put another way, we are asserting that the difference we found is not just a fluke but is real and would be obtained again and again if we repeated the experiment, thus rejecting the null hypothesis.

The null hypothesis amounts to the claim that the mean we actually obtained could have been drawn by chance from a distribution of sample means (that is, the many means of the possible repetitions of our experiment) around a population mean of zero. To test this claim, we have to compute a critical ratio that can tell us how far from zero our own mean actually is. Like all critical ratios, this is a z-score which expresses the distance of a score from a mean in units of the standard deviation (the SD). Thus, $z = (score = M)/SD$. In our present case, the score is our obtained mean (that is, 3); the mean is the hypothetical population mean of zero (assumed by the null hypothesis). But what is the denominator? It is the standard deviation of the distribution of sample means, the means of the many experiments we might have done.

The standard deviation of such a distribution of sample means is called the **standard error** of the mean **(SE).** Its value is determined by two factors: the standard deviation of the sample and the size of that sample. Specifically,

$$SE = \frac{SD}{\sqrt{N-1}} \tag{5}$$

It is clear that the variability of a mean (and this is what the standard error measures) goes down with the increasing sample size. (Why this factor turns out to be $\sqrt{N-1}$ is beyond the scope of this discussion.) A clue as to why comes from the consideration of the effects of an atypical score. Purely by chance, a sample may include an extreme case. But the larger the size of that sample, the less the effect of on extreme case on the average. If a sample of 3 persons includes a midget, the average height will be unusually far from the population mean. But in a sample of 3,000, one midget will not affect the average very markedly.

We can now conclude our analysis of the results of the memorization experiment. The critical ratio to be evaluated is:

$$\text{Critical Ratio} = \frac{\text{obtained sample mean} - \text{population mean}}{\text{SE}}$$

Since the population mean is assumed to be zero (by the null hypothesis), this expression becomes:

$$\text{Critical Ratio} = \frac{\text{obtained sample mean}}{\text{SE}}$$

This critical ratio expresses the mean difference between the two experimental conditions in units of the variability of the sample mean, that is, the standard error.* To compute the standard error, we first find the standard deviation of the

* There are several simplifications in this account. One is that the critical ratio described here does not have an exactly normal distribution. When the sample size is large, this effect is unimportant, but for small samples (like the one in the example) they can be material. To deal with these and related problems, statisticians often utilize measures that refer to distributions other than the normal one. An example is the t-test, a kind of critical ratio based on the so-called t-distribution.

improvement scores; this turns out to be 2.97, as shown in Table A.6. Then equation (5) tells us

$$SE = \frac{SD}{\sqrt{N-1}} = \frac{2.97}{\sqrt{10-1}} = .99$$

The critical ratio is now the obtained mean difference divided by the standard error, or $3/.99 = 3.03$. This is clearly larger than 2.0, so we conclude that the observed difference in memory between the imagery and control conditions is much too great to be attributed to chance factors. Thus using visual imagery evidently does improve recall.

CONFIDENCE INTERVALS

In statistical hypothesis testing we ask whether a certain sample mean could be drawn by chance from a distribution of sample means around some assumed population mean. (When testing the null hypothesis, this assumed population mean is zero.) But there is another way of phrasing this question. Can we be reasonably confident that the mean of the population falls within a certain specified interval? If we know the standard error of the mean, the answer is yes. We have already seen that about 2 percent of the scores in a normal distribution are more than two standard deviations above, and about 2 percent are lower than two standard deviations below the mean of that distribution. Since this is so, we can conclude that the chances are roughly 4 in 100 that the population mean is within an interval whose largest value is two standard errors above the sample mean and whose lowest value is two standard errors below. Because we can be fairly (96 percent) confident that the actual population mean will fall within this specified range, it is often called the **confidence interval.**

As an example, consider the prediction of political elections. During election campaigns, polling organizations report the current standing of various candidates by statements such as the following: "In a poll of 1,000 registered voters, 57 percent favored candidate Smith; the margin of error was 3 percent." This margin of error is the confidence interval around the proportion (that is, ± 3 percent).

To determine this confidence interval, the pollsters compute the standard error of the proportion they found. (In this case, .57). This standard error is analogous to the standard error of a mean we discussed in the previous section. Given an N of 1,000, this standard error happens to be .015.* Since $2 \times .015$ is .03 or 3 percent, the appropriate confidence interval for our example is the interval from 54 to 60 percent. Under the circumstances, candidate Smith can be fairly confident

---

* The standard error of a proportion (e.g., the proportion of polled voters who express pro-X sentiments) is analogous to the standard error of the mean, and measures the precision with which our sample proportion estimates the population proportion. The formula for the standard error of a proportion p is:

$$SE_P = \sqrt{\frac{p \times (1-p)}{N}} \tag{7}$$

In our example, $p = .57$ and $N = 1,000$, so $SE_P = .015$.

that she has the support of at least 50 percent of the electorate since 50 percent is well *below* the poll's confidence interval (see Figure A.10).

Some Implications of Statistical Inference

The methods of testing hypotheses and estimating confidence intervals which we have just described are routinely employed in evaluating the results of psychological research. But they have several characteristics that necessarily affect the interpretation of all such results.

THE PROBABILISTIC NATURE OF HYPOTHESIS TESTING AND CONFIDENCE INTERVALS

Since there is always some unexplained variance in any psychological study, there is always some probability that the conclusions are wrong as applied to the population. If we use a confidence interval of ± 2 SE, the chances that the population mean (or proportion, or whatever) falls outside of that interval are less than 4 or 5 in 100. Do we want to be more confident than this? If so, we might use a confidence interval of ± 3 SE where the equivalent chance is only 1 in 1,000. The same holds for critical ratios. We can say that a critical ratio of 2 means that a difference is statistically significant, but that only means that the chances are less than 2 in 100 that the difference as large or larger than this arose by chance. If we want to be more certain than this, we must insist that the critical ratio be larger—perhaps 3 (a chance factor of 1 in 2,000) or 4 (5 in 100,000), and so on. As long as there is some unexplained variance, there is some chance of error.

The probabilistic nature of statistical reasoning has another consequence. Even if we can come to a correct conclusion about the mean of a population (or a proportion, as in polls), we cannot generalize to individuals. Thus a study which shows that men have higher scores than women on spatial relations tests is not inconsistent with the existence of brilliant female artists or architects. Sample means for the two groups can differ significantly, even though there is considerable overlap in the two distributions of scores.

A.10   A candidate's poll results and their confidence intervals   The results of a mythical poll conducted for a no-less-mythical presidential candidate Smith by randomly sampling 200 persons in each of five regions of the U.S. The figure shows the pro-Smith proportions in each region, together with the confidence intervals around them, and indicates that she is ahead in all five samples. But there are two regions where she cannot be confident that she is ahead in the population—the South and the Southwest, where the confidence intervals of the pro-Smith proportion dip below 50 percent.

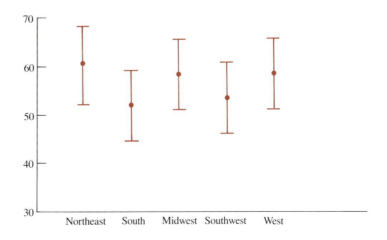

THE CONSERVATIVE NATURE OF HYPOTHESIS TESTING

Another characteristic of statistical hypothesis testing is that it is essentially conservative. This is because of the great stress placed on the null hypothesis in reaching a decision: one has to be quite sure that the null hypothesis is false before one entertains the alternative hypothesis. There are other imaginable strategies for reaching statistical decisions, but the conservative one has a perfectly rational basis. Let's suppose that some independent variable *does* produce a difference between two groups that is quite genuine and not the result of chance, but that the critical ratio is too low to reject the null hypothesis. If so, we will have falsely concluded that no difference exists in the population. As a result, we will have failed to discover a small effect. But what of it? If the effect is interesting enough, someone else may well attempt a similar experiment and manage to find the difference we didn't uncover. On the other hand, suppose we "discover" that some independent variable has an effect when it actually does not (that is, the null hypothesis is true). By falsely rejecting the null hypothesis, we will have added an inaccurate "fact" to the store of scientific knowledge, and run the risk of leading other investigators into a blind alley.

THE ROLE OF SAMPLE SIZE

A last point concerns the role of sample size in affecting the interpretations of results. The larger the sample, the smaller the standard error and the smaller the confidence interval around the mean or the proportion. This can have major effects on hypothesis testing.

Suppose that, in the population, a certain independent variable produces a very small difference. As an example, suppose that the population difference between men and women on a certain test of spatial relations is 1 percent. We would probably be unable to reject the null hypothesis (that there is no sex difference on the test) with samples of moderate size. But if the sample size were sufficiently increased, we could reject the null hypothesis. For such a sizable increase in N would lead to a decrease in the standard errors of the sample means, which in turn would lead to an increase in the critical ratio. Someone who read a report of this experiment would now learn that, by using thousands of subjects, we had discovered a "significant" difference of 1 percent. A fair reaction to this bit of intelligence would be that the null hypothesis can indeed be rejected, but that the *psychological* significance of this finding is rather slight. The moral is simple. Statistical significance is required before a result can be considered reliable, but this statistical significance does not guarantee that the effect discovered is of psychological significance or of any practical importance.

SUMMARY

1. Statistical methods concern the ways in which investigators describe, gather, organize, and interpret collections of numerical data. A crucial concern of statistical endeavors is to deal with the variability that is encountered in all research.

2. An early step in the process is *scaling,* a procedure for assigning numbers to psychological responses. Scales can be *categorical, ordinal, interval,* or *ratio scales.* These differ in the degree to which they can be subjected to arithmetical operations.

3. There are three main methods for conducting psychological research: by means of an *experiment,* an *observational study,* and a *case study.* In an experiment, the investigator manipulates one variable, the *independent variable,* to see how it affects the subject's response, the *dependent variable.* In an observational study, the investigator does not manipulate any variables directly but rather observes them as they occur naturally. A case study is an investigation in which one person is studied in depth.

4. An important distinction in psychological research is that between *sample* and *population.* The population is the entire group about which the investigator wants to draw conclusions. The sample is the subset (usually small) of that population that is actually tested. Generalizations from sample to population are only possible if the one is representative of the other. This requires the use of *random samples.* In some cases a special version of the random sample, the *stratified sample,* may be employed.

5. A first step in organizing the data is to arrange them in a *frequency distribution,* often displayed in graphic form, as in a *histogram.* Frequency distributions are characterized by a *central tendency* and by *variability* around this central tendency. The common measure of central tendency is the *mean,* though sometimes another measure, the *median,* may be preferable, as in cases when the distribution is *skewed.* Important measures of variability are the *variance* and the *standard deviation.*

6. One way of comparing two scores drawn from different distributions is to convert both into *percentile ranks.* Another is to transform them into *z-scores,* which express the distance of a score from its mean in standard deviation units. The percentile rank of a *z*-score can be computed if the shape of that score's distribution is known. An important example is the *normal distribution,* graphically displayed by the *normal curve* which describes the distribution of many psychological variables and is basic to much of statistical reasoning.

7. In observational studies, the relation between variables is often expressed in the form of a *correlation* which may be positive or negative. It is measured by the *correlation coefficient,* a number that can vary from $+1.00$ to -1.00. While correlations reflect the extent to which two variables vary together, they do not necessarily indicate that one of them causes the other.

8. A major task of any investigator is to explain the variability of some dependent variable, usually measured by the variance. One means for doing so is to see whether that variance is reduced when a certain independent variable is controlled. If so, this independent variable is said to account for some of the variability of the dependent variable.

9. One of the main functions of statistical methods is to help test hypotheses about population given information about the sample. An important example is the difference between mean scores obtained under two different conditions. Here the investigator has to decide between the *null hypothesis* which asserts that the difference was obtained by chance, and the *alternative hypothesis* which asserts that the difference is genuine and exists in the population. The decision is made by dividing the obtained mean difference by the *standard error,* a measure of the variability of that mean difference. If the resulting ratio, called the *critical ratio,* is large enough, the null hypothesis is rejected, the alternative hypothesis is accepted, and the difference is said to be *statistically significant.* A related way of making statistical decisions is by using a *confidence interval,* or margin of error. This is based on the variability of the scores from a sample and determines the interval within which the population mean or proportion probably falls.

Glossary

absolute threshold The lowest intensity of some stimulus that produces a response.

accommodation The process by which the lens is thickened or flattened to focus on an object.

acetylcholine A neurotransmitter that acts as an excitatory transmitter at the synaptic junctions between muscle fibers and motor neurons.

achievement motive The desire to meet or exceed some standard of excellence.

action potential A brief change in the electrical potential of an axon which is the physical basis of the nervous impulse.

active sleep (or REM sleep) A stage of sleep during which the EEG is similar to that of waking, during which there are rapid eye movements (REMs), and during which dreams occur.

actor-observer difference The difference in attributions made by actors who describe their own actions and observers who describe another person's. The former emphasizes external, situational causes; the latter, internal, dispositional factors.

adaptive value In biological terms, the extent to which an attribute increases the likelihood of viable offspring. Also, the unit of inheritance.

additive color mixture Mixing colors by stimulating the eye with two sets of wavelengths simultaneously (e.g., by focusing filtered light from two projectors on the same spot).

adrenalin *See* epinephrine.

affective disorders A group of disorders whose primary characteristic is a disturbance of mood. *See also* bipolar disorder, depression, mania, and unipolar affective disorder.

afferent nerves Sensory nerves that carry messages to the brain.

agnosia A serious disturbance in the organization of sensory information produced by lesions in certain cortical association areas. An example is visual agnosia, in which the patient can see, but often does not recognize what it is that he sees.

alarm call Special, genetically pre-programmed cry that impels members of a given species to seek cover. A biological puzzle, since it suggests a form of altruism in which the individual appears to endanger his own survival. *See also* altruism.

algorithm In computer problem-solving, a procedure in which all of the operations are specified step-by-step. *See also* heuristics.

all-or-none law Describes the fact that once a stimulus exceeds threshold, further increases do not increase the amplitude of the action potential.

alpha blocking The disruption of the alpha rhythm by visual stimulation or by active thought with the eyes closed.

alpha waves Fairly regular EEG waves, between eight to twelve per second, characteristic of a relaxed, waking state, usually with eyes closed.

alternative hypothesis In statistics, the hypothesis that the null hypothesis is false; that an obtained difference is so far from zero that one has to assume that the mean difference in the population is greater than zero and that the experimental condition has some effect. *See also* null hypothesis.

altruism As used by sociobiologists, any behavior pattern that benefits individuals that are not one's offspring (e.g., an alarm call). According to the kin-selection hypothesis, such altruism has biological survival value because the altruist's beneficiaries tend to be closely related relatives who carry a high proportion of his own genes. According to the reciprocal-altruism hypothesis, altruism is based on the expectation that today's giver will be tomorrow's taker. *See also* alarm call.

ambiguity (in sentence meaning) The case in which a sentence (i.e., one surface structure) has two meanings (i.e., two underlying structures). (E.g., "These missionaries are ready to eat" overheard in a conversation between two cannibals.)

anal stage In psychoanalytic theory, the stage of psychosexual development during which the focus of pleasure is on activities related to elimination.

androgen Any male sex hormone.

anterograde amnesia A memory deficit suffered after some brain damage. It is an inability to learn and remember any information imparted after the injury, with little effect on memory for information acquired previously. *See also* retrograde amnesia.

antidepressants Drugs (e.g., imipramine, MAO inhibitors) that alleviate depressive symptoms, presumably because of some effect on the availability of certain neurotransmitters at synaptic junctions.

antidiuretic hormone (ADH) A hormone secreted by one of the parts of the pituitary gland. This hormone instructs the kidneys to reabsorb more of the water that passes through them. *See also* pituitary gland.

antisocial personality Also called psychopath or sociopath. The term describes persons who get into continual trouble with society, are indifferent to others, impulsive, with little concern for the future or remorse about the past.

anxiety An emotional state akin to fear. According to Freud, many mental illnesses center around anxiety and on attempts to ward it off by various unconscious mechanisms.

anxiety disorder *See* phobias, generalized anxiety disorder, and obsessive-compulsive disorders.

anxiety hierarchy *See* systematic desensitization.

aphagia Refusal to eat (and in an extreme version, to drink) brought about by lesion of the lateral hypothalamus.

aphasia A disorder of language produced by lesions in certain association areas of the cortex. A lesion in Broca's area leads to expressive aphasia, one in Wernicke's area to receptive aphasia.

apparent movement The perception of movement produced by stimuli that are stationary but flash on and off with appropriate time intervals.

apraxia A serious disturbance in the organization of voluntary action produced by lesions in certain cortical association areas, often in the frontal lobes.

artificial intelligence Some aspect of cognitive processing that is carried out by a computer. Examples are computer programs that recognize patterns or solve certain kinds of problems.

assimilation and accommodation In Piaget's theory, the twin processes by means of which cognitive development proceeds. Assimilation is the process whereby the environment is interpreted in terms of the schemas the child has at the time. Accommodation is the way the child changes his schemas as he continues to interact with the environment.

association A linkage between two psychological processes as a result of past experience in which the two have occurred together. A broad term which subsumes conditioning and association of ideas among others.

association areas Regions of the cortex that are not projection areas. They tend to be involved in the integration of sensory information or of motor commands.

attachment The tendency of the young of many species to stay in close proximity to an adult, usually their mother. *See also* imprinting.

attention A collective label for all the processes by which we perceive selectively.

attitude A fairly stable, evaluative disposition that makes a person think, feel, or behave positively or negatively about some person, group, or social issue.

attribution theory A theory about the process by which we try to explain a person's behavior, attributing it to situational factors or to some inferred dispositional qualities or both.

authoritarian personality A cluster of personal attributes (e.g., submission to persons above and harshness to those below) and social attitudes (e.g., prejudice against minority groups), which is sometimes held to constitute a distinct personality.

automatization A process whereby components of a skilled activity become subsumed under a higher-order organization and are run off automatically.

autonomic nervous system (ANS) A part of the nervous system that controls the internal organs, usually not under voluntary control.

availability heuristic A rule of thumb often used to make probability estimates, which depends on the frequency with which certain events readily come to mind. This can lead to errors since very vivid events will be remembered out of proportion to their actual frequency of occurrence.

aversive therapy A form of behavior therapy in which the undesirable response leads to an aversive stimulus (e.g., the patient shocks himself every time he reaches for a cigarette).

avoidance learning Instrumental learning in which the response averts an aversive stimulus before it occurs. This poses a problem: What is the reinforcement for this kind of learning?

axon Part of a neuron which transmits impulses to other neurons or effectors.

backward pairing *See* simultaneous pairing and forward pairing.

basilar membrane *See* cochlea.

behavior therapy A general approach to psychological treatment which (1) holds that the disorders to which it addresses itself are produced by maladaptive learning and must be remedied by reeducation, (2) proposes techniques for this reeducation based on principles of learning and conditioning, (3) focuses on the maladaptive behaviors as such rather than on hypothetical unconscious processes of which they may be expressions.

belongingness in learning The fact that the ease with which associations are formed depends upon the items to be associated. This holds for classical conditioning in which some CS-UCS combinations are more effective than others (e.g., learned taste aversions) and for instrumental conditioning in which some response-reinforcer combinations work more easily than others (e.g., specific defense reactions in avoidance conditioning of species).

between-group heritability The extent to which variation between groups (as in the difference between the mean IQs of U.S. whites and blacks) is attributable to genetic factors. *See also* heritability and within-group heritability.

biofeedback A procedure by which an individual receives information about some aspect of his involuntary reactions which may enable him to bring these reactions under some measure of voluntary control.

bipolar disorder Affective disorder in which the patient swings from one emotional extreme to another, experiencing both manic and depressive episodes. Formerly called manic-depressive psychosis.

blocking An effect produced when two conditioned stimuli, *A* and *B,* are both presented together with the unconditioned stimulus (UCS). If stimulus *A* has previously been associated with the unconditioned stimulus while *B* has not, the formation of an association between stimulus *B* and the UCS will be impaired (that is, blocked).

bottom-up processes *See* top-down processes.

brightness A perceived dimension of visual stimuli—the extent to which they appear light or dark.

brightness contrast The perceiver's tendency to exaggerate the physical difference in the light intensities of two adjacent regions. As a result, a gray patch looks brighter on a black background, darker on a white background.

brightness ratio The ratio between the light reflected by a region and the light reflected by the area that surrounds it. According to one theory, perceived brightness is determined by this ratio.

British empiricism A school of thought that holds that all knowledge comes by way of empirical experience, that is, through the senses.

Broca's area *See* aphasia.

case study An observational study in which one person is studied intensively.

catatonic schizophrenia A subcategory of schizophrenia. Its main symptoms are peculiar motor patterns such as periods in which the patient is immobile and maintains strange positions for hours on end.

catecholamines A family of neurotransmitters which have an activating function, including epinephrine, norepinephrine and dopamine.

categorical scale A scale that divides the responses into categories that are not numerically related. *See also* interval scale, ordinal scale, and ratio scale.

catharsis An explosive release of hitherto dammed-up emotions that is sometimes believed to have therapeutic effects.

censorship in dreams *See* Freud's theory of dreams.

central nervous system (CNS) The brain and spinal cord.

central tendency The tendency of scores in a frequency distribution to cluster around a central value. *See also* median, mean, and variability.

cerebellum Two small hemispheres that form part of the hindbrain and control muscular coordination and equilibrium.

cerebral cortex The outermost layer of the gray matter of the cerebral hemispheres.

cerebral hemispheres Two hemispherical structures which comprise the major part of the forebrain in mammals and serve as the main coordinating center of the nervous system.

cerebrotonia *See* somatotype theory.

chlorpromazine *See* phenothiazines.

chromosomes Structures in the nucleus of each cell which contain the genes, the units of hereditary transmission. A human cell has 46 chromosomes, arranged in 23 pairs. One of these pairs consists of the sex chromosomes. In males, one member of the pair is an X-chromosome, the other a Y-chromosome. In females, both members are X-chromosomes. *See also* gene.

chunking A process of reorganizing (or recoding) materials in memory which permits a number of items to be packed into a larger unit.

classical conditioning A form of learning in which a hitherto neutral stimulus, the conditioned stimulus (CS) is paired with an unconditioned stimulus (UCS) regardless of what the animal does. In effect, what has to be learned is the relation between these two stimuli. *See also* instrumental conditioning.

client-centered therapy A humanistic psychotherapy developed by Carl Rogers. *See also* humanistic therapies.

closed-class morphemes Consists of all the "little" words and mor-

phemes whose function is grammatical (e.g., *the, and, who, -ed, -s,* etc.). This is in contrast to the open-class morphemes which consist of all the nouns, adjectives, verbs, and adverbs of the language which carry the major meanings in sentences.

closure A factor in visual grouping. The perceptual tendency to fill in gaps in a figure so that it looks closed.

cochlea Coiled structure in the inner ear which contains the basilar membrane whose deformation by sound-produced pressure stimulates the auditory receptors.

cognitive dissonance An inconsistency among some experiences, beliefs, attitudes or feelings. According to dissonance theory, this sets up an unpleasant state which people try to reduce by reinterpreting some part of their experiences to make them consistent with the others.

cognitive interpretation theory of emotions A theory proposed by Schachter and Singer which asserts that emotions are an interpretation of our own autonomic arousal in the light of the situation to which we attribute it. *See also* attribution theory.

cognitive map *See* cognitive theory.

cognitive theory A conception of human and animal learning which holds that both humans and animals acquire items of knowledge (cognitions) such as what is where (cognitive map) or what leads to what (expectancy). This contrasts with theories of instrumental learning such as Thorndike's or Skinner's which assert that learning consists of the strengthening or weakening of particular response tendencies.

cognitive therapy An approach to therapy that tries to change some of the patient's habitual modes of thinking. It is related to behavior therapy because it regards such thought patterns as a form of behavior.

complementary colors Two colors which, when additively mixed with each other in the right proportions, produce the sensation of gray.

compulsions *See* obsessive-compulsive disorders.

concordance The probability that a person who stands in a particular family relationship to a patient (e.g., an identical twin) has the same disorder as the patient.

concrete operational period In Piaget's theory, the period from ages six or seven to about eleven. At this time the child has acquired mental operations that allow her to abstract some essential attributes of reality such as number and substance; but these operations are as yet applicable only to concrete events and cannot be considered entirely in the abstract.

conditioned reflex *See* conditioned response.

conditioned reinforcer An initially neutral stimulus that acquires reinforcing properties through pairing with another stimulus that is already reinforcing.

conditioned response (CR) A response elicited by some initially neutral stimulus, the conditioned stimulus (CS), as a result of pairings between that CS and an unconditioned stimulus. This CR is typically not identical with the unconditioned response though it often is similar to it. *See also* conditioned stimulus, unconditioned response, and unconditioned stimulus.

conditioned stimulus (CS) In classical conditioning, the stimulus which comes to elicit a new response by virtue of pairings with the unconditioned stimulus. *See also* conditioned response, unconditioned response, and unconditioned stimulus.

cones Visual receptors that respond to greater light intensities and give rise to chromatic (color) sensations.

confidence interval An interval around a sample mean or proportion within which the population mean or proportion is likely to fall. In common practice, the largest value of the interval is 2 standard errors above the mean or proportion, and the smallest value is 2 standard errors below it.

confirmation bias The tendency to seek evidence to confirm one's hypothesis rather than to look for evidence to see whether the hypothesis is false.

conservation In Piaget's theory, the understanding that certain attributes such as substance and number remain unchanged despite various transformations (e.g., liquid conservation, the realization that the amount of liquid remains the same when poured from a tall, thin beaker into a wide jar).

construction theory of perception A theory which asserts that visual patterns are constructions based on visual expectations about the consequences of eye movements or of other acts.

construct validity The extent to which performance on a test fits into a theoretical scheme about the attribute the test tries to measure.

context effects *See* top-down processes.

contiguity The togetherness in time of two events, which is sometimes regarded as the condition that leads to association.

contingency A relation between two events in which one is dependent upon another. If the contingency is greater than zero, then the probability of event *A* will be greater when event *B* is present than when it is absent.

convergence The movement of the eyes as they swivel toward each other to focus upon an object.

conversion disorders Formerly called conversion hysteria. A condition in which there are physical symptoms that seem to have no physical basis. They instead appear to be linked to psychological factors and are often believed to serve as a means of reducing anxiety. *See also* hysteria.

conversion hysteria *See* conversion disorders.

corpus callosum A bundle of fibers that connects the two cerebral hemispheres.

correlation The tendency of two variables to vary together. If one goes up as the other goes up, the correlation is positive; if one goes up as the other goes down, the correlation is negative.

correlation coefficient A number, referred to as *r*, that expresses both the size and the direction of a correlation, varying from + 1.00 (perfect positive correlation) through 0.00 (absence of any correlation) to − 1.00 (perfect negative correlation).

counterconditioning A procedure for weakening a classically conditioned CR by connecting the stimuli that presently evoke it to a new response that is incompatible with the CR.

criterion groups Groups whose test performance sets the validity criterion for certain tests (e.g., the Minnesota Multiphasic Personality Inventory, MMPI, which uses several psychiatric criterion groups to define most of its subscales).

critical period Period in the development of an organism when it is particularly sensitive to certain environmental influences. Outside of this period, the same environmental influences have little effect (e.g., the period during which a duckling can be imprinted).

critical ratio A *z*-score used for testing the null hypothesis. It is obtained by dividing an obtained mean difference by the standard error *(SE)* so that critical ratio = obtained mean difference/*SE*. If this ratio is large enough, the null hypothesis is rejected and the difference is said to be statistically significant. *See also* standard error of the mean.

crystallized intelligence The repertoire of information, cognitive skills, and strategies acquired by the application of fluid intelligence to

various fields. This is said to increase with age, in some cases into old age. *See also* fluid intelligence.

cultural anthropology A branch of anthropology that compares the similarities and differences among human cultures.

culture fairness of a test The extent to which test performance does not depend upon information or skills provided by one culture but not another.

curare A drug which completely paralyzes the skeletal musculature but does not affect visceral reactions.

cutoff score A score on a test used for selection below which no individual is accepted.

decay A possible factor in forgetting, producing some loss of the stored information through erosion by some as yet unknown physiological process.

decision making The process of forming probability estimates of events and utilizing them to choose between different courses of action.

declarative knowledge Knowing "what" (e.g., someone's name) as contrasted with procedural knowledge, which is knowing "how" (e.g., riding a bicycle).

deductive reasoning Reasoning in which one tries to determine whether some statement logically follows from certain premises, as in the analysis of syllogisms. This is in contrast with inductive reasoning in which one observes a number of particular instances and tries to determine a general rule that covers them all.

defense mechanism In psychoanalytic theory, a collective term for a number of reactions that try to ward off or lessen anxiety by various unconscious means. *See also* displacement, projection, rationalization, reaction formation, and repression.

definition (of a word) A set of necessary and sufficient features shared by all members of a category which are the criteria for membership in that category.

deindividuation A weakened sense of personal identity in which self-awareness is merged in the collective goals of a group.

delusion Systematized false beliefs, often of grandeur or persecution.

demand characteristics (of an experiment) The cues which tell a subject what the experimenter expects of him.

dendrites A typically highly branched part of a neuron that receives impulses from receptors or other neurons and conducts them toward the cell body and axon.

dependent variable *See* experiment.

depression A state of deep and pervasive dejection and hopelessness, accompanied by apathy and a feeling of personal worthlessness.

descriptive rule *See* prescriptive rules.

deviation IQ A measure of intelligence-test performance based on an individual's standing relative to his own age-mates (e.g., an IQ of 100 is average and IQs of 70 and 130 correspond to percentile ranks of 2 and 98 respectively). *See also* Intelligence Quotient.

diathesis *See* diathesis-stress conception.

diathesis-stress conception The belief that many organic and mental disorders arise from an interaction between a diathesis (a predisposition toward the illness) and some form of precipitating environmental stress.

dichotic listening A procedure by which each ear receives a different message while the listener is asked to attend to one.

difference threshold The amount by which a given stimulus must be increased or decreased so that the subject can perceive a just noticeable difference (j.n.d.).

differentiation A progressive change from the general to the particular and from the simpler to the more complex which characterizes embryological development. According to some theorists, the same pattern holds for the development of behavior after birth.

directed thinking Thinking that is aimed at the solution of a problem.

discrimination A process of learning to respond to certain stimuli that are reinforced and not to others which are unreinforced.

disinhibition An increase of some reaction tendency by the removal of some inhibiting influence upon it (e.g., the increased strength of a frog's spinal reflexes after decapitation).

displacement In psychoanalytic theory, a redirection of an impulse from a channel that is blocked into another, more available outlet (e.g., displaced aggression, as in a child who hits a sibling when punished by her parents).

display Term used by ethologists to describe genetically preprogrammed responses which serve as stimuli for the reaction of others of the same species, and thus serve as the basis of a communication system (e.g., mating rituals).

dissociative disorders Disorders in which a whole set of mental events is stored out of ordinary consciousness. These include psychogenic amnesia, fugue states and, very rarely, cases of multiple personality.

dissonance theory *See* cognitive dissonance.

distal stimulus An object or event outside (e.g., a tree) as contrasted to the proximal stimulus (e.g., the retinal image of the tree), which is the pattern of physical energies that originates from the distal stimulus and impinges on a sense organ.

doctrine of specific nerve energies The assertion that qualitative differences in sensory experience are not attributable to the differences in the stimuli that correspond to different sense modalities (e.g., light versus sound) but rather to the fact that these stimuli excite different nervous structures.

dominant gene *See* gene.

dopamine (DA) A catecholamine which is the neurotransmitter in various brain structures, including some which control motor action. Some writers believe that schizophrenia is based on an oversensitivity to dopamine in some part of the brain.

dopamine hypothesis of schizophrenia Asserts that schizophrenics are oversensitive to the neurotransmitter dopamine and are therefore in a state of overarousal. Evidence for this view comes from the fact that the phenothiazines, which alleviate schizophrenic symptoms, block dopamine transmission. *See also* phenothiazines.

double bind A conflict set up in a person who is told one thing while simultaneously receiving the message that what is meant is the very opposite.

double-blind technique A technique for evaluating drug effects independent of the effects produced by the expectations of patients (placebo effects) and of physicians. This is done by assigning patients to a drug group or a placebo group with both patients and staff members in ignorance of who is assigned to which group. *See also* placebo effect.

drive-reduction theory A theory that claims that all built-in rewards are at bottom reductions of some noxious bodily state. The theory has difficulty in explaining motives in which one seeks stimulation, such as sex and curiosity.

DSM-III The current diagnostic manual of the American Psychiatric Association adopted in 1980. A major distinction between it and its predecessor is that it categorizes mental disorders by their descriptive characteristics rather than by theories about their underlying cause. Thus a number of disorders that were formerly grouped together under the general heading "neurosis" (e.g., phobias, conversion disorders) are now classified under separate headings. *See also* neurosis, phobia, conversion disorders.

ectomorphy *See* somatotype theory.

effectors Organs of action; in humans, muscles and glands.

efferent nerves Nerves that carry messages to the effectors.

ego In Freud's theory, a set of reactions that try to reconcile the id's blind pleasure strivings with the demands of reality. These lead to the emergence of various skills and capacities which eventually become a system that can look at itself—an "I". *See also* id and superego.

egocentrism In Piaget's theory, a characteristic of preoperational children, an inability to see another person's point of view.

eidetic memory A relatively rare kind of memory characterized by relatively long-lasting and detailed images of scenes that can be scanned as if they were physically present.

elaborative rehearsal Rehearsal in which material is actively reorganized and elaborated while being held in short-term memory. In contrast to maintenance rehearsal, this confers considerable benefit. *See also* maintenance rehearsal.

Electra complex *See* Oedipus complex.

electroconvulsive shock treatment (ECT) A somatic treatment, mostly used for cases of severe depression, in which a brief electric current is passed through the brain to produce a convulsive seizure.

electroencephalogram (EEG) A record of the summed activity of cortical cells picked up by wires placed on the skull.

embryo The earliest stage in a developing animal. In humans, up to about eight weeks after conception.

encoding specificity principle The hypothesis that retrieval is most likely if the context at the time of recall approximates that during the original encoding.

endocrine system The system of ductless glands whose secretions are released directly into the bloodstream and affect organs elsewhere in the body (e.g., adrenal gland).

endomorphy *See* somatotype theory.

endorphin A drug produced within the brain itself whose effect and chemical composition are similar to such pain-relieving opiates as morphine.

epinephrine (adrenalin) A catecholamine released into the bloodstream by the adrenal medulla whose effects are similar to those of sympathetic activation (e.g., racing heart).

episodic memory Memory for particular events in one's own life (e.g., I missed the train this morning). *See also* generic memory.

erogenous zones In psychoanalytic theory, the mouth, anus, and genitals. These regions are particularly sensitive to touch. According to Freud, the various pleasures associated with each of them have a common element, which is sexual.

escape learning Instrumental learning in which reinforcement consists of the reduction or cessation of an aversive stimulus (e.g., electric shock).

essential hypertension *See* psychophysiological disorders.

estrogen   A female sex hormone which dominates the first half of the female cycle through ovulation; in animals, estrus performs this function.

estrus   In mammalian animals, the period in the cycle when the female is sexually receptive (in heat).

ethology   A branch of biology that studies the behavior of animals under natural conditions.

expectancy   *See* cognitive theory.

experiment   A study in which the investigator manipulates one (or more than one) variable (the independent variable) to determine its effect on the subject's response (the dependent variable).

expert systems   Computer problem-solving programs with a very narrow scope which only deal with problems in a limited domain of knowledge (e.g., the diagnosis of infectious diseases).

expressive movements   Movements of the face and body in animals and humans that seem to express emotion. They are usually regarded as built-in social displays.

externality hypothesis   The hypothesis that some and perhaps all obese people are relatively unresponsive to their own internal hunger state but are much more susceptible to signals from without.

extinction   In classical conditioning, the weakening of the tendency of CS to elicit CR by unreinforced presentations of CS. In instrumental conditioning, a decline in the tendency to perform the instrumental response brought about by unreinforced occurrences of that response.

extraversion-introversion   In Eysenck's system, a trait dimension that refers to the main direction of a person's energies; toward the outer world of objects and other people (extraversion) or toward the inner world of one's own thoughts and feelings (introversion).

factor analysis   A statistical method for studying the interrelations among various tests, the object of which is to discover what the tests have in common and whether these communalities can be ascribed to one or several factors that run through all or some of these tests.

false alarm   *See* payoff matrix.

familiarity effect   The fact that increased exposure to a stimulus tends to make that stimulus more likable.

family resemblance structure   Overlap of features among members of a category of meaning such that no members of the category have all of the features but all members have some of them.

feature detectors   Neurons in the retina or brain that respond to specific features of the stimulus such as movement, orientation, and so on.

Fechner's law   The assertion that the strength of a sensation is proportional to the logarithm of physical stimulus intensity.

feedback system   A system in which some action produces a consequence which affects (feeds back on) the action. In negative feedback, the consequence stops or reverses the action (e.g., thermostat-controlled furnace). In positive feedback, the consequence strengthens the action (e.g., rocket that homes in on airplanes).

fetus   A later stage in embryonic development. In humans, from about eight weeks until birth.

figure-ground organization   The segregation of the visual field into a part (the figure) which stands out against the rest (the ground).

fixed-action patterns   Term used by ethologists to describe stereotyped, species-specific behaviors triggered by genetically pre-programmed releasing stimuli (e.g., male stickleback's zigzag dance).

flooding   A form of behavior therapy based on classical conditioning in which the patient repeatedly exposes himself to whatever he is afraid of, thus extinguishing his fear.

fluid intelligence   The ability, which is said to decline with age, to deal with essentially new problems. *See also* crystallized intelligence.

forced compliance effect   An individual forced to act or speak publically in a manner contrary to his own beliefs may change his own views in the direction of the public action. But this will happen only if his reward for the false public pronouncement is relatively small. If the reward is large, there is no dissonance and hence no attitude change. *See also* cognitive dissonance.

forebrain   In mammals, the bulk of the brain. Its foremost region includes the cerebral hemispheres; its rear includes the thalamus and hypothalamus.

forward pairing   A classical conditioning procedure in which the conditioned stimulus (CS) precedes the unconditioned stimulus (UCS). This contrasts with simultaneous pairing, in which CS and UCS are presented simultaneously, and backward pairing, in which CS follows UCS. *See also* classical conditioning, conditioned stimulus, and unconditioned stimulus.

fraternal twins   Twins which arise from two different eggs which are (simultaneously) fertilized by different sperm cells. Their genetic similarity is no different than that between ordinary siblings. *See also* identical twins.

free association   Method used in psychoanalytic therapy in which the patient is to say anything that comes to her mind, no matter how apparently trivial, unrelated, or embarrassing.

free recall   A test of memory that asks for as many items in a list as a subject can recall regardless of order.

frequency distribution   An arrangement in which scores are tabulated by the frequency in which they occur.

Freud's theory of dreams   A theory that holds that at bottom all dreams are attempts to fulfill a wish. The wish fulfillment is in the latent dream, which represents the sleeper's hidden desires. This latent dream is censored and reinterpreted to avoid anxiety. It reemerges in more acceptable form as the manifest dream, the dream the sleeper remembers upon awakening.

frontal lobe   A lobe in each cerebral hemisphere which includes the motor projection area.

functional fixedness   A set to think of objects in terms of their normal function.

galvanic skin response (GSR)   A drop in the electrical resistance of the skin, widely used as an index of autonomic reaction.

gender identity   The inner sense of being male or female. *See also* gender role and sexual orientation.

gender role   The set of external behavior patterns a given culture deems appropriate for each sex. *See also* gender identity and sexual orientation.

gene   The unit of hereditary transmission, located at a particular place in a given chromosome. Both members of each chromosome pair have corresponding locations at which there are genes that carry instructions about the same characteristic (e.g., eye color). If one member of a gene pair is dominant and the other is recessive, the dominant gene will exert its effect regardless of what the recessive gene calls for. The characteristic called for by the recessive gene will only be expressed if the other member of the gene pair is also recessive. *See also* chromosomes.

generalization gradient   The curve which shows the relationship between the tendency to respond to a new stimulus and its similarity to the original CS.

generalized anxiety disorder A mental disorder (formerly called anxiety neurosis) whose primary characteristic is an all-pervasive, "free-floating" anxiety. A member of the diagnostic category "anxiety disorders," which also includes phobias and obsessive-compulsive disorders. *See also* phobias and obsessive-compulsive disorders.

general paresis A psychosis characterized by progressive decline in cognitive and motor function culminating in death, reflecting a deteriorating brain condition produced by syphilitic infection.

generic memory Memory for items of knowledge as such, independent of the occasion on which they are learned (e.g., The capital of France is Paris). *See also* episodic memory.

genital stage In psychoanalytic theory, the stage of psychosexual development reached in adult sexuality in which sexual pleasure involves not only one's own gratification but also the social and bodily satisfaction brought to another person.

genotype The genetic blueprint of an organism which may or may not be overtly expressed by its phenotype. *See also* phenotype.

Gestalt An organized whole such as a visual form or a melody.

Gestalt psychology A theoretical approach that emphasizes the role of organized wholes (Gestalten) in perception and other psychological processes.

glove anesthesia A condition sometimes seen in conversion disorders, in which there is an anesthesia of the entire hand with no loss of feeling above the wrist. This symptom makes no organic sense given the anatomical arrangement of the nerve trunks and indicates that the condition has a psychological basis.

glucose A form of sugar which is the major source of energy for most bodily tissues. If plentiful, much of it is converted into glycogen and stored away.

glycogen A stored form of metabolic energy derived from glucose. To be used, it must first be converted back into glucose.

good continuation A factor in visual grouping. Contours tend to be seen in such a way that their direction is altered as little as possible.

gradient of reinforcement The curve that describes the declining effectiveness of reinforcement with increasing delay between the response and the reinforcer.

group-factor theory of intelligence A factor-analytic approach to intelligence-test performance which argues that intelligence is the composite of separate abilities (group factors such as verbal ability, spatial ability, etc.) without a sovereign capacity that enters into each. *See also* factor analysis and Spearman's theory of general intelligence.

group therapy Psychotherapy of several persons at one time.

habituation A decline in the tendency to respond to stimuli that have become familiar due to repeated exposure.

habituation procedure A widely used method for studying infant perception. After some exposure to a visual stimulus, an infant becomes habituated and stops looking at it. The extent to which a new stimulus leads to renewed interest and resumption of looking is taken as a measure of the extent to which the infant regards this new stimulus as different from the old one to which she became habituated.

halo effect The tendency to assume that people who have one positive quality have other positive qualities as well.

hallucination Perceived experiences that occur in the absence of actual sensory stimulation.

heritability As measured by H, the heritability ratio, this refers to the relative importance of heredity and environment in determining the variation of a particular trait. More specifically, H is the proportion of the variance of the trait in a given population that is attributable to genetic factors.

hermaphrodite A person whose reproductive organs are anatomically ambiguous so that they are not exclusively male or female.

heterosexuality A sexual orientation leading to a choice of sexual partners of the opposite sex.

heuristics In computer problem solving, a procedure which has often worked in the past and is likely, but not certain, to work again. *See also* algorithm.

hierarchical organization Organization in which narrower categories are subsumed under broader ones which are subsumed under still broader ones and so on. Often expressed in the form of a tree diagram.

higher-order conditioning In classical conditioning, a procedure by which a new stimulus comes to elicit the CR by virtue of being paired with an effective CS (e.g., first pairings of tone and food, then pairings of bell and tone until finally the bell elicits salivation by itself).

hindbrain The most primitive portion of the brain, which includes the medulla and the cerebellum.

histogram A graphic rendering of a frequency distribution which depicts the distribution by a series of contiguous rectangles. *See also* frequency distribution.

homeostasis The body's tendency to maintain the conditions of its internal environment by various forms of self-regulation.

homogamy The tendency of like to marry like.

homosexuality A sexual orientation leading to a choice of partners of the same sex.

hue A perceived dimension of visual stimuli whose meaning is close to the term *color* (e.g., red, blue).

humanistic therapies Methods of treatment that emphasize personal growth and self-fulfillment. They try to be relatively nondirective since their emphasis is on helping the clients achieve the capacity for making their own choices. *See also* nondirective techniques.

hyperphagia Voracious, chronic overeating brought about by lesion of the ventromedial region of the hypothalamus.

hypnosis A temporary, trancelike state which can be induced in normal persons. During hypnosis, various hypnotic or posthypnotic suggestions sometimes produce effects that resemble some of the symptoms of conversion disorders. *See also* conversion disorders.

hypothalamus A small structure at the base of the brain which plays a vital role in the control of the autonomic nervous system, of the endocrine system, and of the major biological drives.

hysteria An older term for a group of presumably psychogenic disorders that included conversion disorders and dissociative disorders. Since DSM-III, it is no longer used as a diagnostic category, in part because of an erroneous implication that the condition is more prevalent in women (Greek *hystera*—womb). *See also* conversion disorders, dissociative disorders, glove anesthesia.

id In Freud's theory, a term for the most primitive reactions of human personality, consisting of blind strivings for immediate biological satisfaction regardless of cost. *See also* ego and superego.

ideas of reference A characteristic of some mental disorders, notably schizophrenia, in which the patient begins to think that external events are specially related to them personally (e.g., "People walk by and follow me").

identical twins　Twins that originate from a single fertilized egg which then splits into two exact replicas which develop into two genetically identical individuals. *See also* fraternal twins.

identification　In psychoanalytic theory, a mechanism whereby a child models itself (typically) on the same-sexed parent in an effort to become like him or her.

imipramine　*See* antidepressants.

imprinting　A learned attachment that is formed at a particular period in life (the critical period) and is difficult to reverse (e.g., the duckling's acquired tendency to follow whatever moving stimulus it encounters twelve to twenty-four hours after hatching).

incidental learning　Learning without trying to learn (e.g, as in a study in which subjects judge a speaker's vocal quality when she recites a list of words and are later asked to produce as many of the words as they can recall). *See also* intentional learning.

independent variable　*See* experiment.

induced movement　Perceived movement of an objectively stationary stimulus that is enclosed by a moving framework.

inductive reasoning　*See* deductive reasoning.

information processing　A general term for the presumed operations whereby the crude raw materials provided by the senses are refashioned into items of knowledge. Among these operations are perceptual organization, comparison with items stored in memory, and so on.

insightful learning　Learning by understanding the relations between components of the problem; often contrasted with "blind trial and error" and documented by wide and appropriate transfer if tested in a new situation.

instrumental conditioning　(operant conditioning) A form of learning in which a reinforcer (e.g., food) is given only if the animal performs the instrumental response (e.g., pressing a lever). In effect, what has to be learned is the relationship between the response and the reinforcer. *See* classical conditioning.

insulin　A hormone with a crucial role in utilization of nutrients. One of its functions is to help promote the conversion of glucose into glycogen.

Intelligence Quotient (IQ)　A ratio measure to indicate whether a child's mental age (MA) is ahead or behind her chronological age (CA); specifically $IQ = 100 \times MA/CA$. *See also* deviation IQ and mental age.

intentional learning　Learning when informed that there will be a later test of learning. *See also* incidental learning.

intention movements　A term used by ethologists to describe displays that represent anticipations of an impending response (e.g., the bared fangs of a threatening dog).

interference theory of forgetting　The assertion that items are forgotten because they are somehow interfered with by other items learned before or after.

internalization　The process whereby moral codes are adopted by the child so that they control his behavior even where there are no external rewards or punishments.

interneurons　Neurons that receive impulses and transmit them to other neurons.

interval scale　A scale in which equal differences between scores can be treated as equal so that the scores can be added or subtracted. *See also* categorical scale, ordinal scale, and ratio scale.

introversion　*See* extraversion-introversion.

invariant　Some aspect of the proximal stimulus pattern that remains unchanged despite various transformations of the stimulus.

James-Lange theory of emotions　A theory which asserts that the subjective experience of emotion is the awareness of one's own bodily reactions in the presence of certain arousing stimuli.

just noticeable difference (j.n.d.)　*See* difference threshold.

kinesthesis　A general term for sensory information generated by receptors in the muscles, tendons, and joints which informs us of our skeletal movement.

labeling theory of mental disorders　The assertion that the label "mental illness" acts as a self-fulfilling prophecy that perpetuates the condition once the label has been applied. In its extreme form, it asserts that the concept is a myth, mental illness being merely the term by which we designate social deviance that does not fall into other, recognized categories of deviance.

latency　General term for the interval before some reaction occurs.

latency period　In psychoanalytic theory, a stage in psychosexual development in which sexuality lies essentially dormant, roughly from ages five to twelve.

latent dream　*See* Freud's theory of dreams.

latent learning　Learning that occurs without being manifested by performance.

lateral hypothalamus　A region of the hypothalamus which is said to be a "hunger center" and to be in an antagonistic relation to a supposed "satiety center," the ventromedial region of the hypothalamus.

lateral inhibition　The tendency of adjacent neural elements of the visual system to inhibit each other; it underlies brightness contrast and the accentuation of contours. *See also* brightness contrast.

lateralization　An asymmetry of function of the two cerebral hemispheres. In most right-handers, the left hemisphere is specialized for language functions, while the right hemisphere is better at various visual and spatial tasks.

law of effect　A theory which asserts that the tendency of a stimulus to evoke a response is strengthened if the response is followed by reward and is weakened if the response is not followed by reward. Applied to instrumental learning, this theory states that as trials proceed, incorrect bonds will weaken while the correct bond will be strengthened.

learned helplessness　A condition created by exposure to inescapable aversive events. This retards or prevents learning in subsequent situations in which escape or avoidance is possible.

learned helplessness theory of depression　The theory that depression is analogous to learned helplessness effects produced in the laboratory by exposing subjects to uncontrollable aversive events.

learning curve　A curve in which some index of learning (e.g., the number of drops of saliva in Pavlov's classical conditioning experiment) is plotted against trials or sessions.

learning model　As defined in the text, a subcategory of the pathology model that (1) views mental disorders as the result of some form of faulty learning, and (2) believes that these should be treated by behavior therapists according to the laws of classical and instrumental conditioning, or by cognitive therapists who try to affect faulty modes of thinking. *See also* behavior therapy, cognitive therapy, medical model, pathology model, psychoanalytic model.

learning set　The increased ability to solve various problems, especially in discrimination learning, as a result of previous experience with problems of a similar kind.

lexical access The process of recognizing and understanding a word, which is presumably achieved by making contact (accessing) with the word in the mental lexicon.

lightness constancy The tendency to perceive the lightness of an object as more or less the same despite the fact that the light reflected from these objects changes with the illumination that falls upon them.

limbic system A set of brain structures including a relatively primitive portion of the cerebral cortex and parts of the thalamus and hypothalamus; it is believed to be involved in the control of emotional behavior and motivation.

line of best fit A line drawn through the points in a scatter diagram; it yields the best prediction of one variable when given the value of the other variable.

lithium carbonate A drug used in the treatment of mania and bipolar affective disorder.

lobotomy *See* prefrontal lobotomy.

longitudinal study A developmental study in which the same person is tested at various ages.

long-term memory A memory system that keeps memories for long periods, has a very large capacity, and stores items in relatively processed form. *See* sensory registers and short-term memory.

maintenance rehearsal Rehearsal in which material is merely held in short-term memory for a while. In contrast to elaborative rehearsal, this confers little benefit. *See also* elaborative rehearsal.

mania Hyperactive state with marked impairment of judgment, usually accompanied by intense euphoria.

manifest dream *See* Freud's theory of dreams

matching hypothesis The hypothesis that persons of a given level of physical attractiveness will seek out partners of a roughly similar level.

matching to sample A procedure in which an organism has to choose one of two alternative stimuli which is the same as a third sample stimulus.

maturation A pre-programmed growth process based on changes in underlying neural structures that are relatively unaffected by environmental conditions (e.g., flying in sparrows and walking in humans).

mean (M) The most commonly used measure of the central tendency of a frequency distribution. It is the arithmetical average of all the scores. If M is the mean and N the number of cases, then $M =$ sum of the scores/N. *See also* central tendency and median.

median A measure of the central tendency of a frequency distribution. It is the point that divides the distribution into two equal halves when the scores are arranged in ascending order. *See also* central tendency and mean.

medical model As defined in the text, a subcategory of the pathology model that (1) holds that the underlying pathology is organic, and that (2) the treatment should be conducted by physicians. *See also* learning model, pathology model, psychoanalytic model.

medulla The rearmost portion of the brain, just adjacent to the spinal cord. It includes centers which help to control respiration and muscle tone.

memory span The number of items a person can recall after just one presentation.

memory trace The change in the nervous system left by an experi-

ence which is the physical basis of its retention in memory. What this change is, is still unknown.

mental age (MA) A score devised by Binet to represent a child's test performance. It indicates the chronological age at which 50 percent of the children in that age group will perform. If the child's MA is greater than his chronological age (CA), he is ahead of his age mentally; if his MA is lower than his CA, he lags behind.

mental retardation Usually defined as an IQ of 70 and below.

mental set The predisposition to perceive (or remember or think of) one thing rather than another.

mesomorphy *See* somatotype theory.

metacognition A general term for knowledge about knowledge, as in knowing that we do or don't remember something.

midbrain Part of the brain which includes some lower centers for sensory-motor integration (e.g., eye movements) and part of the reticular formation.

middle ear An antechamber to the inner ear which amplifies sound-produced vibrations of the eardrum and imparts them to the cochlea. *See also* cochlea.

Minnesota Multiphasic Personality Inventory (MMPI) *See* criterion groups.

mnemonics Deliberate devices for helping memory. Many of them utilize imagery such as the method of pegs and method of loci.

monoamine oxidase (MAO) inhibitor *See* antidepressants.

monocular depth cues Various features of the visual stimulus which indicate depth, even when viewed with one eye (e.g., linear perspective and motion parallax).

morpheme The smallest significant unit of meaning in a language (e.g., the word *boys* has two morphemes, *boy* + *s*).

Motherese A whimsical term for the speech pattern that mothers and other adults generally employ when talking to infants.

motor projection areas *See* projection areas.

nalaxone A drug that inhibits the effect of morphine and similar opiates and blocks the pain alleviation ascribed to endorphins.

nativism The view that some important aspects of perception and of other cognitive processes are innate.

natural selection The explanatory principle that underlies Darwin's theory of evolution. Some organisms produce offspring which are able to survive and reproduce while other organisms of the same species do not. Thus organisms with these hereditary attributes will eventually outnumber organisms who lack these attributes.

negative feedback *See* feedback system.

neo-Freudians A group of theorists who accept the psychoanalytic conception of unconscious conflict but who differ with Freud in (1) describing these conflicts in social terms rather than in terms of particular bodily pleasures or frustrations, and (2) maintaining that many of these conflicts arise from the specific cultural conditions under which the child was reared rather than being biologically pre-ordained.

neophobia A term used in the study of food selection, where it refers to an animal's tendency to refuse new foods.

nerve impulse *See* action potential.

neuron A nerve cell.

neurosis In psychoanalytic theory, a broad term for mental disorders whose primary symptoms are anxiety or what seem to be defenses against anxiety. Since the adoption of DSM-III, the term has been dropped as the broad diagnostic label it once was. Various disorders that were once diagnosed as subcategories of neurosis (e.g., phobia, conversion disorders, dissociative disorders) are now classified as separate disorders.

neuroticism A trait dimension that refers to emotional instability and maladjustment.

neurotransmitters Chemicals liberated at the terminal end of an axon which travel across the synapse and have an excitatory or inhibitory effect on an adjacent neuron (e.g., norepinephrine).

nondirective techniques A set of techniques for psychological treatment developed by Carl Rogers. As far as possible, the counselor refrains from offering advice or interpretation but only tries to clarify the patient's own feelings by echoing him or restating what he says.

nonsense syllable Two consonants with a vowel between that do not form a word. Used to study associations between relatively meaningless items.

norepinephrine (NE) A catecholamine which is the neurotransmitter by means of which the sympathetic fibers exert their effects on internal organs. It is also the neurotransmitter of various arousing systems in the brain.

normal curve A symmetrical, bell-shaped curve which describes the probability of obtaining various combinations of chance events. It describes the frequency distributions of many physical and psychological attributes of humans and animals.

normal distribution A frequency distribution whose graphic representation has a symmetric, bell-shaped form—the normal curve. Its characteristics are often referred to when investigators test statistical hypotheses and make inferences about the population from a given sample.

null hypothesis The hypothesis that an obtained difference is merely a chance fluctuation from a population in which the true mean difference is zero. *See also* alternative hypothesis.

obesity A condition of marked overweight in animals and humans; it is produced by a large variety of factors including metabolic factors (oversecretion of insulin) and behavioral conditions (overeating, perhaps produced by nonresponsiveness to one's own internal state).

object permanence The conviction that an object remains perceptually constant over time and exists even when it is out of sight. According to Piaget, this does not develop until infants are age eight months or more.

observational study A study in which the investigator does not manipulate any of the variables but simply observes their relationship as they occur naturally.

obsessions *See* obsessive-compulsive disorders.

obsessive-compulsive disorders A disorder whose symptoms are obsessions (persistent and irrational thoughts or wishes) and compulsions (uncontrollable, repetitive acts), which seem to be defenses against anxiety. A member of a diagnostic category called anxiety disorders, which also includes generalized anxiety disorder and phobias. *See also* generalized anxiety disorder and phobia.

occipital lobe A lobe in each cerebral hemisphere which includes the visual projection area.

Oedipus complex In psychoanalytic theory, a general term for a whole cluster of impulses and conflicts which occur during the phallic phase, at around age five. In boys, a fantasied form of intense sexual love is directed at the mother, which is soon followed by hate and fear of the father. As the fear mounts, the sexual feelings are pushed under-

ground and the boy identifies with the father. An equivalent process in girls is called the Electra complex.

open-class morphemes *See* closed-class morphemes.

operant In Skinner's system, an instrumental response. *See also* instrumental conditioning.

operant conditioning *See* instrumental conditioning.

opponent-process theory of color vision A theory of color vision which asserts that there are three pairs of color antagonists: red-green, blue-yellow, and white-black. Excitation of one member of a pair automatically inhibits the other member.

opponent-process theory of motivation A theory which asserts that the nervous system has the general tendency to counteract any deviation from the neutral point of the pain-pleasure dimension. If the original stimulus is maintained, there is an attenuation of the emotional state one is in; if it is withdrawn, the opponent-process reveals itself, and the emotional state swings sharply in the opposite direction.

oral stage In psychoanalytic theory, the earliest stage of psychosexual development during which the primary source of bodily pleasure is stimulation of the mouth and lips, as in sucking at the breast.

ordinal scale A scale in which responses are rank-ordered by relative magnitude but in which the intervals between successive ranks are not necessarily equal. *See also* categorical scale, interval scale, and ratio scale.

orienting response In classical conditioning, an animal's initial reaction to a new stimulus (e.g., turning toward it and looking attentive).

osmoreceptors Receptors that help to control water intake by responding to the concentrations of body fluids. *See also* volume receptors.

overshadowing An effect produced when two conditioned stimuli, *A* and *B,* are both presented together with the unconditioned stimulus (UCS). If *A* is more intense than *B,* it will tend to overshadow it and will prevent the formation of an association between *B* and the UCS.

paired-associate method A procedure in which subjects learn to provide particular response terms to various stimulus items.

paranoid schizophrenia A subcategory of schizophrenia. Its dominant symptom is a set of delusions which are often elaborately systematized, usually of grandeur or persecution.

paraphrase The relation between two sentences whose meanings (underlying structures) are the same but whose surface structures differ (e.g., *the boy hit the ball/The ball was hit by the boy).*

parasympathetic overshoot A rebound effect in which the parasympathetic system responds above its normal level after the inhibition from its sympathetic antagonist is suddenly lifted (e.g., weeping).

parasympathetic system A division of the autonomic nervous system which serves vegetative functions and conserves bodily energies (e.g., slowing heart rate). Its action is antagonistic to that of the sympathetic system.

parietal lobe A lobe in each cerebral hemisphere which includes the somatosensory projection area.

partial reinforcement A condition in which a response is reinforced only some of the time.

partial-reinforcement effect The fact that a response is much harder to extinguish if it was acquired during partial rather than continuous reinforcement.

pathology model A term adopted in the text to describe a general conception of mental disorders which holds that (1) one can generally distinguish between symptoms and underlying causes, and (2) these causes may be regarded as a form of pathology. *See also* learning model, medical model, psychoanalytic model.

payoff matrix A table which shows the costs and benefits for each of the four outcomes in a detection experiment: a hit, reporting the stimulus when it is present; a correct negative, reporting it as absent when it is absent; a miss, failing to report it when it is present; and a false alarm, reporting it when it is absent.

percentile rank The percentage of all the scores in a distribution that lie below a given score.

perceptual adaptation The gradual adjustment to various distortions of the perceptual world, as in wearing prisms which tilt the entire visual world in one direction.

perceptual defense The tendency to perceive anxiety-related stimuli less readily than neutral stimuli.

perceptual differentiation Learning to perceive features of stimulus patterns that were not perceptible at first. A phenomenon central to the theory of perceptual learning proposed by J. J. Gibson and E. J. Gibson.

period of formal operations In Piaget's theory, the period from about age eleven on, when genuinely abstract mental operations can be undertaken (e.g., the ability to entertain hypothetical possibilities).

personality inventories Paper-and-pencil tests of personality that ask questions about feelings or customary behavior. *See also* projective techniques.

phallic stage In psychoanalytic theory, the stage of psychosexual development during which the child begins to regard his genitals as a major source of gratification.

phenothiazines A group of drugs including chlorpromazine which seem to be effective in alleviating the major symptoms of schizophrenia.

phenotype The overt appearance and behavior of an organism, regardless of its genetic blueprint. *See also* genotype.

phenylketonuria (PKU) A severe form of mental retardation determined by a single gene. This disorder can be treated by means of a special diet (if detected early enough), despite the fact that the disorder is genetic.

pheromones Special chemicals secreted by many animals which trigger particular reactions in members of the same species.

phobia One of a group of mental disorders called anxiety disorders which is characterized by an intense and, at least on the surface, irrational fear. *See also* generalized anxiety disorder and obsessive-compulsive disorders.

phoneme The smallest significant unit of sound in a language. In English, it corresponds roughly to a letter of the alphabet (e.g., *apt, tap,* and *pat* are all made up of the same phonemes).

phonology The rules in a language that govern the sequence in which phonemes can be arranged.

phrase A sequence of words within a sentence that function as a unit (e.g., *The ball/rolled/down the hill*).

phrase structure The organization of sentences into phrases. Surface structure is the phrase organization of sentences as they are spoken or written. Underlying structure is the phrase organization that describes the meaning of parts of the sentence, such as doer, action, and done-to.

pituitary gland An endocrine gland heavily influenced by the hypo-

thalamus. A master gland because many of its secretions trigger hormone secretions in other glands.

placebo In medical practice, a term for a chemically inert substance which the patient believes will help him.

placebo effect A beneficial effect of a treatment administered to a patient who believes it has therapeutic powers even though it has none.

pluralistic ignorance A situation in which individuals in a group don't know that there are others in the group who share their feelings.

polygenic inheritance Inheritance of an attribute whose expression is controlled not by one but by many gene pairs.

population The entire group of subjects (or test trials) about which the investigator wants to draw conclusions. *See also* sample.

positive feedback *See* feedback system.

predictive validity A measure of a test's validity based on the correlation between the test score and some criterion of behavior the test predicted (e.g., a correlation between a scholastic aptitude test and college grades).

prefrontal lobotomy A somatic treatment for severe mental disorders which surgically cuts the connections between the thalamus and the frontal lobes; now only rarely used in the U.S.

preoperational period In Piaget's theory, the period from about ages two to six during which children come to represent actions and objects internally but cannot systematically manipulate these representations or relate them to each other; the child is therefore unable to conserve quantity across perceptual transformations and also is unable to take points of view other than her own.

prescriptive rules Rules prescribed by "authorities" about how people *ought* to speak and write that often fail to conform to the facts about natural talking and understanding. This is in contrast to the structural principles of a language which describe (rather than prescribe) the principles according to which native speakers of a language actually arrange their words into sentences. Sentences formed according to these principles are called well-formed or grammatical.

prestige suggestion Approving some statement because a high-prestige person has approved it.

primacy effect (in impression formation) In forming an impression of another person, the phenomenon whereby attributes first noted carry a greater weight than attributes noted later on.

primacy effect (in recall) In free recall, the recall superiority of the items in the first part of a list compared to those in the middle. *See* recency effect.

prisoner's dilemma A particular arrangement of payoffs in a two-person situation in which each individual has to choose between two alternatives without knowing the other's choice. The payoff structure is so arranged that the optimal strategy for each person depends upon whether he can trust the other or not. If trust is possible, the payoffs for each will be considerably higher than if there is no trust.

proactive inhibition Disturbance of recall of some material by other material learned previously. *See* retroactive inhibition.

procedural knowledge *See* declarative knowledge.

progesterone A female sex hormone which dominates the latter phase of the female cycle during which the uterus walls thicken to receive the embryo.

projection In psychoanalytic theory, a mechanism of defense in which various forbidden thoughts and impulses are attributed to another person rather than the self, thus warding off some anxiety (e.g., "I hate you" becomes "You hate me").

projection areas   Regions of the cortex that serve as receiving stations for sensory information or as dispatching stations for motor commands.

projective techniques   Devices for assessing personality by presenting relatively unstructured stimuli which elicit subjective responses of various kinds. Their advocates believe that such tasks allow the person to "project" her own personality into her reactions (e.g., the TAT and the Rorschach inkblot test). *See also* personality inventories.

prototype   The typical example of a category of meaning (e.g., robin is a prototypical bird).

proximal stimulus   *See* distal stimulus.

psychoanalysis   (1) A theory of human personality formulated by Freud whose key assertions include unconscious conflict and psychosexual development. (2) A method of therapy that draws heavily on this theory of personality. Its main aim is to have the patient gain insight into his own, presently unconscious, thoughts and feelings. Therapeutic tools employed toward this end include free association, interpretation, and the appropriate use of the transference relationship between patient and analyst. *See also* free association and transference.

psychoanalytic model   As defined in the text, a subcategory of the pathology model which holds that (1) the underlying pathology is a constellation of unconscious conflicts and defenses against anxiety, usually rooted in early childhood, and (2) treatment should be by some form of psychotherapy based on psychoanalytic principles.

psychogenic disorders   Disorders whose origins are psychological rather than organic (e.g., phobias). *See also* somatogenic mental disorders.

psychometric approach to intelligence   An attempt to understand the nature of intelligence by studying the pattern of results obtained on intelligence tests.

psychopath   *See* antisocial personality.

psychopathology   The study of psychological disorders.

psychophysics   The field which tries to relate the characteristics of physical stimuli to the sensory experience they produce.

psychophysiological disorders   In these disorders (formerly called psychosomatic), the primary symptoms involve genuine organic damage whose ultimate cause is psychological (e.g., essential hypertension, a condition of chronic high blood pressure brought about by the bodily concomitant of chronic emotional stress).

psychosexual development   In psychoanalytic theory, the description of the progressive stages in the way the child gains his main source of pleasure as he grows into adulthood, defined by the zone of the body through which this pleasure is derived (oral, anal, genital) and by the object toward which this pleasurable feeling is directed (mother, father, adult sexual partner). *See also* anal stage, genital stage, oral stage, and phallic stage.

psychosis   A broad category that describes some of the more severe mental disorders in which the patient's thoughts and deeds no longer meet the demands of reality.

psychosocial crises   In Erik Erikson's theory, a series of crises through which all persons must pass as they go through their life cycle (e.g., the identity crisis during which adolescents or young adults try to establish the separation between themselves and their parents).

psychotherapy   As used here, a collective term for all forms of treatment that use psychological rather than somatic means.

quiet sleep   Stages 2 to 4 of sleep during which there are no rapid eye movements and during which the EEG shows progressively less cortical arousal. Also known as non-REM sleep.

random sample   *See* sample.

rationalization   In psychoanalytic theory, a mechanism of defense by means of which unacceptable thoughts or impulses are reinterpreted in more acceptable and thus less anxiety-arousing terms (e.g., the jilted lover who convinces himself he never loved her anyway).

ratio scale   An interval scale in which there is a true zero point, thus allowing ratio statements (e.g., this sound is twice as loud as the other). *See also* categorical scale, interval scale, and ordinal scale.

reaction formation   In psychoanalytic theory, a mechanism of defense in which a forbidden impulse is turned into its opposite (e.g., hate toward a sibling becomes exaggerated love).

reaction time   The interval between the presentation of a signal and the observer's response to that signal.

recall   A task in which some item must be produced from memory. *See* recognition.

recapitulation theory   The now discredited view that in embryological development each organism goes through the evolutionary history of the species of which he is a member.

recency effect   In free recall, the recall superiority of the items at the end of the list compared to those in the middle. *See* primacy effect (in recall).

receptive field   The retinal area in which visual stimulation affects a particular cell's firing rate.

receptors   A specialized cell that can respond to various physical stimuli and transduce them.

recessive gene   *See* gene.

reciprocal altruism   *See* altruism.

reciprocal inhibition   The arrangement by which excitation of some neural system is accompanied by inhibition of that system's antagonist (as in antagonistic muscles).

recognition   A task in which a stimulus has to be identified as having been previously encountered in some context or not. *See also* recall.

reference   The relations between words or sentences and objects or events in the world (e.g., "ball" refers to ball).

reflex   A simple, stereotyped reaction in response to some stimulus (e.g., limb flexion in withdrawal from pain).

rehearsal   *See* elaborative rehearsal and maintenance rehearsal.

reinforced trial   In classical conditioning, a trial on which the CS is accompanied by the UCS. In instrumental conditioning, a trial in which the instrumental response is followed by reward, cessation of punishment, or other reinforcement.

reinforcement   In classical conditioning, the procedure by which the UCS is made contingent on the CS. In instrumental conditioning, the procedure by which the instrumental response is made contingent upon some sought-after outcome.

releasing stimulus   Term used by ethologists to describe a stimulus which is genetically pre-programmed to elicit a fixed-action pattern (e.g., a long, thin, red-tipped beak which elicits a herring gull chick's begging response). *See also* fixed-action patterns.

reliability   The consistency with which a test measures what it measures, as assessed, for example, by the test-retest method.

REM sleep   *See* active sleep.

representational thought   In Piaget's theory, thought that is internalized and includes mental representations of prior experiences with objects and events.

repression In psychoanalytic theory, a mechanism of defense by means of which thoughts, impulses, or memories that give rise to anxiety are pushed out of consciousness.

resistance In psychoanalysis, a collective term for the patient's failures to associate freely and say whatever enters his head.

response bias A preference for one or another response in a psychophysical experiment, independent of the stimulus situation.

restrained-eating hypothesis The hypothesis that the oversensitivity of obese persons to external cues is caused by the disinhibition of conscious restraints on eating. *See also* externality hypothesis, set-point hypothesis.

restructuring A reorganization of a problem, often rather sudden, which seems to be a characteristic of creative thought.

retention The survival of the memory trace over some interval of time.

reticular activating system (RAS) A system that includes the upper portion of the reticular formation and its ascending branches to much of the brain. Its effect is to arouse the brain.

reticular formation A network of neurons extending throughout the midbrain with ramifications to higher parts of the brain. This plays an important role in sleep and arousal.

retina The structure which contains the visual receptors and several layers of neurons further up along the pathway to the brain.

retinal image The image of an object that is projected on the retina. Its size increases with the size of that object and decreases with its distance from the eye.

retrieval The process of searching for some item in memory and of finding it. If retrieval fails, this may or may not mean that the relevant memory trace is not present; it simply may be inaccessible.

retrieval cue A stimulus that helps to retrieve a memory trace.

retroactive inhibition Disturbance of recall of some material by other material learned subsequently. *See* proactive inhibition.

retrograde amnesia A memory deficit suffered after head injury or concussion in which the patient loses memory of some period prior to the injury. *See also* anterograde amnesia.

ROC curve A curve which shows the relationship between hits and false alarms in a detection experiment.

rods Visual receptors that respond to lower light intensities and give rise to achromatic (colorless) sensations.

Rorschach inkblot test A projective technique which requires the person to look at inkblots and say what she sees in them.

safety signal A stimulus that has been contingent with the absence of an electric shock (or another negative reinforcer) in a situation in which such shocks are sometimes delivered. *See also* contingency.

sample A subset of a population selected by the investigator for study. A random sample is one so constructed that each member of the population has an equal chance to be picked. A stratified sample is one so constructed that every relevant subgroup of the population is randomly sampled in proportion to its size. *See also* population.

saturation A perceived dimension of visual stimuli that describes the "purity" of a color—the extent to which it is rich in hue (e.g., green rather than olive).

scaling A procedure for assigning numbers to a subject's responses. *See also* categorical scale, interval scale, ordinal scale, and ratio scale.

schedule of reinforcement A rule that determines the occasions when a response is reinforced. An example is a fixed-ratio schedule, in which reinforcement is given after a fixed number of responses.

schema In Piaget's theory, a mental pattern.

schizophrenia A group of severe mental disorders characterized by at least some of the following: marked disturbance of thought, withdrawal, inappropriate or flat emotions, delusions, and hallucinations. *See also* catatonic schizophrenia and paranoid schizophrenia.

score profile *See* test profile.

self-perception theory The assertion that we don't know ourselves directly but rather infer our own states and dispositions by an attribution process analogous to that we use when we try to explain the behavior of other persons. *See also* attribution theory.

semantic feature The smallest significant unit of meaning within a word (e.g., male, human, and adult are semantic features of the word "man").

semantic memory The component of generic memory that concerns the meaning of words and concepts.

semantics The organization of meaning in language.

sensation According to the British empiricists, the primitive experiences that the senses give us (e.g., green, bitter).

sensory adaptation The decline in sensitivity found in most sensory systems after continuous exposure to the same stimulus.

sensory coding The process by which the nervous system translates various aspects of the stimulus into dimensions of our sensory experience.

sensory-motor intelligence In Piaget's theory, intelligence during the first two years of life which consists mainly of sensations and motor impulses with, at first, little in the way of internalized representations.

sensory projection areas *See* projection areas.

sensory registers A system of memory storage in which material is held for a second or so in its original, unprocessed, sensory form. *See also* long-term memory and short-term memory.

Sentence Analyzing Machinery (SAM) A set of procedures by which listeners comprehend sentences.

set *See* mental set.

set-point A general term for the level at which negative feedback tries to maintain the system. An example is the setting of a thermostat. *See also* set-point hypothesis.

set-point hypothesis The hypothesis that different persons have different set-points for weight. *See also* set-point.

sexual orientation The direction of a person's choice of a sexual partner, which may be heterosexual or homosexual. *See also* gender identity and gender role.

shape constancy The tendency to perceive the shape of objects as more or less the same despite the fact that the retinal image of these objects changes its shape as we change the angle of orientation from which we view them.

short-term memory A memory system that keeps material for intervals of a minute or so, that has a small storage capacity (sometimes said to be 7 ± 2), and that holds material in relatively less processed form than long-term memory. *See also* long-term memory and sensory registers.

signal-detection theory A theory which asserts that observers who are asked to detect the presence or absence of a stimulus try to decide whether an internal sensory experience should be attributed to background noise or to a signal added to background noise.

simultaneous pairing *See* forward pairing and backward pairing.

situationism The view that human behavior is largely determined by the characteristics of the situation rather than those of the person. *See also* trait theory.

size constancy The tendency to perceive the size of objects as more or less the same despite the fact that the retinal image of these objects changes in size whenever we change the distance from which we view them.

social comparison A process of reducing uncertainty about one's own beliefs and attitudes by comparing them to those of others.

socialization The process whereby the child acquires the patterns of behavior characteristic of her society.

social learning theory A theoretical approach that is midway between behavior theories such as Skinner's and cognitive approaches. It stresses learning by observing others who serve as models for the child's behavior. The effect of the model may be to allow learning by imitation and also may be to show the child whether a response he already knows should or should not be performed.

sociobiology A recent movement in biology that tries to trace social behavior to genetically based predispositions; an approach that has led to some controversy when extended to humans.

sociopath *See* antisocial personality.

somatic therapies A collective term for any treatment of mental disorders by means of some organic manipulation. This includes drug administration, any form of surgery, convulsive treatments, etc.

somatogenic mental disorders Mental disorders that are produced by an organic cause. This is the case for some disorders (e.g., general paresis) but almost surely not for all (e.g., phobias). *See also* psychogenic disorders.

somatotonia *See* somatotype theory.

somatotype theory A theory proposed by Sheldon who suggested that there are three body-type (or somatotype) components: endomorphy (soft and round), mesomorphy (hard, rectangular, and well muscled), and ectomorphy (delicate build and lightly muscled). These body types are asserted to go with certain clusters of personality traits, specifically: endomorphy with viscerotonia (loves food and comfort, is sociable, needs affection); mesomorphy with somatotonia (desire for power, delight in physical activity, an indifference to people); and ectomorphy with cerebrotonia (self-consciousness, overreactiveness, desire for privacy).

sound waves Successive pressure variations in the air which vary in amplitude and wave length.

Spearman's theory of general intelligence *(g)* Spearman's account, based on factor analytic studies, ascribes intelligence-test performance to one underlying factor, general intelligence *(g)* which is tapped by all subtests, and a large number of specific skills (*s*'s) which depend on abilities specific to each subtest. *See also* factor analysis and group-factor theory.

split brain A condition in which the corpus callosum and some other fibers are cut so that the two cerebral hemispheres are isolated.

spontaneous recovery An increase in the tendency to perform an extinguished response after a time interval in which neither CS nor UCS are presented.

stabilized image technique A procedure by which the retina receives a stationary image even though the eye is moving.

standard deviation (SD) A measure of the variability of a frequency distribution which is the square root of the variance. If V is the variance and SD the standard deviation, then $SD = \sqrt{V}$. *See also* variance.

standard error of the mean A measure of the variability of the mean whose value depends both on the standard deviation *(SD)* of the distribution and the number of cases in the sample *(N)*. If SE is the standard error, then $SE = SD/\sqrt{N-1}$.

standardization group The group against which an individual's test score is evaluated.

standard score Also called *z*-score. A score which is expressed as a deviation from the mean in standard deviation units, which allows a comparison of scores drawn from different distributions. If M is the mean and SD the standard deviation, then $z = (score - M)/SD$.

stimulus Anything in the environment which the organism can detect and respond to.

stimulus generalization In classical conditioning, the tendency to respond to stimuli other than the original CS. The greater the similarity between the CS and the new stimulus the greater this tendency will be. An analogous phenomenon in instrumental conditioning is a response to stimuli other than the original discriminative stimulus.

Stroop effect A marked decrease in the speed of naming the colors in which various color names (such as green, red, etc.) are printed when the colors and the names are different. An important example of automatization.

structural principles (of language) *See* prescriptive rules.

subtractive color mixture Mixing colors by subtracting one set of wavelengths from another set (as in mixing colors on a palette or superimposing two colored filters).

superego In Freud's theory, a set of reaction patterns within the ego that represent the internalized rules of society and that control the ego by punishing with guilt. *See also* ego and id.

surface structure *See* phrase structure.

sympathetic system A division of the autonomic nervous system which mobilizes the body's energies for emergencies (e.g., increasing heart rate). Its action is antagonistic to that of the parasympathetic system.

symptoms The outward manifestations of an underlying pathology.

synapse The juncture between the axon of one neuron and the dendrite or cell body of another.

syndrome A pattern of symptoms that tend to go together.

systematic desensitization A behavior therapy that tries to remove anxiety connected to various stimuli by a gradual process of counterconditioning to a response incompatible with fear, usually muscular relaxation. The stimuli are usually evoked as mental images according to an anxiety hierarchy whereby the less frightening stimuli are counterconditioned before the more frightening ones.

taste buds The receptor organs for taste.

taxonomy A classification system.

temperament In modern usage, a characteristic level of reactivity and energy, often thought to be based on constitutional factors.

temporal lobe A lobe in each cerebral hemisphere which includes the auditory projection area.

territory Term used by ethologists to describe a region a particular animal stakes out as its own. The territory holder is usually a male, but in some species the territory is held by a mating pair or by a group.

testosterone The principal male sex hormone (androgen) in mammals.

test profile A graphic indication of an individual's performance on several components of a test. This is often useful for guidance or clinical evaluation because it indicates which abilities or traits are relatively high or low in that person.

texture gradient A distance cue based on changes in surface texture which depend on the distance of the observer.

thalamus A part of the lower portion of the forebrain which serves as a major relay and integration center for sensory information.

Thematic Apperception Test (TAT) A projective technique in which persons are shown a set of pictures and asked to write a story about each.

threshold Some value a stimulus must reach to produce a response.

token economy An arrangement for operant behavior modification in hospital settings. Certain responses (e.g., talking to others) are reinforced with tokens which can be exchanged for desirable items.

tolerance *See* opponent-process theory of motivation.

top-down processes Processes in form recognition which begin with higher units and then work down to smaller units (e.g., from phrases to words to letters). This is in contrast with bottom-up processes, which start with smaller component parts and then gradually build up to the higher units on top (e.g., from letters to words to phrases). One demonstration of top-down processing is provided by context effects in which knowledge or expectations affect what one sees.

trace consolidation hypothesis The hypothesis that newly acquired traces undergo a gradual change that makes them more and more resistant to any disturbance.

trait theory The view that people differ in regard to a number of underlying attributes (traits) that partially determine behavior and that are presumed to be essentially consistent from time to time and from situation to situation. *See also* situationism.

transduction The process by which a receptor translates some physical stimulus (e.g., light or pressure) to give rise to an action potential in another neuron.

transference In psychoanalysis, the patient's tendency to transfer emotional reactions that were originally directed to one's own parents (or other crucial figures in one's early life) and redirect them toward the analyst.

transfer of training The effect of having learned one task on learning another. If learning the first task helps in learning the second, the transfer is called positive. If it impedes in learning the second, the transfer is said to be negative.

transposition The phenomenon whereby visual and auditory patterns (i.e., figures and melodies) remain the same even though the parts of which they are composed are changed.

unconditioned reflex *See* unconditioned response.

unconditioned response (UCR) In classical conditioning, the response which is elicited by the unconditional stimulus without prior training. *See* conditioned response, conditioned stimulus, and unconditioned stimulus.

unconditioned stimulus (UCS) In classical conditioning, the stimulus which elicits the unconditioned response and the presentation of which acts as reinforcement. *See* conditioned response, conditioned stimulus, and unconditioned response.

unconscious inference A process postulated by Helmholtz to explain certain perceptual phenomena such as size constancy. An object is perceived to be in the distance and is therefore unconsciously perceived or inferred to be larger than it appears to be retinally. *See also* size constancy.

underlying structure *See* phrase structure.

unipolar affective disorder Affective disorder (usually depression) in which there is no back-and-forth swing between the two emotional extremes.

validity The extent to which a test measures what it is supposed to measure. *See also* construct validity and predictive validity.

variability The tendency of scores in a frequency distribution to scatter away from the central value. *See also* central tendency, standard deviation, and variance.

variance (V) A measure of the variability of a frequency distribution. It is computed by finding the difference between each score and the mean, squaring the result, adding all the squared deviations obtained in this manner and dividing it by the number of cases. If V is the variance, M the mean, and N the number of scores, then $V = $ sum of $(\text{score} - M)^2 / N$.

vasoconstriction The constriction of the capillaries brought on by activation of the sympathetic division of the autonomic nervous system in response to excessive cold.

vasodilatation The dilating of the capillaries brought on by activation of the parasympathetic division of the autonomic nervous system in response to excessive heat.

ventromedial region of the hypothalamus An area in the hypothalamus that is said to be a "satiety center" and in an antagonistic relation to a supposed "hunger center," the lateral hypothalamus.

vestibular senses A set of receptors that provide information about the orientation and movements of the head, located in the semicircular canals and the vestibular sacs of the inner ear. *See also* inner ear, semicircular canals, and vestibular sacs.

vicarious reinforcement According to social learning theorists, a form of reinforcement said to occur when someone watches a model being rewarded or punished.

viscerotonia *See* somatotype theory.

visual cliff A device for assessing depth perception in young organisms; it consists of a glass surface that extends over an apparently deep side (the cliff) and an apparently shallow side.

volume receptors Receptors that help to control water intake by responding to the total volume of fluids in the body. *See also* osmoreceptors.

Weber's law The observation that the size of the difference threshold is proportional to the intensity of the standard stimulus.

Wernicke's area *See* aphasia.

wish fulfillment in dreams *See* Freud's theory of dreams.

withdrawal effects *See* opponent-process theory of motivation.

within-group heritability The extent to which variation within groups (e.g., among U.S. whites) is attributable to genetic factors. *See also* between-group heritability and heritability.

z-score *See* standard score.

References

ABERLE, D. F.; BRONFENBRENNER, U.; HESS, E. H.; MILLER, D. R.; SCHNEIDER, D. M.; AND SPUHLER, J. N. 1963. The incest taboo and the mating pattern of animals. *American Anthropologist* 65:253–65.

ABRAHAM, K. 1927. The influence of oral eroticism on character formation. In Abraham, K., *Selected papers,* pp. 393–406. London: Hogarth Press.

ABRAMSON, L. Y.; SELIGMAN, M. E. P.; AND TEASDALE, J. D. 1978. Learned helplessness in humans: Critique and reformulation. *Journal of Abnormal Psychology* 87:49–74.

ADELSON, E. H., AND JONIDES, J. 1980. The psychophysics of iconic storage. *Journal of Experimental Psychology: Human Perception and Performance* 6:486–93.

ADLER, N. 1969. Effects of the male's copulatory behavior on successful pregnancy of the female rat. *Journal of Comparative and Physiological Psychology* 69:613–22.

ADOLPH, E. F. 1947. Urges to eat and drink in rats. *American Journal of Physiology* 151:110–25.

ADORNO, T. W.; FRENKEL-BRUNSWIK, E.; LEVINSON, D. J.; AND SANFORD, R. N. 1950. *The authoritarian personality.* New York: Harper & Row.

AINSWORTH, M. D. S.; AND BELL, S. M. 1970. Attachment, exploration, and separation: Illustrated by the behavior of one-year-olds in a strange situation. *Child Development* 41: 49–67.

AINSWORTH, M. D. S.; BLEHAR, M. C.; WATERS, E.; AND WALL, S. 1978. *Patterns of attachment.* Hillsdale, N.J.: Erlbaum.

ALBERT, M. S., BUTTERS, N., AND LEVIN, J. 1979. Temporal gradients in the retrograde amnesia of patients with alcoholic Korsakoff's disease. *Archives of Neurology* 36: 211–16.

ALEXANDER, F., AND FRENCH, T. 1946. *Psychoanalytic theory.* New York: Ronald Press.

ALLPORT, G. W. 1937. *Personality: A psychological interpretation.* New York: Henry Holt.

ALLPORT, G. W., AND ODBERT, H. S. 1936. Trait-names: A psychological study. *Psychological Monographs* 47 (Whole No. 211).

ANASTASI, A. 1958. *Differential psychology,* 3rd ed. New York: Macmillan.

ANASTASI, A. 1971. More on heritability: Addendum to the Hebb and Jensen interchange. *American Psychologist* 26:1036–37.

ANDERSON, N. H., AND BARRIOS, A. A. 1961. Primacy effects in personality impression formation. *Journal of Abnormal and Social Psychology* 63:346–50.

ANDERSSON, B.; GRANT, R.; AND LARSSON, S. 1956. Central control of heat loss mechanisms in the goat. *Acta Physiologica Scandinavica* 37:261–80.

ANDRES, R. 1980. Influence of obesity on longevity in the aged. In Borek, C., Fenoglio, C. M., and King, D. W., eds., *Aging, cancer, and cell membranes,* pp. 230–46. New York: Thieme-Stratton.

ANGLIN, J. M. 1975. The child's first terms of reference. In Ehrlich, S., and Tulving, E., eds., *Bulletin de Psychologie,* special issue on semantic memory.

ANGRIST, B.; SATHANANTHAN, G.; WILK, S.; AND GERSHON, S. 1974. Amphetamine psychosis: Behavioral and biochemical aspects. *Journal of Psychiatric Research* 11:13–24.

ANREP, G. V. 1920. Pitch discrimination in the dog. *Journal of Physiology* 53:367–85.

ANSTIS, S. M. 1975. What does visual perception tell us about visual coding? In Gazzaniga, M. S., and Blakemore, C., eds., *Handbook of psychobiology.* New York: Academic Press.

APPADURAI, A. 1981. Gastropolitics in Hindu South Asia. *American Ethnologist* 8: 494–511.

APPEL, L. F.; COOPER, R. G.; MCCARRELL, N.; SIMS-KNIGHT, J.; YUSSEN, S. R.; AND FLAVELL, J. H. 1972. The development of the distinction between perceiving and memorizing. *Child Development* 43:1365–81.

ARBIB, M. A. 1972. *The metaphorical brain.* New York: Wiley.

ARDREY, R. 1966. *The territorial imperative.* New York: Dell.

ARENDT, H. 1965. *Eichmann in Jerusalem: A report on the banality of evil.* New York: Viking Press.

ARIÈS, P. 1962. *Centuries of childhood.* London: Jonathan Cape.

ARIETI, S. 1959. Schizophrenia: The manifest symptomatology, the psychodynamic and formal mechanisms. In Arieti, S., ed., *American handbook of psychiatry,* vol. 1, pp. 455–84. New York: Basic Books.

ARISTOTLE. ca. 330 B.C. On sleep and waking; On dreams; On prophesy in sleep. In *The works of Aristotle,* vol. 3. London: Oxford University Press, 1931.

ARMSTRONG, S. L.; GLEITMAN, L. R.; AND GLEITMAN, H. 1983.

What some concepts might not be. *Cognition* 13: 263–308.

ARNHEIM, R. 1974. *Art and visual perception,* new version. Berkeley, California: University of California Press.

ARONFREED, J. 1968. *Conduct and conscience.* New York: Academic Press.

ARONFREED, J. 1969. The problem of imitation. In Lipsett, L. P., and Reese, H. W., eds., *Advances in child development and behavior,* vol. 4. New York: Academic Press.

ARONSON, E. 1969. The theory of cognitive dissonance: A current perspective. In Berkowitz, L., ed., *Advances in experimental social psychology,* vol. 4, pp. 1–34. New York: Academic Press.

ARONSON, E., AND CARLSMITH, J. M. 1963. The effect of the severity of threat on the devaluation of forbidden behavior. *Journal of Abnormal and Social Psychology* 66: 584–88.

ARONSON, E., AND MILLS, J. 1959. The effect of severity of initiation on liking for a group. *Journal of Abnormal and Social Psychology* 59:177–81.

ASCH, S. E. 1946. Forming impressions of personality. *Journal of Abnormal and Social Psychology* 41:258–90.

ASCH, S. E. 1952. *Social psychology.* New York: Prentice-Hall.

ASCH, S. E. 1955. Opinions and social pressure. *Scientific American* 193:31–35.

ASCH, S. E. 1956. Studies of independence and conformity: A minority of one against a unanimous majority. *Psychological Monographs* 70 (9, Whole No. 416).

ASCH, S. E. 1958. Effects of group pressure upon the modification and distortion of judgments. In Maccoby, E. E.; Newcomb, T. M.; and Hartley, E. L., eds., *Readings in social psychology,* pp. 174–81. New York: Henry Holt.

ASCH, S. E., AND GLEITMAN, H. 1953. Yielding to social pressure as a function of public or private commitment. Unpublished manuscript.

ASHER, E. J. 1935. The inadequacy of current intelligence tests for testing Kentucky Mountain children. *Journal of Genetic Psychology* 46: 480–86.

ATKINSON, J. W., AND McCLELLAND, D. C. 1948. The projective expression of needs. II. The effect of different intensities of the hunger drive on thematic apperception. *Journal of Experimental Psychology* 38:643–58.

AUGUSTINE. 397 A.D. *The confessions.* Translated and annotated by Pilkington, J. G. P. Cleveland: Fine Editions Press, 1876.

AUSTIN, J. L. 1962. *How to do things with words.* London: Oxford University Press.

AX, A. F. 1953. The physiological differentiation of fear and anger in humans. *Psychosomatic Medicine* 15:433–42.

AYLLON, T. 1963. Intensive treatment of psychotic behavior by stimulus satiation and food reinforcement. *Behavior Research and Therapy* 1:53–61.

AYLLON, T., AND AZRIN, N. H. 1968. *The token economy: A motivational system for therapy and rehabilitation.* New York: Appleton-Century-Crofts.

BABIGIAN, H. M. 1975. Schizophrenia: Epidemiology. In Freedman, A. M.; Kaplan, H. I.; and Sadock, B. J., eds., *Comprehensive textbook of psychiatry—II,* vol. 1, pp. 860–66. Baltimore: Williams & Wilkins.

BADDELEY, A. D. 1976. *The psychology of memory.* New York: Basic Books.

BADDELEY, A. 1982. Amnesia: A minimal model and an interpretation. In Cermak, L. S., ed., *Human memory and amnesia,* pp. 305–36. Hillsdale, N.J.: Erlbaum.

BAHRICK, H. P. 1984. Semantic memory content in permastore: Fifty years of memory for Spanish learned in school. *Journal of Experimental Psychology: General* 113: 1–35.

BALTES, P. B., REESE, H. W., AND LIPSITT, L. P. 1980. Life-span developmental psychology. In Rosenzweig, M. R., and Porter, L. W., eds., *Annual Review of Psychology* 31: 65–110.

BALTES, P. B., AND SCHAIE, K. W. 1976. On the plasticity of intelligence in adulthood and old age. *American Psychologist* 31:720–25.

BANDURA, A. 1965. Influence of models' reinforcement contingencies on the acquisition of imitative responses. *Journal of Personality and Social Psychology* 1:589–95.

BANDURA, A.; ROSS, D.; AND ROSS, S. A. 1963. Imitation of film-mediated aggressive models. *Journal of Abnormal and Social Psychology* 66: 3–11.

BANDURA, A., AND WALTERS, R. H. 1963. *Social learning and personality development.* New York: Holt, Rinehart & Winston.

BANUAZIZI, A. 1972. Discriminative shock-avoidance learning of an autonomic response under curare. *Journal of Comparative and Physiological Psychology* 81: 336–46.

BARASH, D. P. 1982. *Sociobiology and behavior,* 2nd ed. New York: Elsevier.

BARBER, T. X. 1969. *Hypnosis: A scientific approach.* New York: Van Nostrand Reinhold.

BARD AND RIOCH, 1937. Quoted in Gallistel, R. C., 1980. *The organization of action.* Hillsdale, N.J.: Erlbaum.

BARNETT, S. A. 1963. *The rat: A study in behavior.* Chicago: Aldine.

BARNOUW, V. 1963. *Culture and personality.* Homewood, Ill.: Dorsey Press.

BARON, R. A., AND BYRNE, D. 1981. *Social psychology: Understanding human interaction,* 3rd ed. Boston: Allyn & Bacon.

BARRERA, M. E., AND MAURER, D. 1981. Recognition of mother's photographed face by the three-month-old infant. *Child Development* 52: 714–16.

BARRY, H., III; CHILD, I. L.; AND BACON, M. K. 1959. Relation of child training to subsistence economy. *American Anthropologist* 61:51–63.

BARTLETT, F. C. 1932. *Remembering: A study in experimental and social psychology.* Cambridge, England: Cambridge University Press.

BARTOSHUK, L. M. 1971. The chemical senses. 1. Taste. In Kling, J. W., and Riggs, L. A., eds., *Experimental psychology,* 3rd ed. New York: Holt, Rinehart & Winston.

BATES, E. 1976. *Language and context: The acquisition of pragmatics.* New York: Academic Press.

BATESON, G.; JACKSON, D. D.; HALEY, J.; AND WEAKLAND, J. 1956. Toward a theory of schizophrenia. *Behavioral Science* 1:251–64.

BAUM, W. M. 1970. Extinction of avoidance response following response prevention. *Psychological Bulletin* 74: 276–84.

BAUMRIND, D. 1967. Child care practices anteceding three patterns of preschool behavior. *Genetic Psychology Monographs* 75: 43–88.

BAUMRIND, D. 1971. Current patterns of parental authority. *Genetic Psychology Monographs* 1.

BAUMRIND, D. 1977. *Socialization determinants of personal agency.* Paper presented at the biennial meetings of the Society for Research in Child Development, New Orleans. (Cited in Maccoby, E. E. 1980. *Social development.* New York: Harcourt Brace Jovanovich.)

BAYER, E. 1929. Beiträge zur Zweikomponententheorie des Hungers. *Zeitschrift der Psychologie* 112:1–54.

BECK, A. T. 1967. *Depression: Causes and treatment.* Philadelphia: University of Pennsylvania Press.

BECK, A. T. 1976. *Cognitive therapy and the emotional disorders.* New York: International Universities Press.

BECK, J. 1966. Effect of orientation and of shape similarity on perceptual grouping. *Perception and Psychophysics* 1:300–2.

BÉKÉSY, G. VON. 1957. The ear. *Scientific American* 197:66–78.

BELL, A. P.; WEINBERG, M. S.; AND HAMMERSMITH, S. K. 1981. *Sexual preference: Its development in men and women.* Bloomington,

Ind.: Indiana University Press.

BELL, R. Q. 1968. A reinterpretation of the direction of effects in studies of socialization. *Psychological Review* 75: 81–95.

BELL, R. Q., AND HARPER, L. V. 1977. *Child effects on adults.* Hillsdale, N.J.: Erlbaum.

BELLUGI, U. 1971. Simplification in children's language. In Huxley, R., and Ingram, E., eds., *Language acquisition: Models and methods.* New York: Academic Press.

BEM, D. J. 1967. Self-perception: An alternative interpretation of cognitive dissonance phenomena. *Psychological Review* 74:183–200.

BEM, D. J. 1972. Self-perception theory. In Berkowitz, L., ed., *Advances in experimental social psychology,* vol. 6, pp. 2–62. New York: Academic Press.

BENBOW, C. P., AND STANLEY, J. C. 1983. Sex differences in mathematical reasoning ability: More facts. *Science* 222: 1029–31.

BEREITER, C., AND ENGLEMANN, S. 1966. *Teaching culturally deprived children in pre-school.* Englewood Cliffs, N.J.: Prentice-Hall.

BERGER, P. A. 1978. Medical treatment of mental illness. *Science* 200: 974–81.

BERGIN, A. E. 1967. An empirical analysis of therapeutic issues. In Arbuckle, D., ed., *Counseling and psychotherapy: An overview,* pp. 175–208. New York: McGraw-Hill.

BERGIN, A. E. 1971. The evaluation of therapeutic outcomes. In Bergin, A. E., and Garfield, S. L., eds., *Handbook of psychotherapy and behavior change,* pp. 217–70. New York: Wiley.

BERKELEY, G. 1709. An essay towards a new theory of vision. In Berkeley, G., *Works on vision,* edited by Turbayne, C. M. Indianapolis, Ind.: Bobbs-Merrill, 1963.

BERKELEY, G. 1710. *The principles of human knowledge.* In Berkeley, G., *The principles of human knowledge,* edited by Warnock, G. J. London: Fontana Library, 1962.

BERLINER, H. J. 1977. Some necessary conditions for a master chess program. In Johnson-Laird, P. N., and Wason, P. C., eds., *Thinking,* pp. 565–79. New York: Cambridge University Press.

BERMANT, G., AND DAVIDSON, J. M. 1974. *Biological bases of sexual behavior.* New York: Harper & Row.

BERNARD, V. W.; OTTENBERG, P.; AND REDL, F. 1965. Dehumanization: A composite psychological defense in relation to modern war. In Schwebel, M., ed., *Behavioral science and human survival,* pp. 64–82. Palo Alto, Calif.: Science and Behavior Books.

BERNHEIM, K. W., AND LEWINE, R. R. J. 1979. *Schizophrenia: Symptoms, causes, treatments.* New York: Norton.

BERNSTEIN, B. 1967. Social structure, language and learning. In Passow, A. H.; Goldberg, M.; and Tannenbaum, A. J., eds., *Education of the disadvantaged,* New York: Holt, Rinehart & Winston.

BERSCHEID, E.; DION, K.; WALSTER, E.; AND WALSTER, G. W. 1971. Physical attractiveness and dating choice: A test of the matching hypothesis. *Journal of Experimental Social Psychology* 7: 173–89.

BERSCHEID, E., AND WALSTER, E. H. 1978. *Interpersonal attraction,* 2nd ed. Reading, Mass.: Addison-Wesley.

BEST, D. L.; WILLIAMS, J. E.; CLOUD, J. M.; DAVIS, S. W.; ROBERTSON, L. S.; EDWARDS, J. R.; GILES, E.; AND FOWLES, J. 1977. Development of sex-trait stereotypes among young children in the United States, England, and Ireland. *Child Development* 48: 1375–84.

BEVER, T. G. 1970. The cognitive basis for linguistic structures. In Hayes, J. R., ed., *Cognition and the development of language,* pp. 279–362. New York: Wiley.

BICKMAN, L. 1971. The effect of another bystander's ability to help on bystander intervention in an emergency. *Journal of Experimental Social Psychology* 7:369–79.

BIEBER, I. 1965. Clinical aspects of male homosexuality. In Marmor, J., ed., *Sexual inversion,* pp. 248–67. New York: Basic Books.

BILSKY, L.; EVANS, R. A.; AND GILBERT, L. 1972. Generalization of associative clustering tendencies in mentally retarded adolescents: Effects of novel stimuli. *American Journal of Mental Deficiency* 77:77–84.

BJORK, R. A. 1970. Positive forgetting: The noninterference of items intentionally forgotten. *Journal of Verbal Learning and Verbal Behavior* 9: 255–68.

BLAKEMORE, C. 1977. *Mechanics of the mind.* New York: Cambridge University Press.

BLASI, A. 1980. Bridging moral cognition and moral action: A critical review of the literature. *Psychological Bulletin* 88: 1–45.

BLASS, E. M., AND EPSTEIN, A. N. 1971. A lateral preoptic osmosensitive zone for thirst in the rat. *Journal of Comparative and Physiological Psychology* 76:378–94.

BLEULER, E. 1911. *Dementia praecox, or the group of schizophrenias.* English translation by Zinkin, J., and Lewis, N. D. C. New York: International Universities Press, 1950.

BLISS, E. L. 1980. Multiple personalities: Report of fourteen cases with implications for schizophrenia and hysteria. *Archives of General Psychiatry* 37: 1388–97.

BLOCK, J. 1971. *Lives through time.* Berkeley, Calif.: Bancroft.

BLOCK, J. 1977. Advancing the psychology of personality: Paradigmatic shift or improving the quality of research. In Magnusson, D., and Endler, N. S., eds., *Personality at the crossroads,* pp. 37–64. New York: Wiley.

BLOOM, L. 1970. *Language development: Form and function in emerging grammars.* Cambridge, Mass.: MIT Press.

BLOOM, L. 1973. *One word at a time.* The Hague: Mouton.

BLOOMFIELD, L. 1933. *Language.* New York: Holt, Rinehart & Winston.

BLUM, J. E.; JARVIK, L. F.; AND CLARK, E. T. 1970. Rate of change on selective tests of intelligence: A twenty-year longitudinal study. *Journal of Gerontology* 25:171–76.

BLURTON-JONES, N. G. 1976. Review of Wilson's *Sociobiology. Animal Behavior* 24:701–3.

BODEN, M. 1977. *Artificial intelligence and natural man.* New York: Basic Books.

BOGEN, J. E. 1969. The other side of the brain II: An appositional mind. *Bulletin of the Los Angeles Neurological Societies* 34:135–62.

BOLES, D. B. 1980. X-linkage of spatial ability: A critical review. *Child Development* 51: 625–35.

BOLLES, R. C. 1970. Species-specific defense reactions and avoidance learning. *Psychological Review* 77:32–48.

BOLLES, R. C., AND FANSELOW, M. S. 1982. Endorphins and behavior. *Annual Review of Psychology* 33:87–102.

BOOTH, D. A. 1980. Acquired behavior controlling energy and output. In Stunkard, A. J., ed., *Obesity,* pp. 101–43. Philadelphia: Saunders.

BORING, E. G. 1930. A new ambiguous figure. *American Journal of Psychology* 42:444–45.

BORING, E. G. 1942. *Sensation and perception in the history of experimental psychology.* New York: Appleton-Century-Crofts.

BORING, E. G. 1964. Size constancy in a picture. *American Journal of Psychology* 77:494–98.

BORING, E. G.; LANGFELD, H. S.; AND WELD, H. P. 1939. *Introduction to psychology.* New York: Wiley.

BORKE, H. 1975. Piaget's mountains revisited: Changes in the egocentric landscape. *Developmental Psychology* 11:240–43.

BOTVIN, G. J., AND MURRAY, F. B. 1975. The efficacy of peer modelling and social conflict in the acquisition of conservation. *Child Development* 46: 796–97.

BOUSFIELD, W. A. 1953. The occurrence of clustering in the recall of randomly arranged associates. *Journal of General Psychology* 49:229–40.

BOWER, G. H. 1970a. Analysis of a mnemonic device. *American Scientist* 58:496–510.

BOWER, G. H. 1970b. Organizational factors in memory. *Cognitive Psychology* 1:18–46.

BOWER, T. G. R. 1966. Slant perception and shape constancy in infants. *Science* 151: 832–34.

BOWER, T. G. R. 1976. Repetitive processes in child development. *Scientific American* 235: 38–47.

BOWER, T. G. R. 1977. *A primer of infant development.* San Francisco: Freeman.

BOWERMAN, M. 1973. *Early syntactic development: A cross-linguistic study with special reference to Finnish.* London: Cambridge University Press.

BOWERMAN, M. 1982. Reorganizational processes in language development. In Wanner, E., and Gleitman, L. R., eds., *Language development: State of the art.* New York: Cambridge University Press.

BOWLBY, J. 1969. *Attachment and loss,* vol. 1. *Attachment.* New York: Basic Books.

BOWLBY, J. 1973. *Separation and loss.* New York: Basic Books.

BRADLEY, D. C.; GARRETT, M. F.; AND ZURIF, E. G. 1979. Syntactic deficits in Broca's aphasia. In Caplan, D., ed., *Biological studies of mental processes.* Cambridge, Mass.: MIT Press.

BRADY, J. P. 1972. Systematic desensitization. In Agras, W. S., ed., *Behavior modification: Principles and clinical applications,* pp. 127–50. Boston: Little, Brown.

BRAIN, L. 1965. *Speech disorders: Aphasia, apraxia, and agnosia.* London: Butterworth.

BRAINE, M. D. S. 1963. The ontogeny of English phrase structure: The first phase. *Language* 39:3–13.

BRAINE, M. D. S. 1976. Children's first word combinations. *Monographs of the Society for Research in Child Development* 41(1, Serial No. 164).

BRAINE, M. D. S., AND HARDY, J. A. 1982. On what case categories there are, why they are, and how they develop: An amalgam of *a priori* considerations, speculations, and evidence from children. In Wanner, E. and Gleitman, L. R., eds., *Language acquisition: State of the art.* New York: Cambridge University Press.

BRAINERD, J. C. 1978. The stage-question in cognitive-developmental theory. *The Behavioral and Brain Sciences* 173–213.

BRANSFORD, J. D., AND FRANKS, J. J. 1971. The abstraction of linguistic ideas. *Cognitive Psychology* 2:331–50.

BRANSFORD, J. D., AND JOHNSON, M. K. 1972. Contextual prerequisites for understanding. *Journal of Verbal Learning and Verbal Behavior* 11: 717–26.

BRAZELTON, T. B. 1962. A child-oriented approach to toilet training. *Pediatrics* 29:121–28.

BRAZELTON, T. B. 1972. Implications of infant development among the Mayan Indians of Mexico. *Human Development* 15: 90–111.

BREGER, L.; HUNTER, I.; AND LANE, R. W. 1971. The effect of stress on dreams. *Psychological Issues* 7(3, Monograph 27):1–213.

BRELAND, K., AND BRELAND, M. 1951. A field of applied animal psychology. *American Psychologist* 6:202–4.

BRETHERTON, I.; MCNEW, S.; AND BEEGHLY-SMITH, M. 1981. Early person knowledge as expressed in gestural and verbal communications. When do infants acquire a "theory of mind"? In Lamb, M. E., and Sherrod, L. R., eds., *Infant social cognition.* Hillsdale, N.J.: Erlbaum.

BRICKMAN, J. C., AND D'AMATO, B. 1975. Exposure effects in a free-choice situation. *Journal of Personality and Social Psychology* 32:415–20.

BRIDGES, K. M. B. 1932. Emotional development in early infancy. *Child Development* 3:324–41.

BROADBENT, D. E. 1958. *Perception and communication.* London: Pergamon Press.

BRODIE, H. K. H.; GARTRELL, N.; DOERING, C.; AND RHUE, T. 1974. Plasma testosterone levels in heterosexual and homosexual men. *American Journal of Psychiatry* 131: 82–83.

BROEN, W. E., JR. 1968. *Schizophrenia: Research and theory.* New York: Academic Press.

BRONSON, W. C. 1966. Central orientations. A study of behavior organization from childhood to adolescence. *Child Development* 37:125–55.

BROWN. A. L. 1974. The role of strategic memory in retardate-memory. In Ellis, N. R., ed., *International Review of Research in Mental Retardation,* vol. 7, pp. 55–108. New York: Academic Press.

BROWN, A. L.; BRANSFORD, J. D.; FERRARA, R. A.; AND CAMPIONE, J. C. 1983. Learning, remembering, and understanding. In Mussen, P., ed., *Carmichael's manual of child psychology: Vol. 3. Cognitive development* (Markman, E. M. and Flavell, J. H., volume editors). New York: Wiley.

BROWN, A. L.; CAMPIONE, J. C.; BRAY, N. W.; AND WILCOX, B. L. 1973. Keeping track of changing variables: Effects of rehearsal training and rehearsal prevention in normal and retarded adolescents. *Journal of Experimental Psychology* 101:123–31.

BROWN, A. L.; CAMPIONE, J. C.; AND MURPHY, M. D. 1974. Keeping track of changing variables: Long-term retention of a trained rehearsal strategy by retarded adolescents. *American Journal of Mental Deficiency* 78:446–53.

BROWN, J. F. 1940. *The psychodynamics of abnormal behavior.* New York: McGraw-Hill.

BROWN, J. K. 1981. Cross-cultural perspectives on the female life cycle. In Monroe, R. H.; Munroe, R. L.; and Whiting, B. B., eds., *Handbook of cross-cultural human development,* pp. 581–610. New York: Garland.

BROWN, J. W. 1972. *Aphasia, apraxia, and agnosia.* Springfield, Ill.: Thomas.

BROWN, R. 1954. Mass phenomena. In Lindzey, G., ed., *Handbook of social psychology,* vol. 2, pp. 833–76. Reading, Mass.: Addison-Wesley.

BROWN, R. 1957. Linguistic determinism and parts of speech. *Journal of Abnormal and Social Psychology* 55: 1–5.

BROWN, R. 1958. *Words and things.* New York: Free Press, Macmillan.

BROWN, R. 1965. *Social psychology.* New York: Free Press, Macmillan.

BROWN, R. 1973. *A first language: The early stages.* Cambridge, Mass.: Harvard University Press.

BROWN, R., AND BELLUGI, U. 1964. Three processes in the child's acquisition of syntax. *Harvard Educational Review* 34:133–51.

BROWN, R.; CAZDEN, C.; AND BELLUGI-KLIMA, U. 1969. The child's grammar from 1 to 11. In Hill, J. P., ed., *Minnesota Symposium on Child Psychology,* vol. 2, pp. 28–73. Minneapolis: University of Minnesota Press.

BROWN, R., AND HANLON, C. 1970. Derivational complexity and order of acquisition in child speech. In Hayes, J. R., ed., *Cognition and the development of language,* pp. 11–53. New York: Wiley.

BROWN R., AND MCNEILL, D. 1966. The tip of the tongue phenomenon. *Journal of Verbal Learning and Verbal Behavior* 5:325–27.

BRUNER, J. S. 1974/75. From communication to language—a psychological perspective. *Cognition* 3:255–78.

BRUNER, J. S., AND KOSLOWSKY, B. 1972. Visually preadative constituents of manipulatory action. *Perception* 1:3–14.

BRYAN, W. L., AND HARTER, N. 1897. Studies in the physiology and psychology of telegraphic language. *Psychological Review* 4:27–53.

BRYAN, W. L., AND HARTER, N. 1899. Studies on the telegraphic language: The acquisition of a hierarchy of habits. *Psychology Review* 6:345–75.

BUGELSKI, B. R., AND ALAMPAY, D. A. 1961. The role of frequency in developing perceptual sets. *Canadian Journal of Psychology* 15:205–11.

BULLOUGH, E. 1912. "Psychical distance" as a factor in art and an aesthetic principle. *British Journal of Psychology* 5:87–118.

BURGESS, E. W., AND WALLIN, P. 1943. Homogamy in social characteristics. *American Journal of Sociology* 49:109–24.

BURTON, R. V. 1963. Generality of honesty reconsidered. *Psychological Review* 70:481–99.

BURTON, R. V., AND WHITING, J. W. M. 1961. The absent father and cross-sex identity. *Merrill-Palmer Quarterly* 7: 85–95.

BURY, J. B. 1932. *The idea of progress.* New York: Macmillan.

BUSS, A. H., AND PLOMIN, R. 1975. *A temperament theory of personality development.* New York: Wiley.

BUTTERS, N., AND ALBERT, M. S. 1982. Processes underlying failures to recall remote events. In Cermak, L. S., ed., *Human memory and amnesia,* pp. 257–74. Hillsdale, N.J.: Erlbaum.

BYRNE, D. 1964. Assessing personality variables and their alteration. In Worchel, P., and Byrne, D., eds., *Personality change,* pp. 38–68. New York: Wiley.

CAIRNS, R. B., AND JOHNSON, D. L. 1965. The development of interspecies social attachments. *Psychonomic Science* 2:337–8.

CANNON, W. B. 1927. The James-Lange theory of emotions: A critical examination and an alternative theory. *American Journal of Psychology* 39:106–24.

CANNON, W. B. 1929. *Bodily changes in pain, hunger, fear and rage,* rev. ed. New York: Appleton-Century.

CANNON, W. B. 1932 and 1960 (revised and enlarged). *The wisdom of the body.* New York: Norton.

CANNON, W. B. 1942. "Voodoo" death. *American Anthropologist* 44:169–81.

CANTOR, N., AND MISCHEL, W. 1979. Prototypes in person perception. In Berkowitz, L., ed., *Advances in experimental social psychology,* vol. 12. New York: Academic Press.

CAPORAEL, L. 1976. Satanism: The satan loosed in Salem? *Science* 192: 21–26.

CAREY, S. 1978. The child as word learner. In Halle, M.; Bresnan, I.; and Miller, G., eds., *Linguistic theory and psychological reality,* pp. 264–93. Cambridge, Mass.: MIT Press.

CAREY, S. 1982. Semantic development: State of the art. In Wanner, E., and Gleitman, L. R., eds., *Language acquisition: State of the art.* New York: Cambridge University Press.

CARLSON, N. R. 1977. *Physiology of behavior.* Boston: Allyn and Bacon.

CARRIGAN, P. M. 1960. Extraversion-introversion as a dimension of personality. A reappraisal. *Psychological Bulletin* 57:329–60.

CARRINGTON, P. 1972. Dreams and schizophrenia. *Archives General Psychiatry* 26:343–50.

CARROLL, L. 1865. *Alice in Wonderland.* Abridged by Frank J. and illustrated by Torrey, M. M. New York: Random House, 1969.

CARTWRIGHT, R. D. 1977. *Night life: Explorations in dreaming.* Englewood Cliffs, N.J.: Prentice-Hall.

CASE, R. 1974. Structures and strictures: Some functional limitations on the course of cognitive growth. *Cognitive Psychology* 6:544–74.

CASE, R. 1978. Intellectual development from birth to adulthood: A neo-Piagetian interpretation. In Siegler, R., ed., *Children's thinking: What develops?* Hillsdale, N.J.: Erlbaum.

CATEL, J. 1953. Ein Beitrag zur Frage von Hirnenentwicklung under Menschwerdung. *Klinische Weisschriften* 31: 473–75.

CATTELL, R. B. 1957. *Personality and motivation structure and measurement.* New York: Harcourt, Brace and World.

CATTELL, R. B. 1963. Theory of fluid and crystallized intelligence: A critical experiment. *Journal of Educational Psychology* 54:1–22.

CAZDEN, U. 1968. The acquisition of noun and verb inflections. *Child Development* 39: 433–48.

CERMAK, L. S., ed. 1982. *Human memory and amnesia.* Hillsdale, N.J.: Erlbaum.

CHASE, W. G., AND SIMON, H. A. 1973. Perception in chess. *Cognitive Psychology* 4:55–81.

CHERRY, E. C. 1953. Some experiments upon the recognition of speech, with one and with two ears. *Journal of the Acoustical Society of America* 25:975–79.

CHI, M. T. H. 1978. Knowledge structures and memory development. In Siegler, R. S., ed., *Children's thinking: What develops?,* pp. 73–96. Hillsdale, N.J.: Erlbaum.

CHILD, I. L. 1950. The relation of somatotype to self-ratings on Sheldon's temperamental traits. *Journal of Personality* 18:440–53.

CHODOFF, P. 1954. A reexamination of some aspects of conversion hysteria. *Psychiatry* 17:75–81.

CHOMSKY, N. 1957. *Syntactic structures.* The Hague: Mouton.

CHOMSKY, N. 1965. *Aspects of the theory of syntax.* Cambridge, Mass.: MIT Press.

CHOMSKY, N. 1975. *Reflections on language.* New York: Pantheon Books.

CHOMSKY, N. 1980. *Rules and representations.* New York: Columbia University Press.

CHRISTIE, R. 1954. Authoritarianism re-examined. In Christie, R., and Jahoda, M., eds., *Studies in the scope and method of "The authoritarian personality."* New York: Free Press, Macmillan.

CHRISTIE, R., AND JAHODA, M., eds. 1954. *Studies in the scope and method of "The authoritarian personality."* New York: Free Press, Macmillan.

CLARK, E. V. 1973. What's in a word?: On the child's acquisition of semantics in his first language. In Moore, T. E., ed., *Cognitive development and the acquisition of language.* New York: Academic Press.

CLARK, E. V. 1982. The young word-maker: A case study of innovation in the child's lexicon. In Wanner, E., and Gleitman, L. R., eds., *Language acquisition: State of the art.* New York: Cambridge University Press.

CLARK, H. H., AND CLARK, E. V. 1977. *Psychology and language: An introduction to psycholinguistics.* New York: Harcourt Brace Jovanovich.

CLARKE, A. C. 1952. An examination of the operation of residual propinquity as a factor in mate selection. *American Sociological Review* 27:17–22.

CLECKLEY, H. 1964. *The mask of sanity,* 4th ed. St. Louis: Mosby.

CLEMENTE, C. D., AND CHASE, M. H. 1973. Neurological substrates of aggressive behavior. *Annual Review of Physiology* 35: 329–56.

COBB, S. 1941. *Foundations of psychiatry.* Baltimore: Williams and Wilkins.

COBB, S., AND ROSE, R. M. 1973. Hypertension, peptic ulcer and diabetes in air traffic controllers. *Journal of the American Medical Association* 224:489–92.

COHEN, D. B., AND WOLFE, G. 1973. Dream recall and repression: Evidence for an alternative hypothesis. *Journal of Consulting and Clinical Psychology* 41: 349–55.

COHEN, H. 1972. Active (REM) sleep deprivation. In Chase, M. H., ed., *The sleeping brain: Perspectives in the brain sciences,* vol. 1, pp. 343–47. Los Angeles: Brain Research Institute, University of California.

COHEN, N. J., AND SQUIRE, L. R. 1980. Preserved learning and retention of pattern-analyzing skill in amnesia: Dissociation of knowing how and knowing what. *Science* 210:207–10.

COHEN, R. A. 1975. Manic-depressive illness. In Freedman, A. M.; Kaplan, H. I.; and Sadock, B. J., eds., *Comprehensive textbook of psychiatry—II,* vol. 1, pp. 1012–24. Baltimore: Williams & Wilkins.

COHEN, Y. A. 1953. A study of interpersonal relations in a Jamaican community. Unpublished doctoral dissertation, Yale University.

COLARUSSO, C. A., AND NEMIROFF, R. A. 1981. *Adult development: A new dimension in psychodynamic theory and practice.* New York: Plenum Press.

COLE, J. O., AND DAVIS, J. M. 1975. Antidepressant drugs. In Freedman, A. M.; Kaplan, H. I.; and Saddock, B. J., eds., *Comprehensive textbook of psychiatry—II,* vol 2. pp. 1941–56. Baltimore: Williams & Wilkins.

COLEMAN, J. C. 1972 AND 1976. *Abnormal psychology and modern life,* 4th and 5th eds. Glenview, Ill.: Scott, Foresman.

COLEMAN, J. C.; BUTCHER, J. N.; AND CARSON, R. C. 1984. *Abnormal psychology and modern life,* 7th ed. Glenview, Ill.: Scott, Foresman.

COLLINS, A. M., AND QUILLIAN, M. R. 1969. Retrieval time from semantic memory. *Journal of Verbal Learning and Verbal Behavior* 8:240–47.

COLLINS, R. L., AND FULLER, J. L. 1968. Audiogenic seizure prone (ASP): A gene affecting behavior in linkage group VIII of the mouse. *Science* 162:1137–39.

COLLIP, P. J. 1980. Obesity in childhood. In Stunkard, A. J., ed., *Obesity.* Philadelphia: Saunders.

COLLIS, G., 1975. The integration of gaze and vocal behavior in the mother-infant dyad. Paper presented at Third International Child Language Symposium, London.

CONEL, J. L. 1939. *The postnatal development of the human cortex,* vol. 1. Cambridge, Mass.: Harvard University Press.

CONEL, J. L. 1947. *The postnatal development of the human cortex,* vol. 3. Cambridge, Mass.: Harvard University Press.

CONEL, J. L. 1955. *The postnatal development of the human cortex,* vol. 5. Cambridge, Mass.: Harvard University Press.

COOLEY, C. H. 1902. *Human nature and the social order.* New York: Scribner's.

COOPER, L. A., AND SHEPARD, R. N. 1973. The time required to prepare for a rotated stimulus. *Memory and Cognition* 1:246–50.

COREN, S., AND GIRGUS, J. S. 1978. *Seeing is deceiving: The psychology of visual illusions.* Hillsdale, N. J.: Erlbaum.

COREN, S.; PORAC, C.; AND WARD, L. M. 1978. *Sensation and perception.* New York: Academic Press.

CORNSWEET, T. M. 1970. *Visual perception.* New York: Academic Press.

CORY, T. L.; ORMISTON, D. W.; SIMMEL, E.; AND DAINOFF, M. 1975. Predicting the frequency of dream recall. *Journal of Abnormal Psychology* 84: 261–66.

COSTA, P. T., JR.; MCCRAE, R. R.; AND ARENBERG, D. 1980. Enduring dispositions in adult males. *Journal of Personality and Social Psychology* 38: 793–800.

COSTELLO, C. G. 1978. A critical review of Seligman's laboratory experiments on learned helplessness and depression in humans. *Journal of Abnormal Psychology* 87:21–31.

COWLES, J. T. 1937. Food-tokens as incentives for learning by chimpanzees. *Comparative Psychology Monographs* 14 (5, Serial No. 71).

CRAIK, F. I. M., AND LOCKHART, R. S. 1972. Levels of processing: A framework for memory research. *Journal of Verbal Learning and Verbal Behavior* 11: 671–84.

CRAIK, F. I. M., AND TULVING, E. 1975. Depth of processing and the retention of words in episodic memory. *Journal of Experimental Psychology: General* 104: 268–94.

CRAIK, F. I. M., AND WATKINS, M. J. 1973. The role of rehearsal in short-term memory. *Journal of Verbal Learning and Verbal Behavior* 12:599–607.

CRANDALL, V. C. 1969. Sex differences in expectancy of intellectual and academic reinforcement. In Smith, C. P., ed., *Achievement-related motives in children.* New York: Russell Sage.

CROMER, R. F. 1976. The cognitive hypothesis of language acquisition and its implications for child language deficiency. In Morehead, D. M., and Morehead, A. E., eds., *Normal and deficient child language,* pp. 283–334. Baltimore: University Park Press.

CRONBACH, L. J. 1970a. *Essentials of psychology testing,* 3rd ed. New York: Harper & Row.

CRONBACH, L. J. 1970b. Test validation. In Thorndike, R. L., ed., *Educational measurement.* Washington: American Council on Education.

CRONBACH, L. J., AND MEEHL, P. E. 1955. Construct validity in psychological tests. *Psychological Bulletin* 52:281–302.

CROWDER, R. G., AND MORTON, J. 1969. Precategorical acoustic storage (PAS). *Perception and Psychophysics* 5:365–73.

CRUTCHFIELD, R. S. 1955. Conformity and character. *American Psychologist* 10:191–99.

CURTISS, S. 1977. *Genie: A linguistic study of a modern-day "wild child."* New York: Academic Press.

CYTRYN, L., AND LOURIE, R. S. 1975. Mental retardation. In Freedman, A. M.; Kaplan, H. I.; and Sadock, B. J., eds., *Comprehensive textbook of psychiatry—II,* vol. 1, pp. 1158–97. Baltimore: Williams & Wilkins.

DALE, A. J. D. 1975. Organic brain syndromes associated with infections. In Freedman, A. M.; Kaplan, H. I.; and Sadock, B. J., eds., *Comprehensive textbook of psychiatry—II,* vol. 1, pp. 1121–30. Baltimore: Williams & Wilkins.

DALY, M., AND WILSON, M. 1978. *Sex, evolution, and behavior.* Belmont, Calif.: Wadsworth.

DARLEY, J., AND LATANÉ, B. 1968. Bystander intervention in emergencies: Diffusion of responsibility. *Journal of Personality and Social Psychology* 10:202–14.

DARWIN, C. 1872a. *The origin of species.* New York: Macmillan, 6th ed., 1962.

DARWIN, C. 1872b. *The expression of the emotions in man and animals.* London: Appleton.

DARWIN, C. 1877. A biographical sketch of a young child. *Kosmos* 1:367–76 (as cited in Bornstein, M. H. 1978. Chromatic vision in infancy. In Reese, H., and Lipsitt, L., eds., *Advances in child development and behavior,* vol. 12. New York: Academic Press.

DARWIN, C. J.; TURVEY, M. T.; AND CROWDER, R. G. 1972. An auditory analogue of the Sperling partial report procedure: Evidence for brief auditory storage. *Cognitive Psychology* 3:255–67.

DAVIDSON, J. M. 1969. Hormonal control of sexual behavior in adult rats. In Raspé, G., ed., *Advances in bioscience,* vol. 1, pp. 119–69. New York: Pergamon.

DAVINCI, LEONARDO, ca. 1500. *Treatise on painting.* In Philosophical Library Edition, *The art of painting.* New York: Philosophical Library, 1957.

DAVIS, D. E. 1964. The physiological analysis of aggressive behavior. In Etkin, W., ed., *Social behavior and organization among vertebrates.* Chicago: University of Chicago Press.

DAVIS, J. M. 1974. A two-factor theory of schizophrenia. *Journal of Psychiatric Research* 11:25–30.

DAVIS, J. M., AND COLE, J. O. 1975. Antipsychotic drugs. In Freedman, A. M.; Kaplan, H. I.; and Sadock, B. J., eds., *Comprehensive textbook of psychiatry—II,* vol. 2, pp. 1921–41. Baltimore: Williams & Wilkins.

DAVIS, K. 1947. Final note on a case of extreme social isolation. *American Journal of Sociology* 52:432–37.

DAVISON, G. C. 1968. Systematic desensitization as a counter-conditioning process. *Journal of Abnormal Psychology* 73:84–90.

DAVISON, G. C., AND NEALE, J. M. 1974, 1978, 1982. *Abnormal psychology: An experimental clinical approach,* 1st, 2nd, 3rd eds. New York: Wiley.

DAY, R. H., AND MCKENZIE, B. E. 1981. Infant perception of the invariant size of approaching and receding objects. *Developmental Psychology* 17:670–77.

DE GROOT, A. D. 1965. *Thought and choice in chess.* The Hague: Mouton.

DEMENT, W. C. 1974. *Some must watch while some must sleep.* San Francisco: Freeman.

DEMENT, W. C., AND KLEITMAN, N. 1957. The relation of eye movements during sleep to dream activity: An objective method for the study of dreaming. *Journal of Experimental Psychology* 53:339–46.

DEMENT, W. C., AND WOLPERT, E. A. 1958. The relationship of

eye-movements, body motility, and external stimuli to dream content. *Journal of Experimental Psychology* 55:543–53.

DENNIS, W. 1940. Does culture appreciably affect patterns of infant behavior? *Journal of Social Psychology* 12:305–17.

DENNIS, W. 1973. *Children of the creche.* New York: Appleton-Century-Crofts.

DEPUE, R. A., AND MONROE, S. M. 1978. Learned helplessness in the perspective of the depressive disorders: Conceptual and definitional issues. *Journal of Abnormal Psychology* 87:3–20.

DESCARTES, R. 1649. Letter (to Morus); ATV, 278. In Eaton, R. M., ed., *Descartes selections,* p. 360. New York: Scribner's, 1927. Cited in Vendler, Z., *Res cogitans: An essay in rational psychology.* Ithaca, N. Y.: Cornell University Press, 1972.

DESCARTES, R. 1662. *Traité de l'homme.* Translated by Haldane, E. S., and Ross, G. R. T. Cambridge, England: Cambridge University Press, 1911.

DEUTSCH, A. 1948. *The shame of the states.* New York: Harcourt and Brace. (Reprint edition, New York: Arno Press, 1973.)

DEUTSCH, J. A. 1960. *The structural basis of behavior.* Chicago: University of Chicago Press.

DEUTSCH, J. A.; ADAMS, D. W.; AND METZNER, R. J. 1964. Choice of intracranial stimulation as a function of the delay between stimulations and competing drive. *Journal of Comparative and Physiological Psychology* 57:241–43.

DEUTSCH, J. A.; PUERTO, A.; AND WANG, M. L. 1978. The stomach signals satiety. *Science* 201:165–67.

DE VALOIS, R. L. 1965. Behavioral and electrophysiological studies of primate vision. In Neff, W. D., ed., *Contributions of sensory physiology,* vol. 1. New York: Academic Press.

DE VALOIS, R. L., AND DE VALOIS, K. K. 1975. Neural coding of color. In Carterette, E. C., and Friedman, M. P., eds., *Handbook of perception,* vol. 5, pp. 117–62. New York: Academic Press.

DE VILLIERS, J. G. 1980. The process of rule learning in child speech: A new look. In Nelson, K., ed., *Child language,* vol. 2. New York: Gardner Press.

DE VILLIERS, J. G., AND DE VILLIERS, P. A. 1973. Development of the use of word order in comprehension. *Journal of Psycholinguistic Research* 2:331–41.

DE VILLIERS, J. G., AND DE VILLIERS, P. A. 1978. *Language acquisition.* Cambridge, Mass.: Harvard University Press.

DE VILLIERS, P. A. 1978. Speech presented at the Boston Child Language Conference.

Diagnostic and statistical manual of mental disorders, 3rd ed. Washington: American Psychiatric Association, 1980.

DICKS, H. V. 1972. *Licensed mass murder: A sociopsychological study of some S. S. killers.* New York: Basic Books.

DIENER, F. 1977. Deindividuation: Causes and consequences. *Social Behavior and Personality* 5:143–55.

DILGER, W. C. 1962. The behavior of lovebirds. *Scientific American* 206:88–98.

DION, K. 1972. Physical attractiveness and evaluations of children's transgressions. *Journal of Personality and Social Psychology* 24:207–13.

DION, K.; BERSCHEID, E.; AND WALSTER, E. 1972. What is beautiful is good. *Journal of Personality and Social Psychology* 24:285–90.

DI VESTA, F. J.; INGERSOLL, G.; AND SUNSHINE, P. 1971. A factor analysis of imagery tests. *Journal of Verbal Learning and Verbal Behavior* 10:471–79.

DODD, B. 1979. Lip reading in infants: Attention to speech presented in- and out-of-synchrony. *Cognitive Psychology* 11:478–84.

DOLGER, H., AND SEEMAN, B. 1985. *How to live with diabetes,* 5th ed. New York: Norton.

DOUVAN, E., AND ADELSON, J. 1958. The psychodynamics of social mobility in adolescent boys. *Journal of Abnormal and Social Psychology* 56:31–44.

DRUCKER-COLÍN, R. R., AND SPANIS, C. W. 1976. Is there a sleep transmitter? *Progress in Neurobiology* 6:1–26.

DUNCKER, K. 1929. Über induzierte Bewegung. *Psychologische Forschung* 12:180–259.

DUNCKER, K. 1945. On problem solving. *Psychological Monographs* (Whole No. 270): 1–113.

DWECK, C. S.; DAVIDSON, W.; NELSON, S.; AND ENNA, B. 1978. Sex differences in learned helplessness: II. The contingencies of evaluative feedback in the classroom. III. An experimental analysis. *Developmental Psychology* 14:268–76.

DWECK, C. S., AND ELLIOT, E. S. 1983. Achievement motivation. In Mussen, P. H., ed., *Carmichael's manual of child psychology: Vol. 4. Socialization, personality and social development* (Hetherington, M. E., volume editor), pp. 643–92. New York: Wiley.

DWECK, C. S.; GOETZ, T. E.; AND STRAUSS, N. L. 1980. Sex differences in learned helplessness: An experimental and naturalistic study of failure generalization and its mediators. *Journal of Personality and Social Psychology* 38:441–52.

DWECK, C. S., AND LICHT, B. G. 1980. Learned helplessness, anxiety and achievement motivation: Neglected parallels in cognitive, affective, and coping responses. In Garber, J., and Seligman, M. E. P., eds. *Human helplessness: Theory and applications.* New York: Academic Press.

DYMOND, R. 1954. Interpersonal perception and marital happiness. *Canadian Journal of Psychology* 8: 164–71.

EAGLY, A. H., AND TELAAK, K. 1972. Width of the latitude of acceptance as a determinant of attitude change. *Journal of Personality and Social Psychology* 23:388–97.

EBBINGHAUS, H. 1885. *Memory.* New York: Teacher's College, Columbia University, 1913. (Reprint edition, New York: Dover, 1964).

ECCLES, J. 1973. *The understanding of the brain.* New York: McGraw-Hill.

EDMONDS, J. M., ed. and trans. 1929. *The characters of Theophrastus.* Cambridge, Mass.: Harvard University Press.

EGGER, M. D., AND FLYNN, J. P. 1963. Effect of electrical stimulation of the amygdala on hypothalamically elicited behavior in cats. *Journal of Neurophysiology* 26:705–20.

EIBL-EIBESFELDT, I. 1970. *Ethology: The biology of behavior.* New York: Holt, Rinehart & Winston.

EIKELBOOM, R., AND STEWART, J. 1982. Conditioning of drug-induced physiological responses. *Psychological Review* 89:507–28.

EIMAS, P. D.; SIQUELAND, E. R.; JUSCZYK, P.; AND VIGORITO, J. 1971. Speech perception in infants. *Science* 171:303–6.

EKMAN, P. 1971. Universals and cultural differences in facial expression. In Cole, J. K., ed., *Nebraska symposium on motivation,* pp. 207–84. Lincoln, Neb.: University of Nebraska Press.

EKMAN, P. 1973. Cross-cultural studies of facial expression. In Ekman, P., ed., *Darwin and facial expression,* pp. 169–222. New York: Academic Press.

EKMAN, P. 1977. Biological and cultural contributions to body and facial movement. In Blacking, J., ed., *The anthropology of the body.* A.S.A. Monograph 15. London: Academic Press.

EKMAN, P. 1985. *Telling lies.* New York: Norton.

EKMAN, P., AND FRIESEN, W. V. 1975. *Unmasking the face.* Englewood Cliffs, N.J.: Prentice-Hall.

EKMAN, P.; LEVENSON, R. W.; AND FRIESEN, W. V. 1983. Emotions differ in autonomic nervous system activity. *Science* 221:1208–10.

EKMAN, P., AND OSTER, H. 1979. Facial expression of emotion. *Annual Review of Psychology* 30:527–54.

ELDER, G. H., JR. 1980. Adolescence in historical perspective. In Adelson, J., ed., *Handbook of adolescent psychology.* New York: Wiley.

ELLENBERGER, H. F. 1970. *The discovery of the unconscious.* New York: Basic Books.

ELLIS, A. 1962. *Reason and emotion in psychotherapy.* Secaucus, N. J.: Lyle Stuart.

EMBER, C. R. 1981. A cross-cultural perspective on sex-differences. In Monroe, R. H.; Munroe, R. L.; and Whiting, B. B., eds., *Handbook of cross-cultural human development,* pp. 531–80. New York: Garland.

EMMELKAMP, P., AND KUIPERS, A. 1979. Agoraphobia: A follow-up study four years after treatment. *British Journal of Psychiatry* 134:352–55.

EMMERICH, W. 1966. Continuity and stability in early social development, II. Teacher ratings. *Child Development* 37:17–27.

ENDLER, N. S., AND HUNT, J. M. 1969. Generalization of contributions from sources of variance in the S-R inventories of anxiousness. *Journal of Personality* 37:1–24.

EPPS, P., AND PARNELL, R. W. 1952. Physique and temperament of women delinquents compared with women undergraduates. *British Journal of Medical Psychology* 25:249–55.

EPSTEIN, A. N.; FITZSIMONS, J. T.; AND ROLLS, B. J. 1970. Drinking induced by injection of angiotensin into the brain of the rat. *Journal of Physiology* 210:457–74.

EPSTEIN, A. W., AND TEITELBAUM, P. 1962. Regulation of food intake in the absence of taste, smell, and other oropharyngeal sensations. *Journal of Comparative and Physiological Psychology* 55:753–59.

EPSTEIN, S. 1979. The stability of behavior: I. On predicting most of the people much of the time. *Journal of Personality and Social Psychology* 37:1097–1126.

EPSTEIN, S. 1980. The stability of behavior. II. Implications for psychological research. *American Psychologist* 35:790–806.

EPSTEIN, S. 1983. The stability of confusion: A reply to Mischel and Peak. *Psychological Review* 90:179–84.

EPSTEIN, S. M. 1967. Toward a unified theory of anxiety. In Maher, B. A., ed., *Progress in experimental personality research,* vol. 4. New York: Academic Press.

EPSTEIN, W. 1961. The influence of syntactical structure on learning. *American Journal of Psychology* 74:80–85.

ERDELYI, M. H. 1974. A new look at the new look: Perceptual defense and vigilance. *Psychological Review* 81:1–25.

ERDELYI, M. H., AND GOLDBERG, B. 1979. Let's not sweep repression under the rug. In Kihlstrom, J. F., and Evans, F. J., eds., *Functional disorders of memory,* pp. 355–402. Hillsdale, N. J.: Erlbaum.

ERICSSON, K. A.; CHASE, W. G.; AND FALOON, S. 1980. Acquisition of a memory skill. *Science* 208:1181–82.

ERIKSEN, C. W., AND PIERCE, J. 1968. Defense mechanisms. In Borgatta, E. F., and Lambert, W. W., eds., *Handbook of personality theory and research,* pp. 1007–40. Chicago: Rand McNally.

ERIKSON, E. H. 1963. *Childhood and society.* New York: Norton.

ERIKSON, E. H. 1974. *Dimensions of a new identity: The Jefferson lectures in the humanities.* New York: Norton.

ERLENMEYER-KIMLING, L., AND JARVIK, L. F. 1963. Genetics and intelligence: A review. *Science* 142:1477–79.

ERON, L. D. 1950. A normative study of the thematic apperception test. *Psychological Monographs* 64 (Whole No. 315).

ERVIN, S., 1964. Imitation and structural change in children's language. In Lenneberg, E. H., ed., *New directions in the study of language.* Cambridge, Mass.: MIT Press.

ETKIN, W. 1964. Reproductive behaviors. In Etkin, W., ed., *Social behavior and organization among vertebrates,* pp. 75–116. Chicago: University of Chicago Press.

EYSENCK, H. J. 1961. The effects of psychotherapy. In Eysenck, H. J., ed., *Handbook of abnormal psychology,* pp. 697–725. New York: Basic Books.

EYSENCK, H. J. 1967. *The biological basis of personality.* Springfield, Ill.: Thomas.

EYSENCK, H. J., AND RACHMAN, S. 1965. *The causes and cures of neurosis.* San Diego, Calif.: Robert R. Knapp.

EYSENCK, H. J.; WAKEFIELD, J. A., JR.; AND FRIEDMAN, A. F. 1983. Diagnosis and clinical assessment: The DSM III. In Rosenzweig, M. R., and Porter, L. W., eds., *Annual Review of Psychology* 34:167–94.

FALLON, A. E., AND ROZIN, P. 1985. Sex differences in perceptions of desirable body shape. *Journal of Abnormal Psychology* 94:102–5.

FANT, L. G. 1972. *Ameslan: An introduction to American Sign Language.* Silver Springs, Md.: National Association of the Deaf.

FANTZ, R. L. 1957. Form preferences in newly hatched chicks. *Journal of Comparative and Physiological Psychology* 50:422–30.

FANTZ, R. L. 1961. The origin of form perception. *Scientific American* 204:66–72.

FANTZ, R. L. 1970. Visual perception and experience in infancy: Issues and approaches. In National Academy of Science, *Early experience and visual information processing in perceptual and reading disorders,* pp. 351–81. New York: National Academy of Science.

FARIS, R. E. L., AND DUNHAM, H. W. 1939. *Mental disorders in urban areas.* Chicago: University of Chicago Press.

FARLEY, F., AND FARLEY, S. V. 1967. Extroversion and stimulus-seeking motivation. *Journal of Consulting Psychology* 31:215–16.

FEARING, F. 1930. *Reflex action: A study in the history of physiological psychology.* Baltimore: Williams & Wilkins.

FELDMAN, H.; GOLDIN-MEADOW, S.; AND GLEITMAN, L. R. 1978. Beyond Herodotus: The creation of language by linguistically deprived deaf children. In Lock, A., ed., *Action, gesture, and symbol: The emergence of language.* London: Academic Press.

FELDMAN, N. S.; KLOSSON, E. C.; PARSONS, J. E.; RHOLES, W. S.; AND RUBLE, D. N. 1976. Order of information presentation and children's moral judgments. *Child Development* 47:556–59.

FELIPE, N. J., AND SOMMER, R. 1966. Invasions of personal space. *Social Problems* 14:206–14.

FENICHEL, O. 1945. *The psychoanalytic theory of neurosis.* New York: Norton.

FERNALD, A. 1984. The perceptual and affective salience of mothers' speech to infants. In Feagans, L.; Garvey, C.; and Golinkoff, R., eds., *The origins and growth of communication.* New Brunswick, N. J.: Ablex.

FERNALD, A., AND SIMON, T. 1984. Expanded intonation contours in mothers' speech to newborns. *Developmental Psychology* 20:104–13.

FERSTER, C. B., AND SKINNER, B. F. 1957. *Schedules of reinforcement.* New York: Appleton-Century-Crofts.

FESHBACH, N. D. 1977. Studies on the empathic behavior of children. In Maher, B. A., ed., *Progress in experimental personality research,* vol. 8. New York: Academic Press.

FESHBACH, N., AND ROE, K. 1968. Empathy in six and seven-year-olds. *Child Development* 39:133–45.

FESHBACH, S. 1970. Aggression. In Mussen, P. H., ed., *Carmichael's manual of child psychology,* 3rd ed., pp. 159–260. New York: Wiley.

FESTINGER, L. 1954. A theory of social comparison processes. *Human Relations* 7:117–40.

FESTINGER, L. 1957. *A theory of cognitive dissonance.* Evanston, Ill.: Row, Peterson.

FESTINGER, L., AND CARLSMITH, J. M. 1959. Cognitive consequences of forced compliance. *Journal of Abnormal and Social Psychology* 58:203–10.

FESTINGER, L.; PEPITONE, A.; AND NEWCOMB, T. 1952. Some consequences of deindividuation in a group. *Journal of Abnormal and Social Psychology* 47:387–89.

FESTINGER, L.; RIECKEN, H.; AND SCHACHTER, S. 1956. *When prophecy fails.* Minneapolis: University of Minnesota Press.

FIEVE, R. R. 1975. Lithium (antimanic) therapy. In Freedman,

A. M.; Kaplan, H. I.; and Sadock, B. J., eds., *Comprehensive textbook of psychiatry—II,* vol. 2, pp. 1982–87. Baltimore: Williams & Wilkins.

FISHER, J. D., AND BYRNE, D. 1975. Too close for comfort: Sex differences in response to invasions of personal space. *Journal of Personality and Social Psychology* 32:15–21.

FITZGERALD, F. T. 1981. The problem of obesity. *Annual Review of Medicine* 32:221–31.

FITZSIMONS, J. T., AND MOORE-GILLOW, M. J. 1980. Drinking and antidiuresis in response to reductions in venous return in the dog: Neural and endocrine mechanisms. *Journal of Physiology* 307:403–16.

FLANAGAN, J. C. 1947. Scientific development of the use of human resources: Progress in the Army Air Forces. *Science* 105:57–60.

FLAVELL, J. H. 1970. Developmental studies of mediated memory. In Reese, H. W., and Lipsitt, L. P., eds., *Advances in child development and behavior,* vol. 5. New York: Academic Press.

FLAVELL, J. H. 1977. *Cognitive development.* Englewood Cliffs, N. J.: Prentice-Hall.

FLAVELL, J. H. 1982. Structures, stages, and sequences in cognitive development. In Collins, W. A., ed., *The concept of development: The Minnesota Symposium on Child Psychology,* vol. 15, pp. 1–28. Hillsdale, N. J.: Erlbaum.

FLAVELL, J. H.; BEACH, D. H.; AND CHINSKY, J. M. 1966. Spontaneous verbal rehearsal in a memory task as a function of age. *Child Development* 37:283–99.

FLAVELL, J. H.; FLAVELL, E. R.; AND GREEN, F. L. 1983. Development of the appearance-reality distinction. *Cognitive Psychology* 15:95–120.

FLAVELL, J. H., AND WELLMAN, H. M. 1977. Metamemory. In Kail, R. V., and Hagen, J. W., eds., *Memory in cognitive development.* Hillsdale, N. J.: Erlbaum.

FLAVELL, J. H., AND WOHLWILL, J. F. 1969. Formal and functional aspects of cognitive development. In Elkind, D., and Flavell, J. H., eds., *Studies in cognitive growth: Essays in honor of Jean Piaget.* New York: Oxford University Press.

FLYNN, J.; VANEGAS, H.; FOOTE, W.; AND EDWARDS, S. 1970. Neural mechanisms involved in a cat's attack on a rat. In Whalen, R. F.; Thompson, M.; Verzeano, M.; and Weinberger, N., eds., *The neural control of behavior.* New York: Academic Press.

FOARD, C. F. 1975. *Recall subsequent to tip-of-the-tongue experience.* Unpublished first-year graduate research paper, University of Pennsylvania, Philadelphia.

FOCH, T. T., AND McCLEARN, G. E. 1980. Genetics, body weight, and obesity. In Stunkard, A. J., ed., *Obesity,* pp. 48–71. Philadelphia: Saunders.

FODOR, J. A. 1972. Some reflections on L. S. Vygotsky's *Thought and language. Cognition* 1:83–95.

FODOR, J. A. 1975. *The language of thought.* New York: Crowell.

FODOR, J. A. 1981. *Representations.* Cambridge Mass.: Harvard University Press.

FODOR, J. 1983. *The modularity of mind.* Cambridge, Mass.: MIT Press, Bradford Books.

FODOR, J. A., AND BEVER, T. G. 1965. The psychological reality of linguistic segments. *Journal of Verbal Learning and Verbal Behavior* 4:414–20.

FODOR, J. A.; BEVER, T. G.; AND GARRETT, M. F. 1974. *The psychology of language.* New York: McGraw-Hill.

FODOR, J. D. 1977. *Semantics: Theories of meaning in generative grammar.* New York: Crowell.

FOLKOW, B., AND RUBENSTEIN, E. H. 1966. Cardiovascular effects of acute and chronic stimulations of the hypothalamic defense area in the rat. *Acta Physiologica Scandinavica* 68:48–57.

FONTANA, A. F. 1966. Familial etiology of schizophrenia: Is a scientific methodology possible? *Psychological Bulletin* 66:214–77.

FORD, C. S., AND BEACH, F. A. 1951. *Patterns of sexual behavior.* New York: Harper & Row.

FOSS, D. J. 1969. Decision processes during sentence comprehension: Effects of lexical item difficulty and position upon decision times. *Journal of Verbal Learning and Verbal Behavior* 8:457–62.

FOUCAULT, M. 1965. *Madness and civilization.* New York: Random House.

FOULKE, E., AND STICHT, T. G. 1969. Review of research on the intelligibility and compression of accelerated speech. *Psychological Bulletin* 72:50–62.

FOUTS, R. S. 1972. Use of guidance in teaching sign language to a chimpanzee *(Pan troglodytes). Journal of Comparative and Physiological Psychology* 80:515–22.

FOWLER, A. 1986. Language acquisition in Down's Syndrome children. In Cichette, D., and Beeghley, M., eds., *Down's Syndrome: The developmental perspective.* New York: Cambridge University Press.

FRANK, G. H. 1965. The role of the family in the development of psychopathology. *Psychological Bulletin* 64:191–205.

FRANKL, V. E. 1966. *The doctor and the soul.* New York: Knopf.

FRAZIER, L., AND FODOR, J. D. 1978. The sausage machine: A new two-stage parsing model. *Cognition* 6:291–325.

FREEDMAN, D. G. 1971. Behavioral assessment in infancy. In Stoeling, G. B. A., and Van Der Weoff Ten Bosch, J. J., eds., *Normal and abnormal development of brain and behavior,* pp. 92–103. Leiden: Leiden University Press.

FREEDMAN, J. L. 1964. Involvement, discrepancy, and change. *Journal of Abnormal and Social Psychology* 64:290–95.

FREEDMAN, J. L., AND FRASER, S. C. 1966. Compliance without pressure: The foot-in-the-door technique. *Journal of Personality and Social Psychology* 4:195–202.

FREEDMAN, J. L.; SEARS, D. O.; AND CARLSMITH, J. M. 1981. *Social psychology,* 4th ed. Englewood Cliffs, N. J.: Prentice-Hall.

FRENCH, J. D. 1957. The reticular formation. *Scientific American* 196:54–60.

FREUD, A. 1946. *The ego and the mechanisms of defense.* London: Hogarth Press.

FREUD, S. 1900. The interpretation of dreams. In Strachey, J., trans. and ed., *The complete psychological works,* vols. 4–5. New York: Norton, 1976.

FREUD, S. 1901. The psychopathology of everyday life. Translated by Tyson, A. New York: Norton, 1971.

FREUD, S. 1905. Three essays on the theory of sexuality. In Strachey, J., trans. and ed., *The complete psychological works,* vol. 7. New York: Norton, 1976.

FREUD, S. 1911. Psychoanalytic notes upon an autobiographical account of a case of paranoia (dementia paranoides). In Strachey, J., trans. and ed., *The complete psychological works,* vol. 12. New York: Norton, 1976.

FREUD, S. 1913a. *Totem and taboo.* Translated by Strachey, J. New York: Norton, 1952.

FREUD, S. 1913b. *Further recommendations in the technique of psychoanalysis.* In Strachey, J., trans. The standard edition, vol. 12. New York: Norton, 1976.

FREUD, S. 1917a. *A general introduction to psychoanalysis.* Translated by Riviere, J. New York: Washington Square Press, 1952.

FREUD, S. 1917b. Introductory lectures on psychoanalysis. In Strachey, J., trans. and ed., *The complete psychological works,* vol. 15. New York: Norton, 1976.

FREUD, S. 1923. *The ego and the id.* Translated by Riviere, J. New York: Norton, 1962.

FREUD, S. 1925. Some psychical consequences of the anatomical distinction between the sexes. In Strachey, J., trans. and ed., *The complete psychological works,* vol. 19. New York: Norton, 1976.

FREUD, S. 1926. *Inhibitions, symptoms, and anxiety.* Translated by Strachey, J. New York: Norton, 1972.

FREUD, S. 1933. *New introductory lectures on psychoanalysis.* Translated by Strachey, J. New York: Norton, 1965.

FREUD, S. 1940. *An outline of psychoanalysis.* Translated by Strachey, J. New York: Norton, 1970.

FREUD, S., AND BREUER, J. 1895. Studies on hysteria. In Strachey, J., trans. and ed., *The complete psychological works,* vol. 2. New York: Norton, 1976.

FRIDLUND, A. J.; EKMAN, P.; AND OSTER, H. 1983. Facial expression of emotion: Review of literature, 1970–1983. In Siegman, A., ed., *Nonverbal behavior and communication.* Hillsdale, N.J.: Erlbaum.

FRIEDMAN, M. I., AND STRICKER, E. M. 1976. The physiological psychology of hunger: A physiological perspective. *Psychological Review* 83:409–31.

FRISCH, H. L. 1977. Sex stereotypes in adult-infant play. *Child Development* 48:1671–75.

FRISHBERG, N. 1975. Arbitrariness and iconicity: Historical change in American Sign Language. *Language* 51:696–719.

FROMKIN, V. A. 1973. *Speech errors as linguistic evidence.* The Hague: Mouton.

FROMKIN, V.; KRASHEN, S.; CURTISS, S.; RIGLER, D.; AND RIGLER, M. 1974. The development of language in Genie: A case of language acquisition beyond the "critical period." *Brain and Language* 1:81–107.

FUNKENSTEIN, D. H. 1956. Nor-epinephrine-like and epinephrine-like substances in relation to human behavior. *Journal of Mental Diseases* 124:58–68.

GALLISTEL, C. R. 1973. Self-stimulation: The neurophysiology of reward and motivation. In Deutsch, J. A., ed., *The physiological basis of memory,* pp. 175–267. New York: Academic Press.

GALLISTEL, C. R. 1980. *The organization of action.* Hillsdale, N.J.: Erlbaum.

GALLISTEL, C. R. 1983. Self-stimulation. In Deutsch, J. A., ed., *The physiological basis of memory,* pp. 269–349. New York: Academic Press.

GALTON, F. 1869. *Hereditary genius: An inquiry into its laws and consequences.* London: Macmillan.

GALTON, F. 1883. *Inquiries into human faculty and its development.* London: Macmillan.

GARCIA, J., AND KOELLING, R. A. 1966. The relation of cue to consequence in avoidance learning. *Psychonomic Science* 4:123–24.

GARDNER, R. A., AND GARDNER, B. T. 1969. Teaching sign language to a chimpanzee. *Science* 165:664–72.

GARDNER, R. A., AND GARDNER, B. T. 1975. Early signs of language in child and chimpanzee. *Science* 187:752–53.

GARDNER, R. A., AND GARDNER, B. T. 1978. Comparative psychology and language acquisition. *Annals of the New York Academy of Science* 309:37–76.

GARRETT, M. F. 1975. The analysis of sentence production. In Bower, G. H., ed., *The psychology of learning and motivation,* vol. 9, pp. 133–77. New York: Academic Press.

GAZZANIGA, M. S. 1967. The split brain in man. *Scientific American* 217:24–29.

GAZZANIGA, M. S. 1970. *The bisected brain.* New York: Appleton-Century-Crofts.

GEFFEN, G.; BRADSHAW, J. L.; AND WALLACE, G. 1971. Interhemispheric effects on reaction time to verbal and nonverbal visual stimuli. *Journal of Experimental Psychology* 87:415–22.

GELDARD, F. A. 1962. *Fundamentals of psychology.* New York: Wiley.

GELDARD, F. A. 1972. *The human senses.* New York: Wiley.

GELMAN, R. 1972. Logical capacity of very young children: Number invariance rules. *Child Development* 43:75–90.

GELMAN, R. 1978. Cognitive development. *Annual Review of Psychology* 29:297–332.

GELMAN, R., AND BAILLARGEON, R. 1983. A review of some Piagetian concepts. In Mussen, P., ed., *Carmichael's manual of child psychology: Vol. 3. Cognitive development* (Markman, E. M. and Flavell, J. H., volume editors), pp. 167–230. New York: Wiley.

GELMAN, R., AND GALLISTEL, C. R. 1978. *The young child's understanding of number: A window on early cognitive development.* Cambridge, Mass.: Harvard University Press.

GERARD, H. B., AND MATHEWSON, G. C. 1966. The effects of severity of initiation on liking for a group: A replication. *Journal of Experimental Social Psychology* 2:278–87.

GERARD, H. B.; WILHELMY, R. A.; AND CONNOLLEY, E. S. 1968. Conformity and group size. *Journal of Personality and Social Psychology* 8:78–82.

GESCHWIND, N. 1970. The organization of language and the brain. *Science* 170:940–44.

GESCHWIND, N. 1972. Language and the brain. *Scientific American* 226:76–83.

GESCHWIND, N. 1975. The apraxias: Neural mechanisms of disorders of learned movement. *American Scientist* 63:188–95.

GESELL, A. L., AND THOMPSON, H. 1929. Learning and growth in identical twins: An experimental study by the method of co-twin control. *Genetic Psychology Monographs,* vol. 6.

GIBSON, E. J. 1969. *Principles of perceptual learning and development.* New York: Appleton-Century-Crofts.

GIBSON, E. J. 1984. Perceptual development from the ecological approach. In Lamb, M. E.; Brown, A. L.; and Rogoff, B., eds., *Advances in developmental psychology,* vol. 3., pp. 243–85. Hillsdale, N.J.: Erlbaum.

GIBSON, E. J.; GIBSON, J. J.; PICK, A. D.; AND OSSER, H. A. 1962. A developmental study of the discrimination of letter-like forms. *Journal of Comparative and Physiological Psychology* 55:897–906.

GIBSON, E. J.; SHURCLIFF, A.; AND YONAS, A. 1970. Utilization of spelling patterns by deaf and hearing subjects. In Levin, H., and Williams, J. P., eds., *Basic studies on reading,* pp. 57–73. New York: Basic Books.

GIBSON, J. J. 1950. *The perception of the visual world.* Boston: Houghton Mifflin.

GIBSON, J. J. 1966. *The senses considered as perceptual systems.* Boston: Houghton Mifflin.

GIBSON, J. J. 1979. *The ecological approach to visual perception.* Boston: Houghton Mifflin.

GIBSON, J. J., AND GIBSON, E. J. 1955. Perceptual learning: Differentiation or enrichment? *Psychological Review* 62:32–41.

GIBSON, R. W.; COHEN, M. B.; AND COHEN, R. A. 1959. On the dynamics of the manic-depressive personality. *American Journal of Psychiatry* 115:1101–7.

GILLIGAN, C. 1982. *In a different voice: Psychological theory and womens' development.* Cambridge, Mass.: Harvard University Press.

GINZBERG, L. 1909. *The legends of the Jews,* vol. 1. Translated by Szold, H. Philadelphia: Jewish Publication Society of America.

GLADUE, B. A.; GREEN, R.; AND HELLMAN, R. E. 1984. Neuroendocrine responses to estrogen and sexual orientation. *Science* 225:1496–99.

GLANZER, M., AND CUNITZ, A. 1966. Two storage mechanisms in free recall. *Journal of Verbal Learning and Verbal Behavior* 5:531–60.

GLEASON, K. K., AND REYNIERSE, J. H. 1969. The behavioral significance of pheromones in vertebrates. *Psychological Bulletin* 71:58–73.

GLEITMAN, H. 1963. Place-learning. *Scientific American* 209:116–22.

GLEITMAN, H. 1971. Forgetting of long-term memories in animals. In Honig, W. K., and James, P. H. R., eds., *Animal memory,* pp. 2–46. New York: Academic Press.

GLEITMAN, H. 1983. Reflections on the psychology of drama and the dramatic experience. Address given at the 1983 meetings of the American Psychological Association, Annaheim, California.

GLEITMAN, H. 1985. Some trends in the study of cognition. In Koch, S., and Leary, D. E., eds., *A century of psychology as science*, pp. 420–36. New York: McGraw-Hill.

GLEITMAN, H., AND GILLETT, E. 1957. The effect of intention upon learning. *Journal of General Psychology* 57:137–49.

GLEITMAN, L. R. 1981. Maturational determinants of language growth. *Cognition* 10:103–14.

GLEITMAN, L. R.; GLEITMAN, H.; AND SHIPLEY, E. F. 1972. The emergence of the child as grammarian. *Cognition* 1(2):137–64.

GLEITMAN, L. R.; SHIPLEY, E. F.; AND SMITH, C. 1978. Old and new ways not to study comprehension. *Journal of Child Language* 5:501–20.

GLEITMAN, L. R., AND WANNER, E. 1982. Language acquisition: The state of the art. In Wanner, E., and Gleitman, L. R., eds., *Language acquisition: State of the art*. New York: Cambridge University Press.

GLEITMAN, L. R., AND WANNER, E. 1984. Current issues in language learning. In Bornstein, M. H., and Lamb, M. E., eds., *Developmental psychology: An advanced textbook*. Hillsdale, N. J.: Erlbaum.

GLICK, J. 1975. Cognitive development in cross-cultural perspective. In Horowitz, F. G., ed., *Review of child development research*, vol. 4. Chicago: University of Chicago Press.

GLORINGEN, I., GLORINGEN, K.; HAUB, G.; AND QUATEMBER, R. 1969. Comparison of verbal behavior in righthanded and non-righthanded patients with anatomically verified lesions of one hemisphere. *Cortex* 5:43–52.

GLUCKSBERG, S. 1962. The influence of strength of drive on functional fixedness and perceptual recognition. *Journal of Experimental Psychology* 63:36–41.

GLUECK, S., AND GLUECK, E. 1956. *Physique and delinquency.* New York: Harper.

GODDEN, D. R. AND BADDELEY, A. D. 1975. Context-dependent memory in two natural environments: On land and underwater. *British Journal of Psychology* 66:325–31.

GOFFMAN, E. 1959. *The presentation of self in everyday life.* Garden City, N. Y.: Anchor Books, Doubleday.

GOFFMAN, E. 1961. *Asylums.* Chicago: Aldine.

GOFFMAN, E. 1974. *Frame-analysis.* New York: Harper & Row.

GOLD, R. 1978. On the meaning of nonconservation. In Lesgold, A. M.; Pellegrino, J. W.; Fokkema, S. D.; and Glaser, R., eds., *Cognitive psychology and instruction.* New York: Plenum.

GOLDBERG, L. R. 1975. Toward a taxonomy of personality descriptive terms: A description of the O. R. I. Taxonomy Project. *Oregon Research Institute Technical Report,* vol. 15 (2).

GOLDBERG, L. R. 1981a. Developing a taxonomy of trait-descriptive terms. In Fiske, D. W., ed., *Problems with language imprecision,* pp. 43–66. San Francisco: Jossey-Bass.

GOLDBERG, L. R. 1981b. Language and individual differences: The search for universals in personality lexicons. In Wheeler, L., ed., *Review of Personality and Social Psychology* 2:141–65.

GOLDFARB, W. 1955. Emotional and intellectual consequences of psychological deprivation in infancy: A reevaluation. In Hock, P. H., and Zubin, eds., *Psychopathology of childhood.* New York: Grune and Stratton.

GOLDIN-MEADOW, S. 1982. Fragile and resilient properties of language learning. In Wanner, E., and Gleitman, L. R., eds., *Language acquisition: State of the art.* New York: Cambridge University Press.

GOLDSTEIN, E. B. 1984. *Sensation and perception,* 2nd ed. Belmont, Calif.: Wadsworth.

GOMBRICH, E. H. 1961. *Art and illusion.* Princeton, N. J.: Bollingen Series, Princeton University Press.

GORDON, H. 1923. Mental and scholastic tests among retarded children. *Educational Pamphlet,* no. 44. London: Board of Education.

GOTTESMAN, I. I., AND SHIELDS, J. 1982. *Schizophrenia: The epigenetic puzzle.* New York: Cambridge University Press.

GOTTLIEB, G. 1976a. Conceptions of prenatal development: Behavioral embryology. *Psychological Review* 83:215–34.

GOTTLIEB, G. 1976b. The role of experience in the development of behavior and the nervous system. In Gottlieb, G., ed., *Neural and behavioral specificity,* pp. 25–56. New York: Academic Press.

GOUGH, H. G. 1957. *California psychological inventory manual.* Palo Alto, Calif.: Consulting Psychologists' Press.

GOULD, S. J. 1977. *Ontogeny and phylogeny.* Cambridge, Mass.: Harvard University Press.

GOULD, S. J. 1978. Sociobiology: The art of storytelling. *New Scientist* 80:530–33.

GOY, R. W. 1968. Organizing effect of androgen on the behavior of rhesus monkeys. In Michael, R. P., ed., *Endocrinology and human behavior.* London: Oxford University Press.

GRAHAM, C. H., AND HSIA, Y. 1954. Luminosity curves for normal and dichromatic subjects including a case of unilateral color blindness. *Science* 120:780.

GRAY, G. W. 1948. The great ravelled knot. *Scientific American* 179:26–38.

GRAY, S. 1977. Social aspects of body image: Perception of normalcy of weight and affect of college undergraduates. *Perceptual and Motor Skills* 45: 1035–40.

GREEN, D. M. 1976. *An introduction to hearing.* New York: Academic Press.

GREEN, D. M., AND SWETS, J. A. 1966. *Signal detection theory and psychophysics.* New York: Wiley.

GREEN, R. 1969. Age-intelligence relationships between ages sixteen and sixty-four: A rising trend. *Developmental Psychology* 1:618–27.

GREENFIELD, P. M. 1976. Cross-cultural research and Piagetian theory: Paradox and progress. In Riegel, K., and Meacham, J., eds., *The developing individual in a changing world,* vol. 1. The Hague: Mouton.

GREENFIELD, P. M., AND SMITH, J. H. 1976. *The structure of communication in early language development.* New York: Academic Press.

GREGORY, R. L. 1963. Distortion of visual space as inappropriate constancy scaling. *Nature* 199:678–80.

GREGORY, R. L. 1966. Visual illusions. In Foss, B., ed., *New horizons in psychology.* Baltimore: Penguin Books.

GREGORY, R. L. 1968. Visual illusions. *Scientific American* 219:66–76.

GREGORY, R. L., AND WALLACE, J. G. 1963. Recovery from early blindness: A case study. *Experimental Psychology Society Monograph,* No. 2.

GREVEN, P. J., JR. 1970. *Four generations: Population, land, and family in colonial Andover, Massachusetts.* Ithaca: N. Y.: Cornell University Press.

GRICE, H. P. 1968. Utterer's meaning, sentence-meaning and word-meaning. *Foundations of Language* 4:225–42.

GRILL, H. J., AND BERRIDGE, K. C. 1985. Taste reactivity as a measure of the neural control of palatability. *Progress in psychobiology and physiological psychology,* vol. 11, pp. 1–61. New York: Academic Press.

GUILFORD, J. P. 1967. *The nature of human intelligence.* New York: McGraw-Hill.

GUTTMAN, N., AND KALISH, H. I. 1956. Discriminability and stimulus generalization. *Journal of Experimental Psychology* 51:79–88.

GUYTON, A. C. 1981. *Textbook of medical physiology.* Philadelphia: Saunders.

HABER, R. N. 1969. Eidetic images. *Scientific American* 220:36–44.

HALL, C. S. 1953. A cognitive theory of dream symbols. *Journal* of General Psychology 48:169–86.

HALL, C. S. 1966. *The meaning of dreams.* New York: McGraw-Hill.

HALL, C. S., AND VAN DE CASTLE, R. 1966. *The content analysis of dreams.* New York: Appleton-Century-Crofts.

HALL, E. T. 1959. *The silent language.* New York: Doubleday.

HALVERSON, H. M. 1931. An experimental study of prehension infants by means of systematic cinema records. *Genetic Psychology Monographs* 47:47–63.

HAMBURG, D. A.; MOOS, R. H.; AND YALOM, I. D. 1968. Studies of distress in the menstrual cycle and the postpartum period. In Michael, R. P., ed., *Endocrinology and human behavior,* pp. 94–116. London: Oxford University Press.

HAMPSON, J. L., AND HAMPSON, J. G. 1961. The ontogenesis of sexual behavior in man. In Young, W. C., ed., *Sex and internal secretions,* 3rd ed. Baltimore: Williams & Wilkins.

HARE, R. D. 1965. Temporal gradients of fear arousal in psychopaths. *Journal of Abnormal Psychology* 70:422–45.

HARE, R. D. 1970. *Psychopathy: Theory and research.* New York: Wiley.

HAREVEN, T. K. 1978. The last stage: Historical adulthood and old age. In Erikson, E. H., ed., *Adulthood,* pp. 201–16. New York: Norton.

HARKINS, S., AND GREEN, R. G. 1975. Discriminability and criterion differences between extraverts and introverts during vigilance. *Journal of Research in Personality* 9:335–40.

HARLOW, H. F. 1949. The formation of learning sets. *Psychological Review* 56:51–65.

HARLOW, H. F. 1950. Learning and satiation of response in intrinsically motivated complex puzzle performance in monkeys. *Journal of Comparative and Physiological Psychology* 43:289–94.

HARLOW, H. F. 1958. The nature of love. *American Psychologist* 13:673–85.

HARLOW, H. F. 1959. Learning set and error factor theory. In Koch, S., ed., *Psychology: A study of a science,* vol. 2, pp. 492–537. New York: McGraw-Hill.

HARLOW, H. F. 1962. The heterosexual affectional system in monkeys. *American Psychologist* 17:1–9.

HARLOW, H. F., AND HARLOW, M. K, 1972. The young monkeys. *Readings in Psychology Today.* Albany, N.Y.: Delmar Publishers, CRM Books.

HARLOW, H. F., AND NOVAK, M. A. 1973. Psychopathological perspectives. *Perspectives in Biology and Medicine* 16:461–78.

HARLOW, H. F., AND ZIMMERMAN, R. R. 1959. Affectional responses in the infant monkey. *Science* 130:421–32.

HARPER, R. A. 1959. *Psychoanalysis and psychotherapy: 36 systems.* Englewood Cliffs, N. J.: Prentice-Hall.

HARRELL, J. P. 1980. Psychological factors and hypertension: A status report. *Psychological Bulletin* 87:482–501.

HARRIS, G. W., AND MICHAEL, R. P. 1964. The activation of sexual behavior by hypothalamic implants of estrogen. *Journal of Physiology* 171:275–301.

HARRIS, L. J. 1978. Sex differences in spatial ability: Possible environmental, genetic, and neurological factors. In Kinsbourne, M., *Asymmetrical functions of the brain.* Cambridge, England: Cambridge University Press.

HARRIS, M. 1974. *Cows, pigs, wars, and witches.* New York: Random House.

HARRIS, P. L. 1983. Infant cognition. In Mussen, P., ed., *Carmichael's manual of child psychology: Vol. 2. Infancy and developmental psychobiology* (Haith, M. M. and Campos, J. J., volume editors), pp. 689–782. New York: Wiley.

HART, B. L., ed. 1976. *Experimental psychobiology.* San Francisco: Freeman.

HARTSHORNE, H., AND MAY, M. A. 1928. *Studies in the nature of character,* vol. 1. New York: Macmillan.

HASE, H. D., AND GOLDBERG, L. R. 1967. Comparative validities of different strategies of constructing personality inventory scales. *Psychological Bulletin* 67:231–48.

HASS, R. G. 1981. Effects of source characteristics on cognitive responses and persuasion. In Petty, R. E.; Ostrom, T. M.; and Brock, T. C., eds., *Cognitive responses in persuasion,* pp. 141–72. Hillsdale, N. J.: Erlbaum.

HEALY, A. F., AND MILLER, G. A. 1970. The verb as the main determinant of sentence meaning. *Psychonomic Science* 20:372.

HEARST, E. 1972. Psychology across the chessboard. In *Readings in Psychology Today,* 2nd ed. Albany, N. Y.: Delmar Publishers, CRM Books.

HEATH, R. 1964. Pleasure response of human subjects to direct stimulation of the brain: Physiologic and psychodynamic considerations. In Heath, R., ed., *The role of pleasure in behavior,* pp. 219–43. New York: Harper and Row.

HEBB, D. O. 1946. On the nature of fear. *Psychological Review* 53:259–76.

HEBB, D. O. 1949. *The organization of behavior: A neuropsychological theory.* New York: Wiley.

HEDIGER, H. 1968. *The psychology and behavior of animals in zoos and circuses.* New York: Dover.

HEIDBREDER, E. 1933. *Seven psychologies.* New York: Appleton-Century-Crofts.

HEIDER, F. 1958. *The psychology of interpersonal relationships.* New York: Wiley.

HEIM, A. W. 1954. *The appraisal of intelligence.* London: Methuen.

HEINICKE, C., AND WESTHEIMER, I. 1966. *Brief separations.* London: Longmans, Green.

HELD, R., AND BOSSOM, J. 1961. Neonatal deprivation and adult rearrangement: Complementary techniques for analyzing plastic sensory-motor coordinations. *Journal of Comparative and Physiological Psychology* 54:33–37.

HELLER, H. C.; CRANSHAW, L. I.; AND HAMMEL, H. T. 1978. The thermostat of vertebrate animals. *Scientific American* 239:102–13.

HELMHOLTZ, H. 1909. *Wissenschaftliche Abhandlungen, II,* pp. 764–843.

HENLE, M. 1962. On the relation between logic and thinking. *Psychological Review* 69:366–78.

HENRY, J. P., AND CASSEL, J. C. 1969. Psychosocial factors in essential hypertension. *American Journal of Epidemiology* 90:171.

HERING, E. 1920. *Outlines of a theory of the light sense,* pp. 150–51. Edited by Hurvich L. M. and Jameson, D. Cambridge, Mass.: Harvard University Press.

HERMAN, C. P., AND POLIVY, J. 1980. Restrained eating. In Stunkard, A. J., ed., *Obesity,* pp. 208–25. Philadelphia: Saunders.

HERMAN, H. C., AND MACK, D. 1975. Restrained and unrestrained eating. *Journal of Personality* 43:647–60.

HERODOTUS. ca. 460 B.C. *The Persian wars.* Translated by G. Rawlinson. Modern Library edition. New York: Random House, 1942.

HESS, E. H. 1958. "Imprinting" in animals. *Scientific American* 198:82.

HESS, E. H. 1959. Imprinting. *Science* 130:133–41.

HESS, E. H. 1973. *Imprinting.* New York: Van Nostrand Rheinhold.

HESS, R. D. 1970. Social class and ethnic influences on socialization. In Mussen, P. H., ed., *Carmichael's manual of child psychology,* 3rd ed., vol. 2, pp. 457–558. New York: Wiley.

HESTON, L. L. 1966. Psychiatric disorders in foster home reared children of schizophrenic mothers. *British Journal of Psychiatry* 112:819–25.

HESTON, L. L., AND DENNEY, D. 1968. Interactions between early life experience and biological factors in schizophrenia. In Rosenthal, D., and Kety, S. S., eds., *The transmission of schizophrenia,* pp. 363–76. New York: Pergamon.

HETHERINGTON, E. M., AND PARKE, R. D. 1979. *Child psychology: A contemporary viewpoint,* 2nd ed. New York: McGraw-Hill.

HILGARD, E. R. 1977. *Divided consciousness: Multiple controls in human thought and action.* New York: Wiley.

HILL, C. T.; RUBIN, L.; AND PEPLAU, L. A. 1976. Breakups before marriage: The end of 103 affairs. *Journal of Social Issues* 32:147–68.

HILL, L. B. 1955. *Psychotherapeutic intervention in schizophrenia.* Chicago: University of Chicago Press.

HINDE, R. A. 1966 and 1970. *Animal behavior,* 1st and 2nd eds. New York: McGraw-Hill.

HINDE, R. A. 1974. *Biological bases of human social behavior.* New York: McGraw-Hill.

HINDE, R. A. 1983. Ethology and child development. In Mussen, P. H., ed., *Carmichael's manual of child psychology: Vol. 2. Infancy and developmental psychobiology* (Haith, M. M. and Campos, J. J., volume editors), pp. 27–94. New York: Wiley.

HINELINE, P. N., AND RACHLIN, H. 1969. Escape and avoidance of shock by pigeons pecking a key. *Journal of the Experimental Analysis of Behavior* 12:533–38.

HINTZMAN, D. L. 1978. *The psychology of learning and memory.* San Francisco: Freeman.

HIROTO, D. S., AND SELIGMAN, M. E. P. 1975. Generality of learned helplessness in man. *Journal of Personality and Social Psychology* 31:311–27.

HIRSCH, J., AND KNITTLE, J. L. 1970. Cellularity of obese and nonobese human adipose tissue. *Federation of American Societies for Experimental Biology: Federation Proceedings* 29:1516–21.

HIRSH-PASEK, K.; GLEITMAN, H.; AND GLEITMAN, L. R. 1978. What did the brain say to the mind? In Sinclair, A.; Jarvella, R. J.; and Levelt, W. J. M., eds., *The child's conception of language.* Berlin: Springer-Verlag.

HIRSH-PASEK, K.; KEMLER-NELSON, D. G.; JUSCZYK, P. W.; WRIGHT, K.; AND DRUSS, B. (forthcoming). Clauses are perceptual units for prelinguistic infants.

HIRSH-PASEK, K., AND TREIMAN, R. 1982. Doggerel: Motherese in a new context. *Journal of Child Language* 9:229–37.

HOBBES, T. 1651. *Leviathan.* Baltimore: Penguin Books, 1968.

HOCHBERG, J. E. 1970. Attention, organization and consciousness. In Mostofsky, D. I., ed., *Attention: Contemporary theory and analysis,* pp. 99–124. New York: Appleton-Century-Crofts.

HOCHBERG, J. E. 1978a. *Perception,* 2nd ed. Englewood Cliffs, N. J.: Prentice-Hall.

HOCHBERG, J. E. 1978b. Art and perception. In Carterette, E. C., and Friedman, M. P., eds., *Handbook of perception,* vol. 10, pp. 225–55. New York: Academic Press.

HOCHBERG, J. E. 1980. Pictorial functions and perceptual structures. In Hagen, M. A., ed., *The perception of pictures,* vol. 2, pp. 47–93. New York: Academic Press.

HODGKINS, A. L., AND HUXLEY, A. F. 1939. Action potentials recorded from inside nerve fiber. *Nature* 144:710–11.

HOEBEL, B. G., AND TEITELBAUM, P. 1976. Weight regulation in normal and hyperphagic rats. *Journal of Physiological and Comparative Psychology* 61:189–93.

HÖHN, E. O. 1969. The phalarope. *Scientific American* 220:104.

HOLLIS, K. I. 1982. Pavlovian conditioning of signal-centered action patterns and autonomic behavior: A biological analysis of function. In Rosenblatt, J. S.; Hinde, R. A.; Beer, C.; and Busnel, M., eds., *Advances in the study of behavior,* vol. 12, pp. 1–64. New York: Academic Press.

HOFFMAN, L. W. 1974. Effects of maternal employment on the child. A review of the research. *Developmental Psychology* 10:204–28.

HOFFMAN, M. L. 1970. Moral development. In Mussen, P. H., ed., *Carmichael's manual of child psychology,* 3rd. ed., vol. 2, pp.

457–558. New York: Wiley.

HOFFMAN, M. L. 1975a. Altruistic behavior and the parent-child relationship. *Journal of Personality and Social Psychology* 31: 937–43.

HOFFMAN, M. L. 1975b. Developmental synthesis of affect and cognition and its implications for altruistic motivation. *Developmental Psychology* 11:607–22.

HOFFMAN, M. L. 1976. Empathy, role-taking, guilt, and the development of altruistic motives. In Lickona, T., ed., *Moral development and behavior,* pp. 124–43. New York: Holt, Rinehart and Winston.

HOFFMAN, M. L. 1977. Empathy, its development and prosocial implications. In Keasey, C. B., ed., *Nebraska Symposium on Motivation* 25:169–217.

HOHN, E. O. 1966. The phalarope. *Scientific American* 220: 104–11.

HOLLINGSHEAD, A. B., AND REDLICH, F. C. 1958. *Social class and mental illness: A community study.* New York: Wiley.

HOLLIS, K. I. 1982. Pavlovian conditioning of signal-centered action patterns and autonomic behavior: A biological analysis of function. In Rosenblatt, J. S.; Hinde, R. A.; Beer, C.; and Busnel, M., eds., *Advances in the study of behavior,* vol. 12, pp. 1–64. New York: Academic Press.

HOOKER, E. 1957. The adjustment of the male overt homosexual. *Journal of Projective Techniques* 21:18–31.

HOOKER, E. 1965. Male homosexuals and their "worlds." In Marmor, J., ed., *Sexual inversion,* pp. 83–107. New York: Basic Books.

HORN, J. L., AND CATTELL, R. B. 1967. Age differences in fluid and crystallized intelligence. *Acta Psychologica* 26:107–29.

HORN, J. L., AND DONALDSON, G. 1976. On the myth of intellectual decline in adulthood. *American Psychologist* 31:701–19.

HORN, J. L.; LOEHLIN, J.; AND WELLERMAN, L. 1975. Preliminary report of Texas adoption project. In Munsinger, H., The adopted child's IQ: A critical review. *Psychological Bulletin* 82:623–59.

HORNE, R. L., AND PICARD, R. S. 1979. Psychosocial risk factors for lung cancer. *Psychosomatic Medicine* 41:503–14.

HORNER, M. S. 1970. Femininity and successful achievement: A basic inconsistency. In Bardwick, J. M.; Dorwan, E.; Horner, M. S.; and Gutmann, D., eds., *Feminine personality and conflict,* pp. 45–74. Belmont, Calif.: Brooks/Cole.

HOVLAND, C. I., AND WEISS, W. 1952. The influence of source credibility on communication effectiveness. *Public Opinion Quarterly* 15:635–50.

HOWARD, D. V. 1983. *Cognitive psychology.* New York: Macmillan.

HOWITT, D., AND MCCABE, J. 1978. Attitudes do predict behavior–In males at least. *British Journal of Social and Clinical Psychology* 106:261–65.

HRDY, S. H. 1981. *The woman that never evolved.* Cambridge, Mass.: Harvard University Press.

HRDY, S. H., AND WILLIAMS, G. C. 1983. Behavioral biology and the double standard. In Wasser, S. K., ed., *The social behavior of female vertebrates,* pp. 3–17. New York: Academic Press.

HUBEL, D. H. 1963. The visual cortex of the brain. *Scientific American* 209:54–62.

HUBEL, D. H., AND WIESEL, T. N. 1959. Receptive fields of single neurones in the cat's visual cortex. *Journal of Physiology* 148:574–91.

HULL, C. L. 1943. *Principles of behavior.* New York: Appleton-Century-Crofts.

HUMPHREY, G. 1951. *Thinking: An introduction to its experimental psychology.* New York: Wiley.

HUMPHREYS, L. G. 1939. The effect of random alternation of reinforcement on the acquisition and extinction of conditioned eyelid reactions. *Journal of Experimental Psychology* 25:141–58.

A57

HUMPHREYS, L. G. 1957. Characteristics of type concepts with special reference to Sheldon's typology. *Psychological Bulletin* 54:218–28.

HUNT, E. 1976. Varieties of cognitive power. In Resnick, L. B., ed., *The nature of intelligence*, pp. 237–60. Hillsdale, N. J.: Erlbaum.

HUNT, E. 1978. Mechanics of verbal ability. *Psychological Review* 85: 109–30.

HUNT, E.; LUNNEBORG, C.; AND LEWIS, J. 1975. What does it mean to be high verbal? *Cognitive Psychology* 7:194–227.

HUNT, J. M. 1961. *Intelligence and experience.* New York: Ronald Press.

HUNTER, R., AND MACALPINE, I. 1974. *Psychiatry for the poor.* Folkestone, KY.: Dawson.

HURVICH, L. M. 1981. *Color vision.* Sunderland, Mass.: Sinauer Associates, Publications.

HURVICH, L. M., AND JAMESON, D. 1957. An opponent-process theory of color vision. *Psychological Review* 64:384–404.

HUTCHINSON, R. R., AND RENFREW, J. W. 1966. Stalking attack and eating behaviors elicited from the same sites in the hypothalamus. *Journal of Comparative and Physiological Psychology* 61:360–67.

HUTTENLOCHER, J. 1974. The origins of language comprehension. In Solso, R. L., ed., *Theories in cognitive psychology.* Hillsdale, N. J.: Erlbaum.

HYDE, D. M. 1959. An investigation of Piaget's theories of the development of the concept of number. Unpublished doctoral dissertation. University of London. (Quoted in Flavell, J. H., *The developmental psychology of Jean Piaget,* p. 383. New York: Van Nostrand Reinhold).

ILYIN, N. A., AND ILYIN, V. N. 1930. Temperature effects on the color of the Siamese cat. *Journal of Heredity* 21:309–18.

IMPERATO-McGINLEY, J.; GUERRERO, L.; GAUTIER, T.; AND PETERSON, R. E. 1974. Steroid 5-alpha reductase deficiency in man: An inherited form of male pseudohermaphroditism. *Science* 186:1213–15.

IMPERATO-McGINLEY, J.; PETERSON, R. E.; GAUTIER, T.; AND STURLA, E. 1979. Androgens and the evolution of male-gender identity among male pseudohermaphrodites with 5-alpha reductase deficiency. *The New England Journal of Medicine* 300:1233–37.

INBAU, F. E., AND REID, J. E. 1953. *Truth and deception: The polygraph ("lie detector") technique.* Baltimore: Williams & Wilkins.

INGVAR, D. H., AND LASSEN, N. A. 1979. Activity distribution in the cerebral cortex in organic dementia as revealed by measurements of regional cerebral blood flow. *Bayer Symposium VII. Brain function in old age,* 268–77.

INHELDER, B., AND PIAGET, J. 1958. *The growth of logical thinking from childhood to adolescence.* New York: Basic Books.

IVINS, W. M., JR. 1975. *On the rationalization of sight.* New York: Da Capo Press.

JACKSON, M., AND McCLELLAND, J. L. 1975. Sensory and cognitive determinants of reading speed. *Journal of Verbal Learning and Verbal Behavior* 14:565–74.

JACKSON, M., AND McCLELLAND, J. L. 1979. Processing determinants of reading speed. *Journal of Experimental Psychology: General* 108:151–81.

JACOBS, A. 1955. Formation of new associations to words selected on the basis of reaction-time-GSR combinations. *Journal of Abnormal and Social Psychology* 51:371–77.

JACOBSON, E. 1932. The electrophysiology of mental activities. *American Journal of Psychology* 44:677–94.

JACOBSON, S. W., AND KAGAN, J. 1979. Interpreting "imitative" responses in early infancy. *Science* 205:215–17.

JAMES, W. 1890. *Principles of psychology.* New York: Henry Holt.

JAMES, W. T. 1941. Morphological form and its relation to behavior. In Stockard, C. R., *The genetic and endocrinic basis for differences in form and behavior,* pp. 525–643. Philadelphia: Wistar Institute.

JAMESON, D., AND HURVICH, L. 1975. From contrast to assimilation: In art and in the eye. *Leonardo* 8:125–31.

JANIS, I. L.; MAHL, G. G.; KAGAN, J.; AND HOLT, R. R. 1969. *Personality: Dynamics, development and assessment.* New York: Harcourt, Brace and World.

JENCKS, C.; SMITH, M.; ACLAND, H.; BANE, M. J.; COHEN, D.; GINTIS, H.; HEYNS, B.; AND MICHELSON, S. 1972. *Inequality: A reassessment of the effect of family and schooling in America.* New York: Basic Books.

JENKINS, H. M., AND MOORE, B. R. 1973. The form of the auto-shaped response with food or water reinforcers. *Journal of the Experimental Analysis of Behavior* 20:163–81.

JENKINS, J. G., AND DALLENBACH, K. M. 1924. Oblivescence during sleep and waking. *American Journal of Psychology* 35:605–12.

JENSEN, A. R. 1965. Scoring the Stroop test. *Acta Psychologica* 24:398–408.

JENSEN, A. R. 1969. How much can we boost I.Q. and scholastic achievement? *Harvard Educational Review* 39:1–123.

JENSEN, A. R. 1973. *Educability and group differences.* New York: Harper & Row.

JOHNSON, J. D.; KRETCHMER, N.; AND SIMOONS, F. J. 1974. Lactose malabsorption: Its biology and history. *Advances in Pediatrics* 21:197–237.

JOHNSON, N. F. 1965. The psychological reality of phrase structure rules. *Journal of Verbal Learning and Verbal Behavior* 5:469–75.

JOHNSON, R. E. 1979. *Juvenile delinquency and its origins.* New York: Cambridge University Press.

JONES, E. 1954. *Hamlet and Oedipus.* New York: Doubleday.

JONES, E. E., AND NISBETT, R. E. 1972. The actor and the observer: Divergent perceptions of the cause of behavior. In Jones, E. E.; Karouse, D. E.; Kelley, H. H.; Nisbett, R. E.; Valins, S.; and Weiner, B., eds., *Attribution: Perceiving the causes of behavior.* Morristown, N. J.: General Learning Press.

JONES, E. E.; DAVIS, K. E.; AND GERGEN, K. J. 1961. Role playing variations and their informational value for person perception. *Journal of Abnormal and Social Psychology* 63:302–10.

JONES, E. E.; KANOUSE, D. E.; KELLEY, H. H.; NISBETT, R. E.; VALINS, S.; AND WEINER, B. 1971. *Attribution: Perceiving the causes of behavior.* Morristown, N. J.: General Learning Press.

JONES, H. E., AND KAPLAN, O. J. 1945. Psychological aspects of mental disorders in later life. In Kaplan, O. J., ed., *Mental disorders in later life,* pp. 69–115. Stanford, Calif.: Stanford University Press.

JONIDES, J., AND BAUM, D. R. 1978. Cognitive maps as revealed by distance estimates. Paper presented at the 18th annual meeting of the Psychonomic Society. Washington D. C.

JORGENSEN, B. W., AND CERVONE, J. C. 1978. Affect enhancement in the pseudorecognition task. *Personality and Social Psychology Bulletin* 4:285–88.

JOSSELSON, R. 1980. Ego development in adolescence. In Adelson, J., ed., *Handbook of adolescent psychology,* pp. 188–211. New York: Wiley.

JOUVET, M. 1967. The stages of sleep. *Scientific American* 216:62–72.

KAGAN, J. 1976. Emergent themes in human development. *American Scientist* 64:186–96.

KAGAN, J.; KEARSLEY, R. B.; AND ZELAZO, P. R. 1978. *Infancy: Its place in human development.* Cambridge, Mass.: Harvard University Press.

KAGAN, J., AND MOSS, H. A. 1962. *Birth to maturity: The Fels study of psychological development.* New York: Wiley.

KALINOWSKY, L. B. 1975. The convulsive therapies. In Freedman, A. M.; Kaplan, H. I.; and Sadock, B. J., eds., *Comprehensive textbook of psychiatry—II,* vol. 2, pp. 1969–75. Baltimore: Williams & Wilkins.

KALLMAN, F. J. 1952. Comparative twin study of genetic aspects of male homosexuality. *Journal of Mental and Nervous Diseases* 15:283–98.

KAMIN, L. J. 1969. Predictability, surprise, attention and conditioning. In Campbell, B. A., and Church, R. M., eds., *Punishment and aversive behavior,* pp. 279–96. New York: Appleton-Century-Crofts.

KAMIN, L. J. 1974. *The science and politics of I.Q.* New York: Wiley.

KANIZSA, G. 1976. Subjective contours. *Scientific American* 234:48–52.

KATZ, B. 1952. The nerve impulse. *Scientific American* 187:55–64.

KATZ, J. J. 1972. *Semantic theory.* New York: Harper & Row.

KATZ, J. J., AND FODOR, J. A. 1963. The structure of a semantic theory. *Language* 39:170–210.

KATZ, N.; BAKER, E.; AND MACNAMARA, J. 1974. What's in a name? A study of how children learn common and proper names. *Child Development* 45:469–73.

KAUFMAN, L., AND ROCK, I. 1962. The moon illusion. *Scientific American* 207:120–30.

KEETON, W. T. 1972 AND 1980. *Biological science,* 2nd and 3rd eds. New York: Norton.

KEIL, F. C. 1979. *Semantic and conceptual development: An ontological perspective.* Cambridge, Mass.: Harvard University Press.

KEIL, F. C., AND BATTERMAN, N. 1984. A characteristic-to-defining shift in the development of word meaning. *Journal of Verbal Learning and Verbal Behavior* 23:221–36.

KELLEY, H. H., AND MICHELA, J. L. 1980. Attribution theory and research. *Annual Review of Psychology* 31:457–501.

KELLMAN, P. J., AND SPELKE, E. S. 1983. Perception of partially occluded objects in infancy. *Cognitive Psychology* 15:483–524.

KESSEL, E. L. 1955. The mating activities of balloon flies. *Systematic Zoology* 4:97–104.

KESSEN, W.; HAITH, M. M.; AND SALAPATEK, P. H. 1970. Infancy. In Mussen, P. H., ed., *Carmichael's manual of child psychology,* 3rd ed., vol. 1, pp. 287–446. New York: Wiley.

KEYNES, R. D. 1958. The nerve impulse and the squid. *Scientific American* 199:83–90.

KIHLSTROM, J. F., AND CANTOR, N. 1984. Mental representations of the self. In Berkowitz, L., ed., *Advances in experimental social psychology,* vol. 17, pp. 1–47. New York: Academic Press.

KIMBLE, G. A. 1961. *Hilgard and Marquis' conditioning and learning.* New York: Appleton-Century-Crofts.

KING, H. E. 1961. Psychological effects of excitation in the limbic system. In Sheer, D. E., ed., *Electrical stimulation of the brain.* Austin: University of Texas Press.

KINSEY, A. C.; POMEROY, W. B.; AND MARTIN, C. E. 1948. *Sexual behavior in the human male.* Philadelphia: Saunders.

KINSEY, A.; POMEROY, W.; MARTIN, C.; AND GEBHARD, P. 1953. *Sexual behavior in the human female.* Philadelphia: Saunders.

KIPARSKY, P. 1968. Linguistic universals and language change. In Bach, E., and Harms, R. T., eds., *Universals in linguistic theory.* New York: Holt, Rinehart & Winston.

KITTRIE, N. N. 1971. *The right to be different: Deviance and enforced therapy.* Baltimore: Penguin Books, 1973.

KLEIN, D. C., AND SELIGMAN, M. E. P. 1976. Reversal of performance deficits in learned helplessness and depression. *Journal of Abnormal Psychology* 85:11–26.

KLEIN, D. F., AND DAVIS, J. M. 1969. *Diagnosis and drug treatment of emotional disorders.* Baltimore: Williams & Wilkins.

KLEITMAN, N. 1960. Patterns of dreaming. *Scientific American* 203:82–88.

KLIMA, E., AND BELLUGI, U.; WITH BATTISON, R.; BOYES-BRAEM, P.; FISCHER, S.; FRISHBERG, N.; LANE, H.; LENTZ, E. M.;

NEWKIRK, D.; NEWPORT, E.; PEDERSEN, C.; AND SIPLE, P. 1979. *The signs of language.* Cambridge, Mass.: Harvard University Press.

KLINEBERG, O. 1940. *Social psychology.* New York: Henry Holt.

KLOPFER, P. H. 1974. *An introduction to animal behavior: Ethology's first century.* Englewood Cliffs, N. J.: Prentice-Hall.

KNITTLE, J. L., AND HIRSCH, J. 1968. Effect of early nutrition on the development of the rat epididymal fat pads: Cellularity and metabolism. *Journal of Clinical Investigations* 47:2091.

KOHLBERG, L. 1963. Development of children's orientations toward a moral order. *Vita Humana* 6:11–36.

KOHLBERG, L. 1966. A cognitive developmental analysis of children's sex-role concepts and attitudes. In Maccoby, E. E., ed., *The development of sex differences,* pp. 82–171. Stanford, Calif.: Stanford University Press.

KOHLBERG, L. 1969. Stage and sequence: The cognitive developmental approach to socialization. In Goslin, D. A., ed., *Handbook of socialization theory of research,* pp. 347–480. Chicago: Rand McNally.

KÖHLER, W. 1925. *The mentality of apes.* New York: Harcourt Brace and World.

KÖHLER, W. 1947. *Gestalt psychology.* New York: Liveright.

KOHLERS, P. A. 1983. Perception and representation. In Rosenzweig, M. R., and Porter, L. W., eds., *Annual Review of Psychology* 34:129–66. Palo Alto, Calif.: Annual Reviews, Inc.

KOHN, M. L. 1968. Social class and schizophrenia: A critical review. In Rosenthal, D., and Kety, S. S., eds., *The transmission of schizophrenia,* pp. 155–74. London: Pergamon.

KOHN, M. L. 1969. *Class and conformity: A study in values.* Chicago: University of Chicago Press.

KOLB, B., AND WHISHAW, I. Q. 1980. *Fundamentals of human neuropsychology.* San Francisco: Freeman.

KOLERS, P. A. 1972. *Aspects of motion perception.* New York: Pergamon.

KOLERS, P. A., AND POMERANTZ, J. R. 1971. Figural change in apparent motion. *Journal of Experimental Psychology* 87:99–108.

KOLODNY, R.; MASTERS, W.; HENDRYX, J.; AND TORO, G. 1971. Plasma testosterone and semen analysis in male homosexuals. *New England Journal of Medicine* 285:1170–74.

KORS, A. C., AND PETERS, E. 1972. *Witchcraft in Europe: 1100–1700. A documentary history.* Philadelphia: University of Pennsylvania Press.

KOSSLYN, S. M. 1973. Scanning visual images: Some structural implications. *Perception and Psychophysics* 14:90–94.

KOSTLAN, A. 1954. A method for the empirical study of psychodiagnosis. *Journal of Consulting Psychology* 18:83–88.

KOTELCHUK, M. 1976. The infant's relationship to the father: Some experimental evidence. In Lamb, M., ed., *The role of the father in child development.* New York: Wiley.

KOULACK, D., AND GOODENOUGH, D. R. 1976. Dream recall and dream recall failure: An arousal-retrieval model. *Psychological Bulletin* 83:975–84.

KRECH, D., AND CRUTCHFIELD, R. 1958. *Elements of psychology.* New York: Knopf.

KUCZAJ, S. A. 1977. The acquisition of regular and irregular past tense forms. *Journal of Verbal Learning and Verbal Behavior* 16:589–600.

KUFFLER, S. W. 1953. Discharge pattern and functional organization of mammalian retina. *Journal of Neurophysiology* 16:37–68.

KURTINES, W., AND GREIF, E. B. 1974. The development of moral thought: Review and evaluation. *Psychological Bulletin* 81:453–70.

LABERGE, D. 1975. Acquisition of automatic processing in perceptual and associative learning. In Rabbitt, P. M. A., and Dormic, S., eds., *Attention and performance,* vol. 5. London: Academic Press.

LABOV, W. 1970a. *Language in the inner city.* Philadelphia: University of Pennsylvania Press.

LABOV, W. 1970b. The logic of nonstandard English. In Williams, F., ed., *Language and poverty: Perspectives on a theme,* pp. 153–89. Chicago: Markham.

LACK, D. 1953. Darwin's finches. *Scientific American* 188:66–72.

LACKNER, J. R. 1976. A developmental study of language behavior in retarded children. In Morehead, D. M., and Morehead, A. E., *Normal and deficient child language,* pp. 181–208. Baltimore: University Park Press.

LAING, R. D. 1967. *The politics of experience.* New York: Ballantine.

LANDAU, B. 1982. Will the real grandmother please stand up? The psychological reality of dual meaning representations. *Journal of Psycholinguistic Research* 11:47–62.

LANDAU, B.; GLEITMAN, H.; AND SPELKE, E. 1981. Spatial knowledge and geometric representation in a child blind from birth. *Science* 213:1275–78.

LANDAU, B., AND GLEITMAN, L. R. 1985. *Language and experience: Evidence from the blind child.* Cambridge, Mass.: Harvard University Press.

LANDAU, B.; SPELKE, E.; AND GLEITMAN, H. 1984. Spatial knowledge in a young blind child. *Cognition* 16:225–60.

LANDIS, C., AND HUNT, W. A. 1932. Adrenalin and emotion. *Psychological Review* 39:467–85.

LANDMAN, J. T. L., AND DAWES, R. M. 1982. Psychotherapy outcome: Smith and Glass' conclusions stand up under scrutiny. *American Psychologist* 37:504–16.

LANDY, D., AND ARONSON, E. 1969. The influence of the characteristics of the criminal and his victim on the decisions of simulated jurors. *Journal of Experimental Social Psychology* 5:141–52.

LANDY, D., AND SIGALL, H. 1974. Beauty is talent. Task evaluation as a function of the performer's physical attractiveness. *Journal of Personality and Social Psychology* 29:299–304.

LANGLOIS, J. H., AND DOWNS, A. C. 1980. Mothers, fathers, and peers as socialization agents of sex-typed play behaviors in young children. *Child Development* 51:1237–1347.

LANYON, R. I., AND GOODSTEIN, L. D. 1971. *Personality assessment.* New York: Wiley.

LAPIERE, R. 1934. Attitudes versus actions. *Social Forces* 13:230–37.

LASHLEY, K. S. 1930. The mechanism of vision: 1. A method for rapid analysis of pattern-vision in the rat. *Journal of Genetic Psychology* 37:453–60.

LASHLEY, K. S. 1951. The problem of serial order in behavior. In Jeffress, L. A., ed., *Cerebral mechanisms in behavior, the Hixon Symposium.* New York: Wiley.

LASKY, J. J.; HOVER, G. L.; SMITH, P. A.; BOSTIAN, D. W.; DUFFENDECK, S. C.; AND NORD, C. L. 1959. Post-hospital adjustment as predicted by psychiatric patients and by their staff. *Journal of Consulting Psychology* 23:213–18.

LASSEN, N. A.; INGVAR, D. H.; AND SKINHOJ, E. 1978. Brain function and blood flow. *Scientific American* 239:62–71.

LAYZER, D. 1972. Science or superstition: A physical scientist looks at the I.Q. controversy. *Cognition* 1:265–300.

LAZARUS, A. A. 1971. *Behavior therapy and beyond.* New York: McGraw-Hill.

LAZARUS, R. S., AND McCLEARY, R. A. 1951. Autonomic discrimination without awareness: A study of subception. *Psychological Review* 58:113–22.

LEASK, J.; HABER, R. N.; AND HABER, R. B. 1969. Eidetic imagery in children: II. Longitudinal and experimental results. *Psychonomic Monograph Supplements* 3(Whole No. 35):25–48.

LE BON, G. 1895. *The crowd.* New York: Viking Press, 1960.

LEE, E. S. 1951. Negro intelligence and selective migration: A Philadelphia test of the Klineberg hypothesis. *American Sociological Review* 16:227–33.

LEEPER, R. W. 1935. A study of a neglected portion of the field of learning: The development of sensory organization. *Journal of Genetic Psychology* 46:41–75.

LEFKOWITZ, M. M.; BLAKE, R. R.; AND MOUTON, J. S. 1955. Status factors in pedestrian violation of traffic signals. *Journal of Abnormal and Social Psychology* 51:704–6.

LEIBOWITZ, H.; BRISLIN, R.; PERLMUTTER, L.; AND HENNESSY, R. 1969. Ponzo perspective illusion as a manifestation of space perception. *Science* 166:1174–76.

LEMPERS, J. S.; FLAVELL, E. R.; AND FLAVELL, J. H. 1977. The development in very young children of tacit knowledge concerning visual perception. *Genetic Psychology Monographs* 95:3–53.

LENNEBERG, E. H. 1967. *Biological foundations of language.* New York: Wiley.

LEPPER, M. R. 1983. Social control processes, attributions of motivation, and the internalization of social values. In Higgins, E. T.; Ruble, D. N.; and Hartup, W. W., eds., *Social cognition and social behavior: Developmental perspectives.* New York: Cambridge University Press.

LEPPER, M. R.; GREENE, D.; AND NISBETT, R. E. 1973. Undermining children's intrinsic interest with extrinsic rewards: A test of the "overjustification" hypothesis. *Journal of Personality and Social Psychology* 28:129–37.

LERNER, M. J. 1971. Observer's evaluation of a victim: Justice, guilt and veridical perception. *Journal of Personality and Social Psychology* 20:127–35.

LERNER, R. M., AND KORN, S. J. 1972. The development of body-build stereotypes in males. *Child Development* 43:908–20.

LEVINE, F. M., AND FASNACHT, G. 1974. Token rewards may lead to token learning. *American Psychologist* 29:816–20.

LEVINE, J. D.; GORDON, N. C.; AND FIELDS, H. L. 1979. The role of endorphins in placebo analgesia. In Bonica, J. J.; Liebesking, J. C.; and Albe-Fessard, D., eds., *Advances in pain research and therapy,* vol. 3. New York: Raven.

LEVINSON, D. J. 1978. *The seasons of a man's life.* New York: Knopf.

LEVY, J. 1974. Psychobiological implications of bilateral asymmetry. In Dimond, S. J., and Beaumont, J. G., eds, *Hemisphere function in the human brain,* pp. 121–83. New York: Wiley.

LEVY, J. 1979. Author's personal communication with Levy.

LEVY, J.; TREVARTHEN, C.; AND SPERRY, R. W. 1972. Perception of bilateral chimeric figures following hemispheric deconnexion. *Brain* 95:61–78.

LEWIS, E. R. ET AL. 1969. Study neural organization in aplysia with the scanning electron microscope. *Science* 165:1140–43.

LEWIS, H. P. 1966. *Child art: The beginnings of self-affirmation.* Emoryville, Calif.: Diablo Press.

LEWONTIN, R. C. 1976. Race and intelligence. In Block, N. J., and Dworkin, G., eds., *The IQ controversy,* pp. 78–92. New York: Pantheon.

LIBERMAN, A. M. 1970. The grammars of speech and language. *Cognitive Psychology* 1:301–23.

LIBERMAN, A. M.; COOPER, F. S.; SHANKWEILER, D. P.; AND STUDDERT-KENNEDY, M. 1967. Perception of the speech code. *Psychological Review* 74:431–61.

LIBERMAN, A. M., AND PISONI, D. B. 1977. Evidence for a special perceiving subsystem in the human. In Bullock, T. H., ed., *Recognition of complex acoustic signals.* Berlin: Dahlem Konferenzen.

LICKLEY, J. D. 1919. *The nervous system.* New York: Longman.

LIDZ, T.; CORNELISON, A.; FLECK, S.; AND TERRY, D. 1957. The intrafamilial environment of schizophrenic patients: II. Marital schism and marital skew. *American Journal of Psychiatry* 114:241–48.

LIEBERMAN, P. L. 1975. *On the origins of language.* New York: Macmillan.

LIEBERMAN, S. 1956. The effects of changes in roles on the attitudes of role occupants. *Human Relations* 9:385–402.

LIEBERT, R. M.; POULOS, R. W.; AND STRAUSS, G. D. 1974. *Developmental psychology.* Englewood Cliffs, N. J.: Prentice-Hall.

LIGHT, L. L., AND CARTER-SOBELL, L. 1970. Effects of changed semantic context on recognition memory. *Journal of Verbal Learning and Verbal Behavior* 9:1–11.

LINDSAY, P. H., AND NORMAN, D. A. 1977. *Human information processing,* 2nd ed. New York: Academic Press.

LINDSLEY, D. B. 1960. Attention, consciousness, sleep, and wakefulness. In *Handbook of physiology,* sect. 1, *Neurophysiology,* vol. 3. Washington, D.C.: American Physiological Society.

LINDSLEY, D. B.; SCHREINER, L. H.; KNOWLES, W. B.; AND MAGOUN, H. W. 1950. Behavioral and EEG changes following chronic brain stem lesions in the cat. *Electroencephalography and Clinical Neurophysiology* 2:483–98.

LIPOWSKI, Z. J. 1975. Psychophysiological cardiovascular disorders. In Freedman, A. M.; Kaplan, H. I.; and Sadock, B. J., eds., *Comprehensive textbook of psychiatry—II,* vol. 2, pp. 1660–68. Baltimore: Williams & Wilkins.

LIPPERT, W. W., AND SENTER, R. J. 1966. Electrodermal responses in the sociopath. *Psychonomic Science* 4:25–26.

LITTLE, K. B., AND SHNEIDMAN, E. S. 1959. Congruencies among interpretations of psychological test and anamnestic data. *Psychological Monographs* 73 (Whole No. 476).

LISKE, E., AND DAVIS, W. J. 1984. Sexual behavior of the Chinese praying mantis. *Animal Behavior* 32:916.

LLOYD, J. E. 1981. Mimicry in the sexual signals of fireflies. *Scientific American* 245:139–45.

LOCKE, J. 1690. *An essay concerning human understanding.* New York: Meridian, 1964.

LOEHLIN, J. C. 1969. Psychological genetics. In Cattell, R. B. *Handbook of modern personality theory.* Chicago: Aldine.

LOEHLIN, J. C.; LINDZEY, G.; AND SPUHLER, J. N. 1975. *Race difference in intelligence.* San Francisco: Freeman.

LOEHLIN, J. C., AND NICHOLS, R. C. 1976. *Heredity, environment and personality: A study of 850 sets of twins.* Austin: University of Texas Press.

LOFTUS, E. F. 1973. Activation of semantic memory. *American Journal of Psychology* 86:331–37.

LOFTUS, E. F. 1975. Leading questions and the eyewitness report. *Cognitive Psychology* 7:560–72.

LOFTUS, E. F., AND LOFTUS, G. R. 1980. On the permanence of stored information in the human brain. *American Psychologist* 35:409–20.

LOFTUS, E. F., AND ZANNI, G. 1975. Eyewitness testimony: The influence of the wording of a question. *Bulletin of the Psychonomic Society* 5:86–88.

LOGAN, F. 1969. The negative incentive value of punishment. In Campbell, B. A., and Church, R. M., eds., *Punishment and aversive behavior.* New York: Appleton-Century-Crofts.

LONDON, P. 1964. *The modes and morals of psychotherapy.* New York: Holt, Rinehart & Winston.

LORENZ, K. Z. 1943. Die angeborenen Formen moeglicher Erfahrung. *Zeitschrift Für Tierpsychologie* 5:276.

LORENZ, K. Z. 1952. *King Solomon's ring.* New York: Crowell.

LORENZ, K. Z. 1966. *On aggression.* London: Methuen.

LUBORSKY, L. 1973. Forgetting and remembering (momentary forgetting) during psychotherapy: A new sample. *Psychological Issues* 8(20):29–55.

LUBORSKY, L.; SACKHEIM, H.; AND CHRISTOPH, P. 1979. The state conducive to momentary forgetting. In Kihlstrom, J. F., and Evans, F. J., eds., *Functional disorders of memory,* pp. 325–54. Hillsdale, N. J.: Erlbaum.

LUCE, R. D., AND RAIFFA, H. 1957. *Games and decisions.* New York: Wiley.

LUCHINS, A. S. 1942. Mechanization in problem-solving: The effect of Einstellung. *Psychological Monographs* 54 (Whole No. 248).

LUND, F. H. 1930. Why do we weep? *Journal of Social Psychology* 1:136–51.

LURIA, A. R. 1966. *Higher cortical functions in man.* New York: Basic Books.

LYKKEN, D. T. 1979. The detection of deception. *Psychological Bulletin* 86:47–53.

LYNN, R., AND EYSENCK, H. J. 1961. Tolerance for pain, extraversion and neuroticism. *Perceptual and Motor Skills* 12:161–62.

MACCOBY, E. E. 1980. *Social development.* New York: Harcourt Brace Jovanovich.

MACCOBY, E. E., AND JACKLIN, C. N. 1974. *The psychology of sex differences.* Stanford, Calif.: Stanford University Press.

MACCOBY, E. E., AND JACKLIN, C. N. 1980. Sex differences in aggression: A rejoinder and reprise. *Child Development* 51:964–80.

MACCOBY, E. E., AND MARTIN, J. A. 1983. Socialization in the context of the family: Parent-child interaction. In Mussen, P. H., ed. *Carmichael's manual of child psychology: vol. 4. Socialization, personality and social development* (Hetherington, M. E., volume editor), pp. 1–102. New York: Wiley.

MacKENZIE, N. 1965. *Dreams and dreaming.* London: Aldus Books.

MacNAMARA, J. 1972. Cognitive basis of language learning in infants. *Psychological Review* 79:1–13.

MacNICHOL, E. F., JR. 1964. Three-pigment color vision: *Scientific American* 211:48–56.

MAGNUS, O., AND LAMMERS, J. 1956. The amygdaloid-nuclear complex. *Folia Psychiatrica Neurologica et Neurochirurgico Neerlandica* 59:552–82.

MAGNUSSON, D., AND ENDLER, N. S. 1977. Interactional psychology: Present status and future prospects. In Magnusson, D., and Endler, N. S., eds., *Personality at the crossroads,* pp. 3–31. New York: Wiley.

MAGOUN, H. W.; HARRISON, F.; BROBECK, J. R.; AND RANSON, S. W. 1938. Activation of heat loss mechanisms by local heating of the brain. *Journal of Neurophysiology* 1:101–14.

MAHER, B. A. 1966. *Principles of psychopathology.* New York: McGraw-Hill.

MAHONEY, M. J. 1976. *Scientist as subject: The psychological imperative.* Cambridge, Mass.: Ballinger.

MAIER, S. F.; LAUDENSLAGER, M. L.; AND RYAN, S. M. 1985. Stressor controllability, immune function, and endogenous opiates.

MAIER, S. F.; SELIGMAN, M. E. P.; AND SOLOMON, R. L. 1969. Pavlovian fear conditioning and learned helplessness: Effects on escape and avoidance behavior of (a) the CS-US contingency and (b) the independence of the US and voluntary responding. In Campbell, B. A., and Church, R. M., ed., *Punishment and aversive behavior,* pp. 299–342. New York: Appleton-Century-Crofts.

MALAN, H. 1963. *A study of brief psychotherapy.* Philadelphia: Lippincott.

MALINOWSKI, B. 1927. *Sex and repression in savage society.* New York: Meridian, 1955.

MANDLER, G. 1967. Organization and memory. In Spence, K. W., and Spence, J. T., eds., *The psychology of learning and motivation,* vol. 1, pp. 327–72. New York: Academic Press.

MANDLER, G. 1975. *Mind and emotion.* New York: Wiley.

MANDLER, G. 1984. *Mind and body: Psychology of emotion and stress.* New York: Norton.

MANDLER, G., AND PEARLSTONE, Z. 1966. Free and constrained concept learning and subsequent recall. *Journal of Verbal Learning and Verbal Behavior* 5:126–31.

MANN, F.; BOWSHER, D.; MUMFORD, J.; LIPTON, S.; AND MILES, J. 1973. Treatment of intractable pain by acupuncture. *Lancet* 2:57–60.

MARCUS, M. 1980. *A theory of syntactic recognition for natural language.* Cambridge, Mass.: MIT Press.

MARIN, O.; SAFFRON, E.; AND SCHWARTZ, M. 1976. Dissociations of language in aphasia: Implications for normal function. *Annals of the New York Academy of Sciences* 280:868–84.

MARKMAN. E. M. 1979. Realizing that you don't understand: Elementary school children's awareness of inconsistencies. *Child Development* 50:643–55.

MARKS, I. 1966. Patterns of meaning in psychiatric patients: Semantic differential responses in obsessives and psychopaths. *Maudsley Monograph* 13. Oxford, England: Oxford University Press.

MARKS, I. M. 1969. *Fears and phobias.* New York: Academic Press.

MARLER, P. R. 1970. A comparative approach to vocal learning: Song development in white-crowned sparrows. *Journal of Comparative and Physiological Psychology Monographs* 71(No. 2, Part 2): 1–25.

MARMOR, J. 1975. Homosexuality and sexual orientation disturbances. In Freedman, A. M.; Kaplan, H. I.; and Sadock, B. J., eds., *Comprehensive textbook of psychiatry—II,* vol. 2, pp. 1510–19. Baltimore: Williams & Wilkins.

MARSHALL, G. D., AND ZIMBARDO, P. G. 1979. Affective consequences of inadequately explained physiological arousal. *Journal of Personality and Social Psychology* 37:970–88.

MARSLEN-WILSON, W. D., AND TEUBER, H. L. 1975. Memory for remote events in anterograde amnesia: Recognition of public figures from news photographs. *Neuropsychologia* 13:353–64.

MASLACH, C. 1979. Negative emotional biasing of unexplained physiological arousal. *Journal of Personality and Social Psychology* 37:953–69.

MASLOW, A. 1968. *Toward a psychology of being,* 2nd ed. New York: Van Nostrand.

MASSERMAN, J. H. 1946. *Principles of dynamic psychiatry.* Philadelphia: Saunders.

MAUGH, T. M. 1981. Biochemical markers identify mental states. *Science* 214:39–41.

MAX, L. W. 1937. An experimental study of the motor theory of consciousness: IV. Action-curved responses in the deaf during awakening, kinaesthetic imagery and abstract thinking. *Journal of Comparative Psychology* 24:301–44.

MAY, R. 1958. Contributions of existential psychotherapy. In May, R.; Angel, E.; and Ellenberger, H. F., eds., *Existence,* pp. 37–91. New York: Basic Books.

MAYER, D. J.; PRICE, D. D.; RAFII, A.; AND BARBER, J. 1976. Acupuncture hypalgesia: Evidence for activation of a central control system as a mechanism of action. In Bonica, J. J., and Albe-Fessard, D., eds., *Advances in pain research and therapy,* vol. 1. New York: Raven Press.

MAYER, J. 1955. Regulation of energy intake and body weight: The glucostatic theory and the lipostatic hypothesis. *Annals of the New York Academy of Sciences* 63:15–43.

McCLEARN, G. E., AND DeFRIES, J. C. 1973. *Introduction to behavioral genetics.* San Francisco: Freeman.

McCLINTOCK, M. K., AND ADLER, N. T. 1978. The role of the female during copulation in wild and domestic Norway rats *(Rattus Norvegicus). Behaviour* 67:67–96.

McCONAGHY, M. J. 1979. Gender constancy and the genital basis of gender: Stages in the development of constancy by gender identity. *Child Development* 50:1223–26.

McCORD, W., AND McCORD, J. 1964. *The psychopath: An essay on the criminal mind.* New York: Van Nostrand.

McGHIE, A., AND CHAPMAN, J. 1961. Disorders of attention and perception in early schizophrenia. *British Journal of Medical Psychology* 34:103–16.

McGRAW, M. B. 1935. *Growth: A study of Johnny and Jimmy.* New York: Appleton-Century.

McGUIGAN, F. J. 1966. Covert oral behavior and auditory hallucinations. *Psychophysiology* 3:421–28.

McKAY, D. G. 1973. Aspects of the theory of comprehension, memory and attention. *Quarterly Journal of Experimental Psychology* 25:22–40.

McKENZIE, B. E.; TOOTELL, H. E.; AND DAY, R. H. 1980. Development of size constancy during the 1st year of human infancy. *Developmental Psychology* 16:163–74.

McNEILL, D. 1966. Developmental psycholinguistics. In Smith, F., and Miller, G. A., eds., *The genesis of language: A psycholinguistic approach.* Cambridge, Mass.: MIT Press.

MEAD, G. H. 1934. *Mind, self, and society.* Chicago: University of Chicago Press.

MEAD, M. 1935. *Sex and temperament in three primitive societies.* New York: Morrow.

MEAD, M. 1937. *Cooperation and competition among primitive peoples.* New York: McGraw-Hill.

MEAD, M. 1939. *From the South Seas: Studies of adolescence and sex in primitive societies.* New York: Morrow.

MEEHL, P. E. 1956. Profile analysis of the MMPI in differential diagnosis. In Welsh, G. S., and Dahlstrom, W. G., eds., *Basic readings on the MMPI in psychology and medicine,* pp. 291–97. Minneapolis: University of Minnesota Press.

MEEHL, P. E. 1959. Some ruminations on the validation of clinical procedures. *Canadian Journal of Psychology* 13:102–28.

MEEHL, P. D. 1962. Schizotaxia, schizotypy, schizophrenia. *American Psychologist* 17:827–38.

MELTZOFF, A. N., AND BORTON, R. W. 1979. Intermodal matching by human neonates. *Nature* 282:403–4.

MELTZOFF, A. N., AND MOORE, M. K. 1977. Imitation of facial and manual gestures by human neonates. *Science* 198:75–78.

MELZACK, R. 1973. *The puzzle of pain.* New York: Basic Books.

MERVIS, C. B., AND CRISAFI, M. 1978. Order acquisition of subordinate, basic, and superordinate level categories. *Child Development* 49:988–98.

MEYER, D. E., AND SCHVANEVELDT, R. W. 1971. Facilitation in recognizing pairs of words: Evidence of a dependence between retrieval operations. *Journal of Experimental Psychology* 90:227–34.

MICHAEL, R. P., AND KEVERNE, E. B. 1968. Pheromones in the communication of sexual status in primates. *Nature* 218:746–49.

MIKAELIAN, H., AND HELD, R. 1964. Two types of adaptation to an optically rotated visual field. *American Journal of Psychology* 77:257–63.

MILGRAM, S. 1963. Behavioral study of obedience. *Journal of Abnormal and Social Psychology* 67:371–78.

MILGRAM, S. 1974. *Obedience to authority.* New York: Harper & Row.

MILGRAM, S., AND TOCH, H. 1969. Collective behavior: Crowds and social movements. In Lindzey, G., and Aronson, E., eds., *Handbook of social psychology,* 2nd ed., vol. 4, pp. 507–610. Reading, Mass.: Addison-Wesley.

MILL, J. S. 1865. *An examination of Sir William Hamilton's philosophy.* London: Longman, Green, Longman, Roberts & Green.

MILLER, G. A. 1956. The magical number seven plus or minus two: Some limits in our capacity for processing information. *Psychological Review* 63:81–97.

MILLER, G. A.; GALANTER, E.; AND PRIBRAM, K. H. 1960. *Plans and the structure of behavior.* New York: Holt, Rinehart & Winston.

MILLER, N. E. 1978. Biofeedback and visceral learning. *Annual Review of Psychology* 29:373–404.

MILLER, N. E.; BAILEY, C. J.; AND STEVENSON, J. A. F. 1950. Decreased "hunger" but increased food intake resulting from hypothalamic lesions. *Science* 112:256–59.

MILLER, N. E., AND BRUCKER, B. S. 1978. Learned large increases in blood pressure apparently independent of skeletal responses in patients paralyzed by spinal lesions. In Birnhaumer, N., and Kimmel, H. O., eds., *Biofeedback and self-regulation.* Hillsdale, N.J.: Erlbaum.

MILLER, R. R., AND MARLIN, N. A. 1979. Amnesia following electroconvulsive shock. In Kihlstrom, J. F., and Evans, F. J., eds., *Functional disorders of memory,* pp. 143–79. Hillsdale, N.J.: Erlbaum.

MILLER, W. R., AND SELIGMAN, M. E. P. 1975. Depression and learned helplessness in man. *Journal of Abnormal Psychology* 84:228–38.

MILLON, T. 1969. *Modern psychopathology.* Philadelphia: Saunders.

MILNER, B. 1966. Amnesia following operation on the temporal lobes. In Whitty, C. W. M., and Zangwill, O. L., eds., *Amnesia,* pp. 109–33. London: Butterworth.

MILNER, B.; CORKIN, S.; AND TEUBER, H. L. 1968. Further analysis of the hippocampal syndrome: 14-year follow-up study of H. M. *Neuropsychologia* 6:215–34.

MINEKA, S. 1979. The role of fear in theories of avoidance learning, flooding, and extinction. *Psychological Bulletin* 86: 985–1010.

MISCHEL, W. 1968. *Personality and assessment.* New York: Wiley.

MISCHEL, W. 1970. Sex-typing and socialization. In Mussen, P. H., ed., *Carmichael's manual of child development,* vol. 1. New York: Wiley.

MISCHEL, W. 1973. Towards a cognitive social learning reconceptualization of personality. *Psychological Review* 80:252–83.

MISCHEL, W. 1979. On the interface of cognition and personality: Beyond the person-situation debate. *American Psychologist* 34:740–54.

MISCHEL, W., AND PEAKE, P. K. 1983. Some facets of consistency. Replies to Epstein, Funder and Bem. *Psychological Review* 90: 394–402.

MISELIS, R. R., AND EPSTEIN, A. N. 1970. Feeding induced by 2-deoxy-D-glucose injections into the lateral ventrical of the rat. *The Physiologist* 13:262.

MISHLER, E. G., AND WAXLER, N. E. 1968. Family interaction and schizophrenia: Alternative frameworks of interpretation. In Rosenthal, D., and Kety, S. S., eds., *The transmission of schizophrenia,* pp. 213–22. New York: Pergamon.

MITA, T. H.; DERMER, M.; AND KNIGHT, J. 1977. Reversed facial images and the mere exposure hypothesis. *Journal of Personality and Social Psychology* 35:597–601.

MITCHELL, D. E.; REARDON, J.; AND MUIR, D. W. 1975. Interocular transfer of the motion after-effect in normal and stereoblind observers. *Experimental Brain Research* 22:163–73.

MITROFF, I. I. 1974. *The subjective side of science.* Amsterdam: Elsevier.

MOELLER, G. 1954. The CS-UCS interval in GSR conditioning. *Journal of Experimental Psychology* 48:162–66.

MONEY, J. 1970. Sexual dimorphism and homosexual gender identity. *Psychological Bulletin* 74: 425–40.

MONEY, J. 1980. *Love and love sickness.* Baltimore: Johns Hopkins University Press.

MONEY, J., AND EHRHARDT, A. A. 1972. *Man and woman, boy and girl.* Baltimore: Johns Hopkins University Press.

MOORE, J. W. 1972. Stimulus control: Studies of auditory generalization in rabbits. In Black, A. H., and Prokasy, W. F., eds., *Classical conditioning II: Current research and theory,* pp. 206–30. New York: Appleton-Century-Crofts.

MORA, G. 1975. Historical and theoretical trends in psychiatry. In Freedman, A. M.; Kaplan, H. I.; and Sadock, B. J., eds., *Comprehensive textbook of psychiatry—II,* vol. 1, pp. 1–75. Baltimore: Williams & Wilkins.

MORAY, N. 1959. Attention in dichotic listening: Affective cues and the influence of instructions. *Quarterly Journal of Experimental Psychology* 11:56–60.

MORGAN, C. D., AND MURRAY, H. A. 1935. A method for investigating fantasies: The thematic apperception test. *Archives of Neurological Psychiatry* 34:289–306.

MORGAN, G. A., AND RICCIUTI, H. N. 1969. Infants' responses to strangers during the first year. In Foss, B. M., *Determinants of infant behavior,* vol. 4. New York: Methuen.

MORRIS, D. 1967. *The naked ape.* New York: McGraw-Hill.

MORRIS, J. 1974. *Conundrum.* New York: Harcourt Brace Jovanovich.

MOSCOVITCH, M. 1972. Choice reaction-time study assessing the verbal behavior of the minor hemisphere in normal adults. *Journal of Comparative and Physiological Psychology* 80: 66–74.

MOSCOVITCH, M. 1979. Information processing and the cerebral hemispheres. In Gazzaniga, M. S., *Handbook of behavioral neurobiology,* vol. 2, pp. 379–446. New York: Plenum.

MOSCOVITCH, M. 1982. Multiple dissociation of function in amnesia. In Cermak, L. S., ed., *Human memory and amnesia,* pp. 337–70. Hillsdale, N.J.: Erlbaum.

MURDOCK, B. 1962. The serial position effect of free recall. *Journal of Experimental Psychology* 64:482–88.

MURPHY, J. M. 1976. Psychiatric labelling in cross-cultural perspective. *Science* 191:1019–28.

MURRAY, F. B. 1978. Teaching strategies and conservation training. In Lesgold, A. M.; Pellegrino, J. W.; Fekkeman, D.; and Glaser, R., eds., *Cognitive psychology and instruction,* vol. 1. New York: Plenum.

MUTER, P. 1980. Very rapid forgetting. *Memory and Cognition* 8: 174–79.

MUUSS, R. E. 1970. Puberty rites in primitive and modern societies. *Adolescence* 5: 109–28.

NEISSER, U. 1963. The imitation of man by machine. *Science* 139:193–97.

NEISSER, U. 1967. *Cognitive psychology.* New York: Appleton-Century-Crofts.

NEISSER, U. 1982. On the trail of the tape-recorder fallacy. Paper presented at a symposium on "The influence of hypnosis and related states on memory: Forensic implications" at the meetings of the American Association for the Advancement of Science, Washington, D. C., in January 1982.

NEL, E.; HELMREICH, R.; AND ARONSON, E. 1969. Opinion change in the advocate as a function of the persuasibility of his audience: A clarification of the meaning of dissonance. *Journal of Personality and Social Psychology* 12:117–24.

NELSON, K. 1973. Structure and strategy in learning to talk. *Monographs of the Society for Research in Child Development* 38:(1–2, Serial No. 149).

NEMIAH, J. C. 1975. Obsessive-compulsive neurosis. In Freedman, A. M.; Kaplan, H. I.; and Sadock, B. J., eds., *Comprehensive textbook of psychiatry—II,* vol. 1, pp. 1241–55. Baltimore: Williams & Wilkins.

NEWCOMB, T. M. 1961. *The acquaintance process.* New York: Holt, Rinehart & Winston.

NEWELL, A.; SHAW, J. C.; AND SIMON, H. A. 1958. Elements of a theory of human problem solving. *Psychological Review* 65:151–66.

NEWELL, A., AND SIMON, H. A. 1972. *Human problem solving.* Englewood Cliffs, N. J.: Prentice-Hall.

NEWPORT, E. L. 1977. Motherese: The speech of mothers to young children. In Castellan, N. J.; Pisoni, D. B.; and Potts, G. R., eds., *Cognitive theory,* vol. 2. Hillsdale, N. J.: Erlbaum.

NEWPORT, E. L. 1984. Constraints on learning: Studies in the acquisition of American Sign Language. *Papers and Reports on Child Language Development* 23:1–22. Stanford, Calif.: Stanford University Press.

NEWPORT, E. L., AND ASHBROOK, E. F. 1977. The emergence of

semantic relations in American Sign Language. *Papers and Reports in Child Language Development* 13.

NEWPORT, E. L., AND SUPPALA, T. (forthcoming). Critical period effects in the acquisition of a primary language.

NEWPORT, E. L.; GLEITMAN, H.; AND GLEITMAN, L. R. 1977. Mother, I'd rather do it myself: Some effects and non-effects of maternal speech style. In Snow, C., and Ferguson, C., eds., *Talking to children: Language input and acquisition.* Cambridge, England: Cambridge University Press.

NILSSON, L. 1974. *Behold man.* Boston: Little, Brown.

NISBETT, R. E. 1968. Taste, deprivation, and weight determinants of eating behavior. *Journal of Personality and Social Psychology* 10:107–16.

NISBETT, R. E. 1972. Eating behavior and obesity in man and animals. *Advances in Psychosomatic Medicine* 7:173–93.

NISBETT, R. E.; CAPUTO, C.; LEGANT, P.; AND MARACEK, J. 1973. Behavior as seen by the actor and as seen by the observer. *Journal of Personality and Social Psychology* 27:154–64.

NISBETT, R., AND ROSS, L. 1980. *Human inference: Strategies and shortcomings of social judgment.* Englewood Cliffs, N. J.: Prentice-Hall.

NISBETT, R. E., AND WILSON, T. D. 1977. Telling more than we can know: Verbal reports on mental processes. *Psychological Review* 84:231–59.

NISSEN, H. 1953. Instinct as seen by a psychologist. *Psychological Review* 60:287–97.

NORMAN, W. T. 1963. Toward an adequate taxonomy of personality attributes: Replicated factor structure in peer nomination personality ratings. *Journal of Abnormal and Social Psychology* 66:574–83.

NOVAK, M. A., AND HARLOW, H. F. 1975. Social recovery of monkeys isolated for the first year of life: I. Rehabilitation and therapy. *Developmental Psychology* 11: 453–65.

ODIORNE, J. M. 1957. Color changes. In Brown, M. E., ed., *The physiology of fishes,* vol. 2. New York: Academic Press.

OHANIAN, H. C. 1985. *Physics.* New York: Norton.

OLDS, J., AND MILNER, P. 1954. Positive reinforcement produced by electrical stimulation of septal areas and other regions of rat brains. *Journal of Comparative and Physiological Psychology* 47:419–27.

OLDS, M. E., AND FOBES, T. 1981. The central basis of motivation: Intracranial self-stimulation. *Annual Review of Psychology* 32:523–74.

OLWEUS, D. 1980. Familial and temperamental determinants of aggressive behavior in adolescent boys: A causal analysis. *Developmental Psychology* 16:644–66.

ORLANSKY, H. 1949. Infant care and personality. *Psychological Bulletin* 46:1–48.

ORNE, M. T. 1951. The mechanisms of hypnotic age regression: An experimental study. *Journal of Abnormal and Social Psychology* 58:277–99.

ORNE, M. T. 1975. Psychotherapy in contemporary America: Its development and context. In Arieti, S., ed., *American handbook of psychiatry,* 2nd ed., vol. 5, pp. 1–33. New York: Basic Books.

ORNE, M. T. 1979. The use and misuse of hypnosis in court. *The International Journal of Clinical and Experimental Hypnosis* 27:311–41.

ORNE, M. T., AND HAMMER, A. G. 1974. Hypnosis, in *Encyclopaedia Brittannica,* 5th ed., pp. 133–40. Chicago: Encyclopaedia Brittannica.

OSOFSKY, J. D., AND DANZGER, B. 1974. Relationships between neo-natal characteristics and mother-infant characteristics. *Developmental Psychology* 10: 124–30.

PAI, M. N. 1946. Sleep-walking and sleep activities. *Journal of Mental Science* 92:756–65.

PARKE, R. D., AND SLABY, R. G. 1983. The development of aggression. In Mussen, P. H., ed., *Carmichael's manual of child psychology: Vol. 4. Socialization, personality and social development* (Hetherington, M. E., volume editor), pp. 547–642. New York: Wiley.

PASCAL-LEONE, J. 1978. Compounds, confounds and models in developmental information processing: A reply to Trabasso and Foellinger. *Journal of Experimental Child Psychology* 26:18–40.

PASSINGHAM, R. 1982. *The human primate.* San Francisco: Freeman.

PAUL, G. L. 1966. *Insight vs. desensitization in psychotherapy: An experiment in anxiety reduction.* Stanford, Calif.: Stanford University Press.

PAUL, G. L. 1967a. Strategy of outcome research in psychotherapy. *Journal of Consulting Psychology* 31:109–18.

PAUL, G. L. 1967b. Insight versus desensitization in psychotherapy two years after termination. *Journal of Consulting Psychology* 31:333–48.

PAVLOV, I. 1927. *Conditioned reflexes.* Oxford, England: Oxford University Press.

PEABODY, D. 1967. Trait inferences: Evaluative and descriptive aspects. *Journal of Personality and Social Psychology Monograph* 7(Whole No. 644).

PELLEGRINO, J. W., AND GLASER, R. 1979. Cognitive correlates and components in the analysis of individual differences. *Intelligence* 3: 187–214.

PENFIELD, W., AND RASMUSSEN, T. 1950. *The cerebral cortex of man.* New York: Macmillan.

PENFIELD, W., AND ROBERTS, L. 1959. *Speech and brain mechanisms.* Princeton, N.J.: Princeton University Press.

PENROSE, L. S., AND PENROSE, R. 1958. Impossible objects: A special type of visual illusion. *British Journal of Psychology* 49: 31–33.

PERIN, C. T. 1943. A quantitative investigation of the delay of reinforcement gradient. *Journal of Experimental Psychology* 32:37–51.

PETERSON, L. B., AND PETERSON, M. J. 1959. Short-term retention of individual items. *Journal of Experimental Psychology* 58:193–98.

PFAFFMAN, C. 1948. Studying the sense of taste and smell. In Andrews T. G., *Methods of psychology,* pp. 268–88. New York: Wiley.

PIAGET, J. 1932. *The moral judgment of the child.* London: Kegan Paul.

PIAGET, J. 1951. *Play, dreams and imitation in childhood.* New York: Norton.

PIAGET, J. 1952. *The origins of intelligence in children.* New York: International University Press.

PIAGET, J. 1954. *The construction of reality in the child.* New York: Basic Books.

PIAGET, J. 1972. *The child's conception of the world.* Totowa, N.J.: Littlefield, Adams.

PIAGET, J., AND INHELDER, B. 1956. *The child's conception of space.* London: Routledge and Kegan Paul.

PIAGET, J., AND INHELDER, B. 1967. *The child's conception of space.* New York: Norton.

PODLESNY, J. A., AND RASKIN, D. C. 1977. Physiological measures and the detection of deception. *Psychological Bulletin,* 84:782–99.

POLIVY, J., AND HERMAN, C. P. 1976. Clinical depression and weight change: A complex relation. *Journal of Abnormal Psychology* 85: 338–40.

PORAC, C. AND COREN, S. 1981. *Lateral preferences and human behavior.* New York: Springer-Verlag.

PORSOLT, R. D.; LE PICHON, M.; AND JALFRE, M. 1977. Depression: A new animal model sensitive to antidepressant treatments. *Nature* 266:730–32.

POSNER, M. I.; BOIES, S.; EICHELMAN, W. H.; AND TAYLOR, R. L. 1969. Retention of visual and name codes of single letters. *Jour-*

nal of Experimental Psychology 79 (1, Pt.2).

POSTAL, P. M. 1968. Epilogue. In Jacobs, R. A., and Rosenbaum, P. S., *English transformational grammar,* pp. 253–89. Waltham, Mass.: Blaisdell.

POTTER, J. M. 1980. What was the matter with Dr. Spooner? In Fromkin, V. A., ed., *Errors in linguistic performance: Slips of the tongue, pen and hand.* New York: Academic Press.

PREMACK, A., AND PREMACK, D. 1983. *The mind of an ape.* New York: Norton.

PREMACK, D. 1976. *Intelligence in ape and man.* Hillsdale, N.J.: Erlbaum.

PREMACK, D. 1978. On the abstractness of human concepts: Why it would be difficult to talk to a pigeon. In Hulse, S. H.; Fowler, H.; and Honig, W. K., eds. *Cognitive processes in animal behavior.* Hillsdale, N.J.: Erlbaum.

PREMACK, D., AND WOODRUFF, G. 1978. Does the chimpanzee have a theory of mind? *The Behavioral and Brain Sciences* 4:515–26.

PRICE-WILLIAMS, D. R. 1981. Concrete and formal operations. In Munroe, R. H.; Munroe, R. L.; and Whiting, B. B., eds., *Handbook of cross-cultural development,* pp. 403–22. New York: Garland.

PRICE-WILLIAMS, D., GORDON, W., AND RAMIREZ, M. 1969. Skill and conservation: A study of pottery-making children. *Developmental Psychology* 1: 769.

PRITCHARD, R. M. 1961. Stabilized images on the retina. *Scientific American* 204:72–78.

PROUST, M. 1913. *Swann's way.* Translated by Moncrieff, C. K. S. New York: Modern Library, 1928.

PROVENCE, S., AND LIPTON, R. C. 1962. *Infants in institutions.* New York: International Universities Press.

PUROHIT, A. D. 1966. Levels of introversion and competitional paired-associate learning. *Journal of Personality* 34:129–43.

PUTNAM, K. E. 1979. Hypnosis and distortions in eye witness memory. *International Journal of Clinical and Experimental Hypnosis* 27: 437–48.

QUAY, L. C. 1971. Language, dialect, reinforcement, and the intelligence test performance of Negro children. *Child Development* 42:5–15.

RACHMAN, S. J., AND TEASDALE, J. 1969. Aversion therapy: An appraisal. In Franks, C. M., ed., *Behavior therapy: Appraisal and status,* pp. 279–320. New York: McGraw-Hill.

RAINER, J. D.; MESNIKOFF, A.; KOLB, L. C.; AND CARR, A. Homosexuality and heterosexuality in identical twins. *Psychosomatic Medicine* 22: 251–58.

READ, C., AND SCHREIBER, P. 1982. Why short subjects are harder to find than long ones. In Wanner, E., and Gleitman, L. R., eds., *Language acquisition: The state of the art.* New York: Cambridge University Press.

REBELSKY, F., AND HANKS, C. 1971. Father's verbal interaction with infants in the first three months of life. *Child Development* 42: 63–68.

REDL, F. 1973. The superego in uniform. In Sanford, N., and Comstock, C., eds., *Sanctions for evil.* San Francisco: Jossey-Bass.

REDLICH, F. C., AND FREEDMAN, D. X. 1966. *The theory and practice of psychiatry.* New York: Basic Books.

REES, L., AND EYSENCK, H. J. 1945. A factorial study of some morphological and psychological aspects of human constitution. *Journal of Mental Science* 91:8–21.

REITMAN, J. S. 1974. Without surreptitious rehearsal, information in short-term memory decays. *Journal of Verbal Learning and Verbal Behavior* 13:365–77.

REITMAN, W. 1965. *Cognition and thought: An information processing approach.* New York: Wiley.

RESCORLA, R. A. 1966. Predictability and number of pairings in Pavlovian fear conditioning. *Psychonomic Science* 4: 383–84.

RESCORLA, R. A. 1967. Pavlovian conditioning and its proper control procedures. *Psychological Review* 74:71–80.

RESCORLA, R. A. 1980. *Pavlovian second-order conditioning.* Hillsdale, N.J.: Erlbaum.

RESCORLA, R. A., AND HOLLAND, P. C. 1982. Behavioral studies of associative learning in animals. *Annual Reviews of Psychology* 33:265–308.

RESCORLA, R. A., AND WAGNER, A. R. 1972. A theory of Pavlovian conditioning: Variations in the effectiveness of reinforcement and non-reinforcement. In Black, A. H., and Prokasy, W. F., eds., *Classical conditioning II.* New York: Appleton-Century-Crofts.

REVLIN, R., AND LEIRER, V. O. 1980. Understanding quantified categorical expressions. *Memory and Cognition* 8: 447–58.

REYNOLDS, G. S. 1968. *A primer of operant conditioning.* Glenview, Ill.: Scott, Foresman.

RHEINGOLD, H. L.; HAY, D. F.; AND WEST, M. J. 1976. Sharing in the second year of life. *Child Development* 47: 1148–58.

RICHTER, C. P. 1957. On the phenomenon of unexplained sudden death in animals and man. *Psychosomatic Medicine* 19:191–98.

RIGGS, L. A.; RATLIFF, F.; CORNSWEET, J. C.; AND CORNSWEET, T. N. 1953. The disappearance of steadily fixated visual test objects. *Journal of the Optical Society of America* 43:495–501.

RINGUETTE, E. L., AND KENNEDY, T. 1966. An experimental study of the double-bind hypothesis. *Journal of Abnormal Psychology* 71:136–42.

RIPS, L. J.; SMITH, E. E.; AND SHOBEN, E. J. 1978. Semantic composition in sentence verification. *Journal of Verbal Learning and Verbal Behavior* 19:705–721.

ROBBIN, A. A. 1958. A controlled study of the effects of leucotomy. *Journal of Neurology, Neurosurgery and Psychiatry* 21:262–69.

ROBINS, L. R. 1966. *Deviant children grown up: A sociological and psychiatric study of sociopathic personality.* Baltimore: Williams & Wilkins.

ROBINSON, H. B., AND ROBINSON, N. M. 1970. Mental retardation. In Mussen, P. H., ed., *Carmichael's manual of child psychology,* vol. 2, pp. 615–66. New York: Wiley.

ROCK, I. 1975. *An introduction to perception.* New York: Macmillan.

ROCK. I. 1983. *The logic of perception.* Cambridge, Mass.: M.I.T. Press.

ROCK. I., AND KAUFMAN, L. 1962. The moon illusion, II. *Science* 136:1023–31.

RODIN, J. 1980. The externality theory today. In Stunkard, A. J., ed., *Obesity,* pp. 226–39. Philadelphia: Saunders.

RODIN, J. 1981. Current status of the internal-external hypothesis for obesity. What went wrong? *American Psychologist* 36:361–72.

ROEDER, K. D. 1935. An experimental analysis of the sexual behavior of the praying mantis. *Biological Bulletin* 69:203–20.

ROEDER, L. 1967. *Nerve cells and insect behavior.* Cambridge, Mass.: Harvard University Press.

ROGERS, C. R. 1942. *Counseling and psychotherapy: New concepts in practice.* Boston: Houghton Mifflin.

ROGERS, C. R. 1961. *On becoming a person: A therapist's view of psychotherapy.* Boston: Houghton Mifflin.

ROLLS, 1975. *The brain and reward.* New York: Pergamon.

ROLLS, B. J., AND ROLLS, E. T. 1982. *Thirst.* New York: Cambridge University Press.

ROMANES, G. J. 1882. *Animal intelligence.* London: Kegan Paul.

ROMANES, G. J. 1901. *Darwin and after Darwin.* Chicago: Open Court Publishing Co.

ROSCH, E. H. 1973a. Natural categories. *Cognitive Psychology* 4:328–50.

ROSCH, E. H. 1973b. On the internal structure of perceptual and semantic categories. In Moore, T. E., ed., *Cognitive development and the acquisition of language.* New York: Academic Press.

ROSCH, E. H. 1978. Principles of categorization. In Rosch, E., and Lloyd, eds., *Cognition and categorization.* Hillsdale, N.J.: Erlbaum.

ROSCH, E. H., AND MERVIS, C. B. 1975. Family resemblances: Studies in the internal structure of categories. *Cognitive Psychology* 7:573–605.

ROSCH, E. H.; MERVIS, C. B.; GRAY, W. D.; JOHNSON, D. M.; AND BOYES-BRAEM, P. 1976. Basic objects in natural categories. *Cognitive Psychology* 8:382–439.

ROSEN, G. 1966. *Madness in society.* Chicago: University of Chicago Press.

ROSENHAN, D. L. 1973. On being sane in insane places. *Science* 179:250–58.

ROSENHAN, D. L., AND SELIGMAN, M. E. P. 1984. *Abnormal psychology.* New York: Norton.

ROSENZWEIG, M. R., AND LEIMAN, A. L. 1982. *Physiological psychology.* Lexington, Mass.: Heath.

ROSENTHAL, A. M. 1964. *Thirty-eight witnesses.* New York: McGraw-Hill.

ROSENTHAL, D. 1970. *Genetic theory and abnormal behavior.* New York: McGraw-Hill.

ROSS, J., AND LAWRENCE, K. Q. 1968. Some observations on memory artifice. *Psychonomic Science* 13:107–8.

ROWELL, T. E. 1966. Hierarchy in the organization of a captive baboon group. *Animal Behavior* 14:430–33.

ROZIN, E. 1982. The structure of cuisine. In Barker, M. L., ed., *The psychobiology of human food selection.* Westport, Conn.: AVI Publ. Co.

ROZIN, P. 1976*a*. The evolution of intelligence and access to the cognitive unconscious. In Stellar, E., and Sprague, J. M., eds., *Progress in psychobiology and physiological psychology,* vol. 6. New York: Academic Press.

ROZIN, P. 1976*b*. The psychobiological approach to human memory. In Rosenzweig, M. R., and Bennett, E. L., *Neural mechanisms of learning and memory,* pp. 3–48. Cambridge, Mass.: MIT Press.

ROZIN, P. 1976*c*. The selection of foods by rats, humans and other animals. *Advances in the study of behavior,* vol. 6, pp. 21–76. New York: Academic Press.

ROZIN, P. 1982. Human food selection: The interaction of biology, culture, and individual experience. In Barker, L. M., ed., *The psychology of human food selection,* pp. 225–54. Westport, Conn.: AVI Publ. Co.

ROZIN, P., AND KALAT, J. W. 1971. Specific hungers and poison avoidance as adaptive specializations of learning. *Psychological Review* 78:459–86.

RUCH, T. C. 1965. The homotypical cortex—the "association areas." In Ruch, T. C.; Palton, H. D.; Woodbury, J. W.; and Towe, A. L., eds., *Neurophysiology,* 2nd ed., pp. 465–79. Philadelphia: Saunders.

RUMBAUGH, D. M., ed. 1977. *Language learning by a chimpanzee: The Lana Project.* New York: Academic Press.

RUNDUS, D. 1977. Maintenance rehearsal and single-level processing. *Journal of Verbal Learning and Verbal Behavior* 16: 665–82.

RUSSEK, M. 1971. Hepatic receptors and the neurophysiological mechanisms controlling feeding behavior. In Ehrenpreis, S., ed., *Neurosciences research,* vol. 4. New York: Academic Press.

RUSSELL, G. V. 1961. Interrelationship within the limbic and centrencephlic systems. In Sheer, D. E., ed., *Electrical stimulation of the brain,* pp. 167–81. Austin, Tex.: University of Texas Press.

RUSSELL, W. R. 1959. *Brain, memory, learning: A neurologist's view.* Oxford, England: Oxford University Press.

SACHS, J. 1967. Recognition memory for syntactic and semantic aspects of connected discourse. *Perception and Psychophysics* 2:437–42.

SACHS, J., AND TRUSWELL, L. 1978. Comprehension of two-word instructions by children in the one-word stage. *Journal of Child Language* 5:17–24.

SADOCK, B. J. 1975. Group psychotherapy. In Freedman, A. M.; Kaplan, H. I.; and Sadock, B. J., eds., *Comprehensive textbook of psychiatry—II,* vol. 2, pp. 1850–76. Baltimore: Williams & Wilkins.

SAGHIR, M. T., AND ROBINS, E. 1973. *Male and female homosexuality.* Baltimore: Williams & Wilkins.

SAGI, A., AND HOFFMAN, M. L. 1976. Empathic distress in the newborn. *Developmental Psychology* 12:175–76.

SAKITT, B. 1975. Locus of short-term visual storage. *Science* 19:1318–19.

SAKITT, B. 1976. Iconic memory. *Psychological Review* 83:257–76.

SALAPATEK, P. 1975. Pattern perception in early infancy. In Cohen, L. B., and Salapatek, P., eds., *Infant perception: From sensation to cognition,* vol. 1, pp. 133–248. New York: Academic Press.

SALAPATEK, P., AND KESSEN, W. 1966. Visual scanning of triangles by the human newborn. *Journal of Experimental Child Psychology* 3:113–22.

SARASON, S. B. 1973. Jewishness, blackness, and the nature-nurture controversy. *American Psychologist* 28:926–71.

SARBIN, T. R., AND ALLEN, V. L. 1968. Role theory. In Lindzey, G., and Aronson, E., eds., *The handbook of social psychology,* 2nd ed., vol. 1, pp. 488–567. Reading, Mass.: Addison-Wesley.

SARNOFF, C. 1957. *Medical aspects of flying motivation—a fear-of-flying case book.* Randolph Air Force Base, Texas: U.S. Air Force, Air University, School of Aviation Medicine.

SATINOFF, E. 1964. Behavioral thermoregulation in response to local cooling of the rat brain. *American Journal of Physiology* 206:1389–94.

SAWREY, W. L.; CONGER, J. J.; AND TURRELL, E. S. 1956. An experimental investigation of the role of psychological factors in the production of gastric ulcers in the rat. *Journal of Comparative and Physiological Psychology* 49:457–61.

SCARR, S., AND CARTER-SALTZMAN, L. 1979. Twin-method: Defense of a critical assumption. *Behavior Genetics* 9:527–42.

SCARR, S., AND CARTER-SALTZMAN, L. 1982. Genetics and intelligence. In Sternberg, R. J., ed., *Handbook of human intelligence,* pp. 792–896. New York: Cambridge University Press.

SCARR, S., AND KIDD, K. K. 1983. Developmental behavior genetics. In Mussen, P. H., ed., *Carmichael's manual of child psychology: Vol. 2. Infancy and developmental psychobiology* (Haith, M. M. and Campos, J. J., volume editors), pp. 345–434. New York: Wiley.

SCARR, S., AND WEINBERG, R. A. 1976. IQ test performance of black children adopted by white families. *American Psychologist* 31:726–39.

SCHACHER, S. 1981. Determination and differentiation in the development of the nervous system. In Kandel, E. R., and Schwartz, J. H., eds., *Principles of neural science.* New York: Elsevier North Holland.

SCHACHTEL, E. G. 1947. On memory and childhood amnesia. *Psychiatry* 10:1–26.

SCHACTER, D. L., AND TULVING, E. 1982. Amnesia and memory research. In Cermak, L. S., ed., *Human memory and amnesia,* pp. 1–32. Hillsdale, N.J.: Erlbaum.

SCHACHTER, S. 1959. *The psychology of affiliation.* Stanford, Calif.: Stanford University Press.

SCHACHTER, S. 1971. Some extraordinary facts about obese humans and rats. *American Psychologist* 26:129–44.

SCHACHTER, S.; GOLDMAN, R.; AND GORDON, A. 1968. Effects of fear, food deprivation, and obesity on eating. *Journal of Personality and Social Psychology* 10:91–97.

SCHACHTER, S., AND RODIN, J. 1974. *Obese humans and rats.* Washington, D.C.: Erlbaum-Halstead.

SCHACHTER, S., AND SINGER, J. 1962. Cognitive, social and physiological determinants of emotional state. *Psychological Review*

69:379–99.

SCHAFFER, H. R. 1966. The onset of fear of strangers and the incongruity hypothesis. *Journal of Child Psychology and Psychiatry* 7:95–106.

SCHAFFER, H. R., AND CALLENDER, W. M. 1959. Psychological effects of hospitalization in infancy. *Pediatrics* 24:528–39.

SCHAIE, K., AND STROTHER, C. 1968. A cross-sequential study of age changes in cognitive behavior. *Psychological Bulletin* 70:671–80.

SCHAPIRO, S., AND VUKOVICH, K. R. 1976. Early experience effects on cortical dendrites: A proposed model for development. *Science* 167:292–94.

SCHEERER, M. 1963. Problem solving. *Scientific American* 208:118–28.

SCHEERER, M.; GOLDSTEIN, K.; AND BORING, E. G. 1941. A demonstration of insight: The horse-rider puzzle. *American Journal of Psychology* 54:437–38.

SCHEFF, T. 1966. *Being mentally ill: A sociological theory.* Chicago: Aldine.

SCHIFFMAN, H. R. 1976. *Sensation and perception: An integrated approach.* New York: Wiley.

SCHILDKRAUT, J. J. 1965. The catecholamine hypothesis of affective disorders: A review of supporting evidence. *American Journal of Psychiatry* 122:509–22.

SCHLEIDT, W. M. 1961. Ueber die Aufloesung der Flucht bor Raubvoeglns bei Truthuenern. *Naturwissenschaften* 48:141–42.

SCHNEIDERMAN, N., AND GORMEZANO, I. 1964. Conditioning of the nictitating membrane of the rabbit as a function of the CS-US interval. *Journal of Comparative and Physiological Psychology* 57:188–95.

SCHOFIELD, W. 1964. *Psychotherapy: The purchase of friendship.* Englewood Cliffs, N.J.: Prentice-Hall.

SCHOPLER, J., AND COMPERE, J. S. 1971. Effects of being kind or harsh to another on liking. *Journal of Personality and Social Psychology* 20:155–59.

SCHULL, J. 1979. A conditioned opponent theory of Pavlovian conditioning and habituation. In Bower, G., ed., *The psychology of learning and motivation,* vol. 13. New York: Academic Press.

SCHWARTZ, B. 1974. On going back to nature: A review of Seligman and Hager's *Biological boundaries of learning. Journal of the Experimental Analysis of Behavior* 21:183–98.

SCHWARTZ, B. 1978. *Psychology of learning and behavior.* New York: Norton.

SCHWARTZ, B. 1984. *Psychology of learning and behavior,* 2nd ed. New York: Norton.

SCHWARTZ, B., AND GAMZU, E. 1977. Pavlovian control of operant behavior. In Honig, W. K., and Staddon, J. E. R., eds., *Handbook of operant behavior.* Englewood Cliffs, N.J.: Prentice-Hall.

SCHWARTZ, S. H., AND CLAUSEN, G. 1970. Responsibility, norms, and helping in an emergency. *Journal of Personality and Social Psychology* 16:299–310.

SCOTT, J. P. 1963. The process of primary socialization in canine and human infants. *Monograph of the Society for Research in Child Development* 28:1–47.

SEARLE, J. R. 1969. *Speech acts: An essay in the philosophy of language.* New York: Cambridge University Press.

SEARS, R. R.; MACCOBY, E. E.; AND LEVIN, H. 1957. *Patterns of child rearing.* Evanston, Ill.: Row, Peterson.

SEAY, B.; ALEXANDER, B. K.; AND HARLOW, H. F. 1964. Maternal behavior of socially deprived rhesus monkeys. *Journal of Abnormal and Social Psychology* 69:345–54.

SEIDENBERG, M. S., AND PETITTO, L. A. 1979. Signing behavior in apes: A critical review. *Cognition* 7:177–215.

SELFRIDGE, O. G. 1955. Pattern recognition and modern computers. In *Proceedings of Western Joint Computer Conference,* Los Angeles, Calif.

SELFRIDGE, O. G. 1959. Pandemonium: A paradigm for learning. In Blake, D. V., and Uttley, A. M., eds. *Proceedings of the Symposium on the Mechanisation of Thought Processes.* London: HM Stationary Office.

SELIGMAN, M. E. P. 1968. Chronic fear produced by unpredictable electric shock. *Journal of Comparative and Physiological Psychology* 66:402–11.

SELIGMAN, M. E. P. 1970. On the generality of the laws of learning. *Psychological Review* 77:406–18.

SELIGMAN, M. E. P. 1975. *Helplessness: On depression, development and death.* San Francisco: Freeman.

SELIGMAN, M. E. P.; KLEIN, D. C.; AND MILLER, W. R. 1976. Depression. In Leitenberg, H., ed., *Handbook of behavior modification and behavior therapy.* Englewood Cliffs, N.J.: Prentice-Hall.

SELIGMAN, M. E. P., AND MAIER, S. F. 1967. Failure to escape traumatic shock. *Journal of Experimental Psychology* 74:1–9.

SELIGMAN, M. E. P.; MAIER, S. F.; AND SOLOMON, R. L. 1971. Unpredictable and uncontrollable aversive events. In Brush, F. R., ed., *Aversive conditioning and learning.* New York: Academic Press.

SENDAK, M. 1963. *Where the wild things are.* New York: Harper & Row.

SENDAK, M. 1979. *Higglety pigglety pop! or There must be more to life.* New York: Harper & Row.

SENDEN, M., VON. 1932. *Raum—und Gestaltauffassung bei operierten Blindgeborenen vor und nach der Operation.* Leipzig: Barth.

SEYFARTH, R. 1978. Social relations among adult male and female baboons. I. Behavior during sexual consortship. *Behavior* 64:204–26.

SHAKOW, D. 1977. Segmental set: The adaptive process in schizophrenia. *American Psychologist* 32:129–39.

SHAPIRO, A. K. 1971. Placebo effects in medicine, psychotherapy, and psychoanalysis. In Bergin, A. E., and Garfield, S. L., eds., *Handbook of psychotherapy and behavior change,* pp. 439–73. New York: Wiley.

SHATZ, M. 1978. The relationship between cognitive processes and the development of communication skills. In Keasey, C. B., ed., *Nebraska Symposium on Motivation.* Lincoln: University of Nebraska Press.

SHEFFIELD, F. D., AND ROBY, T. B. 1950. Reward value of a nonnutritive sweet taste. *Journal of Comparative and Physiological Psychology* 43:471–81.

SHEFFIELD, F. D.; WULFF, J. J.; AND BACKER, R. 1951. Reward value of copulation without sex drive reduction. *Journal of Comparative and Physiological Psychology* 44:3–8.

SHEKELLE, R. B.; RAYNOR, W. J.; OSTFELD, A. M.; GARRON, D. C.; BIELIAVSKAS, L. A.; LIV, S. C.; MALIZA, C.; AND PAUL, O. 1981. Psychological depression and the 17-year risk of cancer. *Psychosomatic Medicine* 43:117–25.

SHELDON, W. H. 1940. *The varieties of human physique.* New York: Harper.

SHELDON, W. H. 1942. *The varieties of temperament.* New York: Harper.

SHEPARD, R. N. 1982. Perceptual and analogical bases of cognition. In Mehler, J., ed., *Perspectives on mental representation,* pp. 49–67. Hillsdale, N.J.: Erlbaum.

SHEPHER, J. 1971. Mate selection among second generation kibbutz adolescents and adults: Incest avoidance and negative imprinting. *Archives of Sexual Behavior* 1:293–307.

SHERRINGTON, C. S. 1906. *The integrative action of the nervous system,* 2nd ed. New Haven, Conn.: Yale University Press, 1947.

SHIMBERG, M. E. 1929. An investigation into the validity of norms with special reference to urban and rural groups. In *Archives of Psychology,* No. 104.

SHIPLEY, E. F., AND KUHN, I. F. 1983. A constraint on comparisons: Equally detailed alternatives. *Journal of Experimental Child Psychology* 35:195–222.

SHIPLEY, E. F.; KUHN, I. F.; AND MADDEN, E. C. 1983. Mothers' use of superordinate terms. *Journal of Child Language* 10:571–88.

SHIPLEY, E. F.; SMITH, C. S.; AND GLEITMAN, L. R. 1969. A study in the acquisition of language: Free responses to commands. *Language* 45: 322–42.

SHIRLEY, M. M. 1933. *The first two years: A study of twenty-five babies,* vol. 1. Minneapolis: University of Minnesota Press.

SHOPSIN, B.; WILK, S.; SATHANANTHAN, G.; GERSHON, S.; AND DAVIS, K. 1974. Catecholamines and affective disorders revised: A critical assessment. *Journal of Nervous & Mental Disease* 158:369–83.

SHORTLIFFE, E. H.; AXLINE, S. G.; BUCHANAN, B. G.; MERIGAN, T. C.; AND COHEN, N. S. 1973. An artificial intelligence program to advise physicians regarding antimicrobial therapy. *Computers and Biomedical Research* 6:544–60.

SHUEY, A. 1966. *The testing of Negro intelligence.* New York: Social Science Press.

SHULTZ, T., AND HORIBE, F. 1974. Development of the appreciation of verbal jokes. *Development Psychology* 10:13–20.

SIEGEL, S. 1977. Morphine tolerance acquisition as an associative process. *Journal of Experimental Psychology: Animal Behavior Processes* 3:1–13.

SIEGEL, S. 1979. The role of conditioning in drug tolerance and addiction. In Keehn, J. D., ed., *Psychopathology in animals: Research and treatment implications.* New York: Academic Press.

SIEGEL, S.; HINSON, R. E.; AND KRANK, M. D. 1979. Modulation of tolerance to the lethal effect of morphine by extinction. *Behav. Neur. Biol.* 25:257.

SIEGLER, M., AND OSMOND, H. 1974. *Models of madness, models of medicine.* New York: Harper & Row.

SILVERMAN, I. 1971. Physical attractiveness and courtship. Cited in Hatfield, E., and Walster, G. W. *A new look at love.* Reading, Mass.: Addison-Wesley, 1981.

SIMNER, M. L. 1971. Newborn's response to the cry of another infant. *Developmental Psychology* 5:136–50.

SIMON, H. A. 1956. Rational choice and the structure of the environment. *Psychological Review* 63:129–38.

SINCLAIR, H. 1970. The transition from sensory-motor behavior to symbolic activity. *Interchange* 1:119–26.

SINCLAIR, H. 1973. Language acquisition and cognitive development. In Moore, T. E., ed., *Cognitive development and the acquisition of language.* New York: Academic Press.

SKEELS, H. 1966. Adult status of children with contrasting early life experiences. *Monograph of the Society for Research in Child Development* 31 (No. 3).

SKINNER, B. F. 1938. *The behavior of organisms.* New York: Appleton-Century-Crofts.

SKINNER, B. F. 1957. *Verbal behavior.* New York: Appleton-Century-Crofts.

SKODAK, M., AND SKEELS, H. M. 1945. A follow-up study of children in adoptive homes. *Journal of Genetic Psychology* 66:21–58.

SKODAK, M., AND SKEELS, H. M. 1947. A follow-up study of the development of one-hundred adopted children in Iowa. *American Psychologist* 2:278.

SKODAK, M., AND SKEELS, H. M. 1949. A final follow-up study of children in adoptive homes. *Journal of Genetic Psychology* 75:85–125.

SLATER, E. 1943. The neurotic constitution. *Journal of Neurological Psychiatry* 6:1–16.

SLATER, E., AND COWIE, V. 1971. *The genetics of mental disorders.* London: Oxford University Press.

SLOANE, R. B.; STAPLES, F. R.; CRISTOL, A. H.; YORKSTON, N. J.; AND WHIPPLE, K. 1975. *Psychotherapy vs. behavior therapy.* Cambridge, Mass.: Harvard University Press.

SLOBIN, D. I. 1966. Grammatical transformations and sentence comprehension in childhood and adulthood. *Journal of Verbal Learning and Verbal Behavior* 5:219–27.

SLOBIN, D. I. 1973. Cognitive prerequisites for the development of grammar. In Ferguson, C., and Slobin D., eds., *Studies of child language development,* pp. 175–208. New York: Holt, Rinehart & Winston.

SLOBIN, D. I. 1977. Language change in childhood and history. In McNamara, J., ed., *Language learning and thought.* New York: Academic Press.

SMEDSLUND, J. 1961. The acquisition of conservation of substance and weight in children. *Scandinavia Journal of Psychology* 2:11–20.

SMELSER, N. J. 1963. *Theory of collective behavior.* New York: Free Press, Macmillan.

SMITH, B. M. 1967. The polygraph. *Scientific American* 216:25–31.

SMITH, C., AND LLOYD, B. 1978. Maternal behavior and perceived sex of infant: Revisited. *Child Development* 49:1263–65.

SMITH, E. E., AND MEDIN, D. L. 1981. *Categories and concepts.* Cambridge, Mass.: Harvard University Press.

SMITH, J. M. 1964. Group selection and kin selection. *Nature* 201:1145–47.

SMITH, J. M. 1965. The evolution of alarm calls. *American Naturalist* 99:59–63.

SMITH, M. L., AND GLASS, G. V. 1977. Meta-analysis of psychotherapy outcome studies. *American Psychologist* 32:752–60.

SMITH, S. M. 1979. Remembering in and out of context. *Journal of Experimental Psychology: Human Learning and Memory* 5:460–71.

SMITH, S. M.; BROWN, H. O.; TOMAN, J. E. P.; AND GOODMAN, L. S. 1947. The lack of cerebral effects of d-tubocurarine. *Anaesthesiology* 8:1–14.

SMITH, W. J. 1977. *The behavior of communicating.* Cambridge, Mass.: Harvard University Press.

SNYDER, M., AND CUNNINGHAM, M. R. 1975. To comply or not comply: Testing the self-perception explanation of the "foot-in-the-door" phenomenon. *Journal of Personality and Social Psychology* 31:64–67.

SNYDER, S. H. 1976. The dopamine hypothesis of schizophrenia. *American Journal of Psychiatry* 133:197–202.

SNYDER, S. H. 1977. Opiate receptors and internal opiates. *Scientific American* 236:44–56.

SNYDER, S. H., AND CHILDERS, S. R. 1979. Opiate receptors and opioid peptides. *Annual Review of Neuroscience* 2:35–64.

SOLOMON, R. L. 1977. An opponent-process theory of acquired motivation: IV. The affective dynamics of addiction. In Maser, J. D., and Seligman, M. E. P., eds., *Psychopathology: Experimental models,* pp. 66–103. San Francisco: Freeman.

SOLOMON, R. L. 1980. The opponent-process theory of acquired motivation: The costs of pleasure and the benefits of pain. *American Psychologist* 35:691–712.

SOLOMON, R. L., AND CORBIT, J. D. 1974. An opponent-process theory of motivation: I. Temporal dynamics of affect. *Psychological Review* 81:119–45.

SOLOMON, R. L., AND WYNNE, L. C. 1953. Traumatic avoidance learning: Acquisition in normal dogs. *Psychological Monographs* 67 (Whole No. 354).

SPEARMAN, C. 1927. *The abilities of man.* London: Macmillan.

SPELKE, E. S. 1976. Infants' intermodal perception of events. *Cognitive Psychology* 8:553–60.

SPELKE, E. S. 1981. The development of intermodal perception. In Cohen, L. B., and Salapatek, P., eds., *Handbook of infant perception.* New York: Academic Press.

SPELKE, E. S. 1982. Perceptual knowledge of objects in infancy. In Meehler, J.; Garrett, M.; and Walker, E. E., eds., *On mental representation.* Hillsdale, N.J.: Erlbaum.

SPELKE, E. S. 1983. Perception of unity, persistence, and identity: Thoughts on infants' conceptions of objects. In Meehler, J., ed., *Infant and neonate cognition.* Hillsdale, N.J.: Erlbaum.

SPEMANN, H. 1967. *Embryonic development and induction*. New York: Hafner Publishing Company.

SPENCE, J. T., AND HELMREICH, R. L. 1983. Achievement-related motives and behaviors. In Spence, J. T., ed., *Achievement and achievement motives: Psychological and sociological approaches*, pp. 7–74. San Francisco: Freeman.

SPERLING, G. 1960. The information available in brief visual presentations. *Psychological Monographs* 74 (Whole No. 11).

SPIES, G. 1965. Food versus intracranial self-stimulation reinforcement in food deprived rats. *Journal of Comparative and Physiological Psychology* 60:153–57.

SPIRO, M. E. 1958. *Children of the kibbutz*. Cambridge, Mass.: Harvard University Press.

SPITZ, R. A. 1945. Hospitalism: An inquiry into the genesis of psychiatric conditions in early childhood. *Psychoanalytic Study of the Child* 1:53–74.

SPRINGER, S. P., AND DEUTSCH, G. 1981. *Left brain, right brain*. San Francisco: Freeman.

SQUIRE, L. R., AND COHEN, N. J. 1982. Remote memory, retrograde amnesia, and the neuropsychology of memory. In Cermak, L. S., ed., *Human memory and amnesia*, pp. 275–304. Hillsdale, N.J.: Erlbaum.

STAMPFL, T. G., AND LEVIS, D. J. 1967. Essentials of implosive therapy: A learning-theory-based psychodynamic behavior therapy. *Journal of Abnormal Psychology* 72:496–503.

STANG, D. J., AND CRANDALL, R. 1977. Familiarity and liking. In Steinfatt, T. M., ed., *Readings in human communication*. Indianapolis: Bobbs-Merrill.

STAUB, E. A. 1970. The influence of age and number of witnesses on children's attempts to help. *Journal of Personality and Social Psychology* 14:130–40.

STEIN, L., AND WISE, C. D. 1971. Possible etiology of schizophrenia: Progressive damage to the noradrenergic reward system by 6-hydroxydopamine. *Science* 171:1032–36.

STEINBERG, B. M., AND DUNN, L. A. 1976. Conservation, competence and performance in Chiapas. *Human Development* 19:14–25.

STEINER, J. E. 1974. The gustafacial response: Observation on normal and anencephalic newborn infants. In Bosma, F. J., ed., *Fourth symposium on oral sensation and perception: Development in the fetus and infant* (DHEW Publication No. NIH 73-546). Washington, D.C.: U.S. Government Printing Office.

STEINER, J. E. 1977. Facial expressions of the neonate infant indicating the hedonics of food-related chemical stimuli. In Weiffenbach, J. M., ed., *Taste and development: The genesis of sweet preference* (DHEW Publication No. NIH 77-1068), pp. 173–88. Washington, D.C.: U.S. Government Printing Office.

STELLAR, E. 1954. The physiology of motivation. *Psychological Review* 61:5–22.

STERNBERG, R. J. 1977. *Intelligence information processing and analogical reasoning: The componential analysis of human abilities*. Hillsdale, N.J.: Erlbaum.

STERNBERG, S. 1969. Memory-scanning: Mental processes revealed by reaction-time experiments. *American Scientist* 57:421–57.

STERNBERG, S. 1970. Memory-scanning: Mental processes revealed by reaction time experiments. In Antrobus, J. S. *Cognition and affect*, pp. 13–58. Boston: Little, Brown.

STERNBERG, S. 1975. Memory scanning: New findings and current controversies. *Quarterly Journal of Experimental Psychology* 27:1–32.

STEVENS, A., AND COUPE, P. 1978. Distortions in judged spatial relations. *Cognitive Psychology* 10:422–37.

STEVENS, S. S. 1955. The measurement of loudness. *Journal of the Acoustical Society of America* 27:815–19.

STEWART, K. 1951. Dream theory in Malaya. *Complex* 6:21–34.

STEWART, T. D. 1957. Stone age surgery: A general review, with emphasis on the New World. *Annual Review of the Smithsonian Institution*. Washington, D.C.: Smithsonian Institute.

STOKOE, W. C., JR.; CASTERLINE, D.; AND CRONEBEG, C. 1965. *A dictionary of American Sign Language*. Washington, D.C.: Gallaudet College Press.

STOLLER, R. J. 1968. *Sex and gender: On the development of masculinity and femininity*. New York: Science House.

STONE, A. 1975. *Mental health and law: A system in transition*. (DHEW Publication No. 75176). Washington, D.C.: U.S. Government Printing Office.

STOTLAND, E.; MATHEWS, K. E., JR.; SHERMAN, S. E.; HANSSON, R. O.; AND RICHARDSON, B. Z. 1978. *Empathy, fantasy, and helping*. Sage Library of Social Research, Volume 65. Beverly Hills, Calif.: Sage Publications.

STRATTON, G. M. 1897. Vision without inversion of the retinal image. *Psychological Review* 4:341–60.

STREET, R. F. 1931. *A gestalt completion test*. New York: Teachers College Press, Columbia University.

STRICKER, E. M., AND ZIGMOND, M. J. 1976. Recovery of function after damage to catecholamine-containing neurons: A neurochemical model for the lateral hypothalamic syndrome. In Sprague, J. M., and Epstein, A. N., eds., *Progress in psychobiology and physiological psychology*, vol. 6, pp. 121–88. New York: Academic Press.

STROOP, J. R. 1935. Studies of interference in serial verbal reactions. *Journal of Experimental Psychology* 18:643–62.

STUART, R. B., AND MITCHELL, C. 1980. Self-help groups in the control of body weight. In Stunkard, A. J., ed., *Obesity*, pp. 354–55. Philadelphia: Saunders.

STUNKARD, A. J. 1975. Obesity. In Freedman, A. M.; Kaplan, H. I.; and Sadock, B. J., eds., *Comprehensive textbook of psychiatry—II*, vol. 2, pp. 1648–54. Baltimore: Williams & Wilkins.

STUNKARD, A. 1980. Psychoanalysis and psychotherapy. In Stunkard, A. J., ed., *Obesity*, pp. 355–68. Philadelphia: Saunders.

SULLIVAN, P. M., AND VERNON, M. 1979. Psychological assessment of hearing impaired children. *School Psychology Digest* 8(3):271–90. Boys Town Institute for Communication Disorders in Children.

SULLY, J. 1910. *Studies of childhood*, 2nd ed. New York: Appleton.

SULS, J. M. 1972. A two-stage model for the appreciation of jokes and cartoons: An information processing analysis. In Goldstein, J. H., and McGhee, P. E., eds., *The psychology of humor*, pp. 81–100. New York: Academic Press.

SUOMI, S. J., AND HARLOW, H. F. 1971. Abnormal social behavior in young monkeys. In Helmuth, J., ed., *Exceptional infant: Studies in abnormalities*, vol. 2, pp. 483–529. New York: Brunner/Mazel.

SUOMI, S. J.; HARLOW, H. F.; AND MCKINNEY, W. T. 1972. Monkey psychiatrist. *American Journal of Psychiatry* 128:41–46.

SUPALLA, I., AND NEWPORT, E. L. 1978. How many seats in a chair? The derivation of nouns and verbs in American Sign Language. In Siple, P., ed., *Understanding language through sign language research*. New York: Academic Press.

SUPER, C. M. 1976. Environmental effects on motor development. *Developmental Medicine and Child Neurology* 18:561–67.

SZASZ, T. S. 1974. *The myth of mental illness: Foundations of a theory of personal conduct*, rev. ed. New York: Harper & Row.

TAKAHASHI, Y. 1979. Growth hormone secretion related to the sleep waking rhythm. In Drucker-Colín, R.; Shkurovich, M.; and Sterman, M.B., eds., *The functions of sleep*. New York: Academic Press.

TANNER, J. M. 1970. Physical growth. In Mussen, P. H., ed., *Carmichael's manual of child psychology*, 3rd ed., pp. 77–105. New York: Wiley.

TAYLOR, S. E., AND FISKE, S. T. 1975. Point of view and perceptions of causality. *Journal of Personality and Social Psychology* 32:439–45.

TEITELBAUM, P. 1955. Sensory control of hypothalamic hyperphagia. *Journal of Comparative and Physiological Psychology* 48: 156–63.

TEITELBAUM, P. 1961. Disturbances in feeding and drinking behavior after hypothalamic lesions. In Jones, M. R., ed., *Nebraska Symposium on Motivation,* pp. 39–65. Lincoln, Nebraska: University of Nebraska Press.

TEITELBAUM, P., AND EPSTEIN, A. N. 1962. The lateral hypothalamic syndrome: Recovery of feeding and drinking after lateral hypothalamic lesions. *Psychological Review* 69:74–90.

TEITELBAUM, P., AND STELLAR, E. 1954. Recovery from failure to eat produced by hypothalamic lesions. *Science* 120:894–95.

TERMAN, L. M., AND MERRILL, M. A. 1972. *Stanford-Binet intelligence scale—manual for the third revision,* form L-M. Boston: Houghton Mifflin.

TERNUS, J. 1938. The problem of phenomenal identity. In Ellis, W. D., ed. and trans., *A source book of Gestalt psychology.* London: Routledge and Kegan Paul.

TERRACE, H. S. 1979. *Nim.* New York: Knopf.

TERRACE, H. S.; PETITTO, L. A.; SANDERS, D. L.; AND BEVER, T. G. 1979. Can an ape create a sentence? *Science* 206:891–902.

TERVOORT, B. T. 1961. Esoteric symbolism in the communication behavior of young deaf children. *American Annals of the Deaf* 106:436–80.

THEOPHRASTUS. 319 B.C. *The characters.* Translated by Edmonds, J. M. Cambridge, Mass.: Harvard University Press, 1929.

THIGPEN, C. H., AND CLECKLEY, H. M. 1957. *The three faces of Eve.* New York: McGraw-Hill.

THOMAS, A.; CHESS, S.; AND BIRCH, H. G. 1970. The origin of personality. *Scientific American* 223:102–9.

THOMPSON, N. L.; McCANDLESS, B. R.; AND STRICKLAND, B. R. 1971. Personal adjustment of male and female homosexuals and heterosexuals. *Journal of Abnormal and Social Psychology* 78:237–40.

THOMPSON, R. F. 1973. *Introduction to biopsychology.* San Francisco: Albion Publishing Co.

THORNDIKE, E. L. 1898. Animal intelligence: An experimental study of the associative processes in animals. *Psychological Monographs* 2 (Whole No. 8).

THORNDIKE, E. L. 1899. The associative processes in animals. *Biological lectures from the Marine Biological Laboratory at Woods Hole.* Boston: Atheneum.

THORNDIKE, E. L. 1911. *Animal intelligence: Experimental studies.* New York: Macmillan.

THORNDIKE, E. L., AND LORGE, I. 1944. *The teacher's word book of 30,000 words.* New York: Teachers College Press, Columbia University.

TINBERGEN, N. 1951. *The study of instinct.* Oxford, England: Clarendon.

TOLMAN, E. C. 1948. Cognitive maps in rats and men. *Psychological Review* 55:189–208.

TOLMAN, E. C., AND GLEITMAN, H. 1949. Studies in learning and motivation: I. Equal reinforcements in both end-boxes, followed by shock in one end-box. *Journal of Experimental Psychology* 39:810–19.

TOLMAN, E. C., AND HONZIK, C. H. 1930. Introduction and removal of reward, and maze performance in rats. *University of California Publications in Psychology* 4:257–75.

TOWNSEND, J. T. 1971. A note on the identifiability of parallel and serial processes. *Perception and Psychophysics* 10:161–63.

TREISMAN, A. M. 1964. Selective attention in man. *British Medical Bulletin* 20:12–16.

TRIVERS, R. L. 1971. The evolution of reciprocal altruism. *Quarterly Review of Biology* 46:35–57.

TULVING, E. 1972. Episodic and semantic memory. In Tulving, E., and Donaldson, W., eds., *Organization and memory.* New York: Academic Press.

TULVING, E., AND OSLER, S. 1968. Effectiveness of retrieval cues in memory for words. *Journal of Experimental Psychology* 77:593–601.

TULVING, E., AND PEARLSTONE, Z. 1966. Availability versus accessability of information in memory for words. *Journal of Verbal Learning and Verbal Behavior* 5:381–91.

TULVING, E., AND THOMSON, D. M. 1973. Encoding specificity and retrieval processes in episodic memory. *Psychological Review* 80:352–73.

TVERSKY, A., AND KAHNEMAN, D. 1973. Availability: A heuristic for judging frequency and probability. *Cognitive Psychology* 5:207–32.

TVERSKY, A., AND KAHNEMAN, D. 1974. Judgment under uncertainty: Heuristics and biases. *Science* 125:1124–31.

TVERSKY, A., AND KAHNEMAN, D. 1983. Extensional vs. intuitive reasoning: The conjunction fallacy in probability judgment. *Psychological Review* 90:293–315.

TYLER, L. E. 1965. *The psychology of human differences.* New York: Appleton-Century-Crofts.

UNGERSTEDT, U., AND LJUNGBERG, T. 1974. Central dopamine neurons and sensory processing. *Journal of Psychiatry Research* 11:149–50.

URWIN, C. 1983. Dialogue and cognitive functioning in the early language development of three blind children. In Mills, A. E., ed., *Language acquisition in the blind child.* London: Croom Helm.

U.S. PUBLIC HEALTH SERVICE, DIVISION OF CHRONIC DISEASES. 1966. *Obesity and health* (Public Health Service Publication No. 1485). Washington, D.C.:U.S. Government Printing Office.

VAILLANT, G. E. 1977. *Adaptation to life.* Boston: Little, Brown.

VALENTA, J. G., AND RIGBY, M. K. 1968. Discrimination of the odor of stressed rats. *Science* 161:599–601.

VALINS, S. 1966. Cognitive effects of false heart-rate feedback. *Journal of Personality and Social Psychology* 4:400–8.

VAN CANTFORT, T. E. 1982. Sign language studies with children and chimpanzees. *Sign Language Studies* 34: 15–72.

VAUGHN, C. E., AND LEFF, J. P. 1976. The influence of family and social factors on the course of psychiatric illness: A comparison of schizophrenic and depressed neurotic patients. *British Journal of Psychiatry* 129:125–37.

VERNON, M., AND BROWN, D. W. 1964. A guide to psychological tests and testing procedures in the evaluation of deaf and hard-of-hearing children. *Journal of Speech and Hearing Disorders* 29:414–23.

VERNON, P. E. 1964. *Personality assessment.* London: Methuen.

VERY, P. S. 1967. Differential factor structure in mathematical ability. *Genetic Psychology Monographs* 75:169–208.

VIATOR. 1505. *De Artifiali Perspectiva,* Toul 1505. In Ivins, W. M., Jr., *On the rationalization of sight.* New York: Da Capo, 1975.

VIERLING, J. S., AND ROCK, J. 1967. Variations of olfactory sensitivity to exaltolide during the menstrual cycle. *Journal of Applied Physiology* 22:311–15.

VISINTAINER, M.; VOLPICELLI, J. R.; AND SELIGMAN, M. E. P. 1982. Tumor rejection in rats after inescapable or escapable shock. *Science* 216:437–39.

VON DOMARUS, E. 1944. The specific laws of logic in schizophrenia. In Kasanin, J., ed., *Language and thought in schizophrenia.* Berkeley, Calif.: University of California Press.

VON HOFSTEN, C. 1980. Predictive reaching for moving objects by human infants. *Journal of Experimental Child Psychology* 30:369–82.

VON HOFSTEN, C. 1982. Eye-hand coordination in the newborn. *Developmental Psychology* 18:450–61.

VON HOFSTEN, C. 1983. Catching skills in infancy. *Journal of Experimental Psychology: Human Perception and Performance* 9:75–85.

VON HOFSTEN, C., AND LINDHAGEN, K. 1979. Observations on the development of reaching for moving objects. *Journal of Experimental Child Psychology* 28:158–73.

WABER, D. P. 1977. Sex differences in mental abilities, hemispheric lateralization, and rate of physical growth at adolescence. *Developmental Psychology* 13:29–38.

WABER, D. P. 1979. Cognitive abilities and sex-related variations in the maturation of cerebral cortical functions. In Wittig, M. A., and Petersen, A. C., eds., *Sex-related differences in cognitive functioning*, pp. 161–89. New York: Academic Press.

WACHTEL, P. L. 1977. *Psychoanalysis and behavior therapy: Toward an integration.* New York: Basic Books.

WALD, G. 1950. Eye and camera. *Scientific American* 183:32–41.

WALK, R. D., AND GIBSON, E. J. 1961. A comparative and analytical study of visual depth perception. *Psychological Monographs* 75 (Whole No. 519).

WALLACE, W. H.; TURNER, S. H.; AND PERKINS, C. C. 1957. Preliminary studies of human information storage. Philadelphia: Signal Corps Project No. 1320, Institute for Cooperative Research, University of Pennsylvania.

WALLAS, G. 1926. *The art of thought.* New York: Harcourt, Brace.

WALSTER, E.; ARONSON, E.; AND ABRAHAMS, D. 1966. On increasing the persuasiveness of a low prestige communicator. *Journal of Experimental Social Psychology* 2:325–42.

WALSTER, E.; ARONSON, E.; ABRAHAMS, D.; AND ROTTMAN, L. 1966. The importance of physical attractiveness in dating behavior. *Journal of Personality and Social Psychology* 4:508–16.

WANNER, E., AND GLEITMAN, L. R., eds. 1982. *Language acquisition: The state of the art.* New York: Cambridge University Press.

WANNER, E., AND MARATSOS, M. 1978. An ATN approach to comprehension. In Halle, M.; Bresnan, J.; and Miller, G. A., eds., *Linguistic theory and psychological reality.* Cambridge, Mass.: MIT Press.

WARREN, R. M. 1970. Perceptual restorations of missing speech sounds. *Science* 167:392–93.

WASMAN, M., AND FLYNN, J. P. 1962. Directed attack elicited from the hypothalamus. *Archives of Neurology* 6:220–27.

WASON, P. C. 1960. On the failure to eliminate hypotheses in a conceptual task. *Quarterly Journal of Experimental Psychology* 12:129–40.

WASON, P. C. 1968. "On the failure to eliminate hypotheses..." —A second look. In Wason, P. C., and Johnson-Laird, P. N., eds., *Thinking and reasoning.* Harmondsworth, England: Penguin Books.

WASON, P. C., AND JOHNSON-LAIRD, P. N. 1972. *Psychology of reasoning.* London: B. T. Batsord, Ltd.

WATERS, E.; WIPPMAN, J.; AND SROUFE, L. A. 1979. Attachment, positive affect, and competence in the peer group: Two studies in construct validation. *Child Development* 50:821–29.

WATSON, J. B. 1925. *Behaviorism.* New York: Norton.

WATSON, J. S. 1967. Memory and "contingency analysis" in infant learning. *Merrill-Palmer Quarterly* 13:55–76.

WEBB, W. B. 1972. Sleep deprivation: Total, partial, and selective. In Chase, M. H., ed., *The sleeping brain*, pp. 323–62. Los Angeles: Brain Information Service, Brain Research Institute.

WEBB, W. B. 1974. Sleep as an adaptive process. *Perceptual and Motor Skills* 38:1023–27.

WEBB, W. B. 1975. *Sleep: The gentle tyrant.* Englewood Cliffs, N.J.: Prentice-Hall.

WECHSLER, D. 1958. *The measurement and appraisal of adult intelligence,* 4th ed. Baltimore: Williams & Wilkins.

WEIGEL, R. H.; VERNON, D. T. A.; AND TOGNACCI, L. N. 1974. Specificity of the attitude as a determinant of attitude-behavior congruence. *Journal of Personality and Social Psychology* 30:724–28.

WEINER, H.; THALER, M.; REISER, M. F.; AND MIRSKY, I. A. 1957. Etiology of duodenal ulcer: I. Relation of specific psychological characteristics to rate of gastric secretion. *Psychosomatic Medicine* 19:1–10.

WEINSTOCK, S. 1954. Resistance to extinction of a running response following partial reinforcement under widely spaced trials. *Journal of Comparative and Physiological Psychology* 47:318–22.

WEISS, B., AND LATIES, V. G. 1961. Behavioral thermoregulation. *Science* 133:1338–44.

WEISS, J. M. 1970. Somatic effects of predictable and unpredictable shock. *Psychosomatic Medicine* 32:397–408.

WEISS, J.M. 1977. Psychological and behavioral influences on gastrointestinal lesions in animal models. In Maser, J. D., and Seligman, M.E.P., eds., *Psychopathology: Experimental models,* pp. 232–69. San Francisco: Freeman.

WEISSMAN, M. M., AND MYERS, J. K. 1978. Affective disorders in a U.S. urban community. *Archives General Psychiatry* 35:1304–10.

WELKER, W. I.; JOHNSON, J. I.; AND PUBOLS, B. H. 1964. Some morphological and physiological characteristics of the somatic sensory system in raccoons. *American Zoologist* 4:75–94.

WELLMAN, H. M.; RITTER, K.; AND FLAVELL, J. H. 1975. Deliberate memory behavior in the delayed reactions of very young children. *Developmental Psychology* 11:780–87.

WENGER, M. A.; JONES, F. N.; AND JONES, M. H. 1956. *Physiological psychology.* New York: Holt, Rinehart & Winston.

WERTHEIMER, M. 1912. Experimentelle Studien über das Gesehen von Bewegung. *Zeitschrift für Psychologie* 61:161–265.

WERTHEIMER, M. 1923. Untersuchungen zur Lehre von der Gestalt, II. *Psychologische Forschung* 4:301–50.

WERTHEIMER, M. 1945. *Productive thinking.* New York: Harper.

WERTHEIMER, MICHAEL. 1961. Psychomotor coordination of auditory and visual space at birth. *Science* 134:1692.

WETZEL, M., AND STUART, D. G. 1976. Ensemble characteristics of cat locomotion and its neural control. *Progress in Neurobiology* 7:1–98.

WEXLER, K., AND CULICOVER, P. 1980. *Formal principles of language acquisition.* Cambridge, Mass.: MIT Press.

WHEELER, L. R. 1942. A comparative study of the intelligence of East Tennessee mountain children. *Journal of Educational Psychology* 33:321–34.

WHITE, R. W., AND WATT, N. F. 1973. *The abnormal personality,* 4th ed. New York: Ronald Press.

WHITE, S. H., AND PILLEMER, D. B. 1979. Childhood amnesia and the development of a socially accessible memory system. In Kihlstrom, J. F., and Evans, F. J. eds., *Functional disorders of memory,* pp. 29–74. Hillsdale, N.J.: Erlbaum.

WHITE, W. A. 1932. *Outlines of psychiatry,* 13th ed. New York: Nervous and Mental Disease Publishing Co.

WHITING, B. B., AND EDWARDS, C. P. 1973. A cross-cultural analysis of the behavior of children aged 3–11. *Journal of Social Psychology* 91:171–88.

WHITING, J. W. M., AND WHITING, B. B. 1975. *Children of six cultures: A psychocultural analysis.* Cambridge, Mass.: Harvard University Press.

WILCOXIN, H. C.; DRAGOIN, W. B.; AND KRAL, P. A. 1971. Illness-induced aversions in rat and quail: Relative salience of visual and gustatory cues. *Science* 171:826–28.

WILLIAMS, C. D. 1959. The elimination of tantrum behavior by extinction procedures. *Journal of Abnormal and Social Psychology* 59:269.

WILLIAMS, D. R., AND WILLIAMS, H. 1969. Automaintenance in the pigeon: Sustained pecking despite contingent non-reinforcement. *Journal of the Experimental Analysis of Behavior* 12:511–20.

WILLIAMS, G. C. 1966. *Adaptation and natural selection.* Princeton, N.J.: Princeton University Press.

WILLIAMS, H. L.; TEPAS, D. I.; AND MORLOCK, H. C. 1962. Evoked responses to clicks and electroencephalographic stages of sleep in man. *Science* 138:685–86.

WILLIAMS, M. D., AND HOLLAN, J. D. 1982. The process of retrieval from very long-term memory. *Cognitive Science* 5:87–119.

WILSON, E. O. 1975. *Sociobiology.* Cambridge, Mass.: Harvard University Press.

WILSON, G. T. 1980. Behavior modification and the treatment of obesity. In Stunkard, A. J., ed., *Obesity,* pp. 325–44. Philadelphia: Saunders.

WINCH, R. F., AND MORE, D. M. 1956. Does TAT add information to interviews? Statistical analysis of the increment. *Journal of Clinical Psychology* 12:316–21.

WINDES, J. D. 1968. Reaction time for numerical coding and naming of numerals. *Journal of Experimental Psychology* 78:318–22.

WISHNER, J. 1960. Reanalysis of "impressions of personality." *Psychological Review* 67:96–112.

WISHNER, J. 1974. *Psychopathology: Defective concept or defective practice?* Invited address delivered at the XVIII International Congress of Applied Psychology, Montreal, Canada.

WITTGENSTEIN, L. 1953. *Philosophical investigations.* Translated by Anscombe, G. E. M. Oxford, England: Blackwell.

WOHLWILL, J. H. 1973. *The study of behavioral development.* New York: Academic Press.

WOLF, S. 1971. Psychosocial influences in gastrointestinal function. In Levi, L., ed., *The psychosocial environment and psychosomatic disease,* vol. 1, pp. 362–68. London: Oxford University Press.

WOLFF, P. H. 1969. The natural history of crying and other vocalizations in early infancy. In Foss, B. M., ed., *Determinants of infant behavior,* vol. 4. London: Methuen.

WOLLEN, K. A.; WEBER, A.; AND LOWRY, D. 1972. Bizarreness versus interaction of mental images as determinants of learning. *Cognitive Psychology* 3:518–23.

WOLPE, J. 1958. *Psychotherapy by reciprocal inhibition.* Stanford, Calif.: Stanford University Press.

WOLPE, J., AND LAZARUS, A. A. 1966. *Behavior therapy techniques: A guide to the treatment of neuroses.* Elmsford, N.Y.: Pergamon.

WOLPE, J., AND LAZARUS, A. A. 1969. *The practice of behavior therapy.* New York: Pergamon.

WOLPERT, E. A., AND TROSMAN, H. 1958. Studies in psychophysiology of dreams: I. Experimental evocation of sequential dream episodes. *Archives of Neurology and Psychiatry* 79:603–6.

WOODS, R. L. 1947. *The world of dreams: An anthology.* New York: Random House.

WOODWORTH, R. S. 1938. *Experimental psychology.* New York: Holt.

WOODWORTH, R. S., AND SELLS, S. B. 1935. An atmosphere effect in formal syllogistic reasoning. *Journal of Experimental Psychology* 18:451–60.

WRIGHTSMAN, L. S., AND DEAUX, K. 1981. *Social psychology in the 80s,* 3rd ed. Monterey, Calif.: Brooks/Cole.

WYERS, E. J.; PEEKE, H. V. S.; AND HERZ, M. J. 1973. Behavioral habituation in invertebrates. In Peeke, H. V. S., and Herz, M. J., eds., *Habituation: Vol. 1. Behavioral studies.* New York: Academic Press.

WYNNE, L. C., AND SINGER, M. T. 1963*a*. Thought disorder and family relations in schizophrenics: I. A research strategy. *Archives of General Psychiatry* 9:191–98.

WYNNE, L. C., AND SINGER, M. T. 1963*b*. Thought disorder and family relations of schizophrenics: II. Classification of forms of thinking. *Archives of General Psychiatry* 9:199–206.

YAGI, N. 1927. Phototropism of *Dixippus murosus. Journal of General Physiology* 11:297–300.

YANDO, R.; SEITZ, V.; AND ZIGLER, E. 1978. *Imitation: A developmental perspective.* Hillsdale, N.J.: Erlbaum.

YARBUS, A. L. 1967. Eye movements and vision. Translated by Riggs, L. A. New York: Plenum Press.

YARROW, L. 1961. Maternal deprivation: Toward an empirical and conceptual reevaluation. *Psychological Bulletin* 58:459–90.

YARROW, L. J., AND GOODWIN, M. S. 1973. The immediate impact of separation reactions of infants to a change in mother figures. In Stone, L. J.; Smith, T. J.; and Murphy, L. B., eds., *The competent infant.* New York: Basic Books.

YARROW, L. J.; GOODWIN, M. S.; MANHEIMER, H.; AND MILESTONE, I. D. 1973. Infant experience and cognitive and personality development. In Stone, L. J.; Smith, T. J.; and Murphy, L. B., eds., *The competent infant.* New York: Basic Books.

YATES, F. A. 1966. *The art of memory.* Chicago: University of Chicago Press.

YERKES, R. M., AND MORGULIS, S. 1909. Method of Pavlov in animal psychology. *Psychological Bulletin* 6:264.

YONAS, A.; CLEAVES, W.; AND PETTERSEN, L. 1978. Development of sensitivity to pictorial depth. *Science* 200: 77–79.

YUSSEN, S. R., AND LEVY, V. M. 1975. Developmental changes in predicting one's own span of memory. *Journal of Experimental Child Psychology* 19:502–8.

ZAJONC, R. B. 1968. Attitudinal effects of mere exposure. *Journal of Personality and Social Psychology Monograph Supplement* 9:1–27.

ZENER, K. 1937. The significance of behavior accompanying conditioned salivary secretion for theories of the conditioned response. *American Journal of Psychology* 50:384–403.

ZENTALL, T., AND HOGAN, D. 1974. Abstract concept learning in the pigeon. *Journal of Experimental Psychology* 102:393–98.

ZIEGLER, F. J.; IMBODEN, J. B.; AND RODGERS, D. A. 1963. Contemporary conversion reactions: III. Diagnostic considerations. *Journal of the American Medical Association* 186:307–11.

ZIGLER, E. 1967. Familial mental retardation: A continuing dilemma. *Science* 155:292–98.

ZIGLER, E., AND CHILD, I. L. 1969. Socialization. In Lindzey, G., and Aronson, E., eds., *The handbook of social psychology,* vol. 3, pp. 450–589. Reading, Mass.: Addison-Wesley.

ZIGLER, E., AND CHILD, I. L. 1972. *Socialization and personality development.* Reading, Mass.: Addison-Wesley.

ZIGLER, E. F.; LAMB, M. E.; AND CHILD, I. L. 1982. *Socialization and personality development,* 2nd ed. New York: Oxford University Press.

ZILBOORG, G., AND HENRY, G. W. 1941. *A history of medical psychology.* New York: Norton.

ZOBRIST, A. L., AND CARLSON, F. R., JR. 1973. Advice taking chess-computer. *Scientific American* 228:92–105.

ZUBIN, J. 1954. Failures of the Rorschach technique. *Journal of Projective Techniques* 18:303–15.

ZUBIN, J.; ERON, L. D.; AND SHUMER, F. 1965. *An experimental approach to projective techniques.* New York: Wiley.

ZUCKERMAN, C. B., AND ROCK, I. 1957. A reappraisal of the roles of past experience and innate organizing processes in visual perception. *Psychological Bulletin* 54:269–96.

ZUCKERMAN, M. 1978. Sensation seeking. In London, H., and Exner, J. E., Jr., eds., *Dimensions of personality,* pp. 487–560. New York: Wiley.

ZUCKERMAN, M. 1979. *Sensation seeking: Beyond the optimum level of arousal.* Hillsdale, N.J.: Erlbaum.

ZUCKERMAN, M., AND WHEELER, L. 1975. To dispel fantasies about the fantasy-based measure of fear of success. *Psychological Bulletin* 82:932–46.

Acknowledgments and Copyrights

E., "Taste, deprivation and weight determinants of eating behavior," *Journal of Personality and Social Psychology* 10 (1968):107–16. Copyright 1968 by the American Psychological Association. Adapted by permission of the author.   3.13 Herman, H. C., and Mack, D., "Restrained and unrestrained eating," *Journal of Personality* 43 (1975):647–60. Copyright 1975 by the American Psychological Association. Adapted by permission of the publisher.   3.14 Andres, R., "Influence of obesity on longevity in the aged," in Borek, C., Fenoglio, C. M., and King, D. W. (eds.), *Aging, cancer, and cell membranes,* pp. 230–46. New York: Thieme-Stratton, 1980.   3.16 Reprinted by permission of Hawthorne Properties (Elsevier-Dutton Publishing Co., Inc.) from *Bodily changes in pain, hunger, fear and rage* by W. B. Cannon. Copyright © 1929 by Appleton-Century Co.; 1957 by W. B. Cannon.   3.18B Inbau, F. E., and Reid, J. E., *Truth and deception: The polygraph ("lie-detector") technique,* 2nd edition. Baltimore, Md.: The Williams & Wilkins Company, 1977. © 1977, The Williams & Wilkins Co., Baltimore.   3.19 Keeton, W. T., *Biological science,* 3rd edition. New York: W. W. Norton & Company, Inc., 1980. Copyright © 1980, 1979, 1972, 1967 by W. W. Norton & Company, Inc.   3.20 Data from "Infants' responses to strangers during the first year" by Morgan, G. A., and Ricciuti, H. N., in *Determinants of infant behavior,* vol. IV, edited by Foss, B. M. New York: Methuen and Company, Ltd., 1969. Copyright © 1969 by Tavistock Institute of Human Relations.   3.23 Guyton, A. C., *Textbook of medical physiology.* Philadelphia, Pa.: W. B. Saunders Company, 1966. Adapted by permission of the publisher.   3.25A,B Kleitman, N., "Patterns of dreaming," *Scientific American* 203 (November 1960): 82–88. Copyright © 1960 by Scientific American, Inc. All rights reserved.   3.26 Data from "Active (REM) sleep deprivation" by Cohen, H., in *The sleeping brain: Perspectives in the brain sciences,* vol. I, edited by Chase, M. H., pp. 343–47. Berkeley, Calif.: University of California Press. Adapted by permission of the publisher.   3.29 Data from Deutsch, J. A., Adams, D. W., and Metzner, R. J., "Choice of intracranial stimulation as a function of the delay between stimulations and competing drive," *Journal of Comparative and Physiological Psychology* 57 (1964):241–43. Copyright 1964 by the American Psychological Association. Adapted by permission of the authors.

4.4 Data from Anrep, G. V., "Pitch discrimination in the dog," *Journal of Physiology* 53 (1920):367–85. Adapted by permission of the publisher.   4.5 Pavlov, I. P., *Lectures on conditioned reflexes,* vol. I. New York: International Publishers Co., Inc., 1928. Adapted by permission of International Publishers Co., Inc.   4.6 Moore, J. W., "Stimulus control: Studies of auditory generalization in rabbits," in Black, A. H., and Prokasy, W. F. (eds.), *Classical conditioning II: Current theory and research.* © 1972. Adapted by permission of Prentice-Hall, Inc., Englewood Cliffs, N.J.   4.9 Spooner, A., and Kellogg, W. N., "The backward conditioning curve," *American Journal of Psychology* 60 (1947):321–34. Copyright © 1947 by Board of Trustees of the University of Illinois. Used with permission of the publisher, The University of Illinois Press.   4.11 Rescorla, R. A., "Pavlovian conditioning and its proper control procedures," *Psychological Review* 74 (1967):71–80.   4.12 Rescorla, R. A. 1966. Predictability and number of pairings in Pavlovian fear conditioning. *Psychonomic Science* 4:383–84.   4.13 Kamin, L. J., "Predictability, surprise, and conditioning," in Campbell, B. A., and Church, R. M. (eds.), *Punishment and aversive behavior,* 1969. Used by permission of Prentice-Hall, Inc., Englewood Cliffs, N. J.   4.19 Reynolds, G. S. *A primer of operant conditioning,* p. 40. Glenview, Ill.: Scott, Foresman and Co., 1968. Copyright © 1968 by Scott, Foresman and Company. Reprinted by permission.   4.23 Ferster, C. B., and Skinner, B. F., *Schedules of reinforcement.* © 1957, pp. 56, 399. Englewood Cliffs, N.J.: Prentice-Hall, Inc., 1957. Adapted by permission of the author.   4.27 Maier, S. F., Seligman, M. E. P., and Solo-

mon, R. L., "Pavlovian fear conditioning and learned helplessness: Effects on escape and avoidance behavior of (a) the CS-US contingency and (b) the independence of the US and voluntary responding," in Campbell, B. A., and Church, R. M. (eds.), *Punishment and aversive behavior,* © 1969, p. 328. Adapted by permission of Prentice-Hall, Inc., Englewood Cliffs, N.J.   4.28 Ayllon, T., "Intensive treatment of psychotic behavior by stimulus satiation and food reinforcement," *Behavior Research and Therapy* 1 (1963):53–61. Copyright 1963 by Pergamon Press, Ltd.   4.32 Tolman, E. C., and Gleitman, H., "Studies in learning and motivation," *Journal of Experimental Psychology* 39 (1949):810–19. Copyright 1949 by the American Psychological Association. Reprinted by permission of the authors.   4.33 and 4.34 Köhler, W., *The mentality of apes.* London: Routledge & Kegan Paul Ltd., 1925. Reprinted by permission.   4.38 Specified illustration from *Why chimps can read* by A. J. Premack. Copyright © 1976 by Ann J. Premack. Used by permission of Harper & Row, Publishers, Inc.   4.39 Premack, D., and Woodruff, G., "Chimpanzee problem-solving: A test for comprehension," *Science* 202 (3 November 1978):533–34. Copyright 1978 by the American Association for the Advancement of Science.

5.2 Coren, S., Porac, C., and Ward, L., *Sensation and perception.* New York: Academic Press, 1978. Adapted by permission of the author and publisher.   5.6 Krech, D., and Crutchfield, R., *Elements of psychology.* New York: Knopf, Inc., 1958. Adapted by permission of Hilda Krech.   5.7 Boring, E. G., *Sensation and perception in the history of experimental psychology,* p. 452. New York: Appleton-Century-Crofts, 1942. Adapted by permission of Mrs. Edwin G. Boring.   5.9 Pfaffman, C., "Studying the sense of taste and smell" in Andrews, T. G., *Methods of psychology,* pp. 268–88. New York: John Wiley & Sons, Inc., 1948. Adapted by permission of the publisher.   5.10 Gibson, James J., *The senses considered as perceptual systems,* p. 80, Fig. 5.4. Boston: Houghton Mifflin Company, 1966. Reprinted by permission of the publisher.   5.11 Thompson, R. F., *Introduction to biopsychology.* San Rafael, Calif.: Albion Publishing Company, 1973. Adapted by permission of the publisher.   5.13, 5.14A, 5.15A Lindsay, P. H., and Norman, D. A., *Human information processing,* 2nd edition, pp. 126, 133, and 136. New York: Academic Press, 1977. Adapted by permission of the author and publisher.   5.14B, 5.15B, 5.17A Coren, S., Porac, C., and Ward, L. M., *Sensation and perception,* pp. 103, 105. New York: Academic Press, 1978. Adapted by permission of the author and publisher.   5.16 Wald, G., "Eye and camera," *Scientific American* 183 (August 1950): 33. Copyright © 1950 by Scientific American, Inc. All rights reserved.   5.18, 5.19 Cornsweet, T. M., *Visual perception.* New York: Academic Press, 1970. Adapted by permission of the author and publisher.   5.22 Hering, E., *Outlines of a theory of the light sense,* 1920 (translated by Hurvich, L. M., and Jameson, D., 1964), pp. 150–51. Cambridge, Mass.: Harvard University Press, 1964. Adapted by permission of Harvard University Press.   5.24 Coren, S., Porac, C., and Ward, L. M., *Sensation and perception,* p. 155. New York: Academic Press, 1978. Adapted by permission of the author and publisher. Also 5.24 Cornsweet, T. M., *Visual perception,* p. 276. New York: Academic Press, 1970. Adapted by permission of the author and publisher.   5.25 Schiffman, H., *Sensation and perception.* New York: John Wiley and Sons, Inc., 1976. Adapted by permission of the publisher.   5.26 Kuffler, S. W., "Discharge pattern and functional organization of mammalian retina," *Journal of Neurophysiology* 16 (1953):37–68.   5.31 Hurvich, L. M., *Color vision.* Sunderland, Mass.: Sinauer Associates, Publications, 1981.   5.41 Hurvich, L. M., and Jameson, D., "An opponent-process theory of color vision," *Psychological Review* 64 (1957):384–404. Copyright 1957 by the American Psychological Association. Adapted by permission of the author.   5.42 DeValois, R. L., and DeValois, K. K., *Neural coding of color,* in Carterette, E. C., and Friedman, M.

P., eds., *Handbook of perception,* vol. 5. New York: Academic Press, 1975. Adapted by permission of the publisher.

6.8 Köhler, W., *Gestalt psychology.* New York: Liveright Publishing Company, 1947. Adapted by permission of the publisher. 6.11 Kanizsa, G., "Subjective contours," *Scientific American* 234 (1976): 48–52. Copyright © 1976 by Scientific American, Inc. All rights reserved. 6.13 Julian Hochberg, *Perception,* 2nd ed., © 1978, p. 56. Adapted by permission of Prentice-Hall, Inc., Englewood Cliffs, N. J. 6.17B Fellig, Arthur (Weegee). *Coney Island.* 1938–39. Gelatin-silver print, 10⁹⁄₁₆″ × 13¹¹⁄₁₆″. Collection, The Museum of Modern Art, New York. Anonymous gift. 6.18 *The perception of the visual world* by James J. Gibson. Copyright © 1950, renewed 1978 by James J. Gibson. Reprinted by permission of Houghton Mifflin Company. 6.19 Yonas, A., et al., "Development of sensitivity to pictorial depth," *Science* 200 (7 April 1978): 77–78, Fig. 1. Copyright 1978 by the American Association for the Advancement of Science. 6.20 Coren, S., Porac, C., and Ward, L. M., *Sensation and perception,* p. 255. New York: Academic Press, 1978. Adapted by permission of the publisher. 6.22 Duncker, K., "Über induzierte Bewegung," *Psychologische Forschung* 12 (1929):180–259. Adapted by permission of Springer-Verlag, Inc., New York. 6.24A,B Yarbus, A. L., *Eye movements and vision,* pp. 179–85. Translated by Riggs, R. A. New York: Plenum Press, 1967. Copyright 1967 by Plenum Press. Reprinted by permission of the publisher. 6.25 Julian Hochberg, "Attention, organization, and consciousness," in *Attention: Contemporary theory and analysis,* edited by D. I. Mostofsky © 1970, p. 115. Adapted by permission of Prentice-Hall, Inc., Englewood Cliffs, N. J. 6.27 Hubel, D. H., "The visual cortex of the brain," *Scientific American* 209 (November 1963): 54–58. Copyright © 1963 by Scientific American, Inc. All rights reserved. 6.30 Gibson, J. J., and Gibson, E. J., "Perceptual learning: Differentiation or enrichment?" *Psychological Review* 62 (1955):32–41. Copyright 1955 by the American Psychological Association. Adapted by permission of the author. 6.31 Street, R. F., *A gestalt completion test.* New York: Teachers College Press, 1931. Reprinted by permission of the publisher. 6.32 From *Sensation and perception,* Second Edition by E. Bruce Goldstein. © 1984 by Wadsworth, Inc. Reprinted by permission of the publisher. 6.33 Boring, E. G. 1930. "A new ambiguous figure," *American Journal of Psychology* 42: 444–45; and Leeper, R. W. 1935. "A study of a neglected portion of the field of learning: The development of sensory organization," *Journal of Genetic Psychology* 46: 41–75. 6.34 Selfridge, O. G., "Pattern recognition and modern computers," in *Proceedings of Western Joint Computer Conference,* Los Angeles, Calif., 1955. 6.36 Reprinted with permission from Kolers, P. A., *Aspects of motion perception.* Copyright 1972, Pergamon Press. 6.37 Kolers, P. A., and Pomerantz, J. R. "Figural change in apparent motion," *Journal of Experimental Psychology* 87 (1971):99–108. Copyright 1971 by the American Psychological Association. Adapted by permission of the author. 6.38 Penrose, L. S., and Penrose, R. "Impossible objects: A special type of visual illusion," *British Journal of Psychology* 49 (1958):31–33. Reprinted by permission of the British Psychological Society. 6.39 Adapted with permission of Macmillan Publishing Co., Inc., from *An introduction to perception* by Irvin Rock. Copyright © 1975 by Irvin Rock. 6.41 *The perception of the visual world* by James J. Gibson. Copyright © 1950, renewed 1978, by James J. Gibson. Reprinted by permission of Houghton Mifflin Company. 6.43 Rock, I., and Kaufman, L., "The moon illusion, II," *Science* 136 (June 1962):1023–31, Figure 22. Copyright 1962 by the American Association for the Advancement of Science. Reprinted by permission of the publisher. 6.44 Coren, S., and Girgus, J.S., 1978. *Seeing is deceiving.* Hillsdale, N.J.: Lawrence Erlbaum Associates, Inc. Reprinted with permission of the publisher. 6.47 Lewis, H. P., *Child art: The beginnings of self-affirmation.* Copyright Diablo Press, Inc., 1973, P. O. Box 7042, Berkeley, Calif.,

94608. Reproduced with permission. 6.48 Ivins, W. M., Jr., *On the rationalization of sight.* New York: Da Capo Press, 1975. 6.52 Picasso, Pablo. *Violin and grapes.* (1912, summer or early fall.) Oil on canvas, 20″ × 24″. Collection, The Museum of Modern Art, New York. Mrs. David M. Levy Bequest.

7.1 Sperling, G., "The information available in brief visual presentations," *Psychological Monographs* 74 (1960): (Whole No. 11). Copyright 1960 by the American Psychological Association. Adapted by permission of the author. 7.2 Peterson, L. R., and Peterson, M. J., "Short-term retention of individual items," *Journal of Experimental Psychology* 58 (1959): 193–98. Copyright 1959 by the American Psychological Association. Reprinted by permission of the author. 7.3 Murdock, B., "The serial position effect of free recall," *Journal of Experimental Psychology* 64 (1962): 482–88. Copyright 1962 by the American Psychological Association. Reprinted by permission of the author. 7.4 Glanzer, M., and Cunitz, A., "Two storage mechanisms in free recall," *Journal of Verbal Learning and Verbal Behavior* 5 (1966): 351–60. Adapted by permission of the author and Academic Press, Inc. 7.5 Murdock, B., "The serial position effect of free recall," *Journal of Experimental Psychology* 64 (1962): 482–88. Copyright 1962 by the American Psychological Association. Reprinted by permission of the author. 7.8 Sternberg, S., "Memory scanning: Mental processes revealed by reaction time experiments," in Antrobus, J. S., *Cognition and affect,* pp. 13–58. Boston: Little, Brown & Company, 1970. Adapted by permission of Saul Sternberg. 7.9 and 7.10 Ebbinghaus, H., *Memory,* p. 47. New York: Dover Publications, 1964. Originally published in 1885. Adapted by permission of the publisher. 7.11 Ericsson, K. A., Chase, W. G., and Faloon, S., "Acquisition of a memory skill." *Science* 208 (June 1980): 1181–82. Copyright 1980 by the American Association for the Advancement of Science. Used with permission of the author and publisher. 7.12 Godden, D. R., and Baddeley, A. D. "Context-dependent memory in two natural environments: On land and underwater," *British Journal of Psychology* 66 (1975): 325–31. Reprinted by permission of the British Psychological Society. 7.14 Bartlett, F. C., *Remembering,* p. 180. Cambridge, England: Cambridge University Press, 1932. Adapted by permission of the publisher. 7.15 Orne, M. T., "The mechanisms of hypnotic age regression: An experimental study," *Journal of Abnormal and Social Psychology* 58 (1951): 277–99. Copyright 1951 by the American Psychological Association. 7.16 Bower, G. H., "Analysis of a mnemonic device," *American Scientist* 58 (1970): 496–510. Used with permission of the publisher. 7.17 Bahrick, H. P., "Semantic memory content in permastore: Fifty years of memory for Spanish learned in school," *Journal of Experimental Psychology: General* 113 (1984): 1–35. Copyright 1984 by the American Psychological Association. Adapted by permission of the author. 7.19 Collins, A. M., and Quillian, M. R., "Retrieval time from semantic memory," *Journal of Verbal Learning and Verbal Behavior* 8 (1969): 240–47. Adapted by permission of the author and Academic Press, Inc. 7.20 From *Alice in wonderland* by Lewis Carroll, illustrated by Marjorie Torrey. Copyright © 1955 by Random House, Inc. Reprinted by permission of Random House, Inc. 7.21 Kosslyn, S. M., "Scanning and visual images: Some structural implications," *Perception and Psychophysics* 14 (1973): 90–94. Adapted by permission of the author and the Psychonomic Society, Inc. 7.22A Top to bottom: *1930s* Marlene Dietrich (Courtesy of Photoworld); Benito Mussolini (Courtesy of the Warder Collection); Al Capone (Courtesy UPI/Bettmann Newsphotos). *1940s* Douglas MacArthur (Courtesy of AP/Wide World Photos); Betty Grable (Courtesy of AP/Wide World Photos); Joe DiMaggio (Photograph by Calvin D. Campbell/Black Star). *1950s* Mamie Eisenhower (Courtesy of Photoworld); Joe McCarthy (Courtesy of AP/Wide World Photos); Adlai Stevenson (Courtesy of UPI/Bettmann Newsphotos). *1960s* Nikita Khrushchev (Courtesy of AP/Wide World Photos); Coretta Scott King (Photograph by Bob Fitch/Black Star); Golda Meir (Photograph by Fred Ward/Black Star). *1970s* Anwar El-

Sadat (Courtesy of United Nations/M. Tzovaras); Betty Ford (Reproduced from The Collection of the Library of Congress); Patty Hearst (Photograph by Owen D. B./Black Star). 7.22B Marslan-Wilson, W. D., and Teuber, H. L. "Memory for remote events in anterograde amnesia: Recognition of public figures from news photographs," *Neuropsychologia* 13 (1975): 353–64. 7.23A From *Fundamentals of human neuropsychology,* 2nd ed., by B. Kolb and I. Q. Wishaw, Figure 20–5, p. 485. San Francisco: W. H. Freeman and Company. Copyright © 1980, 1985. 7.23B Milner, B., Corkin, S., and Teuber, H. L., "Further analysis of the hippocampal amnesic syndrome: Fourteen year follow-up of H. M.," *Psychologia* 6 (1968): 215–34.

8.6 and 8.19 Scheerer, M., "Problem-solving," *Scientific American* (April 1963): 119, 124. Copyright © 1963 by Scientific American, Inc. All rights reserved 8.10 Hearst, E., "Psychology across the chessboard," in *Psychology today: An introduction,* 4th ed., p. 24, edited by Jay Braun and Darwyn E. Linder. Del Mar, Calif.: CRM Books, 1972. Reprinted by permission of Random House, Inc. 8.11 After Figure 73 (p. 109) from *Productive thinking,* enlarged edition, edited by Max Wertheimer and Michael Wertheimer. Copyright © 1945, 1959 by Valentin Wertheimer. Reprinted by permission of Harper & Row Publishers, Inc. 8.17 and 8.20 Scheerer, M., Goldstein, K., and Boring, E. G., "A demonstration of insight: The horse-rider puzzle," *American Journal of Psychology* 54 (1941): 437–38. 8.26 Illustration by Tenniel for Lewis Carroll's *Alice in wonderland,* courtesy of General Research Division, The New York Public Library, Astor, Lenox and Tilden Foundations. 8.22 Suls, J. M. "A two-stage model for the appreciation of jokes and cartoons," in Goldstein, J. H., and McGhee, P. E. (eds.), *The psychology of humor.* New York: Academic Press, 1972, p. 85. Reprinted by permission of the publisher and the author. 8.27 and 8.28 Wason, P. C., and Johnson-Laird, P. N., *Psychology of reasoning.* London: B. T. Batsord, Ltd., 1972.

9.2 Reprinted with permission of Macmillan Publishing Co., Inc., from *On the origins of language: An introduction to the evolution of human language* by Philip Lieberman. Copyright © 1975 by Philip Lieberman. 9.16 Slobin, D. I., "Grammatical transformation and sentence comprehension in childhood and adulthood," *Journal of Verbal Learning and Verbal Behavior* 5 (1966): 219–27. Adapted by permission of the author and the publisher.

10.1A Tinbergen, N., *The study of instinct.* Oxford, England: Oxford University Press, 1951. Adapted by permission of the publisher. 10.2A,B Barnett, S. A., 1963. *The rat: A study in behavior.* Chicago: The University of Chicago Press. Reprinted by permission of the University of Chicago Press. 10.10 Reprinted from "Reproductive behaviors" by Etkin, W., in *Social behavior and organization among vertebrates* by Etkin, W., by permission of The University of Chicago Press. Copyright 1964 by William Etkin; copyright 1967 by the University of Chicago. 10.11 Hohn, E. O., "The phalarope," *Scientific American* 220 (June 1969): 104. Copyright © 1969 by Scientific American, Inc. All rights reserved. 10.12 Keeton, W. T., *Biological science,* 3rd ed. New York: W. W. Norton & Company, Inc., 1980. Copyright © 1980, 1979, 1972, 1967 by W. W. Norton & Company, Inc. 10.13 Bermant, G., and Davidson, J. M., *Biological bases of sexual behavior.* New York: Harper & Row, 1974. In turn adapted from data of Davidson, J. M., Rodgers, C. H., Smith, E. R., and Bloch, G. J., "Relative thresholds of behavioral and somatic responses to estrogen," *Physiology and Behavior* 3 (1968): 227–29. Copyright 1968, Pergamon Press, Ltd. 10.15 Passingham, R., *The human primate.* San Francisco: W. H. Freeman & Co., 1982. Adapted by permission of the publisher. 10.17A Lorenz, K., "Die angeborenen Formen moeglicher Erfahrung." *Zeitschrift Für Tierpsychologie* 5 (1943): 276. Adapted by permission of Paul Parey Verlagsbuchhandlung, Hamburg and

Berlin. 10.21 Darwin, C., *The expression of the emotions in man and animals.* Chicago: The University of Chicago Press. Reprinted by permission of The University of Chicago Press. Originally published 1872. London: Appleton and Company, courtesy of the Meredith Publishing Company. 10.22 Hinde, R. A., *Biological basis of human social behavior,* p. 271. New York: McGraw-Hill, Inc., 1974. Copyright © 1974 by McGraw-Hill, Inc. Adapted by permission of McGraw-Hill, Inc. 10.23 Peter H. Klopfer, *An introduction to animal behavior: Ethology's first century,* 2nd ed., © 1974, p. 208. Adapted by permission of Prentice-Hall, Inc., Englewood Cliffs, N.J. 10.26 Ekman, P., and Friesen, W. V., *Unmasking the face,* Englewood Cliffs, N.J.: Prentice-Hall, 1975.

11.1 Asch, S. E., "Studies of independence and conformity: A minority of one against a unanimous majority," *Psychological Monographs* 70 (9, Whole No. 416), 1956. Copyright 1956 by the American Psychological Association. 11.4 Asch, S. E., "Effects of group pressure upon the modification and distortion of judgments," in Maccoby, E. E., Newcomb, T. M., and Hartley, E. L., eds., *Readings in social psychology.* New York: Henry Holt, 1958. 11.5. Festinger, L., and Carlsmith, J. M., "Cognitive consequences of forced compliance," *Journal of Abnormal and Social Psychology* 58 (1959): 203–10. Copyright 1959 by the American Psychological Association. Reprinted by permission of the author. 11.8 Landy, D., and Sigall, H., "Beauty is talent: Task evaluation as a function of the performer's physical attractiveness," *Journal of Personality and Social Psychology* 29 (1974); 299–304. Copyright 1974 by the American Psychological Association. Adapted by permission of the author. 11.13 Ekman, P., and Friesen, W. V., *Unmasking the face.* Englewood Cliffs, N.J.: Prentice-Hall, 1975.

12.2 Masserman, J. H., *Principles of dynamic psychiatry,* p. 76. Philadelphia: W. B. Saunders & Company, 1946. Adapted by permission of the publisher.

13.2 Liebert, R. M., Poulos, R. W., and Strauss, G. D., *Developmental psychology,* Fig. III–10, p. 81. Englewood Cliffs, N.J.: Prentice-Hall, Inc., 1974. Originally adapted from H. M. Halverston, printed by The Journal Press, 1931. 13.4 Nilsson, Lennart, *Behold man.* Boston: Little, Brown & Company, 1974. 13.5 Tanner, J. M., "Physical growth," in *Carmichael's manual of child psychology,* 3rd ed., vol. 1, Mussen, P. H., ed., Fig. 6, p. 85. New York: John Wiley & Sons, 1970. Copyright 1970 by John Wiley & Sons. 13.6 Liebert, R. M., Poulos, R. W., and Strauss, G. D., *Developmental psychology,* p. 76. Englewood Cliffs, N.J.: Prentice-Hall, Inc., 1974. Originally printed by Jackson, C. M., "Some aspects of form and growth," in Robbins, W. J. et al., *Growth,* Fig. 3.16, p. 118. New Haven, Conn.: Yale University Press, 1929. 13.7 Conel, J. L., *The postnatal development of the human cortex,* vols. 1, 3, 5. Cambridge, Mass.: Harvard University Press, 1939, 1947, 1955. 13.9 Hetherington, E. M., and Parke, R. D., *Child psychology: A contemporary viewpoint,* 2nd ed. New York: McGraw-Hill, 1979. 13.13 Keeton, W. T., *Biological science,* 3rd ed. New York: W. W. Norton & Company, Inc., 1980. Copyright © 1980, 1979, 1972, 1967 by W. W. Norton & Company, Inc.

14.5 Piaget, J., and Inhelder, B., *The child's conception of space.* Humanities Press International Inc., Atlantic Highlands, N.J. Adapted by permission of the publisher and Routledge & Kegan Paul Ltd. 14.11 Kellman, P. J., and Spelke, E. S., "Perception of partially occluded objects in infancy," *Cognitive Psychology* 15 (1983): 483–524. Copyright 1983 by the American Psychological Association. Adapted by permission of the author. 14.12 Borke, H., "Piaget's mountains revisited: Changes in the egocentric landscape," *Developmental Psychology* 11 (1975): 240–43. 14.16 Case, R. 1978. "Intellectual development from birth to adulthood: A neo-Piagetian interpretation," in Siegler, R., ed., *Children's thinking: What develops.* Hillsdale, N.J.: Lawrence Erlbaum Associates, Inc.   14.17 Appel, L. F., Cooper, R. G., McCarrell, N., Sims-Knight, J., Yussen, S. R., and Flavell, J. H., "The development distinction between perceiving and memorizing," *Child Development* 43 (1972): 1365–81. Copyright © 1972 by The Society for Research in Child Development, Inc.

15.1B Eimas, P. D., Siqueland, E. R., Jusczyk, P., and Vigorito, J., Speech perception in infants," *Science* 171 (1971): 303–6. Copyright 1971 by the American Association for the Advancement of Science.   15.3 Three illustrations from *Higglety pigglety pop! Or there must be more to life,* written and illustrated by Maurice Sendak. Copyright © 1967 by Maurice Sendak. Reprinted by permission of Harper & Row, Publishers, Inc.   15.4 Brown, R., Cazden, C., and Bellugi-Klima, U., "The child's grammar from 1 to 3," in Hill, J. P., ed., *Minnesota Symposium on Child Psychology* by The University of Minnesota Press, Minneapolis. Copyright © 1969 by the University of Minnesota.   15.5 Landau, B., and Gleitman, L. R., *Language and experience: Evidence from the blind child.* Cambridge, Mass.: Harvard University Press, 1985. Reprinted by permission of Harvard University Press.   15.7 Frishberg, N., "Arbitrariness and iconicity: Historical change in American Sign Language," *Language* 51 (1975): 696–719.   15.8 Goldin-Meadow, S. "Fragile and resilient properties of language learning," in Wanner, E., and Gleitman, L. R. (eds.), *Language acquisition: State of the art.* New York: Cambridge University Press, 1982.   15.9 Marler, P. R., "A comparative approach to vocal learning: Song development in white crowned sparrows," *Journal of Comparative and Physiological Psychology Monograph* 71 (May 1970): (No. 2, Part 2), pp. 1–25. Copyright 1970 by the American Psychological Association. Reprinted by permission of the author.

16.1A and 16.3 Nina Leen, *Life Magazine* © Time Inc.   16.7 Ainsworth, M., Blehar, M., Waters, E., and Wall, S. 1978. *Patterns of attachment,* p. 34. Hillsdale, N.J.: Lawrence Erlbaum Associates, Inc.   16.11 N. R. Farbman, *Life Magazine* © Time Inc.   16.12 Bandura, A., Ross, D., and Ross, S. A., "Imitation of film-mediated aggressive models," *Journal of Abnormal and Social Psychology* 66 (1963): 8. Copyright 1963 by the American Psychological Association. Reprinted by permission of the author.   16.13B Feshbach, N., and Roe, K., "Empathy in six- and seven-year-olds," *Child Development* 39 (1968): 133–45. Reprinted by permission of The Society for Research in Child Development, Inc.   16.14 Kohlberg, L., "Development of children's orientation towards a moral order in sequence in the development of moral thought," *Vita Humana* 6 (1963): 11–36. Adapted by permission of S. Karger AG, Basel.   16.15 Harlow, H. F., "The heterosexual affectional system in monkeys," *American Psychologist* 17 (1962): 1–9. Copyright 1962 by the American Psychological Association. Reprinted by permission.   16.16 Very, P. S., "Differential factor structure in mathematical ability," *Genetic Psychology Monographs* 75 (1967): 169–208.   16.18 Tanner, J. M., "Physical growth," in Mussen, P. H., ed., *Carmichael's manual of child psychology,* 3rd ed., vol. 1, Fig. 6, p. 85. New York: John Wiley & Sons, 1970. Reprinted by permission of the publisher.

17.1 Reprinted with permission of Macmillan Publishing Co., Inc. from *Differential psychology,* 3rd ed., p. 57, by Ann Anastasi. Copyright © 1958 by Macmillan Publishing Co., Inc.   17.8 Figure 13.7 (p. 432) from *Essentials of psychological testing,* 3rd ed., by Lee J. Cronbach. Copyright © 1949 by Harper & Row, Publishers, Inc. Copyright © 1960, 1970 by Lee J. Cronbach. Reprinted by permission of the publisher.   17.13 Guilford, J. P., *Psychometric methods,* p. 38. New York: McGraw-Hill, 1954.   17.14 Jones, H. E., and Kaplan, O. J., "Psychological aspects of mental disorders in later life," in Kaplan, O. J., ed., *Mental disorders in later life,* 72. Stanford, Calif.:

Stanford University Press, 1945. Adapted by permission of the publisher.   17.15 Schaie, K. and Strother, C., "A cross sequential study of age changes in cognitive behavior," *Psychological Bulletin* 70 (1968): 671–80. Copyright 1968 by the American Psychological Association. Reprinted by permission of the author.   17.18 Jencks, C., Smith, M., Acland, H., Bane, M. J., Cohen, D., Gintis, H., Heyns, B., and Michelson, S., *Inequality: A reassessment of the effect of family and schooling in America.* New York: Basic Books, 1972. Adapted by permission of the publisher. Also 17.18.   Erlenmeyer-Kimling, L., and Jarvik, L. F., "Genetics and intelligence: A review," *Science* 142 (1963): 1477–79. Copyright 1963 by the American Association for the Advancement of Science.

18.1 Lanyon, R. I., and Goodstein, L. D., *Personality assessment,* p. 79. New York: John Wiley & Sons, Inc., 1971. Adapted by permission of the publisher.   18.5 Reprinted by permission of C. P. S., Inc., Box 83, Larchmont, N.Y. 10538, from the *Children's apperception test (C. A. T.).*   18.6 Eysenck, H. J., and Rachman, S., *The causes and cures of neurosis,* p. 16. San Diego, Calif.: Robert R. Knapp, 1965.

19.1 Negative #31568. Courtesy Department of Library Services, American Museum of Natural History.   19.8 Data from Faris, R. E. L., and Dunham, H. W., *Mental disorders in urban areas.* Chicago: University of Chicago Press, 1939. Adapted by permission of the author.   19.11 Hiroto, D. S., and Seligman, M. E. P., "Generality of learned helplessness," *Journal of Personality and Social Psychology* 31 (1975): 311–27. Copyright 1975 by the American Psychological Association. Reprinted by permission of the author. 1912. Folkow, B., and Rubenstein, E. H., "Cardiovascular effects of acute and chronic stimulations of the hypothalamic defense area in the rat," *Acta Physiologica Scandinavica* 68 (1966): 48–57. Adapted by permission of Acta Physiologica Scandinavica.   19.14 Stone, A., "Mental health and law: A system in transition," U.S. Department of Health, Education and Welfare, #75176, p. 7, 1975.   19.15 Hare, R. D., "Temporal gradient of fear arousal in psychopaths," *Journal of Abnormal Psychology* 70 (1965): 442–45. Copyright 1965 by the American Psychological Association. Reprinted by permission of the author.   19.16 Marks, I. "Patterns of meaning in psychiatric patients: Semantic differential responses in obsessives and psychopaths." *Maudsley Monograph* 13. Oxford, England: Oxford University Press, 1966.

TABLES

5.1 Geldard, F. A., *Fundamentals of psychology,* p. 93. New York: John Wiley & Sons, 1962. Reprinted in Schiffman, *Sensation and perception,* p. 15. New York: John Wiley & Sons, 1976. Adapted by permission of the publisher.   5.5 Geldard, F. A., *The human senses.* New York: John Wiley & Sons, 1972. Reprinted by permission of the publisher. 13.1 Lenneberg, E. H., *Biological foundations of language.* New York: John Wiley & Sons, 1967. Reprinted by permission of the publisher.   16.1 Adapted from Kohlberg, L., "Classification of moral judgment into levels and stages of development" in Sizer, Theodore R., *Religion and public education,* pp. 171–73. Copyright © 1967 Houghton Mifflin Company.   16.2 Erikson, E. H., *Childhood and society.* New York: W. W. Norton & Company, Inc., 1963. Adapted by permission.   17.3 Terman, L. M., and Merrill, M. A., *Stanford-Binet intelligence scale-Manual for the third revision,* form L-M. Copyright © 1972, reproduced with the permission of The Riverside Publishing Company, 8420 Bryn Mawr Avenue, Chicago, Ill., 60631.   17.5 Wechsler, D., *The measurement and appraisal of adult intelligence,* 4th edition. Baltimore, Md.: The Williams & Wilkins Co., 1958. © 1958 David Wechsler. Used by permission of Ruth Wechsler, executor David Wechsler estate. Table adapted from the Manual for the Wechsler Adult Intelligence Scale, © 1955 The Psychological Corporation.   18.5 Norman, W. T., "Toward an adequate taxonomy of personality attributes: Replicated factor structure in peer nomination personality ratings," *Journal of Abnormal and Social Psychology* 66 (1963): 577. Copyright 1963 by the American Psychological Association. Adapted by permission of the author.   20.1 Paul, G. L., *Insight vs. desensitization in psychotherapy: An experiment in anxiety reduction.* Stanford, Calif.: Stanford University Press, 1966. Reprinted by permission of the author.

UNNUMBERED PHOTOS AND ART

Page 8 Rousseau, Henri. *The Dream.* 1910. Oil on canvas, 6'8 ½" × 9'9½". Collection, The Museum of Modern Art, New York. Gift of Nelson A. Rockefeller.   Page 12 Two illustrations from *Where the wild things are,* written and illustrated by Maurice Sendak. Copyright 1963 by Maurice Sendak. Reprinted by permission of Harper & Row, Publishers, Inc.   Page 296 Ginzberg, L., *The legends of the Jews,* vol. 1, translated by Szold, H., p. 62. Philadelphia, Pa.: Jewish Publication Society of America, 1909.   Pages 303 and 309 Illustrations by Tenniel for Lewis Carroll's *Alice in wonderland,* courtesy of General Research Division, The New York Public Library, Astor, Lenox and Tilden Foundations.   Page 337 Nina Leen, *Life Magazine* © Time Inc.   Page 453 Babies at: 2 days (photo by Kathy Hirsh-Pasek), 1 month (Photo by Kathy Hirsh-Passek), 5 months (Photo by Erika Stone), 9½ months (Photo by Erika Stone), 12 months (Photo by Suzanne Szasz), and 15 months (Photo by Erika Stone).   Page 454 Carmontell, *Mozart, as child, with father and sister,* Chantilly, Musée Conde. Giraudon/Art Resource.   Page 468 Nina Leen, *Life Magazine* © Time Inc.   Page 567 Nina Leen, *Life Magazine* © 1948 Time Inc.   Page 679 Picasso: *Don quixote,* St. Denis-Siene. Musée Municipal. Scala/Art Resource.   Page 694 Rembrandt: *David playing the harp before Saul,* The Hague, Mauritshuis. Giraudon/Art Resource.

Name Index

Donaldson, G., 593*n*
Dostoevsky, Fyodor M., 413
Douvan, E., 565
Downs, A. C., 548
Dragoin, W. B., 124
Drucker-Colín, R., 78
Druss, B., 500
Duncker, Karl, 270–71
Dunn, L. A., 487
Dweck, Carol, 552–53
Dymond, R., 384

Eagly, A. H., 374
Eaton, R. M., 332
Ebbinghaus, Hermann, 230–31
Edmonds, J. M., 611
Edwards, J. R., 548
Edwards, S., 70
Egger, M. D., 71
Ehrhardt, A. A., 460, 553, 554, 555
Eichelman, W. H., 594
Eichmann, Adolf, 399, 400
Eikelboom, R., 95
Eimas, P. D., 499
Ekman, P., 361, 362, 394
Ellenberger, H. F., 441
Elliott, E. S., 552, 553
Ellis, Albert, 702
Emmelkamp, P., 116
Emmerich, W., 549
Endler, N. S., 626
Engelmann, S., 298
Enna, B., 553
Epps, P., 634
Epstein, A. N., 56, 57, 59
Epstein, A. W., 57
Epstein, Seymour, 624
Epstein, S. M., 82
Epstein, W., 311
Erdelyi, M. H., 431, 432
Ericsson, K. A., 235
Eriksen, C. W., 431
Erikson, Erik, 527, 563, 566–67, 568
Erlenmeyer-Kimling, L., 600
Eron, L. D., 617, 620, 621
Ervin, S., 505
Etkin, W., 346
Eysenck, Hans, 630–32, 647, 706, 707

Fallon, A. E., 67
Faloon, S., 235
Fanselow, M. S., 29
Fant, L. G., 514
Fantz, R. L., 196
Farley, F., 631
Farley, S. V., 631
Fasnacht, G., 119
Fearing, F., 23
Fechner, Gustav Theodor, 141–43, 146
Feldman, H., 514
Feldman, N. S., 545*n*
Felipe, N. J., 345
Fenichel, O., 696
Fernald, A., 500
Ferrara, R. A., 490
Feshbach, N. D., 541
Festinger, Leon, 369, 370–71, 375, 408, 543*n*
Fields, H. L., 30, 691
Fisher, J. D., 345
Fitzsimons, J. T., 56

Flanagan, J. C., 579
Flavell, E. R., 483
Flavell, J. H., 482*n*, 483, 485, 490, 491, 597
Flugel, 387
Flynn, J., 70, 71, 339
Fobes, T., 83
Foch, T. T., 66
Fodor, J. D., 302, 320
Fodor, Jerry A., 266, 302, 303, 485, 506
Fontana, A. F., 657
Foote, W., 70
Ford, C. S., 353, 387, 559
Ford, Gerald, 376
Foss, D. J., 307
Foucault, Michel, 640, 676
Foulke, E., 300
Fowler, A., 329
Fowles, J., 548
Foy, 403
Francis, W. N., A15*n*
Frankl, V. E., 713
Franklin, Benjamin, 389
Franks, J. J., 312
Fraser, S. C., 389
Frazier, L., 320
Freedman, D. G., 452
Freedman, D. X., 693
Freedman, J. L., 196, 374, 376, 389
French, T., 697, 698
Frenkel-Brunswik, E., 397
Freud, Anna, 419
Freud, Sigmund, 11, 12, 376*n*, 410, 412–41, 446*n*, 472, 522–23, 529, 531–32, 535, 538, 539, 542, 556, 558, 561, 562, 563, 564, 616, 635, 643, 645, 668–69, 670, 671, 695–96, 697–99, 705, 711, 715–16, A6
Fridlund, A. J., 361
Friedman, A. F., 647
Friedman, M. I., 58, 60
Friesen, W. V., 394
Frisch, H. L., 548
Fromkin, V. A., 326, 512
Fromm, Erich, 434
Fuller, J. L., 457
Funkenstein, D. H., 394
Fuseli, Henry, 433

Galanter, E., 267
Galen, 17–18
Galileo, Galilei, 15, 16, 288
Gallistel, C. R., 35, 36, 84, 484
Galton, Francis, 253, 572, 574–76, 600
Galvani, Luigi, 18
Gamzu, E., 125*n*
Garcia, J., 123
Gardner, Beatrice D., 330
Gardner, R. Allen, 330
Garrett, M. F., 326, 327
Gartrell, N., 560
Gauss, Karl Friedrich, 273
Gautier, T., 555
Gazzaniga, M. S., 42
Gebhard, P., 559
Geffen, G., 45
Gelman, R., 482, 484, 487
Genovese, Kitty, 408–9
Gerard, H. B., 375
Gergen, K. J., 380
Gershon, S., 662
Geschwind, N., 39, 40, 47
Gesell, A. L., 463

Gibson, Eleanor, J., 195, 201, 448, 476–77, 512
Gibson, James J., 181, 187–88, 201, 209, 448, 476–77
Gibson, R. W., 664
Gilbert, L., 597
Gilbert, Sir William Schwenck, 390
Giles, E., 548
Gillett, E., 235
Girgus, J. S., 211
Gladue, B. A., 561
Glaser, R., 594
Glass, G. V., 706
Gleason, K. K., 150
Gleitman, Henry, 235, 247, 249, 285, 306, 317, 368, 396, 491
Gleitman, Lila R., 306, 317, 319, 491, 500, 503, 504, 506, 507, 514, 518
Glick, J., 487
Gloringen, I., 41
Gloringen, K., 41
Glucksberg, S., 279
Glueck, E., 634
Glueck, S., 634
Godden, D. R., 237
Goetz, T. E., 552, 553
Goffman, Erving, 382, 675, 676
Gold, R., 487
Goldberg, B., 431
Goldberg, L. R., 615, 630
Goldfarb, W., 464, 531
Goldin-Meadow, S., 514, 515, 516
Goldman, R., 66
Goldstein, E. B., 155
Gombrich, E. H., 212, 213–14, 216
Goodenough, D. R., 77
Goodwin, M. S., 533
Gordon, H., 66, 603
Gordon, N. C., 30, 691
Gordon, W., 487
Gormezano, I., 96
Gottesman, I. I., 656
Gottlieb, G., 464
Gough, H. G., 614
Gould, S. S., 446, 447, 451, 567
Goy, R. W., 555
Goya, Francisco, 413
Graham, C. H., 173
Grant, R., 54
Gray, S., 67
Green, D. M., 144, 155, 491
Green, R., 561
Green, R., 593
Green, R. G., 631
Greene, D., 119
Greenfield, P. M., 487, 503
Greif, E. B., 547
Greven, P. J., Jr., 563
Grice, H. P., 329
Grill, H. J., 48
Guerrero, L., 555
Guilford, J. P., 592
Guttman, N., 107

Haber, R. B., 254
Haber, R. N., 254
Haith, M. M., 452
Hall, C. S., 8, 10, 433–34
Hall, E. T., 345
Halverson, H. M., 447

Subject Index

prenatal, 450
presynaptic vs. postsynaptic, 26
in skin receptors, 149
stimulus intensity and, 21–22
structure of, 18–19
synaptic gaps between 19, 23–25, 26–27
temporal and spatial summation effects of, 24–25
types of, 19
neurosis, 637–38, 665*n*
neuroticism, 630, 632
neurotransmitters, 26–30
affective disorders and, 662
drugs' effects on, 28–29
schizophrenia and, 654–55, 658
in transmission process, 27
newborns:
empathic behavior in, 544
environment of, 460–61
equipment of, 451–52, 476, 481
intersensory relations in, 477–78
sex-typing of, 548
vocalization by, 497
see also infants
night vision, 158–59
noise, sound waves and, 153
nondirective techniques, 704
nonsense syllables, 230–31, 310–11
norepinephrine, 28, 30, 68, 69
amphetamine or cocaine use and, 29, 81
affective disorders and, 662, 689, 693
schizophrenia and, 655
normal curve, 573, 574, A13–A15
norms, 578
null hypothesis, A23, A26, A28
number, conservation of, 474, 483–84, 485, 492

obedience, 396–402
cognitive reinterpretations and, 401–2
personality structure and, 397–98
personal responsibility and, 400–401, 402
situational factors in, 398–402
obesity, 63–67
externality hypothesis and, 64–65
restrained-eating hypothesis and, 65–66
treatment of, 66–67
object permanence, 469–70, 471, 492
observational learning, 536–37
observational studies, A5
obsessive-compulsive disorders, 637, 668–70
occipital lobes, 34, 38
occlusion, in infants, 480
Oedipus complex, 425–27, 437, 438–39, 446*n*, 522, 556, 561, 564
cultural differences and, 436
Hamlet and, 439–40
old age, as developmental stage, 562, 568
olfaction, 148, 149–50
open-class words, 308
comprehension and, 328
language learning and, 503, 515
speech errors and, 326–27, 328
operant chambers, 106
operant conditioning, *see* instrumental conditioning
operants, 105
operations, in Piaget's theory, 472, 475–76
opiates, 95
opponent-process theory, 81–82, 95*n*
of color vision, 171–73

of perceptual adaptation, 198
optic nerves, 158
oral stage, in psychoanalytic theory, 424, 426, 522
orgasm, 79, 80, 84
oscilloscope, 20
osmoreceptors, 56
osmosis, 56
ossicles, 153
oval windows (in ears), 153, 154
ovaries, 349, 460
overlearning, 231
overshadowing, in classical conditioning, 100
overweight, 66–67
see also obesity
ovum, 346, 349

pain:
endorphins and alleviation of, 29–30
as fear-evoking stimulus, 71
pleasure vs., 81
as skin sensation, 149
pain receptors, 36
panic, in crowds, 6, 402–3, 404, 405–6
parallax, motion, 189
parallel search, in memory retrieval, 228
paralysis, hysteria and, 415
paranoid schizophrenia, 421, 651, 654
paraphrases, sentence meaning and, 314
parasympathetic overshoot, 72–73
parasympathetic system, 54, 60, 68, 72
parents:
and changing conceptions of childhood, 443–44
child's effect on, 541
home atmosphere and, 437, 539–40
language learning and, 495–97, 499–500, 506
in psychoanalytic thought, 416, 419, 420, 424, 437
self-sacrifices of, 355–56
sex roles and, 462, 548–49, 552, 553, 556, 557, 561
socialization and, 534–35, 539–43
see also child rearing; family; fathers; mothers
parietal lobes, 34, 37
partial-reinforcement effect, 110–11
passive form, in language, 310, 313, 314, 321–22
past tense, language learning and, 501, 505, 508–9, 513
pathology model of mental disorder, 644–48
anxiety disorders and, 668–69
and classification of mental disorders, 559–60, 646–47
diathesis-stress conception of, 647–48, 665, 673–74
homosexuality and, 559–60
schizophrenia and, 648–49, 658–59
sociological critique of, 675–84
sociopathy and, 682
subcategories of, 644–45
pattern recognition, 185–86, 199
as bottom-up vs. top-down process, 202–4
feature analysis and, 201–2
and logic of perception, 205–6
payoff matrices, 144, 145, 405, 406, 580–81
peg method, in mnemonics, 245–46
penis envy, 427–28
peptic ulcers, 119, 671–72, 673, 674

percentile ranks, 584, A12, A13, A14
perception, 179–220, 293, 431–32, 507
adaptation effects in, 200
cognitive development and, 467–93
of depth, 186–89, 195–96, 210–11
differentiation concept and, 200–201, 447–48
empiricism vs. nativism in, 180–82, 209–10
feature detectors in, 197–99
of form, 182–86, 196–97, 199, 201–4, 206, 208–10
Gibsonian approach to, 476–77
grouping factors in, 183–85
illusions in, 210–11, 292
in infants, 189, 195, 196, 209–10
information-processing approach and, 488–93
integration of successive glimpses in, 192–93
and interpersonal nature of reality, 367–70
logic of, 205–6
of movement, 189–91, 198–99, 205
phoneme discrimination and, 498–99
in Piaget's theory, 468–76
of reality, 206–11
and representation of reality in art, 211–18
selective attention in, 191–94, 649–50
after sensory deprivation, 196–97
perceptual constancies, 207–11
of reflectance, 207–8
of size and shape, 208–10
perceptual organization:
innate factors in, 194–99
laws of, 183–85
learned factors in, 199–206
perceptual problem solving, 201–6
bottom-up vs. top-down processing in, 202–4
feature analysis in, 201–2
logic in, 205–6
performance anxiety, therapies for, 707–8
peripheral nervous system, 32–33
see also autonomic nervous system
peripheral vision, 158, 159, 192
permissive pattern, in family life, 539, 540, 543
personality:
antisocial, 546–47, 550, 680–82
assessment of, 611–36
biological classification of, 632–35
differences in, 611
early social deprivation and, 529–34
Freudian theories of, 412–42
genetics and, 634–35
growth of, 703–4
moral development and, 541–47
multiple or split, 648*n*, 670–71
obedience and, 397–98
social development and, 521–34
socialization and, 534–41
taxonomy of, 628–35
trait theory of, 612, 621–27, 628
personality tests, 572
CPI, 614, 615, 635
MMPI, 612–14, 615–16, 635, 680*n*
Rorschach inkblot, 617–18, 620–21, 635
structured, 612–16
TAT, 618–19, 620–21
unstructured (projective techniques), 616–21
validity of, 612, 614–16, 619–21, 622, 628
personality traits, 458, 611

constancy of, 611–12, 621–27, 628
factor analysis in classification of, 628–32
language to describe, 628–29, 630
see also trait theory of personality
personal space, 344–45, 366–67
person-by-situation interaction, 625–27
person constancy, 627
perspective, linear, 138, 187, 211, 213, 217
persuasive communications, 373–74
phallic stage, in psychoanalytic theory, 424, 426, 522
phenothiazines, 653–54, 688–89, 691–92
phenotypes, 456, 599–600
phenylalanine, 457
phenylketonuria (PKU), 457
pheromones, 150
phi phenomenon, 189–90
phobias:
behavioral account of, 94, 112–13, 666–67, 669
behavior therapy for, 116–18, 699–701
psychoanalytic account of, 667, 669
phonemes, 299, 300–301, 498
phonological rules, 498–99
phrases:
meanings of, 302–3
as organizational units for memory, 233
phrase structure, 309–12, 313
see also dual-structure theory of syntax
physical attractiveness, 385–88
halo effect and, 385–86
matching for, 386
standards of, 386–88
physical development, 450, 463, 464, 486
see also embryos; fetuses
physique, personality related to, 632–34
pigeons, pecking response in, 124–25
piloerection, 53
pitch, 151, 152, 154–55, 165
in language learning, 500, 501
pituitary gland, 30, 55, 349
PKU (phenylketonuria), 457
placebo effects, 29, 30, 690–91, 707–8, 713
place theory of pitch, 154–55
play therapy, 710
pleasure, pain vs., 81
pleasure centers in brain, 82–84
pleasure principle, in psychoanalytic theory, 418
pluralistic ignorance, 408
Pointillist art, 169
polarization, of cell membranes, 20
polygamy, 352
polygenic inheritance, 456–57
Ponzo illusion, 211
population, samples and, A6–A7, A26, A28
positive feedback systems, 51–52, 84
positive reinforcers, 106
positive transfer of training, 231
practice, maturation and, 463–65
praying mantis, disinhibitory mechanism in, 25–26
predation, 339, 356–57
predictive validity:
of mental tests, 577
of personality inventories, 615
prefrontal lobotomy, 692
preoperational period, in Piaget's theory, 472–75
preschool programs, 599
primacy effects, 226, 227, 379

primary reinforcers, 108–9
primates, 452
dominance hierarchies in, 343–44
rate of growth in, 451
sexual behavior in, 349–50
see also chimpanzees; monkeys
priming, brain stimulation and, 84
primitive peoples, recapitulation theory and, 446, 447
prisoner's dilemma, 404–6
proactive inhibition, 248
problems, well- vs. ill-defined, 276–77
problem solving, 266–83
algorithms and heuristics in, 274–75
chunking in, 268–70, 272–73
by computer, 273–77
creative thinking in, 280–81
hierarchical organization in, 267–68, 270–73
masters vs. beginners in, 272–73
mental set and, 277–79, 281
obstacles to, 277–79
perceptual, 201–6
restructuring in, 279–83
spatial thinking in, 283–85
procedural knowledge, 259
progesterone, 349, 350
Progressive Matrices Test, 586, 593
prohibitions, internalization of, 542–43
projection, as defense mechanism, 421, 426
projection areas, cortical, 36–38, 148
projective techniques, 616–21
validity of, 619–21
pronouns, 319, 325
proportions, standard error of, A26–A27
propositional thought, in chimpanzees, 330–31
propositions (in abstract thought), 265–66
propositions (in sentence meaning), 311–12
ambiguity and, 315–16
in complex sentences, 318–19
meaning of, 317–18
in paraphrases and opposites, 314
sentences with more than one, 318–19, 320, 321, 322–23
prototypes, in social perception, 378–79
prototype theory of word meaning, 304–7, 502–3
proximal stimuli, 136–37, 140, 180, 207, 211
proximity:
liking and, 383–84
in perceptual grouping, 183
psychoanalysis, 702, 705, 706
classical, 694, 695–97
conceptual difficulties in, 428, 429–30
contributions of, 440–41
culture, myths, and literature interpreted by, 412, 435, 436–40
early experiences and, 529, 531
modern versions of, 697–98
origins of, 412–17
personality theory in, 412–42, 522, 535, 539, 542, 555, 556, 558, 561
phobias as viewed in, 667, 669
psychosexual development theory in, *see* psychosexual development
recapitulation theory and, 446n
reexamination of, 429–37, 440–41, 522
and rejection of cultural absolutism, 435
resistance and repression in, 414, 416–17, 419–20, 423, 426–27, 429, 430–32

separation anxiety and, 523
sex typing and, 435, 555, 556, 558
as therapy, 417, 441, 694, 695–98
psychoanalytic model of psychopathology, 645
psychogenic disorders, 414–15, 643–44
psychological intensity, sensory magnitude and, 141–43
psychological studies:
selection of subjects for, A6–A7
types of, A4–A6
psychology:
defined, 1
general principles vs. unique individuals in, 14
multiple perspectives in, 6–13
scope of, 1–7
task of, 13–14
psychometric approach to intelligence, 588–94
age-intelligence relationship and, 592–93
and structure of mental abilities, 589–92
psychopathology, 637–714
classificatory schemes for, 646–47, 674
conversions and dissociative disorders as, 669–71, 672
demonic possession and, 638–40
of everyday life, 422, 423
and historical conceptions of madness, 638–44, 675
labeling theory and, 676–78, 682–84
as mental rebirth, 678–79
as myth, 677–78
neurosis vs. psychosis in, 637–38
psychophysiological disorders as, 671–74
scope of, 684
sociological perspective on, 675–84
as somatogenic vs. psychogenic disorders, 642–44
symptoms of, 646
treatment of, 640–42, 687–714
see also affective disorders; anxiety disorders; depression; pathology model of mental disorder; schizophrenia
psychopathy, 680n
psychophysics, 139–46
sensory intensity and, 141–43
sensory quality and, 140
signal-detection theory in, 143–46
psychophysiological disorders, 119–21, 671–74
diathesis-stress conception and, 673–74
psychosexual development, 424–29, 434, 441, 522–23, 556, 561, 563
reexamination of, 428, 435–37, 440
stages of, 424, 522–23
psychosis, 638
psychosomatic disorders, *see* psychophysiological disorders
psychosurgery, 692
psychotherapy, 669, 693–713
classical psychoanalysis as, 417, 441, 694, 695–97
client-centered, 703–4
cognitive, 645, 702
common themes in, 704–5
deterioration effect and, 706
evaluation of, 704n, 705–9, 711, 713
existential, 712–13
and expansion of therapeutic goals, 710, 711–12
family, 710
group, 710–11